ENGINEERING MANUAL

OTHER McGRAW-HILL HANDBOOKS OF INTEREST

ENGINEERING MANUAL

*A Practical Reference of Data and Methods
in Architectural, Chemical, Civil, Electrical,
Mechanical, and Nuclear Engineering*

EDITOR-IN-CHIEF

ROBERT H. PERRY, Ph.D.

*Consulting Chemical Engineer; Formerly Project Engineer, Scientific
Design Company; Senior Technologist, Shell Chemical Corporation;
Process Engineer, Shell Development Company*

SECOND EDITION

McGRAW-HILL BOOK COMPANY

New York   San Francisco   Toronto   London   Sydney

ENGINEERING MANUAL

Library of Congress Catalog Card Number 65-28514

49475

345678910 VBVB 765432109

CONTRIBUTORS

William F. Ames, M.S.; Professor, Department of Mechanical Engineering and Department of Statistics and Computer Science, University of Delaware.

Eugene A. Avallone, B.M.E., M.S., M.E., P.E.; Associate Professor of Mechanical Engineering, City University of New York; Member, American Society of Mechanical Engineers.

John W. Bartlett, Ph.D.; Assistant Professor of Chemical and Nuclear Engineering, University of Rochester; Member, American Institute of Chemical Engineers, American Nuclear Society, American Society for Engineering Education, American Association for the Advancement of Science.

Theodore Baumeister, B.S., M.E., P.E.; Stevens Professor Emeritus of Mechanical Engineering, Columbia University; Member, American Society of Mechanical Engineers.

Austin E. Brant, Jr., M.S., P.E.; Associate, Tippetts-Abbett-McCarthy-Stratton, Engineers and Architects; Member, American Society of Civil Engineers, Institute of Traffic Engineers, Highway Research Board, American Road Builders Association, Operations Research Society of America.

Gregory E. Brooks, B.C.E., M.C.E., P.E.; Chief, Structural Division, Smith Haines Lundberg & Waehler; Fellow, American Society of Civil Engineers; Member, American Concrete Institute, American Welding Society, Building Research Institute.

*Kent G. Dedrick, Ph.D.; Research Assistant, University of Michigan.

Leander Economides, B.S., M.E., P.E., R.A.; Economides & Goldberg, Consulting Engineers; Member, American Society of Heating, Air Conditioning and Refrigeration Engineers, Building Research Institute, American Society of Mechanical Engineers, American Institute of Architects.

Richard F. Eisenberg, M.S., Met.E.; Associate Professor of Metallurgy, College of Engineering and Applied Science, University of Rochester; Member, American Society for Metals, American Institute of Metallurgical Engineers.

Owen H. Gailar, Ph.D.; Associate Professor of Nuclear Engineering, Purdue University; Member, American Nuclear Society.

*William A. Hadley, A.B., B.S., M.S., P.E.; Director, Research and Engi-

---

* Contributed to the first edition.

vii

neering Division, Mergenthaler Linotype Company; Member, American Society of Mechanical Engineers.

Arthur E. Hoerl, M.A.; Senior Consultant, Engineering Department, E. I. du Pont de Nemours & Company; Member, Society of Industrial and Applied Mathematics.

*Charles O. Hurd, B.S.; Shell Development Company; Member, American Chemical Society, American Institute of Chemical Engineers.

*Donald L. Katz, Ph.D.; Chairman, Department of Chemical Engineering, University of Michigan; Member, American Chemical Society, American Institute of Chemical Engineers, American Institute of Mining and Metallurgical Engineers, American Petroleum Institute, American Association for the Advancement of Science, American Society of Mechanical Engineers.

*Albert T. Kister, B.S.; Process Engineer, Shell Development Company; Member, American Institute of Chemical Engineers.

*J. G. Lewis, Ph.D.; Associate Research Engineer, Engineering Research Institute, University of Michigan; Member, American Chemical Society, American Institute of Chemical Engineers.

Stuart McLain, Ph.D.; Professor of Nuclear Engineering, Purdue University; President, McLain Associates, Inc., California Nuclear, Inc., Indiana Research and Development, Inc.; Member, American Nuclear Society, American Society for Engineering Education.

Shelby A. Miller, Ph.D., P.E.; Professor and Chairman, Department of Chemical Engineering, University of Rochester; Member, American Association for the Advancement of Science, American Chemical Society, American Institute of Chemical Engineers, Society of Chemical Industry.

*H. A. Ohlgren, D.Sc.; Professor of Chemical Engineering, University of Michigan; Member, American Chemical Society, American Institute of Chemical Engineers, American Society of Mechanical Engineers.

Robert H. Perry, Ph.D.; Consulting Chemical Engineer; Member, American Society for Engineering Education, American Association for the Advancement of Science.

*Carlton P. Roberts, B.S., M.S.; Chief Engineer, Vorhees Walker Smith Smith and Haines; Member, American Physical Society, American Society of Heating and Air Conditioning Engineers, National Society of Professional Engineers.

*Frank L. Rubin, B.A., B.Ch.E.; Downingtown Iron Works; Member, American Institute of Chemical Engineers, American Society of Mechanical Engineers.

*Perry Coke Smith, B.S.; Partner, Vorhees Walker Smith Smith and Haines; Fellow, American Institute of Architects.

*M. E. Weech, B.S., M.S.; Research Engineer, Engineering Research Institute, University of Michigan; Member, American Chemical Society.

D. L. Whitehead, M.S.; Manager, Engineering Laboratories, High Voltage Section, Westinghouse Electric Corporation; Member, American Insti-

* Contributed to the first edition.

tute of Electrical Engineers; Committee Member, National Electrical Manufacturers Association, ASA.

Bronislaus F. Winckowski, B.E.E., P.E.; Chief, Electrical Division, Smith Haines Lundberg & Waehler; Senior Member, The Institute of Electrical and Electronics Engineers; Member, Illuminating Engineering Society, Building Research Institute.

Otto W. Witzell, Ph.D.; Dean of the Graduate School, Drexel Institute of Technology; Member, American Society for Mechanical Engineers, American Society for Engineering Education.

PREFACE

This manual presents in individual sections the commonly used formulas, data, and methods of the principal engineering fields. The first three sections are of broad applicability. Section 1, "Mathematics and Mathematical Tables," contains all of the commonly used mathematical tables and conversion factors. In addition, the basic principles of geometry, trigonometry, algebra, and the calculus are presented. Section 2, "The Engineering Core," covers those areas of engineering interest common to all engineering disciplines; namely, thermodynamics, fluid flow, and heat transfer. Section 3 gives physical and chemical data for a wide variety of elements and compounds. In addition, extensive mechanical and chemical data are given for materials of construction both metallic and plastic.

The final six sections are devoted to the principal engineering professions: Architectural, Chemical, Civil, Electrical, Mechanical, and Nuclear. A recognized authority in each of these fields has summarized the basic relationships and design methods of the profession. The purpose of the book is to provide, in a reasonable number of pages, the data and methods necessary for non-detailed design in any engineering area. The information is presented in a manner to allow use by any technical person even though he is not specifically trained in the area in question.

Section 2 is new in this second edition, and its format is intended to make more accessible information that is applicable to all engineering fields, i.e., fluid flow, heat transfer, and thermodynamics. In the first edition these were arbitrarily assigned to individual professional sections.

Section 3 now includes extensive mechanical and chemical data for materials including the plastics. The performance of materials in the extreme regimes of very high and very low temperature is covered.

Extensive revisions have been made to the final six sections which are devoted to the skills of individual engineering professions. Particular attention was given to changes in legal requirements for the construction of equipment and structures that might affect design procedures. In addition, changes in design methods because of obsolescence of techniques or general acceptance of new techniques are reflected in the content of each section. In two instances, chemical and nuclear engineering, this required a complete rewriting of the section.

The purpose of the manual remains the same as for the first edition. This is a highly *practical* book concerned with everyday problems of *practicing* engineers. Extensive cross referencing and indexing make it possible to quickly find the requisite method, technique, or data appropriate for a large variety of engineering problems.

Robert H. Perry

CONTENTS

SECTION 1

MATHEMATICAL TABLES
AND MATHEMATICS

Arthur E. Hoerl, M.A.; Senior Consultant, Engineering Department, E. I. du Pont de Nemours & Company; Member, Society of Industrial and Applied Mathematics

William F. Ames, M.S.; Professor, Department of Mechanical Engineering and Department of Statistics and Computer Science, University of Delaware

Robert H. Perry, Ph.D.; Consulting Chemical Engineer; Member, American Society for Engineering Education, American Association for the Advancement of Science

CONTENTS

MATHEMATICAL TABLES

Table 1-1. Conversion Factors

To convert from	To	Multiply by
Acres	Square feet	43,560
Acres	Square meters	4,047
Acres	Square miles	0.001563
Acres	Square yards	4,840
Ampere-hours (absolute)	Coulombs (absolute)	3,600
Angstrom units	Inches	3.937×10^{-9}
Angstrom units	Centimeters	1×10^{-8}
Angstrom units	Microns	1×10^{-4}
Atmospheres	Millimeters of mercury at 32°F	760
Atmospheres	Dynes per square centimeter	1.0133×10^{6}
Atmospheres	Feet of water at 39.1°F	33.90
Atmospheres	Grams per square centimeter	1,033.3
Atmospheres	Inches of mercury at 32°F	29.921
Atmospheres	Pounds per square foot	2,116.3
Atmospheres	Pounds per square inch	14.696
Bags (cement)	Pounds (cement)	94
Barrels (cement)	Pounds (cement)	376
Barrels (oil)	Gallons	42
Barrels (cement)	Bags	4
Barrels (U.S. liquid)	Cubic meters	0.11924
Barrels (U.S. liquid)	Gallons	31.5
Barrels per day	Gallons per minute	0.02917
Bars	Atmospheres	0.9869
Bars	Pounds per square inch	14.504
Board feet	Cubic feet	$\frac{1}{12}$
Boiler horsepower	Btu per hour	33,480
Boiler horsepower	Kilowatts	9.803
Btu	Calories (gram)	252
Btu	Centigrade heat units (chu)	0.5556
Btu	Foot-pounds	777.9
Btu	Horsepower-hours	3.929×10^{-4}
Btu	Joules	1,054.6
Btu	Liter-atmospheres	10.41
Btu	Pounds carbon to CO_2	6.88×10^{-5}
Btu	Pounds water evaporated from and at 212°F	0.001036
Btu	Cubic foot–atmospheres	3,676
Btu	Kilowatthours	2.930×10^{-4}
Btu per minute	Horsepower	0.02357
Btu per pound per degree Fahrenheit	Calories per gram per degree centigrade	1
Btu per square foot per minute	Kilowatts per square foot	0.1758
Btu per square foot per second for a temperature gradient of 1°F per inch	Calories, gram (15°C), per square centimeter per second for a temperature gradient of 1°C per centimeter	1.2405
Btu (60°F) per degree Fahrenheit	Calories per degree centigrade	453.6

Table 1-1. Conversion Factors (Continued)

To convert from	To	Multiply by
Bushels (U.S. dry)	Cubic feet	1.2444
Calories, gram	Btu	3.968×10^{-3}
Calories, gram	Foot-pounds	3.087
Calories, gram	Joules	4.185
Calories, gram	Liter-atmospheres	4.130×10^{-2}
Calories, gram	Horsepower-hours	1.5591×10^{-6}
Calories, kilogram	Kilowatthours	0.0011626
Calories, kilogram per second	Kilowatts	4.185
Candle power (spherical)	Lumens	12.556
Carats (metric)	Grams	0.2
Centimeters	Angstrom units	1×10^8
Centimeters	Feet	0.03281
Centimeters	Inches	0.3937
Centimeters	Microns	10,000
Centimeters of mercury at 0°C	Atmospheres	0.013158
Centimeters of mercury at 0°C	Feet of water at 39.1°F	0.4460
Centimeters of mercury at 0°C	Pounds per square foot	27.845
Centimeters of mercury at 0°C	Pounds per square inch	0.19337
Centimeters per second	Feet per minute	1.9685
Circular mils	Square centimeters	5.067×10^{-6}
Circular mils	Square inches	7.854×10^{-7}
Circular mils	Square mils	0.7854
Cords	Cubic feet	128
Cubic centimeters	Cubic feet	3.532×10^{-5}
Cubic centimeters	Gallons	2.6417×10^{-4}
Cubic centimeters	Ounces (U.S. fluid)	0.03381
Cubic centimeters	Quarts (U.S. fluid)	0.0010567
Cubic feet	Bushels (U.S.)	0.8036
Cubic feet	Cubic centimeters	28,317
Cubic feet	Cubic meters	0.028317
Cubic feet	Cubic yards	0.03704
Cubic feet	Gallons	7.481
Cubic feet	Liters	28.316
Cubic foot–atmospheres	Foot-pounds	2,116.3
Cubic foot–atmospheres	Liter-atmospheres	28.316
Cubic feet of water (60°F)	Pounds	62.37
Cubic feet per minute	Cubic centimeters per second	472.0
Cubic feet per minute	Gallons per second	0.1247
Cubic feet per second	Gallons per minute	448.8
Curies	Disintegrations per minute	2.2×10^{12}
Curies	Coulombs per minute	1.1×10^{12}
Degrees	Radians	0.017453
Drams (apothecaries' or troy)	Grams	3.888
Drams (avoirdupois)	Grams	1.7719
Fathoms	Feet	6
Feet	Centimeters	30.48
Feet per minute	Centimeters per second	0.5080
Feet per minute	Miles per hour	0.011364
Foot-poundals	Btu	3.995×10^{-5}
Foot-poundals	Joules	0.04214
Foot-poundals	Liter-atmospheres	4.159×10^{-4}

Table 1-1. Conversion Factors (Continued)

To convert from	To	Multiply by
Foot-pounds	Btu	0.0012856
Foot-pounds	Calories, gram	0.3239
Foot-pounds	Foot-poundals	32.174
Foot-pounds	Horsepower-hours	5.051×10^{-7}
Foot-pounds	Kilowatthours	3.766×10^{-7}
Foot-pounds	Liter-atmospheres	0.013381
Foot-pounds per second	Horsepower	0.0018182
Foot-pounds per second	Kilowatts	0.0013558
Furlongs	Miles	0.125
Gallons	Barrels (U.S. liquid)	0.03175
Gallons	Cubic centimeters	3,785
Gallons	Cubic feet	0.13368
Gallons	Gallons (Imperial)	0.8327
Gallons	Liters	3.785
Gallons	Ounces (U.S. fluid)	128
Gallons per minute	Cubic feet per hour	8.021
Gallons per minute	Cubic feet per second	0.002228
Grains	Grams	0.06480
Grains per gallon	Parts per million	17.118
Grams	Drams (avoirdupois)	0.5644
Grams	Drams (troy)	0.2572
Grams	Pounds (avoirdupois)	0.0022046
Grams	Pounds (troy)	0.002679
Grams per cubic centimeter	Pounds per cubic foot	62.43
Grams per cubic centimeter	Pounds per gallon	8.345
Grams per liter	Grains per gallon	58.42
Grams per liter	Pounds per cubic foot	0.0624
Grams per square centimeter	Pounds per square foot	2.0482
Grams per square centimeter	Pounds per square inch	0.014223
Horsepower (British)	Btu per minute	42.42
Horsepower (British)	Btu per hour	2,545
Horsepower (British)	Foot-pounds per minute	33,000
Horsepower (British)	Foot-pounds per second	550
Horsepower (British)	Kilowatts ($g = 980.665$)	0.74570
Horsepower (British)	Horsepower (metric)	1.0139
Horsepower (British)	Pounds carbon to CO_2 per hour	0.175
Horsepower (British)	Pounds water evaporated per hour at 212°F	2.64
Joules (absolute)	Btu (mean)	9.480×10^{-4}
Joules (absolute)	Calories, gram (mean)	0.2389
Joules (absolute)	Cubic foot–atmospheres	0.3485
Joules (absolute)	Foot-pounds	0.7376
Joules (absolute)	Kilowatthours	2.7778×10^{-7}
Joules (absolute)	Liter-atmospheres	0.009869
Kilograms per square centimeter	Pounds per square inch	14.223
Kilowatthours	Btu	3,414
Kilowatthours	Foot-pounds	2.6552×10^{6}
Kilowatts	Horsepower	1.3410
Knots (nautical miles per hour)	Miles per hour	1.1516
Lamberts	Candles per square inch	2.054

Table 1-1. Conversion Factors (Continued)

To convert from	To	Multiply by
Liter-atmospheres	Cubic foot–atmospheres	0.03532
Liter-atmospheres	Foot-pounds	74.74
Liters	Cubic feet	0.03532
Liters	Gallons	0.26418
Lumens	Watts	0.001496
Microns	Angstrom units	1×10^4
Microns	Centimeters	1×10^{-4}
Miles (nautical)	Feet	6,080
Miles (nautical)	Miles (U.S. statute)	1.1516
Miles	Feet	5,280
Miles per hour	Centimeters per second	44.70
Miles per hour	Feet per second	1.4667
Milliliters	Cubic centimeters	1.000027
Mils	Centimeters	0.00254
Mils	Inches	0.001
Ounces (avoirdupois)	Ounces (troy)	0.9115
Ounces (troy)	Ounces (apothecaries')	1.0000
Poundals	Dynes	13,825
Pounds (avoirdupois)	Grams	453.59
Pounds (avoirdupois)	Pounds (troy)	1.2153
Pounds water evaporated from and at 212°F	Horsepower-hours	0.379
Pound-centigrade units (pcu)	Btu	1.80
Pounds per square foot	Kilograms per square meter	4.882
Pounds per square inch	Kilograms per square centimeter	0.07031
Pounds per cubic foot	Grams per cubic centimeter	0.016018
Pounds per square foot	Atmospheres	4.725×10^{-4}
Pounds per square inch	Atmospheres	0.06805
Radians	Degrees	57.30
Revolutions per minute	Radians per second	0.10472
Slugs	Gee pounds (pounds of mass)	1
Slugs	Kilograms	14.594
Slugs	Pounds	32.17
Square centimeters	Square feet	0.0010764
Square feet	Square centimeters	929.0
Square inches	Square centimeters	6.452
Tons (metric)	Tons (short)	1.1023
Tons (long)	Pounds	2,240
Tons (short)	Pounds	2,000
Tons per square inch	Kilograms per square millimeter	1.5479
Tons (metric)	Pounds	2,204.6
Tons refrigeration	Btu per hour	12,000
Tons (British shipping)	Cubic feet	42.00
Tons (U.S. shipping)	Cubic feet	40.00

Special Conversion Factors

h = heat-transfer coefficient:

Pcu/(hr)(ft²)(°C)	Btu/(hr)(ft²)(°F)	1
Kg-cal/(hr)(m²)(°C)	Btu/(hr)(ft²)(°F)	0.2048
G-cal/(sec)(cm²)(°C)	Btu/(hr)(ft²)(°F)	7,380

Table 1-1. Conversion Factors (Continued)
Special Conversion Factors (Continued)

To convert from	To	Multiply by
Watts/(cm²)(°C)	Btu/(hr)(ft²)(°F)	1,760
Watts/(in.²)(°F)	Btu/(hr)(ft²)(°F)	490
Btu/(hr)(ft²)(°F)	Pcu/(hr)(ft²)(°C)	1
Btu/(hr)(ft²)(°F)	Kg-cal/(hr)(m²)(°C)	4.88
Btu/(hr)(ft²)(°F)	G-cal/(sec)(cm²)(°C)	0.0001355
Btu/(hr)(ft²)(°F)	Watts/(cm²)(°C)	0.000568
Btu/(hr)(ft²)(°F)	Watts/(in.²)(°F)	0.00204
Btu/(hr)(ft²)(°F)	Hp/(ft²)(°F)	0.000394
μ = viscosity:		
Centipoises	G/(sec)(cm) or poise	0.01
Centipoises	Lb/(sec)(ft)	0.000672
Centipoises	Lb/(hr)(ft)	2.42
Centipoises	Kg/(hr)(m)	3.60
Centimeters per second	Square feet per second	929
k = thermal conductivity:		
G-cal/(sec)(cm²)(°C/cm)	Btu/(hr)(ft²)(°F/in.)	2,903.0
Watts/(cm²)(°C/cm)	Btu/(hr)(ft²)(°F/in.)	694.0
G-cal/(hr)(cm²)(°C/cm)	Btu/(hr)(ft²)(°F/in.)	0.8064

Table 1-2. Gas-constant Values

Temp. Scale	Press. units	Vol. units	Wt. units	Energy units	R
Kelvin..........	....	....	g moles	calories	1.9872
	....	....	g moles	joules (abs)	8.3144
	....	....	g moles	joules (int)	8.3130
	atm	cm³	g moles	atm-cm³	82.057
	atm	liters	g moles	atm-liters	0.08205
	mm Hg	liters	g moles	mm Hg–liters	62.361
	bar	liters	g moles	bar-liters	0.08314
	kg/cm²	liters	g moles	kg/(cm²)(liters)	0.08478
	atm	ft³	lb moles	atm-ft³	1.314
	mm Hg	ft³	lb moles	mm Hg–ft³	998.9
	....	....	lb moles	chu or pcu	1.9872
Rankine.........	....	....	lb moles	Btu	1.9872
	....	....	lb moles	hp-hr	0.0007805
	....	....	lb moles	kw-hr	0.0005819
	atm	ft³	lb moles	atm-ft³	0.7302
	in. Hg	ft³	lb moles	in. Hg–ft³	21.85
	mm Hg	ft³	lb moles	mm Hg–ft³	555.0
	lb/in.² abs	ft³	lb moles	lb/(in.²)(ft³)	10.73
	lb/ft² abs	ft³	lb moles	ft-lb	1,545.0

Table 1-3. Fundamental Physical Constants

Name	Symbol	Value	Units
Basic Constants			
Velocity of light............................	c	2.997902×10^{10}	cm/sec
Gravitation constant........................	g	6.66×10^{-8}	cm³/(g)(sec²)
Faraday....................................		96,493.1	coulombs
Absolute temperature of ice point, 0°C..........	$T_{0°C}$	273.160	°K
Pressure-volume product for 1 mole gas at 0°C and zero pressure................................	$(pv)^{p-0}T_{0°C}$	2,271.160	joules/mole
or			
Volume 1 mole gas at 0°C and 1 atm..............		22,411.5	cm³
Atomic weight oxygen........................		16	
P'anck's constant............................	h	6.62377×10^{-27}	
Avogadro's number...........................	N	6.061×10^{23}	molecules/g mole
Pi..	π	3.14159265	
Second......................................	$''$	0.000004848136811095	radian
Minute.....................................	$'$	0.0002908882	radian
Degree.....................................	$°$	0.01745329	radian
Radian.....................................		57.2957795	deg
Napierian-logarithm base.....................	e	2.71828183	
Derivered and Experimental Constants			
Liter.......................................		1,000.027	cm³
Calorie (gram):			
20°C.....................................		4.181	joule
15°C.....................................		4.185	joule
Mean....................................		4.186	joule
Btu			
39°F.....................................		1,060.4	joule
60°F*....................................		1,054.6	joule
Mean....................................		1,054.8	joule
Standard gravity............................	g_0	980.665	cm/sec²
Standard atmosphere.........................	atm	1,013,250	dynes/cm²
Second (mean solar).........................		1.00273791	sec (sidereal)
Joule......................................		0.999835 ± 0.000052	int joule

* Used in conversion tables.

Table 1-4. Five-place Common Logarithms of Numbers
100–155

No.	L	0	1	2	3	4	5	6	7	8	9
100	00	000	043	087	130	173	217	260	303	346	389
101		432	475	518	561	604	647	689	732	775	817
102		860	903	945	988	*030	*072	*115	*157	*199	*242
103	01	284	326	368	410	452	494	536	578	620	662
104		703	745	787	828	870	912	953	995	*036	*078
105	02	119	160	202	243	284	325	366	408	449	490
106		531	572	612	653	694	735	776	816	857	898
107		938	979	*019	*060	*100	*141	*181	*222	*262	*302
108	03	342	383	423	463	503	543	583	623	663	703
109		743	782	822	862	902	941	981	*021	*060	*100
110	04	139	179	218	258	297	336	376	415	454	493
111		532	571	610	650	689	727	766	805	844	883
112		922	961	999	*038	*077	*115	*154	*192	*231	*269
113	05	308	346	385	423	461	500	538	576	614	652
114		690	729	767	805	843	881	918	956	994	*032
115	06	070	108	145	183	221	258	296	333	371	408
116		446	483	521	558	595	633	670	707	744	781
117		819	856	893	930	967	*004	*041	*078	*115	*151
118	07	188	225	262	298	335	372	408	445	482	518
119		555	591	628	664	700	737	773	809	846	882
120		918	954	990	*027	*063	*099	*135	*171	*207	*243
121	08	279	314	350	386	422	458	493	529	565	600
122		636	672	707	743	778	814	849	884	920	955
123		991	*026	*061	*096	*132	*167	*202	*237	*272	*307
124	09	342	377	412	447	482	517	552	587	621	656
125		691	726	760	795	830	864	899	934	968	*003
126	10	037	072	106	140	175	209	243	278	312	346
127		380	415	449	483	517	551	585	619	653	687
128		721	755	789	823	857	890	924	958	992	*025
129	11	059	093	126	160	193	227	261	294	327	361
130		394	428	461	494	528	561	594	628	661	694
131		727	760	793	826	860	893	926	959	992	*024
132	12	057	090	123	156	189	222	254	287	320	353
133		385	418	450	483	516	548	581	613	646	678
134		710	743	775	808	840	872	905	937	969	*001
135	13	033	066	098	130	162	194	226	258	290	322
136		354	386	418	450	481	513	545	577	609	640
137		672	704	735	767	799	830	862	893	925	956
138		988	*019	*051	*082	*114	*145	*176	*208	*239	*270
139	14	301	333	364	395	426	457	489	520	551	582
140		613	644	675	706	737	768	799	829	860	891
141		922	953	983	*014	*045	*076	*106	*137	*168	*198
142	15	229	259	290	320	351	381	412	442	473	503
143		534	564	594	625	655	685	715	746	776	806
144		836	866	897	927	957	987	*017	*047	*077	*107
145	16	137	167	197	227	256	286	316	346	376	406
146		435	465	495	524	554	584	613	643	673	702
147		732	761	791	820	850	879	909	938	967	997
148	17	026	056	085	114	143	173	202	231	260	289
149		319	348	377	406	435	464	493	522	551	580
150		609	638	667	696	725	754	782	811	840	869
151		898	926	955	984	*013	*041	*070	*099	*127	*156
152	18	184	213	241	270	299	327	355	384	412	441
153		469	498	526	554	583	611	639	667	696	724
154		752	780	808	837	865	893	921	949	977	*005
155	19	033	061	089	117	145	173	201	229	257	285
No.	L	0	1	2	3	4	5	6	7	8	9

Proportional parts

	44	43	42
1	4.4	4.3	4.2
2	8.8	8.6	8.4
3	13.2	12.9	12.6
4	17.6	17.2	16.8
5	22.0	21.5	21.0
6	26.4	25.8	25.2
7	30.8	30.1	29.4
8	35.2	34.4	33.6
9	39.6	38.7	37.8

	41	40	39
1	4.1	4.0	3.9
2	8.2	8.0	7.8
3	12.3	12.0	11.7
4	16.4	16.0	15.6
5	20.5	20.0	19.5
6	24.6	24.0	23.4
7	28.7	28.0	27.3
8	32.8	32.0	31.2
9	36.9	36.0	35.1

	38	37	36
1	3.8	3.7	3.6
2	7.6	7.4	7.2
3	11.4	11.1	10.8
4	15.2	14.8	14.4
5	19.0	18.5	18.0
6	22.8	22.2	21.6
7	26.6	25.9	25.2
8	30.4	29.6	28.8
9	34.2	33.3	32.4

	35	34	33
1	3.5	3.4	3.3
2	7.0	6.8	6.6
3	10.5	10.2	9.9
4	14.0	13.6	13.2
5	17.5	17.0	16.5
6	21.0	20.4	19.8
7	24.5	23.8	23.1
8	28.0	27.2	26.4
9	31.5	30.6	29.7

	32	31	30
1	3.2	3.1	3.0
2	6.4	6.2	6.0
3	9.6	9.3	9.0
4	12.8	12.4	12.0
5	16.0	15.5	15.0
6	19.2	18.6	18.0
7	22.4	21.7	21.0
8	25.6	24.8	24.0
9	28.8	27.9	27.0

Proportional parts

* Indicates change in the first two decimal places.

Table 1-4. Five-place Common Logarithms of Numbers (Continued)
155–210

No.	L	0	1	2	3	4	5	6	7	8	9
155	19	033	061	089	117	145	173	201	229	257	285
156		312	340	368	396	424	451	479	507	535	562
157		590	618	645	673	700	728	756	783	811	838
158		866	893	921	948	976	*003	*030	*058	*085	*112
159	20	140	167	194	222	249	276	303	330	358	385
160		412	439	466	493	520	548	575	602	629	656
161		683	710	737	763	790	817	844	871	898	925
162		952	978	*005	*032	*059	*085	*112	*139	*165	*192
163	21	219	245	272	299	325	352	378	405	431	458
164		484	511	537	564	590	617	643	669	696	722
165		748	775	801	827	854	880	906	932	958	985
166	22	011	037	063	089	115	141	168	194	220	246
167		272	298	324	350	376	401	427	453	479	505
168		531	557	583	608	634	660	686	712	737	763
169		789	814	840	866	891	917	943	968	994	*019
170	23	045	070	096	121	147	172	198	223	249	274
171		300	325	350	376	401	426	452	477	502	528
172		553	578	603	629	654	679	704	729	754	776
173		805	830	855	880	905	930	955	980	*005	*030
174	24	055	080	105	130	155	180	204	229	254	279
175		304	329	353	378	403	428	452	477	502	527
176		551	576	601	625	650	674	699	724	748	773
177		797	822	846	871	895	920	944	969	993	*018
178	25	042	066	091	115	139	164	188	212	237	261
179		285	310	334	358	382	406	431	455	479	503
180		527	551	575	600	624	648	672	696	720	744
181		768	792	816	840	864	888	912	935	959	983
182	26	007	031	055	079	102	126	150	174	198	221
183		245	269	293	316	340	364	387	411	435	458
184		482	505	529	553	576	600	623	647	670	694
185		717	741	764	788	811	834	858	881	905	928
186		951	975	998	*021	*045	*068	*091	*114	*138	*161
187	27	184	207	231	254	277	300	323	346	370	393
188		416	439	462	485	508	531	554	577	600	623
189		646	669	692	715	738	761	784	807	830	853
190		875	898	921	944	967	990	*012	*035	*058	*081
191	28	103	126	149	172	194	217	240	262	285	308
192		330	353	375	398	421	443	466	488	511	533
193		556	578	601	623	646	668	691	713	735	758
194		780	803	825	847	870	892	914	937	959	981
195	29	003	026	048	070	092	115	137	159	181	203
196		226	248	270	292	314	336	358	380	403	425
197		447	469	491	513	535	557	579	601	623	645
198		667	688	710	732	754	776	798	820	842	863
199		885	907	929	951	973	994	*016	*038	*060	*081
200	30	103	125	146	168	190	211	233	255	276	298
201		320	341	363	384	406	428	449	471	492	514
202		535	557	578	600	621	643	664	685	707	728
203		750	771	792	814	835	856	878	899	920	942
204		963	984	*006	*027	*048	*069	*091	*112	*133	*154
205	31	175	197	218	239	260	281	302	323	345	366
206		387	408	429	450	471	492	513	534	555	576
207		597	618	639	660	681	702	723	744	765	785
208		806	827	848	869	890	911	931	952	973	994
209	32	015	035	056	077	098	118	139	160	181	201
210		222	243	263	284	305	325	346	366	387	408
No.	L	0	1	2	3	4	5	6	7	8	9

Proportional parts

	29	28
1	2.9	2.8
2	5.8	5.6
3	8.7	8.4
4	11.6	11.2
5	14.5	14.0
6	17.4	16.8
7	20.3	19.6
8	23.2	22.4
9	26.1	25.2

	27	26
1	2.7	2.6
2	5.4	5.2
3	8.1	7.8
4	10.8	10.4
5	13.5	13.0
6	16.2	15.6
7	18.9	18.2
8	21.6	20.8
9	24.3	23.4

	25
1	2.5
2	5.0
3	7.5
4	10.0
5	12.5
6	15.0
7	17.5
8	20.0
9	22.5

	24
1	2.4
2	4.8
3	7.2
4	9.6
5	12.0
6	14.4
7	16.8
8	19.2
9	21.6

	23
1	2.3
2	4.6
3	6.9
4	9.2
5	11.5
6	13.8
7	16.1
8	18.4
9	20.7

	22
1	2.2
2	4.4
3	6.6
4	8.8
5	11.0
6	13.2
7	15.4
8	17.6
9	19.8

Proportional parts

* Indicates change in the first two decimal places.

Table 1-4. Five-place Common Logarithms of Numbers (Continued)
210–265

No.	L	0	1	2	3	4	5	6	7	8	9
210	32	222	243	263	284	305	325	346	366	387	408
211		428	449	469	490	511	531	552	572	593	613
212		634	654	675	695	715	736	756	777	797	818
213		838	858	879	899	919	940	960	980	*001	*021
214	33	041	062	082	102	122	143	163	183	203	224
215		244	264	284	304	325	345	365	385	405	425
216		445	465	486	506	526	546	566	586	606	626
217		646	666	686	706	726	746	766	786	806	826
218		846	866	885	905	925	945	965	985	*005	*025
219	34	044	064	084	104	124	143	163	183	203	223
220		242	262	282	301	321	341	361	380	400	420
221		439	459	479	498	518	537	557	577	596	616
222		635	655	674	694	713	733	753	772	792	811
223		830	850	869	889	908	928	947	967	986	*005
224	35	025	044	064	083	102	122	141	160	180	199
225		218	238	257	276	295	315	334	353	372	392
226		411	430	449	468	488	507	526	545	564	583
227		603	622	641	660	679	698	717	736	755	774
228		793	813	832	851	870	889	908	927	946	965
229		984	*003	*021	*040	*059	*078	*097	*116	*135	*154
230	36	173	192	211	229	248	267	286	305	324	342
231		361	380	399	418	436	455	474	493	511	530
232		549	568	586	605	624	642	661	680	698	717
233		736	754	773	791	810	829	847	866	884	903
234		922	940	959	977	996	*014	*033	*051	*070	*088
235	37	107	125	144	162	181	199	218	236	254	273
236		291	310	328	346	365	383	401	420	438	457
237		475	493	511	530	548	566	585	603	621	639
238		658	676	694	712	731	749	767	785	803	822
239		840	858	876	894	912	931	949	967	985	*003
240	38	021	039	057	075	093	112	130	148	166	184
241		202	220	238	256	274	292	310	328	346	364
242		382	399	417	435	453	471	489	507	525	543
243		561	579	596	614	632	650	668	686	703	721
244		739	757	775	792	810	828	846	863	881	899
245		917	934	952	970	987	*005	*023	*041	*058	*076
246	39	094	111	129	146	164	182	199	217	235	252
247		270	287	305	322	340	358	375	393	410	428
248		445	463	480	498	515	533	550	568	585	602
249		620	637	655	672	690	707	724	742	759	777
250		794	811	829	846	863	881	898	915	933	950
251		967	985	*002	*019	*037	*054	*071	*088	*106	*123
252	40	140	157	175	192	209	226	243	261	278	295
253		312	329	346	364	381	398	415	432	449	466
254		483	500	518	535	552	569	586	603	620	637
255		654	671	688	705	722	739	756	773	790	807
256		824	841	858	875	892	909	926	943	960	976
257		993	*010	*027	*044	*061	*078	*095	*111	*128	*145
258	41	162	179	196	212	229	246	263	280	296	313
259		330	347	364	380	397	414	430	447	464	481
260		497	514	531	547	564	581	597	614	631	647
261		664	681	697	714	731	747	764	780	797	814
262		830	847	863	880	896	913	929	946	963	979
263		996	*012	*029	*045	*062	*078	*095	*111	*127	*144
264	42	160	177	193	210	226	243	259	275	292	308
265		325	341	357	374	390	406	423	439	456	472
No.	L	0	1	2	3	4	5	6	7	8	9

Proportional parts

	21
1	2.1
2	4.2
3	6.3
4	8.4
5	10.5
6	12.6
7	14.7
8	16.8
9	18.9

	20
1	2.0
2	4.0
3	6.0
4	8.0
5	10.0
6	12.0
7	14.0
8	16.0
9	18.0

	19
1	1.9
2	3.8
3	5.7
4	7.6
5	9.5
6	11.4
7	13.3
8	15.2
9	17.1

	18
1	1.8
2	3.6
3	5.4
4	7.2
5	9.0
6	10.8
7	12.6
8	14.4
9	16.2

* Indicates change in the first two decimal places.

Table 1-4. Five-place Common Logarithms of Numbers (Continued)
265–320

No.	L	0	1	2	3	4	5	6	7	8	9
265	42	325	341	357	374	390	406	423	439	456	472
266		488	504	521	537	553	570	586	602	619	635
267		651	667	684	700	716	732	749	765	781	797
268		813	830	846	862	878	894	911	927	943	959
269		975	991	*008	*024	*040	*056	*072	*088	*104	*120
270	43	136	152	169	185	201	217	233	249	265	281
271		297	313	329	345	361	377	393	409	425	441
272		457	473	489	505	521	537	553	569	584	600
273		616	632	648	664	680	696	712	727	743	759
274		775	791	807	823	838	854	870	886	902	917
275		933	949	965	981	996	*012	*028	*044	*059	*075
276	44	091	107	122	138	154	170	185	201	217	232
277		248	264	279	295	311	326	342	358	373	389
278		404	420	436	451	467	483	498	514	529	545
279		560	576	592	607	623	638	654	669	685	700
280		716	731	747	762	778	793	809	824	840	855
281		871	886	902	917	932	948	963	979	994	*010
282	45	025	040	056	071	086	102	117	133	148	163
283		179	194	209	225	240	255	271	286	301	317
284		332	347	362	378	393	408	423	439	454	469
285		484	500	515	530	545	561	576	591	606	621
286		637	652	667	682	697	712	728	743	758	773
287		788	803	818	834	849	864	879	894	909	924
288		939	954	969	984	*000	*015	*030	*045	*060	*075
289	46	090	105	120	135	150	165	180	195	210	225
290		240	255	270	285	300	315	330	345	359	374
291		389	404	419	434	449	464	479	494	509	523
292		538	553	568	583	598	613	627	642	657	672
293		687	702	716	731	746	761	776	790	805	820
294		835	850	864	879	894	909	923	938	953	967
295		982	997	*012	*026	*041	*056	*070	*085	*100	*115
296	47	129	144	159	173	188	202	217	232	246	261
297		276	290	305	319	334	349	363	378	392	407
298		422	436	451	465	480	494	509	524	538	553
299		567	582	596	611	625	640	654	669	683	698
300		712	727	741	756	770	784	799	813	828	842
301		857	871	886	900	914	929	943	958	972	986
302	48	001	015	029	044	058	073	087	101	116	130
303		144	159	173	187	202	216	230	245	259	273
304		287	302	316	330	344	359	373	387	402	416
305		430	444	458	473	487	501	515	530	544	558
306		572	586	601	615	629	643	657	671	686	700
307		714	728	742	756	770	785	799	813	827	841
308		855	869	883	897	911	926	940	954	968	982
309		996	*010	*024	*038	*052	*066	*080	*094	*108	*122
310	49	136	150	164	178	192	206	220	234	248	262
311		276	290	304	318	332	346	360	374	388	402
312		415	429	443	457	471	485	499	513	527	541
313		554	568	582	596	610	624	638	651	665	679
314		693	707	721	734	748	762	776	790	803	817
315		831	845	859	872	886	900	914	927	941	955
316		969	982	996	*010	*024	*037	*051	*065	*079	*092
317	50	106	120	133	147	161	174	188	202	215	229
318		243	256	270	284	297	311	325	338	352	365
319		379	393	406	420	433	447	461	474	488	501
320		515	529	542	556	569	583	596	610	623	637
No.	L	0	1	2	3	4	5	6	7	8	9

Proportional parts

	17		16		15		14
1	1.7	1	1.6	1	1.5	1	1.4
2	3.4	2	3.2	2	3.0	2	2.8
3	5.1	3	4.8	3	4.5	3	4.2
4	6.8	4	6.4	4	6.0	4	5.6
5	8.5	5	8.0	5	7.5	5	7.0
6	10.2	6	9.6	6	9.0	6	8.4
7	11.9	7	11.2	7	10.5	7	9.8
8	13.6	8	12.8	8	12.0	8	11.2
9	15.3	9	14.4	9	13.5	9	12.6

* Indicates change in the first two decimal places.

Table 1-4. Five-place Common Logarithms of Numbers (Continued)
320–375

No.	L	0	1	2	3	4	5	6	7	8	9
320	50	515	529	542	556	569	583	596	610	623	637
321		651	664	678	691	705	718	732	745	759	772
322		786	799	813	826	840	853	866	880	893	907
323		920	934	947	961	974	987	*001	*014	*028	*041
324	51	055	068	081	095	108	121	135	148	162	175
325		188	202	215	228	242	255	268	282	295	308
326		322	335	348	362	375	388	402	415	428	441
327		455	468	481	495	508	521	534	548	561	574
328		587	601	614	627	640	654	667	680	693	706
329		720	733	746	759	772	786	799	812	825	838
330		851	865	878	891	904	917	930	943	957	970
331		983	996	*009	*022	*035	*048	*061	*075	*088	*101
332	52	114	127	140	153	166	179	192	205	218	231
333		244	257	271	284	297	310	323	336	349	362
334		375	388	401	414	427	440	453	466	479	492
335		504	517	530	543	556	569	582	595	608	621
336		634	647	660	673	686	699	711	724	737	750
337		763	776	789	802	815	827	840	853	866	879
338		892	905	917	930	943	956	969	982	994	*007
339	53	020	033	046	058	071	084	097	110	122	135
340		148	161	173	186	199	212	224	237	250	263
341		275	288	301	314	326	339	352	365	377	390
342		403	415	428	441	453	466	479	491	504	517
343		529	542	555	567	580	593	605	618	631	643
344		656	668	681	694	706	719	732	744	757	769
345		782	795	807	820	832	845	857	870	883	895
346		908	920	933	945	958	970	983	995	*008	*020
347	54	033	045	058	070	083	095	108	120	133	145
348		158	170	183	195	208	220	233	245	258	270
349		283	295	307	320	332	345	357	370	382	394
350		407	419	432	444	456	469	481	494	506	518
351		531	543	555	568	580	593	605	617	630	642
352		654	667	679	691	704	716	728	741	753	765
353		777	790	802	814	827	839	851	864	876	888
354		900	913	925	937	949	962	974	986	998	*011
355	55	023	035	047	060	072	084	096	108	121	133
356		145	157	169	182	194	206	218	230	242	255
357		267	279	291	303	315	328	340	352	364	376
358		388	400	413	425	437	449	461	473	485	497
359		509	522	534	546	558	570	582	594	606	618
360		630	642	654	666	678	691	703	715	727	739
361		751	763	775	787	799	811	823	835	847	859
362		871	883	895	907	919	931	943	955	967	979
363		991	*003	*015	*027	*038	*050	*062	*074	*086	*098
364	56	110	122	134	146	158	170	182	194	205	217
365		229	241	253	265	277	289	301	313	324	336
366		348	360	372	384	396	407	419	431	443	455
367		467	478	490	502	514	526	538	549	561	573
368		585	597	608	620	632	644	656	667	679	691
369		703	714	726	738	750	761	773	785	797	808
370		820	832	844	855	867	879	891	902	914	926
371		937	949	961	972	984	996	*008	*019	*031	*043
372	57	054	066	078	089	101	113	124	136	148	159
373		171	183	194	206	217	229	241	252	264	276
374		287	299	310	322	334	345	357	368	380	392
375		403	415	426	438	449	461	473	484	496	507
No.	L	0	1	2	3	4	5	6	7	8	9

Proportional parts

14	
1	1.4
2	2.8
3	4.2
4	5.6
5	7.0
6	8.4
7	9.8
8	11.2
9	12.6

13	
1	1.3
2	2.6
3	3.9
4	5.2
5	6.5
6	7.8
7	9.1
8	10.4
9	11.7

12	
1	1.2
2	2.4
3	3.6
4	4.8
5	6.0
6	7.2
7	8.4
8	9.6
9	10.8

* Indicates change in the first two decimal places.

Table 1-4. Five-place Common Logarithms of Numbers (Continued)
375–430

No.	L	0	1	2	3	4	5	6	7	8	9	Proportional parts
375	57	403	415	426	438	449	461	473	484	496	507	
376		519	530	542	553	565	577	588	600	611	623	
377		634	646	657	669	680	692	703	715	726	738	
378		749	761	772	784	795	807	818	830	841	852	
379		864	875	887	898	910	921	933	944	956	967	
380		978	990	*001	*013	*024	*035	*047	*058	*070	*081	
381	58	093	104	115	127	138	149	161	172	184	195	
382		206	218	229	240	252	263	275	286	297	309	
383		320	331	343	354	365	377	388	399	411	422	
384		433	444	456	467	478	490	501	512	524	535	
385		546	557	569	580	591	602	614	625	636	647	
386		659	670	681	692	704	715	726	737	749	760	
387		771	782	794	805	816	827	838	850	861	872	
388		883	894	906	917	928	939	950	961	973	984	
389		995	*006	*017	*028	*040	*051	*062	*073	*084	*095	11
390	59	106	118	129	140	151	162	173	184	195	207	1 1.1
391		218	229	240	251	262	273	284	295	306	318	2 2.2
392		329	340	351	362	373	384	395	406	417	428	3 3.3
393		439	450	461	472	483	494	506	517	528	539	4 4.4
394		550	561	572	583	594	605	616	627	638	649	5 5.5
395		660	671	682	693	704	715	726	737	748	759	6 6.6
396		770	780	791	802	813	824	835	846	857	868	7 7.7
397		879	890	901	912	923	934	945	956	966	977	8 8.8
398		988	999	*010	*021	*032	*043	*054	*065	*076	*086	9 9.9
399	60	097	108	119	130	141	152	163	173	184	195	
400		206	217	228	239	249	260	271	282	293	304	
401		314	325	336	347	358	369	379	390	401	412	
402		423	433	444	455	466	477	487	498	509	520	
403		531	541	552	563	574	584	595	606	617	627	
404		638	649	660	670	681	692	703	713	724	735	
405		746	756	767	778	788	799	810	821	831	842	
406		853	863	874	885	895	906	917	927	938	949	
407		959	970	981	991	*002	*013	*023	*034	*045	*055	
408	61	066	077	087	098	109	119	130	140	151	162	
409		172	183	194	204	215	225	236	247	257	268	
410		278	289	300	310	321	331	342	352	363	374	10
411		384	395	405	416	426	437	448	458	469	479	1 1.0
412		490	500	511	521	532	542	553	563	574	584	2 2.0
413		595	606	616	627	637	648	658	669	679	690	3 3.0
414		700	711	721	731	742	752	763	773	784	794	4 4.0
												5 5.0
415		805	815	826	836	847	857	868	878	888	899	6 6.0
416		909	920	930	941	951	962	972	982	993	*003	7 7.0
417	62	014	024	034	045	055	066	076	086	097	107	8 8.0
418		118	128	138	149	159	170	180	190	201	211	9 9.0
419		221	232	242	252	263	273	284	294	304	315	
420		325	335	346	356	366	377	387	397	408	418	
421		428	439	449	459	469	480	490	500	511	521	
422		531	542	552	562	572	583	593	603	614	624	
423		634	644	655	665	675	685	696	706	716	726	
424		737	747	757	767	778	788	798	808	818	829	
425		839	849	859	870	880	890	900	910	921	931	
426		941	951	961	972	982	992	*002	*012	*022	*033	
427	63	043	053	063	073	083	094	104	114	124	134	
428		144	155	165	175	185	195	205	215	225	236	
429		246	256	266	276	286	296	306	317	327	337	
430		347	357	367	377	387	397	407	417	428	438	
No.	L	0	1	2	3	4	5	6	7	8	9	Proportional parts

* Indicates change in the first two decimal places.

Table 1-4. Five-place Common Logarithms of Numbers (Continued)
430–485

No.	L	0	1	2	3	4	5	6	7	8	9	Proportional parts
430	63	347	357	367	377	387	397	407	417	428	438	
431		448	458	468	478	488	498	508	518	528	538	
432		548	558	568	579	589	599	609	619	629	639	
433		649	659	669	679	689	699	709	719	729	739	
434		749	759	769	779	789	799	809	819	829	839	
435		849	859	869	879	889	899	909	919	929	939	
436		949	959	969	979	988	998	*008	*018	*028	*038	
437	64	048	058	068	078	088	098	108	118	128	137	
438		147	157	167	177	187	197	207	217	227	237	
439		246	256	266	276	286	296	306	316	326	335	
440		345	355	365	375	385	395	404	414	424	434	
441		444	454	464	473	483	493	503	513	523	532	
442		542	552	562	572	582	591	601	611	621	631	
443		640	650	660	670	680	689	699	709	719	729	
444		738	748	758	768	777	787	797	807	816	826	10
445		836	846	856	865	875	885	895	904	914	924	1 | 1.0
446		933	943	953	963	972	982	992	*002	*011	*021	2 | 2.0
447	65	031	040	050	060	070	079	089	099	108	118	3 | 3.0
448		128	137	147	157	167	176	186	196	205	215	4 | 4.0
449		225	234	244	254	263	273	283	292	302	312	5 | 5.0
450		321	331	341	350	360	369	379	389	398	408	6 | 6.0
451		418	427	437	447	456	466	475	485	495	504	7 | 7.0
452		514	523	533	543	552	562	571	581	591	600	8 | 8.0
453		610	619	629	639	648	658	667	677	686	696	9 | 9.0
454		706	715	725	734	744	753	763	773	782	792	
455		801	811	820	830	839	849	858	868	877	887	
456		896	906	916	925	935	944	954	963	973	982	
457		992	*001	*011	*020	*030	*039	*049	*058	*068	*077	
458	66	087	096	106	115	124	134	143	153	162	172	
459		181	191	200	210	219	229	238	247	257	266	
460		276	285	295	304	314	323	332	342	351	361	
461		370	380	389	398	408	417	427	436	445	455	
462		464	474	483	492	502	511	521	530	539	549	
463		558	567	577	586	596	605	614	624	633	642	
464		652	661	671	680	689	699	708	717	727	736	9
465		745	755	764	773	783	792	801	811	820	829	1 | 0.9
466		839	848	857	867	876	885	894	904	913	922	2 | 1.8
467		932	941	950	960	969	978	987	997	*006	*015	3 | 2.7
468	67	025	034	043	052	062	071	080	090	099	108	4 | 3.6
469		117	127	136	145	154	164	173	182	191	201	5 | 4.5
470		210	219	228	238	247	256	265	274	284	293	6 | 5.4
471		302	311	321	330	339	348	357	367	376	385	7 | 6.3
472		394	403	413	422	431	440	449	459	468	477	8 | 7.2
473		486	495	504	514	523	532	541	550	560	569	9 | 8.1
474		578	587	596	605	614	624	633	642	651	660	
475		669	679	688	697	706	715	724	733	742	752	
476		761	770	779	788	797	806	815	825	834	843	
477		852	861	870	879	888	897	906	916	925	934	
478		943	952	961	970	979	988	997	*006	*015	*024	
479	68	034	043	052	061	070	079	088	097	106	115	
480		124	133	142	151	160	169	178	187	196	205	
481		215	224	233	242	251	260	269	278	287	296	
482		305	314	323	332	341	350	359	368	377	386	
483		395	404	413	422	431	440	449	458	467	476	
484		485	494	502	511	520	529	538	547	556	565	
485		574	583	592	601	610	619	628	637	646	655	
– No.	L	0	1	2	3	4	5	6	7	8	9	Proportional parts

* Indicates change in the first two decimal places.

Table 1-4. Five-place Common Logarithms of Numbers (Continued)
485–540

No.	L	0	1	2	3	4	5	6	7	8	9
485	68	574	583	592	601	610	619	628	637	646	655
486		664	673	682	690	699	708	717	726	735	744
487		753	762	771	780	789	797	806	815	824	833
488		842	851	860	869	878	886	895	904	913	922
489		931	940	949	958	966	975	984	993	*002	*011
490	69	020	028	037	046	055	064	073	082	090	099
491		108	117	126	135	144	152	161	170	179	188
492		197	205	214	223	232	241	249	258	267	276
493		285	294	302	311	320	329	338	346	355	364
494		373	381	390	399	408	417	425	434	443	452
495		461	469	478	487	496	504	513	522	531	539
496		548	557	566	574	583	592	601	609	618	627
497		636	644	653	662	671	679	688	697	705	714
498		723	732	740	749	758	767	775	784	793	801
499		810	819	827	836	845	854	862	871	880	888
500		897	906	914	923	932	940	949	958	966	975
501		984	992	*001	*010	*018	*027	*036	*044	*053	*062
502	70	070	079	088	096	105	114	122	131	140	148
503		157	165	174	183	191	200	209	217	226	234
504		243	252	260	269	278	286	295	303	312	321
505		329	338	346	355	364	372	381	389	398	406
506		415	424	432	441	449	458	467	475	484	492
507		501	509	518	526	535	544	552	561	569	578
508		586	595	603	612	621	629	638	646	655	663
509		672	680	689	697	706	714	723	731	740	749
510		757	766	774	783	791	800	808	817	825	834
511		842	851	859	868	876	885	893	902	910	919
512		927	935	944	952	961	969	978	986	995	*003
513	71	012	020	029	037	046	054	063	071	079	088
514		096	105	113	122	130	139	147	155	164	172
515		181	189	198	206	214	223	231	240	248	257
516		265	273	282	290	299	307	315	324	332	341
517		349	357	366	374	383	391	399	408	416	425
518		433	441	450	458	467	475	483	492	500	508
519		517	525	533	542	550	559	567	575	584	592
520		600	609	617	625	634	642	650	659	667	675
521		684	692	700	709	717	725	734	742	750	759
522		767	775	784	792	800	809	817	825	834	842
523		850	858	867	875	883	892	900	908	917	925
524		933	941	950	958	966	975	983	991	999	*008
525	72	016	024	032	041	049	057	066	074	082	090
526		099	107	115	123	132	140	148	156	165	173
527		181	189	198	206	214	222	230	239	247	255
528		263	272	280	288	296	305	313	321	329	337
529		346	354	362	370	378	387	395	403	411	419
530		428	436	444	452	460	469	477	485	493	501
531		509	518	526	534	542	550	559	567	575	583
532		591	599	607	616	624	632	640	648	656	665
533		673	681	689	697	705	713	722	730	738	746
534		754	762	770	779	787	795	803	811	819	827
535		835	844	852	860	868	876	884	892	900	908
536		916	925	933	941	949	957	965	973	981	989
537		997	*006	*014	*022	*030	*038	*046	*054	*062	*070
538	73	078	086	094	102	111	119	127	135	143	151
539		159	167	175	183	191	199	207	215	223	231
540		239	247	255	264	272	280	288	296	304	312
No.	L	0	1	2	3	4	5	6	7	8	9

Proportional parts

	9
1	0.9
2	1.8
3	2.7
4	3.6
5	4.5
6	5.4
7	6.3
8	7.2
9	8.1

	8
1	0.8
2	1.6
3	2.4
4	3.2
5	4.0
6	4.8
7	5.6
8	6.4
9	7.2

* Indicates change in the first two decimal places.

Table 1-4. Five-place Common Logarithms of Numbers (Continued)
540–595

No.	L	0	1	2	3	4	5	6	7	8	9	Proportional parts
540	73	239	247	255	264	272	280	288	296	304	312	
541		320	328	336	344	352	360	368	376	384	392	
542		400	408	416	424	432	440	448	456	464	472	
543		480	488	496	504	512	520	528	536	544	552	
544		560	568	576	584	592	600	608	616	624	632	
545		640	648	656	664	672	679	687	695	703	711	
546		719	727	735	743	751	759	767	775	783	791	
547		799	807	815	823	830	838	846	854	862	870	
548		878	886	894	902	910	918	926	934	941	949	
549		957	965	973	981	989	997	*005	*013	*020	*028	
550	74	036	044	052	060	068	076	084	092	099	107	
551		115	123	131	139	147	155	162	170	178	186	
552		194	202	210	218	225	233	241	249	257	265	
553		273	280	288	296	304	312	320	327	335	343	
554		351	359	367	374	382	390	398	406	414	421	
555		429	437	445	453	461	468	476	484	492	500	
556		507	515	523	531	539	547	554	562	570	578	
557		586	593	601	609	617	624	632	640	648	656	
558		663	671	679	687	695	702	710	718	726	733	
559		741	749	757	764	772	780	788	796	803	811	
560		819	827	834	842	850	858	865	873	881	889	
561		896	904	912	920	927	935	943	950	958	966	
562		974	981	989	997	*005	*012	*020	*028	*035	*043	
563	75	051	059	066	074	082	089	097	105	113	120	
564		128	136	143	151	159	166	174	182	189	197	
565		205	213	220	228	236	243	251	259	266	274	
566		282	289	297	305	312	320	328	335	343	351	
567		358	366	374	381	389	397	404	412	420	427	
568		435	442	450	458	465	473	481	488	496	504	
569		511	519	526	534	542	549	557	565	572	580	
570		587	595	603	610	618	626	633	641	648	656	
571		664	671	679	686	694	702	709	717	724	732	
572		740	747	755	762	770	778	785	793	800	808	
573		815	823	831	838	846	853	861	868	876	884	
574		891	899	906	914	921	929	937	944	952	959	
575		967	974	982	989	997	*005	*012	*020	*027	*035	
576	76	042	050	057	065	072	080	087	095	103	110	
577		118	125	133	140	148	155	163	170	178	185	
578		193	200	208	215	223	230	238	245	253	260	
579		268	275	283	290	298	305	313	320	328	335	
580		343	350	358	365	373	380	388	395	403	410	
581		418	425	433	440	448	455	462	470	477	485	
582		492	500	507	515	522	530	537	545	552	559	
583		567	574	582	589	597	604	612	619	626	634	
584		641	649	656	664	671	678	686	693	701	708	
585		716	723	730	738	745	753	760	768	775	782	
586		790	797	805	812	819	827	834	842	849	856	
587		864	871	879	886	893	901	908	916	923	930	
588		938	945	953	960	967	975	982	989	997	*004	
589	77	012	019	026	034	041	048	056	063	070	078	
590		085	093	100	107	115	122	129	137	144	151	
591		159	166	173	181	188	195	203	210	218	225	
592		232	240	247	254	262	269	276	283	291	298	
593		305	313	320	327	335	342	349	357	364	371	
594		379	386	393	401	408	415	422	430	437	444	
595		452	459	466	474	481	488	495	503	510	517	
No.	L	0	1	2	3	4	5	6	7	8	9	Proportional parts

Proportional parts:

	9
1	0.9
2	1.8
3	2.7
4	3.6
5	4.5
6	5.4
7	6.3
8	7.2
9	8.1

	8
1	0.8
2	1.6
3	2.4
4	3.2
5	4.0
6	4.8
7	5.6
8	6.4
9	7.2

	7
1	0.7
2	1.4
3	2.1
4	2.8
5	3.5
6	4.2
7	4.9
8	5.6
9	6.3

* Indicates change in the first two decimal places.

Table 1-4. Five-place Common Logarithms of Numbers (Continued)
595–650

No.	L	0	1	2	3	4	5	6	7	8	9	Proportional parts
595	77	452	459	466	474	481	488	495	503	510	517	
596		525	532	539	546	554	561	568	576	583	590	
597		597	605	612	619	627	634	641	648	656	663	
598		670	677	685	692	699	706	714	721	728	735	
599		743	750	757	764	772	779	786	793	801	808	
600		815	822	830	837	844	851	859	866	873	880	
601		887	895	902	909	916	924	931	938	945	952	
602		960	967	974	981	989	996	*003	*010	*017	*025	
603	78	032	039	046	053	061	068	075	082	089	097	
604		104	111	118	125	132	140	147	154	161	168	
605		176	183	190	197	204	211	219	226	233	240	
606		247	254	262	269	276	283	290	297	305	312	
607		319	326	333	340	347	355	362	369	376	383	
608		390	398	405	412	419	426	433	440	447	455	
609		462	469	476	483	490	497	505	512	519	526	
610		533	540	547	554	561	569	576	583	590	597	
611		604	611	618	625	633	640	647	654	661	668	
612		675	682	689	696	704	711	718	725	732	739	
613		746	753	760	767	774	781	789	796	803	810	
614		817	824	831	838	845	852	859	866	873	880	
615		888	895	902	909	916	923	930	937	944	951	
616		958	965	972	979	986	993	*000	*007	*014	*021	
617	79	029	036	043	050	057	064	071	078	085	092	
618		099	106	113	120	127	134	141	148	155	162	
619		169	176	183	190	197	204	211	218	225	232	
620		239	246	253	260	267	274	281	288	295	302	
621		309	316	323	330	337	344	351	358	365	372	
622		379	386	393	400	407	414	421	428	435	442	
623		449	456	463	470	477	484	491	498	505	512	
624		518	525	532	539	546	553	560	567	574	581	
625		588	595	602	609	616	623	630	637	644	651	
626		657	664	671	678	685	692	699	706	713	720	
627		727	734	741	748	754	761	768	775	782	789	
628		796	803	810	817	824	831	837	844	851	858	
629		865	872	879	886	893	900	906	913	920	927	
630		934	941	948	955	962	969	975	982	989	996	
631	80	003	010	017	024	030	037	044	051	058	065	
632		072	079	085	092	099	106	113	120	127	134	
633		140	147	154	161	168	175	182	188	195	202	
634		209	216	223	229	236	243	250	257	264	271	
635		277	284	291	298	305	312	318	325	332	339	
636		346	353	359	366	373	380	387	393	400	407	
637		414	421	428	434	441	448	455	462	468	475	
638		482	489	496	502	509	516	523	530	536	543	
639		550	557	564	570	577	584	591	598	604	611	
640		618	625	632	638	645	652	659	665	672	679	
641		686	693	699	706	713	720	726	733	740	747	
642		754	760	767	774	781	787	794	801	808	814	
643		821	828	835	841	848	855	862	868	875	882	
644		889	895	902	909	916	922	929	936	943	949	
645		956	963	969	976	983	990	996	*003	*010	*017	
646	81	023	030	037	043	050	057	064	070	077	084	
647		090	097	104	111	117	124	131	137	144	151	
648		158	164	171	178	184	191	198	204	211	218	
649		224	231	238	245	251	258	265	271	278	285	
650		291	298	305	311	318	325	331	338	345	351	
No.	L	0	1	2	3	4	5	6	7	8	9	Proportional parts

Proportional parts:

8
1	0.8
2	1.6
3	2.4
4	3.2
5	4.0
6	4.8
7	5.6
8	6.4
9	7.2

7
1	0.7
2	1.4
3	2.1
4	2.8
5	3.5
6	4.2
7	4.9
8	5.6
9	6.3

* Indicates change in the first two decimal places.

Table 1-4. Five-place Common Logarithms of Numbers (Continued)
650–705

No.	L	0	1	2	3	4	5	6	7	8	9	Proportional parts
650	81	291	298	305	311	318	325	331	338	345	351	
651		358	365	371	378	385	391	398	405	411	418	
652		425	431	438	445	451	458	465	471	478	485	
653		491	498	505	511	518	525	531	538	544	551	
654		558	564	571	578	584	591	598	604	611	618	
655		624	631	637	644	651	657	664	671	677	684	
656		690	697	704	710	717	723	730	737	743	750	
657		757	763	770	776	783	790	796	803	809	816	
658		823	829	836	842	849	856	862	869	875	882	
659		889	895	902	908	915	921	928	935	941	948	
660	82	954	961	968	974	981	987	994	*000	*007	*014	
661		020	027	033	040	046	053	060	066	073	079	
662		086	092	099	105	112	119	125	132	138	145	
663		151	158	164	171	178	184	191	197	204	210	
664		217	223	230	236	243	250	256	263	269	276	7
665		282	289	295	302	308	315	321	328	334	341	1 0.7
666		347	354	360	367	374	380	387	393	400	406	2 1.4
667		413	419	426	432	439	445	452	458	465	471	3 2.1
668		478	484	491	497	504	510	517	523	530	536	4 2.8
669		543	549	556	562	569	575	582	588	595	601	5 3.5
												6 4.2
670		607	614	620	627	633	640	646	653	659	666	7 4.9
671		672	679	685	692	698	705	711	718	724	730	8 5.6
672		737	743	750	756	763	769	776	782	789	795	9 6.3
673		802	808	814	821	827	834	840	847	853	860	
674		866	872	879	885	892	898	905	911	918	924	
675		930	937	943	950	956	963	969	975	982	988	
676		995	*001	*008	*014	*020	*027	*033	*040	*046	*052	
677	83	059	065	072	078	085	091	097	104	110	117	
678		123	129	136	142	149	155	161	168	174	181	
679		187	193	200	206	213	219	225	232	238	245	
680		251	257	264	270	276	283	289	296	302	308	
681		315	321	327	334	340	347	353	359	366	372	
682		378	385	391	398	404	410	417	423	429	436	
683		442	448	455	461	468	474	480	487	493	499	
684		506	512	518	525	531	537	544	550	556	563	
												6
685		569	575	582	588	594	601	607	613	620	626	1 0.6
686		632	639	645	651	658	664	670	677	683	689	2 1.2
687		696	702	708	715	721	727	734	740	746	753	3 1.8
688		759	765	771	778	784	790	797	803	809	816	4 2.4
689		822	828	835	841	847	853	860	866	872	879	5 3.0
												6 3.6
690		885	891	898	904	910	916	923	929	935	942	7 4.2
691		948	954	960	967	973	979	986	992	998	*004	8 4.8
692	84	011	017	023	029	036	042	048	055	061	067	9 5.4
693		073	080	086	092	098	105	111	117	123	130	
694		136	142	148	155	161	167	173	180	186	192	
695		198	205	211	217	223	230	236	242	248	255	
696		261	267	273	280	286	292	298	305	311	317	
697		323	330	336	342	348	354	361	367	373	379	
698		386	392	398	404	410	417	423	429	435	442	
699		448	454	460	466	473	479	485	491	497	504	
700		510	516	522	528	535	541	547	553	559	566	
701		572	578	584	590	597	603	609	615	621	628	
702		634	640	646	652	658	665	671	677	683	689	
703		696	702	708	714	720	726	733	739	745	751	
704		757	763	770	776	782	788	794	800	807	813	
705		819	825	831	837	844	850	856	862	868	874	
No.	L	0	1	2	3	4	5	6	7	8	9	Proportional parts

* Indicates change in the first two decimal places.

Table 1-4. Five-place Common Logarithms of Numbers (Continued)
705–760

No.	L	0	1	2	3	4	5	6	7	8	9	Proportional parts
705	84	819	825	831	837	844	850	856	862	868	874	
706		880	887	893	899	905	911	917	924	930	936	
707		942	948	954	960	967	973	979	985	991	997	
708	85	003	009	016	022	028	034	040	046	052	059	
709		065	071	077	083	089	095	101	107	114	120	
710		126	132	138	144	150	156	163	169	175	181	
711		187	193	199	205	211	217	224	230	236	242	
712		248	254	260	266	272	278	285	291	297	303	
713		309	315	321	327	333	339	345	352	358	364	
714		370	376	382	388	394	400	406	412	418	425	
715		431	437	443	449	455	461	467	473	479	485	
716		491	497	503	510	516	522	528	534	540	546	
717		552	558	564	570	576	582	588	594	600	606	
718		612	618	625	631	637	643	649	655	661	667	
719		673	679	685	691	697	703	709	715	721	727	
720		733	739	745	751	757	763	769	775	781	788	
721		794	800	806	812	818	824	830	836	842	848	
722		854	860	866	872	878	884	890	896	902	908	
723		914	920	926	932	938	944	950	956	962	968	
724		974	980	986	992	998	*004	*010	*016	*022	*028	
725	86	034	040	046	052	058	064	070	076	082	088	
726		094	100	106	112	118	124	130	136	141	147	
727		153	159	165	171	177	183	189	195	201	207	
728		213	219	225	231	237	243	249	255	261	267	
729		273	279	285	291	297	303	308	314	320	326	
730		332	338	344	350	356	362	368	374	380	386	
731		392	398	404	410	416	421	427	433	439	445	
732		451	457	463	469	475	481	487	493	499	504	
733		510	516	522	528	534	540	546	552	558	564	
734		570	576	581	587	593	599	605	611	617	623	
735		629	635	641	646	652	658	664	670	676	682	
736		688	694	700	705	711	717	723	729	735	741	
737		747	753	759	764	770	776	782	788	794	800	
738		806	812	817	823	829	835	841	847	853	859	
739		864	870	876	882	888	894	900	906	911	917	
740		923	929	935	941	947	953	958	964	970	976	
741		982	988	994	999	*005	*011	*017	*023	*029	*035	
742	87	040	046	052	058	064	070	075	081	087	093	
743		099	105	111	116	122	128	134	140	146	151	
744		157	163	169	175	181	186	192	198	204	210	
745		216	221	227	233	239	245	251	256	262	268	
746		274	280	286	291	297	303	309	315	320	326	
747		332	338	344	350	355	361	367	373	379	384	
748		390	396	402	408	413	419	425	431	437	442	
749		448	454	460	466	471	477	483	489	495	500	
750		506	512	518	523	529	535	541	547	552	558	
751		564	570	576	581	587	593	599	604	610	616	
752		622	628	633	639	645	651	656	662	668	674	
753		680	685	691	697	703	708	714	720	726	731	
754		737	743	749	754	760	766	772	777	783	789	
755		795	800	806	812	818	823	829	835	841	846	
756		852	858	864	869	875	881	887	892	898	904	
757		910	915	921	927	933	938	944	950	955	961	
758		967	973	978	984	990	996	*001	*007	*013	*018	
759	88	024	030	036	041	047	053	059	064	070	076	
760		081	087	093	099	104	110	116	121	127	133	
No.	L	0	1	2	3	4	5	6	7	8	9	Proportional parts

	6
1	0.6
2	1.2
3	1.8
4	2.4
5	3.0
6	3.6
7	4.2
8	4.8
9	5.4

* Indicates change in the first two decimal places.

Table 1-4. Five-place Common Logarithms of Numbers (Continued)
760–815

No.	L	0	1	2	3	4	5	6	7	8	9
760	88	081	087	093	099	104	110	116	121	127	133
761		138	144	150	156	161	167	173	178	184	190
762		196	201	207	213	218	224	230	235	241	247
763		252	258	264	270	275	281	287	292	298	304
764		309	315	321	326	332	338	343	349	355	360
765		366	372	378	383	389	395	400	406	412	417
766		423	429	434	440	446	451	457	463	468	474
767		480	485	491	497	502	508	514	519	525	530
768		536	542	547	553	559	564	570	576	581	587
769		593	598	604	610	615	621	627	632	638	643
770		649	655	660	666	672	677	683	689	694	700
771		705	711	717	722	728	734	739	745	750	756
772		762	767	773	779	784	790	795	801	807	812
773		818	824	829	835	840	846	852	857	863	868
774		874	880	885	891	897	902	908	913	919	925
775		930	936	941	947	953	958	964	969	975	981
776		986	992	997	*003	*009	*014	*020	*025	*031	*037
777	89	042	048	053	059	064	070	076	081	087	092
778		098	104	109	115	120	126	131	137	143	148
779		154	159	165	170	176	182	187	193	198	204
780		209	215	221	226	232	237	243	248	254	260
781		265	271	276	282	287	293	298	304	310	315
782		321	326	332	337	343	348	354	360	365	371
783		376	382	387	393	398	404	409	415	421	426
784		432	437	443	448	454	459	465	470	476	481
785		487	493	498	504	509	515	520	526	531	537
786		542	548	553	559	564	570	575	581	586	592
787		597	603	609	614	620	625	631	636	642	647
788		653	658	664	669	675	680	686	691	697	702
789		708	713	719	724	730	735	741	746	752	757
790		763	768	774	779	785	790	796	801	807	812
791		818	823	829	834	840	845	851	856	862	867
792		873	878	883	889	894	900	905	911	916	922
793		927	933	938	944	949	955	960	966	971	977
794		982	988	993	998	*004	*009	*015	*020	*026	*031
795	90	037	042	048	053	059	064	069	075	080	086
796		091	097	102	108	113	119	124	129	135	140
797		146	151	157	162	168	173	179	184	189	195
798		200	206	211	217	222	227	233	238	244	249
799		255	260	266	271	276	282	287	293	298	304
800		309	314	320	325	331	336	342	347	352	358
801		363	369	374	380	385	390	396	401	407	412
802		417	423	428	434	439	445	450	455	461	466
803		472	477	482	488	493	499	504	509	515	520
804		526	531	536	542	547	553	558	563	569	574
805		580	585	590	596	601	607	612	617	623	628
806		634	639	644	650	655	660	666	671	677	682
807		687	693	698	704	709	714	720	725	730	736
808		741	747	752	757	763	768	773	779	784	789
809		795	800	806	811	816	822	827	832	838	843
810		849	854	859	865	870	875	881	886	891	897
811		902	907	913	918	924	929	934	940	945	950
812		956	961	966	972	977	982	988	993	998	*004
813	91	009	014	020	025	030	036	041	046	052	057
814		062	068	073	078	084	089	094	100	105	110
815		116	121	126	132	137	142	148	153	158	164
No.	L	0	1	2	3	4	5	6	7	8	9

Proportional parts

	6
1	0.6
2	1.2
3	1.8
4	2.4
5	3.0
6	3.6
7	4.2
8	4.8
9	5.4

	5
1	0.5
2	1.0
3	1.5
4	2.0
5	2.5
6	3.0
7	3.5
8	4.0
9	4.5

* Indicates change in the first two decimal places.

Table 1-4. Five-place Common Logarithms of Numbers (Continued)
815–870

No.	L	0	1	2	3	4	5	6	7	8	9	Proportional parts
815	91	116	121	126	132	137	142	148	153	158	164	
816		169	174	180	185	190	196	201	206	212	217	
817		222	228	233	238	243	249	254	259	265	270	
818		275	281	286	291	297	302	307	312	318	323	
819		328	334	339	344	350	355	360	365	371	376	
820		381	387	392	397	403	408	413	418	424	429	
821		434	440	445	450	455	461	466	471	477	482	
822		487	492	498	503	508	514	519	524	529	535	
823		540	545	551	556	561	566	572	577	582	587	
824		593	598	603	609	614	619	624	630	635	640	
825		645	651	656	661	666	672	677	682	687	693	
826		698	703	709	714	719	724	730	735	740	745	
827		751	756	761	766	772	777	782	787	793	798	
828		803	808	814	819	824	829	834	840	845	850	
829		855	861	866	871	876	882	887	892	897	903	**6**
830		908	913	918	924	929	934	939	944	950	955	1 | 0.6
831		960	965	971	976	981	986	991	997	*002	*007	2 | 1.2 3 | 1.8
832	92	012	018	023	028	033	038	044	049	054	059	4 | 2.4
833		065	070	075	080	085	091	096	101	106	111	5 | 3.0 6 | 3.6
834		117	122	127	132	137	143	148	153	158	163	7 | 4.2 8 | 4.8 9 | 5.4
835		169	174	179	184	189	195	200	205	210	215	
836		221	226	231	236	241	247	252	257	262	267	
837		273	278	283	288	293	298	304	309	314	319	
838		324	330	335	340	345	350	355	361	366	371	
839		376	381	387	392	397	402	407	412	418	423	
840		428	433	438	443	449	454	459	464	469	474	
841		480	485	490	495	500	505	511	516	521	526	
842		531	536	542	547	552	557	562	567	572	578	
843		583	588	593	598	603	609	614	619	624	629	
844		634	639	645	650	655	660	665	670	675	681	
845		686	691	696	701	706	711	717	722	727	732	
846		737	742	747	752	758	763	768	773	778	783	
847		788	793	799	804	809	814	819	824	829	834	
848		840	845	850	855	860	865	870	875	881	886	
849		891	896	901	906	911	916	921	927	932	937	
850		942	947	952	957	962	967	973	978	983	988	**5**
851		993	998	*003	*008	*013	*018	*024	*029	*034	*039	1 | 0.5
852	93	044	049	054	059	064	069	075	080	085	090	2 | 1.0
853		095	100	105	110	115	120	125	131	136	141	3 | 1.5
854		146	151	156	161	166	171	176	181	186	192	4 | 2.0 5 | 2.5
855		197	202	207	212	217	222	227	232	237	242	6 | 3.0
856		247	252	258	263	268	273	278	283	288	293	7 | 3.5
857		298	303	308	313	318	323	328	334	339	344	8 | 4.0
858		349	354	359	364	369	374	379	384	389	394	9 | 4.5
859		399	404	409	414	420	425	430	435	440	445	
860		450	455	460	465	470	475	480	485	490	495	
861		500	505	510	515	520	526	531	536	541	546	
862		551	556	561	566	571	576	581	586	591	596	
863		601	606	611	616	621	626	631	636	641	646	
864		651	656	661	666	671	677	682	687	692	697	
865		702	707	712	717	722	727	732	737	742	747	
866		752	757	762	767	772	777	782	787	792	797	
867		802	807	812	817	822	827	832	837	842	847	
868		852	857	862	867	872	877	882	887	892	897	
869		902	907	912	917	922	927	932	937	942	947	
870		952	957	962	967	972	977	982	987	992	997	
No.	L	0	1	2	3	4	5	6	7	8	9	Proportional parts

*/Indicates change in the first two decimal places.

Table 1-4. Five-place Common Logarithms of Numbers (Continued)
870–925

No.	L	0	1	2	3	4	5	6	7	8	9	Proportional parts
870	93	952	957	962	967	972	977	982	987	992	997	
871	94	002	007	012	017	022	027	032	037	042	047	
872		052	057	062	067	072	077	082	087	091	096	
873		101	106	111	116	121	126	131	136	141	146	
874		151	156	161	166	171	176	181	186	191	196	
875		201	206	211	216	221	226	231	236	240	245	
876		250	255	260	265	270	275	280	285	290	295	
877		300	305	310	315	320	325	330	335	340	345	
878		349	354	359	364	369	374	379	384	389	394	
879		399	404	409	414	419	424	429	433	438	443	
880		448	453	458	463	468	473	478	483	488	493	
881		498	503	507	512	517	522	527	532	537	542	
882		547	552	557	562	567	571	576	581	586	591	
883		596	601	606	611	616	621	626	630	635	640	
884		645	650	655	660	665	670	675	680	685	689	**5**
885		694	699	704	709	714	719	724	729	734	738	1 | 0.5
886		743	748	753	758	763	768	773	778	783	787	2 | 1.0
887		792	797	802	807	812	817	822	827	832	836	3 | 1.5
888		841	846	851	856	861	866	871	876	880	885	4 | 2.0
889		890	895	900	905	910	915	919	924	929	934	5 | 2.5
												6 | 3.0
890		939	944	949	954	959	963	968	973	978	983	7 | 3.5
891		988	993	998	*002	*007	*012	*017	*022	*027	*032	8 | 4.0
892	95	036	041	046	051	056	061	066	071	075	080	9 | 4.5
893		085	090	095	100	105	109	114	119	124	129	
894		134	139	143	148	153	158	163	168	173	177	
895		182	187	192	197	202	207	211	216	221	226	
896		231	236	240	245	250	255	260	265	270	274	
897		279	284	289	294	299	303	308	313	318	323	
898		328	332	337	342	347	352	357	361	366	371	
899		376	381	386	390	395	400	405	410	415	419	
900		424	429	434	439	444	448	453	458	463	468	
901		472	477	482	487	492	497	501	506	511	516	
902		521	525	530	535	540	545	550	554	559	564	
903		569	574	578	583	588	593	598	602	607	612	
904		617	622	626	631	636	641	646	650	655	660	
905		665	670	674	679	684	689	694	698	703	708	**4**
906		713	718	722	727	732	737	742	746	751	756	1 | 0.4
907		761	766	770	775	780	785	789	794	799	804	2 | 0.8
908		809	813	818	823	828	832	837	842	847	852	3 | 1.2
909		856	861	866	871	875	880	885	890	895	899	4 | 1.6
												5 | 2.0
910		904	909	914	918	923	928	933	938	942	947	6 | 2.4
911		952	957	961	966	971	976	980	985	990	995	7 | 2.8
912		999	*004	*009	*014	*019	*023	*028	*033	*038	*042	8 | 3.2
913	96	047	052	057	061	066	071	076	080	085	090	9 | 3.6
914		095	099	104	109	114	118	123	128	133	137	
915		142	147	152	156	161	166	171	175	180	185	
916		190	194	199	204	209	213	218	223	227	232	
917		237	242	246	251	256	261	265	270	275	280	
918		284	289	294	298	303	308	313	317	322	327	
919		332	336	341	346	350	355	360	365	369	374	
920		379	384	388	393	398	402	407	412	417	421	
921		426	431	435	440	445	450	454	459	464	468	
922		473	478	483	487	492	497	501	506	511	515	
923		520	525	530	534	539	544	548	553	558	563	
924		567	572	577	581	586	591	595	600	605	609	
925		614	619	624	628	633	638	642	647	652	656	
No.	L	0	1	2	3	4	5	6	7	8	9	Proportional parts

* Indicates change in the first two decimal places.

Table 1-4. Five-place Common Logarithms of Numbers (Continued)
925–980

No.	L	0	1	2	3	4	5	6	7	8	9
925	96	614	619	624	628	633	638	642	647	652	656
926		661	666	670	675	680	685	689	694	699	703
927		708	713	717	722	727	731	736	741	745	750
928		755	759	764	769	774	778	783	788	792	797
929		802	806	811	816	820	825	830	834	839	844
930		848	853	858	862	867	872	876	881	886	890
931		895	900	904	909	914	918	923	928	932	937
932		942	946	951	956	960	965	970	974	979	984
933		988	993	997	*002	*007	*011	*016	*021	*025	*030
934	97	035	039	044	049	053	058	063	067	072	077
935		081	086	090	095	100	104	109	114	118	123
936		128	132	137	142	146	151	155	160	165	169
937		174	179	183	188	192	197	202	206	211	216
938		220	225	230	234	239	243	248	253	257	262
939		267	271	276	280	285	290	294	299	304	308
940		313	317	322	327	331	336	341	345	350	354
941		359	364	368	373	377	382	387	391	396	400
942		405	410	414	419	424	428	433	437	442	447
943		451	456	460	465	470	474	479	483	488	493
944		497	502	506	511	516	520	525	529	534	539
945		543	548	552	557	562	566	571	575	580	585
946		589	594	598	603	607	612	617	621	626	630
947		635	640	644	649	653	658	663	667	672	676
948		681	685	690	695	699	704	708	713	717	722
949		727	731	736	740	745	750	754	759	763	768
950		772	777	782	786	791	795	800	804	809	813
951		818	823	827	832	836	841	845	850	855	859
952		864	868	873	877	882	887	891	896	900	905
953		909	914	918	923	928	932	937	941	946	950
954		955	959	964	968	973	978	982	987	991	996
955	98	000	005	009	014	019	023	028	032	037	041
956		046	050	055	059	064	069	073	078	082	087
957		091	096	100	105	109	114	118	123	127	132
958		137	141	146	150	155	159	164	168	173	177
959		182	186	191	195	200	205	209	214	218	223
960		227	232	236	241	245	250	254	259	263	268
961		272	277	281	286	290	295	299	304	308	313
962		318	322	327	331	336	340	345	349	354	358
963		363	367	372	376	381	385	390	394	399	403
964		408	412	417	421	426	430	435	439	444	448
965		453	457	462	466	471	475	480	484	489	493
966		498	502	507	511	516	520	525	529	534	538
967		543	547	552	556	561	565	570	574	579	583
968		588	592	597	601	605	610	614	619	623	628
969		632	637	641	646	650	655	659	664	668	673
970		677	682	686	691	695	700	704	709	713	717
971		722	726	731	735	740	744	749	753	758	762
972		767	771	776	780	785	789	793	798	802	807
973		811	816	820	825	829	834	838	843	847	851
974		856	860	865	869	874	878	883	887	892	896
975		900	905	909	914	918	923	927	932	936	941
976		945	949	954	958	963	967	972	976	981	985
977		989	994	998	*003	*007	*012	*016	*021	*025	*029
978	99	034	038	043	047	052	056	061	065	069	074
979		078	083	087	092	096	100	105	109	114	118
980		123	127	131	136	140	145	149	154	158	162
No.	L	0	1	2	3	4	5	6	7	8	9

Proportional parts

	5		4
1	0.5	1	0.4
2	1.0	2	0.8
3	1.5	3	1.2
4	2.0	4	1.6
5	2.5	5	2.0
6	3.0	6	2.4
7	3.5	7	2.8
8	4.0	8	3.2
9	4.5	9	3.6

* Indicates change in the first two decimal places.

Table 1-4. Five-place Common Logarithms of Numbers (Continued)
980–1000

No.	L	0	1	2	3	4	5	6	7	8	9	Proportional parts
980	99	123	127	131	136	140	145	149	154	158	162	
981		167	171	176	180	185	189	193	198	202	207	**5**
982		211	216	220	224	229	233	238	242	247	251	
983		255	260	264	269	273	277	282	286	291	295	1 0.5
984		300	304	308	313	317	322	326	330	335	339	2 1.0
												3 1.5
985		344	348	352	357	361	366	370	374	379	383	4 2.0
986		388	392	397	401	405	410	414	419	423	427	5 2.5
987		432	436	441	445	449	454	458	463	467	471	6 3.0
988		476	480	484	489	493	498	502	506	511	515	7 3.5
989		520	524	528	533	537	542	546	550	555	559	8 4.0
												9 4.5
990		564	568	572	577	581	585	590	594	599	603	
991		607	612	616	621	625	629	634	638	642	647	**4**
992		651	656	660	664	669	673	677	682	686	691	
993		695	699	704	708	712	717	721	726	730	734	1 0.4
994		739	743	747	752	756	760	765	769	774	778	2 0.8
												3 1.2
995		782	787	791	795	800	804	808	813	817	822	4 1.6
996		826	830	835	839	843	848	852	856	861	865	5 2.0
997		870	874	878	883	887	891	896	900	904	909	6 2.4
998		913	917	922	926	930	935	939	944	948	952	7 2.8
999		957	961	965	970	974	978	983	987	991	996	8 3.2
												9 3.6
1000	00	000	004	009	013	017	022	026	030	035	039	
No.	L	0	1	2	3	4	5	6	7	8	9	Proportional parts

* Indicates change in the first two decimal places.

Table 1-5. Natural Trigonometric Functions and Their Logarithms

Deg	Radians	Nat sin	Log sin	Nat cos	Log cos	Nat tan	Log tan	Nat cot	Log cot	Radians	Deg
0° 00'	0.0000	0.0000		1.0000	0.0000	0.0000				1.5708	90° 00'
10	.0029	.0029	7.4637	1.0000	0.0000	.0029	7.4637	343.77	2.5363	1.5679	50
20	.0058	.0058	7.7648	1.0000	0.0000	.0058	7.7648	171.89	2.2352	1.5650	40
30	.0087	.0087	7.9408	1.0000	0.0000	.0087	7.9409	114.59	2.0591	1.5621	30
40	.0116	.0116	8.0658	0.9999	0.0000	.0116	8.0658	85.940	1.9342	1.5592	20
50	.0145	.0145	8.1627	.9999	0.0000	.0146	8.1627	68.750	1.8373	1.5563	10
1° 00'	.0175	.0175	8.2419	.9999	9.9999	.0175	8.2419	57.290	1.7581	1.5533	89° 00'
10	.0204	.0204	8.3088	.9998	9.9999	.0204	8.3089	49.104	1.6911	1.5504	50
20	.0233	.0233	8.3668	.9997	9.9999	.0233	8.3669	42.964	1.6331	1.5475	40
30	.0262	.0262	8.4179	.9997	9.9999	.0262	8.4181	38.188	1.5819	1.5446	30
40	.0291	.0291	8.4637	.9996	9.9998	.0291	8.4639	34.368	1.5362	1.5417	20
50	.0320	.0320	8.5050	.9995	9.9998	.0320	8.5053	31.242	1.4947	1.5388	10
2° 00'	.0349	.0349	8.5428	.9994	9.9997	.0349	8.5431	28.636	1.4569	1.5359	88° 00'
10	.0378	.0378	8.5776	.9993	9.9997	.0378	8.5779	26.432	1.4221	1.5330	50
20	.0407	.0407	8.6097	.9992	9.9996	.0408	8.6101	24.542	1.3899	1.5301	40
30	.0436	.0436	8.6397	.9991	9.9996	.0437	8.6401	22.904	1.3599	1.5272	30
40	.0465	.0465	8.6677	.9989	9.9995	.0466	8.6682	21.470	1.3318	1.5243	20
50	.0495	.0494	8.6940	.9988	9.9995	.0495	8.6945	20.206	1.3055	1.5213	10
3° 00'	.0524	.0523	8.7188	.9986	9.9994	.0524	8.7194	19.081	1.2806	1.5184	87° 00'
10	.0553	.0552	8.7423	.9985	9.9993	.0553	8.7429	18.075	1.2571	1.5155	50
20	.0582	.0581	8.7645	.9983	9.9993	.0582	8.7653	17.169	1.2348	1.5126	40
30	.0611	.0610	8.7857	.9981	9.9992	.0612	8.7865	16.350	1.2135	1.5097	30
40	.0640	.0640	8.8059	.9980	9.9991	.0641	8.8067	15.605	1.1933	1.5068	20
50	.0669	.0669	8.8251	.9978	9.9990	.0670	8.8261	14.924	1.1739	1.5039	10
4° 00'	.0698	.0698	8.8436	.9976	9.9989	.0699	8.8446	14.301	1.1554	1.5010	86° 00'
10	.0727	.0727	8.8613	.9974	9.9989	.0729	8.8624	13.727	1.1376	1.4981	50
20	.0756	.0756	8.8783	.9971	9.9988	.0758	8.8795	13.197	1.1205	1.4952	40
30	.0785	.0785	8.8946	.9969	9.9987	.0787	8.8960	12.706	1.1040	1.4923	30
40	.0814	.0814	8.9104	.9967	9.9986	.0816	8.9119	12.251	1.0882	1.4893	20
50	.0844	.0843	8.9256	.9964	9.9985	.0846	8.9272	11.826	1.0728	1.4864	10
5° 00'	.0873	.0872	8.9403	.9962	9.9983	.0875	8.9420	11.430	1.0581	1.4835	85° 00'
10	.0902	.0901	8.9545	.9959	9.9982	.0904	8.9563	11.059	1.0437	1.4806	50
20	.0931	.0930	8.9683	.9957	9.9981	.0934	8.9701	10.712	1.0299	1.4777	40
30	.0960	.0959	8.9816	.9954	9.9980	.0963	8.9836	10.385	1.0164	1.4748	30
40	.0989	.0987	8.9945	.9951	9.9979	.0992	8.9966	10.078	1.0034	1.4719	20
50	.1018	.1016	9.0070	.9948	9.9978	.1022	9.0093	9.7882	0.9907	1.4690	10

Deg	Radians	Log tan	Nat tan	Log cot	Nat cot	Log sin	Nat sin	Log cos	Nat cos	Radians	Deg
84° 00'	1.4661	.9784	9.5144	9.0216	.1051	9.9976	.9945	9.0192	.1045	.1047	6° 00'
50	1.4632	.9664	9.2553	9.0336	.1081	9.9975	.9942	9.0311	.1074	.1076	10
40	1.4603	.9547	9.0098	9.0453	.1110	9.9973	.9939	9.0426	.1103	.1105	20
30	1.4573	.9433	8.7769	9.0567	.1139	9.9972	.9936	9.0539	.1132	.1134	30
20	1.4544	.9323	8.5556	9.0678	.1169	9.9971	.9932	9.0648	.1161	.1164	40
10	1.4515	.9214	8.3450	9.0786	.1198	9.9969	.9929	9.0755	.1190	.1193	50
83° 00'	1.4486	.9109	8.1443	9.0891	.1228	9.9968	.9926	9.0859	.1219	.1222	7° 00'
50	1.4457	.9005	7.9530	9.0995	.1257	9.9966	.9922	9.0961	.1248	.1251	10
40	1.4428	.8904	7.7704	9.1096	.1287	9.9964	.9918	9.1060	.1276	.1280	20
30	1.4399	.8806	7.5958	9.1194	.1317	9.9963	.9914	9.1157	.1305	.1309	30
20	1.4370	.8709	7.4287	9.1291	.1346	9.9961	.9911	9.1252	.1334	.1338	40
10	1.4341	.8615	7.2687	9.1385	.1376	9.9959	.9907	9.1345	.1363	.1367	50
82° 00'	1.4312	.8522	7.1154	9.1478	.1405	9.9958	.9903	9.1436	.1392	.1396	8° 00'
50	1.4283	.8431	6.9682	9.1569	.1435	9.9956	.9899	9.1525	.1421	.1425	10
40	1.4254	.8342	6.8269	9.1658	.1465	9.9954	.9894	9.1612	.1449	.1454	20
30	1.4224	.8255	6.6912	9.1745	.1495	9.9952	.9890	9.1697	.1478	.1484	30
20	1.4195	.8169	6.5606	9.1831	.1524	9.9950	.9886	9.1781	.1507	.1513	40
10	1.4166	.8085	6.4348	9.1915	.1554	9.9948	.9881	9.1863	.1536	.1542	50
81° 00'	1.4137	.8003	6.3138	9.1997	.1584	9.9946	.9877	9.1943	.1564	.1571	9° 00'
50	1.4108	.7922	6.1970	9.2078	.1614	9.9944	.9872	9.2022	.1593	.1600	10
40	1.4079	.7842	6.0844	9.2158	.1644	9.9942	.9868	9.2100	.1622	.1629	20
30	1.4050	.7764	5.9758	9.2236	.1673	9.9940	.9863	9.2176	.1651	.1658	30
20	1.4021	.7687	5.8708	9.2313	.1703	9.9938	.9858	9.2251	.1679	.1687	40
10	1.3992	.7611	5.7694	9.2389	.1733	9.9936	.9853	9.2324	.1708	.1716	50
80° 00'	1.3963	.7537	5.6713	9.2463	.1763	9.9934	.9848	9.2397	.1737	.1745	10° 00'
50	1.3934	.7464	5.5764	9.2536	.1793	9.9931	.9843	9.2468	.1765	.1774	10
40	1.3904	.7391	5.4845	9.2609	.1823	9.9929	.9838	9.2538	.1794	.1804	20
30	1.3875	.7320	5.3955	9.2680	.1853	9.9927	.9833	9.2606	.1822	.1833	30
20	1.3846	.7250	5.3093	9.2750	.1884	9.9924	.9827	9.2674	.1851	.1862	40
10	1.3817	.7181	5.2257	9.2819	.1914	9.9922	.9822	9.2741	.1880	.1891	50
79° 00'	1.3788	.7114	5.1446	9.2887	.1944	9.9920	.9816	9.2806	.1908	.1920	11° 00'
50	1.3759	.7047	5.0658	9.2954	.1974	9.9917	.9811	9.2871	.1937	.1949	10
40	1.3730	.6981	4.9894	9.3020	.2004	9.9915	.9805	9.2934	.1965	.1978	20
30	1.3701	.6915	4.9152	9.3085	.2035	9.9912	.9799	9.2997	.1994	.2007	30
20	1.3672	.6851	4.8430	9.3149	.2065	9.9909	.9793	9.3058	.2022	.2036	40
10	1.3643	.6788	4.7729	9.3212	.2095	9.9907	.9788	9.3119	.2051	.2065	50
78° 00'	1.3614	.6725	4.7046	9.3275	.2126	9.9904	.9782	9.3179	.2079	.2094	12° 00'
Deg	Radians	Log tan	Nat tan	Log cot	Nat cot	Log sin	Nat sin	Log cos	Nat cos	Radians	Deg

Table 1-5. Natural Trigonometric Functions and Their Logarithms (Continued)

Deg	Radians	Log cot	Nat cot	Log tan	Nat tan	Log cos	Nat cos	Log sin	Nat sin	Radians	Deg
78° 00'	1.3614	0.6725	4.7046	9.3275	0.2126	9.9904	0.9782	9.3179	0.2079	0.2094	12° 00'
50	1.3584	.6664	4.6383	9.3337	.2156	9.9901	.9775	9.3238	.2108	.2123	10
40	1.3555	.6603	4.5736	9.3397	.2186	9.9899	.9769	9.3296	.2136	.2153	20
30	1.3526	.6542	4.5107	9.3458	.2217	9.9896	.9763	9.3353	.2164	.2182	30
20	1.3497	.6483	4.4494	9.3517	.2248	9.9893	.9757	9.3410	.2193	.2211	40
10	1.3468	.6424	4.3897	9.3576	.2278	9.9890	.9750	9.3466	.2221	.2240	50
77° 00'	1.3439	.6366	4.3315	9.3634	.2309	9.9887	.9744	9.3521	.2250	.2269	13° 00'
50	1.3410	.6309	4.2747	9.3691	.2339	9.9884	.9737	9.3575	.2278	.2298	10
40	1.3381	.6252	4.2193	9.3748	.2370	9.9881	.9730	9.3629	.2306	.2327	20
30	1.3352	.6197	4.1653	9.3804	.2401	9.9878	.9724	9.3682	.2335	.2356	30
20	1.3323	.6141	4.1126	9.3859	.2432	9.9875	.9717	9.3734	.2363	.2385	40
10	1.3294	.6086	4.0611	9.3914	.2462	9.9872	.9710	9.3786	.2391	.2414	50
76° 00'	1.3265	.6032	4.0108	9.3968	.2493	9.9869	.9703	9.3837	.2419	.2443	14° 00'
50	1.3235	.5979	3.9617	9.4021	.2524	9.9866	.9696	9.3887	.2447	.2473	10
40	1.3206	.5926	3.9136	9.4074	.2555	9.9863	.9689	9.3937	.2476	.2502	20
30	1.3177	.5873	3.8667	9.4127	.2586	9.9859	.9682	9.3986	.2504	.2531	30
20	1.3148	.5822	3.8208	9.4178	.2617	9.9856	.9674	9.4035	.2532	.2560	40
10	1.3119	.5770	3.7760	9.4230	.2648	9.9853	.9667	9.4083	.2560	.2589	50
75° 00'	1.3090	.5720	3.7321	9.4281	.2680	9.9849	.9659	9.4130	.2588	.2618	15° 00'
50	1.3061	.5669	3.6891	9.4331	.2711	9.9846	.9652	9.4177	.2616	.2647	10
40	1.3032	.5619	3.6471	9.4381	.2742	9.9843	.9644	9.4223	.2644	.2676	20
30	1.3003	.5570	3.6059	9.4430	.2773	9.9839	.9636	9.4269	.2672	.2705	30
20	1.2974	.5521	3.5656	9.4479	.2805	9.9836	.9629	9.4314	.2700	.2734	40
10	1.2945	.5473	3.5261	9.4527	.2836	9.9832	.9621	9.4359	.2728	.2763	50
74° 00'	1.2915	.5425	3.4874	9.4575	.2868	9.9828	.9613	9.4403	.2756	.2793	16° 00'
50	1.2886	.5378	3.4495	9.4622	.2899	9.9825	.9605	9.4447	.2784	.2822	10
40	1.2857	.5331	3.4124	9.4669	.2931	9.9821	.9596	9.4491	.2812	.2851	20
30	1.2828	.5284	3.3759	9.4716	.2962	9.9817	.9588	9.4533	.2840	.2880	30
20	1.2799	.5238	3.3402	9.4762	.2994	9.9814	.9580	9.4576	.2868	.2909	40
10	1.2770	.5192	3.3052	9.4808	.3026	9.9810	.9572	9.4618	.2896	.2938	50
73° 00'	1.2741	.5147	3.2709	9.4853	.3057	9.9806	.9563	9.4659	.2924	.2967	17° 00'
50	1.2712	.5102	3.2371	9.4898	.3089	9.9802	.9555	9.4701	.2952	.2996	10
40	1.2683	.5057	3.2041	9.4943	.3121	9.9798	.9546	9.4741	.2979	.3025	20
30	1.2654	.5013	3.1716	9.4987	.3153	9.9794	.9537	9.4781	.3007	.3054	30
20	1.2625	.4969	3.1397	9.5031	.3185	9.9790	.9528	9.4821	.3035	.3083	40
10	1.2595	.4925	3.1084	9.5075	.3217	9.9786	.9520	9.4861	.3063	.3113	50

Deg	Radians	Log tan	Nat tan	Log cot	Nat cot	Log sin	Nat sin	Log cos	Nat cos	Radians	Deg
72° 00'	1.2566	.4882	3.0777	9.5118	.3249	9.9782	.9511	9.4900	.3090	.3142	18° 00'
50	1.2537	.4839	3.0475	9.5161	.3281	9.9778	.9502	9.4939	.3118	.3171	10
40	1.2508	.4797	3.0178	9.5203	.3314	9.9774	.9492	9.4977	.3145	.3200	20
30	1.2479	.4755	2.9887	9.5245	.3346	9.9770	.9483	9.5015	.3173	.3229	30
20	1.2450	.4713	2.9600	9.5287	.3378	9.9765	.9474	9.5052	.3201	.3258	40
10	1.2421	.4672	2.9319	9.5329	.3411	9.9761	.9465	9.5090	.3228	.3287	50
71° 00'	1.2392	.4630	2.9042	9.5370	.3443	9.9757	.9455	9.5126	.3256	.3316	19° 00'
50	1.2363	.4589	2.8770	9.5411	.3476	9.9752	.9446	9.5163	.3283	.3345	10
40	1.2334	.4549	2.8502	9.5451	.3509	9.9748	.9436	9.5199	.3311	.3374	20
30	1.2305	.4509	2.8239	9.5492	.3541	9.9744	.9426	9.5235	.3338	.3403	30
20	1.2275	.4469	2.7980	9.5532	.3574	9.9739	.9417	9.5271	.3366	.3432	40
10	1.2246	.4429	2.7725	9.5571	.3607	9.9734	.9407	9.5306	.3393	.3462	50
70° 00'	1.2217	.4389	2.7475	9.5611	.3640	9.9730	.9397	9.5341	.3420	.3491	20° 00'
50	1.2188	.4350	2.7228	9.5650	.3673	9.9725	.9387	9.5375	.3448	.3520	10
40	1.2159	.4311	2.6985	9.5689	.3706	9.9721	.9377	9.5409	.3475	.3549	20
30	1.2130	.4273	2.6746	9.5727	.3739	9.9716	.9367	9.5443	.3502	.3578	30
20	1.2101	.4234	2.6511	9.5766	.3772	9.9711	.9357	9.5477	.3529	.3607	40
10	1.2072	.4196	2.6279	9.5804	.3805	9.9706	.9346	9.5510	.3557	.3636	50
69° 00'	1.2043	.4158	2.6051	9.5842	.3839	9.9702	.9336	9.5543	.3584	.3665	21° 00'
50	1.2014	.4121	2.5826	9.5879	.3872	9.9697	.9325	9.5576	.3611	.3694	10
40	1.1985	.4083	2.5605	9.5917	.3906	9.9692	.9315	9.5609	.3638	.3723	20
30	1.1956	.4046	2.5387	9.5954	.3939	9.9687	.9304	9.5641	.3665	.3752	30
20	1.1926	.4009	2.5172	9.5991	.3973	9.9682	.9294	9.5673	.3692	.3782	40
10	1.1897	.3972	2.4960	9.6028	.4007	9.9677	.9283	9.5704	.3719	.3811	50
68° 00'	1.1868	.3936	2.4751	9.6064	.4040	9.9672	.9272	9.5736	.3746	.3840	22° 00'
50	1.1839	.3900	2.4545	9.6100	.4074	9.9667	.9261	9.5767	.3773	.3869	10
40	1.1810	.3864	2.4342	9.6136	.4108	9.9661	.9250	9.5798	.3800	.3898	20
30	1.1781	.3828	2.4142	9.6172	.4142	9.9656	.9239	9.5828	.3827	.3927	30
20	1.1752	.3792	2.3945	9.6208	.4176	9.9651	.9228	9.5859	.3854	.3956	40
10	1.1723	.3757	2.3750	9.6243	.4211	9.9646	.9216	9.5889	.3881	.3985	50
67° 00'	1.1694	.3722	2.3559	9.6279	.4245	9.9640	.9205	9.5919	.3907	.4014	23° 00'
50	1.1665	.3687	2.3369	9.6314	.4279	9.9635	.9194	9.5948	.3934	.4043	10
40	1.1636	.3652	2.3183	9.6348	.4314	9.9629	.9182	9.5978	.3961	.4072	20
30	1.1606	.3617	2.2998	9.6383	.4348	9.9624	.9171	9.6007	.3988	.4102	30
20	1.1577	.3583	2.2817	9.6418	.4383	9.9619	.9159	9.6036	.4014	.4131	40
10	1.1548	.3548	2.2637	9.6452	.4418	9.9613	.9147	9.6065	.4041	.4160	50
66° 00'	1.1519	.3514	2.2460	9.6486	.4452	9.9607	.9136	9.6093	.4067	.4189	24° 00'
Deg	Radians	Log tan	Nat tan	Log cot	Nat cot	Log sin	Nat sin	Log cos	Nat cos	Radians	Deg

Table 1-5. Natural Trigonometric Functions and Their Logarithms (Continued)

Deg	Radians	Log cot	Nat cot	Log tan	Nat tan	Log cos	Nat cos	Log sin	Nat sin	Radians	Deg
66° 00'	1.1519	0.3514	2.2460	9.6486	0.4452	9.9607	0.9136	9.6093	0.4067	0.4189	24° 00'
50	1.1490	.3480	2.2286	9.6520	.4487	9.9602	.9124	9.6121	.4094	.4218	10
40	1.1461	.3447	2.2113	9.6554	.4522	9.9596	.9112	9.6149	.4120	.4247	20
30	1.1432	.3413	2.1943	9.6587	.4557	9.9590	.9100	9.6177	.4147	.4276	30
20	1.1403	.3380	2.1775	9.6620	.4592	9.9584	.9088	9.6205	.4173	.4305	40
10	1.1374	.3346	2.1609	9.6654	.4628	9.9579	.9075	9.6232	.4200	.4334	50
65° 00'	1.1345	.3313	2.1445	9.6687	.4663	9.9573	.9063	9.6260	.4226	.4363	25° 00'
50	1.1316	.3280	2.1283	9.6720	.4699	9.9567	.9051	9.6287	.4253	.4392	10
40	1.1286	.3248	2.1123	9.6752	.4734	9.9561	.9038	9.6313	.4279	.4422	20
30	1.1257	.3215	2.0965	9.6785	.4770	9.9555	.9026	9.6340	.4305	.4451	30
20	1.1228	.3183	2.0809	9.6817	.4806	9.9549	.9013	9.6366	.4331	.4480	40
10	1.1199	.3150	2.0655	9.6850	.4841	9.9543	.9001	9.6392	.4358	.4509	50
64° 00'	1.1170	.3118	2.0503	9.6882	.4877	9.9537	.8988	9.6418	.4384	.4538	26° 00'
50	1.1141	.3086	2.0353	9.6914	.4913	9.9530	.8975	9.6444	.4410	.4567	10
40	1.1112	.3054	2.0204	9.6946	.4950	9.9524	.8962	9.6470	.4436	.4596	20
30	1.1083	.3023	2.0057	9.6977	.4986	9.9518	.8949	9.6495	.4462	.4625	30
20	1.1054	.2991	1.9912	9.7009	.5022	9.9512	.8936	9.6521	.4488	.4654	40
10	1.1025	.2960	1.9768	9.7040	.5059	9.9505	.8923	9.6546	.4514	.4683	50
63° 00'	1.0996	.2928	1.9626	9.7072	.5095	9.9499	.8910	9.6571	.4540	.4712	27° 00'
50	1.0966	.2897	1.9486	9.7103	.5132	9.9492	.8897	9.6595	.4566	.4741	10
40	1.0937	.2866	1.9347	9.7134	.5169	9.9486	.8884	9.6620	.4592	.4771	20
30	1.0908	.2835	1.9210	9.7165	.5206	9.9479	.8870	9.6644	.4618	.4800	30
20	1.0879	.2805	1.9074	9.7196	.5243	9.9473	.8857	9.6668	.4643	.4829	40
10	1.0850	.2774	1.8940	9.7226	.5280	9.9466	.8843	9.6692	.4669	.4858	50
62° 00'	1.0821	.2743	1.8807	9.7257	.5317	9.9459	.8830	9.6716	.4695	.4887	28° 00'
50	1.0792	.2713	1.8676	9.7287	.5355	9.9453	.8816	9.6740	.4720	.4916	10
40	1.0763	.2683	1.8546	9.7318	.5392	9.9446	.8802	9.6763	.4746	.4945	20
30	1.0734	.2652	1.8418	9.7348	.5430	9.9439	.8788	9.6787	.4772	.4974	30
20	1.0705	.2622	1.8291	9.7378	.5467	9.9432	.8774	9.6810	.4797	.5003	40
10	1.0676	.2592	1.8165	9.7408	.5505	9.9425	.8760	9.6833	.4823	.5032	50
61° 00'	1.0647	.2563	1.8041	9.7438	.5543	9.9418	.8746	9.6856	.4848	.5061	29° 00'
50	1.0617	.2533	1.7917	9.7467	.5581	9.9411	.8732	9.6878	.4874	.5091	10
40	1.0588	.2503	1.7796	9.7497	.5619	9.9404	.8718	9.6901	.4899	.5120	20
30	1.0559	.2474	1.7675	9.7526	.5658	9.9397	.8704	9.6923	.4924	.5149	30
20	1.0530	.2444	1.7556	9.7556	.5696	9.9390	.8689	9.6946	.4950	.5178	40
10	1.0501	.2415	1.7438	9.7585	.5735	9.9383	.8675	9.6968	.4975	.5207	50

Deg	Radians	Log tan	Nat tan	Log cot	Nat cot	Log sin	Nat sin	Log cos	Nat cos	Radians	Deg
60° 00'	1.0472	.2386	1.7321	9.7614	.5774	9.9375	.8660	9.6990	.5000	.5236	30° 00'
50	1.0443	.2357	1.7205	9.7644	.5812	9.9368	.8646	9.7012	.5025	.5265	10
40	1.0414	.2328	1.7090	9.7673	.5851	9.9361	.8631	9.7033	.5050	.5294	20
30	1.0385	.2299	1.6977	9.7702	.5891	9.9353	.8616	9.7055	.5075	.5323	30
20	1.0356	.2270	1.6864	9.7730	.5930	9.9346	.8602	9.7076	.5100	.5352	40
10	1.0327	.2241	1.6753	9.7759	.5969	9.9338	.8587	9.7097	.5125	.5381	50
59° 00'	1.0297	.2212	1.6643	9.7788	.6009	9.9331	.8572	9.7118	.5150	.5411	31° 00'
50	1.0268	.2184	1.6534	9.7816	.6048	9.9323	.8557	9.7139	.5175	.5440	10
40	1.0239	.2155	1.6426	9.7845	.6088	9.9315	.8542	9.7160	.5200	.5469	20
30	1.0210	.2127	1.6319	9.7873	.6128	9.9308	.8526	9.7181	.5225	.5498	30
20	1.0181	.2099	1.6213	9.7902	.6168	9.9300	.8511	9.7201	.5250	.5527	40
10	1.0152	.2070	1.6107	9.7930	.6208	9.9292	.8496	9.7222	.5275	.5556	50
58° 00'	1.0123	.2042	1.6003	9.7958	.6249	9.9284	.8481	9.7242	.5299	.5585	32° 00'
50	1.0094	.2014	1.5900	9.7986	.6289	9.9276	.8465	9.7262	.5324	.5614	10
40	1.0065	.1986	1.5798	9.8014	.6330	9.9268	.8450	9.7282	.5348	.5643	20
30	1.0036	.1958	1.5697	9.8042	.6371	9.9260	.8434	9.7302	.5373	.5672	30
20	1.0007	.1930	1.5597	9.8070	.6412	9.9252	.8418	9.7322	.5398	.5701	40
10	0.9977	.1903	1.5497	9.8098	.6453	9.9244	.8403	9.7342	.5422	.5730	50
57° 00'	.9948	.1875	1.5399	9.8125	.6494	9.9236	.8387	9.7361	.5446	.5760	33° 00'
50	.9919	.1847	1.5301	9.8153	.6536	9.9228	.8371	9.7381	.5471	.5789	10
40	.9890	.1820	1.5204	9.8180	.6577	9.9219	.8355	9.7400	.5495	.5818	20
30	.9861	.1792	1.5108	9.8208	.6619	9.9211	.8339	9.7419	.5519	.5847	30
20	.9832	.1765	1.5013	9.8235	.6661	9.9203	.8323	9.7438	.5544	.5876	40
10	.9803	.1737	1.4919	9.8263	.6703	9.9194	.8307	9.7457	.5568	.5905	50
56° 00'	.9774	.1710	1.4826	9.8290	.6745	9.9186	.8290	9.7476	.5592	.5934	34° 00'
50	.9745	.1683	1.4733	9.8317	.6788	9.9177	.8274	9.7494	.5616	.5963	10
40	.9716	.1656	1.4641	9.8344	.6830	9.9169	.8258	9.7513	.5640	.5992	20
30	.9687	.1629	1.4550	9.8371	.6873	9.9160	.8241	9.7531	.5664	.6021	30
20	.9657	.1602	1.4460	9.8398	.6916	9.9151	.8225	9.7550	.5688	.6050	40
10	.9628	.1575	1.4370	9.8425	.6959	9.9143	.8208	9.7568	.5712	.6080	50
55° 00'	.9599	.1548	1.4282	9.8452	.7002	9.9134	.8192	9.7586	.5736	.6109	35° 00'
50	.9570	.1521	1.4193	9.8479	.7046	9.9125	.8175	9.7604	.5760	.6138	10
40	.9541	.1494	1.4106	9.8506	.7089	9.9116	.8158	9.7622	.5783	.6167	20
30	.9512	.1467	1.4020	9.8533	.7133	9.9107	.8141	9.7640	.5807	.6196	30
20	.9483	.1441	1.3934	9.8559	.7177	9.9098	.8124	9.7657	.5831	.6225	40
10	.9454	.1414	1.3848	9.8586	.7221	9.9089	.8107	9.7675	.5854	.6254	50
54° 00'	.9425	.1387	1.3764	9.8613	.7265	9.9080	.8090	9.7692	.5878	.6283	36° 00'
Deg	Radians	Log tan	Nat tan	Log cot	Nat cot	Log sin	Nat sin	Log cos	Nat cos	Radians	Deg

Table 1-5. Natural Trigonometric Functions and Their Logarithms (Continued)

Deg	Radians	Nat sin	Log sin	Nat cos	Log cos	Nat tan	Log tan	Nat cot	Log cot	Radians	Deg
36° 00′	0.6283	0.5878	9.7692	0.8090	9.9080	0.7265	9.8613	1.3764	0.1387	0.9425	54° 0′
10	.6312	.5901	9.7710	.8073	9.9070	.7310	9.8639	1.3680	.1361	.9396	50
20	.6341	.5925	9.7727	.8056	9.9061	.7355	9.8666	1.3597	.1334	.9367	40
30	.6370	.5948	9.7744	.8039	9.9052	.7400	9.8692	1.3514	.1308	.9338	30
40	.6400	.5972	9.7761	.8021	9.9042	.7445	9.8719	1.3432	.1282	.9308	20
50	.6429	.5995	9.7778	.8004	9.9033	.7490	9.8745	1.3351	.1255	.9279	10
37° 00′	.6458	.6018	9.7795	.7986	9.9024	.7536	9.8771	1.3270	.1229	.9250	53° 00′
10	.6487	.6041	9.7811	.7969	9.9014	.7581	9.8797	1.3190	.1203	.9221	50
20	.6516	.6065	9.7828	.7951	9.9004	.7627	9.8824	1.3111	.1176	.9192	40
30	.6545	.6088	9.7845	.7934	9.8995	.7673	9.8850	1.3032	.1150	.9163	30
40	.6574	.6111	9.7861	.7916	9.8985	.7720	9.8876	1.2954	.1124	.9134	20
50	.6603	.6134	9.7877	.7898	9.8975	.7766	9.8902	1.2876	.1098	.9105	10
38° 00′	.6632	.6157	9.7893	.7880	9.8965	.7813	9.8928	1.2799	.1072	.9076	52° 00′
10	.6661	.6180	9.7910	.7862	9.8955	.7860	9.8954	1.2723	.1046	.9047	50
20	.6690	.6202	9.7926	.7844	9.8946	.7907	9.8980	1.2647	.1020	.9018	40
30	.6720	.6225	9.7942	.7826	9.8935	.7954	9.9006	1.2572	.0994	.8988	30
40	.6749	.6248	9.7957	.7808	9.8925	.8002	9.9032	1.2497	.0968	.8959	20
50	.6778	.6271	9.7973	.7790	9.8915	.8050	9.9058	1.2423	.0942	.8930	10
39° 00′	.6807	.6293	9.7989	.7772	9.8905	.8098	9.9084	1.2349	.0916	.8901	51° 00′
10	.6836	.6316	9.8004	.7753	9.8895	.8146	9.9110	1.2276	.0891	.8872	50
20	.6865	.6338	9.8020	.7735	9.8884	.8195	9.9135	1.2203	.0865	.8843	40
30	.6894	.6361	9.8035	.7716	9.8874	.8243	9.9161	1.2131	.0839	.8814	30
40	.6923	.6383	9.8050	.7698	9.8864	.8292	9.9187	1.2059	.0813	.8785	20
50	.6952	.6406	9.8066	.7679	9.8853	.8342	9.9213	1.1988	.0788	.8756	10
40° 00′	.6981	.6428	9.8081	.7660	9.8843	.8391	9.9238	1.1918	.0762	.8727	50° 00′
10	.7010	.6450	9.8096	.7642	9.8832	.8441	9.9264	1.1847	.0736	.8698	50
20	.7039	.6472	9.8111	.7623	9.8821	.8491	9.9289	1.1778	.0711	.8668	40
30	.7069	.6495	9.8125	.7604	9.8811	.8541	9.9315	1.1709	.0685	.8639	30
40	.7098	.6517	9.8140	.7585	9.8800	.8591	9.9341	1.1640	.0659	.8610	20
50	.7127	.6539	9.8155	.7566	9.8789	.8642	9.9366	1.1572	.0634	.8581	10
41° 00′	.7156	.6561	9.8169	.7547	9.8778	.8693	9.9392	1.1504	.0608	.8552	49° 00′
10	.7185	.6583	9.8184	.7528	9.8767	.8744	9.9417	1.1436	.0583	.8523	50
20	.7214	.6604	9.8198	.7509	9.8756	.8796	9.9443	1.1369	.0557	.8494	40
30	.7243	.6626	9.8213	.7490	9.8745	.8847	9.9468	1.1303	.0532	.8465	30
40	.7272	.6648	9.8227	.7470	9.8733	.8899	9.9494	1.1237	.0507	.8436	20
50	.7301	.6670	9.8241	.7451	9.8722	.8952	9.9519	1.1171	.0481	.8407	10

Deg	Radians	Nat cos	Log cos	Nat sin	Log sin	Nat cot	Log cot	Nat tan	Log tan	Radians	Deg
42° 00'	.7330	.6691	9.8255	.7431	9.8711	.9004	9.9544	1.1106	.0456	.8378	48° 00'
10	.7359	.6713	9.8269	.7412	9.8699	.9057	9.9570	1.1041	.0430	.8348	50
20	.7389	.6734	9.8283	.7392	9.8688	.9110	9.9595	1.0977	.0405	.8319	40
30	.7418	.6756	9.8297	.7373	9.8676	.9163	9.9621	1.0913	.0380	.8290	30
40	.7447	.6777	9.8311	.7353	9.8665	.9217	9.9646	1.0850	.0354	.8261	20
50	.7476	.6799	9.8324	.7333	9.8653	.9271	9.9671	1.0786	.0329	.8232	10
43° 00'	.7505	.6820	9.8338	.7314	9.8641	.9325	9.9697	1.0724	.0303	.8203	47° 00'
10	.7534	.6841	9.8351	.7294	9.8630	.9380	9.9722	1.0661	.0278	.8174	50
20	.7563	.6862	9.8365	.7274	9.8618	.9435	9.9747	1.0599	.0253	.8145	40
30	.7592	.6884	9.8378	.7254	9.8606	.9490	9.9773	1.0538	.0228	.8116	30
40	.7621	.6905	9.8391	.7234	9.8594	.9545	9.9798	1.0477	.0202	.8087	20
50	.7650	.6926	9.8405	.7214	9.8582	.9601	9.9823	1.0416	.0177	.8058	10
44° 00'	.7679	.6947	9.8418	.7193	9.8569	.9657	9.9848	1.0355	.0152	.8029	46° 00'
10	.7709	.6968	9.8431	.7173	9.8557	.9713	9.9874	1.0295	.0126	.7999	50
20	.7738	.6988	9.8444	.7153	9.8545	.9770	9.9899	1.0236	.0101	.7970	40
30	.7767	.7009	9.8457	.7133	9.8532	.9827	9.9924	1.0176	.0076	.7941	30
40	.7796	.7030	9.8469	.7112	9.8520	.9884	9.9950	1.0117	.0051	.7912	20
50	.7825	.7051	9.8482	.7092	9.8507	.9942	9.9975	1.0058	.0025	.7883	10
45° 00'	.7854	.7071	9.8495	.7071	9.8495	1.0000	0.0000	1.0000	.0000	.7854	45° 00'
Deg	Radians	Nat cos	Log cos	Nat sin	Log sin	Nat cot	Log cot	Nat tan	Log tan	Radians	Deg

Table 1-6. Values and Logarithms of Exponential and Hyperbolic Functions

x	e^x Value	e^x log₁₀	e^{-x} (value)	sinh x Value	sinh x log₁₀	cosh x Value	cosh x log₁₀	tanh x (value)
0.00	1.0000	0.00000	1.00000	0.0000	$-\infty$	1.0000	0.00000	0.00000
0.01	1.0101	.00434	0.99005	.0100	$\bar{2}$.00001	1.0001	.00002	.01000
0.02	1.0202	.00869	.98020	.0200	$\bar{2}$.30106	1.0002	.00009	.02000
0.03	1.0305	.01303	.97045	.0300	$\bar{2}$.47719	1.0005	.00020	.02999
0.04	1.0408	.01737	.96079	.0400	$\bar{2}$.60218	1.0008	.00035	.03998
0.05	1.0513	.02171	.95123	.0500	$\bar{2}$.69915	1.0013	.00054	.04996
0.06	1.0618	.02606	.94176	.0600	$\bar{2}$.77841	1.0018	.00078	.05993
0.07	1.0725	.03040	.93239	.0701	$\bar{2}$.84545	1.0025	.00106	.06989
0.08	1.0833	.03474	.92312	.0801	$\bar{2}$.90355	1.0032	.00139	.07983
0.09	1.0942	.03909	.91393	.0901	$\bar{2}$.95483	1.0041	.00176	.08976
0.10	1.1052	.04343	.90484	.1002	$\bar{1}$.00072	1.0050	.00217	.09967
0.11	1.1163	.04777	.89583	.1102	$\bar{1}$.04227	1.0061	.00262	.10956
0.12	1.1275	.05212	.88692	.1203	$\bar{1}$.08022	1.0072	.00312	.11943
0.13	1.1388	.05646	.87809	.1304	$\bar{1}$.11517	1.0085	.00366	.12927
0.14	1.1503	.06080	.86936	.1405	$\bar{1}$.14755	1.0098	.00424	.13909
0.15	1.1618	.06514	.86071	.1506	$\bar{1}$.17772	1.0113	.00487	.14889
0.16	1.1735	.06949	.85214	.1607	$\bar{1}$.20597	1.0128	.00554	.15865
0.17	1.1853	.07383	.84366	.1708	$\bar{1}$.23254	1.0145	.00625	.16838
0.18	1.1972	.07817	.83527	.1810	$\bar{1}$.25762	1.0162	.00700	.17808
0.19	1.2092	.08252	.82696	.1911	$\bar{1}$.28136	1.0181	.00779	.18775
0.20	1.2214	.08686	.81873	.2013	$\bar{1}$.30392	1.0201	.00863	.19738
0.21	1.2337	.09120	.81058	.2115	$\bar{1}$.32541	1.0221	00951	.20697
0.22	1.2461	.09554	.80252	.2218	$\bar{1}$.34592	1.0243	.01043	.21652
0.23	1.2586	.09989	.79453	.2320	$\bar{1}$.36555	1.0256	.01139	.22603
0.24	1.2712	.10423	.78663	.2423	$\bar{1}$.38437	1.0289	.01239	.23550
0.25	1.2840	.10857	.77880	.2526	$\bar{1}$.40245	1.0314	.01343	.24492
0.26	1.2969	.11292	.77105	.2629	$\bar{1}$.41986	1.0340	.01452	.25430
0.27	1.3100	.11726	.76338	.2733	$\bar{1}$.43663	1.0367	.01564	.26362
0.28	1.3231	.12160	.75578	.2837	$\bar{1}$.45282	1.0395	.01681	.27291
0.29	1.3364	.12595	.74826	.2941	$\bar{1}$.46847	1.0423	.01801	.28213
0.30	1.3499	.13029	.74082	.3045	$\bar{1}$.48362	1.0453	.01926	.29131
0.31	1.3634	.13463	.73345	.3150	$\bar{1}$.49830	1.0484	.02054	.30044
0.32	1.3771	.13897	.72615	.3255	$\bar{1}$.51254	1.0516	.02187	.30951
0.33	1.3910	.14332	.71892	.3360	$\bar{1}$.52637	1.0549	.02323	.31852
0.34	1.4049	.14766	.71177	.3466	$\bar{1}$.53981	1.0584	.02463	.32748
0.35	1.4191	.15200	.70469	.3572	$\bar{1}$.55290	1.0619	.02607	.33638
0.36	1.4333	.15635	.69768	.3678	$\bar{1}$.56564	1.0655	.02755	.34521
0.37	1.4477	.16069	.69073	.3785	$\bar{1}$.57807	1.0692	.02907	.35399
0.38	1.4623	.16503	.68386	.3892	$\bar{1}$.59019	1.0731	.03063	.36271
0.39	1.4770	.16937	.67706	.4000	$\bar{1}$.60202	1.0770	.03222	.37136
0.40	1.4918	.17372	.67032	.4108	$\bar{1}$ 61358	1.0811	.03385	.37995
0.41	1.5068	.17806	.66365	.4216	$\bar{1}$.62488	1.0852	.03552	.38847
0.42	1.5220	.18240	.65705	.4325	$\bar{1}$.63594	1.0895	.03723	.39693
0.43	1 5373	.18675	.65051	.4434	$\bar{1}$.64677	1.0939	.03897	.40532
0.44	1.5527	.19109	.64404	.4543	$\bar{1}$.65738	1.0984	.04075	.41364
0.45	1.5683	.19543	.63763	.4653	$\bar{1}$.66777	1.1030	.04256	.42190
0.46	1.5841	.19978	.63128	.4764	$\bar{1}$.67797	1.1077	.04441	.43008
0.47	1.6000	.20412	.62500	.4875	$\bar{1}$.68797	1.1125	.04630	.43820
0.48	1.6161	.20846	.61878	.4986	$\bar{1}$.69779	1.1174	.04822	.44624
0.49	1.6323	.21280	.61263	.5098	$\bar{1}$.70744	1.1225	.05018	.45422
0.50	1.6487	.21715	.60653	.5211	$\bar{1}$.71692	1.1276	.05217	.46212

Table 1-6. Values and Logarithms of Exponential and Hyperbolic Functions (Continued)

x	e^x Value	e^x $\log_{10}$	e^{-x} (value)	$\sinh x$ Value	$\sinh x$ $\log_{10}$	$\cosh x$ Value	$\cosh x$ $\log_{10}$	$\tanh x$ (value)
0.50	1.6487	0.21715	0.60653	0.5211	1̄.71692	1.1276	0.05217	0.46212
0.51	1.6653	.22149	.60050	0.5324	1̄.72624	1.1329	.05419	.46995
0.52	1.6820	.22583	.59452	0.5438	1̄.73540	1.1383	.05625	.47770
0.53	1.6989	.23018	.58860	0.5552	1̄.74442	1.1438	.05834	.48538
0.54	1.7160	.23452	.58275	0.5666	1̄.75330	1.1494	.06046	.49299
0.55	1.7333	.23886	.57695	0.5782	1̄.76204	1.1551	.06262	.50052
0.56	1.7507	.24320	.57121	0.5897	1̄.77065	1.1609	.06481	.50798
0.57	1.7683	.24755	.56553	0.6014	1̄.77914	1.1669	.06703	.51536
0.58	1.7860	.25189	.55990	0.6131	1̄.78751	1.1730	.06929	.52267
0.59	1.8040	.25623	.55433	0.6248	1̄.79576	1.1792	.07157	.52990
0.60	1.8221	.26058	.54881	0.6367	1̄.80390	1.1855	.07389	.53705
0.61	1.8404	.26492	.54335	0.6485	1̄.81194	1.1919	.07624	.54413
0.62	1.8589	.26926	.53794	0.6605	1̄.81987	1.1984	.07861	.55113
0.63	1.8776	.27361	.53259	0.6725	1̄.82770	1.2051	.08102	.55805
0.64	1.8965	.27795	.52729	0.6846	1̄.83543	1.2119	.08346	.56490
0.65	1.9155	.28229	.52205	0.6967	1̄.84308	1.2188	.08593	.57167
0.66	1.9348	.28664	.51685	0.7090	1̄.85063	1.2258	.08843	.57836
0.67	1.9542	.29098	.51171	0.7213	1̄.85809	1.2330	.09095	.58498
0.68	1.9739	.29532	.50662	0.7336	1̄.86548	1.2402	.09351	.59152
0.69	1.9937	.29966	.50158	0.7461	1̄.87278	1.2476	.09609	.59798
0.70	2.0138	.30401	.49659	0.7586	1̄.88000	1.2552	.09870	.60437
0.71	2.0340	.30835	.49164	0.7712	1̄.88715	1.2628	.10134	.61068
0.72	2.0544	.31269	.48675	0.7838	1̄.89423	1.2706	.10401	.61691
0.73	2.0751	.31703	.48191	0.7966	1̄.90123	1.2785	.10670	.62307
0.74	2.0959	.32138	.47711	0.8094	1̄.90817	1.2865	.10942	.62915
0.75	2.1170	.32572	.47237	0.8223	1̄.91504	1.2947	.11216	.63515
0.76	2.1383	.33006	.46767	0.8353	1̄.92185	1.3030	.11493	.64108
0.77	2.1598	.33441	.46301	0.8484	1̄.92859	1.3114	.11773	.64693
0.78	2.1815	.33875	.45841	0.8615	1̄.93527	1.3199	.12055	.65271
0.79	2.2034	.34309	.45384	0.8748	1̄.94190	1.3286	.12340	.65841
0.80	2.2255	.34744	.44933	0.8881	1̄.94846	1.3374	.12627	.66404
0.81	2.2479	.35178	.44486	0.9015	1̄.95498	1.3464	.12917	.66959
0.82	2.2705	.35612	.44043	0.9150	1̄.96144	1.3555	.13209	.67507
0.83	2.2933	.36046	.43605	0.9286	1̄.96784	1.3647	.13503	.68048
0.84	2.3164	.36481	.43171	0.9423	1̄.97420	1.3740	.13800	.68581
0.85	2.3396	.36915	.42741	0.9561	1̄.98051	1.3835	.14099	.69107
0.86	2.3632	.37349	.42316	0.9700	1̄.98677	1.3932	.14400	.69626
0.87	2.3869	.37784	.41895	0.9840	1̄.99299	1.4029	.14704	.70137
0.88	2.4109	.38218	.41478	0.9981	1̄.99916	1.4128	.15009	.70642
0.89	2.4351	.38652	.41066	1.0122	0.00528	1.4229	.15317	.71139
0.90	2.4596	.39087	.40657	1.0265	.01137	1.4331	.15627	.71630
0.91	2.4843	.39521	.40252	1.0409	.01741	1.4434	.15939	.72113
0.92	2.5093	.39955	.39852	1.0554	.02341	1.4539	.16254	.72590
0.93	2.5345	.40389	.39455	1.0700	.02937	1.4645	.16570	.73059
0.94	2.5600	.40824	.39063	1.0847	.03530	1.4753	.16888	.73522
0.95	2.5857	.41258	.38674	1.0995	.04119	1.4862	.17208	.73978
0.96	2.6117	.41692	.38289	1.1144	.04704	1.4973	.17531	.74428
0.97	2.6379	.42127	.37908	1.1294	.05286	1.5085	.17855	.74870
0.98	2.6645	.42561	.37531	1.1446	.05864	1.5199	.18181	.75307
0.99	2.6912	.42995	.37158	1.1598	.06439	1.5314	.18509	.75736
1.00	2.7183	.43429	.36788	1.1752	.07011	1.5431	.18839	.76159

Table 1-6. Values and Logarithms of Exponential and Hyperbolic Functions (Continued)

x	e^x Value	e^x $\log_{10}$	e^{-x} (value)	$\sinh x$ Value	$\sinh x$ $\log_{10}$	$\cosh x$ Value	$\cosh x$ $\log_{10}$	$\tanh x$ (value)
1.00	2.7183	0.43429	0.36788	1.1752	0.07011	1.5431	0.18839	0.76159
1.01	2.7456	.43864	.36422	1.1907	.07580	1.5549	.19171	.76576
1.02	2.7732	.44298	.36060	1.2063	.08146	1.5669	.19504	.76987
1.03	2.8011	.44732	.35701	1.2220	.08708	1.5790	.19839	.77391
1.04	2.8292	.45167	.35345	1.2379	.09268	1.5913	.20176	.77789
1.05	2.8577	.45601	.34994	1.2539	.09825	1.6038	.20515	.78181
1.06	2.8864	.46035	.34646	1.2700	.10379	1.6164	.20855	.78566
1.07	2.9154	.46470	.34301	1.2862	.10930	1.6292	.21197	.78946
1.08	2.9447	.46904	.33960	1.3025	.11479	1.6421	.21541	.79320
1.09	2.9743	.47338	.33622	1.3190	.12025	1.6552	.21886	.79688
1.10	3.0042	.47772	.33287	1.3356	.12569	1.6685	.22233	.80050
1.11	3.0344	.48207	.32956	1.3524	.13111	1.6820	.22582	.80406
1.12	3.0649	.48641	.32628	1.3693	.13649	1.6956	.22931	.80757
1.13	3.0957	.49075	.32303	1.3863	.14186	1.7093	.23283	.81102
1.14	3.1268	.49510	.31982	1.4035	.14720	1.7233	.23636	.81441
1.15	3.1582	.49944	.31664	1.4208	.15253	1.7374	.23990	.81775
1.16	3.1899	.50378	.31349	1.4382	.15783	1.7517	.24346	.82104
1.17	3.2220	.50812	.31037	1.4558	.16311	1.7662	.24703	.82427
1.18	3.2544	.51247	.30728	1.4735	.16836	1.7808	.25062	.82745
1.19	3.2871	.51681	.30422	1.4914	.17360	1.7957	.25422	.83058
1.20	3.3201	.52115	.30119	1.5095	.17882	1.8107	.25784	.83365
1.21	3.3535	.52550	.29820	1.5276	.18402	1.8258	.26146	.83668
1.22	3.3872	.52984	.29523	1.5460	.18920	1.8412	.26510	.83965
1.23	3.4212	.53418	.29229	1.5645	.19437	1.8568	.26876	.84258
1.24	3.4556	.53853	.28938	1.5831	.19951	1.8725	.27242	.84546
1.25	3.4903	.54287	.28650	1.6019	.20464	1.8884	.27610	.84828
1.26	3.5254	.54721	.28365	1.6209	.20975	1.9045	.27979	.85106
1.27	3.5609	.55155	.28083	1.6400	.21485	1.9208	.28349	.85380
1.28	3.5966	.55590	.27804	1.6593	.21993	1.9373	.28721	.85648
1.29	3.6328	.56024	.27527	1.6788	.22499	1.9540	.29093	.85913
1.30	3.6693	.56458	.27253	1.6984	.23004	1.9709	.29467	.86172
1.31	3.7062	.56893	.26982	1.7182	.23507	1.9880	.29842	.86428
1.32	3.7434	.57327	.26714	1.7381	.24009	2.0053	.30217	.86678
1.33	3.7810	.57761	.26448	1.7583	.24509	2.0228	.30594	.86925
1.34	3.8190	.58195	.26185	1.7786	.25008	2.0404	.30972	.87167
1.35	3.8574	.58630	.25924	1.7991	.25505	2.0583	.31352	.87405
1.36	3.8962	.59064	.25666	1.8198	.26002	2.0764	.31732	.87639
1.37	3.9354	.59498	.25411	1.8406	.26496	2.0947	.32113	.87869
1.38	3.9749	.59933	.25158	1.8617	.26990	2.1132	.32495	.88095
1.39	4.0149	.60367	.24908	1.8829	.27482	2.1320	.32878	.88317
1.40	4.0552	.60801	.24660	1.9043	.27974	2.1509	.33262	.88535
1.41	4.0960	.61236	.24414	1.9259	.28464	2.1700	.33647	.88749
1.42	4.1371	.61670	.24171	1.9477	.28952	2.1894	.34033	.88960
1.43	4.1787	.62104	.23931	1.9697	.29440	2.2090	.34420	.89167
1.44	4.2207	.62538	.23693	1.9919	.29926	2.2288	.34807	.89370
1.45	4.2631	.62973	.23457	2.0143	.30412	2.2488	.35196	.89569
1.46	4.3060	.63407	.23224	2.0369	.30896	2.2691	.35585	.89765
1.47	4.3492	.63841	.22993	2.0597	.31379	2.2896	.35976	.89958
1.48	4.3929	.64276	.22764	2.0827	.31862	2.3103	.36367	.90147
1.49	4.4371	.64710	.22537	2.1059	.32343	2.3312	.36759	.90332
1.50	4.4817	.65144	.22313	2.1293	.32823	2.3524	.37151	.90515

Table 1-6. Values and Logarithms of Exponential and Hyperbolic Functions (Continued)

x	e^x Value	e^x log₁₀	e^{-x} (value)	sinh x Value	sinh x log₁₀	cosh x Value	cosh x log₁₀	tanh x (value)
1.50	4.4817	0.65144	0.22313	2.1293	0.32823	2.3524	0.37151	0.90515
1.51	4.5267	.65578	.22091	2.1529	.33303	2.3738	.37545	.90694
1.52	4.5722	.66013	.21871	2.1768	.33781	2.3955	.37939	.90870
1.53	4.6182	.66447	.21654	2.2008	.34258	2.4174	.38334	.91042
1.54	4.6646	.66881	.21438	2.2251	.34735	2.4395	.38730	.91212
1.55	4.7115	.67316	.21225	2.2496	.35211	2.4619	.39126	.91379
1.56	4.7588	.67750	.21014	2.2743	.35686	2.4845	.39524	.91542
1.57	4.8066	.68184	.20805	2.2993	.36160	2.5073	.39921	.91703
1.58	4.8550	.68619	.20598	2.3245	.36633	2.5305	.40320	.91860
1.59	4.9037	.69053	.20393	2.3499	.37105	2.5538	.40719	.92015
1.60	4.9530	.69487	.20190	2.3756	.37577	2.5775	.41119	.92167
1.61	5.0028	.69921	.19989	2.4015	.38048	2.6013	.41520	.92316
1.62	5.0531	.70356	.19790	2.4276	.38518	2.6255	.41921	.92462
1.63	5.1039	.70790	.19593	2.4540	.38987	2.6499	.42323	.92606
1.64	5.1552	.71224	.19398	2.4806	.39456	2.6746	.42725	.92747
1.65	5.2070	.71659	.19205	2.5075	.39923	2.6995	.43129	.92886
1.66	5.2593	.72093	.19014	2.5346	.40391	2.7247	.43532	.93022
1.67	5.3122	.72527	.18825	2.5620	.40857	2.7502	.43937	.93155
1.68	5.3656	.72961	.18637	2.5896	.41323	2.7760	.44341	.93286
1.69	5.4195	.73396	.18452	2.6175	.41788	2.8020	.44747	.93415
1.70	5.4739	.73830	.18268	2.6456	.42253	2.8283	.45153	.93541
1.71	5.5290	.74264	.18087	2.6740	.42717	2.8549	.45559	.93665
1.72	5.5845	.74699	.17907	2.7027	.43180	2.8818	.45966	.93736
1.73	5.6407	.75133	.17728	2.7317	.43643	2.9090	.46374	.93906
1.74	5.6973	.75567	.17552	2.7609	.44105	2.9364	.46782	.94023
1.75	5.7546	.76002	.17377	2.7904	.44567	2.9642	.47191	.94138
1.76	5.8124	.76436	.17204	2.8202	.45028	2.9922	.47600	.94250
1.77	5.8709	.76870	.17033	2.8503	.45488	3.0206	.48009	.94361
1.78	5.9299	.77304	.16864	2.8806	.45948	3.0492	.48419	.94470
1.79	5.9895	.77739	.16696	2.9112	.46408	3.0782	.48830	.94576
1.80	6.0496	.78173	.16530	2.9422	.46867	3.1075	.49241	.94681
1.81	6.1104	.78607	.16365	2.9734	.47325	3.1371	.49652	.94783
1.82	6.1719	.79042	.16203	3.0049	.47783	3.1669	.50064	.94884
1.83	6.2339	.79476	.16041	3.0367	.48241	3.1972	.50476	.94983
1.84	6.2965	.79910	.15882	3.0689	.48698	3.2277	.50889	.95080
1.85	6.3598	.80344	.15724	3.1013	.49154	3.2585	.51302	.95175
1.86	6.4237	.80779	.15567	3.1340	.49610	3.2897	.51716	.95268
1.87	6.4883	.81213	.15412	3.1671	.50066	3.3212	.52130	.95359
1.88	6.5535	.81647	.15259	3.2005	.50521	3.3530	.52544	.95449
1.89	6.6194	.82082	.15107	3.2341	.50976	3.3852	.52959	.95537
1.90	6.6859	.82516	.14957	3.2682	.51430	3.4177	.53374	.95624
1.91	6.7531	.82950	.14808	3.3025	.51884	3.4506	.53789	.95709
1.92	6.8210	.83385	.14661	3.3372	.52338	3.4838	.54205	.95792
1.93	6.8895	.83819	.14515	3.3722	.52791	3.5173	.54621	.95873
1.94	6.9588	.84253	.14370	3.4075	.53244	3.5512	.55038	.95953
1.95	7.0287	.84687	.14227	3.4432	.53696	3.5855	.55455	.96032
1.96	7.0993	.85122	.14086	3.4792	.54148	3.6201	.55872	.96109
1.97	7.1707	.85556	.13946	3.5156	.54600	3.6551	.56290	.96185
1.98	7.2427	.85990	.13807	3.5523	.55051	3.6904	.56707	.96259
1.99	7.3155	.86425	.13670	3.5894	.55502	3.7261	.57126	.96331
2.00	7.3891	.86859	.13534	3.6269	.55953	3.7622	.57544	.96403

Table 1-6. Values and Logarithms of Exponential and Hyperbolic Functions (Continued)

x	e^x Value	e^x $\log_{10}$	e^{-x} (value)	$\sinh x$ Value	$\sinh x$ $\log_{10}$	$\cosh x$ Value	$\cosh x$ $\log_{10}$	$\tanh x$ (value)
2.00	7.3891	0.86859	0.13534	3.6269	0.55953	3.7622	0.57544	0.96403
2.01	7.4633	0.87293	.13399	3.6647	.56403	3.7987	.57963	.96473
2.02	7.5383	0.87727	.13266	3.7028	.56853	3.8355	.58382	.96541
2.03	7.6141	0.88162	.13134	3.7414	.57303	3.8727	.58802	.96609
2.04	7.6906	0.88596	.13003	3.7803	.57753	3.9103	.59221	.96675
2.05	7.7679	0.89030	.12873	3.8196	.58202	3.9483	.59641	.96740
2.06	7.8460	0.89465	.12745	3.8593	.58650	3.9867	.60061	.96803
2.07	7.9248	0.89899	.12619	3.8993	.59099	4.0255	.60482	.96865
2.08	8.0045	0.90333	.12493	3.9398	.59547	4.0647	.60903	.96926
2.09	8.0849	0.90768	.12369	3.9806	.59995	4.1043	.61324	.96986
2.10	8.1662	0.91202	.12246	4.0219	.60443	4.1443	.61745	.97045
2.11	8.2482	0.91636	.12124	4.0635	.60890	4.1847	.62167	.97103
2.12	8.3311	0.92070	.12003	4.1056	.61337	4.2256	.62589	.97159
2.13	8.4149	0.92505	.11884	4.1480	.61784	4.2669	.63011	.97215
2.14	8.4994	0.92939	.11765	4.1909	.62231	4.3085	.63433	.97269
2.15	8.5849	0.93373	.11648	4.2342	.62677	4.3507	.63856	.97323
2.16	8.6711	0.93808	.11533	4.2779	.63123	4.3932	.64278	.97375
2.17	8.7583	0.94242	.11418	4.3221	.63569	4.4362	.64701	.97426
2.18	8.8463	0.94676	.11304	4.3666	.64015	4.4797	.65125	.97477
2.19	8.9352	0.95110	.11192	4.4116	.64460	4.5236	.65548	.97526
2.20	9.0250	0.95545	.11080	4.4571	.64905	4.5679	.65972	.97574
2.21	9.1157	0.95979	.10970	4.5030	.65350	4.6127	.66396	.97622
2.22	9.2073	0.96413	.10861	4.5494	.65795	4.6580	.66820	.97668
2.23	9.2999	0.96848	.10753	4.5962	.66240	4.7037	.67244	.97714
2.24	9.3933	0.97282	.10646	4.6434	.66684	4.7499	.67668	.97759
2.25	9.4877	0.97716	.10540	4.6912	.67128	4.7966	.68093	.97803
2.26	9.5831	0.98151	.10435	4.7394	.67572	4.8437	.68518	.97846
2.27	9.6794	0.98585	.10331	4.7880	.68016	4.8914	.68943	.97888
2.28	9.7767	0.99019	.10228	4.8372	.68459	4.9395	.69368	.97929
2.29	9.8749	0.99453	.10127	4.8868	.68903	4.9881	.69794	.97970
2.30	9.9742	0.99888	.10026	4.9370	.69346	5.0372	.70219	.98010
2.31	10.074	1.00322	.09926	4.9876	.69789	5.0868	.70645	.98049
2.32	10.176	1.00756	.09827	5.0387	.70232	5.1370	.71071	.98087
2.33	10.278	1.01191	.09730	5.0903	.70675	5.1876	.71497	.98124
2.34	10.381	1.01625	.09633	5.1425	.71117	5.2388	.71923	.98161
2.35	10.486	1.02059	.09537	5.1951	.71559	5.2905	.72349	.98197
2.36	10.591	1.02493	.09442	5.2483	.72002	5.3427	.72776	.98233
2.37	10.697	1.02928	.09348	5.3020	.72444	5.3954	.73203	.98267
2.38	10.805	1.03362	.09255	5.3562	.72885	5.4487	.73630	.98301
2.39	10.913	1.03796	.09163	5.4109	.73327	5.5026	.74056	.98335
2.40	11.023	1.04231	.09072	5.4662	.73769	5.5569	.74484	.98367
2.41	11.134	1.04665	.08982	5.5221	.74210	5.6119	.74911	.98400
2.42	11.246	1.05099	.08892	5.5785	.74652	5.6674	.75338	.98431
2.43	11.359	1.05534	.08804	5.6354	.75093	5.7235	.75766	.98462
2.44	11.473	1.05968	.08716	5.6929	.75534	5.7801	.76194	.98492
2.45	11.588	1.06402	.08629	5.7510	.75975	5.8373	.76621	.98522
2.46	11.705	1.06836	.08543	5.8097	.76415	5.8951	.77049	.98551
2.47	11.822	1.07271	.08458	5.8689	.76856	5.9535	.77477	.98579
2.48	11.941	1.07705	.08374	5.9288	.77296	6.0125	.77906	.98607
2.49	12.061	1.08139	.08291	5.9892	.77737	6.0721	.78334	.98635
2.50	12.182	1.08574	.08208	6.0502	.78177	6.1323	.78762	.98661

Table 1-6. Values and Logarithms of Exponential and Hyperbolic Functions (Continued)

x	e^x		e^{-x} (value)	$\sinh x$		$\cosh x$		$\tanh x$ (value)
	Value	$\log_{10}$		Value	$\log_{10}$	Value	$\log_{10}$	
2.50	12.182	1.08574	0.08208	6.0502	0.78177	6.1323	0.78762	0.98661
2.51	12.305	1.09008	.08127	6.1118	.78617	6.1931	.79191	.98688
2.52	12.429	1.09442	.08046	6.1741	.79057	6.2545	.79619	.98714
2.53	12.554	1.09877	.07966	6.2369	.79497	6.3166	.80048	.98739
2.54	12.680	1.10311	.07887	6.3004	.79937	6.3793	.80477	.98764
2.55	12.807	1.10745	.07808	6.3645	.80377	6.4426	.80906	.98788
2.56	12.936	1.11179	.07730	6.4293	.80816	6.5066	.81335	.98812
2.57	13.066	1.11614	.07654	6.4946	.81256	6.5712	.81764	.98835
2.58	13.197	1.12048	.07577	6.5607	.81695	6.6365	.82194	.98858
2.59	13.330	1.12482	.07502	6.6274	.82134	6.7024	.82623	.98881
2.60	13.464	1.12917	.07427	6.6947	.82573	6.7690	.83052	.98903
2.61	13.599	1.13351	.07353	6.7628	.83012	6.8363	.83482	.98924
2.62	13.736	1.13785	.07280	6.8315	.83451	6.9043	.83912	.98946
2.63	13.874	1.14219	.07208	6.9008	.83890	6.9729	.84341	.98966
2.64	14.013	1.14654	.07136	6.9709	.84329	7.0423	.84771	.98987
2.65	14.154	1.15088	.07065	7.0417	.84768	7.1123	.85201	.99007
2.66	14.296	1.15522	.06995	7.1132	.85206	7.1831	.85631	.99026
2.67	14.440	1.15957	.06925	7.1854	.85645	7.2546	.86061	.99045
2.68	14.585	1.16391	.06856	7.2583	.86083	7.3268	.86492	.99064
2.69	14.732	1.16825	.06788	7.3319	.86522	7.3998	.86922	.99083
2.70	14.880	1.17260	.06721	7.4063	.86960	7.4735	.87352	.99101
2.71	15.029	1.17694	.06654	7.4814	.87398	7.5479	.87783	.99118
2.72	15.180	1.18128	.06587	7.5572	.87836	7.6231	.88213	.99136
2.73	15.333	1.18562	.06522	7.6338	.88274	7.6991	.88644	.99153
2.74	15.487	1.18997	.06457	7.7112	.88712	7.7758	.89074	.99170
2.75	15.643	1.19431	.06393	7.7894	.89150	7.8533	.89505	.99186
2.76	15.800	1.19865	.06329	7.8683	.89588	7.9316	.89936	.99202
2.77	15.959	1.20300	.06266	7.9480	.90026	8.0106	.90367	.99218
2.78	16.119	1.20734	.06204	8.0285	.90463	8.0905	.90798	.99233
2.79	16.281	1.21168	.06142	8.1098	.90901	8.1712	.91229	.99248
2.80	16.445	1.21602	.06081	8.1919	.91339	8.2527	.91660	.99263
2.81	16.610	1.22037	.06020	8.2749	.91776	8.3351	.92091	.99278
2.82	16.777	1.22471	.05961	8.3586	.92213	8.4182	.92522	.99292
2.83	16.945	1.22905	.05901	8.4432	.92651	8.5022	.92953	.99306
2.84	17.116	1.23340	.05843	8.5287	.93088	8.5871	.93385	.99320
2.85	17.288	1.23774	.05784	8.6150	.93525	8.6728	.93816	.99333
2.86	17.462	1.24208	.05727	8.7021	.93963	8.7594	.94247	.99346
2.87	17.637	1.24643	.05670	8.7902	.94400	8.8469	.94679	.99359
2.88	17.814	1.25077	.05613	8.8791	.94837	8.9352	.95110	.99372
2.89	17.993	1.25511	.05558	8.9689	.95274	9.0244	.95542	.99384
2.90	18.174	1.25945	.05502	9.0596	.95711	9.1146	.95974	.99396
2.91	18.357	1.26380	.05448	9.1512	.96148	9.2056	.96405	.99408
2.92	18.541	1.26814	.05393	9.2437	.96584	9.2976	.96837	.99420
2.93	18.728	1.27248	.05340	9.3371	.97021	9.3905	.97269	.99431
2.94	18.916	1.27683	.05287	9.4315	.97458	9.4844	.97701	.99443
2.95	19.106	1.28117	.05234	9.5268	.97895	9.5791	.98133	.99454
2.96	19.298	1.28551	.05182	9.6231	.98331	9.6749	.98565	.99464
2.97	19.492	1.28985	.05130	9.7203	.98763	9.7716	.98997	.99475
2.98	19.688	1.29420	.05079	9.8185	.99205	9.8693	.99429	.99485
2.99	19.886	1.29854	.05029	9.9177	.99641	9.9680	.99861	.99496
3.00	20.086	1.30288	.04979	10.018	1.00078	10.068	1.00293	.99505

Table 1-6. Values and Logarithms of Exponential and Hyperbolic Functions (Continued)

x	e^x Value	e^x log₁₀	e^{-x} (value)	sinh x Value	sinh x log₁₀	cosh x Value	cosh x log₁₀	tanh x (value)
3.00	20.086	1.30288	0.04979	10.018	1.00078	10.068	1.00293	0.99505
3.05	21.115	1.32460	.04736	10.534	1.02259	10.581	1.02454	0.99552
3.10	22.198	1.34631	.04505	11.076	1.04440	11.122	1.04616	0.99595
3.15	23.336	1.36803	.04285	11.647	1.06620	11.690	1.06779	0.99633
3.20	24.533	1.38974	.04076	12.246	1.08799	12.287	1.08943	0.99668
3.25	25.790	1.41146	.03877	12.876	1.10977	12.915	1.11108	0.99700
3.30	27.113	1.43317	.03688	13.538	1.13155	13.575	1.13273	0.99728
3.35	28.503	1.45489	.03508	14.234	1.15332	14.269	1.15439	0 99754
3.40	29.964	1.47660	.03337	14.965	1.17509	14.999	1.17605	0.99777
3.45	31.500	1.49832	.03175	15.734	1.19685	15.766	1.19772	0.99799
3.50	33.115	1.52003	.03020	16.543	1.21860	16.573	1.21940	0.99818
3.55	34.813	1.54175	.02872	17.392	1.24036	17.421	1.24107	0.99835
3.60	36.598	1.56346	.02732	18.286	1.26211	18.313	1.26275	0.99851
3.65	38.475	1.58517	.02599	19.224	1.28385	19.250	1.28444	0.99865
3.70	40.447	1.60689	.02472	20.211	1.30559	20.236	1.30612	0.99878
3.75	42.521	1.62860	.02352	21.249	1.32733	21.272	1.32781	0.99889
3.80	44.701	1.65032	.02237	22.339	1.34907	22.362	1.34951	0.99900
3.85	46.993	1.67203	.02128	23.486	1.37081	23.507	1.37120	0.99909
3.90	49.402	1.69375	.02024	24.691	1.39254	24.711	1.39290	0.99918
3.95	51.935	1.71546	.01925	25.958	1.41427	25.977	1.41459	0.99926
4.00	54.598	1.73718	.01832	27.290	1.43600	27.308	1.43629	0.99933
4.10	60.340	1.78061	.01657	30.162	1.47946	30.178	1.47970	0.99945
4.20	66.686	1.82404	.01500	33.336	1.52291	33.351	1.52310	0.99955
4.30	73.700	1.86747	.01357	36.843	1.56636	36.857	1.56652	0.99963
4.40	81.451	1.91090	.01227	40.719	1.60980	40.732	1.60993	0.99970
4.50	90.017	1.95433	.01111	45.003	1.65324	45.014	1.65335	0.99975
4.60	99.484	1.99775	.01005	49.737	1.69668	49.747	1.69677	0.99980
4.70	109.95	2.04118	.00910	54.969	1.74012	54.978	1.74019	0.99983
4.80	121.51	2.08461	.00823	60.751	1.78355	60.759	1.78361	0.99986
4.90	134.29	2.12804	.00745	67.141	1.82699	67.149	1.82704	0.99989
5.00	148.41	2.17147	.00674	74.203	1.87042	74.210	1.87046	0.99991
5.10	164.02	2.21490	.00610	82.008	1.91389	82.014	1.91389	0.99993
5.20	181.27	2.25833	.00552	90.633	1.95729	90.639	1.95731	0.99994
5.30	200.34	2.30176	.00499	100.17	2.00074	100.17	2.00074	0.99995
5.40	221.41	2.34519	.00452	110.70	2.04415	110.71	2.04417	0.99996
5.50	244.69	2.38862	.00409	122.34	2.08758	122.35	2.08760	0.99997
5.60	270.43	2.43205	.00370	135.21	2.13101	135.22	2.13103	0.99997
5.70	298.87	2.47548	.00335	149.43	2.17444	149.44	2.17445	0.99998
5.80	330.30	2.51891	.00303	165.15	2.21787	165.15	2.21788	0.99998
5.90	365.04	2.56234	.00274	182.52	2.26130	182.52	2.26131	0.99998
6.00	403.43	2.60577	.00248	201.71	2.30473	201.72	2.30474	0.99999
6.25	518.01	2.71434	.00193	259.01	2.41331	259.01	2.41331	0.99999
6.50	665.14	2.82291	.00150	332.57	2.52188	332.57	2.52189	1.00000
6.75	854.06	2.93149	.00117	427.03	2.63046	427.03	2.63046	1.00000
7.00	1096.6	3.04006	.00091	548.32	2.73903	548.32	2.73903	1.00000
7.50	1808.0	3.25721	.00055	904.02	2.95618	904.02	2.95618	1.00000
8.00	2981.0	3.47436	.00034	1490.5	3.17333	1490.5	3.17333	1.00000
8.50	4914.8	3.69150	.00020	2457.4	3.39047	2457.4	3.39047	1.00000
9.00	8103.1	3.90865	.00012	4051.5	3.60762	4051.5	3.60762	1.00000
9.50	13360.	4.12580	.00007	6679.9	3.82477	6679.9	3.82477	1.00000
10.00	22026.	4.34294	.00005	11013.	4.04191	11013.	4.04191	1.00000

Table 1-7. Capacities of Vertical Cylindrical Tanks

In United States Gallons

Diam Ft	Diam In.	Gal/ft depth	Diam Ft	Diam In.	Gal/ft depth	Diam Ft	Diam In.	Gal/ft depth	Diam Ft	Diam In.	Gal/ft depth
0	0		9	0	475.89	18	0	1,903.6	27	0	4,283.0
	3	0.37		3	502.70		3	1,956.8		3	4,362.7
	6	1.47		6	530.24		6	2,010.8		6	4,443.1
	9	3.31		9	558.51		9	2,065.5		9	4,524.3
1	0	5.88	10	0	587.52	19	0	2,120.9	28	0	4,606.1
	3	9.18		3	617.26		3	2,177.1		3	4,688.8
	6	13.22		6	647.74		6	2,234.0		6	4,772.1
	9	17.99		9	678.95		9	2,291.7		9	4,856.2
2	0	23.50	11	0	710.90	20	0	2,350.1	29	0	4,941.0
	3	29.74		3	743.58		3	2,409.2		3	5,026.6
	6	36.72		6	776.99		6	2,469.1		6	5,112.9
	9	44.43		9	811.14		9	2,529.6		9	5,199.9
3	0	52.88	12	0	846.03	21	0	2,591.0	30	...	5,283
	3	62.06		3	881.64		3	2,653.0	35	...	7,197
	6	71.97		6	918.00		6	2,715.8	40	...	9,400
	9	82.62		9	955.08		9	2,779.3	45	...	11,897
4	0	94.00	13	0	992.91	22	0	2,843.6	50	...	14,688
	3	106.12		3	1,031.5		3	2,908.6	55	...	17,772
	6	118.97		6	1,070.8		6	2,974.3	60	...	21,151
	9	132.56		9	1,110.8		9	3,040.8	70	...	28,788
5	0	146.88	14	0	1,151.5	23	0	3,108.0	80	...	37,601
	3	161.93		3	1,193.0		3	3,175.9	90	...	47,589
	6	177.72		6	1,235.3		6	3,244.6	100	...	58,753
	9	194.25		9	1,278.2		9	3,314.0			
6	0	211.51	15	0	1,321.9	24	0	3,384.1			
	3	229.50		3	1,366.3		3	3,455.0			
	6	248.23		6	1,411.5		6	3,526.6			
	9	267.69		9	1,457.4		9	3,598.9			
7	0	287.88	16	0	1,504.1	25	0	3,672.0			
	3	308.81		3	1,551.4		3	3,745.8			
	6	330.48		6	1,599.5		6	3,820.3			
	9	352.88		9	1,648.4		9	3,895.6			
8	0	376.01	17	0	1,697.9	26	0	3,971.6			
	3	399.88		3	1,748.2		3	4,048.4			
	6	424.48		6	1,799.3		6	4,125.9			
	9	449.82		9	1,851.1		9	4,204.1			

Table 1-8. Capacities of Horizontal Cylindrical Tanks with Flat Ends

Contents Given in United States Gallons for 1 Ft of Length

Tank diam, in.	Contents for various depths of liquid in inches										
	3	6	9	12	15	18	21	24	27	30	33
12	1.15	2.94	4.73	5.88							
18	1.45	3.86	6.61	9.36	11.77	13.22					
24	1.70	4.60	8.05	11.75	15.45	18.90	21.8	23.5			
30	1.91	5.23	9.27	13.72	18.36	23.00	27.5	31.5	34.8	36.7	
36	2.12	5.79	10.34	15.43	20.85	26.44	32.0	37.5	42.5	47.1	50.8
42	2.28	6.31	11.31	16.97	23.07	29.46	36.0	42.5	48.9	55.0	60.7
48	2.45	6.78	12.20	18.38	25.10	32.20	39.5	47.0	54.5	61.8	68.9
54	2.60	7.22	13.04	19.68	26.97	34.72	42.8	51.1	59.5	67.9	76.2
60	2.75	7.64	13.82	20.91	28.72	37.06	45.8	54.9	64.1	73.5	82.8
66	2.89	8.04	14.56	22.07	30.37	39.28	48.7	58.4	68.4	78.6	88.9
72	3.02	8.42	15.26	23.17	31.92	41.36	51.3	61.7	72.5	83.4	94.5
78	3.15	8.78	15.94	24.21	33.41	43.34	53.9	64.9	76.3	88.0	99.9
84	3.26	9.12	16.57	25.24	34.85	45.24	56.3	67.9	79.9	92.3	105.0
90	3.43	9.46	17.20	26.20	36.21	47.05	58.6	70.8	83.4	96.4	109.8
96	3.50	9.79	17.80	27.13	37.52	48.81	60.8	73.5	86.7	100.4	114.4
102	3.61	10.10	18.37	28.01	39.00	50.49	63.0	76.2	89.9	104.2	118.9
108	3.71	10.39	18.94	28.90	40.03	52.14	65.1	78.7	93.0	107.9	123.2

Tank diam, in.	Contents for various depths of liquid, in inches									
	36	39	42	45	48	51	54	57	60	63
36	52.9									
42	65.7	69.7	72.0							
48	75.6	81.8	87.2	91.6	94.0					
54	84.3	92.0	99.3	105.9	111.8	116.4	119.0			
60	92.0	101.1	109.8	118.2	126.0	133.1	139.3	144.1	146.9	
66	99.1	109.3	119.3	129.1	138.5	147.4	155.7	163.2	169.7	174.8
72	105.8	117.0	128.1	139.0	149.8	160.2	170.2	179.6	188.4	196.3
78	112.0	124.1	136.3	148.3	160.3	172.0	183.4	194.4	204.9	214.8
84	117.9	130.9	144.0	157.0	170.1	182.9	195.6	208.0	220.0	231.6
90	123.5	137.3	151.2	165.3	179.3	193.2	207.0	220.7	234.0	247.1
96	128.8	143.4	158.2	173.1	188.0	203.0	217.9	232.6	247.2	261.6
102	133.9	149.3	164.8	180.5	196.4	212.3	228.1	244.0	259.7	275.2
108	138.9	154.9	171.2	187.7	204.4	221.2	238.1	254.8	271.5	288.2

Tank diam, in.	Contents for various depths of liquid, in inches										
	66	69	72	75	78	81	84	90	96	102	108
66	177.7										
72	203.1	209	212								
78	224.0	232	239	245	248						
84	242.7	253	263	271	279	285	288				
90	259.7	272	283	294	304	313	321	330			
96	275.6	289	303	315	327	339	349	366	376		
102	290.6	306	320	335	348	361	374	396	414	424	
108	304.7	321	337	353	368	383	397	424	447	466	476

Table 1-8. Capacities of Horizontal Cylindrical Tanks with Flat Ends (Continued)

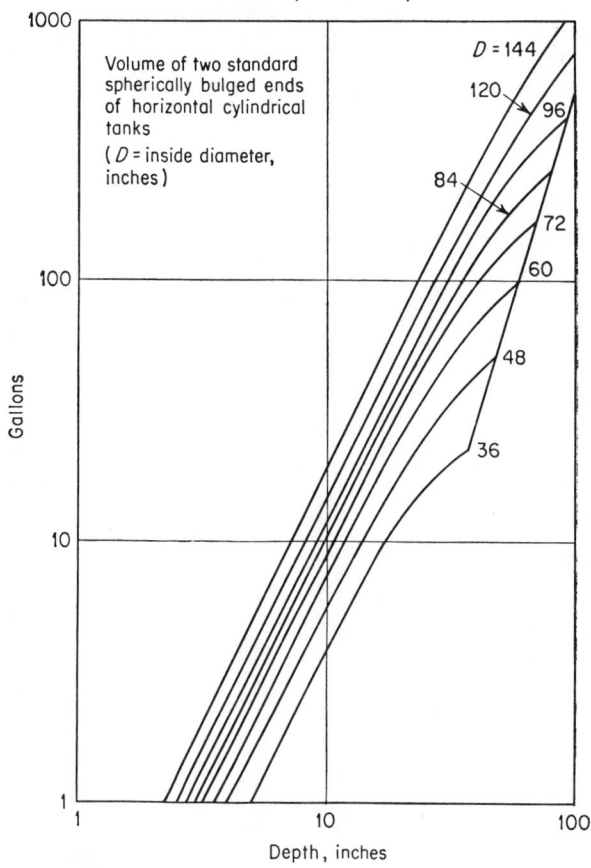

Volume of two standard spherically bulged ends of horizontal cylindrical tanks
(D = inside diameter, inches)

Depth, inches

Gallons

Example

GIVEN: 72 in. ID, horizontal tank, 10 feet long on the straight run with standard, spherically dished heads has a liquid depth of 60 in.

REQUIRED: Volume of liquid in tank.

SOLUTION: Volume in straight run (10 × 188.4)... 1,884 gal
Volume in dished ends...   152
Total volume.. 2,036 gal

Table 1-9. Temperature Conversion Table

The general formulas are

$$°F = (°C \times \tfrac{9}{5}) + 32 \qquad \text{and} \qquad °C = (°F - 32) \times \tfrac{5}{9}$$

The absolute temperature is defined by the statement that it is directly proportional to the pressure-volume product of an ideal gas. On the centigrade scale the absolute temperature is equal to $273.16 + t°C$. A temperature of 50°C is then equal to $273.16 + 50 = 323.16$ degrees centigrade absolute (°C abs) or Kelvin (°K). On the Fahrenheit scale the absolute temperature is equal to $460 + t°F$ and is termed degrees Rankine (°R).

The numbers in bold-face type refer to the temperature (in either centigrade or Fahrenheit degrees) which it is desired to convert into the other scale. If converting from Fahrenheit degrees to centigrade degrees, the equivalent temperature is in the left column, while if converting from degrees centigrade to degrees Fahrenheit, the equivalent temperature is in the column on the right. Interpolation factors are printed in the last two columns.

GIVEN: 200°C.
REQUIRED: Equivalent temperatures in degrees Fahrenheit, Rankine, and Kelvin.
SOLUTION: 200°C = 392°F
200°C = 200 + 273.16 = 473.16°K
200°C = 392 + 460 = 852°R

C		F	C		F	C		F	C		F
−262	−440		−15.0	5	41.0	12.8	55	131.0	66	150	302
−257	−430		−14.4	6	42.8	13.3	56	132.8	71	160	320
−251	−420		−13.9	7	44.6	13.9	57	134.6	77	170	338
−246	−410		−13.3	8	46.4	14.4	58	136.4	82	180	356
−240	−400		−12.8	9	48.2	15.0	59	138.2	88	190	374
−234	−390		−12.2	10	50.0	15.6	60	140.0	93	200	392
−229	−380		−11.7	11	51.8	16.1	61	141.8	99	210	410
−223	−370		−11.1	12	53.6	16.7	62	143.6	104	220	428
−218	−360		−10.6	13	55.4	17.2	63	145.4	110	230	446
−212	−350		−10.0	14	57.2	17.8	64	147.2	116	240	464
−207	−340		−9.44	15	59.0	18.3	65	149.0	121	250	482
−201	−330		−8.89	16	60.8	18.9	66	150.8	127	260	500
−196	−320		−8.33	17	62.6	19.4	67	152.6	132	270	518
−190	−310		−7.78	18	64.4	20.0	68	154.4	138	280	536
−184	−300		−7.22	19	66.2	20.6	69	156.2	143	290	554
−179	−290		−6.67	20	68.0	21.1	70	158.0	149	300	572
−173	−280		−6.11	21	69.8	21.7	71	159.8	154	310	590
−169	−273	−459.4	−5.56	22	71.6	22.2	72	161.6	160	320	608
−168	−270	−454	−5.00	23	73.4	22.8	73	163.4	166	330	626
−162	−260	−436	−4.44	24	75.2	23.3	74	165.2	171	340	644
−157	−250	−418	−3.89	25	77.0	23.9	75	167.0	177	350	662
−151	−240	−400	−3.33	26	78.8	24.4	76	168.8	182	360	680
−146	−230	−382	−2.78	27	80.6	25.0	77	170.6	188	370	698
−140	−220	−364	−2.22	28	82.4	25.6	78	172.4	193	380	716
−134	−210	−346	−1.67	29	84.2	26.1	79	174.2	199	390	734
−129	−200	−328	−1.11	30	86.0	26.7	80	176.0	204	400	752
−123	−190	−310	−0.56	31	87.8	27.2	81	177.8	210	410	770
−118	−180	−292	0	32	89.6	27.8	82	179.6	216	420	788
−112	−170	−274	0.56	33	91.4	28.3	83	181.4	221	430	806
−107	−160	−256	1.11	34	93.2	28.9	84	183.2	227	440	824
−101	−150	−238	1.67	35	95.0	29.4	85	185.0	232	450	842
−95.6	−140	−220	2.22	36	96.8	30.0	86	186.8	238	460	860
−90.0	−130	−202	2.78	37	98.6	30.6	87	188.6	243	470	878
−84.4	−120	−184	3.33	38	100.4	31.1	88	190.4	249	480	896
−78.9	−110	−166	3.89	39	102.2	31.7	89	192.2	254	490	914
−73.3	−100	−148	4.44	40	104.0	32.2	90	194.0	260	500	932
−67.8	−90	−130	5.00	41	105.8	32.8	91	195.8	266	510	950
−62.2	−80	−112	5.56	42	107.6	33.3	92	197.6	271	520	968
−56.7	−70	−94	6.11	43	109.4	33.9	93	199.4	277	530	986
−51.1	−60	−76	6.67	44	111.2	34.4	94	201.2	282	540	1004
−45.6	−50	−58	7.22	45	113.0	35.0	95	203.0	288	550	1022
−40.0	−40	−40	7.78	46	114.8	35.6	96	204.8	293	560	1040
−34.4	−30	−22	8.33	47	116.6	36.1	97	206.6	299	570	1058
−28.9	−20	−4	8.89	48	118.4	36.7	98	208.4	304	580	1076
−23.3	−10	14	9.44	49	120.2	37.2	99	210.2	310	590	1094
−17.8	0	32	10.0	50	122.0	38	100	212	316	600	1112
−17.2	1	33.8	10.6	51	123.8	43	110	230	321	610	1130
−16.7	2	35.6	11.1	52	125.6	49	120	248	327	620	1148
−16.1	3	37.4	11.7	53	127.4	54	130	266	332	630	1166
−15.6	4	39.2	12.2	54	129.2	60	140	284	338	640	1184

Table 1-9. Temperature Conversion Table (Continued)

C	F		C	F		C	F		C	F
343	650	1202	704	1300	2372	1066	1950	3542	1371	2500	4532
349	660	1220	710	1310	2390	1071	1960	3560	1377	2510	4550
354	670	1238	716	1320	2408	1077	1970	3578	1382	2520	4568
360	680	1256	721	1330	2426	1082	1980	3596	1388	2530	4586
366	690	1274	727	1340	2444	1088	1990	3614	1393	2540	4604
371	700	1292	732	1350	2462	1093	2000	3632	1399	2550	4622
377	710	1310	738	1360	2480	1099	2010	3650	1404	2560	4640
382	720	1328	743	1370	2498	1104	2020	3668	1410	2570	4658
388	730	1346	749	1380	2516	1110	2030	3686	1416	2580	4676
393	740	1364	754	1390	2534	1116	2040	3704	1421	2590	4694
399	750	1382	760	1400	2552	1121	2050	3722	1427	2600	4712
404	760	1400	766	1410	2570	1127	2060	3740	1432	2610	4730
410	770	1418	771	1420	2588	1132	2070	3758	1438	2620	4748
416	780	1436	777	1430	2606	1138	2080	3776	1443	2630	4766
421	790	1454	782	1440	2624	1143	2090	3794	1449	2640	4784
427	800	1472	788	1450	2642	1149	2100	3812	1454	2650	4802
432	810	1490	793	1460	2660	1154	2110	3830	1460	2660	4820
438	820	1508	799	1470	2678	1160	2120	3848	1466	2670	4838
443	830	1526	804	1480	2696	1166	2130	3866	1471	2680	4856
449	840	1544	810	1490	2714	1171	2140	3884	1477	2690	4874
454	850	1562	816	1500	2732	1177	2150	3902	1482	2700	4892
460	860	1580	821	1510	2750	1182	2160	3920	1488	2710	4910
466	870	1598	827	1520	2768	1188	2170	3938	1493	2720	4928
471	880	1616	832	1530	2786	1193	2180	3956	1499	2730	4946
477	890	1634	838	1540	2804	1199	2190	3974	1504	2740	4964
482	900	1652	843	1550	2822	1204	2200	3992	1510	2750	4982
488	910	1670	849	1560	2840	1210	2210	4010	1516	2760	5000
493	920	1688	854	1570	2858	1216	2220	4028	1521	2770	5018
499	930	1706	860	1580	2876	1221	2230	4046	1527	2780	5036
504	940	1724	866	1590	2894	1227	2240	4064	1532	2790	5054
510	950	1742	871	1600	2912	1232	2250	4082	1538	2800	5072
516	960	1760	877	1610	2930	1238	2260	4100	1543	2810	5090
521	970	1778	882	1620	2948	1243	2270	4118	1549	2820	5108
527	980	1796	888	1630	2966	1249	2280	4136	1554	2830	5126
532	990	1814	893	1640	2984	1254	2290	4154	1560	2840	5144
538	1000	1832	899	1650	3002	1260	2300	4172	1566	2850	5162
543	1010	1850	904	1660	3020	1266	2310	4190	1571	2860	5180
549	1020	1868	910	1670	3038	1271	2320	4208	1577	2870	5198
554	1030	1886	916	1680	3056	1277	2330	4226	1582	2880	5216
560	1040	1904	921	1690	3074	1282	2340	4244	1588	2890	5234
566	1050	1922	927	1700	3092	1288	2350	4262	1593	2900	5252
571	1060	1940	932	1710	3110	1293	2360	4280	1599	2910	5270
577	1070	1958	938	1720	3128	1299	2370	4298	1604	2920	5288
582	1080	1976	943	1730	3146	1304	2380	4316	1610	2930	5306
588	1090	1994	949	1740	3164	1310	2390	4334	1616	2940	5324
593	1100	2012	954	1750	3182	1316	2400	4352	1621	2950	5342
599	1110	2030	960	1760	3200	1321	2410	4370	1627	2960	5360
604	1120	2048	966	1770	3218	1327	2420	4388	1632	2970	5378
610	1130	2066	971	1780	3236	1332	2430	4406	1638	2980	5396
616	1140	2084	977	1790	3254	1338	2440	4424	1643	2990	5414
621	1150	2102	982	1800	3272	1343	2450	4442	1649	3000	5432
627	1160	2120	988	1810	3290	1349	2460	4460			
632	1170	2138	993	1820	3308	1354	2470	4478			
638	1180	2156	999	1830	3326	1360	2480	4496			
643	1190	2174	1004	1840	3344	1366	2490	4514			
649	1200	2192	1010	1850	3362						
654	1210	2210	1016	1860	3380						
660	1220	2228	1021	1870	3398						
666	1230	2246	1027	1880	3416						
671	1240	2264	1032	1890	3434						
677	1250	2282	1038	1900	3452						
682	1260	2300	1043	1910	3470						
688	1270	2318	1049	1920	3488						
693	1280	2336	1054	1930	3506						
699	1290	2354	1060	1940	3524						

Interpolation Factors

0.56	1	1.8	3.33	6	10.8
1.11	2	3.6	3.89	7	12.6
1.67	3	5.4	4.44	8	14.4
2.22	4	7.2	5.00	9	16.2
2.78	5	9.0	5.56	10	18.0

Table 1-10. Specific-gravity Conversions

See Conversion Formulas at End of Table

Sp gr	°Bé	°API	Lb/gal	Lb/ft³	Sp gr	°Bé	°API	Lb/gal	Lb/ft³
0.60	103.33	104.33	4.993	37.35	0.80	45.00	45.38	6.661	49.83
0.61	99.51	100.47	5.076	37.97	0.81	42.84	43.19	6.744	50.45
0.62	95.81	96.73	5.160	38.60	0.82	40.73	41.06	6.827	51.07
0.63	92.22	93.10	5.243	39.22	0.83	38.67	38.98	6.911	51.70
0.64	88.75	89.59	5.321	39.85	0.84	36.67	36.95	6.994	52.32
0.65	85.38	86.19	5.410	40.47	0.85	34.71	34.97	7.978	52.94
0.66	82.12	82.89	5.493	41.09	0.86	32.79	33.03	7.161	53.57
0.67	78.96	79.69	5.577	41.72	0.87	30.92	31.14	7.244	54.19
0.68	75.88	76.59	5.660	42.34	0.88	29.09	29.30	7.328	54.82
0.69	72.90	73.57	5.743	42.96	0.89	27.30	27.49	7.411	55.44
0.70	70.00	70.64	5.827	43.59	0.90	25.56	25.72	7.491	56.06
0.71	67.18	67.80	5.910	44.21	0.91	23.85	23.99	7.578	56.69
0.72	64.44	65.03	5.994	44.83	0.92	22.17	22.30	7.661	57.31
0.73	61.78	62.34	6.077	45.46	0.93	20.54	20.65	7.745	57.93
0.74	59.19	59.72	6.160	46.08	0.94	18.94	19.03	7.828	58.56
0.75	56.67	57.17	6.234	46.71	0.95	17.37	17.45	7.911	59.18
0.76	54.21	54.68	6.327	47.33	0.96	15.83	15.90	7.995	59.81
0.77	51.82	52.27	6.410	47.95	0.97	14.33	14.38	8.078	60.42
0.78	49.49	49.91	6.494	48.58	0.98	12.86	12.89	8.162	61.05
0.79	47.22	47.61	6.577	49.20	0.99	11.41	11.43	8.250	61.68
					1.00	10.00	10.00	8.328	62.30

Sp gr	°Bé	°Tw	Lb/gal	Lb/ft³	Sp gr	°Bé	°Tw	Lb/gal	Lb/ft³
1.01	1.44	2	8.412	62.92	1.31	34.31	62	10.913	81.63
1.02	2.84	4	8.495	63.55	1.32	35.15	64	10.997	82.26
1.03	4.22	6	8.578	64.17	1.33	35.98	66	11.080	82.88
1.04	5.58	8	8.662	64.80	1.34	36.79	68	11.163	83.50
1.05	6.91	10	8.745	65.41	1.35	37.59	70	11.247	84.13
1.06	8.21	12	8.829	66.04	1.36	38.38	72	11.330	84.75
1.07	9.49	14	8.912	66.67	1.37	39.16	74	11.414	85.37
1.08	10.74	16	8.995	67.29	1.38	39.93	76	11.497	86.00
1.09	11.97	18	9.079	67.91	1.39	40.68	78	11.560	86.62
1.10	13.18	20	9.162	68.54	1.40	41.43	80	11.664	87.25
1.11	14.37	22	9.246	69.16	1.41	42.16	82	11.747	87.88
1.12	15.54	24	9.329	69.79	1.42	42.89	84	11.830	88.49
1.13	16.68	26	9.412	70.41	1.43	43.60	86	11.914	89.12
1.14	17.81	28	9.496	71.03	1.44	44.31	88	11.997	89.74
1.15	18.91	30	9.579	71.66	1.45	45.00	90	12.081	90.36
1.16	20.00	32	9.662	72.28	1.46	45.68	92	12.164	90.99
1.17	21.07	34	9.746	72.90	1.47	46.36	94	12.247	91.61
1.18	22.12	36	9.829	73.53	1.48	47.03	96	12.331	92.24
1.19	23.15	38	9.913	74.15	1.49	47.68	98	12.414	92.86
1.20	24.17	40	9.996	74.78	1.50	48.33	100	12.498	93.49
1.21	25.17	42	10.079	75.40	1.51	48.97	102	12.581	94.11
1.22	26.15	44	10.163	76.02	1.52	49.61	104	12.664	94.79
1.23	27.11	46	10.246	76.65	1.53	50.23	106	12.748	95.36
1.24	28.06	48	10.330	77.27	1.54	50.84	108	12.831	95.98
1.25	29.00	50	10.413	77.89	1.55	51.45	110	12.914	96.61
1.26	29.92	52	10.496	78.51	1.56	52.05	112	12.998	97.23
1.27	30.83	54	10.580	79.14	1.57	52.64	114	13.081	97.85
1.28	31.72	56	10.663	79.76	1.58	53.23	116	13.165	98.48
1.29	32.60	58	10.746	80.38	1.59	53.81	118	13.248	99.10
1.30	33.46	60	10.830	81.01	1.60	54.38	120	13.331	99.73

Table 1-10. Specific-gravity Conversions (Continued)

See Conversion Formulas at End of Table

Sp gr	°Bé	°Tw	Lb/gal	Lb/ft³	Sp gr	°Bé	°Tw	Lb/gal	Lb/ft³
1.61	54.94	122	13.415	100.35	1.81	64.89	162	15.082	112.82
1.62	55.49	124	13.498	100.97	1.82	65.33	164	15.166	113.45
1.63	56.04	126	13.582	101.60	1.83	65.77	166	15.249	114.07
1.64	56.59	128	13.665	102.22	1.84	66.20	168	15.333	114.70
1.65	57.12	130	13.748	102.84	1.85	66.62	170	15.416	115.31
1.66	57.65	132	13.832	103.47	1.86	67.04	172	15.499	115.94
1.67	58.17	134	13.915	104.09	1.87	67.46	174	15.583	116.56
1.68	58.69	136	13.998	104.72	1.88	67.87	176	15.666	117.19
1.69	59.20	138	14.082	105.34	1.89	68.28	178	15.750	117.81
1.70	59.71	140	14.165	105.96	1.90	68.68	180	15.832	118.43
1.71	60.20	142	14.249	106.59	1.91	69.08	182	15.916	119.06
1.72	60.70	144	14.332	107.21	1.92	69.48	184	16.000	110.68
1.73	61.18	146	14.415	107.83	1.93	69.87	186	16.083	120.31
1.74	61.67	148	14.499	108.46	1.94	70.26	188	16.166	120.93
1.75	62.14	150	14.582	109.08	1.95	70.64	190	16.250	121.56
1.76	62.61	152	14.665	109.71	1.96	71.02	192	16.333	122.18
1.77	63.08	154	14.749	110.32	1.97	71.40	194	16.417	122.80
1.78	63.54	156	14.832	110.95	1.98	71.77	196	16.500	123.43
1.79	63.99	158	14.916	111.58	1.99	72.14	198	16.583	124.05
1.80	64.44	160	14.999	112.20	2.00	72.50	200	16.667	124.68

NOTE: The conversion formulas are

$$°Bé = 145 - \frac{145}{\text{sp gr}} \text{ (heavier than } H_2O)$$

$$°Bé = \frac{140}{\text{sp gr}} - 130 \text{ (lighter than } H_2O)$$

$$°Tw = \frac{\text{sp gr } 60°/60°F - 1}{0.005}$$

$$°API = \frac{141.5}{\text{sp gr}} - 131.5$$

Pounds per gallon and pounds per cubic foot are at 60°F, weight in air.

Table 1-11. Wire and Sheet-metal Gauges

Values in Approximate Decimals of an Inch.
As a number of gauges are in use for various shapes and metals, it is advisable to state the thickness in thousandths when specifying gauge number.
Metric wire gauge is ten times the diameter in millimeters.

Gauge no.	(1)*	(2)*	(3)*	(4)*	(5)*	(6)*	Gauge no.
0000000	......	0.4900	.....	0.500	0.6666	0.500	0000000
000000	......	.4615	.....	.469	.6250	.464	000000
00000	......	.4305	.....	.438	.5883	.432	00000
0000	0.460	.3938	0.454	.406	.5416	.400	0000
000	.410	.3625	.425	.375	.5000	.372	000
00	.365	.3310	.380	.344	.4452	.348	00
0	.325	.3065	.340	.312	.3964	.324	0
1	.289	.2830	.300	.281	.3532	.300	1
2	.258	.2625	.284	.266	.3147	.276	2
3	.229	.2437	.259	.250	.2804	.252	3
4	.204	.2253	.238	.234	.2500	.232	4
5	.182	.2070	.220	.219	.2225	.212	5
6	.162	.1920	.203	.203	.1981	.192	6
7	.144	.1770	.180	.188	.1764	.176	7
8	.128	.1620	.165	.172	.1570	.160	8
9	.114	.1483	.148	.156	.1398	.144	9
10	.102	.1350	.134	.141	.1250	.128	10
11	.091	.1205	.120	.125	.1113	.116	11
12	.081	.1055	.109	.109	.0991	.104	,12
13	.072	.0915	.095	.094	.0882	.092	¡13
14	.064	.0800	.083	.078	.0785	.080	¡14
15	.057	.0720	.072	.070	.0699	.072	15
16	.051	.0625	.065	.062	.0625	.064	16
17	.045	.0540	.058	.056	.0556	.056	17
18	.040	.0475	.049	.050	.0495	.048	18
19	.036	.0410	.042	.0438	.0440	.040	19
20	.032	.0348	.035	.0375	.0392	036	20
21	.0285	.0317	.032	.0344	.0349	.032	21
22	.0253	.0286	.028	.0312	.0313	.028	22
23	.0226	.0258	.025	.0281	.0278	.024	23
24	.0201	.0230	.022	.0250	.0248	.022	24
25	.0179	.0204	.020	.0219	.0220	.020	25
26	.0159	.0181	.018	.0188	.0196	.018	26
27	.0142	.0173	.016	.0172	.0175	.0164	27
28	.0126	.0162	.014	.0156	.0156	.0148	28
29	.0113	.0150	.013	.0141	.0139	.0136	29
30	.0100	.0140	.012	.0125	.0123	.0124	30
31	.0089	.0132	.010	.0109	.0110	.0116	31
32	.0080	.0128	.009	.0102	.0098	.0108	32
33	.0071	.0118	.008	.0094	.0087	.0100	33
34	.0063	.0104	.007	.0086	.0077	.0092	34
35	.0056	.0095	.005	.0078	.0069	.0084	35
36	.0050	.0090	.004	.0070	.0061	.0076	36
37	.0045	.0085	.....	.0066	.0054	.0068	37
38	.0040	.0080	.....	.0062	.0048	.0060	38
39	.0035	.0075	.....	......	.0043	.0052	39
40	.0031	.0070	.....	......	.0039	.0048	40

* Gauges are arranged in columns as follows:
1. American (Awg) or Brown & Sharpe (B.&S.), for nonferrous wire and sheet; sometimes used for iron wire.
2. U.S. Steel Wire, Washburn & Moen, Roebling, or American Steel & Wire Co., for steel wire.
3. Birmingham, B.W.G., for steel wire and heat-exchanger tubing, or Stubs Iron Wire, for iron or brass wire; sometimes used for copper plate and for steel plate 12 gauge and heavier and for steel tubes.
4. U.S. Standard, for sheet and plate metal and wrought iron.
5. Standard Birmingham, B.G., for sheet and hoop metal.
6. Imperial Standard Wire Gauge, S.W.G., British legal standard.

Table 1-12. Mathematical Signs, Symbols, and Abbreviations

$\pm(\mp)$	plus or minus (minus or plus)
:	divided by, ratio sign
: :	proportional sign
$<$	less than
$\not<$	not less than
$>$	greater than
$\not>$	not greater than
$\cong$	approximately equals, congruent
$\sim$	similar to
$\rightleftharpoons$	equivalent to
$\neq$	not equal to
$\doteq$	approaches, is approximately equal to
$\propto$	varies as
∞	infinity
$\therefore$	therefore
$\sqrt{}$	square root
$\sqrt[3]{}$	cube root
$\sqrt[n]{}$	nth root
$\angle$	angle
$\perp$	perpendicular to
$\parallel$	parallel to
$|x|$	numerical value of x
log or $\log_{10}$	common logarithm or Briggsian logarithm
$\log_e$ or ln	natural logarithm or hyperbolic logarithm or Napierian logarithm
e	base (2.718) of natural system of logarithms
$a°$	an angle a degrees
a'	a prime, an angle a minutes
a''	a double prime, an angle a seconds, a second
sin	sine
cos	cosine
tan	tangent
ctn or cot	cotangent
sec	secant
csc	cosecant
vers	versed sine
covers	coversed sine
exsec	exsecant
$\sin^{-1}$	anti sine or angle whose sine is
sinh	hyperbolic sine
cosh	hyperbolic cosine
tanh	hyperbolic tangent
$\sinh^{-1}$	anti hyperbolic sine or angle whose hyperbolic sine is
$f(x)$ or $\phi(x)$	function of x
Δx	increment of x
Σ	summation of
dx	differential of x
dy/dx or y'	derivative of y with respect to x
d^2y/dx^2 or y''	second derivative of y with respect to x
d^ny/dx^n	nth derivative of y with respect to x
$\partial y/\partial x$	partial derivative of y with respect to x
$\partial^n y/\partial x^n$	nth partial derivative of y with respect to x
$\dfrac{\partial^n y}{\partial x\,\partial y}$	nth partial derivative with respect to x and y
$\int$	integral of

Table 1-12. Mathematical Signs, Symbols, and Abbreviations (Continued)

$\int_a^b$ integral between the limits a and b

$\dot{y}$ first derivative of y with respect to time
$\ddot{y}$ second derivative of y with respect to time
Δ or ∇^2 the "Laplacian"

$$\left(\frac{\partial^2}{\partial x^2} + \frac{\partial^2}{\partial y^2} + \frac{\partial^2}{\partial z^2}\right)$$

δ sign of a variation
$\oint$ sign of integration around a closed path

Table 1-13. Greek Alphabet

Alpha	= A, α = A, a	Nu	= N, ν = N, n
Beta	= B, β = B, b	Xi	= Ξ, ξ = X, x
Gamma	= Γ, γ = G, g	Omicron	= O, o = O, o
Delta	= Δ, δ = D, d	Pi	= Π, π = P, p
Epsilon	= E, ϵ = E, e	Rho	= P, ρ = R, r
Zeta	= Z, ζ = Z, z	Sigma	= Σ, σ = S, s
Eta	= H, η = E, e	Tau	= T, τ = T, t
Theta	= Θ, θ = Th, th	Upsilon	= Υ, υ = U, u
Iota	= I, ι = I, i	Phi	= Φ, ϕ = Ph, ph
Kappa	= K, κ = K, k	Chi	= X, χ = Ch, ch
Lambda	= Λ, λ = L, l	Psi	= Ψ, ψ = Ps, ps
Mu	= M, μ = M, m	Omega	= Ω, ω = O, o

Table 1-14. Weights and Measures

United States Customary System

Linear Measure

12 inches (in. or $''$)	= 1 foot (ft or $'$)
3 feet	= 1 yard (yd)
16.5 feet $\Big\}$ 5.5 yards	= 1 rod
5,280 feet $\Big\}$ 320 rods	= 1 mile
1 mil	= 0.001 inch

Nautical:

6,080.2	feet	= 1 nautical mile
6	feet	= 1 fathom
120	fathoms	= 1 cable length
1	knot	= 1 nautical mile per hour
60	knots	= 1° (measured at equator)

Table 1-14. Weights and Measures (Continued)
United States Customary System (Continued)
Square Measure

144 square inches (sq in, in.², or □″)	= 1 square foot (sq ft, ft², or □′)
9 square feet	= 1 square yard (sq yd or yd²)
30.25 square yards	= 1 square rod, pole, or perch
160 square rods = $\begin{Bmatrix} 10 \text{ square chains} \\ 43{,}560 \text{ square feet} \end{Bmatrix}$	= 1 acre
640 acres = 1 square mile	= 1 section
1 circular inch (area of circle of 1 inch diameter)	= 0.7854 square inch
1 square inch	= 1.2732 circular inch
1 circular mil	= area of circle of 0.001 inch diameter
1,000,000 circular mils	= 1 circular inch

Circular Measure

60 seconds (sec or ″)	= 1 minute (min or ′)
60 minutes	= 1 degree (deg or °)
90 degrees	= 1 quadrant
360 degrees	= 1 circumference
57.29578 degrees	$\begin{cases} = 1 \text{ radian} \\ = 57°\ 17'\ 44.81'' \end{cases}$

Volume Measure

Solid:

1,728 cubic inches (cu in. or in.³)	= 1 cubic foot (cu ft or ft³)
27 cubic feet	= 1 cubic yard (cu yd or yd³)

Dry Measure:

2 pints	= 1 quart
8 quarts	= 1 peck
4 pecks	= 1 bushel
1 U.S. Winchester bushel	= 2150.42 cubic inches

Liquid:

4 gills	= 1 pint (pt)
2 pints	= 1 quart (qt)
4 quarts	= 1 gallon (gal)
7.4805 gallons	= 1 cubic foot

Apothecaries' liquid:

60 minims (min. or ℳ)	= 1 fluid dram or drachm
8 drams (ʒ)	= 1 fluid ounce
16 ounces (oz. ℥)	= 1 pint

Water measure:
1 miner's inch is the amount of water flowing through an orifice of 1 sq in. cross section under a head varying from 4 to .6.5 in. (as fixed by state law), and thus varies from 0.020 to 0.025 cfs.
1 acre foot = 325,900 U.S. gal.

Table 1-14. Weights and Measures (Continued)
United States Customary System (Continued)

Avoirdupois Weight

16 drams	=	437.5 grains = 1 ounce (oz)	
16 ounces	= 7,000 grains	= 1 pound (lb)	= 453.6 grains
100 pounds	=	1 hundredweight (cwt)	
2,000 pounds	=	1 short ton	
2,240 pounds	=	1 long ton	

Troy Weight (Gold and Precious Stones)

24 grains = 1 pennyweight (dwt)
20 pennyweights = 1 ounce
12 ounces = 5,760 grains = 1 pound = 373.25 grams (g)
1 assay ton = 29,167 milligrams, or as many milligrams as there are troy ounces in a ton of 2,000 lb avoirdupois. Consequently, the number of milligrams of precious metal yielded by an assay ton of ore gives directly the number of troy ounces that would be obtained from a ton of 2,000 lb avoirdupois.

Apothecaries' Weight

20 grains = 1 scruple (℈)
2 scruples = 1 dram (ʒ)
8 drams = 1 ounce (℥)
12 ounces = 1 pound

Board Measure

1 board foot (fbm) is the product of 1 foot length, 1 foot breadth, and 1 inch thickness.

Metric System
Linear Measure

1 micromicron ($\mu\mu$) = 0.000001 micron (μ)
1 Angstrom unit (A) = 0.0001 micron
1 millimicron (mμ) = 0.001 micron
1 micron = 0.001 millimeter (mm)
10 millimeters = 1 centimeter (cm)
10 centimeters = 1 decimeter (dm)
10 decimeters } 100 centimeters } = 1 meter (m) = 39.37 inches
1 dekameter (dkm) = 10 meters
1 hectometer (hm) = 10^2 meters
1 kilometer (km) = 10^3 meters
1 myriameter = 10^4 meters
1 megameter = 10^6 meters

Square Measure

1 square millimeter (sq mm or mm²) = 0.01 square centimeter (sq cm or cm²)
1 square centimeter = 0.01 square decimeter (sq dm or dm²)
1 square decimeter = 0.01 square meter (sq m or m²)
1 square meter (centaire) = 0.01 square dekameter (sq dkm or dkm²)
1 square dekameter (are) = 0.01 square hectometer (sq hm or hm²)
1 hectare = 10,000 square meters
1 square kilometer = 100 square hectometers

Table 1-14. Weights and Measures (Continued)
Metric System (Continued)
Volume Measure

1 cubic millimeter	$= 10^{-6}$ liter $= 0.001$ cm³
1 cubic centimeter	$= 10^{-3}$ liter $= 0.001$ dm³
1 cubic decimeter	$= 1$ liter† $= 0.001$ m³
1 decistere	$= 0.1$ cubic meter
1 stere	$= 1$ cubic meter
1 dekastere	$= 10$ cubic meters
1 microliter (μl or λ)	$= 10^{-6}$ liter
1 milliliter (ml)	$= 10^{-3}$ liter
1 centiliter (cl)	$= 10^{-2}$ liter
1 deciliter (dl)	$= 10^{-1}$ liter
1 dekaliter (dkl)	$= 10$ liters
1 hectoliter (hl)	$= 10^2$ liters

Mass Measure

1 microgram (μg or γ)	$= 10^{-6}$ gram
1 milligram (mg)	$= 10^{-3}$ gram
1 centigram (cg)	$= 10^{-2}$ gram
1 decigram (dg)	$= 10^{-1}$ gram
15.432 grains	$= 1$ gram
1 dekagram (dkg)	$= 10$ grams
1 hectogram (hg)	$= 10^2$ grams
1 kilogram (kg)	$= 10^3$ grams
1 metric ton	$= 10^6$ grams
1 metric carat	$= 200$ milligrams

Surveyor's or Gunther's Measure

7.92 inches	$= 1$ link
100 links ⎫	
66 feet ⎬	$= 1$ chain
4 rods ⎭	
80 chains	$= 1$ mile

Conversion between Systems

1 meter	$= 3.280833$ U.S. feet
1 kilometer	$= 0.6214$ U.S. mile
1 liter	$= 0.2642$ U.S. gallon
1 metric ton	$= 0.9842$ short ton $= 1.1023$ U.S. short tons
1 English ton	$= 1$ U.S. long ton $= 2,240$ pounds
1 Imperial gallon	$= 277.42$ cubic inches $= 1.20094$ U.S. gallons

† Accurately, 1 liter = 1.000028 cubic decimeters.

Table 1-15. Compound Interest Factors

For examples demonstrating use see end of table.

n	Single payment		Uniform annual series				n
	Compound-amount factor	Present-worth factor	Sinking-fund factor	Capital-recovery factor	Compound-amount factor	Present-worth factor	
	Given P, to find S $(1+i)^n$	Given S, to find P $\dfrac{1}{(1+i)^n}$	Given S, to find R $\dfrac{i}{(1+i)^n-1}$	Given P, to find R $\dfrac{i(1+i)^n}{(1+i)^n-1}$	Given R, to find S $\dfrac{(1+i)^n-1}{i}$	Given R, to find P $\dfrac{(1+i)^n-1}{i(1+i)^n}$	
	3 per cent Compound Interest Factors						
1	1.030	0.9709	1.00000	1.03000	1.000	0.971	1
2	1.061	.9426	0.49261	0.52261	2.030	1.913	2
3	1.093	.9151	.32353	.35353	3.091	2.829	3
4	1.126	.8885	.23903	.26903	4.184	3.717	4
5	1.159	.8626	.18835	.21835	5.309	4.580	5
6	1.194	.8375	.15460	.18460	6.468	5.417	6
7	1.230	.8131	.13051	.16051	7.662	6.230	7
8	1.267	.7894	.11246	.14246	8.892	7.020	8
9	1.305	.7664	.09843	.12843	10.159	7.786	9
10	1.344	.7441	.08723	.11723	11.464	8.530	10
11	1.384	.7224	.07808	.10808	12.808	9.253	11
12	1.426	.7014	.07046	.10046	14.192	9.954	12
13	1.469	.6810	.06403	.09403	15.618	10.635	13
14	1.513	.6611	.05853	.08853	17.086	11.296	14
15	1.558	.6419	.05377	.08377	18.599	11.938	15
16	1.605	.6232	.04961	.07961	20.157	12.561	16
17	1.653	.6050	.04595	.07595	21.762	13.166	17
18	1.702	.5874	.04271	.07271	23.414	13.754	18
19	1.754	.5703	.03981	.06981	25.117	14.324	19
20	1.806	.5537	.03722	.06722	26.870	14.877	20
21	1.860	.5375	.03487	.06487	28.676	15.415	21
22	1.916	.5219	.03275	.06275	30.537	15.937	22
23	1.974	.5067	.03081	.06081	32.453	16.444	23
24	2.033	.4919	.02905	.05905	34.426	16.936	24
25	2.094	.4776	.02743	.05743	36.459	17.413	25
26	2.157	.4637	.02594	.05594	38.553	17.877	26
27	2.221	.4502	.02456	.05456	40.710	18.327	27
28	2.288	.4371	.02329	.05329	42.931	18.764	28
29	2.357	.4243	.02211	.05211	45.219	19.188	29
30	2.427	.4120	.02102	.05102	47.575	19.600	30
31	2.500	.4000	.02000	.05000	50.003	20.000	31
32	2.575	.3883	.01905	.04905	52.503	20.389	32
33	2.652	.3770	.01816	.04816	55.078	20.766	33
34	2.732	.3660	.01732	.04732	57.730	21.132	34
35	2.814	.3554	.01654	.04654	60.462	21.487	35
40	3.262	.3066	.01326	.04326	75.401	23.115	40
45	3.782	.2644	.01079	.04079	92.720	24.519	45
50	4.384	.2281	.00887	.03887	112.797	25.730	50
55	5.082	.1968	.00735	.03735	136.072	26.774	55
60	5.892	.1697	.00613	.03613	163.053	27.676	60
65	6.830	.1464	.00515	.03515	194.333	28.453	65
70	7.918	.1263	.00434	.03434	230.594	29.123	70
75	9.179	.1089	.00367	.03367	272.631	29.702	75
80	10.641	.0940	.00311	.03311	321.363	30.201	80
85	12.336	.0811	.00265	.03265	377.857	30.631	85
90	14.300	.0699	.00226	.03226	443.349	31.002	90
95	16.578	.0603	.00193	.03193	519.272	31.323	95
100	19.219	.0520	.00165	.03165	607.288	31.599	100

Table 1-15. Compound Interest Factors (Continued)

For examples demonstrating use see end of table.

	Single payment		Uniform annual series				
	Compound-amount factor	Present-worth factor	Sinking-fund factor	Capital-recovery factor	Compound-amount factor	Present-worth factor	
n	Given P, to find S $(1+i)^n$	Given S, to find P $\dfrac{1}{(1+i)^n}$	Given S, to find R $\dfrac{i}{(1+i)^n-1}$	Given P, to find R $\dfrac{i(1+i)^n}{(1+i)^n-1}$	Given R, to find S $\dfrac{(1+i)^n-1}{i}$	Given R, to find P $\dfrac{(1+i)^n-1}{i(1+i)^n}$	n
			4 per cent Compound Interest Factors				
1	1.040	0.9615	1.00000	1.04000	1.000	0.962	1
2	1.082	.9246	0.49020	0.53020	2.040	1.886	2
3	1.125	.8890	.32035	.36035	3.122	2.775	3
4	1.170	.8548	.23549	.27549	4.246	3.630	4
5	1.217	.8219	.18463	.22463	5.416	4.452	5
6	1.265	.7903	.15076	.19076	6.633	5.242	6
7	1.316	.7599	.12661	.16661	7.898	6.002	7
8	1.369	.7307	.10853	.14853	9.214	6.733	8
9	1.423	.7026	.09449	.13449	10.583	7.435	9
10	1.480	.6756	.08329	.12329	12.006	8.111	10
11	1.539	.6496	.07415	.11415	13.486	8.760	11
12	1.601	.6246	.06655	.10655	15.026	9.385	12
13	1.665	.6006	.06014	.10014	16.627	9.986	13
14	1.732	.5775	.05467	.09467	18.292	10.563	14
15	1.801	.5553	.04994	.08994	20.024	11.118	15
16	1.873	.5339	.04582	.08582	21.825	11.652	16
17	1.948	.5134	.04220	.08220	23.698	12.166	17
18	2.026	.4936	.03899	.07899	25.645	12.659	18
19	2.107	.4746	.03614	.07614	27.671	13.134	19
20	2.191	.4564	.03358	.07358	29.778	13.590	20
21	2.279	.4388	.03128	.07128	31.969	14.029	21
22	2.370	.4220	.02920	.06920	34.248	14.451	22
23	2.465	.4057	.02731	.06731	36.618	14.857	23
24	2.563	.3901	.02559	.06559	39.083	15.247	24
25	2.666	.3751	.02401	.06401	41.646	15.622	25
26	2.772	.3607	.02257	.06257	44.312	15.983	26
27	2.883	.3468	.02124	.06124	47.084	16.330	27
28	2.999	.3335	.02001	.06001	49.968	16.663	28
29	3.119	.3207	.01888	.05888	52.966	16.984	29
30	3.243	.3083	.01783	.05783	56.085	17.292	30
31	3.373	.2965	.01686	.05686	59.328	17.588	31
32	3.508	.2851	.01595	.05595	62.701	17.874	32
33	3.648	.2741	.01510	.05510	66.210	18.148	33
34	3.794	.2636	.01431	.05431	69.858	18.411	34
35	3.946	.2534	.01358	.05358	73.652	18.665	35
40	4.801	.2083	.01052	.05052	95.026	19.793	40
45	5.841	.1712	.00826	.04826	121.029	20.720	45
50	7.107	.1407	.00655	.04655	152.667	21.482	50
55	8.646	.1157	.00523	.04523	191.159	22.109	55
60	10.520	.0951	.00420	.04420	237.991	22.623	60
65	12.799	.0781	.00339	.04339	294.968	23.047	65
70	15.572	.0642	.00275	.04275	364.290	23.395	70
75	18.945	.0528	.00223	.04223	448.631	23.680	75
80	23.050	.0434	.00181	.04181	551.245	23.915	80
85	28.044	.0357	.00148	.04148	676.090	24.109	85
90	34.119	.0293	.00121	.04121	827.983	24.267	90
95	41.511	.0241	.00099	.04099	1,012.785	24.398	95
100	50.505	.0198	.00081	.04081	1,237.624	24.505	100

Table 1-15. Compound Interest Factors (Continued)

For examples demonstrating use see end of table.

	Single payment		Uniform annual series				
	Compound-amount factor	Present-worth factor	Sinking-fund factor	Capital-recovery factor	Compound-amount factor	Present-worth factor	
n	Given P, to find S $(1+i)^n$	Given S, to find P $\dfrac{1}{(1+i)^n}$	Given S, to find R $\dfrac{i}{(1+i)^n-1}$	Given P, to find R $\dfrac{i(1+i)^n}{(1+i)^n-1}$	Given R, to find S $\dfrac{(1+i)^n-1}{i}$	Given R, to find P $\dfrac{(1+i)^n-1}{i(1+i)^n}$	n
			5 per cent Compound Interest Factors				
1	1.050	0.9524	1.00000	1.05000	1.000	0.952	1
2	1.103	.9070	0.48780	0.53780	2.050	1.859	2
3	1.158	.8638	.31721	.36721	3.153	2.723	3
4	1.216	.8227	.23201	.28201	4.310	3.546	4
5	1.276	.7835	.18097	.23097	5.526	4.329	5
6	1.340	.7462	.14702	.19702	6.802	5.076	6
7	1.407	.7107	.12282	.17282	8.142	5.786	7
8	1.477	.6768	.10472	.15472	9.549	6.463	8
9	1.551	.6446	.09069	.14069	11.027	7.108	9
10	1.629	.6139	.07950	.12950	12.578	7.722	10
11	1.710	.5847	.07039	.12039	14.207	8.306	11
12	1.796	.5568	.06283	.11283	15.917	8.863	12
13	1.886	.5303	.05646	.10646	17.713	9.394	13
14	1.980	.5051	.05102	.10102	19.599	9.899	14
15	2.079	.4810	.04634	.09634	21.579	10.380	15
16	2.183	.4581	.04227	.09227	23.657	10.838	16
17	2.292	.4363	.03870	.08870	25.840	11.274	17
18	2.407	.4155	.03555	.08555	28.132	11.690	18
19	2.527	.3957	.03275	.08275	30.539	12.085	19
20	2.653	.3769	.03024	.08024	33.066	12.462	20
21	2.786	.3589	.02800	.07800	35.719	12.821	21
22	2.925	.3418	.02597	.07597	38.505	13.163	22
23	3.072	.3256	.02414	.07414	41.430	13.489	23
24	3.225	.3101	.02247	.07247	44.502	13.799	24
25	3.386	.2953	.02095	.07095	47.727	14.094	25
26	3.556	.2812	.01956	.06956	51.113	14.375	26
27	3.733	.2678	.01829	.06829	54.669	14.643	27
28	3.920	.2551	.01712	.06712	58.403	14.898	28
29	4.116	.2429	.01605	.06605	62.323	15.141	29
30	4.322	.2314	.01505	.06505	66.439	15.372	30
31	4.538	.2204	.01413	.06413	70.761	15.593	31
32	4.765	.2099	.01328	.06328	75.299	15.803	32
33	5.003	.1999	.01249	.06249	80.064	16.003	33
34	5.253	.1904	.01176	.06176	85.067	16.193	34
35	5.516	.1813	.01107	.06107	90.320	16.374	35
40	7.040	.1420	.00828	.05828	120.800	17.159	40
45	8.985	.1113	.00626	.05626	159.700	17.774	45
50	11.467	.0872	.00478	.05478	209.348	18.256	50
55	14.636	.0683	.00367	.05367	272.713	18.633	55
60	18.679	.0535	.00283	.05283	353.584	18.929	60
65	23.840	.0419	.00219	.05219	456.798	19.161	65
70	30.426	.0329	.00170	.05170	588.529	19.343	70
75	38.833	.0258	.00132	.05132	756.654	19.485	75
80	49.561	.0202	.00103	.05103	971.229	19.596	80
85	63.254	.0158	.00080	.05080	1,245.087	19.684	85
90	80.730	.0124	.00063	.05063	1,594.607	19.752	90
95	103.035	.0097	.00049	.05049	2,040.694	19.806	95
100	131.501	.0076	.00038	.05038	2,610.025	19.848	100

Table 1-15. Compound Interest Factors (Continued)

For examples demonstrating use see end of table.

n	Single payment		Uniform annual series				n
	Compound-amount factor	Present-worth factor	Sinking-fund factor	Capital-recovery factor	Compound-amount factor	Present-worth factor	
	Given P, to find S $(1+i)^n$	Given S, to find P $\dfrac{1}{(1+i)^n}$	Given S, to find R $\dfrac{i}{(1+i)^n-1}$	Given P, to find R $\dfrac{i(1+i)^n}{(1+i)^n-1}$	Given R, to find S $\dfrac{(1+i)^n-1}{i}$	Given R, to find P $\dfrac{(1+i)^n-1}{i(1+i)^n}$	
	6 per cent Compound Interest Factors						
1	1.060	0.9434	1.00000	1.06000	1.000	0.943	1
2	1.124	.8900	0.48544	0.54544	2.060	1.833	2
3	1.191	.8396	.31411	.37411	3.184	2.673	3
4	1.262	.7921	.22859	.28859	4.375	3.465	4
5	1.338	.7473	.17740	.23740	5.637	4.212	5
6	1.419	.7050	.14336	.20336	6.975	4.917	6
7	1.504	.6651	.11914	.17914	8.394	5.582	7
8	1.594	.6274	.10104	.16104	9.897	6.210	8
9	1.689	.5919	.08702	.14702	11.491	6.802	9
10	1.791	.5584	.07587	.13587	13.181	7.360	10
11	1.898	.5268	.06679	.12679	14.972	7.887	11
12	2.012	.4970	.05928	.11928	16.870	8.384	12
13	2.133	.4688	.05296	.11296	18.882	8.853	13
14	2.261	.4423	.04758	.10758	21.015	9.295	14
15	2.397	.4173	.04296	.10296	23.276	9.712	15
16	2.540	.3936	.03895	.09895	25.673	10.106	16
17	2.693	.3714	.03544	.09544	28.213	10.477	17
18	2.854	.3503	.03236	.09236	30.906	10.828	18
19	3.026	.3305	.02962	.08962	33.760	11.158	19
20	3.207	.3118	.02718	.08718	36.786	11.470	20
21	3.400	.2942	.02500	.08500	39.993	11.764	21
22	3.604	.2775	.02305	.08305	43.392	12.042	22
23	3.820	.2618	.02128	.08128	46.996	12.303	23
24	4.049	.2470	.01968	.07968	50.816	12.550	24
25	4.292	.2330	.01823	.07823	54.865	12.783	25
26	4.549	.2198	.01690	.07690	59.156	13.003	26
27	4.822	.2074	.01570	.07570	63.706	13.211	27
28	5.112	.1956	.01459	.07459	68.528	13.406	28
29	5.418	.1846	.01358	.07358	73.640	13.591	29
30	5.743	.1741	.01265	.07265	79.058	13.765	30
31	6.088	.1643	.01179	.07179	84.802	13.929	31
32	6.453	.1550	.01100	.07100	90.890	14.084	32
33	6.841	.1462	.01027	.07027	97.343	14.230	33
34	7.251	.1379	.00960	.06960	104.184	14.368	34
35	7.686	.1301	.00897	.06897	111.435	14.498	35
40	10.286	.0972	.00646	.06646	154.762	15.046	40
45	13.765	.0727	.00470	.06470	212.744	15.456	45
50	18.420	.0543	.00344	.06344	290.336	15.762	50
55	24.650	.0406	.00254	.06254	394.172	15.991	55
60	32.988	.0303	.00188	.06188	533.128	16.161	60
65	44.145	.0227	.00139	.06139	719.083	16.289	65
70	59.076	.0169	.00103	.06103	967.932	16.385	70
75	79.057	.0126	.00077	.06077	1,300.949	16.456	75
80	105.796	.0095	.00057	.06057	1,746.600	16.509	80
85	141.579	.0071	.00043	.06043	2,342.982	16.549	85
90	189.465	.0053	.00032	.06032	3,141.075	16.579	90
95	253.546	.0039	.00024	.06024	4,209.104	16.601	95
100	339.302	.0029	.00018	.06018	5,638.368	16.618	100

Table 1-15. Compound Interest Factors (Continued)

For examples demonstrating use see end of table.

| n | Single payment | | Uniform annual series | | | | n |
| | Compound-amount factor | Present-worth factor | Sinking-fund factor | Capital-recovery factor | Compound-amount factor | Present-worth factor | |
	Given P, to find S $(1+i)^n$	Given S, to find P $\dfrac{1}{(1+i)^n}$	Given S, to find R $\dfrac{i}{(1+i)^n-1}$	Given P, to find R $\dfrac{i(1+i)^n}{(1+i)^n-1}$	Given R, to find S $\dfrac{(1+i)^n-1}{i}$	Given R, to find P $\dfrac{(1+i)^n-1}{i(1+i)^n}$	
			8 per cent Compound Interest Factors				
1	1.080	0.9259	1.00000	1.08000	1.000	0.926	1
2	1.166	.8573	0.48077	0.56077	2.080	1.783	2
3	1.260	.7938	.30803	.38803	3.246	2.577	3
4	1.360	.7350	.22192	.30192	4.506	3.312	4
5	1.469	.6806	.17046	.25046	5.867	3.993	5
6	1.587	.6302	.13632	.21632	7.336	4.623	6
7	1.714	.5835	.11207	.19207	8.923	5.206	7
8	1.851	.5403	.09401	.17401	10.637	5.747	8
9	1.999	.5002	.08008	.16008	12.488	6.247	9
10	2.159	.4632	.06903	.14903	14.487	6.710	10
11	2.332	.4289	.06008	.14008	16.645	7.139	11
12	2.518	.3971	.05270	.13270	18.977	7.536	12
13	2.720	.3677	.04652	.12652	21.495	7.904	13
14	2.937	.3405	.04130	.12130	24.215	8.244	14
15	3.172	.3152	.03683	.11683	27.152	8.559	15
16	3.426	.2919	.03298	.11298	30.324	8.851	16
17	3.700	.2703	.02963	.10963	33.750	9.122	17
18	3.996	.2502	.02670	.10670	37.450	9.372	18
19	4.316	.2317	.02413	.10413	41.446	9.604	19
20	4.661	.2145	.02185	.10185	45.762	9.818	20
21	5.034	.1987	.01983	.09983	50.423	10.017	21
22	5.437	.1839	.01803	.09803	55.457	10.201	22
23	5.871	.1703	.01642	.09642	60.893	10.371	23
24	6.341	.1577	.01498	.09498	66.765	10.529	24
25	6.848	.1460	.01368	.09368	73.106	10.675	25
26	7.396	.1352	.01251	.09251	79.954	10.810	26
27	7.988	.1252	.01145	.09145	87.351	10.935	27
28	8.627	.1159	.01049	.09049	95.339	11.051	28
29	9.317	.1073	.00962	.08962	103.966	11.158	29
30	10.063	.0994	.00883	.08883	113.283	11.258	30
31	10.868	.0920	.00811	.08811	123.346	11.350	31
32	11.737	.0852	.00745	.08745	134.214	11.435	32
33	12.676	.0789	.00685	.08685	145.951	11.514	33
34	13.690	.0730	.00630	.08630	158.627	11.587	34
35	14.785	.0676	.00580	.08580	172.317	11.655	35
40	21.725	.0460	.00386	.08386	259.057	11.925	40
45	31.920	.0313	.00259	.08259	386.506	12.108	45
50	46.902	.0213	.00174	.08174	573.770	12.233	50
55	68.914	.0145	.00118	.08118	848.923	12.319	55
60	101.257	.0099	.00080	.08080	1,253.213	12.377	60
65	148.780	.0067	.00054	.08054	1,847.248	12.416	65
70	218.606	.0046	.00037	.08037	2,720.080	12.443	70
75	321.205	.0031	.00025	.08025	4,002.557	12.461	75
80	471.955	.0021	.00017	.08017	5,886.935	12.474	80
85	693.456	.0014	.00012	.08012	8,655.706	12.482	85
90	1,018.915	.0010	.00008	.08008	12,723.939	12.488	90
95	1,497.121	.0007	.00005	.08005	18,701.507	12.492	95
100	2,199.761	.0005	.00004	.08004	27,484.516	12.494	100

Table 1-15. Compound Interest Factors (Continued)

For examples demonstrating use see end of table.

n	Single payment		Uniform annual series				n
	Compound-amount factor	Present-worth factor	Sinking-fund factor	Capital-recovery factor	Compound-amount factor	Present-worth factor	
	Given P, to find S $(1+i)^n$	Given S, to find P $\dfrac{1}{(1+i)^n}$	Given S, to find R $\dfrac{i}{(1+i)^n-1}$	Given P, to find R $\dfrac{i(1+i)^n}{(1+i)^n-1}$	Given R, to find S $\dfrac{(1+i)^n-1}{i}$	Given R, to find P $\dfrac{(1+i)^n-1}{i(1+i)^n}$	

10 per cent Compound Interest Factors

n							n
1	1.100	0.9091	1.00000	1.10000	1.000	0.909	1
2	1.210	.8264	0.47619	0.57619	2.100	1.736	2
3	1.331	.7513	.30211	.40211	3.310	2.487	3
4	1.464	.6830	.21547	.31547	4.641	3.170	4
5	1.611	.6209	.16380	.26380	6.105	3.791	5
6	1.772	.5645	.12961	.22961	7.716	4.355	6
7	1.949	.5132	.10541	.20541	9.487	4.868	7
8	2.144	.4665	.08744	.18744	11.436	5.335	8
9	2.358	.4241	.07364	.17364	13.579	5.759	9
10	2.594	.3855	.06275	.16275	15.937	6.144	10
11	2.853	.3505	.05396	.15396	18.531	6.495	11
12	3.138	.3186	.04676	.14676	21.384	6.814	12
13	3.452	.2897	.04078	.14078	24.523	7.103	13
14	3.797	.2633	.03575	.13575	27.975	7.367	14
15	4.177	.2394	.03147	.13147	31.772	7.606	15
16	4.595	.2176	.02782	.12782	35.950	7.824	16
17	5.054	.1978	.02466	.12466	40.545	8.022	17
18	5.560	.1799	.02193	.12193	45.599	8.201	18
19	6.116	.1635	.01955	.11955	51.159	8.365	19
20	6.727	.1486	.01746	.11746	57.275	8.514	20
21	7.400	.1351	.01562	.11562	64.002	8.649	21
22	8.140	.1228	.01401	.11401	71.403	8.772	22
23	8.954	.1117	.01257	.11257	79.543	8.883	23
24	9.850	.1015	.01130	.11130	88.497	8.985	24
25	10.835	.0923	.01017	.11017	98.347	9.077	25
26	11.918	.0839	.00916	.10916	109.182	9.161	26
27	13.110	.0763	.00826	.10826	121.100	9.237	27
28	14.421	.0693	.00745	.10745	134.210	9.307	28
29	15.863	.0630	.00673	.10673	148.631	9.370	29
30	17.449	.0573	.00608	.10608	164.494	9.427	30
31	19.194	.0521	.00550	.10550	181.943	9.479	31
32	21.114	.0474	.00497	.10497	201.138	9.526	32
33	23.225	.0431	.00450	.10450	222.252	9.569	33
34	25.548	.0391	.00407	.10407	245.477	9.609	34
35	28.102	.0356	.00369	.10369	271.024	9.644	35
40	45.259	.0221	.00226	.10226	442.593	9.779	40
45	72.890	.0137	.00139	.10139	718.905	9.863	45
50	117.391	.0085	.00086	.10086	1,163.909	9.915	50
55	189.059	.0053	.00053	.10053	1,880.591	9.947	55
60	304.482	.0033	.00033	.10033	3,034.816	9.967	60
65	490.371	.0020	.00020	.10020	4,893.707	9.980	65
70	789.747	.0013	.00013	.10013	7,887.470	9.987	70
75	1,271.895	.0008	.00008	.10008	12,708.954	9.992	75
80	2,048.400	.0005	.00005	.10005	20,474.002	9.995	80
85	3,298.969	.0003	.00003	.10003	32,979.690	9.997	85
90	5,313.023	.0002	.00002	.10002	53,120.226	9.998	90
95	8,556.676	.0001	.00001	.10001	85,556.760	9.999	95
100	13,780.612	.0001	.00001	.10001	137,796.123	9.999	100

Table 1-15. Compound Interest Factors (Continued)

Examples in Use of Tables

GIVEN: $2,500 is invested now at 5 per cent.
REQUIRED: Accumulated value in 10 years (i.e., the amount of a given principal).

SOLUTION:
$$S = P(1 + i)^n = \$2,500 \times 1.05^{10}$$
$$\text{Compound-amount factor} = (1 + i)^n = 1.05^{10} = 1.629$$
$$S = \$2,500 \times 1.629 = \$4,062.50$$

GIVEN: $19,500 will be required in 5 years to replace equipment now in use.
REQUIRED: With interest available at 3 per cent, what sum must be deposited in the bank at present to provide the required capital (i.e., the principal which will amount to a given sum).

SOLUTION:
$$P = S \frac{1}{(1 + i)^n} = \$19,500 \frac{1}{1.03^5}$$
$$\text{Present-worth factor} = 1/(1 + i)^n = 1/1.03^5 = 0.8626$$
$$P = \$19,500 \times 0.8626 = \$16,821$$

GIVEN: $50,000 will be required in 10 years to purchase equipment.
REQUIRED: With interest available at 4 per cent, what sum must be deposited each year to provide the required capital (i.e., the annuity which will amount to a given fund).

SOLUTION:
$$R = S \frac{i}{(1 + i)^n - 1} = \$50,000 \frac{0.04}{1.04^{10} - 1}$$
$$\text{Sinking-fund factor} = \frac{i}{(1 + i)^n - 1} = \frac{0.04}{1.04^{10} - 1} = 0.08329$$
$$R = \$50,000 \times 0.08329 = \$4,164$$

GIVEN: $20,000 is invested at 10 per cent interest.
REQUIRED: Annual sum that can be withdrawn over a 20-year period (i.e., the annuity provided by a given capital).

SOLUTION:
$$R = P \frac{i(1 + i)^n}{(1 + i)^n - 1} = \$20,000 \frac{0.10 \times 1.10^{20}}{1.10^{20} - 1}$$
$$\text{Capital-recovery factor} = \frac{i(1 + i)^n}{(1 + i)^n - 1} = \frac{0.10 \times 1.10^{20}}{1.10^{20} - 1} = 0.11746$$
$$R = \$20,000 \times 0.11746 = \$2,349.20$$

GIVEN: $500 is invested each year at 8 per cent interest.
REQUIRED: Accumulated value in 15 years (i.e., amount of an annuity).

SOLUTION:
$$S = R \frac{(1 + i)^n - 1}{i} = \$500 \frac{1.08^{15} - 1}{0.08}$$
$$\text{Compound-amount factor} = \frac{(1 + i)^n - 1}{i} = \frac{1.08^{15} - 1}{0.08} = 27.152$$
$$S = \$500 \times 27.152 = \$13,576$$

GIVEN: $8,000 is required annually for 25 years.
REQUIRED: Sum that must be deposited now at 6 per cent interest.

SOLUTION:
$$P = R \frac{(1 + i)^n - 1}{i(1 + i)^n} = \$8,000 \frac{1.06^{25} - 1}{0.06 \times 1.06^{25}}$$
$$\text{Present-worth factor} = \frac{(1 + i)^n - 1}{i(1 + i)^n} = \frac{1.06^{25} - 1}{0.06 \times 1.06^{25}} = 12.783$$
$$P = \$8,000 \times 12.78 = \$102,264$$

MATHEMATICS

1-16. Miscellaneous Constants and Identities

$\pi = 3.1415926536$ (pi) $\ln \pi = 1.1447298858$
$e = 2.7182818285$ (Napierian) $\log \pi = 0.4971498727$
$\gamma = 0.5772156649$ (Euler) $\log (\log e) = 9.637784311{-}10$
$\log x = 0.4342944819 \ln x$ $\ln x = 2.302585093 \log x$

$\sqrt{2} = 1.4142135624$ $\sqrt{6} = 2.4494897428$ $\sqrt{10} = 3.1622776607$
$\sqrt{3} = 1.7320508076$ $\sqrt{7} = 2.6457513110$ $\sqrt{\gamma} = 0.7597471058$
$\sqrt{5} = 2.2360679775$ $\sqrt{8} = 2.8284271247$ $\sqrt{1/\pi} = 0.5641895385$
$\sqrt{e} = 1.6487212707$ $\sqrt{\pi/2} = 1.2533141373$ $\ln 2 = 0.6931471806$
$\sqrt{\pi} = 1.7724538509$ $\sqrt{\pi/3} = 1.0233267079$ $\ln 10 = 2.302585093$
$\sqrt{2\pi} = 2.5066282746$ $\sqrt{0.1} = 0.3162277660$ $\log e = 0.4342944819$

1 radian = 57.2957795131 degrees   1 degree = 0.0174532925 radian
1 minute = 0.0002908882 radian   1 second = 0.0000048481 radian

		Indeterminants	*Example*
$a^0 = 1$	$(a > 0)$	$(\infty)(0)$	$\lim\limits_{x \to \infty} x e^{-x} = 0$
$0^a = 0$	$(a > 0)$	0^0	$\lim\limits_{x \to 0} x^x = 1$
$a^\infty = 0$	$(a < 1)$	∞^0	$\lim\limits_{x \to 1} \left(\dfrac{1}{1 - x} \right)^{1-x} = 1$
$a^\infty = \infty$	$(a > 1)$		
$\infty^a = 0$	$(a < 0)$	1^∞	$\lim\limits_{x \to 1} (1 - x)^{1/x} = e^{-1}$
$\infty^a = \infty$	$(a > 0)$	$\infty - \infty$	$\lim\limits_{x \to \pi/2} (\sec x - \tan x) = 0$
$1^0 = 1$		$0/0$	$\lim\limits_{x \to 0} \dfrac{\sin x}{x} = 1$
		∞/∞	$\lim\limits_{x \to \pi/2} \dfrac{\ln (\pi/2 - x)}{\tan x} = \infty$

$a^{-n} = 1/a^n$ $(a^n)^m = a^{nm}$ $\sqrt[m]{\sqrt[n]{a}} = a^{1/mn}$
$(ab)^n = a^n b^n$ $\sqrt[n]{a} = a^{1/n}$ $\sqrt[n]{a^m} = a^{m/n}$

For $\dfrac{a}{b} = \dfrac{c}{d}$ then $\dfrac{a + b}{b} = \dfrac{c + d}{d}$ $\dfrac{a - b}{b} = \dfrac{c - d}{d}$

$$\dfrac{a - b}{a + b} = \dfrac{c - d}{c + d} \qquad \dfrac{a + b}{a - b} = \dfrac{c + d}{c - d}$$

$\log ab = \log a + \log b$ $\log a^n = n \log a$

$\log \dfrac{a}{b} = \log a - \log b$ $\log \sqrt[n]{a} = \dfrac{1}{n} \log a$

For $S = x^n$ $S = \sqrt{x}$

        $= e^{n \ln x}$ $S_{i+1} = \dfrac{1}{2} \left(\dfrac{x}{S_i} + S_i \right)$

By iteration

Approximations ($\cong$) When x Is Small

$$\frac{1}{1 \pm x} \cong 1 \mp x \qquad\qquad \sqrt{1 \pm x} \cong 1 \pm \frac{x}{2}$$

$$\frac{1 + y}{1 \pm x} \cong 1 + y \mp x(1 + y) \qquad (1 \pm x)^{-n} \cong 1 \mp nx$$

$$(1 \pm x)^n \cong 1 \pm nx \qquad\qquad (1 \pm x)^{-1/2} \cong 1 \mp x/2$$

$$(a \pm x)^2 \cong a^2 \pm 2ax \qquad\qquad e^x \cong 1 + x$$

$$\sin x \cong x \quad (x \text{ in radians}) \qquad \tan x \cong x$$

$$\sqrt{y(y + x)} \cong \frac{2y + x}{2} \qquad\qquad \sqrt{y^2 + x^2} \cong y + \frac{x^2}{2y} \quad \left(\frac{x}{y} \text{ small}\right)$$

General

$$n! \cong e^{-n} n^n \sqrt{2\pi n}$$

$$n! \cong \sqrt{2\pi} \left(\frac{\sqrt{n^2 + n + \frac{1}{6}}}{e}\right)^{n + \frac{1}{2}}$$

1-17. Mensuration

Let A denote areas and V volumes in the following definitions.

Plane Geometric Figures with Straight Boundaries. *Triangles* (see also Trigonometry). $A = \frac{1}{2}bh$, where b = base, h = altitude.

Rectangle. $A = ab$, where a and b = lengths of sides.

Parallelogram (opposite sides parallel). $A = ah = ab \sin \alpha$, where a, b = lengths of sides, h = height, and α = angle between sides.

Trapezoid (four sides, two parallel). $A = \frac{1}{2}(a + b)h$, where a and b = lengths of parallel sides, and h = height.

Quadrilateral (four sides). $A = \frac{1}{2}ab \sin \theta$, where a, b = lengths of diagonals, and acute angle between them is θ.

Regular Polygon of n sides. $A = \frac{1}{4}nl^2 \cot (180°/n)$, where l = length of each side.

Inscribed and Circumscribed Circles with Regular Polygons of n Sides. Let l = length of one side, and n = number of sides.

Figure	n	Area	Radius of circumscribed circle	Radius of inscribed circle
Equilateral triangle....	3	0.4330l^2	0.5774l	0.2887l
Square..............	4	1.0000l^2	0.7071l	0.5000l
Pentagon............	5	1.7205l^2	0.8507l	0.6882l
Hexagon.............	6	2.5981l^2	1.0000l	0.8660l
Heptagon............	7	3.6339l^2	1.1523l	1.0383l
Octagon.............	8	4.8284l^2	1.3065l	1.2071l

Plane Geometric Figures with Curved Boundaries. *Circle.* Let C = circumference, r = radius, D = diameter, A = area, S = arc length subtended by angle θ in radians, l = cord length subtended by θ, H = rise, $d = r - H$.

$$C = 2\pi r = \pi D \qquad (\pi = 3.14159 \ldots)$$
$$S = r\theta = \tfrac{1}{2}D\theta$$

$$l = 2\sqrt{r^2 - d^2} = 2r\sin\frac{\theta}{2} = 2d\tan\frac{\theta}{2}$$

$$H = r - d$$

$$d = \frac{1}{2}\sqrt{4r^2 - l^2} = \frac{1}{2}l\cot\frac{\theta}{2}$$

$$\theta = \frac{S}{r} = 2\cos^{-1}\frac{d}{r} = 2\sin^{-1}\frac{l}{D}$$

$$A \text{ (circle)} = \pi r^2 = \tfrac{1}{4}\pi D^2$$
$$A \text{ (sector)} = \tfrac{1}{2}rS = \tfrac{1}{2}r^2\theta$$
$$A \text{ (segment)} = A \text{ (sector)} - A \text{ (triangle)} = \tfrac{1}{2}r^2(\theta - \sin\theta)$$
$$= r^2\cos^{-1}\frac{r - H}{r} - (r - H)\sqrt{2rH - H^2}$$

Ring (area between two circles of radius r_1 and r_2). (The circles need not be concentric, but one of the circles must enclose the other.)

$$A = \pi(r_1 + r_2)(r_1 - r_2), \qquad r_1 > r_2$$

Ellipse. Let the semiaxes of the ellipse be a and b. $A = \pi ab$, $C = 4aE(k)$, $k = 1 - b^2/a^2$, and $E(k)$ is the (tabulated) complete elliptic integral of the first kind.

Solid Geometric Figures with Plane Boundaries. *Cube.* Volume = a^3; total surface area = $6a^2$; diagonal = $a\sqrt{3}$, where a = length of one side of cube.

Rectangular Parallelepiped. Volume = abc; surface area = $2(ab + ac + bc)$; diagonal = $\sqrt{a^2 + b^2 + c^2}$, where a, b, c = lengths of sides.

Prism. Volume = (area of base) $\times$ (altitude); lateral surface area = (perimeter of right section) $\times$ (lateral edge).

Pyramid. Volume = $\tfrac{1}{3}$(area of base) $\times$ (altitude); lateral area of regular pyramid = $\tfrac{1}{2}$ (perimeter of base) $\times$ (slant height) = $\tfrac{1}{2}$ (number of sides) $\times$ (length of one side) $\times$ (slant height).

Volume and Surface Area of Regular Polyhedra with Edge l

Type of surface	Name	Volume	Surface area
4 equilateral triangles.......	Tetrahedron	$0.1179l^3$	$1.7321l^2$
6 squares...................	Hexahedron	$1.0000l^3$	$6.0000l^2$
8 equilateral triangles.......	Octahedron	$0.4714l^3$	$3.4641l^2$
12 pentagons...............	Dodecahedron	$7.6631l^3$	$20.6458l^2$
20 equilateral triangles......	Icosahedron	$2.1817l^3$	$8.6603l^2$

Solids Bounded by Curved Surfaces. *Cylinder.* V = (area of base) $\times$ (altitude); lateral surface area = (perimeter of right section) $\times$ (lateral edge).

Right Circular Cylinder. $V = \pi$ (radius)^2 × (altitude); lateral surface area = 2π (radius) × (altitude).

Truncated Right Circular Cylinder. $V = \pi r^2 h$; lateral area = $2\pi rh$; $h = \frac{1}{2}(h_1 + h_2)$.

Hollow Cylinder. Volume = $\pi h(R^2 - r^2)$, where r and R = internal and external radii, and h = height of cylinder.

Sphere

V (sphere) $= \frac{4}{3}\pi R^3 = \frac{1}{6}\pi D^3$

V (spherical sector) $= \frac{2}{3}\pi R^2 h = \frac{1}{6}\pi D^2 h$

V (spherical segment of one base) $= \frac{1}{6}\pi h_1(3r_1^2 + h_1^2)$

A (sphere) $= 4\pi R^2 = \pi D^2$

A (zone) $= 2\pi Rh = \pi Dh$

Cone. $V = \frac{1}{3}$(area of base) × (altitude).

Right Circular Cone. $V = (\pi/3)r^2 h$, where h = altitude, and r = radius of base; curved surface area $= \pi r \sqrt{r^2 + h^2}$, curved surface of *frustum of a right cone* $= \pi(r_1 + r_2)\sqrt{h^2 + (r_1 - r_2)^2}$, where r_1, r_2 = radii of base and top, respectively, and h = altitude; volume of frustum of a right cone = $\pi(h/3)(r_1^2 + r_1 r_2 + r_2^2) = \frac{1}{3}(A_1 + A_2 + \sqrt{A_1 A_2})$, where A_1 = area of base and A_2 = area of top.

Ellipsoid. $V = \frac{4}{3}\pi abc$, where a, b, c = lengths of semiaxes.

Torus (obtained by rotating a circle of radius r about a line whose distance is $R > r$ from the center of the circle). $V = 2\pi^2 R r^2$; surface area $= 4\pi^2 R r$.

Miscellaneous Formulas (see also section on calculus). *Volume of a Solid of Revolution* (the solid generated by rotating a plane area about the x axis).

$$V = \pi \int_a^b [f(x)]^2 \, dx, \text{ where } y = f(x) = \text{equation of place curve, and } a \le x \le b.$$

Area of a Surface of Revolution. $S = 2\pi \int_a^b y \, ds$, where

$$ds = \sqrt{1 + \left(\frac{dy}{dx}\right)^2} \, dx$$

and $y = f(x)$ is the equation of the plane curve rotated about the x axis to generate the surface.

Area Bounded by $f(x)$, the x Axis, and the Lines $x = a$, $x = b$

$$A = \int_a^b f(x) \, dx$$

Length of Arc of a Plane Curve

If $y = f(x)$:   Length of arc $s = \int_a^b \sqrt{1 + \left(\frac{dy}{dx}\right)^2} \, dx$

If $x = g(y)$:   Length of arc $s = \int_c^d \sqrt{1 + \left(\frac{dx}{dy}\right)^2} \, dy$

If $x = f(t)$: $y = g(t)$, $s = \int_{t_0}^{t_1} \sqrt{\left(\frac{dx}{dt}\right)^2 + \left(\frac{dy}{dt}\right)^2} \, dt$

The Theorem of Pappus (for volumes and areas of surfaces of revolution). (1) If a plane area is revolved about a line which lies in its plane but does not intersect the area, then the volume generated is equal to the product of the area and the distance traveled by the area's center of gravity. (2) If an arc of a plane curve is revolved about a line which lies in its plane but does not intersect the arc, then the surface area generated by the arc is equal to the product of the length of the arc and the distance traveled by its center of gravity.

Irregular Areas. Let $y_0, y_1, \ldots, y_n$ be the lengths of a series of equally spaced parallel chords, and h be their distance apart. The area of the figure is given approximately by any of the following equations:

$$A_T = \frac{h}{3}[(y_0 + y_n) + 2(y_1 + y_2 + \cdots + y_{n-1})] \qquad \text{(trapezoidal rule)}$$

$$A_S = \frac{h}{3}[(y_0 + y_n) + 4(y_1 + y_3 + y_5 + \cdots + y_{n-1})$$
$$+ 2(y_2 + y_4 + \cdots + y_{n-2})] \qquad \text{(n even, Simpson's rule)}$$

$$A_W = \frac{3h}{8}[(y_0 + y_n) + 3(y_1 + y_2 + y_4 + y_5 + \cdots) + 2(y_3 + y_6 + \cdots)]$$
$$\left(\text{Weddle's } \frac{3}{8} \text{ rule}\right)$$

The greater the value of n, the greater the accuracy of approximation.

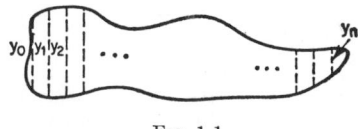

Fig. 1-1

1-18. Dimensions, Units, and Dimensionless Groups

Properties of the physical world are expressed in dimensioned form, and dimensions are expressed in units. Currently, three systems of units are in common use.

Engineering System. Mass M, time t, length L, and force F are considered primary and independent dimensions. None of the four need be defined in terms of the others. However, force F and mass M are related by Newton's second law of motion $F = (1/g_c)Ma$, where a = acceleration resulting from application of force F on mass M, with dimension L/t^2. For this relation to be dimensionally consistent, a constant $(1/g_c)$ must be introduced *for this system.* The constant g_c has the dimension ML/Ft^2, and is numerically equal to the acceleration of gravity at sea level.

Absolute System. Mass M, time t, and length L are considered primary dimensions having independent units. Force is defined in terms of these three, and has the dimension ML/t^2. Since force and mass are not considered to be independent dimensionally, no relating dimensional constant is required.

Gravitational System. Force F, time t, and length L are considered primary dimensions having independent units. Mass is defined in terms of these three, and has the dimension Ft^2/L. As force and mass are not considered to be independent dimensionally, no relating constant is required.

The three systems are compared and dimensions and units for both the English and metric systems given in Tables 1-18A and 1-18B.

Dimensionless Groups. The use of dimensionless numbers or groups of variables is fundamental to many engineering studies. This results in connection with, for example, model and scale-up studies. If all variables affecting a particular operation are known, dimensional analysis can be employed to indicate the groups of variables that are important. Consequently, the number of experiments is reduced by dimensional analysis, since only the effect of each grouping need be explored, rather than the effect of each individual variable. There are a large number of useful dimensionless groups; so only the more commonly occurring ones are given in Table 1-18C. The reader is referred to Boucher and Alves, "A Tabulation of Dimensionless Groups," *Chem. Eng. Progr.*, **55**, 55–64 (September, 1959) for additional listings.

Table 1-18A. Metric System of Units

Quantity	Absolute system		Gravitational system		Engineering system	
	Dimension	Unit	Dimension	Unit	Dimension	Unit
Time.......	t	Second	t	Second	t	Second
Length......	L	Centimeter	L	Centimeter	L	Centimeter
Mass.......	M	Gram	Ft^2/L	Gram	M	Gram
Force.......	ML/t^2	Dyne	F	Gram force	F	Gram force
Work.......	ML^2/t^2	Dyne-centimeter (erg)	FL	Centimeter-gram force	FL	Centimeter-gram force
Temperature	T	Degree centigrade absolute or degree Kelvin	T	Degree centigrade absolute or degree Kelvin	T	Degree centigrade absolute or degree Kelvin
Heat........	ML^2/t^2	Dyne-centimeter (erg)	FL	Centimeter-gram	Q	Calorie
g_c..........	None	None	None	None	ML/Ft^2	980.665 (g mass) (cm) / (g force) (sec²)
J..........	None	None	None	None	FL/Q	42,699 cm-g force/cal

Table 1-18B. English System of Units

Quantity	Absolute system		Gravitational system		Engineering system	
	Dimen-sion	Unit	Dimen-sion	Unit	Dimen-sion	Unit
Time........	t	Second	t	Second	t	Second
Length......	L	Foot	L	Foot	L	Foot
Mass.......	M	Pound mass	Ft^2/L	Slug	M	Pound mass
Force.......	ML/t^2	Poundal	F	Pound force	F	Pound force
Work.......	ML^2/t^2	Foot-poundal	FL	Foot-pound force	FL	Foot-pound force
Temperature	T	Degree Fahrenheit absolute or degree Rankine	T	Degree Fahrenheit absolute or degree Rankine	T	Degree Fahrenheit absolute
Heat........	ML^2/t^2	Foot-poundal	FL	Foot-pound force	Q	Btu
g_c..........	None	None	None	None	ML/Ft^2	32.174 (lb mass)(ft)/ (lb force) (sec^2)
J..........	None	None	None	None	FL/Q	778.26 ft-lb force/Btu

Table 1-18C. Dimensionless Groups

Dimensions Used
[F] force, [H] heat, [L] length, [M] mass, [Q] electric charge, [T] temperature, [t] time.

General Nomenclature
c_p = specific heat, [H/MT]; g_L = gravitational constant, [L/t²]; g_c = conversion factor, [LM/Ft²]; h = heat transfer coefficient, [H/L²Tt]; k = thermal conductivity, [H/LTt]; V = fluid velocity, [L/t]; β = expansion coefficient, [1/T]; ΔT = temperature difference, [T]; μ = viscosity, [M/Lt]; ρ = density, [M/L³]; σ = surface tension, [F/L]; τ_w = shear stress at wall, [F/L²].

Name	Symbol	Formula	Special nomenclature
Fluid mechanics Bingham number.............	N_{Bm}	$\dfrac{\tau_y g_c L}{\mu_p V}$	L = width of channel, [L] μ_p = coeff. of rigidity, [M/tL] τ_y = yield stress, [F/L²] E_b = bulk modulus of fluid, [F/L²].
Cauchy number.............	N_c	$\dfrac{\rho V^2}{g_c E_b}$	
Drag coefficient.............	C_d	$\dfrac{(\rho - \rho')Lg_L}{\rho V^2}$	L = characteristic dimension of object, [L] ρ = object density, [M/L³] ρ' = density of surrounding fluid, [M/L³]
Elasticity number.............	N_{El}	$\dfrac{t_r \mu}{\rho L^2}$	L = radius of pipe, [L] t_r = relaxation time, [t]
Euler number.............	N_{Eu}	$\dfrac{g_c(\Delta p_F/\rho)}{V^2}$	$\dfrac{\Delta p_F}{\rho}$ = friction head, [LF/M]
Fanning friction factor....	f	$\dfrac{g_c D(\Delta p_F/\rho)}{2V^2 L}$	L = length of pipe, [L] D = diameter of cross section, [L] $\Delta p_F/\rho$ = friction head, [LF/M]
Froude number.............	N_{Fr}	$\dfrac{V^2}{g_L L}$	L = characteristic system dimension, [L]
Karmán number.............	N_K	$\dfrac{g_c \rho D^3(-dp/dL)}{\mu^2}$	D = pipe diameter, [L] dp/dL = pressure gradient, [F/L³]
Knudsen number.............	N_{Kn}	$\dfrac{\lambda}{L}$	L = characteristic system dimension, [L] λ = length of mean free path, [L]
Mach number.............	N_{Ma}	$\dfrac{V}{V_c}$	V_c = velocity of sound in fluid, [L/t]

1-68

Pipeline parameter.............	ρ_n	$\dfrac{aV_0}{2g_cH}$
Poiseuille number.............	N_{Po}	$\dfrac{g_cD^2(-dp/dL)}{\mu V}$
Ratio of specific heats........	γ	$\dfrac{c_p}{c_v}$
Reynolds number.............	N_{Re}	$\dfrac{LV\rho}{\mu}$
Weber number................	N_{We}	$\dfrac{V^2\rho L}{g_c\sigma}$
Heat transfer		
Biot number.................	N_{Bi}	$\dfrac{hr_m}{k}$
Fourier number..............	N_{Fo}	$\dfrac{kt}{\rho c_p r_m{}^2}$
Graetz number..............	N_{Gz}	$\dfrac{wc_p}{kL}$
Grashof number.............	N_{Gr}	$\dfrac{L^3\rho^2 g_L\beta\,\Delta T}{\mu^2}$
Nusselt number..............	N_{Nu}	$\dfrac{hL}{k}$
Peclet number...............	N_{Pe}	$\dfrac{LV\rho c_p}{k}$
Prandtl number..............	N_{Pr}	$\dfrac{c_p\mu}{k}$
Mass transfer		
Lewis number................	N_{Le}	$\dfrac{k}{\rho c_p D_V}$
Peclet number...............	$N_{\text{Pe}'}$	$\dfrac{LV}{D'}$

a = water-hammer wave velocity, $[L/t]$
H = static head, $[LF/M]$
V_0 = initial velocity, $[L/t]$

D = diameter of round pipe, $[L]$
dp/dL = pressure gradient, $[F/L^3]$

c_p = specific heat at constant pressure, $[H/MT]$
c_v = specific heat at constant volume, $[H/MT]$
L = characteristic system dimension, $[L]$

L = characteristic system dimension, $[L]$
σ = surface tension, $[F/L]$

r_m = distance from midpoint to surface, $[L]$

r_m = distance from midpoint to surface
t = elapsed time, $[t]$
L = length of heat-transfer channel, $[L]$
w = mass flow rate, $[M/t]$
L = height of surface, $[L]$
ΔT = temperature difference across film, $[T]$
β = expansion coefficient, $[1/T]$
L = heat-transfer-path characteristic length, $[L]$

L = characteristic system dimension, $[L]$

D_V = molecular diffusivity, $[L^2/t]$

L = characteristic length, $[L]$
D' = characteristic diffusion coeff., $[L^2/t]$

Table 1-18C. Dimensionless Groups (Continued)

Name	Symbol	Formula	Special nomenclature
Schmidt number...........	N_{Sc}	$\dfrac{\mu}{\rho D_V}$	D_V = molecular diffusivity, $[L^2/t]$
Sherwood number........	N_{Sh}	$\dfrac{k_c L}{D_V}$	L = characteristic dimension, $[L]$ k_c = mass transfer coeff., $[L/t]$
Rayleigh number........	R'	$\dfrac{L^3 \rho^2 g_L \beta c_p \, \Delta T}{\mu k}$	L = surface height, $[L]$ ΔT = temperature difference across film, $[T]$ β = expansion coefficient, $[1/T]$
Chemical reaction			
Arrhenius group.........		$\dfrac{E}{RT}$	E = activation energy, $[LF/M]$ R = gas constant, $[LF/MT]$ T = absolute temperature, $[T]$
Damkohler group I........		$\dfrac{UL}{V C_A}$ $\dfrac{C_A}{U L^2}$	C_A = concentration, $[M/L^3]$ k = reaction rate constant, $[(L^3/M)^{n-1}/t]$ n = reaction order U = reaction rate, $[M/L^3 t]$
Damkohler group II.......		$\dfrac{D_V C_A}{U L^2}$	D_V = molecular diffusivity, $[L^2/t]$
Damkohler group III......		$\dfrac{Q U L}{\rho c_p V T}$	L = characteristic dimension, $[L]$
Damkohler group IV......		$\dfrac{Q U L^2}{k T}$	Q = heat generated, $[H/M]$ T = temperature, $[T]$

1-19. Significant Figures and Errors

1. The conventional process of *rounding* a number to n digits consists in replacing that number by an n-digit approximation with minimum error. When this requirement leads to two admissible roundings, that one for which the nth digit of the rounded number is *even* is selected. Thus $6.05149 \doteq 6.0515$, 6.051, 6.05, 6.1, and 6; but $6.0515 \doteq 6.052$ and $6.05 \doteq 6.0$. Using this rule, the magnitude of the error is less than or equal to one-half unit of the place of the nth digit in the rounded number.

2. Each correct digit of the approximation, except a zero which serves only to fix the decimal point, is called a *significant figure*. Thus 8.23, 0.0361, and 9.00 each contain three significant figures.

3. If two numbers are rounded to n significant figures, the product of the rounded numbers differs from the true product by less than *four units* in the place of its nth significant digit.

4. When any function $f(x)$, with a continuous derivative, is evaluated, with x replaced by an approximation $\bar{x}$, the mean-value relation $f(x) - f(\bar{x}) = (x - \bar{x})f'(\eta)$, η between x and $\bar{x}$, allows us to deduce that the *error* $E(f(x)) = f(x) - f(\bar{x})$ can be estimated by

$$|E(f(x))| \leq |f'(\eta)|_{\max} |E(x)|$$

The *relative error* $R(f(x)) = [f(x) - f(\bar{x})]/f(x)$ is easily estimated by

$$|R(f(x))| \leq |f'(\eta)|_{\max} |E(x)|/f(x)$$

For example, if $f(x) = \log_{10} x$, then one finds $|E(\log_{10} x)| \leq \dfrac{\log_{10} e}{|\eta|} |E(x)|$, where η lies between $x - E(x)$ and $x + E(x)$. If $x \geq 1$, $|E(x)| \leq \frac{1}{2}$, then $|E(\log_{10} x)| \leq \dfrac{0.44}{1 - |E|} |E(x)| < |E(x)|$. Thus, if the argument exceeds 1, the error in $\log_{10} x$ is less than the error in the argument.

5. By the argument of point 4, for the *sum* or *difference* of two rounded numbers, the error in the result is the algebraic sum of the errors in the separate terms. The magnitude of the maximum error is the sum of the magnitudes of the component errors. If p numbers (positive or negative) are each rounded to n decimal places, that is, each is in error by an amount less than $5 \times 10^{-n-1}$ in magnitude, then the magnitude of the *maximum error* of the *sum* is $5p \times 10^{-n-1}$. Thus the result can be in error by as much as $p/2$ units in the nth decimal place.

6. Most numerical calculations are inexact either as a result of used-data inaccuracies or of inaccuracies introduced in the subsequent analysis of those data. Errors, aside from *gross errors* which arise from unpredictable human or mechanical mistakes, are of two general types. *Roundoff error* arises as a consequence of using a number specified by n correct digits to approximate a number requiring more than n digits (generally, infinitely many) for its exact specification. A *truncation error* is any error which is neither *gross* nor

roundoff. The term is often used to designate that error which occurs wherein an exact result would be obtained by an infinite sequence of steps but the process is "truncated" after a finite number of steps. If a function $f(x)$ has an *infinite* Taylor series, it may be approximated by

$$f(x) = f(a) + \frac{f'(a)}{1!}(x - a) + \frac{f''(a)}{2!}(x - a)^2 + \cdots + \frac{f^{(n)}(a)}{n!}(x - a)^n + E_T,$$

where $|E_T(x_1)| \leq |f^{n+1}(x)|_{max} \dfrac{(x_1 - a)^{n+1}}{(n + 1)!}$, and the maximum value of the derivative is calculated on $a \leq x \leq x_1$. If in a series the terms alternate in sign and if the absolute value of the individual terms is continually decreasing, then the absolute value of the *truncation error* is not greater than the magnitude of the first term omitted.

7. If a quantity $S = F(x_1, x_2, x_3, \ldots, x_n)$ and the x_i are subject to errors $dx_i, i = 1, 2, \ldots, n$, which are *small* in magnitude compared with the magnitude of the x_i, then the error in S, dS, can be approximated by $dS = \displaystyle\sum_{i=1}^{n}(\partial F/\partial x_i)\, dx_i$. However, if the errors Δx_i are large, then the error ΔS should be calculated by $\Delta S = F(x_1 + \Delta x_1, x_2 + \Delta x_2, \ldots, x_n + \Delta x_n) - F(x_1, \ldots, x_n)$.

8. In many cases the data are subject to random errors. Consequently, one cannot guarantee a certain error, but can only *estimate* the *probability* of occurrence. In most cases it is assumed that errors are symmetrically distributed about a zero mean and that, in a sufficiently large set of data, the probability of the occurrence of an error between x and $x + dx$ is $\phi(x)\, dx = (1/\sqrt{2\pi}\,\sigma)e^{-x^2/2\sigma^2}\, dx$, where σ is a parameter, to be estimated from the data. The function $\phi(x)$ (here taken as the given exponential) is called the *frequency function* of the distribution. The probability that an error does not exceed x is given by the *normal distribution function* $\Phi(x) = \displaystyle\int_{-\infty}^{x}\phi(u)\, du = (1/\sqrt{2\pi}\,\sigma)\displaystyle\int_{-\infty}^{x}e^{-u^2/2\sigma^2}\, du$, where $\Phi(\infty) = 1$ is chosen from the (arbitrary) requirement of unit probability that any error lie somewhere in $(-\infty, \infty)$. The probability $P(x)$ that an error, chosen at random, lies between $-|x|$ and $+|x|$ is $P(x) = \sqrt{\dfrac{2}{\pi}}\dfrac{1}{\sigma}\displaystyle\int_{0}^{|x|}e^{-u^2/2\sigma^2}\, du$. The parameter σ is the *standard deviation* (σ^2 is the *variance*) of the distribution. If ϵ is a random variable, the *mean* (*expected*) value of any function $g(\epsilon)$, relative to the assumed distribution ϕ, is given by

$$E[g(\epsilon)] = \int_{-\infty}^{\infty}\phi(u)g(u)\, du = \frac{1}{\sqrt{2\pi}\,\sigma}\int_{-\infty}^{\infty}e^{-u^2/2\sigma^2}g(u)\, du.$$

Thus $E[\epsilon] = 0$, $E[|\epsilon|] = \sqrt{2/\pi}\,\sigma$, $E[\epsilon^2] = \sigma^2$ (variance).

If we specify $\sigma = \epsilon_{\text{rms}} = \sqrt{\dfrac{1}{k-1} \sum\limits_{i=1}^{k} (x_i - \bar{x})^2}$, that is, as the square root of the mean of the squared errors in the true distribution, estimated from a sample of the deviations of k measurements from their mean value, one can then estimate the probability of an error relative to ϵ_{rms}. The following tabulation gives a few estimates in terms of the probability $Q(x) = 1 - P(x)$ that the error exceeds x in magnitude:

$\epsilon/\epsilon_{\text{rms}}$	0.674	0.842	1.000	1.036	1.282	1.645	2.576
$Q(\epsilon)$	0.500	0.400	0.317	0.300	0.200	0.100	0.010

The probability of an error whose magnitude is greater than ϵ_{rms} is 0.317. Only 10 per cent of the errors should exceed $1.645\epsilon_{\text{rms}}$ if the distribution is nearly normal. The number 0.674σ is often called the *probable error* of the distribution.

If ϵ is a random variable representing roundoff error, due to rounding to the nth decimal, then $\epsilon_{\text{rms}} = 0.2887 \times 10^{-n}$.

1-20. Logarithmic and Exponential Relationships

Definitions

Log base $e = \log_e = \ln$ $\ln X = Z \rightarrow X = e^Z$
Log base $10 = \log_{10} = \log$ $\log X = Z \rightarrow X = 10^Z$
Log base $p = \log_p$ $\log_p X = Z \rightarrow X = p^Z$
                 p any positive base except 0 or 1

Antilog$_p$, or $\log_p^{-1}$, is that number whose log value is stated for $\log_p X = Z$, then given Z, find $X \rightarrow X = \log^{-1} Z$.

Conversion

For $\log_p X = Z \rightarrow X = p^Z$
                      $= e^{Z \ln p}$ since $p = e^{\ln p}$
                      $= 10^{Z \log p}$ since $p = 10^{\log p}$

Identities

$\log_p XY = \log_p X + \log_p Y$ $\log_p X^{-n} = -n \log_p X$

$\log_p \dfrac{X}{Y} = \log_p X - \log_p Y$ $\log_p \sqrt[n]{X} = \dfrac{1}{n} \log_p X$

$\log_p X^n = n \log_p X$ $\log_p \sqrt[n]{X^m} = \dfrac{m}{n} \log_p X$

$\log X = (\log e) \ln X$ since $X = e^{\ln X}$
                         $\log X = (\ln X)(\log e)$
       $= 0.434294482 \ln X$
$\ln X = (\ln 10) \log X$
       $= 2.302585093 \log X$

Series

$$\ln x = \begin{cases} \dfrac{x-1}{x} + \dfrac{1}{2}\left(\dfrac{x-1}{x}\right)^2 + \dfrac{1}{3}\left(\dfrac{x-1}{x}\right)^3 + \cdots + \dfrac{1}{n}\left(\dfrac{x-1}{x}\right)^n + \cdots \\ \qquad\qquad\qquad\qquad\qquad\qquad\qquad\qquad\qquad x>0.5 \\[4pt] (x-1) - \tfrac{1}{2}(x-1)^2 + \tfrac{1}{3}(x-1)^3 + \cdots + \dfrac{(-1)^{n+1}}{n}(x-1)^n + \cdots \\ \qquad\qquad\qquad\qquad\qquad\qquad\qquad\qquad\qquad 0<x\le 2.0 \\[4pt] 2\left[\dfrac{x-1}{x+1} + \dfrac{1}{3}\left(\dfrac{x-1}{x+1}\right)^3 + \dfrac{1}{5}\left(\dfrac{x-1}{x+1}\right)^5 + \cdots + \dfrac{1}{2n+1}\left(\dfrac{x-1}{x+1}\right)^{2n+1} + \cdots\right] \\ \qquad\qquad\qquad\qquad\qquad\qquad\qquad\qquad\qquad x>0 \end{cases}$$

Calculation Example. Find $Z = A^B = (0.000273)^{0.074}$.

By Logarithmic Transformation

Define $\log Z = 0.074 \log 0.000273$

$\qquad\qquad = 0.074 \log [(2.73)(0.0001)]$

$\qquad\qquad = 0.074(\log 2.73 + \log 0.0001)$

$\qquad\qquad = 0.074(0.43616 - 4)$

$\qquad\qquad = 0.03225 - 0.296$

$\qquad\qquad = -0.26375$

$\qquad\qquad = 0.73625 - 1$

$\qquad Z = \log^{-1} 0.73625 / \log^{-1} 1$

where $\qquad\qquad \log^{-1} 0.73625 = 5.448 \qquad \log^{-1} 1 = 10$

$\therefore \qquad\qquad\qquad Z = 5.448/10 = 0.5448$

By Exponential Table

For $Z = (0.000273)^{0.074}$

$\qquad = e^{0.074 \ln 0.000273}$

$\qquad = e^{0.074 (\ln 0.001 + \ln 0.273)}$ (most ln tables have minimum arguments to

$\qquad = e^{0.074(-8.20604)}$ 0.001)

$\qquad = e^{-0.60725}$

Most exponential tables are in increments of 0.01.

$\therefore \qquad\qquad e^{-0.60} = 0.548812 \qquad e^{-0.61} = 0.543351$

and $\qquad\qquad Z = 0.548812 - 0.725(0.548812 - 0.543351)$

$\qquad\qquad\qquad = 0.5448$

1-21. Analytic Geometry

The basic concept of analytic geometry is the establishment of a one-to-one correspondence between the points of the plane and number pair (x,y). This correspondence may be done in a number of ways. The *rectangular*, or *cartesian*, coordinate system consists of two straight lines intersecting at right angles. A point is designated by (x,y), where x (the abscissa) is the distance of the point from the y axis measured parallel to the x axis. The ordinate y is the distance of the point from the x axis. The *quadrants* are labeled I, II, III, and IV.

Another common coordinate system is the *polar* system. In this system the position of a point is designated by the pair (r,θ), where

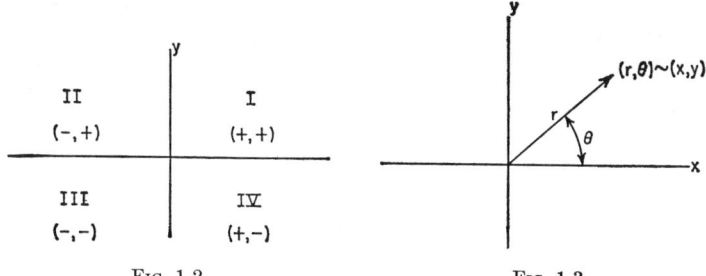

Fig. 1-2   Fig. 1-3

$$r^2 = x^2 + y^2$$

and $x = r \cos \theta$ $y = r \sin \theta$

Distance. The distance between two points (x_1, y_1), (x_2, y_2) is given by

$$d = [(x_1 - x_2)^2 + (y_1 - y_2)^2]^{1/2}$$

or $d = [r_1^2 + r_2^2 - 2r_1 r_2 \cos(\theta_1 - \theta_2)]^{1/2}$

Straight Line. The general equation of a straight line is given by

$$Ax + By + C = 0$$

If a straight line passes through two known points (x_1, y_1) and (x_2, y_2), then

$$y - y_1 = \frac{y_2 - y_1}{x_2 - x_1}(x - x_1)$$

where $\dfrac{y_2 - y_1}{x_2 - x_1} = m$ $(m = \text{slope})$

Two straight lines are parallel if, and only if, they have the same slope. Two lines are perpendicular if, and only if, the product of their slopes is -1 (excluding lines parallel to the coordinate axes).

Linear Transformations. Some nonlinear relationships can be made linear by a suitable transformation:

Function	Transformation	Resultant form
$y = ae^{bx}$	$y' = \ln y$	$y' = a' + bx$ where $a' = \ln a$
$y = ab^x$	$y' = \ln y$	$y' = a' + b'x$ where $a' = \ln a$ $b' = \ln b$
$y = ax^b$	$y' = \ln y$ $x' = \ln x$	$y' = a' + bx'$ where $a' = \ln a$
$y = \dfrac{a}{b + x}$	$y' = 1/y$	$y' = a' + b'x$ where $a' = b/a$ $b' = 1/a$
$y = ae^{bx + cx^2}$	$y' = \ln y$	$y' = a' + bx + cx^2$ where $a' = \ln a$
$y = \dfrac{ax}{b + x}$	$y' = 1/y$ $x' = 1/x$	$y' = a' + b'x'$ where $a' = 1/a$ $b' = b/a$
$y = ax^{bx}$	$y' = \ln y$ $x' = x \ln x$	$y' = a' + bx'$ where $a' = \ln a$
$y = ae^{b/x}$	$y' = \ln y$ $x' = 1/x$	$y' = a' + bx'$ where $a' = \ln a$

Conic Sections. The curves included in this group are obtained from plane sections of the cone. They include the circle, ellipse, parabola, hyperbola, and degeneratively, the point and straight line. A *conic* is the locus of a point whose distance from a fixed point called the *focus* is in a constant ratio to its distance from a fixed line called a *directrix*. The ratio is the *eccentricity e*. If $e = 0$, the conic is a circle; if $0 < e < 1$, the conic is an ellipse; if $e = 1$, the conic is a parabola; if $e > 1$, the conic is a hyperbola. Every conic section is representable by an equation of second degree. Conversely, every equation of second degree in two variables represents a conic. The general equation of the second degree is

$$Ax^2 + Bxy + Cy^2 + Dx + Ey + F = 0$$

Let Δ represent the determinant

$$\Delta = \begin{vmatrix} 2A & B & D \\ B & 2C & E \\ D & E & 2F \end{vmatrix}$$

and

$$Q = D^2 + E^2 - 4(A + C)F$$

	$B^2 - 4AC < 0$	$B^2 - 4AC = 0$	$B^2 - 4AC > 0$
$\Delta \neq 0$	$A\Delta < 0$ $A \neq C$ ellipse $A\Delta < 0$ $A = C$ circle $A\Delta > 0$ no locus	Parabola	Hyperbola
$\Delta = 0$	Point	$Q > 0$ 2 parallel lines $Q = 0$ 1 straight line $Q < 0$ no locus	2 intersecting lines

1-22. Algebra

Addition and Subtraction. Only like terms are added or subtracted:

$$(3 - 5x) + (3x + 4x^2) + (5 + 2x^2) = (3 + 5) + (-5 + 3)x + (4 + 2)x^2$$
$$= 8 - 2x + 6x^2$$

Multiplication. Carried out term by term and corresponding terms are combined:

$$(3xy + 6x)(3y + 2y^2 + 2xy) = 3xy(3y + 2y^2 + 2xy) + 6x(3y + 2y^2 + 2xy)$$
$$= (9xy^2 + 6xy^3 + 6x^2y^2)$$
$$+ (18xy + 12xy^2 + 12x^2y)$$
$$= 18xy + 21xy^2 + 6xy^3 + 6x^2y^2 + 12x^2y$$

Division. Division is carried out with like terms in the same fashion as arithmetic division.

Divisor	Dividend	Quotient
$e^x + 1$	$3e^{2x} + e^x + 1$	$3e^x - 2$
	$-3e^{2x} - 3e^x$	
	$\overline{\qquad - 2e^x + 1}$	
	$+ 2e^x + 2$	
	$\overline{\qquad +3}$ remainder	

Operations with Zero. All operations except division can be carried out with zero and a finite number $a \neq 0$:

$$a + 0 = 0; \quad a(0) = 0; \quad 0/a = 0; \quad a^0 = 1; \quad 0^a = 0 \quad (a > 0)$$

Factoring

$$x^2 - y^2 = (x - y)(x + y) \qquad x^2 + y^2 = (x + yi)(x - yi) \qquad i = \sqrt{-1}$$
$$x^3 - y^3 = (x - y)(x^2 + xy + y^2) \qquad x^3 + y^3 = (x + y)(x^2 - xy + y^2)$$
$$x^4 - y^4 = (x - y)(x + y)(x^2 + y^2)$$

Quadratic Equation

$$ax^2 + bx + c = 0 \qquad x = \frac{-b \pm \sqrt{b^2 - 4ac}}{2a}$$

If $b^2 - 4ac > 0$, the roots are real and unequal.
If $b^2 - 4ac = 0$, the roots are real and equal.
If $b^2 - 4ac < 0$, the roots are imaginary.

Roots for Third- or Higher-order Equations. See numerical methods, page 1-99.

Permutation. A specific sequencing of elements of a set. The number of permutations of n things taken r at a time is written

$$P(n,r) = \frac{n!}{(n - r)!} = n(n - 1)(n - 2) \cdots (n - r + 1)$$

The total permutations of (1,2,3) is

$$P(3,3) = \frac{3!}{0!} = 6, \quad \text{that is,} \quad (123), (132), (213), (231), (321), (312)$$

Combination. A specific subset of a set without regard to sequence. The number of combinations of n things taken r at a time is written

$$_nC_r \quad \text{or} \quad C(n,r) = \frac{n!}{(n - r)!(r)!}$$

The number of combinations of three elements from a set of five is given by $C(5,3) = \frac{5!}{2!3!} = 10$. From the set (1,2,3,4,5) the combinations are (1,2,3), (1,2,4), (1,2,5), (1,3,4), (1,3,5), (1,4,5), (2,3,4), (2,3,5), (2,4,5), (3,4,5).

Binomial Theorem. If n is a positive integer,

$$(x + y)^n = x^n + nx^{n-1}y + \frac{n(n - 1)}{2!} x^{n-2}y^2 + \cdots + {}_nC_rx^{n-r}y^r + \cdots + y^n$$

where

$$_nC_r = \frac{n!}{(n - r)!(r)!} \qquad n! = 1 \times 2 \times 3 \times \cdots \times n, 0! = 1$$

1-23. Trigonometry

Right Triangle

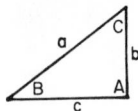

$\sin B = b/a \qquad \cos B = c/a \qquad \tan B = b/c$
$\csc B = 1/\sin B \qquad \sec B = 1/\cos B \qquad \cot B = 1/\tan B$
$A + B + C = 180°$

Inverse function $\theta = \sin^{-1} x$, or the angle θ whose sine is x

FIG. 1-4. Right triangle.

Oblique Triangle

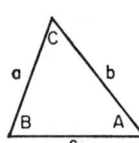

$$\frac{\sin A}{\sin B} = \frac{a}{b} \qquad a^2 = b^2 + c^2 - 2bc \cos A$$

$$\frac{a+b}{a-b} = \frac{\tan \dfrac{A+B}{2}}{\tan \dfrac{A-B}{2}}$$

FIG. 1-5. Oblique triangle.

$$\text{Area} = \frac{bc}{2} \sin A = \sqrt{s(s-a)(s-b)(s-c)}$$

where $2s = a + b + c$

Relations between Functions of a Single Angle

$\sin^2 \theta + \cos^2 \theta = 1 \qquad (1 + \tan^2 \theta) \cos^2 \theta = 1$
$\sin 2\theta = 2 \sin \theta \cos \theta \qquad \cos 2\theta = 2 \cos^2 \theta - 1$
$\sin 3\theta = 3 \sin \theta - 4 \sin^3 \theta \qquad \cos 3\theta = 4 \cos^3 \theta - 3 \cos \theta$
$\sin n\theta = 2 \sin (n-1)\theta \cos \theta - \sin (n-2)\theta$
$\cos n\theta = 2 \cos (n-1)\theta \cos \theta - \cos (n-2)\theta$

$$\sin \frac{x}{2} = \pm\sqrt{0.5(1 - \cos x)} \qquad \cos x/2 = \pm\sqrt{0.5(1 + \cos x)}$$

$$\tan x/2 = \pm\sqrt{\frac{1 - \cos x}{1 + \cos x}} \qquad \begin{array}{l}\text{(signs according to quadrant of } x/2 \text{ for asso-}\\ \text{ciated function)}\end{array}$$

Functions of Two Angles

$\sin (x \pm y) = \sin x \cos y \pm \cos x \sin y$
$\cos (x \pm y) = \cos x \cos y \mp \sin x \sin y$

$$\tan (x \pm y) = \frac{\tan x \pm \tan y}{1 \mp \tan x \tan y} \qquad \sin x \pm \sin y = 2 \sin \frac{x \pm y}{2} \cos \frac{x \mp y}{2}$$

$$\cos x + \cos y = 2 \cos \frac{x+y}{2} \cos \frac{x-y}{2}$$

$$\cos x - \cos y = -2 \sin \frac{x+y}{2} \sin \frac{x-y}{2}$$

$$\tan x \pm \tan y = \frac{\sin (x \pm y)}{\cos x \cos y} \qquad 2 \sin x \sin y = \cos (x - y) - \cos (x + y)$$

$2 \cos x \cos y = \cos (x - y) + \cos (x + y)$
$2 \sin x \cos y = \sin (x + y) + \sin (x - y)$

Magnitude of Trigonometric Functions

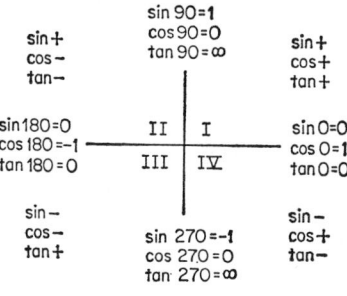

Fig. 1-6

Hyperbolic Trigonometry. The hyperbolic functions are certain combinations of exponentials e^x and e^{-x}.

$$\cosh x = 0.5(e^x + e^{-x}) \qquad \sinh x = 0.5(e^x - e^{-x})$$

$$\sinh x + \cosh x = e^x \qquad \tanh x = \frac{e^x - e^{-x}}{e^x + e^{-x}}$$

1-24. Differential Calculus

Definition of a Function. A function is a quantity which takes on a definite value, or values, when other quantities are specified. If $y = e^x$, then $y = f(x)$; the value of $f(x)$ when x has the value a is represented by $f(a)$.

Definition of Limit. The statement that the *limit* of the function $f(x)$, as x approaches a, is the number N is expressed by writing

$$\lim_{x \to a} f(x) = N$$

and $f(x)$ can be calculated as close to N as desired by making x sufficiently close to a. No restriction is placed on $f(x)$ when $x = a$. For example,

$$\lim_{x \to 0} \frac{\sin x}{x} = 1$$

even though $f(x) = (\sin x)/x$ is undefined at $x = 0$.

Operations with Limits. The following operations are valid for $x \to a$:

(1) $\lim bf(x) = b \lim f(x)$

(2) $\lim [f(x) + g(x)] = \lim f(x) + \lim g(x)$

(3) $\lim [f(x)g(x)] = \lim f(x) \cdot \lim g(x)$

(4) $\lim \dfrac{f(x)}{g(x)} = \dfrac{\lim f(x)}{\lim g(x)} \qquad$ if $\lim_{x \to a} g(x) \neq 0$

Definition of Continuity. A function $f(x)$ is *continuous* at the point $x = a$ if

$$\lim_{h \to 0} [f(a + h) - f(a)] = 0$$

Discontinuities are classified into three types:

Finite: $y = \dfrac{\sin x}{x}$ at $x = 0$

Infinite: $y = \dfrac{1}{x}$ at $x = 0$

Jump: $y = \dfrac{10}{1 + e^{1/x}}$ $\begin{cases} \text{at} & x = 0^+, & y = 0^+ \\ \text{at} & x = 0, & y = 0 \\ \text{at} & x = 0^-, & y = 10 \end{cases}$

Definition of Derivative. The function $f(x)$ has a derivative at $x = a$, which can be denoted as $f'(a)$, if

$$\lim_{h \to 0} \frac{f(a + h) - f(a)}{h}$$

exists. This requires continuity at $x = a$. Conversely, a function may be continuous but not have a derivative. The derivative function

$$f'(x) = \frac{df}{dx} = \lim_{h \to 0} \frac{f(x + h) - f(x)}{h}$$

Differential Operations. The following differential operations are valid; where $f, g, \ldots$, are functions of x, c is a constant; e is the base of the natural logarithms.

$$\frac{dc'}{dx} = 0 \qquad \frac{dx}{dx} = 1 \qquad\qquad \frac{dy}{dx} = \frac{1}{dx/dy}$$

$$\frac{d}{dx}(f + g) = \frac{df}{dx} + \frac{dg}{dx} \qquad\qquad \frac{d}{dx}(f \cdot g) = f\frac{dg}{dx} + g\frac{df}{dx}$$

$$\frac{d}{dx}f^n = nf^{n-1}\frac{df}{dx} \qquad\qquad \frac{df}{dx} = \frac{df}{dv} \cdot \frac{dv}{dx}$$

$$\frac{d}{dx}\frac{f}{g} = \frac{g\,df/dx - f\,dg/dx}{g^2} \qquad\qquad \frac{da^x}{dx} = a^x \ln a$$

$$\frac{df^g}{dx} = gf^{g-1}\frac{df}{dx} + f^g \ln f \frac{dg}{dx}$$

Differentials

$de^x = e^x\,dx$	$d\ln x = \dfrac{1}{x}\,dx$	$d\log x = \dfrac{\log e}{x}\,dx$
$d\sin x = \cos x\,dx$	$d\cos x = -\sin x\,dx$	$d\tan x = \sec^2 x\,dx$
$d\cot x = -\csc^2 x\,dx$	$d\sec x = \tan x \sec x\,dx$	$d\csc x = -\cot x \csc x\,dx$
$d\sin^{-1} x = (1 - x^2)^{-1/2}\,dx$	$d\cos^{-1} x = -(1 - x^2)^{-1/2}\,dx$	$d\tan^{-1} x = (1 + x^2)^{-1}\,dx$
$d\cot^{-1} x = -(1 + x^2)^{-1}\,dx$	$d\sec^{-1} x = x^{-1}(x^2 - 1)^{-1/2}\,dx$	$d\csc^{-1} x = -x^{-1}(x^2 - 1)^{-1/2}\,dx$
$d\sinh x = \cosh x\,dx$	$d\cosh x = \sinh x\,dx$	$d\tanh x = \text{sech}^2 x\,dx$
$d\coth x = -\text{csch}^2 x\,dx$	$d\,\text{sech}\, x = -\text{sech}\, x \tanh x\,dx$	$d\,\text{csch}\, x = -\text{csch}\, x \coth x\,dx$
$d\sinh^{-1} x = (x^2 + 1)^{-1/2}\,dx$	$d\cosh^{-1} x = (x^2 - 1)^{-1/2}\,dx$	$d\tanh^{-1} x = (1 - x^2)^{-1}\,dx$
$d\coth^{-1} x = -(x^2 - 1)^{-1}\,dx$	$d\,\text{sech}^{-1} x = x(1 - x^2)^{-1/2}\,dx$	$d\,\text{csch}^{-1}x = -x^{-1}(x^2 + 1)^{-1/2}\,dx$

Higher Differentials. The first derivative of $f(x)$ with respect to x is denoted as $f'(x)$ or df/dx. The derivative of the first derivative is denoted as f'', $f^{(2)}$, or d^2f/dx^2; similarly for the higher-order derivatives. The differential formulas can be successively applied for the higher-order derivatives.

Indeterminate Forms—L'Hôpital's Theorem. Forms of type $0/0$, ∞/∞, $0 \cdot \infty$, etc., are called *indeterminates*. To find the limiting values of the corresponding functions, L'Hôpital's theorem can be used: If the ratio of two functions $f(x)$ and $g(x)$ is undefined at $x = a$, then the limit of the quotient is equal to the limit of the quotient of their separate derivatives if the limit exists.

For $y = (1 - x)^{1/x}$, then $\ln y = \dfrac{1}{x} \ln (1 - x)$:

$$\lim_{x \to 0} (\ln y) = \lim_{x \to 0} \frac{\ln (1 - x)}{x} = \frac{\lim (d/dx) \ln (1 - x)}{\lim (d/dx)x} = \frac{\lim -1/(1 - x)}{1} = -1$$

Therefore $\lim\limits_{x \to 0} y = e^{-1}$.

Partial Derivative. The abbreviation $Z = f(x,y)$ implies Z is a function of the two independent variables x and y. The derivative of Z with respect to x, treating y as a constant, is called the partial derivative with respect to x and is usually denoted as $\partial Z/\partial x$, or $\partial f/\partial x$, or simply f_x. Partial differentiation is applied like full differentiation for single functions.

Partial Differentiation for Composite Functions. A function of any number of variables x, y, z, which are in turn functions of other independent variables r, s, t, are called composite functions.

1. For $f(x,y)$ with $x = g(t)$ and $y = h(t)$, then the total differential

$$\frac{df}{dt} = \frac{\partial f}{\partial x}\frac{dx}{dt} + \frac{\partial f}{\partial y}\frac{dy}{dt}$$

2. For $x = g(t,s)$ and $y = h(t,s)$,

$$\frac{\partial f}{\partial t} = \frac{\partial f}{\partial x}\frac{\partial x}{\partial t} + \frac{\partial f}{\partial y}\frac{\partial y}{\partial t}$$

The cross-partial derivative

$$\frac{\partial^2 f}{\partial t\, \partial s} = \frac{\partial^2 f}{\partial x^2}\frac{\partial x}{\partial s}\frac{\partial x}{\partial t} + \frac{\partial^2 f}{\partial x\, \partial y}\left(\frac{\partial x}{\partial s}\frac{\partial y}{\partial t} + \frac{\partial x}{\partial t}\frac{\partial y}{\partial s}\right) + \frac{\partial^2 f}{\partial y^2}\frac{\partial y}{\partial s}\frac{\partial y}{\partial t} + \frac{\partial f}{\partial x}\frac{\partial^2 x}{\partial s\, \partial t} + \frac{\partial f}{\partial y}\frac{\partial^2 y}{\partial s\, \partial t}$$

The second partial

$$\frac{\partial^2 f}{\partial t^2} = \frac{\partial^2 f}{\partial x^2}\left(\frac{\partial x}{\partial t}\right)^2 + 2\,\frac{\partial^2 f}{\partial x\, \partial y}\frac{\partial x}{\partial t}\frac{\partial y}{\partial t} + \frac{\partial^2 f}{\partial y^2}\left(\frac{\partial y}{\partial t}\right)^2 + \frac{\partial f}{\partial x}\frac{\partial^2 x}{\partial t^2} + \frac{\partial f}{\partial y}\frac{\partial^2 y}{\partial t^2}$$

1-25. Integral Calculus

Indefinite Integral. If $f'(x)\, dx$ is the differential of $f(x)$, the integral of $f'(x)\, dx$ is $f(x)$. Symbolically,

$$\int f'(x)\, dx = f(x) + C$$

where C is a constant of integration. The following relationships hold (the constant of integration C is implied):

$$\int u\,dv = uv - \int v\,du \qquad\qquad \int a\,dv = a\int dv$$

$$\int (du + dv + dw) = \int du + \int dv + \int dw$$

$$\int v^n\,dv = \frac{v^{n+1}}{n+1} \quad n \neq -1 \qquad\qquad \int \frac{dv}{v} = \ln v$$

$$\int a^v\,dv = \frac{a^v}{\ln a} \qquad\qquad \int e^v\,dv = e^v$$

$$\int \sin v\,dv = -\cos v \qquad\qquad \int \cos v\,dv = \sin v$$

$$\int \sec^2 v\,dv = \tan v \qquad\qquad \int \csc^2 v\,dv = -\cot v$$

$$\int \sec v \tan v\,dv = \sec v \qquad\qquad \int \csc v \cot v\,dv = -\csc v$$

$$\int \frac{dv}{v^2 + a^2} = \frac{1}{a}\tan^{-1}\frac{v}{a} \qquad\qquad \int \frac{dv}{(a^2 - v^2)^{1/2}} = \sin^{-1}\frac{v}{a}$$

$$\int \frac{dv}{v^2 - a^2} = \frac{1}{2a}\ln\frac{v - a}{v + a} \qquad\qquad \int \frac{dv}{(v^2 \pm a^2)^{1/2}} = \ln(v + \sqrt{v^2 \pm a^2})$$

$$\int \sec v\,dv = \ln(\sec v + \tan v) \qquad\qquad \int \csc v\,dv = \ln(\csc v - \cot v)$$

Methods of Integration. Only a relatively small proportion of integrands can be directly integrated. For these, trial and error is required to redefine the integrand to a recognizable form for direct integration. Several general procedures are useful:

Direct Formula. This technique is applicable for transformation of the integrand to a tabled form.

For $\int x\sqrt{ax^2 + b}\,dx$, let $v = ax^2 + b \rightarrow dv = 2ax\,dx$.

$$\therefore \quad \int x\sqrt{ax^2 + b}\,dx = \frac{1}{2a}\int (ax^2 + b)^{1/2}(2ax\,dx) = \frac{1}{2a}\int v^{1/2}\,dv$$

$$= \frac{1}{2a}\frac{v^{3/2}}{3/2} + C = \frac{2}{6a}(ax^2 + b)^{3/2} + C$$

Trigonometric Substitution. This technique is particularly effective for integrands which are in the form of radicals. For these,

$$(x^2 - a^2)^{1/n} \qquad \text{let } x = a\sec\theta$$
$$(x^2 + a^2)^{1/n} \qquad \text{let } x = a\tan\theta$$
$$(a^2 - x^2)^{1/n} \qquad \text{let } x = a\sin\theta$$

Algebraic Substitution. Functions containing elements of the type $(a + bx)^{1/n}$ are best handled by the algebraic transformation $y^n = a + bx$.

Partial Fractions. Rational functions are of the type $f(x)/g(x)$, where $f(x)$ and $g(x)$ are polynomial expressions of degree m and n, respectively. If $m \geq n$, algebraic division can be carried out to define a numerator which is at least one degree less than the denominator. The denominator function is then factored into linear terms and, if necessary, quadratic terms for complex roots. These are expanded to linear and, if necessary, quadratic terms:

$$\frac{8x^2 + 3}{x^3 - x^2 - x - 2} = \frac{8x^2 + 3}{(x^2 + x + 1)(x - 2)} = \frac{Ax + B}{x^2 + x + 1} + \frac{C}{x - 2}$$

Then $\qquad (Ax + B)(x - 2) + C(x^2 + x + 1) = 8x^2 + 3$

or $\qquad A + C = 8 \qquad B + C - 2A = 0 \qquad C - 2B = 3$

$\therefore \qquad\qquad A = 3 \qquad B = 1 \qquad C = 5$

and $\qquad\qquad \dfrac{8x^2 + 3}{x^3 - x^2 - x - 2} = \dfrac{3x + 1}{x^2 + x + 1} + \dfrac{5}{x - 2}$

Algebraic integration formulas can then be used.

Parts. For trigonometric and exponential function, integration by parts is very useful:

$$\int u \, dv = uv - \int v \, du$$

Series Expansion. When an explicit function cannot be found, the integration sometimes can be carried out by expanding the integrand into a power series.

Definite Integral. For the indefinite integral,

$$\int f(x) \, dx = F(x)$$

then for the definite integral,

$$\int_a^b f(x) \, dx = F(b) - F(a)$$

The definite integral is a function of the limits of integration and any variable coefficients of the integrand. It is not a function of the dummy variable of integration x:

$$\int_a^b f(x) \, dx \neq F(x)$$

Properties

$$\int_a^b cf(x) \, dx = c \int_a^b f(x) \, dx \qquad \int_a^b f(x) \, dx = - \int_b^a f(x) \, dx$$

$$\int_a^b [f(x) + g(x)] \, dx = \int_a^b f(x) \, dx + \int_a^b g(x) \, dx$$

$$\int_a^b f(x) \, dx = \int_a^c f(x) \, dx + \int_c^b f(x) \, dx$$

$$\int_a^b f(x)\, dx = (b-a)f(\xi) \qquad a \leq \xi \leq b$$

$$\frac{\partial}{\partial b}\int_a^b f(x)\, dx = f(b) \qquad \frac{\partial}{\partial a}\int_a^b f(x)\, dx = -f(a)$$

$$\frac{\partial}{\partial \alpha}\int_a^b f(x,\alpha)\, dx = \int_a^b \frac{\partial f(x,\alpha)}{\partial \alpha}\, dx$$

$$\int_a^b dx \int_c^d f(x,y)\, dy = \int_c^d dy \int_a^b f(x,y)\, dx$$

Methods of Integration. All the methods of integration for the indefinite integral can be used for the definite integral. In addition, several others are available.

Change of Variable. This substitution is basically the same as indefinite integrals, with the proper change in the limits of integration. For $x = \phi(t)$,

$$\int_a^b f(x)\, dx = \int_{t_0}^{t_1} f[\phi(t)]\phi'\, dt$$

where $\phi(t_1) = b$ and $\phi(t_0) = a$.

Differentiation. Definite integrals can be partially differentiated in respect to the limits or variable parameters contained in the integrand function when the corresponding defined functions satisfy certain properties. See, for example, Courant, "Differential and Integral Calculus," vol. 2, Interscience Publishers, Inc., 1936.

Integration. Comparable theory to that for differentiation of a definite integral also applies for integration of a definite integral.

Complex Variable. Certain definite integrals can be evaluated more readily by the technique of complex variable integration. See, for example, Copson, "Theory of Functions of a Complex Variable," Oxford University Press, 1935.

Numerical Integration. A numerical evaluation of a definite integral can be carried out by using Simpson's or Weddle's rule as shown on page 1–101.

1-26. Infinite Series

Definitions. A succession of numbers or terms which are formed according to some definite rule is called a *sequence*. The indicated sum of a sequence is called a *series*. If the terms of the sequence are variable, the series is called a *power series*. For the geometric progression,

$$S_n = a + ar + ar^2 + \cdots + ar^n$$

Then
$$S_n = a\frac{1-r^n}{1-r}$$

As $n \to \infty$, then

$$S = \lim_{n\to\infty} S_n = a \lim_{n\to\infty} \frac{1-r^n}{1-r}$$

The series is said to *converge* if the limit of S_n approaches a fixed finite value. Otherwise the series is *divergent*.

For $\quad -1 < r < 1 \qquad \lim_{n \to \infty} S_n \qquad$ converges

For $\quad r \geq 1, r < -1 \qquad \lim_{n \to \infty} S_n \qquad$ diverges (unbounded sum)

For $\quad r = -1 \qquad\qquad \lim_{n \to \infty} S_n \qquad$ diverges (sum does not exist)

The latter series is called an *oscillating divergent series*. For the new series

$$S = 1 + \frac{a}{2} + \frac{a^2}{3} + \frac{a^3}{4} + \frac{a^4}{5} + \cdots + \frac{a^n}{n+1} + \cdots$$

$S = \log 2$ for $a = -1$ and S diverges for $a = +1$. This series is called a *conditionally convergent* series. Conversely,

$$e^x = 1 + \frac{x}{1!} + \frac{x^2}{2!} + \frac{x^3}{3!} + \cdots + \frac{x^n}{n!} + \cdots$$

converges for any negative or positive value of $|x| < \infty$, and therefore is said to *converge absolutely*.

Operations with Infinite Series

1. The convergence or divergence of an infinite series is unaffected by the removal of a finite number of finite terms.

2. If a series is conditionally convergent, its sum can be made to take on any arbitrary value by a suitable rearrangement of the series.

3. A series of positive terms, if convergent, has a sum independent of the order of the terms.

4. An oscillatory series always can be made to converge by grouping the terms in brackets.

5. A power series can be inverted, provided the first-degree term is not zero.

6. Two series may be added or subtracted term by term provided each is a convergent series.

7. A power series may be integrated termwise to represent the integral of the function within an interval of convergence.

8. A power series may be differentiated termwise to represent the differential function within the same region of convergence of the function.

Tests for Convergence and Divergence. In general, the problem of determining whether or not a given series will converge can require ingenuity. There is no all-inclusive test which can be applied to all series. There are many special tests.

Comparison Test. A series will converge if the absolute value of each term is less than the corresponding term of a known convergent series.

nth-term Test. A series is divergent unless the nth term of the series approaches zero as n approaches infinity.

Ratio Test. If the absolute ratio of the $(n + 1)$ term divided by the nth term, as n approaches infinity, approaches:

1. A number less than 1, the series is convergent.

2. A number greater than 1, the series is divergent.

3. A number equal to 1, the test is inconclusive.

Summation Test. If the partial summation S_n of a series converges as n becomes unbounded, the series converges, and conversely, it diverges if S_n diverges.

Alternating-series Test. If the terms of a series are alternately positive and negative and never increase in numerical value, the series will converge, provided that the terms tend to zero as a limit.

Cauchy's Root Test. If the nth root of the nth-absolute-value term, as n becomes infinite, approaches

1. A number less than 1, the series is convergent.
2. A number greater than 1, the series is divergent.
3. A number equal to 1, the test is inconclusive.

Maclaurin's Integral Test. A series Σa_n converges or diverges with the integral $\int_1^\infty f(x)\,dx$, where $f(n) = a_n$ and $f(x)$ is defined and continuous for $1 \leq x < \infty$ and $\lim\limits_{x \to \infty} f(x) = 0$.

Series Summation and Identities

$$1 + 2 + 3 + \cdots + n = \frac{n(n + 1)}{2}$$

$$1^2 + 2^2 + 3^2 + \cdots + n^2 = \frac{n(n + 1)(2n + 1)}{6}$$

$$1^3 + 2^3 + 3^3 + \cdots + n^3 = \frac{n^2(n + 1)^2}{4}$$

$$1^4 + 2^4 + 3^4 + \cdots + n^4 = \frac{n(n + 1)(2n + 1)(3n^2 + 3n - 1)}{30}$$

Arithmetic progression:

$$\sum_{m=1}^{n} [a + (m - 1)d] = na + \tfrac{1}{2}n(n - 1)d$$

Geometric progression:

$$\sum_{m=1}^{n} ar^m = a\frac{1 - r^n}{1 - r}$$

Harmonic progression:

$$\sum_{m=1}^{n} \frac{1}{a + md} = S_n \qquad \text{(no general summation formula is known)}$$

Binomial series:

$$(x + y)^n = x^n + nx^{n-1}y + \frac{n(n - 1)}{2!} x^{n-2}y^2 + \cdots + y^n$$

$$(1 \pm x)^n = 1 \pm nx + \frac{n(n - 1)}{2!} x^2 \pm \frac{n(n - 1)(n - 2)}{3!} x^3 + \cdots \qquad x^2 < 1$$

Taylor's series:

$$f(x + h) = f(h) + xf'(h) + \frac{x^2}{2!}f''(h) + \frac{x^3}{3!}f'''(h) + \cdots$$

Maclaurin's series:

$$f(x) = f(0) + xf'(0) + \frac{x^2}{2!}f''(0) + \frac{x^3}{3!}f'''(h) + \cdots$$

Exponential series:

$$e^x = 1 + x + \frac{x^2}{2!} + \frac{x^3}{3!} + \cdots \qquad -\infty < x < \infty$$

Trigonometric series:

$$\sin x = x - \frac{x^3}{3!} + \frac{x^5}{5!} + \cdots + (-1)^n \frac{x^{2n+1}}{(2n+1)!} + \cdots \qquad -\infty < x < \infty$$

$$\cos x = 1 - \frac{x^2}{2!} + \frac{x^4}{4!} + \cdots + (-1)^n \frac{x^{2n}}{(2n)!} + \cdots \qquad -\infty < x < \infty$$

1-27. Vectors

A vector quantity has magnitude and direction; a scalar quantity has magnitude only. Common vector quantities are acceleration, alternating currents, and voltages, force, and velocity. A vector can be represented graphically by a straight line with an arrowhead, as in Fig. 1-7. (Length

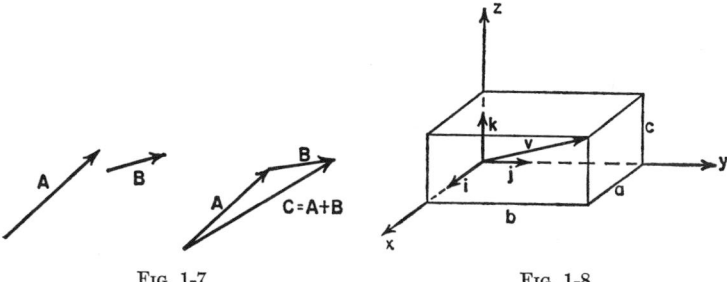

FIG. 1-7   FIG. 1-8

represents magnitude; direction is determined from the position of the line and the arrowhead.)

Vectors are usually indicated by boldface type (**A**), or by an arrow over the symbol $(\vec{A})$, or by a bar $(\overline{A})$.

Representation. A vector **V** in three dimensions can be represented by its projections along three mutually perpendicular lines, the x, y and z axes. Vectors of unit magnitude, directed in the positive sense along these three axes, are denoted by **i**, **j** and **k**, respectively. If a, b, and c represent the lengths of the projections of **V** along these axes, we may represent **V** as **V** $= a\mathbf{i} + b\mathbf{j} + c\mathbf{k}$ (Fig. 1-8). The length (magnitude) of **V** is

$$\mathbf{V} = (a^2 + b^2 + c^2)^{1/2}.$$

Algebra. *Equality.* $\mathbf{A} = \mathbf{B}$ if and only if both have the same magnitude and the same direction.

Addition and Subtraction. $\mathbf{A} + \mathbf{B} = \mathbf{B} + \mathbf{A}$ (commutative law); $\mathbf{A} + \mathbf{B} + \mathbf{C} = (\mathbf{A} + \mathbf{B}) + \mathbf{C} = \mathbf{A} + (\mathbf{B} + \mathbf{C})$ (associative law). If $\mathbf{A} = a_1\mathbf{i} + a_2\mathbf{j} + a_3\mathbf{k}$, $\mathbf{B} = b_1\mathbf{i} + b_2\mathbf{j} + b_3\mathbf{k}$, $\mathbf{A} \pm \mathbf{B} = (a_1 \pm b_1)\mathbf{i} + (a_2 \pm b_2)\mathbf{j} + (a_3 \pm b_3)\mathbf{k}$.

Product of Vector V and Scalar s. $s\mathbf{V} = \mathbf{V}s = (sa)\mathbf{i} + (sb)\mathbf{j} + (sc)\mathbf{k}$.

Scalar Product of Two Vectors V_1, V_2. The scalar (dot or inner) product, indicated by $\mathbf{V}_1 \cdot \mathbf{V}_2$, is a scalar defined by $\mathbf{V}_1 \cdot \mathbf{V}_2 = |\mathbf{V}_1||\mathbf{V}_2| \cos \theta$, where θ = angle between the vectors. $\mathbf{V}_1 \cdot \mathbf{V}_2 = a_1a_2 + b_1b_2 + c_1c_2$; $(\mathbf{V}_1 + \mathbf{V}_2) \cdot \mathbf{V}_3 = \mathbf{V}_1 \cdot \mathbf{V}_3 + \mathbf{V}_2 \cdot \mathbf{V}_3$; $\mathbf{V}_1 \cdot (\mathbf{V}_2 + \mathbf{V}_3) = \mathbf{V}_1 \cdot \mathbf{V}_2 + \mathbf{V}_1 \cdot \mathbf{V}_3 = (\mathbf{V}_2 + \mathbf{V}_3) \cdot \mathbf{V}_1$ (commutative); $\mathbf{i} \cdot \mathbf{i} = \mathbf{j} \cdot \mathbf{j} = \mathbf{k} \cdot \mathbf{k} = 1$; $\mathbf{i} \cdot \mathbf{j} = \mathbf{i} \cdot \mathbf{k} = \mathbf{j} \cdot \mathbf{k} = 0$.

Vector Product. With reference to Fig. 1-9, the vector (outer) product of $\mathbf{V}_1$ and $\mathbf{V}_2$ is defined as the vector $\mathbf{V} = \mathbf{V}_1 \times \mathbf{V}_2$, $\mathbf{V}_1 \times \mathbf{V}_2 = (b_1c_2 - b_2c_1)\mathbf{i} +$

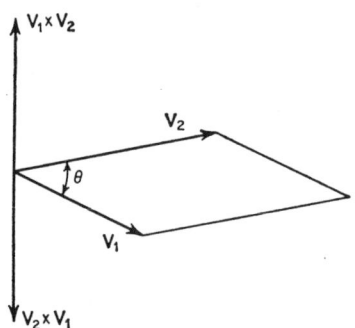

Fɪɢ. 1-9

$(c_1a_2 - c_2a_1)\mathbf{j} + (a_1b_2 - a_2b_1)\mathbf{k}$ illustrated in the figure. $|\mathbf{V}| = |\mathbf{V}_1||\mathbf{V}_2| \sin \theta$; $\mathbf{V}_1 \times \mathbf{V}_2 = -\mathbf{V}_2 \times \mathbf{V}_1$; $\mathbf{V}_1 \times (\mathbf{V}_2 + \mathbf{V}_3) = \mathbf{V}_1 \times \mathbf{V}_2 + \mathbf{V}_1 \times \mathbf{V}_3$; $(\mathbf{V}_1 + \mathbf{V}_2) \times \mathbf{V}_3 = \mathbf{V}_1 \times \mathbf{V}_3 + \mathbf{V}_2 \times \mathbf{V}_3$; $\mathbf{i} \times \mathbf{i} = \mathbf{j} \times \mathbf{j} = \mathbf{k} \times \mathbf{k} = 0$; $\mathbf{i} = \mathbf{j} \times \mathbf{k} = -\mathbf{k} \times \mathbf{j}$; $\mathbf{j} = \mathbf{k} \times \mathbf{i} = -\mathbf{i} \times \mathbf{k}$; $\mathbf{k} = \mathbf{i} \times \mathbf{j} = -\mathbf{j} \times \mathbf{i}$; $\mathbf{V} \times \mathbf{V} = 0$.

Multiple Products. (1) $\mathbf{A}(\mathbf{B} \cdot \mathbf{C})$; here $\mathbf{B} \cdot \mathbf{C}$ is a scalar, so that $\mathbf{A}(\mathbf{B} \cdot \mathbf{C})$ is a vector parallel to A. Clearly, $\mathbf{A}(\mathbf{B} \cdot \mathbf{C}) \neq (\mathbf{A} \cdot \mathbf{B})\mathbf{C}$. (2) $\mathbf{A} \cdot (\mathbf{B} \times \mathbf{C}) = \mathbf{B} \cdot (\mathbf{C} \times \mathbf{A}) = \mathbf{C} \cdot (\mathbf{A} \times \mathbf{B})$. (3) $\mathbf{A} \times (\mathbf{B} \times \mathbf{C}) = \mathbf{B}(\mathbf{A} \cdot \mathbf{C}) - \mathbf{C}(\mathbf{A} \cdot \mathbf{B})$.

1-28. Complex Numbers

The complex-number system z is defined to be made up of an ordered pair of real numbers x and y denoted as $z = x + yi$ and satisfying certain laws of operation. The symbol i is called the imaginary unit and represents $\sqrt{-1}$, where $i^2 = -1$ by definition. If $y \neq 0$, then $x + yi$ is called an imaginary number. Also, the number $x - yi$ is called its complex conjugate. The laws of operation are defined as follows:

Addition. $(x_1 + y_1i) + (x_2 + y_2i) = (x_1 + x_2) + (y_1 + y_2)i$

Multiplication. $(x_1 + y_1i)(x_2 + y_2i) = (x_1x_2 - y_1y_2) + (x_1y_2 + x_2y_1)i$

Division. $\dfrac{x_1 + y_1 i}{x_2 + y_2 i} = \dfrac{x_1 x_2 + y_1 y_2}{x_2{}^2 + y_2{}^2} + \dfrac{x_2 y_1 - x_1 y_2}{x_2{}^2 + y_2{}^2} i \qquad y_2 \neq 0$

It should be noted that numbers of the type $\sqrt{-a}$ should be reduced to the form $x + yi$, or in this instance, to $0 + \sqrt{a}\, i$. Otherwise

$$\sqrt{-8}\,\sqrt{-2} = \sqrt{16} = 4,$$

which is not true. For this case with $\sqrt{-8} = \sqrt{8}\, i$ and $\sqrt{-2} = \sqrt{2}\, i$, it follows that $\sqrt{-8}\,\sqrt{-2} = \sqrt{8}\, i \sqrt{2}\, i = -4$, since $i^2 = -1$.

Utilizing the rectangular coordinates OX and OY, we represent the complex numbers $z = x + yi$ in the complex or Z plane by plotting the ordered pair (x,y). Thus the absolute value or modulus of the number z is given by $r = \sqrt{x^2 + y^2}$, the distance of the point P from the origin. Also the trigonometric form of $x + yi$ is given by $x + yi = r(\cos A + i \sin A)$, where the angle A is measured counterclockwise from OX to OP.

The roots of complex numbers are readily found by means of De Moivre's theorem which states that, if n is any positive whole number, then

$$\cos nA + i \sin nA = (\cos A + i \sin A)^n$$
or $$\cos A + i \sin A = (\cos (1/n)\, A + i \sin (1/n)\, A)^n$$

The cubic roots of $\frac{1}{2} \sqrt{3} + \frac{1}{2}i$ can, therefore, be readily found by writing the three equations corresponding to $\frac{1}{2} \sqrt{3} + \frac{1}{2}i = \cos 30° + i \sin 30°$ and the formula

$$\cos A + i \sin A = [\cos \tfrac{1}{3}(a + 360j) + i \sin \tfrac{1}{3}(A + 360j)]^3 \qquad j = 0, 1, 2$$

Thus:

$$\cos 30 + i \sin 30 = (\cos 10° + i \sin 10°)^3$$
$$\cos 30 + i \sin 30 = [\cos \tfrac{1}{3}(30 + 360) + i \sin \tfrac{1}{3}(30 + 360)]^3$$
$$= (\cos 130 + i \sin 130)^3$$
$$\cos 30 + i \sin 30 = [\cos \tfrac{1}{3}(30 + 720) + i \sin \tfrac{1}{3}(30 + 720)]^3$$
$$= (\cos 250 + i \sin 250)^3$$

and the cube roots

$$\sqrt[3]{\tfrac{1}{2} \sqrt{3} + \tfrac{1}{2}i} = 0.98481 + 0.17365i(\cos 10° = 0.98481, \sin 10° = 0.17365)$$
$$= -0.64279 + 0.76604i$$
$$= -0.34202 - 0.93969i$$

which satisfy

$$(x^3 - \tfrac{1}{2} \sqrt{3} - \tfrac{1}{2}i) = (x - 0.98481 - 0.17365i)(x + 0.64279 - 0.76604i)$$
$$(x + 0.34202 + 0.93969i)$$

Similarly, the roots to the polynomial equation $x^3 - 1 = 0$ are found to be $1,\ -\frac{1}{2} + \frac{1}{2} \sqrt{3}\, i,\ -\frac{1}{2} - \frac{1}{2} \sqrt{3}\, i$.

Certain types of elementary functions of a complex variable find important uses. These are

$$e^z = e^{x+iy} = e^x e^{yi} = e^x(\cos y + i \sin y)$$
$$e^{-yi} = \cos y - i \sin y$$
$$z = x + yi = r(\cos \theta + i \sin \theta) = re^{i\theta}$$
$$\cos z = \tfrac{1}{2}e^{iz} + \tfrac{1}{2}e^{-iz}$$
$$\log z = \log r + i(\theta + 2n\pi) \qquad \text{(multiply valued)}$$
$$z^b = e^{b \log z}$$

Thus to find $(-i)^i$ it follows:

$$\begin{aligned}
(-i)^i = e^{i \log (-i)} &= e^{i \log 1 - i\pi/2} \\
&= e^{i(-i\pi/2)} \\
&= e^{\pi/2}
\end{aligned}$$

which is the principal value of $(-i)^i$ by virtue of the principal value $\sin (\pi/2) = 1$.

The definite integral of the function $f(x)$ is a number given by $\int_b^a f(x)\, dx$, which measures the area under the curve $f(x)$ between b and a; the complex integral $\int_b^a f(z)\, dz$ does not. Rather this integral is a line integral over a specified path between a and b. This follows from the fact that, in the complex plane corresponding to each point (x,y), the function $f(x + iy)$ has a value (real or imaginary), and therefore $\int_b^a f(z)\, dz$ does not have meaning except in the sense of the specified path from $f(b)$ to $f(a)$ in terms of the values $f(z)$.

The selection of different paths will usually give different values to $\int_b^a f(z)\, dz$. Thus, caution should be exercised in carrying out complex integration, since the standard integration formulas do not hold. Nevertheless, this very fact is one of the reasons why complex-variable theory has been found to be extremely useful in engineering and physics in addition to the field of mathematics itself.

1-29. Determinants and Matrices

Determinants. Consider the system of two linear equations

$$a_{11}x_1 + a_{12}x_2 = b_1$$
$$a_{21}x_1 + a_{22}x_2 = b_2$$

If the first equation is multiplied by a_{22} and the second by $-a_{12}$ and the results are added, we obtain

$$(a_{11}a_{22} - a_{21}a_{12})x_1 = b_1a_{22} - b_2a_{12}$$

The expression $a_{11}a_{22} - a_{21}a_{12}$ may be represented by the symbol

$$\begin{vmatrix} a_{11} & a_{12} \\ a_{21} & a_{22} \end{vmatrix} = a_{11}a_{22} - a_{21}a_{12}$$

This symbol is called a *determinant* of second order. The *square* array of n^2 quantities a_{ij}, where $i = 1, \ldots, n$ is the row index, and $j = 1, \ldots, n$ is the column index, written in the form

$$A = |a_{ij}| = \begin{vmatrix} a_{11} & a_{12} & a_{13} & \cdots & a_{1n} \\ a_{21} & a_{22} & a_{23} & \cdots & a_{2n} \\ \cdots & \cdots & \cdots & \cdots & \cdots \\ a_{n1} & a_{n2} & a_{n3} & \cdots & a_{nn} \end{vmatrix}$$

is called a *determinant*. The n^2 quantities a_{ij} are called the *elements* of the determinant. In the determinant A, let the ith row and jth column be deleted and a new determinant be formed having $n - 1$ rows and columns. This new determinant is called the *minor* of a_{ij}, denoted M_{ij}. The *cofactor* A_{ij} of the element a_{ij} is the signed minor of a_{ij}, determined by the rule $A_{ij} = (-1)^{i+j}M_{ij}$.

Fundamental Properties of Determinants

1. The value of a determinant A is not changed if the rows and columns are interchanged.

2. If the elements of one row (or one column) of a determinant are all zero, the value of A is zero.

3. If the elements of one row (or column) of a determinant are multiplied by the same constant factor, the value of the determinant is multiplied by this factor.

4. If one determinant is obtained from another by interchanging any two rows (or columns), the value of either is the negative of the value of the other.

5. If two rows (or columns) of a determinant are identical, the value of the determinant is zero.

6. If two determinants are identical except for one row (or column), the sum of their values is given by a single determinant, obtained by adding corresponding elements of dissimilar rows (or columns) and leaving unchanged the remaining elements.

7. The value of a determinant is not changed if, to the elements of any row (or column), is added a constant multiple of the corresponding elements of any other row (or column).

8. If all elements but one in a row (or column) are zero, the value of the determinant is the product of that element times its cofactor.

The evaluation of determinants, using the definition, is quite laborious. The labor can be reduced by applying the fundamental properties just outlined.

Example: Evaluate $\begin{vmatrix} 2 & 1 & 4 & 3 \\ -1 & 4 & 2 & 1 \\ 5 & 6 & 7 & 2 \\ 1 & 3 & 4 & 5 \end{vmatrix}$

The aim is to transform the determinant so that all elements but one in a given row (or column) are zero, *without changing the determinant* value. This may be done by utilizing property 7. Selecting the element 1 in the fourth column, add -2 times the fourth column to the third column; then -4 times the fourth column to the second column; then add the fourth column to the first column; the result is

$$A = \begin{vmatrix} 5 & -11 & -2 & 3 \\ 0 & 0 & 0 & 1 \\ 7 & -2 & 3 & 2 \\ 6 & -17 & -6 & 5 \end{vmatrix} = 1 \begin{vmatrix} 5 & -11 & -2 \\ 7 & -2 & 3 \\ 6 & -17 & -6 \end{vmatrix}$$

by property 8. Property 7 is now used on this 3×3 determinant. Subtract the elements of the first row from the third row. The result is

$$A = \begin{vmatrix} 5 & -11 & -2 \\ 7 & -2 & 3 \\ 1 & -6 & -4 \end{vmatrix}$$

Now add -7 times the third row to the second row, then -5 times the third row to the first row resulting in

$$A = \begin{vmatrix} 0 & 19 & 18 \\ 0 & 40 & 31 \\ 1 & -6 & -4 \end{vmatrix} = \begin{vmatrix} 19 & 18 \\ 40 & 31 \end{vmatrix} = -131$$

Matrices. A rectangular array of mn quantities, arranged in m rows and n columns,

$$A = (a_{ij}) = \begin{bmatrix} a_{11} & \cdots & a_{1n} \\ a_{21} & \cdots & a_{2n} \\ \cdots\cdots\cdots\cdots \\ a_{m1} & \cdots & a_{mn} \end{bmatrix}$$

is called a *matrix*. The *elements* a_{ij} may be numbers, functions, etc. The notation a_{ij} means the element in the ith row and jth column; i is called the *row index*, j the *column index*. If $m = n$, the matrix is said to be *square* and of *order n*. A matrix, even if it is square, *does not have a numerical value*, as a determinant does. However, if the matrix A is square, a determinant can be formed which has the same elements as the matrix A. This is called the *determinant of the matrix*, and written det (A) or $|A|$. If A is square and det $(A) \neq 0$, A is said to be *nonsingular;* if det $(A) = 0$, A is said to be *singular*. A matrix A has *rank r* if, and only if, it has a nonvanishing determinant of order r and no nonvanishing determinant of order $> r$.

Algebra of Matrices. Let $A = (a_{ij})$, $B = (b_{ij})$.

Equality. Two matrices A and B are *equal* ($=$) if and only if they are identical; that is, they have the same number of rows and the same number of columns and equal corresponding elements ($a_{ij} = b_{ij}$ for all i and j).

Addition and Subtraction. The operations of *addition* ($+$) and subtraction ($-$) of two or more matrices is possible if and only if they have the same number of rows and columns. Thus $A \pm B = (a_{ij} \pm b_{ij})$, that is, addition and subtraction are of corresponding elements.

Multiplication. Let $A = (a_{ij})$, $i = 1, \ldots, m_1$; $j = 1, \ldots, m_2$. Let $B = (b_{ij})$, $i = 1, \ldots, n_1$; $j = 1, \ldots, n_2$. The *product AB* is defined if, and only if, the *number* of *columns* of A (m_2) equals the number of rows of B (n_1), that is, $n_1 = m_2$. For two such matrices the product $P = AB$ is *defined* by

summing the element-by-element products of a row of A by a column of B.
This is the *row-by-column rule*. Thus $p_{ij} = \sum_{k=1}^{n_1} a_{ij}b_{kj}$. The resulting matrix
has m_1 rows and n_2 columns. It is helpful to remember that the element p_{ij}
is formed from the ith row of the first matrix and the jth column of second
matrix. In general, a matrix product is *not commutative;* that is, $AB \neq BA$.

Inverse of a Matrix. A *square* matrix A is said to have an *inverse* if there
exists a matrix B such that $AB = BA = I$, where I is the *identity* matrix
of order n:

$$\begin{bmatrix} 1 & 0 & \cdots & 0 \\ 0 & 1 & \cdot & \cdot \\ \cdot & & & \\ \cdot & & & \\ \cdot & & 1 & 0 \\ 0 & \cdots & 0 & 1 \end{bmatrix}$$

The inverse B is a square matrix of the order of A, designated by A^{-1}. Thus
$AA^{-1} = A^{-1}A = I$. A square matrix A has an inverse if, and only if, A is
nonsingular.

Transposition. The matrix obtained from A by interchanging the rows
and columns of A is called the transpose of A, written A' or A^T.

Scalar Multiplication. For c any real or complex number and A any
matrix, $cA = (ca_{ij})$.

Special Square Matrices

1. A triangular matrix is a matrix all of whose elements above or below the
main diagonal (set of elements $a_{11}, \ldots, a_{nn}$) are zero. If A is triangular,
det $(A) = a_{11} \cdot a_{22} \cdot \cdots \cdot a_{nn}$.

2. A *diagonal matrix* is one such that all elements both above and below
the main diagonal are zero (that is, $a_{ij} = 0$ for all $i \neq j$). If all diagonal
elements are equal, the matrix is called *scalar*. If A is diagonal, $A = (a_{ii})$,
$A^{-1} = (1/a_{ii})$.

3. If $a_{ij} = a_{ji}$ for all i and j (that is, $A = A^T$), the matrix is *symmetric*.

4. If $a_{ij} = -a_{ji}$ for $i \neq j$, but the a_{ii} are not all zero, the matrix is *skew*.

5. If $a_{ij} = -a_{ji}$ for all i and j (that is, $a_{ii} = 0$), the matrix is *skew symmetric*.

6. If $A^T = A^{-1}$, the matrix A is *orthogonal*.

7. If the matrix $A^* = (\bar{a}_{ij})^T$, $\bar{a}_{ij} = $ complex conjugate of a_{ij}, A^* is the
associate of A.

8. If $A = A^{-1}$, A is *involutory*.

9. If $A = A^*$, A is *hermitian*.

10. If $A = -A^*$, A is *skew hermitian*.

11. If $A^{-1} = (A^*)$, A is *unitary*.

If A is any matrix, then AA^T and A^TA are *square symmetric* matrices,
usually of different order.

Important Relations

(1) $(A^{-1})^{-1} = A$. (2) $(A^T)^T = A$. (3) $(AB)^{-1} = B^{-1}A^{-1}$. (4) $(AB)^T =$
B^TA^T. (5) $(A^{-1})^T = (A^T)^{-1}$. (6) $(ABC)^{-1} = C^{-1}B^{-1}A^{-1}$. (7) $ABC = A[BC]$

$= (AB)C$ provided all products have meaning. (8) $A^n = A \cdot \cdots \cdot A$, n times. (9) $(A + B)(A - B) = A^2 + BA - AB + B^2 \neq A^2 + B^2$ since $AB \neq BA$.

1-30. Interpolation and Finite Differences

The practicing engineer finds many opportunities to refer to tables as sources of information. Consequently, interpolation, or that process of "reading between the lines of a table," is useful.

Linear Interpolation. If a function $f(x)$ is approximately linear in a certain range, the ratio $\dfrac{f(x_1) - f(x_0)}{x_1 - x_0} = f[x_0,x_1]$ is approximately independent of x_0, x_1 in the range. The linear approximation to the function $f(x)$, $x_0 < x < x_1$, then leads to the interpolation formula

$$f(x) \approx f(x_0) + (x - x_0)f[x_0,x_1] \approx f(x_0) + \frac{x - x_0}{x_1 - x_0}[f(x_1) - f(x_0)]$$

$$\approx \frac{1}{x_1 - x_0}[(x_1 - x)f(x_0) - (x_0 - x)f(x_1)]$$

Divided Differences of Higher Order and Higher-order Interpolation. Divided differences of second and higher order are defined iteratively by

$$f[x_0,x_1,x_2] = \frac{f[x_1,x_2] - f[x_0,x_1]}{x_2 - x_0}$$

$$\cdots \cdots \cdots \cdots \cdots \cdots \cdots \cdots \cdots \cdots \cdots \cdots \cdots \cdots \cdots$$

$$f[x_0,x_1, \ldots ,x_k] = \frac{f[x_1, \ldots ,x_k] - f[x_0,x_1, \ldots ,x_{k-1}]}{x_k - x_0}$$

and a convenient form for computational purposes is

$$f[x_0,x_1, \ldots ,x_k] = \sum_{j=0}^{k}{}' \frac{f(x_j)}{(x_j - x_0)(x_j - x_1) \cdots (x_j - x_k)}$$

for any $k \geq 0$, where the prime (') means that the term $(x_j - x_j)$ is omitted in the denominator. For example,

$$f[x_0,x_1,x_2] = \frac{f(x_0)}{(x_0 - x_1)(x_0 - x_2)} + \frac{f(x_1)}{(x_1 - x_0)(x_1 - x_2)} + \frac{f(x_2)}{(x_2 - x_0)(x_2 - x_1)}$$

f the accuracy afforded by a linear approximation is inadequate, a generally nore accurate result may be based upon the assumption that $f(x)$ may be pproximated by a polynomial of degree 2 or higher over certain ranges. This ssumption leads to *Newton's interpolation formula* with divided differences,

$$x) \approx f(x_0) + (x - x_0)f[x_0,x_1] + (x - x_0)(x - x_1)f[x_0,x_1,x_2] + \cdots$$
$$+ (x - x_0)(x - x_1) \cdots (x - x_{n-1})f[x_0,x_1, \ldots ,x_n] + E_n(x)$$

here $E_n(x) = $ error $= \dfrac{1}{(n + 1)!} f^{(n+1)}(\epsilon)\pi(x)$, where min $(x_0, \ldots ,x) < \epsilon <$

ax $(x_0,x_1, \ldots ,x_n,x)$, and $\pi(x) = (x - x_0)(x - x_1) \cdots (x - x_n)$. In order to use this result effectively, one may first form a divided-difference table. For example, for third-order interpolation, the difference table is

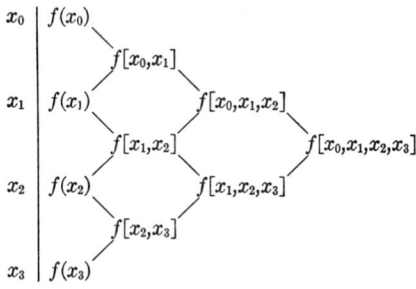

where each entry is obtained by taking the difference between diagonally adjacent entries to the left, divided by the abscissas corresponding to the ordinates, intercepted by the diagonals passing through the calculated entry.

Equally Spaced Forward Differences. If the ordinates are *equally spaced*, that is, $x_j - x_{j-1} = \Delta x$ for all j, then the first differences are denoted by $\Delta f(x_0) = f(x_1) - f(x_0)$, or $\Delta y_0 = y_1 - y_0$, where $y = f(x)$. The differences of these first differences, called second differences, are denoted by $\Delta^2 y_0$, $\Delta^2 y_1$, . . . , $\Delta^2 y_n$. Thus

$$\Delta^2 y_0 = \Delta y_1 - \Delta y_0 = y_2 - y_1 - y_1 + y_0 = y_2 - 2y_1 + y_0$$

and in general,

$$\Delta^j y_0 = \sum_{n=0}^{j} (-1)^n \binom{j}{n} y_{j-n}$$

where
$$\binom{j}{n} = \frac{j!}{n!(j-n)!} = \text{binomial coefficients}$$

Thus

$$\Delta^4 y_0 = \sum_{n=0}^{4} (-1)^n \binom{4}{n} y_{4-n} = \binom{4}{0} y_4 - \binom{4}{1} y_3 + \binom{4}{2} y_2$$

$$- \binom{4}{3} y_1 + \binom{4}{4} y_0 = y_4 - 4y_3 + 6y_2 - 4y_1 + y_0$$

If
$$y = \text{polynomial of degree } n$$
$$= a_n x^n + a_{n-1} x^{n-1} + \cdots + a_0 \qquad \Delta x = \text{constant}$$
then
$$\Delta y = \text{polynomial of degree } n - 1$$
$$\cdots\cdots\cdots\cdots\cdots\cdots\cdots\cdots\cdots$$
$$\Delta^i y = \text{polynomial of degree } n - j \qquad j \leq n$$
$$\Delta^n y = a_n (\Delta x)^n n!$$

That is, if the values of the independent variable are all separated by equal intervals, then the nth differences of a polynomial of the nth degree are constant. Conversely, if the nth differences of a tabulated function are constant when the independent variable is separated by equal intervals, then the function is a polynomial of degree n. This result is quite useful, for it allows one to select a polynomial of appropriate degree to fit data.

Lagrange Interpolation Formulas. The Newton formula is expressed in terms of divided differences. It is often useful to have the interpolation formula expressed explicitly in terms of the ordinates involved. This is accomplished by the Lagrange interpolation polynomial of degree n.

$$y(x) = \sum_{j=0}^{n} \frac{\pi(x)}{(x - x_j)\pi'(x_j)} f(x_j)$$

where $\pi(x) = (x - x_0)(x - x_1) \cdots (x - x_n)$.

$$\pi'(x_j) = (x_j - x_0)(x_j - x_1) \cdots (x_j - x_n)$$

where $(x_j - x_j)$ is the omitted factor. Thus

$$f(x) = y(x) + E_n(x)$$

$$E_n(x) = \frac{1}{(n + 1)!} \pi(x) f^{(n+1)}(\epsilon)$$

Example: The interpolation polynomial of degree 3 is

$$y(x) = \frac{(x - x_1)(x - x_2)(x - x_3)}{(x_0 - x_1)(x_0 - x_2)(x_0 - x_3)} f(x_0) + \frac{(x - x_0)(x - x_2)(x - x_3)}{(x_1 - x_0)(x_1 - x_2)(x_1 - x_3)} f(x_1)$$

$$+ \frac{(x - x_0)(x - x_1)(x - x_3)}{(x_2 - x_0)(x_2 - x_1)(x_2 - x_3)} f(x_2) + \frac{(x - x_0)(x - x_1)(x - x_2)}{(x_3 - x_0)(x_3 - x_1)(x_3 - x_2)} f(x_3)$$

Other Difference Methods (Equally Spaced Ordinates). Backward Differences. The backward differences denoted by

$$\nabla f(x) = f(x) - f(x - h)$$
$$\nabla^2 f(x) = \nabla f(x) - \nabla f(x - h)$$
$$\cdots \cdots \cdots \cdots \cdots \cdots$$
$$\nabla^n f(x) = \nabla^{n-1} f(x) - \nabla^{n-1} f(x - h)$$

are useful for calculation near the end of tabulated data.

Central Differences. The central difference denoted by $\delta f(x) = f(x + h/2) - f(x - h/2)$, $\delta^n f(x) = \delta^{n-1} f(x + h/2) - \delta^{n-1} f(x - h/2)$, is useful for calculating at the interior points of tabulated data.

1-31. Numerical Methods

Numerical Solution of Linear Equations. The methods described here are concerned with a set of n linear equations in n unknowns $x_1, x_2, \ldots, x_n$, expressed in the form

$$a_{11}x_1 + a_{12}x_2 + a_{13}x_3 + \cdots + a_{1n}x_n = b_1$$
$$a_{21}x_1 + a_{22}x_2 + a_{23}x_3 + \cdots + a_{2n}x_n = b_2$$
$$\cdots \cdots \cdots \cdots \cdots \cdots \cdots \cdots \cdots$$
$$a_{n1}x_1 + a_{n2}x_2 + a_{n3}x_3 + \cdots + a_{nn}x_n = b_n$$

$$(1\text{-}1)$$

where the n^2 coefficients a_{ij} and the n right-hand members are given. Equation (1-1) may be written in matrix form as

$$AX = B \qquad (1-2)$$

where

$$A = \begin{bmatrix} a_{11}a_{12} \cdot \cdot \cdot a_{1n} \\ a_{21}a_{22} \cdot \cdot \cdot a_{2n} \\ \cdot \cdot \cdot \cdot \cdot \cdot \cdot \cdot \cdot \\ a_{n1}a_{n2} \cdot \cdot \cdot a_{nn} \end{bmatrix} \qquad X = \begin{bmatrix} x_1 \\ x_2 \\ \cdot \\ \cdot \\ \cdot \\ x_n \end{bmatrix} \qquad B = \begin{bmatrix} b_1 \\ b_2 \\ \cdot \\ \cdot \\ \cdot \\ b_n \end{bmatrix}$$

and in the terminology a_{ij}, i = row index, j = column index. The problem, find the values of $x_1, x_2, \ldots, x_n$ satisfying equation (1-1), may be accomplished numerically from the form (1-1) or from (1-2) by matrix-inversion techniques. In either case the methods are *direct* (meaning "once through") or *iterative* (repeated) procedures.

Direct Methods for Solving (1-1). Suppose that the b_j are not all zero and that the determinant of $A \neq 0$. Then (1-1) has a unique solution.

Gauss Reduction. This method is the simplest practical method for solving (1-1). It consists of dividing the first equation by a_{11} (if $a_{11} = 0$, reorder the equations) and using the result to eliminate x_1 from all succeeding equations. Next, the modified second equation is divided by a'_{22} (if $a'_{22} = 0$, a renumbering of equations and/or variables may again be necessary) and the resulting equation is used to eliminate x_2 from the succeeding equations. This elimination is done n times. The result is of the *triangular* form.

$$
\begin{aligned}
x_1 + a'_{12}x_2 + a'_{13}x_3 + \cdots + a'_{1n}x_n &= b'_1 \\
x_2 + a'_{23}x_3 + \cdots + a'_{2n}x_n &= b'_n \\
\cdots \cdots \cdots \cdots \cdots \cdots \cdots & \\
x_{n-1} + a'_{n-1,n}x_n &= b'_{n-1} \\
x_n &= b'_n
\end{aligned}
$$

where the a'_{ij} and b'_j represent the specific numerical values obtained by the above process. The solution is then obtained by working backward from the last equation.

The Crout Reduction. A modification of the Gauss procedure which is well adapted for use on desk calculators and digital computers is a method devised by Crout. Recording of intermediate steps is minimized in this procedure. The Crout algorithm is summarized by the equations

$$a'_{ij} = a_{ij} - \sum_{k=1}^{j-1} a'_{ik}a'_{kj} \qquad\qquad i \geq j$$

$$a'_{ij} = \frac{1}{a'_{ii}}\left[a_{ij} - \sum_{k=1}^{i-1} a'_{ik}a'_{kj} \right] \qquad i < j \qquad (1-3)$$

$$b'_i = \frac{1}{a'_{ii}}\left[b_i - \sum_{k=1}^{i-1} a'_{ik}b'_k \right]$$

and finally the solution

$$x_i = b'_i - \sum_{k=i+1}^{n} a'_{ik} x_k \tag{1-4}$$

and i and j run from 1 to n unless other restrictions are present.

Iterative Methods for Solving (1-1). In certain systems, for example, in the least-squares problems of statistics, it often happens that the diagonal elements (the elements a_{ii}) of (1-1) dominate strongly over the other elements. In these cases iterative methods may be used to solve the linear system (1-1). The more the diagonal terms dominate, the more rapidly the process converges, and is in many cases superior to the direct processes.

Iteration in Total Steps. Referring to the linear system (1-1), the first set of approximate values is obtained by taking into account only the dominant diagonal terms in each equation. The approximate values are then inserted into the full system to obtain the second approximation. And so on. If the system has been rewritten so that the diagonal terms dominate, then the procedure is to rewrite it as

$$x_1 = \frac{1}{a_{11}} (b_1 - a_{12}x_2 - a_{13}x_3 - \cdots - a_{1n}x_n)$$

$$x_2 = \frac{1}{a_{22}} (b_2 - a_{21}x_1 - a_{23}x_3 - \cdots - a_{2n}x_n) \tag{1-5}$$

$$\cdots\cdots\cdots\cdots\cdots\cdots\cdots\cdots\cdots\cdots$$

$$x_n = \frac{1}{a_{nn}} (b_1 - a_{n1}x_1 - a_{n2}x_2 - \cdots - a_{nn-1}x_{n-1})$$

The initial approximation is

$$x_1{}^{(0)} = \frac{b_1}{a_{11}}, \ x_2{}^{(0)} = \frac{b_2}{a_{22}}, \ \ldots, \ x_n{}^{(0)} = \frac{b_n}{a_{nn}} \tag{1-6}$$

The next approximation is obtained by inserting the initial approximations in (1-5) and repeating until the successive approximations agree to within a specified tolerance.

Iteration in Single Steps. In this method a diagonal unknown, say x_4, is computed approximately, neglecting all others. This value is inserted into all other equations, and from one of them, an approximation for a second diagonal element is obtained. And so forth. Thus at every step all unknowns are computed by means of all components already known.

Matrix Inversion. In some problems, such as those encountered in statistical regression analysis, it is essential that the system (1-1) be solved by matrix inversion of (1-2). Thus $X = A^{-1}B$, where A^{-1} is the inverse of A, defined in the section on algebra.

The number of methods for inverting matrices are many and varied. The methods previously described may be continued to obtain the inverse of the matrix. None of these processes are given here, but the reader is referred to Bodewig, "Matrix Calculus," North Holland Publishing Company, Amsterdam, 1956.

Numerical Solution of Nonlinear Equations in One Variable. *Special Methods for Polynomials.* Consider a polynomial equation of degree n,

$$P(x) = a_0 x^n + a_1 x^{n-1} + a_2 x^{n-2} + \cdots + a_{n-1} x + a_n = 0 \qquad (1\text{-}7)$$

with real coefficients. $P(x)$ has exactly n roots, which may be real or complex. If all the coefficients of $P(x)$ are integers, then any rational root, say r/s (r, s integers, having no common divisors), of $P(x)$ must be such that r is an integral divisor of a_n and s is an integral divisor of a_0. Further, any polynomial with rational coefficients may be converted into one with integral coefficients by multiplying by the lowest common multiple of the denominators of the coefficients. In addition to these results one can obtain an upper and lower bound for the real roots by the following device: If $a_0 > 0$ in Eq. (1-7), and if in (1-7) the first negative coefficient is preceded by k coefficients which are positive or zero, and if G is the greatest of the absolute values of the negative coefficients, then each real root is less than $1 + \sqrt[k]{G/a_0}$.

A lower bound to the real roots may be found by applying the criterion to the equation $P(-x)$.

Descartes Rule. The number of positive real roots of a polynomial with real coefficients is either equal to the number of changes in sign v or is less than v by a positive even integer. The number of negative roots of $f(x)$ is either equal to the number of variations of sign of $f(-x)$ or is less than this by a positive even integer.

General Methods for Nonlinear Equations. *Successive Substitutions.* Let $f(x) = 0$ be the nonlinear equation to be solved. If this is rewritten as $x = F(x)$, then an iterative scheme can be set up in the form $x_{k+1} = F(x_k)$. To start the iteration, an initial guess must be obtained graphically or otherwise. The convergence or divergence of the procedure depends upon the method of writing $x = F(x)$, of which there will usually be several forms. If a is a root of $f(x) = 0$, then a sufficient condition for convergence is that $|F'(x)| < 1$ in that interval about a in which the iteration proceeds. The process is called *first-order* since the error at the $(k + 1)$st step is proportional to the first power of the error at the kth step.

Methods of Perturbation. Let $f(x) = 0$ be the equation. In general, the iterative relation is

$$x_{k+1} = x_k - \frac{f(x_k)}{\alpha_k} \qquad (1\text{-}8)$$

where the iteration begins with x_0 as an initial approximation and α_k as some functional.

1. THE NEWTON-RAPHSON PROCEDURE. This variant chooses $\alpha_k = f'(x_k)$, where $f' = df/dx$ and geometrically consists of replacing the graph of $f(x)$ by the tangent line at $x = x_k$ in each successive step. If $f'(x)$ and $f''(x)$ have the same sign throughout an interval $a \leq x \leq b$ containing the solution, with $f(a)$, $f(b)$ of opposite signs, then the process converges, starting from any x_0 in the interval $a \leq x \leq b$. The process is second-order.

2. THE METHOD OF FALSE POSITION. This variant is commenced by finding

x_0 and x_1 such that $f(x_0)$, $f(x_1)$ are of opposite signs. Then $\alpha_1 = $ slope of secant line joining $(x_0, f(x_0))$ and $(x_1, f(x_1))$ so that

$$x_2 = x_1 - \frac{x_1 - x_0}{f(x_1) - f(x_0)} f(x_1) \tag{1-9}$$

In each following step α_k is the slope of the line joining $(x_k, f(x_k))$ to the most recently determined point, where $f(x_j)$ has the opposite sign from that of $f(x_k)$. This method is of first order. Both of these processes can be immediately generalized to two or more simultaneous equations. For the Newton-Raphson process let the two equations be $f(x,y) = 0$, $g(x,y) = 0$. Begin with an initial approximation (x_0, y_0) and then solve successively the linear equations

$$\Delta x_k \frac{\partial f}{\partial x} (x_k, y_k) + \Delta y_k \frac{\partial f}{\partial y} (x_k, y_k) = -f(x_k, y_k)$$

$$\Delta x_k \frac{\partial g}{\partial x} (x_k, y_k) + \Delta y_k \frac{\partial g}{\partial y} (x_k, y_k) = -g(x_k, y_k) \tag{1-10}$$

for Δx_k and Δy_k. Then the $k + 1$ approximation is given from $x_{k+1} = x_k + \Delta x_k$, $y_{k+1} = y_k + \Delta y_k$. A modification consists in solving Eqs. (1-10), with (x_k, y_k) replaced by (x_0, y_0) (or other suitable pair later on in the iteration) in the derivatives. This means the derivatives (and therefore the coefficients of Δx_k, Δy_k) are independent of k. Hence the results become

$$\Delta x_k = \frac{-f(x_k, y_k) \frac{\partial g}{\partial y} (x_0, y_0) + g(x_k, y_k) \frac{\partial f}{\partial y} (x_0, y_0)}{\frac{\partial f}{\partial x} (x_0, y_0) \frac{\partial g}{\partial y} (x_0, y_0) - \frac{\partial f}{\partial y} (x_0, y_0) \frac{\partial g}{\partial x} (x_0, y_0)}$$

$$\Delta y_k = \frac{-g(x_k, y_k) \frac{\partial f}{\partial x} (x_0, y_0) + f(x_k, y_k) \frac{\partial g}{\partial x} (x_0, y_0)}{\frac{\partial f}{\partial x} (x_0, y_0) \frac{\partial g}{\partial y} (x_0, y_0) - \frac{\partial f}{\partial y} (x_0, y_0) \frac{\partial g}{\partial x} (x_0, y_0)} \tag{1-11}$$

and $x_{k+1} = \Delta x_k + x_k$, $y_{k+1} = \Delta y_k + y_k$. Such an alteration of the basic technique reduces the rapidity of convergence.

Numerical Differentiation. Numerical differentiation should be avoided wherever possible, particularly when data are empirical and subject to appreciable observation errors. Errors in data can affect numerical derivatives quite strongly; i.e., differentiation is a roughening process. When such a calculation must be made, it is usually desirable first to *smooth* the data to a certain extent.

The Use of the Interpolation Formula. If the data are given over equidistant values of the independent variable x, an interpolation formula such as the Newton formula (see Hildebrand) may be used and the resulting formula differentiated analytically. If the independent variable is not at equidistant values, then Lagrange's formulas must be used. By differentiating *three-* and *five-point* Lagrange interpolation formulas, the following differentiation formulas result for equally spaced tabular points:

Three-point Formula. Let x_0, x_1, x_2 be the three points.

$$f'(x_0) = \frac{1}{2h} \left[-3f(x_0) + 4f(x_1) - f(x_2)\right] + \frac{h^2}{3} f'''(\epsilon)$$

$$f'(x_1) = \frac{1}{2h} \left[-f(x_0) + f(x_2)\right] - \frac{h^2}{6} f'''(\epsilon)$$

$$f'(x_2) = \frac{1}{2h} \left[f(x_0) - 4f(x_1) + 3f(x_2)\right] + \frac{h^2}{3} f'''(\epsilon)$$

where the last term is an error term, $\min_j x_j < \epsilon < \max_j x_j$.

Five-point Formula. Let x_0, x_1, x_2, x_3, x_4 be the five values of the equally spaced independent variable and $f_i = f(x_i)$.

$$f'(x_0) = \frac{1}{12h} \left[-25f_0 + 48f_1 - 36f_2 + 16f_3 - 3f_4\right] + \frac{h^4}{5} f^{(v)}(\epsilon)$$

$$f'(x_1) = \frac{1}{12h} \left[-3f_2 - 10f_1 + 18f_2 - 6f_3 + f_4\right] - \frac{h^4}{20} f^{(v)}(\epsilon)$$

$$f'(x_2) = \frac{1}{12h} \left[f_0 - 8f_1 + 8f_3 - f_4\right] + \frac{h^4}{30} f^{(v)}(\epsilon)$$

$$f'(x_3) = \frac{1}{12h} \left[-f_0 + 6f_1 - 18f_2 + 10f_3 + 3f_4\right] - \frac{h^4}{20} f^{(v)}(\epsilon)$$

$$f'(x_4) = \frac{1}{12h} \left[3f_0 - 16f_1 + 36f_2 - 48f_3 + 25f_4\right] + \frac{h^4}{5} f^{(v)}(\epsilon)$$

and the last term is again an error term.

Smoothing Techniques. These techniques involve the approximation of the tabular data by a least-squares fit of the data, using some known functional form, usually a polynomial. In place of approximating $f(x)$ by a single least-squares polynomial of degree n over the entire range of the tabulation, it is often desirable to replace each tabulated value by the value taken on by a least-squares polynomial of degree n relevant to a subrange of $2M + 1$ points centered, where possible, at the point for which the entry is to be modified. Thus each smoothed value replaces a tabulated value. Many methods may be found in the literature.

Numerical Integration. A multitude of formulas have been developed to accomplish numerical integration, which consists of computing the value of a definite integral from a set of numerical values of the integrand.

Newton-Cotes Integration Formulas (Equally Spaced Ordinates) for Functions of One Variable. The definite integral $\int_a^b f(x)\,dx$ is to be evaluated.

Trapezoidal Rule. This formula consists of subdividing the interval $a \leq x \leq b$ into n subintervals a to $a + h$, $a + h$ to $a + 2h$, . . . , and replacing the graph of $f(x)$ by the result of joining the ends of adjacent ordinates by line segments. If $f_j = f(x_j) = f(a + jh)$, $f_0 = f(a)$, $f_n = f(b)$, the integration formula is

$$\int_a^b f(x)\, dx = \frac{h}{2}\,[f_0 + 2f_1 + 2f_2 + \cdots + 2f_{n-1} + f_n] + E_n$$

where

$$|E_n| = \frac{nh^3}{12}\,|f''(\epsilon)| = \frac{(b-a)^3}{12n^2}\,|f''(\epsilon)| \qquad a < \epsilon < b$$

This procedure is not of high accuracy. However, if $f''(x)$ is continuous in $a < x < b$, the error goes to zero as $1/n^2$, $n \to \infty$.

Parabolic Rule (Simpson's Rule). This procedure consists of subdividing the interval $a < x < b$ into $n/2$ subintervals, each of length $2h$, where n is an *even* integer. Using the notation as above, the integration formula is

$$\int_a^b f(x)\, dx$$

$$= \frac{h}{3}\,[f_0 + 4f_1 + 2f_2 + 4f_3 + \cdots + 4f_{n-3} + 2f_{n-2} + 4f_{n-1} + f_n] + E_n$$

where

$$|E_n| = \frac{nh^5}{180}\,|f^{(1v)}(\epsilon)| = \frac{(b-a)^5}{180n^4}\,|f^{(1v)}(\epsilon)| \qquad a < \epsilon < b$$

This method approximates $f(x)$ by a parabola on each subinterval. This rule is more accurate than the trapezoidal rule unless $f(x)$ has wild behavior on $a \leq x \leq b$. It is the most widely used integration formula.

Numerical Solution of Ordinary Differential Equations. By a numerical solution of a differential equation is meant a table of values of the function y and its derivatives over only a limited part of the range of the independent variable. Every differential equation of order n can be rewritten as n first-order differential equations. Therefore the methods given below will be for first-order equations, and the generalization to simultaneous systems will be developed later.

Modified Adam's Method. Let the first-order differential equation be $dy/dx = f(x,y)$ with the initial condition (x_0,y_0); that is, $y = y_0$ when $x = x_0$. The procedure is as follows:

Step 1: From the given initial conditions (x_0,y_0), compute

$$y'_0 = f(x_0,y_0) \qquad \text{and} \qquad y''_0 = \frac{\partial f(x_0,y_0)}{\partial x} + \frac{\partial f(x_0,y_0)}{\partial y}\, y'_0$$

Then determine

$$y_1 = y_0 + hy'_0 + \frac{h^2}{2}\, y''_0$$

where h = subdivision of independent variable.

Step 2: Determine $y'_1 = f(x_1,y_1)$, $(x_1 = x_0 + h)$. These prepare us for the *Predictor Steps*

Step 3: $(y_{n+1})_1 = y_n + \dfrac{h}{24}\,[55y'_n - 59y'_{n-1} + 37y'_{n-2} - 9y'_{n-3}]$ where y'_n,

y'_{n-1}, etc., are calculated in Step 1.

Step 4: $(y'_{n+1})_1 = f[x_{n+1}, (y_{n+1})_1]$

Corrector Steps

Step 5: $(y_{n+1})_2 = y_n + \dfrac{h}{24} [9(y'_{n+1})_1 + 19y'_n - 5y'_{n-1} + y'_{n-2}]$

Step 6: $(y'_{n+1})_2 = f[x_{n+1}, (y_{n+1})_2]$

Step 7: Iterate Steps 5 and 6 if necessary.

Runge-Kutta Methods.   These methods are self-starting and are inherently stable.   Third- and fourth-order procedures are given below for $dy/dx = f(x,y)$, h = interval size.

Third-order (error $\approx h^4$)

$$k_0 = hf(x_n,y_n)$$
$$k_1 = hf(x_n + \tfrac{1}{2}h, y_n + \tfrac{1}{2}k_0)$$
$$k_2 = hf(x_n + h, y_n + 2k_1 - k_0)$$
and $$y_{n+1} = y_n + \tfrac{1}{6}(k_0 + 4k_1 + k_2)$$

for all $n \geq 0$, with initial condition (x_0,y_0).

Fourth-order (error $\approx h^5$)

$$k_0 = hf(x_n,y_n)$$
$$k_1 = hf(x_n + \tfrac{1}{2}h, y_n + \tfrac{1}{2}k_0)$$
$$k_2 = hf(x_n + \tfrac{1}{2}h, y_n + \tfrac{1}{2}k_1)$$
$$k_3 = hf(x_n + h, y_n + k_2)$$
$$y_{n+1} = y_n + \tfrac{1}{6}(k_0 + 2k_1 + 2k_2 + k_3)$$

Equations of Higher Order and Simultaneous Differential Equations.   Any differential equation of second or higher order can be reduced to a simultaneous system of first-order equations by the introduction of auxiliary variables.   A fourth-order Runge-Kutta procedure for

$$\frac{dx}{dt} = f(t,x,y) \qquad \frac{dy}{dt} = g(t,x,y)$$

is given below.

Starting at the initial conditions x_0, y_0, t_0, the next values x_1, y_1 are computed via the equations below (where $\Delta t = h$, $t_j = h + t_{j-1}$).

$k_0 = hf(t_0,x_0,y_0)$ $l_0 = hg(t_0,x_0,y_0)$

$k_1 = hf\left(t_0 + \dfrac{h}{2}, x_0 + \dfrac{k_0}{2}, y_0 + \dfrac{l_0}{2}\right)$ $l_1 = hg\left(t_0 + \dfrac{h}{2}, x_0 + \dfrac{k_0}{2}, y_0 + \dfrac{l_0}{2}\right)$

$k_2 = hf\left(t_0 + \dfrac{h}{2}, x_0 + \dfrac{k_1}{2}, y_0 + \dfrac{l_1}{2}\right)$ $l_2 = hg\left(t_0 + \dfrac{h}{2}, x_0 + \dfrac{k_1}{2}, y_0 + \dfrac{l_1}{2}\right)$

$k_3 = hf(t_0 + h, x_0 + k_2, y_0 + l_2)$ $l_3 = hg(t_0 + h, x_0 + k_2, y_0 + l_2)$

and

$x_1 = x_0 + \tfrac{1}{6}[k_0 + 2k_1 + 2k_2 + k_3]$ $y_1 = y_0 + \tfrac{1}{6}[l_0 + 2l_1 + 2l_2 + l_3]$

To continue the computation, replace t_0, x_0, y_0, in the above formulas, by $t_1 = t_0 + h$, x_1, y_1, just calculated.   Extension of this method to more than two equations follows precisely this same pattern.

SECTION 2

THE ENGINEERING CORE: THERMODYNAMICS, FLUID FLOW, HEAT TRANSFER

Otto W. Witzell, Ph.D.; Dean of the Graduate School, Drexel Institute of Technology; Member, American Society for Mechanical Engineers, American Society for Engineering Education.   (Thermodynamics)

Robert H. Perry, Ph.D.; Consulting Chemical Engineer; Member, American Society for Engineering Education, American Association for the Advancement of Science.   (Fluid Flow and Heat Transfer)

CONTENTS

* Much of this material appeared in Sections 6 and 8 in the first edition of this work.   Authors of those sections: Austin E. Brant, Theodore Baumeister, E. A. Avallone.

THERMODYNAMICS

2-1. Energy Transformations

Transfers of energy are expressed by formulations of the first law of thermodynamics. Several formulations are available, and depend on the manner in which mass enters or leaves the system. Any of the terms in the equations may be obtained, provided all the others are known.

Closed-system Energy Formulation. In a thermodynamic system in which no mass crosses the boundaries, the energy conservation principle takes the form

$$Q_{in} - Q_{out} = E_{final} - E_{initial} + W_{out} - W_{in} \qquad (2\text{-}1)$$

where Q is the heat transfer, W is the work transfer, and E is the stored energy, defined as $U + KE + PE$, with U as the internal energy, KE as the kinetic energy, and PE as the potential energy. Examples of closed systems include batch kettles, calorimeters, and single-expansion or -compression processes.

Steady-flow-system Energy Formulation. For steady-flow systems the equation representing energy interchanges in the system must be written as follows:

$$Q_{in} - Q_{out} + \frac{V_1{}^2}{2} + y_1 + H_1 = \frac{V_2{}^2}{2} + y_2 + H_2 + W_{out} - W_{in} \qquad (2\text{-}2)$$

Here V is the velocity, y is elevation above an arbitrary datum, and H is the enthalpy, defined as $U + pv$, with p as absolute pressure, v as specific volume. Examples of steady-flow machines are boilers, turbines, gas engines, pumps, compressors, refrigerator systems, heat exchangers, throttle valves, and gas burners.

Work. In a closed system the work is often evidenced by pressure-volume changes. Specifically, if there are no changes in either kinetic or potential energies, and no frictional effects are present, the work can be evaluated by the expression

$$W = \int_{initial}^{final} p \, dv \qquad (2\text{-}3)$$

To complete the evaluation of work from this expression, knowledge of the relation between p and v must be available.

Example 1: One pound of an ideal gas expands at constant temperature so that $pv = $ constant from an initial condition of 125 psia and 1.5 ft³ to a final condition of 25 psia. How much work is done?

$$W = \int_{initial}^{final} p \, dv = \int_{initial}^{final} \frac{C}{v} \, dv = C \int_{initial}^{final} \frac{dv}{v} = p_i v_i \int_{initial}^{final} \frac{dv}{v}$$

$$= p_i v_i \ln \frac{v_f}{v_i}$$

The final volume can be found from

$$p_i v_i = p_f v_f \qquad \text{or} \qquad v_f = \frac{p_i v_i}{p_f}$$

Then

$$W = p_i v_i \ln \frac{p_i}{p_f} = 125 \times 144 \times 1.5 \ln \text{}^{125}\!\!/_{25}$$

$$= 43,500 \text{ ft-lb} = 55.9 \text{ Btu}$$

In the case of a steady-flow system, the work must be evaluated using an expression

$$W = \int_{\text{initial}}^{\text{final}} - v \, dp \tag{2-4}$$

The same restrictions apply as in the case of the closed system; i.e., kinetic and potential changes, as well as frictional effects, must be absent.

Heat Transfer. In systems which undergo reversible processes, the heat transfer can be expressed as

$$Q = \int_{\text{initial}}^{\text{final}} T \, dS \tag{2-5}$$

where T is the absolute temperature, and S is the entropy.

Combined First and Second Laws. If Eq. (2-1) is written

$$Q_{\text{net}} - W_{\text{net}} = E_{\text{final}} - E_{\text{initial}}$$

substitution of Eqs. (2-3) and (2-5) results in an equation which expresses the joint statements of both laws:

$$T \, dS = dU + p \, dv \tag{2-6}$$

2-2. Properties

Several convenient relations between properties allow the evaluation of some of the terms in the conservation equations. As an example, the internal energy and enthalpy may be related to the specific heats.

Internal Energy. The specific heat at constant volume is defined by the equation

$$C_V = \left. \frac{\partial U}{\partial T} \right|_v \tag{2-7}$$

This expression can be simplified and rearranged to allow determination of the internal energy. Where temperature changes are small, and for the case where either the system volume is constant or the system material is an ideal gas,

$$U_f - U_i = C_V[T_f - T_i] \tag{2-8}$$

Enthalpy. The enthalpy is related to the specific heat at constant pressure by

$$C_p = \left. \frac{\partial H}{\partial T} \right|_p \tag{2-9}$$

Again, for small temperature changes and where either the pressure of the system is constant or the material is an ideal gas,

$$H_f - H_i = C_p[T_f - T_i] \tag{2-10}$$

In many cases changes of enthalpy or internal energy are desired over ranges of temperature such that the specific heat is not constant. In such cases, it becomes necessary to obtain information as to the variation of the specific heat with the temperature, so that mathematical evaluation of these functions can be obtained. Tabulations and formulations for the variation of specific heats of various substances with temperature are available in such sources as the JANAF Thermochemical Tables, published at the Thermo Laboratory, Dow Chemical Co.

2-3. Equations of State

Ideal Gases. The ideal-gas law represents the property relation for many permanent gases over large ranges of pressure and temperature. It is best expressed in equation form as

$$pv = nRT \tag{2-11}$$

In this equation n represents the number of moles of gas, and R is the universal gas constant. The value of this constant is 1.986 Btu/(mole)(°R), or 1,545 ft-lb/(mole)(°R). The pressure must be expressed as absolute pressure, and similarly, the temperature must also be absolute temperature.

The number of moles of gas is related to the mass of the gas by the expression

$$n = m/M \tag{2-12}$$

where M represents the molecular weight. The molecular weights of various substances, as well as some of the other physical characteristics, are given in Table 2-1. Additional data may be found in Sec. 3.

Real Gases. In many cases, particularly at high pressure, the ideal-gas law will not adequately represent the relationship between the properties. A simple and useful modification of the gas law to include a factor called the compressibility factor results in

$$pv = CnRT \tag{2-13}$$

where C is the compressibility factor, depending on the material, temperature, and pressure.

An approximation called the law of corresponding states makes it possible to determine the compressibility factor in terms of the temperature, pressure, and critical temperature and pressure of the material. We define the reduced temperature and pressure as

$$T_R = T/T_c \quad \text{and} \quad p_R = p/p_c \tag{2-14}$$

where T_c and p_c are the critical values. Figure 3-10 shows how the compressibility factor depends on the reduced temperature and pressure. Tabular values of the critical properties are shown in Table 2-1.

Table 2-1. Properties of Gases*

Gas	Symbol	Approx. mol. wt.	Critical pressure, psia	Critical temp., °F	Enthalpy of formation at 25°C, kcal/mole	Total enthalpy at 25°C, kcal/mole	Entropy at 25°C, cal/mole	Log of equil. const. formation at 25°C
Acetylene	C₂H₂	26	911	96.3	54.19	308.0	48.00	36.64
Air	.....	29	546	-220.3	.....	3.8		2.907
Ammonia	NH₃	17	1640	270.3	-11.04	95.0	45.97	0
Argon	Ar	40	706	-187.7	0	1.5	36.98	-22.714
Benzene	C₆H₆	78	702	551.4	19.82	781.2	64.34	2.752
Butane	C₄H₁₀	58	530	307.4	-29.81	686.1	74.10	69.095
Carbon dioxide	CO₂	44	1073	88.0	-94.05	2.24	51.07	24.029
Carbon monoxide	CO	28	515	-220.3	-26.42	67.82	47.21	75.280
Dichlorodifluoromethane (R12)	CCl₂F₂	121	597	233.6	-112.00	118.83	71.92	5.761
Ethane	C₂H₆	30	718	90.0	-20.24	372.4	54.85	11.934
Ethylene	C₂H₄	28	748	49.3	12.50	335.7	52.45	0
Helium	He	4	33	-450.2	0	1.48	30.13	-1.532
Heptane	C₇H₁₆	100	394	517.1	-44.89	1147	101.64	8.902
Hydrogen	H₂	2	188	-399.8	0	69.4	31.21	0
Methane	CH₄	16	674	-116.5	-17.89	213.2	44.50	8.902
Nitrogen	N₂	28	493	-232.8	0	3.8	45.77	0
Oxygen	O₂	32	731	-181.8	0	4.11	49.00	0
Propane	C₃H₈	44	632	206.3	-24.82	529.5	64.51	4.037
Water	H₂O	18	3106	705.5	-57.80	13.7	45.11	40.048

* Additional physical, chemical, and thermodynamic data are given in Sec. 3.

Example 2: Calculate the volume of 1 mole of refrigerant 12 (dichloro-difluoromethane) at 1,500 psia and 350°F.

The critical properties are $t_c = 233.6°F$, $p_c = 597$ psia. The reduced properties are

$$T_R = \frac{350 + 460}{234 + 460} = 1.17 \qquad p_R = \frac{1,500}{597} = 2.51$$

From Fig. 3-10 $C = 0.5$, and the volume can be obtained from

$$v = \frac{CnRT}{p} = \frac{0.5 \times 1.0 \times 1,545 \times 810}{1,500 \times 144} = 2.9 \text{ ft}^3$$

Tabulations. Where accurate information is desired and where complicated equations of state must be used, it is more convenient, in many cases, to tabulate the relationships between the properties. Such tabulations are available for water vapor, various refrigerants, and for some other gases near their saturation conditions. Tables 3-24 and 3-25 show the properties of water vapor.

Example 3: How much heat must be added to 1 lb of water to change it from a saturated liquid to a saturated vapor at a constant temperature of 212°F?

The heat transfer can be obtained from $Q = \int T \, dS$ and since $T = $ constant

$$Q = T(S_{\text{final}} - S_{\text{initial}})$$

From the tables,

$$S_{\text{final}} = 1.7566 \qquad \text{and} \qquad S_{\text{initial}} = 0.3120$$

so that

$$Q = (212 + 460)(1.7566 - 0.3120) = 1070 \text{ Btu}$$

Since the pressure is constant during the boiling process, we can also calculate the heat transfer from the energy statement, which, when simplified to include only the terms of significance, is

$$Q - W = H_{\text{final}} - H_{\text{initial}}$$

The work can be obtained from $W = \int - v \, dp = 0$, so that $Q = H_{\text{final}} - H_{\text{initial}} = 1,150.4 - 180 = 1,070.4$ Btu.

2-4. Gas Mixtures

Ideal-gas Mixtures. In a mixture of ideal-gas components, the total pressure can be regarded as being equal to the sum of the individual pressures of each component. These individual pressures are called partial pressures, and can be determined from the expression

$$p_i = x_i p_T \qquad (2\text{-}15)$$

where $p_i = $ partial pressure of component,
  $x_i = $ mole fraction $= n_i/n_T$
  $p_T = $ mixture pressure

The components then will each obey the ideal-gas law so that

$$p_i v = n_i RT \tag{2-16}$$

Real-gas Mixtures. Approximations to the pVT behavior of real-gas mixtures may be made using a generalized compressibility factor obtained from the reduced pressure and temperature of the mixture. These properties of the system are expressed in terms of the critical properties of the components of the mixture as follows:

$$p_R = \frac{p_{\text{mix}}}{p_{C,\text{mix}}} \qquad T_R = \frac{T_{\text{mix}}}{T_{C,\text{mix}}} \tag{2-17}$$

where $\qquad\qquad P_{C,\text{mix}} = \Sigma x_i P_{C,i}$
and $\qquad\qquad T_{C,\text{mix}} = \Sigma x_i T_{C,i}$

With these reduced coordinates, the value of the compressibility factor can again be obtained from Fig. 3-10.

2-5. Systems Containing More Than One Phase

In cases where several phases exist in equilibrium together, the thermodynamic condition of equilibrium is described in terms of a system property called the Gibbs function, and defined by

$$G = H - TS \tag{2-18}$$

In the case where a single component exists in several phases, such as ice and steam, the equilibrium condition results in

$$g_{\text{I}} = g_{\text{II}} = g_N \tag{2-19}$$

where g_{I} represents the specific Gibbs function for phase I.

The different conditions of existence are best represented graphically by a phase diagram and pressure-volume diagram. Typical examples of these diagrams are given in Fig. 2-1.

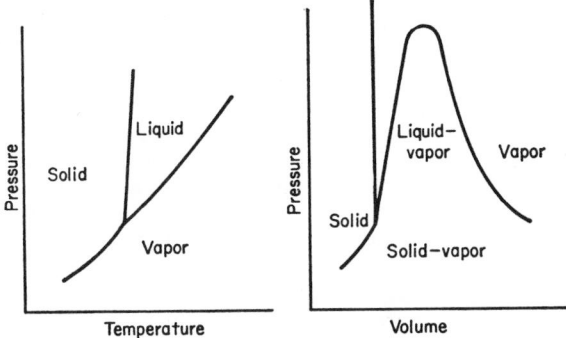

Fig. 2-1. Phase and PV diagram.

Vapor Pressure.   The vapor pressure or saturation pressure at any given temperature can often be obtained from property tables, or may be approximated by an expression of the form

$$\ln p = A/T + B \qquad (2\text{-}20)$$

where A and B are constants that depend on the material. If pressure-temperature information is available for two points on any specific vapor curve, then the vapor pressure at any other temperature can be computed.

Example 4: Determine the saturation pressure of refrigerant 12 at 100°F. The boiling point is −20°F.   Data available are

At p = 14.7 psia t = −20°F
At p = 597 psia t = 234°F   (critical values, Table 2-1)

Substitution of these values into the equation gives

$$\ln 14.7 = \frac{A}{440} + B$$
$$\ln 597 \; = \frac{A}{694} + B$$

from which A = 4,440, B = 12.79.

We can now calculate the saturation pressure from

$$\ln p = -4{,}440/560 + 12.79$$
$$p = 130 \text{ psia}$$

Escaping Tendency and Fugacity.   In the case where the phases are not in equilibrium, the rate at which the system tends to equilibrium is partially determined by a generalized function called the escaping tendency.   To describe this condition in a system containing several components and several phases, a necessary condition for equilibrium is that the escaping tendency must be the same throughout the system.   One convenient measure of the escaping tendency is called the fugacity.   For the gas phase the escaping tendency, and therefore the fugacity, may often be represented satisfactorily by the pressure of the component under consideration.

Where the gas phase deviates considerably from ideal behavior, fugacity must be used as a true measure of the escaping tendency, rather than the pressure.   The fugacity of a substance is a property of that substance, and tabulations of it may be made in the same fashion as other properties of the materials.   For example, the rate at which water vapor will penetrate a porous membrane is dependent on the fugacity of the water vapor on each side of the membrane.

Single-component Systems.   A convenient generalized chart of the fugacity coefficient f/p as it depends on the pressure and temperature of the system is shown in Fig. 3-11.   The correlation is again made in terms of the reduced pressure and reduced temperature, in the same manner as for the compressibility factor.

Example 5: Compare the fugacity to the pressure for saturated water vapor at 3,000 psia.   The critical properties are 3,106 psia and 705°F.   The reduced properties are

$$p_R = \frac{3{,}000}{3{,}106} = 0.966 \qquad T_R = \frac{695 + 460}{705 + 460} = 0.991$$

From Fig. 3-11 we find $f/p = 0.65$.

Thus the fugacity is $0.65 \times 3{,}000 = 1{,}950$ psi.

Systems of Several Components.   The fugacity of a component of a mixture of gases can often be satisfactorily approximated by an expression

$$f_i = x_i f_{pure} \tag{2-21}$$

where f_i = fugacity of component in mixture

x_i = mole fraction = n_i/n_T

f_{pure} = fugacity of pure component at pressure and temperature of mixture

Chemical Equilibrium.   Equilibrium in a chemically reacting system is describable in terms of the equilibrium constant.   Consider the reaction

$$CO + \tfrac{1}{2}O_2 \to CO_2 \tag{2-22}$$

at equilibrium.   Two expressions involving the equilibrium constant for this typical reaction are useful.

$$-\ln K = \frac{G_{final} - G_{initial}}{RT} \tag{2-23}$$

$$K = \frac{f_{CO_2}}{f_{CO}(f_{O_2})^{\frac{1}{2}}} \tag{2-24}$$

where f_{CO_2}, f_{CO}, and f_{O_2} are the fugacities of each of these respective components as they exist in the equilibrium mixture.   The use of the approximation from Eq. (2-21) results in a more manageable relation for Eq. (2-24).

$$K = \frac{\dfrac{f_{CO_2,\,pure}}{p}}{\dfrac{f_{CO,\,pure}}{p}\left(\dfrac{f_{O_2,\,pure}}{p}\right)^{\frac{1}{2}}} \left[\frac{x_{CO_2}}{x_{CO}(x_{O_2})^{\frac{1}{2}}}\right] p^{-\frac{1}{2}} \tag{2-25}$$

The coefficients f/p can now be obtained from Fig. 3-11.   A further simplification is possible if all components of the equilibrium mixture can be considered as ideal gases.   Under this condition $f/p = 1$, and

$$K = \frac{x_{CO_2}}{x_{CO}(x_{O_2})^{\frac{1}{2}}} \, p^{-\frac{1}{2}} \tag{2-26}$$

The equilibrium constant is a temperature function, and tabulations of this function for various reactions and temperatures may be found in the literature. Knowledge of the equilibrium constant makes possible the complete determination of the composition of the equilibrium mixture.   The major portion of the data available for the equilibrium constants is so arranged that the pressure in Eqs. (2-23) and (2-24) must be introduced in atmospheres.   A typical tabulation of this sort is the JANAF Thermochemical Tables, published at the Thermo Laboratory, Dow Chemical Company.

Example 6: A gas stream containing equimolar proportions of CO and H_2O is allowed to come to equilibrium at 1,000°K and 5 atm pressure. What is the composition if only CO, CO_2, H_2O, and H_2 are the important components?

The reaction at equilibrium will be

$$CO + H_2O \leftrightarrows CO_2 + H_2$$

The JANAF tables give the equilibrium constant of formation, i.e., that specific reaction in which the tabulated component is formed from its elements, with these elements occurring in their natural stable state at normal atmospheric conditions.

We can obtain values of the equilibrium constants as follows:

Reaction 1:	$C_{gr} + O_2 \rightarrow CO_2$
Reaction 2:	$C_{gr} + \frac{1}{2}O_2 \rightarrow CO$
Reaction 3:	$H_2 + \frac{1}{2}O_2 \rightarrow H_2O$

The desired reaction

Reaction 4: $CO + H_2O \rightarrow CO_2 + H_2$

can be obtained by subtracting reactions 2 and 3 from 1. The equilibrium constant for reaction 4 is

$$K_4 = \frac{K_1}{K_2 K_3}$$

since the equilibrium constant is exponentially dependent on the Gibbs function. At 1,000°K

$$\log K_1 = 20.680 \qquad \log K_2 = 10.459 \qquad \log K_3 = 10.062$$

and therefore

$$\log K_4 = 0.159 \qquad \text{and} \qquad K_4 = 1.442$$

If we now assume that all components at equilibrium are ideal gases, the fugacity coefficients will all be identical and

$$1.442 = \frac{(x_{CO_2})(x_{H_2})}{(x_{CO})(x_{H_2O})}$$

or

(a) $$1.442 = \frac{(n_{CO_2})(n_{H_2})}{(n_{CO})(n_{H_2O})}$$

We can now write an expression for the reaction, starting with CO and H_2O and ending at equilibrium.

$$CO + H_2O \rightarrow n_{CO}CO + n_{H_2O}H_2O + n_{CO_2}CO_2 + n_{H_2}H_2$$

From this equation we can write three others, one for each elemental type.

(b)	For carbon:	$1 = n_{CO} + n_{CO_2}$
(c)	For oxygen:	$2 = n_{CO} + n_{H_2O} + n_{CO_2}$
(d)	For hydrogen:	$1 = n_{H_2O} + n_{H_2}$

We now have four equations, (a) to (d), which can be used to determine exactly n_{CO}, n_{H_2O}, n_{CO_2}, and n_{H_2}. A trial-and-error solution gives

$$n_{CO} = 0.454 \qquad n_{CO_2} = 0.526$$
$$n_{H_2O} = 0.454 \qquad n_{H_2} = 0.546$$

Heterogeneous Systems. Equilibrium determinations involving more than one phase may also be approximated very satisfactorily by using the mole fraction of the particular component in the phase under consideration for the fugacity in Eq. (2-24). For example, consider the equilibrium reaction

$$C_{gr} + O_2 \rightarrow CO_2$$

Since the condensed phase contains only one component, the mole fraction of the graphitic carbon is unity, and the equilibrium constant for the reaction is

$$K = \frac{x_{CO_2}}{x_{O_2}}$$

if both gas components can be considered ideal.

2-6. Thermochemistry

Property Evaluations. It is desirable to be able to obtain numerical values for various chemical properties of materials involved in processes where chemical reactions occur. For convenience, tabulations of such properties as enthalpy, internal energy, Gibbs function, and the equilibrium constant are made in terms of the reaction of formation.

The formation reaction is the reaction having the component under consideration as the only product, with each reactant in its elemental form and with these elements in their natural stable state at normal atmospheric conditions. For example, the enthalpy of formation of carbon dioxide at 25°C is expressed as follows:

$$C_{gr} + O_2 \rightarrow CO_2 \qquad H_f = -94 \text{ kcal/mole } CO_2 \qquad (2\text{-}27)$$

The negative sign indicates that the reaction is exothermic; i.e., it releases energy. The enthalpies of formation of the elements in their naturally occurring form must then be zero at all temperatures. Table 2-1 lists enthalpies and equilibrium constants of formation for some simple common gases at 25°C. Extensive tabulations of the enthalpy, Gibbs function, and equilibrium constant of formation, as they depend on temperature, can be found in the JANAF Thermochemical Tables. The enthalpy change of reaction for any reaction may be found from the enthalpies of formation of all the components that enter into the reaction.

Example 7: It is desired to find the enthalpy change for the following reaction at 25°C:

$$CO + \tfrac{1}{2}O_2 \rightarrow CO_2 \qquad (2\text{-}28)$$

The enthalpy change is found from

$$H_f - H_i = \Sigma H_{\text{form,products}} - \Sigma H_{\text{form,reactants}} \qquad (2\text{-}29)$$

or

$$H_f - H_i = H_{\text{form},CO_2} - H_{\text{form},CO} - \tfrac{1}{2}H_{\text{form},O_2} \qquad (2\text{-}30)$$

From Table 2-1,

$$H_f - H_i = -94.05 - [-26.42 - \tfrac{1}{2}(O)] = -67.63 \text{ kcal/mole}$$

The same general rule also applies for the internal-energy change of reaction and change in Gibbs function for the reaction. If we represent all these properties by the generalized symbol R, then

$$\Delta R_{\text{reaction}} = \Sigma R_{\text{form,products}} - \Sigma R_{\text{form,reactants}} \tag{2-31}$$

As previously indicated, the equilibrium constant of reaction is related to those of formation by

$$K_{\text{reaction}} = \frac{\pi(K_{\text{form,products}})}{\pi(K_{\text{form,reactants}})} \tag{2-32}$$

An approximation to the variation of the equilibrium constant with temperature can be made from the equation

$$\ln K = \frac{A}{T} + B \tag{2-33}$$

where A and B are constants. Figure 2-2 shows the equilibrium constants for several components as they depend on the inverse temperature.

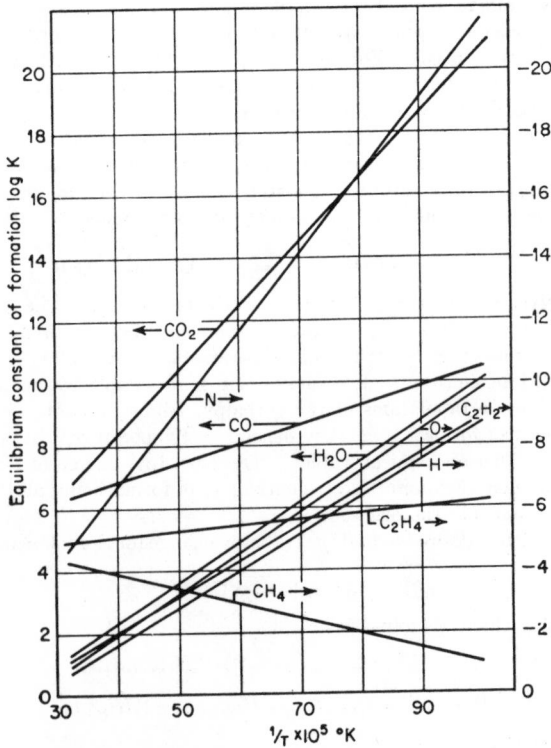

Fig. 2-2. Equilibrium constant of formation.

The entropy change for a reaction may be found from the absolute entropies of the components involved in the reaction. These absolute entropies can be obtained from specific-heat data and the use of the third law of thermodynamics, which, in effect, specifies the state of the component when its entropy is zero. Table 2-1 indicates some of these absolute entropies at 25°C, and a more complete tabulation is given in the JANAF tables.

Since the entropy is an additive property, the change in entropy for any reaction may be found from the absolute entropies of the components of the reaction in the same manner as from the enthalpies of formation. For example, for Eq. (2-28) at 25°C,

$$\Delta S_{\text{reaction}} = S_{CO_2} - S_{CO} - \tfrac{1}{2} S_{O_2}$$
$$\Delta S_{\text{reaction}} = 51.1 - 47.2 - \tfrac{1}{2}(49.0) = -20.6 \text{ cal/(mole)(°K)} \tag{2-34}$$

All components, including the elemental forms, have nonzero values.

It is also convenient to tabulate the total enthalpy of various substances measured above some arbitrary datum. Tabulations of this sort are available, and Table 2-1 shows typical values of this property. Care must be exercised in the use of tabulated total enthalpy values since no universally accepted standard datum is in use. The data in various sources are thus often mutually exclusive.

The total enthalpies may also be used to find the enthalpy change of reaction. As for the entropy for Eq. (2-28) at 25°C,

$$\Delta H_{\text{reaction}} = H_{\text{total},CO_2} - H_{\text{total},CO} - \tfrac{1}{2} H_{\text{total},O_2}$$
$$\Delta H_{\text{reaction}} = 2.24 - 67.82 - \tfrac{1}{2}(4.11) = -67.63 \text{ kcal/mole} \tag{2-35}$$

Here also it is important to recognize that the total enthalpies of all components, including the elemental forms, have nonzero values. The variation of the total enthalpy and absolute entropy with temperature for a representative group of gases is shown in Table 2-2.

It is possible to relate most of the thermochemical properties to each other so that limited data can often be used to construct more extensive information. Some of these formulas have been given elsewhere, but are repeated here for convenience. For any reaction at a given temperature

$$\ln K = -\frac{\Delta G}{RT} \tag{2-23}$$

$$\Delta G = \Delta H - T \Delta S \tag{2-36}$$
$$\Delta H = \Sigma H_{\text{form,products}} - \Sigma H_{\text{form,reactants}} \tag{2-29}$$

or

$$\Delta H = \Sigma H_{T \text{ products}} - \Sigma H_{T \text{ reactants}} \tag{2-37}$$
$$\Delta S = \Sigma S_{\text{products}} - \Sigma S_{\text{reactants}} \tag{2-38}$$

For any component

$$C_p = \frac{\Delta H}{\Delta T} \qquad \text{approximately} \tag{2-39}$$

Flame Temperature at Constant Pressure. The temperature of the flame in a combustion reaction can be satisfactorily approximated by assuming

Table 2-2. Enthalpies and Entropies of Gases

Gas	Symbol	Enthalpy, kcal/mole					Entropy, cal/mole				
		1000°K	1500°K	2000°K	2500°K	3000°K	1000°K	1500°K	2000°K	2500°K	3000°K
Acetylene	C_2H_2	317.9	326.5	336.0	346.0	356.3	64.32	71.34	76.78	81.22	84.97
Ammonia	NH_3	102.5	109.7	117.8	126.5	135.6	58.39	64.17	68.83	72.71	76.01
Argon	Ar	5.0	7.5	9.9	12.4	14.9	42.99	45.01	46.44	47.55	48.45
Benzene	C_6H_6	808.0	835.1	.....	.....	.....	106.73	128.68			
Butane	C_4H_{10}	704.1	712.7	.....	.....	.....	120.31	144.22			
Carbon dioxide	CO_2	10.2	17.0	24.1	31.4	38.8	64.34	69.82	73.90	77.15	79.85
Carbon monoxide	CO	73.0	77.1	81.4	85.8	90.2	56.03	59.35	61.81	63.76	65.37
Dichlorodifluoromethane	CCl_2F_2	134.4	146.8	159.5	172.2	185.1	97.92	107.98	115.27	120.96	125.63
Ethane	C_2H_6	381.2	397.8	416.4	436.2	456.6	79.39	92.46	89.90	96.36	101.79
Ethylene	C_2H_4	347.9	360.3	374.0	388.5	403.4	72.06	82.02	39.59	40.70	41.61
Helium	He	4.97	7.45	9.94	12.4	14.9	36.15	38.16			
Heptane	C_7H_{16}	1178.0	1192.3	.....	.....	.....	180.32	220.45			
Hydrogen	H_2	74.3	78.1	82.1	86.3	90.6	39.70	42.72	45.00	46.88	48.47
Methane	CH_4	222.3	231.9	242.7	254.3	266.3	59.14	66.84	73.08	78.23	82.60
Nitrogen	N_2	8.9	13.0	17.2	21.6	26.0	54.51	57.78	60.22	62.16	63.77
Oxygen	O_2	9.5	13.8	18.3	22.8	27.6	58.19	61.66	64.21	66.25	67.97
Propane	C_3H_8	543.4	550.2	.....	.....	.....	99.77	118.29			
Water	H_2O	19.9	25.2	31.1	37.4	43.9	55.59	59.86	63.23	66.03	68.42

that the enthalpy or internal-energy change for the reaction from initial to final temperature is zero.

Example 8: What temperature can be expected from the reaction of carbon monoxide with air at 1 atm pressure if the reactants are at 25°C?

Since the composition of air is 1 molar part oxygen and 3.78 molar parts nitrogen, the reaction is

$$CO + \tfrac{1}{2}(O_2 + 3.78N_2) = CO_2 + 1.89N_2$$

The enthalpy of the reactants is

$$H_{reactant} = H_{CO} + \tfrac{1}{2}H_{O_2} + 1.89H_{N_2}$$

At 25°C,

$$H_{reactant} = 67.82 + \tfrac{1}{2}(4.11) + 1.89 \times 3.77 = 77.0 \text{ kcal}$$

By trial and error we find that, at $T = 2650°K$,

$$H_{products} = H_{CO_2} + 1.89H_{N_2} = 76.9 \text{ kcal}$$

Thus the flame temperature will be 2650°K.

Example 9: In some cases the flame temperature becomes excessive to the point where dissociation reactions play an important part. What temperature can be expected from the reaction

$$CO + H_2 + O_2 \rightarrow products$$

at 1 atm and initially at 25°C?

We assume that the equilibrium products contain CO, CO_2, H_2, H_2O, and O_2. Thus the reaction is

$$CO + H_2 + O_2 \rightarrow n_{CO}CO + n_{CO_2}CO_2 + n_{H_2}H_2 + n_{H_2O}H_2O + n_{O_2}O_2$$

The equilibrium equations are obtained as follows:

(a)	$C_{gr} + \tfrac{1}{2}O_2 \rightarrow CO$	K_A
(b)	$C_{gr} + O_2 \rightarrow CO_2$	K_B
(c)	$H_2 + \tfrac{1}{2}O_2 \rightarrow H_2O$	K_C

We can combine Eqs. (a) and (b) to give

$$(d) \qquad CO + \tfrac{1}{2}O_2 \rightarrow CO_2 \qquad K_D = \frac{K_B}{K_A}$$

The final statement is the flame-temperature statement:

$$H_{reactants} = H_{products}$$

The set of six simultaneous equations for solution are

$$(1) \qquad K_D = \frac{n_{CO_2}}{n_{CO}(n_{O_2})^{1/2}}(n_T)^{1/2}$$

$$(2) \qquad K_C = \frac{n_{H_2O}}{n_{H_2}(n_{O_2})^{1/2}}(n_T)^{1/2}$$

$$(3) \qquad 1 = n_{CO} + n_{CO_2}$$

$$(4) \qquad 3 = n_{CO} + 2n_{CO_2} + n_{H_2O} + 2n_O$$

$$(5) \qquad 1 = n_{H_2} + n_{H_2O}$$

(6)
$$[n_{CO}H_{CO} + n_{CO_2}H_{CO_2} + n_{H_2}H_{H_2} + n_{H_2O}H_{H_2O} + n_{O_2}H_{O_2}]_{\text{flame temperature}} =$$
$$[H_{CO} + H_{H_2} + H_{O_2}]_{25°C}$$

where $n_T = n_{CO} + n_{CO_2} + n_{H_2} + n_{H_2O} + n_{O_2}$.

If a trial flame temperature is assumed, the equilibrium constants and enthalpies are known, and allow solution for the five composition variables in any five of the equations. The assumed temperature can then be checked from the sixth equation. The results are

$$n_{CO} = 0.633$$
$$n_{CO_2} = 0.368$$
$$n_{H_2} = 0.183$$
$$n_{H_2O} = 0.817$$
$$n_{O_2} = 0.407$$

Substitution of these values into the enthalpy equation shows that

$$H_{\text{reactant}} = H_{\text{products}} = 141.4 \text{ kcal}$$
$$T = 3225°K$$

Heat Released. The energy released as heat in a combustion reaction may be calculated in a manner similar to that for the flame temperature. In this case, the final temperature must be specified, and is not a variable. All equations shown in Example 9 are applicable, with the exception of the enthalpy equation. If the reacting gas flow is steady, the energy equation results in

$$Q = H_{\text{final}} - H_{\text{initial}} \tag{2-40}$$

Thus the composition must first be determined, so that the heat transfer may then be calculated.

Constant-volume Reactions. In instances of this sort where combustion reactions take place in fixed volumes, such as bombs or cylinders of slow-moving internal-combustion engines, a simple modification of the above equations involving only the substitution of the internal energy for the enthalpy is required.

2-7. Mixtures of Ideal Gases and Vapors

Humidity. The relative humidity of an ideal-gas vapor mixture is defined by the equation

$$\text{RH} = \frac{p_v}{p_{\text{sat}}} \tag{2-41}$$

where p_v is the actual pressure of the vapor phase, and p_{sat} is the pressure exerted by the same vapor when saturated at the mixture temperature. For low vapor pressures the vapor may often be considered an ideal gas, so that

$$\text{RH} = \frac{v_{\text{sat}}}{v_V} \tag{2-42}$$

The absolute humidity, or specific humidity, is the ratio of the mass of vapor in the mixture to the mass of the dry gas.

$$\text{SH} = \frac{m_v}{m_g} \tag{2-43}$$

Observations of the concentrations of the two components are usually made in terms of three temperatures: (1) the dew-point temperature, (2) the wet-bulb temperature, and (3) the dry-bulb temperature.

The dew point is the temperature at which condensation of the vapor takes place if the mixture is cooled at constant pressure.

The wet-bulb temperature is the temperature achieved by the mixture if it is saturated by evaporating liquid into it so that the latent heat of vaporization comes from the mixture, thereby depressing its temperature.

The dry-bulb temperature is the normal temperature of the mixture.

Example 10: Calculate the relative humidity of an air–water vapor mixture having a dry-bulb temperature of 80°F and a wet-bulb temperature of 72°F.

The specific humidity may be found from

$$\text{SH} = \frac{c_{p\text{gas}}(t_w - t_d) + \text{SH}_w L_w}{H_{v.d} - H_{L.w}} \tag{2-44}$$

where subscripts w and d refer to the wet- and dry-bulb temperatures, L is the latent heat of the vapor, and H_v and H_L represent, respectively, the enthalpies of the saturated vapor and its corresponding saturated liquid. The specific humidity at the wet-bulb temperature is found from the definition and the assumption of ideal-gas behavior for both components.

$$\text{SH} = \frac{m_v}{m_g} = \frac{M_v}{M_g}\frac{p_v}{p_g} = \frac{18}{29}\left(\frac{0.39}{14.7 - 0.39}\right) = 0.0168 \text{ lb water vapor/lb air}$$

Then

$$\text{SH}_D = \frac{0.24(72 - 80) + 0.0168 \times 1,053}{1,097 - 40} = 0.150 \text{ lb water vapor/lb air}$$

The vapor pressure at the dry-bulb condition can be found by the equation above.

$$\text{SH} = \frac{M_v p_v}{M_g p_g} = \frac{18}{29}\left(\frac{p_v}{p - p_v}\right) \quad \text{or} \quad p_v = \frac{p}{(0.622/\text{SH}) + 1}$$

from which

$$p_v = \frac{14.7}{(0.622/0.0150) + 1} = 0.346 \text{ psia}$$

and

$$\text{RH} = \frac{p_v}{p_{\text{sat}}} = \frac{0.346}{0.507} = 69.2\%$$

Example 11: Calculate the relative humidity of an air–water vapor mixture having a dry-bulb temperature of 80°F and a dew point of 74°F.

From the dew point we find the pressure of the vapor to be 0.416 psia. Thus

$$\text{RH} = \frac{0.416}{0.507} = 82\%$$

The Psychrometric Chart. Solutions to the problems of air–water vapor mixtures are readily available in chart form. Figure 4-14 shows a psychrometric chart for this system. The solutions to Examples 10 and 11 can be taken directly off the chart.

For problems involving the change of conditions, heat exchanges may also be obtained by computing the change in enthalpy read from the psychrometric chart.

Example 12: It is desired to reduce the temperature of air at 80°F dry-bulb and 72°F wet-bulb to a dry-bulb temperature of 65°F. How much heat must be removed for each pound of air cooled?

$$Q = H_f - H_i = 30 - 35.8 = -5.8 \text{ Btu/lb air}$$

2-8. Processes

It is possible to tabulate the equations applicable for the determination of heat, work, and some selected property changes for the simplest processes, where an ideal gas is the medium and in which the conditions throughout the process are idealized. These relations are shown in Table 2-3, and the following example shows the manner in which they have been obtained.

Table 2-3. Relations for Ideal-gas Processes
Reversible Processes with Constant Specific Heats

Process..............	Isothermal $T = $ const	Constant pressure $p = $ const	Constant volume $v = $ const	Isentropic $S = $ const
pvT relations.........	$pv = $ const	$\dfrac{v}{T} = $ const	$\dfrac{p}{T} = $ const	$pv^k = $ const $Tv^{k-1} = $ const $\dfrac{p^{(k-1)/k}}{T} = $ const
Nonflow work $-\int p\,dv$.........	$pv \ln \dfrac{v_f}{v_i}$	$p\,\Delta v$	0	$nC_V \Delta T$
Steady-flow work $-\int v\,dp$.........	$pv \ln \dfrac{p_i}{p_f}$	0	$v\,\Delta p$	$nC_p \Delta T$
Heat $\int T\,dS$.......	$pv \ln \dfrac{p_i}{p_f}$	$nC_p \Delta T$	$nC_V \Delta T$	0
ΔU................	0	$nC_V \Delta T$	$nC_V \Delta T$	$nC_V \Delta T$
ΔH................	0	$nC_p \Delta T$	$nC_p \Delta T$	$nC_p \Delta T$
ΔS................	$nR \ln \dfrac{p_i}{p_f}$	$nC\,p \ln \dfrac{T_f}{T_i}$	$nC_V \ln \dfrac{T_f}{T_i}$	0

Example 13: It is desired to obtain expressions for the heat transfer, work, internal-energy change, enthalpy change, and entropy change for a process which takes place in a steady-flow frictionless machine at constant pressure.

The material may be considered to be an ideal gas. It is further to be assumed that kinetic-energy and potential-energy changes between the inlet and outlet gas streams can be neglected and only one inlet and one outlet stream are present.

The energy statement that applies is Eq. (2-2), which, in consideration of the limitations of the problem, may be written

$$Q_{net} - W_{net} = H_{final} - H_{initial}$$

The work may be obtained from Eq. (2-4).

$$W = \int -v\,dp = 0 \qquad \text{for constant pressure condition}$$

We have, then,

$$Q_{net} = H_{final} - H_{initial}$$

For an ideal gas we find from Eq. (2-10) that

$$H_f - H_i = C_p(T_f - T_i)$$

so that

$$Q = C_p(T_f - T_i)$$

The internal-energy change can be obtained from Eq. (2-8).

$$U_f - U_i = C_v(T_f - T_i)$$

The entropy change can be obtained by using Eq. (2-6).

$$T\,dS = dU + p\,dv$$

In this case, since p is constant, we can write

$$S_f - S_i = \int \frac{dU}{T} + p\int dv \qquad (2\text{-}45)$$

or

$$S_f - S_i = C_V \ln\frac{T_f}{T_i} + R\ln\frac{v_f}{v_i} \qquad (2\text{-}46)$$

We can write the second term as follows:

$$R\ln\frac{v_f}{v_i} = R\ln\frac{T_f}{T_i}$$

so that

$$S_f - S_i = (C_V + R)\ln\frac{T_f}{T_i}$$

Recognizing that, for an ideal gas, $C_V + R = C_p$,   (2-47)

$$S_f - S_i = C_p \ln\frac{T_f}{T_i}$$

2-9. Ideal-gas Power Cycles

The analysis of real power cycles can often be approximated by idealized cycles, using ideal gases in a piston-cylinder arrangement with no transfer of mass. Several such approximations are of interest.

Carnot Cycle. The cycle consists of four processes, two isothermals and two isentropics, as shown in Fig. 2-3. A detailed analysis of the cycle shows that

$$Q_{\text{net}} = W_{\text{net}} = (T_3 - T_4)R \ln \frac{p_2}{p_3}$$

$$Q_{12} = Q_{34} = 0$$

$$Q_{23} = W_{23} = p_2 v_2 \ln \frac{p_2}{p_3}$$

$$W_{12} = C_V(T_2 - T_1)$$
$$W_{34} = C_V(T_4 - T_3)$$
$$U_3 - U_2 = 0 \qquad U_1 - U_4 = 0$$

$$Q_{41} = W_{41} = p_4 v_4 \ln \frac{p_4}{p_1}$$

$$\text{eff} = \frac{T_2 - T_1}{T_2} = \frac{T_3 - T_4}{T_3} \tag{2-48}$$

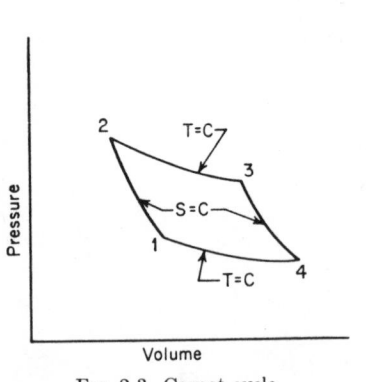

FIG. 2-3. Carnot cycle.   FIG. 2-4. Otto cycle.

Otto Cycle. This cycle consists of two isentropics and two constant-volume processes as shown in Fig. 2-4, and is often used as a representation of a spark-ignition engine.

The cycle analysis indicates

$$Q_{\text{net}} = W_{\text{net}} = C_V[(T_2 + T_4) - (T_1 + T_3)]$$
$$Q_{12} = C_V(T_2 - T_1)$$
$$Q_{34} = C_V(T_4 - T_3)$$
$$Q_{23} = Q_{41} = 0$$
$$W_{12} = W_{34} = 0$$
$$W_{41} = C_V(T_4 - T_1)$$
$$W_{23} = C_V(T_3 - T_2)$$

$$\text{eff} = 1 - \frac{T_4}{T_1} = 1 - \left(\frac{V_4}{V_1}\right)^{k-1} \tag{2-49}$$

Diesel Cycle. The cycle consists of two isentropic, one constant-volume, and one constant-pressure process, as shown in Fig. 2-5. It is representative of a diesel engine.

Results of the cycle analysis are

$$Q_{net} = W_{net} = C_p(T_3 - T_2) - C_V(T_4 - T_1)$$
$$Q_{23} = C_p(T_3 - T_2)$$
$$Q_{41} = C_V(T_4 - T_1)$$
$$Q_{12} = Q_{34} = 0$$
$$W_{23} = p_2(v_3 - v_2)$$
$$W_{41} = 0$$
$$W_{12} = C_V(T_2 - T_1)$$
$$W_{34} = C_V(T_4 - T_3)$$

$$\text{eff} = 1 - \frac{1}{R}\frac{T_4 - T_1}{T_3 T_2} \tag{2-50}$$

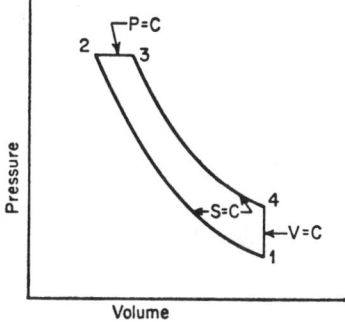

Fig. 2-5. Diesel cycle. Fig. 2-6. Brayton cycle.

Brayton Cycle. This cycle consists of two isentropic and two constant-pressure processes. It is representative of the gas turbine, and is shown in Fig. 2-6.

Results of the cycle analysis are

$$Q_{net} = W_{net} = C_p[(T_4 + T_2) - (T_3 + T_1)]$$
$$Q_{23} = Q_{41} = 0$$
$$Q_{34} = C_p(T_4 - T_3)$$
$$Q_{12} = C_p(T_2 - T_1)$$
$$W_{12} = p_1(v_2 - v_1)$$
$$W_{34} = p_3(v_4 - v_3)$$
$$W_{23} = C_V(T_3 - T_2)$$
$$W_{41} = C_V(T_1 - T_4)$$

$$\text{eff} = 1 - \frac{T_1 - T_2}{T_4 - T_3} \tag{2-51}$$

Stirling Cycle. The Stirling cycle consists of two isothermal and two constant-volume processes. Practical examples of this cycle have been developed recently, and depend on regeneration to achieve practical efficiencies. Figure 2-7 shows this cycle. Practical cycles use the heat rejected in process 41 to partly regenerate the gas during process 23. Cycle analysis must depend on the degree of regeneration.

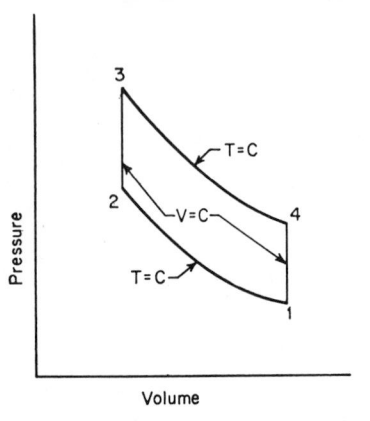

FIG. 2-7. *PV* diagram for Stirling cycle.   FIG. 2-8. Stirling cycle.

Example 14: Calculate the ideal cycle efficiency for a Stirling cycle, using air in which the maximum and minimum temperatures are 2000°R and 500°R and 30 per cent of the heat rejected is regained by regeneration.

The compression ratio is 6.

The temperature-entropy diagram is useful for representation of the problem as shown in Fig. 2-8.

The heat rejected in process 41 is

$$Q_{41} = C_V(T_4 - T_1) = 0.17 \times 1500 = 255 \text{ Btu}$$

The heat supplied in process 23 is

$$Q_{23} = 0.70 C_v(T_3 - T_2) = 0.7 \times 255 = 179 \text{ Btu}$$

The heat supplied in process 34 is

$$Q_{34} = RT_3 \ln \frac{p_3}{p_4} = RT_3 \ln \frac{v_1}{v_2} = \frac{1545}{29} \times \frac{2000}{778} \ln 6 = 245 \text{ Btu}$$

The total heat supply is therefore

$$Q_{23} + Q_{34} = 179 + 245 = 424 \text{ Btu}$$

The net work done as a result of processes 12 and 34 is

$$W_{12} = RT_1 \ln \frac{p_1}{p_2} = -RT_1 \ln \frac{p_2}{p_1}$$

$$W_{34} = RT_3 \ln \frac{p_3}{p_4}$$

Reference to Fig. 2-7 shows that

$$\frac{p_3}{p_4} = \frac{p_2}{p_1} = \frac{v_1}{v_2} = \frac{v_4}{v_3}$$

The total net work is therefore

$$W_{\text{net}} = R(T_3 - T_1) \ln \frac{p_3}{p_4} = \frac{1545}{29} \times \frac{1500}{778} \ln 6 = 184 \text{ Btu}$$

The efficiency is $184/424 = 43.4$ per cent.

2-10. Vapor Cycles

Rankine Cycle. The Rankine cycle is the ideal representation for the **vapor power cycle.** It consists of five processes, two isothermals, two isentropics,

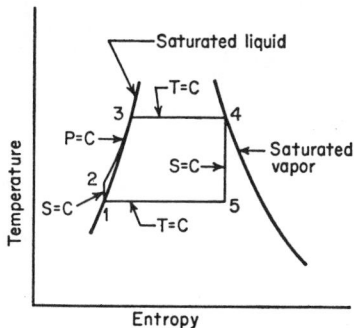

Fig. 2-9. Rankine cycle.

and one constant pressure. The cycle is shown in Fig. 2-9, and the corresponding apparatus diagram in Fig. 2-10.

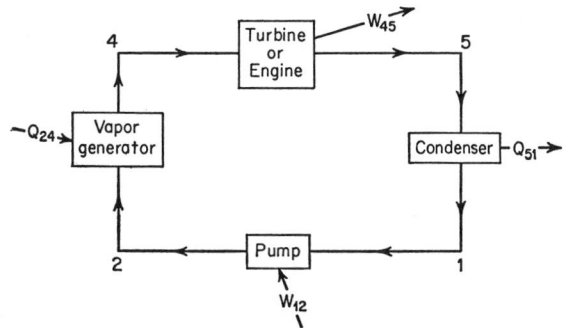

Fig. 2-10. Vapor power system.

The results of a cycle analysis show

$$Q_{24} = H_4 - H_2$$
$$Q_{51} = H_1 - H_5$$
$$W_{45} = H_5 - H_4$$
$$W_{12} = H_1 - H_2 = v'p_1 - p_2) \qquad \text{approx.}$$

$$\text{eff} = \frac{(H_5 - H_4) + W_{12}}{H_4 - H_2} \tag{2-52}$$

In most cases W_{12} is small, so that

$$\text{eff} = \frac{H_5 - H_4}{H_4 - H_2} \tag{2-53}$$

Compression Refrigeration Cycle. The idealized compression refrigeration cycle consists of two constant-pressure processes, an isentropic process, and an irreversible throttling process. The cycle is shown in Fig. 2-11, and the corresponding apparatus in Fig. 2-12.

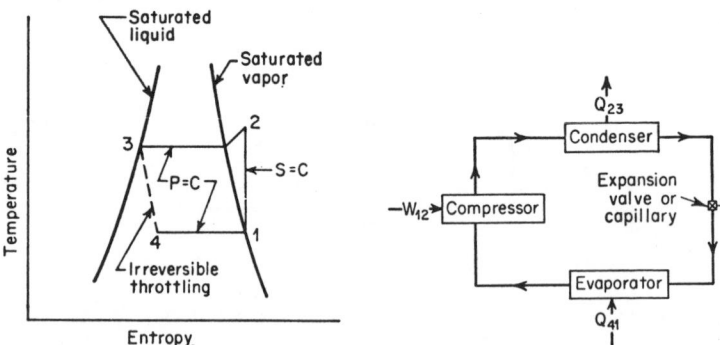

FIG. 2-11. Compression refrigeration cycle.

FIG. 2-12. Compression refrigeration system.

The equations for the cycle are

$$Q_{12} = Q_{34} = 0$$
$$Q_{23} = H_3 - H_2$$
$$Q_{14} = H_4 - H_1$$
$$W_{23} = W_{41} = W_{34} = 0$$
$$H_3 = H_4$$

The coefficient of performance is

$$\text{C.O.P.} = \frac{Q_{41}}{W_{12}} = \frac{H_1 - H_4}{H_2 - H_1} \tag{2-54}$$

FLUID FLOW

2-11. Nomenclature

A = flow-path area normal to flow, ft^2

A_f = wall-effect factor, dimensionless (see Table 2-9)

a = area of jet, ft^2

$\bar{a}$ = transverse tube pitch, ft

b = longitudinal tube pitch, ft

C = pitot-tube coefficient, dimensionless

C_c = jet area/orifice area, dimensionless

C_D = drag coefficient, dimensionless

C_d = coefficient of discharge for orifices

CR = critical-pressure ratio, dimensionless

c_p = specific heat at constant pressure, Btu/(lb)(°F)

c_v = specific heat at constant volume, Btu/(lb)(°F)

D = diameter of pipe, ft (except in Fig. 2-26, in.)

D_c = tube clearance, ft

D_e = hydraulic diameter, ft

D_p = particle diameter, ft

D_t = tube diameter, ft

F = conversion factor, feet of fluid to inches of water = $\frac{1}{12} \times \bar{w}_W/\bar{w}_{HG}$

$\bar{F}$ = force or resistance to force, lb force

f = friction factor, dimensionless

f_c = friction factor for tower packings (Fig. 2-29)

G = quantity of flow, lb/sec

g = gravitational acceleration, ft/sec^2 (32.2 at sea level)

g_c = conversion factor, 32.2 (lb mass)(ft)/(lb force)(sec^2)

H = static head, ft fluid; height above sea level, ft; stack height, ft; with weirs, height above crest, ft

H_m = head in manometric fluid, ft

ΔH = orifice differential, ft fluid flowing

ΔH_f = head loss due to friction, ft

h = enthalpy, Btu/lb

$\bar{h}$ = weir approach velocity head, ft

h'_w = effective draft, in. H$_2$O

K = equivalent number velocity heads (Table 2-7); or elevation, ft

k = ratio of specific heats, c_p/c_v

L = length or linear dimension (with weirs, width), ft

$\bar{L} = N^b$

m = hydraulic radius, ft

N = number of rows of tubes in direction of flow

N_{Re} = Reynolds number (= $Dv\bar{w}/\mu$), dimensionless

p = static pressure, psf

p_i = impact pressure, psf

Δp_f = pressure drop due to friction, psf

Q = quantity of flow, cfs

R = manometer reading, ft

S = cross-sectional area, ft^2

$\overline{S}$ = specific surface, ft^2 particle surface/ft^3 bed

T = absolute temperature, °R

t = time, sec

v = fluid velocity, fps

v_c = acoustical velocity in fluid, fps

v_0 = superficial velocity in packed bed or local velocity as measured by pitot tube, fps

v_{max} = velocity through minimum area of flow, fps

$\overline{v}$ = specific volume $(= 1/\overline{w})$, ft^3/lb

W_a = weight in air, lb

W_f = weight in nonair fluid, lb

$\overline{W}_m$ = density of manometric fluid, lb/ft^3

$\overline{W}_0$ = density of working fluid, lb/ft^3 (also $\overline{W}_A$, $\overline{W}_B$)

$\overline{w}$ = density $(= 1/\overline{v})$, lb/ft^3

$\overline{w}_{CA}$ = density of column of cold air outside stack, lb/ft^3

$\overline{w}_{HG}$ = density of column of hot gas inside stack, lb/ft^3

$\overline{w}_W$ = density of water, 62.4 lb/ft^3

Z = elevational head, ft

ϕ = a mathematical function of — ; in Eq. (2-121) and Fig. 2-29, ϕ = particle-shape factor

μ = viscosity of fluid, lb/(ft)(sec)

ϵ = fraction voids, dimensionless, or in Fig. 2-25, roughness factor

2-12. Hydrostatics

Absolute pressure equals gauge pressure plus atmospheric pressure.

Pascal's principle. An increase in the pressure at any point in a fluid is attended by an equal pressure at every other point in the fluid.

Static pressure at the base of a vertical column of a fluid of uniform density exceeds that at the top by $H\overline{w}g/g_c$ lb force/ft^2. Thus, the pressure equivalent to a head of 18 in. Hg, sp gr 13.6, assuming $g/g_c = 1$, is[1]

$$(18 \times 13.6 \times 62.3)/(12 \times 144) = 8.83 \text{ psi}$$

The absolute pressure and density of the atmosphere at a height H ft above sea level is calculated by the formulas

$$p = p_1(1 - 0.00000687H)^{5.256} \qquad (2\text{-}55)$$
$$\overline{w} = \overline{w}_1(1 - 0.00000687H)^{4.256} \qquad (2\text{-}56)$$

where the subscript 1 refers to sea-level conditions.

Buoyancy. *Archimedes' Principle.* The resultant pressure of a fluid on a body immersed in it acts vertically upward through the center of gravity of the displaced fluid and is equal to the weight of the fluid displaced. The upward force is called the *buoyancy.*

---

[1] For nomenclature see p. 2-25.

Specific gravity and volume of solids by immersion

$$\text{Specific gravity} = W_a/(W_a - W_f) \qquad (2\text{-}57)$$

Pressure Gauges. *U Tube.* (Fig. 2-13). When the interface between the mercury and the fluid for which the pressure is wanted is K ft below the point of attachment A and gives a reading of H_m ft

$$p_A = (H_m\overline{W}_m - K\overline{W}_A) \qquad (2\text{-}58)$$
At A $\qquad\qquad H_A = H_m\overline{W}_m/\overline{W}_A - K \qquad (2\text{-}59)$

where $\overline{W}_A$ = weight density of fluid at A, lb/ft³

$\overline{W}_m$ = density manometric fluid, lb/ft³

p_A = gauge pressure at A, psf

The Differential U Tube.[1] Figure 2-14 shows the difference between the taps A and B to be

$$p_A - p_B = H_m(\overline{W}_m - \overline{W}_A) + K_A\overline{W}_A - K_B\overline{W}_B \qquad (2\text{-}60)$$

where K_A, K_B = vertical distances of upper mercury surface above A and B, ft

$\overline{W}_A$, $\overline{W}_B$ = weight densities of fluid at A and B, lb/ft³

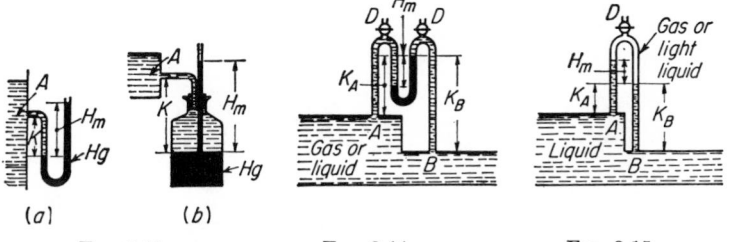

FIG. 2-13   FIG. 2-14   FIG. 2-15

If the differential is that caused by an orifice or other device measuring the flow of a liquid, the orifice differential

$$\Delta H = (p_1v_1 - p_2v_2) + (Z_1 - Z_2) = H_m(\overline{W}_m/\overline{W}_A - 1) \qquad (2\text{-}61)$$

For gases, except at very high pressures, $\overline{W}_A$ and $\overline{W}_B$ are so small compared with $\overline{W}_m$ that Eq. (8-135) reduces to

$$p_A - p_B = H_m\overline{W}_m \qquad (2\text{-}62)$$

The Inverted Differential U Tube (Fig. 2-15)

$$p_A - p_B = H_m(\overline{W}_A - \overline{W}_m) + K_A\overline{W}_A - K_B\overline{W}_B \qquad (2\text{-}63)$$

If the gauge is indicating the orifice differential of a head meter operating with a liquid,

$$\Delta H = H_m(1 - \overline{W}_m/\overline{W}_A) \qquad (2\text{-}64)$$

[1] For nomenclature see p. 2–25.

Closed U Tubes.   These measure directly the absolute pressure p of a fluid (Fig. 2-16).

$$p = H_m \overline{W}_m \qquad (2\text{-}65)$$

where $\overline{W}_m$ = lb mass/ft³ = weight density of manometric fluid
$\quad\quad H_m$ = ft manometric fluid

For liquids and gases under very high pressures, the quantity $K\overline{W}_0$ should be subtracted from Eq. (2-65).

Multiplying Gauges[1]

Inclined U Tube (Fig. 2-18).   If the reading is R (feet), the formula $H_m = (R - R_0) \sin\theta$ is substituted in Eq. (2-60). R_0 = the zero reading.

The Draft Gauge.   Formulas are applied as with an inclined U tube, above (Fig. 2-17).

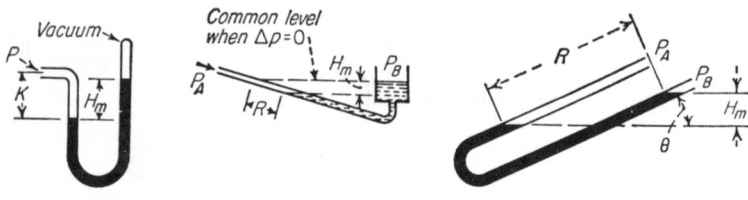

Fɪɢ. 2-16   Fɪɢ. 2-17   Fɪɢ. 2-18

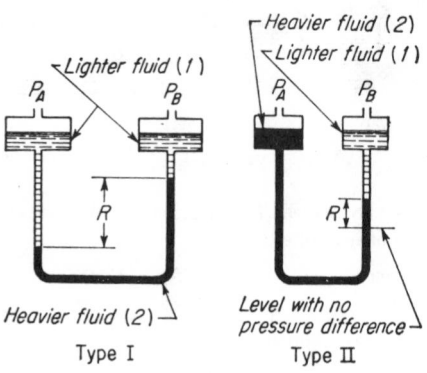

Fɪɢ. 2-19

Two-fluid U Tubes (Fig. 2-19)
For Type I:

$$p_A - p_B = R - R_0[\overline{W}_2 - \overline{W}_1 + (a/A)\overline{W}_1] \qquad (2\text{-}66)$$

For Type II:

$$p_A - p_B = R[\overline{W}_2 - \overline{W}_1 + (a/A)(\overline{W}_2 + \overline{W}_1)] \qquad (2\text{-}67)$$

[1] For nomenclature see p. 2-25.

where A = cross-sectional area of each reservoir, ft^2

a = cross-sectional area of the tube forming the U, ft^2

2-13. Flow Measurement

Nozzle and Orifice Flow.[1] *Free Spouting Jet Velocities. Expansive Fluid, General.* The ideal velocity is derived from

$$v_2{}^2/2g_c - v_1{}^2/2g_c = (h_1 - h_2)778 \qquad (2\text{-}68)$$

If velocity of approach (v_1) is zero or negligibly small, then

$$v_2{}^2/2g_c = (h_1 - h_2)778 \qquad (2\text{-}69)$$

or jet velocity

$$v = 223.7 \sqrt{h_1 - h_2} \qquad (2\text{-}70)$$

For ideal flow without friction and losses the difference in enthalpy is found by use of a Mollier chart with isentropic expansion between initial and final conditions. (This is equal to the Rankine cycle work.) If the path of the expansion is other than isentropic, Eq. (2-70) is equally applicable when the appropriate values of h_1 and h_2 are used.

Expansive Fluids, Fixed and Perfect Gases. If the gas laws of Boyle and Charles can be applied with sufficient accuracy, then the ideal velocity Eq. (2-68) becomes

$$v = 8.02 \sqrt{[k/(k - 1)]p_1\bar{v}_1[1 - (p_2/p_1)^{(k-1)/k}]} \qquad (2\text{-}71)$$

Nonexpansive Fluids. For a nonexpansive fluid like water,

$$v_2{}^2/2g_c - v_1{}^2/2g_c = (p_1 - p_2)\bar{v} \qquad (2\text{-}72)$$

If velocity of approach v_1 is zero or negligibly small, then Eq. (2-72) becomes

$$v_2{}^2/2g_c = (p_1 - p_2)\bar{v} \qquad (2\text{-}73)$$

and the jet velocity,
$$v = 8.02 \sqrt{(p_1 - p_2)\bar{v}}$$
$$= 8.02 \sqrt{\Delta H} \qquad (2\text{-}74)$$

ΔH is the static head on the orifice measured in feet of fluid flowing. If manometric fluid is different from the fluid moving through the orifice, then

$$H = H_m x \overline{W}_m / \overline{W}_0 \qquad (2\text{-}75)$$

Equations (2-72) to (2-75) are applicable to cases of expansive fluids where the density change between initial and final conditions is negligibly small (less than 2 per cent for many engineering calculations).

Continuity Equation

$$Q = Av \qquad (2\text{-}76)$$

or
$$G = Av\bar{w} \qquad (2\text{-}77)$$

Quantity Flow through Orifices and Nozzles, Ideal Conditions. There are no limitations on the applicability of flow equations to nonexpansive fluids, but with expansive fluids a limitation on quantity is imposed by the sonic

---

[1] For nomenclature see p. 2–25.

or acoustic barrier. Thus, if the velocity from Eq. (2-70) or (2-71) is used in the continuity equation (2-76) or (2-77), for an expansive fluid, this critically limits the flow, so that the critical ratio CR between initial and final pressures is defined by

$$CR = p_2/p_1 = [2/(k+1)]^{(k/k-1)} \qquad (2-78)$$

For critical ratios of some common fluids see Table 2-4. This critical ratio is used in Eqs. (2-70) and (2-71) to determine the sonic velocity. If the over-all expansion ratio is such that the final pressure is lower than that given by Eq. (2-78), then p_2 in Eq. (2-71) is made equal to the critical value from Eq. (2-78), and the result is used in the continuity equation (2-76) or

Table 2-4

Fluid	CR
Air ($k = 1.4$)........	0.53
Wet steam..........	.58
Superheated steam...	.55

(2-77), together with the throat area, to determine the volume or weight flow. For a streamlined nozzle with expansion beyond the critical, the weight flow is determined by these values for sonic conditions and constitutes the maximum obtainable. Final pressures, less than the critical, cannot increase the weight flow. The consequences of using these phenomena are the following several equations for flow:

When expansion is beyond the critical ($CR \approx 0.5$) through a 1-in.² orifice,

Saturated steam:

$$G = p_1/70 \qquad\qquad\qquad \text{Napier} \qquad (2-79)$$
$$G = p_1^{0.97}/60 \qquad\qquad\qquad \text{Grashof} \qquad (2-80)$$
$$G = p_1(16.3 - 0.96 \log p_1)/1{,}000 \qquad \text{Rateau} \qquad (2-81)$$

Superheated steam:

$$G = p_1^{0.97}/60(1 + 0.00065 \times \text{deg superheat}) \qquad (2-82)$$

Wet steam:

$$G = p_1^{0.97}/60 \sqrt{\text{dryness fraction}} \qquad (2-83)$$

Air:

$$G = p_1/1.9 \sqrt{T_1} \qquad \text{Fliegner} \qquad (2-84)$$

Orifice and Nozzle Coefficients

A nozzle or orifice coefficient, C_d, must be used as a multiplier in Eqs. (2-70), (2-71), and (2-74) for real-flow situations. For bellmouth or well-rounded nozzles, C_d is essentially unity. For square or sharp-edged orifices, C_d is given by Fig. 2-20 as a function of the location of the pipe taps and the ratio of orifice to pipe diameter β. The continuity equations (2-76) and (2-77) give actual volume or weight flow.

Pitot Tube. If one side of an ordinary differential manometer is connected to the lead from the impact opening and the other leg to the lead from

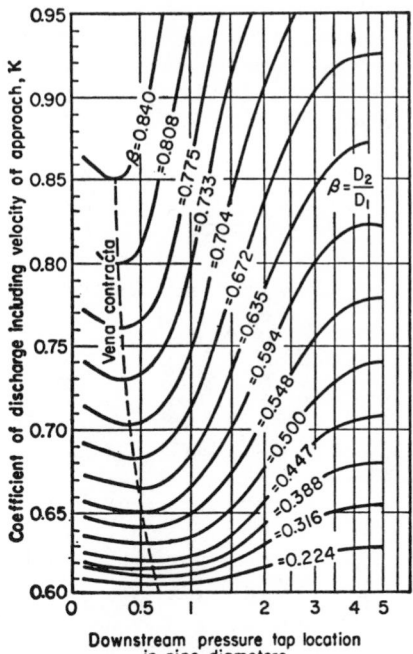

FIG. 2-20. Coefficient of discharge for square-edged circular orifices for $N_{Re} >$ 30,000, with the upstream tap located between one and two pipe diameters from the orifice plate.

the static taps, the manometer will automatically record the velocity pressure $(p_i - p)$ (Figs. 2-21 and 2-22). The local velocity is computed as follows:[1]

1. For liquids or for gases (up to 200 fps)

$$v_0 = C \sqrt{2g_c(p_i - p)/\overline{W}_0} \tag{2-85}$$

2. For gases (200 fps to sonic velocity)

$$v_0 = C \sqrt{\frac{2g_c k}{k - 1} \frac{p}{\overline{W}_0} \left[\left(\frac{p_i}{p} \right)^{\frac{k-1}{k}} - 1 \right]} \tag{2-86}$$

where C is a coefficient, dimensionless, which ranges from 0.98 to 1.00 for a well-made pitot tube.

The pitot tube measures only the local velocity, which means that a traverse has to be made if the flow rate or average velocity in a duct is to be determined by this means. For circular pipe, the most common traverse is the

[1] For nomenclature see p. 2-25.

10-point. Readings are taken at the following distances from the wall: 0.026D, 0.082D, 0.146D, 0.226D, 0.342D, 0.658D, 0.774D, 0.854D, 0.918D, and 0.974D, where D = pipe diameter. An average of the velocities at these points will give a mean velocity which is theoretically only 0.3 per cent high for a normal velocity distribution.

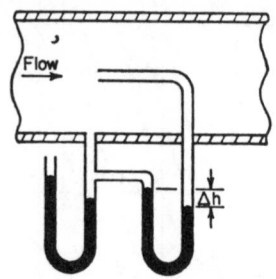

Fig. 2-21. Pitot tube with sidewall static tap.

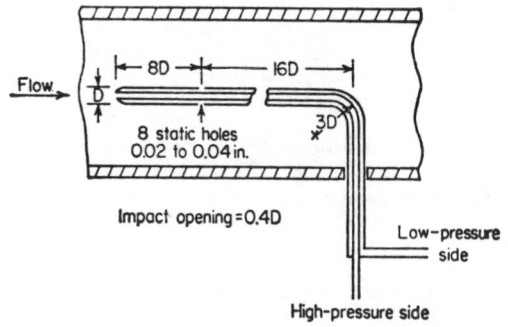

Fig. 2-22. Pitot-static tube.

Weirs. *Rectangular Weirs.* The Francis formula for discharge through rectangular weirs takes the following forms:[1]

1. For a suppressed weir, i.e., a weir so designed by rounding the edges that no contraction of the discharging sheet of liquid occurs,

$$Q = 3.33LH^{3/2} \qquad (2\text{-}87)$$

2. For a suppressed weir considering velocity of approach

$$Q = 3.33L[(H + \bar{h})^{3/2} - \bar{h}^{3/2}] \qquad (2\text{-}88)$$

3. For a contracted, i.e., sharp-edged, weir [see (1)],

$$Q = 3.33(L - 0.2H)H^{3/2} \qquad (2\text{-}89)$$

[1] For nomenclature see p. 2-25.

4. For a contracted weir considering velocity of approach

$$Q = 3.33(L - 0.2H)[(H + \bar{h})^{3/2} - \bar{h}^{3/2}] \qquad (2\text{-}90)$$

The Francis formula agrees with experiment within 3 per cent or less, if (1) L is greater than $2H$, (2) height of crest above bottom of channel is at least $3H$, and (3) H is not less than 0.3 ft. Narrow rectangular notches ($H > L$) have been found to give about 93 per cent of the discharge given by the Francis formula. Thus

$$q = 3.10LH^{3/2} \qquad (2\text{-}91)$$

Triangular or Notch Weirs

For square-edged notches: $q = 2.48H^{5/2}/\tan \alpha$ $\qquad$ (2-92)
For $\theta = 90°$, $\alpha = 45°$: $q = 2.48H^{5/2}$ $\qquad$ (2-93)
For $\theta = 60°$, $\alpha = 60°$: $q = 1.43H^{5/2}$ $\qquad$ (2-94)

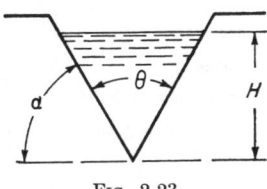

Fig. 2-23

Flow Resistance. The theoretical force of a jet is[1]

$$\bar{F} = (\bar{w}/g_c)av^2 \qquad (2\text{-}95)$$

The actual force, resistance, or drag, in pounds is

$$\bar{F} = C_D av^2 \bar{w}/g_c$$

$$= \bar{W}\frac{av^2}{g_c}\,\phi_1\left(\frac{Dv\bar{w}}{\mu}\right)\phi_2\,\frac{v}{\sqrt{Dg}}\,\phi_3\,\frac{v}{v_c} \qquad (2\text{-}96)$$

where $Dv\bar{w}/\mu$ = Reynolds number $\qquad$ (2-97)
$v/\sqrt{Dg}$ = Froude number $\qquad$ (2-98)
v/v_c = Mach number $\qquad$ (2-99)

Drag coefficient is a function of each of the flow criteria given in Eqs. (2-97), (2-98), and (2-99). These criteria are usually dimensionless for maximum convenience and utility. The Reynolds number is significant in cases of full immersion or completely enclosed flow, as with aircraft wings, pipes, nozzles, pumps, fans. The Froude number is significant in cases of simultaneous motion through two fluids where there are a surface of discontinuity, gravity forces, and wave-making effects, as with ship's hulls. The Mach number is significant in supersonics, as with projectiles and jet propulsion.

Rotameters. The rotameter, an example of which is shown in Fig. 2-24, has become one of the most popular flowmeters in industry. It consists

---

[1] For nomenclature see p. 2-25.

essentially of a plummet, or "float," which is free to move up or down in a vertical, slightly tapered tube having its small end down. The fluid enters the lower end of the tube and causes the float to rise until the annular area between the float and the wall of the tube is such that the pressure drop across this constriction is just sufficient to support the float. Typically, the tapered tube is of glass and carries etched upon it a nearly linear scale on which the position of the float may be visually noted as an indication of the flow.

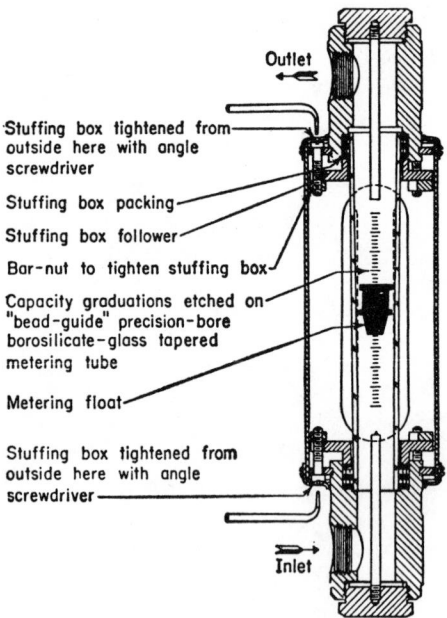

Outlet

Stuffing box tightened from outside here with angle screwdriver

Stuffing box packing

Stuffing box follower

Bar-nut to tighten stuffing box

Capacity graduations etched on "bead-guide" precision-bore borosilicate-glass tapered metering tube

Metering float

Stuffing box tightened from outside here with angle screwdriver

Inlet

Fig. 2-24. Rotameter.

Interchangeable precision-bore glass tubes and metal metering tubes are available. Rotameters have proved satisfactory both for gases and for liquids at high and at low pressures. A single instrument can readily cover a tenfold range of flow, and by providing "floats" of different densities, a 200-fold range is practicable.

Rotameters require no straight runs of pipe before or after the point of installation. Pressure losses are substantially constant over the whole flow range. However, most modern rotameters are precision-made, so that their performance closely corresponds to a master calibration plot for the type in question. Such a plot is supplied with the meter upon purchase.

Flow rate through a rotameter can be obtained from

$$G = Q\overline{W}_0 = KD_f \sqrt{\frac{W_f(\rho_f - \rho)\rho}{\rho_f}} \qquad (2\text{-}100)$$

where K = flow parameter, $ft^{\frac{1}{2}}/sec$
$\quad\quad D_f$ = float diameter at constriction, ft
$\quad\quad W_f$ = float weight, lb
$\quad\quad \rho_f$ = float density, lb/ft^3
and other terms are as defined on page 2-25. The appropriate value of K is obtained from a composite correlation of K versus the parameters corresponding to the float shape being used.

The ratio of flow rates for two different fluids A and B at the same rotameter reading is given by

$$\frac{w_A}{w_B} = \frac{K_A}{K_B} \sqrt{\frac{(\rho_f - \rho_A)\rho_A}{(\rho_f - \rho_B)\rho_B}} \qquad (2\text{-}101)$$

A measure of self-compensation, with respect to weight rate of flow, for fluid-density changes can be introduced through the use of a float with a density twice that of the fluid being metered, in which case an increase of 10 per cent in ρ will produce a decrease of only 0.5 per cent in w for the same reading. The extent of immunity to changes in fluid viscosity depends upon the shape of the float.

2-14. Fluid Dynamics

Bernoulli's Equation.[1] Applied to flow of a noncompressible fluid, such as water, where $\bar{v}_1 = \bar{v}_2$, through a system, Bernoulli's equation is as follows:

$$\frac{Z_1 g}{g_c} + \frac{v_1^2}{2g_c} + p_1\bar{v}_1 = \frac{Z_2 g}{g_c} + \frac{v_2^2}{2g_c} + \Delta H_f + p_2\bar{v}_2 \qquad (2\text{-}102)$$

For compressible fluids the quantity $(p_2 - p_1)\bar{v}$ must be evaluated as an integral, $\int_1^2 \bar{v}\, dp$, which is dependent on the nature of the path followed as the fluid flows through the system. For isothermal flow

$$\int_1^2 \bar{v}\, dp = -\frac{RT}{M} \ln \frac{\bar{v}_2}{\bar{v}_1} = -\frac{RT}{M} \ln \frac{p_1}{p_2} \qquad (2\text{-}103)$$

Flow of Fluids in Pipes. Pressure drop due to friction ΔH_f in circular pipes of diameter D and length L is given by

$$\Delta H_f = fLv^2/2g_c D \qquad (2\text{-}104)$$

Values of f may be obtained from Fig. 2-25. The value of ϵ to be used in calculating the relative roughness is obtained from Table 2-5.

[1] For nomenclature see page 2-25.

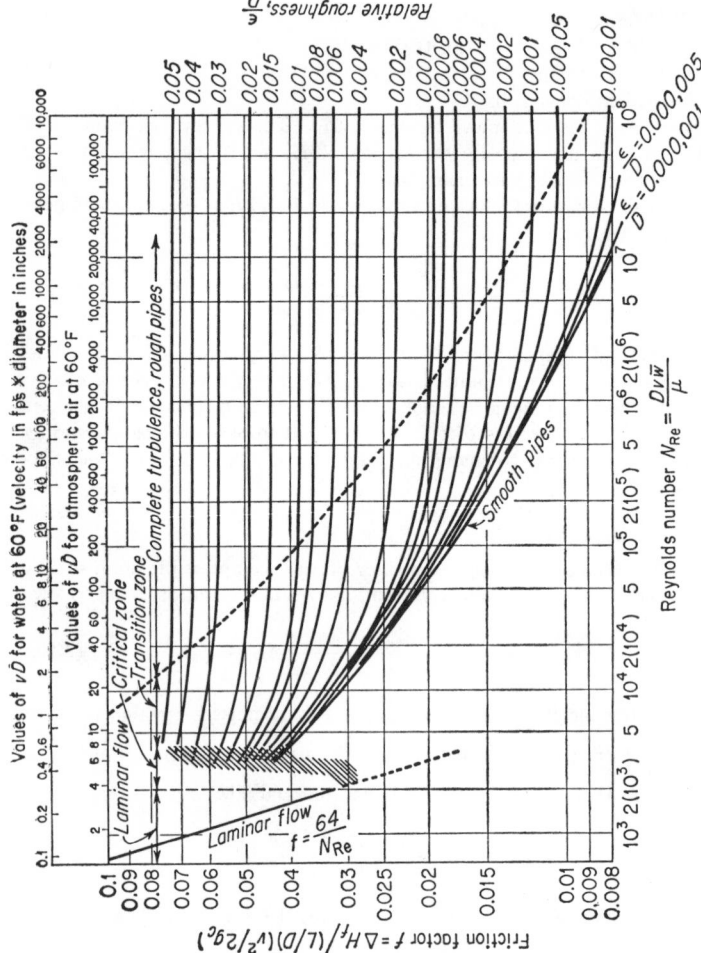

FIG. 2-25. *Source: L. S. Marks, (ed.), "Mechanical Engineers' Handbook," 5th ed., p. 250, McGraw-Hill Book Company, Inc., New York, 1951.*

Table 2-5. Absolute Roughness Classification of Pipe Surfaces for Selection of Friction Factor f in Fig. 2-25

Commercial pipe surf. (new)	Abs roughness ϵ, ft	Commercial pipe surf. (new)	Abs roughness ϵ, ft
Glass, drawn brass, copper, lead...	Smooth	Cast iron.................	0.00085
Wrought iron, steel..............	0.00015	Wood stave...............	0.0006–0.003
Asphalted cast iron..............	.0004	Concrete.................	0.001–0.01
Galvanized iron................	.0005	Riveted steel...............	0.003–0.03

SOURCE: L. S. Marks (ed.), "Mechanical Engineers' Handbook," 5th ed., p. 249, McGraw-Hill Book Company, Inc., New York, 1951.

A convenient nomograph, Fig. 2-26, may be used to solve pipe flow-friction-loss problems. Table 2-6 is used to obtain the necessary coordinates for use of this nomograph.

Table 2-6. Coordinates for Liquids and Aqueous Solutions

	X	Y		X	Y
Acetaldehyde.................	−0.3	3.7	Formic acid.................	1.5	4.5
Acetic acid, 100%...............	1.0	4.0	Glycerol, 100%...............	6.9	1.8
Acetic acid, 77%...............	2.6	3.8	Glycerol, 50%...............	3.0	3.7
Acetic anhydride..............	0.7	4.3	Hydrochloric acid, 31.5%.......	1.1	4.2
Acetone, 100%................	0.9	3.4	Linseed oil, raw..............	3.4	1.8
Acetone, 35%.................	2.7	3.7	Mercury...................	See chart	
Ammonia, anhydrous...........	0.9	3.6	Methanol, 100%..............	0.8	3.3
Ammonia, 26%................	1.9	3.6	Methanol, 40%...............	2.8	3.6
Aniline......................	2.5	3.4	Methyl acetate...............	0.0	4.2
Benzene.....................	0.6	3.6	Methyl chloride..............	−0.8	4.3
Butanol.....................	2.6	2.6	Nitric acid, 95%..............	0.8	5.8
Calcium chloride brine, 25%......	2.6	4.2	Nitric acid, 60%..............	1.5	4.8
Carbon disulfide..............	0.0	5.6	Nitrobenzene................	1.7	4.4
Carbon tetrachloride...........	0.7	6.0	Octane....................	0.4	2.7
Chloroform..................	0.0	6.0	Phenol....................	2.4	3.4
Chlorosulfonic acid............	1.5	5.8	Propionic acid...............	0.6	3.8
Cyclohexanol.................	5.3	2.2	Sodium chloride brine, 25%.....	2.1	4.4
Diphenyl....................	0.0	3.5	Sodium hydroxide, 50%........	5.3	3.7
Ethyl acetate.................	0.2	3.9	Sulfur dioxide...............	−0.2	6.1
Ethyl alcohol, 95%.............	1.9	3.0	Sulfuric acid, 110%...........	3.7	4.7
Ethyl alcohol, 45%.............	3.6	3.4	Sulfuric acid, 98%............	3.5	4.8
Ethyl chloride................	0.2	4.3	Sulfuric acid, 78%............	3.2	4.8
Ethyl ether..................	−0.3	3.2	Tetrachloroethylene...........	0.3	6.2
Ethylene glycol...............	3.5	2.9	Toluene....................	0.4	3.6
Fluorocarbon F-11.............	0.0	6.2	Trichloroethylene.............	0.1	5.9
Fluorocarbon F-12.............	−1.2	5.9	Turpentine..................	1.1	3.1
Fluorocarbon F-21.............	−0.4	5.9	Vinyl acetate................	0.4	4.2
Fluorocarbon F-22.............	−1.7	5.5	Water.....................	2.0	4.2
Fluorocarbon F-113............	0.9	6.2			

The economic pipe diameter for Schedule 40 steel pipe may be found using Fig. 2-27. For pressure drop with noncircular pipe or duct use Eq. (2-104), incorporating the mean hydraulic radius m defined as

$$m = \frac{\text{cross-sectional area of pipe, ft}^2}{\text{wetted perimeter of pipe, ft}} \qquad (2\text{-}105)$$

in place of diameter D.

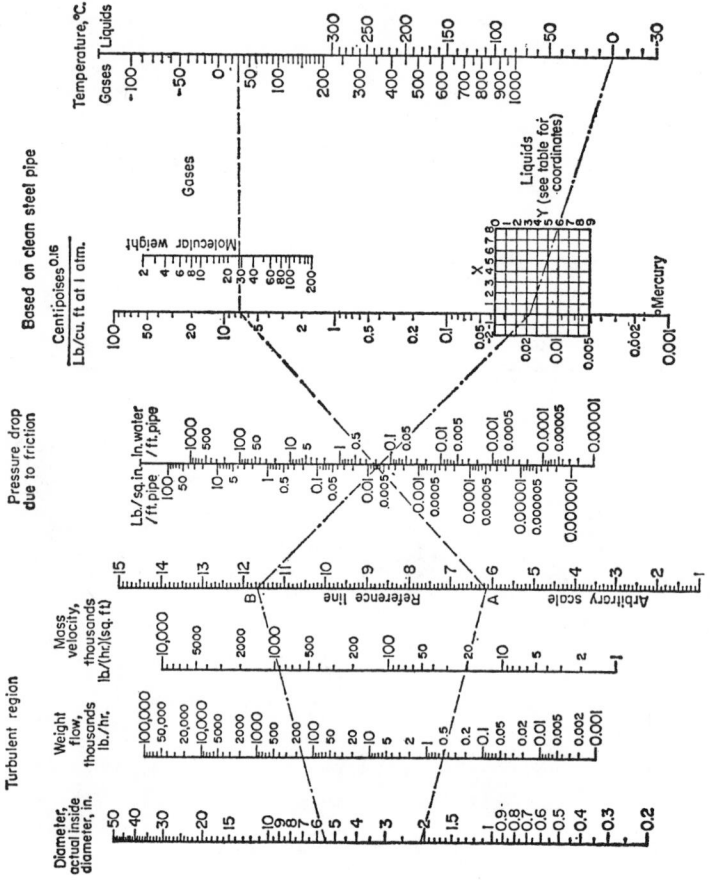

Fig. 2-26. Pipe-flow chart. See Table 2-6 for coordinates. [*Genereaux, Chem. & Met. Eng.,* **44**, 241 (1937).]

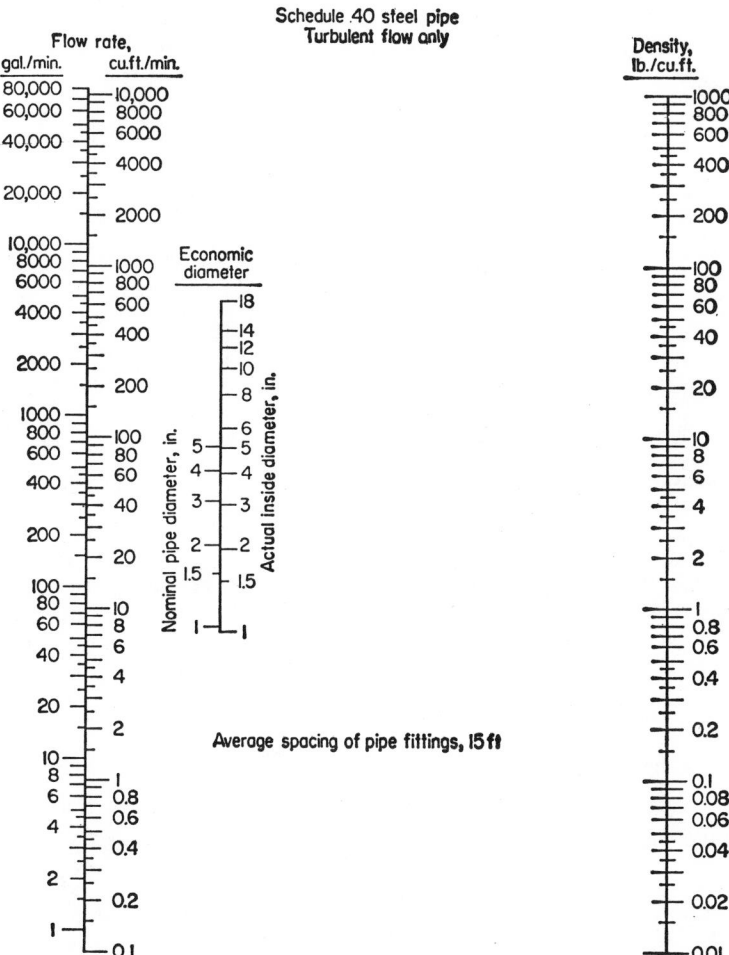

FIG. 2-27. Economic pipe diameter. Connect values of flow rate and density to obtain economic diameter. (*Courtesy of E. I. du Pont de Nemours & Co.*)

For circular pipes
$$m = D/4 \qquad\qquad (2\text{-}106)$$

whence, substituting in Eq. (2-104)

$$\Delta H_f = fLv^2/8mg_c \qquad\qquad (2\text{-}107)$$

Friction Loss through Fittings. The friction loss due to screwed fittings and valves is given in Table 2-7 in terms of equivalent length in number of

Table 2-7. Friction Loss of Screwed Fittings, Valves, Etc.

Fitting	Equiv length in pipe diam, L	No. "velocity heads," K
45° elbows	15	0.3
90° elbows, standard radius	32	0.74
90° elbows, medium radius	26	0.60
90° elbows, long sweep	20	0.46
90° square elbow	60	1.3
180° close return bends	75	1.7
180° medium-radius return bends	50	1.2
Tee (used as elbow, entering run)	60	1.3
Tee (used as elbow, entering branch)	90	1.9
Couplings	Negligible	
Unions	Negligible	
Gate valves, open	7	0.13
Globe valves, open	300	6.0
Angle valves, open	170	3.0
Water meters, disk	400	8.0
Water meters, piston	600	12.0
Water meters, impulse wheel	300	6.0

pipe diameters and in terms of number of velocity heads.   These values are used in conjunction with Eq. (2-104) or Eq. (2-108).

$$\Delta H_f = Kv^2/2g_c \tag{2-108}$$

Miscellaneous Pressure Losses. *Expansion Loss.* For the sudden expansion from an area S_1 to an area S_2 with an average linear velocity from v_1 to v_2, the frictional loss of mechanical energy is[1]

$$\Delta H_f = (v_1 - v_2)^2/2g_c = (v_1^2/2g_c)(1 - S_1/S_2)^2 \tag{2-109}$$

This formula is exact for liquids in turbulent motion and is generally used for gases at moderate velocities.   For viscous flow in the smaller pipe this formula result should be doubled.   For discharge into a large tank,

$$\Delta H_f = v_1^2/2g_c \tag{2-110}$$

For a uniformly divergent duct, for an angle of divergence of $\alpha = 7.5$ to $35°$,

$$\Delta H_f = 3.50[\tan(\alpha/2)]^{1.22}[(v_1 - v_2)^2/2g_c] \tag{2-111}$$

Contraction Loss. For turbulent flow in the smaller pipe, at a sharp-edged entrance to a pipeline, there is a sudden cross-sectional reduction

$$\Delta H_f = K'v_2^2/2g_c$$

where v_2 = linear velocity in smaller pipe, fps

$$K' = 0.4(1.25 - S_2/S_1) \qquad \text{for } S_2/S_1 < 0.715$$
$$= 0.75(1 - S_2/S_1) \qquad \text{for } S_2/S_1 > 0.715$$

Flow of Water in Closed Conduits. For determining the head loss due to friction for the flow of *water under pressure in conduits*, the Hazen-Williams formula may be used

[1] For nomenclature see p. 2–25.

$$v = 1.318CR^{0.63}S^{0.54} \qquad (2\text{-}112)$$
$$h_f = Sl \qquad (2\text{-}113)$$

where h_f = head loss due to friction, ft–lb force/lb mass
S = hydraulic gradient, ft head loss/ft length
l = length of conduit, ft
v = average velocity of flow, fps
R = hydraulic radius (equal to cross-sectional area of conduit divided by perimeter), ft
C = Hazen-Williams coefficient

Values of C commonly used for design purposes for various types of conduit material are given in Table 2-8.

Table 2-8. Values of C in Hazen-Williams Formula

Type of pipe	C^*	Type of pipe	C^*
Cement-asbestos..............	140	Cast iron or wrought iron.....	100
Asphalt-lined iron or steel......	140	Welded or seamless steel......	100
Copper or brass...............	130	Concrete....................	100
Lead, tin, or glass............	130	Corrugated steel.............	60
Wood stave..................	110		

* Values of C commonly used for design. The value of C for pipes made of corrosive materials decreases as the age of the pipe increases; the values given are those that apply at an age of 15 to 20 years. For example, the value of C for cast-iron pipes 30 in. in diameter or greater at various ages is approximately as follows: new, 130; 5 years old, 120; 10 years old, 115; 20 years old, 100; 30 years old, 90; 40 years old, 80; and 50 years old, 75. The value of C for smaller-size pipes decreases at a more rapid rate.

For circular conduits, the Hazen-Williams formula may be written as

$$Q = 0.4322CD^{2.63}S^{0.54} \qquad (2\text{-}114)$$

where Q = quantity of flow, cfs
D = diameter of circular conduit, ft

Figure 2-28 is a nomograph for the solution of Eq. (2-112).

Flow through Beds of Solids. *Granular Solids.* For the flow of a single fluid through a bed of uniform solid granular particles, the pressure drop is given by[1]

$$\Delta p_f = fL\,\bar{w}v_0^2 A_f / 2g_c D_p \qquad (2\text{-}115)$$
and
$$N_{Re} = D_p v_0 \bar{w}/\mu \qquad (2\text{-}116)$$
where
$$f = 3{,}400/N_{Re} \qquad \text{for } N_{Re} < 40 \text{ (viscous)} \qquad (2\text{-}117)$$
$$f = 152/N_{Re}{}^{0.15} \qquad \text{for } N_{Re} > 40 \text{ (turbulent)} \qquad (2\text{-}118)$$

For values of A_f see Table 2-9.

Tower Packings. For solid packings the equations given under granular solids can be used as an approximation if the void content falls between 35 to 45 per cent. If estimates can be made of the percentage of voids and

[1] For nomenclature see p. 2–25.

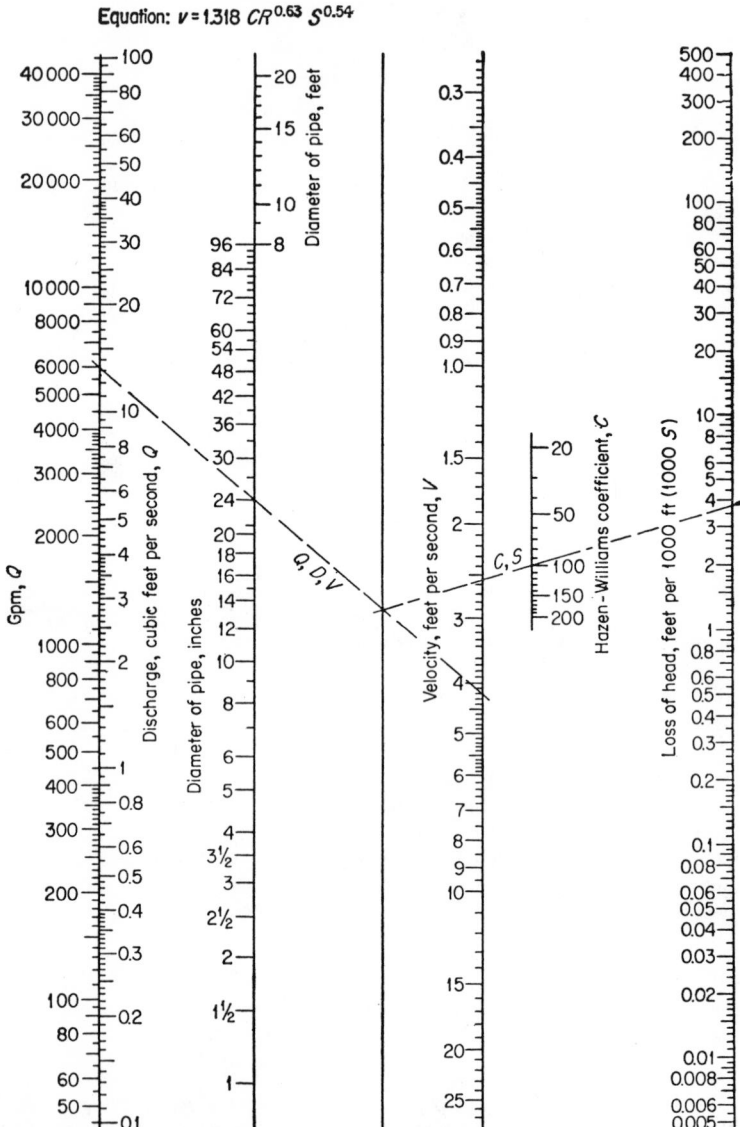

FIG. 2-28. Nomograph for solution of Hazen-Williams equation for circular conduits flowing full of water.

Table 2-9

D_p/D_t	A_f		D_p/D_t	A_f	
	Viscous	Turbulent		Viscous	Turbulent
0.0	1.0	1.0	0.15	0.77	0.65
.05	0.90	0.84	.25	.74	.57
.10	.83	.72			

specific surface, the following equations can be used for both solid and hollow packings.

$$\Delta p_f = f_c L \overline{S} w v_0{}^2 / g_c \qquad (2\text{-}119)$$

and

$$N_{\text{Re}} = \overline{w} v_0 / \mu \overline{S} \qquad (2\text{-}120)$$

The value of f_c may be obtained from Fig. 2-29.

$$\overline{S} = 6(1 - \epsilon)/\phi D_p \qquad (2\text{-}121)$$

where ϕ, the particle-shape factor, equals 1 for spheres and 0.3 for berl saddles.

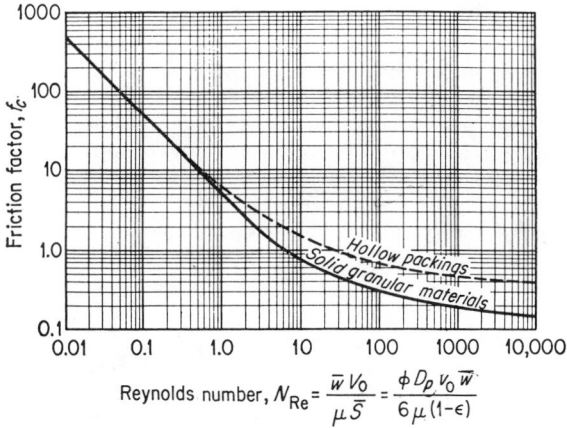

Fig. 2-29. Friction factors for flow through tower packings as a function of Reynolds number.

Flow across Tube Banks. *Viscous Flow.* The pressure drop across a bank of tubes under viscous-flow conditions[1] $(D_e v_{\max}\overline{w}/\mu < 150)$ is given by

$$\Delta p_f = 53\mu \overline{L} v_{\max}/g_c D_e{}^2 \qquad (2\text{-}122)$$

where

$$D_e = (4\bar{a}b - \pi D_t{}^2)/\pi D_t \qquad (2\text{-}123)$$

These equations apply primarily to banks of tubes in equilateral staggered

[1] For nomenclature see p. 2–25.

arrangement.   For staggered-square arrangement multiply the above pressure drop by 2; for an in-line square arrangement, by 1.5.

Turbulent Flow.   The pressure drop across a bank of tubes under turbulent-flow conditions $(D_c v_{max} \bar{w}/\mu > 40)$ can be estimated from[1]

$$\Delta p_f = f N \bar{w} v^2_{max}/2g_c \tag{2-124}$$

where
$$f = 3.0(D_c v_{max} \bar{w}/\mu)^{-0.2} \tag{2-125}$$

These equations apply primarily to banks of tubes in staggered equilateral arrangement.   They will give conservative answers for in-line arrangements.

Draft in Stacks and Chimneys.[2]   The theoretical draft caused by a stack of height H, in feet, is at the base of the vertical column[1]

$$h_w = (H/5.2)(\bar{w}_{CA} - \bar{w}_{HG}) \tag{2-126}$$

The actual, net, or effective draft which is available for overcoming the resistance of any connected load such as a furnace, boiler, still, or heater, is

$$h'_w = \frac{H}{5.2}(\bar{w}_{CA} - \bar{w}_{HG}) - \frac{1}{F}\frac{v^2}{2g_c} - \frac{\text{friction losses}}{F} \tag{2-127}$$

where F = conversion factor from feet of fluid to inches of water =

$$(1/12)(\bar{w}_w/\bar{w}_{HG}) \tag{2-128}$$

Friction losses are given in feet of fluid flowing and must include allowance for pressure drop in straight run of stack and flue, plus losses due to valves, fittings, and changes of section (Table 2-7).

Flow in Open Channels and Nonpressure Flow in Closed Conduits.   For determining the head loss due to friction in open channels and for the *nonpressure flow* of water in noncircular conduits or for partial flow in all types of conduits, Manning's formula is generally used.   For use *with circular conduits flowing full*, the formula may be written as

$$h_f = C_f(l/D)(v^2/2g_c) \tag{2-129}$$
$$C_f = 185n^2/D^{1/3} \tag{2-130}$$

where h_f = head loss due to friction, ft–lb force/lb mass

$\qquad D$ = diameter of circular conduit, ft (*Note:* Hydraulic radius R for a circular conduit running full = $D/4$)

$\qquad n$ = coefficient of roughness for closed conduits (Table 2-10)

$\qquad l$ = length of conduit, ft

$\qquad v$ = average velocity of flow, fps

$\qquad g_c$ = 32.2 (lb mass)(ft)/(lb force)(sec²)

For long conduits where head losses other than the friction head loss are negligible, the Manning formula can be written as

$$Q = (0.4632/n)D^{8/3}S^{1/2} = \text{conveyance factor} \times S^{1/2} \tag{2-131}$$

[1] For nomenclature see p. 2–25.

[2] See also Sect. 4.

where Q = quantity of flow, cfs

$S = h_f/l$ = hydraulic gradient, ft head loss/ft length

Table 2-10. Roughness Coefficients (Manning's n) for Closed Conduits

Type of conduit			Manning's n	
			Good construction*	Fair construction*
Concrete pipe..			0.013	0.015
Corrugated metal pipe or pipe arch, 2⅔- by ½-in. corrugation, riveted:				
Plain...			.024	
Paved invert:				
Per cent of circumference paved........	25	50		
Depth of flow:				
Full.............................	0.021	0.018		
0.8D.............................	.021	.016		
0.6D.............................	.019	.013		
Vitrified clay pipe..................................			.012	.014
Cast-iron pipe, uncoated...........................			.013	
Steel pipe...			.011	
Brick..			.014	.017
Monolithic concrete:				
Wood forms, rough..............................			.015	.017
Wood forms, smooth.............................			.012	.014
Steel forms.....................................			.012	.013
Cemented-rubble masonry walls:				
Concrete floor and top..........................			.017	.022
Natural floor...................................			.019	.025
Laminated treated wood............................			.015	.017
Vitrified-clay liner plates.........................			.015	

* For poor-quality construction use larger values of n.

The head loss due to friction for the flow of water *in an open channel* (*including a closed conduit not flowing full*) is

$$h_f = C_f(l/R)(v^2/2g_c) \qquad (2\text{-}132)$$

The coefficient C_f is given by the Manning formula as

$$C_f = 29.15n^2/R^{1/3} \qquad (2\text{-}133)$$

where $R = A/P$

n = coefficient of roughness (Table 2-12), dimensionless

R = hydraulic radius, ft

A = cross-sectional area of flow, ft²

P = wetted perimeter, ft

h_f = head loss due to friction, ft–lb force/lb mass

l = length of channel or conduit, ft

v = average velocity of flow, fps

g_c = 32.2 (lb mass)(ft)/(lb force)(sec²)

Table 2-12 is taken from "Hydraulic Charts," prepared by the U.S. Bureau of Public Roads.

Equation: $v = \frac{1.486}{n} R^{2/3} S^{1/2}$

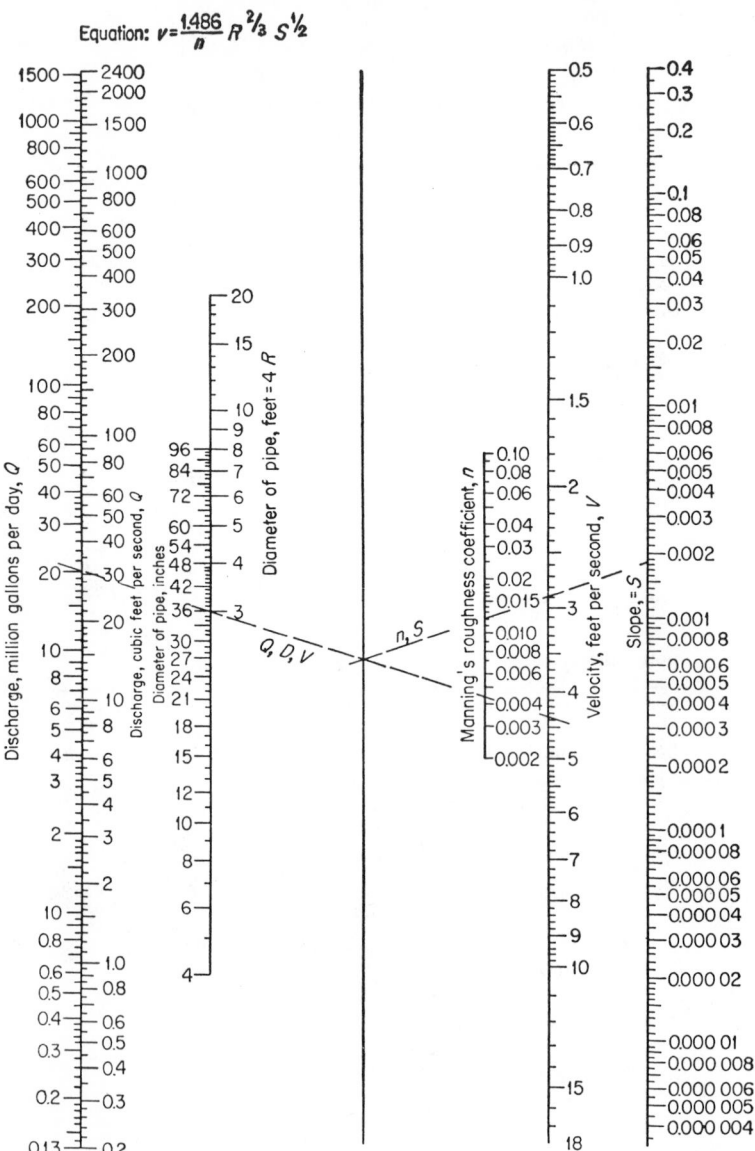

FIG. 2-30. Nomograph for solution of Manning equation for circular conduits for nonpressure flow of water.

Table 2-11. Conveyance Factors

To obtain Q for any diameter pipe, multiply the figure shown under the proper value of n by the square root of the hydraulic gradient expressed in feet of head loss per foot of length.

Diam, in.	Area, ft	Conveyance factors					
		$n = 0.011$	$n = 0.013$	$n = 0.015$	$n = 0.017$	$n = 0.019$	$n = 0.021$
6	0.196	6.62	5.60	4.85	4.28	3.83	3.47
8	0.349	14.32	12.12	10.50	9.27	8.29	7.50
10	0.545	25.80	21.83	18.92	16.70	14.94	13.52
12	0.785	42.15	35.66	30.91	27.27	24.40	22.08
15	1.227	76.46	64.70	56.07	49.48	44.27	40.05
18	1.767	124.2	105.1	91.04	80.33	71.88	65.03
21	2.405	187.1	158.3	137.2	121.1	108.3	98.01
24	3.142	267.4	226.2	196.1	173.0	154.8	140.0
27	3.976	365.8	309.6	268.3	236.7	211.8	191.6
30	4.909	484.7	410.1	355.5	313.6	280.6	253.9
36	7.069	788	667	578	510	456.1	412.7
42	9.621	1,189	1,006	872	770	688	623
48	12.566	1,698	1,436	1,245	1,098	983	889
54	15.904	2,325	1,967	1,705	1,504	1,346	1,218
60	19.635	3,077	2,604	2,256	1,991	1,781	1,612
66	23.758	3,967	3,357	2,909	2,567	2,297	2,078
72	28.274	5,004	4,234	3,669	3,238	2,897	2,621
84	38.495	7,550	6,390	5,540	4,885	4,370	3,954
96	50.27	10,780	9,120	7,900	6,970	6,240	5,640
108	63.62	14,760	12,490	10,820	9,550	8,540	7,730
120	78.54	19,540	16,540	14,330	12,650	11,320	10,240

For long channels where head losses other than the friction head loss are negligible, the Manning formula can be written as:

$$v = (1.486/n)R^{2/3}S^{1/2} \qquad (2\text{-}134)$$

where $S = h_f/l$ = hydraulic gradient, ft head loss/ft length
Figure 2-31 is a nomograph for the solution of Eq. (2-134).

Head Loss at Bend in Channel Alignment. The head loss due to turbulence at a bend in channel alignment is generally taken into account by an increase in the value of the coefficient of roughness n, depending in amount on the degree of curvature (Table 2-12).

Critical Depth. The critical depth for a given flow of water in a channel is the depth for which the total head (total head equals depth plus velocity head) is a minimum; for a given total head, the discharge is therefore a maximum at the critical depth. For a trapezoidal channel cross section, the critical depth is

$$D_c = 4BH_t/(5B + b) \qquad (2\text{-}135)$$

where D_c = critical depth, ft
H_t = total head = $d + v^2/2g$, where d is the measured depth, ft
B = width of channel at water surface, ft
b = width of channel at bottom, ft
For a rectangular channel, the maximum discharge is

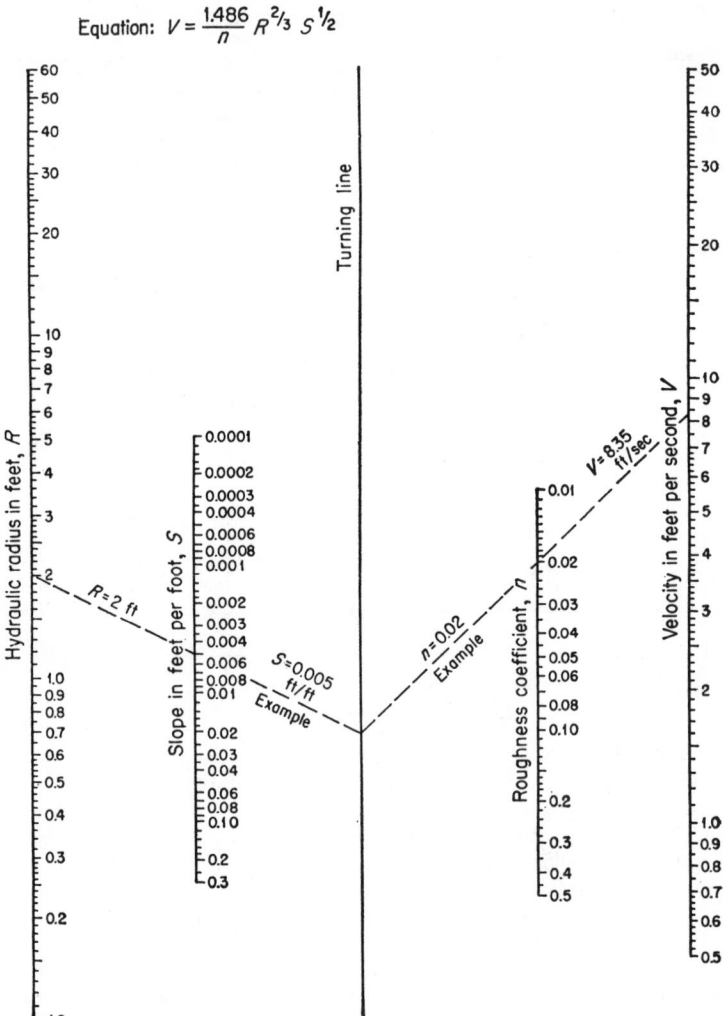

Equation: $V = \dfrac{1.486}{n} R^{2/3} S^{1/2}$

Fig. 2-31. Nomograph for solution of Manning equation for flow of water in open channels.

Table 2-12. Roughness Coefficients (Manning's n) for Open Channels

Channel description	Manning's n	
	Good construction[a]	Fair construction[a]
Open Channels, Nonvegetated Lining, Straight Alignment[b]		
Concrete, with all surfaces:		
Formed, no finish........................	0.013	0.017
Trowel finish.............................	.012	.014
Float finish..............................	.013	.015
Some gravel on bottom....................	.015	.017
Gunite, good section......................	.016	.019
Gunite, wavy section.....................	.018	.022
Concrete bottom, float-finished, sides of:		
Dressed stone in mortar...................	.015	.017
Random stone in mortar...................	.017	.020
Cement rubble masonry....................	.020	.025
Plastered.............................	.016	.020
Dry rubble (riprap).......................	.020	.030
Gravel bottom, sides of:		
Formed concrete........................	.017	.020
Random stone in mortar...................	.020	.023
Dry rubble (riprap).......................	.023	.033
Brick....................................	.014	.017
Asphalt:		
Smooth.................................	.013	
Rough..................................	.016	
Planed wood, clean........................	.011	.013
Concrete-lined excavated rock:		
Good section............................	.017	.020
Irregular section........................	.022	.027
Flumes (steep slope)[b]		
Open Channels, Excavated, Straight Alignment[c], Natural Lining		
Earth, uniform section (best):		
Clean, recently completed..................	0.016	0.018
Clean, after weathering....................	.018	.020
With short grass, few weeds................	.022	.027
Gravel, uniform section, clean..............	.022	.025
Earth, fairly uniform section:		
No vegetation...........................	.022	.025
Grass, some weeds........................	.025	.030
Dense weeds or aquatic plants in deep channels.	.030	.035
Sides clean, gravel bottom.................	.025	.030
Sides clean, cobble bottom.................	.030	.040
Dragline-excavated or dredged:		
No vegetation...........................	.028	.033
Light brush on banks.....................	.035	.050
Rock:		
Based on design section...................	.035	
Based on actual mean section		
a. Smooth and uniform..................	.035	.040
b. Jagged and irregular.................	.040	.045
Channels not maintained, weeds and brush uncut:	Fair condition	Poor condition
Dense weeds, high as flow depth.............	0.08	0.12
Clean bottom, brush on sides...............	.05	.08
highest stage of flow.....................	.07	.11
Dense brush, high stage...................	.10	.14

Table 2-12. Roughness Coefficients (Manning's n) for Open Channels (Continued)

Highway Ditches and Swales with Maintained Vegetation

Type of vegetation	Manning's n			
	Depth 0.7 ft		Depth 0.7–1.5 ft	
	Velocity of flow			
	2 fps	6 fps	2 fps	6 fps
Bermuda; Kentucky bluegrass; buffalo:				
Mowed to 2 in	0.07	0.045	0.05	0.035
Length 4–6 in	.09	.05	.06	.04
Good stand, any grass:				
Length 12 in	.18	.09	.12	.07
Length 24 in	.30	.15	.20	.10
Fair stand, any grass:				
Length 12 in	.14	.08	.10	.06
Length 24 in	.25	.13	.17	.09

Street and Expressway Gutters[d]

Construction	Manning's n
Concrete gutter, troweled finish	0.012
Asphalt pavement:	
Smooth texture	.013
Rough texture	.016
Concrete gutter with asphalt pavement:	
Smooth	.013
Rough	.015
Concrete pavement:	
Float finish	.014
Broom finish	.016
Rough	.020

Channel description	Range in n
Natural Stream Channels, Minor Streams[e] (Surface width at flood stage less than 100 ft)	
Fairly regular section:	
Some grass and weeds, little or no brush	0.030–0.035
Dense growth of weeds, depth of flow materially greater than weed height	0.035–0.05
Some weeds, light brush on banks	0.035–0.05
Some weeds, heavy brush on banks	0.05 –0.07
Some weeds, dense willows on banks	0.06 –0.08
For trees within channel with branches submerged at high stage, increase all above values by	0.01 –0.02
Irregular section, with pools, slight channel meander:	
For channels listed above, increase all values by about	0.01 –0.02
Mountain streams; no vegetation in channel, banks usually steep, trees and brush along banks submerged at high stage:	
Bottom of gravel, cobbles, and few boulders	0.04 –0.05
Bottom of cobbles with large boulders	0.05 –0.07

Natural Stream Channels, Major Streams
(Surface width at flood stage greater than 100 ft)

Roughness coefficient is usually less than for minor streams of similar description on account of less effective resistance offered by irregular banks or vegetation on banks. The value of n for larger streams of most regular section, with no boulders or brush, may be in the range of from 0.028 to 0.033.

Table 2-12. Roughness Coefficients (Manning's n) for
Open Channels (Continued)

Channel description	Range in n
Natural Stream Channels, Flood Plains Adjacent to Natural Streams	
Pasture, no brush:	
Short grass..	0.030–0.035
High grass	0.035–0.05
Cultivated areas:	
No crop..	0.03 –0.04
Mature row crops...	0.035–0.045
Mature field crops..	0.04 –0.05
Heavy weeds, scattered brush.....................................	0.05 –0.07
Light brush and trees:[f]	
Winter...	0.05 –0.06
Summer..	0.06 –0.08
Medium to dense brush:[f]	
Winter...	0.07 –0.11
Summer..	0.10 –0.16
Dense willows, summer, not bent over by current..................	0.15 –0.20
Cleared land with tree stumps, 100-150 per acre:	
No sprouts...	0.04 –0.05
With heavy growth of sprouts.....................................	0.06 –0.08
Heavy stand of timber, a few down trees, little undergrowth:	
Flood depth below branches.......................................	0.10 –0.12
Flood depth reaches branches (n increases with depth)...........	0.12 –0.16

[a] For poor-quality construction, use larger values of n.

[b] With steep slopes, depth of flow will generally be greater than computed by the usual methods for open channels, because of air entrainment and additional resistance offered by air in contact with high-velocity flow. An approximate depth may be calculated by increasing n for the flume material involved by 20 to 30%.

[c] With channel of alignment other than straight, loss of head by resistance forces will be increased. A small increase in value of n may be made to allow for additional loss of energy.

[d] For gutters with small slopes where sediment may accumulate, increase values of n by 0.002 to 0.005.

[e] The values of n shown are principally derived from measurements made on fairly short but straight reaches of natural streams. Where slopes calculated from flood elevations along a considerable length of channel involving meanders and bends, are to be used in velocity calculations, the value of n must be increased by about 3 to 15 per cent to provide for the additional loss of energy caused by bends.

[f] The presence of foliage on trees and brush under flood stage will materially increase the value of n. For trees in channel or on banks, and for brush on banks where submergence of branches increases with depth of flow, n will increase with rising stage.

$$Q_{\max \text{ at } D_c} = 3.087bH_t^{3/2} \qquad \text{cfs} \qquad (2\text{-}136)$$

For a triangular channel, the maximum discharge is

$$Q_{\max \text{ at } D_c} = 1.435BH_t^{3/2} \qquad \text{cfs} \qquad (2\text{-}137)$$

HEAT TRANSFER

There are three fundamental types of heat transfer: conduction, convection, and radiation.

Conduction is the transfer of heat from one part of a body to another part of the same body, or from one body to another in physical contact with it, without appreciable displacement of the particles of the body.

Convection is the transfer of heat from one point to another within a fluid, gas, or liquid by the mixing of one portion of the fluid with another. In natural convection, the motion of the fluid is entirely the result of differences in density resulting from temperature differences; in forced convection, the motion is produced by mechanical means. When the forced velocity is relatively low, it should be realized that "free convection" factors, such as density and temperature difference, may have an important influence.

Radiation is the transfer of heat from one body to another, not in contact with it, by means of wave motion through space.

All three types of heat transfer may occur at the same time, and it is advisable to consider the possibility of heat transfer by each type in any particular case.

2-15. Conduction

Fourier's law is the fundamental differential equation for heat transfer by conduction

$$dQ/d\theta = -kA \, dt/dx \tag{2-138}$$

where $dQ/d\theta$ = rate of heat flow, Btu/hr
  A = area at right angles to direction of heat flow, ft^2
  $-dt/dx$ = rate of change of temperature with distance in direction of heat flow, i.e., temperature gradient, °F/ft

The factor k is called the thermal conductivity, is dependent upon the material through which the heat is flowing and upon the temperature, and has the units Btu per hour per square foot per degree Fahrenheit per foot. (See page 3-23 for data on thermal conductivities.)

Steady Flow of Heat. For the steady flow of heat, the term $dQ/d\theta$ in Eq. (2-138) is constant and may be replaced by Q/θ or q. If k and A are independent of t and x, Eq. (2-138) may be expressed as

$$q = kA(t_1 - t_2)/(x_2 - x_1) = kA \, \Delta t/x \tag{2-139}$$

where Δt = difference in temperatures
  x = distance between points 1 and 2

Usually the thermal conductivity k is not constant, but is a function of the temperature. In most cases, over the ranges of values used, the relation is linear. Integration of Eq. (2-138), with k linear in t, gives

$$q = k_{\text{avg}}A \, \Delta t/x \tag{2-140}$$

where k_{avg} = arithmetic average thermal conductivity between temperatures t_1 and t_2

In case the cross-sectional area A varies with the distance x, A may be expressed in terms of x in order to integrate Eq. (2-138). This may, however, lead to complicated expressions, and it is customary to use Eq. (2-140), substituting the proper average value of A:

1. A flat wall of constant area, $A_{\text{avg}} = A_1 = A_2$ $\tag{2-141}$

2. Area is proportional to first power of distance, as for insulated pipes

$$A_{\text{avg}} = (A_2 - A_1)/2.3 \log (A_2/A_1) \tag{2-142}$$

3. Area is proportional to square of distance, as in a hollow sphere

$$A_{\text{avg}} = \sqrt{A_1 A_2} \tag{2-143}$$

Conduction through Several Bodies in Series. Since the heat flow through each of several walls must be the same,

$$q = k_1 A_1 \, \Delta t_1/x_1 = k_2 A_2 \, \Delta t_2/x_2 = k_3 A_3 \, \Delta t_3/x_3 \tag{2-144}$$

if we let $R_1 = x_1/k_1 A_1$, $R_2 = x_2/k_2 A_2$, etc., then

$$q(R_1 + R_2 + R_3) = \Delta t_1 + \Delta t_2 + \Delta t_3 = \Sigma \, \Delta t \tag{2-145}$$
$$q = \Sigma \, \Delta t/R_T = (t_1 - t_4)/R_T \tag{2-146}$$

where R_T is the over-all resistance and is the sum of the individual resistances in series. Then

$$R_T = R_1 + R_2 + \cdots + R_n \tag{2-147}$$

Conduction through Several Bodies in Parallel. For n resistances in parallel, the rates of heat flow are additive.

$$\begin{aligned} q &= \Delta t/R_1 + \Delta t/R_2 + \cdots + \Delta t/R_n \\ &= (1/R_1 + 1/R_2 + \cdots + 1/R_n) \, \Delta t \\ &= (C_1 + C_2 + \cdots + C_n) \, \Delta t = \Sigma C \, \Delta t \end{aligned} \tag{2-148}$$

where R_1 to R_n = individual resistances

C_1 to C_n = individual conductances, $C = kA/x$

Heat Transfer in the Unsteady State (Heating and Cooling of Solids). In problems involving conduction of heat in the transient state, the temperature of the body varies with both time and the position of points in the body, and the mathematical relations are complicated. However, the basic differential equations for conduction have been integrated for various shapes and boundary conditions (Figs. 2-32 to 2-35) and the results may be plotted as curves involving four ratios defined as follows:

$$Y = (t' - t)/(t' - t_b) \tag{2-149}$$
$$X = k\theta/\rho c_p r_m{}^2 \tag{2-150}$$
$$m = k/h_T r_m \tag{2-151}$$
$$n = r/r_m \tag{2-152}$$

where t' = temperature of surroundings, °F

t_b = initial uniform temperature of body, °F

t = temperature at given point in body at time θ (hours) measured from start of heating or cooling operations, °F

k = uniform thermal conductivity of body, Btu/(hr)(ft²)(°F/ft)

ρ = uniform density of body, lb/ft³

c_p = specific heat of body, Btu/(lb)(°F)

h_T = coefficient of total heat transfer between surroundings and surface of body, Btu/(hr)(°F)(ft²)

r = distance, in direction of heat conduction, from mid-point or mid-plane of body to point under consideration, ft

r_m = radius of sphere or cylinder, one-half the thickness of a slab heated from both faces, the total thickness of a slab heated from one face and insulated perfectly at the other, ft

x = distance, in direction of heat conduction, from surface of semi-infinite body to point under consideration, ft

With the infinite slab, in the early stages of the operation where Fig. 2-35 gives insufficient precision, Fig. 2-34 may be used for points near the surface.

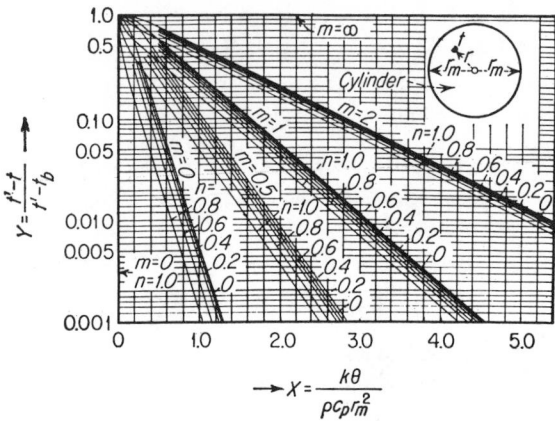

Fig. 2-32. Heating and cooling of a solid cylinder having infinite ratio of length to diameter.

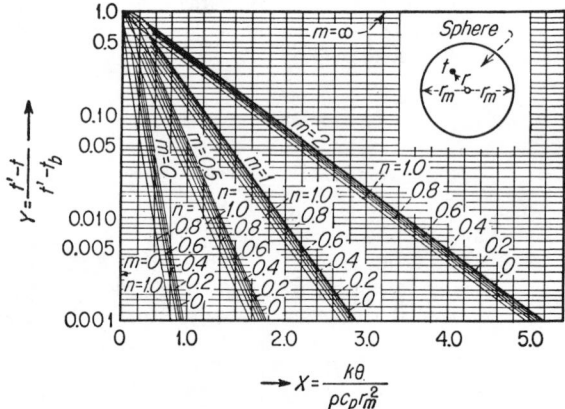

Fig. 2-33. Heating and cooling of a solid sphere.

For a brick-shaped solid having the dimensions $2r_{m1}$, $2r_{m2}$, and $2r_{m3}$ the value of Y at a given time and position may be evaluated as follows: Y equals the product $Y_1 Y_2 Y_3$, where Y_1 is evaluated from Fig. 2-34 at $X_1 = k\theta/\rho c_p r_{m1}^2$, $n_1 = r_1/r_{m1}$, and $m_1 = k/h_T r_{m1}$. Similarly, Y_2 and Y_3 are read for the same θ at X_2, n_2, and m_2 and at X_3, n_3, and m_3, corresponding to r_{m2} and r_{m3}.

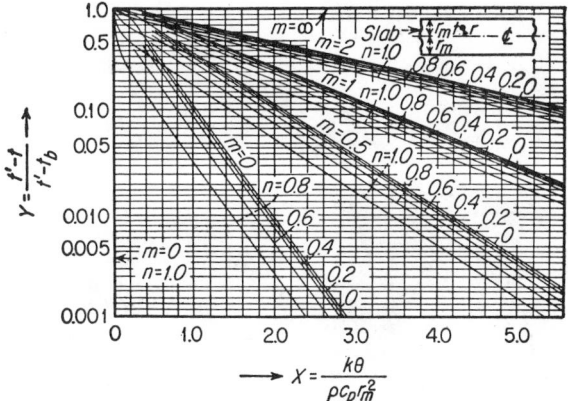

Fig. 2-34. Heating and cooling of a solid slab having a large face area relative to that of the edges.

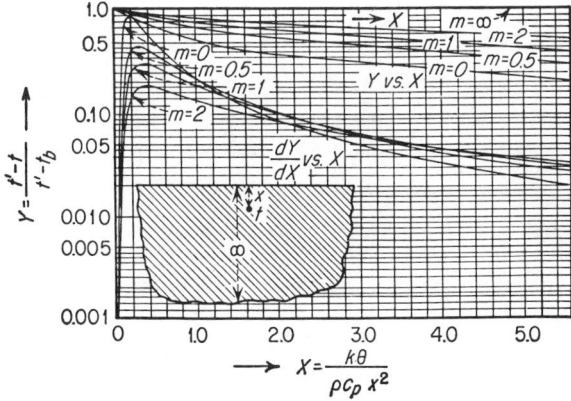

Fig. 2-35. Heating and cooling of a solid of infinite thickness, neglecting edge effects. (This may be used as an approximation in the zone near the surface of a body of finite thickness.)

2-16. Convection

Coefficients of Heat Transfer. In commercial heat-transfer equipment it is not convenient to measure tube-wall temperatures such as t_3 and t_4 in Fig. 2-36, and hence the rate of heat transfer is not easily calculated on the basis of conduction as expressed in Eq. (5-14) and as discussed in the previous section.

$$q = (k/x)A_{\text{avg}}(t_3 - t_4) = (k/x)A_{\text{avg}}\,\Delta t, \qquad (2\text{-}153)$$

where k = thermal conductivity
x = thickness of tube wall

The over-all performance is thus expressed as an over-all coefficient of heat

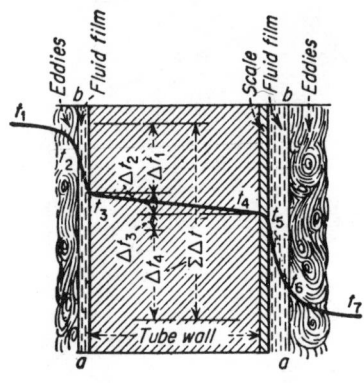

Fig. 2-36. Temperature gradients for steady flow of heat by conduction and convection from a warmer to a colder fluid separated by a solid wall.

transfer U (Btu per hour per square foot per degree Fahrenheit) based on a convenient area such as the inside area A_i (square feet), the outside area A_0 (square feet), or an average of these A_{avg}.   Whence by definition

$$q = UA_{avg}(t_1 - t_7) = UA_{avg}\Sigma \Delta t \qquad (2\text{-}154)$$

The rate of heat transfer through each of the fluid resistances on either side of the tube wall is equal to that shown in Eqs. (2-153) and (2-154) and may be expressed as

$$q = h_i A_i(t_1 - t_3) = h_0 A_0(t_5 - t_7) \qquad (2\text{-}155)$$

where h_i and h_0 = film coefficient of heat transfer inside and outside tube wall, Btu/(hr)(ft²)(°F)

Similarly, the rate of heat transfer through a layer of scale on the tube wall may be expressed as

$$q = h_d A_0(t_4 - t_5) \qquad (2\text{-}156)$$

As was previously noted, it is most convenient to use the over-all coefficient of heat transfer and an over-all Δt such as $t_1 - t_7$.   To do this the individual coefficients are combined by basing the over-all coefficient on one area arbitrarily, let us say in this case A_0.

$$1/U = A_0/A_i h_i + x A_0/k A_{avg} + 1/h_d + 1/h_0 \qquad (2\text{-}157)$$

The second term in the Eq. (2-157), $x A_0/k A_{avg}$, is usually negligible, because of the relatively minor contribution of the tube wall to the over-all resistance to heat transfer.   So the general procedure to evaluate the over-all coefficient U is to evaluate the individual coefficients of heat transfer by the methods of Tables 2-13 and 2-14, use an appropriate scale coefficient from Table 2-15, and combine these with the appropriate physical data (thermal conductivity and dimensions) on the heat-exchanger tubing by means of Eq. (2-157).

Mean Temperature Difference. For parallel or counterflow of fluids

$$q = UA\,\Delta t_{\text{mean}} = UA(\Delta t_1 - \Delta t_2)/\ln(\Delta t_1/\Delta t_2) \qquad (2\text{-}158)$$

where the right-hand term, excluding UA, is the logarithmic mean of the terminal temperature differences, in degrees Fahrenheit, of the exchanger.

Multipass and Cross-flow Exchangers. Here the flow is neither parallel nor countercurrent; the logarithmic-mean temperature difference does not apply. For these exchangers,

$$q = U_m A\,\Delta t'_{\text{mean}} = U_m A Y\,\Delta t_{\text{mean}} \qquad (2\text{-}159)$$

where Y is obtained from Figs. 2-37 or 2-38 and Δt_{mean} is as defined in Eq. (2-158). If one of the temperatures remains constant, as in a condenser or in an evaporative cooler, Eq. (2-158) applies for parallel flow, counterflow, multipass, and cross flow.

If U varies considerably with temperature, the apparatus should be visualized as divided into stages, in each of which variation of U with temperature or temperature difference is linear. Then for parallel or counterflow operation

$$q = A(\Delta t_1 U_2 - \Delta t_2 U_1)/\ln(\Delta t_1 U_2/\Delta t_2 U_1) \qquad (2\text{-}160)$$

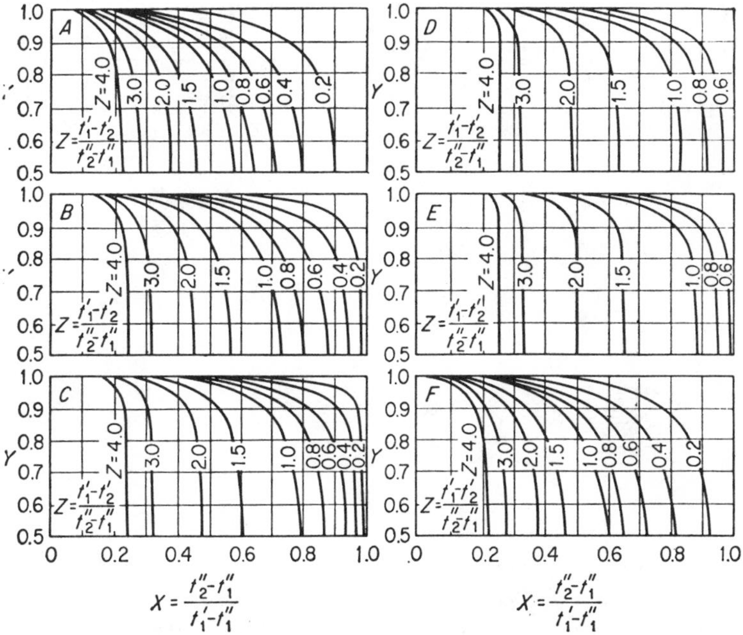

$$X = \frac{t''_2 - t''_1}{t'_1 - t''_1} \qquad\qquad X = \frac{t''_2 - t''_1}{t'_1 - t''_1}$$

Fig. 2-37. Mean temperature difference in reversed-current exchangers. (Shell side well mixed at a given cross section.) (*A*) One shell pass and 2, 4, 6, tube passes. (*B*) Two shell passes and 4, 8, tube passes. (*C*) Three shell passes and 6, 12, tube passes. (*D*) Four shell passes and 8, 16, tube passes. (*E*) Six shell passes and 12, 24, 36, tube passes. (*F*) One shell pass and 3 tube passes. (*Bowman, Mueller, and Nagle.*)

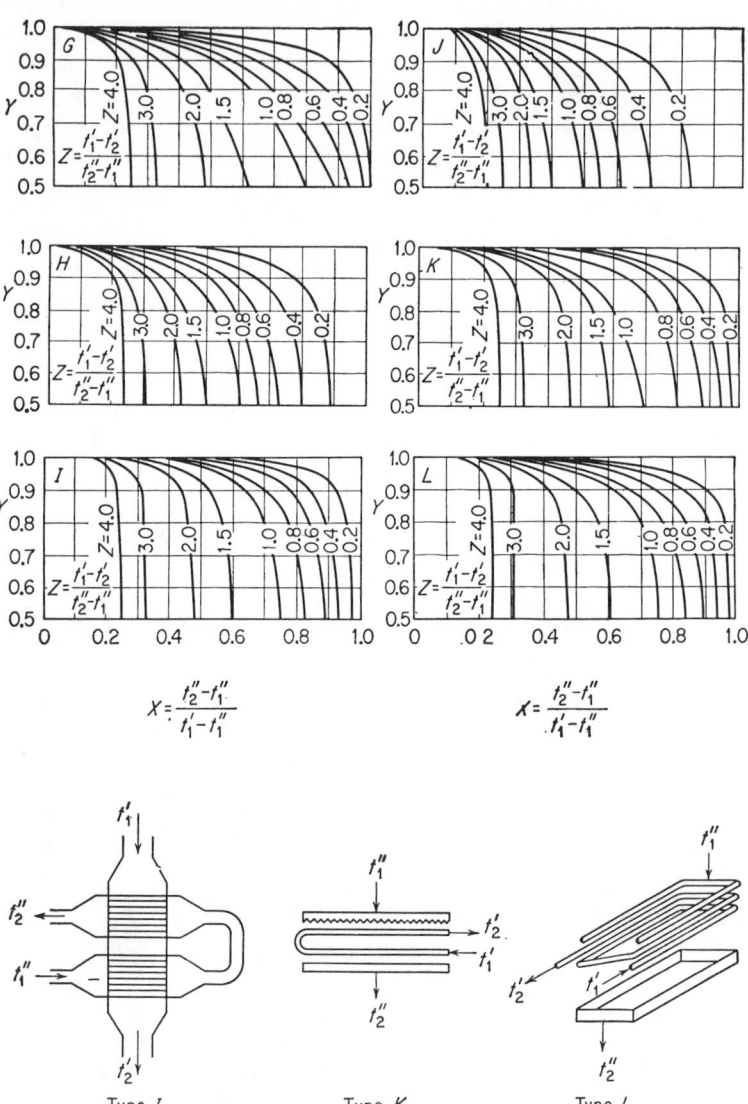

Fig. 2-38. Mean temperature difference in cross-flow exchangers. (*G*) Cross flow, both fluids unmixed, 1 tube pass. (*H*) Cross flow, shell fluid mixed, 1 tube pass. (*I*) Cross flow, shell fluid mixed, 2 tube passes, shell fluid flows across second and first passes in series. (*J*) Cross flow, shell fluid mixed, 2 tube passes, shell fluid flows over first and second passes in series. (*K*) Cross flow (drip type), 2 horizontal passes with U-bend connections (trombone type). (*L*) Cross flow (drip type), helical coils with 2 turns. (*Bowman, Mueller, and Nagle.*)

Conversion Factors for Coefficients of Heat Transfer. Throughout this chapter, values of h and U are expressed in Btu per hour per square foot per degree Fahrenheit. Conversion factors to other units are listed in Table 1.1.

2-17. Radiant-heat Transmission

General. If two small bodies of areas A_1 and A_2 (in square feet) are placed in a large evacuated enclosure perfectly insulated externally, then, when the system has come to thermal equilibrium, the bodies will emit radiation at the rates A_1W_1 and A_2W_2, respectively, where W is the total emissive power: energy per unit time per unit area of the surface (Btu per hour per square foot) emitted throughout the hemisphere above each element of surface. Let the energy impinging on unit area of any small body in the enclosure, due to radiation from the walls of the latter, be I Btu/(hr)(ft²). If the bodies have absorptivities (fraction of incident radiation which is absorbed) of α_1 and α_2, then energy balances on the bodies will have the form $IA_1\alpha_1 = A_1W_1$ and $IA_2\alpha_2 = A_2W_2$, from which

$$W_1/\alpha_1 = W_2/\alpha_2 = W_x/\alpha_x$$

where x is *any* body. This generalization, that at thermal equilibrium the ratio of the emissive power of a surface to its absorptivity is the same for all bodies, is *Kirchhoff's law*. The relation

$$W_B = \sigma T^4 \qquad (2\text{-}161)$$

is the *Stefan-Boltzmann law*, and the proportionality constant σ is the Stefan-Boltzmann constant:

$$0.173 \times 10^{-8} \text{ Btu/(ft}^2)(\text{hr})(°\text{R}^4)$$
$$5.67 \times 10^{-5} \text{ ergs/(cm}^2)(\text{sec})(°\text{K}^4)$$
$$4.88 \times 10^{-8} \text{ kg-cal/(m}^2)(\text{hr})(°\text{K}^4)$$

If $W_{B\lambda}$ is the *monochromatic emissive power* at wavelength λ (centimeters) such that $W_{B\lambda}\, d\lambda$ is the energy emitted from a surface per unit area per unit time in the wavelength interval λ to $d\lambda$, the relation among $W_{B\lambda}$ (Btu per hour per square foot per centimeter), λ, and T is given by *Planck's law*

$$W_{B\lambda} = c_1\lambda^{-5}/(e^{c_2/\lambda t} - 1) \qquad (2\text{-}162)$$

where $c_1 = 1.176 \times 10^{-8}$ Btu/(ft²)(hr)(cm⁴) or 0.885×10^{-12} cal-cm²/sec
$c_2 = 2.58$ cm-°R or 1.433 cm-°K

If α_λ is a constant independent of λ, the surface is called *gray* and its total absorptivity α will be independent of the spectral-energy distribution of the incident radiation; then $\alpha_{1,2} = \alpha_{1,1} = \epsilon_1$; that is, emissivity ϵ may be used in substitution for α even though the temperatures of the incident radiation and the receiver are not the same.

Radiation between Surfaces of Solids Separated by a Nonabsorbing Medium. The net loss of energy by radiation from a body at temperature T_1 in *black* surroundings at T_2 is given by

$$q_{1,\text{net}} = 0.173A_1[\epsilon_1(T_1/100)^4 - \alpha_{1,2}(T_2/100)^4] \qquad (2\text{-}163)$$

where A_1 is in square feet and T is in degrees Rankine.

When $\alpha_{1,2} = \epsilon_1$, that is, when the body is gray, this simplifies to

$$q_{1,\text{net}} = 0.173A_1\epsilon_1[(T_1/100)^4 - (T_2/100)^4] \qquad (2\text{-}164)$$

Values for the emissivity of various surfaces are given in Table 2-16, page 2-71.

Table 2-13. Film Coefficients for Liquids

Units: Btu/(hr)(ft²)(°F)

To obtain the desired film coefficient, a base factor corresponding to the liquid and temperature under consideration is taken from the proper table and multiplied by a correction factor read from the nomograph accompanying that table. The following assumptions apply in each case: (1) the system is in equilibrium, that is, there is no change in temperature gradient with time, (2) radiation is negligible or has been taken into account by other calculations, (3) film temperature is defined as the arithmetic average of the temperatures of the retaining wall and the main body of the liquid. Wall temperature, generally not known, can be estimated or calculated by trial and error. Values of base factors in italics are extrapolated from physical properties.

Case 1. Base Factors for Liquids Heated Inside Horizontal or Vertical Tubes, Turbulent Flow

Average liquid temp, °F	0	50	100	150	200	250
Acetic acid, 100%	....	117	97.2	101	105	109
Acetic acid, 50%	....	122	156	180	203	228
Acetone	104	....	134	137	139	142
Ammonia	330	425	507	599	690	790
Amyl acetate	65.0	66.2	67.7	71.8	78.5	86.0
Amyl alcohol, iso	21.6	35.8	52.7	73.3	96.0	118
Aniline	....	43.8	58.4	76.5	99.2	123
Benzene	....	75.6	94.5	108	121	134
Brine, Ca Cl₂, 25%	139	190	257	332	420	517
n-Butyl alcohol	31.2	45.5	62.4	83.0	107	133
Carbon disulfide	114	119	125	129	132	133
Carbon tetrachloride	57.4	69.2	78.6	82.6	85.8	88.2
Chlorobenzene	64.6	73.3	78.8	80.5	82.0	82.8
Ethyl acetate	126	126	125	123	122	121
Ethyl alcohol, 100%	58.0	73.6	92.3	112	132	161
Ethyl alcohol, 40%	61.5	104	162	228	292	589
Ethyl bromide	97.8	104	110	114	119	122
Ethylene glycol	71.4	105	158	222	299	380
Ethyl ether	100	115	123	130	137	144
Glycerol, 50%	59.0	90.5	131	182	248	302
Heptane	81.4	87.0	94.7	102	112	122
Hexane	85.8	93.8	102	109	114	117
Methyl alcohol, 100%	83.0	110	126	138	149	160
Methyl alcohol, 90%	86.0	114	136	164	172	188
Methyl alcohol, 40%	64.0	110	164	213	264	312
n-Octane	72.0	79.0	85.9	92.0	97.0	102
n-Pentane	103	105	110	115	118	121
Propyl alcohol, iso	25.7	49.3	71.5	94.5	117	139
Sulfur dioxide	167	171	175	180	182	194
Sulfuric acid, 60%	....	65.9	79.4	94.5	110	129
Toluene	77.3	86.9	96.6	104	112	119
Water	....	225	322	408	392	508

Case 2. Base Factors for Liquids Cooled Inside Horizontal or Vertical Tubes, Turbulent Flow

Average liquid temp, °F	0	50	100	150	200	250
Acetic acid, 100%	....	85.2	72.2	75.0	78.7	81.6
Acetic acid, 50%	....	105	118	153	179	201
Acetone	88.4	....	....	121	124	126
Ammonia	314	380	507	650	797	938
Amyl acetate	48.1	50.7	52.3	53.3	54.4	55.5
Amyl alcohol, iso	....	22.7	36.0	53.0	72.3	91.8
Aniline	....	31.6	45.2	63.3	86.9	110
Benzene	106	61.7	79.1	93.5	107	180
Brine, Ca Cl₂, 25%	....	152	217	312	397	510
n-Butyl alcohol	19.2	31.4	45.1	64.0	84.9	107
Carbon disulfide	103	110	110	121	126	128
Carbon tetrachloride	40.4	55.8	67.3	72.0	76.0	78.7
Chlorobenzene	54.5	57.5	60.7	63.8	65.0	65.6
Ethyl acetate	83.3	84.1	84.1	84.1	83.2	82.4
Ethyl alcohol, 100%	41.2	54.8	71.1	89.0	108	128
Ethyl alcohol, 40%	....	70.4	121	176	230	315
Ethyl bromide	84.9	92.9	99.9	106	112	116
Ethylene glycol, 50%	44.2	71.7	120	183	261	135
Ethyl ether	86.0	99.0	109	118	179	222
Glycerol, 50%	54.9	59.5	94.5	184	97.0	104
Heptane	66.8	74.2	81.5	88.8	102	108
Hexane	70.7	78.5	87.2	95.2	132	146
Methyl alcohol, 100%	65.4	88.5	105	118	132	156
Methyl alcohol, 90%	68.5	92.0	112	128	142	292
Methyl alcohol, 40%	38.2	80.0	127	177	236	88.0
n-Octane	56.0	63.8	70.9	77.2	83.2	88.0
n-Pentane	82.8	89.6	96.4	101	106	110
Propyl alcohol, iso	....	32.4	51.5	71.7	92.7	116
Sulfur dioxide	150	155	161	166	174	178
Sulfuric acid, 60%	....	35.3	54.4	66.9	74.0	77.7
Toluene	61.8	71.5	81.4	90.3	97.6	103
Water	....	153	273	355	427	483

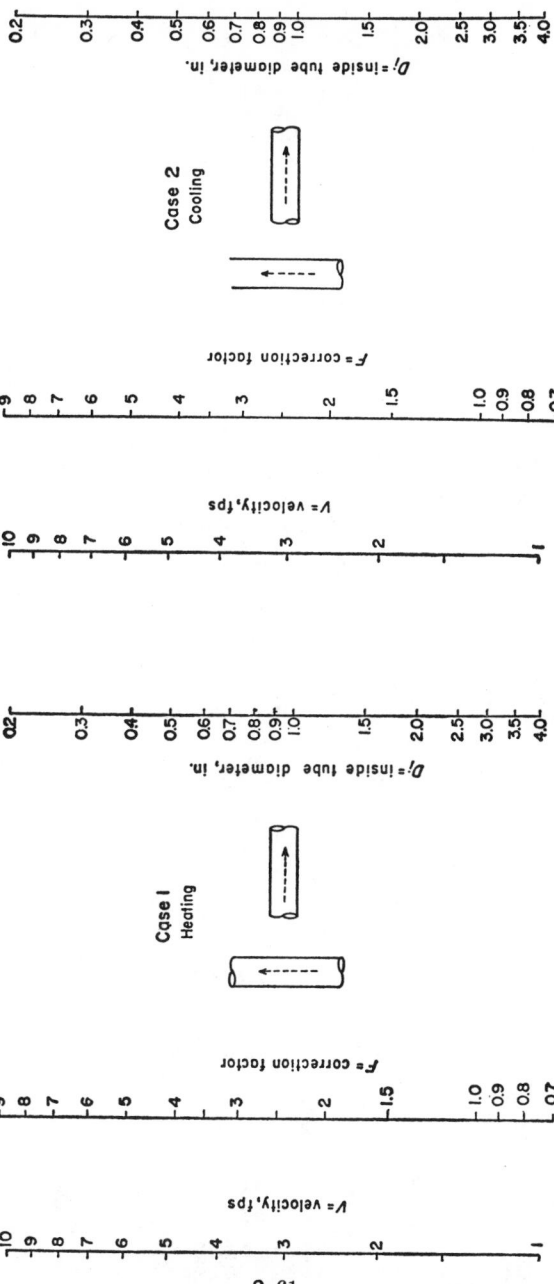

Table 2-13. Film Coefficients for Liquids (Continued)

Case 3. Liquids Heated or Cooled Outside Tube Bundles, Direction of Flow Parallel to Tubes

Film coefficients for liquids flowing outside tube bundles and in a direction parallel to the tubes can be determined from Cases 1 or 2 for liquids inside tubes, if an equivalent inside diameter is used in determining the correction factor. An equivalent diameter can be calculated by $d_e = 4A/P$, where d_e is the equivalent ID in inches, A is the cross-sectional area between tubes in square inches, and P is the sum of the tube-perimeter segments forming the cross-section boundary, in inches.

Case 4. Base Factors for Liquids Heated or Cooled Outside Single Tubes, Direction of Flow Normal to Tube

Average film temp, °F	0	50	100	150	200	250
Acetic acid, 100%		214	142	136	131	125
Acetic acid, 50%		174	260	292	310	321
Acetone	165		184	186	187	189
Ammonia	486	548	616	685	758	827
Amyl acetate	114	106	97.9	91.0	84.8	76.5
Amyl alcohol, iso	54.0	73.0	94.9			
Aniline		124	140	152	163	174
Benzene	264	335	419	508	617	734
Brine, Ca Cl₂, 25%	98.5	100	112	136	167	206
n-Butyl alcohol	164	166	169	171	173	173
Carbon disulfide		105	114	116	117	118
Carbon tetrachloride	115	112	109	106	103	102
Chlorobenzene	154	145	137	129	119	111
Ethyl acetate	108	127	146	165	183	199
Ethyl alcohol, 100%	180	199	277	355	430	508
Ethyl alcohol, 40%	181	137	142	144	146	147
Ethyl bromide	147	209	283	362	447	545
Ethylene glycol, 50%	146	154	161	169	175	188
Ethyl ether	147	192	249	331	431	
Glycerol, 50%	126	133	139	143	147	151
Heptane	128	134	141	147	151	155
Hexane	147	170	187	198	206	212
Methyl alcohol, 100%	159	186	209	226	238	251
Methyl alcohol, 90%	132	201	264	317	359	397
Methyl alcohol, 40%	117	124	129	135	140	146
n-Octane	139	144	148	151	152	154
n-Pentane	62.5	91.0	118	143	163	180
Propyl alcohol, iso	230	225	223	221	221	218
Sulfur dioxide		110	137	150	164	176
Sulfuric acid, 60%						
Toluene	128	135	142	148	152	155
Water		382	497	525	645	700

Case 5. Base Factors for Liquids Heated Outside Single Horizontal Tubes, Natural Convection

Average film temp, °F	0	50	100	150	200	250
Acetic acid, 100%		27.1	19.8	18.8	17.8	17.2
Acetone	85.5		28.0	28.2	28.8	28.8
Ammonia		96.3	108	120	132	144
Benzene	23.9	24.1	20.3	21.9	23.5	23.5
Carbon disulfide		24.7	24.6	24.8	25.1	25.3
Carbon tetrachloride	16.4	15.5	16.6	16.5	16.8	15.9
Chlorobenzene	23.5	21.7	14.8	14.0	13.4	13.0
Ethyl acetate	15.6	18.1	20.1	18.5	17.1	16.6
Ethyl alcohol, 100%	17.9	20.7	20.6	23.1	25.3	27.4
Ethyl alcohol, 40%	20.1	26.6	36.5	47.2	37.8	
Ethyl bromide	22.3	23.9	21.1	25.6	21.7	21.9
Ethyl ether		17.9	24.8	21.8	26.4	26.9
Ethyl iodide	15.9	20.0	19.8		23.0	23.6
Heptane	19.4	19.9	21.0	28.7	21.5	21.9
Hexane	18.7	25.2	27.1	31.8	22.5	22.9
Methyl alcohol, 100%	22.5	25.9	29.1	19.2	34.1	30.9
Methyl alcohol, 90%	21.5	18.1	18.5	23.3	20.0	36.4
n-Octane	17.0	22.8	22.8	36.0	24.0	20.5
n-Pentane	21.9	37.2	36.5	19.2	35.6	24.4
Sulfur dioxide	37.9	11.8	15.5	18.2	22.9	55.2
Sulfuric acid, 98%		12.5	15.6			
Sulfuric acid, 60%	18.1	19.1	16.0	20.9	20.3	21.7
Toluene			20.1		21.5	21.7
Water		36.8	47.9	55.0	60.2	65.0

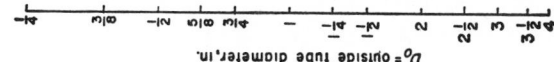

D_o = outside tube diameter, in.

$\frac{1}{4}$ $\frac{3}{8}$ $\frac{1}{2}$ $\frac{5}{8}$ $\frac{3}{4}$ 1 $1\frac{1}{4}$ $1\frac{1}{2}$ 2 $2\frac{1}{2}$ 3 $3\frac{1}{2}$ 4

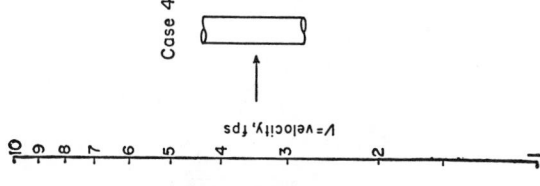

Case 5

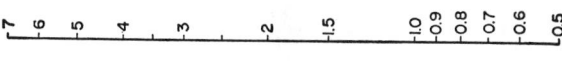

F = correction factor

6 5 4 3 2 1.5 1.0 0.9 0.8 0.7

Δt = temperature difference between retaining wall and liquid, °F

300 200 150 100 80 60 50 40 30 20 15 10 8 6 5 4 3 2 1.5 1

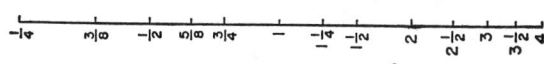

D_o = outside tube diameter, in.

$\frac{1}{4}$ $\frac{3}{8}$ $\frac{1}{2}$ $\frac{5}{8}$ $\frac{3}{4}$ 1 $1\frac{1}{4}$ $1\frac{1}{2}$ 2 $2\frac{1}{2}$ 3 $3\frac{1}{2}$ 4

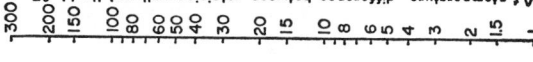

F = correction factor

7 6 5 4 3 2 1.5 1.0 0.9 0.8 0.7 0.6 0.5

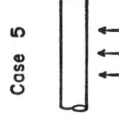

Case 4

V = velocity, fps

10 9 8 7 6 5 4 3 2 1

Table 2-13. Film Coefficients for Liquids (Continued)

Δt = temperature difference between retaining wall and liquid, °F

`1.5  2   3   4   5   6   8  10   15  20  30  40  60  80 100 150 200 300`

`2        3        4        5        6        7`

F = correction factor

Case 6. Base Factors for Liquids Heated Inside or Outside Vertical Tubes or on Vertical Plates, Low Velocities or Natural Convection Only

Average film temp, °F	0	50	100	150	200	250
Acetic acid, 100%	21.0		15.6	15.5	15.5	15.5
Acetone	75.0	22.6	24.1	24.8	25.8	25.8
Ammonia		88.5	103	118	136	155
Benzene	19.7	14.4	16.4	18.2	20.0	21.7
Carbon disulfide	11.4	20.3	21.0	21.6	22.2	22.8
Carbon tetrachloride	12.0	12.7	13.8	14.2	14.4	14.8
Chlorobenzene		12.0	12.0	11.8	11.8	11.7
Ethyl acetate	18.6	18.1	17.4	16.6	15.9	15.0
Ethyl alcohol, 100%	10.8	13.2	15.9	18.6	21.2	23.9
Ethyl alcohol, 40%	10.2	17.4	26.2	25.1	45.4	
Ethyl bromide	17.1	18.0	18.8	19.4	19.8	20.2
Ethyl ether	19.4	21.0	22.3	23.4	24.1	24.6
Ethyl iodide	12.6	15.4	17.7	19.8	21.8	24.0
Heptane	14.8	16.7	16.6	17.2	18.5	19.5
Hexane	15.6	16.5	17.8	18.9	19.4	19.9
Methyl alcohol, 100%	16.7	19.5	21.9	23.9	25.9	27.4
Methyl alcohol, 90%	15.1	19.4	22.6	25.4	27.8	30.3
n-Octane	12.7	13.9	14.8	15.8	16.7	17.7
n-Pentane	18.3	19.3	20.1	20.7	21.1	21.5
Sulfur dioxide	33.6	33.6	33.6	33.6	33.6	33.6
Sulfuric acid, 98%		7.2	9.4	11.6	13.8	15.9
Sulfuric acid, 60%		8.5	11.2	12.3	14.7	16.3
Toluene	13.7	14.9	16.1	17.3	18.5	19.6
Water		23.3	31.9	38.0	42.4	47.9

Case 7. Liquids Heated or Cooled Outside Tube Bundles, Direction of Flow Normal to Tubes

Use data for Case 4 and multiply answer by 1.2 for tubes in line or by 1.3 for staggered tubes. For determining correction factor use velocity at narrowest section between tubes. For baffled heat exchangers, where a small part of the flow is parallel to tubes, use Case 4 data directly, but evaluate correction factor at velocity between tubes at widest part of shell, calculated as $144Q \div (d_s - nd)l$, where Q is rate of flow in cubic feet per second, d_s is inside shell diameter in inches, n is number of tubes across wide part of shell, and l is distance between baffles.

Case 8. Liquids Heated or Cooled in Annular Spaces, Turbulent Flow

Use data for Case 1 (heating) or Case 2 (cooling), but substitute an equivalent diameter equal to $(d_1^2 - d_2^2) \div d_1$ in determining correction factor on nomograph. d_1 is inside diameter of outer pipe and d_2 is outside diameter of inner pipe.

Case 9. Liquids Heated or Cooled Inside Coils, Turbulent Flow

Use data for Case 1 (heating) or Case 2 (cooling) and multiply answer by 1.2

Case 10. Liquids Heated or Cooled Outside Coils, Natural or Forced Convection

Use data for Case 4 (forced convection) or Case 5 (natural convection). SOURCE: H. J. Stoever, Chem. & Met. Eng., 51(5): (1944). Reproduced by permission of H. J. Stoever.

Table 2-14. Film Coefficients for Gases, Condensing Vapors, and Boiling Liquids

Units: Btu/(hr)(ft²)(°F)

Film coefficients for gases, condensing vapors, and boiling liquids are obtained in the same way as was explained for liquids, Table 5-1.

Case 11. Base Factors for Gases Heated or Cooled Inside Horizontal or Vertical Tubes, Turbulent Flow

Average gas temp, °F	−100	0	100	200	300	400	500
Acetone	….	….	3.98	4.58	5.26	6.33	7.56
Acetylene	4.47	4.90	5.32	5.75	6.15	6.55	6.89
Air	3.52	3.76	3.92	4.08	4.19	4.27	4.39
Ammonia	4.87	5.68	6.25	6.69	7.06	7.36	7.64
Benzene	….	….	3.61	4.33	5.20	6.10	7.00
Butane	2.57	4.61	5.48	5.98	6.42	6.74	7.05
Carbon dioxide	3.53	2.89	3.14	3.33	3.49	3.64	3.83
Carbon monoxide	1.69	3.77	3.97	4.17	4.33	4.49	4.65
Chlorine	….	1.66	1.73	1.78	1.83	1.88	1.92
Chloroform	….	….	1.90	2.07	2.26	2.45	2.64
Ethane	4.06	4.83	5.31	6.28	7.00	7.72	8.46
Ethyl acetate	….	….	3.81	4.49	5.14	5.75	6.32
Ethyl alcohol	….	….	5.22	5.44	5.64	5.85	6.06
Ethyl chloride	….	3.08	3.50	3.75	3.89	4.03	4.13
Ethylene	3.89	4.56	5.19	5.75	6.33	6.90	7.46
Ethyl ether	….	4.71	5.30	5.93	6.68	7.47	8.78
Helium	20.6	21.2	21.9	22.6	23.2	23.9	24.6
Hydrogen	45.1	47.7	49.6	51.6	53.6	55.6	57.5
Hydrogen sulfide	2.68	2.90	3.15	3.37	3.60	3.79	3.98
Methane	6.68	7.49	8.06	8.47	8.79	9.11	9.35
Methyl chloride	1.88	2.36	2.85	3.31	3.74	4.16	4.56
Nitric oxide	3.43	3.62	3.77	3.89	3.99	4.07	4.16
Nitrogen	3.83	3.95	4.11	4.24	4.33	4.41	4.49
Nitrous oxide	2.87	2.94	3.00	3.06	3.12	3.18	3.24
Oxygen	3.38	3.57	3.71	3.82	3.93	4.01	4.09
Pentane, iso	….	4.73	5.37	6.13	6.93	8.02	9.24
Steam	….	….	5.82	6.00	6.18	6.41	6.64
Sulfur dioxide	….	1.88	2.00	2.10	2.20	2.28	2.36

Case II

D = inside tube diameter, in. — 0.2 · 0.3 · 0.4 · 0.5 · 0.6 · 0.7 · 0.8 · 0.9 · 1.0 · 1.5 · 2.0 · 2.5 · 3.0 · 3.5 · 4.0

F = correction factor — 30 · 25 · 20 · 15 · 10 · 9 · 8 · 7 · 6 · 5 · 4 · 3 · 2 · 1.5 · 1.0 · 0.9 · 0.8

G = rate of flow, lb/sec; $\dfrac{v}{\phi} = \dfrac{\text{velocity} \times \text{density}}{\text{cross-sect. area, sq ft}}$ = (fps × lb/ft³) — 50 · 40 · 30 · 20 · 15 · 10 · 9 · 8 · 7 · 6 · 5 · 4 · 3 · 2 · 1.5 · 1

Table 2-14. Film Coefficients for Gases, Condensing Vapors, and Boiling Liquids (Continued)

Case 12. Base Factors for Gases Heated or Cooled Outside Single Tubes, Direction of Flow Normal to Tube, Turbulent Flow

Average film temp, °F	-100	0	100	200	300	400	500
Acetone	7.16	8.54	6.69	8.09	9.63	11.4	13.1
Acetylene	6.97	7.71	9.92	11.2	12.4	13.6	
Air	8.34	10.4	8.38	8.96	9.46	9.88	10.2
Ammonia			12.1	13.4	14.6	15.7	16.8
Benzene		8.05	9.47	10.0	12.4	13.9	16.4
Butane	4.62	5.57	6.32	6.95	7.59	8.15	8.73
Carbon dioxide	6.91	7.68	8.42	9.10	9.79	10.4	11.0
Carbon monoxide	2.85	3.12	3.39	3.63	3.86	4.06	4.27
Chlorine			3.46	3.94	4.46	5.02	5.53
Chloroform	6.82	8.46	3.94	4.46	4.94		
Ethane			10.2	12.3	14.4	10.0	12.6
Ethyl acetate			6.42	7.85	9.38	11.1	11.7
Ethyl alcohol			9.10	9.75	10.5	7.16	8.37
Ethyl chloride	6.40	4.80	5.59	6.30	6.98	7.16	15.4
Ethylene	8.02	8.02	9.54	11.0	12.5	14.1	16.1
Ethyl ether	7.78	7.78	8.95	10.3	12.0	14.1	58.6
Helium	41.8	45.2	48.1	50.9	53.8	56.5	105
Hydrogen	75.5	82.4	88.8	94.2	97.7	101	7.75
Hydrogen sulfide	4.94	5.55	6.10	6.59	7.08	7.58	11.3
Methane	7.61	8.32	8.95	9.67	10.1	10.7	9.84
Methyl chloride	2.98	4.09	5.25	6.30	7.40	8.37	10.2
Nitric oxide	6.64	7.36	8.00	8.56	9.04	9.44	6.66
Nitrogen	7.38	8.06	8.67	9.18	9.63	9.87	9.89
Nitrous oxide	5.49	5.72	5.90	6.01	6.32	6.49	9.50
Oxygen	6.83	7.54	8.12	8.60	9.09	9.50	
Pentane, iso		7.40	8.91	10.6	12.1	14.4	14.0
Steam			9.97	11.1	12.1	13.1	5.10
Sulfur dioxide		3.42	3.83	4.21	4.52	4.79	

Case 13. Base Factors for Gases Heated Outside Single Horizontal Tubes, Natural Convection

Average film temp, °F	-100	0	100	200	300	400	500
Acetone	0.83	0.90	0.94	1.06	1.19	1.32	1.45
Acetylene	0.91	0.89	0.96	1.02	1.07	1.13	1.18
Air	0.82	0.88	0.88	0.87	0.85	0.84	0.83
Ammonia			0.94	0.99	1.04	1.08	1.12
Benzene		1.25	1.36	1.47	1.58	1.68	1.80
Butane	0.71	0.76	0.80	0.82	0.84	0.86	0.87
Carbon dioxide	0.86	0.86	0.80	0.82	0.84	0.86	0.87
Carbon monoxide		0.56	0.86	0.85	0.84	0.83	0.82
Chlorine			0.55	0.55	0.55	0.54	0.53
Chloroform	0.85	0.95	0.72	0.77	0.82	0.86	0.91
Ethane			1.06	1.16	1.26	1.36	1.45
Ethyl acetate			1.12	1.29	1.45	1.60	1.76
Ethyl alcohol			1.17	1.16	1.13	1.12	1.10
Ethyl chloride	0.79	0.86	0.84	0.89	0.94	0.98	1.08
Ethylene			0.95	1.04	1.11	1.19	1.26
Ethyl ether		1.94	1.42	1.57	1.72	1.88	2.02
Helium	2.02	1.94	1.88	1.84	1.82		
Hydrogen	2.44	2.39	2.34	2.30	2.25	2.21	2.16
Hydrogen sulfide		0.66	0.67	0.68	0.68		
Methane	1.04	1.15	1.21	1.27	1.33	1.39	1.44
Methyl chloride		0.61	0.71	0.79	0.87	0.95	1.03
Nitric oxide	0.86	0.91	0.85	0.84	0.82	0.81	0.79
Nitrogen	0.92	0.79	0.89	0.87	0.85	0.84	0.81
Nitrous oxide	0.86	0.91	0.75	0.71	0.68	0.65	
Oxygen	0.92	1.26	0.90	0.89	0.87	0.85	0.84
Pentane, iso			1.40	1.56	1.74	1.42	2.14
Steam			0.80	0.81	0.83	0.85	0.86
Sulfur dioxide			0.59	0.60	0.61	0.61	0.61

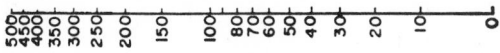

P = pressure, psig

F = correction factor

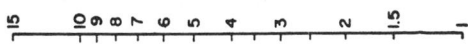

Case 13

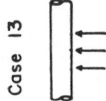

$\dfrac{\Delta t}{D_0} = \dfrac{\text{temperature difference between retaining wall and gas, °F}}{\text{outside tube diameter, in.}}$

D_0 = outside tube diameter, in.

Case 12

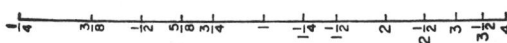

F = correction factor

$G = \dfrac{\text{rate of flow, lb/sec}}{\text{cross-sect. area ft}^2} = V\rho$ = velocity x density, (fps X lb/ft^3)

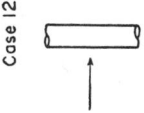

2–67

Table 2-14. Film Coefficients for Gases, Condensing Vapors, and Boiling Liquids (Continued)

Case 14. Gases Heated or Cooled Outside Tube Bundles, Direction of Flow Parallel to Tubes

Use Case 11 data, but substitute an equivalent diameter in determining correction factor as in Case 3.

Case 15. Gases Heated or Cooled Outside Tube Bundles, Direction of Flow Normal to Tubes

See Case 7. Instead of using data for Case 4 as directed in Case 7, use data from Case 12 and correct in the same way.

Case 16. Gases Heated or Cooled in Annular Spaces, Turbulent Flow

Use data for Case 11 but substitute an equivalent diameter as described in Case 8.

Case 17. Gases Heated or Cooled Outside Coils, Natural or Forced Convection

Coefficients for these cases are approximately the same as for Cases 12 or 13, and these data should be used.

Case 18. Base Factors for Gases Heated Inside or Outside Vertical Tubes or on Vertical Plates, Natural Convection

Average film temp., °F	−100	0	100	200	300	400	500
Acetone	0.56	0.55	0.65	0.69	0.73	0.78	0.83
Acetylene	0.53		0.54	0.53	0.53	0.53	0.52
Air	0.50	0.49	0.46	0.43	0.41	0.39	0.38
Ammonia	0.50	0.50	0.50	0.49	0.49	0.48	0.48
Benzene		0.83	0.72	0.79	0.88	0.97	1.06
Butane			0.93	0.94	0.96	0.97	0.98
Carbon dioxide	0.49	0.48	0.47	0.46	0.45	0.44	0.43
Carbon monoxide	0.51	0.48	0.45	0.42	0.40	0.38	0.36
Chlorine		0.38	0.36	0.34	0.32	0.31	0.30
Chloroform			0.53	0.53	0.54	0.55	0.56
Ethane	0.57	0.59	0.61	0.63	0.65	0.67	0.69
Ethyl acetate			0.83	0.89	0.95	1.02	1.06
Ethyl alcohol			0.76	0.71	0.67	0.62	0.58
Ethyl chloride			0.56	0.55	0.54	0.54	0.53
Ethylene	0.62	0.54	0.55	0.56	0.58	0.59	0.60
Ethyl ether			1.03	1.05	1.11	1.17	1.24
Helium	0.83	0.74	0.69	0.65	0.62		
Hydrogen sulfide	1.04	0.95	0.88	0.82	0.77	0.72	0.68
Methane	0.46	0.41	0.39	0.37	0.35		
Methyl chloride		0.45	0.44	0.43	0.42	0.41	0.40
Nitric oxide	0.52	0.48	0.45	0.42	0.40	0.37	0.35
Nitrogen	0.54	0.49	0.46	0.43	0.40	0.38	0.35
Nitrous oxide	0.55	0.49	0.44	0.40	0.37	0.34	
Oxygen	0.54	0.50	0.47	0.44	0.41	0.39	0.37
Pentane, iso		0.99	1.01	1.05	1.18	1.20	1.30
Steam				0.42	0.41	0.40	0.39
Sulfur dioxide			0.38	0.36	0.35	0.34	0.33

Case 19. Base Factors for Condensation of Pure Saturated Vapors on Horizontal Tubes

Temperature of condensate film (assume equal to tube wall), °F	50	100	150	200	250	300
Acetic acid		511	495	470	424	373
Acetone	772	789	805	805	795	780
Ammonia	2,768	3,145	3,459	3,711	3,875	3,965
Aniline	375	405	544	685	830	977
Benzene	554	609	658	706	755	798
Carbon disulfide	924	933	933	924	905	868
Carbon tetrachloride	551	580	569	482		
Chloroform	735	791	847	895	950	997
Ethyl acetate	702	772	835	889	936	990
Ethyl alcohol	495	556	618	678	745	807
Ethyl ether	620	646	665	678	691	705
Heptane	488	537	580	607	628	645
Hexane	595	552	576	592	608	614
Methyl alcohol	695	772	850	920	972	103
Octane	488	513	538	554	575	585
Propyl alcohol, iso	284	400	488	548	596	632
Steam	1,830	2,440	3,020	3,590	4,120	4,660
Sulfur dioxide	1,260	1,200	1,115	1,010	900	780

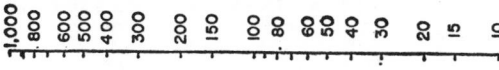

W= rate of condensation per sq ft of tube surface, $lb/(ft^2)(hr)$

Case 19
Condensing

F= correction factor

ND_o= number of tubes arranged directly over each other X outside tube diameter, in.

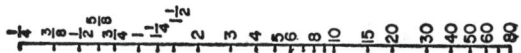

P= pressure, psig

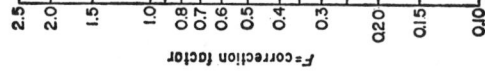

F= correction factor

Case 18

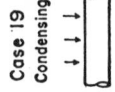

Δt= temperature difference between refilming wall and gas, °F

Table 2-14. Film Coefficients for Gases, Condensing Vapors, and Boiling Liquids (Continued)

Case 20. Liquids Boiling on Horizontal or Vertical Plates

Use nomograph for Case 20. For water boiling at pressures other than atmospheric multiply by the following correction factor:

Abs press., atm...	0.2	0.4	0.6	0.8	1.0	2.0	4.0	6.0	8.0	10.5	15.0
Correction factor...	0.62	0.78	0.88	0.94	1.00	1.16	1.32	1.40	1.46	1.51	1.60

Case 21. Gases Heated or Cooled Inside Coils, Turbulent Flow

Use the following equation: $h_{coils} = [1 + 3.54 (d/d_c)] \times h_{tubes}$, where d is the inside diameter of the pipe or tube in inches, d_c is the diameter of the coil in inches, and h_{tubes} is the straight-tube coefficient, from Case 11.

Case 22. Air Heated on Horizontal Plates, Natural Convection

For large plates (3 ft² or more) get coefficient from Case 18 and multiply by 1.27 for horizontal plates facing downward or by 0.67 for plates facing upward. If radiation is an important factor, a combined coefficient can be obtained by adding the product of the emissivity of the surface and the radiation coefficient, which is defined as $h_1 = 0.173 \times 10^{-8} (T_1^4 - T_2^4) \div (T_1 - T_2)$, where T_1 is the temperature of the emitting surface and T_2 is the temperature of the absorbing surface, both in degrees Fahrenheit absolute.

Case 23. Liquids Boiling Inside Tubes

When liquid moves by natural convection only, use coefficient from Case 20 and multiply by 1.25. If liquid moves at high velocity, use coefficient from Case 1, since conditions then are as if there were no evaporation.

SOURCE: H. J. Stoever, *Chem. & Met. Eng.*, 51(5): (1944). Reproduced by permission of H. J. Stoever.

Use the h for free convection on vertical surfaces if it is larger than the h obtained from this nomograph.

Case 20 Boiling

h = film coefficient, Btu/(ft²)(hr)(°F)

Δt = temperature difference between retaining wall and liquid, °F

Water · Ammonia · Ethyl acetate · Carbon disulfide · Carbon tetrachloride · Methyl alcohol · Ethyl alcohol

Table 2-15. Heat-transfer Coefficients h_d for Scale Deposits from Water

Fluid	Scale coefficient h_d
Sea water....	2,000
Brackish water....	500
Cooling tower with treated make-up....	1,000
Cooling tower with untreated make-up....	333
City water, Great Lakes water, well water....	1,000
River water....	500
Mississippi, Delaware, Schuylkill, and East Rivers, New York Bay....	333
Muddy or silty water....	333
Hard water (>15 grains/gal)....	333
Engine jacket or treated boiler feed water....	1,000
Distilled water....	2,000
Boiler blowdown....	500
Fuel oil....	200
Clean recirculating oil....	1,000
Quenching oil....	250
Organic vapors and non-oil-bearing steam....	2,000
Exhaust steam with oil from reciprocating engines....	1,000
Air....	500
Organic liquids....	1,000
Refrigerating liquids, brine....	1,000

SOURCE: "Standards of Tubular Exchanger Manufacturers Association," TEMA, New York, 1952.

Table 2-16. The Normal Total Emissivity of Various Surfaces

Metals and Their Oxides

Surface	t, °F*	Emissivity*
Aluminum:		
Highly polished plate, 98.3% pure	440–1,070	0.039–0.057
Polished plate	73	0.040
Rough plate	78	0.055
Oxidized at 1110°F	390–1,110	0.11–0.19
Al-surfaced roofing	100	0.216
Calorized surfaces, heated at 1110°F:		
Copper	390–1,110	0.18–0.19
Steel	390–1,110	0.52–0.57
Brass:		
Highly polished:		
73.2 Cu, 26.7 Zn	476–674	0.028–0.031
62.4 Cu, 36.8 Zn, 0.4 Pb, 0.3 Al	494–710	0.033–0.037
82.9 Cu, 17.0 Zn	530	0.030
Polished	100–600	0.096
Rolled plate, natural surface	72	0.06
Rolled plate, rubbed with coarse emery	72	0.20
Dull plate	120–660	0.22
Oxidized by heating at 1110°F	390–1,110	0.61–0.59
Chromium (see nickel alloys for Ni-Cr steels)	100–1,000	0.08–0.26
Copper:		
Carefully polished electrolytic	176	0.018
Plate, heated long time, covered with thick oxide layer	77	0.78
Plate heated at 1110°F	390–1,110	0.57
Cuprous oxide	1,470–2,010	0.66–0.54
Molten copper	1,970–2,330	0.16–0.13
Gold:		
Pure, highly polished	440–1,160	0.018–0.035
Iron and steel:		
Metallic surfaces (or very thin oxide layer):		
Electrolytic iron, highly polished	350–440	0.052–0.064
Polished iron	800–1,880	0.144–0.377
Oxidized surfaces:		
Iron plate, pickled, then rusted red	68	0.612
Iron plate, pickled, then completely rusted	67	0.685
Rolled sheet steel	70	0.657
Oxidized iron	212	0.736
Cast iron, oxidized at 1100°F	390–1,110	0.64–0.78
Steel, oxidized at 1100°F	390–1,110	0.79
Smooth oxidized electrolytic iron	260–980	0.78–0.82
Iron oxide	930–2,190	0.85–0.89
Rough ingot iron	1,700–2,040	0.87–0.95
Wrought iron, dull oxidized	70–680	0.94
Steel plate, rough	100–700	0.94–0.97
High-temp alloy steels (see nickel alloys)		
Molten metal:		
Cast iron	2,370–2,550	0.29
Mild steel	2,910–3,270	0.28
Lead:		
Pure (99.96%), unoxidized	260–440	0.057–0.075
Gray oxidized	75	0.281
Oxidized at 390°F	390	0.63
Mercury	32–212	0.09–0.12
Molybdenum filament	1,340–4,700	0.096–0.292
Monel metal, oxidized at 1110°F	390–1,110	0.41–0.46
Nickel:		
Electroplated on polished iron, then polished	74	0.045
Technically pure (98.9 Ni + Mn), polished	440–710	0.07–0.087
Electroplated on pickled iron, not polished	68	0.11
Wire	368–1,844	0.096–0.186
Plate, oxidized by heating at 1110°F	390–1,110	0.37–0.48
Nickel oxide	1,200–2,290	0.59–0.86
Nickel alloys:		
Chromnickel	125–1,894	0.64–0.76
Nickelin (18–32 Ni, 55–68 Cu, 20 Zn), gray oxidized	70	0.262
Platinum:		
Pure, polished plate	440–1,160	0.054–0.104
Strip	1,700–2,960	0.12 –0.17
Filament	80–2,240	0.036–0.192
Wire	440–2,510	0.073–0.182

Table 2-16. The Normal Total Emissivity of
Various Surfaces (Continued)

Metals and Their Oxides

Surface	t, °F*	Emissivity*
Silver:		
Polished, pure..	440–1,160	0.0198–0.0324
Polished...	100–700	0.0221–0.0312
Steel, see iron.		
Tantalum filament......................................	2,420–5,430	0.194–0.31
Tin, bright tinned iron sheet.............................	76	0.043 and 0.064
Tungsten:		
Filament, aged..	80–6,000	0.032–0.35
Filament...	6,000	0.39
Zinc:		
Commercial, 99.1%, polished..........................	440–620	0.045–0.053
Oxidized by heating at 750°F..........................	750	0.11
Galvanized sheet iron, fairly bright....................	82	0.228
Galvanized sheet iron, gray oxidized...................	75	0.276

Refractories, Building Materials, Paints, and Miscellaneous

Surface	t, °F*	Emissivity*
Asbestos:		
Board..	74	0.96
Paper..	100–700	0.93–0.945
Brick:		
Red, rough, but no gross irregularities..................	70	0.93
Silica, unglazed, rough...............................	1,832	0.80
Silica, glazed, rough..................................	2,012	0.85
Grog brick, glazed....................................	2,012	0.75
See also refractory materials		
Carbon:		
T carbon (Gebr. Siemens) 0.9% ash. This started with emissivity at 260°F of 0.72, but on heating changed to values given...	260–1,160	0.81–0.79
Carbon filament......................................	1,900–2,560	0.526
Candle soot..	206–520	0.952
Lampblack, waterglass coating........................	209–362	0.959–0.947
	260–440	0.957–0.952
Thin layer on iron plate............................	69	0.927
Thick coat...	68	0.967
Lampblack, 0.003 in. or thicker........................	100–700	0.945
Enamel, white fused, on iron...........................	66	0.897
Glass, smooth...	72	0.937
Gypsum, 0.02 in. thick on smooth or blackened plate.......	70	0.903
Marble, light gray, polished...........................	72	0.931
Oak, planed..	70	0.895
Oil layers on polished nickel (lub. oil)...................	68	
Polished surface, alone...............................	....	0.045
+0.001-in. oil......................................	....	0.27
+0.002-in. oil......................................	....	0.46
+0.005-in. oil......................................	....	0.72
∞ thick oil layer....................................	....	0.82
Oil layers on aluminum foil (linseed oil):		
Aluminum foil.......................................	212	0.087
+1 coat oil..	212	0.561
+2 coats oil.......................................	212	0.574
Paints, lacquers, varnishes		
Snow-white enamel varnish on rough iron plate..........	73	0.906
Black shiny lacquer, sprayed on iron...................	76	0.875
Oil paints, sixteen different, all colors.................	212	0.92–0.96
Aluminum paints and lacquers		
10% Al, 22% lacquer body, on rough or smooth surface.	212	0.52
Paper, thin:		
Pasted on tinned iron plate...........................	66	0.924
Pasted on rough iron plate............................	66	0.929
Pasted on black lacquered plate.......................	66	0.944

Table 2-16. The Normal Total Emissivity of Various Surfaces (Continued)

Refractories, Building Materials, Paints and Miscellaneous

Surface	t, °F*	Emissivity*
Plaster, rough lime....................................	50–190	0.91
Porcelain, glazed.....................................	72	0.924
Quartz, rough, fused..................................	70	0.932
Refractory materials, 40 different.......................	1,110–1,830	
Poor radiators.....................................	....	0.65–0.70 to 0.75
Good radiators.....................................	....	0.80–0.85 to 0.85–0.90
Roofing paper..	69	0.91
Rubber:		
Hard, glossy plate.................................	74	0.945
Soft, gray, rough (reclaimed)......................	76	0.859
Serpentine, polished.................................	74	0.900
Water...	32–212	0.95–0.963

* When two temperatures and two emissivities are given, they correspond, first to first and second to second, and linear interpolation is permissible.

PHYSICAL, CHEMICAL, AND MECHANICAL PROPERTIES

Richard F. Eisenberg, M.S. Met. E.; Associate Professor of Metallurgy, College of Engineering and Applied Science, University of Rochester; Member, American Society for Metals, American Institute of Metallurgical Engineers

Robert H. Perry, Ph.D.; Professor of Chemical Engineering, University of Rochester; Member, American Society for Engineering Education, American Association for the Advancement of Science

CONTENTS

PHYSICAL PROPERTIES OF ELEMENTS AND COMPOUNDS
Abbreviations used in Tables 3–1 and 3–2

alk.	alkali (i.e., aqueous NaOH or KOH)	g.	gas
aq.	aqueous	gly.	glycerol (glycerin)
bz.	benzene	h.	hot
c.	crystalline	i.	insoluble
cc	cubic centimeter	l.	liquid
chl.	chloroform	s.	soluble
conc.	concentrated	sl.	slightly
d.	decomposes	subl.	sublimes
dil.	dilute	v.	very
et.	ethyl ether	∞	soluble in all proportions

Formula weights are based upon the International Atomic Weights of 1941 and are computed to the nearest hundredth.

Melting point is recorded in certain cases as d. 82 to indicate that decomposition occurs at 82°F. Where a value such as $-2H_2O$, 82 is given, it indicates loss of 2 moles of water per formula weight of the compound at a temperature of 82°F.

Boiling point is given at atmospheric pressure unless otherwise indicated, thus $82^{15\,mm}$ indicates the boiling point is 82°F when the pressure is 15 mm Hg.

Solubility is given in parts by weight (of the formula shown at the extreme left) per 100 parts by weight of the solvent; the small superscript indicates the temperature. In the case of gases the solubility is often expressed in the manner of $5cc^{70}$, which indicates that, at 70°F, 5 cc of the gas is soluble in 100 g of the solvent. The symbols of the common mineral acids represent dilute aqueous solutions of the acids.

Table 3-1. Physical Properties of Inorganic Elements and Compounds
Common Synonyms

Common Name	Chemical Name	Common Name	Chemical Name
Anhydrite.............	Calcium sulfate	Lunar caustic .	Silver nitrate
Arcanite..............	Potassium sulfate	Mascagnite ...	Ammonium sulfate
Barytes...............	Barium sulfate	Nitrobarite....	Barium nitrate
Blue vitriol	Cupric sulfate	Nitrocalcite ...	Calcium nitrate
Calcite...............	Calcium carbonate	Paramelaconite	Cupric oxide
Caustic (soda or potash)	Sodium hydroxide	Prussic acid ...	Hydrocyanic acid
Celestite..............	Strontium sulfate	Rutile	Titanium oxide
Chalcanthite..........	Cupric sulfate	Salammoniac..	Ammonium chloride
Chromic acid..........	Chromium trioxide	Sal soda	Sodium carbonate (hydrated)
Epsomite (epsom salts).	Magnesium sulfate		
Fluorite..............	Calcium fluoride	Soda ash.	Sodium carbonate (anhydrous)
Glauber salt...........	Sodium sulfate		
Glucinum.............	Beryllium	Soda niter	Sodium nitrate
Gypsum..............	Calcium sulfate	Titania	Titanium oxide (di-)
Hydrophilite..........	Calcium chloride	Witherite	Barium carbonate

3–4

Table 3-1. Physical Properties of Inorganic Elements and Compounds (Continued)

Compound	Formula	Mol wt	Sp gr 60°/60°	Mp, °F	Heat of fusion, Btu/lb	Bp, °F	Heat of vaporization at bp, Btu/lb
Aluminum	Al	26.97	2.702	1220	170.2	3272	3591
Ammonia	NH₃	17.03	0.771	-107.9	142.9	-28.03	589.9
Ammonium bicarbonate	NH₄HCO₃	79.06	1.58	225.5		subl.	
Ammonium carbonate	(NH₄)₂CO₃·H₂O	114.11		d. 136			
Ammonium chloride	NH₄Cl	53.05	1.527	subl. 635			
Ammonium formate	NH₄CHO₂	63.06	1.266	241		d. 356	
Ammonium hydroxide	NH₄OH	35.05		-107			
Ammonium nitrate	NH₄NO₃	80.05	1.725	337	32.8	d. 410	
Ammonium phosphate:							
Monobasic	(NH₄)₂HPO₄	132.11	1.619	d.		d.	
Dibasic	NH₄H₂PO₄	115.08	1.803				
Meta	NH₄PO₃	388.08	2.21				
Ammonium sulfamate	NH₄SO₃NH₂	114.12	1.769	d. 212		d. 320	
Ammonium sulfate	(NH₄)₂SO₄	132.14		270			
Antimony	Sb	121.76	6.684	1167	70.5	2516	671
Argon	A	39.94		-308.5	13.07	-302.2	71.66
Arsenic	As	299.64	5.7	subl. 1497 (36 atm)	9.9	subl. 1139	199
Arsenious oxide	As₄O₆	395.64	3.865	subl.	36.4	-208.4	467.4
Barium	Ba	137.36	3.5	1562	18.34		
Barium carbonate	BaCO₃	197.37	4.29		40.6	d. 2642	
Barium nitrate	Ba(NO₃)₂	261.38	3.244	1098	74.8	d.	
Barium sulfate	BaSO₄	233.42	4.499	d. 2876			
Beryllium	Be	9.02	1.816	2343	499.	5013	397
Bismuth	Bi	209.00	9.80	520	21.57	2642	
Boric acid	H₃BO₃	61.84	1.435	d. 365			
Boron	B	10.82	2.32	4172		4622	
Bromine	Br₂	159.83	3.119	19.04	29.05	137.8	83.6
Cadmium	Cd	112.41	8.65	610	23.4	1413	382.2
Calcium	Ca	40.08	1.55	1490	100.1	2192	1,643
Calcium acetate	Ca(C₂H₃O₂)₂·H₂O	176.18		d.			
Calcium carbonate	CaCO₃	100.09	2.711	2442			
Calcium chloride	CaCl₂	110.99	2.152	1422	228.3	>2900	
Calcium fluoride	CaF₂	78.08	3.180	2426	98.9		
Calcium hydroxide	Ca(OH)₂	74.10	2.2	-H₂O 1075	94.5		
Calcium nitrate	Ca(NO₃)₂	236.16	1.82	108.9	39.0		
Calcium phosphate:							
Monobasic	CaH₄(PO₄)₂·H₂O	252.09	2.22	-H₂O 212			
Dibasic	CaHPO₄·2 H₂O	172.10	2.306	d.		d. 392	
Tribasic	Ca₃(PO₄)₂	310.20	3.14	3038			

3-5

Table 3-1. Physical Properties of Inorganic Elements and Compounds (Continued)

Compound	Heat of formation Btu/lb mole at 77°F	Free energy of formation Btu/lb mole at 77°F	Solubility, g/100 ml solvent — Water	Alcohol	Ether, etc.	Critical temp, °F	Critical press, atm	Critical density lb/ft³
Aluminum	0 (c.)	0 (c.)	i.	i.	s. HCl, H_2SO_4, alk.			
Ammonia	−19,728 (g.)	−6,665 (g.)	89.9^{32}	13.2^{68}	s. et.	270.1	111.3	14.7
Ammonium bicarbonate	.....	.....	11.9^{32}	i.	i. acetone			
Ammonium carbonate	−402,120 (aq.)	−295,380 (aq.)	100^{59}	i.	i. CS_2, NH_3			
Ammonium chloride	−135,400 (c.)	−87,460 (c.)	29.7^{32}	0.06^{66}	s. NH_3			
Ammonium formate	.....	.....	102^{52}	s.	s. NH_3			
Ammonium hydroxide	−157,660 (aq.)	.....	s.		17.1^{68} methanol; i. et.			
Ammonium nitrate	−157,320 (c.)	.....	118.3^{32}	3.8^{68}				
Ammonium phosphate:								
Monobasic	.....	.....	42.9^{32}	i.	i. acetone			
Dibasic	.....	.....	22.7^{32}		i. acetone			
Meta	.....	.....	s.					
Ammonium sulfamate	.....	.....	134^{32}	i.	i. NH_3, acetone			
Ammonium sulfate	−507,130 (c.)	−387,108 (c.)	76.6^{32}	i.	s. hot conc. H_2SO_4			
Antimony	0 (c.)	0 (c.)	i.	i.				
Argon	0 (g.)	0 (g.)	$5.06\ cc^{32}$		s. HNO_3, hot alk.	−188	48.0	33.2
Arsenic	0 (c.)	0 (c.)	i.	i.	i. et.			
Arsenious oxide	−554,760 (c.)	−485,280 (c.)	sl.s.	d.				
Barium	0 (c.)	0 (c.)	d.	i.	s. dil. acid			
Barium carbonate	−511,560 (c.)	−488,520 (c.)	0.0022^{34}	i.	s. HNO_3			
Barium nitrate	−426,582 (c.)	−341,890 (c.)	5.0^{32}	i.	0.24^{77} et, 22.2^{86} gly.			
Barium sulfate	−612,360 (c.)	−564,120 (c.)	0.000115^{32}		s. HNO_3			
Beryllium	0 (c.)	0 (c.)	i.		s. et, alk.			
Bismuth	0 (c.)	0 (c.)	i.		s. acid			
Boric acid	.....	.....	6.35^{32}	s.	s. acid			
Boron	0 (c.)	0 (c.)	i.	i.				
Bromine	0 (l.)	0 (l.)	4.22^{32}	s.		592	102	73.7
Cadmium	0 (c.)	0 (c.)	i.		s. acid, NH_4Cl			
Calcium	0 (c.)	0 (c.)	d.	sl.s.				
Calcium acetate	−655,380 (aq.)	−560,340 (aq.)	37.4^{32}	sl.s.				
Calcium carbonate	−521,100 (c.)	−487,440 (c.)	0.0014^{77}		s. acid, NH_4Cl			
Calcium chloride	−343,100 (c.)	−323,600 (c.)	59.5^{32}	s.				
Calcium fluoride	−522,400 (c.)	.....	0.0016^{64}		s. NH_4Cl			
Calcium hydroxide	−424,040 (c.)	−385,000 (c.)	0.1852^{32}					
Calcium nitrate	−403,290 (c.)	−319,280 (c.)	266^{32}	s.				
Calcium phosphate:								
Monobasic	.....	.....						
Dibasic	.....	.....	0.02^{76}					
Tribasic	.....	.....	0.0025	i.	i. acetic acid			

Table 3-1. Physical Properties of Inorganic Elements and Compounds (Continued)

Compound	Formula	Mol wt	Sp gr 60/60°	Mp, °F	Heat of fusion, Btu/lb	Bp, °F	Heat of vaporization at bp, Btu/lb
Calcium sulfate (anhydrite)	CaSO$_4$	136.14	2.96	2642	88.6	$-2\ H_2O$ 325	
Calcium sulfate (gypsum)	CaSO$_4$·2 H$_2$O	172.17	2.32	$-1\frac{1}{2}\ H_2O$ 262		7600	
Carbon, amorphous	C	12.01	1.8–2.1	>6300	1649	7600	
Carbon, graphite	C	12.01	2.26	>6300			
Carbon dioxide	CO$_2$	44.01	1.10^{-35}	-69.9	77.7	subl. -109.3	246.6
Carbon disulfide	CS$_2$	76.13	1.261	-163.5	24.8	115.3	92.8
Carbon monoxide	CO	28.01	0.814^{-319}	-341	12.85	-314	123.8
Cerium	Ce	140.13	6.9	1193	27.2	2552	
Chlorine	Cl$_2$	70.91	$1.56^{-28.5}$	-150.9	38.9	-30.3	
Chromium	Cr	52.01	7.1	2939	136.0	3992	
Chromium trioxide	CrO$_3$	100.01	2.70	d. 386.6			
Cobalt	Co	58.94	8.9	2696	111.8	5250	2,061
Copper	Cu	63.59	8.92	1981	88.03	4172	
Cupric oxide	CuO	79.57	6.40	d. 1880	63.8		
Cupric sulfate	CuSO$_4$·5 H$_2$O	249.71	2.286	$-4\ H_2O$ 230		$-5\ H_2O$ 480	
Ferric chloride	FeCl$_3$·6 H$_2$O	270.32		99		536	
Ferric sulfate	Fe$_2$(SO$_4$)$_3$	399.88	3.097	d. 900			747
Gold	Au	197.20	19.3	1945	27.6	4700	
Hydrazine	N$_2$H$_4$	32.05	1.011	34.5		236.3	
Hydrazine hydrate	N$_2$H$_4$·H$_2$O	50.06	1.03	-40		245.3	
Hydrobromic acid	HBr	80.92		-123	12.8	-89	93.6
Hydrochloric acid	HCl	36.47		-168	23.49	-121	190.5
Hydrocyanic acid	HCN	27.03	0.697	6.8	133.8	78.8	401.4
Hydrofluoric acid	HF	20.01	0.988	-117	98.4	66.9	671
Hydrogen	H$_2$	2.016	0.0709^{-423}	-434.4	25.00	-422.9	192.8
Hydrogen peroxide	H$_2$O$_2$	34.02	1.438	30.4	133	304.5	543
Hydrogen sulfide	H$_2$S	34.08		-117.2	30	-75.3	235.7
Hydroxylamine	NH$_2$OH	33.03	1.35	93.2			
Iodine	I$_2$	253.84	4.93	236.3	25.9	363.8	73.7
Iron	Fe	55.85	7.86	2795	86.4	5432	2926
Lead	Pb	207.21	11.337	621.5	10.6	2948	365
Lead chromate	PbCrO$_4$	323.22	6.12	1551		d.	
Lead formate	Pb(HCO$_2$)$_2$	297.25	4.56	d. 375			
Lead nitrate	Pb(NO$_3$)$_2$	331.23	4.53	d. 880			
Lithium	Li	6.94	0.53	367	285	2435	8,364
Magnesium	Mg	24.32	1.74	1204	160	2030	2,407
Magnesium sulfate	MgSO$_4$·7 H$_2$O	246.49	1.68	d. 158			
Manganese	Mn	54.93	7.20	2300	113	3450	1,807
Mercury	Hg	200.61	13.546	-38	5.00	674.4	125.4
Molybdenum	Mo	95.95	10.2	4750	124	6690	2,400
Nickel	Ni	58.69	8.90	2645	129	5250	2,677
Nickel sulfate	NiSO$_4$·6 H$_2$O	262.85	2.07			$-6\ H_2O$ 536	
Nitric acid	HNO$_3$	63.02	1.52	-44	17.1	187	85.8
Nitrogen	N$_2$	28.02	0.808^{-320}	-345.8	11.05	-320	85.8
Nitric oxide	NO	30.01	$1.269^{-238.4}$	-258	33.0	-240	198.3

Table 3-1. Physical Properties of Inorganic Elements and Compounds (Continued)

Compound	Heat of formation Btu/lb mole at 77°F	Free energy of formation at 77°F	Solubility, g/100 ml solvent			Critical temp., °F	Critical press., atm	Critical density lb/ft²
			Water	Alcohol	Ether, etc.			
Calcium sulfate (anhydrite)	−605,840 (c.)	−557,640 (c.)	0.298^{68}	....	s. acid			
Calcium sulfate (gypsum)	−862,790 (c.)	−765,850 (c.)	0.223^{32}	....	s. acid			
Carbon, amorphous	0 (c.)	0	i.	i.				
Carbon, graphite	0 (c.)	0	i.	i.				
Carbon dioxide	−169,294 (g.)	−169,668 (g.)	$179.7\ cc^{32}$	....	s. acid, alk.	87.8	72.9	29.2
Carbon disulfide	+50,600 (g.)	+29,030 (g.)	0.2^{12}	s.	s. et.	221	61	18.8
Carbon monoxide	−47,549 (g.)	−59,054 (g.)	0.0044^{32}	s.	s. Cu_2Cl_2	−220	34.5	
Cerium	0 (g.)	0 (g.)	i.	....	s. dil. acid			
Chlorine	0 (g.)	0 (g.)	1.46^{32}	s.	s. alk.	291	76.1	35.8
Chromium	0 (c.)	0 (c.)	i.	....	s. HCl			
Chromium trioxide	−250,740 (c.)		164.9^{32}	s.	s. H_2SO_4, et.			
Cobalt	0 (c.)	0 (c.)	i.	....	s. acid			
Copper	0 (c.)	0 (c.)	i.	....	s. HNO_3			
Cupric oxide	−69,300 (c.)	−57,400 (c.)	i.	....	s. acid			
Cupric sulfate	−361,400 (aq.)	−288,340 (aq.)	24.3^{32}	$1.1^{37.4}$	s. acetone			
Ferric chloride	−231,300 (aq.)	−173,700 (aq.)	246^{32}	s.	i. H_2SO_4, NH_3			
Ferric sulfate	−1,176,000 (aq.)	−960,100 (c.)	sl.s.	i.	s. aqua regia		145	
Gold	0 (c.)	0 (c.)	i.	i.	i. et.	716		
Hydrazine	+21,710 (l.)		∞	∞				
Hydrazine hydrate	−104,330 (l.)		∞	∞				
Hydrobromic acid	−15,590 (g.)	−22,900 (g.)	221^{12}	s.	s. et.	194.0	84.0	26
Hydrochloric acid	−39,710 (g.)	−41,000 (g.)	82.3^{32}	s.	∞ et.	124.5	81.5	12.2
Hydrocyanic acid	+55,980 (g.)	+50,290 (g.)	∞	∞		362.3	53.2	
Hydrofluoric acid	−115,600 (g.)	−116,500 (g.)	∞	i.		446.4		
Hydrogen	0 (g.)	0 (g.)	$2.1\ cc^{32}$	i.	sl.s. Fe, Pd, Pt	−399.8	12.8	1.94
Hydrogen peroxide	−81,290 (l.)	−50,810 (g.)	∞	∞	i. et.			
Hydrogen sulfide	−8,590 (g.)	−14,130 (g.)	$437\ cc^{32}$	$9.54\ cc^{59}$	s. CS_2	212.7	88.9	21.8
Hydroxylamine			s.	s.	s. acid	954		
Iodine	0 (c.)	0 (c.)	0.0162^{22}	s.	s. et.			
Iron	0 (c.)	0 (c.)	i.	i.	s. acid; i. alk.			
Lead	0 (c.)	0 (c.)	i.		s. HNO_3			
Lead chromate			0.0000076^{68}	....	s. acid, alk.			
Lead formate			1.6^{91}	....				
Lead nitrate	−192,380 (c.)		38.8^{32}	i.	s. acid, NH_3			
Lithium	0 (c.)	0 (c.)	d.	8.8^{72}	s. acid			
Magnesium	0 (c.)	0 (c.)	i.	i.				
Magnesium sulfate	−585,700 (aq.)	−510,980 (aq.)	72.4^{32}	s.				
Manganese	0 (c.)	0 (c.)	d.	....	s. dil. acid			
Mercury	0 (l.)	0 (l.)	i.	....	s. HNO_3			
Molybdenum	0 (c.)	0 (c.)	i.	....	s. hot conc. H_2SO_4			
Nickel	0 (c.)	0 (c.)	i.	....	s. dil. HNO_3			
Nickel sulfate	−416,340 (aq.)	−337,680 (aq.)	131^{22}	....	v.s. NH_4OH			
Nitric acid	−74,430 (l.)	−34,290 (l.)	∞	v.s., explodes				
Nitrogen	0 (g.)	0 (g.)	$2.35\ cc^{32}$	sl.s.		−232.6	33.5	14.4
Nitric oxide	+38,880 (g.)	+37,294 (g.)	$7.34\ cc^{32}$	26.6 cc				

Table 3-1. Physical Properties of Inorganic Elements and Compounds (Continued)

Compound	Formula	Mol wt	Sp gr 60°/60°	Mp, °F	Heat of fusion, Btu/lb	Bp, °F	Heat of vaporization at bp, Btu/lb
Nitrogen dioxide	NO_2	46.01	1.448^{68}	15.3	108.4	70.3	137.7
Nitrous oxide	N_2O	44.02	1.226^{-128}	-152.1	63.91	-131	161.5
Oxygen	O_2	32.00	1.14^{-297}	-361.1	5.96	-297	91.63
Ozone	O_3	48.00	1.71^{-297}	-420		-170	108
Phosphoric acid, meta	HPO_3	79.99	2.2-2.5	subl.			
Phosphoric acid, ortho	H_3PO_4	98.00	1.834	108.23	46.3	-½ H_2O 415	182
Phosphorous, yellow	P_4	123.92	1.82	111.4	8.93	536	131
Phosphoric oxide	P_2O_5	141.96	2.387	subl. 480	11.3		986
Platinum	Pt	195.23	21.45	3190	43.3	7770	921
Potassium	K	39.10	0.86	144	26.4	1400	
Potassium sulfate	K_2SO_4	174.25	2.662		83.7		
Silicic acid, ortho	H_4SiO_4	99.09	1.576				
Silicon	Si	28.06	2.4	2590	607.5	4700	72.7
Silicon chloride	$SiCl_4$	169.89	1.50	-94	19.5	135.7	1,013
Silver	Ag	107.88	10.5	1761	45.0	3542	
Silver nitrate	$AgNO_3$	169.89	4.352	414	29.2	d. 820	
Sodium	Na	22.997	0.97	207.5	49.3	1616	1,810
Sodium bicarbonate	$NaHCO_3$	84.01	2.20	$-CO_2$ 520			
Sodium carbonate (sal soda)	$Na_2CO_3 \cdot 10\ H_2O$	286.16	1.46	1564		d.	
Sodium carbonate (soda ash)	Na_2CO_3	106.00	2.533	1473	119	2575	1,257
Sodium chloride	$NaCl$	58.45	2.163	605	222	2534	
Sodium hydroxide	$NaOH$	40.00	2.13	586	90	d. 716	
Sodium nitrate	$NaNO_3$	85.01	2.257	1990	79.6		
Sodium silicate, meta	Na_2SiO_3	122.05		1864	152		
Sodium silicate, ortho	Na_4SiO_4	184.05					
Sodium sulfate	$Na_2SO_4 \cdot 10\ H_2O$	322.21	1.464	90.3		-10 H_2O 212	
Strontium nitrate	$Sr(NO_3)_2$	211.65	2.986	1058			
Strontium sulfate	$SrSO_4$	183.69	3.96	28.76			
Sulfamic acid	NH_2SO_3H	97.09	2.03	d. 400			
Sulfur, amorphous	S	32.06	2.046	248		832.3	
Sulfur, monoclinic	S_8	256.48	1.96	246		832.3	
Sulfur, rhombic	S_8	256.48	2.07	235	23.76	832.3	141.8
Sulfur dioxide	SO_2	64.06	1.434	-103.9	49.7	14.0	167.5
Sulfuric acid	H_2SO_4	98.08	0.834	50.88	43.3	d. 644	
Sulfurous acid	H_2SO_3	66.08					
Tantalum	Ta	180.88	16.6	5160		>7400	
Tellurium	Te	127.64	α 6.24 β 6.00	845	45.5	2534	

3-9

Table 3-1. Physical Properties of Inorganic Elements and Compounds (Continued)

Compound	Heat of formation Btu/lb mole at 77°F	Free energy of formation Btu/lb mole at 77°F	Solubility, g/100 ml solvent			Critical temp, °F	Critical press., atm	Critical density lb/ft³
			Water	Alcohol	Ether, etc.			
Nitrogen dioxide	+14,330 (g.)	+22,068 (g.)	d.	....	s. HNO_3			
Nitrous oxide	+35,190 (g.)	+44,680 (g.)	130.52 cc^{32}	s.	s. H_2SO_4	-181.1	50.1	26
Oxygen	0 (g.)	0 (c.)	4.89 cc^{32}	sl.s.	....	23	67	33.5
Ozone	+60,980 (g.)	+69,950 (g.)	0.494 cc^{32}	....	....			
Phosphoric acid, meta	....	....	s.	....	....			
Phosphoric acid, ortho	-536,780 (aq.)	-486,000 (aq.)	2340^{78}	0.04	1,000^{50} CS_2			
Phosphorous acid, yellow	-648,000 (c.)	....	0.0003	....	i. NH_3			
Phosphorous oxide	....	....	forms H_3PO_4	s.	s. aqua regia			
Platinum	0 (c.)	0 (c.)	i.	....	s. acid			
Potassium	0 (c.)	0 (c.)	d.	....	i. acetone			
Potassium sulfate	-605,660 (aq.)	-559,730 (aq.)	7.35^{32}	i.	s. alk.			
Silicic acid, ortho	-613,100 (c.)	....	sl.s.	....	....			
Silicon	....	0 (c.)	i.	d.	....			
Silicon chloride	-270,000 (l.)	-241,000 (c.)	d.	....	d. conc. H_2SO_4	451		
Silver	0 (c.)	0 (c.)	i.	v.sl.s.	s. HNO_3			
Silver nitrate	-52,900 (c.)	-13,790 (c.)	122^{32}	d.	s. gly.			
Sodium	0 (c.)	0 (c.)	forms NaOH	i.	i. bz.			
Sodium bicarbonate	-399,800 (aq.)	-365,166 (aq.)	6.9^{32}	i.	....			
Sodium carbonate (sal soda)	-495,230 (aq.)	-452,450 (aq.)	21.5^{32}	i.	i. et.			
Sodium carbonate (soda ash)	-485,030 (c.)	-449,190 (c.)	7.1^{22}	sl.s.	i. conc. HCl			
Sodium chloride	-176,980 (c.)	-165,409 (c.)	35.7^{32}	v.s.	v.s. et.			
Sodium hydroxide	-183,530 (c.)	-163,080 (c.)	42^{32}	sl.s.	s. NH_3			
Sodium nitrate	-210,780 (c.)	-157,720 (c.)	73^{32}	i.	....			
Sodium silicate, meta	....	....	s.	....	....			
Sodium silicate, ortho	....	....	....	i.	s. NH_3			
Sodium sulfate	-594,900 (c.)	-544,280 (c.)	3.6^{59}	0.012	sl.s. acids			
Strontium nitrate	-411,710 (aq.)	-334,260 (aq.)	40^{32}	i.	sl.s. acetone; i. et.			
Strontium sulfate	-621,000 (aq.)	-556,700 (aq.)	0.0113^{32}	sl.s.	sl.s. CS_2			
Sulfamic acid	....	....	20^{32}	s.	s. CS_2			
Sulfur, amorphous	-128 (c.)	-41 (c.)	i.	....	24^{22} CS_2	1,904	116	
Sulfur, monoclinic	....	....	i.	s.	s. acetone			
Sulfur, rhombic	....	....	i.	....	s. et.			
Sulfur dioxide	-127,690 (g.)	-129,025 (g.)	28.8^{32}	s.	i. HNO_3	315.5	77.8	32.7
Sulfurous acid	-381,650 (aq.)	....	∞	s.	s. HNO_3			
Sulfuric acid	-264,380 (aq.)	-231,370 (aq.)	s.	d.				
Tantalum	0 (c.)	0 (c.)	i.	....				
Tellurium	0 (c.)	0 (c.)	i.	....				

Table 3-1. Physical Properties of Inorganic Elements and Compounds (Continued)

Compound	Formula	Mol wt	Sp gr, 60°/60°	Mp, °F	Heat of fusion, Btu/lb	Bp, °F	Heat of vaporization at bp, Btu/lb
Tin...........	Sn	118.70	7.31	449.3	6.52	4100	258
Titanium.......	Ti	47.90	4.50	3270	.....	>5400	.....
Titanium dioxide..	TiO₂	79.90	4.26	d. 2980	257	.....	.....
Tungsten.......	W	183.92	19.3	6100	82.2	10,650	1,722
Uranium........	U	238.07	18.7	<3362	.....	.....	.....
Water..........	H₂O	18.016	1.00	32	143.5	212	972
Water, heavy....	D₂O	20.029	1.107	38.88	.....	214.56	.....
Zinc...........	Zn	65.38	7.140	787	43.9	1665	755
Zinc oxide.......	ZnO	81.38	5.47	>3270	98.9	.....	.....
Zirconium.......	Zr	91.22	6.4	3100	.....	>5250	.....

Table 3-1. Physical Properties of Inorganic Elements and Compounds (Continued)

Compound	Heat of formation Btu/lb mole at 77°F	Free energy of formation Btu/lb mole at 77°F	Solubility, g/100 ml solvent			Critical temp, °F	Critical press., atm	Critical density lb/ft³
			Water	Alcohol	Ether, etc.			
Tin............................	0 (c.)	0 (c.)	i.	.....	s. HCl			
Titanium.....................	0 (c.)	0 (c.)	i.	.....	s. acids			
Titanium dioxide...........	−405,000 (c.)	−381,400 (c.)	i.	.....	s. H_2SO_4			
Tungsten.....................	0 (c.)	0 (c.)	i.	.....	s. hot conc. KOH			
Uranium......................	0 (c.)	0 (c.)	i.	.....	s. acid; i. alk.			
Water.........................	−122,971 (l.)	−102,042 (l.)	∞	∞	s l.s. et.	705.6	218.3	20.
Water, heavy................	.... 0 (c.)	.... 0 (c.)	i.	.....	s l.s. et.			
Zinc..........................	0 (c.)	0 (c.)	i.	.....	s. acids, alk.			
Zinc oxide..................	−150,050 (c.)	−137,140 (c.)	0.0004[24]	.....	s. acids, alk.			
Zirconium..................	0 (c.)	0 (c.)	i.	.....	s. l.F			

Table 3-2. Physical Properties of Organic Compounds

Compound	Formula	Mol. wt	Sp gr, 60°/60°	Mp, °F	Heat of fusion, Btu/lb	Bp, °F	Heat of vaporization at bp, Btu/lb
Acetic acid	CH₃COOH	60.05	1.049	61.9	84.0	244.6	174.2
Acetic anhydride	(CH₃CO)₂O	102.09	1.087	-99.6		284.0	119.1
Acetone	CH₃COCH₃	58.08	0.792	-139.0	42.2	141.8	223
Acetylene	CH:CH	26.04	Gas	-114	41.5	-118.5 subl.	
Acrylonitrile	CH₂:CHCN	53.06	0.797	-115.6		173.0	
Adipic acid	COOH(CH₂)₄COOH	146.14	1.366	306		509.0	
Aniline	C₆H₅NH₂	93.12	1.022	-11.2	48.8	363.9	186.6
Anthracene	C₆H₄:(CH)₂:C₆H₄	178.22	1.25	423	69.7	669	
Benzene	C₆H₆	78.11	0.879	41.9	54.2	176.2	169.5
Butadiene-1,3	(CH:CH₂)₂	54.09	0.65	-164.0		24.1	
Butane	CH₃(CH₂)₂CH₃	58.12	0.60	-217	34.5	31.1	165.8
Butyl cellosolve	C₄H₉OCH₂CH₂OH	118.17	0.903			339	
Carbon dioxide	CO₂	44.01	Gas	-69.9	77.6	-109.3 subl.	246.6
Carbon monoxide	CO	28.01	Gas	-341	12.8	-310	93.8
Carbon tetrachloride	CCl₄	153.84	1.595	-9.1	74.8	168.8	83.6
Cellosolve	C₂H₅OCH₂CH₂OH	90.12	0.931			275.2	
Cellulose	(C₆H₁₀O₅)x	(162.14)x	1.27-1.61				
o-Cresol	CH₃C₆H₄OH	108.13	1.047	86		376.7	
m-Cresol	CH₃C₆H₄OH	108.13	1.034	52.7		397	181
p-Cresol	CH₃C₆H₄OH	108.13	1.035	96.8		396.5	
Cyclohexane	C₆H₁₂	84.16	0.779	43.8	47.3	177.3	153.7
Cyclohexanol	C₆H₁₁OH	100.16	0.962	75.2	13.6	322.7	194.8
Cyclohexene	C₆H₁₀	82.14	0.810	-154.7	7.5	181.4	
Dimethyl amine	(CH₃)₂NH	45.08	0.680	-140.8		45.3	
Dimethyl aniline	(CH₃)₂NC₆H₅	121.18	0.956	36.5		379	145.4
Dimethyl phthalate	C₆H₄(CO₂CH₃)₂	194.18	1.189			536	
Diphenyl	(C₆H₅)₂	154.20	1.18	158	51.8	490.1	
Diphenyl amine	(C₆H₅)₂NH	169.22	1.159	127	45.4	576	
Ethyl acetate	CH₃CO₂C₂H₅	88.10	0.901	-116.4	37.1	170.8	183.6
Ethyl benzene	C₆H₅C₂H₅	106.16	0.867	-138.9		277.2	145.8
Ethyl chloride	C₂H₅Cl	64.52	0.916	-218		55.4	166.5
Ethylene	C₂H₄	28.05	Gas	-272.4	51.4	-153.7	207.6
Ethylene dibromide	CH₂BrCH₂Br	187.88	2.180	50	24.3	268.7	83.2
Ethylene oxide	(CH₂)₂ > O	44.05	0.887	-168.4		56.3	249.4
Formaldehyde	HCHO	30.3	Gas	-133.6		5.8	
Formamide	HCONH₂	45.04	1.139	35.6		379.4	

Table 3-2. Physical Properties of Organic Compounds (Continued)

Compound	Heat of formation, Btu/lb mole at 77°F	Free energy of formation, Btu/lb mole at 77°F	Solubility, g/100 ml solvent			Critical temp, °F	Critical press, atm	Critical density, lb/ft³
			Water	Alcohol	Ether, etc.			
Acetic acid	−209,160	−168,408	∞	∞	∞ et., i. CS₂.	610.9	57.1	21.9
Acetic anhydride			13.6 d.	∞	∞ et.; s. chl.; s. bz.	565	46.2	
Acetone	−106,780	−66,890	∞	∞	∞ et.; s. chl.	455.9	46.6	17.0
Acetylene			100 cc[54]	600 cc[54]	2,500 cc acetone[64]; s. bz.; s. chl.	97	61.6	14.4
Acrylonitrile			s.	v.s.	∞ et.			
Adipic acid	−423,920	−318,910	1.5[59]	v.s.	v.sl. et.			
Aniline			3.4[48]	∞	∞ et.; bz.	798.1	52.3	21.2
Anthracene	+21,090	+53,560		0.076[61]	1.189 et.; 1.767 chl.			
Benzene			0.082[72]	v.s.	∞ et.; s. chl.	552	48.6	18.7
Butadiene-1,3					∞ et.	306	42.7	15.3
Butane	−53,660 (g.)	−6,760 (g.)	15 cc[63]	1,813 cc[63]	2,980 cc et.[63]	305.5	37.5	14.2
Butyl cellosolve			∞	∞				
Carbon dioxide	−169,294 (g.)	−169,668 (g.)	90.1 cc[68]	31 cc[59]	s. bz.	87.8	72.9	29.2
Carbon monoxide	−47,550 (g.)	−59,050 (g.)	3.5 cc[32]	20 cc[68]	∞ et., bz.	−220	34.5	18.8
Carbon tetrachloride			0.086[8]	∞		541.8	45.0	34.8
Cellosolve			∞	∞				
Cellulose			i.	i.	i. et.			
o-Cresol			2.35[68]	∞	∞ >[86] et.	792	49.4	
m-Cresol			2.4[04]	∞	∞ et.>[97]	810	45.0	22
p-Cresol				∞	∞ et.	799	50.8	
Cyclohexane	−67,210	+11,500		s.	s. et.	536	40.0	17.0
Cyclohexanol			5.67[99]	s.	v.s. et.			
Cyclohexene				s.	s. et.			
Dimethyl amine			v.s.		s. et.	328.1	52.4	
Dimethyl aniline			0.43		s. et.	778.5	35.8	
Dimethyl phthalate					s. et.			
Diphenyl			0.03[77]	10	s. et.			
Diphenyl amine	−199,300	−137,000		44	v.s. et.	482.2	37.8	19.2
Ethyl acetate	−5,360	+51,500	8.5[9]	∞	∞ et.	655.5	38	
Ethyl benzene			0.01[49]	∞	∞ et.	369.0	52	
Ethyl chloride			0.45[32]	360 cc	s. et.	48.6	50.0	14.2
Ethylene	+22,490 (g.)	+29,310 (g.)	26 cc[32]	∞	∞ et.			
Ethylene dibromide			0.43[98]	∞	∞ et.			
Ethylene oxide	−29,000	−12,500	∞	v.s.	v.s. et.	383	71.0	20
Formaldehyde	−50,920 (g.)	−48,380 (g.)	v.s.	∞	v.s. et.			
Formamide	−80,350	−65,880	∞		v.sl.s. et.			

Table 3-2. Physical Properties of Organic Compounds (Continued)

Compound	Formula	Mol. wt	Sp gr 60°/60°	Mp, °F	Heat of fusion, Btu/lb	Bp, °F	Heat of vaporization at bp, Btu/lb
Furfural	C_4H_3OCHO	96.08	1.159	-37.7		323.1	193.5
Glycerol	$CH_2OHCHOHCH_2OH$	92.09	1.260	64.2	85.5	554	
Glycerol nitrate	$CH_2NO_2CHNO_2CH_2NO_2$	227.09	1.601	55.9		320 (16 mm)	
Glycerol tristearate	$[CH_3(CH_2)_{16}CO_2]_3C_3H_5$	891.45	0.862	159.4			
Glycol	$(CH_2OH)_2$	62.07	1.113	3.9	77.8	387.3	
Hexamethylene-tetramine	$(CH_2)_6N_4$	140.19		subl.	65.0		143.9
n-Hexane	C_6H_{14}	86.17	0.659	-139.6		155.7	
Isoprene	$CH_2{:}CH(CH_3){:}CH_2$	68.11	0.681	-230.8		93.3	
Ketene	$H_2C{:}CO$	42.04	Gas	-240		-69	
Lauryl alcohol	$CH_3(CH_2)_{10}CH_2OH$	186.33	0.831	75		495	
Linoleic acid	$C_{17}H_{31}COOH$	280.44	0.903	14.9		445	
Maleic anhydride	$(CHCO)_2 > O$	98.06	1.5	137		396	
Methane	CH_4	16.04	Gas	-296.5	25.2	-258.6	219.2
Methyl alcohol	CH_3OH	32.04	0.792	-144	42.7	148.5	473.0
Methyl amine	CH_3NH_2	31.06	0.699	-134.5		19.9	
Methyl cellosolve	$CH_3OCH_2CH_2OH$	76.09	0.965			256	135.9
Naphthalene	$C_{10}H_8$	128.16	1.145	176.4	64.8	424.2	
α-Naphthol	$C_{10}H_7OH$	114.16	1.224	205	70.1	534	142.4
β-Naphthol	$C_{10}H_7OH$	114.16	1.217	252	56.3	546	131.6
Nitrobenzene	$C_6H_5NO_2$	123.11	1.205	42.3	40.5	411.6	175.5
n-Octane	C_8H_{18}	114.22	0.703	-70.2		258.2	
n-Octyl alcohol	$C_8H_{17}OH$	130.22	0.827	3.2	77.7	382	
Oxalic acid	$(COOH)_2{\cdot}2H_2O$	126.07	1.653	214.7		subl.	153.6
n-Pentane	C_5H_{12}	72.15	0.630	-201.5	50.2	96.9	
Phenol	C_6H_5OH	94.11	1.071	108.5	52.2	358.5	
Phthalic anhydride	$C_6H_4 < (CO)_2 > O$	148.11	1.527	267.4		544.1	
Propane	C_3H_8	44.09	Gas	-305.7	34.4	-43.7	183.0
Propylene	C_3H_6	42.08	Gas	-301.4	30.7	-53.9	118.2
Styrene	$C_6H_5CH{:}CH_2$	104.14	0.911	-23.1		293.4	
Toluene	$C_6H_5CH_3$	92.13	0.866	-139	30.9	231.1	156.2
Urea	H_2NCONH_2	60.06	1.355	270.9		d.	
Vinyl (poly-)	$(CH_2CO_2CH{:}CH_2)_x$	(86.09)x	1.19	210-260			
Vinyl chloride	$CH_2{:}CHCl$	62.50	0.908	-256		10.4	
o-Xylene	$C_6H_4(CH_3)_2$	106.16	0.881	-13.3	55.1	291.9	149.2
m-Xylene	$C_6H_4(CH_3)_2$	106.16	0.867	-54.2	46.9	282.4	147.6
g-Xylene	$C_6H_4(CH_3)_2$	106.16	0.861	55.9	69.3	281.0	146.2

Table 3-2. Physical Properties of Organic Compounds (Continued)

Compound	Heat of formation, Btu/lb mole at 77°F	Free energy of formation, Btu/lb mole at 77°F	Solubility, g/100 ml solvent — Water	Alcohol	Ether, etc.	Critical temp, °F	Critical press, atm	Critical density, lb/ft³
Furfural	-286,520	-204,600	9.1^{55}	∞	∞ et.			
Glycerol	....	....	∞	∞	i. et.			
Glycerol nitrate	....	....	0.18^{68}	50^{68}	∞ et.			
Glycerol tristearate	-194,270	-137,620	i.	s.h.	s.h. et.			
Glycerol	-55,030 (g.)	-53,040 (g.)	∞	3	1.0 et.			
Hexamethylenetetramine	-85,540	-1,640	81^{54}	50^{91}	v.sl.s. et.	454.5	29.9	14.6
n-Hexane	....		i.	∞	∞ et.			
Isoprene	-26,600 (g.)	-25,740 (g.)	d.	d.	∞ et.			
Ketene	....		d.	s.	s. et.			
Lauryl alcohol	....		i.		s. et.			
Linoleic acid	....		i.	s.	s. et.			
Maleic anhydride	-32,200 (g.)	-21,850 (g.)	16.3^{86}	$47\ cc^{68}$	$104\ cc^{50}$ et.	-115.8	45.8	10.1
Methane	-102,670	-71,640	$0.4\ cc^{68}$	∞	∞ et.	464.0	78.5	17.0
Methyl alcohol	-12,060 (g.)	+11,880 (g.)	v.s.	v.s.	∞ et.	314.4	73.6	
Methyl amine	....		∞	v.s.	....			
Methyl cellosolve	....		0.003^{77}	9.5^{48}	∞ et.			
Naphthalene	....		sl.s.h.	v.s.	v.s. et.			
α-Naphthol	....		0.074^{77}	v.s.	v.s. et.			
β-Naphthol	....		0.19^{68}	v.s.	v.s. et.			
Nitrobenzene	-107,530	+3,190	0.002^{61}	sl.s.	s. et.	565.2	24.6	14.5
n-Octane	....		0.054^{77}	∞	∞ et.			
n-Octyl alcohol	....		s.	s.	1.3 et.			
Oxalic acid	....		0.036^{61}	∞	∞ et.			
n-Pentane	-74,450	-3,980	8.2^{9}		∞ et.	385.9	33.3	14.5
Phenol	-68,040	-19,840	v.l.s.	s.	sl.s. et.	786.6	60.5	
Phthalic anhydride	....		$6.5\ cc^{64}$		v.s. et.			
Propane	-44,680 (g.)	-10,110 (g.)	44.6 cc	1.200 cc		206.2	42.0	13.7
Propylene	+8,780 (g.)	+26,940 (g.)	v. l.s.	∞		197.2	45.6	14.5
Styrene	....		0.05^{61}	s.	∞ et.			
Toluene	+5,160	+31,110	100^{63}	20^{68}	∞ et.	609.4	41.6	18
Urea	-143,340	-84,810	i.		sl.s. et.			
Vinyl chloride	....		sl.s.	s.	v.s. et.			
Vinyl (poly-)	....		i.	s.	∞ et.			
o-Xylene	-10,510	+47,470	i.	s.	∞ et.	677.1	36.9	
m-Xylene	-10,940	+46,310	i.	s.	v.s. et.	655	36	
p-Xylene	-10,510	+47,360	i.			653	35	

Table 3-3. Densities of Miscellaneous Materials

Approximate Values at Ordinary Temperature

Name	Sp gr	Lb/ft³	Name	Sp gr	Lb/ft³
Aluminum bronze.............	7.7	481	Marble*.....................	2.6–2.86	170
Anthracite..................	1.4–1.7	97	Mica.......................	2.65–3.2	182
Asbestos*...................	2.1–2.8	153	Oats, bulk.................	0.51	32
Asphalt.....................	1.1–1.5	81	Oil:		
Ashes (cinders).............	....	45	Vegetable.................	0.91–0.94	58
Barytes*....................	4.5	281	Fuel......................	1.0	63
Bituminous.................	1.2–1.5	84	Lubricant.................	0.9	56
Bluestone*..................	2.5–2.6	159	Paper.....................	0.70–1.15	58
Borax*......................	1.7–1.8	109	Paraffin..................	0.87–0.91	56
Brass (70 Cu, 30 Zn).........	8.53	532	Phosphate rock (apatite)*.....	3.2	200
Brick, common..............	1.8–2.0	120	Pitch.....................	1.07–1.15	69
Bronze (90 Cu, 10 Zn).......	8.80	550	Plaster:		
Cast iron..................	7.2	450	On lath.................	....	100
Cement, loose..............	....	90	On masonry.............	....	60
Cement, set................	2.7–3.2	183	Potatoes, piled...........	0.67	44
Charcoal...................	0.4	25	Pumice, natural*...........	0.37–0.9	40
Clay:			Rubber:		
Dry.....................	1.0	63	Goods....................	1.0–2.0	93
Damp, plastic.............	1.8	110	Raw......................	0.92–0.96	59
Coke.......................	1.0–1.4	75	Salt, granulated, piled........	0.77	48
Concrete:			Sand:		
Plain....................	....	144	Dry.....................	....	100
Reinforced...............	....	150	Wet.....................	....	120
Cinder...................	....	100	Sandstone*.................	2.0–2.6	143
Cork.......................	0.24	15	Shale and slate*...........	2.6–2.9	172
Corn, bulk.................	0.73	45	Slag, blast furnace...........	2.5–3.0	172
Cotton, flax, hemp...........	1.47–1.50	93	Snow, loose................	0.125	8
Earth:			Stainless steel (18:8).........	7.93	493
Dry, loose..............	1.2	76	Steel......................	7.87	490
Dry, packed.............	1.5	95	Sugar.....................	1.61	100
Moist, loose.............	1.3	78	Tile, hollow...............	....	55
Moist, packed............	1.6	96	Water:		
Flour, loose...............	0.4–0.5	28	Fresh....................	1.00	62.3
Gasoline...................	0.75	46.8	Salt.....................	1.02	64
Glass, common..............	2.4–2.8	162	Wheat, bulk..............	0.77	48
Granite*....................	2.6–2.7	165	Wood, seasoned:		
Gravel:			Birch....................	0.71	44
Dry.....................	....	100	Cedar....................	0.35	22
Wet.....................	....	120	Cypress..................	0.48]	30
Greenstone (trap)*...........	2.8–3.2	187	Elm......................	0.56	35
Gypsum*....................	2.3–2.8	159	Mahogany.................	0.56–0.85	44
Hay and straw (bales)........	0.32	20	Maple, white..............	0.53	33
Hematite (iron ore)..........	5.2	325	Oak, red or black..........	0.64–0.71	42
Leather....................	0.86–1.02	59	Oak, white...............	0.77	48
Lignite....................	1.1–1.4	78	Pine, white...............	0.43	27
Limestone*.................	2.1–2.86	155	Pine, yellow..............	0.71	44
Limonite (iron ore)..........	3.6–4.0	237	Redwood.................	0.42	26
Magnesite*.................	3.0	187	Spruce...................	0.45	28
Magnetite (iron ore).........	4.9–5.2	315	Walnut...................	0.59	37

* Density for the mineral is specified.   Most minerals, when quarried and piled are about 35 to 45 per cent less dense.   Masonry is generally 5 to 10 per cent less dense than the mineral.

SPECIFIC HEATS

Specific heat = P.c.u. /(lb)(deg.C) = Btu /(lb)(deg F)
= calories /(gm)(deg C)

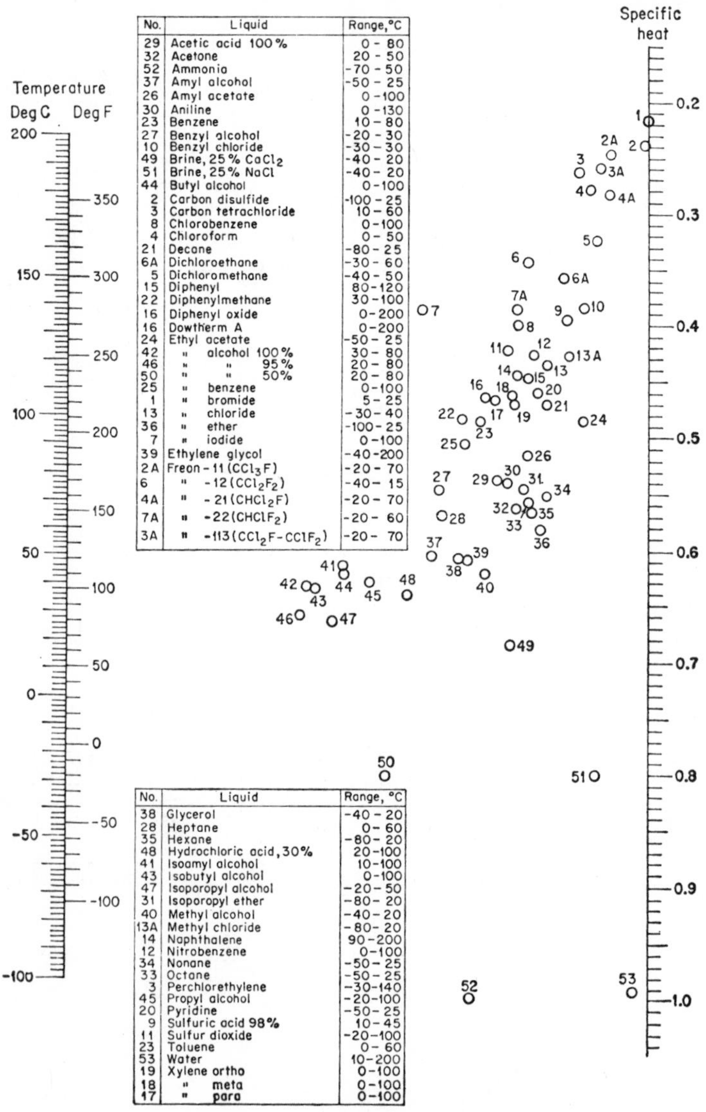

Temperature
Deg C   Deg F

Specific heat

No.	Liquid	Range,°C
29	Acetic acid 100%	0 – 80
32	Acetone	20 – 50
52	Ammonia	-70 – 50
37	Amyl alcohol	-50 – 25
26	Amyl acetate	0 –100
30	Aniline	0 –130
23	Benzene	10 – 80
27	Benzyl alcohol	-20 – 30
10	Benzyl chloride	-30 – 30
49	Brine, 25% CaCl$_2$	-40 – 20
51	Brine, 25% NaCl	-40 – 20
44	Butyl alcohol	0 –100
2	Carbon disulfide	-100 – 25
3	Carbon tetrachloride	10 – 60
8	Chlorobenzene	0 –100
4	Chloroform	0 – 50
21	Decane	-80 – 25
6A	Dichloroethane	-30 – 60
5	Dichloromethane	-40 – 50
15	Diphenyl	80 –120
22	Diphenylmethane	30 –100
16	Diphenyl oxide	0 –200
16	Dowtherm A	0 –200
24	Ethyl acetate	-50 – 25
42	" alcohol 100%	30 – 80
46	" " 95%	20 – 80
50	" " 50%	20 – 80
25	" benzene	0 –100
1	" bromide	5 – 25
13	" chloride	-30 – 40
36	" ether	-100 – 25
7	" iodide	0 –100
39	Ethylene glycol	-40 –200
2A	Freon – 11 (CCl$_3$F)	-20 – 70
6	" – 12 (CCl$_2$F$_2$)	-40 – 15
4A	" – 21 (CHCl$_2$F)	-20 – 70
7A	" –22 (CHClF$_2$)	-20 – 60
3A	" – 113 (CCl$_2$F–CClF$_2$)	-20 – 70

No.	Liquid	Range, °C
38	Glycerol	-40 – 20
28	Heptane	0 – 60
35	Hexane	-80 – 20
48	Hydrochloric acid, 30%	20 –100
41	Isoamyl alcohol	10 –100
43	Isobutyl alcohol	0 –100
47	Isopropyl alcohol	-20 – 50
31	Isoporopyl ether	-80 – 20
40	Methyl alcohol	-40 – 20
13A	Methyl chloride	-80 – 20
14	Naphthalene	90 –200
12	Nitrobenzene	0 –100
34	Nonane	-50 – 25
33	Octane	-50 – 25
3	Perchlorethylene	-30 –140
45	Propyl alcohol	-20 –100
20	Pyridine	-50 – 25
9	Sulfuric acid 98%	10 – 45
11	Sulfur dioxide	-20 –100
23	Toluene	0 – 60
53	Water	10 –200
19	Xylene ortho	0 –100
18	" meta	0 –100
17	" para	0 –100

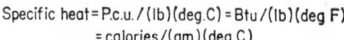

Fig. 3-1. Specific heats of liquids.

3–18

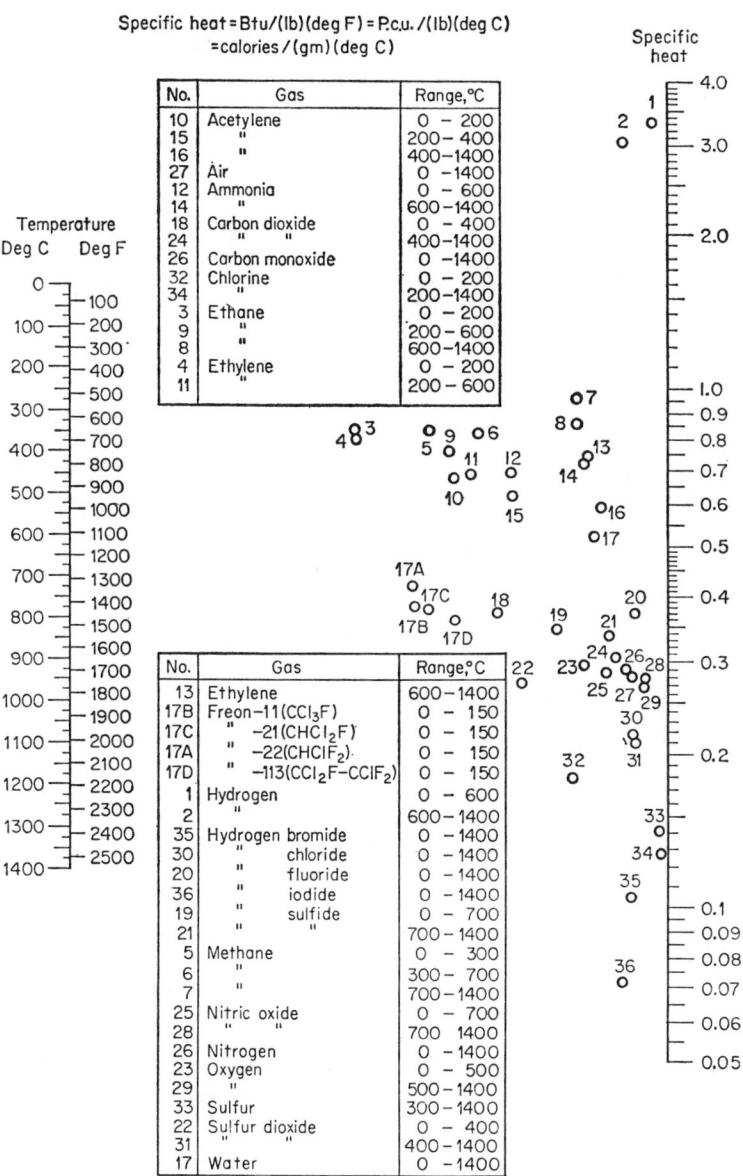

Specific heat = Btu/(lb)(deg F) = P.c.u. /(lb)(deg C)
           = calories /(gm)(deg C)

No.	Gas	Range,°C
10	Acetylene	0 – 200
15	"	200 – 400
16	"	400 – 1400
27	Air	0 – 1400
12	Ammonia	0 – 600
14	"	600 – 1400
18	Carbon dioxide	0 – 400
24	" "	400 – 1400
26	Carbon monoxide	0 – 1400
32	Chlorine	0 – 200
34	"	200 – 1400
3	Ethane	0 – 200
9	"	200 – 600
8	"	600 – 1400
4	Ethylene	0 – 200
11	"	200 – 600

No.	Gas	Range,°C
13	Ethylene	600 – 1400
17B	Freon–11(CCl$_3$F)	0 – 150
17C	" –21(CHCl$_2$F)	0 – 150
17A	" –22(CHClF$_2$)	0 – 150
17D	" –113(CCl$_2$F–CClF$_2$)	0 – 150
1	Hydrogen	0 – 600
2	"	600 – 1400
35	Hydrogen bromide	0 – 1400
30	" chloride	0 – 1400
20	" fluoride	0 – 1400
36	" iodide	0 – 1400
19	" sulfide	0 – 700
21	" "	700 – 1400
5	Methane	0 – 300
6	"	300 – 700
7	"	700 – 1400
25	Nitric oxide	0 – 700
28	" "	700 – 1400
26	Nitrogen	0 – 1400
23	Oxygen	0 – 500
29	"	500 – 1400
33	Sulfur	300 – 1400
22	Sulfur dioxide	0 – 400
31	" "	400 – 1400
17	Water	0 – 1400

FIG. 3-2. Specific heats (C_p) of gases at 1 atm pressure.

Table 3-4. Specific Heats of Miscellaneous Materials

Material	Sp ht, cal/(g)(°C) or Btu/(lb)(°F)	Material	Sp ht, cal/(g)(°C) or Btu/(lb)(°F)
Alumina....................	0.2 (212°F)	Gypsum....................	0.26
	.274 (2730°F)	Iron......................	.117 (212°F)
Aluminum..................	.223 (212°F),		.151 (2372°F)
	.259 (1832°F)	Kerosene..................	.47
Asbestos..................	.25	Lead......................	.032 (212°F)
Asphalt...................	.22		.033 (1652°F)
Bakelite..................	.3–0.4	Limestone.................	.22
Brickwork.................	.2	Litharge..................	.055
Carbon....................	.168 (80–170°F)	Magnesia..................	.234 (212°F)
	.314 (100–1630°F)		.188 (2730°F)
	.387 (130–2640°F)	Marble....................	.21
Cellulose.................	.32	Nickel....................	.113 (212°F)
Charcoal, wood............	.24		.143 (2372°F)
Clay......................	.22	Plastics..................	.3–0.45
Coal......................	.26–0.37	Polyethylene plastics........	.55
Coal tar..................	.35 (100°F),	Porcelain.................	.18 (68–212°F)
	.45 (400°F)		.22 (68–930°F)
Cobalt....................	.108 (212°F),	Pyrites, copper............	.13
	.176 (2372°F)	Pyrites, iron..............	.14
Coke......................	.265 (70–750°F)	Pyroxylin plastics...........	.34–0.38
	.403 (70–2400°F)	Quartz....................	.17 (32°F)
Concrete..................	.156		.28 (660°F)
Copper....................	.094 (212°F),	Rubber, vulcanized.........	.42
	.118 (2372°F)	Sand......................	.19
Fireclay brick.............	.2 (212°F),	Silica....................	.32
	.3 (2730°F)	Silk......................	.33
Fluorspar.................	.21	Steel.....................	.12
Gasoline..................	.53	Stone.....................	.2, approx.
Glass:		Turpentine................	.42
Crown..................	.16–0.20	Wood:	
Flint...................	.12	Oak..................	.57
Pyrex..................	.20	Most others..............	.45–0.65
Fiber insulating wool......	.20	Wool.....................	.33
Granite...................	.20	Zinc......................	.096 (212°F)
Graphite..................	.165 (80–170°F)		.126 (1652°F)
	.39 (130–2650°F)		

Table 3-5. Specific Heats of Aqueous Solutions at 68°F

Substance and formula	Wt, %	Sp ht, cal/(g)(°C) or Btu/(lb)(°F)	Substance and formula	Wt, %	Sp ht, cal/(g)(°C) or Btu/(lb)(°F)
Acetic acid, CH_3COOH......	20	0.91*	Phosphoric acid, H_3PO_4		
	60	0.73*	(Continued)...............	40	0.70
	80	0.63*		56	0.60
	100	0.54*		72	0.50
Ammonia, NH_3..............	35	1.00		88	0.43
	72	0.99	Potassium chloride, KCl......	4	0.95
Aniline, $C_6H_5NH_2$...........	94	0.58		14	0.83
	98	0.53		20	0.78
	100	0.50		25	0.73
Copper sulfate, $CuSO_4$.......	2	0.98	Potassium hydroxide, KOH....	2	0.97
	4	0.95		5	0.93
	15	0.85		14	0.81
Ethyl alcohol, C_2H_5OH........	10	1.02		24	0.75
	25	1.03	n-Propyl alcohol, C_3H_7OH.....	5	1.02
	60	0.86		15	1.06
	80	0.73		30	1.03
	100	0.58		50	0.90
Glycerol, $C_3H_5(OH)_3$..........	10	0.96†		70	0.78
	20	0.93†		90	0.65
	40	0.85†		100	0.57
	60	0.77†	Sodium carbonate, Na_2CO_3....	3	0.96‡
	80	0.67†		8	0.92‡
	100	0.56†		12	0.90‡
Hydrochloric acid, HCl.......	17	0.74	Sodium chloride, $NaCl$........	1	0.99
	29	0.63		8	0.91
	34	0.59		25	0.81
Methyl alcohol, CH_3OH.......	10	1.0	Sodium hydroxide, $NaOH$.....	2	0.97
	20	0.98		18	0.84
	40	0.92		29	0.80
	60	0.81		58	0.78
	80	0.71	Sulfuric acid, H_2SO_4..........	2	0.98
	100	0.60		15	0.88
Nitric acid, HNO_3............	10	0.90		28	0.78
	30	0.73		40	0.68
	50	0.65		65	0.50
	70	0.62		85	0.44
	90	0.52		100	0.34
Phosphoric acid, H_3PO_4.......	5	0.97	Zinc sulfate, $ZnSO_4$...........	4	0.95
	14	0.90		15	0.84
	26	0.80			

* 100°F.   † 60°F.   ‡ 63.5°F.

Table 3-6. Specific Heats of Air at High Pressures

Temp, °C	C_p, Specific heat, cal/(g)(°C) or Btu/(lb)(°F)						Temp, °F
	1 atm	10 atm	20 atm	40 atm	70 atm	100 atm	
100	0.237	0.239	0.240	0.245	0.250	0.258	212
0	.238	.242	.247	.251	.277	.298	32
−50	.238	.246	.257	.279	.332	.412	−58
−100	.239	.259	.285	.370	.846	.....	−148
−150	.240	.311	.505	.....	.....	.....	−238

Table 3-7. C_p/C_v: Ratios of Specific Heats of Gases at 1 Atm Pressure

Compound	Formula	Temp, °F	Ratio of sp ht, $\gamma = C_p/C_v$	Compound	Formula	Temp, °F	Ratio of sp ht, $\gamma = C_p/C_v$
Acetaldehyde	C_2H_4O	86	1.14	Hydrogen cyanide	HCN	149	1.31
Acetic acid	$C_2H_4O_2$	275	1.15			284	1.28
Acetylene	C_2H_2	59	1.26			410	1.24
		−96	1.31	Hydrogen iodide	HI	68–212	1.40
Air		1697	1.36	Hydrogen sulfide	H_2S	59	1.32
		63	1.403			−49	1.30
		−108	1.408			−71	1.29
		−180	1.415	Iodine	I_2	365	1.30
Ammonia	NH_3	59	1.310	Isobutane	C_4H_{10}	59	1.11
Argon	A	59	1.668	Krypton	Kr	66	1.68
		−292	1.76	Mercury	Hg	680	1.67
		32–212	1.67	Methane	CH_4	1112	1.113
Benzene	C_6H_6	194	1.10			572	1.15
Bromine	Br_2	68–662	1.32			59	1.31
Carbon dioxide	CO_2	59	1.304			−112	1.34
		−103	1.37			−175	1.41
Carbon disulfide	CS_2	212	1.21	Methyl acetate	$C_5H_6O_2$	59	1.14
Carbon monoxide	CO	59	1.404	Methyl alcohol	CH_4O	171	1.203
		−292	1.41	Methyl ether	C_2H_6O	43–86	1.11
Chlorine	Cl_2	59	1.355	Methylal	$C_3H_8O_2$	55	1.06
Chloroform	$CHCl_3$	212	1.15			104	1.09
Cyanogen	$(CN)_2$	59	1.256	Neon	Ne	66	1.64
Cyclohexane	C_6H_{12}	176	1.08	Nitric oxide	NO	59	1.400
Dichlorodifluoromethane	CCl_2F_2	77	1.139			−49	1.39
Ethane	C_2H_6	212	1.19			−112	1.38
		59	1.22	Nitrogen	N_2	59	1.404
		−116	1.28			−294	1.47
Ethyl alcohol	C_2H_6O	194	1.13	Nitrous oxide	N_2O	212	1.28
Ethyl ether	$C_4H_{10}O$	95	1.08			59	1.303
		176	1.086			−22	1.31
Ethylene	C_2H_4	212	1.18			−94	1.34
		59	1.255	Oxygen	O_2	59	1.401
		−132	1.35			−105	1.415
Helium	He	−292	1.660			−294	1.45
n-Hexane	C_6H_{14}	176	1.08	n-Pentane	C_5H_{12}	187	1.086
Hydrogen	H_2	59	1.410	Phosphorus	P	572	1.17
		−105	1.453	Potassium	K	1562	1.77
		−294	1.597	Sodium	Na	1382–1688	1.68
Hydrogen bromide	HBr	68	1.42	Sulfur dioxide	SO_2	59	1.29
Hydrogen chloride	HCl	59	1.41	Xenon	Xe	66	1.66
		212	1.40				

Table 3-8. Ratios of Specific Heats of Air at High Pressures

Pressure, atm	Ratio of specific heats, $\gamma = C_p/C_v$		Pressure, atm	Ratio of specific heats, $\gamma = C_p/C_v$	
	32°F	−110°F		32°F	−110°F
25	1.47	1.57	125	1.69	2.40
50	1.53	1.77	150	1.74	2.47
75	1.59	2.00	175	1.78	2.41
100	1.65	2.20	200	1.83	2.33

TRANSPORT PROPERTIES

Table 3-9. Effect of Temperature upon Thermal Conductivity of Metals and Alloys

t, °F	k, Btu/(hr)(ft²)(°F/ft)							Mp, °F
	32	212	392	572	752	932	1112	
Aluminum	117	119	124	133	144	155	...	1220
Brass (70–30)	56	60	63	66	67	...	...	1724
Cast iron	32	30	28	26	25	...	...	2327
Cast high-silicon iron	30	...	...	...	...	...	...	2300
Copper, pure	224	218	215	212	210	207	204	1981
Lead	20	19	18	18	...	...	...	621
Nickel	36	34	33	32	...	...	...	2646
Silver	242	238	...	...	...	...	...	1761
Sodium	81	...	...	...	...	...	...	208
Steel, mild	...	26	26	25	23	22	21	2507
Tantalum at 64°F	32	...	...	...	...	...	...	5162
Tin	36	34	33	...	...	...	...	450
Wrought iron, Swedish	...	32	30	28	26	23	...	2741
Zinc	65	64	62	59	54	...	...	787

Table 3-10. Thermal Conductivities of Metals

$k = $ Btu/(hr)(ft²)(°F/ft)

Substance	t, °F	k	Substance	t, °F	k
Metals:			Metals (cont.):		
Antimony	32	10.6	Steel (1 % C)	64	26.2
	212	9.7		212	25.9
Bismuth	64	4.7	Magnesium	32–212	92.0
	212	3.9	Mercury	32	4.8
Cadmium	64	53.7	Nickel alloy (62 Ni, 12 Cr, 26 Fe)	68	7.8
	212	52.2	Platinum	64	40.2
Gold	64	169.0		212	41.9
	212	170.0	Alloys:		
Iron, pure	64	39.0	Constantan (60 Cu, 40 Ni)	64	13.1
	212	36.6		212	15.5
Iron, wrought	64	34.9	Nickel silver	32	16.9
	212	34.6		212	21.5
Iron, cast	129	27.6	Manganin (84 Cu, 4 Ni, 12 Mn)	64	12.8
	216	26.8		212	15.2
			Platinoid (54 Cu, 25 Ni, 20 Zn)	64	14.5

Table 3-11. Thermal Conductivities of Alloy Steels

Type of steel	k, Btu/(hr)(ft²)(°F/ft)	
	400°F	1000°F
Carbon	26.8	23.2
2 Cr, 0.5 Mo	16.9	16.9
5 Cr, 0.5 Mo	15.8	16.3
5 Cr, 0.5 Mo, 1.5 Si	13.0	14.8
18 Cr, 8 Ni (stainless 304, 316, 321, 347)	10.9	13.7
25 Cr, 20 Ni (stainless 310)	9.5	12.9

Table 3-12. Thermal Conductivities of Building and Insulating Materials

Material	Apparent density ρ, lb/ft³ at room temp	t, °F	k, Btu/(hr)(ft²)(°F/ft)
Aerogel, silica, opacified	8.5	248	0.013
		554	0.026
Aluminum foil (7 air spaces per 2.5 in.)	0.2	100	0.025
		350	0.038
Asbestos	29	−300	0.055
	29	32	0.090
	36	32	0.087
	36	400	0.121
	36	800	0.130
	44	−300	0.100
	44	32	0.135
Cement boards	120	68	0.43
Felt:			
40 laminations/in	.....	100	0.033
40 laminations/in	.....	500	0.048
20 laminations/in	.....	100	0.045
20 laminations/in	.....	500	0.065
Sheets	55.5	124	0.096
Slate	112	32	0.087
	112	140	0.114
Asphalt	132	68	0.43
Bricks:			
Alumina (92–99% Al_2O_3 by wt) fused	.....	800	1.8
Alumina (64–65% Al_2O_3 by wt)	.....	2400	2.7
Building brickwork	.....	68	0.4
Carbon	96.7	.....	3.0
Chrome (32% Cr_2O_3 by wt)	200	392	0.67
	200	1200	0.85
	200	2400	1.0
Diatomaceous earth:			
1600°F service	.....	300	0.058
1600°F service	.....	1000	0.073
2500°F service	.....	300	0.135
2500°F service	.....	1000	0.163
2500°F service	.....	2000	0.203
Fire clay (Missouri)	.....	392	0.58
	.....	1112	0.85
	.....	1832	0.95
	.....	2550	1.02
Kaolin insulating brick	27	932	0.15
	27	2100	0.26
Kaolin insulating firebrick	19	392	0.050
	19	1400	0.113
Magnesite (86.8% MgO, 6.3% Fe_2O_3, 3% CaO, 2.6% SiO_2 by wt)	158	400	2.2
	158	1200	1.6
	158	2200	1.1

Table 3-12. Thermal Conductivities of Building and Insulating Materials (Continued)

Material	Apparent density ρ, lb/ft^3 at room temp	t, °F	k, Btu/(hr)(ft^2)(°F/ft)
Silicon carbide, recrystallized	129	1112	10.7
	129	1832	8.0
	129	2550	6.3
Calcium carbonate:			
Natural	162	86	1.3
White marble	.....	......	1.7
Chalk	96	......	0.4
Calcium sulfate (4H$_2$O):			
Artificial	84.6	104	0.22
Plaster:			
Artificial	132	167	0.43
Building	77.9	77	0.25
Cambric, varnished	.....	100	0.091
Cardboard, corrugated	.....	......	0.037
Celluloid	87.3	86	0.12
Charcoal flakes	11.9	176	0.043
Clinker, granular	.....	0–1200	0.27
Coke, petroleum	.....	212	3.4
		932	2.9
20–100 mesh	62	750	0.55
Coke, powdered	.....	32–212	0.11
Concrete:			
Cinder	.....	......	0.20
Stone	.....	......	0.54
1:4 dry	.....	......	0.44
Cotton	5	60	0.033
Cotton wool	5	86	0.024
Cork:			
Board	10	86	0.025
Regranulated	8.1	86	0.026
Diatomaceous earth, powder	18	100	0.039
	18	500	0.051
	18	1000	0.068
Enamel, silicate	38	......	0.5–0.75
Felt, wool	20.6	86	0.03
Fiber insulating board	14.8	70	0.028
Glass:			
Borosilicate type	139	......	0.63
Window	.....	......	0.3–0.61
Soda	.....	......	0.3–0.44
Glass, insulating:			
Cellular, slab	9	75	0.035
Fiberglass wool	3	100	0.0225
	3	300	0.0342
	9	100	0.0188
	9	500	0.0375
Granite	.....	......	1.0–2.3
Graphite:			
Longitudinal	.....	68	95.
Powdered (through 100 mesh)	30	104	0.104
Gypsum:			
Plaster	.....	......	0.27
Cellular	8	......	0.029
	30	......	0.083
Powdered	26–34	......	0.043–0.05
Hair felt between layers of paper	17	86	0.021
Ice	57.5	32	1.3
Kapok	0.88	68	0.020
Lampblack	10	104	0.038
Lava	.....	......	0.49
Leather, sole	62.4	......	0.092
Limestone (15.3% H$_2$O by vol)	103	73	0.54
Linen	.....	86	0.05

Table 3-12. Thermal Conductivities of Building and Insulating Materials (Continued)

Material	Apparent density ρ, lb/ft³ at room temp	t, °F	k, Btu/(hr)(ft²)(°F/ft)
Magnesia:			
Powdered..	49.7	117	0.35
85%..	13	100	0.034
	13	400	0.040
Magnesium oxide, compressed...............................	49.9	68	0.32
Marble..	....	......	1.2–1.7
Mica (perpendicular to planes).............................	....	122	0.25
Mill shavings...	....	......	0.033–0.05
Mineral wool:			
Fibrous..	9.4	86	0.0225
	19.7	86	0.024
Block, with binder.......................................	16.7	......	0.031
Blanket..	4.5	......	0.022
Paper...	....	......	0.075
Paper and asbestos fiber with emulsified asphalt binder.....	4.2	94	0.023
Paraffin wax..	....	32	0.14
Porcelain...	....	392	0.88
Portland cement (see also concrete)........................	....	194	0.17
Pumice stone..	....	70–150	0.14
Pyroxylin plastics..	....	......	0.075
Rock wool...	....	100	0.030
	....	600	0.057
Rubber:			
Hard..	74.8	32	0.087
Para..	....	70	0.109
Soft..	....	70	0.075–0.092
Sand, dry...	94.6	68	0.19
Sandstone...	140	104	1.06
Sawdust...	12	70	0.034
Silk..	6.3	60	0.026
Varnished..	....	100	.096
Slag wool...	12	86	.022
Slate...	....	200	.86
Snow..	34.7	32	.27
Sugar-cane-fiber insulation blocks encased in asphalt membrane.......	13.8	70	.025
Wallboard:			
Insulating type..	14.8	70	.028
Stiff pasteboard...	43	86	.04
Wood shavings...	8.8	86	.034
Wood:			
Douglas fir, 0% moisture.................................	30	75	.056
Longleaf yellow pine, 0% moisture........................	40	75	.072
Wood lath and plaster.....................................	....	70	.27
Wood pulp in sheet form...................................	16.5	......	.028
Wool, animal..	6.9	86	.021

Table 3-13. Thermal Conductivities of Liquids

Liquid	k, Btu/(hr)(ft²)(°F/ft)			
	50°F	100°F	200°F	300°F
Acetic acid:				
100%..	0.099			
50%..	0.20			
Ammonia..	0.29			
Ammonia, aqueous, 26%.............................	0.253	0.274	0.315	
Amyl acetate.......................................	0.083			
n-Amyl alcohol.....................................	0.096	0.094	0.0895	
Isoamyl alcohol....................................	0.089	0.088	0.087	
Aniline..	0.100			
Benzene..	0.096	0.091	0.081	
Bromobenzene.......................................	0.075	0.074	0.071	
Butyl acetate......................................	0.078	0.074	0.068	
n-Butyl alcohol....................................	0.098	0.097	0.094	
Isobutyl alcohol...................................	0.091			
Calcium chloride brine:				
30%..	......	0.32		
15%..	......	0.34		
Carbon disulfide...................................	0.095	0.092	0.086	
Carbon tetrachloride...............................	0.067	0.065	0.062	
Chloroform...	0.073	0.071	0.067	
Decane...	0.0865	0.0843	0.0805	0.0775
Dibutyl phthalate..................................	0.079	0.078	0.073	
Dichlorodifluoromethane............................	0.054	0.048	0.035	
Dowtherm A...	......	0.082	0.079	0.077
Dowtherm E...	......	0.073	0.071	0.064
Ethane...	0.056			
Ethyl acetate......................................	0.085	0.080	0.068	
Ethyl alcohol......................................	0.106	0.092	0.068	
Ethyl benzene......................................	0.088	0.085	0.077	
Ethyl ether..	......	0.080	0.077	
Ethylene glycol....................................	0.145	0.144	0.142	0.140
Glycerine (USP)....................................	0.156	0.159	0.164	
Heptane..	0.083	0.0815	0.0765	0.071
Hexane...	0.0820	0.0795	0.0745	0.068
Mercury..	4.7	......	......	6.7
Methyl alcohol.....................................	0.128	0.117	0.095	
Nitrobenzene.......................................	0.097	0.093	0.089	
Nitromethane.......................................	0.128	0.124	0.115	
Octane...	0.0845	0.0825	0.078	0.073
Olive oil (USP)....................................	0.097	0.096	0.094	
Paraldehyde..	0.086	0.083	0.0785	
Pentane..	0.080	0.0775	0.071	0.0615
Propane..	0.072	0.0675	0.056	
n-Propyl alcohol...................................	0.101	0.099	0.094	
Propylene glycol...................................	0.116	0.115	0.113	0.110
Sodium...	......	......	14.8	15.0
Sodium chloride brine:				
25%..	0.34			
12.5%..	0.35			
Sulfuric acid:				
90%..	0.22			
60%..	0.26			
30%..	0.31			
Sulfur dioxide.....................................	0.116	0.108		
Trichlorethylene...................................	0.072	0.068	0.060	
Toluene..	0.087	0.086	0.084	
Vinyl acetate......................................	0.095	0.083	0.075	
Water..	0.331	0.363	0.393	0.395
Dow Corning silicone DC-200 (500,000 centistokes)..	......	0.090	0.085	
GE silicones SF-96:				
40 centistokes.................................	......	0.085	0.080	
100 centistokes.................................	......	0.086	0.081	
300 centistokes.................................	......	0.090	0.084	
1,000 centistokes.................................	......	0.091	0.086	

NOTE: Viscosities, where specified, are at 85°F.

Table 3-14. Thermal Conductivities of Gases and Vapors

$$k = Btu/(hr)\,(ft^2)\,(°F/ft)$$

The extreme temperature values given constitute the experimental range. For extrapolation to other temperatures, it is suggested that the data given be plotted as log k vs. log T, or that use be made of the assumption that the ratio $c_p\mu/k$ is practically independent of temperature (or of pressure, within moderate limits).

Substance	t, °F	k	Substance	t, °F	k	Substance	t, °F	k
Acetone	32	0.0057		−29	0.0086	20	32	0.0170
	115	.0074		32	.0106	40	32	.0270
	212	.0099		212	.0175	60	32	.0410
	363	.0147	Ethyl acetate	115	.0072	80	32	.0650
Acetylene	−103	.0068		212	.0096	Hydrogen sulfide	32	.0076
	32	.0108		363	.0141	Mercury	392	.0197
	122	.0140	Ethyl alcohol	68	.0089	Methane	−148	.0100
	212	.0172		212	.0124		−58	.0145
Air	−148	.0095	Ethyl chloride	32	.0055		32	.0175
	32	.0140		212	.0095		122	.0215
	212	.0183		363	.0135	Methyl alcohol	32	.0083
	392	.0226		413	.0152		212	.0128
	572	.0265	Ethyl ether	32	.0077	Methyl acetate	32	.0059
Ammonia	−76	.0095		115	.0099		68	.0068
	32	.0128		212	.0131	Methyl chloride	32	.0053
	122	.0157		363	.0189		115	.0072
	212	.0185		413	.0209		212	.0094
Benzene	32	.0052	Ethylene	−96	.0064		363	.0130
	115	.0073		32	.0101		413	.0148
	212	.0103		122	.0131	Methylene chloride	32	.0039
	363	.0152		212	.0161		115	.0049
	413	.0176	n-Heptane	392	.0112		212	.0063
n-Butane	32	.0078		212	.0103		413	.0095
	212	.0135	n-Hexane	32	.0072	Nitric oxide	−94	.0103
Isobutane	32	.0080		68	.0080		32	.0138
	212	.0139	Hexene	32	.0061	Nitrogen	−148	.0095
Carbon dioxide	−58	.0068		212	.0109		32	.0140
	32	.0085	Hydrogen	−148	.065		122	.0160
	212	.0133		−58	.083		212	.0180
	392	.0181		32	.100	Nitrous oxide	−98	.0067
	572	.0228		122	.115		32	.0087
Carbon disulfide	32	.0040		212	.129		212	.0128
	45	.0042		572	.178	Oxygen	−148	.0095
Carbon monoxide	−312	.0041	Hydrogen and carbon dioxide (by % H₂):				−58	.0119
	−294	.0046					32	.0142
	32	.0135	0	32	.0083		122	.0164
Carbon tetrachloride	115	.0041	20	32	.0165		212	.0185
	212	.0052	40	32	.0270	n-Pentane	32	.0074
	363	.0065	60	32	.0410		68	.0083
Chlorine	32	.0043	80	32	.0620	Isopentane	32	.0072
Chloroform	32	.0038	100	32	.10		212	.0127
	115	.0046	Hydrogen and nitrogen (by % H₂):			Propane	32	.0087
	212	.0058					212	.0151
	363	.0077	0	32	.0133	Sulfur dioxide	32	.0050
Cyclohexane	216	.0095	20	32	.0212		212	.0069
Dichlorodifluoro-			40	32	.0313	Water vapor, zero		
methane	32	.0048	60	32	.0438	pressure*	32	.0132
	122	.0064	80	32	.0635		200	.0159
	212	.0080	Hydrogen and nitrous oxide (by % H₂):				400	.0199
	302	.0097					600	.0256
Ethane	−94	.0066	0	32	.0092		800	.0306
							1000	.0495

* For saturated vapor:

Lb/in.² abs	250	500	1000	1500	2000
t, °F	401	467	545	596	636
k	0.0248	0.0299	0.0395	0.0486	0.0578

Table 3-15. Viscosities of Gases

Coordinates for Use with Fig. 3-3

No.	Gas	X	Y	No.	Gas	X	Y
1	Acetic acid...................	7.7	14.3	29	Freon-113....................	11.3	14.0
2	Acetone......................	8.9	13.0	30	Helium......................	10.9	20.5
3	Acetylene....................	9.8	14.9	31	Hexane......................	8.6	11.8
4	Air.........................	11.0	20.0	32	Hydrogen....................	11.2	12.4
5	Ammonia....................	8.4	16.0	33	$3H_2 + 1N_2$...................	11.2	17.2
6	Argon.......................	10.5	22.4	34	Hydrogen bromide...........	8.8	20.9
7	Benzene.....................	8.5	13.2	35	Hydrogen chloride...........	8.8	18.7
8	Bromine.....................	8.9	19.2	36	Hydrogen cyanide............	9.8	14.9
9	Butene......................	9.2	13.7	37	Hydrogen iodide.............	9.0	21.3
10	Butylene....................	8.9	13.0	38	Hydrogen sulfide.............	8.6	18.0
11	Carbon dioxide..............	9.5	18.7	39	Iodine......................	9.0	18.4
12	Carbon disulfide.............	8.0	16.0	40	Mercury.....................	5.3	22.9
13	Carbon monoxide............	11.0	20.0	41	Methane....................	9.9	15.5
14	Chlorine....................	9.0	18.4	42	Methyl alcohol..............	8.5	15.6
15	Chloroform..................	8.9	15.7	43	Nitric oxide.................	10.9	20.5
16	Cyanogen...................	9.2	15.2	44	Nitrogen....................	10.6	20.0
17	Cyclohexane.................	9.2	12.0	45	Nitrosyl chloride.............	8.0	17.6
18	Ethane.....................	9.1	14.5	46	Nitrous oxide...............	8.8	19.0
19	Ethyl acetate................	8.5	13.2	47	Oxygen.....................	11.0	21.3
20	Ethyl alcohol................	9.2	14.2	48	Pentane....................	7.0	12.8
21	Ethyl chloride...............	8.5	15.6	49	Propane....................	9.7	12.9
22	Ethyl ether.................	8.9	13.0	50	Propyl alcohol...............	8.4	13.4
23	Ethylene....................	9.5	15.1	51	Propylene...................	9.0	13.8
24	Fluorine....................	7.3	23.8	52	Sulfur dioxide...............	9.6	17.0
25	Freon-11....................	10.6	15.1	53	Toluene....................	8.6	12.4
26	Freon-12....................	11.1	16.0	54	2,3,3-Trimethylbutane........	9.5	10.5
27	Freon-21....................	10.8	15.3	55	Water......................	8.0	16.0
28	Freon-22....................	10.1	17.0	56	Xenon......................	9.3	23.0

Table 3-16. Viscosity of Steam

Pressure, psia	Temp, °F	Viscosity, centipoises	Pressure, psia	Temp, °F	Viscosity, centipoises
0	32	0.0096	1,000	545	0.029
	200	.013		600	.029
	600	.021		1000	.033
	1000	.028			
			2,000	636	.039
500	467	.022		1000	.039
	600	.024			
	1000	.030	3,000	695	.048
				1000	.045

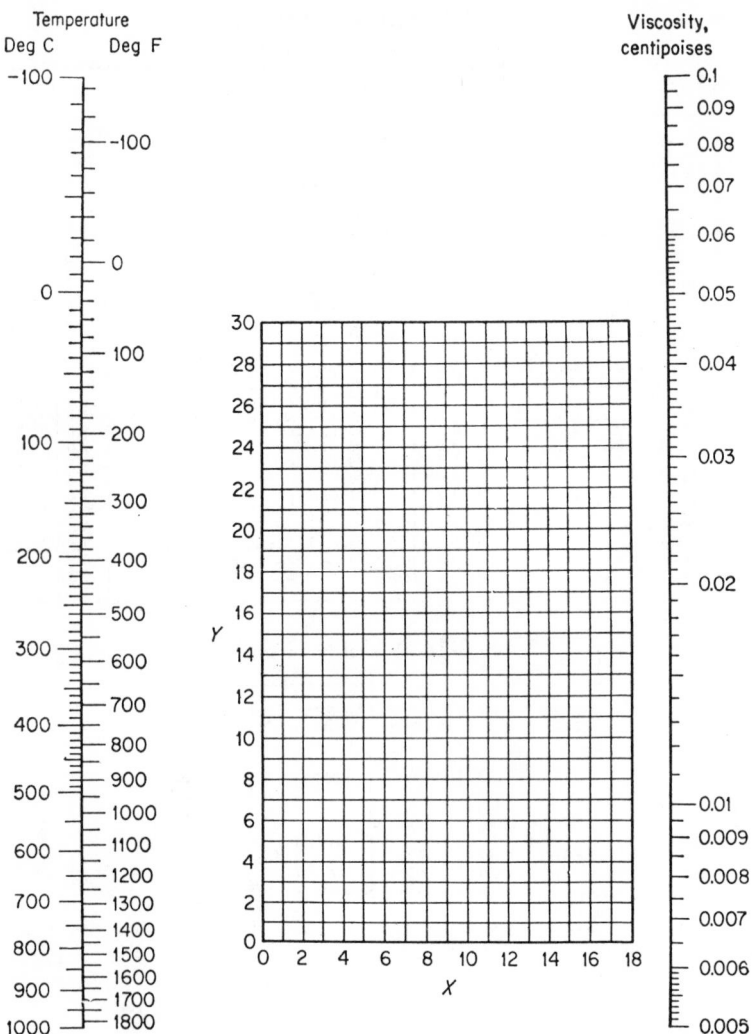

Fɪɢ. 3-3. Viscosities of gases at 1 atm.   For coordinates, see Table 3-15.

Table 3-17. Viscosities of Liquids

Coordinates for Use with Fig. 3-4

No.	Liquid	X	Y	No.	Liquid	X	Y
1	Acetaldehyde..............	15.2	4.8	56	Freon-22..................	17.2	4.7
2	Acetic acid, 100%..........	12.1	14.2	57	Freon-13..................	12.5	11.4
3	70%..........	9.5	17.0	58	Glycerol, 100%.............	2.0	30.0
4	Acetic anhydride............	12.7	12.8	59	50%.............	6.9	19.6
5	Acetone, 100%..............	14.5	7.2	60	Heptene...................	14.1	8.4
6	35%..............	7.9	15.0	61	Hexane....................	14.7	7.0
7	Allyl alcohol...............	10.2	14.3	62	Hydrochloric acid, 31.5%......	13.0	16.6
8	Ammonia, 100%............	12.6	2.0	63	Isobutyl alcohol.............	7.1	18.0
9	26%............	10.1	13.9	64	Isobutyric acid.............	12.2	14.4
10	Amyl acetate..............	11.8	12.5	65	Isopropyl alcohol...........	8.2	16.0
11	Amyl alcohol..............	7.5	18.4	66	Kerosene..................	10.2	16.9
12	Aniline...................	8.1	18.7	67	Linseed oil, raw.............	7.5	27.2
13	Anisole...................	12.3	13.5	68	Mercury...................	18.4	16.4
14	Arsenic trichloride..........	13.9	14.5	69	Methanol, 100%............	12.4	10.5
15	Benzene..................	12.5	10.9	70	90%............	12.3	11.8
16	Brine, CaCl₂, 25%..........	6.6	15.9	71	40%............	7.8	15.5
17	NaCl, 25%..........	10.2	16.6	72	Methyl acetate.............	14.2	8.2
18	Bromine..................	14.2	13.2	73	Methyl chloride.............	15.0	3.8
19	Bromotoluene.............	20.0	15.9	74	Methyl ethyl ketone.........	13.9	8.6
20	Butyl acetate.............	12.3	11.0	75	Naphthalene...............	7.9	18.1
21	Butyl alcohol.............	8.6	17.2	76	Nitric acid, 95%............	12.8	13.8
22	Butyric acid..............	12.1	15.3	77	60%............	10.8	17.0
23	Carbon dioxide............	11.6	0.3	78	Nitrobenzene...............	10.6	16.2
24	Carbon disulfide...........	16.1	7.5	79	Nitrotoluene...............	11.0	17.0
25	Carbon tetrachloride........	12.7	13.1	80	Octane....................	13.7	10.0
26	Chlorobenzene............	12.3	12.4	81	Octyl alcohol..............	6.6	21.1
27	Chloroform...............	14.4	10.2	82	Pentachloroethane..........	10.9	17.3
28	Chlorosulfonic acid.........	11.2	18.1	83	Pentane...................	14.9	5.2
29	Chlorotoluene, ortho........	13.0	13.3	84	Phenol....................	6.9	20.8
30	meta.........	13.3	12.5	85	Phosphorus tribromide.......	13.8	16.7
31	para.........	13.3	12.5	86	Phosphorus trichloride.......	16.2	10.9
32	Cresol, meta..............	2.5	20.8	87	Propionic acid.............	12.8	13.8
33	Cyclohexanol..............	2.9	24.3	88	Propyl alcohol.............	9.1	16.5
34	Dibromoethane............	12.7	15.8	89	Propyl bromide.............	14.5	9.6
35	Dichloroethane............	13.2	12.2	90	Propyl chloride.............	14.4	7.5
36	Dichloromethane...........	14.6	8.9	91	Propyl iodide..............	14.1	11.6
37	Diethyl oxalate............	11.0	16.4	92	Sodium...................	16.4	13.9
38	Dimethyl oxalate...........	12.3	15.8	93	Sodium hydroxide, 50%......	3.2	25.8
39	Diphenyl.................	12.0	18.3	94	Stannic chloride............	13.5	12.8
40	Dipropyl oxalate...........	10.3	17.7	95	Sulfur dioxide.............	15.2	7.1
41	Ethyl acetate.............	13.7	9.1	96	Sulfuric acid, 110%.........	7.2	27.4
42	Ethyl alcohol, 100%........	10.5	13.8	97	98%.........	7.0	24.8
43	95%........	9.8	14.3	98	60%.........	10.2	21.3
44	40%........	6.5	16.6	99	Sulfuryl chloride...........	15.2	12.4
45	Ethyl benzene.............	13.2	11.5	100	Tetrachloroethane...........	11.9	15.7
46	Ethyl bromide.............	14.5	8.1	101	Tetrachloroethylene.........	14.2	12.7
47	Ethyl chloride.............	14.8	6.0	102	Titanium tetrachloride.......	14.4	12.3
48	Ethyl ether...............	14.5	5.3	103	Toluene...................	13.7	10.4
49	Ethyl formate.............	14.2	8.4	104	Trichloroethylene...........	14.8	10.5
50	Ethyl iodide..............	14.7	10.3	105	Turpentine................	11.5	14.9
51	Ethylene glycol............	6.0	23.6	106	Vinyl acetate..............	14.0	8.8
52	Formic acid...............	10.7	15.8	107	Water....................	10.2	13.0
53	Freon-11..................	14.4	9.0	108	Xylene, ortho..............	13.5	12.1
54	Freon-12..................	16.8	5.6	109	meta..............	13.9	10.6
55	Freon-21..................	15.7	7.5	110	para..............	13.9	10.9

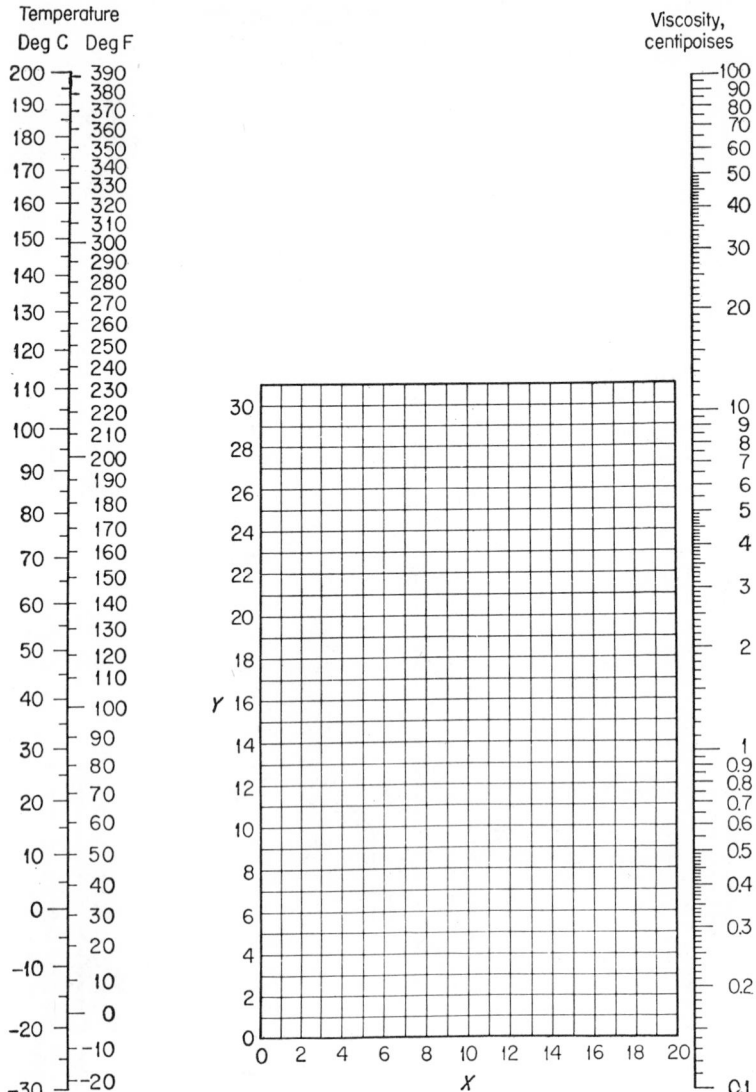

Fɪɢ. 3–4. Viscosities of liquids at 1 atm. For coordinates, see Table 3–17.

Table 3-18. Diffusivities of Pairs of Gases and Vapors (1 Atm)

D_v in Cm²/Sec *

Substance	Temp., °C	Air	A	H₂	O₂	N₂	CO₂
Acetic acid	0	0.1064	......	0.416	......	......	0.0716
Acetone	0	.109	......	.361	......	......	
n-Amyl alcohol	0	.0589	......	.235	......	......	.0422
sec-Amyl alcohol	30	.072					
Amyl butyrate	0	.040					
Amyl formate	0	.0543					
i-Amyl formate	0	.058					
Amyl isobutyrate	0	.0419		.171			
Amyl propionate	0	.046	......	.1914	......	......	.0347
Aniline	0	.0610					
	30	.075					
Anthracene	0	.0421					
Argon	20	......	......	......	......	0.194	
Benzene	0	.077	......	.306	0.0797	......	.0528
Benzidine	0	.0298					
Benzyl chloride	0	.066					
n-Butyl acetate	0	.058					
i-Butyl acetate	0	.0612	......	.2364	......	......	.0425
n-Butyl alcohol	0	.0703	......	.2716	......	......	.0476
	30	.088					
i-Butyl alcohol	0	.0727	......	.2771	......	......	.0483
Butyl amine	0	.0821					
i-Butyl amine	0	.0853					
i-Butyl butyrate	0	.0468	......	.185	......	......	.0327
i-Butyl formate	0	.0705					
i-Butyl isobutyrate	0	.0457	......	.191	......	......	.0364
i-Butyl propionate	0	.0529	......	.203	......	......	.0366
i-Butyl valerate	0	.0424	......	.173	......	......	.0308
Butyric acid	0	.067	......	.264	......	......	.0476
i-Butyric acid	0	.0679	......	.271	......	......	.0471
Cadmium	0	......	......	......	......	.17	
Caproic acid	0	.050					
i-Caproic acid	0	.0513					
Carbon dioxide	0	.138	......	.550	.139		
	20	......	......	......	......	.163	
	500	......	......	......	.9		
Carbon disulfide	0	.0892	......	.369	......	......	.063
Carbon monoxide	0	......	......	.651	.185	......	.137
	450	......	......	......	1.0		
Carbon tetrachloride	0	......	......	.293	0.0636		
Chlorobenzene	30	.075					
Chloroform	0	.091					
Chloropicrin	25	.088					
m-Chlorotoluene	0	.054					
o-Chlorotoluene	0	.059					
p-Chlorotoluene	0	.051					
Cyanogen chloride	0	.111					
Cyclohexane	15	......	0.0719	.319	.0744	.0760	
	45	.086					
n-Decane	90	......	......	.306	......	.0841	
Diethylamine	0	.0884					
2,3-Dimethyl butane	15	......	.0657	.301	.0753	.0751	
Diphenyl	0	.0610					
n-Dodecane	126	......	......	.308	......	.0813	
Ethane	0	......	......	.459			
Ethanol	0	......	......	.377	......	......	.0686
Ether (diethyl)	0	.0778	......	.298	......	......	.0546
Ethyl acetate	0	.0715	......	.273	......	......	.0487
	30	.089					
Ethyl alcohol	0	.102	......	.375	......	......	.0685
Ethyl benzene	0	.0658					
Ethyl n-butyrate	0	.0579	......	.224	......	......	.0407
Ethyl i-butyrate	0	.0591	......	.229	......	......	.0413
Ethylene	0	......	......	.486			
Ethyl formate	0	.0840	......	.337	......	......	.0573
Ethyl propionate	0	.068	......	.236	......	......	.0450

* To convert to square feet per hour, multiply by 0.388.

Table 3-18. Diffusivities of Pairs of Gases and Vapors (1 Atm)
(Continued)

D, in Cm^2/Sec*

Substance	Temp., °C	Air	A	H_2	O_2	N_2	CO_2
Ethyl valerate..........	0	0.0512	......	0.205	......	......	0.0367
Eugenol...............	0	.0377					
Formic acid............	0	.1308	......	.510	......	......	.0874
Helium................	0	......	0.641				
	20	......					0.705
n-Hexane..............	15	......	.0663	.290	0.0753	.0757	
Hexyl alcohol..........	0	.0499	......	.200			.0351
Hydrogen..............	0	.611	......	......	.697	.674	.550
	25	......	......	......	......	......	.646
	500	......	......	......	4.2		
Hydrogen cyanide......	0	.173					
Hydrogen peroxide......	60	.188					
Iodine.................	0	.07	......	......	......	.070	
Mercury...............	0	.112	......	.53	......	.13	
Mesitylene.............	0	.056					
Methane...............	500	......	......	......	1.1		
Methyl acetate.........	0	.084	......	.333	......	......	.0567
Methyl alcohol.........	0	.132	......	.506	......	......	.0879
Methyl butyrate........	0	.0633	......	.242	......	......	.0446
Methyl i-butyrate......	0	.0639	......	.257	......	......	.0451
Methyl cyclopentane....	15	......	.0731	.318	0.0742	.0758	
Methyl formate........	0	.0872					
Methyl propionate......	0	.0735	......	.295	......	......	.0528
Methyl valerate........	0	.0569					
Naphthalene...........	0	.0513					
Nitrogen...............	0	......	......	......	.181		
	25	......	......	......	......	......	.165
Nitrous oxide..........	0	.0505	......	.535	......	......	.096
n-Octane..............	0	.0505					
	30	......	.0642	.271	.0705	.0710	
Oxygen................	0	.178	......	.697	......	.181	.139
Phosgene..............	0	.095					
Propionic acid..........	0	.0829	......	.330	......	......	.0588
Propyl acetate.........	0	.067					
n-Propyl alcohol.......	0	.085	......	.315	......	......	.0577
i-Propyl alcohol........	0	.0818					
	30	.101					
n-Propyl benzene.......	0	.0481					
i-Propyl benzene.......	0	.0489					
n-Propyl bromide.......	0	.085					
i-Propyl bromide.......	0	.0902					
Propyl butyrate........	0	.0530	......	.206	......	......	.0364
Propyl formate.........	0	.0712	......	.281	......	......	.0490
n-Propyl iodide.........	0	.079					
i-Propyl iodide.........	0	.0802					
n-Propyl isobutyrate....	0	.0549	......	.212	......	......	.0388
i-Propyl isobutyrate.....	0	.059					
Propyl propionate......	0	.057	......	.212	... ..	......	.0395
Propyl valerate.........	0	.0466	......	.189	......	......	.0341
Safrol.................	0	.0434					
i-Safrol................	0	.0455					
Sulfur hexafluoride......	25	......	......	.418			
Toluene...............	0	.076	.071				
	30	.088					
Trimethyl carbinol......	0	.087					
2,2,4-Trimethyl pentane...............	30	......	.0618	.288	.0688	.0705	
2,2,3-Trimethyl heptane	90	......	......	.270	......	.0684	
n-Valeric acid..........	0	.050					
i-Valeric acid...........	0	.0544	......	.212	......	......	.0376
Water.................	0	.220	......	.75	......	......	.138
	450	......	......	......	1.3		

* To convert to square feet per hour, multiply by 0.388.

Table 3-19. Diffusivities in Liquids (25°C)

Dilute solutions and 1 atm unless otherwise noted; use $D_L \mu / T$ = constant to estimate effect of temperature; * indicates that reference gives effect of concentration.

Solute	Solvent	$D_L \times 10^5$, cm²/sec [†]	Estimated possible error, $\pm$ %
Acetal*.............................	Ethanol	1.25	5
Acetamide*...........................	Ethanol	0.68	5
Acetamide*...........................	Water	1.19	3
Acetic acid...........................	Acetone	3.31	
Acetic acid...........................	Benzene	2.11	
Acetic acid...........................	Carbon tetrachloride	1.49	
Acetic acid...........................	Ethylene glycol	0.13	
Acetic acid...........................	Toluene	2.26	
Acetic acid*..........................	Water	1.24	3
Acetonitrile..........................	Water	1.66	5
Acetylene............................	Water	1.78, 2.11	
Allyl alcohol*........................	Ethanol	1.06	5
Allyl alcohol.........................	Water	1.19	6
Ammonia*.............................	Water	1.7, 2.0, 2.3	
i-Amyl alcohol*......................	Ethanol	0.87	5
i-Amyl alcohol.......................	Water	1.0	8
Benzene..............................	Carbon tetrachloride	1.53	
Benzene (50 mole %)..................	n-Decane	1.72	
Benzene (50 mole %)..................	2,4-Dimethyl pentane	2.49	
Benzene (50 mole %)..................	n-Dodecane	1.40	
Benzene (50 mole %)..................	n-Heptane	2.47	
Benzene (50 mole %)..................	n-Hexadecane	0.96	
Benzene (50 mole %)..................	n-Octadecane	0.86	
Benzoic acid.........................	Acetone	2.62	
Benzoic acid.........................	Benzene	1.38	
Benzoic acid.........................	Carbon tetrachloride	0.91	
Benzoic acid.........................	Ethylene glycol	0.043	
Benzoic acid.........................	Toluene	1.49	
Bromine..............................	Benzene	2.7	
Bromine..............................	Carbon disulfide	4.1	
Bromine..............................	Water	1.3	
Bromobenzene........................	Benzene	2.30	
Bromoform*..........................	Acetone	2.90	
Bromoform...........................	i-Amyl alcohol	0.53	
Bromoform...........................	Ethanol	1.08	5
Bromoform*..........................	Ethyl ether	3.62	
Bromoform...........................	Methanol	2.20	
Bromoform...........................	n-Propanol	0.94	
n-Butanol............................	Water	0.96	5
Caffeine.............................	Water	0.63	6
Carbon dioxide.......................	Ethanol	4.0	6
Carbon dioxide.......................	Water	1.96	1
Carbon disulfide (50 mole %, 200 atm).......	n-Butanol	3.57	
Carbon disulfide (50 mole %, 200 atm).......	i-Butanol	2.42	
Carbon disulfide (50 mole %, 218 atm).......	Chlorobenzene	3.00	
Carbon disulfide (50 mole %, 200 atm).......	2,4-Dimethyl pentane	3.63	
Carbon disulfide (50 mole %, 100 atm).......	n-Heptane	3.0	
Carbon disulfide (50 mole %, 50 atm)........	Methyl cyclohexane	3.5	
Carbon disulfide (50 mole %, 200 atm).......	n-Octane	3.10	
Carbon disulfide (50 mole %)...............	Toluene	2.06	
Carbon tetrachloride..................	Benzene	2.04	3
Carbon tetrachloride*.................	Cyclohexane	1.49	2
Carbon tetrachloride..................	Decalin	0.776	2
Carbon tetrachloride..................	Dioxane	1.02	2
Carbon tetrachloride*.................	Ethanol	1.50	2
Carbon tetrachloride..................	n-Heptane	3.17	2
Carbon tetrachloride..................	Kerosene	0.961	2
Carbon tetrachloride..................	Methanol	2.30	2
Carbon tetrachloride..................	i-Octane	2.57	2
Carbon tetrachloride..................	Tetralin	0.735	2
Chloral*.............................	Ethanol	0.68	5
Chloral hydrate.......................	Water	0.77	7
Chlorine.............................	Water	1.44	4
Chlorobenzene........................	Benzene	2.66	

† To convert to square feet per hour, multiply by 0.388.

Table 3-19. Diffusivities in Liquids (25°C) (Continued)

Solute	Solvent	$D_L \times 10^5$, cm²/sec †	Estimated possible error, ± %
Chloroform	Benzene	2.50	6
Chloroform	Ethanol	1.38	
Cinnamic acid	Acetone	2.41	
Cinnamic acid	Benzene	1.12	
Cinnamic acid	Carbon tetrachloride	0.76	
Cinnamic acid	Toluene	2.41	
1,1'-Dichloropropanol	Water	1.0	6
Dicyanodiamide*	Water	1.18	4
Diethyl ether	Benzene	2.73	
Diethyl ether	Water	0.85	
2,4-Dimethyl pentane (50 mole %)	n-Dodecane	1.44	
2,4-Dimethyl pentane (50 mole %)	n-Hexadecane	0.88	
Ethanol*	Water	1.28	4
Ethyl acetate	Ethyl benzoate	0.94	
Ethylene dichloride	Benzene	2.8	
Formic acid	Acetone	3.77	
Formic acid	Benzene	2.28	
Formic acid	Carbon tetrachloride	1.89	
Formic acid	Ethylene glycol	0.094	
Formic acid	Toluene	2.65	
Formic acid	Water	1.37	10
Glucose	Water	0.69	6
Glycerol	i-Amyl alcohol	0.12	
Glycerol	Ethanol	0.56	
Glycerol*	Water	0.94	6
n-Heptane (50 mole %)	n-Dodecane	1.58	
n-Heptane (50 mole %)	n-Hexadecane	1.00	
n-Heptane (50 mole %)	n-Octadecane	0.92	
n-Heptane (50 mole %)	n-Tetradecane	1.29	
Hexamethylene tetramine	Water	0.67	
Hydrogen chloride*	Water	3.10	3
Hydrogen	Water	5.85 (4.4?)	
Hydrogen sulfide	Water	1.61	
Hydroquinone*	Ethanol	0.53	5
Hydroquinone*	Water	0.88, 1.12	
Iodine	Acetic acid	1.13	
Iodine	Anisole	1.25	
Iodine	Benzene	1.98	
Iodine	Bromobenzene	1.25	10
Iodine	Carbon disulfide	3.2	
Iodine	Carbon tetrachloride	1.45	8
Iodine	Chloroform	2.30	3
Iodine	Cyclohexane	1.80	
Iodine	Dioxane	1.07	
Iodine*	Ethanol	1.30	
Iodine	Ethyl acetate	2.2	
Iodine	Ethyl ether	3.61	
Iodine	Ethylene bromide	0.93	
Iodine	n-Heptane	3.4, 2.5	
Iodine	n-Hexane	4.15	
Iodine	Mesitylene	1.49	
Iodine	Methanol	1.74	
Iodine	Methyl cyclohexane	2.1	
Iodine	n-Octane	2.76	
Iodine	Tetrabromoethane	2.0	
Iodine	n-Tetradecane	0.96	
Iodine	Toluene	2.1	
Iodine	m-Xylene	1.82	
Iodobenzene	Ethanol	1.09	3
Lactose*	Water	0.49	5
Maltose*	Water	0.48	5
Mannitol*	Water	0.65	5
Methanol	Water	1.6	
Micotine*	Water	0.60	8
Nitric acid*	Water	2.98	2
Nitrobenzene	Carbon tetrachloride	1.00	
Nitrogen	Water	1.9	
Nitrous oxide	Water	1.8	
Oxalic acid*	Water	1.61	2
Oxygen	Glycerol*-water (106 poise)	0.24	

† To convert to square feet per hour, multiply by 0.388.

Table 3-19. Diffusivities in Liquids (25°C) (Continued)

Solute	Solvent	$D_L \times 10^6$, cm²/sec †	Estimated possible error, ± %
Oxygen	Sucrose*-water (125 poise)	0.25	
Oxygen	Water	2.5	20
Pentaerythritol*	Water	0.77	4
Phenol	i-Amyl alcohol	0.2	
Phenol	Benzene	1.68	
Phenol	Carbon disulfide	3.7	
Phenol	Chloroform	2.0	
Phenol	Ethanol	0.89	
Phenol	Ethyl ether	3.9	
n-Propanol	Water	1.1	
Pyridine*	Ethanol	1.24	3
Pyridine	Water	0.76	7
Pyrogallol	Water	0.74	7
Raffinose*	Water	0.41	4
Resorcinol*	Ethanol	0.46	5
Resorcinol*	Water	0.87	4
Saccharose*	Water	0.49	4
Stearic acid*	Ethanol	0.65	5
Succinic acid*	Water	0.94	
Sucrose	Water	0.56	6
Sulfur dioxide	Water	1.7	
Sulfuric acid*	Water	1.97	3
Tartaric acid*	Water	0.80	10
1,1,2,2-Tetrabromoethane	1,1,2,2-Tetrachloroethane	0.61	4
Toluene	n-Decane	2.09	
Toluene	n-Dodecane	1.38	
Toluene	n-Heptane	3.72	
Toluene	n-Hexane	4.21	
Toluene	n-Tetradecane	1.02	
Urea	Ethanol	0.73	
Urea	Water	1.37	2
Urethane	Water	1.06	
Water	Glycerol	0.021	

† To convert to square feet per hour, multiply by 0.388.

VAPOR PRESSURES

Table 3-20. Vapor Pressures of Inorganic Compounds, above 1 Atm

Name	Formula	Pressure, atm — Temperature, °C									Critical point	
		1	2	5	10	20	30	40	50	60	t_c, °C	P_c, atm
Ammonia	NH_3	−33.6	−18.7	+4.7	25.7	50.1	66.1	78.9	89.3	98.3	132.4	111.5
Carbon monoxide	CO	−191.3	−183.5	−170.7	−161.0	−149.7	−141.9				−138.7	34.6
Carbon dioxide	CO_2	−78.2	−69.1	−56.7	−39.5	−18.9	−5.3	+5.9	14.9	22.4	31.1	73.0
disulfide	CS_2	46.5	69.1	104.8	136.3	175.5	201.5	222.8	240.0	256.0	273.0	72.9
Chlorine	Cl_2	−33.8	−16.9	+10.3	35.6	65.0	84.8	101.6	115.2	127.1	144.0	76.1
para-Hydrogen	H_2	−252.5	−250.2	−246.0	−241.6						−240.0	12.8
Hydrogen bromide	HBr	−66.5	−51.5	−29.1	−8.4	+16.8	33.9	48.1	60.0	70.6	90.0	84.4
chloride	HCl	−84.8	−71.4	−50.5	−31.7	−8.8	+5.9	17.8	27.9	36.2	51.4	81.6
cyanide	HCN	25.9	45.8	75.8	102.7	135.0	153.8	169.9	183.5		183.5	50.0
Water	H_2O	100.0	120.1	152.4	180.5	213.1	234.6	251.1	264.7	276.5	374.2	218.0
Hydrogen sulfide	H_2S	−60.4	−45.9	−22.3	0.4	+25.5	41.9	55.8	66.7	76.3	100.3	88.9
Krypton	Kr	−152.0	−143.5	−130.0	−118.0	−101.7	−88.8	−78.4	−66.5		−63	54
Nitrogen	N_2	−195.8	−189.2	−179.1	−169.8	−157.6	−148.3				−147.2	33.5
Oxygen	O_2	−183.1	−176.0	−164.5	−153.2	−140.0	−130.7	−124.1			−118.9	49.7
Sulfur dioxide	SO_2	−10.0	+6.3	32.1	55.5	83.8	102.6	118.0	130.2	141.7	157.2	77.7
trioxide	SO_3	44.8	60.0	82.5	104.0	138.0	157.8	175.0	187.8	198.0	218.3	83.6

SOURCE: Compiled from the extended tables by D. R. Stull, *Ind. Eng. Chem.*, 39, 517 (1947).

Table 3-21. Vapor Pressures of Inorganic Compounds, up to 1 Atm

Compound		Pressure, mm Hg — Temperature, °C										Melting point, °C
Name	Formula	1	5	10	20	40	60	100	200	400	760	
Ammonia	NH_3	-109.1	-97.5	-91.9	-85.8	-79.2	-74.3	-68.4	-57.0	-45.4	-33.6	-77.7
heavy	ND_3	—	—	—	—	—	-74.0	-67.4	-57.0	-45.4	-33.4	-74.0
Carbon (graphite)	C	3586	3828	3946	4069	4196	4273	4373	4516	4660	4827	—
dioxide	CO_2	-134.3	-124.4	-119.5	-114.4	-108.6	-104.8	-100.2	-93.0	-85.7	-78.2	-57.5
disulfide	CS_2	-73.8	-54.3	-44.7	-34.3	-22.5	-15.3	-5.1	+10.4	+28.0	+46.5	-110.8
monoxide	CO	-222.0	-217.2	-215.0	-212.8	-210.0	-208.1	-205.7	-201.3	-196.3	-191.3	-205.
Chlorine	Cl_2	-118.0	-106.7	-101.6	-93.3	-84.5	-79.0	-71.7	-60.2	-47.3	-33.8	-100.7
fluoride	ClF	—	-143.4	-139.0	-134.3	-128.8	-125.3	-120.8	-114.4	-107.0	-100.5	-145
p-Hydrogen	H_2	-263.3	-261.9	-261.3	-260.4	-259.6	-258.9	-257.9	-256.3	-254.5	-252.5	-259.1
Hydrogen bromide	HBr	-138.8	-127.4	-121.8	-115.4	-108.3	-103.8	-97.7	-88.1	-78.0	-66.5	-87.0
chloride	HCl	-150.8	-140.7	-135.6	-130.0	-123.8	-119.6	-114.0	-105.2	-95.3	-84.8	-114.3
cyanide	HCN	-71.0	-55.3	-47.7	-39.7	-30.9	-25.1	-17.8	-5.3	+10.2	+25.9	-13.2
sulfide	H_2S	-134.3	-122.4	-116.3	-109.7	-102.3	-97.9	-91.6	-82.3	-71.8	-60.4	-85.5
Krypton	Kr	-199.3	-191.3	-187.2	-182.9	-178.4	-175.7	-171.8	-165.9	-159.0	-152.0	-156.7
Nitrogen	N_2	-226.1	-221.3	-219.1	-216.8	-214.0	-212.3	-209.7	-205.6	-200.9	-195.8	-210.0
Nitric oxide	NO	-184.5	-180.6	-178.2	-175.3	-171.7	-168.9	-166.0	-162.3	-156.8	-151.7	-161
Nitrogen dioxide	NO_2	-55.6	-42.7	-36.7	-30.4	-23.9	-19.9	-14.7	-5.0	+8.0	+21.0	-9.3
Oxygen	O_2	-219.1	-213.4	-210.6	-207.5	-204.1	-201.9	-198.8	-194.0	-188.8	-183.1	-218.7
Sulfur	S	183.8	223.0	243.8	264.7	288.3	305.5	327.2	359.7	399.6	444.6	112.8
dioxide	SO_2	-95.5	-83.0	-76.8	-69.7	-60.5	-54.6	-46.9	-35.4	-23.0	-10.0	-73.2
trioxide (α)	SO_3	-39.0	-23.7	-16.5	-9.1	-1.0	4.0	10.5	20.5	32.6	44.8	16.8
trioxide (β)	SO_3	-34.0	-19.2	-12.3	-4.9	3.2	8.0	14.3	23.7	32.6	44.8	32.5
trioxide (γ)	SO_3	-15.3	+2.0	+4.3	11.1	17.9	21.4	28.0	35.8	44.0	51.6	62.1
Water	H_2O	-17.3	+1.2	+11.2	22.1	34.0	41.5	51.6	66.5	83.0	100.0	0.0

Table 3-22. Vapor Pressures of Organic Compounds, above 1 Atm

Name	Formula	Pressure, atm — Temperature, °C									Critical point t_c, °C	P_c, atm
		1	2	5	10	20	30	40	50	60		
Acetic acid	$C_2H_4O_2$	118.1	143.5	180.3	214.0	252.0	276.5	297.0	312.5	....	321.6	57.2
anhydride	$C_4H_6O_3$	139.6	162.0	194.0	221.5	253.0	272.8	288.5	....	....	296	46
Acetone	C_3H_6O	56.5	78.6	113.0	144.5	181.0	205.0	214.5	....	....	235.0	47.0
Acetylene	C_2H_2	−84.0	−71.6	−50.2	−32.7	−10.0	+4.8	16.8	26.8	34.8	36.0	62.0
Allene (propadiene)	C_3H_4	−35.0	−18.4	+8.0	32.2	64.5	85.5	103.5	118.0	....	120.7	51.8
Aniline	C_6H_7N	184.4	212.8	254.8	292.7	342.0	375.5	400.0	422.4	....	426	52.4
Benzene	C_6H_6	80.1	103.8	142.5	178.8	221.5	249.5	272.3	290.3	....	290.5	50.1
Bromobenzene	C_6H_5Br	156.2	186.2	232.5	274.5	327.0	359.8	387.5	....	....	397	44.6
1,3-Butadiene	C_4H_6	−4.5	+15.3	47.0	76.0	114.0	139.8	158.0	....	....	161.8	42.6
iso-Butane (2-methylpropane)	C_4H_{10}	−11.7	+7.5	39.0	68.6	99.5	120.5	....	....	....	134.0	37.0
n-Butane	C_4H_{10}	−0.5	+18.8	50.0	79.5	116.0	140.6	....	....	....	152.8	36.0
iso-Butyl alcohol (2-methylpropanol-1)	$C_4H_{10}O$	108.0	127.3	156.2	182.0	212.5	232.0	251.0	....	....	265	48
n-Butyl alcohol (1-butanol)	$C_4H_{10}O$	117.5	139.8	172.5	203.0	237.0	259.0	277.0	....	....	287	48.4
sec-Butyl alcohol (2-butanol)	$C_4H_{10}O$	99.5	118.2	147.5	172.0	204.0	230.0	251.0	....	....	265	48
tert-Butyl alcohol (trimethyl carbinol)	$C_4H_{10}O$	82.9	102.0	130.0	147.2	184.5	207.0	222.5	....	....	235	49
iso-Butyl formate	$C_5H_{10}O_2$	98.2	121.8	157.8	192.4	234.0	261.0	....	....	....	278.0	38.0
Butyric acid	$C_4H_8O_2$	163.5	188.3	225.0	257.0	295.0	319.0	338.0	352.0	....	355	52.0
iso-Butyric acid	$C_4H_8O_2$	154.5	179.8	217.0	250.0	289.0	315.0	336.0	....	....	336	40.0
Carbon dioxide	CO_2	−78.2	−69.1	−56.7	−39.5	−18.9	−5.3	+5.9	14.9	22.4	31.1	73.0
disulfide	CS_2	46.5	69.1	104.8	136.3	175.5	201.5	222.8	240.0	256.0	273.0	72.9
monoxide	CO	−191.3	−183.5	−170.7	−161.0	−149.7	−141.9	....	....	....	−138.7	34.6
tetrachloride	CCl_4	76.7	102.0	141.7	178.0	222.0	251.2	276.0	....	....	283.1	45.0
Chlorobenzene	C_6H_5Cl	132.2	160.2	205.0	245.3	292.8	324.4	349.8	....	....	359.2	44.6
Chlorodifluoromethane	$CHClF_2$	−40.8	−24.7	+0.3	24.0	52.0	70.3	85.3	....	....	96	48.7
Chloroform (trichloromethane)	$CHCl_3$	61.3	83.9	120.0	152.3	191.8	216.5	237.5	254.0	....	260	54.9
1-Chloro-1,2,2-trifluoroethylene	C_2ClF_3	−27.9	−11.1	+15.5	40.0	71.1	91.9	....	....	....	107.0	39.0
Chlorotrifluoromethane	$CClF_3$	−81.2	−66.7	−42.7	−18.5	+12.0	34.8	52.8	....	....	53	40.3
Cyanogen	C_2N_2	−21.0	+4.4	21.4	44.6	72.6	91.6	106.5	118.2	....	126.6	58.2
Cyclohexane	C_6H_{12}	80.7	106.0	146.4	184.0	228.4	257.5	....	....	....	279.9	39.8
1,2-Dibromoethane	$C_2H_4Br_2$	131.5	157.7	200.0	237.0	269.0	286.0	295.0	300.0	304.5	309.8	70.6
Dichlorodifluoromethane	CCl_2F_2	−29.8	−12.2	+16.1	42.4	74.0	95.6	....	....	....	111.5	39.6
1,1-Dichloroethane	$C_2H_4Cl_2$	57.3	80.2	117.3	150.3	192.7	220.0	243.0	261.5	....	261.5	50.0
1,2-Dichloroethane	$C_2H_4Cl_2$	83.7	108.1	147.8	183.5	226.5	254.0	272.0	285.0	....	288.4	50.0
cis-1,2-Dichloroethylene	$C_2H_2Cl_2$	59.0	82.1	119.3	152.3	194.0	221.5	244.5	260.0	....	271.0	57.9

The following is a large data table of physical constants (temperatures at increasing pressures, with critical temperature and critical pressure) for organic compounds. Column headers are not printed on this page. Values shown as `...` are blank (dotted) in the original. A leading `—` indicates a negative value and `+` a small positive value as printed.

Compound	Formula										t_c	P_c
trans-1,2-Dichloroethylene	C₂H₂Cl₂	47.8	69.8	104.0	135.7	174.0	199.8	220.0	236.5	242.0	243.3	54.5
Dichlorofluoromethane	CHCl₂F	8.9	28.4	59.0	87.0	121.2	144.0	162.6	177.5	...	178.5	51.0
1,2-Dichloro-1,1,2,2-tetrafluoroethane	C₂Cl₂F₄	3.5	22.8	54.0	82.3	117.5	140.9	...	...	...	145.7	32.3
Diethylamine	C₄H₁₁N	55.5	77.8	113.0	145.3	184.5	210.0	...	...	...	223.3	36.6
Diethyl ether	C₄H₁₀O	34.6	56.0	90.0	122.0	159.0	183.3	...	...	...	193.8	35.5
sulfide	C₄H₁₀S	88.0	112.0	153.8	190.2	234.0	263.0	...	...	...	283.8	39.1
Dimethylamine	C₂H₇N	7.4	25.0	53.9	80.0	111.7	132.2	149.8	162.6	...	164.5	52.4
2,3-Dimethylbutane	C₆H₁₄	58.0	82.0	120.3	155.7	198.7	225.5	...	...	...	227.4	52.0
Dimethyl ether	C₂H₆O	—23.7	6.4	20.8	45.5	75.7	96.0	112.1	125.2	...	126.9	9.5
oxalate	C₂H₆O₄	163.3	189.6	228.7	124.5	163.8	188.5	209.0	224.5	...	260	54.6
sulfide	C₂H₆S	36.0	57.8	92.3	345.8	...	...	...	...	...	229.9	17.5
n-Dodecane	C₁₂H₂₆	216.2	249.2	300.0	32.0	...	...	...	...	...	385	48.2
Ethane	C₂H₆	—88.6	—75.0	—52.8	6.4	10.0	23.6	...	...	...	32.3	37.9
Ethyl acetate	C₄H₈O₂	77.1	100.6	136.6	169.7	209.5	235.0	218.0	230.0	...	250.1	63.1
alcohol (ethanol)	C₂H₆O	78.4	97.5	126.0	151.8	183.0	203.0	218.0	230.0	...	243.5	55.5
Ethylamine	C₂H₇N	16.6	35.7	65.3	91.8	124.0	146.0	163.0	176.0	...	183.2	38.1
Ethyl benzene	C₈H₁₀	136.2	163.5	207.5	246.3	294.5	326.5	206.5	220.0	229.5	346.4	61.5
bromide	C₂H₅Br	28.4	60.2	95.0	126.8	164.3	188.0	167.0	180.5	...	230.8	52.0
chloride	C₂H₅Cl	12.3	32.5	64.0	92.6	127.3	149.5	90.0	...	...	187.2	49.6
fluoride	C₂H₅F	32.0	16.7	7.7	30.2	57.5	75.7	...	...	...	102.2	46.8
formate	C₃H₆O₂	54.3	76.0	110.5	142.2	180.0	205.0	225.0	...	...	235.3	30.0
isobutyrate	C₆H₁₂O₂	110.1	135.5	174.2	210.0	253.0	280.0	...	...	...	280.0	54.2
mercaptan (ethanethiol)	C₂H₆S	35.0	56.6	90.7	121.9	159.5	184.3	204.7	220.0	...	225.5	43.4
methyl ether	C₃H₈O	7.5	26.5	56.4	84.0	108.0	141.4	160.0	176.0	...	164.7	33.2
propionate	C₅H₁₀O₂	99.1	123.8	162.7	197.8	240.0	264.5	...	...	...	272.8	32.1
propyl ether	C₆H₁₄O	61.7	85.3	123.1	156.2	197.2	223.0	...	...	...	227.4	50.7
Ethylene	C₂H₄	—103.7	90.8	71.1	52.8	29.1	14.2	+1.5	+8.9	...	9.6	44.7
Fluorobenzene	C₆H₅F	84.7	109.9	148.5	184.4	227.6	257.0	279.3	...	...	286.8	26.9
n-Heptane	C₇H₁₆	98.4	124.8	165.7	202.8	247.5	...	...	...	...	266.8	29.6
n-Hexane	C₆H₁₄	68.7	93.0	131.7	166.6	209.4	...	...	...	...	234.8	50.0
Hydrogen cyanide (hydrocyanic acid)	CHN	25.9	45.8	75.0	102.7	135.0	153.8	169.9	183.5	...	183.5	44.7
Iodobenzene	C₆H₅I	188.6	220.0	270.0	315.7	371.5	406.0	437.2	...	...	448	45.8
Methane	CH₄	—161.5	—152.3	—138.3	—124.8	—108.5	96.3	225.0	...	...	82.1	46.3
Methyl acetate	C₃H₆O₂	57.8	79.5	113.1	144.2	181.0	205.0	225.0	...	...	233.7	52.8
acetylene (propyne)	C₃H₄	23.3	7.1	19.5	43.8	74.0	94.0	111.5	125.0	...	128	78.7
alcohol	CH₄O	64.7	84.0	112.5	138.0	167.8	186.5	203.5	214.0	224.0	240.0	73.6
Methylamine	CH₅N	—6.3	10.1	36.0	59.5	87.8	106.3	121.8	133.7	144.6	156.9	51.6
Methyl bromide	CH₃Br	3.6	23.3	54.8	84.0	121.7	147.5	170.2	190.0	...	194	34.2
butyrate	C₅H₁₀O₂	102.3	127.5	166.7	203.0	244.5	272.0	...	...	...	281.2	65.8
chloride	CH₃Cl	—24.0	6.4	22.0	47.3	77.3	97.5	113.8	126.0	137.5	143.8	62.0
fluoride	CH₃F	—78.2	64.5	42.0	21.0	2.6	15.5	26.5	36.0	43.5	44.9	59.1
formate	C₂H₄O₂	32.0	51.9	83.5	112.0	147.2	169.7	188.5	213.0	...	214.0	54.6
iodide	CH₃I	42.4	101.8	155.9	138.0	176.5	206.0	228.5	248.0	185.0	255	33.9
isobutyrate	C₄H₈O₂	92.6	116.7	155.2	190.2	232.0	259.5	...	...	...	267.5	71.4
mercaptan (methanethiol)	CH₄S	6.8	26.1	55.9	83.4	117.5	140.0	157.7	172.0	...	196.8	—
propionate	C₄H₈O₂	79.8	103.0	139.8	172.6	212.5	239.0	157.7	172.0	...	257.4	39.3

Table 3-22. Vapor Pressures of Organic Compounds, above 1 Atm (Continued)

| Name | Formula | Pressure, atm — Temperature, °C | | | | | | | | | Critical point | |
		1	2	5	10	20	30	40	50	60	t_c, °C	P_c, atm
n-Octane	C_8H_{18}	125.6	152.7	196.2	235.8	281.4	......	......	......	......	296.2	24.7
iso-Pentane (2-methylbutane)	C_5H_{12}	27.8	48.8	82.8	114.5	154.0	180.3	......	......	......	187.8	32.8
n-Pentane	C_5H_{12}	36.1	58.0	92.4	124.7	164.3	191.3	......	......	......	197.2	33.0
neo-Pentane (2,2-dimethylpropane)	C_5H_{12}	+ 9.5	29.5	61.1	90.7	127.6	152.5	......	......	......	159.0	33.0
Phenol	C_6H_6O	181.9	208.0	248.2	283.8	328.7	358.0	382.1	400.0	418.7	419	60.5
Phosgene (carbonyl chloride)	CCl_2O	8.3	27.3	57.2	85.0	119.0	141.8	159.8	174.0	......	181.7	56.0
Propane	C_3H_8	− 42.1	− 25.6	+ 1.4	26.9	58.1	78.7	94.8	......	......	96.8	42.0
Propionic acid	$C_3H_6O_2$	141.1	160.0	186.0	203.5	220.0	228.0	233.0	238.0	......	239.5	53.0
Propyl acetate	$C_5H_{10}O_2$	101.8	126.8	165.7	200.5	242.8	269.0	......	......	......	276.2	33.2
iso-Propyl alcohol (2-propanol)	C_3H_8O	82.5	101.3	130.2	155.7	186.0	205.0	220.2	232.0	......	235	53
n-Propyl alcohol (1-propanol)	C_3H_8O	97.8	117.0	149.0	177.0	210.8	232.3	250.0	......	......	263.7	49.9
Propylamine	C_3H_9N	48.5	69.8	102.8	133.4	170.0	194.3	214.5	......	......	223.8	46.8
Propyl formate	$C_4H_8O_2$	81.3	104.3	142.0	176.4	217.5	245.0	......	......	......	264.8	39.5
Propylene	C_3H_6	− 47.7	− 31.4	+ 4.8	+ 19.8	49.5	70.0	85.0	......	......	91.4	45.4
Tetramethylsilane	$C_4H_{12}Si$	− 27.0	48.0	82.0	113.0	152.0	178.0	......	......	......	185	33
Toluene	C_7H_8	110.6	136.5	178.0	215.8	262.5	292.8	319.0	......	......	320.6	41.6
Trichlorofluoromethane	CCl_3F	23.7	44.1	77.3	108.2	146.7	172.0	194.0	......	......	198.0	43.2

SOURCE: Compiled from the extended tables by D. R. Stull, *Ind. Eng. Chem.*, 39, 517 (1947). For data on gasoline and aircraft fuels see Hibbard, *NACA Research Mem.*, E56I21, 1956 (declassified 1956). Extensive data for aqueous solutions of ethylene glycol, diethylene glycol, triethylene glycol, and propylene glycol from −20 to 300°F are contained in "Glycols," Union Carbide Corp. publ. F4763F, 1958. For vapor-pressure curves of the Freon compounds to 300°F, 1,000 psia, see E. I. du Pont De Nemours & Co., Inc., *Tech. Bull.* B-2, 1957; for methane data see Johnson (ed.), WADD-TR-56-60, 1960.

Table 3-23. Vapor Pressure of Organic Compounds, up to 1 Atm

Compound		Pressure, mm Hg — Temperature, °C										Melting point, °C
Name	Formula	1	5	10	20	40	60	100	200	400	760	
Acetic acid	$C_2H_4O_2$	−17.2	+6.3	17.5	29.9	43.0	51.7	63.0	80.0	99.0	118.1	16.7
anhydride	$C_4H_6O_3$	1.7	24.8	36.0	48.3	62.1	70.8	82.2	100.0	119.6	139.6	−73
Acetylene	C_2H_2	−142.9	−133.0	−128.2	−122.8	−116.7	−112.8	−107.9	−100.3	−92.0	−84.0	−81.5
Allene (propadiene)	C_3H_4	−120.6	−108.0	−101.0	−93.4	−85.2	−78.8	−72.5	−61.3	−48.5	−35.0	−136
Aniline	C_6H_7N	34.8	57.9	69.4	82.0	96.7	106.0	119.9	140.1	161.9	184.4	+6.2
Benzene	C_6H_6	−36.7	−19.6	−11.5	−2.6	7.6	15.4	26.1	42.2	60.6	80.1	5.5
Bromobenzene	C_6H_5Br	2.9	27.8	40.0	53.8	68.6	78.1	90.8	110.1	132.3	156.2	−30.7
1,3-Butadiene	C_4H_6	−102.8	−87.6	−79.7	−71.0	−61.3	−55.1	−46.8	−33.9	−19.3	−4.5	−108.9
n-Butane	C_4H_{10}	−101.5	−85.7	−77.8	−68.9	−59.1	−52.8	−44.2	−31.2	−16.3	−0.5	−135
iso-Butane (2-methylpropane)	C_4H_{10}	−109.2	−94.1	−86.4	−77.9	−68.4	−62.4	−54.1	−41.5	−27.1	−11.7	−145
n-Butyl alcohol	$C_4H_{10}O$	1.2	20.0	30.2	41.5	53.4	60.3	70.1	84.3	100.8	117.5	−79.9
iso-Butyl alcohol	$C_4H_{10}O$	−9.0	+11.6	21.7	32.4	44.1	51.7	61.5	75.9	91.4	108.0	−108
sec-Butyl alcohol	$C_4H_{10}O$	−12.2	+7.2	16.9	27.3	38.1	45.2	54.1	67.9	83.9	99.5	−114.7
tert-Butyl alcohol	$C_4H_{10}O$	−20.4	+3.0	5.5	14.3	24.5	31.0	39.8	52.7	68.0	82.9	25.3
iso-Butyl formate	$C_5H_{10}O_2$	−32.7	−11.4	0.8	+11.0	24.1	32.4	43.4	60.0	79.0	98.2	−95.3
Butyric acid	$C_4H_8O_2$	25.5	49.8	61.5	74.0	88.0	96.5	108.0	125.5	144.5	163.5	−74
iso-Butyric acid	$C_4H_8O_2$	14.7	39.3	51.2	64.0	77.8	86.3	98.0	115.8	134.5	154.5	47
Carbon dioxide	CO_2	−134.3	−124.4	−119.5	−114.4	−108.6	−104.8	−100.2	−93.0	−85.7	−78.2	−57.5
disulfide	CS_2	−73.8	−54.3	−44.7	−34.3	−22.5	−15.3	−5.1	+10.4	28.0	46.5	−110.8
monoxide	CO	−222.0	−217.2	−215.0	−212.8	−210.0	−208.1	−205.7	−201.3	−196.3	−191.3	−205.0
Carbon tetrachloride	CCl_4	−50.0	−30.0	−19.6	−8.2	+4.3	12.3	23.0	38.3	57.8	76.7	−22.6
Chlorobenzene	C_6H_5Cl	13.0	+10.6	22.2	35.3	49.7	58.3	70.7	89.4	110.0	132.2	−45.2
Chlorodifluoromethane	$CHClF_2$	−122.8	−110.2	−103.7	−96.5	−88.6	−83.4	−76.4	−65.8	−53.6	−40.8	−160
Chloroform (trichloromethane)	$CHCl_3$	−58.0	−39.1	−29.7	−19.0	−7.1	+0.5	10.4	25.9	42.7	61.3	−63.5
1-Chloro-1,2,2-trifluoroethylene	C_2ClF_3	−116.0	−102.5	−95.9	−88.2	−79.7	−74.1	−66.7	−55.0	−41.7	−27.9	−157.5
Chlorotrifluoromethane	$CClF_3$	−149.5	−139.2	−134.1	−128.5	−121.9	−117.3	−111.7	−102.5	−92.7	−81.2	—
Cyanogen	C_2N_2	−95.8	−83.2	−76.8	−70.1	−62.7	−57.9	−51.8	−42.6	−33.0	−21.0	−34.4
Cyclohexane	C_6H_{12}	−45.3	−25.4	−15.9	−5.0	+6.7	14.7	25.5	42.0	60.8	80.7	+6.6
Dichlorofluoromethane	$CHCl_2F$	−91.3	−75.5	−67.5	−58.6	−48.8	−42.6	−33.9	−20.9	−6.2	8.9	−135
1,2-Dichloro-1,1,2,2-tetrafluoroethane	$C_2Cl_2F_4$	−95.4	−80.0	−72.3	−63.5	−53.7	−47.5	−39.1	−26.3	−12.0	+3.5	−94
Diethylamine	$C_4H_{11}N$	—	—	−33.0	−22.6	−11.3	−4.0	+6.0	21.0	38.0	55.5	−38.9
Diethyl ether	$C_4H_{10}O$	−74.3	−56.9	−48.1	−38.5	−27.7	−21.8	−11.5	+2.2	17.9	34.6	−116.3
sulfide	$C_4H_{10}S$	−39.6	−18.6	−8.0	+3.5	16.1	24.2	35.0	51.3	69.7	88.0	−99.5
Dimethylamine	C_2H_7N	−87.7	−72.2	−64.6	−56.0	−46.7	−40.7	−32.6	−20.4	−7.1	+7.4	−96
2,3-Dimethylbutane	C_6H_{14}	−63.7	−44.5	−34.9	−24.1	−12.4	−4.9	+5.4	21.1	39.0	58.0	−128.4
Dimethylether	C_2H_6O	−115.7	−101.1	−93.3	−85.2	−76.2	−70.4	−62.7	−50.9	−37.8	−23.7	−138.5
oxalate	$C_4H_6O_4$	20.0	44.0	56.0	69.4	83.6	92.8	104.8	123.3	143.3	163.3	—
sulfide	C_2H_6S	−75.6	−58.0	−49.2	−39.4	−28.4	−21.4	−12.0	2.6	18.7	37.3	−83.2
n-Dodecane	$C_{12}H_{26}$	47.8	75.8	90.0	104.6	121.7	132.1	146.2	167.2	191.0	216.2	−9.6
Ethane	C_2H_6	−159.5	−148.5	−142.9	−136.7	−129.8	−125.4	−119.3	−110.2	−99.7	−88.6	−183.2
Ethyl acetate	$C_4H_8O_2$	−43.4	−23.5	−13.5	−3.0	+9.0	16.6	27.0	42.0	59.3	77.1	−82.4
Ethyl alcohol (ethanol)	C_2H_6O	−31.3	−12.0	−2.3	+8.0	19.0	26.0	34.9	48.4	63.5	78.4	−112
Ethylamine	C_2H_7N	−82.3	−66.4	−58.3	−48.6	−39.8	−33.4	−25.1	−12.3	+2.0	16.6	−80.6

Table 3-23. Vapor Pressure of Organic Compounds, up to 1 Atm (Continued)

Compound		Pressure, mm Hg — Temperature, °C										Melting point, °C
Name	Formula	1	5	10	20	40	60	100	200	400	760	
Ethylbenzene	C_8H_{10}	-9.8	13.9	25.9	38.6	52.8	61.8	74.1	92.7	113.8	136.2	-94.9
Ethyl bromide	C_2H_5Br	-74.3	-56.4	-47.5	-37.8	-26.7	-19.5	-10.0	4.5	21.0	38.4	-117.8
chloride	C_2H_5Cl	-89.8	-73.9	-65.8	-56.8	-47.0	-40.6	-32.0	-18.6	+3.9	12.3	-139
Ethylene	C_2H_4	-168.3	-158.3	-153.2	-147.6	-141.3	-137.3	-131.8	-123.4	-113.9	-103.7	-169
Ethyl fluoride	C_2H_5F	-117.0	-103.8	-97.7	-90.0	-81.8	-76.4	-69.3	-58.0	-45.5	-32.0	
formate	$C_3H_6O_2$	-60.5	-42.2	-33.0	-22.7	-11.5	-4.3	5.4	20.0	37.1	54.3	-79
mercaptan (ethanethiol)	C_2H_6S	-76.7	-59.1	-50.2	-40.1	-29.8	-22.4	-13.0	1.5	17.7	35.0	-121
methyl ether	C_2H_6O	-91.0	-75.6	-67.8	-59.1	-49.4	-43.3	-34.8	-22.0	-7.7	7.5	
propionate	$C_5H_{10}O_2$	-28.0	-7.2	3.4	14.3	27.2	35.1	45.2	61.7	79.8	99.1	-72.6
propyl ether	$C_6H_{14}O$	-64.3	-45.0	-35.0	-24.0	-11.5	-4.0	+6.8	23.3	41.6	61.7	
Fluorobenzene	C_6H_5F	-43.4	-22.8	-12.4	-1.2	+11.5	19.6	30.4	47.2	65.7	84.7	-42.1
n-Heptane	C_7H_{16}	-34.0	-12.7	-2.1	9.5	22.3	30.6	41.8	58.7	78.0	98.4	-90.6
n-Hexane	C_6H_{14}	-53.9	-34.5	-25.0	-14.1	-2.3	5.4	15.8	31.6	49.6	68.7	-95.3
Hydrogen cyanide (hydrocyanic acid)	CHN	-71.0	-55.3	-47.7	-39.7	30.9	25.1	17.8	5.3	10.2	25.9	-13.2
Iodobenzene	C_6H_5I	24.1	50.6	64.0	78.3	94.4	105.0	118.3	139.8	163.9	188.6	-28.5
Methane	CH_4	-205.9	-199.0	-195.5	-191.8	-187.7	-185.1	-181.4	-175.5	-168.8	-161.5	-182.5
Methyl acetate	$C_3H_6O_2$	-57.2	-38.6	-29.3	-19.1	-7.9	0.5	9.4	24.0	40.0	57.8	-98.7
acetylene (propyne)	C_3H_4	-111.0	-97.5	-90.5	-82.9	-74.3	-68.8	-61.3	-49.8	-37.2	23.3	-102.7
alcohol (methanol)	CH_4O	-44.0	-25.3	-16.2	-6.0	5.0	12.1	21.2	34.8	49.9	64.7	-93.9
Methylamine	CH_5N	-95.8	-81.3	-72.8	-65.9	-56.9	-51.3	-43.7	-32.4	-19.7	-6.3	-93.5
Methyl bromide	CH_3Br	-96.3	-80.6	-72.8	-64.0	-54.2	-48.0	-39.4	-26.5	-11.9	3.6	93
n-butyrate	$C_5H_{10}O_2$	-26.8	-5.5	+5.0	16.7	29.6	37.4	48.0	64.3	83.1	102.3	
isobutyrate	$C_5H_{10}O_2$	-34.1	-13.0	-2.9	8.4	21.0	28.9	39.6	55.7	73.6	92.6	-84.7
chloride	CH_3Cl	-147.3	-137.0	-131.6	-125.9	-119.1	-115.0	-109.0	-99.9	-89.5	-24.0	-97.7
fluoride	CH_3F	-74.2	-57.0	-48.6	-39.2	-28.7	-21.9	-12.9	+0.8	16.0	-78.2	
formate	$C_3H_6O_2$	-42.0	-21.5	-11.8	-1.0	+11.0	16.9	7.0	8.0	25.3	32.0	-99.8
iodide	CH_3I	-14.0	+8.3	19.2	31.5	45.1	18.7	29.0	44.2	61.8	42.4	-64.4
propionate	$C_4H_8O_2$	-76.6	-62.5	-50.1	-40.2	29.2	53.8	65.7	83.6	104.0	79.8	-87.5
n-Octane	C_8H_{18}	-82.9	-65.8	-57.0	-47.3	36.5	22.2	12.6	1.9	18.5	125.6	-56.8
n-Pentane	C_5H_{12}	-102.0	-85.4	-76.7	-67.2	56.1	29.6	20.2	5.9	10.5	36.1	-129.7
iso-Pentane (2-methylbutane)	C_5H_{12}	-40.1	-62.5	-73.8	-86.0	100.1	49.0	39.1	23.7	7.1	27.8	-159.7
neo-Pentane (2,2-dimethylpropane)	C_5H_{12}	-92.9	-77.0	-69.3	-60.3	50.3	108.4	121.4	139.0	160.0	9.5	-16.6
Phenol	C_6H_6O	-128.9	-115.4	-108.5	-100.9	92.4	44.0	35.6	22.3	7.6	181.9	40.6
Phosgene (carbonyl chloride)	CCl_2O	4.6	28.0	39.7	52.0	65.8	87.0	79.6	68.4	55.6	7.6	-104
Propane	C_3H_8	26.7	5.4	5.0	16.0	28.8	74.1	85.8	102.5	122.0	-42.1	-187.1
Propionic acid	$C_3H_6O_2$	-15.0	-5.0	14.7	25.3	36.4	37.0	47.8	64.0	82.0	141.1	-22
n-Propyl acetate	$C_5H_{10}O_2$	-26.1	+7.0	2.4	12.7	23.8	43.5	52.8	66.8	82.0	101.8	-92.5
alcohol (1-propanol)	C_3H_8O	-64.4	46.3	37.2	27.1	16.0	30.5	0.5	53.0	67.8	97.8	-127
iso-Propyl alcohol (2-propanol)	C_3H_8O	131.9	120.7	112.1	104.7	96.5	9.0	84.1	15.0	31.5	82.5	-85.8
n-Propylamine	C_3H_9N	43.0	22.7	12.6	1.7	10.8	91.3	29.5	73.3	60.9	48.5	-83
Propylene	C_3H_6	-26.7	4.4	6.4	18.4	31.8	18.8	51.9	45.3	62.6	-47.7	-185
n-Propyl formate	$C_4H_8O_2$	-84.3	67.6	59.0	49.7	39.0	40.3	23.0	69.5	89.5	81.3	-92.9
Toluene	C_7H_8										110.6	-92.9
Trichlorofluoromethane	CCl_3F									+6.8	23.7	-95.0

3-44

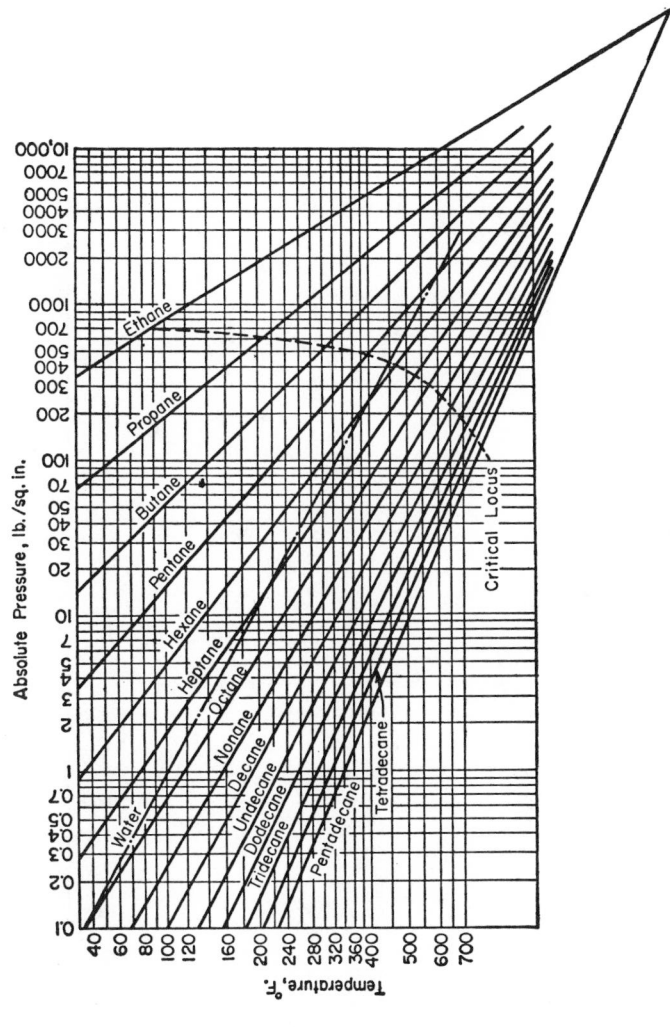

FIG. 3-5. Cox chart of vapor pressures of normal paraffin hydrocarbons. *(Sage and Lacey, "Volumetric and Phase Behavior of Hydrocarbons," Stanford University Press, Stanford, Calif., 1939.)*

LATENT HEATS

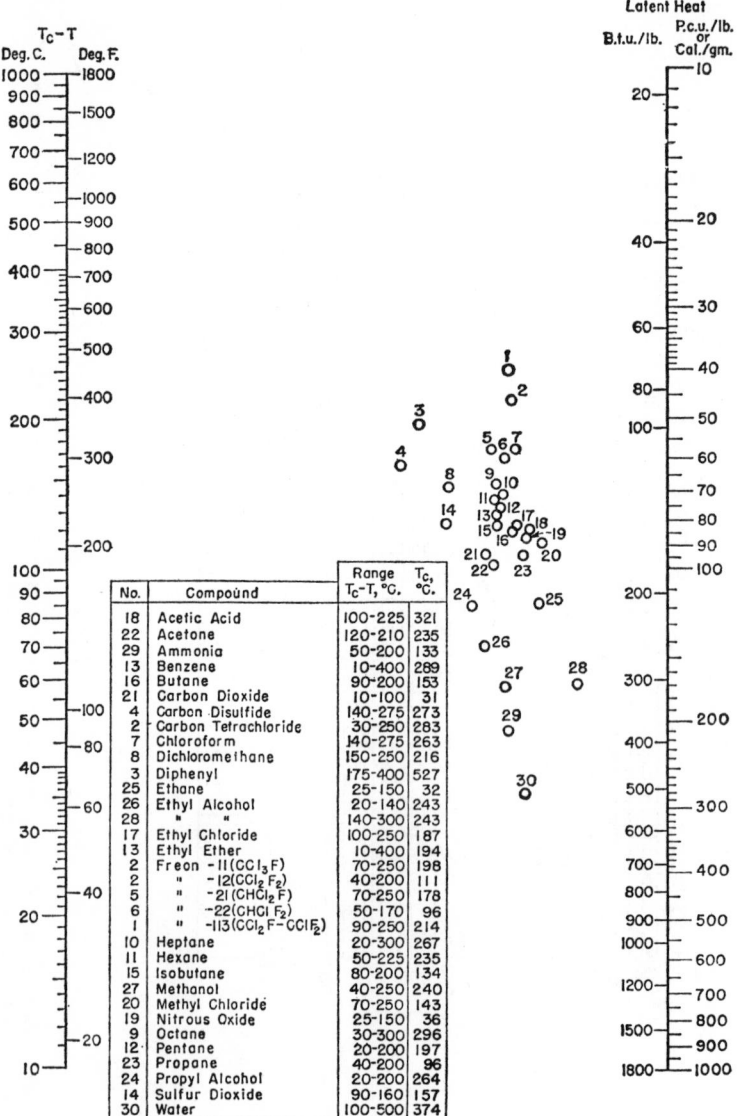

No.	Compound	Range T_c-T, °C.	T_c, °C.
18	Acetic Acid	100-225	321
22	Acetone	120-210	235
29	Ammonia	50-200	133
13	Benzene	10-400	289
16	Butane	90-200	153
21	Carbon Dioxide	10-100	31
4	Carbon Disulfide	140-275	273
2	Carbon Tetrachloride	30-250	283
7	Chloroform	140-275	263
8	Dichloromethane	150-250	216
3	Diphenyl	175-400	527
25	Ethane	25-150	32
26	Ethyl Alcohol	20-140	243
28	" "	140-300	243
17	Ethyl Chloride	100-250	187
13	Ethyl Ether	10-400	194
2	Freon -11(CCl₃F)	70-250	198
2	" -12(CCl₂F₂)	40-200	111
5	" -21(CHCl₂F)	70-250	178
6	" -22(CHCl F₂)	50-170	96
1	" -113(CCl₂F-CClF₂)	90-250	214
10	Heptane	20-300	267
11	Hexane	50-225	235
15	Isobutane	80-200	134
27	Methanol	40-250	240
20	Methyl Chloride	70-250	143
19	Nitrous Oxide	25-150	36
9	Octane	30-300	296
12	Pentane	20-200	197
23	Propane	40-200	96
24	Propyl Alcohol	20-200	264
14	Sulfur Dioxide	90-160	157
30	Water	100-500	374

FIG. 3-6. Latent heat of vaporization.

STEAM TABLES

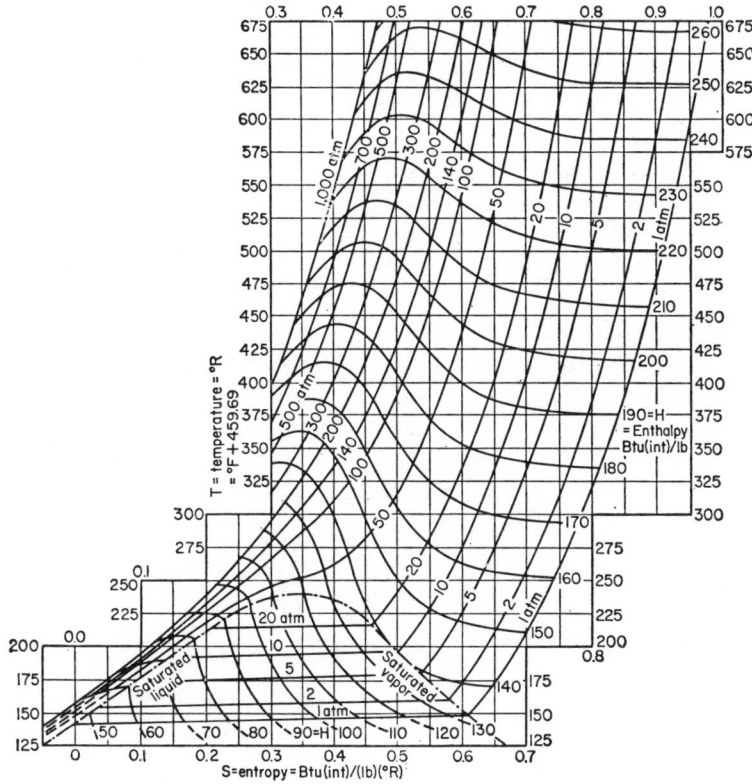

FIG. 3-7. Temperature-entropy diagram for air.

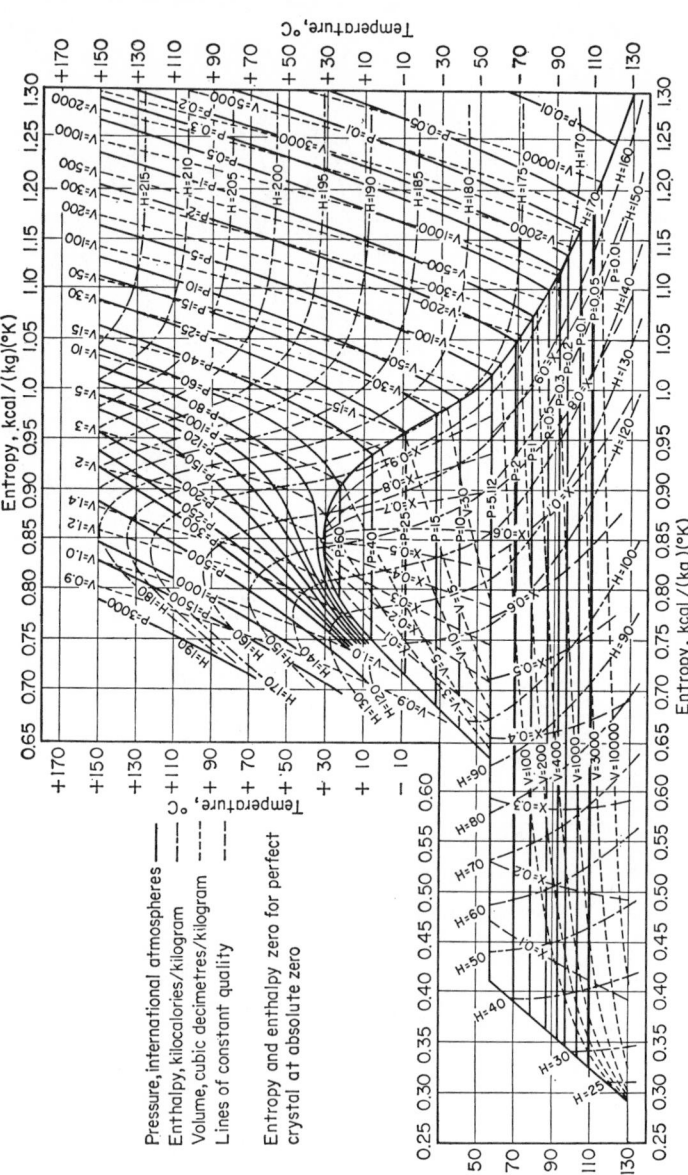

Fig. 3-8. Temperature-entropy diagram for carbon dioxide.

Pressure, international atmospheres ——
Enthalpy, kilocalories/kilogram ——·——
Volume, cubic decimetres/kilogram ———
Lines of constant quality ————

Entropy and enthalpy zero for perfect
crystal at absolute zero

3-48

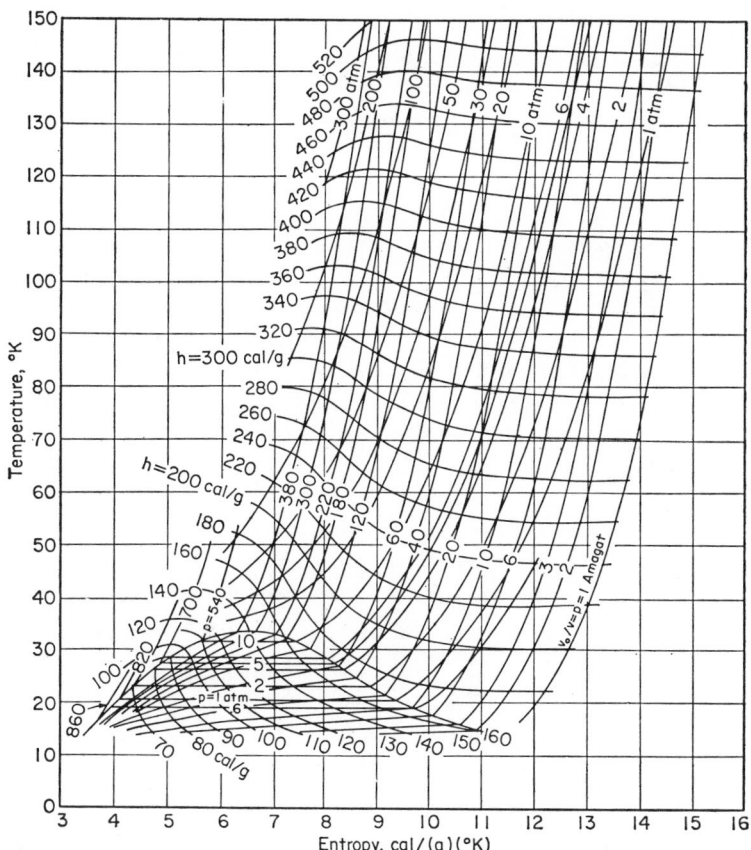

Fig. 3-9. Temperature-entropy diagram for hydrogen.

Table 3-24. Properties of Saturated Steam, Pressure Table

Abs press., lb/in.² p	Temp, °F t	Volume, ft³/lb		Enthalpy, Btu/lb		Entropy, Btu/(lb)(°R)		Internal energy, Btu/lb	
		Liquid v_f	Vapor v_g	Liquid h_f	Vapor h_g	Liquid s_f	Vapor s_g	Liquid u_f	Vapor u_g
1	101.74	0.01614	333.6	69.70	1,106.0	0.1326	1.9782	69.70	1,044.3
2	126.08	.01623	173.73	93.99	1,116.3	0.1749	1.9200	93.98	1,051.9
3	141.48	.01630	118.71	109.37	1,122.6	0.2008	1.8863	109.36	1,056.7
4	152.97	.01636	90.63	120.86	1,127.3	0.2198	1.8625	120.85	1,060.2
5	162.24	.01640	73.52	130.13	1,131.1	0.2347	1.8441	130.12	1,063.1
6	170.06	.01645	61.98	137.96	1,134.2	0.2472	1.8292	137.94	1,065.4
7	176.85	.01649	53.64	144.76	1,136.9	0.2581	1.8167	144.74	1,067.4
8	182.86	.01653	47.34	150.79	1,139.3	0.2674	1.8057	150.77	1,069.2
9	188.28	.01656	42.40	156.22	1,141.4	0.2759	1.7962	156.19	1,070.8
10	193.21	.01659	38.42	161.17	1,143.3	0.2835	1.7876	161.14	1,072.2
14.696	212.00	.01672	26.80	180.07	1,150.4	0.3120	1.7566	180.02	1,077.5
15	213.03	.01672	26.29	181.11	1,150.8	0.3135	1.7549	181.06	1,077.8
20	227.96	.01683	20.089	196.16	1,156.3	0.3356	1.7319	196.10	1,081.9
25	240.07	.01692	16.303	208.42	1,160.6	0.3533	1.7139	208.34	1,085.1
30	250.33	.01701	13.746	218.82	1,164.1	0.3680	1.6993	218.73	1,087.8
35	259.28	.01708	11.898	227.91	1,167.1	0.3807	1.6870	227.80	1,090.1
40	267.25	.01715	10.498	236.03	1,169.7	0.3919	1.6763	235.90	1,092.0
45	274.44	.01721	9.401	243.36	1,172.0	0.4019	1.6669	243.22	1,093.7
50	281.01	.01727	8.515	250.09	1,174.1	0.4110	1.6585	249.93	1,095.3
55	287.07	.01732	7.787	256.30	1,175.9	0.4193	1.6509	256.12	1,096.7
60	292.71	.01738	7.175	262.09	1,177.6	0.4270	1.6438	261.90	1,097.9
65	297.97	.01743	6.655	267.50	1,179.1	0.4342	1.6374	267.29	1,099.1
70	302.92	.01748	6.206	272.61	1,180.6	0.4409	1.6315	272.38	1,100.2
75	307.60	.01753	5.816	277.43	1,181.9	0.4472	1.6259	277.19	1,101.2
80	312.03	.01757	5.472	282.02	1,183.1	0.4531	1.6207	281.76	1,102.1
85	316.25	.01761	5.168	286.39	1,184.2	0.4587	1.6158	286.11	1,102.9
90	320.27	.01766	4.896	290.56	1,185.3	0.4641	1.6112	290.27	1,103.7
95	324.12	.01770	4.652	294.56	1,186.2	0.4692	1.6068	294.25	1,104.5
100	327.81	.01774	4.432	298.40	1,187.2	0.4740	1.6026	298.08	1,105.2
110	334.77	.01782	4.049	305.66	1,188.9	0.4832	1.5948	305.30	1,106.5
120	341.25	.01789	3.728	312.44	1,190.4	0.4916	1.5878	312.05	1,107.6
130	347.32	.01796	3.455	318.81	1,191.7	0.4995	1.5812	318.38	1,108.6
140	353.02	.01802	3.220	324.82	1,193.0	0.5069	1.5751	324.35	1,109.6
150	358.42	.01809	3.015	330.51	1,194.1	0.5138	1.5694	330.01	1,110.5
160	363.53	.01815	2.834	335.93	1,195.1	0.5204	1.5640	335.39	1,111.2
170	368.41	.01822	2.675	341.09	1,196.0	0.5266	1.5590	340.52	1,111.9
180	373.06	.01827	2.532	346.03	1,196.9	0.5325	1.5542	345.42	1,112.5
190	377.51	.01833	2.404	350.79	1,197.6	0.5381	1.5497	350.15	1,113.1
200	381.79	.01839	2.288	355.36	1,198.4	0.5435	1.5453	354.68	1,113.7
250	400.95	.01865	1.8438	376.00	1,201.1	0.5675	1.5263	375.14	1,115.8
300	417.33	.01890	1.5433	393.84	1,202.8	0.5879	1.5104	392.79	1,117.1
350	431.72	.01913	1.3260	409.69	1,203.9	0.6056	1.4966	408.45	1,118.0
400	444.59	.0193	1.1613	424.0	1,204.5	0.6214	1.4844	422.6	1,118.5
450	456.28	.0195	1.0320	437.2	1,204.6	0.6356	1.4734	435.5	1,118.7
500	467.01	.0197	0.9278	499.4	1,204.4	0.6487	1.4634	447.6	1,118.6
550	476.94	.0199	.8424	460.8	1,203.9	0.6608	1.4542	458.8	1,118.1
600	486.21	.0201	.7698	471.6	1,203.2	0.6720	1.4454	469.4	1,117.7
650	494.90	.0203	.7083	481.8	1,202.3	0.6826	1.4374	479.4	1,117.1
700	503.10	.0205	.6554	491.5	1,201.2	0.6925	1.4296	488.8	1,116.3
750	510.86	.0207	.6092	500.8	1,200.0	0.7019	1.4223	598.0	1,115.4

Table 3-24. Properties of Saturated Steam, Pressure Table (Continued)

Abs press., lb/in.^{2} p	Temp, °F t	Volume, ft^3/lb		Enthalpy, Btu/lb		Entropy, Btu/ (lb)(°R)		Internal energy, Btu/lb	
		Liquid v_f	Vapor v_g	Liquid h_f	Vapor h_g	Liquid s_f	Vapor s_g	Liquid u_f	Vapor u_g
800	518.23	.0209	.5687	509.7	1,198.6	0.7108	1.4153	506.6	1,114.4
850	525.26	.0210	.5327	518.3	1,197.1	0.7194	1.4085	515.0	1,113.3
900	531.98	.0212	.5006	526.6	1,195.4	0.7275	1.4020	523.1	1,112.1
950	538.43	.0214	.4717	534.6	1,193.7	0.7355	1.3957	530.9	1,110.8
1,000	544.61	.0216	.4456	542.4	1,191.8	0.7430	1.3897	538.4	1,109.4
1,100	556.31	.0220	.4001	557.4	1,187.8	0.7575	1.3780	552.9	1,106.4
1,200	567.22	.0223	.3619	571.7	1,183.4	0.7711	1.3667	566.7	1,103.0
1,300	577.46	.0227	.3293	585.4	1,178.6	0.7840	1.3559	580.0	1,099.4
1,400	587.10	.0231	.3012	598.7	1,173.4	0.7963	1.3454	592.7	1,095.4
1,500	596.23	.0235	.2765	611.6	1,167.9	0.8082	1.3351	605.1	1,091.2
2,000	635.82	.0257	.1878	671.7	1,135.1	0.8619	1.2849	662.2	1,065.6
2,500	668.13	.0287	.1307	730.6	1,091.1	0.9126	1.2322	717.3	1,030.6
3,000	695.36	.0346	.0858	802.5	1,020.3	0.9731	1.1615	783.4	972.7
3,206.2	705.40	.0503	.0503	902.7	902.7	1.0580	1.0580	872.9	872.9

SOURCE: Abridged from Keenan and Keyes, "Thermodynamic Properties of Steam," John Wiley & Sons Inc., New York, 1936. Copyright, 1937, by Joseph H. Keenan and Frederick G. Keyes.

Table 3-25. Properties of Superheated Steam

Abs press., psi (sat. temp)		200°F	300°F	400°F	500°F	600°F	700°F	800°F	900°F	1000°F	1100°F	1200°F	1400°F	1600°F
1 (101.74)	v^*	392.6	452.3	512.0	571.6	631.2	690.8	750.4	809.9	869.5	929.1	988.7	1107.8	1227.0
	h^*	1150.4	1195.8	1241.7	1288.3	1335.7	1383.8	1432.8	1482.7	1533.5	1585.2	1637.7	1745.7	1857.5
	s^*	2.0512	2.1153	2.1720	2.2233	2.2702	2.3137	2.3542	2.3923	2.4283	2.4625	2.4952	2.5566	2.6137
5 (162.24)	v	78.16	90.25	102.26	114.22	126.16	138.10	150.03	161.95	173.87	185.79	197.71	221.6	245.4
	h	1148.8	1195.0	1241.2	1288.0	1335.4	1383.6	1432.7	1482.6	1533.4	1585.1	1637.7	1745.7	1857.4
	s	1.8718	1.9370	1.9942	2.0456	2.0927	2.1361	2.1767	2.2148	2.2509	2.2851	2.3178	2.3792	2.4363
10 (193.21)	v	38.85	45.00	51.04	57.05	63.03	69.01	74.98	80.95	86.92	92.88	98.84	110.77	122.69
	h	1146.6	1193.9	1240.6	1287.5	1335.1	1383.4	1432.5	1482.4	1533.2	1585.0	1637.6	1745.6	1857.3
	s	1.7927	1.8595	1.9172	1.9689	2.0160	2.0596	2.1002	2.1383	2.1744	2.2086	2.2413	2.3028	2.3598
14.696 (212.00)	v	....	30.53	34.68	38.78	42.86	46.94	51.00	55.07	59.13	63.19	67.25	75.37	83.48
	h	....	1192.8	1239.9	1287.1	1334.8	1383.2	1432.3	1482.3	1533.1	1584.8	1637.5	1745.5	1857.3
	s	....	1.8160	1.8743	1.9261	1.9734	2.0170	2.0576	2.0958	2.1319	2.1662	2.1989	2.2603	2.3174
20 (227.96)	v	....	22.36	25.43	28.46	31.47	34.47	37.46	40.45	43.44	46.42	49.41	55.37	61.34
	h	....	1191.6	1239.2	1286.6	1334.4	1382.9	1432.1	1482.1	1533.0	1584.7	1637.4	1745.4	1857.2
	s	....	1.7808	1.8396	1.8918	1.9392	1.9829	2.0235	2.0618	2.0978	2.1321	2.1648	2.2263	2.2834
40 (267.25)	v	....	11.040	12.628	14.168	15.688	17.198	18.702	20.20	21.70	23.20	24.69	27.68	30.66
	h	....	1186.8	1236.5	1284.8	1333.1	1381.9	1431.3	1481.4	1532.4	1584.3	1637.0	1745.1	1857.0
	s	....	1.6994	1.7608	1.8140	1.8619	1.9058	1.9467	1.9850	2.0212	2.0555	2.0883	2.1498	2.2069
60 (292.71)	v	....	7.259	8.357	9.403	10.427	11.441	12.449	13.452	14.454	15.453	16.451	18.446	20.44
	h	....	1181.6	1233.6	1283.0	1331.8	1380.9	1430.5	1480.8	1531.9	1583.8	1636.6	1744.8	1856.7
	s	....	1.6492	1.7135	1.7678	1.8162	1.8605	1.9015	1.9400	1.9762	2.0106	2.0434	2.1049	2.1621
80 (312.03)	v	....	....	6.220	7.020	7.797	8.562	9.322	10.077	10.830	11.582	12.332	13.830	15.325
	h	....	....	1230.7	1281.1	1330.5	1379.9	1429.7	1480.1	1531.3	1583.4	1636.2	1744.5	1856.5
	s	....	....	1.6791	1.7346	1.7836	1.8281	1.8694	1.9079	1.9442	1.9787	2.0115	2.0721	2.1303
100 (327.81)	v	....	....	4.937	5.589	6.218	6.835	7.446	8.052	8.656	9.259	9.860	11.060	12.258
	h	....	....	1227.6	1279.1	1329.1	1378.9	1428.9	1479.5	1530.8	1582.9	1635.7	1744.2	1856.2
	s	....	....	1.6518	1.7085	1.7581	1.8029	1.8443	1.8829	1.9193	1.9538	1.9867	2.0484	2.1056
120 (341.25)	v	....	....	4.081	4.636	5.165	5.683	6.195	6.702	7.207	7.710	8.212	9.214	10.213
	h	....	....	1224.4	1277.2	1327.7	1377.8	1428.1	1478.8	1530.2	1582.4	1635.3	1743.9	1856.0
	s	....	....	1.6287	1.6869	1.7370	1.7822	1.8237	1.8625	1.8990	1.9335	1.9664	2.0281	2.0854

140 (353.02) v* r* h* s*													
140 (353.02) v	⋯	⋯	3.468	3.954	4.413	4.861	5.301	5.738	6.172	6.604	7.035	7.895	8.752
h	⋯	⋯	1221.1	1275.2	1326.4	1376.8	1427.3	1478.2	1529.7	1581.9	1634.9	1743.5	1855.7
s	⋯	⋯	1.6087	1.6683	1.7190	1.7645	1.8063	1.8451	1.8817	1.9163	1.9493	2.0110	2.0663
160 (363.53) v	⋯	⋯	3.008	3.443	3.849	4.244	4.631	5.015	5.396	5.775	6.152	6.906	7.656
h	⋯	⋯	1217.6	1273.1	1325.0	1375.7	1426.4	1477.5	1529.1	1581.4	1634.5	1743.2	1855.5
s	⋯	⋯	1.5908	1.6519	1.7033	1.7491	1.7911	1.8301	1.8667	1.9014	1.9344	1.9962	2.0535
180 (373.06) v	⋯	⋯	2.649	3.044	3.411	3.764	4.110	4.452	4.792	5.129	5.466	6.136	6.804
h	⋯	⋯	1214.0	1271.0	1323.5	1374.7	1425.6	1476.8	1528.6	1581.0	1634.1	1742.9	1855.2
s	⋯	⋯	1.5745	1.6373	1.6894	1.7355	1.7776	1.8167	1.8534	1.8882	1.9212	1.9831	2.0404
200 (381.79) v	⋯	⋯	2.361	2.726	3.060	3.380	3.693	4.002	4.309	4.613	4.917	5.521	6.123
h	⋯	⋯	1210.3	1268.9	1322.1	1373.6	1424.8	1476.2	1528.0	1580.5	1633.7	1742.6	1855.0
s	⋯	⋯	1.5594	1.6240	1.6767	1.7232	1.7655	1.8048	1.8415	1.8763	1.9094	1.9713	2.0287
220 (389.86) v	⋯	⋯	2.125	2.465	2.772	3.066	3.352	3.634	3.913	4.191	4.467	5.017	5.565
h	⋯	⋯	1206.5	1266.7	1320.7	1372.6	1424.0	1475.5	1527.5	1580.0	1633.3	1742.3	1854.7
s	⋯	⋯	1.5453	1.6117	1.6652	1.7120	1.7545	1.7939	1.8308	1.8656	1.8987	1.9607	2.0181
240 (397.37) v	⋯	⋯	1.9276	2.247	2.533	2.804	3.068	3.327	3.584	3.839	4.093	4.597	5.100
h	⋯	⋯	1202.5	1264.5	1319.2	1371.5	1423.2	1474.8	1526.9	1579.6	1632.9	1742.0	1854.5
s	⋯	⋯	1.5319	1.6003	1.6546	1.7017	1.7444	1.7839	1.8209	1.8558	1.8889	1.9510	2.0084
260 (404.42) v	⋯	⋯	⋯	2.063	2.330	2.582	2.827	3.067	3.305	3.541	3.776	4.242	4.707
h	⋯	⋯	⋯	1262.3	1317.7	1370.4	1422.3	1474.2	1526.3	1579.1	1632.5	1741.7	1854.2
s	⋯	⋯	⋯	1.5897	1.6447	1.6922	1.7352	1.7748	1.8118	1.8467	1.8799	1.9420	1.9995
280 (411.05) v	⋯	⋯	⋯	1.9047	2.156	2.392	2.621	2.845	3.066	3.286	3.504	3.938	4.370
h	⋯	⋯	⋯	1260.0	1316.2	1369.4	1421.5	1473.5	1525.8	1578.6	1632.1	1741.4	1854.0
s	⋯	⋯	⋯	1.5796	1.6354	1.6834	1.7265	1.7662	1.8033	1.8383	1.8716	1.9337	1.9912
300 (417.33) v	⋯	⋯	⋯	1.7675	2.005	2.227	2.442	2.652	2.859	3.065	3.269	3.674	4.078
h	⋯	⋯	⋯	1257.6	1314.7	1368.3	1420.6	1472.8	1525.2	1578.1	1631.7	1741.1	1853.7
s	⋯	⋯	⋯	1.5701	1.6268	1.6751	1.7184	1.7582	1.7954	1.8305	1.8638	1.9260	1.9835
350 (431.72) v	⋯	⋯	⋯	1.4923	1.7036	1.8980	2.084	2.266	2.445	2.622	2.798	3.147	3.493
h	⋯	⋯	⋯	1251.8	1310.9	1365.5	1418.5	1471.1	1523.8	1577.0	1630.7	1740.3	1853.1
s	⋯	⋯	⋯	1.5481	1.6070	1.6563	1.7002	1.7403	1.7777	1.8130	1.8463	1.9086	1.9663
400 (444.59) v	⋯	⋯	⋯	1.2851	1.4770	1.6508	1.8161	1.9767	2.134	2.290	2.445	2.751	3.055
h	⋯	⋯	⋯	1245.1	1306.9	1362.7	1416.4	1469.4	1522.4	1575.8	1629.6	1739.5	1852.5
s	⋯	⋯	⋯	1.5281	1.5894	1.6398	1.6842	1.7247	1.7623	1.7977	1.8311	1.8936	1.9513

Table 3-25. Properties of Superheated Steam (Continued)

Abs. press., psi (sat. temp)		500°F	550°F	600°F	620°F	640°F	660°F	680°F	700°F	800°F	900°F	1000°F	1200°F	1400°F	1600°F
450 (456.28)	v^*	1.1231	1.2155	1.3005	1.3332	1.3652	1.3967	1.4278	1.4584	1.6074	1.7516	1.8928	2.170	2.443	2.714
	h^*	1238.4	1272.0	1302.8	1314.6	1326.2	1337.5	1348.8	1359.9	1414.3	1467.7	1521.0	1628.6	1738.7	1851.9
	s^*	1.5095	1.5437	1.5735	1.5845	1.5951	1.6054	1.6153	1.6250	1.6699	1.7108	1.7486	1.8177	1.8803	1.9381
500 (467.01)	v	0.9927	1.0800	1.1591	1.1893	1.2188	1.2478	1.2763	1.3044	1.4405	1.5715	1.6996	1.9504	2.197	2.442
	h	1231.3	1266.8	1298.6	1310.7	1322.6	1334.2	1345.7	1357.0	1412.1	1466.0	1519.6	1627.6	1737.9	1851.3
	s	1.4919	1.5280	1.5588	1.5701	1.5810	1.5915	1.6016	1.6115	1.6571	1.6982	1.7363	1.8056	1.8683	1.9262
550 (476.94)	v	0.8852	0.9686	1.0431	1.0714	1.0989	1.1259	1.1523	1.1783	1.3038	1.4241	1.5414	1.7706	1.9957	2.219
	h	1223.7	1261.2	1294.3	1306.8	1318.9	1330.8	1342.5	1354.0	1409.9	1464.3	1518.2	1626.6	1737.1	1850.6
	s	1.4751	1.5131	1.5451	1.5568	1.5680	1.5787	1.5890	1.5991	1.6452	1.6868	1.7250	1.7946	1.8575	1.9155
600 (486.21)	v	0.7947	0.8753	0.9463	0.9729	0.9988	1.0241	1.0489	1.0732	1.1899	1.3013	1.4096	1.6208	1.8229	2.033
	h	1215.7	1255.5	1289.9	1302.7	1315.2	1327.4	1339.3	1351.1	1407.7	1462.5	1516.7	1625.5	1736.3	1850.0
	s	1.4586	1.4990	1.5323	1.5443	1.5558	1.5667	1.5773	1.5875	1.6343	1.6762	1.7147	1.7846	1.8476	1.9056
700 (503.10)	v	. . . .	0.7277	0.7934	0.8177	0.8411	0.8639	0.8860	0.9077	1.0108	1.1082	1.2024	1.3853	1.5641	1.7405
	h	. . . .	1243.2	1280.6	1294.3	1307.5	1320.3	1332.8	1345.0	1403.2	1459.0	1513.9	1623.5	1734.8	1848.8
	s	. . . .	1.4722	1.5084	1.5212	1.5333	1.5449	1.5559	1.5665	1.6147	1.6573	1.6963	1.7666	1.8299	1.8881
800 (518.23)	v	. . . .	0.6154	0.6779	0.7006	0.7223	0.7433	0.7635	0.7833	0.8763	0.9633	1.0470	1.2088	1.3662	1.5214
	h	. . . .	1229.8	1270.7	1285.4	1299.4	1312.9	1325.9	1338.6	1398.6	1455.4	1511.0	1621.4	1733.2	1847.5
	s	. . . .	1.4467	1.4863	1.5000	1.5129	1.5250	1.5366	1.5476	1.5972	1.6407	1.6801	1.7510	1.8146	1.8729
900 (531.98)	v	. . . .	0.5264	0.5873	0.6089	0.6294	0.6491	0.6680	0.6863	0.7716	0.8506	0.9262	1.0714	1.2124	1.3509
	h	. . . .	1215.0	1260.1	1275.9	1290.9	1305.1	1318.8	1332.1	1393.9	1451.8	1508.1	1619.3	1731.6	1846.3
	s	. . . .	1.4216	1.4653	1.4800	1.4938	1.5066	1.5187	1.5303	1.5814	1.6257	1.6656	1.7371	1.8009	1.8595
1000 (544.61)	v	. . . .	0.4533	0.5140	0.5350	0.5546	0.5733	0.5912	0.6084	0.6878	0.7604	0.8294	0.9615	1.0893	1.2146
	h	. . . .	1198.3	1248.8	1265.9	1281.9	1297.0	1311.4	1325.3	1389.2	1448.2	1505.1	1617.3	1730.0	1845.0
	s	. . . .	1.3961	1.4450	1.4610	1.4757	1.4893	1.5021	1.5141	1.5670	1.6121	1.6525	1.7245	1.7886	1.8474
1100 (556.31)	v	. . . .	. . . .	0.4532	0.4738	0.4929	0.5110	0.5281	0.5445	0.6191	0.6866	0.7503	0.8716	0.9885	1.1031
	h	. . . .	. . . .	1236.7	1255.3	1272.4	1288.5	1303.7	1318.3	1384.3	1444.5	1502.2	1615.2	1728.4	1843.8
	s	. . . .	. . . .	1.4251	1.4425	1.4583	1.4728	1.4862	1.4989	1.5535	1.5995	1.6405	1.7130	1.7775	1.8363
1200 (567.22)	v	. . . .	. . . .	0.4016	0.4222	0.4410	0.4586	0.4752	0.4909	0.5617	0.6250	0.6843	0.7967	0.9046	1.0101
	h	. . . .	. . . .	1223.5	1243.9	1262.4	1279.6	1295.7	1311.0	1379.3	1440.7	1499.4	1613.1	1726.9	1842.5
	s	. . . .	. . . .	1.4062	1.4243	1.4413	1.4568	1.4710	1.4843	1.5409	1.5879	1.6293	1.7025	1.7672	1.8263
1400 (587.10)	v	. . . .	. . . .	0.3174	0.3390	0.3580	0.3753	0.3912	0.4062	0.4714	0.5281	0.5805	0.6789	0.7727	0.8640
	h	. . . .	. . . .	1193.0	1218.4	1240.4	1260.3	1278.5	1295.5	1369.1	1433.1	1493.2	1608.9	1723.7	1840.0
	s	. . . .	. . . .	1.3639	1.3877	1.4079	1.4258	1.4419	1.4567	1.5177	1.5666	1.6093	1.6836	1.7489	1.8083

Pressure (sat. temp)		C1	C2	C3	C4	C5	C6	C7	C8	C9	C10	C11					
1600 (604.90)	v^*	0.7545	0.6738	0.5906	0.5027	0.4553	0.4034	0.3417	0.3271	0.3112	0.2936	0.2733	……	……	……	……	……
	h^*	1837.5	1720.5	1604.6	1487.0	1425.3	1358.4	1278.7	1259.6	1238.7	1215.2	1187.8					
	s^*	1.7926	1.7328	1.6669	1.5914	1.5476	1.4964	1.4303	1.4137	1.3952	1.3741	1.3489					
1800 (621.03)	v	0.6693	0.5968	0.5218	0.4421	0.3986	0.3502	0.2907	0.2760	0.2597	0.2407	……	……	……	……	……	……
	h	1835.0	1717.3	1600.4	1480.8	1417.4	1347.2	1260.3	1238.5	1214.0	1185.1						
	s	1.7786	1.7185	1.6520	1.5752	1.5301	1.4765	1.4044	1.3855	1.3638	1.3377						
2000 (635.82)	v	0.6011	0.5352	0.4668	0.3935	0.3532	0.3074	0.2489	0.2337	0.2161	0.1936	……	……	……	……	……	……
	h	1832.5	1714.1	1596.1	1474.5	1409.2	1335.5	1240.0	1214.8	1184.9	1145.6						
	s	1.7660	1.7055	1.6384	1.5603	1.5139	1.4576	1.3783	1.3564	1.3300	1.2945						
2500 (668.13)	v	0.4784	0.4244	0.3678	0.3061	0.2710	0.2294	0.1686	0.1484	……	……	……	……	……	……	……	……
	h	1826.2	1706.1	1585.3	1458.4	1387.8	1303.6	1176.8	1132.3								
	s	1.7389	1.6775	1.6088	1.5273	1.4772	1.4127	1.3073	1.2687								
3000 (695.36)	v	0.3966	0.3505	0.3018	0.2476	0.2159	0.1760	0.0984	……	……	……	……	……	……	……	……	……
	h	1819.9	1698.0	1574.3	1441.8	1365.0	1267.2	1060.7									
	s	1.7163	1.6540	1.5837	1.4984	1.4439	1.3690	1.1966									
3206.2 (705.40)	v	0.3703	0.3267	0.2806	0.2288	0.1981	0.1583	……	……	……	……	……	……	……	……	……	……
	h	1817.2	1694.6	1569.8	1434.7	1355.2	1250.5										
	s	1.7080	1.6452	1.5742	1.4874	1.4309	1.3508										
3500	v	0.3381	0.2977	0.2546	0.2058	0.1762	0.1364	0.0306	……	……	……	……	……	……	……	……	……
	h	1813.6	1689.8	1563.3	1424.5	1340.7	1224.9	780.5									
	s	1.6968	1.6336	1.5615	1.4723	1.4127	1.3241	0.9519									
4000	v	0.2943	0.2581	0.2192	0.1743	0.1462	0.1052	0.0287	……	……	……	……	……	……	……	……	……
	h	1807.2	1681.7	1552.2	1406.8	1314.4	1174.8	763.8									
	s	1.6795	1.6154	1.5417	1.4482	1.3827	1.2757	0.9347									
4500	v	0.2602	0.2273	0.1917	0.1500	0.1226	0.0798	0.0276	……	……	……	……	……	……	……	……	……
	h	1800.9	1673.5	1540.8	1388.4	1286.5	1113.9	753.5									
	s	1.6640	1.5990	1.5235	1.4253	1.3529	1.2204	0.9235									
5000	v	0.2329	0.2027	0.1696	0.1303	0.1036	0.0593	0.0268	……	……	……	……	……	……	……	……	……
	h	1794.5	1665.3	1529.5	1369.5	1256.5	1047.1	746.4									
	s	1.6499	1.5839	1.5066	1.4034	1.3231	1.1622	0.9152									
5500	v	0.2106	0.1825	0.1516	0.1143	0.0880	0.0462	0.0262	……	……	……	……	……	……	……	……	……
	h	1788.1	1637.0	1518.2	1349.3	1224.1	985.0	741.3									
	s	1.6369	1.5699	1.4908	1.3821	1.2930	1.1093	0.9090									

$*$ v = volume, ft³/lb
h = enthalpy, Btu/lb
s = entropy, Btu/(lb)(°R)
SOURCE: Abridged from Keenan and Keyes, "Thermodynamic Properties of Steam," John Wiley & Sons, Inc., New York, 1936. Copyright, 1937, by Joseph H. Keenan and Frederick G. Keyes.

Table 3-26. Properties of Freon-21 (Dichloromonofluoromethane)*, Saturated

Temp., °F t	Abs. pressure, psi p	Volume, ft³/lb		Enthalpy, Btu/lb		Entropy, Btu/(lb)(°R)	
		Liquid v_f	Vapor v_g	Liquid h_f	Vapor h_g	Liquid s_f	Vapor s_g
−40	1.358	.01058	32.09	0.00	114.56	.0000	.2730
−30	1.888	.01066	23.61	2.36	115.76	.0055	.2695
−20	2.578	.01075	17.66	4.71	116.96	.0109	.2663
−10	3.463	.01084	13.43	7.07	118.17	.0162	.2633
0	4.582	.01093	10.35	9.44	119.37	.0214	.2606
5	5.243	.01097	9.132	10.63	119.97	.0240	.2593
10	5.978	.01102	8.085	11.81	120.57	.0265	.2581
20	7.699	.01112	6.392	14.21	121.78	.0316	.2559
30	9.793	.01122	5.112	16.61	122.98	.0365	.2538
40	12.32	.01132	4.130	19.04	124.19	.0414	.2519
50	15.33	.01142	3.370	21.49	125.39	.0463	.2502
60	18.90	.01153	2.773	23.98	126.60	.0511	.2486
70	23.08	.01164	2.300	26.49	127.79	.0559	.2471
80	27.96	.01176	1.923	29.03	128.98	.0606	.2458
86	31.23	.01183	1.733	30.56	129.68	.0634	.2450
90	33.58	.01188	1.619	31.59	130.14	.0652	.2445
100	40.04	.01200	1.371	34.18	131.29	.0699	.2434
110	47.40	.01213	1.169	36.79	132.42	.0745	.2424
120	55.75	.01226	1.001	39.46	133.53	.0791	.2411
130	65.15	.01240	0.8623	42.13	134.61	.0837	.2405
140	75.72	.01254	0.7457	44.86	135.66	.0882	.2395
150	87.51	.01269	0.6476	47.62	136.68	.0927	.2388
160	100.6	.01284	0.5646	50.43	137.69	.0972	.2331

*Courtesy Kinetic Chemicals, Inc.

Table 3-27. Properties of Freon-21 (Dichloromonofluoromethane)*, Superheated

v, volume, ft³/lb; *h*, enthalpy, Btu/lb; *s*, entropy, Btu/(lb)/(°R)
Parenthetic figures after pressures are saturation temperatures.

Abs. pressure 1.2 psi (−43.6°F)

Temp., °F	v	h	s
Sat.	36.02	114.13	.2744
−40	36.34	114.57	.2754
−30	37.21	115.80	.2783
−20	38.08	117.03	.2812
−10	38.95	118.28	.2840
0	39.83	119.54	.2867
10	40.70	120.80	.2894
20	41.57	122.08	.2921
30	42.44	123.38	.2948
40	43.32	124.69	.2975
50	44.19	126.01	.3001
60	45.06	127.35	.3027
70	45.93	128.71	.3053
80	46.80	130.09	.3079
90	47.67	131.48	.3104
100	48.54	132.88	.3129
110	49.42	134.29	.3154
120	50.29	135.71	.3179
130	51.16	137.14	.3203
140	52.03	138.59	.3228
150	52.90	140.06	.3252
160	53.77	141.55	.3276
170	54.64	143.05	.3300
180	55.51	144.56	.3324
190	56.38	146.08	.3348
200	57.25	147.61	.3371
210	58.12	149.16	.3394
220	58.99	150.73	.3418
230	59.86	152.31	.3441
240	60.73	153.90	.3464
250	61.60	155.51	.3486

Abs. pressure 2 psi (−28.2°F)

Temp., °F	v	h	s
Sat.	22.37	115.98	.2689
−20	22.80	116.99	.2712
−10	23.33	118.24	.2740
0	23.85	119.49	.2768
10	24.38	120.76	.2795
20	24.90	122.04	.2822
30	25.43	123.34	.2849
40	25.95	124.65	.2876
50	26.47	125.98	.2902
60	27.00	127.33	.2928
70	27.52	128.69	.2954
80	28.05	130.07	.2979
90	28.57	131.45	.3005
100	29.09	132.85	.3030
110	29.62	134.26	.3055
120	30.14	135.68	.3080
130	30.66	137.12	.3104
140	31.19	138.57	.3129
150	31.71	140.03	.3153
160	32.23	141.52	.3177
170	32.76	143.00	.3201
180	33.28	144.53	.3225
190	33.80	146.05	.3249
200	34.33	147.59	.3272
210	34.85	149.14	.3296
220	35.37	150.71	.3319
230	35.89	152.29	.3342
240	36.42	153.88	.3365
250	36.94	155.59	.3388

Abs. pressure 4 psi (−4.9°F)

Temp., °F	v	h	s
Sat.	11.74	118.78	.2619
0	11.87	119.40	.2633
10	12.14	120.66	.2660
20	12.40	121.95	.2687
30	12.66	123.25	.2714
40	12.93	124.57	.2741
50	13.19	125.90	.2767
60	13.45	127.25	.2793
70	13.72	128.61	.2819
80	13.98	129.99	.2845
90	14.24	131.37	.2870
100	14.51	132.77	.2895
110	14.77	134.18	.2920
120	15.03	135.61	.2945
130	15.29	137.04	.2970
140	15.56	138.49	.2994
150	15.82	139.96	.3019
160	16.08	141.45	.3043
170	16.35	142.95	.3067
180	16.61	144.46	.3091
190	16.87	145.98	.3114
200	17.13	147.52	.3138
210	17.39	149.08	.3161
220	17.66	150.65	.3184
230	17.92	152.23	.3207
240	18.18	153.82	.3230
250	18.44	155.43	.3253
260	18.70	157.05	.3276
270	18.97	158.68	.3298

Abs. pressure 10 psi (30.9°F)

Temp., °F	v	h	s
Sat.	5.014	123.10	.2536
40	5.112	124.30	.2561
50	5.219	125.63	.2587
60	5.326	126.99	.2613
70	5.443	128.36	.2639
80	5.540	129.74	.2665
90	5.646	131.13	.2691
100	5.753	132.54	.2716
110	5.860	133.95	.2741
120	5.966	135.38	.2766
130	6.072	136.82	.2791
140	6.178	138.28	.2815
150	6.285	139.75	.2840
160	6.391	141.24	.2864
170	6.497	142.75	.2888
180	6.603	144.27	.2912
190	6.709	145.79	.2936
200	6.815	147.33	.2959
210	6.921	148.89	.2983
220	7.027	150.46	.3006
230	7.133	152.05	.3029
240	7.239	153.65	.3052
250	7.344	155.26	.3075
260	7.450	156.88	.3098
270	7.555	158.52	.3120
280	7.661	160.17	.3143
290	7.767	161.84	.3165
300	7.872	163.52	.3187
310	7.978	165.21	.3210

* Courtesy of Kinetic Chemicals, Inc.

Table 3-27. Superheated Freon-21 (Dichloromonofluoromethane) (Continued)

Abs. pressure 20 psi (62.8°F)

Temp., °F t	v	h	s
Sat.	2.630	126.94	.2482
60			
70	2.670	127.94	.2501
80	2.725	129.33	.2527
90	2.780	130.73	.2552
100	2.834	132.14	.2578
110	2.889	133.56	.2603
120	2.943	135.00	.2628
130	2.998	136.45	.2653
140	3.052	137.91	.2678
150	3.106	139.39	.2702
160	3.160	140.90	.2727
170	3.214	142.41	.2751
180	3.268	143.93	.2775
190	3.322	145.46	.2799
200	3.376	147.01	.2822
210	3.430	148.58	.2846
220	3.484	150.16	.2869
230	3.537	151.75	.2892
240	3.591	153.36	.2915
250	3.645	154.97	.2938
260	3.698	156.60	.2961
270	3.752	158.24	.2984
280	3.805	159.90	.3007
290	3.859	161.57	.3029
300	3.912	163.25	.3051
310	3.965	164.95	.3074
320	4.019	166.67	.3096
330	4.072	168.40	.3118
340	4.125	170.14	.3140
...	.....	.....	.....

Abs. pressure 50 psi (113.3°F)

Temp., °F t	v	h	s
Sat.	1.111	132.79	.2421
120	1.127	133.78	.2438
130	1.150	135.26	.2463
140	1.173	136.75	.2488
150	1.197	138.26	.2513
160	1.220	139.79	.2538
170	1.243	141.33	.2563
180	1.265	142.88	.2587
190	1.288	144.43	.2612
200	1.311	146.00	.2636
210	1.334	147.59	.2659
220	1.356	149.19	.2683
230	1.379	150.80	.2707
240	1.401	152.42	.2730
250	1.424	154.06	.2753
260	1.446	155.71	.2776
270	1.469	157.37	.2799
280	1.491	159.05	.2822
290	1.513	160.74	.2845
300	1.535	162.44	.2867
310	1.558	164.16	.2890
320	1.580	165.89	.2912
330	1.602	167.63	.2934
340	1.624	169.38	.2956
350	1.646	171.14	.2978
360	1.668	172.92	.3000
370	1.690	174.72	.3022
380	1.712	176.52	.3044
390	1.734	178.34	.3065

Abs. pressure 100 psi (159.6°F)

Temp., °F t	v	h	s
Sat.	.5680	137.66	.2381
160	.5685	137.72	.2382
170	.5815	139.32	.2408
180	.5945	140.92	.2433
190	.6073	142.53	.2458
200	.6200	144.16	.2483
210	.6326	145.80	.2508
220	.6540	147.45	.2532
230	.6574	149.10	.2556
240	.6698	150.76	.2580
250	.6820	152.44	.2604
260	.6942	154.13	.2628
270	.7063	155.83	.2651
280	.7183	157.54	.2674
290	.7303	159.26	.2698
300	.7423	161.00	.2721
310	.7542	162.75	.2743
320	.7660	164.51	.2766
330	.7777	166.28	.2789
340	.7894	168.06	.2811
350	.8011	169.85	.2833
360	.8128	171.66	.2856
370	.8244	173.48	.2878
380	.8360	175.31	.2900
390	.8475	177.16	.2922
400	.8590	179.02	.2943

REDUCED PROPERTIES

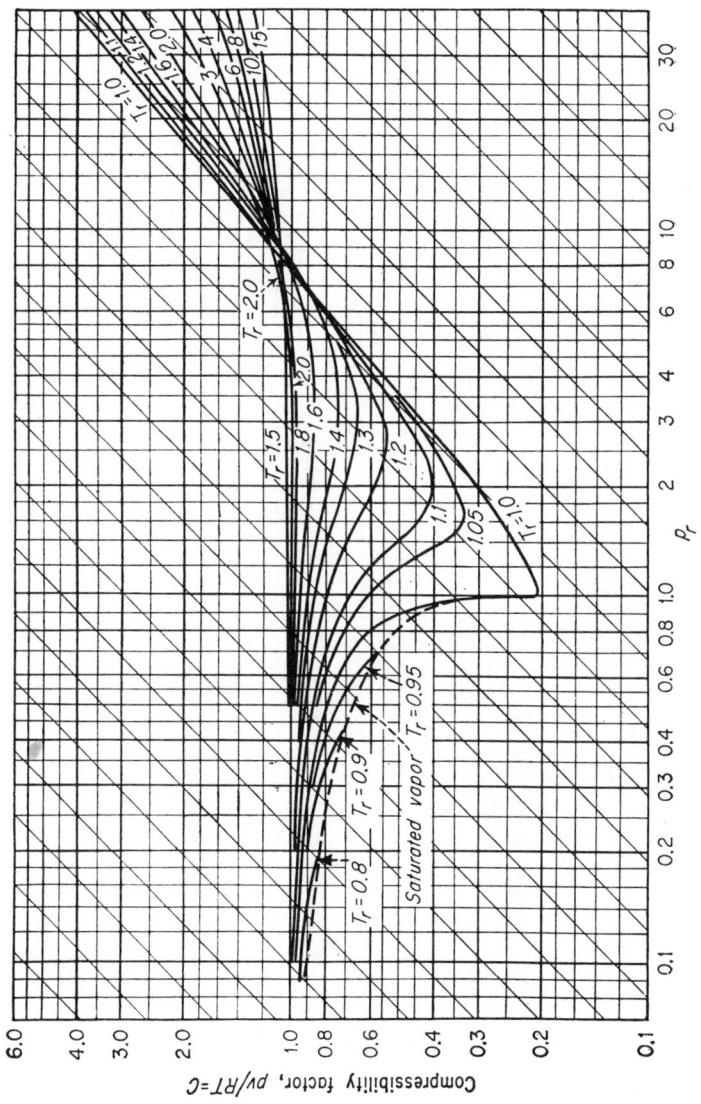

Fig. 3-10. Compressibility factors of gases,

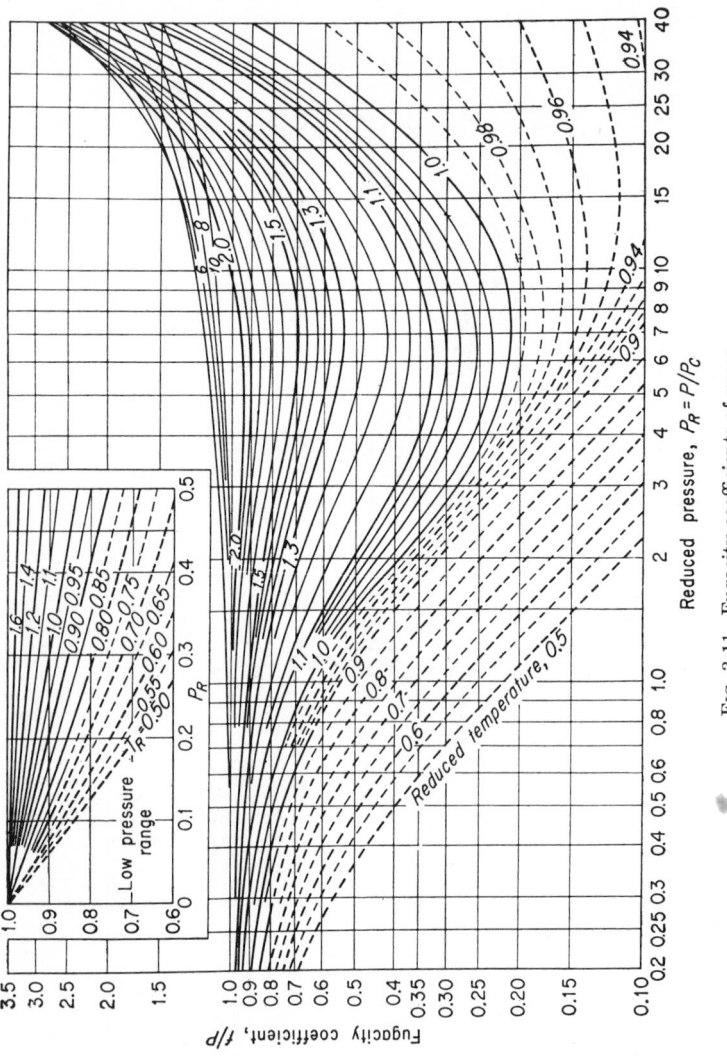

Fig. 3-11. Fugacity coefficients of gases.

GAS DENSITY — Based on the assumption that the gas laws hold over the ranges of temperature and pressure below (Example shown for air at 100°F and 50 lb/sq in. gage)

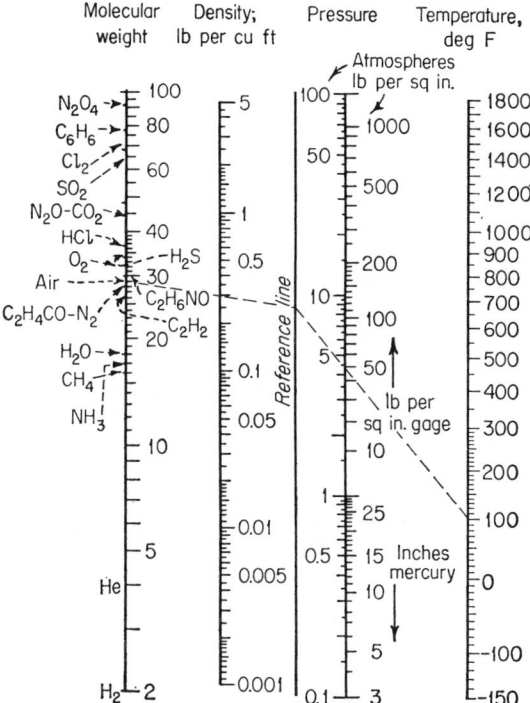

Fig. 3-12. Gas-density nomograph.

Table 3-28. Coefficients of Thermal Expansion of Gases

Substance	Initial pressure, mm Hg	$10^6\alpha$	Substance	Initial pressure, mm Hg	$10^6\alpha$
Coefficient at Constant Volume for Temperatures from 32 to 212°F $\alpha_p = (1/\rho_0)(dp/dt)_v$						

Substance	Initial pressure, mm Hg	$10^6\alpha$	Substance	Initial pressure, mm Hg	$10^6\alpha$
Air............	760	3,671.6	Hydrogen.........	760	3,662.7
	1,000	3,675		1,000	3,662.6
Ammonia.........	760	3,767.8	Hydrogen chloride.....	760	3,721
Argon...........	517	3,668	Krypton..........	1,000	3,689.9
	760	3,672	Methane..........	760	3,679
	1,000	3,675	Neon.............	760	3,662.8
Carbon dioxide....	760	3,711		1,362.8	3,662.3
	1,000	3,726	Nitrogen.........	760	3,672
Carbon monoxide...	760	3,673		994	3,674
Chlorine.........	760	3,803	Nitrous oxide.....	760	3,719
Cyanogen.........	760	3,830	Oxygen...........	760	3,673.5
Ethylene.........	760	3,722		1,000	3,675.7
Helium..........	760	3,661.3	Sulfur dioxide.....	760	3,840
	1,000	3,660.7	Xenon............	1,000	3,720

Coefficient at Constant Pressure for Temperatures from 32 to 212°F
$$\alpha_v = (1/v_0)(dv/dt)_p$$

Substance	Initial pressure, mm Hg	$10^6\alpha$	Substance	Initial pressure, mm Hg	$10^6\alpha$
Air............	760	3,671.1	Krypton..........	862	3,691.6
	1,000	3,674		1,000	3,696.7
Ammonia.........	760	3,790	Methane..........	760	3,682
Argon...........	760	3,672.4	Neon.............	760	3,660.6
	1,000	3,676		1,000	3,660.2
Carbon dioxide....	760	3,725	Nitrogen.........	760	3,671
Carbon monoxide...	760	3,672		994	3,673.4
Chlorine.........	760	3,830	Nitrous oxide.....	760	3,732
Cyanogen.........	760	3,870		1,000	3,706.7
Ethylene.........	760	3,735	Oxygen...........	760	3,674
Helium..........	760	3,659.1		1,000	3,676.3
	994	3,657.9	Sulfur dioxide.....	760	3,880
Hydrogen.........	760	3,660.3	Sulfur hexafluoride.....	760	3,808
	1,095	3,659.0	Xenon............	1,000	3,739.5
Hydrogen chloride.....	760	3,734			

Table 3-29. Linear Expansion of Metallic Elements

Element	Temp, °F	Coef/°F × 10^6	Element	Temp, °F	Coef/°F × 10^6
Aluminum...........	68	12.4	Lead.............	212	16.2
	572	15.8		536	19.0
Carbon (graphite)......	122	3.3	Nickel...........	68	7.0
Chromium...........	140	3.8	Platinum.........	68	4.9
Copper............	68	9.0	Silver...........	68	10.5
	392	9.4	Tantalum.........	68	3.6
Iron, cast..........	68	6.6	Tin..............	32–212	12.8
			Zinc.............	68–482	22.1

GIVEN: 1,000 ft copper pipe installed at 58°F and heated to 78°F.
REQUIRED: The expansion.
SOLUTION: Expansion = (78 − 58) × 1,000 × 9.0 × 10^{-6}
= 0.18 ft

Table 3-30. Linear Expansion of Miscellaneous Substances*

	Temp, °F	Coef/°F × 10⁶		Temp, °F	Coef/°F × 10⁶
Amber...	32–194	34	Quartz:		
Bakelite, bleached...	68–140	12	With axis...	32–176	4.4
Brass, cast...	32–212	10.4	Against axis...	32–176	7.4
Bronze (75 Cu, 25 Sn)...	62–212	10.2	Rubber, hard...	32	38
Fluorspar, CaF₂...	32–212	10.8	Solder (66⅔ Pb, 33⅓ Sn)...	32–212	14
Glass:			Steel...	0–400	6.8
Plate...	32–212	4.95	Wood with fiber:		
Tube...	32–212	4.6	Mahogany...	36	2.0
Flint...	122–140	4.4	Maple...	36	3.5
Quartz...	60–930	0.32	Oak...	36	2.7
Ice...	−4–31	28	Pine...	36	3.0
Limestone...	77–212	5	Wood across fiber:		
Marble...	59–212	6.5	Mahogany...	36	2.2
Monel metal...	77–212	7.8	Maple...	36	2.7
Paraffin...	32–60	59	Oak...	36	3.0
	60–100	72	Pine...	36	1.9
	100–120	265	Wax, white...	50–79	127
Porcelain...	68–1450	2.3		79–111	242
				111–135	850

* For an example of use, see Table 3-29.

Table 3-31. Cubical Expansion of Solids

Substance	Temp, °F	Coef/°F × 10⁶	Substance	Temp, °F	Coef/°F × 10⁶
Antimony...	32–212	17.6	Iron...	32–212	19.7
Beryl...	32–212	0.58	Lead...	32–212	46.5
Copper...	32–212	27.8	Paraffin...	86	326
Galena...	32–212	31.0	Quartz...	32–212	21.4
Glass:			Rubber...	68	270
Common tube...	32–212	15.3	Silver...	32–212	32.4
Hard...	32–212	11.9	Tin...	32–212	38.2
Silica...	32–176	0.72	Zinc...	32–212	49.5
Ice...	−4–31	62.5			

Given: 3,000 ft³ ice at 11°F.
Required: Total volume at 31°F.
Solution: Total volume = 3,000 [1 + (31 − 11) × 62.5 × 10⁻⁶]
= 3,000 [1 + 0.00135]
= 3,000 + 3.75 = 3,003.75 ft³

Table 3-32. Cubical Expansion of Liquids*

Liquid	Coef/°F × 10³	Liquid	Coef/°F × 10³
Acetic acid...	0.595	Hydrochloric acid, 33.2%...	0.253
Acetone...	.825	Mercury...	.109
Alcohol, ethyl...	.622	Olive oil...	.400
Alcohol, methyl...	.666	Pentane (93°API)...	.74
Benzene...	.686	Petroleum:	
Bromine...	.630	15°API...	.35
Calcium chloride:		35°API...	.44
5.8% solution...	.139	Phenol...	.605
40.9% solution...	.260	Sodium chloride, 20.6% solution...	.230
Carbon disulfide...	.676	Sulfuric acid:	
Carbon tetrachloride...	.686	10.9%...	.215
Chloroform...	.707	100.0%...	.31
Ether...	.920	Turpentine...	.541
Glycerin...	.280	Water...	.115

* For an example of use, see Table 3-31.

Table 3-33. General Corrosion Pro

Ratings: 0 unsuitable. Not available in form required or not suitable for fabrication requirements or not
    1 poor to fair.
    2 fair. For mild conditions or where periodic replacement is possible. Restricted use.
    3 fair to good.
    4 good. Suitable when superior alternatives are uneconomic.
    5 good to excellent.
    6 normally excellent.
Small variations in service conditions may appreciably affect corrosion resistance. Choice of materials is

Material	Nonoxidizing or reducing media				Liquids		
					Oxidizing media		
	Acid solutions, excluding hydrochloric, e.g., phosphoric, sulfuric, most conditions, many organics	Neutral solutions, e.g., many non-oxidizing salt solutions, chlorides, sulfates	Alkaline solutions, e.g.		Acid solutions, e.g., nitric	Neutral or alkaline solutions, e.g., persulfates, peroxides, chromates	Pitting media,† acid ferric chloride solutions
			Caustic and mild alkalies, excluding ammonium hydroxide	Ammonium hydroxide and amines			
Cast iron, flake graphite, plain or low alloy.....	1	3	4	5	0	4	0
Ductile iron (higher strength and hardness may be attained by composition and heat-treatment or both)....	1	3	4	5	0	4	0
Ni-Resist corrosion-resistant cast iron, type 1 (14 Ni; 7 Cu; 2 Cr; bal. Fe).........	4	5	5	5	0	5	0
Ni-Resist corrosion-resistant cast iron, type 2 Cu free (20–30 Ni; 2–3 Cr; bal. Fe)...	4	5	5	6	0	5	0
Ni-Resist corrosion-resistant cast iron, ductile (24 Ni; bal. Fe)...	4	5	5	6	0	5	0
14% silicon iron........	6	6	2	5	6	6	3
Mild steel, also low-alloy irons and steels.......	1	3	4	5	0	4	0
Stainless steel, ferritic 17% Cr type........	2	4	4	6	5	6	0
Stainless steel, austenitic 18 Cr; 8 Ni type......	3	4	5	6	6	6	0
Stainless steel, austenitic 18 Cr; 12 Ni; 2.5 Mo type.................	4	5	5	6	5	6	1
Stainless steel, austenitic 20 Cr; 29 Ni; 2.5 Mo; 3.5 Cu type..........	5	6	5	6	5	6	2
Ni-o-nel nickel-iron-chromium alloy (40 Ni; 21 Cr; 3 Mo; 1.5 Cu; bal. Fe)..............	6	6	5	6	5	6	2
Hastelloy alloy C[a] (55 Ni; 17 Mo; 16 Cr; 6 Fe; 4 W).............	5	6	5	6	4	6	5
Hastelloy alloy B[b] (61 Ni; 28 Mo; 6 Fe).....	6	5	4	4	0	3	0
Hastelloy alloy D (82 Ni; 10 Si; 4 Cu)..........	6	6	3	4	2	5	1
Inconel nickel-chromium alloy (78 Ni; 15 Cr; 7 Fe).................	3	6	6	6	3	6	1

[a] Also Chlorimet 3. [b] Also Chlorimet 2.

perties of Some Metals and Alloys

suitable for corrosion conditions.

therefore guided wherever possible by a combination of experience and laboratory and site tests.

Liquids				Gases				
Natural waters				Common industrial media				
Fresh-water supplies		Sea water		Steam		Furnace gases with incidental sulfur content		Ambient air, city or industrial
Static or slow-moving	Turbu-lent	Static or slow-moving	Turbu-lent	Moist, conden-sate	Dry at high temp., promoting slight dissociation	Reducing, e.g., heat-treatment furnace gases	Oxidizing, e.g., flue gases	
4	3	4	2	4	4	1	1	3
4	4	4	3	4	4	1	1	3
5	5	5	5	5	5	3	2	4
5	5	5	5	5	5	3	2	4
5	5	5	5	5	5	3	2	4
5	5	5	5	6	4	4	3	6
4	3	4	2	4	4	1	1	3
4	6	1	4	5	6	3	2	4
6	6	2	5	6	6	2	3	5
6	6	3	5	6	6	2	4	6
6	6	4	6	6	6	2	4	6
6	6	4	6	6	6	2	5	6
6	6	6	6	6	6	3	4	6
6	6	4	4	6	5	3	2	5
6	6	6	6	6	6	4	2	6
6	6	4	6	6	6	2	4	6

Table 3-33. General Corrosion Properties

Ratings: 0 unsuitable. Not available in form required or not suitable for fabrication requirements or not
1 poor to fair.
2 fair. For mild conditions or where periodic replacement is possible. Restricted use.
3 fair to good.
4 good. Suitable when superior alternatives are uneconomic.
5 good to excellent.
6 normally excellent.
Small variations in service conditions may appreciably affect corrosion resistance. Choice of materials is

Material	Nonoxidizing or reducing media				Liquids		
					Oxidizing media		
	Acid solutions, excluding hydrochloric, e.g., phosphoric, sulfuric, most conditions, many organics	Neutral solutions, e.g., many non-oxidizing salt solutions, chlorides, sulfates	Alkaline solutions, e.g.		Acid solutions, e.g., nitric	Neutral or alkaline solutions, e.g., persulfates, peroxides, chromates	Pitting media,† acid ferric chloride solutions
			Caustic and mild alkalies, excluding ammonium hydroxide	Ammonium hydroxide and amines			
Copper-nickel alloys up to 30% nickel.......	4	5	5	0	0	4	1
Monel nickel-copper alloy (68 Ni; 30 Cu; 2 Fe)...	5	6	6	1	0	5	1
S Monel nickel-copper cast alloy (66 Ni; 30 Cu; 4 Si).............	5	6	6	1	0	5	1
K Monel age hardenable Ni-Cu alloy (67 Ni; 30 Cu; 3 Al)............	5	6	6	1	0	5	1
A nickel—commercial (99.4 Ni).............	4	5	6	1	0	5	0
Copper and silicon bronze	4	4	4	0	0	4	0
Aluminum brass (76 Cu; 22 Zn; 2 Al)..........	3	4	2	0	0	3	0
Nickel-aluminum-bronze (80 Cu; 10 Al; 5 Ni; 5 Fe).................	4	4	2	0	0	3	0
Bronze, type A (88 Cu; 5 Sn; 5 Ni; 2 Zn).....	4	5	4	0	0	4	0
Aluminum and its alloys	1	3	0	6	0–5	0–4	0
Lead, chemical or anti-monial..............	5	5	2	2	0	2	0
Silver..................	4	6	6	0	0	2	0
Titanium..............	3	6	2	6	6	6	6
Zirconium..............	3	6	2	6	6	6	2

of Some Metals and Alloys (Continued)

suitable for corrosion conditions.

therefore guided wherever possible by a combination of experience and laboratory and site tests.

Liquids				Gases				
Natural waters				Common industrial media				
Fresh-water supplies		Sea water		Steam		Furnace gases with incidental sulfur content		Ambient air, city or industrial
Static or slow-moving	Turbulent	Static or slow-moving	Turbulent	Moist, condensate	Dry at high temp., promoting slight dissociation	Reducing, e.g., heat-treatment furnace gases	Oxidizing, e.g., flue gases	
6	6	6	6	6	5	2	2	5
6	6	4	6	6	6	2	3	5
6	6	4	6	6	6	2	3	5
6	6	4	6	6	6	2	3	5
6	6	3	5	6	6	2	2	4
6	5	4	1	6	5	2	2	5
6	6	4	5	6	5	2	2	5
6	6	4	5	6	5	2	3	5
6	6	5	5	6	5	2	2	5
4	5	0–5	4	5	2	5	4	5
6	5	5	3	2	0	4	3	5
6	6	5	5	6	5	4	4	4
6	6	6	6	6	5	3	5	6
6	6	6	6	6	6	3	5	6

Table 3-33. General Corrosion Properties

Ratings: **0** unsuitable. Not available in form required or not suitable for fabrication requirements or not
       1 poor to fair.
       2 fair. For mild conditions or where periodic replacement is possible. Restricted use.
       3 fair to good.
       4 good. Suitable when superior alternatives are uneconomic.
       5 good to excellent.
       6 normally excellent.
Small variations in service conditions may appreciably affect corrosion resistance. Choice of materials is

	Gases (Cont'd)				
	Halogens and derivatives				
Material	Halogens		Halide acids, moist, e.g., hydrochloric hydrolysis products of organic halides	Hydrogen halides, dry,† e.g., dry hydrogen chloride, °F	Available forms
	Moist, e.g., chlorine below dew point	Dry, e.g., fluorine above dew point			
Cast iron, flake graphite, plain or low alloy	0	2	0	2 < 400 1 < 750	Cast
Ductile iron (higher strength and hardness may be attained by composition and heat-treatment or both)	0	2	0	2 < 400 1 < 750	Cast
Ni-Resist corrosion-resistant cast iron, type 1 (14 Ni; 7 Cu; 2 Cr; bal. Fe)	0	2	3	3 < 400 2 < 750	Cast
Ni-Resist corrosion-resistant cast iron, type 2 Cu free (20–30 Ni; 2–3 Cr; bal. Fe)	0	2	3	3 < 400 2 < 750	Cast
Ni-Resist corrosion-resistant cast iron, ductile (24 Ni; bal. Fe)	0	2	3	3 < 400 2 < 750	Cast
14% silicon iron....................	0	0	4	1 < 400	Cast
Mild steel, also low-alloy irons and steels	0	3	0	3 < 400 1 < 750	Wrought, cast
Stainless steel, ferritic 17% Cr type....	0	2	0	2 < 400	Wrought, cast, clad
Stainless steel, austenitic 18 Cr; 8 Ni types	0	2	0	3 < 400	Wrought, cast, clad
Stainless steel, austenitic 18 Cr; 12 Ni; 2.5 Mo type	0	3	2	4 < 400 3 < 750	Wrought, cast, clad
Stainless steel, austenitic 20 Cr; 29 Ni; 2.5 Mo; 3.5 Cu type	1	3	3	4 < 400 3 < 750	Wrought, cast
Ni-o-nel nickel-iron-chromium alloy (40 Ni; 21 Cr; 3 Mo; 1.5 Cu; bal. Fe)	2	3	3	4 < 400 3 < 750	Wrought, cast, clad
Hastelloy alloy C^a (55 Ni; 17 Mo; 16 Cr; 6 Fe; 4 W)	5	4	4	4 < 750 3 < 900	Wrought, cast, clad
Hastelloy alloy B^b (61 Ni; 28 Mo; 6 Fe)	1	3	5	4 < 750 3 < 900	Wrought, cast, clad
Hastelloy alloy D (82 Ni; 10 Si; 4 Cu)	1	1	2	3 < 400 2 < 750 1 < 900	Cast
Inconel nickel-chromium alloy (78 Ni; 15 Cr; 7 Fe)	2	5	3	5 < 400 4 < 900	Wrought, cast, clad

† On suitable materials these media may promote potentially dangerous pitting.
‡ Many of these materials are suitable for resisting dry corrosion at elevated temperatures.
§ Special precautions required.
^a Also Chlorimet 3. ^b Also Chlorimet 2.

of Some Metals and Alloys (Continued)

suitable for corrosion conditions.

therefore guided wherever possible by a combination of experience and laboratory and site tests.

Cold formability in wrought and clad form	Weldability	Max. strength annealed condition × 1,000 psi	Coeff. of thermal expansion, millionths per °F 70–212°F	Remarks‡
No	Fair§	45	6.7	ASTM A48-48
No	Good§	67	7.5	ASTM A339, A396-55 MIL-I-1466 (ORD), MIL-I-17166 (Ships), A.M.S. 5313, 5316
No	Good§	22–31	10.3	AMS-5392 MIL-G-858A Hyd. Inst. No. 115
No	Good§	22–31	9.6	MIL-G-858A Hyd. Inst. No. 115 Type 3 Ni-Resist has same corrosion resistance
No	Good§	56	10.4	AMS-5394 MIL-I-18397 (Ships)
No	No	22	7.4	Very brittle, susceptible to cracking by mechanical and thermal shock
Good	Good	67	6.7	High strengths obtainable by alloying, also improved atmospheric corrosion resistance. See ASTM specifications for particular grade
Good	Good§	78	6.0	AISI type 430 ASTM corrosion- and heat-resisting steels
Good	Good	90	9.6	AISI type 304 ASTM corrosion- and heat-resisting steels. Stabilized or ELC types used for welding
Good	Good	90	8.9	AISI type 316 ASTM corrosion- and heat-resisting steel. ELC type used for welding
Good	Good	90	9.4	ACI Cn-7M. Good resistance to sulfuric, phosphoric, and fatty acids at elevated temperatures
Good	Good	100	7.3	Special alloy with good resistance to sulfuric, phosphoric, and fatty acids. Resistant to chlorides in some environments
Fair	Good	145	6.3	Excellent resistance to wet chlorine gas and sodium hypochlorite solutions
Fair	Good	135	5.6	Resistant to solutions of hydrochloric and sulfuric acids
No	§	90–110	6.1	Greatest application in hot concentrated solutions of sulfuric acid
Good	Good	90	8.9	Wide application in food and pharmaceutical industries

Table 3-33. General Corrosion Properties

Ratings: 0 unsuitable. Not available in form required or not suitable for fabrication requirements or not
1 poor to fair.
2 fair. For mild conditions or where periodic replacement is possible. Restricted use.
3 fair to good.
4 good. Suitable when superior alternatives are uneconomic.
5 good to excellent.
6 normally excellent.
Small variations in service conditions may appreciably affect corrosion resistance. Choice of materials is

Material	Gases (Cont'd)				Available forms
	Halogens and derivatives				
	Halogens		Halide acids, moist, e.g., hydrochloric hydrolysis products of organic halides	Hydrogen halides, dry,† e.g., dry hydrogen chloride, °F	
	Moist, e.g., chlorine below dew point	Dry, e.g., fluorine above dew point			
Copper-nickel alloys up to 30% nickel	1	5	2	4 < 400 3 < 750	Wrought, cast, clad
Monel nickel-copper alloy (68 Ni; 30 Cu; 2 Fe)	2	6	3	6 < 400 3 < 750 2 < 900	Wrought, cast, clad
S Monel nickel-copper cast alloy (66 Ni; 30 Cu; 4 Si)	2	4	3	6 < 400 3 < 750 2 < 900	Cast
K Monel age hardenable Ni-Cu alloy (67 Ni; 30 Cu; 3 Al)	2	6	3	6 < 400 3 < 750 2 < 900	Wrought, cast
A nickel—commercial (99.4 Ni).......	2	6	2	6 < 400 5 < 750 4 < 900	Wrought, cast, clad
Copper and silicon bronze...........	0	5	2	3 < 400 2 < 750	Wrought, cast, clad
Aluminum brass (76 Cu; 22 Zn; 2 Al)	0	4	2	2 < 400	Wrought, cast
Nickel-aluminum-bronze (80 Cu; 10 Al; 5 Ni; 5 Fe)	0	4	3	3 < 400 2 < 750	Wrought, cast
Bronze, type A (88 Cu; 5 Sn; 5 Ni; 2 Zn)	0	4	3	3 < 400 2 < 750	Cast
Aluminum and its alloys.............	0	6	0	3 < 400 1 < 750	Wrought, cast, clad
Lead, chemical or antimonial........	0	1	3	0	Wrought, cast, clad
Silver.............................	5	5	3	4 < 400 2 < 750	Wrought, cast, clad
Titanium...........................	6	0	1	0	Wrought, cast
Zirconium.........................	6	1	6	0	Wrought, cast

† On unsuitable materials these media may promote potentially dangerous pitting.
‡ Many of these materials are suitable for resisting dry corrosion at elevated temperatures.
§ Special precautions required.
SOURCE: Data courtesy of International Nickel Co., in "Perry's Chemical Engineer's Handbook," Sec. 23, by Perry, Chilton, and Kirkpatrick. Copyright © 1963, McGraw-Hill, Inc.

of Some Metals and Alloys (Concluded)

suitable for corrosion conditions.

therefore guided wherever possible by a combination of experience and laboratory and site tests.

Cold formability in wrought and clad form	Weldability	Max. strength annealed condition $\times$ 1,000 psi	Coeff. of thermal expansion, millionths per °F 70–212°F	Remarks‡
Good	Good	38–62	9.3–8.5	High-iron types excellent for resisting high-velocity effects in condenser tubes
Good	Good	77	7.5	Widely used for sulfuric acid pickling equipment. Also for propeller shafts in motor boats. Take precautions to avoid sulfur attack during fabrication
No	No	100	8.8	Nongalling characteristics. Excellent for bearings or bushings. High strength developed by heat-treatment
Fair	Good	99–155	7.4	High strength obtainable by heat-treatment. Take precautions to avoid sulfur attack during fabrication
Good	Good	54	6.6	Widely used for hot concentrated caustic solutions. Take precautions to avoid sulfur attack during fabrication
Excellent	Fair	29	9.3–9.5	Unsuitable for hot concentrated mineral acids or for high-velocity HF
Good	Fair	60	10.3	May develop localized corrosion in sea water
Good	Fair	60–80	9.4	Ship propellers an excellent application
No	§	45	11.0	High strengths obtainable by heat-treatment. Not susceptible to dezincification
Good	Good	9–90	11.5–13.7	Extent of corrosion dependent upon type and concentration of acidic ions. Wide range of mechanical properties obtainable by alloying and heat-treatment
Excellent	Good	2	16.4–15.1	High purity "chemical lead" preferred for most applications
Excellent	Good	21	10.6	Used as a lining
Fair	Good§	6–90	5.0	Red fuming HNO₃ may initiate explosions. Good resistance to solutions containing chlorides
Fair	Good§			

Table 3-34. Chemical Resistance of Important Plastics

Ratings are for Long-term Exposures at Ambient Temperatures (Less Than 100°F)

	Poly-propylene poly-ethylene	CAB*	ABS†	PVC‡	Saran§	Polyester glass¶	Epoxy glass	Phenolic asbestos	Fluoro-carbons	Chlorinated polyether (Penton)	Poly-carbonate
10% H_2SO_4	Excel.	Good	Excel.	Excel.	Excel.	Excel.	Excel.	Excel.	Excel.	Excel.	Excel.
50% H_2SO_4	Excel.	Poor	Excel.	Excel.	Excel.	Good	Excel.	Excel.	Excel.	Excel.	Excel.
10% HCl	Excel.	Excel.	Excel.	Excel.	Excel.	Excel.	Excel.	Excel.	Excel.	Excel.	Excel.
10% HNO_3	Excel.	Poor	Good	Excel.	Excel.	Good	Good	Fair	Excel.	Excel.	Excel.
10% Acetic	Excel.	Good	Excel.	Excel.	Excel.	Excel.	Excel.	Excel.	Excel.	Excel.	Excel.
10% NaOH	Excel.	Fair	Excel.	Good	Fair	Fair	Excel.	Poor	Excel.	Excel.	Excel.
50% NaOH	Excel.	Poor	Excel.	Excel.	Fair	Poor	Good	Poor	Excel.	Excel.	Excel.
NH_4OH	Excel.	Poor	Excel.	Excel.	Poor	Fair	Excel.	Poor	Excel.	Excel.	Excel.
NaCl	Excel.	Excel.	Excel.	Excel.	Excel.	Excel.	Excel.	Excel.	Excel.	Excel.	Excel.
$FeCl_3$	Excel.	Excel.	Excel.	Excel.	Excel.	Excel.	Excel.	Excel.	Excel.	Excel.	Excel.
$CuSO_4$	Excel.	Excel.	Excel.	Excel.	Excel.	Excel.	Excel.	Excel.	Excel.	Excel.	Excel.
NH_4NO_3	Excel.	Excel.	Excel.	Excel.	Excel.	Excel.	Excel.	Good	Excel.	Excel.	Excel.
Wet H_2S	Excel.	Excel.	Excel.	Excel.	Excel.	Excel.	Excel.	Excel.	Excel.	Excel.	
Wet Cl_2	Poor	Poor	Excel.	Good	Poor	Poor	Poor	Excel.	Excel.	Excel.	
Wet SO_2	Excel.	Poor	Excel.	Excel.	Good	Excel.	Excel.	Excel.	Excel.	Excel.	
Gasoline	Poor	Excel.	Excel.	Excel.	Excel.	Excel.	Excel.	Excel.	Excel.	Excel.	Excel.
Benzene	Poor	Poor	Poor	Poor	Fair	Good	Excel.	Excel.	Excel.	Fair	Fair
CCl_4	Poor	Poor	Poor	Fair	Fair	Excel.	Good	Excel.	Excel.	Fair	Poor
Acetone	Poor	Poor	Poor	Poor	Fair	Poor	Good	Poor	Excel.	Good	Good
Alcohol	Poor	Poor	Excel.	Excel.	Excel.	Excel.	Excel.	Excel.	Excel.	Excel.	Excel.

* Cellulose acetate butyrate.
† Acrylonitrile butadiene styrene polymer.
‡ Polyvinyl chloride, type I.
§ Chemical resistance of Saran-lined pipe is superior to extruded Saran in some environments.
¶ Refers to general-purpose polyesters. Special polyesters have superior resistance, particularly in alkalies.
SOURCE: "Perry's Chemical Engineer's Handbook," Sec. 23, by Perry, Chilton, and Kirkpatrick. Copyright © 1963, McGraw-Hill, Inc.

MECHANICAL PROPERTIES

Table 3-35. Chemical Ranges and Limits of AISI Carbon Steels

AISI No.	Chemical composition limits, %			
	C	Mn	P, max.	S, max.
C 1008	0.10 max.	0.25/0.50	0.040	0.050
C 1010	.08/0.13	0.30/0.60	.040	.050
C 1011	.08/0.13	0.60/0.90	.040	.050
C 1012	.10/0.15	0.30/0.60	.040	.050
C 1015	.13/0.18	0.30/0.60	.040	.050
C 1016	.13/0.18	0.60/0.90	.040	.050
C 1017	.15/0.20	0.30/0.60	.040	.050
C 1018	.15/0.20	0.60/0.90	.040	.050
C 1019	.15/0.20	0.70/1.00	.040	.050
C 1020	.18/0.23	0.30/0.60	.040	.050
C 1021	.18/0.23	0.60/0.90	.040	.050
C 1022	.18/0.23	0.70/1.00	.040	.050
C 1023	.20/0.25	0.30/0.60	.040	.050
C 1024	.19/0.25	1.35/1.65	.040	.050
C 1025	.22/0.28	0.30/0.60	.040	.050
C 1026	.22/0.28	0.60/0.90	.040	.050
C 1027	.22/0.29	1.20/1.50	.040	.050
C 1029	.25/0.31	0.60/0.90	.040	.050
C 1030	.28/0.34	0.60/0.90	.040	.050
C 1031	.28/0.34	0.30/0.60	.040	.050
C 1033	.30/0.36	0.70/1.00	.040	.050
C 1035	.32/0.38	0.60/0.90	.040	.050
C 1036	.30/0.37	1.20/1.50	.040	.050
C 1037	.32/0.38	0.70/1.00	.040	.050
C 1038	.35/0.42	0.60/0.90	.040	.050
C 1039	.37/0.44	0.70/1.00	.040	.050
C 1040	.37/0.44	0.60/0.90	.040	.050
C 1041	.36/0.44	1.35/1.65	.040	.050
C 1042	.40/0.47	0.60/0.90	.040	.050
C 1043	.40/0.47	0.70/1.00	.040	.050
C 1045	.43/0.50	0.60/0.90	.040	.050
C 1046	.43/0.50	0.70/1.00	.040	.050
C 1049	.46/0.53	0.60/0.90	.040	.050
C 1050	.48/0.55	0.60/0.90	.040	.050
C 1051	.45/0.56	0.85/1.15	.040	.050
C 1052	.47/0.55	1.20/1.50	.040	.050
C 1053	.48/0.55	0.70/1.00	.040	.050
C 1055	.50/0.60	0.60/0.90	.040	.050
C 1060	.55/0.65	0.60/0.90	.040	.050
C 1070	.65/0.75	0.60/0.90	.040	.050
C 1078	.72/0.85	0.30/0.60	.040	.050
C 1080	.75/0.88	0.60/0.90	.040	.050
C 1084	.80/0.93	0.60/0.90	.040	.050
C 1085	.80/0.93	0.70/1.00	.040	.050
C 1086	.80/0.93	0.30/0.50	.040	.050
C 1090	.85/0.98	0.60/0.90	.040	.050
C 1095	.90/1.03	0.30/0.50	.040	.050

Table 3-36. Chemical Ranges and Limits of AISI Standard Alloys

Open-hearth and electric-furnace alloy steels, bars, billets, blooms, and slabs
Ranges and limits apply to steel not exceeding 200 in.[2] in cross-sectional area.

AISI No.	Chemical composition ranges and limits, %							
	C	Mn	P, max.	S, max.	Si	Ni	Cr	Mo
1330	0.28/0.33	1.60/1.90	0.040	0.040	0.20/0.35			
1335	.33/0.38	1.60/1.90	.040	.040	.20/0.35			
1340	.38/0.43	1.60/1.90	.040	.040	.20/0.35			
1345	.43/0.48	1.60/1.90	.040	.040	.20/0.35			
3140	.38/0.43	0.70/0.90	.040	.040	.20/0.35	1.10/1.40	0.55/0.75	
E3310	.08/0.13	.45/0.60	.025	.025	.20/0.35	3.25/3.75	1.40/1.75	
4012	.09/0.14	.75/1.00	.040	.040	.20/0.35	....	....	0.15/0.25
4023	.20/0.25	.70/0.90	.040	.040	.20/0.35	....	....	.20/0.30
4024	.20/0.25	.70/0.90	.040	.035/.050	.20/0.35	....	....	.20/0.30
4027	.25/0.30	.70/0.90	.040	.040	.20/0.35	....	....	.20/0.30
4028	.25/0.30	.70/0.90	.040	.035/.050	.20/0.35	....	....	.20/0.30
4037	.35/0.40	.70/0.90	.040	.040	.20/0.35	....	....	.20/0.30
4042	.40/0.45	.70/0.90	.040	.040	.20/0.35	....	....	.20/0.30
4047	.45/0.50	.70/0.90	.040	.040	.20/0.35	....	....	.20/0.30
4063	.60/0.67	.75/1.00	.040	.040	.20/0.35	....	....	.20/0.30
4118	.18/0.23	.70/0.90	.040	.040	.20/0.35	....	0.40/0.60	.08/0.15
4130	.28/0.33	.40/0.60	.040	.040	.20/0.35	....	.80/1.10	.15/0.25
4135	.33/0.38	.70/0.90	.040	.040	.20/0.35	....	.80/1.10	.15/0.25
4137	.35/0.40	.70/0.90	.040	.040	.20/0.35	....	.80/1.10	.15/0.25
4140	.38/0.43	.75/1.00	.040	.040	.20/0.35	....	.80/1.10	.15/0.25
4142	.40/0.45	.75/1.00	.040	.040	.20/0.35	....	.80/1.10	.15/0.25
4145	.43/0.48	.75/1.00	.040	.040	.20/0.35	....	.80/1.10	.15/0.25
4147	.45/0.50	.75/1.00	.040	.040	.20/0.35	....	.80/1.10	.15/0.25
4150	.48/0.53	.75/1.00	.040	.040	.20/0.35	....	.80/1.10	.15/0.25
4320	.17/0.22	.45/0.65	.040	.040	.20/0.35	1.65/2.00	.40/0.60	.20/0.30
4337	.35/0.40	.60/0.80	.040	.040	.20/0.35	1.65/2.00	.70/0.90	.20/0.30
E4337	.35/0.40	.65/0.85	.025	.025	.20/0.35	1.65/2.00	.70/0.90	.20/0.30
4340	.38/0.43	.60/0.80	.040	.040	.20/0.35	1.65/2.00	.70/0.90	.20/0.30
E4340	.38/0.43	.65/0.85	.025	.025	.20/0.35	1.65/2.00	.70/0.90	.20/0.30
4422	.20/0.25	.70/0.90	.040	.040	.20/0.35	....	....	.35/0.45
4427	.24/0.29	.70/0.90	.040	.040	.20/0.35	....	....	.35/0.45
4520	.18/0.23	.45/0.65	.040	.040	.20/0.35	....	....	.45/0.60
4615	.13/0.18	.45/0.65	.040	.040	.20/0.35	1.65/2.00	....	.20/0.30
4617	.15/0.20	.45/0.65	.040	.040	.20/0.35	1.65/2.00	....	.20/0.30
4620	.17/0.22	.45/0.65	.040	.040	.20/0.35	1.65/2.00	....	.20/0.30
4621	.18/0.23	.70/0.90	.040	.040	.20/0.35	1.65/2.00	....	.20/0.30
4718	.16/0.21	.70/0.90	.040	.040	.20/0.35	0.90/1.20	.35/0.55	.30/0.40
4720	.17/0.22	.50/0.70	.040	.040	.20/0.35	0.90/1.20	.35/0.55	.15/0.25
4815	.13/0.18	.40/0.60	.040	.040	.20/0.35	3.25/3.75	....	.20/0.30
4817	.15/0.20	.40/0.60	.040	.040	.20/0.35	3.25/3.75	....	.20/0.30
4820	.18/0.23	.50/0.70	.040	.040	.20/0.35	3.25/3.75	....	.20/0.30
5015	.12/0.17	.30/0.50	.040	.040	.20/0.35	....	.30/0.50	
5046	.43/0.50	.75/1.00	.040	.040	.20/0.35	....	.20/0.35	
5115	.13/0.18	.70/0.90	.040	.040	.20/0.35	....	.70/0.90	
5120	.17/0.22	.70/0.90	.040	.040	.20/0.35	....	.70/0.90	
5130	.28/0.33	.70/0.90	.040	.040	.20/0.35	....	.80/1.10	
5132	.30/0.35	.60/0.80	.040	.040	.20/0.35	....	.75/1.00	
5135	.33/0.38	.60/0.80	.040	.040	.20/0.35	....	.80/1.05	
5140	.38/0.43	.70/0.90	.040	.040	.20/0.35	....	.70/0.90	
5145	.43/0.48	.70/0.90	.040	.040	.20/0.35	....	.70/0.90	

Table 3-36. Chemical Ranges and Limits of AISI Standard Alloys (Continued)

AISI No.	Chemical composition ranges and limits, %							
	C	Mn	P, max.	S, max.	Si	Ni	Cr	Mo
5147	0.45/0.52	0.70/0.95	0.040	0.040	0.20/0.35	....	0.85/1.15	
5150	.48/0.53	.70/0.90	.040	.040	0.20/0.35	....	0.70/0.90	
5155	.50/0.60	.70/0.90	.040	.040	0.20/0.35	....	0.70/0.90	
5160	.55/0.65	.75/1.00	.040	.040	0.20/0.35	....	0.70/0.90	
E50100	.95/1.10	.25/0.45	.025	.025	0.20/0.35	....	0.40/0.60	
E51100	.95/1.10	.25/0.45	.025	.025	0.20/0.35	....	0.90/1.15	
E52100	.95/1.10	.25/0.45	.025	.025	0.20/0.35	....	1.30/1.60	
								V
6118	.16/0.21	.50/0.70	.040	.040	0.20/0.35	....	0.50/0.70	.10/0.15
6120	.17/0.22	.70/0.90	.040	.040	0.20/0.35	....	0.70/0.90	.10 min.
6150	.48/0.53	.70/0.90	.040	.040	0.20/0.35	....	0.80/1.10	.15 min.
								Mo
8115	.13/0.18	.70/0.90	.040	.040	0.20/0.35	0.20/0.40	0.30/0.50	.08/0.15
8615	.13/0.18	.70/0.90	.040	.040	0.20/0.35	0.40/0.70	0.40/0.60	.15/0.25
8617	.15/0.20	.70/0.90	.040	.040	0.20/0.35	0.40/0.70	0.40/0.60	.15/0.25
8620	.18/0.23	.70/0.90	.040	.040	0.20/0.35	0.40/0.70	0.40/0.60	.15/0.25
8622	.20/0.25	.70/0.90	.040	.040	0.20/0.35	0.40/0.70	0.40/0.60	.15/0.25
8625	.23/0.28	.70/0.90	.040	.040	0.20/0.35	0.40/0.70	0.40/0.60	.15/0.25
8627	.25/0.30	.70/0.90	.040	.040	0.20/0.35	0.40/0.70	0.40/0.60	.15/0.25
8630	.28/0.33	.70/0.90	.040	.040	0.20/0.35	0.40/0.70	0.40/0.60	.15/0.25
8637	.35/0.40	.75/1.00	.040	.040	0.20/0.35	0.40/0.70	0.40/0.60	.15/0.25
8640	.38/0.43	.75/1.00	.040	.040	0.20/0.35	0.40/0.70	0.40/0.60	.15/0.25
8642	.40/0.45	.75/1.00	.040	.040	0.20/0.35	0.40/0.70	0.40/0.60	.15/0.25
8645	.43/0.48	.75/1.00	.040	.040	0.20/0.35	0.40/0.70	0.40/0.60	.15/0.25
8650	.48/0.53	.75/1.00	.040	.040	0.20/0.35	0.40/0.70	0.40/0.60	.15/0.25
8655	.50/0.60	.75/1.00	.040	.040	0.20/0.35	0.40/0.70	0.40/0.60	.15/0.25
8660	.55/0.65	.75/1.00	.040	.040	0.20/0.35	0.40/0.70	0.40/0.60	.15/0.25
8720	.18/0.23	.70/0.90	.040	.040	0.20/0.35	0.40/0.70	0.40/0.60	.20/0.30
8735	.33/0.38	.75/1.00	.040	.040	0.20/0.35	0.40/0.70	0.40/0.60	.20/0.30
8740	.38/0.43	.75/1.00	.040	.040	0.20/0.35	0.40/0.70	0.40/0.60	.20/0.30
8742	.40/0.45	.75/1.00	.040	.040	0.20/0.35	0.40/0.70	0.40/0.60	.20/0.30
8822	.20/0.25	.75/1.00	.040	.040	0.20/0.35	0.40/0.70	0.40/0.60	.30/0.40
9255	.05/0.60	.70/0.95	.040	.040	1.80/2.20			
9260	.55/0.65	.70/1.00	.040	.040	1.80/2.20			
9262	.55/0.65	.75/1.00	.040	.040	1.80/2.20	....	0.25/0.40	
E9310	.08/0.13	.45/0.65	.025	.025	0.20/0.35	3.00/3.50	1.00/1.40	.08/0.15
9840	.38/0.43	.70/0.90	.040	.040	0.20/0.35	0.85/1.15	0.70/0.90	.20/0.30
9850	.48/0.53	.70/0.90	.040	.040	0.20/0.35	0.85/1.15	0.70/0.90	.20/0.30

NOTES:

1. Grades shown with prefix letter E generally are manufactured by the basic electric-furnace process. All others are normally manufactured by the basic open-hearth process, but may be manufactured by the basic electric-furnace process with adjustments in phosphorus and sulfur.

2. The phosphorus and sulfur limitations for each process are as follows:

> Basic electric furnace........ 0.025 max. %
> Basic open hearth........... .040 max. %
> Acid electric furnace......... .050 max. %
> Acid open hearth............ .050 max. %

3. Minimum silicon limit for acid open-hearth or acid electric-furnace alloy steel is 0.15 per cent.

4. Small quantities of certain elements are present in alloy steels which are not specified or required. These elements are considered as incidental, and may be present to the following maximum amounts: copper, 0.35 per cent; nickel, 0.25 per cent; chromium, 0.20 per cent; and molybdenum, 0.06 per cent.

5. Where minimum and maximum sulfur content is shown, it is indicative of resulfurized steels.

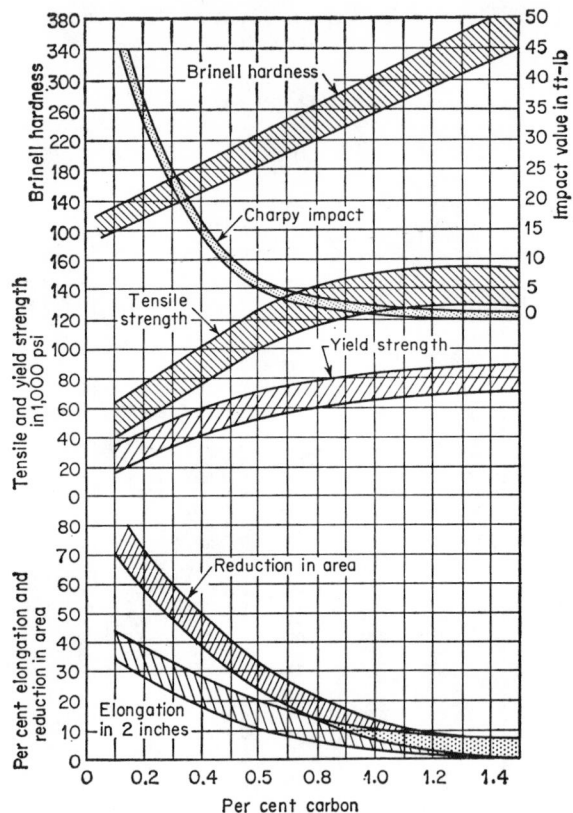

FIG. 3-13. Effect of carbon content on mechanical properties of hot-worked steels. (After F. T. Sisco, *Alloys of Iron and Carbon*, vol. 2, McGraw-Hill Book Company, New York.) Properties of annealed and normalized steels would be approximately the same as hot-worked steels.

Table 3-37. Typical Mechanical Properties of Some AISI Steels with Various Heat-treatments

Sections up to 1½ in. Diam or Thickness

Draw temp, °F	Tensile strength, kpsi	Yield strength, kpsi	Reduction of area, %	Elong. in 2 in., %	Brinell hardness	Tensile strength, kpsi	Yield strength, kpsi	Reduction of area, %	Elong. in 2 in., %	Brinell hardness
	AISI C 1040 quenched in water at 1500°F					AISI 1340 normalized at 1585°F, quenched in oil at 1550°F				
600	125	104	46	11	260	227	206	43	11	448
800	119	91	53	13	250	181	166	51	13	372
1000	110	78	58	15	220	140	121	58	17.5	297
1100	108	71	60	17	216	125	103	62	20	270
1200	104	66	62	20	210	115	88	65	23	250
1300	98	60	64	22	205	110	78	68	25.5	234
	AISI 2340 normalized at 1600°F, quenched in oil at 1425°F					AISI 3140 normalized at 1600°F, quenched in oil at 1500°F				
600	222	205	43	11	437	228	209	42	11	448
800	180	165	50	14	372	187	168	51	13	372
1000	139	122	58	19	297	140	128	59	18	352
1100	121	108	62	22	270	125	112	63	21.5	332
1200	110	95	65	25	250	112	100	66	24	297
1300	99	85	67	27	240	105	90	68	27.5	283
	AISI 4042 normalized at 1600°F, quenched in oil at 1500°F					AISI 4140 normalized at 1600°F, quenched in oil at 1500°F				
600	231	210	41	12	448	225	208	42.5	10	426
800	175	158	50	14	372	180	163	49	13	372
1000	140	125	58	19	297	135	120	57	18	283
1100	125	110	62	23	260	120	105	61	20	250
1200	113	99	65	26	234	108	195	62	22.5	228
1300	105	92	68	30	210	100	88	63	25	216
	AISI 4340 normalized at 1600°F, quenched in oil at 1525°F					AISI 4640 normalized at 1600°F, quenched in oil at 1500°F				
600	250	230	40	9	484	225	208	43	11	448
800	211	200	44	10	426	182	168	50	13	372
1000	173	160	52	12.5	352	141	125	58	19	283
1100	158	140	56	15	313	125	109	62	22.5	260
1200	140	123	60	18	283	110	93	64	26	234
1300	123	108	63	22.5	250	100	81	66	27.5	222
	AISI 5140 normalized at 1575°F, quenched in oil at 1500°F					AISI 8640 normalized at 1600°F, quenched in oil at 1525°F				
600	232	211	43	11	448	240	220	42	10	472
800	190	162	49	12.5	372	202	188	45	12.5	415
1000	140	124	58	17.5	283	165	148	53	16	332
1100	123	108	62	21	250	145	130	57	18	297
1200	110	95	65	24	228	130	113	61	21	283
1300	100	88	68	29	210	116	100	63	22.5	250

SOURCE: "Mechanical Engineer's Handbook," 6th ed., by Marks and Baumeister. Copyright © 1958, McGraw-Hill Inc. Used by permission of McGraw-Hill Book Company.

Table 3-38. Mechanical and Physical Properties of Metals and Alloys

Material	Nominal composition (essential elements), %	Form and condition	Typical mechanical properties				Typical physical constants								
			Yield strength (0.2% offset), 1,000 psi	Tensile strength, 1,000 psi	Elongation in 2 in., %	Hardness, Brinell	Density, lb/in.³	Specific gravity	Melting point, °F	Specific heat (32-212°F) Btu/(lb)(°F)	Thermal expansion coefficient (32-212°F) × 10^{-6} in./(in.)(°F)	Thermal conductivity (32-212°F) Btu/(ft²)(hr)(°F)(in.)	Electrical resistivity (68°F), ohms/cir mil ft	Tensile modulus of elasticity × 10^6 psi
Ferrous Alloys														
Carbon steel[a] AISI-SAE 1020	Fe bal., Mn 0.45, Si 0.25, C 0.20	Annealed; Hot-rolled; Hardened (water quench 1000°F temper)	38 / 42 / 62	65 / 68 / 90	30 / 32 / 25	130 / 135 / 179	0.284	7.86	2760	0.107	6.7	360	60	30
300-M[b]	C 0.43, Mn 0.80, Si 1.60, Ni 1.85, Cr 0.85, Mo 0.38, V 0.08	Hardened (oil quench, 600°F temper)	240	290	10	535	.283	7.84	2740	.107	6.5	400	70	30
Wrought iron	Fe bal., Slag 2.5	Hot-rolled	30	48	30 (in 8 in.)	100	.278	7.70	2750	.11	6.35	418	70	29
Ingot iron	Fe 99.9 plus	Hot-rolled; Annealed	29 / 19	45 / 38	26 / 45	90 / 67	.284	7.86	2795	.108	6.8	490	57	30.1
Cast gray iron (ASTM A48-48, Class 25)	C 3.4, Si 1.8, Mn 0.5, Fe bal.	Cast (as cast)	......	25 min.	0.5 max.	180	.260	7.20	2150	......	6.7	310	400	13 ±1.5
Malleable iron	C 2.5, Si 1, Mn 0.55 max.	Cast (annealed)	33	52	12	130	.264	7.32	2250	.122	6.6	......	180	25
Ductile iron (Mg-containing)	C 3.4, Si 2.5, Mn 0.40, P 0.1 max., Ni 0-1, Mg 0.06, Fe bal.	Cast; Cast (as cast); Cast (quench, temper)	53 / 68 / 108	70 / 90 / 135	18 / 7 / 5	170 / 235 / 310	.26	7.2	2100	......	7.5	228	360	25

Nickel and Nickel Alloys

Nickel (pure)	Ni 99.99	Annealed	8.5	46	30	.....	.322	8.91	2650	.11	7.4	543	41	30
Nickel (cast)	Ni 95.6, Cu 0.5, Fe 0.5, Mn 0.8, Si 1.5, C 0.8	As-cast	25	57	22	110	.301	8.34	2450–2600	.13	8.85 (70–1400°F)	410	125	21.5
A nickel Rods, bars, forgings ASME SB-160 ASTM B160 Plate, sheet, strip ASME SB-162 ASTM B162 Seamless pipe, tubing ASME SB-161 ASTM B161	Ni(+Co) 99.40, C 0.06, Mn 0.25, Fe 0.15, S 0.005, Si 0.05, Cu 0.05	Annealed Hot-rolled Cold-drawn Cold-rolled	20 25 70 95	70 75 95 105	40 40 25 5	100 110 170 210	.321	8.89	2615–2635	.13	6.6	420	53 57	30
Low-carbon nickel Rods, bars, forgings ASME SB-160 ASTM B160 Plate, sheet, strip ASME SB-162 ASTM B162 Seamless pipe, tubing ASME SB-161 ASTM B161	Ni(+Co) 99.50, C 0.02, Mn 0.20, Fe 0.15, S 0.005, Si 0.05, Cu 0.05	Annealed Hot-rolled Cold-drawn Cold-rolled	15 25 65	60 60 95	50 45 15	90 105 150	.321	8.89	2615–2635	.11	7.2	420	50	30
E nickel	Ni(+Co) 97.85, C 0.05, Mn 1.95, Fe 0.05, S 0.005, Si 0.04, Cu 0.03	Annealed Hot-rolled Cold-drawn	35 50 80	75 90 100	40 35 25	140 150 190	.319	8.86	2600	.11	7.4	335	85	30
D nickel	Ni(+Co) 95.00, C 0.10, Mn 4.75, Fe 0.05, S 0.005, Si 0.05, Cu 0.02	Annealed Hot-rolled Cold-drawn	35 50 80	75 90 100	40 35 25	140 150 190	.315	8.78	2600	.11	7.4	335	110	30

a Carbon-steel mechanical properties are strongly influenced by the carbon level; the physical properties will not be appreciably changed. See Fig. 3-13.
b Type of ultra-high-strength steel, attaining tensile strengths of 220,000 to 300,000 psi.

Table 3-38. Mechanical and Physical Properties of Metals and Alloys (Continued)

Material	Nominal composition (essential elements), %	Form and condition	Typical mechanical properties				Typical physical constants								
			Yield strength (0.2% offset), 1,000 psi	Tensile strength, 1,000 psi	Elongation in 2 in., %	Hardness, Brinell	Density, lb/in.³	Specific gravity	Melting point, °F	Specific heat Btu/(lb)(°F) (32-212°F)	Thermal expansion coefficient ×10⁻⁶ in./(in.)(°F) (32-212°F)	Thermal conductivity (32-212°F) Btu/(ft²)(hr) (°F)(in.)	Electrical resistivity (68°F), ohms/cir mil ft	Tensile modulus of elasticity ×10⁶ psi
Hastelloy Alloy B (ASME Code, UPV case 1173) (MIL–R–5031–A Amendment 1, Class 10, welding wire)	Ni bal., Mo 28, Fe 5, Mn, Si	Sand-cast (anneal)	50	80	8	199	.....	.....	.....	.....	.....	.....	.....	26.5
		Rolled (anneal)	56	120	50	215	.334	9.24	2410–2460	.091	5.6	72	812	30.8
	....	Investment cast	54	85	14	209	.....	.....	.....	.....	.....	.....	.....	28.5
Hastelloy Alloy C (ASME Code, UPV Case 1194) AMS-5530-C (sheet)[e] AMS-5750 (bars and forgings) AMS-5388-B (invest-ment castings) AMS-5389-A (sand castings)	Ni bal., Mo 16, Cr 16, Fe 5, W 4, Mn, Si	Sand-cast (anneal)	50	78	5	199	.....	.....	.....	.....	.....	.....	.....	26
	....	Rolled (anneal)	71	130	45	204	.323	8.94	2320–2380	.092	6.3	61	834	30.9
	....	Investment cast	50	80	10	215	.....	.....	.....	.....	.....	.....	.....	24.5
Hastelloy Alloy D	Ni bal., Si 10, Cu 3, Mn	Sand-cast (anneal)	118	118	0–2	321	.282	7.80	2030–2050	.108	6.1	145 (at 72°F)	680	28.9
Hastelloy Alloy F	Ni 46, Cr 22, Fe 21, Mo 6.5, Cb + Ta 2, Mn, Si	Hot-rolled (anneal)	50	110	50	255	.296	8.2	2350	.1025	8.7 (70–600°F)	.....	676	29
Nimonic 90	Ni(+Co) 57.00, C 0.05, Mn 0.50, Fe 0.45, S 0.007, Si 0.20, Cu 0.05, Cr 20.55, Al 1.65, Ti 2.60, Co 16.90	Annealed	90	155	.....	260	.298	8.25	2470–2530	.....	6.5	86.5	690	31

Material	Composition	Condition												
G nickel	Ni(+Co) 94.2, Cu 0.5, Fe 0.5, Mn 0.8, Si 1.5, C 1.5	As-cast	30	55	20	105	.301	8.34	2400–2600	.....	8.75 (70–1400°F)	.....	125	22
S nickel	Ni(+Co) 91.5, Cu 0.5, Fe 0.5, Mn 0.8, Si 6.0, C 0.8	As-cast	62	85	2	220	0.288	8.01	2400–2600	.....	8.76 (70–1400°F)	.....	180	24
		Annealed, aged	65	90	2	240								
Inconel X Rods, bars, forgings AMS 5667, 5668 Sheet AMS 5542 Wire AMS 5698, 5699	Ni(+Co) 72.85, C 0.04, Mn 0.65, Fe 6.80, S 0.007, Si 0.30, Cu 0.05, Cr 15.15, Al 0.75, Ti 2.50, Cb(+Ta) 0.85	Annealed	50	115	50	150	.298	8.25	2540–2600	.105	6.7	102 212°F	735 (76°F)	31.0
		Annealed, age-hardened	115	175	25	300	.....	.....	.....	.....	.....			
330 nickel	Ni(+Co) 99.55, C 0.09, Mn 0.20, Fe 0.05, S 0.005, Si 0.05, Cu 0.02	Annealed	20	70	40	100	.321	8.85	2615–2635	.110	7.2	420	57	31
Monel Plate, sheet, strip AMS 4544 ASTM B127 Rods, bars, forgings ASTM B164 (Cl. A) MIL-N-894C (Cl. A) Wire AMS 4730 MIL-N-894C (Cl. A)	Ni(+Co) 66.15, C 0.12, Mn 0.90, Fe 1.35, S 0.005, Si 0.15, Cu 31.30	Annealed	35	75	40	125	.319	8.83	2370–2460	.127	7.5	174 (212°F)	290	26
		Hot-rolled	50	90	35	150								
		Cold-drawn	80	110	25	190								
		Cold-rolled	100	110	5	240								
Monel (cast) QQ-N-288 (Comp. A)	Ni(+Co) 64.0, Cu 31.5, Fe 1.0, Mn 0.8, Si 1.5, C 0.20	As-cast	35	75	35	140	.312	8.63	2400–2450	.13	9.17	186	320	23
K Monel Rods, bars, forgings, plate, sheet, strip, wire QQ-N-286a (Cl. A), Am. 1 MIL-N-17506A (Cl. A) Wire MIL-W-4471 (Comp. A)	Ni(+Co) 65.25, C 0.15, Mn 0.60, Fe 1.00, S 0.005, Si 0.15, Cu 29.60, Al 2.75, Ti 0.45	Annealed	45	100	40	155	.305	8.47	2400–2460	.127	7.4	130	350	26
		Annealed, age-hardened	100	155	25	270								
		Spring	140	150	5	300								
		Spring, age-hardened	160	185	10	335								

^a AMS is Aeronautical Material Specification (SAE).

Table 3-38. Mechanical and Physical Properties of Metals and Alloys (Continued)

Material	Nominal composition (essential elements), %	Form and condition	Typical mechanical properties				Typical physical constants								
			Yield strength (0.2% offset), 1,000 psi	Tensile strength, 1,000 psi	Elongation in 2 in., %	Hardness, Brinell	Density, lb/in.³	Specific gravity	Melting point, °F	Specific heat (32-212°F), Btu/(lb)(°F)	Thermal expansion coefficient (32-212°F), × 10⁻⁶ in./(in.)(°F)	Thermal conductivity (32-212°F), Btu/(ft³)(hr)(°F)(in.)	Electrical resistivity (68°F), ohms/cir mil ft	Tensile modulus of elasticity × 10⁶ psi
Inconel (wrought) Rods, bars, forgings AMS 5665B ASTM B166 Plate, sheet, strip AMS 5540D ASTM M168 Seamless pipe, tubing AMS 5580C ASTM B167 Wire AMS 5687B QQ-W-390a	Ni(+Co) 76.40, C 0.04, Mn 0.20, Fe 7.20, S 0.007, Si 0.20, Cu 0.10, Cr 15.85	Annealed	35	90	45	150	.304	8.43	2540–2600	.109	7.0	104 113 (212°F)	623 (76°F)	31.0
		Cold-drawn	100	130	20	200	…	…	…	…	…	…		

Stainless Steels

Stainless steel type 201	C 0.15 max., Mn 5.5-7.5, Cr 16.0-18.0, Ni 3.5-5.5, N 0.25 max.	Mill-annealed strip	50	115	60	194	.28	7.7	2550–2650	.12	…	113	414	28.6
Stainless steel type 202	C 0.15 max., Mn 7.5-10.0, Cr 17.0-19.0, Ni 4.0-6.0, N 0.25 max.	Mill-annealed strip	50	100	60	184	.28	7.7	2550–2650	.12	…	113	414	28.6
Stainless steel type 301	Fe bal., Cr 17, Ni 7, C 0.08-0.20	Annealed Cold-rolled[4]	30 up to 165	100 up to 200	72 15*	160 385	.29	8.02	2550–2590	.12	9.4	112.8	435	28

Material	Composition	Condition												
Stainless steel type 302 AMS 5515-6-7-8-9 (plate, sheet, strip) AMS 5637 (bars) AMS 5688 (wire)	Fe bal, Cr 18, Ni 8 C 0.08–0.20	Annealed	30 up to 165	90 up to 190	60	160 up to 400	0.29	8.02	2550–2590	0.12	9.6	112.8	435	28
		Cold-rolled[d]			8*									
Stainless steel type 304 AMS 5639 (bars, forgings, tubing) AMS 5697 (wire)	Fe bal, Cr 19, Ni 9.0, C 0.08 max.	Annealed	30 up to 160	85 up to 185	62	160 up to 400	.29	8.02	2550–2650	.12	9.6	113	435	28
		Cold-rolled[e]			8*									
Stainless steel type 304L	Fe bal, Cr 19, Ni 10, C 0.03 max.	Annealed	30	80	60	150	.29	8.02	2550–2650	.12	9.6	113	435	28
		Cold-drawn	95	125	25	277								
Stainless steel type 309 AMS 5523 (plate, sheet, strip) AMS 5574 (tubing) AMS 5650 (bars, forgings)	Fe bal, Cr 23, Ni 13, C 0.20 max.	Annealed	30 up to 120	82 up to 150	50	165	.29	8.02	2550–2650	.12	8.3	96	470	29
		Cold-rolled[d]			4*	275								
Stainless steel type 310 AMS 5572-7 (tubing) AMS 5651 (bars, forgings)	Fe bal, Cr 25, Ni 20, C 0.25 max.	Annealed	40	100	50	165	.29	8.02	2550–2650	.12	8.0	96	470	29
Stainless steel type 316 AMS 5524 (plate, sheet, strip) AMS 5573 (tubing) AMS 5548 (bars, forgings)	Fe bal, Cr 18, Ni 11, Mo 25, C 0.10 max.	Annealed	30 up to 120	90 up to 150	50	165	.29	8.02	2500–2550	.12	8.9	113	445	28
		Cold-rolled[f]			8*	275								
Stainless steel type 316L	Fe bal, Cr 17, Ni 12, C 0.03 max., Mo 2	Annealed	30	80	60	150	.29	8.02	2500–2550	.12	8.9	113	445	28
		Cold-drawn	60	90	45	190								
Stainless steel types 321 and 347 AMS 5570-71 (tubing) (321 has Ti) (347 has Cb)	Fe bal, Cr 18, Ni 10, C 0.10 max., Ti 4 × carbon min. or Cb 8 × carbon min.	Annealed	30 up to 120	85 up to 150	50	160	.286	7.92	2550–2600	.12	9.3	110	435	28
		Cold-rolled			5*	300								

[d] The cold-rolled properties depend upon composition; types 302 and 304 are not rolled often in excess of 175,000 psi tensile strength.

[e] The values for elongation (per cent in 2 in.) are obtainable in the steel cold-rolled to *the maximum stated* yield strength and tensile strength. For lower values of tensile strength, elongation will be correspondingly higher.

[f] Types 316, 321, and 347 are used chiefly in the annealed condition.

Table 3-38. Mechanical and Physical Properties of Metals and Alloys (Continued)

Material	Nominal composition (essential elements), %	Form and condition	Yield strength (0.2% offset), 1,000 psi	Tensile strength, 1,000 psi	Elongation in 2 in., %	Hardness, Brinell	Density, lb/in.³	Specific gravity	Melting point, °F	Specific heat (32–212°F) Btu/(lb)(°F)	Thermal expansion coefficient (32–212°F) × 10⁻⁶ in./in./(°F)	Thermal conductivity (32–212°F) Btu/(ft²)(hr)(°F)(in.)	Electrical resistivity (68°F), ohms/cir mil ft	Tensile modulus of elasticity × 10⁶ psi
Stainless steel type 330	Fe bal., Ni 36, Cr 16	Hot-rolled	55	100	35	200	.284	7.86	2515	.11	6.3 8.8 (68–932°F)	90	600	
		Cold-drawn (annealed)		80										
		Cold-drawn (heat-treated)		150										
Stainless steel AM 350	Fe bal., Cr 17, Ni 4 Mo 3, C 0.08	Annealed	45	156	21	205	.286				9.0			30
		Hardened	153	195	12	382								
Stainless steel type 410 AMS 5591 (tubing) AMS 5613 (bars, forgings)	Fe bal., Cr 12.5, C 0.15 max.	Annealed	40	75	30	150	.28	7.75	2700–2790	.11	5.5	173	340	29
		Heat-treated	115	150	15	300								
Stainless steel type 414 AMS 5615 (bars, forgings)	Fe bal., Cr 12.5, Ni 2.5	Annealed	80	100	22	217	.28	7.75	2600–2700	.11	6.1	173	420	29
		Heat-treated	150	200	17	387								
Stainless steel type 420 AMS 5621 (bars, forgings) AMS 5506 (plate, sheet, and strip)	Fe bal., Cr 13, C 0.35	Annealed	60	98	28	180	.28	7.75	2650–2750	.11	5.7	173	330	29
		Heat-treated	200	250	8	480								
Stainless steel type 430	Fe bal., Cr 16, C 0.12 max.	Annealed	40	70	35	165	.28	7.75	2600–2750	.11	6.0	180	360	29
		Cold-rolled	95	110	10	225								
Stainless steel type 431 AMS 5628 (bars, forgings)	Fe bal., Cr 16, Ni 2	Annealed	85	120	25	250	.280	7.75	2600–2700	.11	6.5	140	430	29
		Heat-treated	150	195	20	400								
Stainless steel type 446	Fe bal., Cr 25, C 0.35 max.	Annealed	50	80	30	165	0.27	7.45	2600–2750	0.12	5.8	145	405	29

Material	Composition	Condition												
Stainless steel 17-4 PH AMS 5673 (bars, forgings)	Fe bal., Cr 17, Ni 4, Cu 4, Co 0.35, C 0.07	Annealed Hardened	110 180	150 195	12 13	363 404	.28	…	…	…	6	124	…	28.5
Stainless steel 17-7 PH AMS 5673 (wire) AMS 5644 (bars and forgings) AMS 5668 (tubing) AMS 5628-9 (plate, sheet, strip)	Fe bal., Cr 17, Ni 7, Al 1, C 0.09	Annealed Hardened	40 185	130 200	30 9	165 404	.282	…	…	…	8.5	128	…	29
Stainless steel, stainless W	Fe bal., Cr 17, Ni 7, Ti 0.7, Al 0.2, C 0.07	Annealed Hardened	75-115 150-185	120-150 170-210	8-15 8-16	255 365	.28	…	…	…	6	…	…	28
Carpenter stainless No. 20ᵃ	C 0.07 max., Mn 0.75, Si 1.00, Cr 20.00, Ni 29.00, Mo 2.00 min., Cu 3.00 min.	Annealed	35	85	50	160	.289	8.02	…	.12	9.4	145.2 (212°F)	451	28.0
Cast 12 Cr Alloy (CA-15)ᵇ (C means corrosion-resistant casting, Alloy Casting Institute designations)	C 0.15 max., Mn 1.00 max., Si 1.50 max., Cr 11.5-14, Ni 1.00 max., Fe bal.	Air-cooled from 1800°F. Tempered at 600°F. Air-cooled from 1800°F. Tempered at 1400°F.	150 75	200 100	7 30	390 185	.275	7.61	2750	.11	6.4 (70-1000°F)	14.5 (212°F)	468	29
Cast 20 Cr Alloy (CB-30)	C 0.30 max., Mn 1.00 max., Si 1.00 max., Cr 18-22, Ni 2 max.	Annealed	60	95	15	195	.272	7.53	2725	.11	6.5 (70-1000°F)	12.8 (212°F)	456	29
Cast 20-10 Alloy (CF-8)	C 0.08 max., Mn 1.50 max., Si 2.00 max., Cr 18-21, Ni 8-11, Fe bal.	Water-quenched (1950-2050°F)	37	77	55	140	.280	7.75	2600	.12	10.0 (70-1000°F)	9.2 (212°F)	457.2	28
Cast 20-10-2, 5 Alloy (CF-8M)	C 0.08 max., Mn 1.50 max., Si 1.50 max., Cr 18-21, Ni 9-12, Mo 2.5, Fe bal.	Water-quenched (1950-2050°F)	42	80	50	156-170	.280	7.75	2550	.12	9.7 (70-1000°F)	9.4 (212°F)	492	28

ᵃ Carpenter stainless No. 20-Cb same composition except for columbium + tantalum, eight times the carbon minimum.
ᵇ American Casting Institute (ACI) designations.

Table 3-38. Mechanical and Physical Properties of Metals and Alloys (Continued)

Material	Nominal composition (essential elements), %	Form and condition	Yield strength (0.2% offset), 1,000 psi	Tensile strength, 1,000 psi	Elongation in 2 in., %	Hardness, Brinell	Density, lb/in.³	Specific grav.	Melting point, °F	Specific heat Btu/(lb)(°F) (32-212°F)	Thermal expansion coefficient × 10⁻⁶ in./(in.)(°F) (32-212°F)	Thermal conductivity (32-212°F) Btu/(ft²)(hr)(in.)(°F)	Electrical resistivity (68°F), ohms/cir mil ft	Tensile modulus of elasticity × 10⁶ psi
Cast 29-9 Alloy (HE)	C 0.20-0.50, Mn 2.00 max., Si 2.00 max., Cr 26-30, Ni 8-11, Fe bal.	As-cast	45	95	20	200	.277	7.68	2650	.14	11.1 (70-2000°F)	10.0 (70-1500°F)	510	25
		Aged	55	90	10	270								
Cast 25-12 Alloy (HH)	C 0.20-0.50, Mn 2.00 max., Si 2.00 max., Cr 24-28, Ni 11-14, Fe bal.	As-cast—Type 1	50	80	25	185	.279	7.72	2500	.12	10.8 (70-2000°F)	10.9 (70-1000°F)	450-510	27
		Type 2	40	85	15	180								
		Aged—Type 1	55	86	11	200								
		Type 2	45	92	8	200								
Cast 25-20 Alloy (HK)	C 0.20-0.60, Mn 2.00 max., Si 2.00 max., Cr 24-28, Ni 18-22, Fe bal.	As-cast	50	75	17	170	.280	7.75	2550	.12	10.1 (70-2000°F)	10.9 (70-1000°F)	540	29
		Aged	50	85	10	190								
Cast 30-20 Alloy (HL)	C 0.20-0.60, Mn 2.00 max., Si 2.00 max., Cr 28-32, Ni 18-22, Fe bal.	As-cast	52	82	19	192	0.279	7.72	2600	0.12	10.1 (70-2000°F)	10.9 (70-1000°F)	574	29

Cast Alloys (Miscellaneous)

Material	Nominal composition (essential elements), %	Form and condition	Yield strength (0.2% offset), 1,000 psi	Tensile strength, 1,000 psi	Elongation in 2 in., %	Hardness, Brinell	Density, lb/in.³	Specific grav.	Melting point, °F	Specific heat Btu/(lb)(°F) (32-212°F)	Thermal expansion coefficient × 10⁻⁶ in./(in.)(°F) (32-212°F)	Thermal conductivity (32-212°F) Btu/(ft²)(hr)(in.)(°F)	Electrical resistivity (68°F), ohms/cir mil ft	Tensile modulus of elasticity × 10⁶ psi
Durimet 20	C 0.07, Mn 1.5, Si 1.5, Cr 20.0, Ni 29.0, Mo 2.0, Cu 3.0	Cast, annealed	30	65	48	130	.286	.....	.....	.....	8.6	145 (212°F)	.....	.....
Iron-silicon Alloy (Duriron)	Si 14.50, C 0.85, Mn 0.65, Mo nil, Fe bal.	Cast only	.....	16	Nil	520	.255	7.0	2300	.13	7.4 (68-392°F)	.....	.....	23

Aluminum and Alloys

Alloy	Composition	Condition												
Fe-Si-Mo Alloy (Duriclor)	Si 14.50, C 0.85, Mn 0.65, Mo 3.00, Fe bal.	Cast only	.....	16	Nil	520	.255	7.0	2300	.13	7.2	......	.....	23
Ni-Mo Alloy (Chlorimet 2)	Ni 62.00, Mo 32.00, Fe 3.00 max., Si 1.00, C 0.10	Cast	55	80	5	230	.333	9.24	2460	.....	4.7	......	.....	27
Ni-Cr-Mo Alloy (Chlorimet 3)	Ni 60.00, Cr 18.00, Mo 18.00, Fe 3.00 max., Si 1.00, C 0.07	Cast only	50	75	10	220	.325	8.94	2380	.092	7.0 (68–392°F)	......	.....	24.5
Aluminum Alloy No. 1100 QQ-A-411C; ASTM B211 wire, rod, and bar	Al 99 plus	Annealed-0 Cold-rolled-H14 Cold-rolled-H18	5 17 22	13 18 24	45 20 15	23 32 44	.098	2.71	1190–1215	.23	13.1 (68°F)	1540 1510 (68°F)	18 19	10
3003 QQ-A-357; ASTM B221 bar, rod, and shapes extruded	Al bal., Mn 1.2	Annealed-0 Cold-rolled-H14 Cold-rolled-H18	6 21 27	16 22 29	40 16 10	28 40 55	.099	2.73	1190–1210	.23	12.9 (68°F)	1340 1100 1075 (68°F)	21 25 26	10
2014 ASTM B211 QQ-A-266 rod, bar, extrusions, forgings	Al bal., Cu 4.4, Si 0.8, Mn 0.8, Mg 0.4	Annealed-0 Heat-treated T4 Heat-treated and artificially aged—T6	14 42 60	27 62 70	18 20 13	45 105 135	.101	2.8	950–1215	.23	12.5	1335 840 1075	21 34 26.5	10.6

Temper designations:
O annealed temper of wrought alloys.
F wrought alloys—as fabricated. Cast alloys—as cast.
T Heat-treated alloys. First numeral following T is the type of heat-treatment. The second numeral, if there is one, indicates a variation to produce desired results.
  T3 Solution treatment followed by strain hardening. Different amount of straining is indicated by the second digit.
  T4 Solution treatment and natural aging.
  T5 Artificial aging after casting or extruding.
  T6 Solution treatment and artificial aging.
  T7 Solution treatment and stabilization.
H Cold-worked wrought alloy:
  H1 Cold-worked to desired dimensions. Second digit indicates degree of hardness: H18 full hard, H14 half hard.
  H3 Strain-hardened and stabilized.

3–87

Table 3-38. Mechanical and Physical Properties of Metals and Alloys (Continued)

Material	Nominal composition (essential elements), %	Form and condition	Typical mechanical properties				Typical physical constants								
			Yield strength (0.2% offset), 1,000 psi	Tensile strength, 1,000 psi	Elongation in 2 in., %	Hardness, Brinell	Density, lb/in.³	Specific gravity	Melting point, °F	Specific heat (32–212°F) Btu/(lb)(°F)	Thermal expansion coefficient (32–212°F) × 10⁻⁶ in./(in.)(°F)	Thermal conductivity (32–212°F) Btu/(ft²)(hr)(°F)(in.)	Electrical resistivity (68°F), ohms/cir mil ft	Tensile modulus of elasticity × 10⁶ psi
2024 Alclad QQ-A-268; ASTM B211 bar, rod, and wire	Core: 2024, Al bal., Cu 4.5, Mn 0.6, Mg 1.5, Coating: Al 99.3	Heat-treated–T4 Heat-treated and strain hardened–T36 Heat-treated, strain hardened, and artificially aged–T86[i]	42 53 66	64 67 70	18 11 6	...	...	...	935–1215	.23	12.9 (68°F)	...	...	10.6
2218 ASTM B247 QQ-A-367 forgings	Al bal., Cu 4.0, Mg 1.5, Ni 2.0	Heat-treated–T72[i]	37	48	11	95	0.102	2.8	940–1175	0.23	12.4	1075	26.5	10.8
5052 QQ-A-315a; ASTM B211 bar, rod, and wire QQ-A-381b; ASTM B209 sheet and plate	Al bal., Mg 2.5, Cr 0.25	Annealed–0 Cold-rolled and stabilized–H34 Cold-rolled and stabilized–H38[i]	13 31 37	28 38 42	30 14 8	47 68 77	.097	2.68	1100–1200	.23	13.2 (68°F)	960 (68°F) 960 (68°F)	30 30	10.2
6061 ASTM B221 QQ-A-325 all wrought products	Al bal., Mg 1.0, Cu 0.25, Si 0.6, Cr 0.25	Annealed–0 Heat-treated–T4 Heat-treated and artificially aged–T6[i]	8 21 40	18 35 45	30 25 17	30 65 95	.098	2.7	1080–1200	.23	13.0	1185 1075 1075	23 26.5 26.5	10.0

Alloy	Composition	Condition													
6063 MIL-A-18593; ASTM B221 bar, rod, and shapes extruded	Al bal., Si 0.4, Mg 0.7	Annealed-0 Artificially aged–T5 Heat-treated and artificially aged–T6[i]	7 21 31	13 27 35	30 12 12	25 60 73	.098	2.70	1140–1205	.....	13.0 (68°F)	1390 (68°F)	20	10.0
7075 QQ-A-282; ASTM B211 bar, rod, wire, and shapes; rolled or drawn	Al bal., Zn 5.6, Cu 1.6, Mg 2.5, Cr 0.3	Annealed-0 Heat-treated and artificially aged–T6[i]	15 73	33 83	17 11	60 150	.101	2.80	890–1180	.23	12.9 (68°F)	840 (68°F)	34	10.4
13 ASTM S12A S12B	Al bal., Si 12	Die-cast-F[i]	21	39	2.0	.....	.096	2.65	1065–1080	.23	11.5 (68°F)	840 (68°F)	33	10.3
360 ASTM B85 QQ-A-591	Al bal., Si 9.5, Mg 0.5	Die-cast-F[i]	27	44	3	.....	.095	2.64	1035–1105	.23	11.6	780	37	10.3
380 ASTM SC84B	Al bal., Cu 3.5, Si 9.0	Die-cast-F[i]	26	43	2.0	.....	.098	2.72	1000–1100	.....	11.6 (68°F)	670 (68°F)	45	10.3
43 ASTM S5A S5B S5C	Al bal., Si 5.0	Sand-cast-F Permanent mold-cast-F Die-cast-F[i]	8 9 16	19 23 30	8 10 7	40 45	.097	2.69	1065–1170	.23	12.3 (68°F)	990 (68°F)	27	10.3

[i] Temper designations:

O   annealed temper of wrought alloys.

F   wrought alloys—as fabricated. Cast alloys—as cast.

T   Heat-treated alloys. First numeral following *T* is the type of heat-treatment. The second numeral, if there is one, indicates a variation to produce desired results.

    T3   Solution treatment followed by strain hardening. Different amount of straining is indicated by the second digit.

    T4   Solution treatment and natural aging.

    T5   Artificial aging after casting or extruding.

    T6   Solution treatment and artificial aging.

    T7   Solution treatment and stabilization.

H   Cold-worked wrought alloy.

    H1   Cold-worked to desired dimensions. Second digit indicates degree of hardness: H18 full hard, H14 half hard,

    H3   Strain-hardened and stabilized.

Table 3-38. Mechanical and Physical Properties of Metals and Alloys (Continued)

Material	Nominal composition (essential elements), %	Form and condition	Typical mechanical properties				Typical physical constants							
			Yield strength (0.2% offset), 1,000 psi	Tensile strength, 1,000 psi	Elongation in 2 in., %	Hardness, Brinell	Density, lb/in.³	Specific gravity	Melting point, °F	Specific heat Btu/(lb)(°F) (32-212°F)	Thermal expansion coefficient × 10^{-6} in./(in.)(°F) (32-212°F)	Thermal conductivity (32-212°F) Btu/(ft²)(hr)(in.)(°F)	Electrical resistivity (68°F), ohms/cir mil ft	Tensile modulus of elasticity × 10^6 psi
195 ASTM C4A	Al bal, Cu 4.5, Si 0.8	Sand-cast; heat-treated-4	16	32	8.5	60	.102	2.81	970–1190	.23	12.7 (68°F)	960 (68°F)	30	10.3
		Sand-cast; heat-treated and artificially aged–T6	24	36	5	75	...	...	...	...	...	960 (68°F)		
319 ASTM B179 SAE 329	Al bal, Cu 3.5, Si 6.3	Sand-cast As cast–F	18	27	2	70	0.101	2.79	960–1120	0.23	11.9	750	38.5	10.3
		Heat-treated and artificially aged–T6	24	36	2	80								
355 ASTM B26 QQ-A-601 Sand-cast ASTM B108 QQ-A-596 Perm. mold	Al bal, Cu 1.3, Si 5.0, Mg 0.5	Sand-cast Artificially aged–T51	23	28	1.5	65	...	...	...	...	...	1160	24	10.3
		Heat-treated and artificially aged–T6	25	35	3.0	80	...	...	1015–1150	...	...	985	29	
		Perm. mold Artificially aged–T51	24	30	2	75	.098	2.71	...	.23	12.4	1160	...	
		Heat-treated and artificially aged–T6	27	42	4	90	...	...	...	...	...	985	26.5	

Material	Composition	Condition												
356 QQ-A-601 Sand-cast · ASTM B108 QQ-A-596 Perm. mold	Al bal., Si 7.0, Mg 0.3	Sand-cast Artificially aged—T51	20	25	2	60	.....	.....	.....	.....	.....	1160	24	.....
		Heat-treated and artificially aged—T6	24	33	3.5	70	.097	2.68	1035–1135	.23	11.9	1040	26.5	10.3
		Perm. mold Heat-treated and artificially aged—T6	27	38	5	85	.....	.....	.....	.....	.....	1040	25	.....
Copper and Alloys														
Cupronickel 10% Tube ASTM B111 Plate ASTM B171	Cu 88.35, Ni 10, Fe 1.25, Mn 0.4	Annealed	22	44	45	.....	.323	8.94	2090	.09	9.3	310	113	18
		Cold-drawn tube	57	60	15									
Cupronickel 30% Sheet ASTM B122 Plate ASTM B171 Tube ASTM B111	Cu 68.90, Ni 30, Mn 0.60, Fe 0.50	Annealed	22	55	45	70	.323	8.94	2240	.09	8.5	200	220	22
		Cold-drawn	60	75	20	150								
		Cold-rolled	70	77	5	155								
Cupronickel 55–45 (Constantan)	Cu 55, Ni 45	Annealed	30	60	45	.....	.321	8.89	2300	.....	8.1	155	290	24
		Cold-drawn	50	65	30									
		Cold-rolled	65	85	20									
Copper Sheet ASTM B152 Rod ASTM B124, B133 Wire ASTM B1, B2, B3	Cu 99.9 plus	Annealed	10	32	45	42	.322	8.91	1980	.092	9.3	2700	10.3	17
		Cold-drawn	40	45	15	90								
		Cold-rolled (HT)[i]	40	46	5	100								

† Temper designations:

O   annealed temper of wrought alloys.
F   wrought alloys—as fabricated. Cast alloys—as cast.
T   Heat-treated alloys. First numeral following T is the type of heat-treatment. The second numeral, if there is one, indicates a variation to produce desired results.
    T3   Solution treatment followed by strain hardening. Different amount of straining is indicated by the second digit.
    T4   Solution treatment and natural aging.
    T5   Artificial aging after casting or extruding.
    T6   Solution treatment and artificial aging.
    T7   Solution treatment and stabilization.
H   Cold-worked wrought alloy.
    H1   Cold-worked to desired dimensions. Second digit indicates degree of hardness: H18 full hard, H14 half hard,
    H2   Strain-hardened and stabilized.
    H3   Strain-hardened and stabilized.

i Hard temper (H1). Hard temper and heat-treated (strip) (HT, HT).

Table 3-38. Mechanical and Physical Properties of Metals and Alloys (Continued)

Material	Nominal composition (essential elements), %	Form and condition	Typical mechanical properties				Typical physical constants								
			Yield strength (0.2% offset), 1,000 psi	Tensile strength, 1,000 psi	Elongation in 2 in., %	Hardness, Brinell	Density, lb/in.^{3}	Specific gravity	Melting point, °F	Specific heat (32-212°F), Btu/(lb)(°F)	Thermal expansion coefficient (32-212°F), $\times 10^{-6}$ in./(in.)(°F)	Thermal conductivity (32-212°F), Btu/(ft^2)(hr)(°F)(in.)	Electrical resistivity (68°F), ohms/cir mil ft	Tensile modulus of elasticity $\times 10^6$ psi
Red brass (wrought) Sheet, strip, and plate, ASTM B36 Wire ASTM B134 Tubes ASTM B135	Cu 85, Zn 15	Annealed Cold-drawn Cold-rolled	15 55 60	40 70 75	50 15 7	50 120 135	.316	8.75	1875	.09	9.8	1100	28	17
Red brass (cast)	Cu 85, Zn 5, Pb 5, Sn 5	Cast (as cast)	17	35	25	60	.317	8.75	1810–1840	……	10.2	500	63	13
Gilding metal Sheet ASTM B36	Cu 95.0, Zn 5.0	Cold-rolled	50	56	5	114	.320	……	1950	……	10.0	1600	……	17
Commercial bronze Sheet ASTM B36 Wire ASTM B134	Cu 90.0, Zn 10.0	Cold-rolled	54	61	5	125	.318	……	1910	……	10.2	1300	……	17
Cartridge 70-30 brass Sheet ASTM B19 Plate ASTM B36 Wire ASTM B134 Tube ASTM B14 Tube ASTM B135	Cu 70.0, Zn 30.0	Cold-rolled	63	76	8	155	0.308	……	1750	……	11.1	840	……	16
Architectural bronze	Cu 57.0, Zn 40.0, Pb 3.0	Annealed	20	60	30	95	.306	……	1630	……	11.6	850	……	14
Phosphor bronze 10% Sheet ASTM B103 Rod ASTM B139 Wire ASTM B159	Cu 90, Sn 10, P 0.25	Spring temper	……	122	4	241	.317	……	1830	……	10.2	350	……	16

Properties of copper alloys (column headings not shown on this page):

Material and specification	Composition	Condition												
Phosphor bronze 5% Sheet ASTM B103 Rod ASTM B139 Wire ASTM B159	Cu 94.75, Sn 5, P 0.25	Annealed Cold-drawn wire (HT) Cold-rolled (HT)	20 ⋮ 65	50 ⋮ 130	50 ⋮ 2	60 ⋮ 160	.320	8.86	1920	0.09	9.4	480	69	16
Aluminum brass Tube ASTM B111	Cu 76.0, Zn 22.0, Al 2.0, As trace	Annealed	27	60	55	82	.301	⋮	1780	⋮	10.3	700	⋮	16
Yellow brass (high brass) Sheet, strip, and plate ASTM B36 Wire ASTM B134 Tubes ASTM B135	Cu 65, Zn 35	Annealed Cold-drawn Cold-rolled (HT)	18 55 60	48 70 74	60 15 10	55 115 180	.306	8.47	1710	.09	10.5	830	40	15
Naval brass Rods, bars, and shapes ASTM B21; AMS 4611B; 4612C	Cu 60, Zn 39.25, Sn 0.75	Annealed Cold-drawn	22 40	56 65	40 35	90 150	.304	8.41	1625	.09	11.0	810	40	15
Admiralty brass (inhibited) Plates ASTM B171 Tubes ASTM B111	Cu 71, Zn 28, Sn 1, As, Sb, or P present	Annealed	20	53	65	60	.308	8.53	1720	.09	10.2	770	42	16
Muntz metal Tubes ASTM B135, B111	Cu 60, Zn 40	Annealed	20	54	45	80	.303	8.39	1660	.09	10.8	870	37	15
Manganese bronze rods, bars, and shapes ASTM B138	Cu 58.5, Zn 39.2, Fe 1, Sn 1, Mn 0.3	Annealed Cold-drawn	30 50	60 80	30 20	95 180	.302	8.36	1645	.09	11.2	700	45	15
High-silicon bronze A Sheet ASTM B96, B97 Rod ASTM B98, B124 Wire ASTM B99	Cu 96, Si 3, Mn, Zn, or Fe	Annealed Cold-drawn Cold-rolled	22 60 60	58 90 95	60 20 7	70 180 190	.308	8.53	1865	.09	9.5	225	160	15
Low-silicon bronze B	Cu 96, Si 0.8–2.0, Mn 0.7 max., Fe 0.8 max	Annealed Hardened	15 55	40 70	50 15	F55 B80 (Rockwell)	.316	⋮	⋮	.09	9.9	360		
Aluminum bronze Sheet ASTM B169 Rod ASTM B124, B150	Cu 92, Al 8	Annealed Hard	25 65	70 105	60 7	80 210	.281	7.78	1900	.09	9.2	490	70	17

Table 3-38. Mechanical and Physical Properties of Metals and Alloys (Continued)

Material	Nominal composition (essential elements), %	Form and condition	Typical mechanical properties				Typical physical constants							
			Yield strength (0.2% offset), 1,000 psi	Tensile strength, 1,000 psi	Elongation in 2 in., %	Brinell Hardness	Density, lb/in.³	Specific gravity	Melting point, °F	Specific heat Btu/(lb)(°F) (32–212°F)	Thermal expansion coefficient (32–212°F) ×10⁻⁶ in./(in.)(°F)	Thermal conductivity (32–212°F) Btu/(ft²)(hr)(in.)(°F)	Electrical resistivity (68°F), ohms/cir mil ft	Tensile modulus of elasticity ×10⁶ psi
Copper beryllium 25 Sheet and strip ASTM B194 Wire ASTM B197 Rod ASTM B196	Be 1.9, Co 0.25, Cu bal.	Annealed (SA)[k]	……	70	45	B60 (Rockwell)	……	……	……	……	……	……	……	17
		Annealed (SA, HT)	……	175	6	C38	.298	8.26	1600–1800	.10[l]	9.3	750–900	……	19
		Cold-rolled (HT)	……	110	5	B99	……	……	……	……	……	……	……	17
		Cold-rolled (HT, HT)	……	200	2	C42	……	……	……	……	……	……	……	19
Lead and Alloys														
Chemical lead	Pb 99.9, Cu 0.06, Bi 0.005 max.	Rolled	1.9	2.5	50	5	0.410	11.35	621	0.030	16.4	240	124	2
Antimonial lead	Pb 94, Sb 6	Cast Rolled	…… ……	6.8 4.1	22 47	12 9	.393	10.90	554	.032	15.1	200	140	3
Tellurium lead	Pb 99.85, Te 0.04, Cu 0.06	Rolled	2.2	3	45	6	.410	11.35	621	.030	16.4	240	124	2
Soft solder 50-50	Sn 50, Pb 50	Cast	……	6.8	50	14	.321	8.89	421	.051	13.1	310	93	
Magnesium and Alloys														
Magnesium alloy AZ92A AMS 4434E	Mg bal., Al 9.0, Zn 2.0, Mn 0.10 min.	Sand-cast (as cast) Sand-cast (solution heat-treated)	14 14	24 40	6 12	50 55	.066	1.83	1100	.245	14.5	360 310	84 101	6.5
		Sand-cast (solution heat-treated and aged)	19	40	5	83	……	……	……	……	……	410	74	
		Sand-cast (age-hardened)	16	30	4	66	……	……	……	……	……	410	74	

Alloy	Composition	Condition												
AZ31B AMS 4375-76 (plate, sheet)	Mg bal., Al 3.0, Mn 1.0, Zn 0.20 min.	Rolled-plate (strain hardened then partially annealed)	24	37	18	……	.064	1.77	1160	.245	14.5	540	55	6.5
		Rolled-sheet (strain hardened then partially annealed)	32	42	15	73	……	……	……	……	……	540	55	……
		Annealed	22	37	21	56	……	……	……	……	……	540	55	……
		Extruded	28	38	14	……	……	……	……	……	……	540	55	……
Magnesium alloy AZ80A AMS 4360 (forgings)	Mg bal., Al 8.5, Zn 0.5, Mn 0.15 min.	Extruded	36	49	11	60	……	……	……	……	……	……	……	……
		Extruded (age-hardened)	39	53	6	82	……	……	……	……	……	……	……	……
		Forged (age-hardened)	34	50	6	72	.065	1.80	1130	.245	14.5	350	87	6.5
Magnesium alloy AZ91A and AZ91B AMS 4490 (casting)	Mg bal., Al 9.0, Zn 0.6, Mn 0.13 min.	Die-cast (as cast)	22	33	3	67	.065	1.81	1105	.245	14.5	370	83	6.5
Magnesium alloy AZ91C	Mg bal., Al 8.7, Zn 0.7, Mn 0.13 min.	Sand-cast (as cast)	14	24	2	52	……	……	……	……	……	370	82	……
		Sand-cast (solution heat-treated)	14	40	11	55	.065	1.81	1105	.245	14.5	320	97	6.5
		Sand-cast (solution heat-treated and aged)	19	40	5	73	……	……	……	……	……	390	78	……
Magnesium alloy BZ33A	Mg bal., Zn 2.6, Zr 0.7, other elements 3.0	Sand-cast (age-hardened)	15	23	3	50	.066	1.83	1189	.245	14.5	690	42	.65
Magnesium alloy HK31A AMS 4445	Mg bal., Th 3.0, Zr 0.7	Sand-cast (solution heat-treated and aged)	15	30	8	55	.065	1.79	1200	.245	14.5	640	46	6.5
		Rolled-sheet (strain-hardened then partially annealed)	29	37	8	57	……	……	……	……	……	780	37	……
Magnesium alloy HZ32A	Mg bal., Th 3.0, Zn 2.1, Zr 0.7	Sand-cast (age-hardened)	14	29	7	57	.066	1.83	1198	.245	14.5	740	39	6.5

Solution annealed, heat-treated (SA, HT).

k Solution annealed (SA).
l Cal/(g)(°C)(30–100°C).

Table 3-38. Mechanical and Physical Properties of Metals and Alloys (Continued)

Material	Nominal composition (essential elements), %	Form and condition	Yield strength (0.2% offset), 1,000 psi	Tensile strength, 1,000 psi	Elongation in 2 in., %	Hardness, Brinell	Density, lb/in.³	Specific gravity	Melting point, °F	Specific heat (32-212°F), Btu/(lb)(°F)	Thermal expansion coefficient (32-212°F), $\times 10^{-6}$ in./(in.)(°F)	Thermal conductivity (32-212°F), Btu/(ft²)(hr)(in.)(°F)	Electrical resistivity (68°F), ohms/cir mil ft	Tensile modulus of elasticity $\times 10^6$ psi
Magnesium alloy ZK60A AMS 4370 (sheet)	Mg bal., Zn 5.7, Zr 0.55	Extruded Extruded (age-hardened) Forged	37 43 38	49 52 49	14 12 13	75 82	.066	1.83	1175	.245	14.5	800 850	36 34	6.5

Titanium and Alloys

Material	Nominal composition (essential elements), %	Form and condition	Yield strength (0.2% offset), 1,000 psi	Tensile strength, 1,000 psi	Elongation in 2 in., %	Hardness, Brinell	Density, lb/in.³	Specific gravity	Melting point, °F	Specific heat (32-212°F), Btu/(lb)(°F)	Thermal expansion coefficient (32-212°F), $\times 10^{-6}$ in./(in.)(°F)	Thermal conductivity (32-212°F), Btu/(ft²)(hr)(in.)(°F)	Electrical resistivity (68°F), ohms/cir mil ft	Tensile modulus of elasticity $\times 10^6$ psi
Titanium (commercially pure)	Ti bal., Fe 0.2 max., N_2 0.05 max., C 0.08 max., H_2 0.015 max.	Annealed	70	90	23	200	.163	4.54	3300	.129	5.0 (70-1000°F)	118	480	16.5
Titanium-chromium-iron-molybdenum alloy (Ti-140A)	Ti bal., Fe 2.0, Cr 2.0, Mo 2.0, C 0.08 max., N_2 0.05 max., H_2 0.015 max.	Annealed Heat-treated	125 145	135 155	14 10	35 (Rockwell C) 37 (Rockwell C)	.166	4.60	3000	.....	5.6 (70-1000°F)	.....	780	16.5
Titanium-aluminum-iron-chromium-molybdenum alloy (Ti-155A)	Ti bal., Al 5.0, Fe 1.4, Cr 1.4, Mo 1.2, H_2 0.0125 max., C 0.08 max., N_2 0.05 max.	Annealed Heat-treated	135 150	150 160	15 10	36 (Rockwell C) 39 (Rockwell C)	.165	4.59	3000	.....	5.7 (70-1000°F)	60	990	16.5

Material	Composition	Condition												
Titanium-aluminum-vanadium alloy (Ti-6 Al-4V)	Ti bal., Al 6.0, V 4.0, Fe 0.25 max., C 0.08 max., H_2 0.0125 max., N_2 0.05 max.	Annealed Heat-treated	130 145	135 155	15 12	32 (Rockwell C) 37 (Rockwell C)	.161	4.46	3000	....	5.7 (70-1000°F)	....	1020	16.5
Other Nonferrous Alloys														
Antimony	Sb 100	As-cast	....	1.56	....	42	.249	6.62	1166	.092	5.5	131	234	11.3
Columbium	....	....	35	40	....	....	.31	....	4474	.06	3.8	375	....	
Gold	Au 100	Hard Annealed	....	30 17.5	2 40	48 28	.692	19.3	1945	.056	7.9	2060	14.7	10.8
18K white gold	Au 75 Ni 18.5, Zn 5.25, Cu 1.25	Hard Annealed	 93	178 115	.. 25	323 211	.53	14.61	1886	....	....	....	210.3	16.6
Haynes Stellite Alloy 21 AMS 5385 (cast)	C 0.25, Cr 28, Ni 2.5, Mo 5.5, Co bal.	As investment cast	82.0	103	8.0	313 max.	0.299	8.30	2465	0.1006	7.83 (70-600°F)	100.6 (at 392°F)	527	36.0
Haynes Stellite Alloy 31 (X-40 Cast) AMS 5382 (cast)	C 0.50, Cr 25.5, Ni 11, W 7.5, Co bal.	As investment cast	80.0	113	8.0	313 max.	.311	8.61	2500	.0981	7.84 (70-600°F)	102.7 (at 392°F)	....	36.0
Molybdenum	Mo 99.9 plus	As-rolled Stress-relieved Recrystallized	75 75 50	100 100 70	30 30 45	250 240 190	.369	10.22	4730	.061	2.67	900	31.3	46.0
0.5% titanium molybdenum alloy	Mo bal., Ti 0.5	As-rolled Stress-relieved Recrystallized	90 90 60	120 120 80	30 30 40	290 280 200	.369	10.22	4730	.061	3.06	816	31.3	46.0
Platinum	Pt (commercial)	Hard Annealed	....	65 27	2 28	101 65	.773	21.4	3215	.057	5.0	465	65	22.0
Platinum-iridium	Pt 90, Ir 10	Hard Annealed	.. 34	80 53	2 23	169 104	.776	21.5	3299	....	5.0	....	146	25.0

Table 3-38. Mechanical and Physical Properties of Metals and Alloys (Continued)

Material	Nominal composition (essential elements), %	Form and condition	Yield strength (0.2% offset), 1,000 psi	Tensile strength, 1,000 psi	Elongation in 2 in., %	Hardness, Brinell	Density, lb/in.³	Specific gravity	Melting point, °F	Specific heat (32–212°F), Btu/(lb)(°F)	Thermal expansion coefficient (32–212°F) × 10⁻⁶ in./(in.)(°F)	Thermal conductivity (32–212°F) Btu/(ft²)(hr)(°F)(in.)	Electrical resistivity (68°F), ohms/cir mil ft	Tensile modulus of elasticity × 10⁶ psi
Platinum-rhodium	Pt 90, Rh 10	Hard / Annealed	…… / 18.3	93 / 50	3 / 36	169 / 79	.720	19.93	3353	……	……	……	117	21.2
Platinum-ruthenium	Pt 90, Ru 10	Hard / Annealed	…… / 47.6	145 / 91	2 / 28	210 / 156	.713	19.8	3344	……	……	……	255	31.5
Palladium	Pd (commercial)	Hard / Annealed	…… / 7.6	55 / 30	… / 30	91 / 47	.433	12.0	2829	……	6.5	488	63.5	16.3
Rhodium	Rh 100	Annealed	……	80	…	119	.448	12.44	3571	……	4.6	611	27	50
Silver (pure)	Ag 99.9 plus	Annealed / Cold-rolled	12 / 38	23 / 43	45 / 6	30 / 90	.379	10.50	1760	.056	10.6	2900	9.8	10.5
Sterling silver	Ag 92.5, Cu bal.	Hard / Annealed	50 / 20	64 / 41	4 / 26	125 / 65	.376	……	1635	……	10.5	2510	12.08	10.5
Silver, coin	Ag 90, Cu bal.	Hard / Annealed	53 / 23	65 / 42	4 / 26	125 / 70	.374	……	1615	……	10.5	2490	12.13	11
Tantalum	Ta 99.9 plus	Annealed sheet / Unannealed sheet	45 / 100	60 / 110	37 / 3	55 / 123	.60	16.6	5425	.036	3.6	377	74.6	
Tantalum 10W	W 10, Ta bal.	Annealed	158	160	…	……	.61	……	5516	……	……	……		
Tin	Sn 100	As-cast	……	2.1	70	3.9	.263	7.29	449	.0954	12.8	428	66	6

Material	Composition (W)	Condition												
Tungsten		Hard (sheet) / Annealed / Hard (wire)	360 / 540	400 / 600	... / 0-8	... / 290	.697 / .697	19.3 / 19.3	6092 / 6092	.034 / .034	2.4 / 2.4	1390 / 1390	33.08 / 33.08	53.0 / 53.0
Waspaloy	C 0.10 max., Mn 0.50, S 0.030 max., Si 0.75 max., Cr 18.00–21.00, Co 12.00–15.00, Mo 3.50–5.00, Ti 2.75–3.25, Al 1.00–1.50, Zr 0.05–0.12, B 0.008 max., Fe 2.00 max., Cu 0.10, Ni remainder	Vacuum melted forgings	115	185	25	298–346	.295	8.18	2400	...	8.92 (70–1500°F)	80–160 (70–1500°F)	...	31.4
Udimet 500	C 0.15 max., Mn 0.75 max., Si 0.75 max., S 0.015 max., Cr 15.0–20.0, Ti 2.50–3.25, Al 2.50–3.25, Co 13.0–20.0, Mo 3.0–5.0, Fe 4.0 max., Cu 0.15 max., Ni bal.	Forged and heat-treated	125	195	12-18 (in 1 in.)	346–363	.290	8.03	2550–2600	...	6.8–8.8 (32–1800°F)	75.6 (32–1700°F) 177.6	...	31.05
Zinc ASTM B69	Zn bal., Pb 0.08	Hot-rolled (long.) / Hot-rolled (transv.) / Cold-rolled (long.) / Cold-rolled (transv.)	... / ... / ... / ...	19.5 / 23 / 21 / 27	65 / 50 / 50 / 40	38 / ...	0.258 / ...	7.14 / ...	786 / ...	0.094 / ...	18 / 12.8	746.07	36.56	...
Zinc-aluminum alloy ASTM 23	Zn (99.99% pure remainder), Al 3.5–4.3, Mg 0.03–0.08, Cu 0.25 max.	Die-cast	...	41	10	82	.24	6.6	727.9	.10	15.2	783.81	38.2	...

Table 3-38. Mechanical and Physical Properties of Metals and Alloys (Continued)

Material	Nominal composition (essential elements), %	Form and condition	Typical mechanical properties				Typical physical constants							
			Yield strength (0.2% offset), 1,000 psi	Tensile strength, 1,000 psi	Elongation in 2 in., %	Hardness, Brinell	Density, lb/in.^{3}	Specific gravity	Melting point, $^\circ$F	Specific heat (32–212°F), Btu/(lb)($^\circ$F)	Thermal expansion coefficient (32–212°F), in./(in.)($^\circ$F) $\times 10^{-6}$	Thermal conductivity (32–212°F), Btu/(ft^2)(hr)($^\circ$F)(in.)	Electrical resistivity (68°F), ohms/cir mil ft	Tensile modulus of elasticity, $\times 10^6$ psi
Zinc-aluminum-copper alloy ASTM 25	Zn (99.99% pure remainder), Al 3.5–4.3, Mg 0.03–0.08, Cu 0.75–1.25	Die-cast	.....	47.6	7	91	.24	6.7	727.0	.10	15.2	754.78	39.2	
Zirconium, commercial	O$_2$ 0.07, C 0.15, Hf 1.90, Zr bal.	Annealed	40	65	27	B80 (Rockwell)	.245	6.5	3380	.118	2.9	95	246	11
Zircaloy 2	Hf 0.02, Sn 1.46, Fe 0.12, Ni 0.05, Zr bal., other 0.25	Annealed	50	75	22	B90 (Rockwell)	.237	.....	.....	.....	3.6	95		
Zircaloy 3	Hf 0.02, Sn 0.25, Fe 0.25, Ni 0.05, Zr bal., other 0.20	Annealed	45	70	25	B85 (Rockwell)								

SOURCE: Based on material from International Nickel Co., adopted from Perry's Chemical Engineer's Handbook, Sec. 23, by Perry, Chilton, and Kirkpatrick. Copyright © 1963, McGraw-Hill, Inc.

At subzero temperatures materials of construction can exhibit drastic changes in mechanical properties. Metals, for example, generally show a marked increase in tensile strength with decreasing temperature. In particular, the tensile strength of certain copper and aluminum alloys can increase 35,000 psi as the temperature decreases from 100° to −415°F. Austenitic stainless steels can show an increase in tensile strength of as much as 150,000 psi over the same temperature range. More important than tensile strength, however, is the change in toughness. Materials tend to become brittle at cryogenic temperatures. Although some metals maintain good toughness at low temperatures, certain grades of structural steel undergo a sharp transition from tough to brittle properties, and some grades become brittle at temperatures as high as 32°F. Low-temperature toughness of metals is conveniently measured by a notched-bar impact test. Impact toughness is sensitive to a number of structural and compositional variables, giving a wide scatter of data points. Therefore the information in Fig. 3-14 should be used only to select possible acceptable alloys. Final selection for a given application must be based on more complete information.

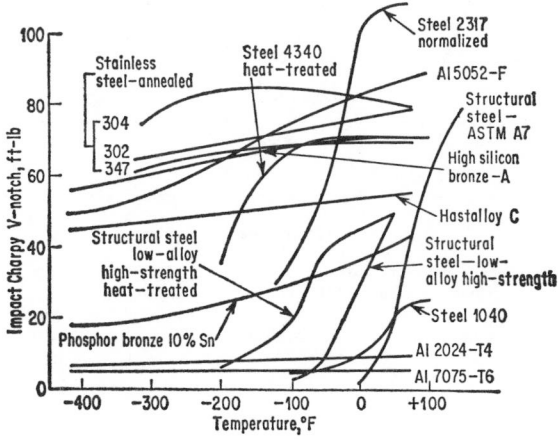

Fig. 3-14. Cryogenic properties.

Stress-rupture properties give the stress to rupture a test bar in a specified number of hours and at a given temperature. Stress-rupture data do not indicate the creep rate, although, in general, a metal with good stress-rupture properties also has good creep resistance.

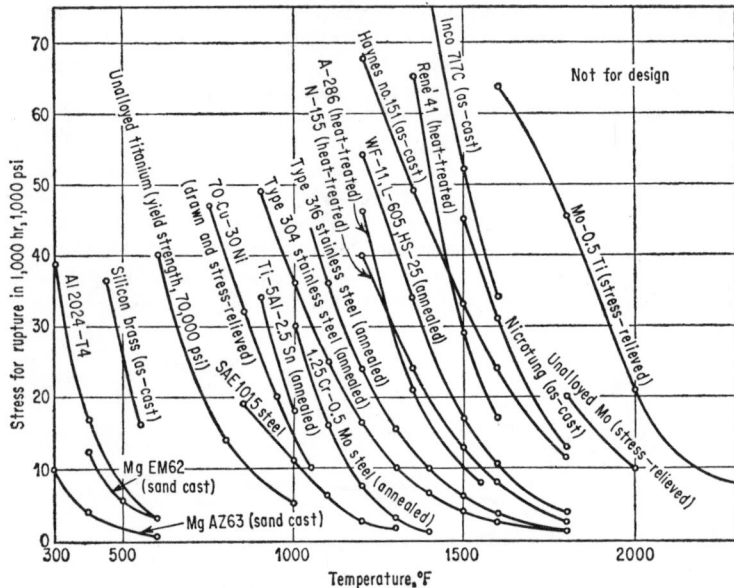

FIG. 3-15. Typical curves of stress for rupture in 1,000 hr versus temperature for selected engineering alloys. (Based on *D. P. Moon and W. F. Simmons, DMIC Memo 92, Battelle Memorial Institute, Mar.* 23, 1961 in "Mechanical Metallurgy" by George Dieter, Jr. Copyright © 1961, McGraw-Hill, Inc. Used by permission.)

Table 3-39. Compositions of Typical High-temperature Alloys

(See also Fig. 3-15)

Alloy	C	Cr	Ni	Mo	Co	W	Cb	Ti	Al	Fe	Other
					Ferritic Steels						
1.25 Cr, Mo	.10	1.25	....	0.50	....	...	....	....	....	Balance	
5 Cr, Mo	.20	5.00	....	0.50	....	...	....	....	....	Balance	
"17-22-A" S	.30	1.25	....	0.50	....	...	....	....	....	Balance	
410	.10	12.0	....	.....	....	...	....	....	....	Balance	
					Austenitic Steels						
316	.08	17.0	12.0	2.50	....	...	....	....	....	Balance	
347	.06	18.0	12.0	.....	....	...	0.70	....	....	Balance	
16-25-6	.10	16.0	25.0	6.00	....	...	....	....	....	Balance	
A-286	.05	15.0	26.0	1.25	....	...	....	1.95	0.20	Balance	
					Nickel-base Alloys						
Inconel	.04	15.5	76.0	.....	....	...	....	....	....	7.0	
Inconel X	.04	15.0	75.0	.....	....	...	....	2.5	0.6	7.0	
Nimonic 90	.08	20.0	58.0	.....	16	...	....	2.3	1.4	0.5	
Hastelloy B	.10	1.0	65.0	28	....	...	....	....	....	5.0	
René 41	.10	19.0	53.0	10	11	...	....	3.2	1.6	2.0	
Udimet 500	.10	19.4	55.6	4	14	...	....	2.9	2.9	0.6	
					Cobalt-base Alloys						
Vitallium (HS-21)	.25	27.0	3.0	5	62	...	....	....	....	1.0	
X-40 (HS-31)	.40	25.0	10.0	.....	55	8	....	....	....	1.0	
					Complex Superalloys						
N-155 (Multimelt)	.15	21.0	20.0	3	20	2.5	1.0	....	....	Balance	0.15N
S-590	.40	20.0	20.0	4	20	4.0	4.0	....	....	Balance	
S-816	.40	20.0	20.0	4	Bal.	4.0	4.0	....	....	3.0	
K 42 B	.05	18.0	43.0	.....	22	...	....	2.5	0.2	13	
Refractaloy 26	.05	18.0	37.0	3	20	...	....	2.8	0.2	18	

SOURCE: "Mechanical Metallurgy" by Dieter. Copyright © 1961, McGraw-Hill, Inc. Used by permission of McGraw-Hill Book Company.

Table 3-40. Mechanical and Phys

Material	Specific gravity	Thermal conductivity, Btu/(hr)(ft²)(°F)(ft)	Coefficient of thermal expansion, $10^{-5}/°F$	Specific heat, Btu/(lb)(°F)	Flammability, in./min	Modulus of elasticity in tension, 10^6 psi
Acrylonitrile butadiene styrene (ABS):						
High-impact...............	1.04–1.06	0.08–0.12	4.7	0.35–0.38	1.3	2.6–2.9
Extra-high impact..........	1.01–1.06	0.08–0.12	4.7–5.6	0.35–0.38	1.3	2.1–2.6
Low-temperature impact......	1.02	0.08–0.12	4.7–5.6	0.35–0.38	1.3	1.0
Acetal polymer...............	1.425	0.13	4.5	0.35	1.1	4.1
Acrylics, cast:						
General-purpose, type 1......	1.17–1.19	0.12	4.5	0.35	0.5–2.2	3.5–4.5
General-purpose, type 2......	1.18–1.20	0.12	4.5	0.35	0.5–1.8	4.0–5.0
Alkyds, molded...............	2.22–2.24	0.35–0.60	1–3	....	Self-ext.	....
Cellulose acetate:						
Medium, type 1.............	1.23–1.34	0.10–0.19	4.4–9.0	0.3–0.4	0.5–2.0	....
Hard, type 2................	1.29–1.34	0.10–0.19	4.4–9.0	0.3–0.4	0.5–2.0	....
Soft, type 3.................	1.27–1.34	0.10–0.19	4.4–9.0	0.3–0.4	....	....
Cellulose acetate butyrate (CAB):						
Medium, type 1.............	1.16–1.24	0.10–0.19	6–9	0.3–0.4	0.5–1.5	....
Hard, type 2................	1.19–1.25	0.10–0.19	6–9	0.3–0.4	0.5–1.5	....
Soft, type 3.................	1.15–1.22	0.10–0.19	6–9	0.3–0.4	0.5–1.5	....
Chlorinated polyether (Penton)	1.4	11.0	6.6	....	Self-ext.	....
Epoxies, cast:						
General-purpose.............	1.12–2.4	0.1–0.8	1.7–5.0	....	0.3 to self-ext.	....
Heat-resistant...............	1.15–3.2	0.1–0.8	2.8–3.3	....		....
Fluorocarbons:						
Polytrifluorochlorethylene.....	2.15	0.145	3.88	0.22	Non	1.9–3.0
Polytetrafluoroethylene........	2.1–2.3	0.14	5.5	0.25	Non	0.38–0.65
Fluorinated ethylene-propylene	2.14–2.17	0.11	8.3–10.5	0.28	Non	0.5–0.7
Melamines, unfilled...........	1.48	....	....	....	Self-ext.	....
Polyamides, molded:						
Nylon 66 (0.2% water).......	1.14	0.14	5.5	0.3–0.5	Self-ext.	4.1
Nylon 6....................	1.14	0.10–0.14	4.6–5.4	0.4	Self-ext.	2.5–3.4
Nylon 11...................	1.1	....	5.5	0.58	Self-ext.	1.8–1.9
Polycarbonates...............	1.20	0.11	3.9	....	Self-ext.	3.2
Phenolics, molded (no filler).....	1.24–1.90	....	2.4	....	Self-ext.	7–15
Phenolics, cast:						
Type 1, mechanical and chemical.................	1.31	....	3.3–4.4	....	Self-ext.	4–5
Polyester, cast:						
Allyl type...................	1.30–1.45	0.12	2.8–5.6	0.26–0.55	....	2–3
Styrene type, rigid..........	1.12–1.46	0.10–0.12	3.9–5.6	0.30–0.55	....	1.5–6.5
Silicones, molded:						
Mineral filler...............	1.8–2.0	0.09–0.97	2.78–3.23	....	0–78	....

ical Properties of Plastics (73.4°F)

Tensile strength, 1,000 psi	Elongation (in 2 in.), %	Hardness, Rockwell	Impact strength (Izod notched), ft-lb/in. notch	Modulus of elasticity in flex, 10^5 psi	Flexural strength, 1,000 psi	Compression strength (0.1% offset), 1,000 psi	Maximum recommended service temperature, °F	Heat distortion temperature, °F (264 psi)
4.5–8.5	5–100	R85–118	3–6	37–45	7.5–11	....	150	185–215
8	20–50	R85–100	5–9	....	6.8–8.0	....	....	185
5	30–200	R30–65	6–10	....	3–4	....	....	175–185
10.0	15 (total)	M94, R120	1.4	4.1	14.1	5.2	185	212
6–9	2–7	M8C–90	0.4	3.5–4.5	12–14	12–14	140–160	150–180
8–10	2–7	M96–102	0.4	4.0–5.0	15–17	14–18	180–200	190–225
3–4	....	....	0.30–0.35	....	7–10	16–20	350	350–400
2.7–6.5	18–54	R68–115	1.1–4.0	1.1–3.5	....	14–25		
6–8.5	6–31	R112–123	0.4–1.9	2.6–4.0	....	25–36		
4.6–7.5	17–40	R106–121	0.6–2.3	1.9–3.4	....	22–33		
2.9–5.7	47–66	R79–112	1.0–4.3	0.93–1.7	No break	....	....	130–172
5.0–6.8	38–54	R108–114	0.6–2.4	1.5–2.0	No break	....	....	158–210
1.9–3.8	60–74	R59–95	2.5–5.4	0.74–1.3	No break	....	....	121–137
6	130 (total)	R100	0.4	1.3	5	....	255	185
2–12	2–6	M75–110	0.2–0.7	0.4–1.5	8–20	20–40	175	250
5–14	2–5	M90–110	0.2–1.5	0.4–1.5	8–20	25–40	400	500
4.6–5.7	125–175	R110–115	3.5–3.6	2–2.5	3.5	2.0	380	150–178
2.5–3.5	250–350	J75–95	2.5–4.0	0.6	1.6	0.7–1.8	500	
2.5–3.5	300–900	D55	No break	0.8	....	1.6	400	
....	....	....	....	13	11–14	40–45	210	295
11.8	60	M79, R118	0.9	4.1	13.8	....	275–300	
10.2–12	300	R105–118	1.2–3.0	....	....	7–9.7	225–250	145
8.5	100–120	A50	3.3–3.6	....	....	....	212–250	
9–10.5	60–100 (total)	M70, R118	12–16	3.8	11–13	11	250–300	280–290
4.5–7.5	....	M105–120	0.2–0.6	7–15	7–12	18–32	300–425	300–350
6–9	....	M93–120	0.30–0.45	3–5	11–17	14–18	....	170–195
4.5–7	....	M92–118	0.18–0.32	3–8	6–14	20–26	300	120–320
4–10	<5	M65–115	0.18–0.40	3–9	7–19	12–37	250–300	120–420
4–4.3	....	M89	0.25–0.30	10–13	6.8–7.5	16–20	>700	>900

Table 3-40. Mechanical and Physical

Material	Specific gravity	Thermal conductivity, Btu/(hr)(ft²)(°F)(ft)	Coefficient of thermal expansion, $10^{-6}/°F$	Specific heat, Btu/(lb)(°F)	Flammability, in./min	Modulus of elasticity in tension, 10^5 psi
Polystyrenes:						
General-purpose...........	1.04–1.07	0.058–0.09	3.3–4.8	0.30	1–1.5	4–5
Heat, chemical resistant......	1.05–1.11	0.046–0.09	3.6–3.8	0.30	0.4–1.0	4–6
Polyethylene:						
Type I, low density..........	0.91–0.925	0.19	8.9–11.0	0.55	1.0	0.21–0.27
Type II, medium density.....	0.926–0.940	0.19	8.3–16.7	0.55	1.0	....
Type III, high density.......	0.942–0.960	0.19	8.3–16.7	0.46–0.55	1.0	....
Polypropylene................	0.89–0.91	0.08	6.2	0.46	....	1.4–1.7
Polyvinyl butyral:						
Rigid......................	1.08–1.12	....	4.4–12.7	0.4	Slow	3.5–4.0
Flexible...................	1.05	....	....	....	....	....
Polyvinyl dichloride...........	1.5	....	....	....	....	0.40
Polyvinyl chloride:						
Type I, rigid................	1.32–1.44	0.07–0.10	2.8–3.3	....	Self-ext.	3.5–4.0
Type II, flexible.............	1.20–1.55	0.07–0.10	....	....	Self-ext.	0.004–0.03
Polyvinylidene chloride (saran)..	1.68–1.75	0.053	8.78	0.32	Self-ext.	0.4–0.8
Ureas, molded:						
Cellulose-filled..............	1.52	....	....	....	Self-ext.	13–16
						Reinforced
Phenolic						
Glass fabric filled............	1.80–1.95	0.15	5.0–6.0	0.23	Self-ext.	34
Asbestos fiber..............	1.908	0.17	....	0.30	Self-ext.	55
Polyester:						
Glass fiber reinforced........	1.6–2.0	0.15	1.2–4	0.3	Self-ext.	....
Silicones:						
Glass fabric reinforced........	1.6–1.93	....	....	....	....	....
Epoxies:						
Woven-glass filled............	1.6–1.85	....	....	....		....
Filament-wound..............	1.7–2.2	20–60	....	....	Self-ext.	....

NOTE: ASTM test results referring to thermoplastics: sp gr, D792; thermal conductivity, C177; coefficient of thermal expansion, D696; flammability, D635; modulus of elasticity, D638, D790; tensile strength, D638, D651; elongation, D638; hardness, D785; impact strength, D256; flexibility strength, D790; compression strength, D695; heat distortion temperature, D648.

SOURCE: "Perry's Chemical Engineer's Handbook," sec. 23, by Perry, Chilton, and Kirkpatrick. Copyright © 1963 McGraw-Hill, Inc.

Properties of Plastics (73.4°F) (Continued)

Tensile strength, 1,000 psi	Elongation (in 2 in.), %	Hardness, Rockwell	Impact strength (Izod notched), ft-lb/in. notch	Modulus of elasticity in flex, 10^5 psi	Flexural strength, 1,000 psi	Compression strength (0.1% offset), 1,000 psi	Maximum recommended service temperature, °F	Heat distortion temperature, °F (264 psi)
5-8 10-11	1.5-2.5 1-4	M68-80 M78-88	0.25-0.35 0.25-0.50	4-5 4-6	8-15 11-17	11.5-16 12-17	140-160 175-190	165-190 200-220
1.4-2.5 2.0 2.9-4.0	500-725 200 25-400	C73 (Shore) D55 (Shore) D60 (Shore)	.... 0.4-6.0	13-27 43 90-125	....	....	250 250 250	175-200 (soft pt.) 215 (soft pt.) 250 (soft pt.)
5.0	500-700 (total)	R85-95	1.02	1.4-1.7	8.1	....	275-320	130-140
4-8.5 0.5-3	5-60 150-450	L95 10-100 (Shore)	1.2	....	10	....	115	61.5
7.5-9.0	4.5	R117	0.8-5.0	....	14-17	....	210	
5.5-9.0 1-3.5	5-25 200-450	R117	0.25-1.2 Variable	3.8-5.4	12-16	11-12	150-165 150-220	140-170
3-5	15-25	M50-65	0.3-1.0	....	4-7	7.5-8.5	150-212	130-150
5-10	1.0	E94	0.24-0.35	....	10-18	25-38	....	266-280
Plastics								
58 46.1	....	....	15	48 49.8	87 52.5	47.5 20.8	525 >350	500-600 500-600
25-55	....	M100	13-18	20-38	40-75	25-45	250-400	390-550
20-40	....	....	....	18-32	23-47	9-24	450-500	
40-85 80-250	....	M100 M98-120	12-18 40-60	30-46 50-70	65-120 100-270	45-52 45-70	250-400 500	350-400

Table 3-41. Standard Pipe Tables

Chemical and Tensile-strength Requirements for Several ASTM and API Specificities

Continuous-weld (Furnace-welded) Pipe

Specification	Steel	% manganese Min.	% manganese Max.	% phosphorus Min.	% phosphorus Max.	% sulfur Max.	Yield point or yield strength (min. psi)	Tensile strength (min. psi)
ASTM A120	Open hearth	ASTM A120 does not specify chemical or tensile requirements; it specifies mill hydrostatic tests.						
ASTM A53	Open hearth	.....	.....	.....	0.08	0.060	25,000	45,000
API 5 L	Class I	0.30	0.60	.....	.045	0.060	25,000	45,000
	Class II	.30	.60	0.045	.080	.060	28,000	48,000

Electric Resistance-welded Pipe

Specification	Grade	% carbon (max.)	% manganese (max.)	% phosphorus (max.)	% sulfur (max.)	Yield point or yield strength (min. psi)	Tensile strength (min. psi)
ASTM A120		ASTM A120 does not specify chemical or tensile requirements; it specifies mill hydrostatic tests.					
ASTM A53	A	....	....	0.050	....	30,000	48,000
	B	....	....	.050	....	35,000	60,000
ASTM A135	A	....	....	.050	0.060	30,000	48,000
	B	....	....	.050	.060	35,000	60,000
ASTM A252	1	....	....	....	....	30,000	50,000
	2	....	....	....	....	35,000	60,000
API 5 L	A	0.21	0.90	.04	.05	30,000	48,000
	B	.26	1.15	.04	.05	35,000	60,000
API 5 LX* nonexpanded	X-42	.28	1.25	.04	.05	42,000	60,000
	X-46	.31	1.35	.04	.05	46,000	63,000
	X-52	.31	1.35	.04	.05	52,000	66,000
API 5 LX* expanded	X-42	.28	1.25	.04	.05	42,000	60,000
	X-46	.28	1.25	.04	.05	46,000	63,000
	X-52	.28	1.25	.04	.05	52,000	66,000

* All grades listed in API 5 LX are shown for information purposes only.

Table 3-41. Standard Pipe Tables (Continued)

Seamless Pipe

Specification	Grade	Specified chemical requirements						Specified tensile requirements	
		% carbon (max.)	% manganese (min.)	% manganese (max.)	% phosphorus (max.)	% sulfur (max.)	% silicon (min.)	Yield point or yield strength (min. psi)	Tensile strength (min. psi)
ASTM A120		ASTM A120 does not specify chemical or tensile requirements; it specifies mill hydrostatic tests.							
ASTM A53	A							30,000	48,000
	B				0.048			35,000	60,000
ASTM A106	A	0.25	.27	.93	.048	0.058	0.10	30,000	48,000
	B	.30	.29	1.06	.048	.058	.10	35,000	60,000
	C	.35	.29	1.06	.048	.058	.10	40,000	70,000
ASTM A252	1							30,000	50,000
	2							35,000	60,000
	3							45,000	66,000
API 5 L	A	.22		.90	.04	.05		30,000	48,000
	B	.27		1.15	.04	.05		35,000	60,000
API 5 LX*	X-42	.29		1.25	.04	.05		42,000	60,000
	X-46	.32		1.35	.04	.05		46,000	63,000
	X-52	.32		1.35	.04	.05		52,000	66,000

* All grades listed in API 5 LX are shown for information purposes only.
SOURCE: Adapted from "Youngstown Engineering Data Oil Country and Line Pipe," sec. G, Youngstown Sheet and Tube Co., Youngstown, Ohio, 1964.

Table 3-41. Standard Pipe Tables (Continued)

Standard-weight Pipe

Dimensions, Weights, and Test Pressures—Plain Ends and Threads and Couplings

Size: nominal, in.	Weight per foot		Wall thickness, in.	Diameter		No. of threads per inch	Coupling		Test pressure, psi		
	Nom., thds. and cplg., lb	Calculated plain ends, lb		Outside, in.	Inside, in.		Length, in.	Outside diameter, in.	Butt-welded	Grade A	Grade B
1/8	0.24	0.24	0.068	0.405	0.269	27	13/16	0.563	700	700	700
1/4	0.42	0.42	.088	0.540	0.364	18	1 3/16	0.719	700	700	700
3/8	0.57	0.57	.091	0.675	0.493	18	1 3/16	0.875	700	700	700
1/2	0.85	0.85	.109	0.840	0.622	14	1 9/16	1.063	700	700	700
3/4	1.13	1.13	.113	1.050	0.824	14	1 5/8	1.313	700	700	700
1	1.68	1.68	.133	1.315	1.049	11 1/2	2	1.576	700	700	700
1 1/4	2.28	2.27	.140	1.660	1.380	11 1/2	2 1/16	1.900	1000	1000	1100
1 1/2	2.73	2.72	.145	1.900	1.610	11 1/2	2 1/16	2.200	1000	1000	1100
2	3.68	3.65	.154	2.375	2.067	11 1/2	2 1/8	2.750	1000	1000	1100
2 1/2	5.82	5.79	.203	2.875	2.469	8	3 1/8	3.250	1000	1000	1100
3	7.62	7.58	.216	3.500	3.068	8	3 1/4	4.000	1000	1000	1100
3 1/2	9.20	9.11	.226	4.000	3.548	8	3 3/8	4.625	1200	1200	1300
4	10.89	10.79	.237	4.500	4.026	8	3 1/2	5.000	1200	1200	1300
5	14.81	14.62	.258	5.563	5.047	8	3 3/4	6.296	....	1200	1300
6	19.18	18.97	.280	6.625	6.065	8	4	7.390	....	1200	1300

NOTES: The customary weight tolerance is ±5 per cent.
Taper of threads on all sizes of pipe and in couplings in sizes 2½ in. and over is ¾ in./ft on diameter. Couplings 2 in. and smaller are straight-tapped.

Table 3-41. Standard Pipe Tables (Continued)

Extra-strong Pipe

Dimensions, Weights, and Test Pressures—Plain Ends and Threads and Couplings

Size: nominal, in.	Weight per foot calculated plain ends, lb	Wall thickness, in.	Diameter		Test pressure, psi		
			Outside, in.	Inside, in.	Butt-welded	Grade A	Grade B
1/8	0.31	0.095	0.405	0.215	850	850	850
1/4	0.54	.119	0.540	0.302	850	850	850
3/8	0.74	.126	0.675	0.423	850	850	850
1/2	1.09	.147	0.840	0.546	850	850	850
3/4	1.47	.154	1.050	0.742	850	850	850
1	2.17	.179	1.315	0.957	850	850	850
1 1/4	3.00	.191	1.660	1.278	1300	1500	1600
1 1/2	3.63	.200	1.900	1.500	1300	1500	1600
2	5.02	.218	2.375	1.939	1300	1500	1600
2 1/2	7.66	.276	2.875	2.323	1300	1500	1600
3	10.25	.300	3.500	2.900	1300	1500	1600
3 1/2	12.51	.318	4.000	3.364	1700	1700	1800
4	14.98	.337	4.500	3.826	1700	1700	1800
5	20.78	.375	5.563	4.813	....	1700	1800
6	28.57	.432	6.625	5.761	....	1700	1800
8	43.39	.500	8.625	7.625	....	1700	2400
10	54.74	.500	10.750	9.750	....	1600	1900
12	65.42	.500	12.750	11.750	....	1600	1900

NOTES: The customary weight tolerance is ±5 per cent.
Taper of threads is ¾ in./ft on diameter for all sizes.

3-111

Table 3-41. Standard Pipe Tables (Continued)

Double Extra-strong Pipe

Dimensions, Weights, and Test Pressures—Plain Ends and Threads and Couplings

Size: nominal, in.	Weight per foot calculated plain ends, lb	Wall thickness, in.	Diameter			Test pressure, psi		
			Outside, in.	Inside, in.	Butt-welded	Grade A	Grade B
½	1.71	0.294	0.840	0.252	1,000	1,000	1,000
¾	2.44	.308	1.050	0.434	1,000	1,000	1,000
1	3.66	.358	1.315	0.599	1,000	1,000	1,000
1¼	5.21	.382	1.660	0.896	1,400	1,800	1,900
1½	6.41	.400	1.900	1.100	1,400	1,800	1,900
2	9.03	.436	2.375	1.503	.....	1,800	1,900
2½	13.70	.552	2.875	1.771	.....	1,800	1,900
3	18.58	.600	3.500	2.300	.....	1,800	1,900
4	27.54	.674	4.500	3.152	.....	2,000	2,100
5	38.55	.750	5.563	4.063	.....	2,000	2,100
6	53.16	.864	6.625	4.897	.....	2,000	2,100
8	72.42	.875	8.625	6.875	.....	2,800	2,800

NOTES: The customary weight tolerance is ±10 per cent.

Taper of threads is ¾ in./ft on diameter for all sizes.

SOURCE: Adapted from "Youngstown Engineering Data Oil Country and Line Pipe," sec. G, Youngstown Sheet and Tube Co., Youngstown, Ohio, 1964.

SECTION 4

ARCHITECTURAL ENGINEERING

Gregory E. Brooks, B.C.E., M.C.E., P.E.; Chief, Structural Division, Smith Haines Lundberg & Waehler; Fellow, American Society of Civil Engineers; Member, American Concrete Institute, American Welding Society, Building Research Institute

Leander Economides, B.S.M.E., P.E., R.A.; Economides & Goldberg, Consulting Engineers; Member, American Society of Heating, Air Conditioning and Refrigeration Engineers, Building Research Institute, American Society of Mechanical Engineers, American Institute of Architects

Bronislaus F. Winckowski, B.E.E., P.E.; Chief, Electrical Division, Smith Haines Lundberg & Waehler; Senior Member, The Institute of Electrical and Electronics Engineers; Member, Illuminating Engineering Society, Building Research Institute

CONTENTS

STRUCTURAL

4-1. Loads

Structural Design. All structures are designed to sustain safely the weight of all permanent stationary construction (dead load) entering into a structure and the greatest loads induced by the intended occupancy (live load) or other uses.

Design Loads. The weights of materials most commonly used in building construction are tabulated and are classified as dead loads. Live loads are generally considered to be uniformly distributed and are classified according to occupancy.

Dead Load. Dead load is usually determined by the use of the weights given in Table 4-1.

Table 4-1

Building materials	Wt., lb/ft³	Building materials	Wt., lb/ft³
Aluminum	175	Fir	32
Ash, white	40	Granite, limestone, marble	165
Ashes, cinders	45	Iron, cast	450
Brass	534	Iron, wrought	485
Brick	120	Lead	710
Bronze	509	Maple	43
Cedar	22	Oak	59
Clay, dry	63	Paper	58
Clay, damp	110	Pine, white	26
Clay and gravel	100	Pine, yellow, long leaf	44
Concrete, lightweight aggregates	90	Poplar	30
Concrete, normal aggregates	150	Redwood	26
Concrete block, hollow, lightweight aggregates	65	Sand, gravel, dry, loose	90–105
		Sand, gravel, dry, packed	100–120
Concrete block, hollow, normal aggregates	85	Sandstone, bluestone	140
Copper	556	Spruce	27
Earth, loose	76	Steel	490
Earth, packed	95	Tin	459
Elm	45	Zinc	440

Table 4-1 (Continued)

Partitions and walls	Thick., in.	Wt., psf
Partitions:*		
Hollow plaster partition	4	22
Plaster on metal lath	¾	7
Steel studs—metal lath and plaster (2 sides)	4¾	15
Wood studs—wood lath and plaster (2 sides)	5⅜	14
Wood studs—metal lath and plaster (2 sides)	5⅜	16
Wood studs—sheetrock	4⅜	5
Interior walls:*		
Brick	4	40
Clay tile, hollow block	3	17
	4	18
	6	25
	8	31
Concrete block, hollow-normal	3	26
	4	35
	6	50
	8	59
Interior walls (continued):		
Concrete block, hollow-normal	12	97
Concrete block, hollow-cinder	3	17
	4	24
	6	33
	8	39
	12	63
Gypsum block, solid	2	10
	3	13
Exterior walls:*		
Brick	4	40
	8	80
	12	120
Block, cinder, hollow	8	38
	12	61
Block, cinder, solid	8	48
	12	72
Block, normal aggregate	8	59
	12	97

Floors, ceilings, & roofing	Thick., in.	Wt., psf
Floors:		
Asphalt—mastic	1	12
Asphalt—tile	⅛	1
Cement or terr. finish	1	13
Cinder concrete fill	2	10
Cinder concrete plank	2	15
Concrete, lightweight	1	8
Concrete, normal	1	12
Floor plate	⅜	16
Grating (1-1¼ × 3/16)	1¼	9
Cellular metal flooring	1½	5
	3	7
Ceilings:		
Insulation	1	2
Plaster on concrete	½	3
Plaster on metal lath	¾	7
Plaster on suspended metal lath	...	10
Plaster on wood lath	⅞	6
Pressed steel (No. 18 gauge)	...	3
Sheetrock	½	2
Roofing:		
Cinder fill	1	5
Concrete channel slab, lightweight, precast	3½	14
Roofing (continued):		
Cooper sheet	...	2
Concrete plank	2	13
	2¾	18
Felt, 4 layers	...	1
Foamglass (insulation)	1	1
Gypsum (fill)	1	3
Gypsum slab, precast	2	12
	3	14
Lead	⅛	8
3-ply roofing	...	1
4-ply felt and gravel	...	6
5-ply felt and gravel	...	7
Sheathing	1	3
Shingle, asbestos	...	4
Shingle, wood	...	2
Slag roofing	...	5
Slate	¼	10
Steel (No. 20 gauge)	...	4
Tile, flat	...	18
Tile, Spanish	...	8
Tin	...	1
Transite	...	4
Wood roofers (av)	...	3

* Weights given do not include plaster on any surface. Add 5 psf for plaster applied directly on each face. Add 7 psf for metal lath and plaster applied on each face.

Live Load.   Live loads generally used for buildings are shown in Table 4-2.

Table 4-2

Occupancy	Live load, psf	Occupancy	Live load, psf
Public buildings:		Hospitals, etc. (*Continued*):	
Armories..........................	150	Operating rooms...................	60
Auditoriums, churches, etc.:		Corridors, laboratories............	100
Fixed seats......................	60	Residential buildings:	
Movable seats....................	100	Living areas......................	40
Exhibition buildings:		Corridors.........................	100
Restaurants, etc..................	100	Business buildings:	
Schools:		Office buildings...................	80
Classrooms......................	40	Light manufacturing...............	125
Corridors.......................	100	Heavy manufacturing..............	175 min
Other public buildings...............	80	Storage buildings:	
Theaters (stage floor)..............	150	Garages...........................	100
Institutional buildings:		Light warehouses..................	125
Hospitals, etc.:		Heavy warehouses.................	250 min
Private rooms and wards..........	40		

Wind Load.   Vertical walls should be designed to resist a wind load, acting either inward or outward, as shown in Table 4-3.

Table 4-3

Height, ft	Wind press., psf	Height, ft	Wind press., psf
Less than 50........................	20	100–199............................	28
50–99...............................	24	200 and above......................	30

Roof Wind and Snow Loads.   Roofs should be designed for a combined wind and snow load of from 25 to 45 psf.   The lesser value would be used for flat roofs in no-snow areas, and the greater values for flat roofs in heavy-snow areas.   Intermediate values would be used for sloping roofs in all areas.

Other Loads.   Other types of loading that should be considered in particular cases include earthquake loads, excessive wind loads, and impact loads.

4-2. Structural Framing Systems

The most economical structural framing system for a particular building is predicated on many variable conditions: use, locale, availability of material, fire resistivity, and magnitude of construction, to mention a few.   The cost per square foot of floor area of an interior bay cannot be assumed as the average cost of the whole area, since the exterior-wall spandrels, elevator shafts, and wind-bracing and foundation conditions are not reflected in this single area, and these factors assume greater proportions of total building cost for smaller buildings than for larger buildings.   Cost of various modes of design, however, can be determined by the design of an interior bay, which will indicate to some degree the most economical system to be chosen for a particular use and occupancy.

The unit prices used in this comparison of necessity reflect average prices for a certain locality. Any one unit price might be subject to variation. However, it is believed that the relationship between systems will not be materially affected. For the purpose of such a comparison, eight different designs of an interior bay are shown and described in Fig. 4-1 as schemes 1 to 8.

The designs are made for an office load of $80 + 20$ psf, the 20 psf being an allowance for lightweight movable partitions, as required by most building codes. Weight in pounds per square foot includes floor fills, floor arches, beams, girders, and the average column weight for a 10-story structure, plus 85 per cent of the live load.

Indicated cost includes only the separately listed parts, and does not include contractor's profit, sales tax, and overhead charges.

The table of relative cost (Table 4-4) is so arranged to show:

Table 4-4. Construction Cost Analysis

Construction	Structural steel framing					Reinforced concrete		
	Scheme 1	Scheme 2	Scheme 3	Scheme 4	Scheme 5	Scheme 6	Scheme 7	Scheme 8
Live + dead load, psf*.......	160	163	182	203	150	192	222	208
Depth of construction.......	1'11"	2'¼"	2'2½"	2'2⅝"	2'7½"	2'1½"	2'1½"	1'2"
1 Concrete................	0.33	0.31	0.54	0.52	0.27	0.79	0.93	0.74
2 Reinforcing steel.........	0.10	.....	0.21	0.25	0.04	0.94	0.79	0.97
3 Structural steel..........	1.36	1.49	1.47	1.71	1.07			
4 Open web joist...........	.....	.....	.....	.....	0.84			
5 Metal cellular deck.......	0.64	1.30						
6 Forms...................	.....	.....	1.43	1.43	0.15	1.43	1.57	1.12
7 Monolithic fl. finish......	0.13	0.13	0.13	0.13	0.13	0.13	0.13	0.13
8 Subtotal................	2.56	3.23	3.78	4.04	2.50	3.29	3.42	2.96
9 Cost ratio...............	100	126	147	158	98	128	134	116
10 Fire retardant...........	0.55	0.52	0.10	0.10	1.10			
11 Subtotal................	3.11	3.75	3.88	4.14	3.60	3.29	3.42	2.96
12 Cost ratio...............	100	120	125	133	116	106	110	95
13 Elect. service ducts.......	0.59	0.40	2.64	2.64	2.64	2.64	2.64	2.64
14 Hung ceiling.............	0.85	0.85	0.85	0.85	0.85	0.85	0.85	0.85
15 Total...................	4.55	5.00	7.37	7.63	7.09	6.78	6.91	6.45
16 Cost ratio...............	100	110	162	167	156	149	152	142

* Load includes floor arches, beams, girders and columns, plus 85 per cent of live load. Depth of construction is from finished floor to underside of girders.

1. A complete structural floor capable of supporting the design loads, but not containing underfloor electrical ducts or hung ceiling and with no fire protection rating (lines 8 and 9).

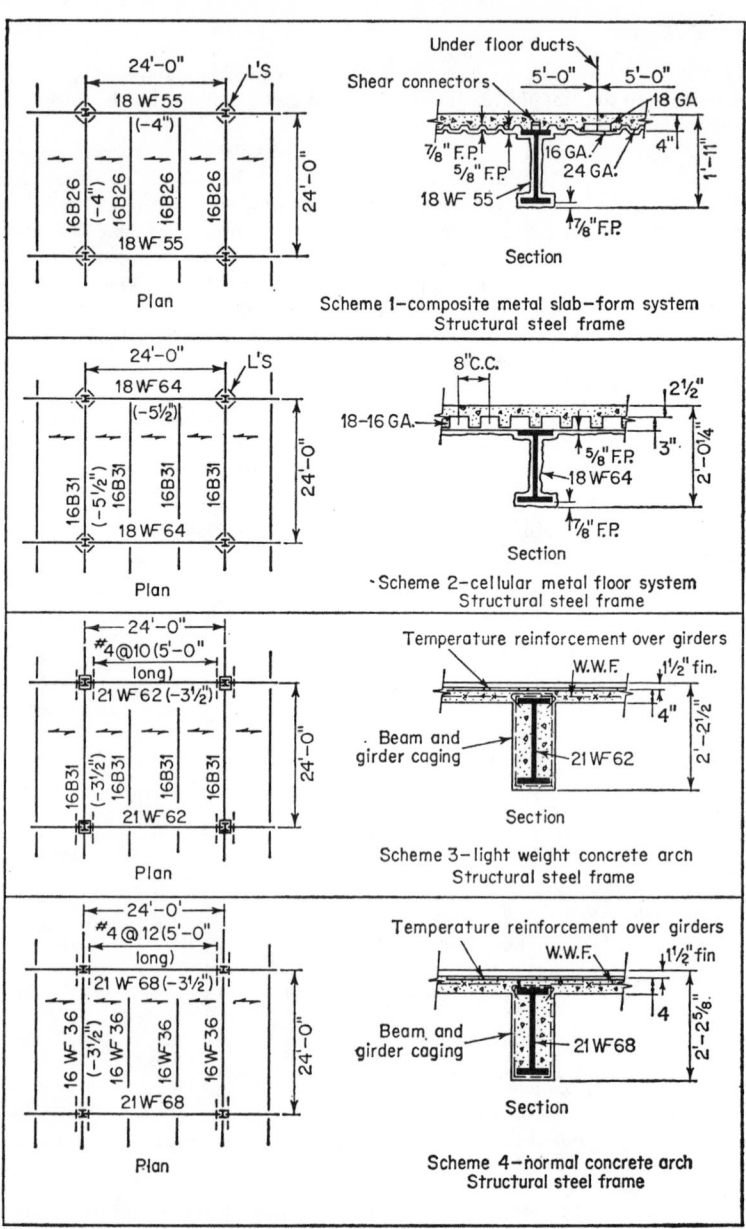

FIG. 4-1. Alternative construction schemes for interior bays.

4-6

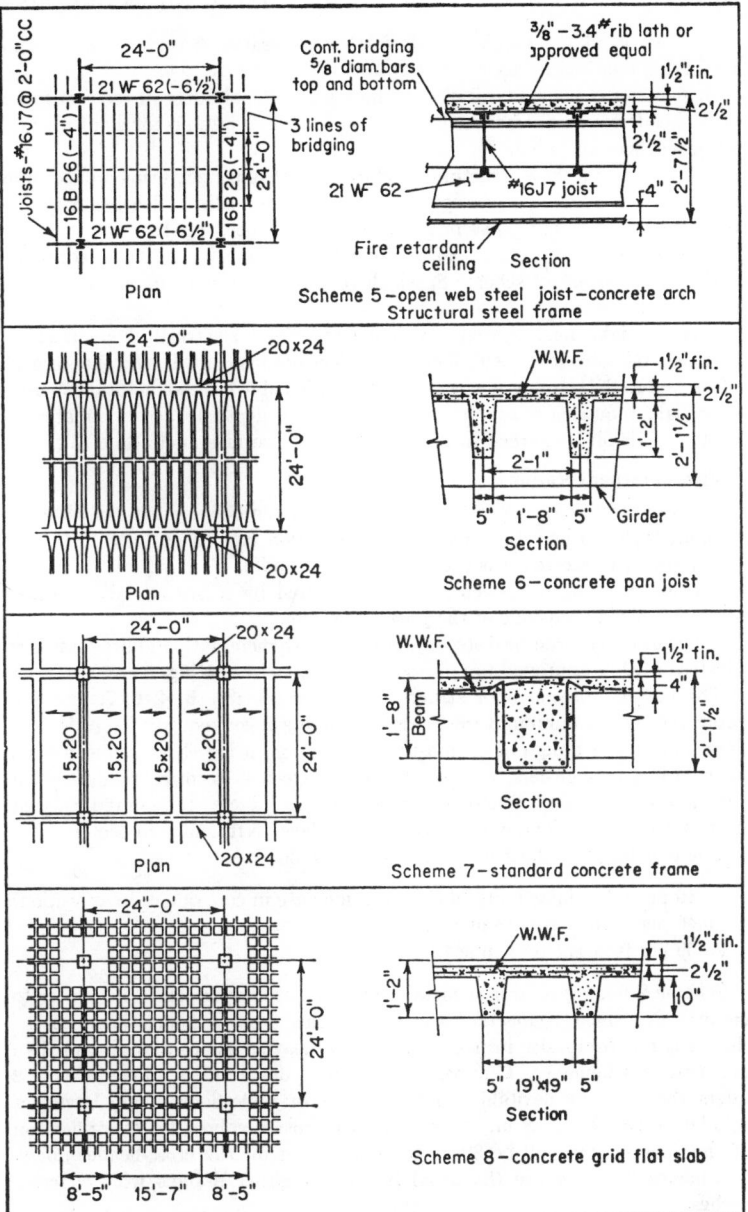

FIG. 4-1. Alternative construction schemes for interior bays. (*Continued*)

2. Cost of adding required materials (if necessary) to give the maximum fire rating required by code (lines 11 and 12).

3. Cost for electrical flexibility, including additional ducts (if required) and cross headers. A finished ceiling is also included, but no mechanical duct work has been included.

Schemes 1 to 5 show structural steel framing of A36 steel, using a maximum unit stress of 24,000 psi, except for schemes 3 and 4, in which beam caging is used to allow a unit stress of 27,000 psi (AISC spec. sec. 1.11.2).

Schemes 6 to 8 are designs in reinforced concrete, using 3,000 psi concrete, with the exception of scheme 8, which requires 4,000 psi concrete to satisfy shear conditions.

For all eight floor systems without underfloor electrical ducts a steel-troweled monolithic cement floor finish has been included. In the case of schemes 3 to 8, the underfloor ducts are installed above the structural concrete floor slab, requiring a concrete fill of $1\frac{1}{2}$ in. in depth to accommodate the ducts. This fill is charged to the cost of electric service ducts (line 13).

Fire Retardant Rating

A fire retardant rating of 3 hr is attained in the floor systems of all eight designs, with a 4-hr rating for column protection (shown on lines 10 to 12). Sprayed-on fire retardant is used in schemes 1 and 2.

Scheme 5, using open-web joist, is protected by a fire retardant ceiling attached to the underside of the joist and girders.

All columns of structural steel are covered with metal lath and fire retardant plaster or other approved fire protection giving a 4-hr rating.

The bar reinforcement or structural steel of schemes 3, 4, 6, 7, and 8 is protected by the minimum thickness of concrete cover required by code.

Scheme 1 is a design of composite construction, using shear connectors on both beams and girders, utilizing a light-gauge-steel form as reinforcement for the concrete slab. Where underfloor electrical ducts are required, cellular units are utilized. These units are usually placed 5 ft center to center.

The cost for electrification is estimated as follows:

$0.19 per ft² cellular units (differential increase in cost due cellular section)
  0.40 per ft² for cross-header ducts
$0.59 per ft² (scheme 1, line 13)

Scheme 2 floor system uses metal cellular flooring with cells 8 in. center to center. No shear connectors are used in this type of floor; therefore the design is not composite in nature, requiring heavier beams and girders than are used in scheme 1. If underfloor electrical ducts are required, scheme 2 offers the greatest flexibility in the layout of underfloor ducts, having a cellular section every 8 in. The only extra cost involved for electrification of the floor system will be $0.40 per square foot for the cross-header ducts.

Schemes 3 and 4 are the usual beam and girder designs with concrete arches.

Scheme 3 was included to show a comparison between lightweight and normal-weight concrete. An underfloor electrical-duct system for schemes 3 to 8 requires 1½ in. of concrete fill to accommodate the ducts.

The estimated cost for underfloor ducts will be:

> $0.22 for concrete fill (the difference in unit cost)
> 2.42 for grid system of ducts (including headers)
> $2.64 (schemes 3 to 8, line 13)

The details of these floor systems of construction are clearly shown in the plans and sections of their particular reference.

Table 4-4 clearly demonstrates that a given framing system can change its relative economic position, depending on the design criteria established for the particular building being analyzed.

Whereas scheme 5 is the most economical for a building requiring no fire protection, it drops to fifth place when fire protection is required. Scheme 8 at no extra cost now becomes the most economical. However, when electrification of the floor becomes a design criterion, scheme 1 or 2 becomes the economical choice.

MECHANICAL

This section includes design criteria, data, and physical laws and formulas applicable to the design of building heating, ventilating, air-conditioning, and plumbing systems.

4-3. Heating

Heating Load

$$Q_t = Q_{tr} + Q_{inf} + Q_{vent} \tag{4-1}$$

where Q_t = total heating load, Btu/hr

$$Q_{tr} = \text{transmission load} = AU(t_i - t_o) \qquad \text{Btu/hr} \tag{4-2}$$

$$Q_{inf} = \text{infiltration load} = 1.08 \,(\text{cfm})(t_i - t_o) \qquad \text{Btu/hr} \tag{4-3}$$

$$Q_{vent} = \text{ventilation load} = 1.08 \,(\text{cfm})(t_i - t_o) \qquad \text{Btu/hr} \tag{4-4}$$

where

A = area through which heat flow occurs, ft²
U = over-all heat transfer coefficient = $1/R_t$ Btu/(hr)(ft²)(°F)   (4-5)
t_o = outside-air design dry-bulb temperature, °F (Fig. 4-2)
t_i = inside design dry-bulb temperature, °F (Table 4-5)
cfm = cubic feet per minute, air
R_t = thermal resistance, °F/(Btu)(hr)(ft²)

$$R_t = R_1 + R_2 + R_3 + \cdots + R_n \tag{4-6}$$

where $R_1, R_2, \ldots,$ are the resistances to heat flow of the individual components of a composite construction.

Design Conditions—Outdoor

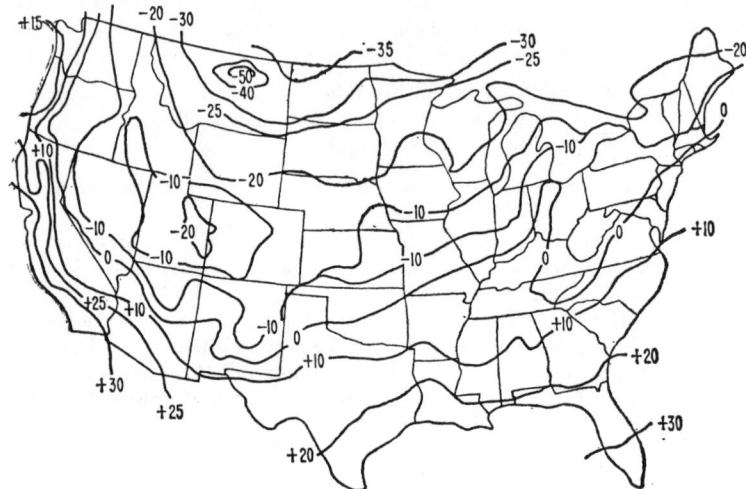

Fig. 4-2. Isotherms of winter outdoor design temperatures. ("*ASHRAE Guide and Data Book*," *chap*. 12, *fig*. 1, *ASHRAE*, 1958.)

Table 4-5. Winter Indoor Dry-bulb Temperatures, Usually Specified

Type of building	°F	Type of building	°F
Schools:		Theaters:	
Classrooms...........................	72–74	Seating space........................	68–72
Assembly rooms......................	68–72	Lounge rooms........................	68–72
Gymnasiums.........................	55–65	Toilets..............................	68
Toilets and baths.....................	70	Hotels:	
Wardrobe and locker rooms............	65–68	Bedrooms and baths.................	75
Kitchens.............................	66	Dining rooms.......................	72
Dining and lunch rooms...............	65–70	Kitchens and laundries..............	66
Playrooms...........................	60–65	Ballrooms..........................	65–68
Natatoriums.........................	75	Toilets and service rooms............	68
Hospitals:		Homes..............................	73–75
Private rooms........................	72–74	Stores..............................	65–68
Private rooms (surgical)..............	70–80	Public buildings	72–74
Operating rooms.....................	70–95	Warm-air baths......................	120
Wards...............................	72–74	Steam baths.........................	110
Kitchens and laundries................	66	Factories and machine shops...........	60–65
Toilets..............................	68	Foundries and boiler shops	50–60
Bathrooms...........................	70–80	Paint shops.........................	80

SOURCE: "ASHRAE Guide and Data Book," chap. 25, table 3, ASHRAE, New York, 1963.

Transmission Load

Table 4-6. Over-all Heat Transfer Coefficient *U*

Air-to-air heat transfer, Btu/(hr)(ft²)(°F)
Outside air 15-mph wind, inside still air

Example	Construction	*U*
Frame walls...............	Wood siding, building paper, air space, gypsum lath, plaster	0.24
	Wood siding, insulation board, air space, gypsum board	0.19
Frame partition............	Gypsum board, air space, gypsum board	0.34
Frame construction ceilings and floors	Linoleum or tile, felt, plywood, wood subfloor, air space, metal lath, plaster	0.23
Pitched roofs..............	Asphalt shingles, building paper, wood sheathing, air space, gypsum lath, plaster	0.28
Masonry wall..............	Face brick 4″, common brick 4″	0.48
	Face brick 4″, common brick 4″, air space, gypsum lath, plaster	0.29
	Face brick 4″, concrete block 4″, air space, gypsum lath, plaster	0.26
Masonry partition...........	Cement block (cinder aggregate), plaster on both sides	0.31
Concrete floor and ceiling....	Tile, felt, plywood ⅜″, air space, metal lath, plaster	0.23
Flat masonry roof..........	Built-up roofing, roof insulation 1″, concrete slab 4″, air space, metal lath, plaster	0.18

Table 4-7. Coefficient of Heat Transmission *U* for Windows and Skylights

Air-to-air heat transfer, Btu/(hr)(ft²)(°F)
Outside air 0°F, 15-mph wind, no solar radiation; inside still air

Construction	Vertical glass sheets		Horizontal glass sheets	
	Outdoor exposure	Indoor exposure	Outdoor exposure	Indoor exposure
Common window glass, single sheet................	1.13	0.75	1.40	0.96
Common window glass, two sheets, 1″ air space.......	0.53	0.45	0.63	0.56

Table 4-8. Coefficient of Heat Transmission *U* for Wood Doors

Air-to-air heat transfer, Btu/(hr)(ft²)(°F)
Outside air 0°F, 15-mph wind, no solar radiation; inside still air

Construction	Outdoor exposure	
	Single	With glass storm door
1″-thick solid door (²⁵⁄₃₂″)...............	0.64	0.37
2″-thick solid door (1⅝″)...............	.43	.28
Door containing wood or glass panels......	.85	.39

Table 4-9. Heat Loss of Concrete Floors at or Near Grade Level per Foot of Exposed Edge

Outdoor design temperature, °F	Heat loss per foot of exposed edge, Btu/hr	
	Recommended 2-in. edge insulation	1-in. edge insulation
−20 to −30	50	55
−10 to −20	45	50
0 to −10	40	45
Outdoor design temperature, °F	1-in. edge insulation	No edge insulation*
−20 to −30	60	75
−10 to −20	55	65
0 to −10	50	60

*This construction not recommended; shown for comparison only.

SOURCE: "Heating, Ventilating, Air Conditioning Guide," chap. 12, table 6, ASHRAE, New York, 1960.

Table 4-10. Infiltration through Windows
Cubic Feet per Foot of Crack per Hour

Type of window	Wind velocity, mph					
	5	10	15	20	25	30
Double-hung wood-sash windows (unlocked):						
Total for average window, nonweatherstripped, $\frac{1}{16}$-in. crack and $\frac{3}{64}$-in. clearance. Includes wood-frame leakage	7	21	39	59	80	104
Weatherstripped	4	13	24	36	49	63
Double-hung metal windows:						
Nonweatherstripped, locked	20	45	70	96	125	154
Nonweatherstripped, unlocked	20	47	74	104	137	170
Weatherstripped, unlocked	6	19	32	46	60	76
Rolled-section steel-sash windows:						
Industrial pivoted, $\frac{1}{16}$-in. crack	52	108	176	244	304	372
Architectural projected, $\frac{1}{32}$-in. crack	15	36	62	86	112	139
Residential casement, $\frac{1}{32}$-in. crack	14	32	52	76	100	128
Heavy casement section, projected, $\frac{1}{32}$-in. crack	8	24	38	54	72	92
Hollow-metal, vertically pivoted window	30	88	145	186	221	242

SOURCE: "ASHRAE Guide and Data Book," chap. 24, table 2, ASHRAE, New York, 1963.

Table 4-11. Infiltration through Walls[a]
Cubic Feet per Square Foot per Hour

Type of wall	Wind velocity, mph					
	5	10	15	20	25	30
Brick wall[b]						
8½ in. plain....................	2	4	8	12	19	23
plastered[c]...............	0.02	0.04	0.07	0.11	0.16	0.24
13 in. plain....................	1	4	7	12	16	21
plastered[c]...............	0.01	0.01	0.03	0.04	0.07	0.10
plastered[d]...............	0.03	0.10	0.21	0.36	0.53	0.72
Frame wall, lath and plaster[e]......	0.03	0.07	0.13	0.18	0.23	0.26

[a] The values given in this table are 20 per cent less than test values to allow for building up of pressure in rooms.

[b] Constructed of porous brick and lime mortar—workmanship poor.

[c] Two coats prepared gypsum plaster on brick.

[d] Furring, lath, and two coats prepared gypsum plaster on brick.

[e] Wall construction: bevel siding painted or cedar shingles, sheathing, building paper, wood lath, and three coats gypsum plaster.

SOURCE: "ASHRAE Guide and Data Book," chap. 24, table 3, ASHRAE, New York, 1963.

Table 4-12. Infiltration through Doors—Winter*
15 Mph Wind Velocity†
Doors on One or Adjacent Windward Sides‡

Description	Cfm/ft² area§				
	Infrequent use	Average use			
		1- and 2-story building	Tall buildings, ft		
			50	100	200
Revolving door.......................	1.6	10.5	12.6	14.2	17.3
Glass door (³⁄₁₆″ crack)...............	9.0	30.0	36.0	40.5	49.5
Wood door 3′ × 7′...................	2.0	13.0	15.5	17.5	21.5
Small factory door....................	1.5	3.0			
Garage and shipping-room door.........	4.0	9.0			
Ramp garage door....................	4.0	13.5			

* All values are based on the wind blowing directly at the window or door. When the prevailing wind direction is oblique to the window or doors, multiply the values by 0.60 and use the total window and door area on the windward side(s).

† Based on a wind velocity of 15 mph. For design wind velocities different from the base, multiply the table values by the ratio of velocities.

‡ Stack effect in tall buildings may also cause infiltration on the leeward side. To evaluate this, determine the equivalent velocity (V_e) and subtract the design velocity (V). The equivalent velocity is

$$V_e = \sqrt{V^2 - 1.75a} \text{ (upper section)}$$
$$= \sqrt{V^2 + 1.75b} \text{ (lower section)}$$

where a and b are the distances above and below the mid-height of the building, respectively, in feet.

Multiply the table values by the ratio $(V_e - V)/15$ for one-half of the windows and doors on the leeward side of the building. (Use values under one- and two-story building for doors on leeward side of tall buildings.)

§ Doors on opposite sides increase values 25 per cent.

SOURCE: "Carrier Corporation System Design Manual," Part I, Load Estimating, 1960.

Ventilation Load

Table 4-13. Minimum Outdoor Air Requirements to Remove Objectionable Body Odors under Laboratory Conditions

Type of occupants	Air space per person, ft³	Outdoor air supply, cfm per person
Heating season with or without recirculation. Air not conditioned.		
Sedentary adults of average socioeconomic status.......	100	25
	200	16
	300	12
	500	7
Laborers..	200	23
Grade school children of average socioeconomic status...	100	29
	200	21
	300	17
	500	11
Grade school children of lower socioeconomic status.....	200	38
Children attending private grade schools..............	100	22

Heating season. Air humidified by means of centrifugal humidifier. Water atomization rate 8 to 10 gph. Total air circulation 30 cfm per person.

Sedentary adults...................................	200	12

Summer season. Air cooled and dehumidified by means of a spray dehumidifier. Spray water changed daily. Total air circulation 30 cfm per person.

Sedentary adults...................................	200	<4

SOURCE: "ASHRAE Guide and Data Book," chap. 8, table 1, ASHRAE, New York, 1963.

Table 4-14. Outdoor Air Requirements

Application	Smoking	Cfm per person — Recommended	Cfm per person — Min.	Cfm/ft² of floor, min.
Apartment:				
Average	Some	20	10	
Deluxe	Some	20	10	
Banking space	Occasional	10	7½	
Barber shops	Considerable	15	10	
Beauty parlors	Occasional	10	7½	
Brokers' board rooms	Very heavy	50	20	
Cocktail bars	....	40	25	
Corridors (supply or exhaust)	....	....	....	0.25
Department stores	None	7½	5	0.05
Directors' rooms	Extreme	50	30	
Drugstores	Considerable	10	7½	
Factories	None	10	7½	0.10
Five and ten cent stores	None	7½	5	
Funeral parlors	None	10	7½	
Garages	....	....	....	1.0
Hospitals:				
Operating rooms	None	....	....	2.0
Private rooms	None	30	25	0.33
Wards	None	20	10	
Hotel rooms	Heavy	30	25	0.33
Kitchens:				
Restaurant	....	....	....	4.0
Residence	....	....	....	2.0
Laboratories	Some	20	15	
Meeting rooms	Very heavy	50	30	1.25
Offices:				
General	Some	15	10	
Private	None	25	15	0.25
	Considerable	30	25	0.25
Restaurants:				
Cafeteria	Considerable	12	10	
Dining-room	Considerable	15	12	
Schoolrooms	None			
Shop, retail	None	10	7½	
Theater	None	7½	5	
	Some	15	10	
Toilets (exhaust)	....	....	....	2.0

SOURCE: "ASHRAE Guide and Data Book," chap. 26, table 2, ASHRAE, New York, 1963.

Radiator and Convector Ratings. To determine the rating of a radiator or a convector for a given space, multiply the heat loss of the space by the proper factor from Table 4-15 and select the radiator or convector having an equivalent Btu per hour rating. Thus, for a 75°F room with 1000 Btu heat loss, a convector fed with 1 psig steam should be selected for a 1110-Btu rating.

Table 4-15. Correction Factors for Radiators and Convectors

Top section

Steam pressure (approx.) Gage vacuum in. Hg	Psia	Heating-medium temp., °F, steam or water	Factors for finned-tube—inlet air temperature, °F							Factors for direct cast-iron radiators—room temperature, °F						
			80	75	70	65	60	55	50	80	75	70	65	60	55	50
22.4	3.7	150	2.80	2.50	2.20	1.95	1.81	1.67	1.54	2.58	2.36	2.17	2.00	1.86	1.73	1.62
20.3	4.7	160	2.34	2.14	1.94	1.75	1.62	1.50	1.37	2.17	2.00	1.86	1.73	1.62	1.52	1.44
17.7	6.0	170	2.01	1.86	1.70	1.56	1.46	1.36	1.26	1.86	1.73	1.62	1.52	1.44	1.35	1.28
14.6	7.5	180	1.76	1.65	1.53	1.42	1.32	1.24	1.15	1.62	1.52	1.44	1.35	1.28	1.21	1.15
10.9	9.3	190	1.53	1.45	1.36	1.28	1.20	1.12	1.03	1.44	1.35	1.28	1.21	1.15	1.10	1.05
6.5	11.5	200	1.38	1.31	1.24	1.16	1.09	1.02	0.95	1.28	1.21	1.15	1.10	1.05	1.00	0.95
Psi																
1	15.6	215	1.17	1.12	1.06	1.00	0.95	0.90	0.85	1.10	1.05	1.00	0.96	0.92	0.88	0.85
6	21	230	1.00	0.97	0.93	0.90	0.86	0.82	0.78	0.96	0.92	0.88	0.85	0.81	0.78	0.76
15	30	250	0.88	0.85	0.82	0.78	0.75	0.71	0.67	0.81	0.78	0.76	0.73	0.70	0.68	0.66
27	42	270	0.75	0.73	0.70	0.68	0.65	0.62	0.59	0.70	0.68	0.66	0.64	0.62	0.60	0.58
52	67	300	0.62	0.60	0.58	0.56	0.54	0.52	0.50	0.58	0.57	0.55	0.53	0.52	0.51	0.49

Bottom section

Steam pressure (approx.) Gage vacuum in. Hg	Psia	Heating-medium temp., °F, steam or water	Factors for baseboard—inlet air temperature, °F							Factors for convectors—inlet air temperature, °F						
			80	75	70	65	60	55	50	80	75	70	65	60	55	50
22.4	3.7	150	2.86	2.61	2.38	2.20	2.03	1.89	1.76	3.14	2.83	2.57	2.35	2.15	1.93	1.84
20.3	4.7	160	2.38	2.20	2.03	1.89	1.76	1.64	1.56	2.57	2.35	2.15	1.98	1.84	1.71	1.59
17.7	6.0	170	2.03	1.89	1.76	1.64	1.54	1.44	1.38	2.15	1.98	1.84	1.71	1.59	1.49	1.43
14.6	7.5	180	1.76	1.64	1.55	1.44	1.38	1.29	1.23	1.84	1.71	1.59	1.49	1.40	1.32	1.24
10.9	9.3	190	1.54	1.44	1.37	1.29	1.22	1.16	1.09	1.59	1.49	1.40	1.32	1.24	1.17	1.11
6.5	11.5	200	1.38	1.29	1.23	1.16	1.09	1.05	1.00	1.40	1.32	1.24	1.17	1.11	1.05	1.03
Psi																
1	15.6	215	1.16	1.10	1.05	1.00	0.95	0.92	0.88	1.17	1.11	1.05	1.00	0.95	0.91	0.87
6	21	230	1.00	0.96	0.92	0.88	0.84	0.81	0.77	1.00	0.95	0.91	0.87	0.83	0.79	0.76
15	30	250	0.86	0.82	0.79	0.76	0.73	0.70	0.68	0.83	0.79	0.76	0.73	0.70	0.68	0.65
27	42	270	0.73	0.70	0.68	0.66	0.63	0.61	0.59	0.70	0.68	0.65	0.63	0.60	0.58	0.56
52	67	300	0.58	0.57	0.55	0.53	0.52	0.51	0.49	0.56	0.54	0.53	0.51	0.49	0.48	0.47

SOURCE: "ASHRAE Guide and Data Book," chap. 46, p. 721, ASHRAE, New York, 1963.

Example of Use of Basic and Velocity Multiplier Charts

GIVEN:

Weight flow rate = 6,700 lb/hr

Initial steam pressure = 100 psig

Pressure drop = 11 psi/100 ft

FIND: Size of Schedule 40 pipe required and velocity of steam in pipe.

SOLUTION: The following steps are illustrated by the broken line in Fig. 4-3.

Step 1. Enter diagram at a weight flow rate of 6,700 lb/hr and move vertically to the horizontal line at 100 psig.

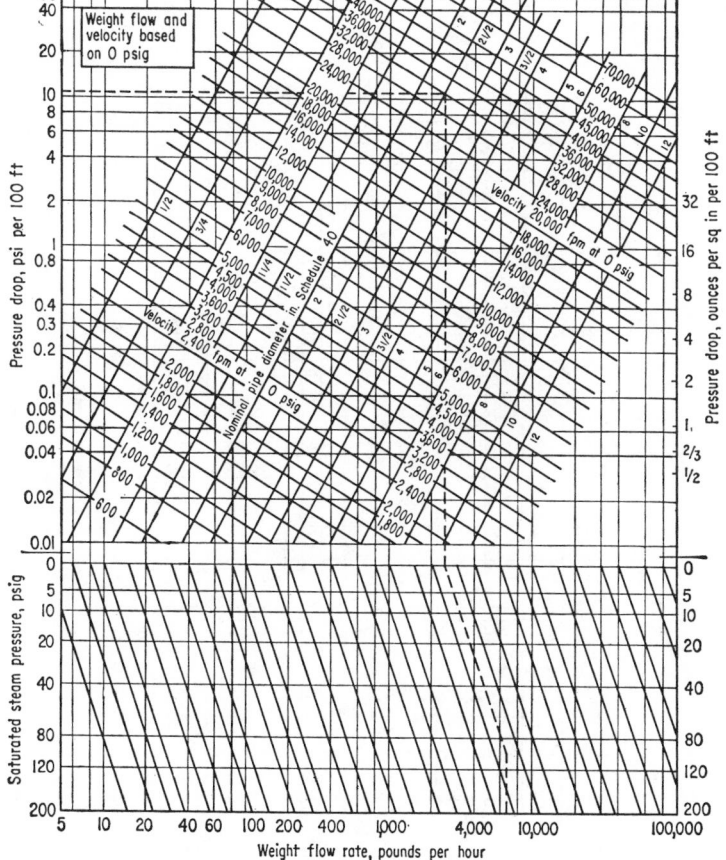

FIG. 4-3. Basic chart for weight flow rate and velocity of steam in Schedule 40 pipe based on saturation pressure of 0 psig. ("*ASHRAE Guide and Data Book*," chap. 8, fig. 22, *ASHRAE*, 1964.)

Step 2. Follow along inclined multiplier line (upward and to the left) to horizontal 0-psig line. The equivalent weight flow at 0 psig is about 2,500 lb/hr.

Step 3. Follow the 2,500-lb/hr line vertically until it intersects the horizontal line at 11 psi/100 ft pressure drop. The nominal pipe size is 2½ in. The equivalent steam velocity at 0 psig is about 32,700 fpm.

Step 4. To find the steam velocity at 100 psig, locate the value of 32,700 fpm on the ordinate of the velocity multiplier chart at 0 psig.

Step 5. Move along the inclined multiplier line (downward and to the right) until it intersects the vertical 100-psig pressure line. The velocity as read from the right (or left) scale is about 13,000 fpm.

Note: The preceding steps 1 to 5 would be rearranged or reversed if different data were given.

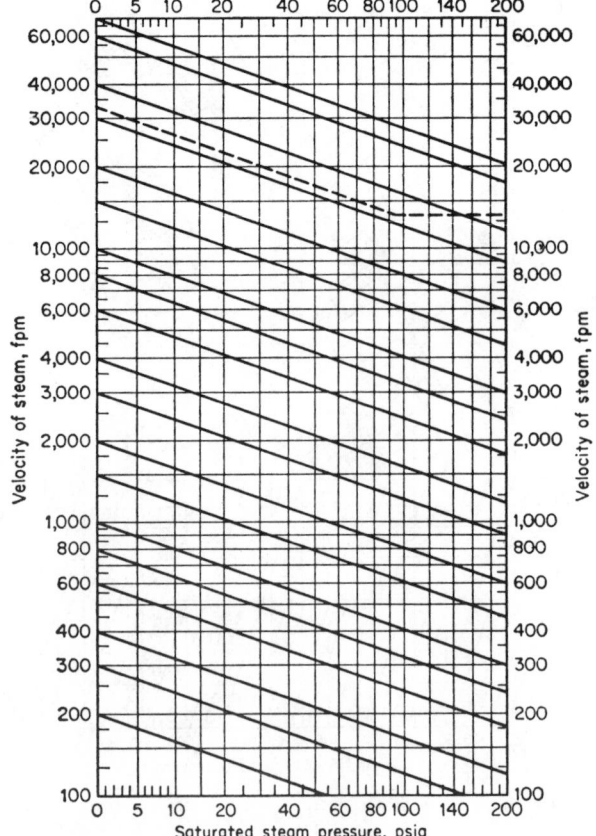

Fig. 4-4. Velocity multiplier chart for use with Fig. 4-3. ("*ASHRAE Guide and Data Book*," chap. 8, fig. 22, *ASHRAE*, 1964.)

Table 4-16. Weight Flow Rate of Steam in Schedule 40 Pipe[a] at Initial Saturation Pressures of 3.5 and 12 Psig[b,c]

Weight Flow Rate in Pounds per Hour

Pressure drop, psi per 100 ft in length

Saturation pressure, psig

Nom. pipe size, in.	1/16 psi (1 oz)		1/8 psi (2 oz)		1/4 psi (4 oz)		1/2 psi (8 oz)		3/4 psi (12 oz)		1 psi		2 psi	
	3.5	12	3.5	12	3.5	12	3.5	12	3.5	12	3.5	12	3.5	12
¾	9	11	14	16	20	24	29	35	36	43	42	50	60	73
1	17	21	26	31	37	46	54	66	68	82	81	95	114	137
1¼	36	45	53	66	78	96	111	138	140	170	162	200	232	280
1½	56	70	84	100	120	147	174	210	218	260	246	304	360	430
2	108	134	162	194	234	285	336	410	420	510	480	590	710	850
2½	174	215	258	310	378	460	540	660	680	820	780	950	1,150	1,370
3	318	380	465	550	660	810	960	1,160	1,190	1,430	1,380	1,670	1,950	2,400
3½	462	550	670	800	990	1,218	1,410	1,700	1,740	2,100	2,000	2,420	2,950	3,450
4	640	800	950	1,160	1,410	1,690	1,980	2,400	2,450	3,000	2,880	3,460	4,200	4,900
5	1,200	1,430	1,680	2,100	2,440	3,000	3,570	4,250	4,380	5,250	5,100	6,100	7,500	8,600
6	1,920	2,300	2,820	3,350	3,960	4,850	5,700	7,000	7,200	8,600	8,400	10,000	11,900	14,200
8	3,900	4,800	5,570	7,000	8,100	10,000	11,400	14,300	14,500	17,700	16,500	20,500	24,000	29,500
10	7,200	8,800	10,200	12,600	15,000	18,200	21,000	26,000	26,200	32,000	30,000	37,000	42,700	52,000
12	11,400	13,700	16,500	19,500	23,400	28,400	33,000	40,000	41,000	49,500	48,000	57,500	67,800	81,000

[a] Based on Moody friction factor, where flow of condensate does not inhibit the flow of steam.

[b] The weight flow rates at 3.5 psi can be used to cover saturation pressure from 1 to 6 psig, and the rates at 12 psig can be used to cover saturation pressure from 8 to 16 psig with an error not exceeding 8 per cent.

[c] The steam velocities corresponding to the weight flow rates given in this table can be found from the basic chart and velocity multiplier chart, Fig. 4-3.

SOURCE: "ASHRAE Guide and Data Book," chap. 8, table 5, ASHRAE, New York, 1964.

Table 4-17. Return Main and Riser Capacities for Low-pressure Systems, Pounds per Hour

This table is based on pipe size data developed through the research investigations of The American Society of Heating, Refrigerating and Air-Conditioning Engineers.

Pipe size, in.	1/32 psi or 1/2 oz drop per 100 ft			1/24 psi or 2/3 oz drop per 100 ft			1/16 psi or 1 oz drop per 100 ft			1/8 psi or 2 oz drop per 100 ft			1/4 psi or 4 oz drop per 100 ft			1/2 psi or 8 oz drop per 100 ft		
	Wet	Dry	Vac.	Wet	Dry	Vac.	Wet	Dry	Vac.	Wet	Dry	Vac.	Wet	Dry	Vac.	Wet	Dry	Vac.
G	H	I	J	K	L	M	N	O	P	Q	R	S	T	U	V	W	X	Y
Mains																		
¾	……	……	……	……	……	42	……	……	100	……	……	142	……	……	200	……	……	283
1	125	62	……	145	71	143	175	80	175	250	103	249	350	115	350	……	……	494
1¼	213	130	……	248	149	244	300	168	300	425	217	426	600	241	600	……	……	848
1½	338	206	……	393	236	388	475	265	475	675	340	674	950	378	950	……	……	1,340
2	700	470	……	810	535	815	1,000	575	1,000	1,400	740	1,420	2,000	825	2,000	……	……	2,830
2½	1,180	760	……	1,580	868	1,360	1,680	950	1,680	2,350	1,230	2,380	3,350	1,360	3,350	……	……	4,730
3	1,880	1,460	……	2,130	1,560	2,180	2,680	1,750	2,680	3,750	2,250	3,800	5,350	2,500	5,350	……	……	7,560
3½	2,750	1,970	……	3,300	2,200	3,250	4,000	2,500	4,000	5,500	3,250	5,680	8,000	3,580	8,000	……	……	11,300
4	3,880	2,930	……	4,580	3,350	4,500	5,500	3,750	5,500	7,750	4,830	7,810	11,000	5,380	11,000	……	……	15,500
5	……	……	……	……	……	7,880	……	……	9,680	……	……	13,700	……	……	19,400	……	……	27,300
6	……	……	……	……	……	12,600	……	……	15,500	……	……	22,000	……	……	31,000	……	……	43,800
Risers																		
¾	……	48	……	……	48	143	……	48	175	……	48	249	……	48	350	……	……	494
1	……	113	……	……	113	244	……	113	300	……	113	426	……	113	600	……	……	848
1¼	……	248	……	……	248	388	……	248	475	……	248	674	……	248	950	……	……	1,340
1½	……	375	……	……	375	815	……	375	1,000	……	375	1,420	……	375	2,000	……	……	2,830
2	……	750	……	……	750	1,360	……	750	1,680	……	750	2,380	……	750	3,350	……	……	4,730
2½	……	……	……	……	……	2,180	……	……	2,680	……	……	3,800	……	……	5,350	……	……	7,560
3	……	……	……	……	……	3,250	……	……	4,000	……	……	5,680	……	……	8,000	……	……	11,300
3½	……	……	……	……	……	4,480	……	……	5,500	……	……	7,810	……	……	11,000	……	……	15,500
4	……	……	……	……	……	7,880	……	……	9,680	……	……	13,700	……	……	19,400	……	……	27,300
5	……	……	……	……	……	12,600	……	……	15,500	……	……	22,000	……	……	31,000	……	……	43,800

SOURCE: "ASHRAE Guide and Data Book," chap. 8, table 7, ASHRAE, New York, 1964.

Boiler Load. *Net Load* is the sum of direct-connected load components. These include direct radiation, infiltration, air tempering, humidification, hot water, process steam, and snow melting.

Design Load is the sum of the *net load* and the *piping tax*. Piping tax is the estimated heat emission in Btu per hour of the piping connecting the radiation and other apparatus to the boiler. In average heating systems it is common practice to consider the piping tax to be 20 per cent of the net load.

Gross, or Maximum, Load is the sum of the *design load* and the *pickup allowance*. Pickup allowance is the estimated increase in the normal load in

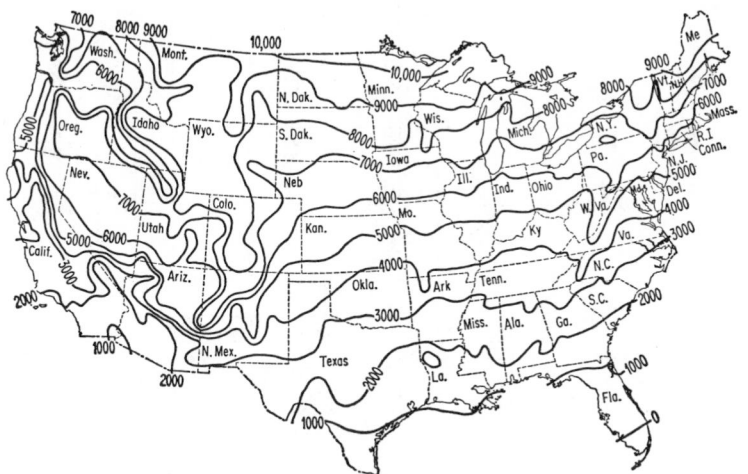

FIG. 4-5. Number of degree-days in a normal heating season. (*Clifford Strock*, "*Engineering Data Book*," *The Industrial Press*, 1948.)

Btu per hour, caused by the heating up of the cold system. For automatically fired boilers the sum of the piping tax and pickup allowance varies from 33.3 to 28.8 per cent of the *net load*. The larger percentage should be applied to smaller boilers.

Information on *boiler performance* and the *heating value of various fuels* may be found in Sec. 8.

Chimneys. Equations (4-7) to (4-10) are simplified equations for chimney sizes if the following typical values for boiler plants are assumed:

Average chimney gas temperature:	$T_c = 500°F$ (960°F abs)
Average atmospheric temperature:	$T_0 = 62°F$ (522°F abs)
Average coefficient of friction:	$f = 0.016$
Average chimney gas density at 0°F and 1 atm:	0.09 lb/ft³
Barometer reading, sea level:	$B_0 = 29.92$ in. Hg

Required height of chimney above inlet, in feet:

$$H = 190D_r \qquad (4\text{-}7)$$

Required minimum diameter of chimney, in feet:

$$d = 1.5W^{2/5} \tag{4-8}$$

Chimney gas velocity, in feet per second:

$$V_c = 13.7W^{1/5} \tag{4-9}$$

Stack draft, in inches of water:

$$D_r = 0.256HB_0\left(\frac{1}{T_0\text{ abs}} - \frac{1}{T_c\text{ abs}}\right) \tag{4-10}$$

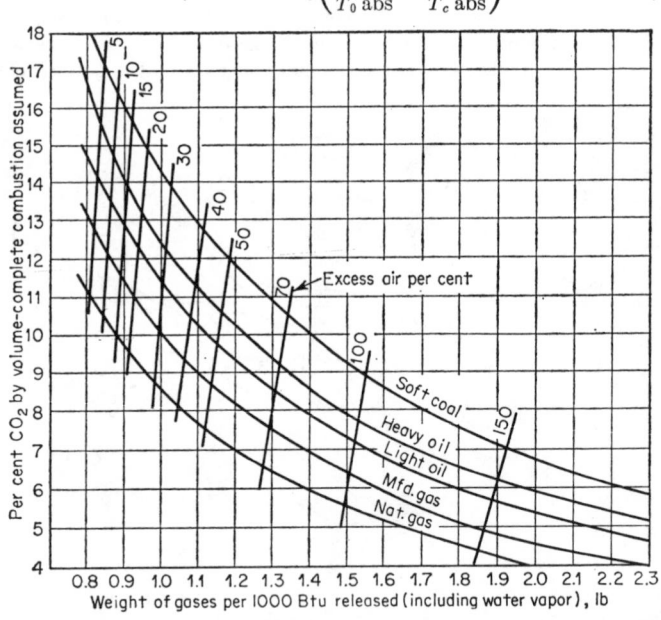

FIG. 4-6. Graphical evaluation and rate of flue gas flow from per cent CO_2 and fuel rate. ("*ASHRAE Guide and Data Book*," chap. 44, fig. 4, *ASHRAE*, 1963.)

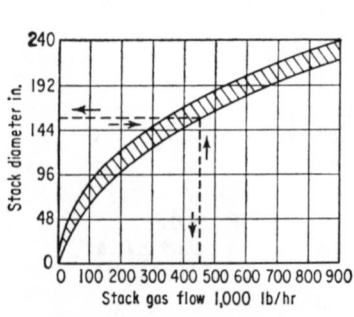

FIG. 4-7. Economical stack size based on approximately 5 per cent draft loss.

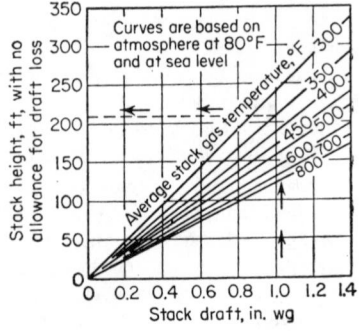

FIG. 4-8. Stack height as a function of stack draft.

where D_r = total required draft, in. of water

W = flue gas flow rate, lb/sec

Total required draft is the sum of draft loss through the breeching and through the boiler and the required draft in the firebox.

4-4. Moisture

The moisture entering a building as water vapor may be expressed as

$$W_t = W_{\text{trans}} + W_{\text{inf}} + W_{\text{vent}} \qquad (4\text{-}11)$$

where W_t = total weight of vapor, g

$$W_{\text{trans}} = \text{transmitted vapor} = MA\theta \, \Delta\rho \qquad \text{g} \qquad (4\text{-}12)$$

$$W_{\text{inf}} = \text{air infiltrated vapor} = W(M_o - M_i) \qquad \text{g} \qquad (4\text{-}13)$$

$$W_{\text{vent}} = \text{ventilation air vapor} = W(M_o - M_i) \qquad \text{g} \qquad (4\text{-}14)$$

where M = permeance coefficient, perms

$$= \bar{\mu}/l, \text{ g/(ft}^2)(\text{hr})(\text{Hg } \Delta\rho) \qquad (4\text{-}15)$$

A = area of flow path, ft^2

θ = time of transmission, hr

$\Delta\rho$ = vapor-pressure difference through flow path, in. Hg

W = weight of air, lb

M_o = moisture content of outside air, g/lb

where 1 perm = 1 g/(ft^2)(hr)(in. Hg $\Delta\rho$)

$\bar{\mu}$ = permeability, perm-in., g-in./(ft^2)(hr)(Hg $\Delta\rho$)

l = length of flow path, in.

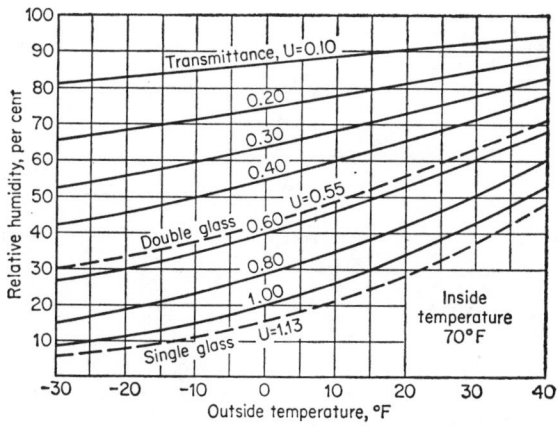

FIG. 4-9. Relative humidity at which visible condensation will appear on inside surface. ("*ASHRAE Guide and Data Book*," chap. 6, fig. 4, *ASHRAE*, 1963.)

Table 4-18. Permeance and Permeability of Materials to Water Vapor

Material	Permeance, perms	%RH₁–RH₂	Method†
Air (still)	120*	92–73	b
Insulation:			
Cellular glass	0.0*	.....	d
Corkboard	2.1–2.6*	75–0	d
	9.5*	100–45	w
Structural insulating board (vegetable, uncoated)	20–50*	40–x	t
Mineral wool (unprotected)	116*	100–30	w
Interior finish:			
Plaster on wood lath	11	100–30	w
Plaster on metal lath, ¾ in.	15	40–x	t
Plaster on plain gypsum lath (with studs)	20	40–85	t
Gypsum wallboard—plain, ⅜ in.	50	50–20	v
Insulating wallboard (uncoated), ½ in.	50–90	40–x	t
Hardboard, ⅛ in.	11		
Tempered, ⅛ in.	5		
** Paint—2 coats:			
Asphaltic paint on plywood	0.4	100–30	w
Aluminum in varnish on wood	0.3–0.5	95–0	d
Enamels, brushed on smooth plaster	0.5–1.5	92–0	b
Primers or sealers on insulating wallboard	0.9–2.1	40–x	t
Various primers + 1 coat flat paint on plaster	1.6–3	40–x	t
Flat paint (alone) on insulating wallboard	4	40–x	t
Water emulsion on insulating wallboard	30–85	40–x	t
** Paint—exterior, 3 coats:			
White lead and oil prepared paint on wood siding	0.3–1.0	50–0	d
White lead-zinc oxide and linseed oil on wood	0.9	95–0	d
Wood:			
Sugar pine	0.4–5.4*	various	tv
Plywood (exterior type 3 ply D.F.), ¼ in.	0.72	50–	4
Plywood (interior type 3 ply D.F.), ¼ in.	1.86	50–	4
Masonry:			
Concrete (1:2:4 mix)	3.2*	100–45	w
Concrete (8-in. cored block wall, limestone aggrt.)	2.4	79–68	t
Brick wall—with mortar, 4 in.	0.8	50–x	t
Tile wall—with mortar, 4 in.	0.12	50–x	t
Films:			
Aluminum foil, 1 mil	0.0	100–0	d
0.35 mil	0.05	100–0	d
Polyethylene, 2 mil	0.16	50–0	d
4 mil	0.08	50–0	d
Polyester, 1 mil	0.72	50–0	d
Cellulose acetate, 10 mil	4.1	50–0	d

Material	Lb per 500 ft²	Permeance, perms	
		Dry cup	Wet cup
** Building papers, felts:			
Duplex sheet, asphalt laminae, aluminum foil one side	43	0.002	0.176
Saturated and coated felt heavy roll roofing	326	0.05	0.24
Kraft and asphalt laminae, Reinforced 30-120-30	34	0.3	1.8
Insulation back up, asphalt-sat., one side glossy	31	0.4	0.6–4.2
Asphalt-saturated and coated sheathing paper	43	0.3	0.6
Asphalt-saturated sheathing paper	22	3.3	20.2
15-lb asphalt felt	70	1.0	5.6
15-lb tar felt	70	4.0	18.2
Single-sheet Kraft, double-infused	16	30.8	41.9

* These values are permeability in perm-inches.
** Description is a guide only, and does not ensure permeance.
† Methods: d—dry cup; w—wet cup; t—two temperatures; b—special cell; v—air velocity both sides; 4—average of four methods.
SOURCE: "ASHRAE Guide and Data Book," chap. 6, table 1, ASHRAE, New York, 1963.

Table 4-19. Grams of Moisture per Pound of Dry Air vs. Dew-point Temperature, °F

DP	Grams	DP	Grams	DP	Grams	DP	Grams	DP	Grams
0	5.50	16	12.36	32	26.40	48	49.50	64	89.18
1	5.79	17	12.99	33	27.52	49	51.42	65	92.40
2	6.10	18	13.63	34	28.66	50	53.38	66	95.76
3	6.43	19	14.30	35	29.83	51	55.45	67	99.19
4	6.77	20	15.01	36	31.07	52	57.58	68	102.8
5	7.12	21	15.75	37	32.33	53	59.74	69	106.4
6	7.50	22	16.53	38	33.62	54	61.99	70	110.2
7	7.89	23	17.33	39	34.97	55	69.34	71	114.2
8	8.30	24	18.17	40	36.36	56	66.75	72	118.2
9	8.73	25	19.05	41	37.80	57	69.23	73	122.4
10	9.18	26	19.97	42	39.31	58	71.82	74	126.6
11	9.65	27	20.94	43	40.88	59	74.48	75	131.1
12	10.15	28	21.93	44	42.48	60	77.21	76	135.7
13	10.66	29	22.99	45	44.14	61	80.08	77	140.4
14	11.20	30	24.07	46	45.87	62	83.02	78	145.3
15	11.77	31	25.21	47	47.66	63	86.03	79	150.3

Table 4-19A. Vapor Pressure of Saturated Air, Inches of Hg, vs. Dry-bulb Temperature, °F

T	P_{sat}	T	P_{sat}	T	P_{sat}	T	P_{sat}	T	P_{sat}
0	.03764	16	.08461	32	.18035	48	.33629	64	.60073
1	.03966	17	.08884	33	.18778	49	.34913	65	.62209
2	.04178	18	.09326	34	.19546	50	.36240	66	.64411
3	.04400	19	.09789	35	.20342	51	.37611	67	.66681
4	.04633	20	.10272	36	.21166	52	.39028	68	.69019
5	.04877	21	.10777	37	.22020	53	.40492	69	.71430
6	.05133	22	.11305	38	.22904	54	.42004	70	.73915
7	.05402	23	.11856	39	.23819	55	.43565	71	.76475
8	.05683	24	.12431	40	.24767	56	.45176	72	.79112
9	.05977	25	.13032	41	.25748	57	.46480	73	.81828
10	.06285	26	.13659	42	.26763	58	.48558	74	.84624
11	.06608	27	.14313	43	.27813	59	.50330	75	.87504
12	.06946	28	.14966	44	.28889	60	.52159	76	.90470
13	.07299	29	.15707	45	.30023	61	.54047	77	.93523
14	.07669	30	.16452	46	.31185	62	.55994	78	.96665
15	.08056	31	.17227	47	.32386	63	.58002	79	.99899

SOURCE: "ASHRAE Guide and Data Book," chap. 3, table 2, ASHRAE, New York, 1963.

4-5. Cooling

Cooling Load. Q_t, the total simultaneous cooling load, Btu/hr.

$$Q_t = Q_{ext} + Q_{int} + Q_{outside\ air} \tag{4-16}$$

where

$$Q_{ext} = \text{external heat gains} = Q_{transmission} + Q_{solar} \tag{4-17}$$

$$Q_{int} = \text{internal heat gains} = Q_{lights} + Q_{people} + Q_{equipment} + Q_{transmission} \tag{4-18}$$

$$Q_{tr\text{-}sol} = AU(sa\ \Delta t) \qquad \text{for walls and roofs, Btu/hr} \tag{4-19}$$

where $sa\ \Delta t$ = sol-air equivalent temperature differential, °F

$$Q_{\text{glass}} = Q_{\text{solar}} + Q_{\text{tr}} \tag{4-20}$$

$$= \text{SHGF (SF)}A_1 + A_2 U(t_o - t_i) \tag{4-21}$$

where SHGF = solar heat gain factor (Tables 4-23 and 4-24)
         SF = shading factor (Tables 4-25 to 4-28)
         A_1 = area of sunlit glass, ft²
         A_2 = area of total glass, ft²
         U = over-all coefficient (Tables 4-22 and 4-29)
         t_o = outside design temp, °F (Fig. 4-12)
         t_i = inside design temp, °F (Table 4-33)

$$Q_{\text{lights}} = 3.41 \times \text{wattage input to conditioned space, Btu/hr} \tag{4-22}$$
(Figs. 4-10 and 4-11)

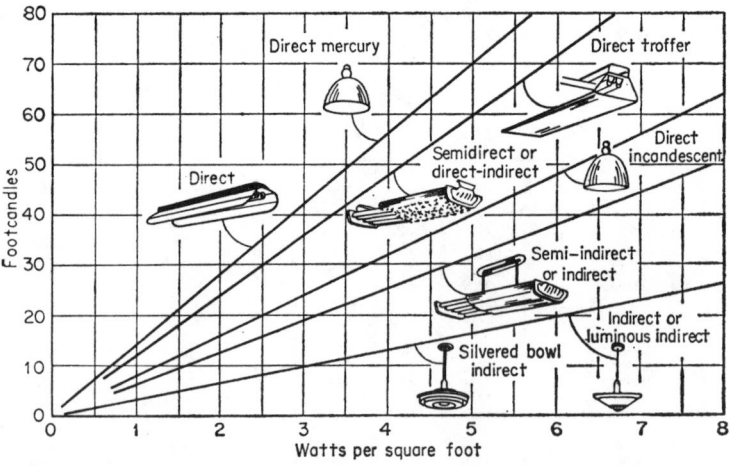

FIG. 4-10. Typical heat-gain lighting fixtures. On the curve above, follow the horizontal line, beginning at the maintained foot-candle value selected in (1), until it intersects the curve corresponding to the fixture type to be installed.

$$Q_{\text{people}} = \text{number of people } (q_{\text{sensible}} + q_{\text{latent}}), \text{Btu/hr} \tag{4-23}$$
(Table 4-30)

$$Q_{\text{equipment}} = q_{\text{sensible}} + q_{\text{latent}} \quad \text{Btu/hr (Tables 4-31 and 4-32)} \tag{4-24}$$

$$Q_{\text{outside air}} = q_{\text{sensible}} + q_{\text{latent}} \quad \text{Btu/hr}$$
$$= 1.08(t_o - t_i) \text{ cfm} + 0.68(M_o - M_i) \text{ cfm} \quad \text{Btu/hr} \tag{4-25}$$

where M_o = outside moisture content at design wet bulb °F, g/lb
         M_i = inside moisture content at design relative humidity, g/lb
         Q_{tr} = $AU(t_o - t_i)$ for partitions, floors, ceilings, Btu/hr $\tag{4-26}$

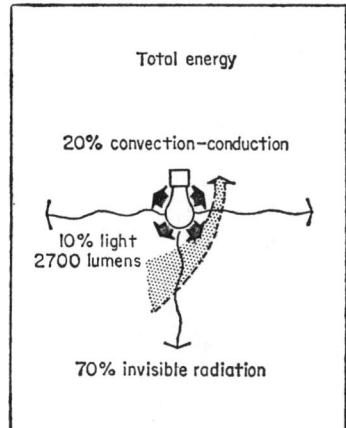

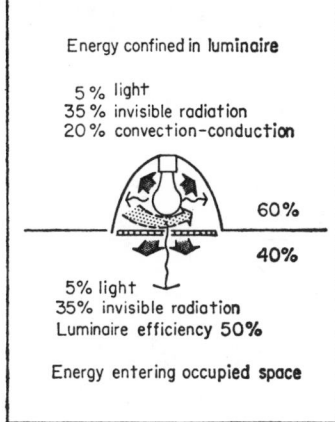

Energy output for 150-watt Incandescent lamp

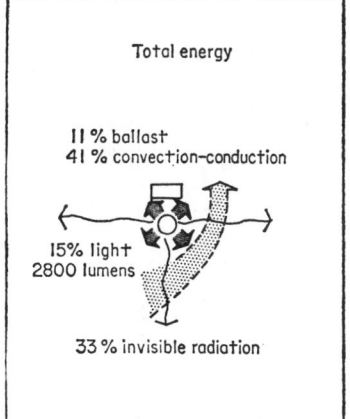

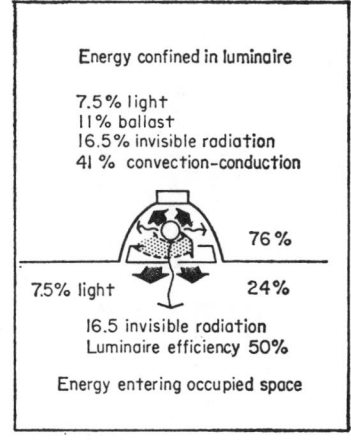

Energy output for 40-watt Fluorescent lamp and ballast

Fig. 4-11. Distribution of energy output of incandescent and fluorescent lamps. (*Light Magazine*, vol. 29, fig. 1.)

Table 4-20. Total Equivalent Temperature Differentials for Calculating Heat Gain through Sunlit and Shaded Walls

Exterior Color of Wall—D = dark, L = light

North latitude wall facing	Sun time A.M. 8 D	8 L	10 D	10 L	12 D	12 L	P.M. 2 D	2 L	4 D	4 L	6 D	6 L	8 D	8 L	10 D	10 L	12 D	12 L	South latitude wall facing
Frame																			
NE	22	10	24	12	14	10	12	10	14	14	14	14	10	10	6	4	2	2	SE
E	30	14	36	18	32	16	12	12	14	14	14	14	10	10	6	6	2	2	E
SE	13	6	26	16	28	18	24	16	16	14	14	14	10	10	6	4	2	2	NE
S	−4	−4	4	0	22	12	30	20	26	20	16	14	10	10	6	6	2	2	N
SW	−4	−4	0	−2	6	4	26	22	40	28	42	28	24	20	6	4	2	2	NW
W	−4	−4	0	0	6	6	20	12	40	28	48	34	22	22	8	8	2	2	W
NW	−4	−4	0	−2	6	4	12	10	24	20	40	26	34	24	6	4	2	2	SW
N (shade)	−4	−4	−2	−2	4	4	10	10	14	14	12	12	8	8	4	4	0	0	S (shade)
4-in. Brick or Stone Veneer + Frame																			
NE	−2	−4	24	12	20	10	10	6	12	10	14	14	12	12	10	10	6	4	SE
E	2	0	30	14	31	17	14	14	12	12	14	14	12	12	10	8	6	6	E
SE	2	−2	20	10	28	16	26	16	14	14	14	14	12	12	10	8	6	6	NE
S	−4	−4	−2	−2	12	6	24	16	26	18	20	16	12	12	8	8	4	4	N
SW	0	−2	0	−2	2	2	12	8	32	22	36	26	34	24	10	8	6	6	NW
W	0	−2	0	0	4	2	10	8	26	18	40	28	42	28	16	14	6	6	W
NW	−4	−4	−2	−2	2	2	6	6	12	12	30	22	34	24	12	10	6	6	SW
N (shade)	−4	−4	−2	−2	0	0	6	6	10	10	12	12	12	12	8	8	4	4	S (shade)
8-in. Hollow Tile or 8-in. Cinder Block																			
NE	0	0	0	0	20	10	16	10	10	6	12	10	14	12	12	10	8	8	SE
E	4	2	12	4	24	12	26	14	20	12	12	10	14	12	14	10	10	8	E
SE	2	0	2	0	16	8	20	12	20	14	14	12	14	12	12	10	8	6	NE
S	0	0	0	0	2	0	12	6	24	14	26	16	20	14	12	10	8	6	N
SW	2	0	2	0	2	0	6	4	12	10	26	18	30	20	26	18	8	6	NW
W	4	2	4	2	4	2	6	4	10	8	18	14	30	22	32	22	18	14	W
NW	0	0	0	0	2	0	4	2	8	6	12	10	22	18	30	22	10	8	SW
N (shade)	−2	−2	−2	−2	−2	−2	0	0	6	6	10	10	10	10	10	10	6	6	S (shade)
8-in. Brick or 12-in. Hollow Tile or 12-in. Cinder Block																			
NE	2	2	2	2	10	2	16	8	14	8	10	6	10	8	10	10	10	8	SE
E	8	6	8	6	14	8	18	10	18	10	14	8	14	10	14	10	12	10	E
SE	8	4	6	4	6	4	14	10	18	12	16	12	12	10	12	10	12	10	NE
S	4	2	4	2	4	2	4	2	10	6	16	10	16	12	12	10	10	8	N
SW	8	4	6	4	6	4	8	4	10	6	12	8	20	12	24	16	20	14	NW
W	8	4	6	4	6	6	8	4	10	6	14	8	20	16	24	16	24	16	W
NW	2	2	2	2	2	2	4	2	6	4	8	6	10	8	16	14	18	14	SW
N (shade)	0	0	0	0	0	0	0	0	2	2	6	6	8	8	8	8	6	6	S (shade)

Table 4-20. Total Equivalent Temperature Differentials for Calculating Heat Gain through Sunlit and Shaded Walls (Continued)

North latitude wall facing	8		10		12		2		4		6		8		10		12		South latitude wall facing
	D	L	D	L	D	L	D	L	D	L	D	L	D	L	D	L	D	L	
12-in. Brick																			
NE	8	6	8	6	8	4	8	4	10	4	12	6	12	6	10	6	10	6	SE
E	12	8	12	8	12	8	10	6	12	8	14	10	14	10	14	8	14	8	E
SE	10	6	10	6	10	6	10	6	10	6	12	8	14	10	14	10	12	8	NE
S	8	6	8	6	6	4	6	4	6	4	8	4	10	6	12	8	12	8	N
SW	10	6	10	6	10	6	10	6	10	6	10	8	10	8	12	8	14	10	NW
W	12	8	12	8	12	8	10	6	10	6	10	6	10	6	12	8	16	10	W
NW	8	6	8	6	8	4	8	4	8	4	8	4	8	6	10	6	10	6	SW
N (shade)	4	4	2	2	2	2	2	2	2	2	2	2	2	2	4	4	6	6	S (shade)
8-in. Concrete or Stone or 6- or 8-in. Concrete Block																			
NE	4	2	4	0	16	8	14	8	10	6	12	8	12	10	10	8	8	6	SE
E	6	4	14	8	24	12	24	12	18	10	14	10	14	10	12	10	10	8	E
SE	6	2	6	4	16	10	18	12	18	12	14	12	12	12	10	10	8	6	NE
S	2	1	2	1	4	1	12	6	16	12	18	12	14	12	10	8	8	6	N
SW	6	2	6	2	6	2	8	4	14	10	22	16	24	16	22	16	10	8	NW
W	6	4	6	4	6	4	8	6	12	8	20	14	28	18	26	18	14	10	W
NW	4	2	4	0	4	2	4	4	6	6	12	10	20	14	22	16	8	6	SW
N (shade)	0	0	0	0	0	0	2	2	4	4	6	6	8	8	6	6	4	4	S (shade)
12-in. Concrete or Stone																			
NE	6	4	6	2	6	2	14	8	14	8	10	8	10	8	12	10	10	8	SE
E	10	6	8	6	10	6	18	10	18	12	16	10	12	10	14	10	14	10	E
SE	8	4	8	4	6	4	14	8	16	10	16	10	14	10	12	10	12	10	NE
S	6	4	4	2	4	2	4	2	10	6	14	10	16	12	14	10	10	8	N
SW	8	4	8	4	6	4	6	4	6	4	10	8	18	14	20	14	18	12	NW
W	10	6	8	6	8	6	10	6	10	6	12	8	16	10	24	14	22	14	W
NW	6	4	6	2	6	2	6	4	6	4	8	6	10	8	18	12	20	14	SW
N (shade)	0	0	0	0	0	0	0	0	2	2	4	4	6	6	8	8	6	6	S (shade)

SOURCE: "ASHRAE Guide and Data Book," chap. 26, table 9, ASHRAE, New York, 1963.

Table 4-21. Total Equivalent Temperature Differentials for Calculating Heat Gain through Sunlit and Shaded Roofs

Description of roof construction	Sun time								
	A.M.			P.M.					
	8	10	12	2	4	6	8	10	12
Light-construction Roofs—Exposed to Sun									
1″ wood or 1″ wood + 1″ or 2″ insulation	12	38	54	62	50	26	10	4	0
Medium-construction Roofs—Exposed to Sun									
2″ concrete or 2″ concrete + 1″ or 2″ insulation or 2″ wood	6	30	48	58	50	32	14	6	2
2″ gypsum or 2″ gypsum + 1″ insulation 1″ wood or 2″ wood or } + 4″ rock wool in furred ceiling 2″ concrete or 2″ gypsum	0	20	40	52	54	42	20	10	6
4″ concrete or 4″ concrete with 2″ insulation	0	20	38	50	52	40	22	12	6
Heavy-construction Roofs—Exposed to Sun									
6″ concrete	4	6	24	38	46	44	32	18	12
6″ concrete + 2″ insulation	6	6	20	34	42	44	34	20	14
Roofs Covered with Water—Exposed to Sun									
Light-construction roof with 1″ water	0	4	16	22	18	14	10	2	0
Heavy-construction roof with 1″ water	−2	−2	−4	10	14	16	14	10	6
Any roof with 6″ water	−2	0	0	6	10	10	8	4	0
Roofs with Roof Sprays—Exposed to Sun									
Light construction	0	4	12	18	16	14	10	2	0
Heavy construction	−2	−2	2	8	12	14	12	10	6
Roofs in Shade									
Light construction	−4	0	6	12	14	12	8	2	0
Medium construction	−4	−2	2	8	12	12	10	6	2
Heavy construction	−2	−2	0	4	8	10	10	8	4

NOTE: For 0 to 50°N or S latitude in the hottest weather, 95°F maximum day outdoor temperature, 75°F minimum night temperature, 20°F daily range, 84°F 24-hr average, 80°F room temperature; all roofs assumed dark with 90 per cent absorbence.

SOURCE: "ASHRAE Guide and Data Book," chap. 26, table 8, ASHRAE, New York, 1963.

Table 4-22. Summer Coefficients of Heat Transmission U of Flat Roofs Covered with Built-up Roofing

Btu/(hr)(ft²)(°F difference between the air on the two sides)

Type of roof deck (ceiling not shown)	Thickness of roof deck, in.	No ceiling—underside of roof exposed					Furred ceiling with air space, metal lath, and plaster				
		No insulation	Insulating board thickness, in.				No insulation	Insulating board thickness, in.			
			½	1	1½	2		½	1	1½	2
Flat metal roof deck	4-ply felt roof	.73	.35	.23	.17	.13	.40	.25	.18	.14	.12
	+ ½-in. slag	.54	.30	.20	.16	.13	.34	.22	.16	.13	.11
Precast cement tile	4-ply felt roof 1⅝	.67	.33	.22	.17	.13	.38	.24	.18	.14	.12
	+ ½-in. slag 1⅝	.50	.28	.20	.15	.12	.32	.21	.17	.13	.11
Concrete	4-ply felt roof 2	.65	.33	.22	.16	.13	.37	.24	.18	.14	.12
	4	.59	.31	.21	.16	.13	.36	.23	.17	.13	.12
	6	.54	.30	.20	.16	.13	.33	.22	.17	.13	.11
	+ ½-in. slag 2	.49	.28	.20	.15	.12	.31	.21	.16	.13	.11
	4	.46	.27	.19	.15	.12	.30	.21	.16	.13	.11
	6	.42	.26	.19	.14	.12	.29	.20	.16	.13	.10
Gypsum and wood fiber on ½-in. gypsum board	4-ply felt roof 2½	.34	.23	.17	.13	.12	.25	.18	.14	.12	.097
	3½	.28	.20	.15	.12	.11	.21	.16	.13	.11	.094
	+ ½-in. slag 2½	.29	.20	.16	.13	.11	.22	.16	.13	.11	.093
	3½	.25	.18	.14	.12	.10	.19	.15	.13	.10	.090
Wood	4-ply felt roof 1	.43	.26	.19	.15	.12	.29	.20	.15	.13	.11
	1½	.33	.22	.17	.13	.11	.24	.18	.14	.12	.097
	2	.29	.20	.16	.13	.11	.20	.16	.13	.11	.094
	3	.22	.16	.13	.11	.09	.17	.13	.12	.10	.085
	+ ½-in. slag 1	.35	.23	.17	.14	.11	.25	.18	.14	.12	.10
	1½	.29	.20	.15	.12	.10	.21	.17	.13	.11	.093
	2	.26	.19	.14	.12	.10	.20	.15	.13	.10	.090
	3	.20	.15	.12	.10	.09	.16	.13	.11	.09	.081

SOURCE: "ASHRAE Guide and Data Book," chap. 26, table 10, ASHRAE, New York, 1963.

Table 4-23. Solar Heat Gain Factors,[a] Btu/(hr)(ft²), for August 21

Latitude	Sun time[b] A.M. ↓→	N	NE	E	SE	S	SW	W	NW	Horiz.	Sun time[c]
24°N	6 A.M.	7	46	56	31	2	2	2	2	8	6 P.M.
	7	12	130	173	116	9	9	9	9	54	5
	8	14	136	203	146	15	14	14	14	124	4
	9	18	104	185	148	27	18	18	18	188	3
	10	20	55	136	128	43	20	20	20	234	2
	11	22	23	65	89	54	22	22	22	264	1
	12 N	23	23	23	43	59	43	23	23	273	12 N
32°N	6 A.M.	8	60	74	41	3	3	3	3	11	6 P.M.
	7	9	126	173	124	9	9	9	9	55	5
	8	14	122	202	158	21	14	14	14	121	4
	9	18	84	184	166	46	18	18	17	179	3
	10	20	36	133	152	71	20	20	20	223	2
	11	21	21	64	115	91	25	21	21	250	1
	12 N	22	22	22	64	97	64	22	22	259	12 N
40°N	6 A.M.	8	70	88	51	3	3	3	4	13	6 P.M.
	7	9	120	174	127	9	9	9	9	55	5
	8	13	108	199	169	32	13	13	13	114	4
	9	17	65	180	183	69	17	17	17	168	3
	10	19	23	130	172	102	19	19	19	207	2
	11	20	20	62	141	126	37	20	20	231	1
	12 N	21	21	21	89	134	89	21	21	240	12 N
48°N	6 A.M.	8	79	100	59	4	4	4	4	16	6 P.M.
	7	9	113	174	129	11	9	9	9	56	5
	8	13	92	193	175	44	13	13	13	105	4
	9	16	46	175	195	91	16	16	16	152	3
	10	18	18	126	188	131	18	18	18	187	2
	11	19	19	60	155	156	56	19	19	209	1
	12 N	19	19	19	111	165	111	19	19	216	12 N
		N	NW	W	SW	S	SE	E	NE	Horiz.	←↑ P.M.

[a] Values in boldface are for hours when sun is striking fenestration.

[b] Values for *morning* hours must be selected by reading *down* for the proper direction listed at the *top* of the columns.

[c] Values for *afternoon* hours must be selected by reading *up* for the proper direction listed at the *bottom* of the columns.

SOURCE: "ASHRAE Guide and Data Book," chap. 26, table 13, ASHRAE, New York, 1963.

Table 4-24. Solar Heat Gain Factors,[a] Btu(hr)(ft²), for October 21

Latitude	Sun time[b] A.M. ↓→	N	NE	E	SE	S	SW	W	NW	Horiz.	Sun time[c]
24°N	6 A.M. 7 8 9 10 11 12 N	... **7** 13 16 18 19 19	... **53** 63 37 20 20 20	... **106** 174 172 128 64 21	... **97** 179 203 193 158 109	... **26** 70 107 135 153 160	... **7** 13 17 20 51 109	... **6** 12 15 18 20 21	... **6** 12 15 17 19 20	... **16** 72 131 185 217 229	6 P.M. 5 4 3 2 1 12 N
32°N	6 A.M. 7 8 9 10 11 12 N	... **5** 12 15 17 17 18	... **38** 51 25 18 19 18	... **84** 162 166 122 61 19	... **73** 167 202 202 175 126	... **22** 72 118 156 180 186	... **5** 12 16 23 69 126	... **4** 11 14 17 19 19	... **4** 11 13 16 18 18	... **10** 54 102 154 188 197	6 P.M. 5 4 3 2 1 12 N
40°N	6 A.M. 7 8 9 10 11 12 N	... **3** 10 13 15 16 16	... **23** 39 18 17 17 17	... **55** 141 150 115 57 19	... **40** 153 194 202 182 139	... **15** 71 127 167 194 202	... **3** 10 14 28 82 139	... **3** 9 13 16 18 19	... **3** 9 12 14 16 17	... **5** 37 81 122 151 161	6 P.M. 5 4 3 2 1 12 N
48°N	6 A.M. 7 8 9 10 11 12 N	... **2** 8 11 13 14 14	... **12** 29 14 15 15 15	... **22** 113 134 106 53 17	... **25** 126 181 196 181 143	... **7** 62 122 168 195 205	... **2** 8 13 37 90 143	... **1** 7 11 14 16 17	... **1** 7 10 13 14 15	... **2** 22 63 90 109 115	6 P.M. 5 4 3 2 1 12 N
		N	NW	W	SW	S	SE	E	NE	Horiz.	←↑ P.M.

[a] Values in boldface are for hours when sun is striking fenestration.
[b] Values for *morning* hours must be selected by reading *down* for the proper direction listed at the *top* of the columns.
[c] Values for *afternoon* hours must be selected by reading *up* for the proper direction listed at the *bottom* of the columns.
SOURCE: "ASHRAE Guide and Data Book," chap. 26, table 15, ASHRAE, New York, 1963.

Table 4-25. Shading Coefficients—Single Glass and Insulating Glass^a—No Shading

Single glass

Type of glass	Nominal thickness, in.	Solar transmittance^b	Glass in sun	Glass in shade
Regular sheet	7/32–1/8	0.86	1.00	1.00
Regular plate	1/4	.80	.95	.95
	3/8	.75	.91	.91
	1/2	.71	.88	.88
Heat-abs^d sheet	7/32	.51	.71	.78
Heat-abs^d plate	1/4	.46	.67	.74
	3/8	.34	.57	.64
Gray^e sheet	1/8	.59	.78	.78
	3/16	.74	.90	.90
	7/32	.45	.66	.66
	7/32	.71	.88	.88
Gray^e plate	1/4	.67	.88	.88
	13/64	.52	.72	.72
	1/4	.47	.70	.70
	3/8	.33	.56	.56
	1/2	.24	.50	.50

Insulating glass^a

Type of glass	Nominal thickness,^b,c in.	Solar transmittance^b Outer pane	Inner pane	Glass in sun	Glass in shade
Regular sheet out, regular sheet in	7/32–7/8	0.86	0.86	0.90	0.84
Regular plate out, regular plate in	1/4	.80	.80	.83	.77
Heat-abs.^d plate out, regular plate in	1/4	.46	.80	.56	.53
Gray^e plate out, regular plate in	1/4	.46	.80	.56	.53
Gray^e plate with sun control film out, regular plate in	1/4	.23	.80	.36	.36

^a Refers to factory-fabricated units with 3/16, 1/4, or 1/2 in. air space or to prime windows plus storm windows.

^b Refer to manufacturer's literature for values.

^c Thickness of each pane of glass, not thickness of assembled unit.

^d Heat-absorbing sheet does not meet radiant-transmittance requirements of Federal Specification DD-G-451a. Heat-absorbing plate meets these requirements. Consult manufacturer's data for specific solar transmittances.

^e Glare-reducing glasses other than gray in color will have approximately equal shading coefficients for equal solar transmittances. Consult manufacturer's data for specific product values.

Table 4-26. Shading Coefficients—Single Glass with Indoor Shading

Type of glass	Nominal thickness,[a] in.	Solar transmittance[a]	Type of shading													
			Venetian blinds				Draperies						Roller shade, opaque			
			Light		Medium		Light		Medium		Dark		Light		Dark	
			Glass in sun	Glass in shade	Glass in sun	Glass in shade	Glass in sun	Glass in shade	Glass in sun	Glass in shade	Glass in sun	Glass in shade	Glass in sun	Glass in shade	Glass in sun	Glass in shade
Regular sheet	3/32–1/4	0.87–0.80	0.55	0.60	0.64	0.66	0.56	0.51	0.61	0.55	0.66	0.60	0.25	0.22	0.59	0.61
Regular plate	1/4–1/2	0.80–0.71														
Regular pattern	1/8–9/32	0.87–0.79														
Heat-abs. pattern	1/8	0.74, 0.71														
Gray sheet	3/16, 7/32															
Heat-abs.[b] sheet	7/32	0.51	.53	.52	.57	.58	.48	.43	.52	.47	.56	.51	.30	.30	.45	.42
Heat-abs.[b] plate	1/4	0.46														
Heat-abs. pattern	3/16, 7/32	0.59, 0.45														
Gray[c] sheet	19/64, 1/4	0.52, 0.45														
Gray[c] plate																
Heat-abs.[b] sheet, plate, or pattern	.....	0.44–0.30	.52	.52	.54	.53	.44	.40	.48	.43	.52	.47	.28	.26	.40	.36
Heat-abs.[b] plate	3/8	0.34														
Gray[d] plate	3/8	0.33														
Heat-abs.[b] sheet, plate, or pattern	.....	0.29–0.15	.50	.50	.51	.51	.42	.38	.46	.41	.50	.45	.28	.25	.36	.32
Gray[c] plate	1/2	0.24														

[a] Refer to manufacturer's literature for values.
[b] See footnote d, Table 4-25.
[c] See footnote e, Table 4-25.

SOURCE: "ASHRAE Guide and Data Book," chap. 26, table 20, ASHRAE, New York, 1963.

Table 4-27. Shading Coefficients—Insulating Glass[a] with Indoor Shading

Type of glass	Nominal thickness[d]	Solar transmittance[c] Outer pane	Solar transmittance[c] Inner pane	Venetian blinds — Light, Glass in sun	Venetian blinds — Light, Glass in shade	Venetian blinds — Medium, Glass in sun	Venetian blinds — Medium, Glass in shade	Draperies — Light, Glass in sun	Draperies — Light, Glass in shade	Draperies — Medium, Glass in sun	Draperies — Medium, Glass in shade	Draperies — Dark, Glass in sun	Draperies — Dark, Glass in shade	Roller shade, opaque — Light, Glass in sun	Roller shade, opaque — Light, Glass in shade	Roller shade, opaque — Dark, Glass in sun	Roller shade, opaque — Dark, Glass in shade
Regular sheet out, regular sheet in	3/32, 1/8	0.86	0.86	0.51	0.51	0.57	0.55	0.54	0.49	0.59	0.53	0.64	0.58	0.25	0.22	0.60	0.55
Regular plate out, regular plate in	1/4	.80	.80														
Heat-abs.[e] plate out, regular plate in	1/4	.46	.80	.36	.36	.39	.38	.41	.37	.43	.39	.45	.41	.22	.20	.40	.37
Gray[f] plate out, regular plate in	1/4	.46	.80														

[a] Refers to factory-fabricated units with 3/16, 1/4, or 1/2 in. air space, or to prime windows plus storm windows.
[b] See text section basic data for properties of types of shading.
[c] Refer to manufacturer's literature for values.
[d] Thickness of each pane of glass, not thickness of assembled unit.
[e] See footnote d, Table 4-25.
[f] See footnote e, Table 4-25.
SOURCE: "ASHRAE Guide and Data Book," chap. 26, table 21, ASHRAE, New York, 1963.

Table 4-28. Shading Coefficients—Double Glazing with Between-glass Shading

Type of glass	Nominal thickness[c]	Solar transmittance[b]		Description of air space	Type of shading[a]					
					Venetian blinds				Louvered sun screen	
					Light		Medium			
		Outer pane	Inner pane		Glass in sun	Glass in shade	Glass in sun	Glass in shade	Glass in sun	Glass in shade
Regular sheet out, regular sheet in	3/32, 1/8	0.86	0.86	Shade in contact with glass or shade separated from glass by air space	0.33	0.37	0.36	0.40	0.43[d]	0.43
Regular plate out, regular plate in	1/4	.80	.80	Shade in contact with glass-voids filled with plastic	....	....	....	....	.49[d]	.48
Heat-abs.[e] plate out, regular plate in	1/4	.46	.80	Shade in contact with glass or shade separated from glass by air space	.28	.30	.30	.31	.37[d]	.4)
Gray[f] plate out, regular plate in	1/4	.46	.80	Shade in contact with glass-voids filled with plastic	....	....	....	....	.41[d]	.42

[a] See text section basic data for properties of types of shading.
[b] Refer to manufacturer's literature for values.
[c] Thickness of each pane of glass, not thickness of assembled unit.
[d] See text section basic data for limitations of values.
[e] See footnote d, Table 4-25.
[f] See footnote e, Table 4-25.
SOURCE: "ASHRAE Guide and Data Book," chap. 26, table 22, ASHRAE, New York, 1963.

Table 4-29. U Values for Various Fenestration (for 7½-mph Wind)
Btu/(ft²)(°F)

Type of glass	U value	
	No shading	Shading[a]
Any single glass............................	1.06	0.81
Insulating glass:		
³⁄₁₆ in. air space...........................	0.64	.54
¼ in. air space...........................	.61	.52
½ in. air space...........................	.56	.48
Prime window plus storm window, air space 1 in.		
or more.................................	.54[b]	.47[b]

Type of glass	No supplementary shading
Double glazing with between-glass shading:	
Louvered sun screen:	
In contact with glass.....................	0.95
Separated by air space....................	.63
Venetian blinds...........................	.44

[a] Values apply to tightly closed venetian blinds, draperies, and roller shades.
[b] Values apply to storm sash with a tight air space. Air leakage present in virtually all storm windows will, in effect, increase this value.
SOURCE: "ASHRAE Guide and Data Book," chap. 26, table 18, ASHRAE, New York, 1963.

Table 4-30. Rates of Heat Gain from Occupants
Based on 80°F Dry-bulb Conditioned Space Temperature

Degree of activity	Typical application	Heat gain from occupants based on normal percentage of men, women, and children present, Btu/hr		
		Total heat	Sensible heat	Latent heat
Seated at rest	Theater	350	195	155
Seated, very light work	Offices, apartments	400	195	205
Moderately active work, standing, walking slowly	Offices, apartments, stores	450	200	250
Light bench work	Factory	750	220	530
Dancing	Dance hall	850	245	605
Moderately heavy work	Factory	1,000	300	700
Heavy work	Factory	1,450	465	985

Table 4-31. Internal Heat Gains for Electric Motors and Domestic Appliances

Electric Motors

Nameplate rating of motor, hp	Average motor efficiency in continuous operation	Btu/hr to room air per rated hp of motor		
		Motor outside of room, driven device inside room	Motor in room, driven device outside of room	Motor and driven device both inside room
⅛–½	0.60	2546	1700	4246
½–3	.69	2546	1100	3646
3–20	.85	2546	400	2946

General rule for motors: if H_m = Btu/hr of motor input,

$$H_m = \frac{2{,}546 \times hp \text{ (connected load)}}{\text{motor efficiency}}$$

NOTE: Where possible obtain actual value of motor efficiency. Where not possible: for motors, use average efficiencies as listed above; for motor generators, use average efficiency for sets up to 3 hp as 0.55; for larger sets, use average efficiency as 0.80.

Electric Motor-driven Appliances
Motor and Driven Appliance Both in Same Room

Fans (blade diameters, in.)	Btu/hr	Appliances	Btu/hr
Ceiling 32	340	Clock.........................	7
52	410	Hair dryer.....................	1900
56	600	Drink mixer....................	240
Desk or wall 8	120	Sewing machine (domestic).......	220
10	140	Vacuum cleaner (domestic).......	250
12	200	Hair clipper...................	78
16	300	Vibrator (beauty)..............	11

NOTE: Figures are thermal equivalents of nameplate rating, corrected for motor efficiency.

NOTE: Figures are thermal equivalents of nameplate ratings.

Electric Refrigerators

Electric motor and air-cooled condenser in cabinet in room air		Cold Cabinet in Room (compressor and condenser remote) With well-insulated cabinet in 80°F air and 40°F inside cabinet allow a cooling effect as follows:	
Cabinet volume, ft³	Btu/hr (thermal equivalent of motor input)	Cabinet volume, ft³	Btu/(hr)(ft³) of cabinet volume
2–4	530	2–4	100–75
5	710	5–6	70–65
6–10	850	7–10	60–55
12–18	1060	12, 14, 16	55–50
		20, 25, 30	50, 45, 40

Table 4-31. Internal Heat Gains for Electric Motors and Domestic Appliances (Continued)

Miscellaneous Electric Appliances

Type of appliance	Btu/hr	Type of appliance	Btu/hr
Domestic electric irons:		Radio (6 to 8 tubes)................	340
Small..........................		Infrared lamp (heat)................	850
Medium.......................	2300	Sun lamp.........................	1350
Large..........................	3400	Neon lights (15 mm), per ft..........	12
Tumbler water heaters...............	1200	Neon lights (11 mm), per ft..........	18
Curling irons........................	70	Permanent waver (beauty)..........	4240

NOTE: Figures are thermal equivalent of nameplate rating of typical example of appliance listed.

SOURCE: Clifford Strock, "Engineering Data Book," The Industrial Press, New York, 1948.

Table 4-32. Rate of Heat Gain from Miscellaneous Appliances

Appliance	Manufacturer's rating		Recommended rate of heat gain, Btu/hr		
	Watts	Btu/hr	Sensible	Latent	Total
Electrical Appliances					
Hair dryer:					
Blower type.............................	1,580	5,400	2,300	400	2,700
Helmet type.............................	705	2,400	1,870	330	2,200
Permanent-wave machine, 60 heaters at 25 w, 36 in normal use.........................	1,500	5,000	850	150	1,000
Neon sign, per linear foot of tube:					
½″ diam...............................	.....	.....	30	.....	30
⅜″ diam...............................	.....	.....	60	.....	60
Sterilizer, instrument........................	1,100	3,750	650	1,200	1,850
Gas-burning Appliances					
Lab burners:					
Bunsen, ⁷⁄₁₆″ barrel.......................	.....	3,000	1,680	420	2,100
Fishtail, 1½″ wide........................	.....	5,000	2,800	700	3,500
Meeker, 1″ diam..........................	.....	6,000	3,360	840	4,200
Gaslight, per burner, mantle type............	.....	2,000	1,800	200	2,000
Cigar lighter, continuous flame................	.....	2,500	900	100	1,000

SOURCE: "ASHRAE Guide and Data Book," chap. 26, table 32, ASHRAE, New York, 1963.

Table 4-33. Design Room Conditions Usually Specified for Summer Average Peak Load in Comfort Air Conditioning[a]

Type of installation	Dry-bulb temp.	Wet-bulb temp.[$'$]	Relative humidity per cent	Grains/lb[b]	Effective temp.
Ample capacity.................	78	65	50	72.7	72.2
Practical application...........	80	67	51	78.5	74.0
Occupancy 15 to 40 min.......	82	68	49	80.0	75.3

[a] Values are for *peak load* conditions. It is general practice to operate a system at approximately 75°F and 50 per cent relative humidity at other than peak load.

[b] Psychrometric data for standard barometric pressure.

SOURCE: "ASHRAE Heating, Ventilating, and Air Conditioning Guide," chap. 13, table 1, ASHRAE, New York. 1960.

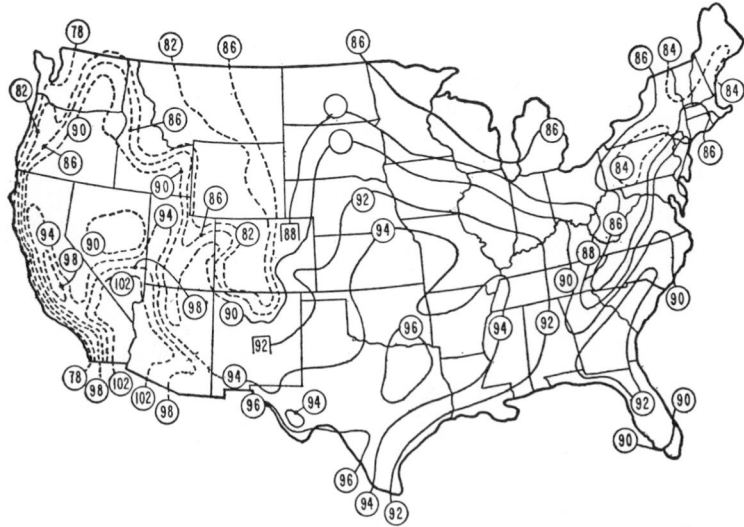

FIG. 4-12. Design dry-bulb temperatures at the 5 per cent level. Each line passes through the localities at which the noted dry-bulb temperature is equaled or exceeded 5 per cent of the time during the average 4-month summer season.

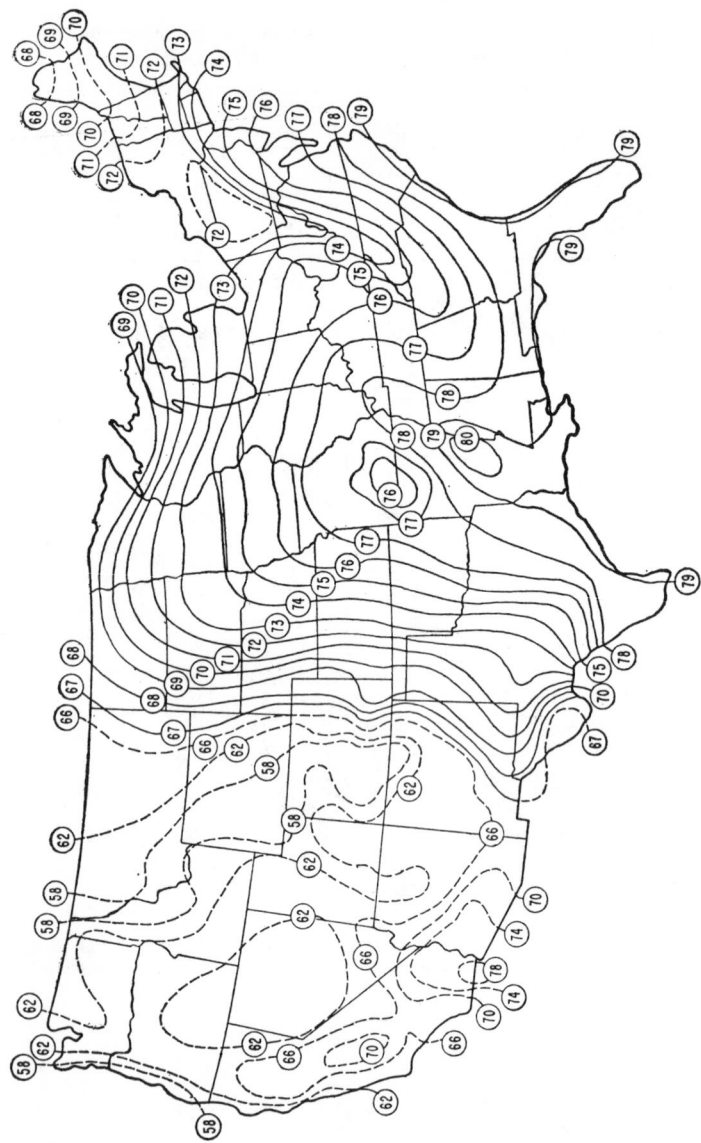

Fig. 4-13. Design wet-bulb temperatures at the 5 per cent level. Each line passes through the localities at which the noted wet-bulb temperature is equaled or exceeded 5 per cent of the time during the average 4-month summer season.

Supply Air Temperature. The room cooling load is the sum of external and internal sensible and latent heat gains plus the difference in enthalpy between outside and room air for that portion of outside air that does not contact the cooling-coil surfaces. The percentage of air that passes through a cooling coil untreated is the numerical value of the *coil bypass factor;* e.g., a bypass factor of 20 per cent represents a cooling-coil saturation efficiency of 80 per cent.

The ratio of room sensible heat gains to total room sensible and latent heat gains is the room *sensible heat ratio* (RSHR).

$$\text{RSHR} = Q_{rs}/Q_{rs} + Q_{rl} \tag{4-27}$$

It represents the ratio of sensible cooling capacity to the total cooling capacity required of the supply air to satisfy room conditions. It is used to plot the slope of the *room-condition line* on a psychrometric chart (Fig. 4-14) for the determination of the *apparatus dew point* (ADP).

The actual supply air temperature and off coil wet-bulb temperature will depend on the bypass characteristic of the selected cooling coil (Fig. 4-15).

Supply Air Rate. The rate of supply air required is expressed by

$$Q_{sa} = Q_{rs}/1.08(t_r - t_s) \tag{4-28}$$

where Q_{sa} = supply air, cfm

t_r = room design temperature, °F

t_s = supply air temperature, °F

$1.08 = (60 \text{ min})[0.244 \text{ Btu}/(\text{lb})(°F)](0.075 \text{ lb/ft}^3) \tag{4-29}$

4-6. Air Distribution

Outlets. *Purpose.* Outlets are designed:

1. To control air motion, noise level, and temperature gradients caused by the introduction of air to and the removal of air from a space

2. To counteract the natural convection and radiation effects within the room

Supply Outlets. Supply outlets should be selected on the basis of manufacturers' data. Factors which usually affect the selection of supply outlets are (1) noise, (2) location of outlet, (3) temperature of supply air, and (4) area of diffusion.

Return Outlets. Selection of return registers or grilles is usually governed by face velocity.

Table 4-34. Recommended Return Intake Face Velocities

Intake Location	Velocity over Gross Area, FPM
Above occupied zone	800 up
Within occupied zone, not near seats	600–800
Within occupied zone, near seats	400–600
Door or wall louvers	200–300
Undercutting of doors (through undercut area)	200–300

SOURCE: "Heating, Ventilating, Air Conditioning Guide," chap. 31, table 2, ASHRAE New York, 1955.

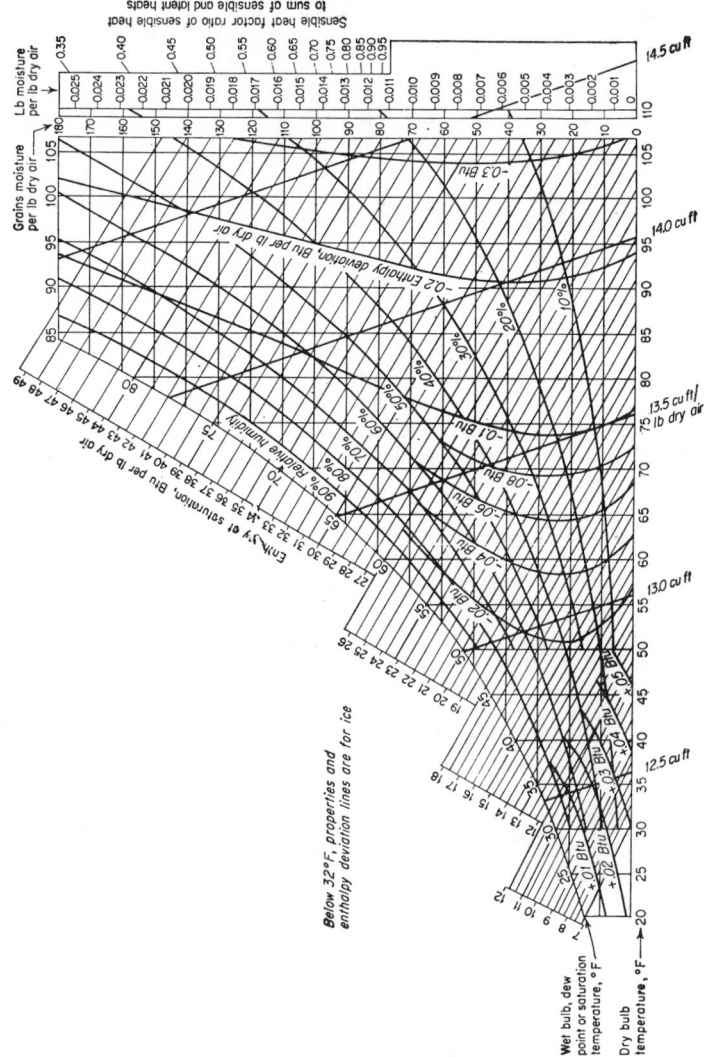

FIG. 4-14. Psychrometric chart—normal temperatures.

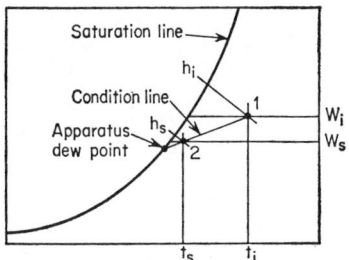

Fig. 4-15. Apparatus dew-point and condition line.

Ductwork. *Air Velocity.* Supply and return air ducts and apparatus are sized on the basis of air quantity, within the limitations of allowable friction losses, velocity, and noise.

Table 4-35. Recommended and Maximum Duct Velocities for Conventional Systems

Designation	Residences	Schools, theaters, public buildings	Industrial buildings
Recommended velocities, fpm			
Outdoor air intakes*.........	500	500	500
Filters*....................	250	300	350
Heating coils*..............	450	500	600
Air washers................	500	500	500
Fan outlets.................	1,000–1,600	1,300–2,000	1,600–2,400
Main ducts.................	700–900	1,000–1,300	1,200–1,800
Branch ducts..............	600	600–900	800–1,000
Branch risers..............	500	600–700	800
Maximum velocities, fpm			
Outdoor air intakes*.........	800	900	1,200
Filters*....................	300	350	350
Heating coils*..............	500	600	700
Air washers................	500	500	500
Fan outlets.................	1,700	1,500–2,200	1,700–2,800
Main ducts.................	800–1,200	1,100–1,600	1,300–2,200
Branch ducts..............	700–1,000	800–1,300	1,000–1,800
Branch risers..............	650–800	800–1,200	1,000–1,600

*These velocities are for total face area, not the net free area; other velocities in the table are for net free area.

SOURCE: "ASHRAE Guide and Data Book," chap. 12, table 6, ASHRAE, New York, 1963.

High-velocity air distribution (2,000 to 6,000 fpm) using much smaller ducts and operating at greater pressures is used when space is critical.

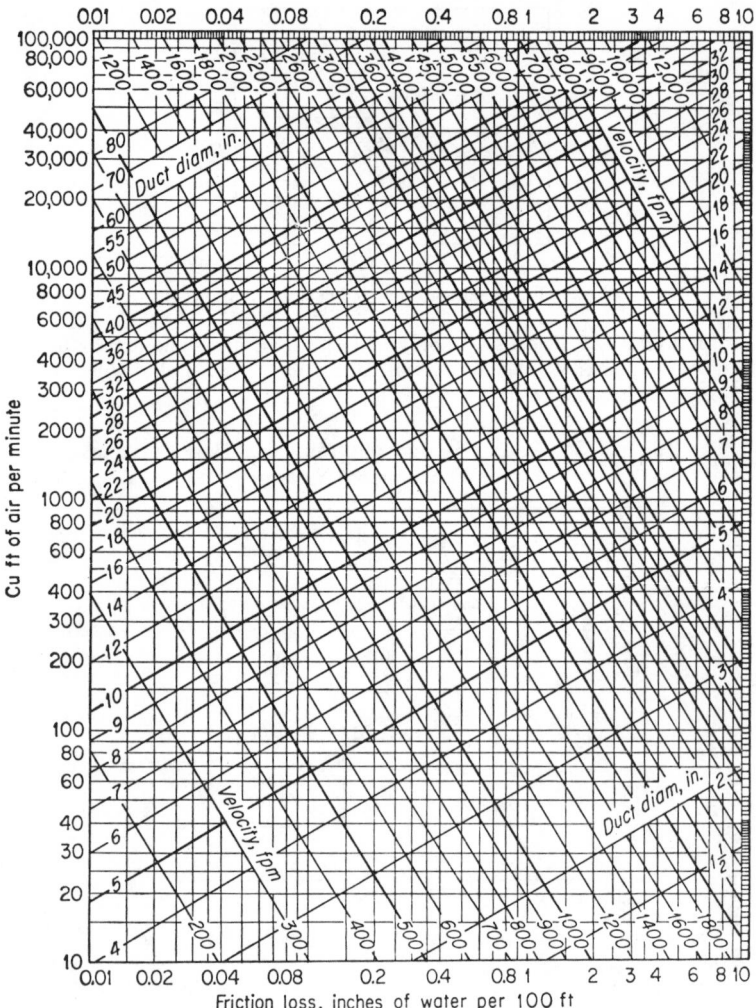

Fig. 4-16. Friction loss for usual air conditions. This chart applies to smooth round galvanized-iron ducts, and is based on air at 70°F and 29.96 in. Hg abs pressure. For air of different density the friction may be assumed to vary directly with the density.

Pressure Losses in Duct Systems. Pressure losses in duct systems are due to friction of the air in contact with the sides of the duct and dynamic losses caused by changes of duct shape or direction and by obstructions to flow.

Friction:
$$H_f = \frac{fL/D}{V^2/4,005} \tag{4-30}$$

where H_f = head loss due to friction, in. H_2O

L = length of duct, ft

D = diameter of duct, ft

V = velocity of air, fpm

f = nondimensional friction coefficient

Dynamic losses: $H_v = CV^2/4,005$

where H_v = velocity-head loss, in. H_2O

C = experimentally determined constant

V = air velocity, fpm

Design Methods. The *equal-friction method* is applicable primarily to systems using low or moderate velocities where the velocity head is not an important factor. A friction drop per 100 ft of length is chosen, and the duct mains and branches are all sized on the basis of this friction drop. This will invariably result in higher velocities in the mains, where they can be tolerated, and low velocities in the branches, where they are desirable.

Table 4-36. Friction Drops

Application	Friction Drop, In. H_2O/100 Ft
Noise critical, low velocity	0.05–0.07
Average application	0.08–0.1
Equipment rooms, industrial applications	0.11–0.13

The *static-regain method* is used for both conventional and high-velocity systems. It is especially applicable in the latter, where the velocity head may be appreciable. In the static-regain method, the static pressure required to give proper air flow through the system outlets is determined, and this pressure is maintained by reducing the velocity at each branch or takeoff, so that the recovery in pressure due to reduction of velocity balances the friction loss in the preceding section of duct. This is possible because of the convertibility of static and velocity pressures. For practical applications it is usually assumed that 50 per cent of the velocity pressure available will be converted to static pressure.

$$H_R = 0.5V_1^2/4,005 - V_2^2/4,005 \tag{4-31}$$

where H_R = head recovered, in. H_2O

V_1 = system inlet velocity, fpm

V_2 = system outlet velocity, fpm

Fans. *Fan Laws*

Quantity required	Cfm	Total head delivered by wheel	Rpm	Hp	Wheel diam*
Cfm..........................	....	$H_t^{1/2}$	rpm†	$hp^{1/3}$	D
Total head delivered by wheel.....	cfm^2	.....	rpm^2	$hp^{2/3}$	D^2
Rpm..........................	cfm	$H_t^{1/2}$	.....	$hp^{1/3}$	
Hp...........................	cfm^3	$H_t^{3/2}$	rpm^3	....	D^3

* Constant speed.
† Constant head.

Equations

$$\text{Mechanical efficiency} = \frac{0.0001575 \times cfm \times \text{total pressure, in. } H_2O}{\text{horsepower input}} \qquad (4\text{-}32)$$

Equation (4-32) is applicable to fans operating with high outlet velocity pressure relative to static pressure.

$$\text{Static efficiency} = \frac{0.0001573 \times cfm \times \text{static pressure, in. } H_2O}{\text{horsepower input}} \qquad (4\text{-}33)$$

Equation (4-33) is more applicable to fans with high static pressure relative to velocity pressure.

Characteristics

Table 4-37. Relative Characteristics of Centrifugal Fans

Characteristic	Backward	Radial	Forward
First cost................	High	Medium	Low
Efficiency...............	High	Medium	Poor
Stability of operation......	Good	Good	Poor
Space required...........	Medium	Medium	Small
Tip speed...............	High	Medium	Low
Resistance to abrasion.....	Medium	Good	Poor

Table 4-38. Outlet Velocities for Optimum Performance of Typical Ventilating Fans

Static pressure, in. water	Centrifugal fans— outlet velocity, fpm	Tube-axial and vane-axial fans— outlet velocity at wheel diam., fpm
¼	400–1,100	950–1,500
½	550–1,300	1,350–1,900
¾	700–1,500	1,650–2,350
1	800–1,750	1,900–2,700
1½	1,000–2,450	2,350–3,300
2	1,150–2,800	2,700–3,800
2½	1,250–3,200	3,000–4,300
3	1,400–3,500	3,300–4,700
4	1,600–4,000	
6	2,000–4,900	
8	2,300–5,650	
10	2,500–6,300	

SOURCE: "ASHRAE Guide and Data Book," chap. 40, fig. 1, ASHRAE, New York, 1963.

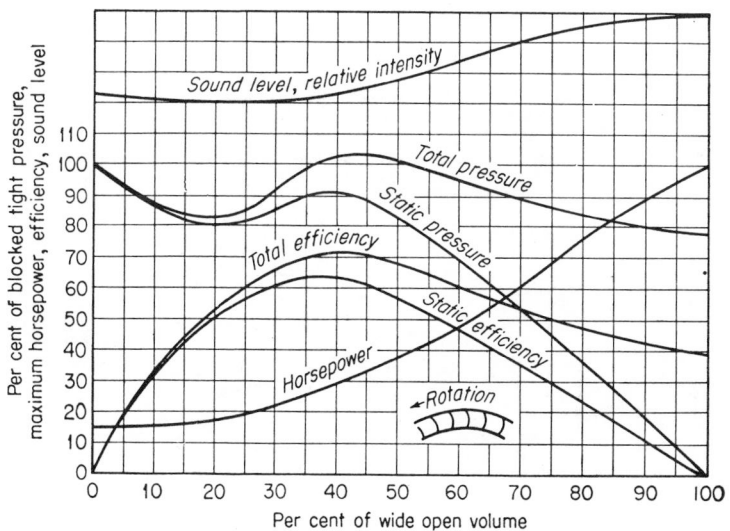

FIG. 4-17. Percentage performance curves of a forward-blade centrifugal fan.

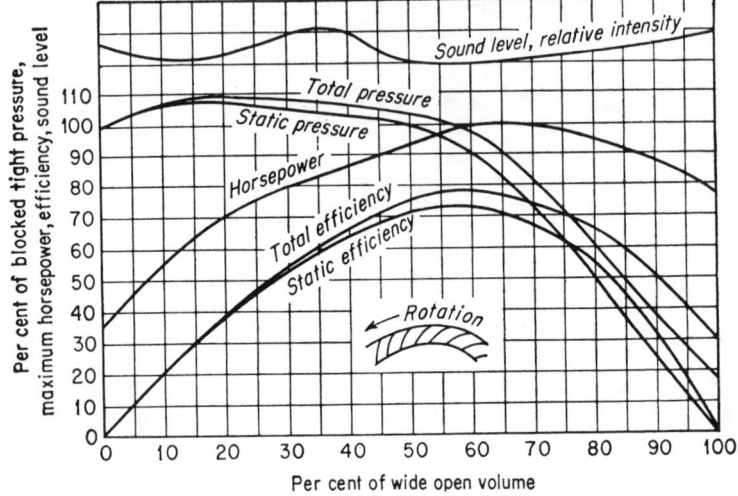

Fig. 4-18. Percentage performance curves of a backward-curved-blade centrifugal fan.

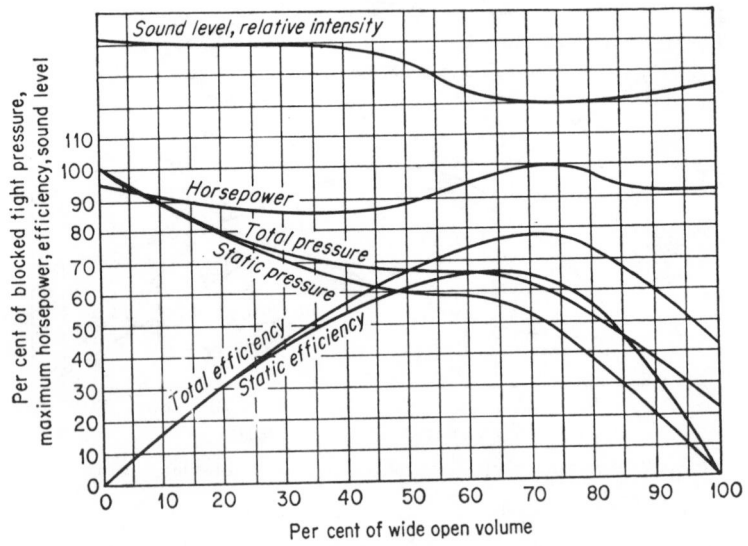

Fig. 4-19. Percentage performance curves of an axial-flow fan.

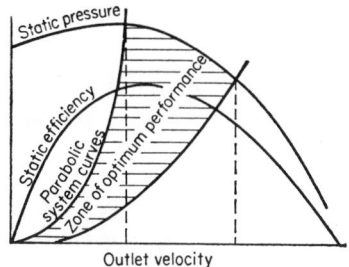

Fig. 4-20. Zone of optimum performance for fans.

Correction Factors for Temperature and Altitude

Table 4-39. Correction Factor for Altitude and Temperature to Air Volume

Altitude, ft above sea level....	0	1,000	2,000	3,000	4,000	5,000	6,000	7,000	8,000
Barometric pressure, in. Hg...	29.92	28.86	27.82	26.81	25.84	24.89	23.98	23.09	22.22
Air temp, °F	Correction factors								
70	1.040	1.003	0.967	0.932	0.898	0.865	0.833	0.803	0.772
100	0.984	0.948	.915	.882	.850	.818	.788	.759	.731
150	.904	.872	.840	.801	.781	.752	.724	.698	.672
200	.835	.805	.777	.749	.722	.694	.668	.645	.620
250	.777	.749	.722	.696	.671	.647	.622	.599	.577
300	.725	.699	.674	.649	.628	.603	.580	.560	.538
350	.680	.656	.632	.609	.588	.566	.545	.525	.505
400	.641	.618	.596	.574	.553	.533	.512	.495	.476
450	.605	.583	.564	.543	.523	.503	.485	.467	.450
500	.574	.553	.534	.515	.496	.477	.460	.443	.426
550	.546	.526	.508	.490	.472	.454	.438	.421	.406
600	.520	.501	.484	.466	.449	.433	.416	.401	.387
650	.496	.478	.462	.444	.428	.413	.397	.383	.368
700	.475	.458	.442	.426	.411	.395	.381	.367	.354

NOTE: Equivalent cfm = $\dfrac{\text{cfm at actual conditions}}{\text{correction factor}}$

SOURCE: "Bulletin 3576-B, Correction Factors for Temperature and Altitude," Buffalo Forge Co., Buffalo, N.Y.

4-7. Refrigeration

Refrigeration cycles are discussed in Sec. 8. Thermodynamic data for typical refrigerants are given in Secs. 3 and 8.

4-8. Water Distribution

Chilled-water Systems

Temperature differential

Application	Temperature rise, °F
Close-coupled system on one floor..............	5–8
Two- or three-story building.................	8–11
Multistory building........................	12–20

$$\text{Gpm} = \frac{\text{total load Btu/hr} + \text{piping heat gains} + \text{pump heat}}{500 \times \text{temperature differential}} \quad (4\text{-}34)$$

Condenser Water Systems. For electrically driven refrigeration compressors a temperature differential of 10°F may be assumed, and for steam-driven equipment a temperature differential of 20°F is usual. In the latter case the refrigeration and steam condensers are piped in series with a temperature rise of approximately 10°F each.

Table 4-40. Heat Rejection of Typical Processes

Equipment	Btu/min/ton	Btu/kwhr	Btu/bhp-hr
Refrigeration compressors, open drive..........	250		
Refrigeration compressors, hermetic............	300		
Refrigeration absorption system................	550		
Steam jet refrigerating system................	550		
Steam electric power plant, kw:			
500...................................	...	11,210	
1,000..................................	...	10,750	
5,000..................................	...	8,150	
7,500..................................	...	7,700	
10,000.................................	...	7,020	
Diesel engine jacket and lube oil:			
Four-cycle, supercharged....................	...	.....	2,600
Four-cycle, nonsupercharged.................	...	.....	3,000
Two-cycle, crank-case compressor............	...	.....	2,000
Two-cycle, pump-scavenging (large unit)......	...	.....	2,500
Two-cycle, pump-scavenging (high-speed).....	...	.....	2,200
Natural-gas engine:			
Four-cycle...............................	...	.....	4,500
Two-cycle................................	...	.....	4,000

SOURCE: "ASHRAE Guide and Data Book," chap. 37, table 4, ASHRAE, New York, 1961.

Atmospheric Cooling Equipment. The lowest temperature to which water can be cooled in atmospheric cooling equipment is the wet-bulb temperature of the ambient air.

Water Cooling Effectiveness in Per Cent

$$E = \frac{(\text{hot-water temperature—cold-water temperature}) \times 100}{\text{hot-water temperature—wet-bulb temperature of entering air}} \quad (4\text{-}35)$$

The cold-water temperature must be chosen to place the requirement within the effectiveness range of the equipment used.

Table 4-41. Effectiveness of Water Cooling Equipment

Cooling equipment	Water cooling effectiveness, %		
	Minimum	Typical	Maximum
Spray ponds..........................	30	40–50	68
Spray-filled atmospheric towers......	40	45–55	60
Atmospheric deck towers.............	50	50–60	90
Mechanical draft towers.............	50	55–75	93

SOURCE: "Heating, Ventilating, and Air Conditioning Guide," chap. 34, table 3, ASHRAE, New York, 1958

Makeup Water. Makeup water is introduced to replace losses due to evaporation, drift, and blowdown.

If all water were cooled by evaporation, the loss by evaporation for the usual 10°F cooling range would be

$$\text{Evaporation } \% = \frac{Q \times 100}{8.3 \times \text{gpm} \times h_{fg}} \qquad (4\text{-}36)$$

where Q = total heat rejected, Btu/hr

gpm = total condenser water circulated, gpm

h_{fg} = evaporation heat of water, Btu/lb, at ambient design temperature

In practice, the loss of circulating water by evaporation due to additional cooling by sensible heat transfer will vary from about 0.64 per cent in winter to 0.88 per cent in the summer for a water-cooling range of 10°F.

Drift losses depend on the tower design, but generally, from the cooling tower, they are limited to 0.2 per cent of the circulated rate.

The makeup water replacing losses due to evaporation, drift, and blowdown introduces dissolved solids into the system.

To prevent excessive concentration, a portion of the circulating water is wasted. The quantity of blowdown depends on the original quantity of dissolved solids in the makeup water and the permissible concentration.

For larger installation, chemical water-treatment processes are used, which also require a controlled blowdown rate.

4-9. Pumps

The performance of pumps is discussed in Sec. 8. Methods for calculating pressure drop in pipe and fittings are presented in Sec. 2.

4-10. Drainage

Sanitary Load

Table 4-42. Fixture Units per Fixture or Group

Fixture type	Fixture-unit value as load factors	Min size trap, in.
Bathroom group consisting of water closet, lavatory, and bathtub or shower stall:		
Tank water closet..............................	6	
Flush-valve water closet.........................	8	
Bathtub (with or without overhead shower)..........	2	1½
Bathtub...	3	2
Bidet..	3	1½*
Combination sink and tray........................	3	1½
Combination sink and tray with food-disposal unit.....	4	1½†
Dental unit or cuspidor...........................	1	1¼
Dental lavatory...................................	1	1¼
Drinking fountain.................................	½	1
Dishwasher, domestic.............................	2	1½
Floor drains......................................	1	2
Kitchen sink, domestic............................	2	1½
Kitchen sink, domestic with food-disposal unit........	3	1½
Lavatory, small P.O..............................	1	1¼
Lavatory, large P.O..............................	2	1½
Lavatory, barber, beauty parlor....................	2	1½
Lavatory, surgeon's...............................	2	1½
Laundry tray (1 or 2 compartments)................	2	1½
Shower stall, domestic............................	2	2
Showers (group) per head.........................	3	
Sinks:		
Surgeon's......................................	3	1½
Flushing rim (with valve)........................	8	3
Service (trap standard)..........................	3	3
Service (P trap).................................	2	2
Pot, scullery, etc...............................	4	1½
Urinal, pedestal, syphon jet, blowout................	8	3
Urinal, wall lip...................................	4	1½
Urinal stall, washout..............................	4	2
Urinal trough (each 2-ft section)...................	2	1½
Wash sink (circular or multiple), each set of faucets....	2	1½
Water closet:		
Tank-operated..................................	4	3
Valve-operated.................................	8	3

* Nominal.
† Separate traps.
SOURCE: U.S. Department of Commerce, "National Plumbing Code," table 11.4.2, 1951.

Table 4-43. Fixture Units per Drain or Trap Size

Fixture drain or trap size, in.	Fixture-unit value	Fixture drain or trap size, in.	Fixture-unit value
1¼ and smaller............	1	2½.......................	4
1½......................	2	3.......................	5
2.......................	3	4.......................	6

SOURCE: U.S. Department of Commerce, "National Plumbing Code," table 11.4.3, 1951.

Table 4-44. Size and Length of Vents

Diam of vent required, in		1¼	1½	2	2½	3	4	5	6	8
Size of soil or waste stack, in.	Fixture units connected	Maximum length of vent, ft								
1¼	2	30								
1½	8	50	150							
1½	10	30	100							
2	12	30	75	200						
2	20	26	50	150						
2½	42	..	30	100	300					
3	10	..	30	100	200	600				
3	30	..	...	60	200	500				
3	60	..	...	50	80	400				
4	100	..	...	35	100	260	1,000			
4	200	..	...	30	90	250	900			
4	500	..	...	20	70	180	700			
5	200	..	...	...	35	80	350	1,000		
5	500	..	...	...	30	70	300	900		
5	1,100	..	...	...	20	50	200	700		
6	350	..	...	...	25	50	200	400	1,300	
6	620	..	...	...	15	30	125	300	1,100	
6	960	..	...	...	...	24	100	250	1,000	
6	1,900	..	...	...	...	20	70	200	700	
8	600	..	...	...	...	...	50	150	500	1,300
8	1,400	..	...	...	...	...	40	100	400	1,200
8	2,200	..	...	...	...	...	30	80	350	1,100
8	3,600	..	...	...	...	...	25	60	250	800
10	1,000	..	...	...	...	...	.....	75	125	1,000
10	2,500	..	...	...	...	...	.....	50	100	500
10	3,800	..	...	...	...	...	.....	30	80	350
10	5,600	..	...	...	...	...	.....	25	60	250

SOURCE: U.S. Department of Commerce, "National Plumbing Code," table 12.21.5, 1951.

Table 4-45. Distance of Fixture Trap from Vent

Size of fixture drain, in.	Distance trap to vent		Size of fixture drain, in.	Distance trap to vent	
	Ft	In.		Ft	In.
1¼	2	6	3	6	0
1½	3	6	4	10	0
2	5	0			

SOURCE: U.S. Department of Commerce, "National Plumbing Code," table 12.9.3, 1951.

Storm-water Load

$$S = ARC/96 \tag{4-37}$$

where S = storm-water quantity, gpm
A = area being drained, ft^2
R = design rate of rainfall, in./hr
C = ratio of runoff to rainfall

Design rate of rainfall varies with locality but is usually between 3 and 6 in./hr.

Table 4-46. Runoff Coefficients for Rational Formula

Type of area	Flat: slope $<2\%$	Rolling: slope $2-10\%$	Hilly: slope $>10\%$
Pavements, roofs, etc..........	0.90	0.90	0.90
City business areas............	.80	.85	.85
Suburban residential areas.....	.45	.50	.55
Dense residential areas........	.60	.65	.70
Grassed areas................	.25	.30	.30
Earth areas.................	.60	.65	.70
Cultivated land:			
Impermeable (clay, loam)....	.50	.55	.60
Permeable (sand)...........	.25	.30	.35
Meadows and pasture lands....	.25	.30	.35
Forests and wooded areas......	.10	.15	.20

Pipe Sizing

Table 4-47. Pipe Size vs. Fixture Units, Building Drains and Sewers

Pipe diam, in.	Maximum number fixture units that may be connected to any portion* of building drain or building sewer at various falls per foot			
	$\frac{1}{16}$ in.	$\frac{1}{8}$ in.	$\frac{1}{4}$ in.	$\frac{1}{2}$ in.
2	.....	......	21	26
2½	.....	......	24	31
3	.....	20†	27†	36†
4	.....	180	216	250
5	.....	390	480	575
6	.....	700	840	1,600
8	1,400	1,600	1,920	2,300
10	2,500	2,900	3,500	4,200
12	3,900	4,600	5,600	6,700

* Includes branches of the building drain.
† Not over two water closets.
SOURCE: U.S. Department of Commerce, "National Plumbing Code," table 11.5.2, 1951.

Size of Combined Drains and Sewers.   For combined storm and sanitary systems, drain sizing is based on fixture units and the storm drainage area is converted to equivalent fixture units.

Where the total fixture-unit load on the combined drain is less than 256 fixture units, the equivalent drainage area in horizontal projection is taken as 1,000 ft².

When the total fixture-unit load exceeds 256 fixture units, each fixture unit is considered the equivalent of 3.9 ft² of drainage area.

If the rainfall to be provided for is more or less than 4 in./hr, the 1,000-ft² equivalent and the 3.9 ft² are adjusted by multiplying by 4 and dividing by the rainfall in inches per hour to be provided for.

Table 4-48. Sizes of Semicircular Gutters

| Diameter of gutter,* in. | Maximum projected roof area for roofs of various slopes | | | |
	¹⁄₁₆ in.	⅛ in.	¼ in.	½ in.
	Square Feet			
3	170	240	340	480
4	360	510	720	1,020
5	625	880	1,250	1,770
6	960	1,360	1,920	2,770
7	1,380	1,950	2,760	3,900
8	1,990	2,800	3,980	5,600
10	3,600	5,100	7,200	10,000

* Gutters other than semicircular may be used provided they have an equivalent cross-sectional area.
SOURCE: U.S. Department of Commerce, "National Plumbing Code," tables 13.6 and 13.6.3, 1951.

Table 4-49. Size of Vertical Leaders

Leader or conductor diam,* in.	Max projected roof area, ft²	Leader or conductor diam,* in.	Max projected roof area, ft²
2	720	5	8,650
2½	1,300	6	13,500
3	2,200	8	29,000
4	4,600		

* The equivalent diameter of a square or rectangular leader may be taken as the diameter of that circle which may be inscribed within the cross-sectional area of the leader.
NOTE: Based on 4 in. rainfall per hour.
SOURCE: U.S. Department of Commerce, "National Plumbing Code," table 13.6.1, 1951.

Table 4-50. Horizontal Fixture Branches and Stacks

Pipe diam, in.	Maximum number fixture units			
	Any horiz* fixture branch	1 stack of 3 stories or 3 intervals	More than 3 stories	
			Total for stack	Total at 1 story or branch interval
1¼	1	2	2	1
1½	3	4	8	2
2	6	10	24	6
2½	12	20	42	9
3	20†	30‡	60‡	16†
4	160	240	500	90
5	360	540	1,100	200
6	620	960	1,900	350
8	1,400	2,200	3,600	600
10	2,500	3,800	5,600	1,000
12	3,900	6,000	8,400	1,500

* Does not include branches of the building drain.
† Not over two water closets.
‡ Not over six water closets.
SOURCE: U.S. Department of Commerce, "National Plumbing Code," table 11.3.3, 1951.

Table 4-51. Size of Horizontal Storm Drains

Drain diam, in.	Max projected roof area for drains for various slopes, ft²			Drain diam, in.	Max projected roof area for drains for various slopes, ft²		
	⅛ in.	¼ in.	½ in.		⅛ in.	¼ in.	½ in.
3	822	1,160	1,644	8	11,500	16,300	23,000
4	1,880	2,650	3,760	10	20,700	29,200	41,400
5	3,340	4,720	6,680	12	33,300	47,000	66,600
6	5,350	7,550	10,700	15	59,500	84,000	119,000

NOTE: Based on 4 in. rainfall per hour.
SOURCE: U.S. Department of Commerce, "National Plumbing Code," table 13.6.2, 1951.

4-11. Cold Water

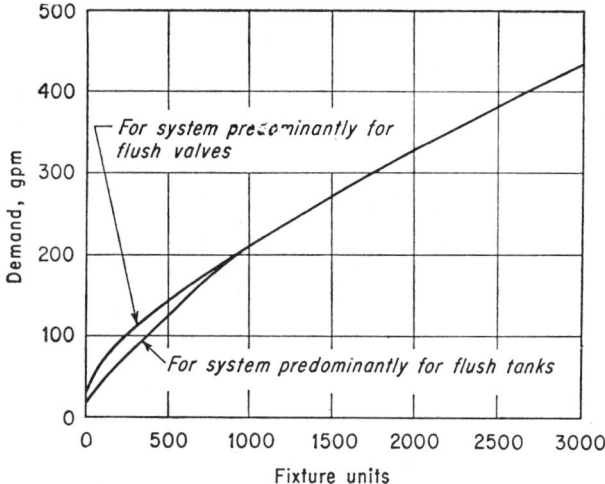

Fig. 4-21. Estimate curves for demand-load–cold-water drainage.

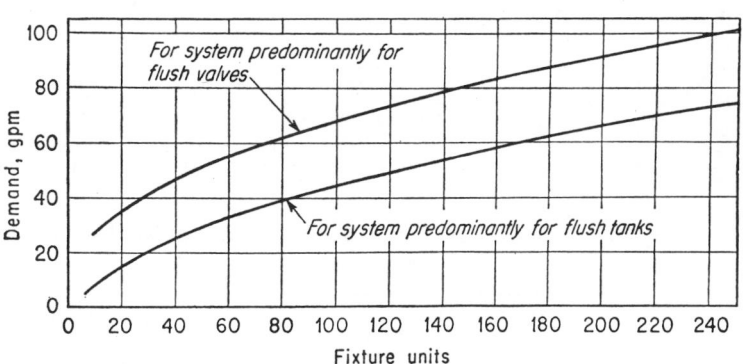

Fig. 4-22. Enlarged-scale demand-load–cold-water drainage.

Table 4-52. Water Consumption per Capita

Occupancy	Gal as stated or gpcpd	Occupancy	Gal as stated or gpcpd
Office buildings.............	27–45	Laundries, per pound.......	3–5.7
Grade schools..............	5–10	Hotels, per room...........	300–525
High schools...............	15–20	Hospitals, per bed..........	125–350
Restaurants, per meal.......	0.5–4		

Table 4-53. Demand Weight of Fixtures in Fixture Units*

Fixture or group†	Occupancy	Supply-control type	Wt in fixture units‡
Water closet	Public	Flush valve	10
Water closet	Public	Flush tank	5
Pedestal urinal	Public	Flush valve	10
Stall or wall urinal	Public	Flush valve	5
Stall or wall urinal	Public	Flush tank	3
Lavatory	Public	Faucet	2
Bathtub	Public	Faucet	4
Shower head	Public	Mixing valve	4
Service sink	Office, etc	Faucet	3
Kitchen sink	Hotel or restaurant	Faucet	4
Water closet	Private	Flush valve	6
Water closet	Private	Flush tank	3
Lavatory	Private	Faucet	1
Bathtub	Private	Faucet	2
Shower head	Private	Mixing valve	2
Bathroom group	Private	Flush valve for closet	8
Bathroom group	Private	Flush tank for closet	6
Separate shower	Private	Mixing valve	2
Kitchen sink	Private	Faucet	2
Laundry trays (1 to 3)	Private	Faucet	3
Combination fixture	Private	Faucet	3

* For supply outlets likely to impose continuous demands, estimate continuous supply separately and add to total demand for fixtures.

† For fixtures not listed, weights may be assumed by comparing the fixture to a listed one using water in similar quantities and at similar rates.

‡ The given weights are for total demand. For fixtures with both hot- and cold-water supplies, the weights for maximum separate demands may be taken as three-fourths the listed demand for supply.

SOURCE: U.S. Department of Commerce, "National Plumbing Code," table D3.5, 1951.

Table 4-54. Rate of Flow and Required Pressure during Flow for Different Fixtures

Fixture	Flow press.,* psi	Flow rate, gpm	Fixture	Flow press.,* psi	Flow rate, gpm
Ordinary basin faucet	8	3.0	Shower	12	5.0
Self-closing basin faucet	12	2.5	Ball cock for closet	15	3.0
Sink faucet, ⅜ in	10	4.5	Flush valve for closet	10–20	15–40†
Sink faucet, ½ in	5	4.5	Flush valve for urinal	15	15.0
Bathtub faucet	5	6.0	Garden hose, 50 ft and sill		
Laundry-tub cock, ½ in	5	5.0	cock	30	5.0

* Flow pressure is the pressure in the pipe at the entrance to the particular fixture considered.

† Wide range due to variation in design and type of flush-valve closets.

SOURCE: U.S. Department of Commerce, "National Plumbing Code," table D3.2, 1951.

4-12. Hot Water

Table 4-55. Maximum Daily Requirements for Hot Water

No. bathrooms.....	1	2	3	4	5
No. rooms	Gal/24 hr				
1	60				
2	70				
3	80				
4	90	120			
5	100	140			
6	120	160	200		
7	140	180	220		
8	160	200	240	250	
9	180	220	260	275	
10	200	240	280	300	
11	...	260	300	340	
12	...	280	325	380	450
13	...	300	350	420	500
14	...	...	375	460	550
15	...	...	400	500	600
16	...	...	...	540	650
17	...	...	...	580	700
18	...	...	...	620	750
19	...	...	...	...	800
20	...	...	...	...	850

Hotels

	Gal/24 hr
Room with basin....................................	10
Room with bath—transient...........................	50
Room with bath—resident...........................	60
Two rooms with bath..............................	80
Three rooms with bath.............................	100
Public shower....................................	200
Public basins....................................	150
Slop sink.......................................	30

Office Buildings

White collar worker (per person).......................	2.0
Other workers (per person)...........................	4.0
Cleaning per 10,000 ft;.............................	30.0

Hospitals

Per bed..	80–100

source: "Heating, Ventilating, Air Conditioning Guide," chap. 49, table 8, ASHRAE, New York, 1955.

Table 4-56. Estimated Hot-water-demand Characteristics for Various Types of Building

Type of building	Hot water* required, gpcpd	Max hourly demand in relation to day's use	Duration of peak load, hr	Storage capacity in relation to day's use	Heating capacity in relation to day's use
Residences, apartments, hotels, etc.....	40	1/7	4	1/5	1/7
Office buildings......................	2	1/5	2	1/5	1/6
Factory buildings....................	5	1/3	1	2/5	1/8
Restaurants..........................	...	...	...	1/10	1/10
Restaurants, 3 meals/day..............	...	1/10	8	1/5	1/10
Restaurants, 1 meal/day..............	...	1/5	2	2/5	1/6

* At 140°F.

source: "Heating, Ventilating, Air Conditioning Guide," chap. 49, table 9, ASHRAE, New York, 1955.

Table 4-57. Hot-water Demand per Fixture for Various Types of Building

Gallons of Water per Hour per Fixture, Calculated at a Final Temperature of 140°F

Fixture	Apartment house	Club	Gymnasium	Hospital	Hotel	Industrial plant	Office building	Private residence	School	YMCA
Basins, private lavatory	2	2	2	2	2	2	2	2	2	2
Basins, public lavatory	4	6	8	6	8	12	6	....	15	8
Bathtubs	20	20	30	20	20	30	....	20	......	30
Dishwashers	15	50–150	....	50–150	50–200	20–100	....	15	20–100	20–100
Foot basins	3	3	12	3	3	12	....	3	3	12
Kitchen sink	10	20	....	20	20	20	....	10	10	20
Laundry, stationary tubs	20	28	....	28	28	......	....	20	......	28
Pantry sink	5	10	....	10	10	......	....	5	10	10
Showers	75	150	225	75	75	225	....	75	225	225
Slop sink	20	20	....	20	30	20	15	15	20	20
Demand factor	0.30	0.30	0.40	0.25	0.25	0.40	0.30	0.30	0.40	0.40
Storage capacity factor*	1.25	0.90	1.00	0.60	0.80	1.00	2.00	0.70	1.00	1.00

* Ratio of storage-tank capacity to probable maximum demand per hour.
SOURCE: "Heating, Ventilating, Air Conditioning Guide," chap. 49, table 10, ASHRAE, New York, 1955.

Hot Water for Kitchens. Although, in private dwellings, a water temperature of 140°F is reasonable for dishwashing, in public places sanitation regulations call for 180°F water. Most of the dishwashing machines now available on the market require 180°F water. The amount of 180°F water needed in restaurants per day may be determined according to the American Gas Association method outlined in the following paragraphs:

1. Multiply the number of meals per day by the number of dishes per meal (6 for low-price restaurants, 8 for medium-price restaurants, and 10 for high-price restaurants) to determine the total number of dishes per day.

2. Divide the total number of dishes per day by the average number of dishes per rack to find the number of racks per day.

3. Multiply the number of racks per day by the gallons of 180°F water (using 1.5 gal for single-tank machines and 0.75 gal for two-tank machines). This product will give the gallons of 180°F water per day for rinse sprays.

4. Multiply the number of meal periods per day (one, two, or three) by the dishwashing tank capacity in gallons, giving the gallons of 180°F water per day necessary to fill the tanks.

5. Add values from (3) and (4) to obtain the total number of gallons of 180°F water required per day.

For purposes other than dishwashing, a considerable amount of 140°F water is used. To find the daily 140°F water requirement in a restaurant, multiply the total number of meals served per day by the gallons of 140°F water per meal. Low-price restaurants on the average utilize 0.9 gal of 140°F water per meal; medium- and high-price restaurants use 1.2 and 1.5 gal per meal, respectively.

4-13. Gas Piping

Table 4-58. Capacity of Gas Piping

Pipe length, ft	Capacity at various nominal pipe diam, ft³/hr*				
	¾ in.	1 in.	1¼ in.	1½ in.	2 in.
15	172	345	750		
30	120	241	535	850	
45	99	199	435	700	
60	86	173	380	610	
75	77	155	345	545	
90	70	141	310	490	
105	65	131	285	450	920
120	...	120	270	420	860
150	...	109	242	380	780
180	...	100	225	350	720

* With a 0.6-sp gr gas and a pressure drop of 0.3 in. H_2O. For a gas of specific gravity other than 0.6 use a multiplier from table 4.59.
SOURCE: "Heating, Ventilating, Air Conditioning Guide," chap. 15, table 1, ASHRAE, New York, 1955.

Table 4-59. Multipliers for Various Specific Gravities

Sp gr	Multiplier	Sp gr	Multiplier	Sp gr	Multiplier
0.35	1.31	0.75	0.895	1.40	0.655
.40	1.23	0.80	.867	1.50	.633
.45	1.16	0.85	.841	1.60	.612
.50	1.10	0.90	.817	1.70	.594
.55	1.04	1.00	.775	1.80	.577
.60	1.00	1.10	.740	1.90	.565
.65	0.962	1.20	.707	2.00	.547
.70	.926	1.30	.680	2.10	.535

SOURCE: "Heating, Ventilating, Air Conditioning Guide," chap. 15, table 2, ASHRAE, New York, 1955.

Table 4-60. Common Gas Appliances
Maximum Gas Consumption in Ft³/Hour

Appliance	Natural gas 1050 Btu/ft³	Mixed gas 800 Btu/ft³	Manufactured gas 550 Btu/ft³
Range, domestic, 4 top, 1 oven burners..............	60	80	115
Range, domestic, 6 top, 2 oven burners..............	100	135	200
Hot plate, domestic or laundry stove per burner......	8.5	11	16
Room heater, radiant type, single, domestic..........	2	2.5	4
Water heater, instantaneous, automatic, per 1 gpm capacity....................................	36	47	68
Refrigerator....................................	2.6	3.1	4.5

ELECTRICAL

4-14. Power Systems

The typical circuit arrangements of power systems found in buildings may be classified as follows: radial, secondary selective, secondary (spot) network, and primary selective.

The radial arrangement employs a single power source and one circuit to each load. An equipment failure will result in a power outage until difficulty is corrected. The high quality of modern distribution equipment provides the service reliability which justifies the use of the radial arrangement for a majority of applications.

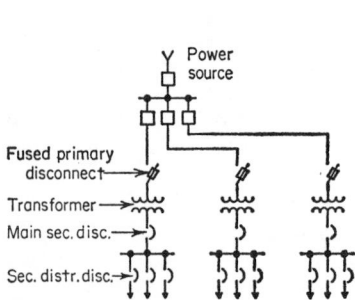

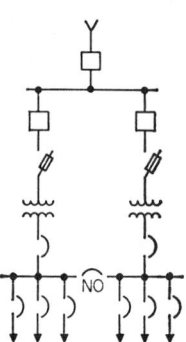

FIG. 4-23. Radial-circuit arrangement.

FIG. 4-24. Secondary-selective-circuit arrangement.

The secondary selective arrangement is in effect two radial systems with a secondary tie between them. It is provided in buildings where a greater degree of reliability is desired. This arrangement permits any secondary bus to be energized from either of two sources.

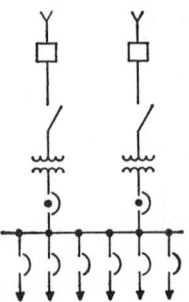

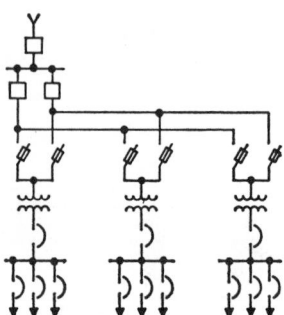

FIG. 4-25. Simple spot-network-circuit arrangement.

FIG. 4-26. Primary-selective-circuit arrangement.

The secondary-network arrangement is one where a high degree of service continuity is desired, as in large institutional buildings. The arrangement consists of two or more transformers energized by separate primary circuits, with the respective secondaries joined together.

The primary-selective arrangement provides an alternative power source to the substation transformers, but does not provide an alternative source of power to the secondary loads in event of a transformer outage.

The local prevailing rules of the Electric Service Company will usually determine the type and voltage of service available, regardless of the building size. This service may be from the secondary-network system in the street or for buildings of large magnitude, a spot network being instituted for the specific building load. The service voltage may be either 208Y/120 or 460Y/265 volts. In some of the current taller buildings, spot-network vaults are established by the Electric Service Company on intermediate floors in addition to the basement. In areas where buildings can be served at voltages greater than the utilization voltage, in the range of 2,400 to 13,800 volts, greater flexibility is available for circuit arrangements and in the selection and establishment of the utilization voltage.

4-15. System Voltages

Distribution systems may be classified according to voltage, levels used to carry the power directly to the branch circuits, or to load-center transformers or substations at which feeders to branch circuits originate. Preferred voltage ratings for a-c equipment are outlined in Table 4-61. Typical voltage-level utilization and application are outlined in Table 4-62.

Table 4-61. Preferred Voltage Ratings for A-C Equipment

Preferred nominal system voltage	Generator rated voltage	Transformer secondary rated voltage	Transformer primary rated voltage	Switchgear nominal rated voltage	Capacitor rated voltage	Motor and control rated voltage	Ballast rated voltage
Single-phase Systems and Single-phase Components Applied on Three-phase Systems							
120	120	120	120	120	....	115	120
120/240	120/240	120/240	240	240	230 or 240	230	236 or 240
208Y/120, 3-phase	125/216Y, 3-phase	216Y/125, 3-phase	120	240	230 or 240	115*	120*
460Y/265, 3-phase	277/480Y, 3-phase	480Y/277, 3-phase	480	480	460 or 480	....	265* or 277*
Three-phase Low-voltage Systems							
208Y/120	125/216Y	216Y/125	208	240	216 or 230 or 240	208 or 220	208†
230	139/240Y	240Y/139 or 240	240	240	230 or 240	220	235† or 240†
460Y/265	277/480Y	480Y/277	480	480	460 or 480	440	460† or 430†
460	277/480Y	480Y/277	480	480	460 or 480	440	450† or 430†
575	346/600Y	600Y/346 or 600	600	600	575 or 600	550	
Three-phase Medium-voltage Systems							
2,400	1,388/2,400Y	2,400Y/1,388 or 2,400	2,400	2,400	2,400	2,300	
4,160	2,400/4,160Y	4,160Y/2,400	4,160	4,160	2,400 or 4,160	4,000	
4,800	2,770/4,800Y	4,800Y/2,770 or 4,800	4,800		2,770 or 4,800	4,600	
6,900	3,980/6,900Y	6,900Y/3,980	6,900	7,200	4,160 or 6,640	6,600	
7,200	3,980/6,900Y	7,200Y/4,160	7,200	7,200	4,160 or 7,200	6,600	
12,000	7,210/12,500Y	12,000Y/6,920	12,000	13,800 or 7,200	7,200 or 12,470	11,000	
7,200/12,470Y	7,210/12,500Y	12,470Y/7,200	12,000	13,800 or 7,200	7,200 or 12,470		
13,200	7,970/13,800Y	13,200Y/7,610	13,200	13,800	7,620 or 13,800	13,200	
13,800	7,970/13,800Y	13,800Y/7,970	13,800	13,800	7,960 or 13,800	13,200	
14,400	8,320/14,400Y	13,800Y/7,970	13,800	14,400	7,960 or 13,800 or 14,400	13,200	

* Line-to-neutral rating.
† Line-to-line rating.
SOURCE: "Electric Systems for Commercial Buildings," IEEE 241, p. 41, October, 1964.

Table 4-62. Voltage Levels—Utilization and Application

Typical nominal voltage levels	Utilization	Application
120/240	Light and power (light at 120 volts, power at 120 and 240 volts)	Small loads such as individual homes, multi-family dwellings, and small commercial occupancies
208Y/120, 3 phase	Light and power (light at 120 volts, power at 120 volts and 208 volts, 1 phase, and 208 volts, 3 phase)	Commercial buildings and small industrial shops with limited electrical load
230	Power	Commercial and industrial buildings
460	Power	Commercial and industrial buildings with substantial motor loads
575		
460Y/265, 3 phase	Light and power (light at 277 volts, 1 phase, and power at 480 volts, 3 phase)	Commercial and industrial buildings
2,400	Distribution	Industrial, heavy motor loads directly and lighting through transformation
4,160	Distribution	Large-area, spread-out commercial and institutional buildings such as shopping centers, schools, and motels; supply load centers and transformers for lighting and power
4,800	Distribution	Industrial, with substations for stepping voltage to lower levels for lighting and power
6,900		
7,200		
12,000	Distribution	Large industrial plants with substations for stepping voltage to lower levels for lighting and power
7,200/12,470Y		
13,200		
13,800		
14,400		

4-16. Building Loads

This subsection contains tables which permit the establishment of the anticipated electrical load for the building. With the area and the knowledge of the building utilization, the building-load density can be formulated. Total building load can be estimated by application of pertinent factors in Table 4-63. Individual building-load densities are obtained by application of pertinent items and factors in Tables 4-64 to 4-67. The demand load is obtained by application of items and factors contained in Table 4-68.

Table 4-63. Load Density in Representative Plants and Buildings

Type of industry	Light and power, volt-amp demand/ft²	Type of industry	Light and power, volt-amp demand/ft²
Commercial		Manufacturing	
Bank..	6–8	Appliance...................	7–12
Department store.............	8–11	Automotive..................	7.5–12
Hotel........................	6–9	Beet sugar refinery...........	19
Office building................	6–14	Cigarette manufacture........	11
Restaurant...................	12–18	Chemical....................	10–15
Small store..................	5–8	Electronics, industrial.........	6–10
Shopping center...............	7–10	Foundry*....................	11–15
School.......................	4–7	Glass.......................	1.5–8.5
		Heavy machinery.............	7–13
		Light machinery..............	11–15
		Metal fabricating and assembly	3–8
		Small device, industrial.......	4.5–10
		Textile.....................	12

* Large electric furnace loads are not included. They should be considered separately.
SOURCE: "Electrical Equipment Specifications Manual," Book III, Load Estimating Data Table 5.3, p. 2, General Electric Co., 1959.

Table 4-64. Lighting Load Density

Based on IES Foot-candle Standards, IES "Lighting Handbook," 3d ed.

Location	Maintained foot-candles	Va/ft²
Factories:		
General fabrication and assembly, automatic machining, medium inspection..	150	7.5–15
Rough bench and machine work, shearing foundry work. rough inspection....	70	2.5–3.5
Washrooms, storage..	30	2–2.5
Finishing and inspecting, engraving, alterations and repairs (tailoring), textile (sewing, grading dark goods), shoe manufacturing, extra-fine bench work, toolmaking..	1000	50–70
Proofreading, typesetting, machining, sewing (light goods), fine assembly, inspection, fine hand painting..	300	15–20
Office:		
Designing, detailed drafting...	200	10–20
Auditing, accounting, rough layout......................................	150	7.5–15
Regular office work, active filing..	100	5–10
Conferring, interviewing, washrooms.....................................	30	2–2.5
Corridors, elevators, stairways..	20	1–5.2
Schools:		
Sewing, regular classwork performed by visually handicapped pupils.........	150	7.5–15
Drafting, fine shop work...	100	5–10
Reading, study, observation in classrooms, lecture rooms, laboratories, etc....	70	3–4.5
Simple bench work, choral work..	50	2.5–3
Locker rooms, storerooms, washrooms....................................	30	2–2.5
Stores:		
Circulation areas..	20	2–2.5
Display and selling zone:		
Service shops..	100	4–6
Self-service..	200	8–12
Displays..	1000	50–80
Show windows:		
General...	200	15–20
Spotlighting...	500–2000	25–60
Public buildings:		
Banks:		
Lobby—general...	50	2–4
Tellers' cages...	150	6–9
Libraries:		
Reading and stockrooms...	50	2.5–3.5
Research, study areas...	100	5–7
Museums:		
General (environmental)...	30	2–2.5
Special displays...	100	4–7

SOURCE: "Electrical Equipment Specifications Manual," Book III, Load Estimating Data Table 5.8, p. 3, General Electric Co., 1959.

Table 4-65. Air-conditioning Load Density

Based on 1.5 Kva/Ton, Air-cooled Units*

Application	Demand	
Banks	4.5–6	va/ft²
Barber shops	5–6	va/ft²
Bars and taverns	165–210	va/seat
Beauty parlors	750	va/booth
Department stores:		
Main floor	7.5–10	va/ft²
Upper floors	4.5–6	va/ft²
Top floors	5–7.5	va/ft²
Bargain basement	6–10	va/ft²
Normal basement	4.5–6	va/ft²
Dress shops	4.5–10	va/ft²
Drugstores	4.5–10	va/ft²
Funeral parlors	3.75–5	va/ft²
Grocery stores	3.75–5	va/ft²
Night clubs:		
Convention type	190–210	va/seat
Week-end peak	165–190	va/seat
Offices:		
Multistory	3–3.75	va/ft²
Single floor	3.75–4.5	va/ft²
Top floor	5–6	va/ft²
Restaurants:		
Cafeterias	165–210	va/seat
Hotel dining-rooms	130	va/seat
Family restaurants	125–150	va/seat
Shoe shops	4.5–9.0	va/ft²
Supermarkets	3.75–5.25	va/ft²
Theaters:		
Continuous performances	82.5–100	va/seat
Neighborhood	75–82.5	va/seat

* For water-cooled units multiply load by 0.75.

Table 4-66. Air-conditioning Equipment

Kva Demand (Air-cooled)

Type of drive	Tons	Btu	Equipment kva demand
Induction-motor drive	1	12,000	1.5
0.8 PF synchronous-motor drive	1	12,000	1.65
1.0 PF synchronous-motor drive	1	12,000	1.3

SOURCE: "Electrical Equipment Specifications Manual," Book III, Load Estimating Data Tables 5.6 and 5.7, p. 3, General Electric Co., 1959.

Table 4-67. Kva-demand Material-handling Loads

Load	Kva demand*	Load	Kva demand*
Conveyors...............	1–15	Escalators..............	10–40
Cranes:		Hoists:	
Gantry................	25–200	Ash and cinder........	1–5
Traveling bridge.......	5–200	Tramrail 1-ton........	1.5–3
Dumbwaiters...........	1/2–5	Tramrail 5-ton........	6–10
Elevators:		Warehouse loading....	1–3
1-ton freight...........	3–20		
5-ton freight...........	7.5–20		
10-passenger..........	7.5–30		
20-passenger..........	7.5–50		
27-passenger..........	10–60		

* Demand depends upon rate of travel as well as size of load.
SOURCE: "Electrical Equipment Specifications Manual," Book III, Load Estimating Data Table 5.4, p. 2, General Electric Co., 1959.

Table 4-68. Demand Factors of Utilization Equipment

Equipment	Range, per unit	Equipment	Range, per unit
Arc furnaces....................	0.90–0.100	Hand tools..................	0.20–0.40
Arc welders....................	.20–.50	Induction furnaces and heating	
Compressors...................	.20–.50	equipment...................	.80–1.0
Conveyors.....................	.90–.100	Lighting.....................	.75–1.0
Cranes........................		Paper mills..................	.50–.70
		Resistance ovens, heaters,	
Elevators (quantity)		furnaces....................	.80–1.0
		Resistance welders...........	.05–.40
1–2	1.0	Rubber mills.................	.50–.70
3	0.9	Pumps......................	.20–.50
4	.775	Rolling mills.................	.20–.50
6	.55	Refineries...................	.50–.70
10	.48	Textile mills.................	.70–1.0
20	.44	Ventilation, blower motors.......	.20–.50

SOURCE: "Electrical Equipment Specifications Manual," Book III, Load Estimating Data Table 5.5, p. 2, General Electric Co., 1959.

4-17. Distribution

The purpose of any electric system is to provide a continuous supply of energy to the utilization equipment at reasonable cost. A typical power distribution system consisting of transformer, switchboard, motor control center, panelboards, feeders, lighting and power arrangements, and their relationship in an integrated system is outlined in Fig. 4-27.

Wire and cables in conduit and busways are used as feeders and capable of carrying large and small blocks of power from main switchboard to load centers to loads.

The feeder-conductor volt-drop limitations to building loads are outlined in Table 4-69.

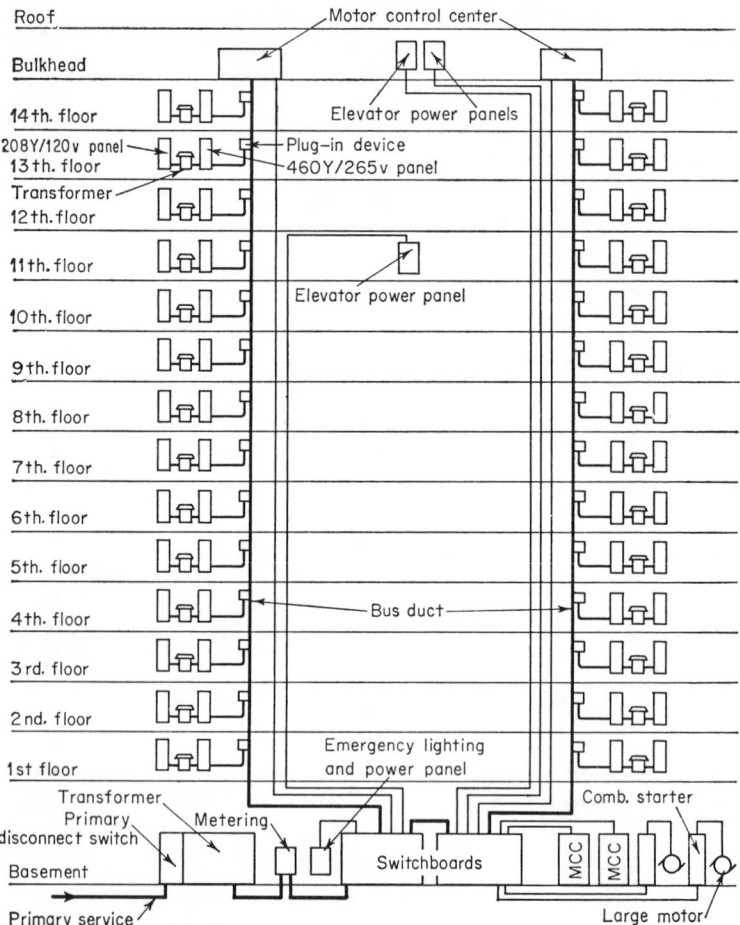

Fig. 4-27. Typical power-riser diagram.

Table 4-69. Feeder-conductor Volt-drop Limitations

Load	Limitations,* %
Power, heating or lighting or combination thereof...................	3
Max. total drop for conductors for feeders and branch circuits......	5

* Recommended by National Electrical Code 1965.

The IPCEA has published ampere ratings of cables insulated with oil-impregnated paper, varnished cambric, and rubber compounds. The National

Electric Code publishes current ratings of low-voltage cables for most applications in commercial buildings. Wiring in insured buildings must be installed at rated values which do not exceed those in the NEC or other local codes which are more restrictive than IPCEA ratings.

Because of the versatility, flexibility, and economic feasibility for the method of electrical distribution in large commercial and institutional buildings, feeder and plug-in busways are being widely accepted. Various bus ducts are listed in Table 4-70.

Table 4-70. Bus Ducts

Type	Volt rating	Ampere rating	Conductor
Plug-in	600 ac	100	Copper
Plug-in	600 ac-dc	225, 400, 600, 800, 1000	Copper or aluminum
Plug-in or feeder, low impedance	600 ac-dc	600, 800, 1000, 1350, 1600, 2000, 2500, 3000, 4000, 5000	Copper or aluminum
Plug-in or feeder, high frequency, 120 to 10,000 cycles/sec	800 ac	400, 500, 700	Copper or aluminum
Feeder	600 dc	225, 400, 600, 800, 1000, 1350, 1600, 2000, 2500, 3000, 4000, 5000	Copper or aluminum
Feeder, current limiting	600 ac	1000, 1350, 1600, 2000, 2500, 3000, 4000	Copper

Circuit breakers, fuses, safety switches, and combinations of these devices provide protection in a building distribution system against short circuits, overloads, and undervoltage by controlling the flow of current up to their respective rating. These devices may be contained in switchboards, panelboards, control centers, or in individual enclosures. Typical devices are listed in Table 4-71.

Table 4-71. Ampere Rating of Standard Fuses. Safety Switches, Pressure Switches, and Circuit Breakers (600 Volts or Less)

Single-element Fuses*

15	70	225	1,000
20	80	250	1,200
25	90	300	1,600
30	100	350	2,000
35	110	400	2,500
40	125	450	3,000
45	150	500	4,000
50	175	600	5,000
60	200	800	6,000

Enclosed General-purpose Safety Switches

30	100	400	800
60	200	600	1,200

Enclosed Pressure Switches

800	1,600	2,500	4,000
1,200	2,000	3,000	5,000

Nonadjustable Trip Circuit Breakers

15	70	200	400
20	100	225	500
30	125	250	600
40	150	300	700
50	175	350	800

* Dual-element fuses that provide both motor-running protection and short-circuit protection are available in a much greater range of sizes.

Table 4-72 outlines a basis for selection of panelboards.

Table 4-72. Panelboards

Usage	Type	Max. circuits per panel	Remarks
Lighting........	Switch and fuse or circuit breaker	42*	Includes lighting and appliance panelboards†
Power..........	Switch and fuse or circuit breaker	None	Physical size is limiting factor

* Where more than 42 circuits originate at one location, use two panels. Not more than 42 overcurrent devices shall be installed in a lighting and/or lighting and appliance panelboard, or cabinet.
† Lighting and appliance panelboard is defined as having more than 10 per cent of its overcurrent devices rated 30 amp or less, for which neutral connections are provided.

4-18. Motors and Controls

The general requirements for motor provisions are outlined in the National Electric Code (NEC). The design of motor installations must conform to the code requirements and should include considerations for adequacy, flexibility, voltage drop, and safety.

Motors can be classified as outlined in Table 4-74 (see page 4-76).

The full-load currents (amperes) of representative motors at typical voltages are outlined in Tables 4-73 and 4-75. These data are useful in determining the wiring and setting of protective devices.

Table 4-73. Full-load-current D-C and Single-phase A-C Motors

Horsepower of motor	D-c motors		Single-phase motors		
	120V	240V	115V	230V	440V
⅛	....	.....	4.4	2.2	
¼	2.9	1.5	5.8	2.9	
½	5.2	2.6	9.8	4.9	
½	3.6	1.8	7.2	3.6	
¾	7.4	3.7	13.8	6.9	
1	9.4	4.7	16	8	
1½	13.2	6.6	20	10	
2	17	8.5	24	12	
3	25	12.2	34	17	
5	40	20	56	28	
7½	58	29	80	40	21
10	76	38	100	50	26
15	....	55			
20	....	72			
25	....	89			
30	....	106			
40	....	140			
50	....	173			
60	....	206			
75	....	255			
100	....	341			
125	....	425			
150	....	506			
200	....	675			

NOTE: The voltages listed are rated motor voltages. Corresponding nominal system voltages are 110 to 220, 220 to 240, 440 to 480, and 550 to 600 volts.
SOURCE: National Electrical Code 1965, p. 70–232.

Table 4-74. Classification of Motors

	Type	Speed characteristics	Full voltage		Hp range	Application— see footnotes (a) to (e)
			Starting torque	Starting current		
	Constant-speed Drive					
Polyphase a-c	Squirrel-cage general-purpose Design A	Constant	Normal 1–2.5 times^f	High 6–8 times	All	(a) Fans and centrifugal pumps and centrifugal compressors (c)
	Squirrel-cage Design B	Constant	Normal 1–2.5 times^f	Normal 5–6 times	Medium small	(a) Fans and centrifugal pumps and centrifugal compressors
	Squirrel-cage Design C	Constant	High 2–2.5 times^f	Normal 5–6 times	Medium small	(b) Reciprocating pumps and compressors (e) started loaded
	Squirrel-cage Design F	Constant	Low 1.25	Low 4 times	Medium large	Fans, centrifugal pumps, and compressors
	Wound rotor	Constant or variable	High 1–2.5 times (with secondary control)	Low 1–3 times (with secondary control)	All	(a) Hoists (b) reciprocating pumps and compressors (c) and frequent (e) or hard start
	Synchronous high speed	Exactly constant	Normal 0.75–1.75 times	Normal 5–7 times	Medium large	(a) Fans and centrifugal pumps and centrifugal compressors
	Synchronous low speed	Exactly constant	Low 0.3–0.4 times	Low 3–4 times	Medium large	(a) Reciprocating compressors starting unloaded
	Two-value capacitor	Constant	High	Normal	Small	(b) Pumps and compressors
	Permanent split capacitor	Constant	Low	Normal	Fractional	(a) Fans, blowers

Class	Type	Speed	Starting torque	Speed regulation	hp rating	Applications
Single-phase a-c	Capacitor start	Constant	Moderate	Normal	Small fractional	(a) Fans and pumps
	Repulsion induction	Constant	High	Normal	Medium small	(a) Fans; (b) pumps and compressors
	Split phase	Constant and adjustable	Normal	Normal	Fractional	(a) Fans; (b) pumps and compressors; (d) fans—direct
			Adjustable-speed Drive			
Polyphase a-c	Squirrel-cage high slip; transformer adjustment	Variable	Normal	Normal	Medium small	(a) Fans
	Squirrel-cage separate winding or regrouped poles	Constant multispeed	Normal or high	Normal or low	All	(a) Fans, pumps, and compressors
	Wound rotor	Variable	High (with secondary control)	Low (with secondary control)	All	(a) Fans; (b) centrifugal pumps and compressors
Single-phase a-c	Repulsion	Variable	High	Normal	Low and fractional	(a) Fans, centrifugal pumps; (b) compressors
	Capacitor low-torque tapped winding	Variable two-speed	Low	Normal	Fractional	(d) Fans, direct
	Capacitor low-torque transformer adjustment	Variable	Low	Low	Fractional	(d) Fans
	Split-phase regrouped poles	Constant	Normal	Normal	Fractional	(d) Fans

[a] Drives having medium or low starting torque and inertia WR^2 such as fans and centrifugal pumps or reciprocating pumps and compressors started unloaded.
[b] Drives having high starting torques, such as reciprocating pumps and compressors started loaded.
[c] Similar to (a) except where frequent or hard starting (large WR^2) requires a higher starting and accelerating torque.
[d] Fans direct-connected.
[e] Stoker drives.
[f] Torque depends on hp rating and speed. See *NEMA Standard* MG1-4.10, Motors and Generators.
SOURCE: "Heating, Ventilating, Air Conditioning Guide," vol. 37, pp. 642 and 643, ASHRAE, New York, 1959.

Table 4-75. Full-load-current Three-phase A-C Motors

Hp	Induction-type squirrel-cage and wound-rotor,* amp					Synchronous type, unity power factor,† amp			
	110V	220V	440V	550V	2300V	220V	440V	550V	2300V
½	4	2	1	0.8					
¾	5.6	2.8	1.4	1.1					
1	7	3.5	1.8	1.4					
1½	10	5	2.5	2.0					
2	13	6.5	3.3	2.6					
3	....	9	4.5	4					
5	....	15	7.5	6					
7½	....	22	11	9					
10	....	27	14	11					
15	....	40	20	16					
20	....	52	26	21					
25	....	64	32	26	7	54	27	22	5.4
30	....	78	39	31	8.5	65	33	26	6.5
40	....	104	52	41	10.5	86	43	35	8
50	....	125	63	50	13	108	54	44	10
60	....	150	75	60	16	128	64	51	12
75	....	185	93	74	19	161	81	65	15
100	....	246	123	98	25	211	106	85	20
125	....	310	155	124	31	264	132	106	25
150	....	360	180	144	37	...	158	127	30
200	....	480	240	192	48	...	210	168	40

NOTE: For full-load currents of 208- and 200-volt motors, increase the corresponding 220-volt-motor full-load current by 6 and 10 per cent, respectively.
* These values of full-load current are for motors running at speeds usual for belted motors and motors with normal torque characteristics. Motors built for especially low speeds or high torques may require more running current, in which case the nameplate current rating should be used.
† For 90 and 80 per cent PF the figures should be multiplied by 1.1 and 1.25, respectively.
The voltages listed are rated motor voltages. Corresponding nominal system voltages are 110 to 120, 220 to 240, 440 to 480 and 550 to 600 volts.
SOURCE: National Electrical Code 1965, p. 70–232.

4-19. Telephones

Well-planned communication facilities for both present and future needs incorporated into buildings during initial construction or major alterations will be beneficial throughout the life of the building.

Modern buildings may require teletypewriter service, data-transmission service—connections between data-processing machines over telephone facilities, centrex service—permitting the dialing of outgoing calls as well as receiving incoming calls without attendant, and public telephone service.

Communication needs of the building include:

Raceway. Underfloor ducts or cellular floor systems to serve as a telephone cable distribution facility.

Apparatus Closets. To house relay cabinets and auxiliary apparatus of modern key telephone systems.

PBX Equipment Rooms. To house the large equipment required for PBX service.

Cable Riser Systems. For bringing cables from the main terminal room to the various building floors.

Main Terminal Room. Connecting point between building and outside facilities.

Service from the Street. Aerial or underground service into the building.

A desirable distribution arrangement for commercial buildings is to divide the floor space into zones of no more than 10,000 ft², and preferably from 4,000 to 6,000 ft², to handle the distribution cables. The size of the raceway in each zone should be one square inch for every 100 ft² of office area, which is predicated upon the average allocation of one desk and telephone per 100 ft² of floor area. The raceway for the distribution cables can be provided as follows:

Underfloor Ducts. Spaced $4\frac{1}{2}$ to 6 ft between parallel runs or feeds with cross runs and junction boxes located every 40 ft or less.

Cellular Floor. Appropriate cell utilization with header ducts connected to cell area at intervals for maximum coverage, usually no greater than 50 ft.

The communications equipment in each zone is connected to relay cabinets and other apparatus in a central closet in each zone. The type and size closet is outlined in Table 4-76.

Table 4-76. Telephone Zone Closets

Specification	Walk-in closet	Shallow closet
Depth:		
Minimum...................	3 ft	$1\frac{1}{2}$ ft
Maximum...................	None	$2\frac{1}{2}$ ft
Width:		
Minimum...................	5 ft	3 ft
Maximum...................	None	None
Floor area per 100 ft² served......	4 ft²	None
Length of walls per 1,000 ft² served	$2\frac{1}{2}$ ft	$2\frac{1}{2}$ ft
Minimum height of doors........	6 ft 8 in.	6 ft 8 in.*
Minimum width of doors.........	3 ft	3 ft†

* When shallow closets are used, the center post between double doors should be eliminated, if possible.
† Minimum for single door, $2\frac{1}{2}$ ft for double doors.
SOURCE: Bell Telephone System, Telephone-planning Fact File, AIA File 31-i-5.

4-20. Signal and Communications Systems

Different types of buildings require a variety of signal and communications systems.

Industrial Buildings. *Burglar Alarm.* Burglar alarm system may be used to protect all doors, windows, elevator openings, skylights, etc.

Clock and Program Systems. These are used for indicating the time of day and operating signal devices such as bells or horns at predetermined times, such as starting and stopping work, rest periods, lunch periods, etc.

Door Alarm. Door alarm system is used to signal the guard room when certain restricted areas have been entered or vacated by individuals.

Fire Alarm. Fire alarm systems should be of the closed-circuit supervised type. Generally, noncoded systems are limited to small plants, since they only transmit a general alarm and do not indicate the location of the operated station. Coded systems are preferable.

Fire Detection. Automatic fire detection system may be used separately or combined with the manual fire alarm systems.

Intercom. Intercommunicating system may be provided in various forms.

P.A. Public address sound system may be used throughout the plant for paging, radio programs, recordings, announcements, and entertainment.

Paging. Paging system is used to call and locate individuals.

Smoke Detection. This system is used to detect smoke in ventilating, air-conditioning, and dust-collecting ducts.

Sprinkler System. This alarm system is used to signal when sprinkler heads open, when noticeable leaks occur, when water flow valves operate in either dry or wet systems, when post indicator valves operate or are left open, or when the shutoff valves are placed in any subnormal position.

Watchman's System. Watchman's supervisory system should be of a type which will require the watchmen on the various tours to produce a record in the superintendent's or chief guard's quarters at the start and at the finish of each tour.

Commercial Buildings. *Fire Systems.* Fire alarm system of the manual type should be provided for the protection of the general public and the employees within the building.

A fire alarm system of the automatic type should be provided where records or files are kept or stored. A fire-line signal system is used exclusively by members of the fire department to transmit signals to the pump room.

A fire-line telephone system consists of a master station telephone located in the pump room, submaster station telephones located in the auxiliary pump room and at the building entrance, and outlying telephones located on each of the other floors. This system is of the common-talking type.

Schools. *Clock and Program System.* Clock and program system provides the means of showing correct time throughout the premises and to denote the different periods in a day's schedule.

Fire Alarms. Any fire signal should be distinctive from all other signals and should be audible to everyone in the building.

A fire alarm system for use in schools is one of four types, having a common characteristic: they are all closed-circuit, electrically supervised.

In small schools, either the noncoded or master-coded type is frequently used.

In large schools and colleges, the coded types of system are used.

Intercom System. Telephones are used for intercommunication between the principal's office and the main office and the classrooms.

Sound and Radio Distribution System. A sound and radio distribution system enables the distribution of radio programs, recordings, lectures, and announcements.

Hospitals. *Clock System.* A clock system is important in hospitals, both for keeping time and administering anesthesia.

Emergency Call. An emergency feature may be added to any nurse-call system. This is used by the nurse to call assistance to a patient's room when the occasion requires.

Fire Alarm System. A fire alarm system for use in hospitals is usually of the presignal type.

Nurse Call. A nurse-call system is used by patients to call a nurse to the bedside. There are two general types of such systems, the visual and the audio.

Paging Systems. Paging systems are used to locate doctors and other members of the staff throughout the building. The visual system uses lamp annunciators throughout and also incorporates an audible signal such as a buzzer or chime.

The sound system consists of loudspeakers throughout one or more hospital buildings.

"In" and "out" systems are used by the doctors and other members of the staff to designate whether or not they are in the building.

Sound and Radio System. Sound and radio systems enable patients to listen in on one or more channels of radio programs, TV, recordings, announcements, etc.

4-21. Grounding

Grounding refers to both system and equipment grounding. A *system ground* is a connection to ground from one of the current-carrying conductors of a distribution system or of an interior wiring system. An *equipment ground* is a solid connection to ground from one or more of the non-current-carrying metal parts of the wiring system such as metal conduits, outlet boxes, motor frames, and control cabinets.

The principal types of system grounding are (1) solid, (2) low-resistance, (3) high-resistance, (4) reactance, (5) resonant, and (6) ungrounded (capacitance).

The ungrounded system has only the relatively high inherent system capacitive-reactance connection between current-carrying parts and ground. Resonant grounding is a special case of reactance grounding in which the neutral grounding reactance is approximately equal to the line-to-ground capacitive reactance of the system at power-system frequency.

A comparison of the grounding methods is outlined in Table 4-77. The grounding practice for various voltage systems is outlined in Table 4-78.

Table 4-77. Grounding Methods

	Solid grounding	Resistance grounding		Reactance* grounding	Ungrounded
		Low resistance	High resistance		
Degree of grounding, line-to-ground fault in per cent of three-phase fault current magnitude	Varies, may be 100% or slightly greater	5 to 10%	Less than 0.1%	Usually between 25 and 100%	Less than 0.1%, but not less than system charging current
Transient overvoltage	Not excessive; does not exceed 1½ to 2 times normal	Not excessive; does not exceed 1½ to 2 times normal	Not excessive; does not exceed 1½ to 2 times normal	Not excessive; does not exceed 1½ to 2 times normal	Excessive, up to 6 times normal
Immediate and automatic removal of faulted circuit by conventional relays	Yes	Yes	No	Yes	No
Circuit outage for one line-to-ground fault	Yes	Yes	No	Yes	No
Multiple faults	Insignificant number of multiple failures	Insignificant number of multiple failures	Insignificant number of multiple failures	Insignificant number of multiple failures	Many cases of multiple failures
Lightning-arrester ratings	Grounded neutral	Ungrounded neutral	Ungrounded neutral	Grounded neutral for 60% current or more	Ungrounded neutral
General areas of application	Low-voltage industrial and commercial building systems; residential and rural primary distribution systems; some 4-wire systems where high ground fault may be tolerated; systems above 15 kv	Medium-voltage industrial power and commercial building systems with motor loads; not used in utility-type distribution systems	Applied on low- or medium-voltage industrial power systems not permitted to be tripped for first ground fault	Limited use in large 12-kv class utility-type distribution substations and in generator neutrals directly supplying 4-wire systems; also occasional application above 15 kv	Used in approximately 50% of the residential and rural primary distribution systems in the 4-kv class; decreasing use in industrial power systems because of excessive transient overvoltages

* This degree of grounding is sometimes called low-reactance grounding. High-reactance grounding (5 to 25 per cent) is not listed because of its associated very high transient overvoltages.

Table 4-78. Industrial and Commercial Systems Grounding

Condition	*Grounding Practice*
	Low-voltage systems*
Wye-connected generators on system	Ground generator through low value of reactance to limit ground fault current to not more than its three-phase value.†
System supplied by transformer with wye-connected secondary winding	Solidly grounded transformer neutral.†
No wye-connected transformer or generator on system	Use solidly grounded grounding transformer.† Check adequacy of ground fault current for breaker and fuse operation.
	Medium-voltage systems*
Wye-connected generators on system	Use low-resistance grounding.‡ In four-wire distribution system, use low-value neutral reactance to limit ground fault current to 100% of generator three-phase value.
Wye-connected transformers	Use low-resistance grounding of supply transformers (avoid grounding of load transformers).§
No wye-connected generators or transformers on system	Use one or more grounding transformers with neutral resistor to effect low-resistance grounding.

* In all cases where tripping on first ground fault is not permitted, use high-resistance grounding.

† Solid- and reactance-grounded systems must have ground fault currents not less than 25 per cent of three-phase fault current to avoid excessive transient overvoltages. This may set minimum size of grounded apparatus.

‡ In small limited fault current systems, reactance grounding may be used if more economical. See footnote † above.

§ In small systems of limited fault current, solid grounding may be used in interest of economy. See footnote † above.

SOURCE: "Electrical Equipment Specifications Manual," Book III, table 2.33, Grounding of Industrial and Commercial Systems, p. 54, General Electric Co., 1959.

SECTION 5

CHEMICAL ENGINEERING

Shelby A. Miller, Ph.D., P.E.; Professor and Chairman, Department of Chemical Engineering, University of Rochester; Member, American Association for the Advancement of Science, American Chemical Society, American Institute of Chemical Engineers, and Society of Chemical Industry

CONTENTS

INTRODUCTION

Chemical engineering is concerned with processes in which material is upgraded by virtue of physical and chemical changes, or energy is made available through chemical transformation. The upgrading may be related to form, state of aggregation, purity, or chemical composition. Usually, one or more chemical reactions are involved. The energy conversions most frequently dealt with are combustions (or other controlled oxidations) and recovery of the liberated thermal energy and electrochemical reactions and recovery of the liberated chemical energy. Although nuclear processes, of increasing importance as sources of energy and products, often employ the chemical engineer, they are generally considered the subject matter of *nuclear engineering* (Sec. 9).

Whether the process goal is a product or an energy supply, the material involved (called the process stream) is likely to undergo not only obvious chemical change, but a series of physical or physicochemical transformations as well. These usually are effected in discrete stages or steps, called *unit operations*. Their purpose is the assembly and preparation of raw materials (reactants) and the recovery, purification, and dispensing of products or by-products.

In the course of a process, the material of the process stream may be in the form of more than one of the several *phases* possible (gas, liquid, and one or more solid phases). Often two or more phases coexist. Multiphase dispersion to provide a desired physical mixture, to promote interphase transport, or to abet chemical reaction is an important objective of the unit operations, as is the collection and separation of phases. In addition to their mechanical aspects, then, the unit operations also depend heavily on *phase equilibria* (thermodynamics) and the *transfer of material, energy, and momentum* within or among phases (transport phenomena).

At the heart of almost every process is equipment, called a *reactor*, in which chemical transformation occurs. *Reactor design* (which is based on chemical kinetics, thermodynamics, and transport behavior), reactor control and operation, and the diffusional unit operations are virtually the exclusive responsibility of chemical engineers.

This section presents design and computation methods for the most important unit operations dealing with diffusive transfer, phase contacting, and phase separation and for reactors.

A list of nomenclature for symbols used in this section follows.

Nomenclature

A = area of filter surface, ft^2

= area of heat transfer and evaporation, ft^2

= frequency factor in Arrhenius equation; units depend on order of reaction

$\overline{A}_a, \overline{A}_L$ = arithmetic and logarithmic means of areas at base and surface of a centrifuge filter cake, ft^2

a = agitation Froude-number parameter (Fig. 5-20 and Table 5-3)

= agitation heat-transfer parameter (Table 5-5)

= bed-drying area, ft^2/ft^3 bed volume

= effective specific surface of packing, ft^2/ft^3

= empirical constant of Eqs. (5-29) and (5-30), hr/(lb mass)^2

= per cent coarser than designated size in screen feed

= stoichiometric coefficient of reactant A

B = coefficient of cross-circulation drying, hr [defined by Eq. (5-27)]

= distance of impeller above tank bottom, ft

= empirical coefficient of Eq. (5-72)

= molal boiling rate, lb moles/hr

B' = coefficient of through-circulation drying, hr [defined by Eq. (5-28)]

B_c = cyclone dimension (Fig. 5-28), ft

b = agitation Froude-number parameter (Fig. 5-20 and Table 5-3)

= empirical constant of Eqs. (5-29) and (5-30), (hr/lb mass)^2

= per cent finer than designated size in screen feed

= stoichiometric coefficient of reactant B

C = concentration (when subscripted), lb moles/ft^3 or g moles/liter

= experimental parameter of constant-pressure filtration = $\mu r/\Delta P$, hr/ft

C' = plate-spacing-adjustment parameter (Fig. 5-5)

C_1 = annual cost for power and depreciation of column, \$/(ft^3)(yr)

C_2 = value of solute at concentration of exit gas, \$/lb mole pure solute

C_3 = annual cost of column packing and shell, \$/(ft^3)(yr)

C_4 = cost of delivered energy, \$/kwhr

c = heat capacity, Btu/(lb mass)(°F)

= mass fraction of solids in prefilt

= per cent coarser than designated size in screen oversize

= stoichiometric coefficient of reactant C

= volume of liquid holdup in centrifuge bowl, cm^3

c_s = humid heat, Btu/(lb mass dry air)(°F)

D = disk diameter, ft

= inside column diameter, ft

= molal product or distillate rate, lb moles/hr

D_a = impeller diameter, ft

D'_a = impeller diameter, in.

D_e = cyclone dimension (Fig. 5-28), ft

D_i = fluid-phase diffusion coefficient

D_0 = diameter on disk atomizer where liquid is fed, ft

D_p = particle diameter, ft

D_{pc} = particle cut size in cyclone (diameter of particles of which 50 per cent of those present are collected), ft

D_t = inside diameter of tank, ft

$\mathfrak{D}$ = molecular diffusivity, cm²/sec

d = per cent finer than designated size in screen fines

d_F = packing size, ft

d_l = liquid density in column at point of maximum vapor flow, lb mass/ft³ (Fig. 5-5)

d_v = vapor density in column at point of maximum vapor flow, lb mass/ft³ (Fig. 5-5)

E = energy of activation, cal/g mole

  = extract flow rate, lb mass/hr

  = specific atomization energy requirement, ft-lb force/lb mass liquid

E_c = column efficiency, ideal plates/actual plate

e = base of natural logarithms

F = centrifugal force, lb force or g force

  = evaporator or solvent extractor feed rate, lb mass/hr

  = reactor feed rate, lb moles/hr

F_{cv} = friction loss across a cyclone inlet, velocity heads

f = amount of vapor found in a flash still or rectifying column per unit of feed, lb mole/lb mole

G = mass velocity of gas or vapor, lb mass/(hr)(ft²); in Eqs. (5-23) and (5-28), G is evaluated on a moisture-free basis

  = rate of solute-free solvent removed in solvent separator, lb mass/hr

G_M = molal mass velocity of gas or vapor, lb moles/(hr)(ft²)

$G_{M,\text{opt}}$ = optimum molar mass velocity of gas, lb moles/(hr)(ft²)

g = acceleration due to gravity, ft/sec² or cm/sec²

g_c = gravitational conversion factor, (lb mass)(ft)/(lb force)(sec²) or (g mass)(cm)/(g force)(sec²)

H = head of liquid over weir on a plate, in.

  = height of transfer unit (transfer through a single-phase film), ft

H_0 = height of over-all transfer unit (transfer from one phase to another), ft

H_c = cyclone dimension (Fig. 5-28), ft

h = film heat transfer coefficient, Btu/(hr)(ft²)(°F)

h_t = over-all heat transfer coefficient for combined convection and radiation between drying slab and air, Btu/(hr)(ft²)(°F)

j = number of equal size ideal continuous stirred tank reactors in series

K = coefficient of drying [Eqs. (5-25) and (5-26)]

  = coefficient of cyclone pressure drop [Eq. (5-56)]

K' = distribution coefficient for liquid-liquid equilibrium, [Eq. (5-20)]

$K_G a$ = volumetric over-all coefficient of mass transfer based on gas-phase driving-force units, lb moles/(hr)(ft³)(atm)

$K_L a$ = volumetric over-all coefficient of mass transfer based on liquid-phase driving-force units, lb moles/(hr)(ft³)(unit concentration)

K_c = chemical equilibrium constant based on concentrations; dimensions depend on the stoichiometry of the equilibrium reaction

K_{CK} = Carman-Kozeny permeability

K_p = constant-pressure filtration resistance coefficient, hr/(lb mass)(ft³)

K'_p = constant-pressure filtration resistance coefficient, hr/ft²

K''_p = constant-pressure filtration resistance coefficient, hr/ft²

K_r = constant-rate filtration resistance coefficient, lb force/ft³

k = coefficient of thermal conductivity, Btu/(hr)(ft²)(°F/ft)

= specific reaction rate constant, dimensions depending on order of reaction

k' = specific reaction rate constant for reverse reaction, dimensions depending on order of reaction

k_G = individual gas film coefficient of mass transfer, lb moles/(hr)(ft²)(atm)

$k_G a, k_L a$ = volumetric individual film coefficients of mass transfer based on gas-phase and liquid-phase driving-force units, respectively, same units as $K_G a$ and $K_L a$

k_K = Kozeny coefficient

k_L = individual liquid film coefficient of mass transfer, lb moles/(hr)(ft²)(unit concentration)

L = thickness of slab or cake, ft

= mass velocity of liquid, lb mass/(hr)(ft²) (Figs. 5-9 and 5-10)

= rate of liquid flow in column, lb mass/hr

L_E = rate of liquid flow in enriching section of column, lb mass/hr

L_M = molal mass velocity of liquid, lb moles/(hr)(ft²)

L_s = rate of liquid flow in stripping section of column, lb mass/hr

l = nominal length of pore in catalyst (radius of spherical particle; one-half thickness of plate-shaped particle or flake), ft

M_m = mean molecular weight of gas

m = effectiveness factor correlation modulus (Fig. 5-33)

= mass, lb mass or g mass

= mass of air, lb mass [Eq. (5-37)]

= mass ratio of wet cake to washed dry cake

= slope of gas-liquid equilibrium line (plot of y against x)

= slope of line in mass-transfer correlation [Eq. (5-72)]

m_c = mass of cake in centrifuge, lb mass

N = number of moles of a species (usually designated by subscript) present

= rotation speed of impeller or disk, rpm

N_0 = number of transfer units of height H_0

N_M = molal flux between phases in mass transfer, lb moles/(ft³)(hr)

N_{Re} = Reynolds number, $D_p G/\mu$ or $D_a^2 N \rho/\mu$

N_T = number of theoretical plates required at total reflux

N_{act} = number of real or actual plates in column

N_e = number of turns made by gas stream in cyclone (5 to 10 for design of Fig. 5-28)

N_{id} = number of ideal or theoretical plates required by a column design

n = agitation-power Froude-number exponent (Table 5-3)

= number of spaces between centrifuge disks in stack

= order of a chemical reaction

P = agitator shaft power, ft-lb force/min or ft-lb force/sec

= liquid content of still pot, lb moles

= pressure in fluid being filtered, lb force/in.^{2}

ΔP = pressure drop across filter or nozzle, lb force/in.^{2}

P' = power to pump through a pressure nozzle, or to drive a rotating nozzle, hp

P_1^0 = vapor pressure of pure component 1

P_s = agitator shaft power to produce complete suspension of solids, ft-lb force/min or ft-lb force/sec

P_v = agitator shaft power per unit volume of stirred liquid, hp/1,000 gal

p = partial pressure of a subscripted component in a gas mixture, atm

Δp = pressure drop in column, lb force/in.^{2}

p_{BM} = mean partial pressure of inert gas in a mixture, atm

p_f = pressure film factor in gas diffusing to a catalyst surface (analagous to p_{BM}), atm

Q = rate of feed of solute-free solvent to raffinate end of extractor, lb mass/hr

= throughput capacity of settling centrifuge when separating half of feed particles, cm^3/sec

= volumetric film rate through pressure nozzle, gpm

q = rate of heat transfer, Btu/hr

R = raffinate rate from extraction, lb mass/hr

= reflux ratio = L/D (Fig. 5-3)

= reflux stream rate, lb moles/hr

= universal gas constant, ft-lb force/(lb mass)(°R) in Eq. (5-37); cal/(g mole)(°K)

R_m = flow resistance of filter medium, ft^{-1}

R_{min} = minimum reflux ratio (i.e., with an infinite column)

$\mathfrak{R}_c$ = constant rate of filtrate flux, ft^3/(hr)(ft^2)

r = radius of rotation, ft or cm

= rate of a chemical reaction, lb moles reacted/(ft^3)(hr), usually subscripted for a particular participant

= stoichiometric coefficient of product R

r' = rate of reverse chemical reaction, lb moles/(ft^3)(hr)

$\bar{r}$ = average pore radius in a catalyst, angstroms (A)

r_2 = radius of centrifuge bowl or filtering surface, ft or cm

r_{net} = net forward rate of a reversible reaction, lb moles/(ft^3)(hr)

r_0 = radius of liquid level in a centrifuge, ft or cm

S = amount of material distilled in a Rayleigh distillation, lb moles

= mass of dry solids in a bed of drying material, lb mass

$\quad\quad$ = solvent content of extract layer, lb mass/lb mass total dissolved material

S_g = catalyst specific surface, m²/g

s = effective thickness of liquid layer in a centrifuge, cm

$\quad$ = solvent content of raffinate layer, lb mass/lb mass total dissolved material

$\quad$ = stoichiometric coefficient of product S

S_0 = specific surface of filter cake, ft²/ft³

T = absolute temperature, °R or °K

t = temperature, °F

Δt_m = logarithmic mean temperature difference, °F; in Eq. (5-28), $(t_a - t_w)_m$

t_a = dry-bulb temperature of air, °F

t_s = temperature of surface during constant-rate drying, °F

t_w = wet-bulb temperature of air, °F

U = over-all heat transfer coefficient, Btu/(hr)(ft²)(°F)

U_{shell} = maximum allowable superficial vapor velocity in column, fps

u_t = actual terminal setting velocity of a particle in air, fps

u_{ts} = theoretical Stokes settling velocity of a particle in air [Eq. (5-55)] or in a liquid, fps

V = reactor or tank volume, ft³

$\quad$ = superficial velocity of phase subscripted, ft/hr

$\quad$ = vapor rate in column, lb moles/hr

$\quad$ = volume of filtrate, ft³

$\quad$ = volumetric flow rate of vapor at column conditions, ft³/sec

V_e = rate of extract layer removal from last extract stage, lb mass/hr

V_g = specific pore volume of catalyst, cm³/g

$\quad$ = terminal settling velocity in gravitational field, cm/sec

V_r = rate of raffinate layer removal from last raffinate stage, lb mass/hr

V_s = molal vapor flow in stripping sector of column, lb moles/hr

$\quad$ = superficial gas velocity, ft/min [Eq. (5-33)] or ft/hr

$\quad$ = terminal settling velocity in centrifugal field, cm/sec

$\quad$ = volume of solids-containing portion of an agitated suspension, ft³

W = mass of dry filter cake formed, lb mass

$\quad$ = moisture content of wet solids, lb mass water/lb mass dry solids

$\quad$ = rate of bottoms removal from still, lb moles/hr

W_c = critical moisture content, lb mass water/lb mass dry solids

W_e = equilibrium moisture content, lb mass water/lb mass dry solids

w = mass of filter cake deposited per unit filtrate, lb mass/ft³

$\quad$ = mass of water evaporated, lb mass

$\quad$ = equilibrium composition of raffinate phase, lb mass solute/lb mass solute-free phase

w' = equilibrium composition of extract phase, lb mass solute/lb mass solute-free solvent

X = mass fraction of solute in raffinate layer, solvent-free basis

X_A = moles of reactant A converted per mole of feed

x = mole fraction, usually of subscripted component, in liquid phase

x^* = mole fraction in liquid phase in equilibrium with vapor or gas

$(1 - x)_{lm}$ = logarithmic mean of $1 - x$ and $1 - x^*$

Y = length of liquid column in a tubular centrifuge, cm

= mass fraction of solute in extract layer, solvent-free basis

y = mole fraction, usually of subscripted component, in vapor or gas phase

y^* = mole fraction in vapor or gas phase in equilibrium with liquid

$(1 - y)_{lm}$ = logarithmic mean of $1 - y$ and $1 - y^*$

Z = height of column (packed section), ft

Z_f = solvent content of feed, lb mass solvent/lb mass solvent-free total solute

Z_s = depth of uniform suspension of solids above tank bottom, ft

Z_t = spacing between trays or plates, ft

Z'_t = spacing between trays or plates, in.

α = index of kinetic order of reactant A

= specific resistance of filter cake, ft/lb mass

α, α_{12} = relative volatility = $(y_1/x_1)/(y_2/x_2)$ at equilibrium

β = index of kinetic order of reactant B

γ = activity coefficient = $\Pi y/P^0 x$

= index of kinetic order of reactant C

ϵ = porosity = volume-fraction voids in a bed (volume-fraction liquid in a solid-liquid suspension)

η = effectiveness factor, ratio of actual reaction rate to rate if no diffusional resistance exists

θ = conical half angle of centrifuge disk stack

= time, hr

θ_c = drying time for constant-rate period, hr

= time for emptying, cleaning, and refilling, hr

θ_f = drying time for falling-rate period, hr

θ_m = boiling time for maximum average productivity, hr

θ_t = total drying time, hr

θ_y = annual operating time, hr/year

λ = latent heat of vaporization, Btu/lb mass

μ = viscosity of fluid, lb mass/(ft)(hr), lb mass/(ft)(min), or centipoises

μ_B = viscosity in bulk of fluid, lb mass/(ft)(hr), lb mass/(ft)(min), or centipoises

μ_W = viscosity of film at heated or cooled wall, centipoises

Π = total pressure, atm

π = 3.1416

ρ = density, lb mass/ft^3

= index of kinetic order of product R

$\Delta\rho$ = density difference between continuous and disperse phases, or between liquid and solids of slurry, lb mass/ft^3

ρ_1 = density of liquid, lb mass/ft³

ρ_m = density of slurry, lb mass/ft³

ρ_s = true density of solids, lb mass/ft³

ρ'_s = bulk density of a bed or cake of solids, lb mass/ft³

Σ = centrifuge throughput capacity factor, cm² [Eqs. (5-50), (5-52), (5-53)]

σ = index of kinetic order of product S

$\quad$ = interfacial tension, lb mass/hr²

σ' = interfacial tension, dynes/cm

ϕ = density correction factor = $\sqrt{\rho_m/0.075}$, where ρ_m = mean gas density, lb mass/ft³

τ = space time, time required to process one reactor volume of feed

ω = angular velocity, radians/sec

Subscripts

A = reactant A

a = streams entering or leaving top of a column

B = reactant B

C = reactant C

$\quad$ = continuous phase

D = disperse phase

$\quad$ = distillate or overhead stream

F = feed

G = gas phase

i = at the interface

L = liquid phase

m = mean value

$\quad$ = plate number or designation, usually in stripping section; material flowing from plate m

$m + 1$ = plate above the mth plate; material flowing from plate $m + 1$

n = plate number or designation, usually in enriching section; material flowing from plate n

$n + 1$ = plate above the nth plate; material flowing from plate $n + 1$

P = still or pot contents in batch distillation

R = product R

S = product S

W = bottoms or waste stream

0 = at time zero, initial value

1 = initial value; value at point or time 1; component 1

2 = final value; value at point or time 2; component 2

DIFFUSIONAL OPERATIONS

5-1. Mass-transfer Fundamentals

In the course of a process, it is frequently necessary to transfer a molecularly dispersed ingredient from one phase to another. Such transfer is accomplished by those unit operations, called *diffusional operations*, all of which are based on the same principles of material and energy conservation, equilibria, and transport rates.

Equilibria. *Equilibrium data* consist of sets of corresponding concentrations of the same component obtaining in different phases that are in equilibrium. Although they sometimes are reasonably estimable, they generally must be obtained from experiment. Many such data are reported in the literature (e.g., in "International Critical Tables" and in "Perry's Chemical Engineers' Handbook," 4th ed., McGraw-Hill Book Company, New York, 1963).

Staged Operations. *Staged operations* (e.g., in plate columns) are calculated on the assumption of *equilibrium stages* (also called perfect, or ideal, plates) with subsequent adjustment for their nonequilibrium performance by application of an experience factor called *stage efficiency.* In addition to equilibria and efficiencies, the *operating lines* of the operation must be known. A different operating line applies to each portion of the operation between entering or exiting streams, and each is described by an equation based on a material balance, of the form

$$y_n = \frac{L_{n+1}}{V_n}\, x_{n+1} + \frac{V_a y_a - L_a x_a}{V_n} \tag{5-1}$$

When V and L are constant, as is often substantially so, Eq. (5-1) is a straight line of slope L/V.

Unstaged Equipment. For *differential-stage* or continuous apparatus (for example, a packed column), the rate of transfer between phases is calculated by an expression obtained from the diffusion equations:

$$N_M = k_L a(x - x_i) = k_G a(y_i - y) \tag{5-2}$$

The *individual film coefficients* k_L and k_G, which are inferred experimentally, customarily are determined as volumetric coefficients $k_G a$ and $k_L a$ because the exact interfacial area of columns is seldom known. Involvement with interface concentrations x_i and y_i is avoided by use of *over-all transfer coefficients* $K_G a$ and $K_L a$:

$$N_M = K_L a(x - x^*) = K_G a(y^* - y) \tag{5-3}$$

Equation (5-3) is applicable strictly only if the equilibrium line is straight (i.e., the relationship between equilibrium concentrations is linear); otherwise values of the coefficients are unreliable for conditions other than the exact ones under which they were measured. When the equilibrium line is substantially straight, the following expressions relate over-all and film coefficients:

$$\frac{1}{K_G a} = \frac{1}{k_G a} + \frac{m}{k_L a} \tag{5-4}$$

$$\frac{1}{K_L a} = \frac{1}{k_L} + \frac{1}{m k_G a} \tag{5-5}$$

The *height of a transfer unit* (HTU), which is the height of apparatus required to accomplish a separation of standard difficulty, is often used instead of a transfer coefficient to describe the rate with which diffusive transfer occurs. The HTU has the advantage of virtual independence of fluid rates in the equipment, whereas coefficients may vary strongly with flow rates. Over-all HTU's are related to over-all coefficients and to individual-phase HTU's thus:

$$H_{OG} = \frac{G_M \Pi}{K_G a p_{BM} (1 - y)_{lm}} = H_G + H_L \frac{mG_M}{L_M} \frac{(1 - x)_f}{(1 - y)_f} \tag{5-6}$$

$$H_{OL} = \frac{L_M}{K_L a (1 - x)_{lm}} = H_L + H_G \frac{L_M}{mG_M} \frac{(1 - y)_f}{(1 - x)_f} \tag{5-7}$$

The *number of transfer units* represented by a separation is defined as

$$\frac{Z}{H_{OG}} = N_{OG} = \int_{y_2}^{y_1} \frac{(1 - y)_{lm} \, dy}{(1 - y)(y - y^*)} \cong \int_{y_2}^{y_1} \frac{dy}{y - y^*} \tag{5-8}$$

The right-hand member of Eq. (5-8) is strictly correct only for cases of equimolar diffusion. A comparable liquid-phase number N_{OL} is defined similarly in terms of liquid concentrations.

5-2. Distillation

Definitions. *Distillation* is the separation of the constituents of a liquid mixture by partial vaporization of the mixture and separate recovery of vapor and residue. The more volatile constituents of the original mixture are obtained in increased concentration in the vapor, the less volatile in greater concentration in the liquid residue. Completeness of separation depends upon certain properties of the components involved and upon arrangement of the distillation process.

Rectification is a distillation in which a vapor is continuously and countercurrently contacted with a condensed portion of the vapor. This process secures a greater enrichment of the vapor in the more volatile components than could be secured with a single distillation operation using the same amount of heat. The condensate returned to accomplish this object is termed *reflux.*

Fractional distillation, or *fractionation,* is synonymous with rectification.

Rectifying columns are most commonly fed at or near the center of the column, in which case the section above the feed is known as the *rectifying section,* and the part below the feed is the *stripping section.*

Equilibrium Data. Vapor-liquid equilibrium data are required for the design of stills. In general, these must be observed experimentally. For binary systems, they are reported usually as tables or graphs of corresponding x and y values. Many such data are summarized by Chu ("Vapor-liquid Equilibrium Data," J. W. Edwards Publisher, Incorporated, Ann Arbor, Mich., 1956), by Gerster ("Perry's Chemical Engineers' Handbook," 4th ed., sec. 13, McGraw-Hill Book Company, New York, 1963), and by Hala, Pick, Fried, and Vilim ("Vapour-liquid Equilibrium," 2d ed., Pergamon Press, New York, 1958).

If equilibrium data are not available, they may be estimated for a binary by a modification of Raoult's law:

$$y_1 = \frac{p_1}{\Pi} = \frac{\gamma_1 x_1 P_1^0}{\Pi} = \frac{\alpha_{12} x_1}{1 + (\alpha_{12} - 1)x_1} \tag{5-9}$$

For ideal mixtures $\gamma_1 = \gamma_2 = 1.0$; as a system departs from ideality, use of Eq. (5-9) becomes less reliable. Values of γ may be estimated for a number of binaries by a method summarized by Gerster (*loc. cit.*).

Simple Batch (Rayleigh, Differential) Distillation. In this case a batch of material is charged to a still pot, boiling is initiated, and the vapors are then continuously removed, condensed, and collected until their average composition has reached a desired value. If the vapor is at all times in equilibrium with the liquid boiling in the still, the relationship of amount distilled to average composition of distilling liquid is

$$2.3 \log \frac{S_1}{S_2} = \int_{x_2}^{x_1} \frac{dx}{y - x} \tag{5-10}$$

The cycle time depends on the molal boil-up rate B:

$$\theta = \int_{S_1}^{S_2} \frac{dS}{B} = \frac{S_2 - S_1}{B_m} \tag{5-11}$$

Equilibrium Flash Distillation. Liquid feed heated under pressure is

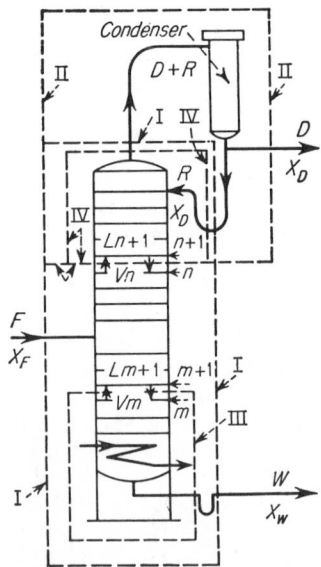

throttled into a flash chamber, in which a certain molal fraction $f = V/F = (F - L)/F$ is vaporized. Equilibrated vapor and liquid streams are led separately from the still. From material and energy balances

$$(1 - f)x + fy = x_F \tag{5-12}$$

$$(t_F - t)c_F = f\lambda_m \tag{5-13}$$

where f is the moles of vapor formed per mole of feed. Equation (5-13) assumes adiabatic vaporization in the chamber; otherwise additional heat terms must be included. As a reasonable approximation, c_F and λ_m may be assumed constant over the range of temperatures and concentrations involved. Equations (5-12) and (5-13) and an equilibrium relationship [e.g., Eq. (5-9) or a set of experimental data] are solved simultaneously by trial and error.

Continuous Binary Rectification. *Plate Columns.* *Plate-to-plate Calculations.* The simultaneous solution of material balance, energy balance, and equilibrium relation-

Fig. 5-1. Schematic of continuous distillation column.

ships between each successive two stages in a column permits the exact computation of the column from one terminal stream to another. Until recently a generally impractical procedure, it now may be followed economically if the need for repeated designs is sufficient to justify its being programmed for a digital computer. This method is beyond the scope of this manual (see Gerster, *loc. cit.*).

McCabe-Thiele Graphical Method. If *constant molal overflow* and *no heat losses* may be assumed (L and V constant unless material enters or leaves the column), the following useful graphical method is acceptable:

1. Plot the vapor-liquid equilibrium data as y against x.

2. Write and plot the operating-line (material-balance) equations for each section of the column between entrance-exit streams. With reference to Fig. 5-1, these equations are, for section II (enriching section),

$$y_n = x_{n+1} \frac{L_{n+1}}{V_n} + x_D \frac{D}{V_n}$$

$$= x_{n+1} \frac{L_E}{L_E + D} + x_D \frac{D}{L_E + D} = \frac{R}{R+1} x_n + \frac{x_D}{R+1} \quad (5\text{-}14)$$

and for section III (stripping section),

$$y_m = x_{m+1} \frac{L_{m+1}}{V_m} - x_W \frac{W}{V_m} = x_{m+1} \frac{L_s}{V_s} - x_W \frac{W}{V_s} \quad (5\text{-}15)$$

The upper and lower operating lines intersect on a *feed line* described by Eq. (5-12) if f is the moles of vapor formed in the rectifying section per mole of feed because of the introduction of the feed. In Fig. 5-2a, five different feed lines are shown with the same upper operating line. Each feed line represents feed of a different quality: C_1, cold liquid ($f < 0$); C_2, saturated liquid ($f = 0$); C_3, wet vapor ($0 < f < 1$); C_4, saturated vapor ($f = 1$); C_5, superheated vapor ($f > 1$).

Three sets of operating lines are shown in Fig. 5-2b.

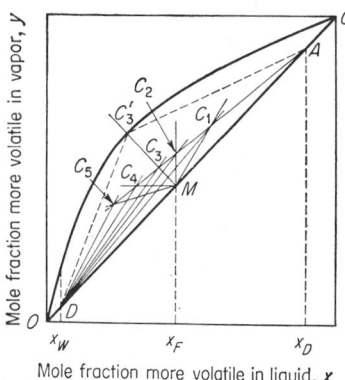

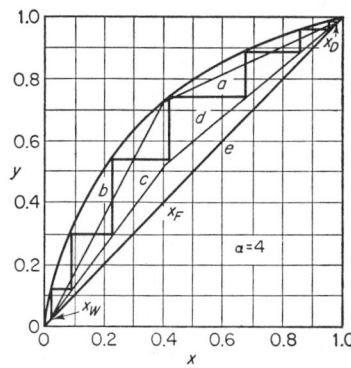

Fig. 5-2a. Effect of thermal condition of feed on operating lines and minimum reflux ratio.

Fig. 5-2b. McCabe-Thiele graphical method for determining number of theoretical stages.

a. Lines *a* and *b*, intersecting on the equilibrium line, represent minimum reflux and require an infinite number of plates to achieve the finite separation represented by compositions x_D and x_W.

b. Line *e*, the coincidence of both operating lines with the diagonal, represents total reflux, the condition of minimum number of plates, but no product.

c. Lines *c* and *d* represent practical operating lines between the extremes of minimum and total reflux. The operating lines chosen should represent the economic optimum. In practice, the slope of the upper operating line often is established by taking a reflux ratio 1.2 to 2.0 times the minimum, or such that the number of ideal plates required is about twice the minimum. In Fig. 5-2*b*, line *d* actually represents a reflux ratio about six times the minimum represented by line *a*.

3. Step off the number of ideal plates required to progress between x_D and x_W. The number shown in Fig. 5-2*b* is about seven (the minimum, stepped between the equilibrium line and line *c*, would be about five).

4. Calculate the required number of actual plates from Eq. (5-16):

$$N_{\text{act}} = N_{\text{id}}/E_c \tag{5-16}$$

The column efficiency E_c may be taken as the average of individual plate efficiencies.

Analytical Method for Mixtures of Constant Relative Volatility

1. Solve for the number of theoretical plates necessary at "total" reflux (the condition when vapor and liquid rates within the column are infinitely large compared to feed, overhead, and bottom drawoff rates), using the Fenske-Underwood equation

$$N_T + 1 = \log\ (x_1/x_2)_D(x_2/x_1)_W/\log\ \alpha \tag{5-17}$$

2. Estimate the minimum reflux ratio (the ratio of liquor to distillate rates if the column were infinitely tall) by using

$$\frac{R}{R_{\min}} = \frac{x_D[1 + (\alpha - 1)x_F] - \alpha x_F}{(\alpha - 1)x_F(1 - x_F)} \tag{5-17a}$$

3. By use of Fig. 5-3, estimate the number of theoretical trays necessary for the reflux ratio to be employed.

Batch Binary Rectification. In batch distillations, generally three "products" are withdrawn from the still. These are an initial product high in purity with regard to the more volatile or light-key component, an intermediate product which will usually be recycled for redistillation, and

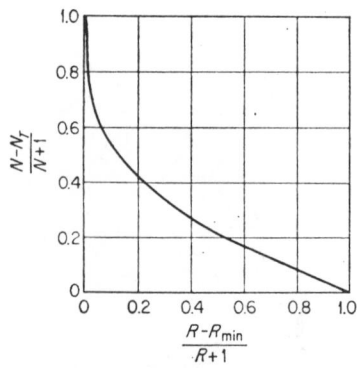

FIG. 5-3. Correlation of Gilliland for number of theoretical stages.

finally a product high in purity with regard to the heavy or less volatile component. Obviously a desirable separation is one which will minimize the middle or recycle cut. For most batch distillations found satisfactory in this latter regard the following rule of thumb will hold and is useful in setting the reflux to be used.

$$(L/D)(\alpha - 1) \geqq 10 \qquad (5\text{-}18)$$

If a constant reflux ratio is maintained, the product purity of the more volatile component will drop off as the distillation proceeds. The speed at which this decline in purity occurs will be a function of the particular reflux ratio employed, the relative volatility, and the amount of volatile component originally present.

It must be remembered that the practicing engineer is most often confronted with a different problem in designing for continuous operation as opposed to batch distillation. In the former a column is usually designed and built for a given separation; in the latter the usual problem is how a given piece of equipment should be operated to effect a desired separation. We shall therefore assume that the equipment and the number of plates are specified.

Of importance in designing for the use of any batch distillation are answers to the following questions:

1. What is the overhead-product composition as a function of still-pot composition?

2. How many moles of steam (as a heating medium) will be required to effect the separation?

For the constant-reflux case the vapor requirement, and thus the steam requirement, is obtained from

$$V = (L/D + 1)D \qquad (5\text{-}18a)$$

The relation between still-pot and overhead compositions is obtained by plotting on a y-x diagram (as shown in Fig. 5-4) lines of constant slope equal to

$$L/V = (L/D)/(L/D + 1) \qquad (5\text{-}19)$$

and stepping off the number of theoretical plates in the column. To obtain the relation between the *amount* distilled and the still-pot composition plot x_P vs. $1/(x_P - x_D)$. The area under the curve is equal then to P/D, where P represents the amount of liquid in the still pot.

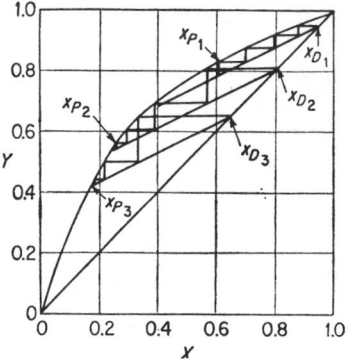

Fig. 5-4. Diagram for batch distillation at constant reflux ratio.

A second method of operating batch-distillation columns is to maintain product purity over a period of time by constantly increasing the reflux ratio. The relation between amount distilled and still-pot composition is now found by a simple material balance. The steam requirement is obtained by finding the area under a curve of $\dfrac{P_0(x_0 - x_P)}{(x_P - x_D)^2(1 - L/V)}$ versus x_P. Appropriate values of x_P are read as a function of L/V from a y-x plot.

Multicomponent Rectification. This subject is too complicated for treatment here. The interested reader should refer to a more comprehensive source (e.g., Gerster, *op. cit.*, p. 32).

Plate Efficiency. The estimation of plate efficiencies is empirical. In a properly designed column, the value should exceed 0.60 and may exceed 0.95. Teller presents estimation methods and typical values ("Perry's Chemical Engineers' Handbook," 4th ed., sec. 18, pp. 16–23, McGraw-Hill Book Company, New York, 1963).

Tower Diameter. In many distillations and absorptions the liquid entrainment on each tray may be controlling in fixing the tower diameter. In this event the nomograph presented as Fig. 5-5 is helpful.

5-3. Solvent Extraction

Definitions. Solvent extraction consists of the transfer of a component dissolved in a liquid (called the *feed* solution) to a second liquid (called the *solvent*) to form an *extract* solution of the transferred component and to leave a *raffinate* solution relatively lean in the transferred component. Solvent extraction is used when distillation is impractical, as with close-boiling or temperature-sensitive mixtures. There is a strong analogy between extraction and distillation, solubility being the counterpart of volatility and the solvent that of heat (Fig. 5-6).

Equilibrium Data. Phase equilibria for liquids are so specific that it is best to refer to laboratory data for the system in question. Emmert and Pigford ("Perry's Chemical Engineers' Handbook," 4th ed., sec. 14, McGraw-Hill Book Company, New York, 1963) cite many such data.

For some systems the equilibrium is well approximated by the ideal-distribution law

$$K' = w/w' \tag{5-20}$$

with consequent simplification of design procedures. In solvent extraction fewer theoretical plates and much lower plate efficiencies are encountered than in distillation or absorption, with corresponding aggravation of inaccuracies implicit in simplified methods. For this reason, short-cut approximations should be used with caution.

Countercurrent Extraction with Reflux. The method of operation is outlined schematically in Fig. 5-6. A feed mixture of two completely miscible liquid components A and B is to be separated into its components by isothermal extraction with a solvent. The solvent is partly miscible with each component of the feed and preferentially selects component A. Reflux is furnished to the top of the column by removing sufficient solvent from the saturated-extract layer to reduce it to a saturated-raffinate phase, and a portion of this is returned to the column. Raffinate reflux is supplied at the bottom of the column by adding solvent to a portion of the raffinate layer

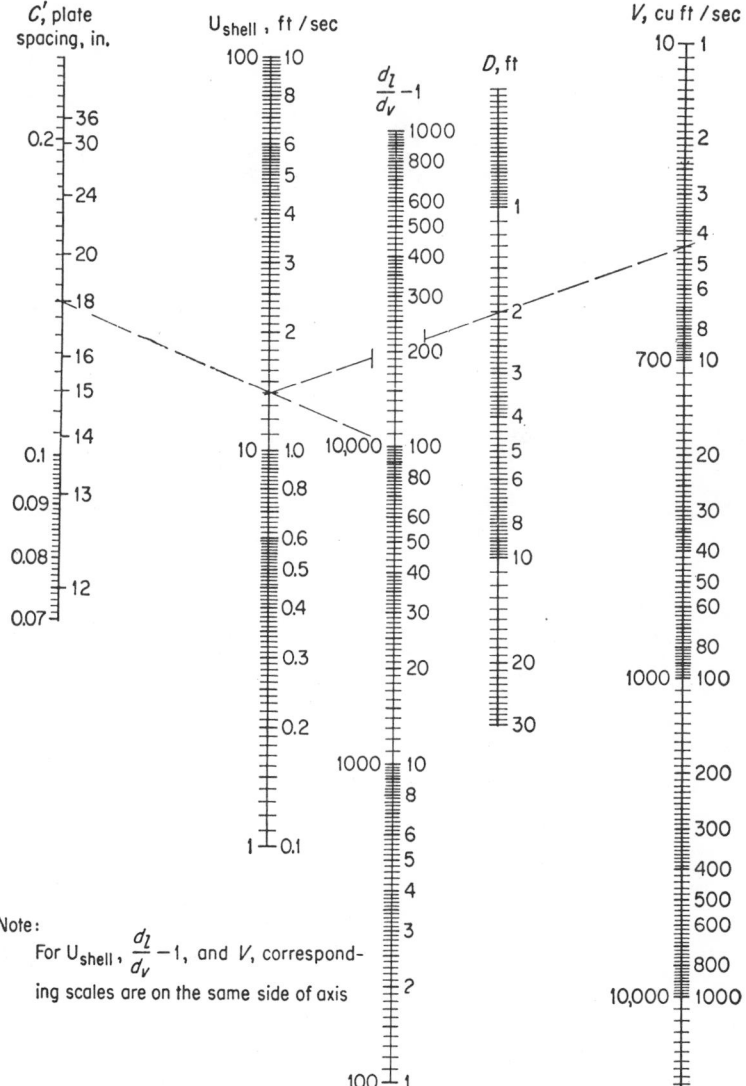

FIG. 5-5a. Vapor velocity of bubble-cap columns, entrainment-controlling.

$$\text{Linear velocity: } U_{\text{shell}} = C' \sqrt{\frac{d_1}{d_v} - 1} \qquad V = \frac{\pi D^2}{4} U_{\text{shell}}$$

where U_{shell} = maximum allowable superficial vapor velocity, entrainment-controlling, fps; G_{shell} = maximum allowable superficial vapor-mass velocity, entrainment-controlling, lb/(hr)(ft²); V = total vapor flow at column conditions, ft³/sec; W = total vapor flow at column conditions, lb/hr; d_1, d_v = liquid, vapor density at point of maximum vapor flow, lb/ft³; D = inside diameter of column shell, ft; C' = a constant (see Fig. 5-5b). (*Reproduced with permission of the Shell Development Co., Inc., Emeryville, California.*)

C' shown applies for $H \leq 2$ in. If $H > 2$ in., obtain C' approximately from curve at plate spacing = (actual plate spacing) $-3(H-2)$ where H = head over weir in inches

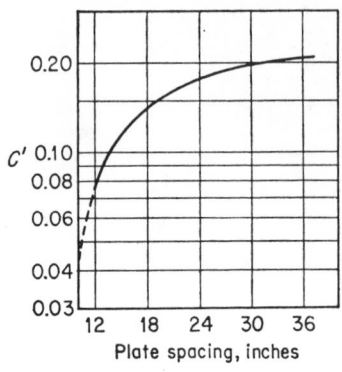

FIG. 5-5b. Correction to plate spacing for liquid depth on plate.

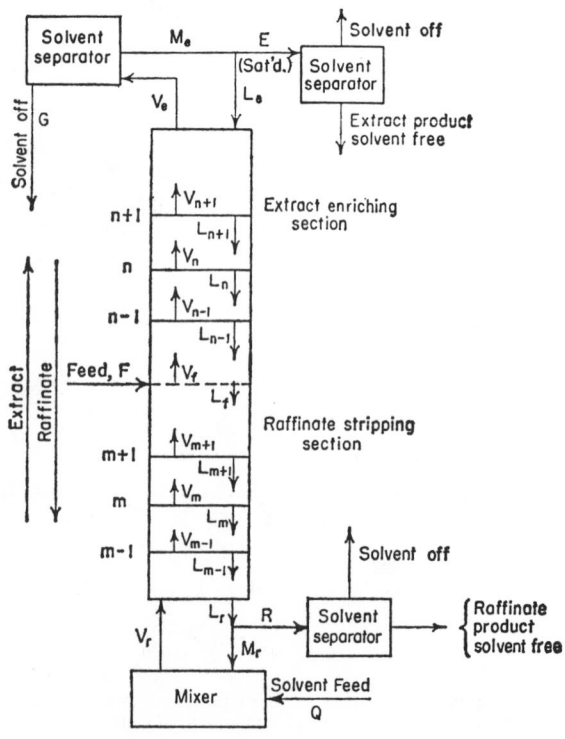

FIG. 5-6. Flow diagram for countercurrent multistage extraction with reflux.

leaving the column. Equilibrium is assumed on each tray and the feed is assumed to enter saturated with solvent.

A simplified design procedure similar to the McCabe-Thiele method for distillation may be used.

1. Equilibrium data are plotted as mass fraction of A in the extract layer (ordinate) against mass fraction of A in the raffinate layer (abscissa), *both fractions being on a solvent-free basis.*

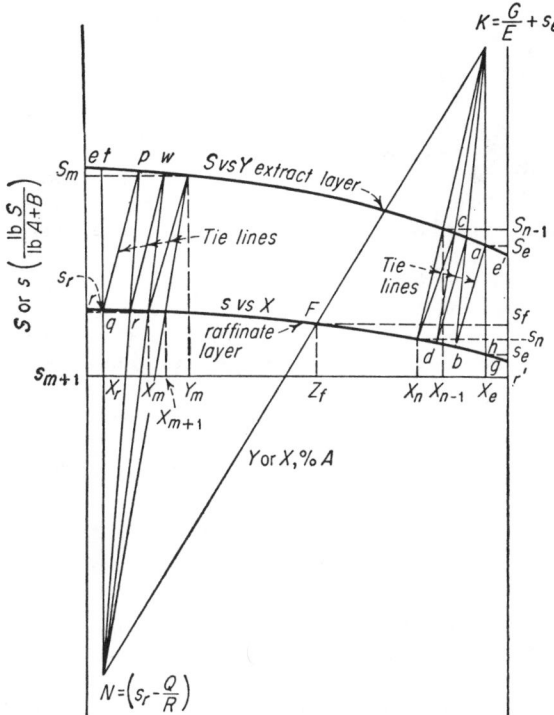

Fig. 5-7. Graphical stepwise calculation of equilibrium stages on a solvent content-concentration diagram for operation with reflux.

2. Extract and raffinate products are located on the $Y = X$ line.

3. Operating lines through these points and of slope L_e/V_e and L_r/V_r are drawn.

4. Plates are stepped off as in the McCabe-Thiele method previously described.

A more precise design procedure is illustrated in Fig. 5-7 and is outlined below. All flow rates and concentrations are on a solvent-free basis, unless otherwise noted.

1. From known equilibrium relationships construct the S vs. Y (extract layer) and s vs. X (raffinate layer) lines on working diagram.

2. Locate the operating point K at an abscissa of X_e (extract-product composition) and an ordinate of $G/E + s_e$.

3. Locate the operating point N at an abscissa of X_r (the A content of the raffinate product) and an ordinate of $s_r - Q/R$. A line joining K and N will intersect the s vs. X line at Z_f (solvent content of the feed).

It is now possible to "walk" across the diagram to determine the number of theoretical stages necessary to effect the separation. A line is drawn from K to X_e intersecting the S vs. Y curve at a. Line ab is an equilibrium tie line wherein the composition represented by b is that in equilibrium with the composition represented by a. Another line from K can then be drawn to the point b so established, and another equilibrium tie line cd is drawn. The procedure is repeated until a ray from K coincides with the line joining K and N. To the left of this dividing line the same procedure is followed, using point N where point K was used before. The number of theoretical stages is then obtained by counting the total number of rays drawn from the two operating points.

Minimum reflux on this type of diagram is obtained by moving K vertically downward and N vertically upward (at such a relative rate that F always lies on a line joining them) until the line between them coincides with a tie line through F. The ordinate of K then corresponds to a point of minimum reflux. Economic balances of column size vs. heat loads in solvent recovery of course determine the optimum degree of departure from this minimum-reflux point in actual operation.

Column Efficiency. For perforated-plate columns, the over-all efficiency may be estimated as the fraction E_c:

$$E_c = \frac{89,500 Z_t^{0.5}}{\sigma} \left(\frac{V_D}{V_C}\right)^{0.42} = \frac{0.9 Z'_t{}^{0.5}}{\sigma'} \left(\frac{V_D}{V_C}\right)^{0.42} \tag{5-20a}$$

For packed columns, the efficiency is expressed in the height assigned to a transfer unit (HTU) or theoretical stage (HETS). Ellis [*Ind. Chemist*, **28,** 483 (1952)] shows that, for *rough estimates*, the following empirical relationships are useful for towers packed with Raschig rings larger than ⅜ in.

1. Transfer of solute from aqueous continuous to dispersed organic phase,

$$\text{HETS} = \frac{94.5 \mu_C (12 d_F)^b (V_C/V_D)^{0.5}}{10^{0.0683 s} \, \Delta\rho} \tag{5-20b}$$

2. Transfer of solute from dispersed organic to aqueous continuous phase,

$$\text{HETS} = \frac{69 \mu_C (12 d_F)^b}{10^{0.0535 s} \, \Delta\rho} \tag{5-20c}$$

where $b = 2.15/10^{0.096 s}$. Here s is the average of the mutual solubilities of the solute-free contacted liquids in each other, expressed as weight per cent, and provides a rough measure of interfacial tension. For liquid pairs as insoluble as toluene and water, s may be taken as zero.

Extraction-tower Diameter. Limiting flows, and hence minimum allowable diameters, in liquid-liquid extraction columns may be calculated by using Fig. 5-8. While strictly applicable only to packed towers, the figure may also be applied to bubble-cap columns in the absence of better data.

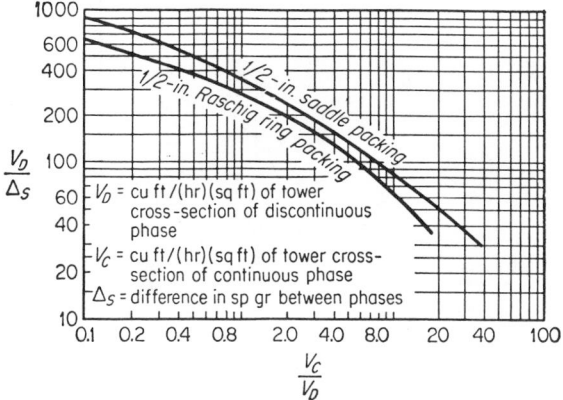

FIG. 5-8. Colburn correlation of flooding data for packed extraction columns.

5-4. Gas Absorption

Definitions. Gas absorption consists of the transfer of a component from a gas phase to a liquid phase. The liquid phase is called the *solvent*, or *absorbant*; the transferred gas is called the *solute*, or *absorbate*. Usually, the solute is selectively absorbed from a carrier gas. Fundamental considerations and design methods that apply to absorption are useful generally for the reverse operation of *desorption*, or *stripping*.

Equilibrium Data. Gas solubility in a liquid is measured as a function of partial pressure or concentration of the gas in the equilibrium vapor phase. Solubilities sometimes are reported in the form of Henry's-law constants. Equilibrium data for many systems may be found in standard reference sources (e.g., "Perry's Chemical Engineers' Handbook," 4th ed., sec. 14, McGraw-Hill Book Company, New York, 1963).

Equipment. Gas absorption or stripping is accomplished in three principal types of equipment: *absorption columns*, packed or plate; *spray chambers* or towers; *bubble-sparged tanks*, frequently agitated. Only absorption columns, by far the most important, will be treated here.

Column Height. The height of a *packed column* is determined by the degree of separation to be achieved and by a characteristic contacting effectiveness of the packing. The former may be expressed by stream compositions or by number of transfer units [Eq. (5-8)]; the latter, by the appropriate transfer coefficient [Eq. (5-3)] or HTU [Eqs. (5-6) and (5-7)]. Typical values of HTU are shown in Figs. 5-9 and 5-10.

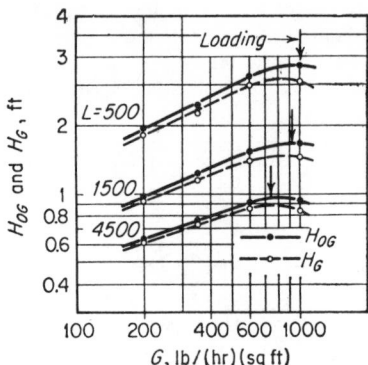

Fig. 5-9. Absorption of ammonia in water—1.5-in. ceramic Raschig rings. (*Data of Fellinger, Sc.D. Thesis, Massachusetts Institute of Technology*, Cambridge, Mass., 1941.)

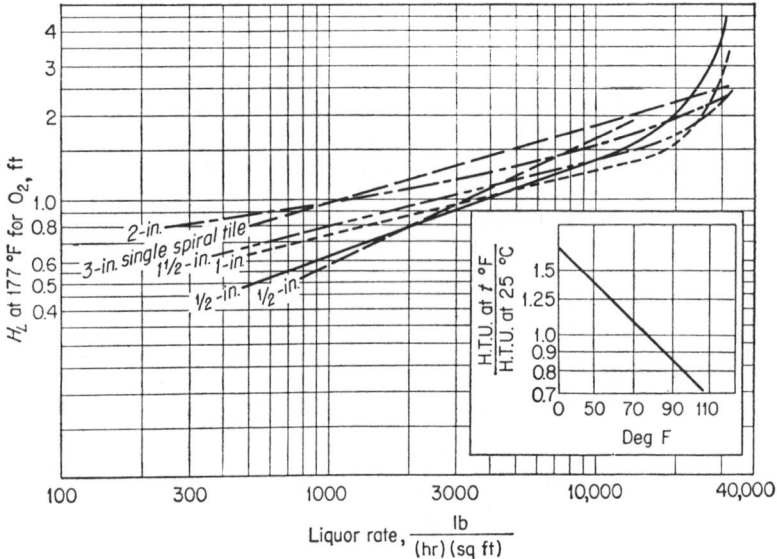

Fig. 5-10. Desorption of O_2, H_2, and CO_2 from water, compiled by Sherwood and Holloway (*Trans. AIChE*, **36**, 39 (1940), using a 20-in. diameter column with packaged heights from 13 to 49 in. The plot gives values of H_L for oxygen at 25°C; values at other temperatures may be obtained from the small ratio plot. The curves apply to dumped rings, except for 2-in. and 3-in. spiral tile, which apply to dumped or stacked staggered.

The number of transfer units required may be calculated from Eq. (5-8) or, if operating and equilibrium lines are approximately straight, by Fig. 5-11, use of which requires knowledge of the slope of the equilibrium line m and stipulation of G_M/L_M. The latter should be an economic selection. For most columns, 0.7 is an acceptable value for mG_M/L_M, but something less may be used if the solute is of low economic value.

If the concentration of solute left in the exit gas stream (hence, the column height) is simply an economic choice, the effluent composition y_2 may be calculated thus:

$$y_2 - mx_2 = \frac{C_1H_{OG}}{C_2\theta_y G_M(1 - mG_M/L_M)} \tag{5-21}$$

The number of ideal plates in a *plate column* may be determined by the McCabe-Thiele procedure (Sec. 5-2).

Once the values of HTU_L and HTU_G are estimated for the particular

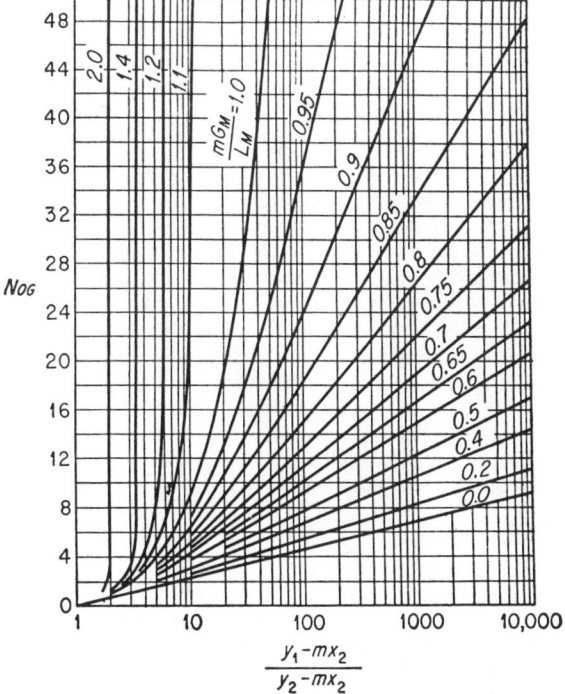

FIG. 5-11. Number of transfer units in an absorption column. Subscripts 1 and 2 refer to the concentrated and dilute ends, respectively.

conditions under consideration and then combined to give a value for HTU_{OG}, the total packed-tower height is obtained from

$$Z = HTU_{OG} \, N_{OG} \qquad (5\text{-}21a)$$

The estimation of N_{OG} may be obtained from Fig. 5-11, assuming that the operating and equilibrium lines are both straight or, at worst, only slightly curved.

Emmert and Pigford ("Perry's Chemical Engineers' Handbook," 4th ed., sec. 14, p. 38, McGraw-Hill Book Company, New York, 1963) list plate efficiencies for absorption.

Column Diameter. For packed columns, a final economic consideration results from compromising power cost (to overcome gas pressure drop) with the cost of added column diameter. This balance results in an optimum gas velocity

$$GM_{,\text{opt}} = 2{,}680\phi^{\frac{4}{9}}(C_3/C_4\theta_y b')^{\frac{1}{9}} \qquad (5\text{-}22)$$

For plate columns, the diameter usually is limited by entrainment considerations. In this case, Fig. 5-5 may be used.

5-5. Humidification

Definitions. A system comprising a noncondensable gas in contact adiabatically with a liquid will equilibrate, so that at the equilibrium temperature the amount of vapor contained in the gas contributes a partial pressure equal to vapor pressure of the liquid. The process of approaching such an equilibrium is called humidification. The equilibrium temperature is the *adiabatic-saturation temperature*. The equilibrium gas-vapor mixture is said to be *saturated* and at its *dew-point temperature*. The degree of saturation of the mixture is indicated by the difference between its measured temperature (called the *dry-bulb temperature*) and the steady-state temperature assumed by a small amount of liquid (e.g., a film or surface) that is evaporating into a large amount of the mixture; this temperature is called the *wet-bulb temperature*. For the system air-water, wet-bulb and adiabatic-saturation temperatures are equal, a fortuity not shared by other gas-vapor systems.

The composition of gas-vapor mixtures is described by four alternative quantities: *absolute humidity*, the mass of vapor carried by unit mass of dry gas; *percentage absolute* humidity, the ratio of absolute humidity to absolute humidity at saturation at the same temperature and pressure, expressed as a percentage; *molal humidity*, the mole ratio of vapor to gas; and *relative humidity*, the ratio of partial pressure of vapor to its vapor pressure. The properties of air-water mixtures are so frequently of interest that the humidity and related values are commonly summarized in a *humidity chart*. Figure 5-12 is a section of such a chart for 1 atm. The unmarked lines that slope upward to the left are adiabatic-cooling lines. If a total pressure other than 1 atm is involved, Fig. 5-12 may be used only if properly corrected (see "Perry's Chemical Engineers' Handbook," 4th ed., page 15–10, McGraw-Hill Book Company, New York, 1963).

Humidification and dehumidification are important to cooling-tower and

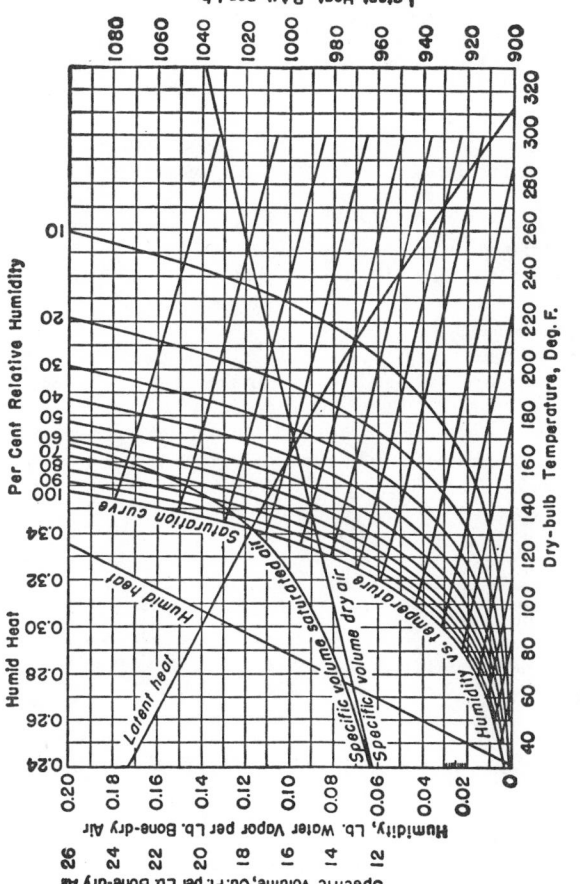

Fig. 5-12. Humidity chart for air–water vapor mixtures.

5–25

spray-pond operation, air conditioning, and drying. Air conditioning is not appropriate for treatment here. Drying is the subject of Sec. 5-6.

Cooling Towers. A cooling tower is a structure in which water is sprayed or trickled to provide extensive contact with air that is circulated through the tower to effect evaporative cooling of the water. Cooling towers are of four major types: *forced-draft* (air blown in at the bottom), *induced-draft* (air withdrawn by a fan at the top), *atmospheric* (air circulation dependent on wind), and *natural-draft* (air flown dependent on density difference between entrance and exit). Induced-draft towers are the most widely used in the United States.

Design of Induced-draft Counterflow Towers. Performance of a cooling tower is determined by mass ratio of air to water circulated, the wet-bulb temperature of the air, and the time of contact provided. In good design practice, the water is cooled no more than to within 5°F of the wet-bulb temperature of the air.

The time of contact required determines the height of the tower. It is fixed by the approach to wet-bulb temperature required and by the contacting effectiveness of the tower (usually characterized by an over-all transfer coefficient). The exact height of a tower that will achieve a particular approach should be established by consultation with a reputable manufacturer. For estimation, the following figures may be applied when a cooling range (difference between entrance and exit water temperatures) of 25 to 35°F is required:

Approach to wet-bulb, °F	20–15	15–8	8–4
Height of contact section, ft	15–20	25–30	35–40

The air-water ratio and the rate of water treatment required establish the cross section of the tower. Air velocity is commonly fixed at about 350

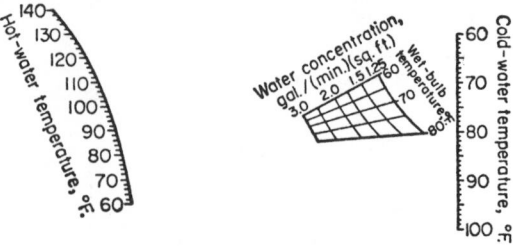

Fig. 5-13. Sizing chart for counterflow induced-draft cooling tower. For induced-draft towers with (1) upspray distributing system and 24 ft of filling or (2) flume-type distributing system and 32 ft of filling. (Chart will give approximations for towers of any height.) (*Courtesy of Fluor Corp.*)

ft³/(ft² active tower volume)(min). For this air rate, the appropriate water rate may be estimated from Fig. 5-13. Knowledge of the water rate then permits calculation of tower cross section.

As a rule of thumb, one may estimate the fan-power requirement of a well-designed tower as 0.04 hp/ft² tower cross section.

Spray Ponds. A spray pond produces evaporative cooling by spraying water upward through a number of nozzles into contact with the air circulating across the pond. With proper design, the water may approach to within 5°F of the air wet-bulb temperature. The nozzles should provide fine drops, but not mist that will be carried away to cause excessive loss.

Table 5-1 provides design data that will assist in the layout of a spray pond. A long narrow pond is more effective than a square one, and the pond should be placed with its long axis perpendicular to the direction of the prevailing summer wind.

Table 5-1. Spray-pond Engineering Data and Design

Recommendations	Usual	Minimum	Maximum
Nozzle capacity, gpm each	35–50	10	60
Nozzles per 12-ft length of pipe	5–6	4	8
Height of nozzles above sides of basin, ft	7–8	2	10
Nozzle pressure, psi	5–7	4	10
Size of nozzles and nozzle arms, in.	2	1¼	2½
Distance between spray lateral piping, ft	25	13	38
Distance of nozzles from side of pond, unfenced, ft	25–35	20	50
Distance of nozzles from side of pond, fenced, ft	12–18	10	25
Height of louver fence, ft	12	6	18
Depth of pond basin, ft	4–5	2	7
Friction loss per 100 ft pipe, in. of water	1–3	....	6
Design wind velocity, mph	5	3	10

SOURCE: *Spray Pond Bull.* SP-51, p. 3, Marley Co., Kansas City, Mo.

5-6. Drying

Definitions. Drying is the evaporative removal of liquid from a solid. The solid usually is particulate or porous, and the liquid may be merely physically contained by voids in the solid or physicochemically bound to the solid. During drying, heat must be transferred to the solid-liquid system as evaporating material simultaneously is transferred through and away from the solid.

Drying generally occurs at a rate that depends on the degree of dryness accomplished. As illustrated in Fig. 5-14, an erratic *warmup*

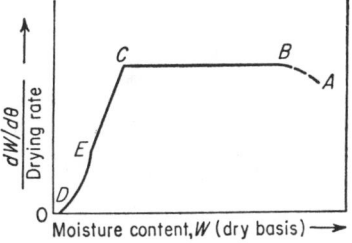

FIG. 5-14. Typical drying-rate curve.

period (*AB*) leads to a *constant-rate* period (*BC*), which is followed by one or more regimes of *falling rate* (two are shown, *CE* and *ED*). The value of *W* at point C is known as the *critical moisture content*. The drying process is limited in that it can proceed no further than to the *equilibrium moisture content* of the solids, a characteristic value for every solid that depends on temperature and humidity of the gas in contact with it.

Determination of Drying Rates and Drying Cycles. Drying rates generally must be determined experimentally, with representative samples of the material of interest being dried under the conditions anticipated for the operation. If the liquid being removed is water, if the drying gas is air, and if there is negligible heat transferred by conduction through the solid or by radiation, the rate of drying during the constant-rate period may be estimated as

$$\frac{dw}{d\theta} = \frac{0.0128G^{0.8}A(t_a - t_w)}{\lambda} = \frac{0.128G^{0.8}S(t_a - t_w)}{\rho'_s L\lambda} \tag{5-23}$$

The rate during the falling-rate period frequently is approximated by one of two expressions. If liquid diffusion within the solid controls,

$$\left(\frac{dW}{d\theta}\right)_f = -(\pi^2 D/4L^2)(W - W_e) \tag{5-24}$$

Otherwise, many cases are satisfied by the expression

$$\left(\frac{dW}{d\theta}\right)_f = -K(W - W_e) \tag{5-25}$$

where K is a function of the constant rate:

$$K = (-dW/d\theta)_c/(W_c - W_e) \tag{5-26}$$

Examples of materials obeying Eqs. (5-24) and (5-25) are given in Table 5-2.

Table 5-2. Materials Obeying Eqs. (5-24) and (5-25)

Materials Obeying Eq. (5-24)	*Materials Obeying Eq.* (5-25)
1. Single-phase solid systems, such as soap, gelatin, glue	1. Coarse granular solids, such as sand, paint pigments, minerals
2. Wood and similar solids below the fiber-saturation point	2. Materials in which moisture flow occurs at concentrations above the equilibrium moisture content at atmospheric saturation, or above the fiber-saturation point
3. Last stages of drying starches, textiles, paper, clay, hydrophilic solids, and other materials when bound water is being removed	

From Eqs. (5-23) and (5-25), the time to dry a material obeying these relations may be calculated simply:

$$\theta_t = \theta_c + \theta_f = \frac{(W_0 - W_c)\lambda L\rho_s}{h_t(t_a - t_s)} + \frac{\rho_s L\lambda(W_c - W_e)}{h_t(t_a - t_s)} \ln \frac{W_c - W_e}{W - W_e}$$

$$= B\left(\frac{W_0 - W_c}{W_c - W_e} + \ln \frac{W_c - W_e}{W - W_e}\right) \tag{5-27}$$

Through-circulation Drying. In some types of dryers, the hot gas is circulated through a granular bed rather than over a massive slab or surface.

The time to complete a through-circulation cycle may be approximated by Eq. (5-27) if the coefficient B is replaced by B', defined

$$B' = \frac{2.7\rho_s\lambda D_p{}^{0.41}(W_c - W_e)}{c_s a G^{0.59}\,\Delta t_m} \tag{5-28}$$

5-7. Evaporation

Definitions. Evaporation is the *separation of liquid* from a solution or suspension *by vaporization*. The separation usually is not complete, but may be; the removed vapor may not be condensed, but usually is; and the condensate may or may not be recovered, depending on its material value.

An *evaporator* usually consists of an array of tubes in parallel so placed in a surrounding vessel called the body that liquid contained in the body has access to the interior of the tubes. The tubes are heated, usually by steam, so that the liquid boils within them. Circulation in the tubes may be forced

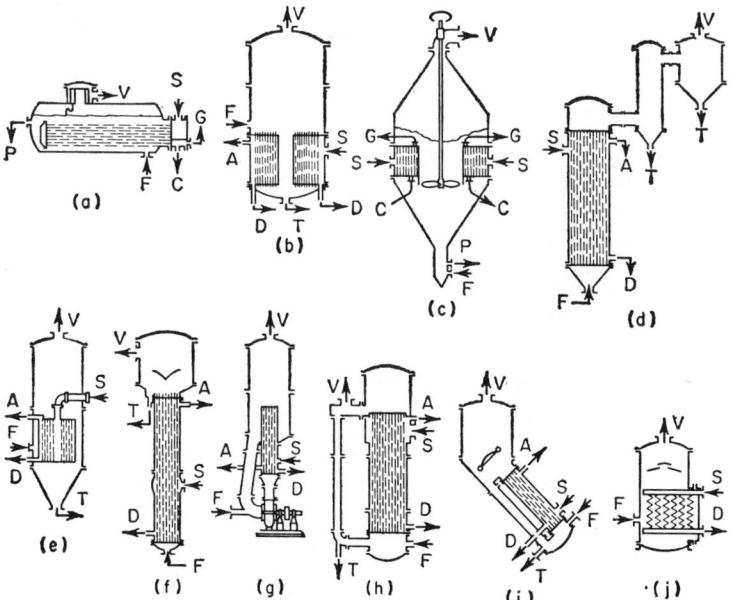

Fig. 5-15. Typical evaporator designs. (*a*) Horizontal tube. (*b*) Short tube vertical. (*c*) Propeller calandria. (*d*) Long tube vertical without vapor head. (*e*) Basket type. (*f*) Long tube vertical. (*g*) Forced circulation. (*h*) Long tube vertical with downtake. (*i*) Buflovac inclined tube. (*j*) Coiled tube.

by a pump or agitator or may be natural. Figure 5-15 shows some popular types of evaporators.

Heat Transfer in Evaporators. Heat transfer is the most important single factor in evaporator design, for the heating surface represents the largest part

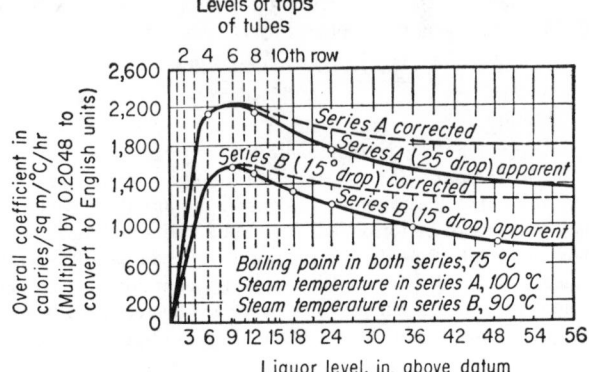

Fig. 5-16. Heat transfer coefficients in a horizontal-tube evaporator. [*Badger, Trans. AIChE,* **13**, pt II, 148 (1920).]

of evaporator cost. Equipment costs usually are correlated as functions only of heating area, materials of construction, and evaporator type.

The rate of heat transfer is conveniently calculated in terms of an over-all coefficient by the usual expression $q = UA \Delta t$, but special considerations obtain. The over-all coefficient is composited from individual coefficients for the boiling liquid, the condensing heating medium, the tube wall, and scale collected on the tube wall. In good practice the latter three will be large

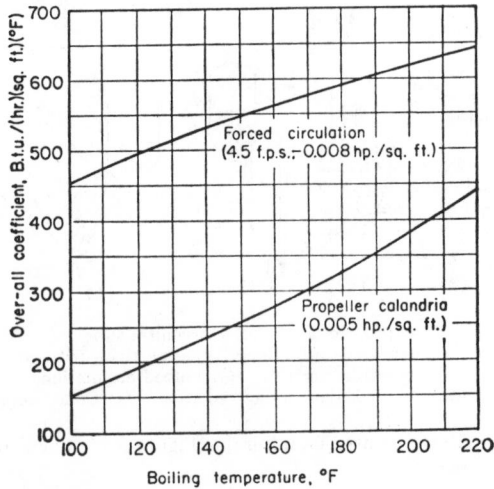

Fig. 5-17. Heat transfer coefficients in salt evaporators.

relative to the first, and the over-all coefficient is substantially equal to the boiling-liquid film coefficient. The area employed, therefore, is that of the liquid side.

The values of U used are nearly always derived from experimentally observed rate of evaporation and Δt. The temperature difference observed, however, is more often apparent than real because it is inferred from pressure measurements, and these correspond to temperature values that do not reflect boiling-point rise of the liquid due to dissolved solute, or temperature shifts on the steam side due to vapor superheat or condensate subcooling. Such Δt values are known as *apparent temperature differences,* and the values of U corresponding to them are known as *apparent coefficients.*

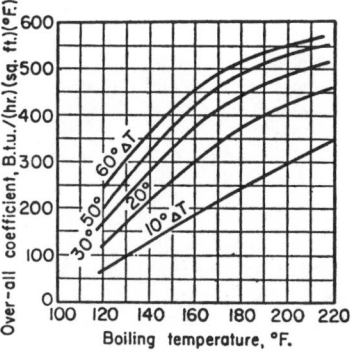

FIG. 5-18. Heat transfer coefficients for water in short tube.

Error on the steam side usually is small. When the boiling-point rise is known, therefore, and the temperature difference can be adjusted for it, nearly correct values of Δt and U result; such values are known as *temperature difference and coefficient corrected for boiling-point rise.* When not otherwise stipulated, the values reported for evaporators usually are these.

Illustrative over-all coefficients are given in Figs. 5-16 to 5-19. These

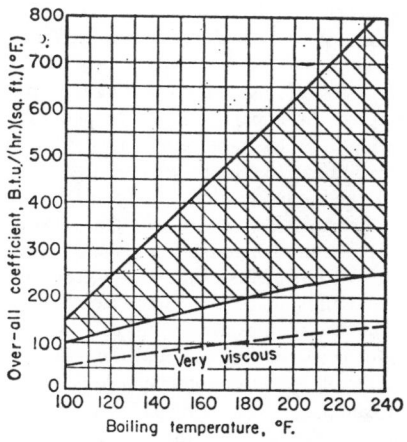

FIG. 5-19. General range of LTV coefficients.

coefficients are intended only for high-spot estimation; they are unreliable for close design calculation. Final designs should be based on tests of the actual material or on the judgment of experts.

Scale Formation and Optimum Cycle. When the evaporating liquid deposits a scale on the heating surface, the over-all heat transfer coefficient diminishes and finally becomes so low that the evaporator must be shut down for cleaning. If the scale thickness is proportional to the amount of liquid evaporated, the feed rate to the evaporator (which is proportional to the evaporation rate and hence to U) will be related to time elapsed since last cleaning, thus:

$$1/F^2 = a\theta + b \qquad (5\text{-}29)$$

The length of cycle θ_m to give maximum average productivity of the evaporator then is

$$\theta_m = \theta_c + (2/a) \sqrt{ab\theta_c} \qquad (5\text{-}30)$$

Multiple-effect Evaporation. A multiple-effect evaporator is merely a series of evaporator bodies so connected that the vapor from one body is the heating medium for the next. Passing from single to multiple effect does not alter the major features of body construction; it merely affects the interconnecting piping and the operation.

The purpose of multiple-effect evaporation is to reduce the steam consumption. One pound of steam entering the first effect will evaporate approximately 1 lb of water in that effect. This pound of water vapor will then pass to the steam space of the second effect and, in condensing, will evaporate approximately another pound of water, and so on, so that in N effects, 1 lb of steam will evaporate approximately (but somewhat less than) N lb of water. The pressure must be progressively reduced from effect to effect in order to produce a temperature difference between the boiling liquid of that effect and the vapor from the preceding one.

If it is assumed that the terminal temperatures (temperature of heating steam available and temperature corresponding to the vacuum that can be produced in the condenser) are fixed, then passing from a single to a multiple effect does not increase the capacity of an evaporator. If a single-effect evaporator is operating between these terminal conditions and requires A ft^2 heating surface to accomplish the desired evaporation, an N-effect evaporator to be used between the same terminal conditions for the same weight of water evaporated will require N bodies of approximately A ft^2 each to accomplish the same result. In short, passing from single- to multiple-effect operation decreases steam cost but increases apparatus cost.

The effects are commonly made the same size. The total area required may be calculated from the simultaneous solution of heat and material balance statements written for the several effects and the entire evaporator (e.g., see McCabe and Smith, "Unit Operations of Chemical Engineering," pp. 563–569, McGraw-Hill Book Company, New York, 1956).

Thermocompression. The simplest, though not the least expensive, means of reducing the energy requirements of evaporation is to compress the vapor from a single-effect evaporator so that the vapor can be used as the heating medium in the same evaporator. The compression may be accomplished by mechanical means or by a steam jet. In order to keep the compressor cost and power requirements within reason, the evaporator must work with a fairly narrow temperature difference, usually from about 10 to 20°F. This means that a large evaporator heating surface is needed, partially offsetting the advantages of thermocompression.

MULTIPHASE CONTACTING AND PHASE DISTRIBUTION

5-8. Disperse Systems

In chemical processing, it is often desirable to subdivide a phase and distribute it throughout a second continuous phase (1) to promote interphase transfer of mass or energy or (2) to produce or approach a uniform dispersion as an end goal. The subdivided phase may be solid, liquid, or gas; the continuous phase is nearly always fluid. The dispersion of gases, liquids, and particulate solids into liquids and of liquids and particulate solids into gases are all of processing importance. The more important unit operations whereby energy is directed to multiphase contacting and phase distribution are treated in this section.

5-9. Agitation

Definitions. Agitation is motion imparted to material to promote heat or mass transfer to, from, or within the material or to distribute another phase through the material. The terms "agitation" and "mixing" are popularly, if unprecisely, interchanged; because the operation achieves many important functions besides mixing, the more general name *agitation* is preferred.

The most important process applications of agitation involve a freely fluid liquid as the primary phase. The key equipment is almost always a rotating element (sometimes more than one) called the *agitator*, or *impeller*. Turbines, paddles, propellers, and special shapes are used, the choice depending somewhat upon the viscosity or consistency of the agitated material, somewhat upon the function being performed, and somewhat upon the whim of the designer. Over wide ranges of conditions, the effectiveness of an agitator depends more on the power that it delivers and the way in which it is used than on the particulars of its shape.

The significant process design considerations related to the stipulation of an agitator are its performance with respect to the process function required and its power-delivery capability.

Agitation Power. The power required by a rotating impeller cannot be calculated directly; rather it must be measured for an accurate model of the agitator and its surroundings and then scaled up or down by the principle of dimensional similitude, involving in this case the numerics Reynolds number $D_a^2 N \rho / \mu$, power number $P g_c / D_a^5 \rho N^3$, and Froude number $g / N^2 D_a$. A great many data have been so reported for a variety of impeller designs. The most extensive and useful are those of Fig. 5-20. Given the diameter of one of the impellers described by Fig. 5-20 and the properties of the agitated

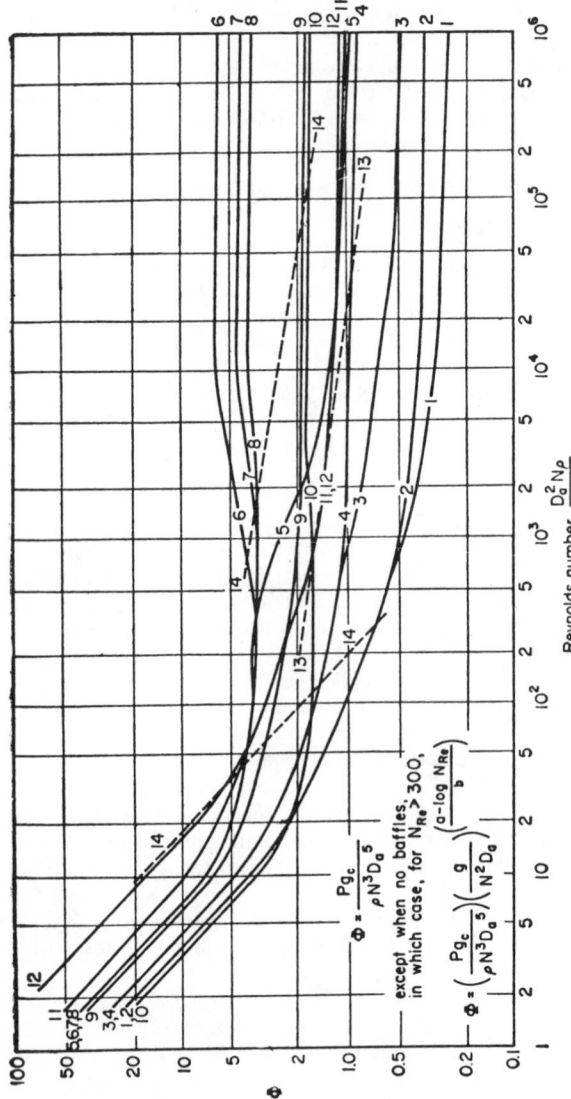

FIG. 5-20. Power characteristics of various mixing propellers.

$$\Phi = \frac{Pg_c}{\rho N^3 D_a{}^5}$$

except when no baffles,
in which case, for $N_{Re} > 300$,

$$\Phi = \left(\frac{Pg_c}{\rho N^3 D_a{}^5}\right)\left(\frac{g}{N^2 D_a}\right)^{\left(\frac{a - \log N_{Re}}{b}\right)}$$

Reynolds number, $\dfrac{D_a{}^2 N \rho}{\mu}$

liquid, one can calculate the power delivered at any impeller speed. The values of a and b depend on impeller design (Table 5-3).

Table 5-3. Values of Parameters for the Agitation-power Froude-number Exponent n†

Impeller	Tank-to-impeller ratio, D_t/D_a	a	b
Square-pitch marine propeller, three blades..	2.1	2.6	18
	2.7	2.3	18
	3.0	2.1	18
	3.3	1.7	18
	4.5	0	18
Flat-blade Mixco turbine, six blades.........	3.3	1.0	40
	3.0	1.0	40

† $n = (a - \log N_{Re})/b$. In baffled tanks, or in unbaffled tanks when $N_{Re} > 300$, $n = 0$.
SOURCE: Rushton, Costich, and Everett, *Chem. Eng. Progr.*, **46**, 401 (1950).

In the use of an agitation-power-number chart, *care must be exercised that the exact geometry of the system of the chart be preserved.* A 20 per cent increase in impeller diameter, for example, can result in a 2.5-fold increase in power, and the presence of dip legs and coil supports may baffle the tank sufficiently to cause a 5-fold increase in power over that for an unbaffled tank.

Functional Performance of Agitators. The degree or effectiveness of agitation is related to the intensity of shear, the level of turbulence, and the circulation rate produced by the impeller. For an impeller of given design, these quantities are determined by the agitator speed and power delivery.

Agitator design generally must be based on model tests in which the desired performance is achieved and on a reliable scale-up method. For many functions for which a scale-up correlation has not been established, an inexact but satisfactory basis consists of *maintaining geometrical similarity and constant power input per unit volume of agitated material in model and scaled-up design.* Workable designs have resulted from this procedure for miscible-liquid blending, immiscible-liquid dispersion, and solids-in-liquid suspension. The method tends to be conservative for scale-up; i.e., as scale size increases, agitation intensity increases rather than remaining constant.

As a rough guide to degree of agitation developed by rotating impellers in water, Table 5-4 may be used. For material more dense than water, the power levels should be increased proportionately.

Table 5-4. Agitation Intensity in Water

Degree of Agitation	Power/Input, $Hp/1.000$ Gal
Mild....................	0.05–0.2
Moderate..............	0.2–0.8
Vigorous*..............	0.8–4.0
Violent*...............	>4

* Power input greater than 1 hp/1,000 gal generally requires a baffled tank.

It should be noted that the power referred to in Table 5-4 and in the preceding discussion is that actually delivered to the material by the impeller, and not the input to the motor or drive.

Suspension of Solids. Equations (5-31) and (5-32), due to Weisman and Efferding, [*AIChE J.*, **6**, 419 (1960)], are guides to the power input to a baffled tank to remove the last particle of heavy solid from the tank bottom [Eq. (5-31)] and to produce a uniform suspension of height Z_s above the tank bottom [Eq. (5-32)].

$$P_s = \frac{1.2(g\,\Delta\rho)^{1.5}VD_p{}^{0.5}}{g_c\rho_l{}^{0.5}}\left(\frac{1-\epsilon}{\epsilon}\right)^{0.5} \tag{5-31}$$

$$\frac{Z_s - B}{D_t} = 0.23 \ln\left[\frac{g_cP}{g\rho_m V_s u_{ls}}\left(\frac{D_a}{D_t}\right)^{0.5}(1-\epsilon)^{-0.67}\right] + 0.1 \tag{5-32}$$

Gas Dispersion. When gas is dispersed in a liquid, it is usually to promote mass transfer between the gas and liquid phases. An absorption coefficient then becomes a proper performance parameter. The Bernard equation predicts coefficients for oxygen absorption in water promoted by a flat paddle in a baffled tank:

$$\log k_La = 0.0425 - 0.0939\log D'_a + 0.5690\log P_V - 0.0457\,(\log P_V)^2$$
$$+ 0.4190\log V_S - 0.1699\,(\log V_S)^2 \tag{5-33}$$

For other liquid-phase controlled systems and other agitator geometries, the form of correlation presumably would hold with different constants. Over considerable ranges of power and equipment size the simpler correlation of $\log (K_La/V_S{}^{0.67})$ against $\log P_V$ should be satisfactory. Use of this scale-up scheme or of Eq. (5-33) is difficult because the power delivered by the agitator at a given speed varies with gas input rate in a complicated way (see "Perry's Chemical Engineers' Handbook," 4th ed., page 18–80, McGraw-Hill Book Company, New York, 1963).

Heat Transfer in Agitated Tanks. Heat transfer coefficients to jacket and coil walls inside agitated tanks may be calculated from a Sieder-Tate type of relation:

$$\frac{hD_t}{k} = a\left(\frac{D_a{}^2 N\rho}{\mu}\right)^{0.67}\left(\frac{c\mu}{k}\right)^{0.33}\left(\frac{\mu_B}{\mu_W}\right)^{0.14} \tag{5-34}$$

where a depends on agitator and surface geometry, as shown in Table 5-5.

Table 5-5. Coefficient for Agitation Sieder-Tate Equation

Agitator	Surface	a
Turbine..........	Jacket	0.62
	Coil	1.50
Paddle..........	Jacket	0.36
	Coil	0.87
Anchor..........	Jacket	0.46
Propeller.........	Jacket	0.54
	Coil	0.83

SOURCE: Ackley, *Chem. Eng.*, **67** (16), 133 (1960).

5-10. Spray Generation

Definitions. A spray is a mechanically produced, unstable suspension of liquid drops in a gas. Mists and fogs, on the other hand, are formed by condensation and usually are relatively stable. Sprays are generated from

Table 5-7. Discharge Rates and Included Angle of Spray of Typical Pressure Nozzles

Nozzle type	Orifice diam., in.	Discharge, gpm, and included angle of spray							
		10 psi		25 psi		50 psi		100 psi	
		Discharge	Angle, deg	Discharge	Angle, deg	Discharge	Angle, deg	Discharge	Angle, deg
Hollow cone......	0.046	.....	..	0.10	65	0.135	68	0.183	75
	.140	0.535	82	0.81	88	1.10	90	1.50	93
	.218	1.25	83	1.88	86	2.55	89	3.45	92
	.375	7.2	62	11.8	70	16.5	70		
Solid cone........	.047	.....	..	0.167	65	0.235	70	0.34	70
	.188	1.60	55	2.46	58	3.42	60	4.78	60
	.250	3.35	65	5.40	70	7.50	70	10.4	75
	.500	17.5	86	27.5	84	38.7	73		
Fan..............	.031	0.085	40	0.132	90	0.182	110	0.252	110
	.093	0.70	70	1.12	76	1.57	80	2.25	80
	.187	2.25	50	3.70	59	5.35	65	7.70	65
	.375	9.50	66	15.40	74	22.10	75	30.75	75

SOURCE: Data furnished through the courtesy of the Spray Engineering Co., Cambridge, Mass.

Table 5-8. Drop-size Distributions Produced by Three Hollow-cone Nozzles of the Same Design

Nominal drop diam., μ	Number of drops in each size group					
	0.063-in. orifice diam.			0.086-in. orifice diam.		0.128-in. orifice diam., 200 psi
	50 psi	100 psi	200 psi	100 psi	200 psi	
10	375	800	1700	100	300	100
25	200	280	580	60	150	50
50	160	180	260	41	100	45
100	50	60	70	26	34	27
150	27	31	35	14	18	15
200	19	23	27	9	12	11
300	8	9	11	5	8	6
400	2	4	4	4	7	3
500	1	1	....	2	1	2
600	1	...	....	1	...	1

NOTE: $1\mu = 10^{-4}$ cm $= 0.0000394$ in. The nominal diameter is the mid-diameter of a drop group which includes a finite range of sizes. The 25 group includes drops from 17.5 to 37.5 μ; the 50 group contains drops rom 37.5 to 75μ, etc. The number of drops has been adjusted in each case so that the total amount of fluid sprayed is the same for each size distribution.

Table 5-6. Common Applications for Spray Nozzles

First number:* type most used.
Second number: type frequently used.
Third number: type sometimes used.

Types
1. Solid-cone wide-angle spray
2. Hollow-cone wide-angle spray
3. Narrow-angle spray
4. Pressure atomizing spray
5. Tangential spray
6. Flat spray
7. Deflector or impact spray
8. Air- or gas-atomizing spray
9. Rotating-disk spray

Pressure Nozzles
Cooling circulating water for condenser (5, 1, 6)
Spray-type condensers (1, 4, 3)
Aerating and purifying water supplies (5, 1, 6)
Scrubbing and washing gases (1, 3, 9)
Humidification and dehumidification (4, 8, 3)
Spray refrigeration (5, 1)
Gas absorption and adsorption (1, 3, 5)
Spray drying (4, 8)
Chemical processes where a large free surface is required (1, 4, 8)
Distributing oil over the fuel bed in gas machines (1)
Enriching gas with a liquid distillate (1, 4)
Oil burners (4, 8, 9)
Desuperheaters (4)
Washing or coating materials in process (4, 2, 8)
Washing liquids (1, 4)
Washing automobiles, railway coaches, etc. (6, 3)
Washing coal, sand, gravel, etc. (2, 6)
Beating down foam (1, 3, 6)
Cooling mill rolls (1, 4, 6)
Descaling hot billets (3, 6)
Quenching coke and pig iron (5, 1)
Settling dust (4, 1)
Applying insecticides, weed killers, etc. (1, 7, 8)
Applying asphalt to highways (1, 7, 6)
Fire protection (7)
Ornamental sprays

Rotating Nozzles
Spraying viscous liquids and slurries (7, 9, 8)
Oil burners (4, 8, 9)
Small air moisteners (8)
Spray drying (4, 8)
Air washing (4, 1, 9)

Gas-atomizing Nozzles
Spray painting (8)
Oil burners (4, 8, 9)
Spray drying (4, 8)
Air moistening (8, 4)
Moistening materials with water or other fluids (8, 4)
Spraying small quantities of insecticides, etc. (8, 4)
Metal coating (8)
Applying cements, refractories, etc. (8, 7)

* Classification kindly supplied by S. G. Ketterer.

continuous liquid by nozzles, of which there are three principal types: *pressure nozzles, rotating nozzles* (or spinning atomizers), and *gas-atomizing nozzles* (or two-fluid nozzles).

Spray nozzles of all kinds are widely applied both inside and outside the process industries, as indicated by Table 5-6.

Pressure Nozzles. In pressure nozzles, classified as *hollow-cone, solid-cone, fan,* or *impact types,* the fluid is throttled and is broken up by its inherent instability or by its impact with the atmosphere, another jet, or a solid surface. Discharge rates and drop-size distributions typical of pressure nozzles are given in Tables 5-7 and 5-8. The power to pump through a pressure nozzle is calculated as

$$P' = 5.82 \times 10^{-4} Q \, \Delta P \tag{5-35}$$

Rotating Nozzles. A rotating nozzle is a spinning disk or cup which disintegrates by centrifugal force a liquid fed to it at low pressure. The drop-size distribution produced by a rotating nozzle may be estimated from

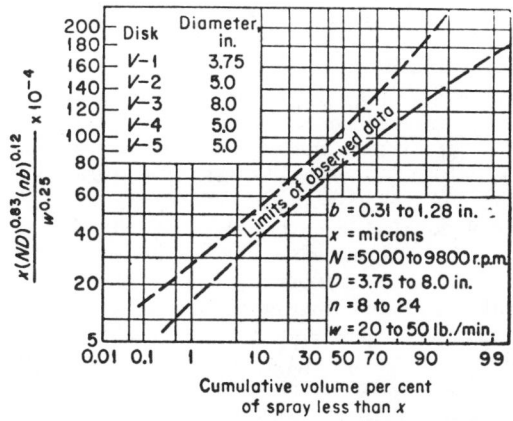

FIG. 5-21. Generalized drop-size distribution for vaned-disk atomizers. [*From Chem. Eng. Progr. Monograph Ser.,* **50** (2), 69 (1954), *with permission.*]

Fig. 5-21. The power consumed by the disk, if there is no slip and if air pumping is negligible, is

$$P' = 1.8 \times 10^{-11} \omega N^2 \frac{D^2 - D_0{}^2}{2} \tag{5-36}$$

Gas-atomizing Nozzles. These nozzles disintegrate a stream of liquid by contact with a high-velocity stream of gas. The liquid usually is pressure-fed, but need not be. The discharge capacity is small, usually less than 10 gal/hr. They produce very fine drops at the price of high-energy consumption. A typical drop-size distribution is shown in Table 5-9. The energy

Table 5-9. Drop-size Distribution of a Small Atomizing Nozzle

Drop diam., μ	Number of drops	Drop diam., μ	Number of drops
2	390,000	35	1,730
5	340,000	40	1,080
10	165,000	45	650
15	40,200	50	430
20	11,680	60	350
25	4,970	70	220
30	2,160		

NOTE: The fluid pressure and the gas pressure were each 15 psi. The total quantity of fluid represented by this size distribution is the same as that in Table 5-8, so that the numbers of drops are directly comparable.

requirement to atomize 1 lb of liquid by use of m lb of air expanding isothermally from p_1 to p_2 is

$$E = mRT \ln \frac{p_1}{p_2} \tag{5-37}$$

where R is in ft-lb/(lb mass)(°R), and T is in °R.

5-11. Gas Sparging

Definitions. A sparger is a distributor that disperses gas into the body of a liquid by emitting bubbles or jets of gas through an individual orifice, an array of orifices, or a porous structure. Spargers are used to promote gas-liquid mass transfer or to produce dispersions; sometimes they are used as gentle agitators.

Simple Bubblers. Open-end pipes or perforated tubes or plates with orifices ⅛ to ½ in. in diameter are used as spargers. A perforated tube should be so designed that the pressure drop across the air orifice is large compared with the pressure drop down the tube. At practical operating rates, simple bubblers produce jets rather than bubbles; the jets disintegrate, but the resulting cloud of bubbles may include some as large as 0.5 in. Their effectiveness as mass-transfer promoters is orders of magnitude below that of vigorously agitated tanks or packed columns, and they are used only for very easy transport operations (e.g., air humidification) or for gentle mechanical agitation.

Porous Septa. Porous plates, tubes, or disks are made by bonding or sintering carefully sized particles of carbon, ceramic, metal, or polymer. The resulting septa may be used as spargers to produce much smaller bubbles than will result from a simple bubbler. Table 5-10 lists typical grades of some commercially available porous material.

The gas flux through a porous septum is limited on the lower side by the requirement that, for good performance, the whole sparger surface should bubble uniformly, and on the higher side by the onset of serious bubble coalescence. In a practical range of fluxes, the size of bubbles produced is a direct function of both pore size and pressure drop. Figure 5-22 shows the recommended limit of flux density for carbon spargers.

Table 5-10. Characteristics of Porous Septa

Grade	Average per cent porosity	Average pore diameter	Air-permeability data		
			Diaphragm thickness, in.	Pressure differential, in. water	Air flow, ft³/(ft²)(min)
Alundum porous alumina*					
P2220	....	25	1	2	0.35
P2120	36	60	1	2	2
P260	35	164	1	2	15
P236	34	240	1	2	40
P216	....	720	1	2	110
National porous carbon†					
60	48	33	1	2	
45	48	58	1	2	2
25	48	120	1	2	13
Filtros porous silica‡					
Extra fine	26.0	55	1.5	2	1–3
Fine	28.8	110	1.5	2	4–8
Medium fine	31.1	130	1.5	2	9–12
Medium	33.7	150	1.5	2	13–20
Medium coarse	33.8	200	1.5	2	21–30
Coarse	34.5	250	1.5	2	31–59
Extra coarse	36.5	300	1.5	2	60–100
Porous plastic§					
Teflon	....	9	0.125	1.38	5
Kel-F	....	15	0.125	1.38	13
Micrometallic porous stainless steel§¶					
H	45	5	0.125	1.38	1.8
G	50	10	0.125	1.38	3
F	50	20	0.125	1.38	5
E	50	35	0.125	1.38	18
D	50	65	0.125	1.38	60
C	55	165	0.125	27.7	990

* Data by courtesy of Norton Co., Worcester, Mass. A number of other grades between the extremes listed are available.
† Data by courtesy of National Carbon Co., Cleveland, Ohio.
‡ Data by courtesy of Filtros Inc., East Rochester, N.Y.
§ Data by courtesy of Pall Corp., Glen Cove, N.Y.
¶ Similar septa made from other metals are available.

Figure 5-22 also indicates the working pressure drop across typical porous media, much higher than the dry-permeability values of Table 5-10. The wet permeability should be used for design calculations.

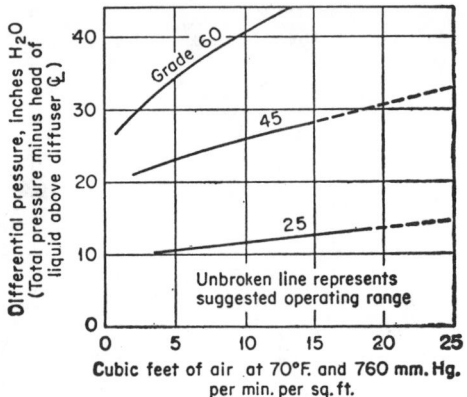

FIG. 5-22. Pressure drop across porous carbon diffusers submerged in water at 70°F. (*National Carbon Co.*)

Porous spargers are used generally to promote gas absorption. They are of the same order of effectiveness as packed or tray columns or agitated vessels, but no generalized data or methods are available for their specification as mass-transfer devices. Their advantages of simplicity and inexpensiveness are balanced by their susceptability to plugging and their awkwardness for countercurrent operations.

5-12. Fluidization

Definitions. If a gas is passed upward through an unrestrained and unconsolidated bed of granular solids with ever-increasing velocity, the pressure drop across the bed due to friction will increase until it becomes equivalent to the weight of the bed plus the friction between bed and walls. With further increase in the gas velocity, the bed tends to rise as a unit, but its unconsolidated character causes it instead to expand until the increased porosity allows the friction again just to balance the pressure drop. As the bed becomes more expanded, individual particles achieve freedom to interchange position, and the bed can circulate. Such a bed is said to be *fluidized*.

Fluidized beds sometimes are called *boiling beds*. Indeed, the expanded suspended mass of the bed does resemble a boiling liquid. This mass has a zero angle of repose, seeks its own level, and assumes the shape of the containing vessel. Just as in a vessel designed for boiling a liquid, space must be provided for vertical expansion of the solids and for disengaging splashed and entrained material.

Conditions for Fluidization. The size of solid particles which can be fluidized varies greatly, from less than 1 micron to 2½ in. It is generally concluded that particles distributed in size between 65 mesh and 10 microns are the best for smooth fluidization (least formation of large bubbles). Large particles cause instability and result in slugging or massive surges. Small particles (less than 10 microns) frequently, even though dry, act as if damp, forming agglomerates or fissures in the bed, or spouting. Adding finer-sized particles to a coarse bed or coarser-sized particles to a bed of fines usually results in better fluidization.

The upward velocity of the gas is usually between 0.5 and 10 fps. This velocity is based upon the flow through the empty vessel, and is frequently referred to as the *superficial velocity*. Its upper limit is fixed by the terminal free-settling velocity of the smallest particles in the bed that should not be carried over. The velocity used is best determined by test in equipment where visual observations of the action of the bed can be made. The flow required to maintain a completely homogeneous bed of solids, whereby coarse or heavy particles will not segregate from the fluidized portion, is very different from the minimum fluidizing velocity discussed in many papers.

Bed height is determined by a number of factors, either individually or collectively, such as:

1. Space-time yield
2. Gas-contact time
3. L/D ratio required to provide staging
4. Space required for internal heat exchangers
5. Solids-retention time

Generally, bed heights are not less than 12 in. or more than 50 ft.

For details beyond the scope of this section, references should be made to Leva ("Fluidization," McGraw-Hill Book Company, New York, 1959), Othmer ("Fluidization," Reinhold Publishing Corporation, New York, 1960), and Wells ("Perry's Chemical Engineers' Handbook," 4th ed., sec. 20, pp. 42–53, McGraw-Hill Book Company, New York, 1963).

Heat Transfer and Mixing in Fluidized Beds. Heat-exchange surfaces have been used to provide means of removing or adding heat to fluidized beds. Usually, these surfaces are provided in the form of vertical tubes manifolded at top and bottom. Other shapes have been used such as horizontal bayonets. In any such installations adequate provision must be made for abrasion of the exchanger surface by the bed. Normally, the transfer rate is 5 to 25 times that for solids-free gas.

Heat transfer from solids to gas and gas to solids usually results in a coefficient of about 3 to 10 Btu/(hr)(ft²)(°F). However, the large area of the solids per cubic foot of bed (15,000 ft²/ft³ for 60-micron particles of 40 lb/ft³ bulk density) results in the rapid approach of gas and solids temperatures. With a fairly good distributor, essential equalization of temperatures occurs within 1 to 3 in. of the top of the distributor.

Bed thermal conductivities in the vertical direction have been measured in the laboratory in the range of 20,000 to 30,000 Btu/(hr)(ft²)(°F/ft). Horizontal conductivities for ⅛-in. particles in the range of 1000 Btu/(hr) (ft²)(°F/ft) have been measured in large-scale experiments.

Except in extreme L/D ratios, the temperature in the fluidized bed is uniform, the temperature at any point being, generally, within 10°F of any other point. The solids, too, will be well mixed. For all practical purposes, beds with L/D ratios of from 4 to 0.1 can be considered to be completely mixed continuous-reaction vessels as far as the solids are concerned.

Equipment. The use of the fluidization technique requires in almost all cases the employment of a fluidized-bed system rather than an isolated piece of equipment. Figure 5-23 illustrates the arrangement of components of a

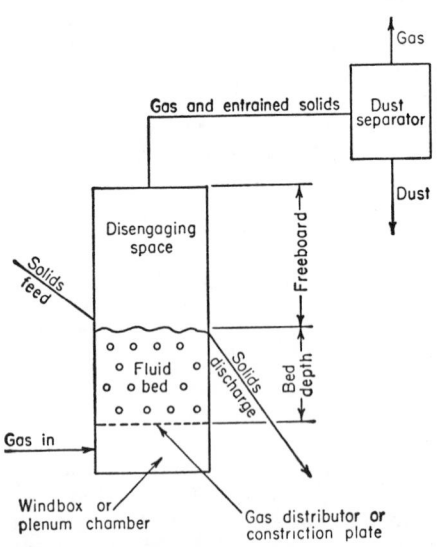

FIG. 5-23. Non-catalytic fluidized-bed system.

system used in cases where the flow of solids is small, such as is generally encountered in noncatalytic usages of the fluidized bed or in catalytic units where there is little or no deactivation of the catalyst. Figure 5-24 illustrates a catalytic-type unit such as is used for petroleum cracking where large quantities of solids flow into and out of the reactor, and to and from the catalyst regenerator, which also is usually a fluidized bed. It is obvious that, in the simplified form, the only difference between a fluidized catalytic-cracking unit and fluidized-bed units used in most other cases is the method and point of solids feed.

The major parts of a fluidized-bed system can be listed as follows:

1. Reaction vessel

    a. Fluidized-bed portion
    b. Disengaging space or freeboard
    c. Gas distributor
2. Solids feeder or flow control
3. Solids discharge
4. Dust separator for the exit gases
5. Instrumentation
6. Gas supply

The reactor is usually a vertical cylinder; however, there is no real limitation on shape. The specific design features vary with operating conditions, available space, and use. The lack of moving parts lends toward simple, clean design.

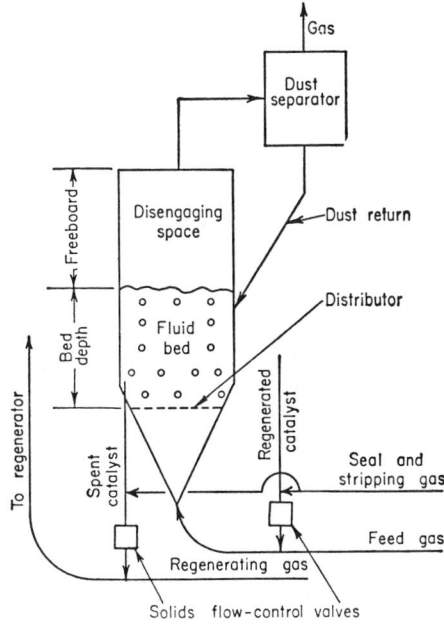

Fig. 5-24. Catalytic fluidized-bed system.

The freeboard or disengaging height is frequently chosen rather arbitrarily or based on experience. It has been established that carry-over of solids entrained by the gases is reduced as the vertical distance between the top of the dense-phase fluidized bed and gas-outlet port is increased. Small-scale experiments have also shown that the size distribution of the solids entrained by the gases is reduced as the freeboard height or cross-sectional area is increased. However, for some distance (from a few inches to a number of feet) the size distribution of the solids in the dilute suspension just above the fluid bed is the same as the size distribution of the solids in the fluid bed.

The gas distributor has a considerable effect on proper operation of the fluidized bed. Basically, there are two types: (1) for use where the inlet gas contains solids, (2) for use where the inlet gas is clean. In most cases, the distributor is designed to prevent backflow of solids during normal operation, and in many cases it is designed to prevent backflow during shutdown. In order to provide distribution, it is necessary to restrict the gas or gas and solids flow so that pressure drops across the restriction amount to from a few inches of water to a few psi. As a general rule, pressure drops in excess of 2 psi are not used.

In cases where both solids and gases pass through the distributor, such as in catalytic-cracking units, a number of variations are or have been used, such as concentric rings in the same plane, with the annuli open, concentric rings in the form of a cone, grids of T-bars or other structural shapes, flat metal perforated plates supported or reinforced with structural members, and dished and perforated plates concave both upward and downward. The last two forms are generally more economical.

Fluidized-bed reactors usually are designed by scaling up a laboratory or pilot unit. Considerable difficulty has been encountered in such scale-up because of the staging effect achieved in high L/D ratio units used in the laboratory or semiworks as compared with the lower L/D ratios used in commercial units.

Generalized correlations based upon specific reactions and catalysts or catalyst supports indicate reduced conversion and yield as the L/D ratio is decreased. Both gas and solids mixing increase as the L/D ratio is decreased [May, *Chem. Eng. Progress,* **55,** 49–56 (December, 1959); Reman, *Chem. & Ind.* (*London*), **1955,** pp. 46–51]. If adsorption of products and reactants is insignificant, a reduction in conversion will result as reactor diameter is increased. If adsorption of products and reactants is significant, a reduction of both conversion and yield will result as reactor diameter is increased.

Evidence of improved conversion by restricting mixing is presented by Ruthuff [*Petrol. Refiner,* **32** (10), 113–114 (1953); also *World Petrol.,* **24,** 42–44 (1953)]. When means to stop or hinder the circulation of solids (i.e., baffles) are incorporated in the design, care must be exercised lest heat transfer be hindered to the point that "hot spots" may develop.

MECHANICAL SEPARATIONS AND PHASE COLLECTION

5-13. Introduction

In addition to the separations achieved by mass transport between phases, the mechanical collection and separation of phases is of great importance to chemical processing. Indeed, the usefulness of diffusive separations is dependent on the ability to separate quickly, cleanly, and inexpensively the phases that have been brought into intimate contact with one another to abet the mass-transfer operation.

Although most mechanical separations consist of phase segregation, some consist the fractionation of particulate solids on the basis of size, shape, density, or some other characteristic besides phase identification.

5-14. Filtration

Definitions. Filtration is the separation of undissolved, particulate, suspended solids from a fluid mixture by passage of most of the fluid through a septum or membrane that retains the solids on or within itself. The mixture to be separated is called the *feed* slurry, or *prefilt,* the fluid that passes through the septum is called the *filtrate,* and the septum is called the *filter medium;* when the separated solids accumulate in amounts that visibly cover the medium, they are called the *filter cake,* or simply the cake. The housing for the medium and the accumulated solids is called a *filter.*

In the broadest sense of filtration the fluid may be a liquid, a gas, or a mixture of the two. In practice, however, liquid filtration and gas clarification are treated as distinct unit operations, each served by its own technical experts and equipment designers that only infrequently work simultaneously in both fields.

The driving force effecting filtration may be hydrostatic head, superatmospheric pressure applied upstream of the septum, subatmospheric pressure applied downstream of the septum, or centrifugal force across the septum. Centrifugal filtration is customarily associated with centrifugal sedimentation in the general subject of centrifugation, a separate unit operation.

Filtration Theory. Filters are designed by scaling up tests. The scale-up is considerably empirical. Nevertheless, filtration theory is useful in interpreting the tests, in seeking the optimum conditions for filtration, and in predicting effects of changes in operating conditions.

The fundamental rate equation for cake filtration may be written as a modification of Darcy's law:

$$\frac{dV}{A\,d\theta} = \frac{\Delta P}{\mu(\alpha W/A + R_m)} \tag{5-38}$$

W may be related to V by a material balance:

$$W = wV = \frac{\rho c V}{1 - mc} \tag{5-39}$$

In many operations, α may be replaced by $\alpha'P^s$, where α' is a constant determined largely by the size of the particles forming the filter cake, and s is the cake compressibility varying from 0 for incompressible material like sand and kieselguhr to 1.0 for highly compressible cakes.

Equation (5-38) may be integrated easily for constant-pressure and constant-rate filtrations. At constant pressure,

$$\frac{\theta}{V/A} - \frac{\mu R_m}{\Delta P} = \frac{\mu\alpha W}{2\,\Delta PA} = \frac{\mu\alpha wV}{2\,\Delta PA} = \frac{\mu\alpha\rho c V}{2\,\Delta PA(1 - mc)} \tag{5-40}$$

which may be rewritten as

$$\frac{\theta}{V/A} = \frac{K_p W}{A} + C = K'_p \frac{V}{A} + C = K''_p \frac{V}{A} + C \qquad (5\text{-}41)$$

where K_p, K'_p, K''_p, and C are constants, depending on the filtering pressure. At constant rate. Eq. (5-38) integrates

$$\frac{\theta}{V/A} = \frac{\mu \alpha W}{(P - P_1)A} = \frac{\mu \alpha w V}{(P - P_1)A} = \frac{\mu \alpha \rho c V}{(P - P_1)A(1 - mc)} \qquad (5\text{-}42)$$

where P_1 is the pressure at the face of the filter medium, and P is the filtering pressure, no longer constant. For incompressible solids (α independent of pressure) and calling the constant rate $\Re_c$,

$$\frac{V}{A} = \Re_c \theta = \frac{P}{K_r} + C' \qquad (5\text{-}43)$$

where the values of the constants K_r and C' may depend on the rate of filtration.

The filtration-rate equations may also be written in terms of the Carman-Kozeny permeability and the porosity of the cake, ϵ, as illustrated by the constant-pressure equation

$$\frac{\theta}{V/A} - \frac{\mu R_m}{\Delta P} = \frac{\mu W}{2\,\Delta P} \frac{k_K S_0^2 (1 - \epsilon)}{\epsilon^3 \rho_s} = \frac{\mu W}{2 K_{CK}\,\Delta P\, \rho_s (1 - \epsilon)} \qquad (5\text{-}44)$$

Equation (5-44) permits one to interpret the results from a permeability-compression experiment as the equivalent of a series of constant-pressure filtration experiments, thus simplifying test-data collection.

The insertion of test data into whichever integrated rate equation is appropriate permits the evaluation of the constants.

Equation (5-38) and its several integrated forms do not apply to filtrations in which solids collect within the medium rather than build a cake on its surface. Such conditions arise when the prefilt contains < 0.1 per cent solids; the operation is termed *clarification*, or *filter-medium filtration*. For the theory and laws of filter-medium filtration, reference should be made to Grace, *AIChE J.*, **2**, 323 (1956).

Effect of Temperature and Pressure on Filtering Rates. Theoretically, an increase in temperature will increase the filtering rate in proportion to the reduction in filtrate viscosity, but in practice the effect is modified by temperature effects on particle size and form, especially with soft, hydrated flocs. Usually this effect is favorable (i.e., an increase in temperature reduces α). On the other hand, high temperatures may shorten the life of the filter medium and may cause filtrate evaporation losses.

With completely incompressible cakes, filtering rate is proportional to the pressure but with many slurries encountered in industry, the effect is reduced to a square-root relationship or even less. With very highly compressible cakes, filtration rate is virtually independent of filtering pressure; a low operating pressure is then advisable to minimize filter medium plugging.

Typical Filter Performance. Examples of filtration rates with industrial materials are given in Table 5-11.

Table 5-11. Typical Filter Performance

Typical materials	Character	In. Hg vacuum or psi pressure	Approx filter capacity
Cyanide slime	Finely ground quartz ores	18–25 in.	400–2,000*
Flotation concentrates	Minerals, finely ground	18–25 in.	400–1,800*
Gravity concentrates and sand	Metallic and nonmetallic minerals almost free from slime	2– 6 in.	10,000–70,000*
Cement slurry	Finely ground limestone and shale, or clay, etc.	18–25 in.	400–2,000*
Pulp and paper	Free-filtering fibers	6–20 in.	200–1,200; 1½ –20†
Crystals, salt, etc	Granular, crystalline	2– 6 in.	3,000–12,000*
Cane-sugar-liquor clarification, beverages, etc.	Sirups and solution with small percentage of solids with filter aid	40–50 lb	36–1,400‡
Pigments	Smeary, sticky, finely divided, noncrystalline	20–27 in. 40–50 lb	200–500* Batch operation
Sewage sludge	Colloidal and slimy	22–24 in.	25–250*
Varnish	Cloudy viscous liquid, filter aid used for clarification, filtered hot	15–16 lb	5¶
Mineral oils, with or without wax	Removal of bleaching clay from petroleum products, 1 to 20% clay used	50 lb max	3–30¶ (lube oils) 25–75¶ (gasoline)

* Lb/(ft²)(day). † Gal/(ft²)(min). ‡ Gal/(ft²)(day). ¶ Gal/(ft²)(hr).

5-15. Centrifugation

Definitions. Centrifugation is the subjection of a liquid-solid or liquid-liquid suspension to a centrifugal force field to accomplish sedimentary separation or filtration. *Centrifugal force* is the force produced by any moving mass that is compelled to depart from the rectilinear path which it tends to follow; it is exerted in the direction away from the center of curvature of the path of motion.

A *centrifuge* is a machine designed to subject material held in it, or being passed through it, to centrifugal force. Centrifuges may be classified as *settlers* (clarifiers, separators) and *filters*. The former are solid-bowl, or disk, machines; the latter are perforate-bowl machines.

Theory. The centrifugal force on a mass m having an angular velocity ω is calculated by the equation

$$F = mr\omega^2/g_c \qquad (5\text{-}45)$$

where $r\omega^2$ is the centripetal acceleration. The dynamics of a centrifugal field are similar to those of the gravitational field, with the centrifugal force substituted for the gravitational. Thus the Stokes settling velocity of a particle in a centrifugal field is

$$V_s = (\rho_s - \rho_l)D_p{}^2 r\omega^2/18\mu \qquad (5\text{-}46)$$

Likewise, the filtration-rate equation may be rewritten as

$$\frac{dV}{d\theta} = \frac{\rho\omega^2(r_2{}^2 - r_0{}^2)}{2\mu[(\alpha m_c/\overline{A}_L\overline{A}_A) + (R_m/A_2)]} \qquad (5\text{-}47)$$

where $\overline{A}_L$ and $\overline{A}_A$ are the logarithmic and arithmetic means, respectively, of A_1 and A_2.

Performance of Centrifugal Settlers.[1] The throughput capacity Q of a settling centrifuge at the "cutoff point" (50 per cent of feed particles removed and 50 per cent passed) is given by

$$Q = 2V_g\Sigma \qquad \text{cm}^3/\text{sec} \tag{5-48}$$

with
$$V_g = (\rho_s - \rho_1)D_p^2 g/18\mu \qquad \text{cm/sec} \tag{5-49}$$

$$\Sigma = c\omega^2 r/gs \qquad \text{cm}^2 \tag{5-50}$$

where c = volume of liquid in bowl at any instant, cm^3

ω = angular velocity, radians/sec

r = effective distance from center of rotation to settling point, cm

s = effective thickness of liquid layer in which settling is occurring, cm

It may be shown that

$$r/s = 1/\ln(2r_2^2/r_2^2 r_0^2) \cong (\tfrac{3}{2}r_2^2 + \tfrac{1}{2}r_0^2)/(r_2^2 - r_0^2) \tag{5-51}$$

where r_0 and r_2 = inner and outer radii of liquid layer, cm.

All elements concerned with the system are included in Eq. (5-49), whereas Eqs. (5-50) and (5-51) are concerned with elements relating to the centrifuge.

For tubular bowls the approximation

$$\Sigma = (\pi Y \omega^2/g)(\tfrac{3}{4}r_2^2 + \tfrac{1}{4}r_0^2) \qquad \text{cm}^2 \tag{5-52}$$

applies, where Y is the length of the liquid column in centimeters and r_0, r_2, and ω are as defined for Eq. (5-51).

For disk-type centrifuge bowls, the following approximation applies:

$$\Sigma = 2n\pi(r_2^3 - r_0^3)\omega^2/3g \tan\theta \qquad \text{cm}^2 \tag{5-53}$$

where n = number of spaces between disks in stack

r_0, r_2 = inner and outer radii of disk stack, cm

θ = conical half angle of the disk stack

and other terms are as defined above.

In general, the performance of any two centrifuges treating the same system will be the same if the quantity Q/Σ is held constant. The relationship

$$Q_1 = Q_2\Sigma_1/\Sigma_2 \tag{5-54}$$

where subscripts 1 and 2 refer to plant and laboratory centrifuges, respectively, forms a basis for estimating commercial-centrifuge performance from laboratory and pilot-plant tests.

Basket Centrifuges. Basket centrifuges with perforated walls find a considerable use in chemical plants for recovery of crystals precipitated from their mother liquor. The screening medium may be laid over a grid work or corrugated backing to allow a free flow-discharge path for the liquid after passing through the screen. Monel or other corrosion-resisting metal wires may also be woven in close mesh for screening out fine crystals. Such wire cloth may be rolled to flatten the wires and so reduce the mesh opening. For very coarse nonporous particles, 5 to 10 mm minimum dimension in any direction, less than 1 per cent by weight of liquid may be left after centrifuging.

[1] See Ambler, *Chem. Eng. Progr.*, **48**, 150–158 (1952).

Finer particles necessarily carry more liquid with them in proportion to the surface-volume relation, which increases linearly with decrease of dimension of particles. Basket centrifuges cannot readily be rated in terms of throughput, but are usually rated by basket diameters. The curves in Fig. 5-25 give

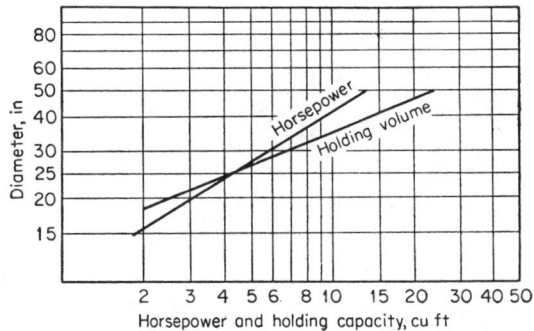

Fig. 5-25. Power and holding capacity of basket centrifugals.

representative figures, showing the relation of holding capacity and the horsepower required for such standard work as laundry drying, dry cleaner's solvent drying, and the handling of simple chemicals. The throughputs must be estimated from the drying characteristics of the materials handled and the dryness required.

5-16. Dust and Mist Collection

Definition. Dust and mist collection is concerned with the removal or collection of solid or liquid dispersoids in gases. The principles are generally the same, whether the dispersoids are solid (dust) or liquid (mist).

The primary distinguishing feature of dispersoids in gases is particle diameter. Dust and mist removal is concerned principally with particles $< 100\mu$ in diameter. In discussions of small particles, a convenient unit of length is the micron, abbreviated by the symbol μ. One micron $= 0.001$ mm. Figure 5-26 shows the size of a number of typical particles, methods of analysis for them, and appropriate removal equipment.

Particle Dynamics. Particles of the size encountered in dust and mist usually are sufficiently small so that, when they settle in air, they obey Stokes' law or are in the transition region not far from Stokes behavior. Inasmuch as the criterion of Stokes behavior is the Reynolds number, itself a function of velocity, a trial-and-error procedure is involved. Use of Fig. 5-27 is recommended. A velocity first is calculated from Stokes' law:

$$u_{ts} = gD_p{}^2(\rho_s - \rho_L)/18\mu \qquad (5\text{-}55)$$

From u_t a hypothetical Reynolds number, $D_p u_t \rho/\mu$, is calculated, which provides the necessary correction factor to u_t from Fig. 5-27.

Particle diameter, μ

| (1 mµ) 0.001 | 0.01 | 0.1 | 1 | 10 | 100 | (1 mm) 1,000 | (1 cm) 10,000 |

Angström units, Å.

| 0.0001 | 0.001 | 0.01 | 0.1 | 1 | 10 | 100 | 1,000 | 10,000 |

Equivalent sizes

Theoretical mesh (used very infrequently): 11,5000 1250 625 ; 10,000 2500

Tyler screen mesh: 325 250 170 150 100 65 48 35 28 20 14 10 8 6 4 3
U.S. screen mesh: 325 270 200 140 100 60 50 40 30 20 16 12 8 6 4 3/8" 1/2" 3/4"

Electromagnetic waves

X-rays — Ultraviolet — Solar radiation — Visible — Near infrared — Far infrared — Microwaves (radar, etc.)

Technical definitions

Gas dispersoids — Solid: — Fume — Dust
Liquid: — Mist — Spray

Soil: Atterberg or International Std. Classification System adopted by Internat. Soc. Soil Sci. since 1934
Clay — Silt — Fine sand — Coarse sand — Gravel

Common atmospheric dispersoids

Smog — Clouds and fog — Mist — Drizzle — Rain

Typical particles and gas dispersoids

Gas Molecules*

H_2 F_2
O_2 CO_2 C_6H_6
CO H_2O HCl C_4H_{10}
N_2 CH_4 SO_2 Cl_2

Viruses
Aitken nuclei
Sea salt nuclei
Atmospheric dust
Combustion nuclei
Colloidal silica
Zinc oxide fumes
Carbon black
Rosin smoke
Oil smokes
Tobacco smoke
Metallurgical dusts and fumes
Ammonium chloride fumes
Sulfuric concentrator mist
Contact sulfuric mist
Paint pigments
Insecticide dusts
Ground talc
Spray dried milk
Alkali fume
Milled flour
Lung-damaging dust
Nebulizer drops
Pneumatic nozzle drops
Hydraulic nozzle drops
Red-blood-cell diameter (adults): 7.5µ±0.3µ
Bacteria
Human hair
Combustion
Plant spores
Pollens
Fertilizer, ground limestone
Fly ash
Coal dust
Cement dust
Pulverized coal
Flotation ores
Beach sand

Molecular diameters calculated from viscosity data at 0°C.

5-52

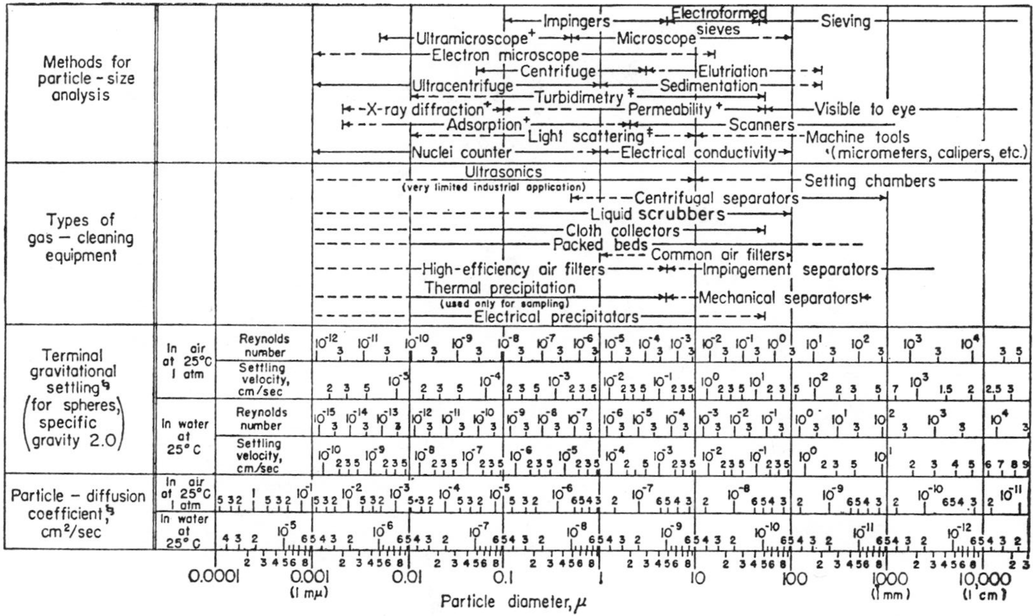

Fig. 5-26. Characteristics of particles and particle dispersoids. (Courtesy of Stanford Research Institute, Palo Alto, California; prepared by C. E. Lapple.)

* Molecular diameters calculated from viscosity data at 0°C.
+ Furnishes average particle diameter but no size distribution.
‡ Size distribution may be obtained by special calibration.
§ Stokes–Cunningham factor included in values given for air but not included for water.

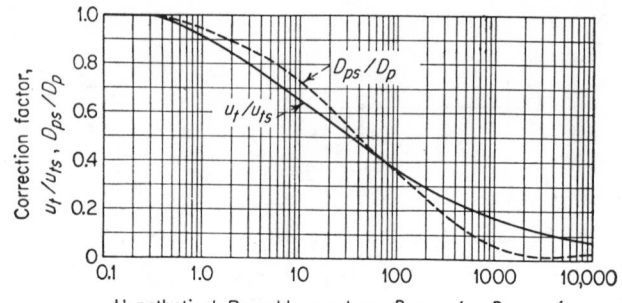

FIG. 5-27. Correction factor for deviation from Stokes' law.

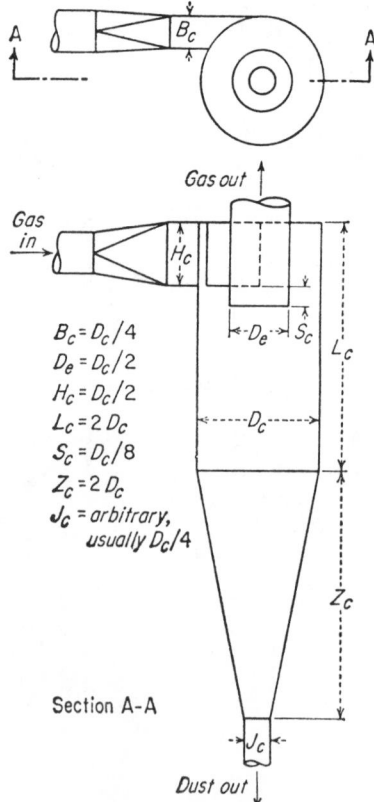

$B_c = D_c/4$

$D_e = D_c/2$

$H_c = D_c/2$

$L_c = 2\,D_c$

$S_c = D_c/8$

$Z_c = 2\,D_c$

J_c = arbitrary, usually $D_c/4$

Section A-A

FIG. 5-28. Cyclone separator proportions.

Dust and Mist Separators. The most important types of equipment used are indicated in Fig. 5-26. Only four of these are treated briefly in this section. Those interested in equipment details are referred to a discussion by Lucas ("Perry's Chemical Engineers' Handbook," 4th ed., sec. 20, McGraw-Hill Book Company, New York, 1963).

Cyclone Separators. The most widely used type of dust-collection equipment is the cyclone, in which dust-laden gas enters a cylindrical or conical chamber tangentially and leaves through a central opening, as shown in Fig. 5-28.

Cyclones for removing solids or liquids from gases are generally applicable when particles of over 5 μ diameter are involved. Unless very small cyclones are used, the efficiency will be low if much of the suspended material is finer than 5 μ.

Cyclone friction loss is a direct measure of the static pressure and power that a fan must develop. Cyclone friction loss for the design shown in Fig. 5-28 may be expressed empirically

$$F_{cv} = KB_cH_c/D_e^2 \tag{5-56}$$

in which F_{cv} is the number of cyclone inlet velocity heads. The value of K is 16, with the normal arrangement in which the rectangular inlet terminates at the outer elements of the cyclone body or cylinder.

Theoretical collection efficiency is compared with actual efficiency for a cyclone (of the design given in Fig. 5-28) in Fig. 5-29. The graph gives the collection efficiency for a given particle size expressed as a ratio to the cut size D_{pc}, that is, the particle diameter of which 50 per cent of those present are collected.

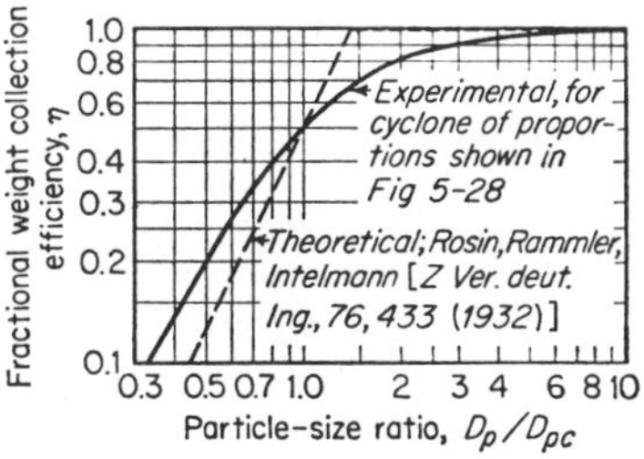

$$D_{pc} = \sqrt{9\mu B_c/2\pi N_e V_c(\rho_s - \rho)} \tag{5-57}$$

where N_e is the number of turns made by gas stream in cyclone separator (5 to 10 for design of Fig. 5-28), and B_c is as defined in Fig. 5-28.

FIG. 5-29. Separation efficiency of cyclones.

Electrical Precipitators. When particles suspended in a gas are exposed to gas ions in an electrostatic field, they will become charged, and migrate under the action of the field. The functional mechanisms of electrical precipitation may be listed as follows:

1. Gas ionization
2. Particle collection
   a. Production of electrostatic field to cause charging and migration of dust particles
   b. Gas retention to permit particle migration to a collection surface
   c. Prevention of reentrainment of collected particles
   d. Removal of collected particles from the equipment

There are two general classes of electrical precipitators: (1) single-stage, in which ionization and collection are combined; (2) two-stage, in which ionization is achieved in one portion of the equipment, followed by collection in another. Various types in each class differ essentially in the method by which each function is accomplished. Details design, construction, and operation are given by Lucas (*loc. cit.*).

In practice, precipitators are usually operated at the highest voltage practicable without sparking, since this increases both the particle charge and the electrical precipitating field. The sparking potential is generally higher with a negative charge on the discharge electrode and is less erratic in behavior than a positive corona discharge. It is the consensus, however, that ozone formation with a positive discharge is considerably less than with a negative discharge. For these reasons negative discharge is generally used in industrial precipitators, and a positive discharge is utilized in air-conditioning applications.

Performance data for single-stage precipitators are presented in Table 5-12.

Table 5-12. Performance Data on Typical Single-stage Electrical Precipitator Installations*

Type of precipitator	Type of dust	Gas volume, ft³/min	Average gas velocity, fps	Collecting electrode area, ft²	Over-all collection efficiency, %	Average particle migration velocity, fps
Rod curtain........	Smelter fume	180,000	6	44,400	85	0.13
Tulip type.........	Gypsum from kiln	25,000	3.5	3,800	99.7	.64
Perforated plate.....	Fly ash	108,000	6	10,900	91	.40
Rod curtain........	Cement	204,000	9.5	26,000	91	.31

* Courtesy Research Corp.

Bag Filters. Bag filters, or cloth collectors, are the industrial counterparts of air filters; they process industrial dusts of much higher concentration than those of the atmosphere. A bag filter is for dust suspensions the equivalent of a cake filter for liquid slurries. The filter medium (bag), however, usually is discharged *in situ* without the filter's being opened.

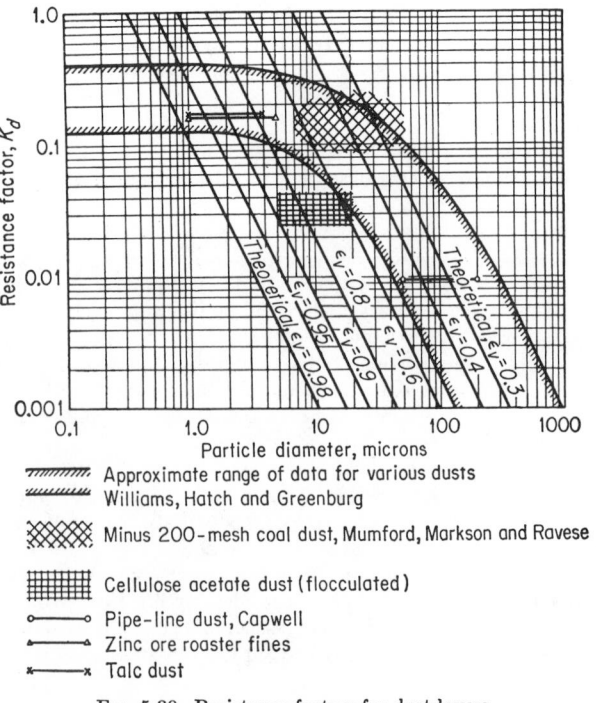

Fig. 5-30. Resistance factors for dust layers.

For properly selected bag filters, the resistance of the cloth is negligible compared with that of the collecting dust layer after the first $\frac{1}{16}$ in. of dust has collected. The pressure drop, then, is calculated in terms of the dust concentration in the feed stream (c_d), the superficial velocity of gas through the cloth (V_f), and a resistance factor (K_d):

$$\Delta p_i = K_d \mu c_d V_f{}^2 \theta \tag{5-58}$$

The value of K_d must be determined experimentally. Its range of magnitude is indicated in Fig. 5-30. The values of Fig. 5-30 may be used in Eq. (5-58) if μ is in centipoises, V_f in ft/min, θ in min, c_d in grains/ft^3, and Δp_i in in. H$_2$O.

Air Filters. Air filters are employed in the elimination of atmospheric dust. They differ in application from bag filters more in the quantity than in the quality of the dust. Whereas process-dust concentrations may be as high as several hundred grains per cubic foot, atmospheric dust concentrations generally are less than 0.005 grain/ft^3.

Air filters are classified in three groups: viscous filters (so called because the filter medium is coated with a high-viscosity liquid), dry filters, and automatic filters (which employ either a viscous-coated or dry medium, but in which the cleaning is automatic and essentially continuous). The characteristics of the various types are compared in Table 5-13.

5-17. Screening

Definitions. Screening is the separation of a mixture of particulate solids into two or more fractions by means of a surface, called a screen, that acts as a multiple go and no-go gauge; the fractions consist of grains of a more uniform size than the feed. The screen may consist of cloth woven from wire, silk, or polymer fibers; of perforated or punched plate; or of an assembly of spaced parallel bars (grizzly).

Regardless of its grain size, material remaining on a screen is called oversize ($+$); that passing through is called undersize ($-$).

Screens are specified by (1) the number of openings per linear inch, called *mesh count*, and (2) the dimension, in inches or millimeters, of the clear opening measured between and normal to adjacent wires or bars, called *aperture*, or *clear opening*. Mesh is generally favored for screens 2 mesh and finer.

The fraction of open area (P) of an M-mesh screen of known aperture (D_A) and wire (D_W) sizes is

$$P = D_A{}^2/(D_A + D_W)^2 = (D_A M)^2 = (1 - D_W M)^2 \tag{5-59}$$

Sieve Scales. A sieve scale is a series of screens having apertures in a fixed size succession. In the original Tyler standard series, each two adjacent screens have openings with the ratio $\sqrt{2}$. The Tyler scale has been enlarged by the inclusion of intermediate sizes such that successive members of the series have apertures in the ratio $\sqrt[4]{2}$. An alternative scale (U.S. Standard) adopted by the National Bureau of Standards, American Society for Testing Materials, American Standards Association, and many foreign countries is

Table 5-13. Comparative Air-filter Characteristics

	Unit filters				Automatic filters
	Viscous type		Dry type		
	Cleanable	Throwaway	Throwaway	Cleanable	
Dust capacity	1. Well adapted for heavy dust loads (up to 2 grains/1,000 ft³) due to high dust capacity.		1. Well adapted to light or moderate dust loads of less than 1 grain/1,000 ft³.		1. Well adapted for heavy dust loads (>2 grains/1,000 ft³) since it is serviced automatically.
Filter size			1. Common size of unit filter is 20- × 20-in, face area handling 800 ft³/min at rated capacity. 2. Face velocity is generally 300–400 ft/min for all types.		1. Automatic viscous units supplied to handle 1,000 ft³/min and over. 2. Face velocity is 350–750 ft/min.
Air velocity	1. Rated velocity is 300–400 ft/min through the filter medium. 2. Entrainment of oil may occur at very high velocities.		1. Rated velocity is 10–50 ft/min through the medium. (Some dry glass types run as high as 300 ft/min.) 2. Higher velocities may result in rupture of filter medium.		1. Rated velocity is 350–750 ft/min through the filter medium for viscous types. For dry types, it is 10–50 ft/min.
Resistance		4. High resistance due to excessive dust loading results in channeling and poor efficiency.	1. Resistance ranges from 0.05–0.30 in. when clean to 0.4–0.5 in. when dirty. 2. When the resistance exceeds a given value, the cells should be replaced or reconditioned. 3. Cycling cells in large installations will serve to maintain a nearly constant resistance. 4. Excessive pressure drops resulting from high dust loading may result in rupture of filter medium.		1. Resistance runs about 0.3–0.4 in. water.
Efficiency	1. Commercial makes are found in a variety of efficiencies, these depending roughly on filter resistance for similar types of medium. 2. Efficiency decreases with increased dust load and increases with increased velocity up to certain limits.		1. In general, give higher efficiency than viscous type, particularly on fine particles. 2. Efficiency increases with increased dust load and decreases with increased velocity.		
Operating cycle	2. Operating cycle is 1–2 months for general "average" industrial air conditioning.	1. Well adapted for short-period operations (less than 10 hr/day) because of relatively low investment cost.	2. Operating cycle is 2–4 weeks for general "average" industrial air conditioning.		1. Well adapted for continuous operation.
Method of cleaning	1. Washed with steam, hot water, or solvents and given fresh oil coating.		1. Filter cell replaced. Life may in some cases be lengthened by shaking or vacuum cleaning but this is not often successful.	1. Vacuum-cleaned, blown with compressed air, or dry-cleaned.	1. Automatic. Filter may clog in time, and cleaning by blowing with compressed air may be necessary.

Characteristic					
Space requirement	1. Well adapted for low headroom requirements. 2. Form of banks can be chosen to fit any shaped space. 3. Space should be allowed for a man to remove filter cells for cleaning or replacement. 4. Requires space for washing, reoiling, and draining tanks.	4. Requires space for mechanical loader in some cases.			1. Have a high headroom requirement. 2. Take up less floor space than other types.
Type of filter medium	1. Crimped, split, or woven metal, glass fibers, wood shavings, hair—all oil-coated.	1. Cellulose pulp, felt, cotton gauze, spun glass. 2. Dry medium cannot stand direct wetting. Oil-impregnated mediums are available to resist humidity and prevent fluff entrainment.			1. Metal screens, packing, or baffling. One type uses cellulose pulp.
Character of dust	1. Not well suited for linty materials. 2. Well adapted for make-up air and granular materials.	1. Not well suited for handling oily dusts. 2. Well adapted for linty material. 3. Better adapted for fine dust than other types.			1. Not suited for linty material if of viscous types.
Temperature limitations	1. All metal types may be used up as high as 250°F if suitable oil or grease is used. Those utilizing cellulosic materials are limited to 180°F.	1. Limited to 180°F except for glass types which may be used up to 700°F if suitable frames and gaskets are used.			1. Viscous may be used up to 250°F if suitable oil is used; dry type limited to 180°F.
Initial cost	1. Higher first cost than throwaway.	1. First cost is relatively low. Frames are generally permanent, but cells are replaced.	1. Higher first cost than throwaway.		1. Highest first cost of all.
Operating cost	2. Labor cost to remove, clean, and replace the cells is comparable with the cost of replacement of throwaway-type cells for medium-sized installations of 10,000–50,000 ft^3/min.	1. Power costs are comparable for all unit-type filters. 2. Replacement costs are comparable to cleanable types for medium-sized installations (10,000–50,000 ft^3/min).	2. Same as for Viscous Cleanable.		1. Power costs are somewhat higher for automatic types. 2. Little labor required to inspect, replace oil, or hand-crank filter.
Purchase cost (including frames), cost per 1,000 ft^3/min (1960)	3. Maintenance exclusive of filter cells and depreciation are roughly comparable and vary more between different commercial makes in these groups than between different types. $10 to $35	$5 to $10	$5 to $10 for complete throwaway unit. $8 to $30 for units with replaceable medium.	$7 to $40	3. Depreciation and maintenance costs are the highest for automatic filters. $35 to $100

Table 5-14. U.S. Sieve Series and Tyler Equivalents
ASTM—E-11-61

Sieve designation		Sieve opening		Nominal wire diam.*		Tyler equivalent designation
Standard	Alternatively	Mm	in. (approx. equivalents)	Mm	in. (approx. equivalents)	
107.6 mm	4.24 in.	107.6	4.24	6.40	0.2520	
101.6 mm	4 in.†	101.6	4.00	6.30	.2480	
90.5 mm	3½ in.	90.5	3.50	6.08	.2394	
76.1 mm	3 in.	76.1	3.00	5.80	.2283	
64.0 mm	2½ in.	64.0	2.50	5.50	.2165	
53.8 mm	2.12 in.	53.8	2.12	5.15	.2028	
50.8 mm	2 in.†	50.8	2.00	5.05	.1988	
45.3 mm	1¾ in.	45.3	1.75	4.85	.1909	
38.1 mm	1½ in.	38.1	1.50	4.59	.1807	
32.0 mm	1¼ in.	32.0	1.25	4.23	.1665	
26.9 mm	1.06 in.	26.9	1.06	3.90	.1535	1.050 in.
25.4 mm	1 in.†	25.4	1.00	3.80	.1496	
22.6 mm ‡	⅞ in.	22.6	0.875	3.50	.1378	0.883 in.
19.0 mm	¾ in.	19.0	.750	3.30	.1299	.742 in.
16.0 mm‡	⅝ in.	16.0	.625	3.00	.1181	.624 in.
13.5 mm	0.530 in.	13.5	.530	2.75	.1083	.525 in.
12.7 mm	½ in. †	12.7	.500	2.67	.1051	
11.2 mm‡	⁷⁄₁₆ in.	11.2	.438	2.45	.0965	.441 in.
9.51 mm	⅜ in.	9.51	.375	2.27	.0894	.371 in.
8.00 mm‡	⁵⁄₁₆ in.	8.00	.312	2.07	.0815	2½ mesh
6.73 mm	0.265 in.	6.73	.265	1.87	.0736	3 mesh
6.35 mm	¼ in. †	6.35	.250	1.82	.0717	
5.66 mm‡	No. 3½	5.66	.223	1.68	.0661	3½ mesh
4.76 mm	No. 4	4.76	.187	1.54	.0606	4 mesh
4.00 mm‡	No. 5	4.00	.157	1.37	.0539	5 mesh
3.36 mm	No. 6	3.36	.132	1.23	.0484	6 mesh
2.83 mm‡	No. 7	2.83	.111	1.10	.0430	7 mesh
2.38 mm	No. 8	2.38	.0937	1.00	.0394	8 mesh
2.00 mm ‡	No. 10	2.00	.0787	0.900	.0354	9 mesh
1.68 mm	No. 12	1.68	.0661	.810	.0319	10 mesh
1.41 mm‡	No. 14	1.41	.0555	.725	.0285	12 mesh
1.19 mm	No. 16	1.19	.0469	.650	.0256	14 mesh
1.00 mm‡	No. 18	1.00	.0394	.580	.0228	16 mesh
841 μ	No. 20	0.841	.0331	.510	.0201	20 mesh
707 μ‡	No. 25	.707	.0278	.450	.0177	24 mesh
595 μ	No. 30	.595	.0234	.390	.0154	28 mesh
500 μ‡	No. 35	.500	.0197	.340	.0134	32 mesh
420 μ	No. 40	.420	.0165	.290	.0114	35 mesh
354 μ‡	No. 45	.354	.0139	.247	.0097	42 mesh
297 μ	No. 50	.297	.0117	.215	.0085	48 mesh
250 μ‡	No. 60	.250	.0098	.180	.0071	60 mesh
210 μ	No. 70	.210	.0083	.152	.0060	65 mesh
177 μ‡	No. 80	.177	.0070	.131	.0052	80 mesh
149 μ	No. 100	.149	.0059	.110	.0043	100 mesh
125 μ‡	No. 120	.125	.0049	.091	.0036	115 mesh
105 μ	No. 140	.105	.0041	.076	.0030	150 mesh
88 μ‡	No. 170	.088	.0035	.064	.0025	170 mesh
74 μ	No. 200	.074	.0029	.053	.0021	200 mesh
63 μ‡	No. 230	.063	.0025	.044	.0017	250 mesh
53 μ	No. 270	.053	.0021	.037	.0015	270 mesh
44 μ‡	No. 325	.044	.0017	.030	.0012	325 mesh
37 μ	No. 400	.037	.0015	.025	.0010	400 mesh

* These specifications are primarily for testing sieves. Many commercial screen cloths employ wire diameters considerably different from those of the standard series.

† These sieves are not in the fourth-root-of-2 series, but they have been included because they are in common usage.

‡ These sieves correspond to those proposed as an international (ISO) standard. It is recommended that wherever possible these sieves be included in all sieve analysis data or reports intended for international publication.

based also on the $\sqrt[4]{2}$ module and is fully compatible with the Tyler scale even though the mesh designations may differ.   Table 5-14 compares the two scales.

Screen Efficiency.   There is confusion concerning the meaning of screen efficiency, since a uniform definition has never been accepted.   A useful and popular method of evaluating efficiency is that of the W. S. Tyler Co., Cleveland, Ohio:

When screen throughput is the desired product:

$$E = Rd/b \tag{5-60}$$

When screen oversize is the desired product:

$$E = Oc/a \tag{5-61}$$

The Taggart efficiency is also widely used.   It is defined as

$$E = 100(b - v)/b(100 - v) \tag{5-62}$$

5-18. Classification

Definitions.   Classification is the separation of a mixture of particulate solids into two or more fractions according to particle size, density, shape, or other distinguishing characteristic, by some method other than screening. The *coarsest fraction* is sometimes called the *sand;* the *finest* is called the *slimes;* and the *intermediate* fractions are the *middlings*.   Most classifiers employ a fluid, usually a liquid, in their operation.

A few of the most important methods of classification are outlined here. For others and for details of operation, reference should be made to a comprehensive source such as Taggart, "Handbook of Mineral Dressing," John Wiley & Sons, Inc., New York, 1945.

Wet Classification.   Wet classification is carried out in a liquid-solid suspension confined in a tank so as to allow coarse or heavy solids to settle while fine or light ones overflow.   It depends on settling-rate differences identified with size or density of particles.

Classifier types fall into three basic categories: (1) nonmechanical, (2) mechanical, and (3) hydraulic.   Functionally, the first two are similar and differ only in the means of sand removal.   In hydraulic types the character of separation is different because of the hindered settling induced by the hydraulic water.

The applications and most important characteristics of wet classifiers are summarized in Table 5-15.

Jigging.   Jigging is the separation of materials of different specific gravities by the pulsation of a stream of liquid flowing through a bed of the materials. The liquid pulsates, or "jigs," up and down, causing the heavy material to work down to the bottom of the bed and the lighter material to rise to the top. Each product is then drawn off separately.

The throughput capacity and power requirements of jigs depend upon the character of the feed, the separation required, and the type of equipment

Table 5-15. Sizes, Limitations, and Major Applications of Wet Classification Machines

Type of classifier	Normal size range, ft			Normal mesh of separation range*	Normal feed tonnage range	Max. oversize in feed	Normal overflow, % solids range	Normal sand product, % solids range	Motor range, hp	Typical applications
	Width	Diam.	Max. length							
Nonmechanical:										
Cone classifier	......	2–12	....	28–325	2–100 tons/hr	¼ in.	5–30	35–60	None	For desliming and primary dewatering
Liquid cyclone	......	10 mm to 4 ft	9	48 mesh to 5 μ	½–1500 gpm	14–325 mesh	5–30	55–70	Power for pressure head 5–60 psi	For medium or fine separations and closed-circuit grinding
Mechanical:										
Drag classifier	1–10	....	Not critical	28–200	5–350 tons/hr	1½ in.	5–30	70–83	1–10	For desliming, conveying, and closed-circuit grinding
Rake and spiral classifiers	1–20	....	40	20–200	5–350 tons/hr	1 in.	5–30	75–83	½–25	Closed-circuit grinding, washing and dewatering, desliming, process feed control
Bowl classifier	1½–20	4–28	40	100–325	5–200 tons/hr	½ in.	5–25	75–80	Bowl: 1–7½ Rake: 1–25	Closed-circuit grinding usually in secondary circuits
Bowl desiltor	4–16	20–50	40	100–325	5–250 tons/hr	½ in.	1–15	75–83	Bowl: 1–10 Rake: 5–25	Recovery of fine sand, limestone, coal, and fine phosphate rock from large flow volumes
Hydroseparator	......	10–150	....	100–325	5–700 tons/hr	¼ in.	1–20	30–50	1–15	For fine separation where large feed volumes are involved and drainage not critical
Solid-bowl centrifuge	......	18–54 in.	70 in.	200 mesh to 1 μ	10–600 gpm	¼ in.	1–40	10–70	15–150	For fine-size fractionating
Sand washer	......	7–12	....	28–65	25–125 tons/hr	1 in.	5–15	75–80	5–10	For desliming and dewatering large tonnages of solids
Countercurrent classifier	......	1½–10	40	35–100	1–600 tons/hr	3 in.	5–30	75–83	¼–25	Sand-slime separations, washing, closed-circuit grinding
Hydraulic:										
Sizer	1½–20	....	5–20	8–150	2–100 tons/hr	3⁄16 in.	1–10	40–60	1–2 for air pressure	Multiproduct unit for exceptionally clean sands fractionated into narrow size ranges; min. 3 tons hydraulic water per ton sand
Super Sorter†	6	....	40	8–150	40–150 tons/hr	⅜ in.	1–10	40–60	1 to operate pincer valves	Multiproduct unit for exceptionally clean sands fractionated into narrow size ranges; min. 3 tons hydraulic water per ton sand
Siphon Sizer‡	......	3–30	....	14–150	1–100 tons/hr	1 in.	1–10	40–60	None	Two-product unit efficient for desliming and exceptionally clean sands, washing, closed-circuit grinding; min. 2 tons hydraulic water per ton sand
Hydroscillator‡	4–12	4–14	40	20–150	5–250 tons/hr	½ in.	5–30	75–83	Oscillator: 3–10 Rakes: 5–20	Two-product unit for exceptionally clean sand having low moisture content; closed-circuit grinding, washing; min. 0.5 ton hydraulic water per ton sand

* Size of screen retaining 1½ per cent of the overflow solids. † Trademark of Deister Concentrator Co., Inc. ‡ Trademark of Dorr-Oliver Inc.

used. The water consumption is high, 1,200 to 2,500 gal water/ton of solids processed.

Tabling. Tabling is the classification of particulate solids by means of an inclined, riffled, shaking surface (called a table) across which water or air is flowed. The particles are classified principally on the basis of density difference.

Wet tables require finer feed (dense ore, 6 to 150 mesh; light material, such as coal, < 1 in.) than air tables (which handle ore up to $\frac{1}{4}$ in. and coal up to 3 in.).

Froth Flotation. Froth flotation is the fractionation of particulate solids based on the interfacial tension between the surface of the solids, water, and air. It is employed most importantly on the beneficiation of ore, but is finding increasing use in the process industries.

In flotation machines the ore is suspended in water at a pulp density generally from 15 to 35 per cent solids by means of mechanical or air agitation. The surfaces of specific mineral particles are treated with chemicals called promoters, or collectors, which render those particles air-avid and water-repellent. With vigorous agitation and aeration in the presence of a frother, a layer of froth or foam forms at the top of the flotation machine. The air-avid minerals become attached to air bubbles and rise to the surface, where they collect in the froth and are skimmed off.

The valuable concentrates from froth flotation may be either the froth product which collects at the top or the underflow product. In the case of metallic sulfide ores of copper, lead, zinc, nickel, mercury, and molybdenum and native gold and silver, the values collect in the froth. In glass-sand flotation, iron-bearing minerals are floated off in the froth, while high-grade silica values appear as underflow.

CHEMICAL KINETICS AND REACTOR DESIGN

5-19. Introduction

At one or more stages in every industrial chemical process, chemical transformation of the process stream occurs. Usually, such changes are induced, but in any event they must be predicted and controlled for the entire process and its products to be under control.

The Chemical Reactor. The environment in which planned chemical reactions are confined as they proceed is called a *reactor*. *Reactor design,* the goal of which is the specification of a well-controlled, efficient reactor of adequate production capacity, is based on the application of chemical rate data, thermodynamic data, and such physical principles as may affect the reactor performance; for example, the principles of heat transfer are important in almost all reactions, and those of mass transfer (such as gas absorption) are important in many.

Chemical Kinetics. The principles relevant to the mechanisms of chemical reactions and to the rates at which such reactions proceed are those of *chemical kinetics,* and they are of great practical importance to the chemical engineer.

Although the theory of chemical kinetics is imperfect, it is useful as a guide to the interpretation of experimental observations that are essential in kinetic applications. Applied kinetics makes possible rational reactor design and the chemical control of industrial processes.

The rate of a chemical reaction is most simply described as the number of moles of a particular participant converted or formed per unit time. As such, it is an *extensive* quantity. A more useful *intensive* quantity is the *specific rate of reaction*, defined as the rate of molar conversion of a component per unit of reactor volume. Thus, for the reaction

$$aA + bB + cC \leftrightharpoons rR + sS \qquad (5\text{-}63)$$

the rate may be described in terms of the disappearance of A or B or C or the formation of R or S. Any one of these descriptions must be equivalent to any other, being related through the stoichiometric coefficients:

$$r_A = \frac{-dN_A}{V\,d\theta} = -\frac{a}{b}\frac{dN_B}{V\,d\theta} = -\frac{a}{c}\frac{dN_C}{V\,d\theta} = \frac{a}{r}\frac{dN_R}{V\,d\theta} = \frac{a}{s}\frac{dN_S}{V\,d\theta} \qquad (5\text{-}64)$$

If the volume of the reacting system is constant,

$$r_A = \frac{-d(N_A/V)}{d\theta} = -\frac{dC_A}{d\theta} \qquad (5\text{-}65)$$

This condition is approximated by virtually all liquid-phase reactions taking place in a tank where material is not added or removed in the course of the reaction or where no more than a 5 per cent change in level occurs even if there are material interchanges. It may be met exactly by nonflow gas reactions (which, however, are uncommon).

For a steady-state flow reactor with no longitudinal mixing, there will be no change in composition with time at any given point in the reactor. The reaction rate in such an environment is conveniently described as the change of conversion with *position* along the reactor:

$$r_A = F\,dX_A/dV \qquad (5\text{-}66)$$

where X_A is the moles of reactant A converted per mole of total feed F at a point, and V is the reactor volume upstream from that point.

5-20. Homogeneous Reactions

Definition. A chemical reaction is homogeneous if the reactants and products are simultaneously present in the same phase, or if the system may be treated as if they were. (A reaction that results in a precipitated product, for example, may be treated as a homogeneous reaction during which the product concentration is constant at its solubility level.) Practically, homogeneous reactions must occur in either a gas or a liquid phase.

Order of Reaction. In general, reaction rates have been found to be proportional to simple powers of the concentrations of some or all of the reacting components; that is, for a reaction involving reactants A, B, and C,

$$r = kC_A{}^\alpha C_B{}^\beta C_C{}^\gamma \qquad (5\text{-}67)$$

The exponents α, β, and γ are empirically determined, and are not to be confused with the stoichiometric coefficients of the reaction [for example, a, b, and c of Eq. (5-63)]. In general, they have values between zero and 3, and usually the values are integers.

The reaction kinetically described by Eq. (5-67) is said to be αth order with respect to A, βth order with respect to B, and γth order with respect to C; as a whole, its order is $(\alpha + \beta + \gamma)$th. Theory suggests that order may be related to molecularity and, if so, that the order of homogeneous reactions with respect to each component should be finite and represented by an integer. Most, in fact, are of first, second, or third order, the latter being rare. Under certain conditions, however, reactions appear to be of zeroth order with respect to some reactants and of fractional order with respect to others.

To postulate a reaction mechanism and order without reference to actual rate data is speculative and dangerous if a reactor design is to be based on the postulate. The order assigned a reaction must rationalize reliable experimental kinetic data. On the other hand, data that indicate a homogeneous reaction to be of exotic order should be critically examined, or the method of their treatment should be questioned, or both.

Equation (5-67) gives the rate of a reaction proceeding irreversibly among three components. If the reaction of interest were, instead, a reversible one (as, strictly speaking, all reactions are), such as

$$A + B + C \leftrightarrows R + S$$

Eq. (5-67) would describe only the rate of the forward half-reaction. The reverse might be expected to exhibit a rate proportional to simple powers of the concentrations of the products R and S:

$$r' = k'C_R{}^\rho C_S{}^\sigma \tag{5-68}$$

Thus the reverse half-reaction would be ρth order with respect to R, σth order with respect to S, and $(\rho + \sigma)$th order over-all.

It should be noted that the net rate of a reversible reaction is the algebraic sum of its forward and reverse rates. For the reaction described by Eqs. (5-67) and (5-68),

$$r_{\text{net}} = r - r' \tag{5-69}$$

The coefficients k and k' of Eqs. (5-67) and (5-68) are known as specific rate constants, peculiar to a particular reaction and temperature but independent of concentrations of reactants.

Integrated Rate Equations. Substitution of the appropriate order statement [such as Eq. (5-67)] into the appropriate fundamental rate equation [such as Eq. (5-65)] and relation of the concentrations involved by means of a material balance will permit the integration of the resulting differential equation. For irreversible reactions of low order, the integrated equations are of simple form. Table 5-16 presents equations for irreversible constant-volume reactions.

Table 5-16. Rate Equations for Reactions of Simple Order

Order	Differential equation	Constant-volume process
Zero	$-\dfrac{dN_A}{Vd\theta} = k$	$k(\theta - \theta_0) = C_A^0 - C_A$
One-half	$-\dfrac{dN_A}{Vd\theta} = kC_A^{1/2}$	$k(\theta - \theta_0) = 2(C_A^{01/2} - C_A^{1/2})$
First	$-\dfrac{dN_A}{Vd\theta} = kC_A$	$k(\theta - \theta_0) = \ln \dfrac{C_A^0}{C_A}$
Second	$-\dfrac{dN_A}{Vd\theta} = kC_A^2$	$k(\theta - \theta_0) = \dfrac{1}{C_A} - \dfrac{1}{C_A^0}$
	$-\dfrac{dN_A}{Vd\theta} = kC_A C_B$	$k(\theta - \theta_0) = \dfrac{1}{C_B^0 - C_A^0} \ln \dfrac{C_A C_A^0 + C_A^0 C_B^0 - C_A^{02}}{C_A C_B^0} \qquad C_A^0 \neq C_B^{0*}$
Third	$-\dfrac{dN_A}{Vd\theta} = kC_A^3$	$2k(\theta - \theta_0) = \dfrac{1}{C_A^2} - \dfrac{1}{C_A^{02}}$
	$-\dfrac{dN_A}{Vd\theta} = kC_A C_B C_C$	$k(\theta - \theta_0) = \dfrac{1}{(C_B^0 - C_A^0)(C_C^0 - C_A^0)} \ln \dfrac{C_A^0}{C_A} + \dfrac{1}{(C_B^0 - C_C^0)(C_B^0 - C_A^0)} \ln \left(\dfrac{C_B^0}{C_A + C_B^0 - C_A^0}\right)$ $+ \dfrac{1}{(C_C^0 - C_B^0)(C_C^0 - C_A^0)} \ln \left(\dfrac{C_C^0}{C_A + C_C^0 - C_A^0}\right) \qquad C_B^0 \neq C_C^0 \neq C_A^0$

NOTE: C^0 and θ_0 are initial conditions for time and concentration, respectively.
* If $C_A^0 = C_B^0$, use expression for $-dN_A/Vd\theta = kC_A^2$.
† If $C_A^0 = C_B^0 = C_C^0$, use expression for $-dN_A/Vd\theta = kC_A^3$.

Reversible reactions, consecutive reactions $(A \to B \to D)$, and parallel reactions $\left(A \begin{smallmatrix} \nearrow B \\ \searrow D \end{smallmatrix} \right)$ require much more complicated rate equations for their description. Whereas the formulation of an appropriate rate statement usually is simple, the solution of the resulting differential equations is likely to be difficult and is beyond the scope of this section. Typical solutions are presented in monographs on applied kinetics (e.g., Walas, "Reaction Kinetics for Chemical Engineers," McGraw-Hill Book Company, New York, 1959). Many rate equations previously considered too difficult to solve because of their demand for awkward or tedious numerical approximation methods now are tractable by virtue of their amenability to electronic analog or digital computers.

Equilibrium and Kinetics. Inasmuch as all chemical reactions are limited by a chemical equilibrium, reaction kinetics really describes the rate of approach to that equilibrium rather than to a stoichiometric completeness of the reaction. At equilibrium, the net rate of reaction [Eq. (5-69)] is zero; whence it follows that an equilibrium constant for the reaction is related to the forward and reverse specific rate constants, thus:

$$K_c = \frac{k}{k'} \tag{5-70}$$

It is clear that the larger the value of K_c, the larger the magnitude of the forward rate constant relative to the reverse and the closer to stoichiometric completeness the equilibrium conversion. Also, for a given concentration of reactant greater than the equilibrium concentration, the faster the progress of the reaction toward equilibrium. *All other things being equal,* conditions that increase the value of the equilibrium constant are favorable to the net kinetics of the reaction. Equilibrium constants are discussed in Sec. 2.

Effect of Temperature. Homogeneous reactions are strongly temperature-dependent. Their specific reaction rate always increases with increasing temperature. The effect of temperature is described by the semitheoretical relation of Arrhenius:

$$k = Ae^{-E/RT} \tag{5-71}$$

The coefficient A (called the frequency factor) and the exponent E (called the energy of activation) have theoretical connections, but they are best regarded by the process designer as empirical quantities peculiar to a particular chemical reaction and evaluable from experimental rate data. Thus a plot of $\ln k$ against $1/T$ should be linear and should have a slope of $-E/R$ and an intercept of $\ln A$ †, provided A and E are independent of temperature. In fact, both the frequency factor and energy of activation vary slightly with temperature, but over the temperature ranges normally encountered, they may be assigned constant average values without serious error. Figure 5-31

† A plot of $\log_{10} k$ against $1/T$ will have a slope of $-0.434E/R$ and an intercept of $\log_{10} A$.

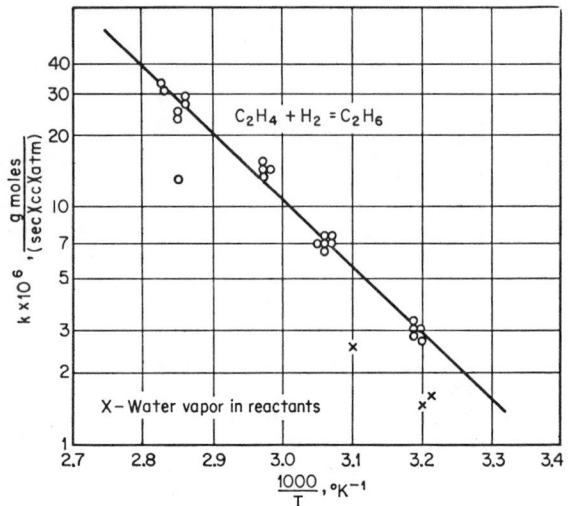

Fɪɢ. 5-31. Arrhenius plot for hydrogenation of ethylene. (*Smith*, *"Chemical Engineering Kinetics,"* p. 74, *McGraw-Hill Book Company, New York,* 1956.)

shows an Arrhenius plot for a second-order reaction. The activation energy represented by the line drawn through the data is 10,100 cal/g mole.

The failure of rate data to fit Eq. (5-71) may be accepted as evidence that:

1. A reversible reaction has been treated as if it were irreversible, and the effect of temperature on the equilibrium is significant.

2. An otherwise incorrect mechanism has been assigned to the reaction.

3. The specific rate constant has been evaluated from the experimental data incorrectly.

4. The reaction is heterogeneous, and its rate is influenced by adsorption or by some other physical process.

Energies of activation have been measured less than 1,000 and greater than 100,000 cal/g mole. For most reactions, the value will be between 10,000 and 70,000 cal/g mole.

Table 5-17. Temperature Rise Needed to Double the Rate of Reaction

Temperature, °C	Activation energy E, cal		
	10,000	40,000	70,000
0	11	3	2
400	70	17	9
1000	273	62	37
2000	1037	197	107

A long-popular rule of thumb states that the rate of a reaction approximately doubles for each 10°C rise in temperature. Such an approximation is consistent with the Arrhenius equation in the range of normal ambient temperatures and with moderate activation energies (Levenspiel, "Chemical Reaction Engineering," pp. 28–30, John Wiley & Son, Inc., New York, 1962). Above 200°C it can be considerably in error unless the activation energy is very large. Table 5-17 shows the calculated temperature rise necessary for reaction-rate doubling for several activation energies and at several temperature levels.

Effect of Concentration. At constant temperature, the specific rate constant is assumed to be independent of the concentration of reactants and products, so that equations like (5-67) or (5-68) show explicitly the effect of concentration on the progress of the reaction. In general, this is a valid assumption for homogeneous uncatalyzed reactions. If there seems to be a dependency of k on concentration, the most likely reasons are that the wrong order (or mechanism) has been postulated, that a catalyst is influencing the reaction, or that the temperature has not remained constant. Heterogeneous reactions may yield apparent rate constants that reflect complex combinations of physical and chemical processes, and hence may vary with concentration.

Homogeneous Catalyzed Reactions. A catalyst is a substance which affects the rate of a chemical reaction without entering the reaction in any stoichiometric sense. The catalyst may undergo net physical or chemical change in the course of the reaction, but often it does neither. Trace amounts of a catalyst can greatly influence the reaction rate and mechanism. A catalyst can be positive (increase the rate) or negative (decrease the rate). If not otherwise stipulated, a positive effect is implied. Negative catalysts are called inhibitors.

Some homogeneous gas-phase and liquid-phase (most commonly the latter) reactions can be catalyzed by materials that are soluble in the reacting mass and therefore do not destroy the homogeneity of the system. Sometimes homogeneous catalysis occurs without the prior knowledge of the kinetic experimenter. In such a case, grossly incorrect conclusions can be drawn about the kinetics of the reaction. Usually, catalytic behavior will be signaled by one or more of the following phenomena:

1. Irrationally rapid or accelerating rate of reaction
2. Irrationally slow rate of reaction
3. Apparent zero or fractional order with respect to known reactants
4. Abnormal temperature dependency of the rate

Although homogeneous catalysts are likely to be effective in very small amounts, most catalyzed reactions will exhibit a definite order with respect to the catalyst below a particular concentration. This order should be determined experimentally for the most reliable statement of the kinetics of the reaction. In some instances, however, the catalyst concentration is kept constant, and the reaction may be described satisfactorily for design purposes by the assignment of apparent orders to the reactants and products, with no explicit ordering of the catalyst.

5-21. Heterogeneous Reactions

Definition. A chemical reaction is heterogeneous if more than one phase is an active participant. It is not necessary that the reaction occur in more than one phase (often it is impossible to tell, in fact) or that reactants or products be distributed among phases (although they often are) for the reaction to be classified as heterogeneous, nor does the presence of two or more phases in the reacting mixture ensure such classification. *The criterion is whether more than one phase is required for the reaction to occur in an expected way.*

Heterogeneous reactions may be catalyzed or uncatalyzed.

Uncatalyzed Heterogeneous Reactions. Many uncatalyzed chemical reactions of industrial importance are heterogeneous. Two-phase systems having at least one of the phases a fluid are encountered in all possible combinations: gas-liquid (as in the chlorination of benzene), liquid-liquid (as in the nitration of toluene), liquid-solid (as in the pickling of steel), and gas-solid (as in the combustion of coke). Reactions involving more than two phases simultaneously are less common but not unknown.

In an uncatalyzed heterogeneous reaction, chemical action occurs among components that are simultaneously being transferred physically from phase to phase. The apparent rate of the reaction is in fact the rate of the whole more complicated process. It will be influenced not only by factors affecting chemical kinetics, but also by those affecting the rate of interphase mass transfer. Among the latter are:

1. Amount of interfacial surface
2. Concentration of reactants in each phase
3. Concentration of products in each phase (if the reaction is importantly reversible)
4. Relative velocity at the interface
5. Temperature (in its effect on phase equilibrium and diffusivities)
6. Presence of a solid resistance at the interface (as an ash layer formed on a reacting solid)

Sometimes the conditions of a heterogeneous process are such that the chemical reaction is relatively rapid, whence the rate of physical transport becomes effectively that of the over-all process. Sometimes the reverse is true. More generally, the rates of physical transfer and chemical reaction are of the same order of magnitude, in which case each contributes significantly to the kinetics of the over-all process.

Inasmuch as temperature effects in chemical and physical processes usually are quite different, the selection of operating temperature in a heterogeneous reaction may determine which component process is controlling. Figure 5-32 shows the rate of a gas-solid reaction, in which an ash film is formed, as a function of temperature. Over section AB the process rate is essentially that of the chemical reaction; over section CD, that of the diffusion of reactant through the gas film; and over EF, that of diffusion through the ash layer. Over sections BC and DE more than one phenomenon controls. *It should be noted that the over-all rate never can be greater than that of the slowest component process.*

Whenever more than one phenomenon determines the effective reaction rate, the rate equation becomes a difficult one to solve.   Listed below are a number of special cases for which solutions have been formulated, and references to their treatment:

1. Gas absorption and simultaneous simple-order reaction between absorbed gas and absorbant liquid. Enhancement factors for the physical mass transfer coefficient are calculated as functions of the chemical rate and equilibrium constants (Emmert and Pigford in "Perry's Chemical Engineers' Handbook," 4th ed., sec. 14, pp. 15–17, McGraw-Hill Book Company, New York, 1963).

2. Absorption of two gases that react with one another immediately after absorption. Method similar to case 1 (Emmert and Pigford, *loc. cit.*).

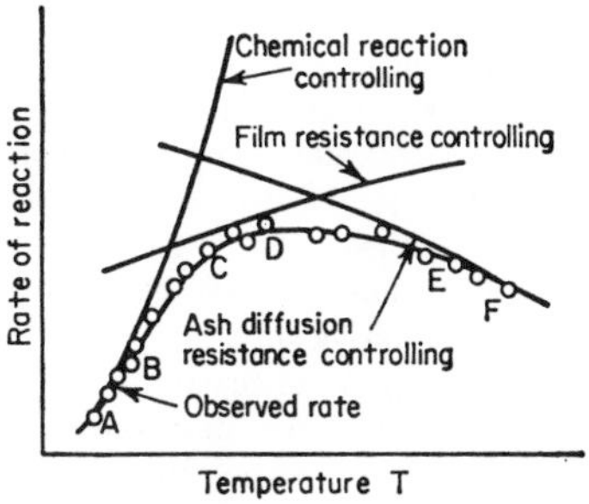

FIG. 5-32. Rate of reaction as affected by combined resistances. (*Levenspiel,* "*Chemical Reaction Engineering,*" *p. 355, John Wiley & Sons, Inc., New York,* 1962.)

3. Reaction between components of two substantially immiscible liquids, taking place significantly in only one of the phases.   An analysis similar to that of case 1 is appropriate (Perry and Green, in "Perry's Chemical Engineers' Handbook," 4th ed., sec. 4, p. 16, McGraw-Hill Book Company, New York, 1963).

4. Reaction between components of two substantially immiscible liquids, taking place in both phases.   Concentrations of reactants must be calculated so that their displacement from physical-equilibrium values will balance physical and chemical rates (Perry and Green, *loc. cit.*).

5. Fluid-solid systems involving reaction at the solid surface.   Modified methods of treatment developed for catalyzed heterogeneous reactions are appropriate (see following discussion under this topic).

6. Fluid-solid systems involving reaction in the fluid phase.   Methods similar to those for case 1 should apply, but have been less well established (Perry and Green, *op. cit.*, p. 17).

The design equations derived for the preceding special cases have as yet been supported by few data.   Meanwhile, a number of empirical scale-up correlations exist for one or another application of uncatalyzed heterogeneous reaction, useful within the restrictions of the experimental conditions under which they were established.   Generally, they are treated as modifications of a mass-transfer phenomenon.

Catalyzed Heterogeneous Reactions.   Although heterogeneous reactions responsive to catalysis may involve any combination of phases, the examples most common and industrially most important are solid-fluid systems in which the catalyst is the solid phase. The reactants and products may be gaseous, liquid, or both. The solid catalyst may be a container wall, a metal gauze, or a granular mass. Usually it is the latter, in either fixed or fluidized bed form, with particles seldom larger than 0.25 in. A reaction catalyzed by a solid is believed to take place at the surface of the solid (the surface may be internal, i.e., interstitial within a porous particle) and to involve activated adsorption or chemisorption on that surface.

The mechanism of a fluid-phase reaction catalyzed by a solid is extremely complex, and may comprise as many as seven sequential steps:

1. Diffusion of reactants to the outside catalyst surface from the body of the fluid phase

2. Diffusion of reactants into the catalyst pores (or through an inert deposit to active surface regions)

3. Adsorption of reactants

4. Chemical reaction in the adsorbed state

5. Desorption of products

6. Diffusion of products from the catalyst pores

7. Diffusion of products from the outside catalyst surface into the body of the fluid phase

Any one or more of these steps may be slow enough to control the rate of the entire sequence. Often control can be ascribed to a single step, and an adequate design procedure can be based on this premise.

Analysis of a catalyzed heterogeneous process, then, consists in examining the data for evidence of the rate-controlling step (the experimental program must have been planned to yield such evidence) and applying the data to evaluate coefficients and indices of whatever equations appropriately describe the rate. The procedure is outlined as follows:

1. If the degree of conversion depends on the linear velocity of reacting fluid with respect to the catalyst (at constant space velocity), mass transfer between the body of the fluid and the external surface of the catalyst is controlling. The rate of the process is then the rate of diffusion to or from the catalyst, and the transfer coefficient may be calculated from established correlations such as

$$\frac{k_G M_m p_f}{G} \left(\frac{\mu}{\rho \mathfrak{D}}\right)^{0.67} = B \left(\frac{D_p G}{\mu}\right)^m \tag{5-72}$$

When $(D_p G/\mu) \leq 350$, $B = 1.82$ and $m = -0.51$; for higher Reynolds numbers, $B = 0.99$ and $m = -0.41$. The calculated value of k_G and the observed rate of reaction will permit calculation of the concentration of the significant component at the interface.

2. If the degree of conversion is independent of fluid velocity but depends on size of the catalyst pellets, diffusion of reactants or products within the pores of the catalyst is the rate-controlling step. In such a case, the data should be treated to evaluate an effectiveness factor, defined as the ratio of observed reaction rate to that which would obtain if pore diffusional resistance were negligible.

Figure 5-33 is a typical plot of effectiveness factor against a modulus

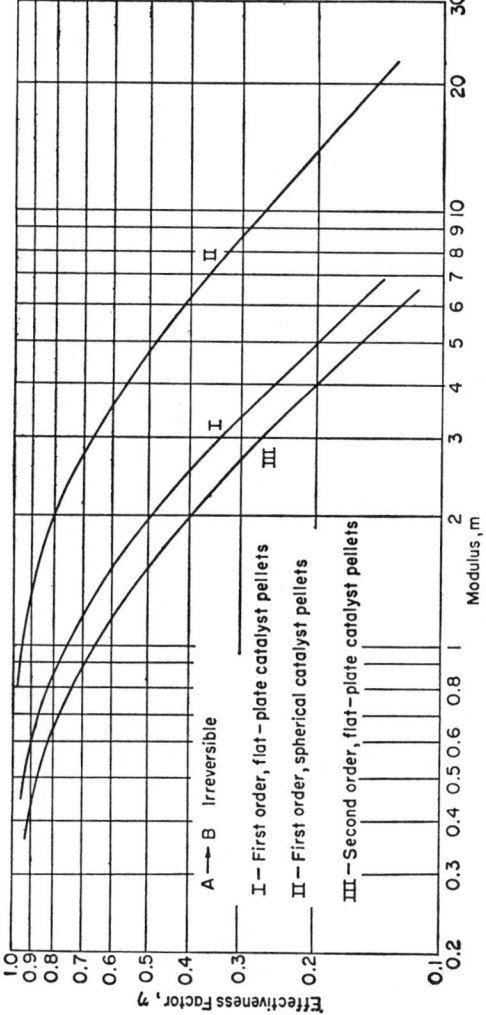

Fig. 5-33. Effectiveness factor for equations of simple order.

A → B   Irreversible

I — First order, flat–plate catalyst pellets

II — First order, spherical catalyst pellets

III — Second order, flat–plate catalyst pellets

Effectiveness Factor, η

Modulus, m

Table 5-18. Values of Internal Surface Area, Pore Volume, and Average Pore Radius for Typical Catalysts

Catalyst	S_g, m²/g	V_g, cc/g	$\bar{r} = 2V_g/S_g$, A
Activated carbons...	500–1500	0.6–0.8	10–20
Silica gels..	200–700	0.4	15–100
Silica-alumina cracking catalysts ~10–20% Al₂O₃........	200–700	0.2–0.7	15–150
Silica-alumina (steam-deactivated)......................	67	0.519	155
Silica-magnesia microsphere:			
Nalco, 25% MgO......................................	630	0.451	14.3
Nalco, steam treated, 621°C, 400 psig for 24 hr.........	322	0.283	17.6
Da-5 silica-magnesia...................................	656	0.365	11.1
Activated clays..	150–225	0.4–0.52	~100
TCC clay pellets (MgO, CaO, Fe₂O₃, SO₄) = ~10%......	276	0.363	26.3
Clays:			
Montmorillonite (raw)...............................	214	0.297–0.306	~28
Montmorillonite (heated 550°C)......................	212	0.268	25.2
Vermiculite..	35	0.063–0.057	~314
Activated alumina (Alorico)..........................	175	0.388	45
CoMo on alumina.....................................	168–251	0.261–0.331	20–40
Kieselguhr (Celite 296)................................	4.2	1.14	11,000
Fe-synthetic NH₃ catalyst............................	4–13	0.12	200–1000
Co-ThO₂-Kieselguhr 100:18:100 (reduced) pellets.........	42.3	0.73	345
Co-ThO₂-MgO (100:6:12) (reduced) granular.............	84.1	0.80	190
Co-Kieselguhr 100:200 (reduced) granular..............	22.8	2.31	2030
Porous plate (Coors No. 760).........................	1.6	0.172	2150
Pumice..	0.38		
Fused copper catalyst.................................	0.23		
Ni film...	8.4		
Ni on pumice, 91.8% pumice...........................	1.27		

S_g = catalyst surface area
V_g = catalyst pore volume
$\bar{r}$ = average radius of pore
A = angstrom unit = 1×10^{-8} cm

$m = l\sqrt{2k(C_i^0)^{n-1}/(\bar{r}D_i)}$, in which C^0 is the concentration of reactant at the external catalyst surface, and $\bar{r}$, the average pore radius, is calculated as $2V_g/S_g$ (Table 5-18 gives examples). Perry and Green (*op. cit.*, pp. 11 and 12) describe the method of calculation.

3. If adsorption-desorption or chemical reaction at the catalyst surface is the controlling process, a mechanism must be found that will identify which of the possibilities is rate-controlling and which are equilibrium steps. For example, for the stoichiometric reaction

$$A \leftrightarrows R \qquad (5\text{-}73)$$

the following mechanistic steps involving the participants A and R and a catalyst site s may be postulated:

$$A + s \leftrightarrows As \qquad (5\text{-}73a)$$
$$As \leftrightarrows Rs \qquad (5\text{-}73b)$$
$$Rs \leftrightarrows R + s \qquad (5\text{-}73c)$$

Assumption of each of these in order as the controlling step results in a different rate equation, which may be validated against experimental kinetic data. If none meet the test, a new mechanism must be tried. Perry and Green (*op. cit.*, pp. 13–16) give a good summary of the calculation procedure. The resulting controlling-rate equations for a number of simple examples are summarized in Table 5-19.

Table 5-19. Mechanisms and Their Corresponding Rate Equations

Chemical equation	Catalytic steps	Rate equation*
$A \rightleftharpoons R$	$A + s \rightleftharpoons As$	$r = \dfrac{k(C_A - C_R/K)}{1 + K_R C_R}$
	$As \rightleftharpoons Rs$	$r = \dfrac{k(C_A - C_R/K)}{1 + K_A C_A + K_R C_R}$
	$Rs \rightleftharpoons R + s$	$r = \dfrac{k(C_A - C_R/K)}{1 + K_A C_A}$
$A \rightleftharpoons R$	$2A + s \rightleftharpoons A_2 s$	$r = \dfrac{k(C_A^2 - C_R^2/K^2)}{1 + K_R C_R + K_R C_R^2}$
	$A_2 s + s \rightleftharpoons 2As$	$r = \dfrac{k(C_A^2 - C_R^2/K^2)}{(1 + K_R C_R + K_A C_A^2)^2}$
	$As \rightleftharpoons Rs$	$r = \dfrac{k(C_A - C_R/K)}{1 + K_A C_A^2 + K_A' C_A + K_R C_R}$
	$Rs \rightleftharpoons R + s$	$r = \dfrac{k(C_A - C_R/K)}{1 + K_A C_A^2 + K_A' C_A}$
$A \rightleftharpoons R$	$A + 2s \rightleftharpoons 2A_{\frac{1}{2}}s$	$r = \dfrac{k(C_A - C_R/K)}{(1 + \sqrt{K_R C_R} + K_R' C_R)^2}$
	$2A_{\frac{1}{2}}s \rightleftharpoons Rs + s$	$r = \dfrac{k(C_A - C_R/K)}{(1 + \sqrt{K_A C_A} + K_R C_R)^2}$
	$Rs \rightleftharpoons R + S$	$r = \dfrac{k(C_A - C_R/K)}{1 + \sqrt{K_A C_A} + K_A' C_A}$
$A \rightleftharpoons R + S$	$A + s \rightleftharpoons As$	$r = \dfrac{k(C_A - C_R C_S/K)}{1 + K_{RS} C_R C_S + K_R C_R + K_S C_S}$
	$As + s \rightleftharpoons Rs + Ss$	$r = \dfrac{k(C_A - C_R C_S/K)}{(1 + K_A C_A + K_R C_R + K_S C_S)^2}$
	$\left.\begin{array}{l} Rs \rightleftharpoons R + s \\ Ss \rightleftharpoons S + s \end{array}\right\}$	$r = \dfrac{k(C_A - C_R C_S/K)}{C_S(1 + K_A C_A + (K_{AS} C_A/C_S) + K_S C_S)}$
$A \rightleftharpoons R + S$	$A + s \rightleftharpoons As$	$r = \dfrac{k(C_A - C_R C_S/K)}{1 + K_R C_R + K_{RS} C_R C_S}$
	$As \rightleftharpoons Rs + s$	$r = \dfrac{k(C_A - C_R C_S/K)}{1 + K_A C_A + K_R C_R}$
	$Rs \rightleftharpoons R + s$	$r = \dfrac{k(C_A - C_R C_S/K)}{C_S(1 + K_A C_A + K_{AS} C_A/C_S)}$
$A + B \rightleftharpoons R$	$A + s \rightleftharpoons As$	$r = \dfrac{k(C_A - C_R/KC_B)}{1 + (K_{RB} C_R/C_B) + K_B C_B + K_R C_R}$
	$B + s \rightleftharpoons Bs$	$r = \dfrac{k(C_B - C_R/KC_A)}{1 + K_A C_A + (K_{RA} C_R/C_A) + K_R C_R}$
	$As + Bs \rightleftharpoons Rs + s$	$r = \dfrac{k(C_A C_B - C_R/K)}{(1 + K_A C_A + K_B C_B + K_R C_R)^2}$
	$Rs \rightleftharpoons R + s$	$r = \dfrac{k(C_A C_B - C_R/K)}{1 + K_A C_A + K_B C_B + K_{AB} C_A C_B}$
$A + B \rightleftharpoons R + S$	$A + s \rightleftharpoons As$	$r = \dfrac{k(C_A - C_R C_S/KC_B)}{1 + (K_{RS} C_R C_S/C_B) + K_B C_B + K_R C_R + K_S C_S}$
	$B + s \rightleftharpoons Bs$	$r = \dfrac{k(C_B - C_R C_S/KC_A)}{1 + (K_{RS} C_R C_S/C_A)^{\frac{1}{2}} + K_A C_A + K_R C_R + K_S C_S}$
	$As + Bs \rightleftharpoons Rs + Ss$	$r = \dfrac{k(C_A C_B - C_R C_S/K)}{(1 + K_A C_A + K_B C_B + K_R C_R + K_S C_S)^2}$
	$\left.\begin{array}{l} Rs \rightleftharpoons R + s \\ Ss \rightleftharpoons S + s \end{array}\right\}$	$r = \dfrac{k[(C_A C_B/C_S) - C_R/K]}{1 + K_A C_A + K_B C_B + K_S C_S + K_{AB} C_A C_B/C_S}$

Table 5-19. Mechanisms and Their Corresponding Rate Equations
(Continued)

Chemical equation	Catalytic steps	Rate equation*
$A + B \rightleftharpoons R + S$	$A + 2s \rightleftharpoons 2A_{1/2}s$	$r = \dfrac{k(C_A - C_RC_S/KC_B)}{[1 + K_{RS}C_RC_S/C_B + K_BC_B + K_RC_R + K_SC_S]^2}$
	$B + s \rightleftharpoons Bs$	$r = \dfrac{k(C_B - C_RC_S/KC_A)}{1 + \sqrt{K_AC_A} + (K_{RS}C_RC_S/C_A) + K_RC_R + K_SC_S}$
	$2A_{1/2}s + Bs \rightleftharpoons Rs + Ss + s$	$r = \dfrac{k(C_AC_B - C_RC_S/K)}{(1 + \sqrt{K_AC_A} + K_BC_B + K_RC_R + K_SC_S)^3}$
	$Rs \rightleftharpoons R + s$	$r = \dfrac{k(C_AC_B/C_S - C_R/K)}{1 + K_A\sqrt{C_A} + K_BC_B + (K_{AB}C_AC_B/C_S) + K_SC_S}$
	$Ss \rightleftharpoons S + s$	$r = \dfrac{k(C_AC_B/C_R - C_S/K)}{1 + \sqrt{K_AC_A} + K_BC_B + K_RC_R + K_{AB}C_AC_B/C_R}$
$A + B \rightleftharpoons R + S$	$B + s \rightleftharpoons Bs$	$r = \dfrac{k(C_B - C_SC_R/KC_A)}{1 + K_RC_R + K_{RS}C_RC_S/C_A}$
	$A + Bs \rightleftharpoons Rs + S$	$r = \dfrac{k(C_AC_B - C_RC_S/K)}{1 + K_RC_R + K_BC_B}$
	$Rs \rightleftharpoons R + s$	$r = \dfrac{k[(C_AC_B/C_S) - C_R/K]}{1 + (K_{AB}C_AC_B/C_S) + K_BC_B}$

NOTE: $K_{AB}\ldots$ = combined equilibrium constants; K = over-all equilibrium constant for the chemical equation; k = constant.
* The rate equation is opposite the catalytic step assumed to be rate-controlling.

The discovery of a suitable rate equation by the methods described does not constitute establishment of the true mechanism by which the heterogeneous catalytic reaction is occurring. Nevertheless, whenever the true mechanism is unknown—and it usually is—a rate-equation formulation by the kind of semitheoretical approach outlined offers the most reliable device for rationalizing kinetic data and extending them to conditions not exactly covered in the experiment that yielded them.

5-22. Interpretation of Chemical Kinetic Data and Design of Reactors

Analysis of Experimental Data. The confident design of plant-scale chemical reactors requires properly collected laboratory or pilot-plant kinetic data. The data in general will be of one of the following types:

1. Measurements of composition as a function of time in a batch reactor of constant volume operated at various temperatures and pressures

2. Measurements of composition as a function of feed rate to a flow reactor of constant volume operated at various pressure and temperature levels

3. Measurements of composition as a function of time in a variable-volume batch reactor operated at constant temperature and substantially constant pressure

The third type of data is much less common than the other two, and the experimental technique is more difficult. Data of the second type are generally the most dependable and simple to obtain. This method has the advantage of direct applicability to flow-type reactors. Data of the first type should not be used for the design of flow reactors unless it is certain that the extent of mixing is the same in both the batch and flow systems. In all cases it is important that the temperature does not vary with time in the batch reactor or with position in the flow reactor.

Once collected, the data at one temperature should be treated to determine the order of the reaction with respect to each participant. This treatment consists, generally, of testing the validity of the rate equations, differential or integrated, suspected to be appropriate, until one is found that fits the data. The use of differential rate equations requires the direct measurement of reaction rates in the laboratory (usually not feasible) or the differentiation of composition-time data (a procedure highly susceptible to error). Differential equations are useful for a quick tentative assessment of a reaction, but integrated equations are preferred for final evaluation.

Specific methods for determining the order of the reaction of Eq. (5-63), with the simplifying assumptions that it is substantially irreversible, that $a = b$, that A and B are present initially in equal concentration, and that the rate is independent of C, are illustrated below:

1. *Differential rate equation.* A logarithmic plot of $dC_A/d\theta$ (or, by approximation, $\Delta C_A/\Delta\theta$) against C_A yields a straight line, of which the slope is n, the order of the reaction (Fig. 5-34).

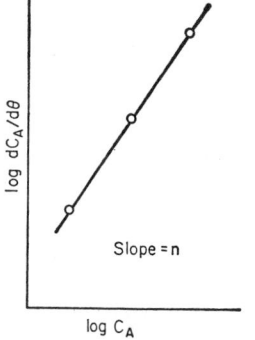

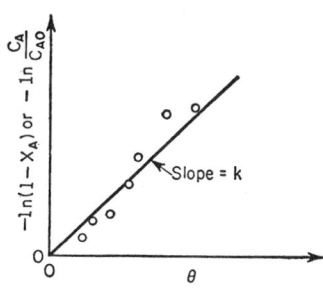

FIG. 5-34. Determining reaction order: differentiation. (*Walas, "Reaction Kinetics for Chemical Engineers," Fig. 2-1, McGraw-Hill Book Company, New York, 1959.*)

FIG. 5-35. Test for the first-order reaction. (*Levenspiel, op. cit., Fig. 3, p. 48*).

2. *Integrated rate equation, first order.* A plot of $-\log (C_A/C_{A0})$ against θ yields a straight line through the origin (Fig. 5-35).

3. *Integrated rate equation, other than first order.* When $n \neq 1$, the general rate equation

$$-\frac{dC_A}{d\theta} = kC_A{}^n \qquad (5\text{-}74)$$

is integrated between the limits C_{A0} and C_A to give

$$\left(\frac{1}{C_A}\right)^{n-1} - \left(\frac{1}{C_{A0}}\right)^{n-1} = (n-1)k\theta \qquad (5\text{-}75)$$

From Eq. (5-75), a plot of $(1/C_A)^{n-1}$ against θ yields a straight line with the intercept $(1/C_{A0})^{n-1}$ and the slope $k(n-1)$ (Fig. 5-36).

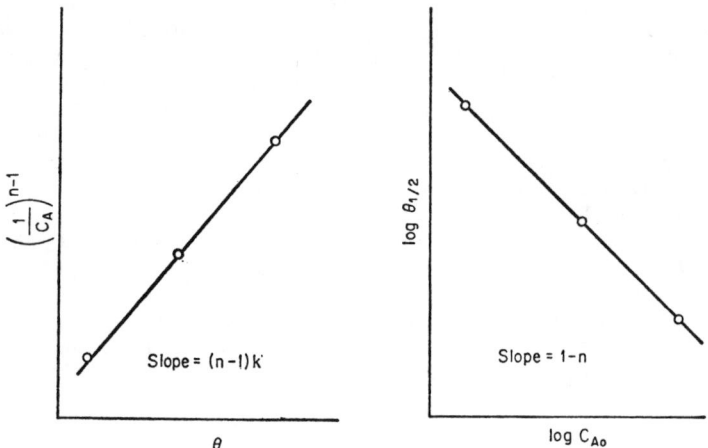

FIG. 5-36. Determining order of reaction: integrated equation. (*Walas, op. cit., Fig. 2-2.*)

FIG. 5-37. Determining order of reaction: half-lives. (*Walas, op. cit., Fig. 2-3.*)

4. *Integrated rate equation: method of half-life.* The half-life, or time for 50 per cent conversion, is a useful criterion for order. Integration of Eq. (5-74) between the limits C_{A0} and $0.5C_{A0}$ yields the following values for half-life, $\theta_{1/2}$:

$$\theta_{1/2} = \begin{cases} \dfrac{1}{2k}\,C_{A0} & n = 0 \\[2ex] \dfrac{0.69}{k} & n = 1 \\[2ex] \dfrac{1}{kC_{A0}} & n = 2 \\[2ex] \dfrac{2^{n-1}-1}{k(n-1)C_{A0}^{\,n-1}} & n = \text{any value (except 1)} \end{cases}$$

Hence, if experiments are run at different initial concentrations and $\log \theta_{1/2}$ is plotted against $\log C_{A0}$, a straight line of slope $1-n$ results (Fig. 5-37).

5. *Integrated rate equation: method of reference curves.* Inspection of the integrated rate equations indicates that the ratio of times required for any two degrees of conversion is dependent only on those conversion fractions

and on the reaction order. Walas (*op. cit.*, p. 35) has calculated such ratios, taking 90 per cent conversion as the arbitrary convenient reference, to give the useful curves of Fig. 5-38. If one plots per cent conversion, $100C_A/C_{A_0}$ against $\theta/\theta_{0.9}$, to the same scale as in Fig. 5-38, comparison of the two graphs will reveal the order of the reaction.

It is emphasized that the five preceding methods of testing for order are predicated on the assumptions of irreversibility, equimolar stoichiometry, equal concentration of reactants, and constant volume. For other irreversible constant-volume reactions, the data may be tested against the integrated expressions of Table 5-16.

If the reaction is substantially irreversible and the experiment was

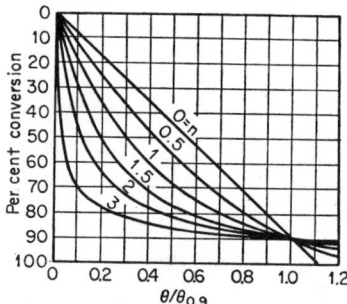

Fraction of time required for 90% conversion

FIG. 5-38. Generalized curves for determining order of reaction. (*Walas, op. cit., Fig. 2-4.*)

carried out batchwise at constant volume, the expressions of Table 5-16 are easily employed. Thus a logarithmic plot of C_A against θ will be linear for a first-order reaction, a Cartesian plot of $1/C_A$ against θ will be linear for a reaction that is of second order with respect to a single reactant, and so on. For more complicated homogeneous reactions, the equation that best approximates the actual mechanism should be tried. If the equation involves many parameters, enough data must be collected to allow the solution of a sufficient number of simultaneous equations to evaluate them all. Digital computers permit the solution of equations of otherwise prohibitive complexity. Perry and Green (*op. cit.*, pp. 18–21) explain the approach to complex reaction evaluation.

Sometimes complicated reactions can be simplified in their analysis by approximations permitted in the way experimental data are taken. For example, the early stages of reversible reaction among initially pure reactants will act substantially as if the reaction were irreversible, and the data may be so treated. Again the order of each of several reactants sometimes can be determined individually from experiments in which all but the reactant of interest is present in large stoichiometric excess. Extreme care must be taken in such approximations, however, inasmuch as sampling and analysis problems can induce large experimental error.

After establishment of the order of the reaction, the specific rate constant is easily evaluated from the data by use of the appropriate integrated equation. A value of k must be calculated for each temperature investigated.

Reactor Design. Once a suitable rate equation that fits the experimental kinetic data has been discovered, design of the plant reactor can proceed. Five steps are involved:

1. Selection of the type of reactor
2. Selection of the shape or proportions of reactor
3. Sizing the reactor
4. Selection of materials of construction
5. Design of reactor auxiliaries

Type of Reactor. Reactors generally are of four basic types: batch, semi-continuous stirred tank, continuous stirred tank, and tubular (plug-flow). The choice of type depends on the state of the reactants and products, the nature of the reaction, the rate of production, and the character of the rest of the process of which the reaction is a part. The choice is considerably economic. Table 5-20 indicates some of the conditions for which each type may be suitable.

Table 5-20. Types of Reactors and Their Applications

Type	*Conditions Suitable*
Batch..................	Intermittent operation
	Holdup of charge for testing required
	Individual fine adjustment necessary
	Small production rate
	Liquid-liquid or liquid-solid reactions
	Long induction period involved
Semicontinuous.........	Gas-liquid reactions
	Large excess of one reagent desired, for liquid-liquid or liquid-solid reactions
Continuous stirred tank..	Homogeneous liquid-phase reactions best
	Steady availability of all reactants
	Steady demand for product
	Liquid-solid reactions satisfactory if solids are easily suspended
	Gas-solid reactions satisfactory if fluidization is feasible
Tubular (plug-flow)......	Solid-catalyzed gas-phase reactions appropriate
	Homogeneous fluid-phase reactions best
	Steady availability of reactants
	Steady demand for product

Shape of Reactor. Except for the simplest of reactions, it is desirable that a plant reactor be of the same type and generally of the same shape as the laboratory unit from which the kinetic data for the reaction were obtained. In extremely complicated cases a pilot prototype of the plant unit should be operated. Even in the latter instance, however, rational scale-up of the pilot unit will be required, and may lead to a plant reactor of different proportions from the prototype.

For perfect scale-up, complete similarity (geometrical, kinematic, dynamic, thermodynamic, and chemical) should be preserved between small and large models. If one is to operate with the same process stream in both models, as he must, complete similarity is impossible. A compromise must then be made, frequently requiring longer reaction times or lower reactor productivity (rate of production per unit volume) in the large unit than in the small, but meeting the most critical demands of the system—good mixing, catalyst distribution, or temperature control, for example.

Walas (*op. cit.*, chap. 10) and Perry and Green (*op. cit.*, pp. 17–18) give excellent discussions of reactor scale-up.

Sizing the Reactor.   The volume of a reactor is calculated directly from the rate equation, such as Eq. (5-64), which may be rewritten as

$$\int_0^\theta V \, d\theta = \int_{N_{A_2}}^{N_{A_1}} dN_A/r_A \tag{5-76}$$

the correct-order expression being inserted for r_A.   For flow reactors, a more useful form of Eq. (5-76) is

$$\int_0^V \frac{dV}{F} = \int_0^{X_A} \frac{dX_A}{r_A} \tag{5-77}$$

written in terms of the molal flow rate F and degree of conversion X_A, moles of A converted per mole of °F.   For steady-state continuous stirred tanks, the rate expression is simply

$$r_A = (F/V)(C_{A_1} - C_{A_2}) \tag{5-78}$$

where the subscripts 1 and 2 refer to the concentration of reactant A in the entering and leaving streams, respectively.

A plug-flow reactor (no longitudinal mixing) and a batch reactor (no concentration or temperature gradients) require the shortest residence time possible for a given reaction of finite order to proceed to the desired extent. The residence time is identical for these two types.   The productivity (average rate of product availability per unit of reactor volume) is reduced for the batch reactor by the outage time (time required for emptying, cleaning, and refilling between batches).

Single-stage continuous stirred-tank reactors, which provide a reaction environment of the constant composition of the effluent or completed-reaction stream, have the lowest productivity of all reactors.   As the total volume of the continuous stirred-tank reactor is subdivided into equal-volume series stages, the productivity increases, approaching that of a plug-flow reactor as the number of stages approaches infinity.   Figure 5-39 shows a comparison of residence times in stirred-tank reactors of j equal stages and in plug-flow reactors for second-order irreversible reactions of various specific reaction constants and initial concentrations.

In actual practice, the assumptions of perfect mixing in continuous-stirred tanks and of no longitudinal mixing in tubular reactors are only approximations.   For stirred tanks of proper design with vigorous agitation and for small-diameter, high-velocity tubular reactors, the approximations are well within the limits of design accuracy.   For large-diameter tubes and for packed beds, the effect of longitudinal mixing can be appreciable, resulting in a larger requirement of reactor volume.   Figure 5-40 gives an idea of the effect

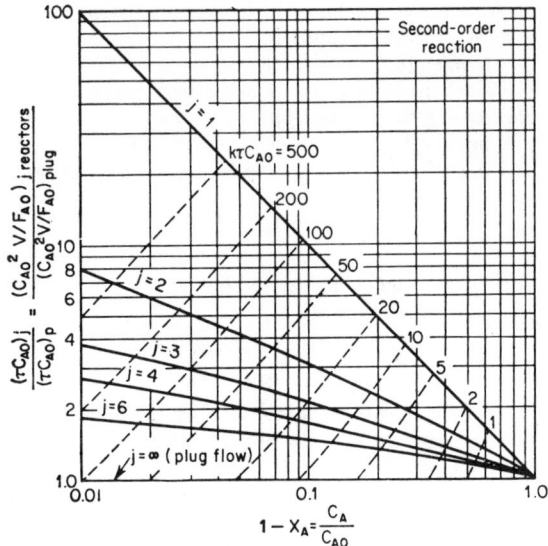

Fig. 5-39. Comparison of plug-flow and a series of j equal-size backmix reactors.

$$2A \rightarrow R$$

$$A + B \rightarrow R \qquad C_{A0} = C_{B0}$$

with negligible expansion. For the same processing rate of identical feed, the ordinate measures the volume ratio V_j/V_p or space-time ratio τ_j/τ_p directly. (*Levenspiel, op. cit.*, Fig. 7, p. 141.)

of longitudinal mixing on the required reactor volume for irreversible second-order reactions. The axial dispersion coefficient D must be determined experimentally for a given reactor.

Materials of Construction. Materials for the fabrication of all process equipment are selected, first for their ability to withstand chemical attack and thus avoid process-stream contamination, and second for their economic life. Resistance to corrosion is especially important in reactors because (1) the combination of composition, temperature, and mechanical conditions is likely to be more severe there than in most other pieces of process equipment, and (2) trace contamination due to dissolved metal can be disastrous in its catalytic effect. The high pressures, high or low temperatures, and rapid temperature changes that obtain in many reactors also make their mechanical and structural integrity difficult.

Detailed tables summarizing the chemical and mechanical characteristics of materials are available in a number of review sources (for example, Norden, Honnaker, and Holmberg, in "Perry's Chemical Engineers' Handbook," sec. 23, McGraw-Hill Book Company, New York, 1963).

Reactor Auxiliaries. The reactor designer is responsible for the provision of such auxiliaries essential to the success of the reactor's operation as agitators, pumps, heat exchangers, shafts and bearings, transfer lines, nozzles and ports, stuffing boxes, and controllers. Each of these is too specialized and extensive a subject to be treated here. The interested reader is referred to other sections of this manual or to "Perry's Chemical Engineers' Handbook" (*op cit.*).

Optimal Design. The optimization of reaction conditions and of the reactor design is highly complicated, because of the many variables that are involved, and is seldom achieved or even attempted. Certain aspects of the optimization must be considered, however, to arrive at a reasonable, if not optimal, operation.

The temperature of the reaction is chosen with regard to the following considerations: (1) reaction rates increase with temperature, and high temperatures favor low residence time in a reactor; (2) undesirable side reactions may be minimized by the proper choice of temperature; (3) equilibrium of exothermic reactions is less favorable, the higher the temperature; (4) maintaining high reactor temperatures may require high thermal costs; (5) temperature must be chosen with regard to its effect on catalysts; (6) high temperatures are identified with high corrosion rates and with costly materials of construction. To achieve a compromise between kinetic and equilibrium effects in an exothermic reaction, a programmed temperature change during

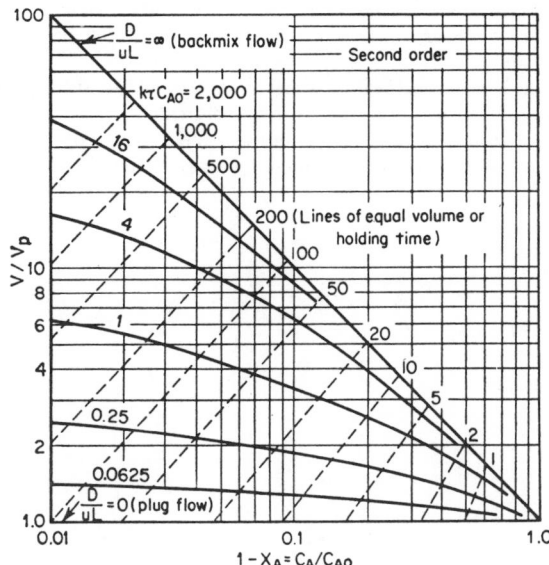

Fig. 5-40. Comparison of real and ideal (plug-flow) reactors. (*Levenspiel, op. cit.,* Fig. 24, p. 280.)

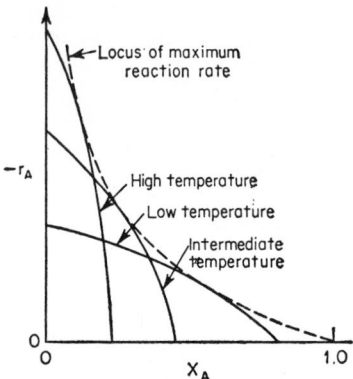

FIG. 5-41. Reaction rate as a function of conversion and temperature for reversible exothermic reactions, using a given feed material. Dashed line shows the temperature to use at each composition for optimum operations. (*Levenspiel, op. cit., Fig.* 6, *p.* 217.)

the course of the reaction may be used, as in sulfuric acid converters. Figure 5-41 shows how such programming can achieve the maximum average rate of reaction.

Reactant concentrations are selected in such a way as to allow maximum conversion of the most expensive or critical reactant, with due regard to product isolation and reactant-recovery costs. Pressure is generally the equivalent of concentration in a gas-phase reaction, and must be selected with additional regard for the equipment costs associated with high-pressure reactors. Pressure does not affect liquid-phase reactions.

Degree of conversion must be chosen, keeping separation, recycle, and subsequent processing steps and their costs in mind. In general, these costs are balanced against the cost of the reactor and its operation; the former are high for low conversion, whereas the latter may be high for high conversion.

The optimization of reactor type, proportion, size, and materials of construction is extremely complicated and cannot be treated here. The interested reader is referred to special literature on the subject (e.g., Aris, "The Optimal Design of Chemical Reactors," Academic Press Inc., New York, 1961).

CIVIL ENGINEERING

Austin E. Brant, Jr., M.S., P.E.; Associate, Tippetts-Abbett-McCarthy-Stratton, Engineers and Architects; Member, American Society of Civil Engineers, Institute of Traffic Engineers, Highway Research Board, American Road Builders Association, Operations Research Society of America.

CONTENTS

SURVEYING

6-1. Measurement of Distance

Units of Measurement. Distances are usually measured in feet and tenths, hundredths, and (for accurate work) thousandths of feet. For many older surveys, distances were measured in chains and links. A chain is 66 ft in length and is divided into 100 links, each 7.92 in. long.

Three methods used for the direct measurement of distance are pacing, stadia measurement, and tape measurement.

Pacing. Pacing is a rapid means of checking more accurate measurements of distance. The precision of pacing under average conditions is from 1 : 100 to 1 : 200.

Stadia Measurement. The use of stadia furnishes a rapid method of determining distances with a fair degree of accuracy. Under average conditions, a precision of from 1 : 300 to 1 : 1,000 can be obtained (Sec. 6-4).

Measurement with Tape. The most accurate and commonly used method of determining distance is by measurement with a tape. Steel tapes, ranging in length from 50 to 300 ft, are generally used, but tapes of other materials may be used where accuracy is not essential. The precision of a tape measurement depends on the degree of refinement with which the measurement is made. The precision of taping ordinarily used in surveys is from 1 : 3,000 to 1 : 5,000.

For ordinary taping, a tape accurate to 0.01 ft should be used. The tension of the tape should be about 15 lb. The temperature should be determined within 10°F, and the slope of the ground within 2 per cent, and the proper corrections applied. The correction to be applied for temperature when using a steel tape is

$$C_t = 0.0000065s(T - T_0) \tag{6-1}$$

The correction to be made to measurements on a slope is

$$C_h = s(1 - \cos \theta) \qquad \text{exact} \tag{6-2}$$

or

$$= 0.00015s\theta^2 \qquad \text{approximate} \tag{6-2a}$$

or

$$= h^2/2s \qquad \text{approximate} \tag{6-2b}$$

where C_t = temperature correction to measured length, ft

C_h = correction to be subtracted from slope distance, ft

s = measured length, ft

T = temperature at which measurements are made, °F

T_0 = temperature at which tape is standardized, °F

h = difference in elevation at ends of measured length, ft

θ = slope angle, deg

In more accurate taping, using a tape standardized when fully supported

6–3

throughout, corrections should also be made for tension and for support conditions. The correction for tension is

$$C_p = \frac{(P_m - P_s)s}{SE} \tag{6-3}$$

The correction for sag when not fully supported is

$$C_s = \frac{w^2 L^3}{24 P_m{}^2} \tag{6-4}$$

where C_p = tension correction to measured length, ft
   C_s = sag correction to measured length for each section of unsupported tape, ft
   P_m = actual tension, lb
   P_s = tension at which tape is standardized, lb (usually 10 lb)
   S = cross-sectional area of tape, in.²
   E = modulus of elasticity of tape, psi (29 million psi for steel)
   w = weight of tape, lb/ft
   L = unsupported length, ft

6-2. Measurement of Difference in Elevation

Difference in elevation may be measured by three methods: barometric leveling, stadia leveling, and direct leveling. Barometric methods are used for rough or preliminary work. Stadia is a rapid method and will give results having an error, in feet, of 1.0 $\sqrt{\text{distance in miles}}$ (Sec. 6-4). Direct leveling is the most accurate and most commonly used method for determining difference in elevation.

Rough Leveling. Rough leveling is practiced on preliminary or reconnaissance surveys. Sights are permitted up to 1,000 ft in length, and rod readings are made to 0.1 ft. Precision in feet is 0.4 $\sqrt{\text{distance in miles}}$.

Ordinary Leveling. Ordinary leveling is used in the construction and location of highways, railroads, and the like. Sights are permitted up to 500 ft in length, and rod readings are made to 0.01 ft. Precision in feet is 0.1 $\sqrt{\text{distance in miles}}$.

Accurate Leveling. Accurate leveling is used for establishing important bench marks. Sights are limited to 300 ft in length, and rod readings are made to 0.001 ft. Precision in feet is 0.05 $\sqrt{\text{distance in miles}}$.

Precise Leveling. Precise leveling is used for establishing bench marks at widely separated locations. Sights are limited to 300 ft in length, and rod readings are made to 0.001 ft. Special equipment and extreme care are used, and several runs are usually made. Precision in feet is 0.02 $\sqrt{\text{distance in miles}}$.

6-3. Measurement of Angles

Angles may be measured with either a compass or a transit. The precision of compass measurement is from 30' to 1°. The precision of transit measurements is from 1″ to 2′, depending on the type of instrument used and the care exercised. Angle measurements should have a precision consistent with distance measurements. Surveys in which distances are measured to 0.01 ft should have angles measured to 15″, with a resulting accuracy of better than 1 : 10,000, and surveys with distances measured to 0.1 ft and angles measured to 1′ should have an accuracy of about 1 : 5,000.

6-4. Stadia Surveying

In stadia surveying, a transit having horizontal stadia cross hairs above and below the central horizontal cross hair is used. The difference in the rod readings at the stadia cross hairs is termed the rod intercept. The intercept may be converted to the horizontal and vertical distances between the instrument and the rod by the following formulas:

$$H = Ki(\cos a)^2 + (f + c) \cos a \qquad (6\text{-}5)$$

$$V = \tfrac{1}{2}Ki(\sin 2a) + (f + c) \sin a \qquad (6\text{-}6)$$

where H = horizontal distance between center of transit and rod, ft
V = vertical distance between center of transit and point on rod intersected by middle horizontal cross hair, ft
K = stadia factor (usually 100)
i = rod intercept, ft
a = vertical inclination of line of sight, measured from the horizontal, deg
$f + c$ = instrument constant, ft (usually taken as 1 ft)

In the use of these formulas, distances are usually calculated to feet and differences in elevation to tenths of feet.

6-5. Latitudes and Departures

The latitude of a line is the projection of the line upon a true or assumed north-south meridian. The latitude of a line of length s is $s \cos \beta$ where β is the bearing of the line (the angle between the direction of the line and the direction of the north-south axis). If the line is considered as running from the southerly end to the northerly end, the latitude is positive; if from the northerly end to the southerly end, the latitude is negative.

The departure of a line is the projection of the line upon a parallel at right angles to the meridian. The departure of a line of length s is $s \sin \beta$. If the line is considered as running from the westerly end to the easterly end, the departure is positive; if from the easterly end to the westerly end, the departure is negative.

6-6. Balancing a Closed Traverse

The geometry of a closed traverse requires that the algebraic sum of the latitudes and of the departures be zero. If these sums are not zero, but are small enough to indicate that the discrepancy is not the result of an actual error, the traverse may be balanced by adjusting each line. The compass rule is usually used in balancing. The rule states: The correction to be applied to the latitude (or departure) of any line in the traverse is to the total error in latitude (or departure) as the length of the line is to the length of the traverse.

6-7. Calculation of Areas of Land

Areas of land within the limits of a balanced traverse are usually calculated by the method of double meridian distances. For convenience in the use of this method, a meridian is assumed to pass through one corner (usually the most westerly corner) of the traverse. The meridian distance of any point in the traverse is then the departure of the point, departures to the east of the meridian being considered positive and departures to the west, negative. The double meridian distance of a line in the traverse is the sum of the departures (or meridian distances) of the two ends of the line. Double meridian distances (DMD) may be calculated by the following rules:

1. The DMD of the first line in the traverse (the line one end of which is on the reference meridian) is equal to the departure of that line.

2. The DMD of any other line is equal to the DMD of the preceding line, plus the departure of the preceding line, plus the departure of the line itself.

3. The DMD of the last line is the same as the departure of that course with opposite sign.

Algebraic values should be used with due regard for signs. The area of the traverse is equal to one-half the algebraic sum of the products of the DMD and the latitude of each line.

The area of irregular tracts of land may be determined by the trapezoidal method or by Simpson's method. Both of these methods require that a straight line enclose one side of the area and that offsets from this line be measured at regular intervals to the irregular boundary. In addition, Simpson's method requires that the number of offsets be odd (or the number of regular intervals be even). The trapezoidal method states: The area is equal to the product of the interval between offsets and the sum of the intermediate offsets and one-half each end offset. Simpson's method states: The area is equal to one-third the product of the interval between offsets and the sum of the end offsets, twice each odd intermediate offset, and four times each even intermediate offset.

6-8. Circular Curves

Circular curves are the most common type of horizontal curve used to connect intersecting tangent (or straight) sections of highways or railroads. In the United States, two methods of defining circular curves are in use: the first, in general use in railroad work, defines the degree of curve as the central angle subtended by a *chord* of 100 ft in length; the second, used in highway work, defines the degree of curve as the central angle subtended by an *arc* of 100 ft in length.

The terms and symbols generally used in reference to circular curves are listed below and shown in Figs. 6-1 and 6-2.

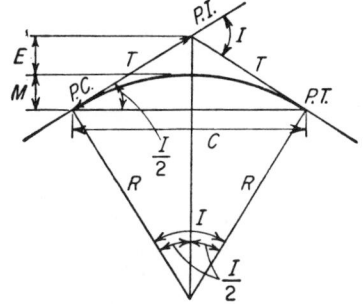

FIG. 6-1. Circular curve.   FIG. 6-2. Offsets to circular curve.

PC = point of curvature, beginning of curve
PI = point of intersection of tangents
PT = point of tangency, end of curve
 R = radius of curve, ft
 D = degree of curve (see above)
 I = deflection angle between tangents at PI, also central angle of curve
 T = tangent distance, distance from PI to PC or PT, ft
 L = length of curve from PC to PT measured on 100-ft chord for chord definition, on arc for arc definition, ft
 C = length of long chord from PC to PT, ft
 E = external distance, distance from PI to mid-point of curve, ft
 M = mid-ordinate, distance from mid-point of curve to mid-point of long chord, ft
 d = central angle for portion of curve ($d < D$)
 l = length of curve (arc) determined by central angle d, ft
 c = length of curve (chord) determined by central angle d, ft
 a = tangent offset for chord of length c, ft
 b = chord offset for chord of length c, ft

Equations of Circular Curves

$$R = 5{,}729.578/D \qquad \text{exact for arc definition, approximate for} \qquad (6\text{-}7)$$
$$\text{chord definition}$$
$$= 50/\sin \tfrac{1}{2}D \qquad \text{exact for chord definition} \qquad (6\text{-}8)$$
$$T = R \tan \tfrac{1}{2}I \qquad \text{exact} \qquad (6\text{-}9)$$
$$E = R \operatorname{exsec} \tfrac{1}{2}I = R(\sec \tfrac{1}{2}I - 1) \qquad \text{exact} \qquad (6\text{-}10)$$
$$M = R \operatorname{vers} \tfrac{1}{2}I = R(1 - \cos \tfrac{1}{2}I) \qquad \text{exact} \qquad (6\text{-}11)$$
$$C = 2R \sin \tfrac{1}{2}I \qquad \text{exact} \qquad (6\text{-}12)$$
$$L = 100I/D \qquad \text{exact} \qquad (6\text{-}13)$$
$$L - C = L^3/24R^2 = C^3/24R^2 \qquad \text{approximate} \qquad (6\text{-}14)$$
$$d = Dl/100 \qquad \text{exact for arc definition} \qquad (6\text{-}15)$$
$$Dc/100 \qquad \text{approximate for chord definition} \qquad (6\text{-}16)$$

$$\sin \tfrac{1}{2}d = c/2R \qquad \text{exact for chord definition} \qquad (6\text{-}17)$$
$$a = c^2/2R \qquad \text{approximate} \qquad (6\text{-}18)$$
$$b = c^2/R \qquad \text{approximate} \qquad (6\text{-}19)$$

Layout of Circular Curve. The field layout of a circular curve depends

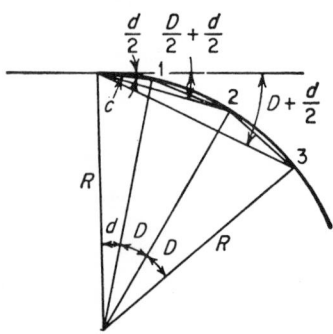

on the geometric property of a circle that the angle between a tangent and a chord is one-half the included angle. The procedure is shown in Fig. 6-3, where the length of the first chord (or arc) is so chosen that point 1 is at an even 100-ft station. Point 1 is located by measurement of the chord distance c from the PC and by the deflection angle $\tfrac{1}{2}d$ from the tangent. Point 2 is then located by measurement of the 100-ft chord (or the chord corresponding to the 100-ft arc) from point 1 and by the total deflection angle $(\tfrac{1}{2}D + \tfrac{1}{2}d)$ from the tangent. Succeeding points

FIG. 6-3. Layout of a circular curve.

are similarly located. The entire curve can be laid out with the transit set at the PC.

6-9. Parabolic Curves

Parabolic curves are used to connect sections of highways or railroads of differing gradient. The use of a parabolic curve provides a gradual change in direction along the curve. The terms and symbols generally used in reference to parabolic curves are listed below and shown on Fig. 6-4.

PVC = point of vertical curvature, beginning of curve

PVI = point of vertical intersection of grades on either side of curve

PVT = point of vertical tangency, end of curve

G_1 = grade at beginning of curve, ft/ft

G_2 = grade at end of curve, ft/ft

L = length of curve, ft

R = rate of change of grade, ft/ft²

V = elevation of PVI, ft

E_0 = elevation of PVC, ft

E_t = elevation of PVT, ft

x = distance of any point on the curve from the PVC, ft

E_x = elevation of point x distant from PVC, ft

x_s = distance from PVC to lowest point on a sag curve or highest point on a summit curve, ft

E_s = elevation of lowest point on a sag curve or highest point on a summit curve, ft

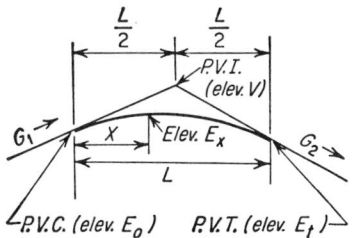

Fig. 6-4. Vertical parabolic curve (summit curve).

Equations of Parabolic Curves. In the parabolic-curve equations given below, algebraic quantities should always be used. Upward grades are positive and downward grades are negative.

$$R = (G_2 - G_1)/L \qquad \text{\textit{Note: } } K \text{ as used on Figs. 6-10 and 6-11 is} \qquad (6\text{-}20)$$
$$\text{equal to } 1/100R.$$

$$E_0 = V - \tfrac{1}{2}LG_1 \tag{6-21}$$
$$E_x = E_0 + G_1x + \tfrac{1}{2}Rx^2 \tag{6-22}$$
$$x_s = -G_1/R \qquad \text{\textit{Note: } If } x_s \text{ is negative or if } x_s > L, \text{ the curve} \tag{6-23}$$
$$\text{does not have a high point or a low point.}$$
$$E_s = E_0 - G_1^2/2R \tag{6-24}$$

SOIL MECHANICS AND FOUNDATIONS

6-10. Grain Size

The grain size classification of soils used by the U.S. Department of Agriculture is given as follows.

Soil type	Particle diam, mm	Soil type	Particle diam, mm
Gravel	>2.0	Sand, very fine	0.10–0.05
Gravel, fine	2.0–1.0	Silt	0.05–0.005
Sand, coarse	1.0–0.5	Clay	0.005–0.0002
Sand, medium	0.5–0.25	Colloids	<0.0002
Sand, fine	0.25–0.10		

6-11. Bureau of Public Roads Soil Classification

The U.S. Bureau of Public Roads has developed a detailed method for classifying soils for use as highway subgrades. Soils are classified in seven major groups as shown in Table 6-1 and described below.

Granular Materials

Group A-1. This group includes granular materials with or without non-plastic or feebly plastic soil binders. Subgroup A-1-a includes materials con-

Table 6-1. U.S. Bureau of Public Roads Classification of Highway Subgrade Materials *

General classification	Granular materials (35% or less passing no. 200 sieve)							Silt-clay materials (more than 35% passing no. 200 sieve)			
	A-1		A-3	A-2				A-4	A-5	A-6	A-7**
Group classification	A-1-a	A-1-b		A-2-4	A-2-5	A-2-6	A-2-7				A-7-5, A-7-6
Sieve analysis, % passing:											
No. 10	50 max										
No. 40	30 max	50 max	51 min								
No. 200	15 max	25 max	10 max	35 max	35 max	35 max	35 max	36 min	36 min	36 min	36 min
Characteristics of fraction passing no. 40:											
Liquid limit				40 max	41 min	40 max	41 min	40 max	41 min	40 max	41 min
Plasticity index	6 max	6 max	NP	10 max	10 max	11 min	11 min	10 max	10 max	11 min	11 min
Group index	0	0	0	0	0	4 max	4 max	8 max	12 max	16 max	20 max
Usual types of significant constituent materials	Stone fragments, gravel, and sand		Fine sand	Silty or clayey gravel and sand				Silty soils		Clayey soils	
General rating as subgrade	Excellent to good							Fair to poor			

* Classification procedure: With required test data available, proceed from left to right on above chart and correct group will be found by process of elimination. The first group from the left into which the test data will fit is the correct classification. **Plasticity index of A-7-5 subgroup is equal to or less than LL minus 30. Plasticity index of A-7-6 subgroup is greater than LL minus 30.

sisting predominantly of stone fragments or gravel, either with or without a well-graded binder of fine material. Subgroup A-1-b includes materials consisting predominantly of coarse sand either with or without a well-graded soil binder.

Group A-3. This group includes fine beach sand or fine desert blow sand without silty or clay fines or with a very small amount of nonplastic silt and stream-deposited mixtures of poorly graded fine sand with limited amounts of coarse sand and gravel.

Group A-2. This group includes a wide variety of "granular" materials which are at the border line between materials falling in groups A-1 and A-3 and the silt-clay materials of groups A-4, A-5, A-6, and A-7. Subgroups A-2-4 and A-2-5 include such materials as gravel and coarse sand with silt content or plasticity index in excess of the limitations of group A-1 and fine sand with nonplastic silt content in excess of the limitations of group A-3. Subgroups A-2-6 and A-2-7 include materials similar to those described under subgroups A-2-4 and A-2-5, except that the fine portion contains plastic clay having the characteristics of the A-6 or A-7 group.

Silt-Clay Materials

Group A-4. The typical material of this group is a nonplastic or moderately plastic silty soil. The group also includes mixtures of fine silty soil and sand and gravel.

Group A-5. The typical material of this group is similar to that described under group A-4, except that it is usually of diatomaceous or micaceous character and may be highly elastic as indicated by the high liquid limit.

Group A-6. The typical material of this group is a plastic clay soil. The group also includes mixtures of fine clayey soil and sand and gravel. Materials of this group usually have a high volume change between wet and dry states.

Group A-7. The typical material of this group is similar to that described under group A-6, except that it has the high-liquid-limit characteristics of the A-5 group and may be elastic as well as subject to high volume change. Subgroup A-7-5 includes those materials with moderate plasticity indexes which may be highly elastic as well as subject to considerable volume change. Subgroup A-7-6 includes those materials with high plasticity indexes in relation to liquid limit which are subject to extremely high volume change.

Group Index

The group index is used as an approximate within-group evaluation of the materials of the A-2-6, A-2-7, A-4, A-5, A-6, and A-7 groups.

$$\text{Group index} = 0.2a + 0.005ac + 0.01bd$$

where a = that portion of the percentage passing the no. 200 sieve greater than 35 and not exceeding 75 per cent, expressed as a positive whole number (1 to 40)

b = that portion of the percentage passing the no. 200 sieve greater than 15 and not exceeding 55 per cent, expressed as a positive whole number (1 to 40)

c = that portion of the numerical liquid limit greater than 40 and not exceeding 60, expressed as a positive whole number (1 to 20)

d = that portion of the numerical plasticity index greater than 10 and not exceeding 30, expressed as a positive whole number (1 to 20)

Under average conditions of good drainage and thorough compaction, the supporting value of a material as a subgrade is in inverse ratio to its group index; that is, a group index of 0 indicates a good subgrade material and a group index of 20 indicates a very poor subgrade material.

6-12. Relationship among Soil Classifications

Other important soil classifications and measures of supporting strength include the following:

1. California bearing ratio, the ratio (expressed as a percentage) of the load required to cause a specified penetration in a given soil to the load required to cause the same penetration in a compacted gravel
2. Casagrande soil classification
3. Civil Aeronautics Administration soil classification
4. Resistance value R
5. Bearing value

The approximate relationships among these classifications are shown in Fig. 6-5.

In the Casagrande soil classification, the following symbols are used:

G = gravel, gravelly soil
S = sand, sandy soil
O = organic silt or clay
C = clay
M = silt or very fine sand
F = fine
P = poorly graded
W = well graded
L = low to medium compressibility
H = high compressibility

6-13. Relationship of Weights and Volumes in Soil

The unit weight of soil varies, depending on the amount of water contained in the soil. Three unit weights are in general use: the saturated unit weight γ_{sat}, the dry unit weight γ_{dry}, and the buoyant unit weight γ_b.

$$\gamma_{sat} = (G + e)\gamma_0/(1 + e) = (1 + w)G\gamma_0/(1 + e) \qquad S = 100\% \qquad (6\text{-}25)$$
$$\gamma_{dry} = G\gamma_0/(1 + e) \qquad\qquad\qquad\qquad\qquad\qquad S = 0\% \qquad (6\text{-}26)$$
$$\gamma_b = (G - 1)\gamma_0/(1 + e) \qquad\qquad\qquad\qquad\quad S = 100\% \qquad (6\text{-}27)$$

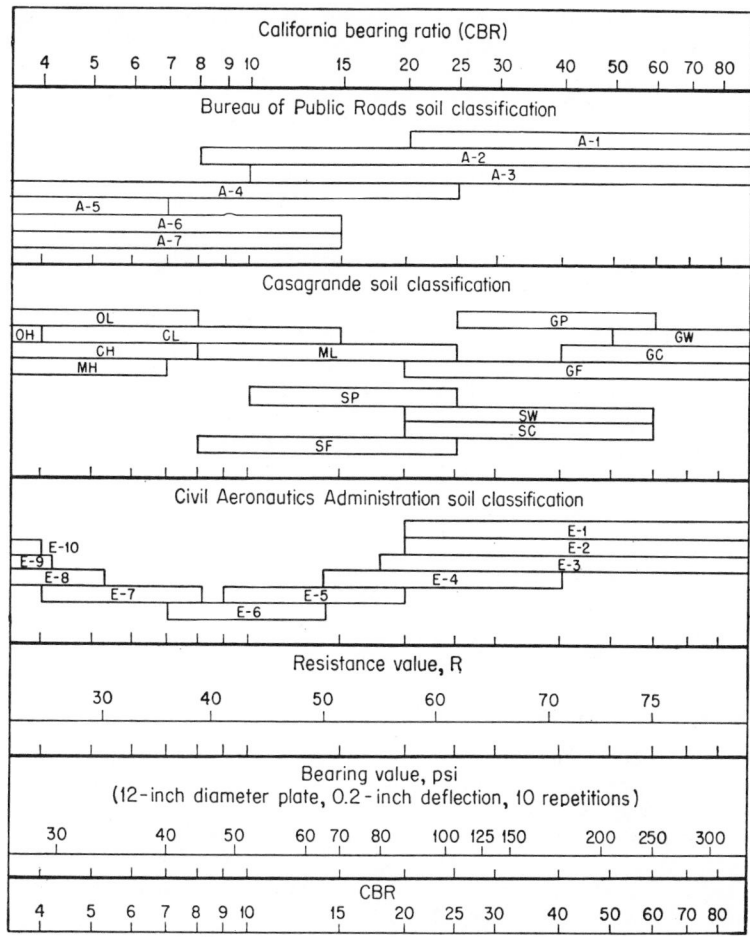

Fig. 6-5. Approximate relationship among soil classifications.

Unit weights are generally expressed in pounds per cubic foot or grams per cubic centimeter. Representative values of unit weights for a soil with a specific gravity of 2.73 and a void ratio of 0.80 are

$$\gamma_{sat} = 122 \ lb/ft^3 = 1.96 \ g/cm^3$$
$$\gamma_{dry} = \ \ 95 \ lb/ft^3 = 1.52 \ g/cm^3$$
$$\gamma_b = \ \ 60 \ lb/ft^3 = 0.96 \ g/cm^3$$

The symbols used in Eqs. (6-25) to (6-27) and in Fig. 6-6 are

G = specific gravity of soil solids (specific gravity of quartz is 2.67; for majority of soils specific gravity ranges between 2.65 and 2.85; organic soils would have lower specific gravities)

γ_0 = unit weight of water (62.4 lb/ft³ or 1.0 g/cm³)

e = voids ratio, volume of voids in mass of soil divided by volume of solids in same mass [also equal to $n/(1 - n)$, where n is porosity—volume of voids in mass of soil divided by total volume of same mass]

S = degree of saturation, volume of water in mass of soil divided by volume of voids in same mass

w = water content, weight of water in mass of soil divided by weight of solids in same mass (also equal to Se/G)

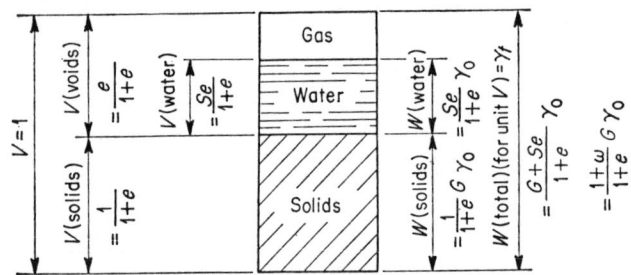

Total volume (solids + water + gas) = 1

FIG. 6-6. Relationship of weights and volumes in soil.

6-14. Atterberg Limits

The Atterberg limits are used to define the change in the strength properties of fine-grained soils with a change in water content. The *liquid limit* w_l is the highest water content at which the soil has a small but definite shear resistance. At the liquid limit, the cohesion of the soil is practically zero. The *plastic limit* w_p is the lowest water content at which the soil is plastic. The *shrinkage limit* w_s is the lowest water content that can occur in a soil when it is completely saturated.

The *plasticity index* I_p is the liquid limit minus the plastic limit and is the range of water content throughout which the soil is plastic. When the plastic limit is equal to the liquid limit, the plasticity index is zero and the soil is entirely lacking in plasticity.

6-15. Permeability

The coefficient of permeability of a soil is the volume of water which would be forced through a mass of soil having a unit cross-sectional area and a unit length by a unit head of water. The permeability of sand usually ranges from 20×10^{-4} to $3,000 \times 10^{-4}$ cm/sec (5 to 850 ft/day). The permeability of clays is usually less than 10×10^{-4} cm/sec (2.8 ft/day).

Natural soils occurring in stratified formations have a permeability in the direction of stratification much greater than in the direction perpendicular to the stratification.

6-16. Internal Friction and Cohesion

The angle of *internal friction* for a soil is expressed by

$$\tan \phi = \tau/\sigma \tag{6-28}$$

where ϕ = angle of internal friction
  $\tan \phi$ = coefficient of internal friction
  σ = normal force on given plane in cohesionless soil mass
  τ = shearing force on same plane when sliding on plane is impending
For medium and coarse sands, the angle of internal friction is about 30 to 35°. The angle of internal friction for clays ranges from practically 0 to 20°.

The *cohesion* of a soil is the shearing strength which the soil possesses by virtue of its intrinsic pressure. The value of the ultimate cohesive resistance of a soil is usually designated by c. Average values for c are given below.

General soil type	Cohesion c, psf	General soil type	Cohesion c, psf
Almost liquid clay........	100	Medium clay...........	1,000
Very soft clay............	200	Damp, muddy sand......	400
Soft clay................	400		

6-17. Vertical Pressures in Soils

The vertical stress in a soil caused by a vertical, concentrated surface load may be determined with a fair degree of accuracy by the use of elastic theory. Two equations are in common use, the Boussinesq and the Westergaard. The Boussinesq equation applies to an elastic, isotropic, homogeneous mass which extends infinitely in all directions from a level surface. The vertical stress at a point in the mass is

$$\sigma_z = 3P/2\pi z^2[1 + (r/z)^2]^{5/2} \tag{6-29}$$

The Westergaard equation applies to an elastic material laterally reinforced with horizontal sheets of negligible thickness and infinite rigidity, which prevent the mass from undergoing lateral strain. The vertical stress at a point in the mass, assuming a Poisson's ratio of zero, is

$$\sigma_z = P/\pi z^2[1 + 2(r/z)^2]^{3/2} \tag{6-30}$$

where σ_z = vertical stress at a point, psf
  P = total concentrated surface load, lb
  z = depth of point at which σ_z acts, measured vertically downward from surface, ft
  r = horizontal distance from projection of surface load P to point at which σ_z acts, ft
For values of r/z between 0 and 1, the Westergaard equation gives stresses

appreciably lower than those given by the Boussinesq equation. For values of r/z greater than 2.2, both equations give stresses less than $P/100z^2$.

The Westergaard equation is somewhat preferable for use in analyses in sedimentary soils because the assumptions on which it is based are probably nearer to the conditions existing in stratified soils.

Equations (6-29) and (6-30) may be used for loads spread over an area, provided that the area of loading has a maximum dimension less than one-third the depth z at which the stress is to be computed. Areas having greater dimensions should be subdivided for purposes of the computation, and the resulting stresses added.

6-18. Lateral Pressures in Soils, Forces on Retaining Walls

The Rankine theory of lateral earth pressures, used for estimating approximate values for lateral pressures on retaining walls, assumes that the pressure on the back of a vertical wall is the same as the pressure that would exist on a vertical plane in an infinite soil mass. Friction between the wall and the soil is neglected. The pressure on a wall consists of (1) the lateral pressure of the soil held by the wall, (2) the pressure of the water, if any, behind the wall, and (3) the lateral pressure from any surcharge on the soil behind the wall.

Symbols used in this section are as follows:

γ = unit weight of soil, lb/ft³ (saturated unit weight, dry unit weight, or buoyant unit weight, depending on conditions)

P = total thrust of soil, lb/linear ft of wall

H = total height of wall, ft

ϕ = angle of internal friction of soil, deg

i = angle of inclination of ground surface behind wall with horizontal; also angle of inclination of line of action of total thrust P and pressures on wall with horizontal

K_A = coefficient of active pressure

K_P = coefficient of passive pressure

c = cohesion, psf

Lateral Pressure of Cohesionless Soils. For walls that retain cohesionless soils and are free to move an appreciable amount, the total thrust from the soil is

$$P = \frac{1}{2}\gamma H^2 \cos i \, \frac{\cos i - \sqrt{(\cos i)^2 - (\cos \phi)^2}}{\cos i + \sqrt{(\cos i)^2 - (\cos \phi)^2}} \tag{6-31}$$

When the surface behind the wall is level, the thrust is

$$P = \frac{1}{2}\gamma H^2 K_A \tag{6-32}$$

$$K_A = [\tan (45° - \phi/2)]^2 \tag{6-33}$$

The thrust is applied at a point $H/3$ above the bottom of the wall, and the pressure distribution is triangular, with the maximum pressure of $2P/H$ occurring at the bottom of the wall.

For walls that retain cohesionless soils and are free to move only a slight amount, the total thrust is $1.12P$, where P is as given above. The thrust is applied at the mid-point of the wall and the pressure distribution is trapezoidal with the maximum pressure of $1.4P/H$ extending over the middle six-tenth of the height of the wall.

For walls that retain cohesionless soils and are completely restrained (very rare), the total thrust from the soil is

$$P = \frac{1}{2}\gamma H^2 \cos i \cdot \frac{\cos i + \sqrt{(\cos i)^2 - (\cos \phi)^2}}{\cos i - \sqrt{(\cos i)^2 - (\cos \phi)^2}} \qquad (6\text{-}34)$$

When the surface behind the wall is level, the thrust is

$$P = \frac{1}{2}\gamma H^2 K_P \qquad (6\text{-}35)$$
$$K_P = [\tan (45° + \phi/2)]^2 \qquad (6\text{-}36)$$

The thrust is applied at a point $H/3$ above the bottom of the wall, and the pressure distribution is triangular, with the maximum pressure of $2P/H$ occurring at the bottom of the wall.

Lateral Pressure of Cohesive Soils. For walls that retain cohesive soils and are free to move a considerable amount over a long period of time, the total thrust from the soil (assuming a level surface) is

$$P = \frac{1}{2}\gamma H^2 K_A - 2cH \sqrt{K_A} \qquad (6\text{-}37)$$

or, since highly cohesive soils generally have small angles of internal friction,

$$P = \frac{1}{2}\gamma H^2 - 2cH \qquad (6\text{-}38)$$

The thrust is applied at a point somewhat below $H/3$ from the bottom of the wall, and the pressure distribution is approximately triangular.

For walls that retain cohesive soils and are free to move only a small amount or not at all, the total thrust from the soil is

$$P = \frac{1}{2}\gamma H^2 K_P \qquad (6\text{-}39)$$

since the cohesion would be lost through plastic flow.

Water Pressure. The total thrust from water retained behind a wall is

$$P = \frac{1}{2}\gamma_0 H^2 \qquad (6\text{-}40)$$

where H = height of water above bottom of wall, ft
γ_0 = unit weight of water, lb/ft³ (62.4 lb/ft³ for fresh water and 64 lb/ft³ for salt)

The thrust is applied at a point $H/3$ above the bottom of the wall, and the pressure distribution is triangular, with the maximum pressure of $2P/H$ occurring at the bottom of the wall. Regardless of the slope of the surface behind the wall, the thrust from water is always horizontal.

Lateral Pressure from Surcharge. The effect of a surcharge on a wall retaining a cohesionless soil or an unsaturated cohesive soil can be accounted for by applying a uniform horizontal load of magnitude $K_A p$ over the entire height of the wall, where p is the surcharge in pounds per square foot. For saturated cohesive soils the full value of the surcharge p should be considered as acting over the entire height of the wall as a uniform horizontal load. K_A is defined in list of nomenclature, above.

6-19. Stability of Slopes

Cohesionless Soils. A slope in a cohesionless soil without seepage of water is stable if

$$i < \phi \qquad (6\text{-}41)$$

With seepage of water parallel to the slope, and assuming the soil to be saturated, an infinite slope in a cohesionless soil is stable if

$$\tan i < (\gamma_b/\gamma_{\text{sat}}) \tan \phi \qquad (6\text{-}42)$$

where i = slope of ground surface
ϕ = angle of internal friction of soil
$\gamma_b, \gamma_{\text{sat}}$ = unit weights, lb/ft³ (Sec. 6-13)

Cohesive Soils. A slope in a cohesive soil is stable if

$$H < C/\gamma N \qquad (6\text{-}43)$$

where H = height of slope, ft
C = cohesion, lb/ft²
γ = unit weight, lb/ft³
N = stability number, dimensionless

For failure on the slope itself, without seepage water,

$$N = (\cos i)^2(\tan i - \tan \phi) \qquad (6\text{-}44)$$

Similarly, with seepage of water,

$$N = (\cos i)^2[\tan i - (\gamma_b/\gamma_{\text{sat}}) \tan \phi] \qquad (6\text{-}44a)$$

where terms are as defined for Eq. (6-42).

For failure encompassing all or part of the slope, together with soil at the top or toe of the slope, approximate values of the stability number N are given in Table 6-2. In the use of formula (6-44a) and Table 6-2, appropriate values must be used for ϕ and γ. When the slope is submerged, ϕ is the angle

Table 6-2. Stability Numbers for Simple Slopes

i	N for various values of ϕ			
	0°	5°	15°	25°
90°	0.261	0.239	0.199	0.165
75°	.219	.196	.154	.118
60°	.191	.165	.120	.082
45°	.170	.141	.085	.048
30°	.156	.114	.048	.012
15°	.145	.072		

of internal friction of the soil and γ is equal to γ_b. When the surrounding water is removed from a submerged slope in a short time (sudden drawdown), ϕ is the weighted angle of internal friction [equal to $(\gamma_b/\gamma_{sat})\phi$] and γ is equal to γ_{sat}.

6-20. Bearing Capacity of Soils

The approximate ultimate bearing capacity under a long footing at the surface of a soil is given by Prandtl's equation as

$$q_u = (c/\tan \phi + \tfrac{1}{2}\gamma_{dry}b\sqrt{K_p})(K_p e^{\pi \tan \phi} - 1) \tag{6-45}$$

where q_u = ultimate bearing capacity of soil, lb/ft²

c = cohesion, lb/ft²

ϕ = angle of internal friction, deg

γ_{dry} = unit weight of dry soil, lb/ft³ (Sec. 6-13)

b = width of footing, ft

d = depth of footing below surface, ft

K_p = coefficient of passive pressure = $[\tan (45 + \phi/2)]^2$

e = 2.718 . . .

For footings below the surface, the ultimate bearing capacity of the soil may be modified by the factor $1 + Cd/b$. The coefficient C is about 2 for cohesionless soils and about 0.3 for cohesive soils. The increase in bearing capacity with depth for cohesive soils is often neglected.

Typical values of the allowable bearing capacity of various soils as given in the National Building Code of the National Board of Fire Underwriters are shown in Table 6-3. These values represent the ultimate bearing capacity divided by an appropriate safety factor.

Table 6-3. Allowable Bearing Capacity of Soils

Soil	Allowable Bearing Capacity, Tons/Ft²
Medium soft clay	1.5
Medium stiff clay	2.5
Sand, fine, loose	2
Sand, coarse, loose; compact fine sand; loose sand-gravel mixture	3
Gravel, loose; compact coarse sand	4
Sand-gravel mixture, compact	6
Hardpan and exceptionally compacted or partially cemented gravels or sands	10
Sedimentary rocks, such as hard shales, sandstones, limestones, and silt stones, in sound condition	15
Foliated rocks, such as schist or slate, in sound condition	40
Massive bedrock, such as granite, diorite, gneiss, and trap rock, in sound condition	100

6-21. Settlement under Foundations

The approximate relationship between loads on foundations and settlement is

$$\frac{q}{P} = C_1 \left(1 + \frac{2d}{b}\right) + \frac{C_2}{b} \tag{6-46}$$

where q = load intensity, lb/ft²

P = settlement, in.

d = depth of foundation below ground surface, ft

b = width of foundation, ft
C_1 = coefficient dependent on internal friction
C_2 = coefficient dependent on cohesion

The coefficients C_1 and C_2 are usually determined by bearing-plate loading tests.

6-22. Allowable Loads on Piles

A dynamic formula extensively used in the United States to determine the allowable static load on a pile is the *Engineering News* formula. For piles driven by a drop hammer, the allowable load is

$$P_a = 2WH/(p + 1) \tag{6-47}$$

For piles driven by a steam hammer, the allowable load is

$$P_a = 2WH/(p + 0.1) \tag{6-48}$$

where P_a = allowable pile load, tons
W = weight of hammer, tons
H = height of drop, ft
p = penetration of pile per blow, in.

Equations (6-47) and (6-48) include a factor of safety of 6.

For a group of piles penetrating a soil stratum of good bearing characteristics and transferring their loads to the soil by point bearing on the ends of the piles, the total allowable load would be the sum of the individual allowable loads for each pile. For piles transferring their loads to the soil by skin friction on the sides of the piles, the total allowable load would be less than the sum on the individual allowable loads for each pile, because of the interaction of the shearing stresses and strains caused in the soil by each pile.

HIGHWAY AND TRAFFIC ENGINEERING

For detailed data on the geometric design of highways, reference should be made to "A Policy on Geometric Design of Rural Highways"[1] and "A Policy on Arterial Highways in Urban Areas."[1] Information on the capacity of highways will be found in the "Highway Capacity Manual."[2] Much of the material herein was taken from these publications.

6-23. Highway Design Controls

Vehicle Characteristics. Dimensions of the four design vehicles recommended for use by AASHO[1] as controls for geometric design are shown in Table 6-4. Minimum turning paths for these vehicles are shown in Fig. 6-7. The vehicle which should be used in design is the largest one which represents a significant percentage of the traffic. For design of most highways accommodating truck traffic, one of the design semitrailer combinations should be used. A design check should be made for the largest vehicle expected, in order to ensure that such a vehicle can negotiate the designated turns, particularly if pavements are curbed.

[1] American Association of State Highway Officials (AASHO).
[2] Highway Research Board, U.S. Bureau of Public Roads.

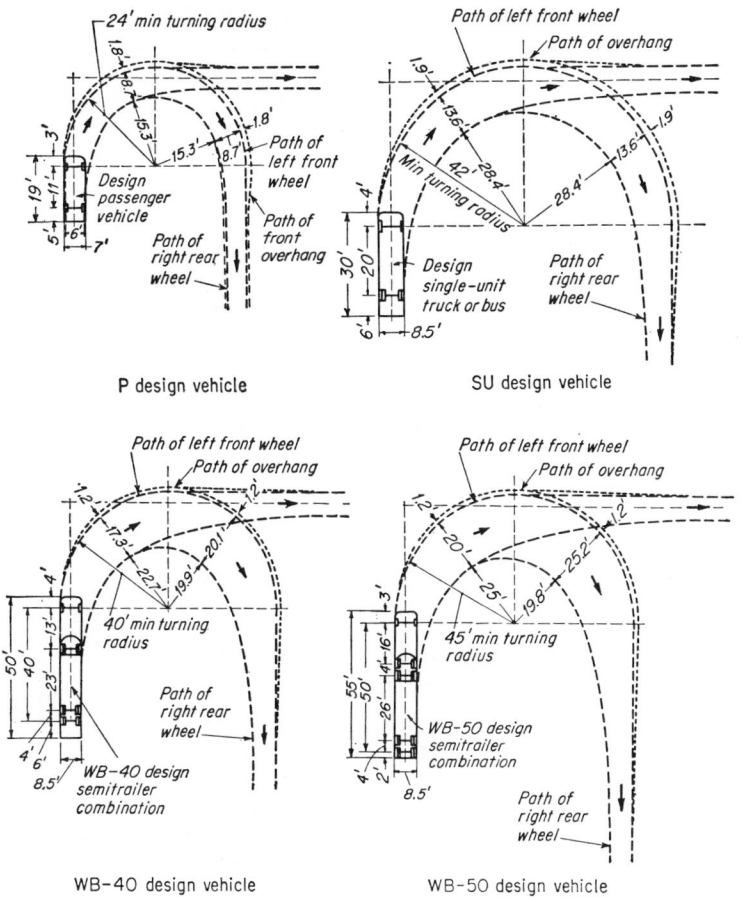

FIG. 6-7. Minimum turning paths for design vehicles.

Design Speed. The design speed of a highway is the maximum safe speed that can be maintained over a specified section when conditions are favorable, so that the design features of the highway govern the speed.

Traffic. The principal measures of traffic volume and character and the relationship between the various elements for rural highways are shown in Table 6-5. Determination of the relationship between the traffic elements for urban highways usually requires special study.

Types of Arterial Highways. A major street is an arterial highway with intersections at grade and direct access to abutting property and on which

Table 6-4. Dimensions of Design Vehicles

Design vehicle type and symbol	Dimensions. ft					
	Wheelbase	Overhang		Over-all length	Over-all width	Height
		Front	Rear			
Passenger car, P............................	11	3	5	19	7	13.5
Single-unit truck, SU......................	20	4	6	30	8.5	13.5
Semitrailer combination, intermediate, WB-40..	13 + 27 = 40	4	6	50	8.5	13.5
Semitrailer combination, large, WB-50........	20 + 30 = 50	3	2	55	8.5	13.5

geometric design and traffic control measures are used to expedite the safe movement of through traffic. An expressway is a divided arterial highway with full or partial control of access and generally with grade separations at intersections. A freeway is an expressway with full control of access. A parkway is a type of arterial highway provided for noncommercial traffic, with full or partial control of access and usually located within a park or ribbon of parklike development.

Table 6-5. Traffic Elements and Their Relation for Rural Highways

Traffic Element	*Explanation and Nationwide Percentage or Factor*
Average daily traffic, ADT...	Average 24-hr volume for a given year; total for both directions of travel, unless otherwise specified
DHV.....................	Design hour volume (two-way unless otherwise specified), usually the thirtieth highest hourly volume of the design year (30HV)
K.......................	DHV expressed as a percentage of ADT, both two-way: normal range 12 to 18%
D.......................	Directional distribution of DHV, one-way volume in predominant direction of travel expressed as a percentage of two-way DHV: general range 55 to 80%, average 67%
T.......................	Trucks (exclusive of light delivery trucks) expressed as a percentage of DHV: normal range 5 to 12%, average 8%.

6-24. Elements of Geometric Design

Stopping Sight Distance. Design stopping sight distance is the minimum distance required for a vehicle traveling at or near the design speed to stop before reaching an object in its path. It is the sum of the distances traveled during perception and brake reaction time and the distance traveled while braking to a stop. Stopping sight distance is measured from a point 3.75 ft above the road surface to a point 6 in. above the road surface. The sight distance at every point on a highway should be at least as great as the minimum distances shown in Table 6-6.

Table 6-6. Stopping Sight Distance

Design Speed, Mph	Min Stopping Sight Distance, Ft	Design Speed, Mph	Min Stopping Sight Distance, Ft
15	80	40	275
20	120	50	350
25	160	60	475
30	200	70	600
		80	750

Passing Sight Distance. Design passing sight distance is the minimum distance required to make safely a normal passing maneuver on two- and three-lane highways at passing speeds representative of nearly all drivers, commensurate with design speed. Passing sight distance is measured from a point 3.75 ft above the road surface to a second point 4.5 ft above the road surface. The minimum passing sight distance is shown in Table 6-7.

Maximum Horizontal Curvature and Superelevation. The maximum horizontal curvature for a given design speed is limited by the maximum rate of superelevation and the allowable side friction. The maximum superelevation that is considered generally desirable is 0.10 ft/ft pavement width. Values from 0.06 to 0.12 are used for maximum superelevation rates, depending on local conditions such as ice formation, frequency of intersection, and similar factors. For a maximum superelevation rate of 0.10 ft/ft, the design

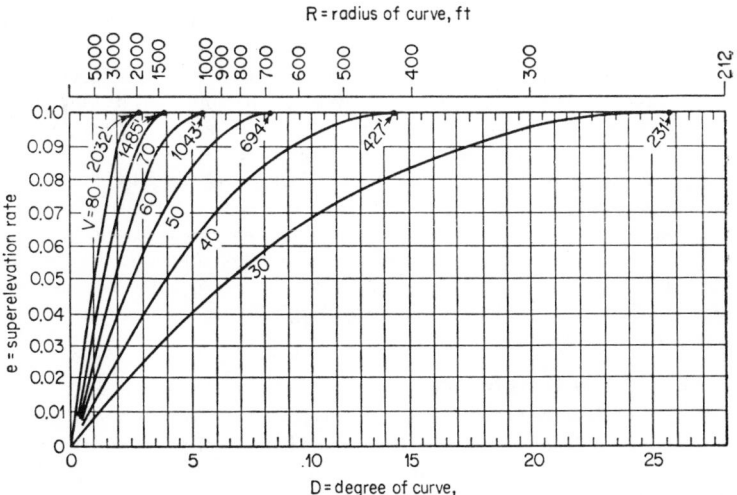

FIG. 6-8. Design superelevation rates for maximum superelevation rate of 0.10 ft/ft.

Table 6-7. Passing Sight Distance
for Two-lane Highways

Design Speed, Mph	Min Passing Sight Distance, Ft
30	1100
40	1500
50	1800
60	2100
70	2500
80	2700

superelevation rates recommended by AASHO for various speeds are shown on Fig. 6-8. The figure also indicates the maximum curvature for various design speeds at the maximum superelevation rate of 0.10.

Maximum Grades. The maximum grades recommended by AASHO for main highways are shown in Table 6-8. Maximum grades for secondary highways may be about 2% steeper than those shown in the table.

Table 6-8. Maximum Grades, Per Cent

Topography	Design speed, mph					
	30	40	50	60	70	80
Flat...............	6	5	4	3	3	3
Rolling............	7	6	5	4	4	4
Mountainous........	9	8	7	6	5	

Sight Distance on Horizontal Curves. Stopping sight distance must be provided on all horizontal curves. Figure 6-9 shows the required clearance from the center line of the inside lane to provide the minimum stopping sight distance. Design of two-lane highways for passing sight distance must in general be confined to tangent or very flat alignment conditions because of the excessive clearances that would be required on curves.

Sight Distance on Vertical Curves. Vertical curves must be designed to provide stopping sight distance. Other factors that enter into the determination of the length of a vertical curve are rider comfort and drainage control. It is generally impractical to design vertical curves for passing sight distance. The minimum length of vertical curve L for various algebraic differences in grade A is shown in Fig. 6-10 for crest vertical curves and in Fig. 6-11 for sag vertical curves.

6-25. Highway Cross Sections

Pavement Type and Cross Slope. The type of pavement is determined by the volume and composition of traffic, the availability of materials, the initial cost, and the extent and cost of maintenance. *High-type* pavements have smooth riding qualities and good antiskid properties in all weather, and should support adequately the expected volume and weight of vehicles without fatigue. *Intermediate-type* pavements vary from those only slightly less

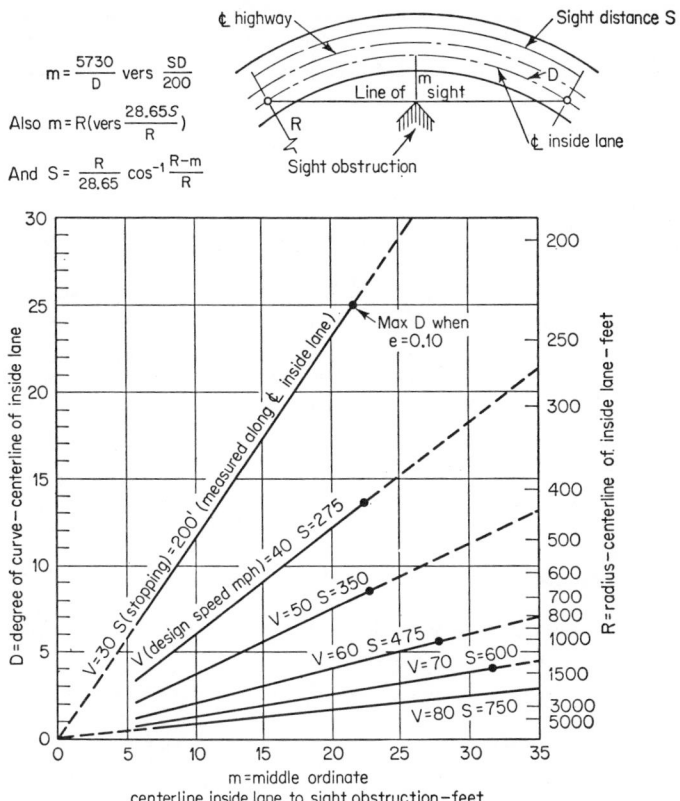

$$m = \frac{5730}{D} \text{ vers } \frac{SD}{200}$$

Also $m = R(\text{vers } \frac{28.65S}{R})$

And $S = \frac{R}{28.65} \cos^{-1} \frac{R-m}{R}$

FIG. 6-9. Stopping sight distance on horizontal curves (open road conditions).

costly than the high type to surface treatments. *Low-type* surfaces range from surface-treated earth to loose surfaces such as earth, shell, or gravel.

The range of cross slopes applicable to each type of pavement for adequate drainage is as follows:

Surface Type	Cross Slope, Ft/Ft
High	0.01 –0.02
Intermediate	0.015–0.03
Low	0.02 –0.04

When curbs are located at the pavement edge, the above values should be increased slightly.

Vertical Clearance. Clear heights of 14 ft should be provided over all highways, except for routes limited to noncommercial traffic, where 12.5 ft is adequate. In many states, 16 ft is required on interstate highway routes.

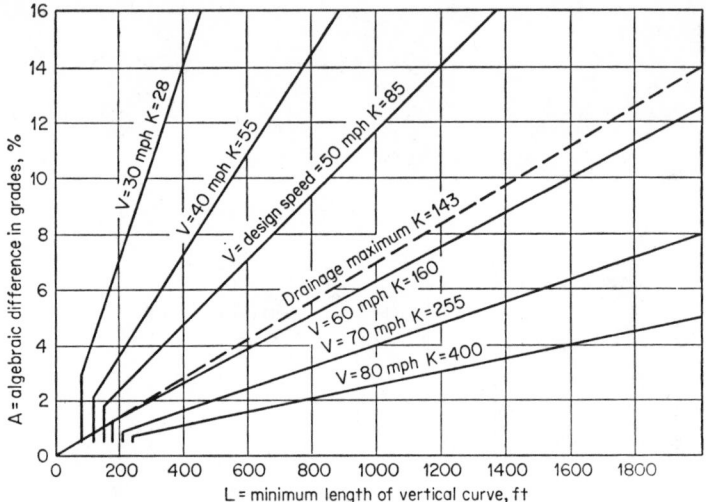

FIG. 6-10. Design controls for crest vertical curves (stopping sight distance).

These clearances are often increased by 4 to 6 in. to provide for future resurfacing.

Pavement Width. The desirable width of pavement on a highway is 12 ft per lane. This width may be reduced where traffic is light or speed is low.

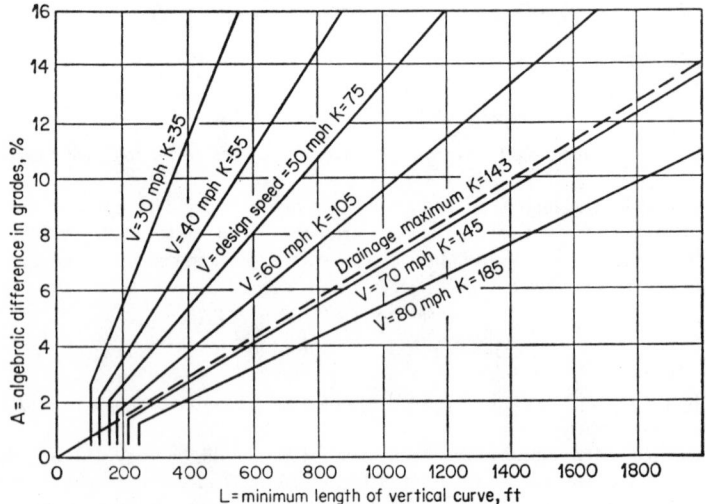

FIG. 6-11. Design controls for sag vertical curves.

Shoulder Width. The usable width of shoulder is that which can be used when a driver makes an emergency stop. The over-all width of shoulder, the dimension between the edge of pavement and the intersection of the shoulder and side-slope planes, is 1 to 3 ft greater than the usable shoulder width, except where the side slopes are 4 : 1 or flatter. Usable shoulders 10 to 12 ft wide are desirable on all highways, but narrower shoulders may be used in low-volume highways.

Table 6-9. Design Guides for Two-lane Rural Highways

Cross-section element	Element dimension, ft		
	Low	Intermediate	High
Surfacing............	18–20	20–24	24
Usable shoulder......	4–8	8	10
Roadway............	26–36	36–40	44
Border. each side.....	18–25*	20– 30*	25– 35*
Right of way........	66–80*	80–100*	100–120*

* Preferably more.

Design Guides. Design guides for cross-section elements for two-lane rural highways are shown in Table 6-9.

Four-lane highways should, if possible, be designed as divided highways. Design guides for cross-section elements for various types of four-lane divided rural highways are shown in Table 6-10. These cross-section elements should provide a balanced total section. Where restrictions are necessary, the border width should be reduced before decreasing the median, and both should be cut to a minimum before considering a reduction in shoulder or lane width.

Table 6-10. Design Guides for Four-lane Divided Rural Highways

Cross-section element	Element dimension, ft		
	Restricted	Intermediate	Desirable
Pavement, each......	24	24	24
Usable shoulder......	8– 10	10	10– 12
Median.............	4– 15	20*	40*
Border, each side.....	12– 15*	25– 40*	50– 80*
Right of way........	90–110*	140–180*	210–310*

* Preferably more.

Design guides for major streets in urban areas are shown in Table 6-11. Design speeds for major streets are 30 mph in built-up districts and as high as 50 mph in outlying areas.

Table 6-11. Design Guides for Major Urban Streets

Section	Type of urban area	Through traffic lanes		Median—width, ft		Shoulders, pavement widening at curbs, or parking lanes—width, ft		Border—width, ft		Right of way—width, ft	
		No.	Width, ft*								
			A	B	A	B	A	B	A	B	A	B
Shoulders—no curbs	Res.	2	11	12	0	0	10	10	12	20	66	84
	Res.	4	11	12	0	14	10	10	8	12	80	106
Curbed—no parking	Com.	4	11	12	0	4	1	2	8	12	62	80
	Res.	4	11	12	0	4	1	2	12	16	70	88
	Com.	6	11	12	0	4	1	2	8	12	84	104
	Res.	6	11	12	0	4	1	2	12	16	92	112
Curbed with parking lanes	Com.	4	11	12	0	4	10	11	8	12	80	98
	Res.	4	11	12	0	4	10	10	12	16	88	104
	Com.	6	11	12	0	4	10	11	8	12	102	122
	Res.	6	11	12	0	4	10	10	12	16	110	128
Divided with parking lanes†	Com.	4	11	12	4	14	10	12	8	12	84	110
	Res.	4	11	12	4	14	10	11	12	16	92	116
	Com.	6	11	12	4	14	10	12	8	12	106	134
	Res.	6	11	12	4	14	10	11	12	16	114	140

NOTE: A = acceptable minimum, B = desirable minimum, Res. = residential, Com. = commercial.
* Ten-foot widths may be considered in special cases, but not on two-lane streets.
† Without parking lanes, deduct 20 ft from right of way.

Table 6-12. Design Guides for Expressways-at-grade

Cross-section element	Element dimension, ft		
	Restricted	Intermediate	Desirable
Pavement, each:			
Four-lane.........	24	24	24
Six-lane..........	36	36	36
Shoulder...........	10	10	10
Median.............	4	14–25	40*
Border, each side.....	12	20	30*
Right of way:			
Four-lane.........	96	120–130	170*
Six-lane..........	120	145–155	195*

* Preferably more.

An expressway-at-grade is intermediate between a major street and a freeway with respect to design features. The expressway-at-grade is a surface facility practically free from roadside interference and on which crossing or entering traffic from minor streets is eliminated. Design speeds range from 40 mph in built-up districts to 60 mph in outlying areas. Design guides for expressways-at-grade are shown in Table 6-12.

Design guides for freeways are similar to those for expressways-at-grade. Design speeds range from 50 mph in built-up districts to 60 or 70 mph in outlying areas. Frontage roads are often required for depressed freeways to provide continuity in the local street system. Grade separations for cross-streets may occur at intervals of one to two blocks in downtown areas, three to five blocks in intermediate areas, and at greater distances in outlying areas. Interchanges are generally located about 2 miles apart in urban areas, 4 miles apart in suburban areas, and 8 miles apart in rural areas.

6-26. Highway Capacity and Levels of Service

The capacity of a highway is the maximum number of vehicles which has a reasonable expectation of passing over a given section of a lane or a roadway in one direction (or in both directions for a two-lane or a three-lane highway) during a given time period under prevailing roadway and traffic conditions.

Table 6-13. Operating Speeds and Service Volumes, Two-lane Highway

(Uninterrupted Flow Conditions; Rural)

Level of service	Operating speed, mph	% of length with passing sight distance of 1,500 ft or more	Maximum service volume under ideal conditions (total passenger cars per hour, both directions)			
			For 70-mph design speed	For 60-mph design speed	For 50-mph design speed	For 40-mph design speed
A	60 or more	100	400	1	1	1
		50	270	1	1	1
		0	80	1	1	1
B	50 or more	100	900	800	1	1
		50	720	540	1	1
		0	480	240	1	1
C	40 or more	100	1,400	1,320	1,120	1
		50	1,270	1,070	850	1
		0	1,080	760	360	1
D	35 or more	100	1,700	1,660	1,500	1,160
		50	1,650	1,550	1,350	960
		0	1,600	1,320	1,020	380
E[2]	30±	n.p.[3]	2,000	2,000	2,000	2,000
F	Less than 30	n.p.[3]	Variable	Variable	Variable	Variable

[1] This level of service not attainable at this design speed.
[2] Capacity.
[3] No passing at this level.

Table 6-14. Operating Speeds and Service Volumes, Freeways and Expressways

(Uninterrupted Flow Conditions; Rural or Small Metropolitan Areas)

Level of service	Operating speed, mph	Maximum service volume under ideal conditions (total passenger cars per hour, one direction)			
		For 70-mph design speed		For 60-mph design speed per lane in one direction	For 50-mph design speed per lane in one direction
		For two lanes in one direction	Each additional lane in one direction		
A	60 or more	1,400	1,000	1	1
B	55 or more	2,000	1,500	500	1
C	50 or more	2,300	1,400	700	1
D	40 or more	2,800	1,400	1,200	700
E²	30 to 35	4,000	2,000	2,000	2,000
F	Less than 30	Variable	Variable	Variable	Variable

¹ This level of service not attainable at this design speed.
² Capacity.

Table 6-15. Effects of Narrow Traffic Lanes and Restricted Lateral Clearances

Clearance from pavement edge to obstruction	Percentage of service volume*							
	Lanes with obstruction on one side				Lanes with obstruction on both sides			
	12-ft	11-ft	10-ft	9-ft	12-ft	11-ft	10-ft	9-ft
Two-lane Highways								
6	100	86	77	70	100	86	77	70
4	96	83	74	68	92	79	71	65
2	91	78	70	64	81	70	63	57
0	85	73	66	60	70	60	54	49
Freeways and Expressways, Two Lanes Each Direction								
6	100	97	91	81	100	97	91	81
4	99	96	90	80	98	95	89	79
2	97	94	88	79	94	91	86	76
0	90	87	82	73	81	79	74	66

* Applies to level of service B for two-lane highways and to all levels for freeways and expressways.

Capacity is equivalent to level of service E, defined below with other levels of service:

A—free flow, low volumes, high speeds, little or no restriction in maneuverability

B—stable flow, operating speeds somewhat restricted by traffic conditions (level B suitable for design of rural highways)

C—stable flow, operating speeds satisfactory but closely controlled by traffic conditions (level C suitable for urban design)

D—approaching unstable flow, tolerable operating speed, little freedom to maneuver

E—unstable flow, momentary stoppages (level E is capacity)

F—forced flow, congestion (volumes below capacity)

Service volumes for two-lane highways and for freeways and expressways under uninterrupted flow conditions are shown in Tables 6-13 and 6-14. These service volumes must be adjusted for roadway and traffic conditions. Adjustments for lane widths and lateral clearances are given in Table 6-15. Adjustments for trucks may be made by converting trucks to equivalent passenger cars using the factors from Table 6-16. The service volumes shown do not apply at intersections or in the vicinity of ramp termini.

Table 6-16. Average Passenger Car Equivalent of Trucks over Extended Lengths of Highways

Type of route	Level of service	Level terrain	Rolling terrain	Mountainous terrain
Freeway and expressways.......	All	2	4	8
Two-lane highways............	A	3	4	7
	B and C	2.5	5	10
	D and E	2	5	12

Typical design service volumes per lane for urban arterial routes with allowances for the factors discussed above and for roadside and intersection interferences are shown in Fig. 6-12.

6-27. Intersection Capacity and Levels of Service

The capacity of a signalized intersection approach is the maximum number of vehicles that the approach can reasonably accommodate under the existing geometric, environmental, and traffic characteristics and controls. Capacity is equivalent to level of service E, defined below with other levels of service:

A—free operation, no vehicle waits longer than one red indication: load factor = 0.0

B—stable operation, occasional approach cycle fully utilized, many drivers somewhat restricted by traffic conditions: load factor = 0.1 or less (level B suitable for design of rural intersections)

C—stable operation, intermittent loading, most drivers somewhat restricted by traffic conditions: load factor = 0.3 or less (level C suitable for design of urban intersections)

D—approaching instability, substantial delays during short peaks within peak period: load factor = 0.7 or less

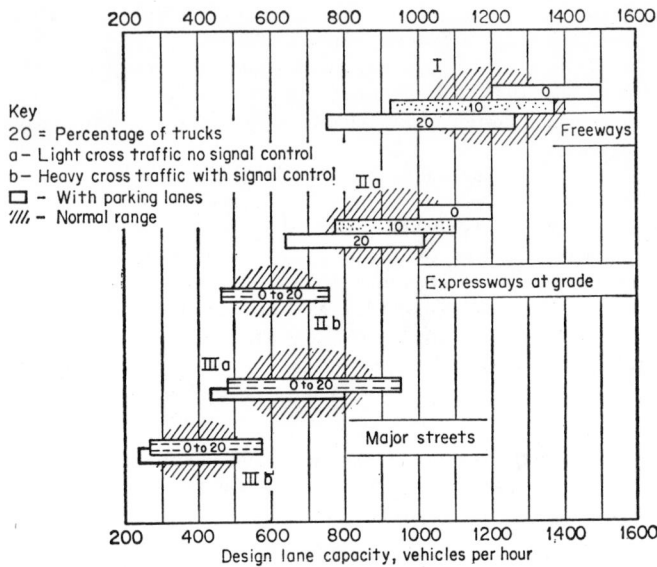

FIG. 6-12. Lane capacities for urban routes.

E—delays of several cycles, queues developing: load factor = 0.7 to 1.0,
    depending on conditions, with an average of 0.85 (level *E* is capacity)

F—jammed conditions, traffic flow controlled by downstream conditions,
    volumes unpredictable

Load factor is the proportion of green-signal intervals that are fully utilized.

Service volumes at intersections on two-way and one-way urban streets
with parking are shown on Figs. 6-13 and 6-14. Service volumes of intersections are expressed as vehicles per hour of green signal time, and the service
volume for an approach must be adjusted for the proportion of total time
allocated to the approach. Adjustments must also be made for metropolitan-
area size, the peak-hour factor (for intersections, the ratio of the volume during
the peak hour to four times the volume during the peak 15 minutes: range
0.25 to 1.00), the location within the metropolitan area, and the effects of
commercial-vehicle traffic, turning movements, and parking prohibitions.

Peak-hour factors of 1.00 are rarely found. Where long lines of waiting
vehicles are typically present, a peak-hour factor of 0.90 or 0.95 may be used.
The usual conditions in a metropolitan area are equivalent to a peak-hour
factor of 0.85, but where a high rate of flow occurs over a period shorter than
an hour, factors of 0.75, 0.70, or less should be used. Adjustments to service
volumes for various peak hours are combined on Figs. 6-13 and 6-14 with
adjustments for metropolitan-area size. The figures also indicate adjustments for the location of the intersection within the metropolitan area.

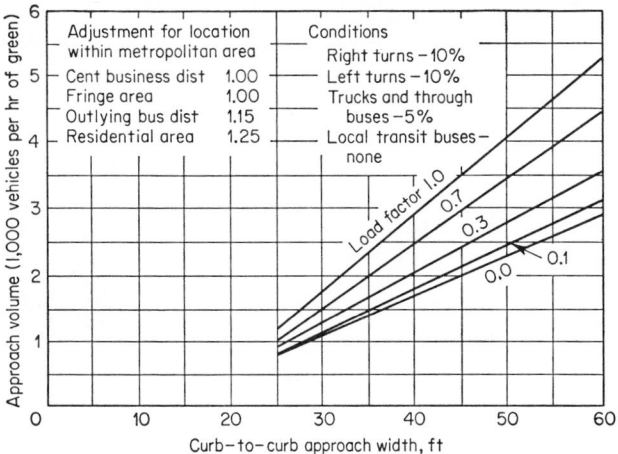

Adjustment for Peak-hour Factor and Metropolitan-area Size

Metropolitan-area pop. (1,000's)	Peak-hour factor						
	0.70	0.75	0.80	0.85	0.90	0.95	1.00
Over 1,000	1.00	1.05	1.09	1.14	1.19	1.24	1.29
1,000	0.97	1.02	1.07	1.11	1.16	1.21	1.26
750	0.94	0.99	1.04	1.09	1.14	1.18	1.23
500	0.91	0.96	1.01	1.06	1.11	1.16	1.21
375	0.88	0.93	0.98	1.03	1.08	1.13	1.18
250	0.85	0.90	0.95	1.00	1.05	1.10	1.15
175	0.82	0.87	0.92	0.97	1.02	1.07	1.12
100	0.80	0.85	0.89	0.94	0.99	1.04	1.09
75	0.77	0.82	0.87	0.92	0.96	1.01	1.06

Fig. 6-13. Urban intersection approach service volume, in vehicles per hour of green-signal time, for one-way streets with parking both sides.

For streets with approach widths of 21 to 29 ft where turning movements differ from 10 per cent right and 10 per cent left, multiply the service volume by
$[1.00 - (0.005)(R - 10)]$ $[1.00 - (0.010)(L - 10)]$ [for two-way streets]
$[1.00 - (0.005)(R - 10)]$ $[1.00 - (0.005)(L - 10)]$ [for one-way streets]
where R = percentage of right turns (maximum $R = 30$)
     L = percentage of left turns (maximum $L = 30$)
Special adjustments must be made for intersections having separate lanes and/or separate signal indications for turning movements.

For intersections where the percentage of trucks and through buses differs from 5 per cent, multiply the service volume by $[1.00 - (0.010)(T - 5)]$ where T is the percentage of trucks and through buses. Adjustments for buses which stop in the vicinity of the intersection require special procedures.

Prohibition of parking can result in increases of 30 to 50 per cent over the service volumes shown on Fig. 6-14 for two-way streets and 20 per cent to as much as 100 per cent over the volumes shown on Fig. 6-13 for one-way streets.

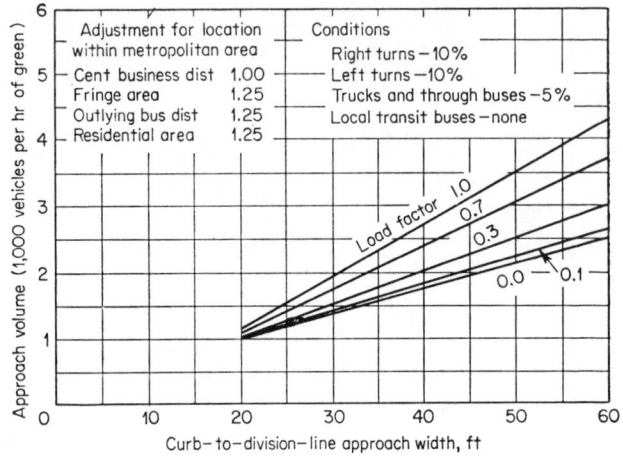

Adjustment for Peak-hour Factor and Metropolitan-area Size

Metropolitan-area pop. (1,000's)	Peak-hour factor						
	0.70	0.75	0.80	0.85	0.90	0.95	1.00
Over 1,000	1.00	1.05	1.10	1.14	1.19	1.24	1.29
1,000	0.97	1.02	1.07	1.11	1.16	1.21	1.27
750	0.94	0.99	1.04	1.09	1.13	1.18	1.23
500	0.91	0.96	1.01	1.06	1.11	1.15	1.20
375	0.89	0.93	0.98	1.03	1.08	1.12	1.17
250	0.86	0.91	0.95	1.00	1.05	1.10	1.14
175	0.83	0.88	0.92	0.97	1.02	1.07	1.11
100	0.80	0.85	0.90	0.94	0.99	1.04	1.09
75	0.77	0.82	0.87	0.91	0.96	1.01	1.06

Fig. 6-14. Urban intersection approach service volume, in vehicles per hour of green-signal time, for two-way streets with parking.

6-28. Parking Requirements

Curb Parking. The street space used for curb parking is shown in Fig. 6-15 and Table 6-17.

RAILROADS

6-29. Track Gage

Standard railroad gage in North America is 4 ft 8½ in. between inside of rails, measured ⅝ in. below top of rail. The gage may be varied from 4 ft 8⅜ in. on some high-speed tangent track to 4 ft 9⅛ in. on curves of small radius.

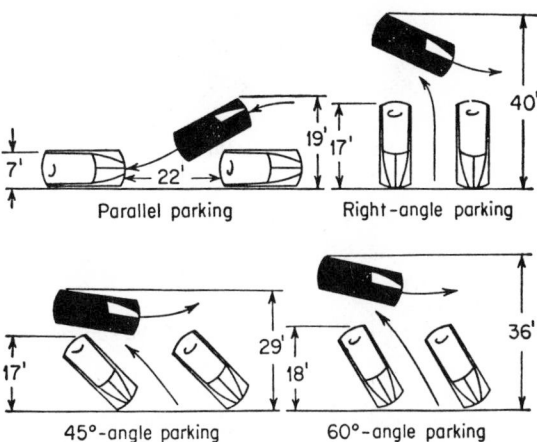

Fig. 6-15. Street space and maneuvering space used for various parking positions.

Table 6-17. Street Space Used for Parking

Angle of parking at curb	Width of street used when parked, ft	Width needed for parking plus maneuvering, ft	Length of curb per car, ft
Parallel....	7	19	22.0
45°	17	29	11.3
60°	18	36	9.2
90°	17	40	8.0

The 4 ft 8½ in. gage is also used in parts of Europe, Asia, and Africa. Other gages in use include 30 in., 36 in., 1 m, 42 in., 5 ft, and 5 ft 3 in.

6-30. Track Materials

Ties are usually oak, pine, or fir, but concrete ties are in use. Ties are generally 8 ft 6 in. or 9 ft (recommended) in length for standard gage and range from 6 in. deep and 6 in. wide for yard and sidetracks to 7 in. deep and 10 in. wide for principal main lines. Tie spacing varies from 19½ in. on centers for main lines to 24 in. for secondary tracks.

Rail is designated by weight per yard and section. Weights up to 155 lb/yd are used for high-speed track, but rail ranging from 100 to 130 lb/yd is in more common use. Rail is usually rolled in 39-ft lengths, but 78-ft lengths are often provided.

Rails are connected by means of joint bars which hold adjoining rails in horizontal and vertical alignment. Tie plates are placed under rails to distribute rail loads and reduce wear. Both rail and tie plates are held to the ties by means of spikes. Longitudinal rail movement is prevented by rail anchors.

6-31. Curvature and Superelevation

Minimum degree of curves for railroads are usually determined by train operating speeds and allowable superelevation. Maximum superelevation is 6 to 7 in., but may be less on a particular railroad. The equilibrium superelevation is

$$e = 0.00066DV^2 \qquad (6\text{-}49)$$

where e = superelevation, in.

D = degree of curve, deg

V = speed, mph

For high-speed trains, as much as 3 in. of unbalanced superelevation may be permitted, so that

$$e = 0.00066DV^2 - 3 \qquad (6\text{-}49a)$$

Curvature may also be limited because of coupling difficulties on curves of more than 6°. Some railroads have established an absolute maximum curvature of 16° because of dimensions of the rigid wheelbase of cars and engines and permissible swing of couplers. Reverse curves should be separated by at least two car lengths.

Vertical curves should be of sufficient length to limit gradient changes to 0.05 ft/100 ft for sags and 0.10 ft/100 ft for crests on main lines; secondary lines may have vertical curves one-half the lengths required for main lines.

6-32. Clearances

Track clearances are established from center line of track for horizontal dimensions and from top of rail for vertical dimensions. Track spacings vary among railroads, but the following are common centerline spacings:

Main track–main track	13 ft 6 in.
Main track–yard or passing tracks	15 ft 0 in.
Yard track–yard track	13 ft 6 in.
Ladder track–yard track	18 ft 0 in.
Ladder track–ladder track	19 ft 0 in.

Track spacings are increased on curves at a rate of 2 in./deg. Where adjacent tracks have different superelevation, additional clearance is provided of 3 in./in. of difference in superelevation.

Clearances from track to fixed structures vary by railroad and by state. Generally, vertical clearances of 22 ft are required, except at building entrances, where 17 ft may be permitted. Horizontal clearances of 8 ft and 8 ft 6 in. are standard for tangent track, with additional allowances of 1 in./deg of curve and 3 in./in. of superelevation for curved track. Loading platforms are generally located 5 ft 8 in. from track center line and 3 ft 10½ in. above top of rail.

6-33. Turnouts and Crossovers

Turnouts, used to divert trains from one track to another, consist of a switch, a frog to carry the wheel flanges over crossing rails, closure rails connecting the switch rails and the frog, and guard rails to guide the flanges at the frog.   Control points for turnouts are the actual or ⅛-in. point of the switch (ground to a width of ⅛ in.) and the actual or ½-in. point of frog. Standard turnouts, shown on Fig. 6-16, are identified by the frog number.

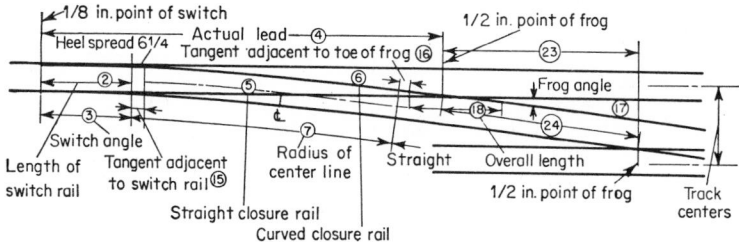

FIG. 6-16. Standard turnouts and crossovers.

Turnouts with No. 16 to No. 20 frogs are used for high-speed main-line movements, No. 10 to No. 12 for slow-speed main-line movements, and No. 8 for yards and sidings.

Crossovers, used to transfer trains between parallel tracks, consist of two turnouts and connecting rails.   Data for crossovers are also shown on Fig. 6-16.

WATER SUPPLY, SEWERAGE AND DRAINAGE

6-34. Water Supply and Treatment

Quantity of Water.   Average annual water requirements in metropolitan areas with metered systems generally range from 100 gallons per capita per day (gpcpd) to 200 gpcpd, with a median value of about 150 gpcpd.   Unmetered supply systems have considerably higher consumption, and large water-using industries require special determination of demand.

Seasonal variations in water demand occur largely because of irrigation, lawn sprinkling, and air-conditioning loads, and maximum monthly consumption is generally about 125 per cent of average annual demand but may range up to 200 per cent of average annual demand.   Maximum daily demands of 150 per cent of average annual demand and maximum hourly demands of from 200 to 250 per cent of annual average demand are commonly used for design.

Fire demand is often the determining factor in the design of mains, distribution storage tanks, and pumps, even though the total quantity of water required for fire fighting is small during a long period.   For communities of less than 200,000 population, the fire demand is given by the National Board of Fire Underwriters as

Turnout and Crossover Data

(1) Frog number	Properties of switches		(4) Actual lead	Closure distance		Lead curve	
	(2) Length of switch rail	(3) Switch angle		(5) Straight closure rail	(6) Curved closure rail	(7) Radius of center line	(8) Degree of curve
	Ft In.	Deg Min Sec	Ft In.	Ft In.	Ft In.	Ft	Deg Min Sec
5	11-0	2-39-34	42-6½	28-0	28-4	177.80	32-39-56
6	11-0	2-39-34	47-6	32-9	33-0	258.57	22-17-58
7	16-6	1-46-22	62-1	40-10½	41-1¼	365.59	15-43-16
8	16-6	1-46-22	68-0	46-5	46-7½	487.28	11-46-44
9	16-6	1-46-22	72-3½	49-5	49-7¼	615.12	9-19-30
10	16-6	1-46-22	78-9	55-10	56-0	779.39	7-21-24
11	22-0	1-19-46	91-10¼	62-10¼	63-0	927.27	6-10-56
12	22-0	1-19-46	96-8	66-10½	67-0	1104.63	5-11-20
14	22-0	1-19-46	107-0¾	76-5¼	76-6¾	1581.20	3-37-28
15	30-0	0-58-30	126-4½	86-11½	87-0¾	1720.77	3-19-48
16	30-0	0-58-30	131-4	91-11	92-0	2007.12	2-51-18
18	30-0	0-58-30	140-11½	99-11	100-0	2578.79	2-13-20
20	30-0	0-58-30	151-11½	110-11	111-0	3289.29	1-44-32

$$Q = 1,020 \sqrt{P}(1 - 0.01 \sqrt{P}) \qquad (6\text{-}50)$$

where Q = fire demand, gpm

P = population in thousands

The fire demand is added to the normal demand on the maximum day to determine the total maximum demand.

(for Use with Fig. 6-16)

		Properties of frogs		Data for crossovers			
				13' 0" track centers		For change of 1' 0" of track centers	
(15) Tangent adjacent to switch rail	(16) Tangent adjacent to toe frog	(17) Frog angle	(18) Over-all length	(23) Straight track	(24) Crossover track	Straight track	Crossover track
Ft	Ft	Deg Min Sec	Ft In.	Ft In.	Ft In.	Ft In.	Ft In.
0.00	0.78	11-25-16	9-0	16-10 5/16	18-1 7/8	4-11 7/16	5-0 5/8
0.00	1.75	9-31-38	10-0	20-5 1/2	21-6 1/2	5-11 1/2	6-0 1/2
0.01	0.00	8-10-16	12-0	24-0 3/4	24-11 5/8	6-11 9/16	7-0 7/16
0.64	0.00	7-09-10	13-0	27-7 1/8	28-4 7/8	7-11 7/8	8-0 7/8
0.00	0.17	6-21-35	16-0	31-1 5/8	31-10 3/8	8-11 11/16	9-0 5/16
2.08	0.00	5-43-29	16-6	34-8 1/8	35-3 3/8	9-11 11/16	10-0 5/16
0.00	0.13	5-12-18	18-8 1/2	38-2 1/2	38-9 1/2	10-11 3/4	11-0 1/4
0.00	0.50	4-46-19	20-4	41-8 3/4	42-3 1/4	11-11 3/4	12-0 1/4
0.24	0.00	4-05-27	23-7	48-9 1/4	49-2 13/16	13-11 13/16	14-0 1/4
1.56	0.00	3-49-06	24-4 1/2	52-3 7/16	52-8 5/8	14-11 13/16	15-0 3/16
0.66	0.00	3-34-47	26-0	55-9 5/8	56-2 1/2	15-11 13/16	16-0 3/16
0.57	0.00	3-10-56	29-3	62-9 7/8	63-2 3/16	17-11 13/16	18-0 3/16
2.47	0.00	2-51-51	30-10 1/2	69-10	70-2	19-11 7/8	20-0 1/8

Design Period. Pipes less than 12 in. in diameter are generally designed to be adequate for the full development of the area served; pipes more than 12 in. in diameter and wells, distribution systems, and filtration and treatment plants are generally designed for the flow expected 15 to 25 years in the future; and large dams and conduits are generally designed to be adequate for 25 to 50 years.

Quality of Water. The outstanding requirement for a domestic water supply is freedom from pathogenic bacteria. In addition, there are reasonable limits for certain impurities, as listed in Table 6-18.

Table 6-18. Limits for Certain Impurities in Water Supplies

Impurity	Limit, ppm	Impurity	Limit, ppm
Turbidity...............	10	Iron plus manganese.....	0.3
Color...................	20	Magnesium..............	125
Lead....................	0.1	Total solids.............	500
Fluoride................	1.0	Total hardness (calcium	
Copper.................	3.0	plus magnesium salts)..	100

Water Treatment. Water treatment usually consists of filtration through either a slow or a rapid sand filter and disinfection with chlorine. In addition, water may be softened to remove hardness and aerated to remove iron and manganese.

The slow sand filter operates at a rate of 2 to 4 million gal/(acre)(day) and is effective in removing tastes and odors from raw water. About 99 per cent of the bacterial content is also removed.

The rapid sand filter operates at a rate of 125 to 190 million gal/(acre)(day). However, preliminary treatment of the raw water is required, including chemical coagulation and sedimentation. The entire treatment process is effective in removing about 99.98 per cent of the bacterial content, but removal of the color and turbidity is less dependable than for the slow sand filter and requires particular attention to the coagulation process.

Softening is accomplished by the addition of lime, or lime and soda ash, and sedimentation. The addition of lime and passage through a zeolite softener is also used. Iron and manganese may be removed by aeration and sedimentation.

Disinfection by the addition of chlorine is the final stage of any treatment process. Common practice is to add sufficient chlorine so that a small free chlorine residual is maintained.

6-35. Water Distribution

Transmission mains connecting the source of supply to the distribution system must be large enough to supply at least the maximum daily demand plus fire flow. If the distribution system does not include storage, supply mains must also be adequate to deliver maximum hourly demands.

Both transmission and distribution mains are usually designed by using the Hazen-Williams formula. This equation with factors necessary for its use and a nomograph to facilitate its application are presented in Sec. 2.

6-36. Sewage Collection and Treatment

Quantity of Sewage. The average flow of sewage from a metropolitan area is about 100 gpcpd (gallons per capita per day). This rate may vary from

240 gpcpd in a maximum hour, 160 gpcpd on a maximum day, 70 gpcpd on a minimum day, and 40 gpcpd in a minimum hour. In addition, infiltration of ground water into sewers may be taken at about 600 gal/(day)(in. diam) (mile).

Design Period. Laterals and submains less than 15 in. in diameter are generally designed to be adequate for the full development of the area served; main sewers, outfalls, and intercepter sewers are generally designed for the flow expected from 40 to 50 years in the future; and treatment works are generally designed for the flow expected from 10 to 25 years in the future.

Sewer Design. Sewers should be at least 8 in. in diameter and should be laid on a grade sufficient to produce a velocity of 2 fps when flowing full, to prevent the deposition of suspended solids. Sewer lines should be designed with straight alignment and uniform grade between manholes, which should have a maximum spacing of 400 ft.

Quality of Sewage. Sewage is approximately 99.92 per cent water, with the remaining 0.08 per cent (800 ppm by weight) composed of organic and mineral matter, as shown below:

	Organic matter, ppm	Mineral matter, ppm
Suspended solids....	100	50
Colloidal solids......	140	60
Dissolved solids.....	160	290

The "biochemical oxygen demand" of sewage, BOD, is the quantity of oxygen which must be supplied during the aerobic stabilization of sewage, and thus is a direct measure of the pollutional effect. Residential sewage has an average BOD of 0.24 lb oxygen per capita.

Sewage Treatment. The degree of sewage treatment required should be based on the size, characteristics, and usage of the receiving body of water and upon the amount and quality of sewage to be treated. Complete sewage treatment might include preliminary treatment, such as screening to remove large suspended solids, grit removal, and grease removal; primary treatment, such as plain sedimentation or chemical precipitation; secondary treatment of a biological nature, such as the trickling filter or the activated sludge process; final treatment by chlorination; and finally disposal by dilution in a body of water. Approximate values of the BOD and suspended-solids removal of primary and secondary treatment are shown below:

Treatment process	Percentage removal		Treatment process	Percentage removal	
	BOD	Suspended solids		BOD	Suspended solids
Plain sedimentation.........	25–40	40–70	Trickling filter.............	80–95	80–90
Chemical precipitation.......	50–75	70–90	Activated sludge...........	85–95	85–95

6·37. Sizes and Slopes of Sewers

Sewer sizes and slopes are usually designed by using the Manning formula

$$v = \frac{1.486}{n} R^{2/3} S^{1/2} \tag{6-51}$$

where v = average velocity of flow, fps

n = coefficient of roughness

R = hydraulic radius, ft = A/P = $D/4$ for circular conduit flowing full

S = hydraulic gradient, ft head loss/ft length

A = cross-sectional area of flow, ft^2

P = wetted perimeter, ft

D = diameter of circular conduit, ft

For circular sewers flowing full, the Manning formula can be written as

$$Q = (0.4632/n)D^{8/3}S^{1/2} = \text{conveyance factor} \times S^{1/2} \tag{6-52}$$

where Q = quantity of flow, cfs.

The factors necessary for the use of this equation and nomographs to facilitate its application are presented in Sec. 2.

6-38. Quantity of Runoff

The rational method for the determination of the quantity of storm water which appears as runoff involves the use of

$$Q = ciA \tag{6-53}$$

where Q = runoff from rainfall, cfs

c = coefficient of runoff, dimensionless

i = rainfall intensity, expressed as a rate, in. rain/hr

A = tributary area, acres

These factors are discussed below.

Coefficient of Runoff. The coefficient of runoff for a particular area depends on the character of the surface, the type and extent of vegetation, the slope of the surface, and other less important factors. Approximate values of the coefficient of runoff c are given in Table 6-19.

Table 6-19. Runoff Coefficients for Rational Formula

Type of area	Flat: slope <2%	Rolling: slope 2-10%	Hilly: slope >10%
Pavements, roofs, etc..........	0.90	0.90	0.90
City business areas...........	.80	.85	.85
Suburban residential areas.....	.45	.50	.55
Dense residential areas........	.60	.65	.70
Grassed areas................	.25	.30	.30
Earth areas..................	.60	.65	.70
Cultivated land:			
Impermeable (clay, loam)....	.50	.55	.60
Permeable (sand)..........	.25	.30	.35
Meadows and pasture lands....	.25	.30	.35
Forests and wooded areas.....	.10	.15	.20

Rainfall Intensity. The rainfall intensity is dependent on the recurrence interval and the time of concentration. The recurrence interval is the period of time within which, on the average, a rainfall of a given intensity will be equaled or exceeded only once. Recurrence intervals of from 5 to 25 years are generally used, but for important structures periods of 100 years have been used.

For a particular area and a given recurrence interval, a study of rainfall records will permit the determination of an intensity-duration curve, which gives the rainfall intensity (in inches per hour) as a function of the duration of rainfall. The rainfall intensity is greatest for short periods and decreases sharply as the duration of rainfall becomes greater. The intensity to use for a particular design is that for which the duration is equal to the time of concentration.

Time of Concentration. The time of concentration for a particular inlet to a drainage system is the time required for rainfall falling on the most remote part of the tributary area drained by the inlet to reach the inlet. At this time, the entire area tributary to the inlet will be contributing to the runoff and the total runoff will be a maximum. The time for water to flow overland from the most remote part of the tributary area to the inlet may be approximated by

$$t = C(L/Si^2)^{1/3} \qquad (6\text{-}54)$$

where t = time of overland flow, min

L = distance of overland flow, ft

S = slope of land, ft/ft

i = rainfall intensity, in./hr

C = coefficient: 0.5 for paved areas, 1.0 for bare earth, 2.5 for turf

For any portions of the flow carried in ditches, the time of flow to the inlet may be computed by means of the Manning formula.

6-39. Flow in Drainage Channels

Drainage channels are usually of such lengths that head losses other than those due to friction are negligible. Design of drainage channels is generally by the Manning formula:

$$v = (1.486/n)R^{2/3}S^{1/2} \qquad (6\text{-}55)$$

where $S = h_f/l$ = hydraulic gradient, ft head loss/ft length

n = coefficient of roughness, dimensionless

R = hydraulic radius, ft = A/P

A = cross-sectional area of flow, ft^2

P = wetted perimeter, ft

h_f = head loss due to friction, ft

l = length of channel or conduit, ft

v = average velocity of flow, fps

Factors necessary for the use of this equation and nomographs to facilitate its application are presented in Sec. 2.

STRUCTURAL ANALYSIS AND DESIGN[1]

The four basic types of load-carrying members are *ties*, which carry axial tension; *columns*, which carry axial compression; *beams*, which carry transverse loads; and *shafts*, which carry torsional loads. Many structural members have as their primary loading a combination of the basic types of loading, and most have secondary loadings of a type other than their primary loading.

6-40. Ties

The stress in a tie carrying axial tension or tension applied at the centroid of the cross section of the tie is

$$f_a = P/A \tag{6-56}$$

and the total strain, or total elongation, of a tie under load is

$$e = Pl/AE = f_a l/E \tag{6-57}$$

where f_a = tensile unit stress, psi
P = total axial[2] load, lb
A = cross-sectional area of tie, in.[2]
e = total elongation, in. or ft
l = total length of member, in. or ft
E = modulus of elasticity, psi

6-41. Columns

The stress and strain in a short column, sometimes called a strut, carrying an axial compressive load is the same as given above for a tie, except that the stress is compressive and the strain is a shortening. Long, slender columns usually fail by buckling, and the strength of these columns is not determined by the strength of the material of which the column is made. The critical elastic buckling load for a long, slender column axially loaded is given by Euler's formula as

$$P_c = \pi^2 EI/l^2 = \pi^2 AE/(l/r)^2 \tag{6-58}$$

The critical buckling load for a column intermediate between the short column and the long, slender column is given by the secant formula as

$$P_c = \frac{f_y A}{1 + \dfrac{ec}{r^2} \sec\left(\dfrac{l}{2r}\sqrt{\dfrac{P_c}{AE}}\right)} \tag{6-59}$$

where P_c = critical buckling load, lb
I = least moment of inertia of cross-sectional area, in.[4]
A = cross-sectional area, in.[2]
r = least radius of gyration of cross-sectional area $(r = \sqrt{I/A})$, in.
f_y = yield-point stress of material, psi

[1] The properties of various cross sections, such as moment of inertia, section modulus, and radius of gyration, are given in Sec. 8.

ec/r^2 = factor introducing effect of column crookedness and unintentional eccentricity of loading (generally taken as 0.25)

l = effective length of column (see below), in.

E = modulus of elasticity, psi

The ratio of the effective length of columns to their actual length is approximately as follows:

End Conditions	Effective Length as Percentage of Actual Length
One end fixed, one end free	200
One end fixed, one end free to turn but not move	70
Both ends free to turn but not move	100
Both ends fixed	50
Pin-ended columns	87½
Riveted-end columns	75

6-42. Beams

Shear and Moment. The vertical *shear* for a section of a beam is the algebraic sum of the external forces acting perpendicularly to the beam's longitudinal axis to either side of the section. For convenience, the forces that lie to the left of the section are usually used. When the sum of these forces is upward, the shear at the section is positive. The bending *moment* for a section of a beam is the algebraic sum of the moments, about the centroid of the section, of the external forces and moments that act on the beam to either side of the section. For convenience, the forces and moments that lie to the left of the section are usually used. When the sum of these moments is clockwise, the upper fibers of the beam are in compression and the bending moment at the section is positive. Shears and bending moments for beams with loading conditions of frequent occurrence are shown in Fig. 6-17.

List of Symbols Used for Fig. 6-17

R_1, R_2 = reactions at left and right ends of beam, respectively, lb

V = shear, lb

M = moment, lb-in.

Δ = deflection, in.

w = intensity of distributed load on beam, lb/in.

l = length of beam, in. (x, a, and b in same units)

W = total load on beam, lb

P = concentrated load on beam, lb

E = modulus of elasticity, psi

I = moment of inertia of beam cross section, in.[4]

Statically Determinate Beams. The reactions, shears, and moments in statically determinate beams (those having only three unknown reaction components) can be determined by the three equations of statics which can be applied to a beam:

$$\Sigma H = 0 \qquad (6\text{-}60)$$

$$\Sigma V = 0 \tag{6-61}$$
$$\Sigma M = 0 \tag{6-62}$$

where ΣH = algebraic sum of all horizontal forces acting on beam, including horizontal reaction forces

ΣV = algebraic sum of all vertical forces acting on beam, including vertical reaction forces

ΣM = algebraic sum of all moments acting on beam and of moments of all forces, including reactions, acting on beam, about any point in beam (generally chosen as at one of reactions)

The reactions, shears, and moments for beams with loading conditions of frequent occurrence are shown in Fig. 6-17.

Statically Indeterminate Beams. The moments at the points of support of statically indeterminate beams may be determined by either the three-moment equation or the slope-deflection equations. The three-moment equation for a beam with a constant moment of inertia between supports is

$$M_{AB}\frac{l_{AB}}{I_{AB}} + 2M_{BA}\left(\frac{l_{AB}}{I_{AB}} + \frac{l_{CB}}{I_{CB}}\right) + M_{CB}\frac{l_{CB}}{I_{CB}} = -\left(\frac{6A_{AB}a_{AB}}{I_{AB}l_{AB}} + \frac{6A_{CB}a_{CB}}{I_{CB}l_{CB}}\right)$$
$$+ \left(\frac{6Eh_{AB}}{l_{AB}} + \frac{6Eh_{CB}}{l_{CB}}\right) \tag{6-63}$$

The symbols used in the three-moment equation are shown in Fig. 6-18 and listed below.

M_{AB}, M_{BA}, M_{CB} = moments in statically indeterminate beam at points A, B, and C, respectively, lb-in.

l_{AB}, l_{CB} = lengths of spans AB and CB, in.

I_{AB}, I_{CB} = moments of inertia of beam cross section between A and B and between C and B, in.[4]

A_{AB}, A_{CB} = areas of moment diagrams, considering sections of beam between supports to be simply supported, between A and B and between C and B, lb-in.[2]

a_{AB}, a_{CB} = distance from A and C, respectively, to the centroids of areas A_{AB} and A_{CB}, in.

h_{AB}, h_{CB} = deflection of A and C above B, in.

E = modulus of elasticity of beam material, psi

In using the three-moment equation, moments are considered positive when they cause a compressive stress in the upper fibers of the beam. Beams of more than two spans may be analyzed by this method by writing the three-moment equation for successive, overlapping two-span sections.

The slope-deflection equations for a beam with a constant moment of inertia between supports are

$$M_{AB} = M_{FAB} + (EI_{AB}/l_{AB})(4\theta_A + 2\theta_B - 6R) \tag{6-64}$$
$$M_{BA} = M_{FBA} + (EI_{AB}/l_{AB})(4\theta_B + 2\theta_A - 6R) \tag{6-65}$$

The terminology is the same as that used for the three-moment equation, with the following additions:

1. Simple Beam—Uniformly Distributed Load

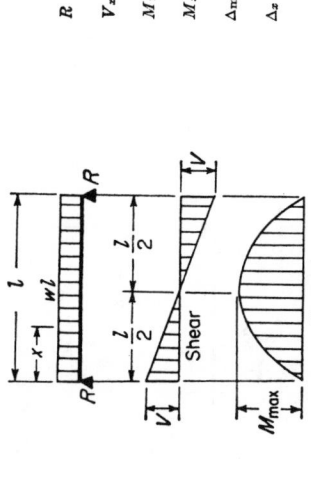

$$R = V = \frac{wl}{2}$$

$$V_x = w\left(\frac{l}{2} - x\right)$$

$$M_{max} \text{ (at center)} = \frac{wl^2}{8}$$

$$M_x = \frac{wx}{2}(l - x)$$

$$\Delta_{max} \text{ (at center)} = \frac{5wl^4}{384EI}$$

$$\Delta_x = \frac{wx}{24EI}(l^3 - 2lx^2 + x^3)$$

2. Simple Beam—Load Increasing Uniformly to One End

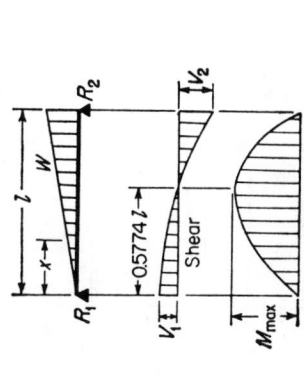

$$R_1 = V_1 = \frac{W}{3}$$

$$R_2 = V_{2max} = \frac{2W}{3}$$

$$V_x = \frac{W}{3} - \frac{Wx^2}{l^2}$$

$$M_{max}\left(\text{at } x = \frac{l}{\sqrt{3}} = .5774l\right) = \frac{2Wl}{9\sqrt{3}} = .1283Wl$$

$$M_x = \frac{Wx}{3l^2}(l^2 - x^2)$$

$$\Delta_{max}\left(\text{at } x = l\sqrt{1 - \sqrt{\frac{8}{15}}} = .5193l\right) = .01304\frac{Wl^3}{EI}$$

$$\Delta_x = \frac{Wx}{180EIl^2}(3x^4 - 10l^2x^2 + 7l^4)$$

FIG. 6-17. Beam diagrams and formulas for various static loading conditions.

3. Simple Beam—Load Increasing Uniformly to Center

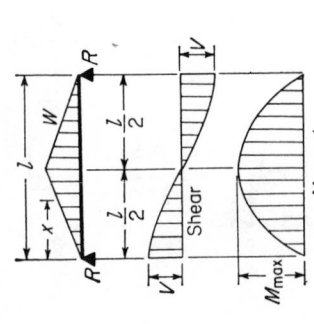

$$R = V = \frac{W}{2}$$

$$V_x \left(\text{when } x < \frac{l}{2}\right) = \frac{W}{2l^2}(l^2 - 4x^2)$$

$$M_{max} \text{ (at center)} = \frac{Wl}{6}$$

$$M_x \left(\text{when } x < \frac{l}{2}\right) = Wx\left(\frac{1}{2} - \frac{2x^2}{3l^2}\right)$$

$$\Delta_{max} \text{ (at center)} = \frac{Wl^3}{60EI}$$

$$\Delta_x = \frac{Wx}{480EI\, l^2}(5l^2 - 4x^2)^2$$

4. Simple Beam—Uniform Load Partially Distributed

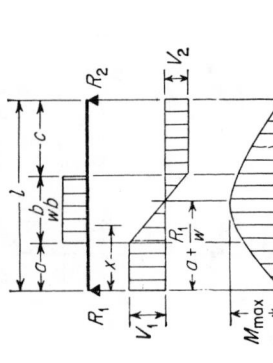

$$R_1 = V_1 \text{ (max when } a < c) = \frac{wb}{2l}(2c + b)$$

$$R_2 = V_2 \text{ (max when } a > c) = \frac{wb}{2l}(2a + b)$$

$$V_x \left[\text{when } x < a \text{ and } > (a + b)\right] = R_1 - w(x - a)$$

$$M_{max} \left(\text{at } x = a + \frac{R_1}{w}\right) = R_1\left(a + \frac{R_1}{2w}\right)$$

$$M_x \text{ (when } x < a) = R_1 x$$

$$M_x \left[\text{when } x > a \text{ and } < (a + b)\right] = R_1 x - \frac{w}{2}(x - a)^2$$

$$M_x \text{ (when } x > (a + b)) = R_2(l - x)$$

Fig. 6-17. (*Continued*)

5. Simple Beam—Uniform Load Partially Distributed at One End

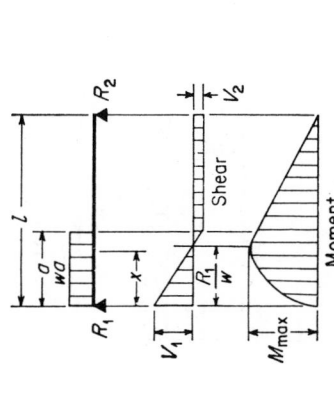

$$R_1 = V_{1\max} = \frac{wa}{2l}(2l - a)$$

$$R_2 = V_2 = \frac{wa^2}{2l}$$

$$V \text{ (when } x < a) = R_1 - wx$$

$$M_{\max}\left(\text{at } x = \frac{R_1}{w}\right) = \frac{R_1^2}{2w}$$

$$M_x \text{ (when } x < a) = R_1 x - \frac{wx^2}{2}$$

$$M_x \text{ (when } x > a) = R_2(l - x)$$

$$\Delta_x \text{ (when } x < a) = \frac{wx}{24EIl}[a^2(2l - a)^2 - 2ax^2(2l - a) + lx^3]$$

$$\Delta_x \text{ (when } x > a) = \frac{wa^2(l - x)}{24EIl}(4xl - 2x^2 - a^2)$$

6. Simple Beam—Concentrated Load at Center

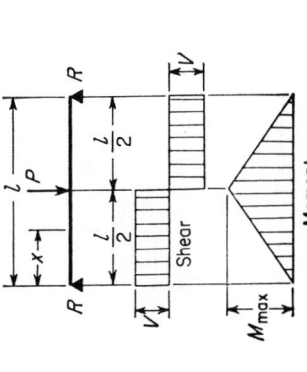

$$R = V = \frac{P}{2}$$

$$M_{\max} \text{ (at point of load)} = \frac{Pl}{4}$$

$$M_x\left(\text{when } x < \frac{l}{2}\right) = \frac{Px}{2}$$

$$\Delta_{\max} \text{ (at point of load)} = \frac{Pl^3}{48EI}$$

$$\Delta_x\left(\text{when } x < \frac{l}{2}\right) = \frac{Px}{48EI}(3l^2 - 4x^2)$$

Fig. 6-17. (*Continued*)

7. Simple Beam—Concentrated Load at Any Point

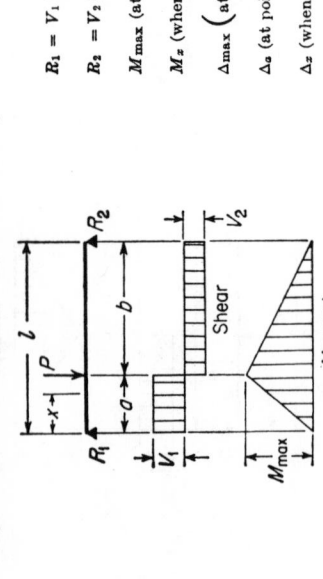

$R_1 = V_1$ (max when $a < b$) $= \dfrac{Pb}{l}$

$R_2 = V_2$ (max when $a > b$) $= \dfrac{Pa}{l}$

M_{max} (at point of load) $= \dfrac{Pab}{l}$

M_x (when $x < a$) $= \dfrac{Pbx}{l}$

$\Delta_{max}\left(\text{at } x = \sqrt{\dfrac{a(a+2b)}{3}} \text{ when } a > b\right) = \dfrac{Pab(a+2b)\sqrt{3a(a+2b)}}{27EIl}$

Δ_a (at point of load) $= \dfrac{Pa^2b^2}{3EIl}$

Δ_x (when $x < a$) $= \dfrac{Pbx}{6EIl}(l^2 - b^2 - x^2)$

8. Cantilever Beam—Load Increasing Uniformly to Fixed End

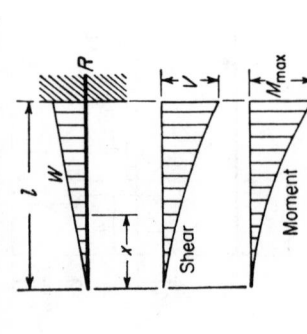

$R = V = W$

$V_x = W\dfrac{x^2}{l^2}$

M_{max} (at fixed end) $= \dfrac{Wl}{3}$

$M_x = \dfrac{Wx^3}{3l^2}$

Δ_{max} (at free end) $= \dfrac{Wl^3}{15EI}$

$\Delta_x = \dfrac{W}{60EIl^2}(x^5 - 5l^4x + 4l^5)$

Fig. 6-17. (*Continued*)

9. Cantilever Beam—Uniformly Distributed Load

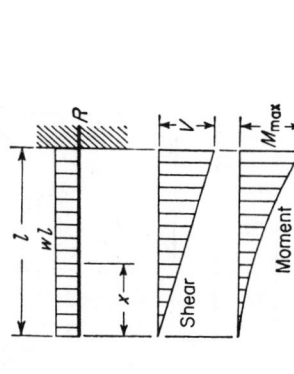

$$R = V \qquad\qquad = wl$$
$$V_x \qquad\qquad = wx$$
$$M_{\max} \text{ (at fixed end)} = \frac{wl^2}{2}$$
$$M_x \qquad\qquad = \frac{wx^2}{2}$$
$$\Delta_{\max} \text{ (at free end)} = \frac{wl^4}{8EI}$$
$$\Delta_x \qquad\qquad = \frac{w}{24EI}(x^4 - 4l^3x + 3l^4)$$

10. Cantilever Beam—Concentrated Load at Any Point

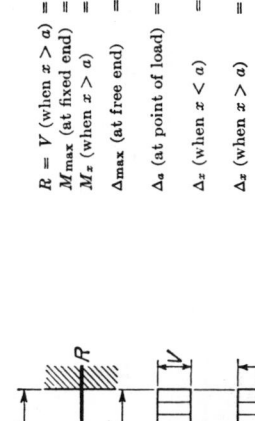

$$R = V \text{ (when } x > a) = P$$
$$M_{\max} \text{ (at fixed end)} = Pb$$
$$M_x \text{ (when } x > a) = P(x - a)$$
$$\Delta_{\max} \text{ (at free end)} = \frac{Pb^2}{6EI}(3l - b)$$
$$\Delta_a \text{ (at point of load)} = \frac{Pb^3}{3EI}$$
$$\Delta_x \text{ (when } x < a) = \frac{Pb^2}{6EI}(3l - 3x - b)$$
$$\Delta_x \text{ (when } x > a) = \frac{P(l - x)^2}{6EI}(3b - l + x)$$

Fig. 6-17. (*Continued*)

11. Cantilever Beam—Concentrated Load at Free End

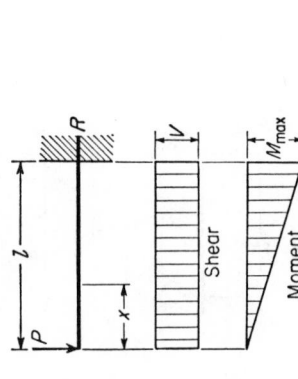

$$R = V \qquad\qquad\qquad = P$$
$$M_{max} \text{ (at fixed end)} = Pl$$
$$M_x \qquad\qquad\qquad = Px$$
$$\Delta_{max} \text{ (at free end)} = \frac{Pl^3}{3EI}$$
$$\Delta_x \qquad\qquad\qquad = \frac{P}{6EI}(2l^3 - 3l^2x + x^3)$$

12. Beam Fixed at Both Ends—Uniformly Distributed Loads

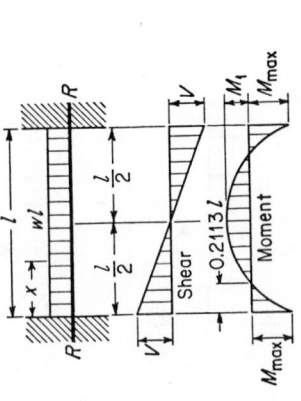

$$R = V \qquad\qquad\quad = \frac{wl}{2}$$
$$V_x \qquad\qquad\qquad = w\left(\frac{l}{2} - x\right)$$
$$M_{max} \text{ (at ends)} = \frac{wl^2}{12}$$
$$M_1 \text{ (at center)} = \frac{wl^2}{24}$$
$$M_x \qquad\qquad\qquad = \frac{w}{12}(6lx - l^2 - 6x^2)$$
$$\Delta_{max} \text{ (at center)} = \frac{wl^4}{384EI}$$
$$\Delta_x \qquad\qquad\qquad = \frac{wx^2}{24EI}(l - x)^2$$

Fig. 6-17. (*Continued*)

13. Beam Fixed at Both Ends—Concentrated Load at Center

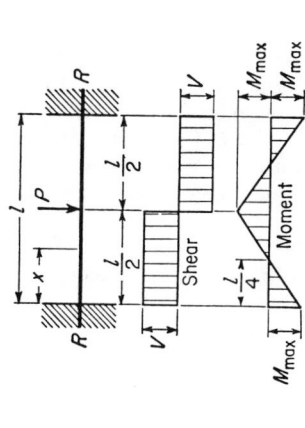

$$R = V = \frac{P}{2}$$

$$M_{max} \text{ (at center and ends)} = \frac{Pl}{8}$$

$$M_x \left(\text{when } x < \frac{l}{2}\right) = \frac{P}{8}(4x - l)$$

$$\Delta_{max} \text{ (at center)} = \frac{Pl^3}{192EI}$$

$$\Delta_x = \frac{Px^2}{48EI}(3l - 4x)$$

14. Beam Fixed at Both Ends—Concentrated Load at Any Point

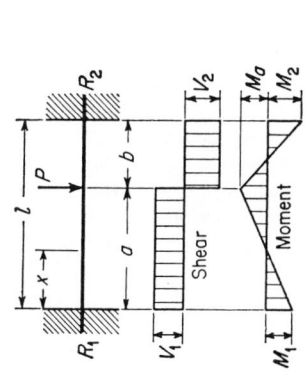

$$R_1 = V_1 \text{ (max when } a < b) = \frac{Pb^2}{l^3}(3a + b)$$

$$R_2 = V_2 \text{ (max when } a > b) = \frac{Pa^2}{l^3}(a + 3b)$$

$$M_1 \text{ (max when } a < b) = \frac{Pab^2}{l^2}$$

$$M_2 \text{ (max when } a > b) = \frac{Pa^2b}{l^2}$$

$$M_a \text{ (at point of load)} = \frac{2Pa^2b^2}{l^3}$$

$$M_x \text{ (when } x < a) = R_1 x - \frac{Pab^2}{l^2}$$

$$\Delta_{max}\left(\text{when } a > b \text{ at } x = \frac{2al}{3a + b}\right) = \frac{2Pa^3b^2}{3EI(3a + b)^2}$$

$$\Delta_a \text{ (at point of load)} = \frac{Pa^3b^3}{3EIl^3}$$

$$\Delta_x \text{ (when } x < a) = \frac{Pb^2x^2}{6EIl^3}(3al - 3ax - bx)$$

Fig. 6-17. (*Continued*)

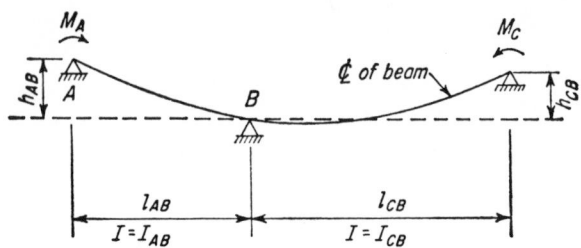

Diagram of statically indeterminate beam

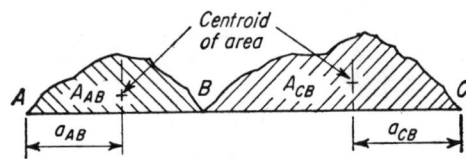

Moment diagram for each section of beam
considered to be simply supported

FIG. 6-18. Statically indeterminate beam.

M_{FAB}, M_{FBA} = moments in member AB at end A and end B, respectively, with both ends of member considered to be fixed, lb-in.

θ_A, θ_B = slopes of statically indeterminate beam at end A and end B, radians

R = ratio of deflection of one end of beam, with respect to the other end, to length of beam, with both measured in same units, radians

In the use of the slope-deflection equations, all moments and slopes should be considered positive when clockwise (R is considered to be a slope). The equations are written for each section of the beam and are solved simultaneously for the slopes. These slopes are then substituted in the original equations to determine the moments at the points of support. After the signs of these moments are revised to conform to the normal beam convention (positive moment causes compression in the upper fibers of the beam) shears and reactions may be determined.

Stresses. The stress in a beam due to moment is

$$f = My/I \qquad f_{\max} = Mc/I \qquad (6\text{-}66) \quad (6\text{-}67)$$

and the stress due to shear is

$$s = VQ/It \qquad (6\text{-}68)$$

where f = fiber stress, psi

y = distance from neutral axis to point at which stress is f, in.

c = distance from neutral axis to outermost surface of beam, in.

s = horizontal (and vertical) shearing stress, psi

Q = statical moment, or first moment, about neutral axis of cross-sectional area of beam between plane on which s occurs and outer face of beam, in.[3]

t = thickness of beam at plane on which s occurs, in.

M = moment, lb-in.

I = moment of inertia of beam cross section, in.[4]

V = shear, lb

When the bending moment is positive, the fiber stress is compression at the top of the beam and tension at the bottom.

Deflection. The general equation for the deflection of a beam is

$$\Delta = \int_0^l \int_0^l \frac{M}{EI}\, dx\, dx + \int_0 \frac{s}{G}\, dx \qquad (6\text{-}69)$$

where Δ = deflection of beam from its longitudinal axis, in.

x = distance measured parallel to beam axis, in.

M = moment, expressed as a function of x, lb-in.

s = shearing unit stress, expressed as a function of x, psi

G = shearing modulus of elasticity, psi

E = modulus of elasticity, psi

l = length of beam, in.

The first term of Eq. (6-69) expresses the deflection due to moment; the second term, the deflection due to shear.

The deflection of a beam due to moment is shown in Fig. 6-17 for beams with loading conditions of frequent occurrence. The deflection of a beam due to shear is negligible in the usual case where the length of the beam is great in comparison with the depth of the beam. In short deep beams, however, the deflection due to shear may require consideration.

6-43. Shafts and Torsion Members

The shearing stress in a cylindrical shaft carrying a twisting moment is

$$s = T\rho/J \qquad (6\text{-}70)$$

Since the maximum stress occurs at the outer edge of the shaft and J for a solid cylindrical shaft is $\pi d^4/32$,

$$s = 16T/\pi d^3 \qquad (6\text{-}71)$$

The angle of twist in a cylindrical shaft is

$$\theta = Tl/JG \qquad (6\text{-}72)$$

where s = shearing stress, psi

T = twisting moment or torque, lb-in.

J = polar moment of inertia of cross-sectional area of shaft with respect to center, in.[4]

hp = horsepower transmitted by shaft

n = shaft speed, rpm

d = shaft diameter, in.

l = shaft length, in.

θ = angle of twist in length l, radians

G = shearing modulus of elasticity, psi

ρ = distance from center to point in shaft, in.

6-44. Stress Due to Temperature Change

Material subjected to a temperature increase expands in length a total of

$$e = l\epsilon \Delta t \qquad (6\text{-}73)$$

For a straight member so restrained that the ends are unable to move, the compressive stress caused by a temperature increase is

$$f_t = E\epsilon \Delta t \qquad (6\text{-}74)$$

where e = total change in length, in.

l = length of member, in.

ϵ = coefficient of thermal expansion, dimensionless

Δt = change in temperature, °F

f_t = stress due to temperature change, psi

E = modulus of elasticity, psi

For a decrease in temperature, a tensile stress would be set up in the member. Average values of ϵ for several structural materials, expressed as the change in length per unit of length and related to the Fahrenheit scale, are as follows:

Aluminum...	0.0000125	Concrete...	0.0000062
Brick.......	.0000050	Steel.......	.0000065
Cast iron....	.0000062	Timber.....	.0000025

6-45. Combined Stresses

When an element of a body is subjected to stresses, either direct or shearing, on a given plane, the stresses on other planes may be determined by the following equations. (For nomenclature see Fig. 6-19; all stresses have units of pounds per square inch.)

$$f_n = \tfrac{1}{2}(f_1 + f_2) + \tfrac{1}{2}(f_1 - f_2)\cos 2\theta + s_s \sin 2\theta \qquad (6\text{-}75)$$

$$s_t = \tfrac{1}{2}(f_1 - f_2)\sin 2\theta - s_s \cos 2\theta \qquad (6\text{-}76)$$

The maximum and minimum normal stresses are

$$f_n = \tfrac{1}{2}(f_1 + f_2) \pm \tfrac{1}{2}[(f_1 - f_2)^2 + 4s_s^2]^{1/2} \qquad (6\text{-}77)$$

These maximum stresses occur when

$$\tan 2\theta = 2s_s/(f_1 - f_2) \qquad (6\text{-}78)$$

The maximum shearing stress is

$$s_t = \tfrac{1}{2}[(f_1 - f_2)^2 + 4s_s^2]^{1/2} \qquad (6\text{-}79)$$

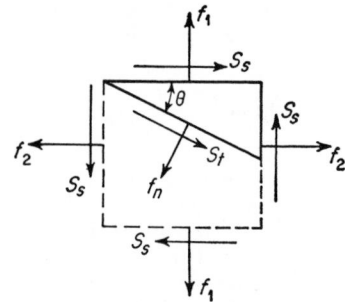

FIG. 6-19. Combined stresses.

The maximum shear occurs on planes at 45° to the planes of the maximum and minimum normal stresses. There is no shearing stress on the planes of maximum and minimum normal stress. However, there are usually normal stresses on the planes of maximum shear.

6-46. Timber Design

Grading of Lumber. Stress-grade lumber consists of three classifications:

1. *Beams and stringers.* Lumber of rectangular cross section, 5 in. or more thick and 8 in. or more wide, graded with respect to its strength in bending when loaded on the narrow face.

2. *Joists and planks.* Lumber of rectangular cross section, 2 in. to, but not including, 5 in. thick and 4 in. or more wide, graded with respect to its strength in bending when loaded either on the narrow face as a joist or on the wide face as a plank.

3. *Posts and timbers.* Lumber of square, or approximately square, cross section 5 by 5 in. or larger, graded primarily for use as posts or columns carrying longitudinal load but adapted for miscellaneous uses in which the strength in bending is not especially important.

Allowable unit stresses apply only for loading for which lumber is graded.

Size of Lumber. Lumber is usually designated by a nominal size. The size of unfinished lumber is the same as the nominal size, but the dimensions of dressed or finished lumber are from $\frac{3}{8}$ to $\frac{1}{2}$ in. smaller. The standard dressed sizes and the properties of standard lumber cross sections are given in Table 6-20.

Working Stresses. The allowable unit stresses and the modulus of elasticity for some of the commonly used species of lumber, as recommended by the National Lumber Manufacturers Association, are shown in Table 6-21. These stresses are for normal conditions of loading, and should be decreased by 10 per cent for lumber fully stressed to working load for many years. For short-term loading, the maximum allowable stress should be increased as follows:

Loading Conditions	Percentage Increase in Allowable Unit Stress
Loading of 2 months' duration (snow)	15
Loading of 7 days' duration	25
Wind or earthquake loading	33⅓
Impact loading	100

The allowable unit stresses in Table 6-21 apply to lumber used under conditions continuously dry. These stresses also apply to lumber used under conditions where the moisture content of the wood is at or above the fiber saturation point, as when continuously submerged, except that, under such conditions of use, the allowable unit stresses in compression parallel to grain is reduced one-tenth, in compression perpendicular to the grain is reduced one-third, and the values of the modulus of elasticity are reduced one-eleventh. Allowable unit stresses for lumber pressure-impregnated with preservative are the same as shown in Table 6-21, but these stresses should be reduced by 10 per cent for lumber pressure-impregnated with fire-retardant chemicals.

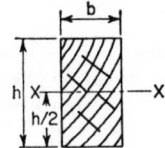

Table 6-20. Properties of Sections for Standard Lumber Sizes

Dressed (S4S) Sizes

Moment of inertia and section modulus are given with respect to xx axis, with dimensions b and h as shown on sketch.

Nominal size $b \quad h$	Standard dressed size S4S $b \quad h$	Area of section $A = bh$	Moment of inertia $I = \dfrac{bh^3}{12}$	Section modulus $S = \dfrac{bh^2}{6}$	Board feet per linear foot of piece
2 × 4	1⅝ × 3⅝	5.89	6.45	3.56	⅔
2 × 6	1⅝ × 5½	8.93	22.53	8.19	1
2 × 8	1⅝ × 7½	12.19	57.13	15.23	1⅓
2 × 10	1⅝ × 9½	15.44	116.10	24.44	1⅔
2 × 12	1⅝ × 11½	18.69	205.95	35.82	2
3 × 4	2⅝ × 3⅝	9.52	10.42	5.75	1
3 × 6	2⅝ × 5½	14.43	36.40	13.23	1½
3 × 8	2⅝ × 7½	19.69	92.29	24.61	2
3 × 10	2⅝ × 9½	24.94	187.55	39.48	2½
3 × 12	2⅝ × 11½	30.19	332.69	57.86	3
4 × 6	3⅝ × 5½	19.95	50.25	18.28	2
4 × 8	3⅝ × 7½	27.19	127.44	33.98	2⅔
4 × 10	3⅝ × 9½	34.44	259.00	54.43	3⅓
4 × 12	3⅝ × 11½	41.69	459.43	79.90	4
4 × 14	3⅝ × 13½	48.94	743.24	110.11	4⅔
4 × 16	3⅝ × 15½	56.19	1,124.92	145.15	5⅓
6 × 6	5½ × 5½	30.25	76.26	27.73	3
6 × 8	5½ × 7½	41.25	193.36	51.56	4
6 × 10	5½ × 9½	52.25	392.96	82.73	5
6 × 12	5½ × 11½	63.25	697.07	121.23	6
6 × 14	5½ × 13½	74.25	1,127.67	167.06	7
6 × 16	5½ × 15½	85.25	1,706.78	220.23	8
6 × 18	5½ × 17½	96.25	2,456.38	280.73	9
8 × 8	7½ × 7½	56.25	263.67	70.31	5⅓
8 × 10	7½ × 9½	71.25	535.86	112.81	6⅔
8 × 12	7½ × 11½	86.25	950.55	165.31	8
8 × 14	7½ × 13½	101.25	1,537.73	227.81	9⅓
8 × 16	7½ × 15½	116.25	2,327.42	300.31	10⅔
8 × 18	7½ × 17½	131.25	3,349.61	382.81	12
8 × 20	7½ × 19½	146.25	4,625.00	475.00	13⅓
10 × 10	9½ × 9½	90.25	678.76	142.90	8⅓
10 × 12	9½ × 11½	109.25	1,204.03	209.40	10
10 × 14	9½ × 13½	128.25	1,947.80	288.56	11⅔
10 × 16	9½ × 15½	147.25	2,948.07	380.40	13⅓
10 × 18	9½ × 17½	166.25	4,242.84	484.90	15
10 × 20	9½ × 19½	185.25	5,870.11	602.06	16⅔
12 × 12	11½ × 11½	132.25	1,457.51	253.48	12
12 × 14	11½ × 13½	155.25	2,357.86	349.31	14
12 × 16	11½ × 15½	178.25	3,568.71	460.48	16
12 × 18	11½ × 17½	201.25	5,136.07	586.98	18
12 × 20	11½ × 19½	224.25	7,105.92	728.81	20
12 × 22	11½ × 21½	247.25	9,530.00	887.50	22
12 × 24	11½ × 23½	270.25	12,435.00	1,057.50	24

Decking (Based on Strip 1 Ft Wide and of Thickness Indicated)

1′0 × 2	12 × 1⅝	19.50	4.29	5.28	2
1′0 × 3	12 × 2⅝	31.50	18.00	13.76	3
1′0 × 4	12 × 3½	42.00	42.88	24.50	4

SOURCE: National Lumber Manufacturers Association.

The stresses indicated in Table 6-21 are reduced for Douglas fir and western hemlock when the lumber contains splits parallel to the grain.

The deflection of wood beams may be calculated by the standard methods of mechanics discussed in Sec. 6-42. Under long-term loading, lumber acquires a permanent set about equal to the deflection, but the strength is not reduced.

Bearing. The allowable unit stresses given for compression perpendicular to the grain apply to bearings of any length at the ends of beams, and to all bearings 6 in. or more in length at other locations. When calculating the required bearing area at the ends of beams, no allowance should be made for the fact that, as the beam bends, the pressure upon the inner edge of the bearing is greater than at the end of the beam. For bearings of less than 6 in. in length and not nearer than 3 in. to the end of the member, the allowable stress for compression perpendicular to the grain should be modified by multiplying by the factor $(l + \frac{3}{8})/l$, where l is the length of the bearing in inches measured along the grain of the wood.

Beams. The extreme fiber stress in bending for a rectangular beam is

$$f = 6M/bh^2 = M/S \tag{6-80}$$

A beam of circular cross section is assumed to have the same strength in bending as a square beam having the same cross-sectional area.

The horizontal shearing stress in a rectangular beam is

$$H = 3V/2bh \tag{6-81}$$

For a rectangular beam with a notch in the lower face at the end, the horizontal shearing stress is

$$H = (3V/2bd_1)(h/d_1) \tag{6-82}$$

A gradual change in cross section rather than a square notch decreases the shearing stress nearly to that computed for the actual depth above the notch.

Nomenclature for Eqs. (6-80) to (6-84)

f = maximum fiber stress, psi
M = bending moment, lb-in.
h = depth of beam, in.
b = width of beam, in.
S = section modulus ($= bh^2/6$ for rectangular section), in.[3]
H = horizontal shearing stress, psi
V = total shear, lb
d_1 = depth of beam above notch, in.
l = span of beam, in.
P = concentrated load, lb
V^1 = modified total end shear, lb
W = total uniformly distributed load, lb
x = distance from reaction to concentrated load, in.

For simple beams, the span should be taken as the distance from face to face of supports plus one-half the required length of bearing at each end, and

Table 6-21. Allowable Unit Stresses, Stress-grade Lumber for Normal Loading Conditions

Species, commercial grade, and modulus of elasticity	Allowable unit stresses, psi					
	Extreme fiber in bending, f, and tension parallel to grain, t		Horizontal shear, H	Compression perpendicular to grain, $c\perp$	Compression parallel to grain, c	
	J and P B and S	P and T			J and P P and T	B and S
Douglas fir						
$E = 1,760,000$ psi						
Dense select structural.........	2,050	1,900	120	455	1,650	1,500
Select structural....	1,900	1,750	120	415	1,500	1,400
Dense construction.............	1,750	1,500	120	455	1,400	1,200
Construction..................	1,500	1,200	120	390	1,200	1,000
Standard (J and P only).......	1,200	.....	95	390	1,000	
Pine, southern, 5 in. thick and up						
$E = 1,760,000$ psi						
Dense structural 86.............	2,400	2,400	150	455	1,800	1,800
Dense structural 72.............	2,000	2,000	135	455	1,550	1,550
Dense structural 65.............	1,800	1,800	120	455	1,400	1,400
Dense structural 58.............	1,600	1,600	105	455	1,300	1,300
No. 1 dense SR................	1,600	1,600	120	455	1,500	1,500
No. 1 SR.....................	1,400	1,400	120	390	1,300	1,300
No. 2 dense SR................	1,400	1,400	105	455	1,050	1,050
No. 2 SR.....................	1,200	1,200	105	390	900	900
Pine, Norway (J and P only)						
$E = 1,320,000$						
Prime structural...............	1,200	.....	75	360	900	
Common structural.............	1,100	.....	75	360	775	
Utility structural..............	950	.....	75	360	650	
Spruce, eastern (J and P only)						
$E = 1,320,000$						
1450 f structural grade.........	1,450	.....	110	300	1,050	
1300 f structural grade.........	1,300	.....	95	300	975	
1200 f structural grade.........	1,200	.....	95	300	900	
Redwood						
$E = 1,320,000$ psi						
Dense structural...............	1,700	.....	110	320	1,450	1,450
Heart structural...............	1,300	.....	95	320	1,100	1,100
Hemlock, eastern						
$E = 1,210,000$						
Select structural...............	1,300	.....	85	360	850	850
Prime structural (J and P only)..	1,200	.....	60	360	775	
Common structural (J and P only)	1,100	.....	60	360	650	
Utility structural (J and P only).	950	.....	60	360	600	
Hemlock, western						
$E = 1,540,000$						
Select structural (J and P only)..	1,600	.....	100	365	1,200	
Construction..................	1,500	1,200	100	365	1,100	1,000
Standard (J and P only)........	1,200	.....	80	365	1,000	

NOTE: J and P = joists and planks, B and S = beams and stringers, P and T = posts and timbers.

for continuous beams the span should be taken as the distance between the centers of bearing on supports.

When determining V, neglect all loads within a distance from either support equal to the depth of the beam.

In the stress grade of solid-sawn beams, allowances for checks, end splits, and shakes have been made in the assigned unit stresses. For such members,

Eq. (6-81) does not indicate the actual shear resistance because of the redistribution of shear stress that occurs in checked beams. For a solid-sawn beam which does not qualify using Eq. (6-81) and the H values in Table 6-21, the modified reaction V^1 should be determined as follows:

For concentrated loads:
$$V^1 = \frac{10P(l-x)(x/h)^2}{9l[2+(x/h)^2]} \tag{6-83}$$

For uniform loading:
$$V^1 = \frac{W}{2}\left(1 - \frac{2h}{l}\right) \tag{6-84}$$

The sum of the V^1 values from Eqs. (6-83) and (6-84) should be substituted for V in Eq. (6-81), and the resulting H values checked against those given in Table 6-22. Shear values in Table 6-22 should be adjusted for duration of loading as described under working stresses in this section.

Table 6-22. Modified Allowable Horizontal Shear

H in Pounds per Square Inch
For Use When Total Shear Is Determined Using Eqs. (6-83) and (6-84)

Douglas fir	145
Pine, southern	175
Pine, Norway	130
Spruce, eastern	130
Redwood	110
Hemlock, eastern	110
Hemlock, western	120

Columns. The allowable unit stress on timber columns consisting of a single piece of lumber or a group of pieces glued together to form a single member is

$$\frac{P}{A} = \frac{3.619E}{(l/r)^2} \tag{6-85}$$

For columns of square or rectangular cross section, this formula becomes

$$\frac{P}{A} = \frac{0.30E}{(l/d)^2} \tag{6-86}$$

For columns of circular cross section, the formula becomes

$$\frac{P}{A} = \frac{0.22E}{(l/d)^2} \tag{6-87}$$

The allowable unit stress P/A may not exceed the allowable compressive stress c. The ratio l/d must not exceed 50. Values of P/A are subject to the duration of loading adjustment given previously.

Nomenclature for Eqs. (6-85) to (6-87)

P = total allowable load, lb
A = area of column cross section, in.^{2}
c = allowable unit stress in compression parallel to grain, psi
d = dimension of least side of column, in.
l = unsupported length of column between points of lateral support, in.

E = modulus of elasticity, psi

r = least radius of gyration of column, in.

For members loaded as columns, the allowable unit stresses for bearing on end grain (parallel to grain) are given in Table 6-23. These allowable stresses

Table 6-23. Allowable Unit Stresses for End Grain in Bearing, Psi

Species	Sawn lumber 4 in. and less in thickness and glued laminated lumber	Sawn lumber more than 4 in. in thickness
Douglas fir, dense........	2,600	2,050
Douglas fir.............	2,200	1,750
Pine, dense.............	2,600	2,050
Pine, southern..........	2,200	1,750
Pine, Norway...........	1,600	1,250
Spruce, eastern.........	1,600	1,250
Redwood..............	2,050	1,650
Hemlock, eastern.......	1,450	1,150
Hemlock, western.......	1,800	1,450

apply provided there is adequate lateral support and end cuts are accurately squared and parallel. When stresses exceed 75 per cent of values given, bearing must be on a snug-fitting metal plate. These stresses apply under conditions continuously dry, and must be reduced by 27 per cent for glued laminated lumber and lumber 4 in. or less in thickness and by 9 per cent for sawn lumber more than 4 in. in thickness, for lumber exposed to weather.

Combined Bending and Axial Load. Members under combined bending and axial load should be so proportioned that the quantity

$$P_a/P + M_a/M < 1 \tag{6-88}$$

where P_a = total axial load on member, lb

P = total allowable axial load, lb

M_a = total bending moment on member, lb-in.

M = total allowable bending moment, lb-in.

Compression at Angle to Grain. The allowable unit compressive stress when the load is at an angle to the grain is

$$c' = c(c\perp)/[c(\sin\theta)^2 + (c\perp)(\cos\theta)^2] \tag{6-89}$$

where c' = allowable unit stress at angle to grain, psi

c = allowable unit stress parallel to grain, psi

$c\perp$ = allowable unit stress perpendicular to grain, psi

θ = angle between direction of load and direction of grain

Timber Connections. *Split Rings and Bolts.* Split rings are available in two sizes: $2\frac{1}{2}$ in. diameter with a $\frac{1}{2}$-in. bolt and 4 in. diameter with a $\frac{3}{4}$-in. bolt. The allowable single-shear load for a split ring and bolt connector varies widely depending on the type of wood, the thickness of material, the edge distance, and other factors. With adequate edge distances, the allowable load on the $2\frac{1}{2}$-in. ring ranges up to 3,160 lb and on the 4-in. ring to

6,140 lb. Detailed data on loads for these and other timber connectors can be found in the "National Design Specification for Stress-Grade Lumber and its Fastenings," recommended by the National Lumber Manufacturers Association.

Toothed Rings and Bolts. Toothed rings are available in four sizes: 2 in. diameter with a ½-in. bolt, 2⅝ in. diameter with a ⅝-in. bolt, 3⅜ in. diameter with a ¾-in. bolt, and 4 in. diameter with a ¾-in. bolt. The allowable single-shear load for a 2-in. ring ranges up to 1,330 lb, for the 2⅝-in. ring to 2,270 lb, for the 3⅜-in. ring to 3,180 lb, and for the 4-in. ring to 3,700 lb. The reference cited above should be consulted for further data.

Shear Plates and Bolts. Shear plates are available in two sizes: 2⅝ in. diameter with a ¾-in. bolt and 4 in. diameter with either a ¾- or a ⅞-in. bolt. The allowable single-shear load for a 2⅝-in. plate ranges up to 2,900 lb and for the 4-in. plate up to 5,090 lb. The reference cited above should be consulted for further data.

Bolts. The allowable double-shear load for a bolt loaded at both ends depends on the factors discussed under split rings and bolts and also on the ratio of the length of the bolt in the wood member to the bolt diameter. Allowable loads in Douglas fir and southern Pine range from a maximum of 1,290 lb for a ½-in. bolt to a maximum of 8,040 lb for a 1¼-in. bolt.

Nails and Spikes. The allowable withdrawal load per inch of penetration of a common nail or spike driven into side grain (perpendicular to fibers) of seasoned wood, or unseasoned wood which will remain wet, is

$$p = 1,380G^{5/2}D \qquad (6\text{-}90)$$

where p = allowable load per inch of penetration into member receiving point, lb

D = diameter of nail or spike, in.

G = specific gravity of wood, oven-dry (see Table 6-24)

Table 6-24. Specific Gravity and Group Number for Common Species of Lumber

Species	Group number	Specific gravity G	G^2	$G^{5/2}$
Douglas fir.............	II	0.51	0.260	0.186
Pine, southern.........	iI	.59	.348	.267
Hemlock, western......	III	.44	.194	.128
Hemlock, eastern......	IV	.43	.185	.121
Pine, Norway.........	III	.47	.221	.151
Redwood.............	III	.42	.176	.114
Spruce...............	IV	.41	.168	.108

When nails or spikes are driven into side grain in unseasoned wood which will season subsequently under load, or in wood pressure-impregnated with fire-retardant chemicals, the allowable withdrawal load is one-fourth that given. Nails and spikes should not be loaded in withdrawal from end grain of wood.

The total allowable lateral load for a nail or spike driven into side grain of seasoned wood is

$$p = CD^{3/2} \qquad (6\text{-}91)$$

where p = allowable load per nail or spike, lb

D = diameter of nail or spike, in.

C = coefficient dependent on group number of wood (see Table 6-24)

Values of C for the four groups into which stress-grade lumber is classified are

Group I: $C = 2,040$
Group II: $C = 1,650$
Group III: $C = 1,350$
Group IV: $C = 1,080$

The loads apply where the nail or spike penetrates into the member receiving its point at least 10 diameters for Group I species, 11 diameters for Group II species, 13 diameters for Group III species, and 14 diameters for Group IV species. Allowable loads for lesser penetrations are directly proportional to the penetration, but the penetration must be at least one-third that specified. When nails or spikes are driven into side grain in unseasoned wood which will remain wet or will be loaded before seasoning, or in wood pressure-impregnated with fire-retardant chemicals, the allowable lateral load per nail or spike is three-fourths that given above. The allowable lateral load for nails or spikes driven into end grain is two-thirds that given above for side grain.

Nails and spikes are usually designated by pennyweight sizes. The diameters and lengths of common sizes are shown in Table 6-25.

Wood Screws. The allowable withdrawal load per inch of penetration of the threaded portion of a wood screw into side grain of seasoned wood which remains dry is

$$p = 2,850G^2D \qquad (6\text{-}92)$$

where p = allowable load per inch of penetration of threaded portion into member receiving point, lb

D = diameter of wood screw, in.

G = specific gravity of wood, oven-dry (see Table 6-24)

Wood screws should not be loaded in withdrawal from end grain.

The total allowable lateral load for wood screws driven into the side grain of seasoned wood which remains dry is

$$p = CD^2 \qquad (6\text{-}93)$$

where p = allowable load per wood screw, lb

D = diameter of wood screw, in.

C = coefficient dependent on group number of wood (Table 6-24)

Table 6-25. Nail and Spike Sizes

Size (pennyweight)	Length, in.	Diam D, in.	$D^{3/2}$
Nails			
6	2	0.113	0.038
8	2½	.131	.047
10	3	.148	.057
12	3¼	.148	.057
16	3½	.162	.065
20	4	.192	.084
30	4½	.207	.094
40	5	.225	.107
50	5½	.244	.122
60	6	.263	.135
Spikes			
10	3	.192	.084
12	3¼	.192	.084
16	3½	.207	.094
20	4	.225	.107
30	4½	.244	.122
40	5	.263	.135
50	5½	.283	.150
60	6	.283	.150
⁵⁄₁₆ in.	7	.312	.175
⅜ in.	8–12	.375	.230

Values of C for the four groups into which stress-grade lumber is classified are

Group I: $C = 4,800$
Group II: $C = 3,960$
Group III: $C = 3,240$
Group IV: $C = 2,520$

The allowable lateral load for wood screws driven into end grain is two-thirds that given for side grain.

Allowable loads for withdrawal and lateral resistance apply where the wood screw penetrates at least seven times its diameter. For penetration between seven and four times the diameter, the allowable load should be reduced proportionately; a screw should not be used with a penetration of less than 4 diam. When the screw is driven into wood which is exposed to the weather, or wood pressure-impregnated with fire-retardant chemicals, 75 per cent, and when always wet, 67 per cent of the load determined above should be used.

Wood screws are usually designated by a gauge number. The diameter of common sizes is shown in Table 6-26.

6-47. Steel Design

Working Stresses. Structural steel has a weight of 490 lb/ft³, a modulus

Table 6-26. Wood-screw Sizes

Gauge no.	Diam D, in.	D^2	Gauge no.	Diam D, in.	D^2
0	0.060	0.0036	10	0.190	0.0361
1	.073	.0053	11	.203	.0412
2	.086	.0074	12	.216	.0467
3	.099	.0098	14	.242	.0586
4	.112	.0125	16	.268	.0718
5	.125	.0156	18	.294	.0864
6	.138	.0190	20	.320	.1024
7	.151	.0228	24	.372	.1384
8	.164	.0269			
9	.177	.0313			

of elasticity of 29 million psi, and a shearing modulus of 12 million psi. Structural steels used in buildings and the minimum yield points are listed in Table 6-27.

Table 6-27. Designations and Yield Points for Structural Steels

ASTM Specification	Designation	Specified minimum yield point F_y, psi
"Steel for Bridges and Buildings"...............	A7	33,000
"Structural Steel for Welding"..................	A373	33,000
"Structural Steel"............................	A36	36,000
"High-strength Low-alloy Structural Steel"......	A242	42,000*
"High-strength Structural Steel"...............	A440	42,000*
"High-strength Low-alloy Structural Magnesium Vanadium Steel"...........................	A441	42,000*

* Yield point for steel over 1½ to 4 in. inclusive in thickness; $F_y = 46,000$ psi for steel ¾ to 1½ in. inclusive in thickness; $F_y = 50,000$ psi for steel ¾ in. and less in thickness.

The allowable unit working stresses for structural steel as given in the "Specification for the Design, Fabrication and Erection of Structural Steel for Buildings" of the American Institute of Steel Construction are shown below. Somewhat lower stresses than those shown are used for bridges, in recognition of the more severe service and the greater possibility of overloading such structures.

Tension

Tension on net section, except at pinholes: $F_t = 0.60F_y$ (6-94)

Tension on net section at pinholes: $F_t = 0.45F_y$ (6-95)

where F_t = allowable tensile stress, psi.
The slenderness ratio Kl/r [defined following Eq. (6-101)] preferably should not exceed 240 for main members or 300 for bracing or other secondary members, other than rods.

Shear

Shear on gross section: $F_v = 0.40F_y$ (6-96)

where F_v = allowable shear stress, psi.

Compression

Compression on the gross section of axially loaded compression members when Kl/r is less than C_c:

$$F_a = \frac{\left[1 - \dfrac{(Kl/r)^2}{2C_c^2}\right]F_y}{\text{FS}}$$ (6-97)

Compression on the gross section of axially loaded columns when Kl/r exceeds C_c:

$$F_a = \frac{149,000,000}{(Kl/r)^2}$$ (6-98)

Compression on the gross section of axially loaded bracing and secondary members when l/r exceeds 120:

$$F_{as} = \frac{F_a \text{ [from Eq. (6-97) or (6-98), depending on } C_c]}{1.6 - l/200r}$$ (6-99)

Compression on the gross area of plate girder stiffeners:

$$F_a = 0.60F_y$$ (6-100)

Compression on the web of rolled shapes at the toe of the fillet:

$$F_a = 0.75F_y$$ (6-101)

where F_a = allowable comprehensive stress permitted in absence of bending moment, psi

F_{as} = allowable comprehensive stress permitted in absence of bending moment for bracing and other secondary members, psi

K = effective-length factor (suggested design values shown in Fig. 6-20)

l = actual unbraced length, in.

r = radius of gyration corresponding to K and l, in. ($= \sqrt{I/A}$)

I = moment of inertia, in.[4]

A = gross cross-sectional area, in.[2]

C_c = slenderness ratio separating elastic and inelastic buckling

$$C_c = \sqrt{\frac{2\pi^2 E}{F_y}}$$ (6-102)

Fs = factor of safety

$$Fs = 1.67 + \frac{3(Kl/r)}{8C_c} - \frac{(Kl/r)^3}{8C_c^3}$$ (6-103)

The slenderness ratio Kl/r of compression members must not exceed 200.

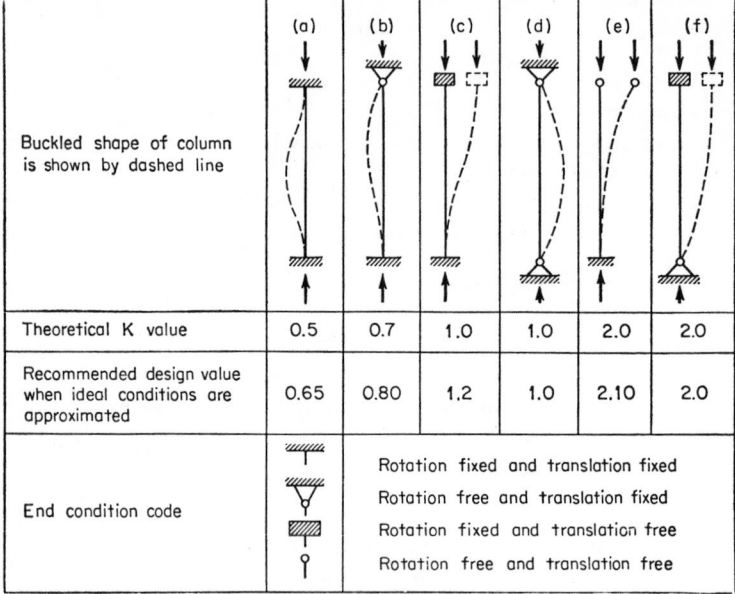

	(a)	(b)	(c)	(d)	(e)	(f)
Buckled shape of column is shown by dashed line						
Theoretical K value	0.5	0.7	1.0	1.0	2.0	2.0
Recommended design value when ideal conditions are approximated	0.65	0.80	1.2	1.0	2.10	2.0
End condition code		Rotation fixed and translation fixed				
		Rotation free and translation fixed				
		Rotation fixed and translation free				
		Rotation free and translation free				

Fig. 6-20. Effective-length factors for members subject to axial load.

Bending

Tension and compression on extreme fibers of laterally supported compact shapes[1] having an axis of symmetry in the plane of loading:

$$F_b = 0.66F_y \qquad (6\text{-}104)$$

where F_b = allowable bending stress in absence of axial load, psi
Laterally supported members have transverse movement of the compression flange prevented at points of support not more than $2,400b_f/\sqrt{F_y}$, or $20,000,000A_f/dF_y$ in. apart.

[1] A compact shape has the flanges continuously connected to the web or webs; the width of projecting elements of the compression flange does not exceed $1,600/\sqrt{F_y}$ times the flange thickness for built-up members and $1,648/\sqrt{F_y}$ times the flange thickness for rolled members; the width of flange plates between longitudinal lines of rivets, welds, or high-strength bolts does not exceed $6,000/\sqrt{F_y}$ times the flange-plate thickness; and the depth of the web does not exceed $13,300/\sqrt{F_y}$ times the web thickness for bending alone and $[13,300 (1 - 1.43f_a/F_a)]/\sqrt{F_y}$ times the web thickness or $8,000/\sqrt{F_y}$ times the web thickness, whichever is larger, for bending combined with axial force, where f_a/F_a is the ratio of computed axial stress to allowable axial stress in the absence of bending moment.

b_f = compression flange width, in.
A_f = cross-sectional area of compression flange, in.^{2}
d = depth of member, in.

Tension and compression on extreme fibers of laterally supported unsymmetrical members (except channels) or box-type members, and tension on other rolled shapes or built-up members:

$$F_b = 0.60F_y \qquad (6\text{-}105)$$

Compression on extreme fibers of other rolled shapes and built-up members (except box-type members), the larger value from Eqs. (6-106) and (6-107), but not more than $0.60F_y$:

$$F_b = \left[1.0 - \frac{(l/r)^2}{2C_c^2} \right] 0.60F_y \qquad (6\text{-}106)$$

$$F_b = \frac{12,000,000}{ld/A_f} \qquad (6\text{-}107)$$

where l = unsupported length of compression flange, in.
r = radius of gyration of compression flange plus one-sixth web about an axis in plane of web, in.
d = depth of member, in.
A_f = cross-sectional area of compression flange, in.^{2}
$C_c = \sqrt{2\pi^2 E/F_y}$

Equation (6-106) may be further modified in certain cases by consideration of the moments at each end of the unsupported length.

Compression on extreme fibers of channels, the value from Eq. (6-107) but not more than $0.60F_y$.

Tension and compression on extreme fibers of pins:

$$F_b = 0.90F_y \qquad (6\text{-}108)$$

Tension and compression on extreme fibers of rectangular bearing plates:

$$F_b = 0.75F_y \qquad (6\text{-}109)$$

Bearing

Bearing on milled surfaces and pins in reamed, drilled, or bored holes:

$$F_p = 0.90F_y \qquad (6\text{-}110)$$

Bearing on bolts or rivets:

$$F_p = 1.35F_y \qquad (6\text{-}111)$$

where F_p = allowable bearing stress, psi.

Columns and Tension Members. Columns are designed on the basis of the gross area of the section used. Tension members, however, are designed on the basis of net area, with deductions made for rivet and other holes. In determining net area, net width is obtained by deducting from the gross width the sum of the diameters of all the holes in any chain of holes in any diagonal or zigzag direction and adding for each gauge space in the chain the quantity $s^2/4g$, where s is the longitudinal spacing (pitch) in inches of any two successive holes, and g is the transverse spacing (gauge) in inches of the same two holes. Several chains of holes should be tried until the one giving the least net width is found. The net area of a tension member taken through a hole is limited to 85 per cent of the gross area. The diameter of a rivet or bolt hole is taken as $\frac{1}{8}$ in. greater than the nominal diameter of the rivet or bolt.

Beams. The extreme fiber stress in bending for a steel beam is computed as

$$f_b = M/S \tag{6-112}$$

where f_b = maximum fiber stress, psi
M = bending moment, lb-in.
S = section modulus $(= I/c)$, in.[3]
I = moment of inertia of cross-sectional area, in.[4]
c = distance from extreme fiber to neutral axis, in. (c = one-half the depth for a symmetrical cross section)

The section moduli for standard rolled-steel sections are shown in Table 6-28. For beams requiring greater section moduli, built-up sections or plate girders are generally used.

The shearing stress in a steel beam with flanges is relatively constant over the depth of the web, and may be computed as

$$f_v = V/d_w t \tag{6-113}$$

where f_v = shearing stress in web, psi
V = total shear at section, lb
d_w = depth of web, in.
t = thickness of web, in.

Built-up sections will usually require stiffeners to prevent web buckling.

6-48. Steel Connections

Rivets. Rivets vary in size from $\frac{3}{8}$ to $1\frac{1}{4}$ in. in diameter, with the $\frac{3}{4}$- and $\frac{7}{8}$-in. sizes most commonly used. The standard sizes and cross-sectional areas of rivets are shown in Table 6-29. Rivet holes are considered to be $\frac{1}{8}$ in. larger in diameter than the rivet.

Bolts. Both turned and unfinished bolts are available in the same sizes as rivets. Larger sizes are also available. Cross-sectional areas are as shown in Table 6-29.

Welds. The allowable loads on butt welds of the same size as the connected members are the same as for the members. The allowable load per inch of fillet weld is determined on the minimum cross section; for an equal leg weld, the minimum section at the throat is 0.707 times the dimension of the weld leg.

Working Stresses. *Rivets.* Allowable stresses for A141 hot-driven rivets are 20,000 psi in tension and 15,000 psi in shear; for A195 and A406 hot-driven rivets, stresses are 27,000 psi in tension and 20,000 psi in shear.

Bolts. Allowable stresses for A307 bolts and threaded parts of A7 and A373 steels are 14,000 psi in tension and 10,000 psi in shear; for other threaded

Table 6-28

S_x — ELASTIC SECTION MODULUS TABLE
For shapes used as beams

Elastic Modulus	Shape	Elastic Modulus	Shape	Elastic Modulus	Shape
1105.1	**36 WF 300**	242.8	**27 WF 94**	109.7	**‡21 WF 55**
1031.2	**36 WF 280**	234.3	24 I 105.9	107.8	18 WF 60
951.1	**36 WF 260**	222.2	12 WF 161	107.1	‡12 WF 79
892.5	**36 WF 245**	220.9	**24 WF 94**	104.2	16 WF 64
835.5	**36 WF 230**	220.1	18 WF 114	103.0	14 WF 68
811.1	33 WF 240	216.0	14 WF 136	101.9	18 I 70
740.6	**33 WF 220**	211.7	**‡27 WF 84**	99.7	10 WF 89
669.6	**33 WF 200**	202.2	18 WF 105	98.2	**18 WF 55**
663.6	**36 WF 194**	202.0	14 WF 127	97.5	†12 WF 72
649.9	30 WF 210	197.6	21 WF 96	94.1	16 WF 58
621.2	**36 WF 182**	197.6	24 I 100	92.2	‡14 WF 61
586.1	30 WF 190	196.3	**24 WF 84**	89.0	**18 WF 50**
579.1	**36 WF 170**	189.4	‡14 WF 119	88.4	18 I 54.7
541.0	**36 WF 160**	185.8	24 I 90	88.0	†12 WF 65
528.2	30 WF 172	184.4	18 WF 96	86.1	10 WF 77
502.9	**36 WF 150**	182.5	12 WF 133	80.7	**16 WF 50**
492.8	27 WF 177	176.3	‡14 WF 111	80.1	10 WF 72
486.4	33 WF 152	175.4	**24 WF 76**	78.9	**‡18 WF 45**
446.8	**33 WF 141**	173.9	24 I 79.9	78.1	‡12 WF 58
444.5	27 WF 160	168.0	21 WF 82	77.8	14 WF 53
438.6	**‡36 WF 135**	166.1	16 WF 96	74.5	*18 [58
413.5	24 WF 160	163.6	†14 WF 103	73.7	10 WF 66
404.8	**33 WF 130**	163.4	12 WF 120	72.4	**16 WF 45**
402.9	27 WF 145	160.0	20 I 95	70.7	‡12 WF 53
379.7	**30 WF 132**	156.1	18 WF 85	70.2	14 WF 48
372.5	24 WF 145	153.1	**‡24 WF 68**	69.1	*18 [51.9
358.3	**‡33 WF 118**	151.3	16 WF 88	67.1	‡10 WF 60
354.6	30 WF 124	150.7	21 WF 73	64.7	12 WF 50
330.7	‡24 WF 130	150.6	†14 WF 95	64.4	**16 WF 40**
327.9	**30 WF 116**	150.2	20 I 85	64.2	15 I 50
317.2	21 WF 142	144.5	12 WF 106	63.7	*18 [45.8
299.2	**30 WF 108**	141.7	18 WF 77	62.7	‡14 WF 43
299.2	27 WF 114	139.9	**21 WF 68**	61.0	*18 [42.7
299.1	24 WF 120	138.1	†14 WF 87	60.4	‡10 WF 54
284.1	21 WF 127	134.7	12 WF 99	60.4	8 WF 67
274.4	24 WF 110	130.9	‡14 WF 84	58.9	15 I 42.9
269.1	**‡30 WF 99**	128.2	18 WF 70	58.2	12 WF 45
266.3	27 WF 102	127.8	16 WF 78	56.3	**‡16 WF 36**
263.2	12 WF 190	126.4	**21 WF 62**	54.6	14 WF 38
250.9	24 I 120	126.3	20 I 75	54.6	†10 WF 49
249.6	‡21 WF 112	126.3	10 WF 112	53.6	*15 [50
248.9	‡24 WF 100	125.0	12 WF 92	52.0	8 WF 58
		121.1	‡14 WF 78	51.9	‡12 WF 40
		117.0	18 WF 64	50.3	12 I 50
		116.9	20 I 65.4	49.1	10 WF 45
		115.9	16 WF 71	48.5	**‡14 WF 34**
		115.7	‡12 WF 85		
		112.4	10 WF 100		
		112.3	14 WF 74		

Table 6-28. (Continued)

ELASTIC SECTION MODULUS TABLE
For shapes used as beams

$$S_x$$

Elastic Modulus	Shape	Elastic Modulus	Shape	Elastic Modulus	Shape
47.0	16 B 31	21.0	‡14 B 17.2	9.3	*12 JR C 10.6
46.2	*15 C 40	20.8	‡ 8 WF 24	9.0	* 8 C 13.75
45.9	12 WF 36	20.6	*10 C 30	8.7	6 I 17.25
44.8	12 I 40.8	18.8	10 B 19	8.5	5 WF 16
43.2	8 WF 48	18.1	*10 C 25	8.1	* 8 C 11.5
42.2	‡10 WF 39				
		17.5	‡12 B 16.5	7.8	‡10 JR 9
41.8	‡14 WF 30	17.1	‡ 8 M 22.5	7.8	† 8 B 10
41.7	*15 C 33.9	17.0	8 WF 20	7.7	* 7 C 14.75
39.4	12 WF 31	16.8	6 WF 25	7.3	6 I 12.5
		16.2	10 B 17	7.2	6 B 12
38.1	‡16 B 26	16.0	8 I 23	6.9	* 7 C 12.25
37.8	12 I 35	15.7	*10 C 20		
36.0	12 I 31.8	15.7	6 M 25	6.5	*10 JR C 8.4
35.5	8 WF 40	15.5	‡ 8 M 18.5	6.0	* 7 C 9.8
35.0	†10 WF 33	15.2	‡ 8 M 20	6.0	5 I 14.75
				5.8	* 6 C 13
34.9	14 B 26	14.8	†12 B 14	5.4	4 WF 13
34.1	‡12 WF 27	14.2	8 I 18.4	5.2	4 M 13
31.1	‡ 8 WF 35	14.1	‡ 8 WF 17	5.1	† 6 B 8.5
30.8	10 WF 29	14.0	‡ 8 M 17	5.0	* 6 C 10.5
29.2	10 I 35	13.8	‡10 B 15	4.8	5 I 10
		13.7	‡ 6 M 22.5		
28.8	‡14 B 22	13.5	‡ 9 C 20	4.7	8 JR 6.5
28.9	‡ 8 M 34.3	13.4	*10 C 15.3	4.4	*10 JR C6.5
28.2	‡ 8 M 32.6	13.4	‡ 6 WF 20	4.3	* 6 C 8.2
27.4	† 8 WF 31	12.9	‡ 6 M 20		
26.9	*12 C 30			3.5	7 JR 5.5
26.6	‡10 M 29.1	12.0	‡12 JR 11.8	3.5	* 5 C 9
		12.0	7 I 20	3.3	4 I 9.5
26.4	10 WF 25	11.8	8 B 15	3.0	* 5 C 6.7
		11.3	* 9 C 15	3.0	4 I 7.7
25.3	12 B 22	10.9	* 8 C 13.75		
24.4	10 I 25.4			2.4	6 JR 4.4
24.3	8 WF 28	10.5	†10 B 11.5	2.3	* 4 C 7.25
23.9	*12 C 25	10.5	* 9 C 13.4	1.9	* 4 C 5.4
23.6	‡10 M 22.9	10.4	7 I 15.3	1.9	3 I 7.5
22.5	‡ 8 M 28	10.1	† 6 WF 15.5	1.7	3 I 5.7
		10.1	6 B 16	1.4	* 3 C 6
21.5	‡10 WF 21	9.9	‡ 8 B 13		
		9.9	5 WF 18.5	1.2	* 3 C 5
21.4	12 B 19	9.5	5 M 18.9		
21.4	*12 C 20.7			1.1	* 3 C 4.1
21.1	‡10 M 21				
21.0	‡ 8 M 24				

* Bending stress F_b may not exceed $0.60F_y$.

† Identifies noncompact shapes for which bending stress F_b may not exceed $0.60F_y$ in A36, A242, A440, and A441 steels.

‡ Identifies noncompact shapes for which bending stress F_b may not exceed $0.60F_y$ in A242, A440, and A441 steels.

NOTES: Shapes subject to combined axial force and bending moment may not be compact, and should be checked to determine bending stress F_b.

Section modulus in cubic inches.   In shape column, initial figures indicate nominal depth of section in inches, final figures indicate weight in pounds per foot, and center symbol indicates type of section, as follows:

WF = wide-flange shapes   M = miscellaneous shapes
I = American Standard beams   JR = junior beams
B = light beams   C = American Standard channels

SOURCE: "Specifications for Design of Structural Steel for Buildings," American Institute of Steel Construction, 1961.

Table 6-29. Rivet and Bolt Diameters and Areas

Rivets and bolts		Bolts only		Rivets and bolts		Bolts only	
Nominal diam, in.	Cross-sec area, in.²	Cross-sec area, thread root, in.²	Threads/in.	Nominal diam, in.	Cross-sec area, in.²	Cross-sec area, thread root, in.²	Threads/in.
⅜	0.110	0.068	16	⅞	0.601	0.419	9
½	.196	.126	13	1	0.785	.551	8
⅝	.307	.202	11	1⅛	0.994	.693	7
¾	.442	.302	10	1¼	1.227	.890	7

parts of other steels, stresses are $0.40F_y$ in tension and $0.30F_y$ in shear. Allowable stresses for A325 and A354, Grade BC, bolts are shown below:

Allowable Bolt Stresses, Psi

Bolts	Tension	Shear		
		Friction-type connections	Bearing-type connections	
			Threading excluded from shear planes	Threading not excluded from shear planes
A325................	40,000	15,000	22,000	15,000
A354, (Grade BC).....	50,000	20,000	24,000	20,000

Welds. The allowable stress for welds on A7 and A373 steels is 13,600 psi; on A36, A242, and A441 steels is 15,800 psi; except that complete-penetration groove welds with any type of loading and partial-penetration groove welds loaded in compression, bearing, or tension parallel to the axis of the weld may be stressed to the full allowable stress of the connected material.

6-49. Reinforced-concrete Design

Strength and Durability of Concrete. The most important factor affecting the strength and durability of concrete is the water-cement ratio. For concrete made from average materials, compressive strengths to be used for design are shown in Table 6-30. Strengths greater than those shown may be used, based on compressive-strength tests. Water-cement ratios for various types of construction and exposure conditions are shown in Table 6-31, but any concrete subject to freezing temperatures while wet should have a water-cement ratio not more than 6 gal per bag and should contain entrained air.

Design Methods. Reinforced concrete may be designed by either one of two methods: working-stress design or ultimate-strength design. Both methods are permitted under current codes, and the selection of a method is left to the designer. Only working-stress design is discussed herein; reference should be made to the American Concrete Institute Building Code for information on ultimate-strength design.

Table 6-30. Maximum Permissible Water-cement Ratios for Concrete

Specified compressive strength at 28 days, psi f'_c	Maximum permissible water-cement ratio*			
	Non-air-entrained concrete		Air-entrained concrete	
	U.S. gal per 94-lb bag of cement	Absolute ratio by weight	U.S. gal per 94-lb bag of cement	Absolute ratio by weight
2,500	7¼	0.642	6¼	0.554
3,000	6½	.576	5¼	.465
3,500	5¾	.510	4½	.399
4,000	5	.443	4	.354

* Including free surface moisture on aggregates.
SOURCE: "Building Code Requirements for Reinforced Concrete (ACI 318-63)," American Concrete Institute, 1963.

Table 6-31. Maximum Permissible Water-cement Ratios (Gal per Bag) for Different Types of Structures and Degrees of Exposure

Type of structure	Exposure conditions*						
	Severe wide range in temperature or frequent alternations of freezing and thawing (air-entrained concrete only)			Mild temperature, rarely below freezing, or rainy, or arid			
	In air	At the water line or within the range of fluctuating water level or spray		In air	At the water line or within the range of fluctuating water level or spray		
		In fresh water	In sea water or in contact with sulfates†		In fresh water	In sea water or in contact with sulfates†	
Thin sections, such as railings, curbs, sills, ledges, ornamental or architectural concrete, reinforced piles, pipe, and all sections with less than 1 in. concrete cover over reinforcing..............	5.5	5.0	4.5‡	6	5.5	4.5‡	
Moderate sections, such as retaining walls, abutments, piers, girders, beams.......	6.0	5.5	5.0‡	§	6.0	5.0‡	
Exterior portions of heavy (mass) sections	6.5	5.5	5.0‡	§	6.0	5.0‡	
Concrete deposited by tremie under water	...	5.0	5.0	...	5.0	5.0	
Concrete slabs laid on the ground........	6.0	...	....	§			
Concrete protected from the weather, interiors of buildings, concrete below ground......................	§	...	....	§			
Concrete which will later be protected by enclosure or backfill but which may be exposed to freezing and thawing for several years before such protection is offered.........................	6.0	...	....	§			

* Air-entrained concrete should be used under all conditions involving severe exposure, and may be used under mild exposure conditions to improve workability of the mixture.
† Soil or ground water containing sulfate concentrations of more than 0.2 per cent.
‡ When sulfate-resisting cement is used, maximum water-cement ratio may be increased by 0.5 gal per bag.
§ Water-cement ratio should be selected on the basis of strength and workability requirements.
SOURCE: "Recommended Practice for Selecting Proportions for Concrete (ACI 613-54)," American Concrete Institute, 1954.

Reinforcing Bars. Steel bars for concrete reinforcement are available in the sizes shown in Table 6-32.

Table 6-32. Deformed-steel Reinforcing Bars

Bar size no.)	Wt, lb/ft	Diam, in.	Cross-sectional area, in.[6]	Perimeter, in.
2	0.167	0.250	0.05	0.786
3	0.376	0.375	0.11	1.178
4	0.668	0.500	0.20	1.571
5	1.043	0.625	0.31	1.963
6	1.502	0.750	0.44	2.356
7	2.044	0.875	0.60	2.749
8	2.670	1.000	0.79	3.142
9	3.400	1.128	1.00	3.544
10	4.303	1.270	1.27	3.990
11	5.313	1.410	1.56	4.430
14S	7.650	1.693	2.25	5.319
18S	13.600	2.257	4.00	7.091

Design Loadings. In working-stress design, members should be designed to withstand actual service loads, consisting of dead loads, live loads, wind loads, and earthquake loads in any combination. Members subject to stress produced by wind or earthquake may be proportioned for stresses one-third greater than those given in Tables 6-33 and 6-34, provided that the section thus required is not less than required for dead plus live loads.

Working Stresses. Allowable unit stresses for concrete and reinforcing steel are given in Tables 6-33 and 6-34.

Beams. Concrete beams may be considered to be of three principal types: rectangular beams with tensile reinforcing only, T beams with tensile reinforcing only, and beams with tensile and compressive reinforcing.

Rectangular Beams with Tensile Reinforcing Only. This type of beam includes slabs (for which $b = 12$ in. when the moment and shear are expressed per foot of width). The stresses in the concrete and steel are

$$f_c = 2M/kjbd^2 \tag{6-114}$$

$$f_s = M/A_s jd = M/pjbd^2 \tag{6-115}$$

where b = width of beam (equals 12 in. for slab), in.
  d = effective depth of beam, measured from compressive face of beam to centroid of tensile reinforcing (Fig. 6-21), in.
  M = bending moment, lb-in.
  f_c = compressive stress in extreme fiber of concrete, psi
  f_s = stress in reinforcement, psi
  A_s = cross-sectional area of tensile reinforcing, in.[2]
  j = ratio of distance between centroid of compression and centroid of tension to depth d

Table 6-33. Allowable Stresses in Concrete

Description		For any strength of concrete	For strength of concrete shown below			
			$f'_c = 2,500$ psi	$f'_c = 3,000$ psi	$f'_c = 4,000$ psi	$f'_c = 5,000$ psi
Modulus of elasticity ratio: n		$\dfrac{29,000,000}{w^{1.5}33\sqrt{f'_c}}$				
For concrete weighing 145 lb per cu ft	n	....	10	9	8	7
Flexure: f_c						
Extreme fiber stress in compression...	f_c	$0.45f'_c$	1,125	1,350	1,800	2,250
Extreme fiber stress, in tension in plain concrete footings and walls........	f_c	$1.6\sqrt{f'_c}$	80	88	102	113
Shear: v (as a measure of diagonal tension at a distance d from the face of the support)						
Beams with no web reinforcement....	v_c	$1.1\sqrt{f'_c}$	55	60	70	78
Joists with no web reinforcement.....	v_c	$1.2\sqrt{f'_c}$	61	66	77	86
Members with vertical or inclined web reinforcement or properly combined bent bars and vertical stirrups.....	v	$5\sqrt{f'_c}$	250	274	316	354
Slabs and footings (peripheral shear)..	v_c	$2\sqrt{f'_c}$	100	110	126	141
Bearing: f_c						
On full area......................		$0.25f'_c$	625	750	1,000	1,250
On one-third area or less*..........		$0.375f'_c$	938	1,125	1,500	1,875

* This increase is permitted only when the least distance between the edges of the loaded and unloaded areas is a minimum of one-fourth of the parallel side dimension of the loaded area. The allowable bearing stress on a reasonably concentric area greater than one-third but less than the full area is to be interpolated between the values given.

NOTE: f'_c = compressive strength of concrete, psi; n = ratio of modulus of elasticity of steel to that of concrete; w = weight of concrete, lb/ft³.

SOURCE: "Building Code Requirements for Reinforced Concrete (ACI 318-63)," American Concrete Institute, 1963.

Table 6-34. Allowable Stresses in Steel for Concrete Reinforcement

In tension   *Psi*

For billet-steel or axle-steel concrete-reinforcing bars of structural grade........................ 18,000
For main reinforcement, ⅜ in. or less in diameter, in one-way slabs of not more than 12-ft span, 50% of the minimum yield strength specified by the American Society for Testing Materials for the reinforcement used, but not to exceed... 30,000
For deformed bars with a yield strength of 60,000 psi or more and in sizes No. 11 and smaller....... 24,000
For all other reinforcement... 20,000

In compression, vertical column reinforcement
Spiral columns, 40% of the minimum yield strength, but not to exceed........................... 30,000
Tied columns, 85% of the value for spiral columns, but not to exceed............................ 25,500
Composite and combination columns:
    Structural steel sections:
        For ASTM A36 Steel.. 18,000
        For ASTM A7 Steel... 16,000
    Cast-iron sections.. 10,000

Spirals [yield strength for use in Eq. (6-129)]
Hot-rolled rods, intermediate grade.. 40,000
Hot-rolled rods, hard grade... 50,000
Hot-rolled rods, ASTM A432 grade and cold-drawn wire....................................... 60,000

SOURCE: "Building Code Requirements for Reinforced Concrete (ACI 318-63)," American Concrete Institute, 1963.

k = ratio of depth of compression area to depth d

p = ratio of cross-sectional area of tensile reinforcing to area of the beam ($= A_s/bd$)

For approximate design purposes, j may be assumed to be $\frac{7}{8}$ and k $\frac{1}{3}$. For average structures, the following guides to the depth d of a reinforced concrete beam may be used.

Member	d
Roof and floor slabs..........	$l/25$
Light beams................	$l/15$
Heavy beams and girders.....	$l/12$–$l/10$

where l is the span of the beam or slab in inches. The width of a beam should be at least $l/32$.

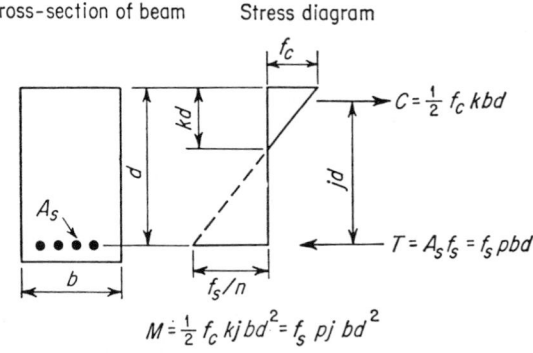

FIG. 6-21. Rectangular concrete beam with tensile reinforcing only.

For a balanced design, one in which both the concrete and the steel are stressed to the maximum allowable stress, the following formulas may be used.

$$bd^2 = M/K \qquad (6\text{-}116)$$

$$K = \tfrac{1}{2}f_c kj = pf_s j \qquad (6\text{-}117)$$

Values of K, k, j, and p for commonly used stresses are given in Table 6-35.

T Beams with Tensile Reinforcing Only. When a concrete slab is constructed monolithically with the supporting concrete beams, a portion of the slab acts as the upper flange of the beam. The effective flange width should not exceed (1) one-fourth the span of the beam, (2) the width of the web portion of the beam plus 16 times the thickness of the slab, or (3) the center-to-center distance between beams. T beams where the upper flange is not a portion of a slab should have a flange thickness not less than one-half the width of the web and a flange width not more than 4 times the width of the web. For preliminary designs, the formulas given above for rectangular beams with tensile reinforcing only can be used, since the neutral axis is usually in or near the flange. The area of tensile reinforcing will usually be critical.

Beams with Tensile and Compressive Reinforcing. Beams with compressive reinforcing are generally used when the size of the beam is limited. The allowable beam dimensions are used in the formulas given above to determine the moment which could be carried by a beam without compressive reinforcement. The reinforcing requirements may then be approximately determined from

$$A_s = 8M/7f_s d \tag{6-118}$$

$$A_{sc} = (M - M')/nf_c d \tag{6-119}$$

where A_s = total cross-sectional area of tensile reinforcing, in.^{2}

A_{sc} = cross-sectional area of compressive reinforcing, in.^{2}

M = total bending moment, lb-in.

M' = bending moment which would be carried by beam of balanced design and same dimensions with tensile reinforcing only, lb-in.

n = ratio of modulus of elasticity of steel to that of concrete

Check of Stresses in Beam. Beams designed by the above approximate formulas should be checked to ensure that the actual stresses do not exceed the allowable, and that the reinforcing is not excessive. This can be accomplished by determining the moment of inertia of the beam. In this determination, the concrete below the neutral axis should not be considered as stressed, while the reinforcing steel should be transformed into an equivalent concrete section. For tensile reinforcing, this transformation is made

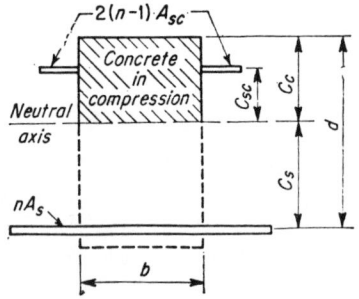

Fig. 6-22. Transformed section of concrete beam.

by multiplying the area A_s by n, the ratio of the modulus of elasticity of steel to that of concrete. For compressive reinforcing, the area A_{sc} is multiplied by $2(n - 1)$. This factor includes allowances for the concrete in compression replaced by the compressive reinforcing and for the plastic flow of concrete. The neutral axis is then located by solving

$$\tfrac{1}{2}bc_c{}^2 + 2(n - 1)A_{sc}c_{sc} = nA_s c_s \tag{6-120}$$

for the unknowns c_c, c_{sc}, and c_s (Fig. 6-22). The moment of inertia of the transformed beam section is

$$I = \tfrac{1}{3}bc_c{}^3 + 2(n - 1)A_{sc}c_{sc}{}^2 + nA_s c_s{}^2 \tag{6-121}$$

and the stresses are

$$f_c = Mc_c/I \tag{6-122}$$

$$f_{sc} = 2nMc_{sc}/I \tag{6-123}$$

$$f_s = nMc_s/I \tag{6-124}$$

where f_c, f_{sc}, f_s = actual unit stresses in extreme fiber of concrete, in compressive reinforcing steel, and in tensile reinforcing steel, respectively, psi

c_c, c_{sc}, c_s = distances from neutral axis to face of concrete, to compressive reinforcing steel, and to tensile reinforcing steel, respectively, in.

I = moment of inertia of transformed beam section, in.^{4}

b = beam width, in.

and A_s, A_{sc}, M, and n are as defined for Eqs. (6-118) and (6-119).

Table 6-35. Coefficients K, k, j, p for Rectangular Sections

f'_c	n	f_c	K	k	j	p
			$f_s = 16,000$ psi			
2,000	15	900	175	0.458	0.847	0.0129
2,500	12	1,125	218	.458	.847	.0161
3,000	10	1,350	262	.458	.847	.0193
3,750	8	1,700	331	.460	.847	.0244
			$f_s = 18,000$ psi			
2,000	15	900	165	.429	.857	.0107
2,500	12	1,125	207	.429	.857	.0134
3,000	10	1,350	248	.429	.857	.0161
3,750	8	1,700	313	.430	.857	.0203
			$f_s = 20,000$ psi			
2,000	15	900	157	.403	.866	.0091
2,500	12	1,125	196	.403	.866	.0113
3,000	10	1,350	236	.403	.866	.0136
3,750	8	1,700	298	.405	.865	.0172

Shear and Diagonal Tension in Beams. The shearing unit stress, as a measure of diagonal tension, in a reinforced concrete beam is

$$v = V/bd \qquad (6-125)$$

where v = shearing unit stress, psi

V = total shear, lb

b = width of beam (for T beam use width of stem), in.

d = effective depth of beam

If the value of the shearing unit stress as computed above exceeds the allowable shearing unit stress (v_c in Table 6-33) web reinforcement should be provided. Such reinforcement will usually consist of stirrups. The cross-sectional area required for a stirrup placed perpendicular to the longitudinal reinforcement is

$$A_v = (V - V')s/f_v d \qquad (6-126)$$

where A_v = cross-sectional area of web reinforcement in distance s (measured parallel to longitudinal reinforcement), in.^{2}

f_v = allowable unit stress in web reinforcement, psi
V = total shear, lb
V' = shear which concrete alone could carry ($= v_c bd$), lb
s = spacing of stirrups in direction parallel to that of longitudinal reinforcing, in.
d = effective depth, in.

Stirrups should be so spaced that every 45° line extending from the mid-depth of the beam to the longitudinal tension bars is crossed by at least one stirrup. If the total shearing unit stress is in excess of 3 $\sqrt{f'_c}$ psi, every such line should be crossed by at least two stirrups. The shear stress at any section should not exceed 5 $\sqrt{f'_c}$ psi.

Bond and Anchorage for Reinforcing Bars. In beams in which the tensile reinforcing is parallel to the compression face, the bond stress on the bars is

$$u = \frac{V}{jd\Sigma_0} \tag{6-127}$$

where u = bond stress on surface of bar, psi
V = total shear, lb
d = effective depth of beam, in.
Σ_0 = sum of perimeters of tensile reinforcing bars, in.

For preliminary design, the ratio j may be assumed to be $\frac{7}{8}$. Bond stresses may not exceed the values shown in Table 6-36. To provide sufficient anchor-

Table 6-36. Allowable Bond Stresses, Psi

	Horizontal bars with more than 12 in. of concrete cast below the bar	Other bars
Tension bars with sizes and deformations conforming to ASTM A305...	$\dfrac{3.4\sqrt{f'_c}}{D}$ or 350, whichever is less	$\dfrac{4.8\sqrt{f'_c}}{D}$ or 500, whichever is less
Tension bars with sizes and deformations conforming to ASTM A408....	$2.1\sqrt{f'_c}$	$3\sqrt{f'_c}$
Deformed compression bars..........	$6.5\sqrt{f'_c}$ or 400, whichever is less	$6.5\sqrt{f'_c}$ or 400, whichever is less
Plain bars.........................	$1.7\sqrt{f'_c}$ or 160, whichever is less	$2.4\sqrt{f'_c}$ or 160, whichever is less

NOTE: f'_c = compressive strength of concrete, psi; D = nominal diameter of bar, in.

age to develop the strength of reinforcing steel, tensile bars should be extended beyond the point at which they are needed to resist stress and should be terminated in a compression region, over a support, or with a hook.

Columns. The principal columns in a structure should have a minimum diameter of 10 in. or, for rectangular columns, a minimum thickness of 8 in. and a minimum gross cross-sectional area of 96 in.²

Short Columns, Spiral Reinforcing. For short columns with closely spaced spiral reinforcing enclosing a circular concrete core reinforced with vertical bars, the maximum allowable load is

$$P = A_g(0.25f'_c + f_s p_g) \tag{6-128}$$

where P = total allowable axial load, lb

A_g = gross cross-sectional area of column, in.^{2}

f'_c = compressive strength of concrete, psi

f_s = allowable stress in vertical concrete reinforcing, psi, equal to 40 per cent of the minimum yield strength, but not to exceed 30,000 psi

p_g = ratio of cross-sectional area of vertical reinforcing steel to gross area of column A_g

The ratio p_g should not be less than 0.01 nor more than 0.08. The minimum number of bars to be used is six, and the minimum size is no. 5. The spiral reinforcing to be used in a spirally reinforced column is

$$p_s = 0.45(A_g/A_c - 1)f'_c/f_y \qquad (6\text{-}129)$$

where p_s = ratio of spiral volume to concrete-core volume (out-to-out spiral)

A_c = cross-sectional area of column core (out-to-out spiral), in.^{2}

f_y = yield strength of spiral reinforcement, psi, but not to exceed 60,000 psi

The center-to-center spacing of the spirals should not exceed one-sixth of the core diameter. The clear spacing between spirals should not exceed one-sixth the core diameter, or 3 in., nor be less than $1\frac{3}{8}$ in., or $1\frac{1}{2}$ times the maximum size of coarse aggregate used.

Short Columns with Ties. The maximum allowable load on short columns reinforced with longitudinal bars and separate lateral ties is 85 per cent of that given in Eq. (6-128) for spirally reinforced columns. The ratio p_g for a tied column should not be less than 0.01 nor more than 0.08. The longitudinal reinforcing should consist of at least four bars, and the minimum size is no. 5.

Ties should be at least $\frac{1}{4}$ in. in diameter, and should be spaced apart not over 16 bar diameters, 48 tie diameters, or the least dimension of the column.

Long Columns. Allowable column loads where compression governs design must be adjusted for column length, as follows:

1. If the ends of the column are fixed so that a point of contraflexure occurs between the ends, applied axial loads and moments should be divided by R from Eq. (6-130) (R cannot exceed 1.0).

$$R = 1.32 - 0.006h/r \qquad (6\text{-}130)$$

2. If relative lateral displacement of the ends of the column is prevented and the member is bent in single curvature, applied axial loads and moments should be divided by R from Eq. (6-131) (R cannot exceed 1.0).

$$R = 1.07 - 0.008h/r \qquad (6\text{-}131)$$

where h = unsupported length of column, in.

r = radius of gyration of gross concrete area, in.

= 0.30 times depth for rectangular column

= 0.25 times diameter for circular column

R = long-column load reduction factor

Applied axial load and moment when tension governs design should be similarly adjusted, except that the factor R varies linearly with the axial load from the values given by Eqs. (6-130) and (6-131) at the balanced condition, as defined by Eq. (6-137) to a value of 1.0 when the axial load is 0.

Combined Bending and Compression. The strength of a symmetrical column is controlled by compression if the equivalent axial load N has an eccentricity e in each principal direction no greater than given by Eq. (6-132) or (6-133) and by tension if e exceeds these values in either principal direction.

For spiral columns: $e_b = 0.43p_gmD_s + 0.14t$ (6-132)

For tied columns: $e_b = (0.67p_gm + 0.17)d$ (6-133)

where e = eccentricity, in.

   e_b = maximum permissible eccentricity, in.

   N = eccentric load normal to cross section of column

   p_g = ratio of area of vertical reinforcement to gross concrete area

   $m = f_y/0.85f'_c$

   D_s = diameter of circle through centers of longitudinal reinforcement, in.

   t = diameter of column or over-all depth of column, in.

   d = distance from extreme compression fiber to centroid of tension reinforcement, in.

   f_y = yield point of reinforcement, psi

Design of columns controlled by compression is based on Eq. (6-134), except that the allowable load N may not exceed the allowable load P [Eq. (6-128)] permitted when the column supports axial load only.

$$\frac{f_a}{F_a} + \frac{f_{bx}}{F_b} + \frac{f_{by}}{F_b} \leq 1.0 \tag{6-134}$$

where f_a = axial load divided by gross concrete area, psi

f_{bx}, f_{by} = bending moment about x and y axes, divided by section modulus of corresponding transformed uncracked section, psi

   F_b = allowable bending stress permitted for bending alone, psi

   $F_a = 0.34(1 + p_gm)f'_c$

The allowable bending moment on columns controlled by tension varies linearly with the axial load from M_0 when the section is in pure bending to M_b when the axial load is N_b.

For spiral columns: $M_0 = 0.12A_{st}f_yD_s$ (6-135)

For tied columns: $M_0 = 0.40A_sf_y(d - d')$ (6-136)

where A_{st} = total area of longitudinal reinforcement, in.[2]

   f_y = yield strength of reinforcement, psi

   D_s = diameter of circle through centers of longitudinal reinforcement, in.

   A_s = area of tension reinforcement, in.[2]

   d = distance from extreme compression fiber to centroid of tension reinforcement, in.

d' = distance from extreme compression fiber to centroid of compression reinforcement, in.

N_b and M_b are the axial load and moment at the balanced condition, i.e., when the eccentricity e equals e_b as determined from Eq. (6-132) or (6-133). At this condition, N_b and M_b should be determined from Eq. (6-134) so that

$$M_b = N_b e_b \qquad (6\text{-}137)$$

When bending is about two axes,

$$\frac{M_x}{M_{0x}} + \frac{M_y}{M_{0y}} \le 1 \qquad (6\text{-}138)$$

where M_x and M_y are bending moments about the x and y axes, and M_{0x} and M_{0y} are the values of M_0 for bending about these axes.

Concrete Protection for Reinforcing Steel. The concrete protection for reinforcing steel should not be less than that given in Table 6-37.

Table 6-37. Minimum Concrete Protection for Reinforcement

	Minimum Concrete Protection, In.
Concrete placed directly against the ground....	3
Concrete exposed to weather:	
Bars less than no. 5 in size.................	1½
Bars no. 5 in size or larger.................	2
Concrete not exposed to ground or weather:	
Slabs and walls............................	¾
Beams, girders, and columns..............	1½

SECTION 7

ELECTRICAL ENGINEERING

D. L. Whitehead, M.S.; Manager, Engineering Laboratories, High Voltage Section, Westinghouse Electric Corporation; Fellow, Institute of Electrical and Electronics Engineers; Committee Member, National Electrical Manufacturers Association, ASA

CONTENTS

UNITS

Three distinct sets of units are used in the electrical engineering field: the centimeter-gram-second electrostatic units, cgs esu; the centimeter-gram-second electromagnetic units, cgs emu; and the meter-kilogram-second, mks or practical, units. From geometrical relationships the factor 4π inherently appears in some of the basic equations. If 4π is arbitrarily placed in the denominator of Coulomb's law expressions, the more commonly used formulas in engineering do not contain the 4π term. The three systems of units are then called *rationalized* in contrast to the *unrationalized* systems that carry the 4π term separately. The cgs esu system of units is commonly used when working electrostatic-field problems, the cgs emu units when working magnetic-field problems and related problems in physics, and the mks units when working practical-circuit problems. All of the systems

Table 7-1. Conversion Factors between MKS (Practical), CGS Electrostatic (ESU), and CGS Electromagnetic (EMU) Systems of Units

Quantity	Symbol	Mks unit	Conversion factors		Cgs (esu) unit	Conversion factors		Cgs (emu) unit	Conversion factors	
			To cgs (esu)	To cgs (emu)		To cgs (emu)	To mks		To cgs (esu)	To mks
Acceleration	a	Meter per second per second	10^2	10^2	Centimeter per second per second	1	10^{-2}	Centimeter per second per second	1	10^{-2}
Area	A	Square meter	10^4	10^4	Square centimeter	1	10^{-4}	Square centimeter	1	10^{-4}
Capacitance	C	Farad	9×10^{11}	10^{-9}	Statfarad	$\frac{1}{9} \times 10^{-20}$	$\frac{1}{9} \times 10^{-11}$	Abfarad	9×10^{20}	10^9
Charge	Q	Coulomb	3×10^9	10^{-1}	Statcoulomb	$\frac{1}{3} \times 10^{-10}$	$\frac{1}{3} \times 10^{-9}$	Abcoulomb	3×10^{10}	10
Charge density: Linear	q	Coulomb per meter	3×10^7	10^{-3}	Statcoulomb per centimeter	$\frac{1}{3} \times 10^{-10}$	$\frac{1}{3} \times 10^{-7}$	Abcoulomb per centimeter	3×10^{10}	10^3
Area	σ	Coulomb per square meter	3×10^5	10^{-5}	Statcoulomb per square centimeter	$\frac{1}{3} \times 10^{-10}$	$\frac{1}{3} \times 10^{-5}$	Abcoulomb per square centimeter	3×10^{10}	10^5
Volume	ρ	Coulomb per cubic meter	3×10^3	10^{-7}	Statcoulomb per cubic centimeter	$\frac{1}{3} \times 10^{-10}$	$\frac{1}{3} \times 10^{-3}$	Abcoulomb per cubic centimeter	3×10^{10}	10^7
Conductance	G	Mho	9×10^{11}	10^{-9}	Statmho	$\frac{1}{9} \times 10^{-20}$	$\frac{1}{9} \times 10^{-11}$	Abmho	9×10^{20}	10^9
Conductivity	γ	Mho per meter	9×10^9	10^{-11}	Statmho per centimeter	$\frac{1}{9} \times 10^{-20}$	$\frac{1}{9} \times 10^{-9}$	Abmho per centimeter	9×10^{20}	10^{11}
Current	I	Ampere	3×10^9	10^{-1}	Statampere	$\frac{1}{3} \times 10^{-10}$	$\frac{1}{3} \times 10^{-9}$	Abampere	3×10^{10}	10
Current density	ρ	Ampere per square meter	3×10^5	10^{-5}	Statampere per square centimeter	$\frac{1}{3} \times 10^{-10}$	$\frac{1}{3} \times 10^{-5}$	Abampere per square centimeter	3×10^{10}	10^5
Elastance	S	Daraf	$\frac{1}{9} \times 10^{-11}$	10^9	Statdaraf	9×10^{20}	9×10^{11}	Abdaraf	$\frac{1}{9} \times 10^{-20}$	10^{-9}
Electric intensity	E	Volt per meter	$\frac{1}{3} \times 10^{-4}$	10^6	Statvolt per centimeter	3×10^{10}	3×10^4	Abvolt	$\frac{1}{3} \times 10^{-10}$	10^{-6}
Electrostatic flux	ψ	......	3×10^9	10^{-1}	......	$\frac{1}{3} \times 10^{-10}$	$\frac{1}{3} \times 10^{-9}$	......	3×10^{10}	10
Electrostatic flux density	D	......	3×10^5	10^{-5}	......	$\frac{1}{3} \times 10^{-10}$	$\frac{1}{3} \times 10^{-5}$	......	3×10^{10}	10^5
Energy	W	Joule	10^7	10^7	Erg	1	10^{-7}	Erg	1	10^{-7}
Force	f	Newton	10^5	10^5	Dyne	1	10^{-5}	Dyne	1	10^{-5}
Inductance	L	Henry	$\frac{1}{9} \times 10^{-11}$	10^9	Stathenry	9×10^{20}	9×10^{11}	Abhenry	$\frac{1}{9} \times 10^{-20}$	10^{-9}
Length	l	Meter	10^2	10^2	Centimeter	1	10^{-2}	Centimeter	1	10^{-2}
Magnetic flux	Φ	Weber	$\frac{1}{3} \times 10^{-2}$	10^8	......	3×10^{10}	3×10^2	Maxwell	$\frac{1}{3} \times 10^{-10}$	10^{-8}
Magnetic flux density	B	Weber per square meter	$\frac{1}{3} \times 10^{-6}$	10^4	......	3×10^{10}	3×10^6	Gauss	$\frac{1}{3} \times 10^{-10}$	10^{-4}
Magnetic intensity	H	Praoersted	3×10^7	10^{-3}	......	$\frac{1}{3} \times 10^{-10}$	$\frac{1}{3} \times 10^{-7}$	Oersted	3×10^{10}	10^3
Magnetic linkages	λ	Weber-turn	$\frac{1}{3} \times 10^{-2}$	10^8	......	3×10^{10}	3×10^2	Maxwell-turn	$\frac{1}{3} \times 10^{-10}$	10^{-8}
Magnetomotive force	F	Pragilbert	3×10^9	10^{-1}	......	$\frac{1}{3} \times 10^{-10}$	$\frac{1}{3} \times 10^{-9}$	Gilbert	3×10^{10}	10

Table 7-1. Conversion Factors between MKS (Practical), CGS Electrostatic (ESU), and CGS Electromagnetic (EMU) Systems of Units (Continued)

Quantity	Symbol	Mks unit	Conversion Factors — To cgs (esu)	Conversion Factors — To cgs (emu)	Cgs (esu) unit	Conversion factors — To cgs (emu)	Conversion factors — To mks	Cgs (emu) unit	Conversion factors — To cgs (esu)	Conversion factors — To mks
Mass	m	Kilogram	10^{3}	10^{3}	Gram	1	10^{-3}	Gram	1	10^{-3}
Permeability	μ	10^{-7}	$\frac{1}{9}\times10^{-13}$	10^{7}	……	9×10^{20}	9×10^{13}	Gauss per oersted	$\frac{1}{9}\times10^{-20}$	10^{-7}
Permeability of free space	μ_{0}	……	$\frac{1}{9}\times10^{-13}$	10^{7}	……	9×10^{20}	9×10^{13}	……	$\frac{1}{9}\times10^{-20}$	10^{-7}
Permeance	P	Weber per pragilbert	$\frac{1}{9}\times10^{-11}$	10^{9}	……	9×10^{20}	9×10^{11}	Maxwell per gilbert	$\frac{1}{9}\times10^{-20}$	10^{-9}
Permittivity	ϵ	Farads per meter	9×10^{9}	10^{-11}	……	$\frac{1}{9}\times10^{-20}$	$\frac{1}{9}\times10^{-9}$	……	9×10^{20}	10^{11}
Permittivity of free space	ϵ_{0}	$\frac{1}{9}\times10^{-9}$	9×10^{9}	10^{-11}	$\frac{1}{9}\times10^{-20}$	$\frac{1}{9}\times10^{-20}$	$\frac{1}{9}\times10^{-9}$	$\frac{1}{9}\times10^{-20}$	9×10^{20}	10^{11}
Potential difference	p	Volt	$\frac{1}{3}\times10^{-2}$	10^{8}	Statvolt	3×10^{10}	3×10^{8}	Abvolt	$\frac{1}{3}\times10^{-10}$	10^{-8}
Power	P	Watt	10^{7}	10^{7}	Erg per second	1	10^{-7}	Erg per second	1	10^{-7}
Reluctance	$\mathcal{R}$	Pragilbert weber	9×10^{11}	10^{-9}	……	$\frac{1}{9}\times10^{-20}$	$\frac{1}{9}\times10^{-11}$	Gilbert per maxwell	9×10^{20}	10^{9}
Reluctivity	ν	……	9×10^{13}	10^{-7}	……	$\frac{1}{9}\times10^{-20}$	$\frac{1}{9}\times10^{-13}$	Oersted per gauss	9×10^{20}	10^{7}
Resistance	R	Ohm	$\frac{1}{9}\times10^{-11}$	10^{9}	Statohm	9×10^{20}	9×10^{11}	Abohm	$\frac{1}{9}\times10^{-20}$	10^{9}
Resistivity	ρ	Ohm-meter	$\frac{1}{9}\times10^{-9}$	10^{11}	Statohm centimeter	9×10^{20}	9×10^{9}	Abohm centimeter	$\frac{1}{9}\times10^{-20}$	10^{-11}
Time	t	Second	1	1	Second	1	1	Second	1	1

have some units that are of inconvenient size; however, the mks system has the advantage of using units of practical size in the expressions most commonly used in engineering. Table 7-1 gives the conversion factors between the three systems of units.

ELECTRIC-CIRCUIT THEORY

7-1. D-C Circuits

The flow of direct current in any circuit is determined only by the resistance of that circuit for a given applied direct voltage other than initial transients when the voltage is applied or changed. The resistance of a pure inductance is zero, and the resistance of a pure capacitance is infinite.

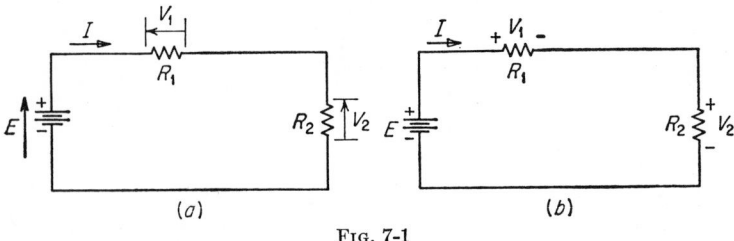

Fɪɢ. 7-1

Applied voltages are indicated by E, current by I, and resistance by R. In contrast to applied voltages, voltage drops are indicated by V. Arrow directions are assigned to the voltages and currents. Although arbitrary, one convenient system for designating voltage and current directions is the use of closed heads on the arrows for currents and open heads for voltage rises, with the head of the arrow the point of higher potential. Plus and minus symbols can also be used, the heads of arrows being $+$ and the tails $-$ (Fig. 7-1a and b).

Ohm's law states that, for a steady current, the current through a given circuit is directly proportional to the total electromotive force in the circuit and inversely proportional to the total resistance in the circuit. Expressed in equation form,

$$I = E/R \qquad \text{or} \qquad E = IR \tag{7-1}$$

where I is in amperes, E is in volts, and R is in ohms.

Resistors in series (Fig. 7-2) are added to obtain the total resistance

$$R = R_1 + R_2 + R_3 + \cdots \qquad \text{ohms} \tag{7-2}$$

Fɪɢ. 7-2

Resistors in parallel (Fig. 7-3) can be lumped to a single equivalent resistor by

$$1/R = 1/R_1 + 1/R_2 + 1/R_3 + \cdots \quad \text{ohms}^{-1} \quad (7\text{-}3)$$

or $\quad\quad\quad G = G_1 + G_2 + G_3 + \cdots \quad \text{mhos} \quad (7\text{-}3a)$

where G is the reciprocal of resistance, or conductance.

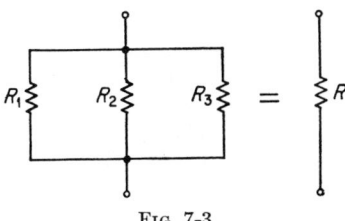

FIG. 7-3

Two resistors in parallel (Fig. 7-4) are equivalent to

$$R = R_1R_2/(R_1 + R_2) \quad \text{ohms} \quad (7\text{-}4)$$

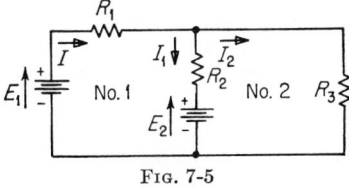

FIG. 7-4

Kirchhoff's voltage law states that the sum of the voltage drops around any closed loop in a circuit is equal to the sum of the emfs or driving voltages around the same loop (Fig. 7-5).

For loop 1 $\quad\quad R_1I + R_2I_1 = E_1 - E_2 \quad \text{volts}$
and for loop 2 $\quad\quad -R_2I_1 + R_3I_2 = E_2 \quad \text{volts} \quad (7\text{-}5)$

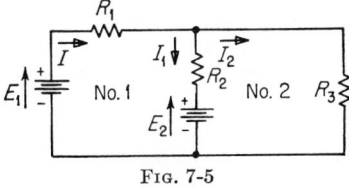

FIG. 7-5

Kirchhoff's current law states that the sum of all the currents flowing into or out of a junction is equal to zero. In Fig. 7-6

$$I - I_1 - I_2 = 0 \quad \text{amp} \quad (7\text{-}6)$$

Current I flowing into two resistors in parallel (Fig. 7-7) divides in the proportion

$$I_1 = I\,R_2/(R_1 + R_2) \text{ (7)} \qquad \text{and} \qquad I_2 = I\,R_1/(R_1 + R_2) \qquad \text{(7-7)}$$

where $I = E(R_1 + R_2)/R_1R_2$ amp, E is in volts, and R is in ohms.

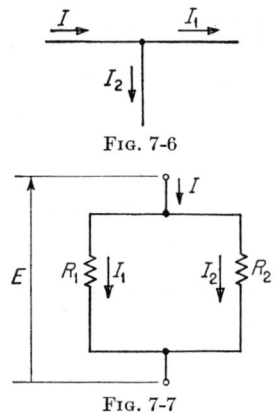

Fig. 7-6

Fig. 7-7

Resistance R of a homogeneous material of uniform cross section varies directly as its length and inversely as its cross section

$$R = \rho\,l/A \qquad \text{ohms} \qquad \text{(7-8)}$$

where ρ = specific resistance of conductor
      l = conductor length
      A = conductor cross section

l and A must be in consistent units, feet and square feet, centimeters and square centimeters, etc. ρ must correspondingly be in ohms per cubic foot, per cubic centimeter, etc.   A convenient consistent set of units for calculating the resistance of wires is to express ρ in ohms per circular mil–foot, l in feet, and A in circular mils.

Resistivity ρ at 20°C for 100 per cent conductivity copper and 61 per cent conductivity aluminum is as follows:

ρ		Unit
Copper	Aluminum	
1.724×10^{-6}	2.828×10^{-6}	ohms/cm.³
0.6788×10^{-6}	1.113×10^{-6}	ohms/in.³
10.37	17.01	ohms/(cir mil)(ft)

A *circular mil* is the area of a circle whose diameter is 1 mil (0.001 in.).

To obtain the number of circular mils in a solid cylindrical wire, express the diameter in mils and then square it, or cir mils = $(1,000 \times \text{in. diam})^2$.

Temperature change causes change in the resistance of a conductor

$$R_t = R_0(1 + \alpha t) \qquad \text{ohms} \qquad (7\text{-}9)$$

where R_t = resistance at desired temperature t, °C

R_0 = resistance at 0°C

α = temperature coefficient of resistance at 0°C

For copper $\alpha = 0.00427$, for aluminum $\alpha = 0.0039$ at 0°C. For most other pure metals $\alpha = 0.004$ approximately. Generally the resistance of a conductor will be known at one temperature and it is desired to find its resistance at some other temperature. The following general formula may be used:

$$R_{t2}/R_{t1} = (M + t_2)/(M + t_1) \qquad (7\text{-}10)$$

where R_{t2} = d-c resistance at t_2°C, ohms

R_{t1} = d-c resistance at t_1°C, ohms

M = constant for type of conductor material: 234.5 for annealed 100 per cent conductivity copper, 241.5 for hard-drawn 97.3 per cent conductivity copper, 228.1 for aluminum

Skin effect will cause an increase of the resistance of a conductor if current other than direct is passed through it. For any alternating current of frequency f the resistance can be expressed by

$$R_f = KR_{dc} \qquad \text{ohms} \qquad (7\text{-}11)$$

where R_f = a-c resistance at desired frequency f cps, ohms

R_{dc} = d-c resistance at any known temperature, ohms

K = a value taken from Table 7-2

In Table 7-2 K is shown as a function of X and

$$X = 0.063598 \sqrt{\mu f/R_{dc}} \qquad (7\text{-}12)$$

where μ = permeability of conductor (1.0 for nonmagnetic materials)

f = frequency of alternating current, cps

Table 7-2. Skin-effect Table

X	K	X	K	X	K	X	K	X	K	X	K	X	K	X	K
0.0	1.00000	0.5	1.00032	1.0	1.00519	1.5	1.02582	2.0	1.07816	2.5	1.17538	3.0	1.31809	3.5	1.49202
0.1	1.00000	0.6	1.00067	1.1	1.00758	1.6	1.03323	2.1	1.09375	2.6	1.20056	3.1	1.35102	3.6	1.52879
0.2	1.00001	0.7	1.00124	1.2	1.01071	1.7	1.04205	2.2	1.11126	2.7	1.22753	3.2	1.38504	3.7	1.56587
0.3	1.00004	0.8	1.00212	1.3	1.01470	1.8	1.05240	2.3	1.13069	2.8	1.25620	3.3	1.41999	3.8	1.60314
0.4	1.00013	0.9	1.00340	1.4	1.01969	1.9	1.06440	2.4	1.15207	2.9	1.28644	3.4	1.45570	3.9	1.64051

Network reduction can be accomplished in d-c circuits by combining in series and in parallel various branches. When delta or star branches are present (Fig. 7-8), it is necessary to be able to convert from delta to star and from star to delta. The following equations are used, with all resistances in ohms.

From delta to star:

$$R_a = \frac{R_{ab}R_{ca}}{R_{ab} + R_{bc} + R_{ca}} \qquad R_b = \frac{R_{ab}R_{bc}}{R_{ab} + R_{bc} + R_{ca}}$$

$$R_c = \frac{R_{bc}R_{ca}}{R_{ab} + R_{bc} + R_{ca}} \qquad (7\text{-}13)$$

From star to delta:

$$R_{ab} = \frac{R_aR_b + R_bR_c + R_cR_a}{R_c} \qquad R_{bc} = \frac{R_aR_b + R_bR_c + R_cR_a}{R_a}$$

$$R_{ca} = \frac{R_aR_b + R_bR_c + R_cR_a}{R_b} \qquad (7\text{-}14)$$

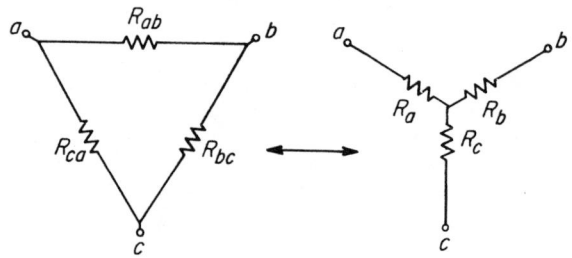

Fig. 7-8

Network theorems used in d-c circuits are similar to those used in a-c circuits (Sec. 7-2) with resistance substituted for impedance. Circuits are usually solved by reduction, series and parallel combinations, star-delta and delta-star transformations, or by mesh current calculations (Sec. 7-2). If there is more than one voltage source and the solution is to be made by reduction, it is desirable to use the *superposition theorem*, which states: In any network consisting of voltage sources and linear resistances (or impedances for a-c circuits) the current flowing at any point is the sum of the currents which would flow if each voltage source were considered separately, all other sources being replaced at the time by resistances (impedances) equal to their internal resistances (impedances). For example (Fig. 7-9),

$$I_1 = I'_1 + I''_1 \qquad I_2 = I'_2 + I''_2 \qquad I_3 = I'_3 + I''_3 \qquad \text{amp} \qquad (7\text{-}15)$$

It is assumed that the internal resistances of E_1 and E_2 have been combined with R_1 and R_2. The theorem is valid for any number of sources.

The *d-c power through a conductor* is given by

$$P = EI \quad \text{watts} \qquad (7\text{-}16)$$

where E = voltage across terminals of circuit, volts

I = current through conductor, amp

The *energy delivered to a conductor* carrying direct current during a time T is

$$W = PT = EIT \qquad \text{watt-sec or joules} \qquad (7\text{-}17)$$

where P is expressed in watts, E in volts, I in amperes, and T in seconds. If E is expressed in kilovolts, I in amperes, and T in hours, the power is expressed in kilowatts and the energy in kilowatthours.

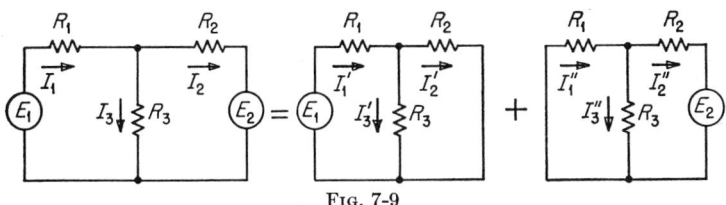

FIG. 7-9

7-2. A-C Circuits

Kirchhoff's and Ohm's laws apply to a-c as well as d-c circuits. Impedance must be used instead of resistance in the defining equations, and the numerical work is accomplished by complex numbers. Voltages and currents are represented by planars (vectors lying in one plane) which can be plotted on a single plane, commonly called the complex plane, with real portions of the complex number plotted along the abscissa and the j or imaginary numbers plotted as ordinates. Root mean square (rms) values of current and voltage are plotted as the magnitude of the planars; the planar positions are located by the real and imaginary components. The origin of *imaginary numbers* stems from equations of the form $X^2 + K^2 = 0$. The solution takes the form

$$X = \pm \sqrt{-K^2} = \pm K \sqrt{-1}$$
$$= \pm jK$$

where $j = \sqrt{-1}$ and is called an imaginary number. Some of the unique properties of j are

$$
\begin{array}{ccc}
j = \sqrt{-1} & j^3 = -j & j^5 = j \\
j^2 = -1 & j^4 = +1 & j^6 = -1
\end{array}
$$

If we consider an equation of the form $X^2 - 2X + 10 = 0$, we get

$$X = (2 \pm \sqrt{4 - 40})/2 = 1 \pm j3 \qquad \text{or} \qquad X = a + jb$$

which is known as a *complex number* and can be plotted on the complex plane, a units along the real axis and b units along the imaginary axis, as shown in

Fig. 7-10.   A complex number can be represented in four common forms:

Orthogonal:	$A = a + jb$	(7-18)
Vectorial:	$A = \bar{A}\,\underline{\lvert\theta}$	(7-19)
where	$\bar{A} = \sqrt{a^2 + b^2}$	
	$\theta = \tan^{-1}(b/a)$	
Trigonometric:	$A = \bar{A}(\cos\theta + j\sin\theta)$	(7-20)
Exponential:	$A = \bar{A}\epsilon^{j\theta}$	(7-21)

Alternating voltages and currents, being sinusoidal in nature, can be represented in any of the four forms.   For example, 100 volts is applied to

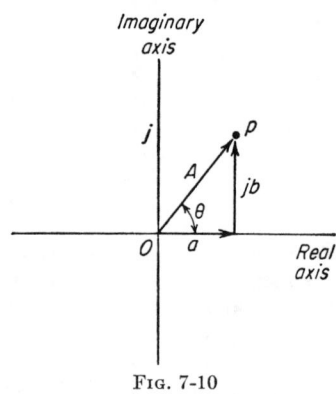

Fig. 7-10

a circuit which takes a current at 80 per cent power factor ($\theta = \cos^{-1} 0.80$). The voltage can be represented in each of the four forms, using current as a reference.

1. $a + jb = 100(\cos\theta + j\sin\theta) = 80.0 + j\,60.0$ volts
2. $\bar{A}\,\underline{\lvert\theta} = 100\underline{\lvert 36.9°}$ volts
3. $\bar{A}(\cos\theta + j\sin\theta) = 100(\cos 36.9° + j\sin 36.9°)$ volts
4. $\bar{A}\epsilon^{j\theta} = 100\epsilon^{j36.9°}$

Addition and subtraction can best be done in the orthogonal form.   Multiplication, division, powers, and roots can best be done in the exponential form or vector form.

Orthogonal addition and subtraction:

$$(a + jb) + (c + jd) = (a + c) + j(b + d) \tag{7-22}$$
$$(a + jb) - (c + jd) = (a - c) + j(b - d) \tag{7-23}$$

Exponential multiplication, division, powers and roots:

$$\bar{A}\epsilon^{j\theta_1} \cdot \bar{B}\epsilon^{j\theta_2} = \overline{AB}\epsilon^{j(\theta_1 + \theta_2)} = \overline{AB}\,\underline{\lvert \theta_1 + \theta_2} \tag{7-24}$$

$$\frac{\bar{A}\epsilon^{j\theta_1}}{\bar{B}\epsilon^{j\theta_2}} = \frac{\bar{A}}{\bar{B}}\,\epsilon^{j(\theta_1-\theta_2)} = \frac{\bar{A}}{\bar{B}}\,\underline{|\theta_1 - \theta_2} \tag{7-25}$$

$$(\bar{A}\epsilon^{j\theta})^n = (\bar{A})^n\epsilon^{jn\theta} = \bar{A}^n\underline{|n\theta} \tag{7-26}$$

$$\sqrt[n]{\bar{A}\epsilon^{j\theta}} = \sqrt[n]{\bar{A}}\,\epsilon^{j\theta/n} = \sqrt[n]{\bar{A}}\,\underline{|\theta/n} \tag{7-27}$$

Circuit Parameters. A-c circuits are made up of resistance, self-inductance, mutual inductance, and capacitance. The units of impedance in ohms are R, $+j2\pi fL$, $\pm j2\pi fM$, and $-j/2\pi fC$, where R is the resistance in ohms, L is the self-inductance in henrys, M is the mutual inductance in henrys, C is the capacitance in farads, and f is the frequency in cycles per second. A circuit may contain any or all of the above parameters with a total impedance of

$$\begin{aligned} Z &= R + j2\pi fL \pm j2\pi fM - j/2\pi fC \qquad \text{ohms} \\ &= R + jX_L \pm jX_M - jX_c \qquad \text{ohms} \end{aligned} \tag{7-28}$$

Impedances can be added directly in series. For parallel circuits the reciprocals of the impedance elements can be added to give the total *admittance*

$$Y = 1/Z = g - jb \qquad \text{mhos} \tag{7-29}$$

where g is the *conductance* and b is the *susceptance* in mho units.

The *sign of the mutual M* is determined by the direction of the mutual flux relative to the direction of the flux of the self-inductance of the circuit into

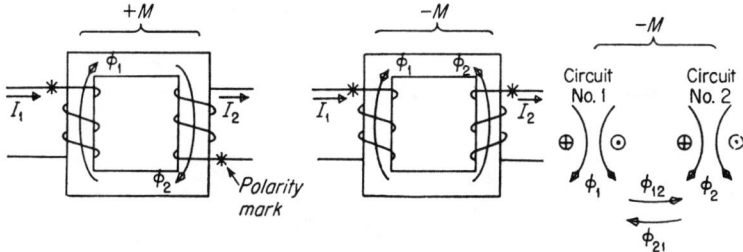

FIG. 7-11

which the mutual is being considered. If the mutual flux *adds* to the flux of self-inductance, the sign of the mutual is *plus*. If the mutual flux is in *opposition* to or *subtracts* from the self-inductance flux, the sign of the mutual is *minus*. The *right-hand rule* is useful in determining the direction of self and mutual fluxes. Grasp the conductor in the right hand with the thumb in the direction of the current and the fingers will surround the conductor in the direction of the flux (Fig. 7-11).

The *impedance of a circuit* is expressed in ohms, per cent, or per unit (p.u.). When working in ohms, all the impedance values must be on the same *voltage* basis. When working in per cent or per unit, all impedance values must be on the same kva base. To convert from per cent to ohms use

$$\text{Ohms} = \frac{10 \times \text{per cent} \times \text{kv}^2_{L-L}}{\text{kva}} \qquad \text{per phase} \qquad (7\text{-}30)$$

$$\text{Per cent} = \frac{\text{ohms} \times \text{kva}}{10 \times \text{kv}^2_{L-L}} \qquad \text{per phase} \qquad (7\text{-}31)$$

$$\text{Per unit (pu)} = \text{per cent}/100 \qquad\qquad\qquad\qquad (7\text{-}32)$$

Per cent is expressed in numerical form, i.e., one hundred per cent = 100 per cent = 1.00 per unit. kv_{L-L} is line-to-line voltage in kilovolts and kva is the three-phase kilovolt-ampere base. The equations are equally valid if line-to-neutral voltage in kilovolts and single-phase kilovolt amperage is used.

Transformer turns ratio are squared and multiplied by the ohms when transferring ohms from one side of a transformer to the other. Per cent impedance is moved from one side of a transformer to the other unchanged (Fig. 7-12). Unequal transformer turns ratio in circuits involving step-up and step-down transformers can be readily solved by first converting to ohms on a common kv base as viewed from the point of greatest interest in the circuit and then converting to per cent (Fig. 7-13). The per-phase impedance diagram in ohms on n kv base as viewed from F is shown in Fig. 7-14, the per-phase diagram in per unit in Fig. 7-15.

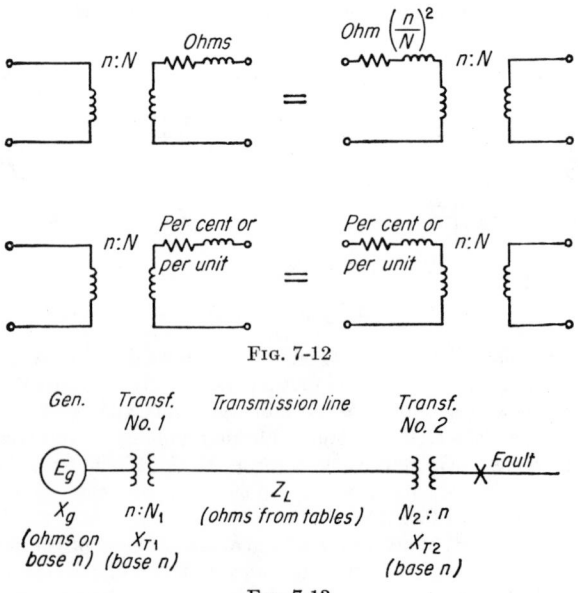

Fig. 7-12

Fig. 7-13

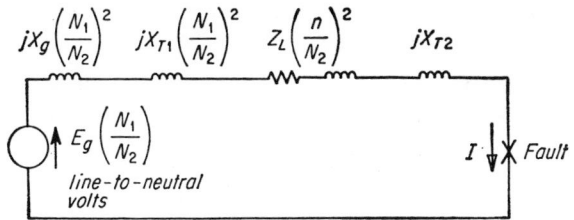

FIG. 7-14

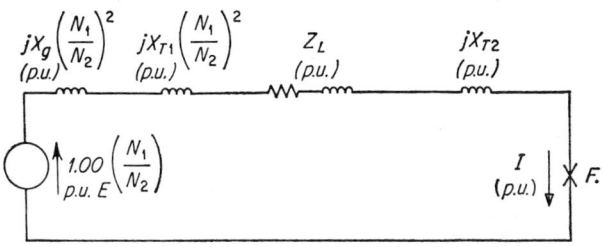

FIG. 7-15

Per unit current I_{pu} is given by

$$I_{pu} = E_{pu}/Z_{pu} \qquad \text{per unit} \tag{7-33}$$

where $Z_{pu} = jX_{g\ pu}(N_1/N_2)^2 + jX_{T1\ pu}(N_1/N_2)^2 + Z_{L\ pu} + jX_{T2\ pu}$

per unit, ohms

The individual per unit reactances and impedances must be on the same arbitrary kva base.

Normal current I_n is defined as

$$I_n = \frac{\text{three-phase base kva}}{\sqrt{3}\ \text{line-to-line kv}} \qquad \text{amp} \tag{7-34}$$

$$I = I_{pu} \times I_n \qquad \text{amp} \tag{7-35}$$

Name-plate data for heavy generators and transmission equipment give nominal kv, kva, and per cent impedance based on nominal ratings from which equivalent ohms at any desired kv base can be obtained by using Eq. (7-30).

Capacitors are usually built with an average $+5$ per cent kva tolerance, and the equivalent ohms can be found from

$$X_c = 1{,}000\ \text{kv}^2/1.05\ \text{kva} \qquad \text{ohms} \tag{7-36}$$

where kv = rated voltage of capacitor, line-to-line for three-phase kva and line-to-neutral for one-phase kva

Shunt reactors have 100 per cent reactance, and the equivalent ohms are given by

$$X_L = 1,000 \text{ kv}^2/\text{kva} \qquad \text{ohms} \qquad (7\text{-}37)$$

Series reactors have a name-plate per cent reactance based on the through-circuit kva. The kva of reactor parts is also given. For example, a 5 per cent, 1,000-kva, series reactor will have 5 per cent reactance based on 20,000 kva circuit kva (1,000 kva is 5 per cent of 20,000 kva).

$$X_{L \text{ series}} = (10 \times \text{per cent} \times \text{kv}^2_{L-L})/\text{circuit kva} \qquad \text{ohms} \qquad (7\text{-}38)$$

Loads can be converted to equivalent ohms by

$$Z = 1,000 \text{ kv}^2/(P - jQ) = [1,000 \text{ kv}^2/(P^2 + Q)](P + jQ) \qquad \text{ohms} \qquad (7\text{-}39)$$

where kv = the line-to-line voltages, kv

$\quad P$ = three-phase kw = kva $\times \cos \theta$

$\quad Q$ = reactive kva lagging (three-phase) kvar

$\qquad$ = kva $\times \sin \theta$

$\quad \theta$ = power-factor angle

Network Solutions. The solution of electrical circuits is based on the application of Ohm's and Kirchhoff's laws. For circuits of any complexity the solution can be systematized by the use of mesh currents, voltages, and impedances. The following steps are suggested in setting up any given circuit:

1. Label individual impedances in any consistent manner.

2. Set up arrow direction of voltages (establish direction of voltage rise).

3. Number the meshes and set up arrow directions for the branch and mesh currents.

Mesh impedances are defined in general as: Z_{pq} is the voltage drop in volts in the reference direction in mesh q due to 1 amp of current in the reference direction in mesh p. Curved current arrows show the reference direction in each mesh. In linear circuits the current is directly proportional to the voltage, and in bilateral circuits the impedance is independent of the direction of current flow. In such circuits $Z_{pq} = Z_{qp}$.

Self-impedance is defined as Z_{pp}, which is equal to the sum of all the individual impedances around mesh p, and p is any one of the meshes in a given circuit. For example in the three-mesh circuit of **Fig. 7-16**

$$Z_{11} = Z_a + Z_c + Z_d$$
$$Z_{22} = Z_b + Z_c + Z_e$$
$$Z_{33} = Z_d + Z_e + Z_f$$

Mutual impedance is defined as Z_{pq}, which is equal to the sum of the individual impedances that are common to meshes p and q where p and q are any two meshes of a given circuit. The signs of the mutuals are determined by the arbitrary current direction; when mesh currents are in the same direction in a common branch, the mutual is $+$, when in opposite directions, the sign is $-$. In Fig. 7-16 the mutuals are given by

$$Z_{12} = -Z_c \qquad Z_{13} = -Z_d \qquad Z_{23} = -Z_e$$

Mesh emf is defined as the sum of the voltages around a given mesh in the reference direction:

$$E_{11} = E_a - E_b \qquad E_{22} = E_b - E_c \qquad E_{33} = E_d$$

Mesh-voltage equations are obtained by applying Kirchhoff's voltage law around the various meshes:

$$Z_{11}I_1 + Z_{21}I_2 + Z_{31}I_3 = E_{11}$$
$$Z_{12}I_1 + Z_{22}I_2 + Z_{32}I_3 = E_{22}$$
$$Z_{13}I_1 + Z_{23}I_2 + Z_{33}I_3 = E_{33}$$

These three independent equations can be solved in any desired manner for

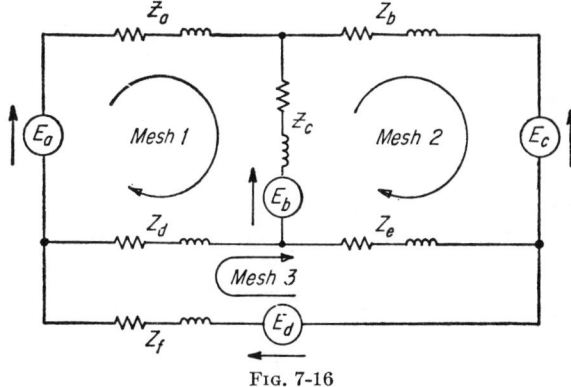

Fig. 7-16

the currents; one of the best methods when two or more meshes are involved is by means of determinants. For example

$$I_1 = E_{11}A_{11}/D + E_{22}A_{12}/D + E_{33}A_{13}/D \qquad \text{amp} \qquad (7\text{-}40)$$

where

$$D = \begin{vmatrix} Z_{11} & Z_{21} & Z_{31} \\ Z_{12} & Z_{22} & Z_{32} \\ Z_{13} & Z_{23} & Z_{33} \end{vmatrix} = Z_{11}Z_{22}Z_{33} - Z_{23}{}^2 Z_{11} + 2Z_{12}Z_{23}Z_{13} - Z_{13}{}^2 Z_{22}$$

and

$$A_{11} = + \begin{vmatrix} Z_{22} & Z_{32} \\ Z_{23} & Z_{33} \end{vmatrix} = Z_{22}Z_{33} - Z_{23}{}^2$$

$$A_{12} = - \begin{vmatrix} Z_{21} & Z_{31} \\ Z_{23} & Z_{33} \end{vmatrix} = - Z_{21}Z_{33} + Z_{31}Z_{23}$$

$$A_{13} = + \begin{vmatrix} Z_{21} & Z_{31} \\ Z_{22} & Z_{32} \end{vmatrix} = Z_{21}Z_{32} - Z_{31}Z_{22}$$

The *general solution for the current in any mesh p* of a network consisting of n meshes is given by

$$I_p = E_{11}A_{p1}/D + E_{22}A_{p2}/D + \cdots + E_{nn}A_{pn}/D \qquad \text{amp} \qquad (7\text{-}41)$$

where D is given by

$$D = \begin{vmatrix} Z_{11} & Z_{21} & \cdots & Z_{n1} \\ Z_{12} & Z_{22} & \cdots & Z_{n2} \\ \cdots & \cdots & \cdots & \cdots \\ Z_{1n} & Z_{2n} & \cdots & Z_{nn} \end{vmatrix}$$

and the A's are the cofactors of D formed from D by drawing intersecting lines through the row and column intersecting on the element whose cofactor is being found.   For example, in a three-mesh circuit

$$D = \begin{vmatrix} Z_{11} & Z_{21} & Z_{31} \\ Z_{12} & Z_{22} & Z_{32} \\ Z_{13} & Z_{23} & Z_{33} \end{vmatrix}$$

From which cofactor A_{11} corresponding to element Z_{11} is seen to be

$$A_{11} = \begin{vmatrix} Z_{22} & Z_{32} \\ Z_{23} & Z_{33} \end{vmatrix}$$

The *sign of the cofactor* is determined from its position in the original determinant.   If the sum of the row and the column is even, the sign is $+$, if odd, the sign is $-$.   The sign can also be determined by multiplying the cofactor by $(-1)^{r+c}$, where r is the number of the row and c the number of the column from which the cofactor is being formed.   For example, the second row and first column would give $(-1)^{2+1} = -1$.

Driving-point impedance is the ratio of the voltage applied to two terminals of a network to the current that flows through those two terminals with all other voltage sources in the network replaced by their internal impedance. The driving-point admittance is the reciprocal of the driving-point impedance.   The driving point-impedance, Z'_{nn} and the driving-point admittance Y'_{nn} can be readily found by using determinants

$$Z'_{nn} = D/A_{nn} \text{ ohms} \qquad \text{and} \qquad Y'_{nn} = A_{nn}/D \qquad \text{mhos} \qquad (7\text{-}42)$$

where n denotes the driving-point mesh.

Transfer impedance Z'_{pq} is the ratio of the voltage in one mesh, say mesh p, to the current in a second mesh q.

$$Z'_{pq} = D/A_{pq} \qquad \text{ohms} \qquad\qquad (7\text{-}43)$$

The transfer admittance is given by

$$Y'_{pq} = A_{pq}/D \qquad \text{mhos} \qquad\qquad (7\text{-}44)$$

Solution of a-c networks by reduction is accomplished by taking a single source of voltage and then reducing the network to a single impedance by means of series and parallel combinations as shown for direct current, Sec.

7-1, with impedance substituted for resistance. Star-delta impedance conversions are made as shown on page 7-8 and in Fig. 7-8. Other voltage sources are similarly treated, and the final currents are obtained by superposing or adding the results of the individual solutions to obtain the total solution. Some star-connected impedances have mutuals between star branches which must be eliminated before further reduction can be made.

A *star circuit with mutuals* can be converted to a star without mutuals, as shown in Fig. 7-17, where

$$Z_A = Z_a + Z_{bc} - Z_{ab} - Z_{ca} \qquad \text{ohms}$$
$$Z_B = Z_b + Z_{ca} - Z_{bc} - Z_{ab} \qquad \text{ohms}$$
$$Z_C = Z_c + Z_{ab} - Z_{ca} - Z_{bc} \qquad \text{ohms}$$

Polarity marks as shown require that, with all reference directions from the center outward as shown, all self and mutual drops are from center out-

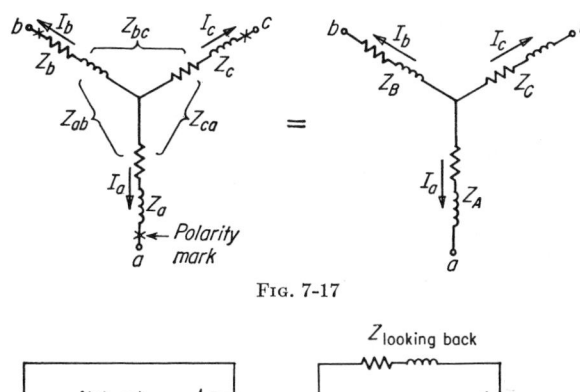

Fig. 7-17

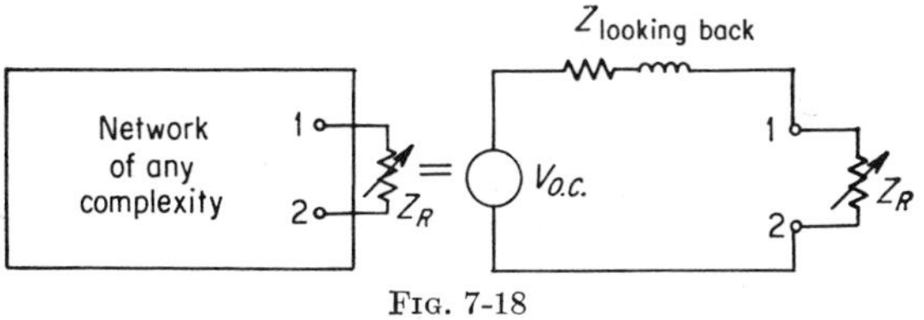

Fig. 7-18

ward. Polarity marks on a two-winding transformer indicate a $-M$ mutual for current into one polarity mark and out the other as shown in Fig. 7-11.

Network Theorems. *Thévenin's Theorem.* The current in any impedance (including short-circuit) connected to any two terminals of a network is the same as if that impedance were connected to a simple generator whose generated voltage is the open-circuit voltage of the terminals in question, and whose impedance is the impedance of the network looking back from the terminals with all generators replaced by impedances equal to their internal impedance. See Fig. 7-18, where

$V_{o\text{-}c}$ = open-circuit voltage at terminals 1-2

$Z_{l.b.}$ = impedance looking back from terminals 1-2

Norton's Theorem. The current in any impedance (including short-circuit) connected to any two terminals of a network is the same as if the impedance were connected to a constant-current generator whose current is equal to the current which flows through the two terminals when these terminals are short-circuited, the constant-current generator being in shunt with an impedance equal to the impedance looking back into the network from the terminals in question. See Fig. 7-19, where

I_{s-c} = short circuit current at terminals 1-2

$Z_{l.b.}$ = looking-back impedance from terminals 1-2

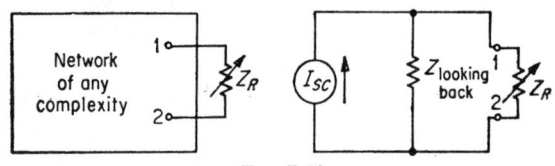

Fɪɢ. 7-19

Maximum-power-transfer Theorem. Maximum power will be absorbed by one network from another connected to it at two terminals if the impedances looking into the two networks from the junction are conjugates of each other $(a + jb$ and $a - jb)$.

Reciprocal Theorem. If a voltage E is applied between any two terminals of a passive linear network and the current I is measured in any branch, the ratio E/I will be unchanged if the location of the voltage source and measuring point of the current are interchanged.

Equivalent Circuits. Equivalent circuits at all frequencies can be found for some of the simple configurations. These circuits are equivalent at the input terminals only and are enclosed in a dotted box to indicate terminal equivalence only. They are useful in designing circuits such as filters and computer elements to have a given response with a choice of elements used to make up the circuit. All resistance is in ohms, inductance in henrys, and capacitance in farads.

Resistance and Inductance Circuits. The circuits of Fig. 7-20 are equivalent when

$$R_1 = R_B{}^2/(R_A + R_B) \qquad\qquad R_B = R_1 + R_2$$
$$L_1 = L_A/(1 + R_A/R_B)^2 \qquad\qquad R_A = R_2 + R_2{}^2/R_1$$
$$R_2 = R_A R_B/(R_A + R_B) \qquad\qquad L_A = L_1(1 + R_2/R_1)^2$$

The circuits of Figs. 7-21 are equivalent when

$$L_1 = L_B{}^2/(L_A + L_B) \qquad\qquad L_A = (L_2/L_1)(L_1 + L_2)$$
$$R_1 = R_A/(1 + L_A/L_B)^2 \qquad\qquad L_B = L_1 + L_2$$
$$L_2 = L_A L_B/(L_A + L_B) \qquad\qquad R_A = R_1(1 + L_2/L_1)^2$$

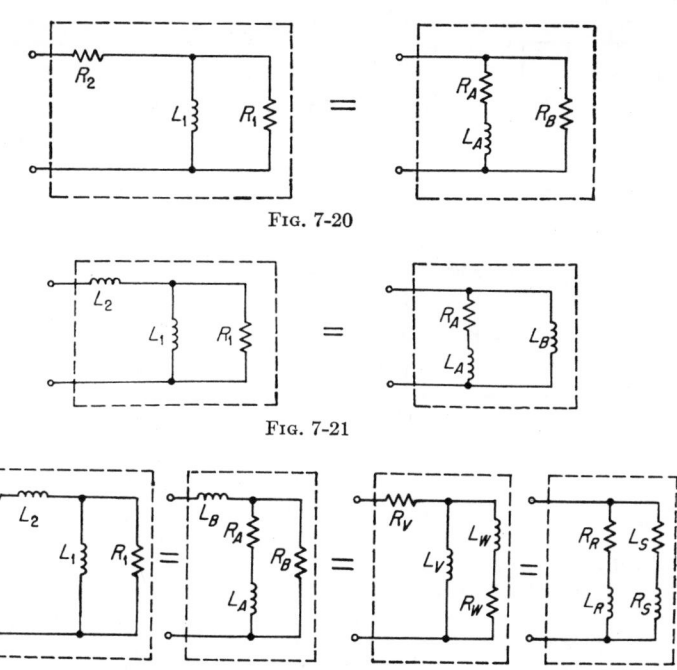

Fig. 7-20

Fig. 7-21

Fig. 7-22

All four of the circuits of Fig. 7-22 are equivalent when

$$R_1 = \frac{R_B{}^2}{R_A + R_B} = \frac{R_w}{(1 + L_w/L_v)^2} = \frac{(L_R R_s - L_s R_R)^2}{(L_R + L_s)^2(R_R + R_s)}$$

$$R_2 = R_A R_B/(R_A + R_B) = R_v = R_R R_s/(R_R + R_s)$$

$$L_2 = L_B = L_v L_w/(L_v + L_w) = L_R L_s/(L_R + L_s)$$

$$L_1 = L_A/(1 + R_A/R_B)^2 = L_v{}^2/(L_v + L_w)$$

$$\qquad\qquad\qquad = (L_R R_s - L_s R_R)^2/(R_R + R_s)^2(L_R + L_s)$$

$R_A = R_2 + R_2{}^2/R_1$	$R_B = R_1 + R_2$
$L_B = L_2$	$L_A = L_1(1 + R_2/R_1)^2$
$R_v = R_2$	$R_w = R_1(1 + L_2/L_1)^2$
$L_v = L_1 + L_2$	$L_w = \dfrac{L_2}{L_1}(L_1 + L_2)$

$$L_s = (R_2{}^2/2L_1)[K + \sqrt{K^2 - 4L_1L_2K/R_2{}^2}]$$

$$K = (L_1/R_1 + L_1/R_2 + L_2/R_2)^2 - 4L_1L_2/R_1R_2$$

$$L_R = L_sL_2/(L_s - L_2) \qquad\qquad R_s = \frac{(L_s - L_R)}{(L_1/R_1 + L_1/R_2 + L_2/R_2 - L_R/R_2)}$$

$$R_R = R_2R_s/(R_s - R_2)$$

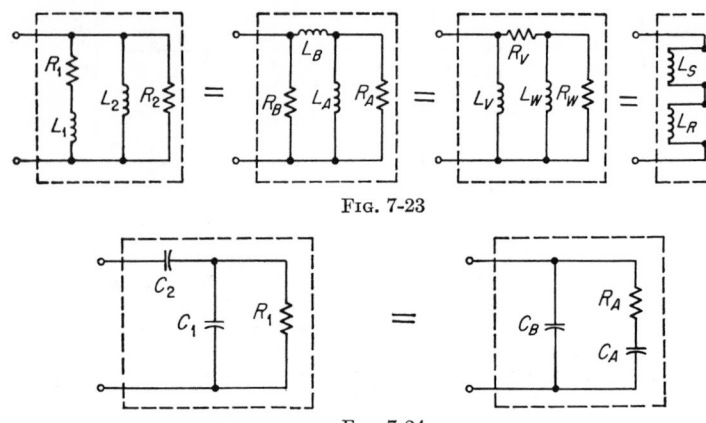

FIG. 7-23

FIG. 7-24

The four-element circuits of Fig. 7-23 are equivalent when

$$L_1 = (L_B/L_A)(L_A + L_B) = L_w(1 + R_v/R_w)^2$$
$$= L_A L_s (L_R + L_s)(R_R + R_s)^2/(L_R R_s - L_s R_R)^2$$
$$L_2 = L_A + L_B = L_v = L_R + L_s$$
$$R_1 = R_A(1 + L_B/L_A)^2 = R_v + R_v^2/R_w$$
$$= R_R R_s (R_R + R_s)(L_R + L_s)^2/(L_R R_s - L_s R_R)^2$$
$$R_2 = R_B = R_v + R_w = R_R + R_s$$

$$L_A = L_2^2/(L_1 + L_2) \qquad\qquad L_B = L_1 L_2/(L_1 + L_2)$$
$$R_A = R_1/(1 + L_1/L_2)^2 \qquad\qquad R_B = R_2$$
$$L_v = L_2 \qquad\qquad\qquad L_w = L_1/(1 + R_1/R_2)^2$$
$$R_v = R_1 R_2/(R_1 + R_2) \qquad\qquad R_w = R_2^2/(R_1 + R_2)$$

$$R_s = \frac{2L_2^2}{R_1} \frac{1}{K + \sqrt{K^2 - 4L_2^2 K/R_1 R_2}}$$
$$K = (L_1/R_1 + L_2/R_1 + L_2/R_2)^2 - 4L_1 L_2/R_1 R_2$$
$$R_R = R_2 - R_s$$
$$L_s = (L_1/R_1 + L_2/R_1 + L_2/R_2 - L_2/R_R) R_R R_s/(R_R - R_s)$$
$$L_R = L_2 - L_s$$

Equivalent Resistance and Capacitance Circuits. The circuits of Fig. 7-24 are equivalent when

$$C_2 = C_A + C_B \qquad\qquad C_B = C_1 C_2/(C_1 + C_2)$$
$$R_1 = R_A/(1 + C_B/C_A)^2 \qquad\qquad C_A = C_2^2/(C_1 + C_2)$$
$$C_1 = (C_B/C_A)(C_A + C_B) \qquad\qquad R_A = R_1(1 + C_1/C_2)^2$$

The circuits of Fig. 7-25 are equivalent when

$$R_1 = R_B^2/(R_A + R_B) \qquad\qquad R_B = R_1 + R_2$$
$$C_1 = C_A(1 + R_A/R_B)^2 \qquad\qquad R_A = (R_2/R_1)(R_1 + R_2)$$
$$R_2 = R_A R_B/(R_A + R_B) \qquad\qquad C_A = C_1/(1 + R_2/R_1)^2$$

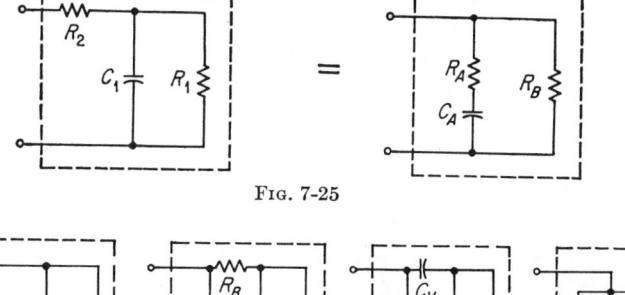

FIG. 7-25

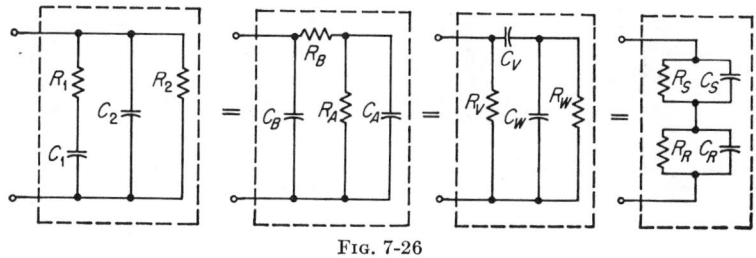

FIG. 7-26

The circuits of Fig. 7-26 are equivalent when

$$R_1 = (R_B/R_A)(R_A + R_B) = R_w(1 + C_w/C_v)^2$$
$$= R_R R_s (R_R + R_s)(C_R + C_s)^2/(R_R C_R - R_s C_s)^2$$
$$R_2 = R_A + R_B = R_v = R_R + R_s$$
$$C_1 = C_A/(1 + R_B/R_A)^2 = C_v^2/(C_v + C_w)$$
$$= (R_R C_R - R_s C_s)^2/(R_R + R_s)^2(C_R + C_s)$$
$$C_2 = C_B = C_v C_w/(C_v + C_w) = C_R C_s/(C_R + C_s)$$
$$R_A = R_2^2/R_1 + R_2 \qquad R_B = R_1 R_2/(R_1 + R_2)$$
$$C_A = C_1(1 + R_1/R_2)^2 \qquad C_B = C_2$$
$$R_v = R_2 \qquad R_w = R_1/(1 + C_2/C_1)^2$$
$$C_v = C_1 + C_2 \qquad C_w = (C_2/C_1)(C_1 + C_2)$$
$$C_s = (K + \sqrt{K^2 - 4R_2^2 C_1 C_2 K}/2R_2^2 C_1$$
$$K = (R_1 C_1 + R_2 C_1 + R_2 C_2)^2 - 4R_1 C_1 R_2 C_2$$
$$C_R = C_s C_2/(C_s - C_2) \qquad R_s = (R_1 C_1 + R_2 C_1 + R_2 C_2 - R_2 C_R)/(C_s - C_R)$$
$$R_R = R_2 - R_s$$

Each of the circuits of Fig. 7-27 will be equivalent at all frequencies when

$$C_1 = (C_B/C_A)(C_A + C_B) = C_w(1 + R_w/R_v)^2$$
$$= C_R C_s (C_R + C_s)(R_R + R_s)^2/(R_R C_R - L_s C_s)^2$$
$$C_2 = C_A + C_B = C_v = C_R + C_s$$
$$R_1 = R_A/(1 + C_B/C_A)^2 = R_v^2/(R_v + R_w)$$
$$= (R_R C_R - R_s C_s)^2/(C_R + C_s)^2(R_R + R_s)$$
$$R_2 = R_B = (R_v R_w/(R_v + R_w) = R_R R_s/(R_R + R_s)$$

$$C_A = C_2{}^2/(C_1 + C_2) \qquad\qquad C_B = C_1C_2/(C_1 + C_2)$$
$$R_A = R_1(1 + C_1/C_2)^2 \qquad\qquad R_B = R_2$$
$$C_v = C_2 \qquad\qquad\qquad\qquad C_w = C_1/(1 + R_2/R_1)^2$$
$$R_v = R_1 + R_2 \qquad\qquad\qquad R_w = (R_2/R_1)(R_1 + R_2)$$
$$R_s = (K + \sqrt{K^2 - 4R_1R_2C_2{}^2K})/2R_1C_2{}^2$$
$$K = (R_1C_1 + R_1C_2 + R_2C_2)^2 - 4R_1R_2C_1C_2$$
$$R_R = R_sR_2/(R_s - R_2) \qquad C_s = R_1C_1 + R_1C_2 + R_2C_2 - R_RC_2/(R_s - R_R)$$
$$C_R = C_2 - C_s$$

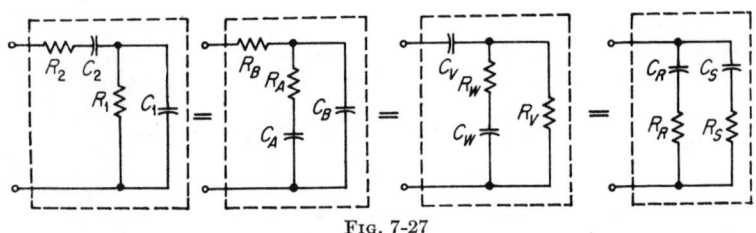

Fig. 7-27

Power Transmission. *Transmission-line Representation.* Three-phase power circuits are usually solved on a per-phase basis, since in a balanced system the only difference between the voltages and currents in the different

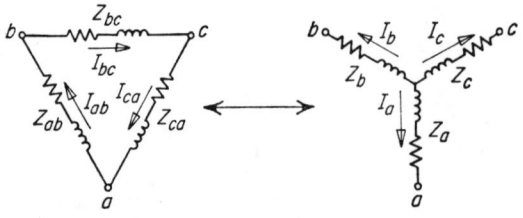

Fig. 7-28

phases is that the b and c phases are displaced 120° lagging and leading from the a phase quantities. Delta (pi) systems are solved by first converting to an equivalent wye (T).

Delta to star (pi to T) transformation of impedances are made by the rule: Star impedances are the product of adjacent delta impedances divided by the sum of all the delta impedances (Fig. 7-28).

$$Z_a = Z_{ca}Z_{ab}/D \qquad\qquad I_{ab} = -(Z_{ca}/D)I_a + (Z_{bc}/D)I_b$$
$$Z_b = Z_{ab}Z_{bc}/D \qquad\qquad I_{bc} = -(Z_{ab}/D)I_b + (Z_{ca}/D)I_c$$
$$Z_c = Z_{bc}Z_{ca}/D \qquad\qquad I_{ca} = -(Z_{bc}/D)I_c + (Z_{ab}/D)I_a$$
$$D = Z_{ab} + Z_{bc} + Z_{ca}$$

Star to delta transformation of impedances can be made as follows:

$Z_{ab} = D'Z_aZ_b$ $I_a = I_{ca} - I_{ab}$

$Z_{bc} = D'Z_bZ_c$ $I_b = I_{ab} - I_{bc}$

$Z_{ca} = D'Z_cZ_a$ $I_c = I_{bc} - I_{ca}$

$D' = 1/Z_a + 1/Z_b + 1/Z_c$

ABCD constants of a linear bilateral circuit having distinct input (sending end) and output (receiving end) terminals can be defined as:

A = voltage impressed at sending end per volt at open-circuited receiving end; a dimensionless voltage ratio

B = voltage impressed at sending end per ampere in short-circuited receiving end, same as transfer impedance; also, equal to voltage impressed at receiving end per ampere in short-circuited sending-end terminals

C = current in amperes into sending end per volt on open-circuited receiving end; has dimensions of admittance

D = current in amperes into sending end per ampere in short-circuited receiving end; a dimensionless current ratio

For all passive networks

$$AD - BC = 1 \qquad (7\text{-}45)$$

Voltage and current relationships in terms of *ABCD* constants for transmission-type network are

$E_s = AE_R + BI_R$ volts $E_R = DE_s - BI_s$ volts

$I_s = CE_R + DI_R$ amp $I_R = AI_s - CE_s$ amp

The values of A, B, C, and D can be determined for typical networks by referring to Tables 7-3 and 7-4.

Power-circle Diagrams. Power-circle diagrams can be drawn by using the equations of Table 7-5. *Real and reactive* power is expressed by

$$P + jQ = E\hat{I} \qquad \text{va} \qquad (7\text{-}46)$$

where P = real power

Q = reactive power

E = vector voltage

$\hat{I}$ = conjugate current in vector form (if $I = a + jb$, then $\hat{I} = a - jb$)

Two-station systems can be analyzed by means of circle diagrams obtained from equations in Table 7-5. A step-by-step procedure is as follows:

1. Calculate vector to center, and locate C_s or C_R.

2. Calculate radius vector R_{SO} or R_{RO} for $\theta = 0$ ($\epsilon^{j\theta} = 1$).

3. Add (1) and (2) to obtain real and reactive power for sending and receiving voltages in phase. Plot this as power for $\theta = 0$.

4. Draw circle using center from (1) and passing through power for $\theta = 0$. Draw reference radius vector from center to power for $\theta = 0$ point to serve as reference from which angles are measured.

5. Corresponding sending and receiving conditions are found at the same angle on the corresponding circles.

Type of network		A
Series impedance		1
Shunt admittance		1
Transformer		$1 + \dfrac{Z_T Y_T}{2}$
Transformer ratio		$\dfrac{1}{N}$
Transmission line*		$\cosh \sqrt{ZY} =$ $\left(1 + \dfrac{ZY}{2} + \dfrac{Z^2 Y^2}{24} + \cdots\right)$
$A_1 B_1 C_1 D_1$ in series with impedance		A_1
Impedance in series with $A_1 B_1 C_1 D_1$		$A_1 + C_1 Z$
Sending-end impedance in series with $A_1 B_1 C_1 D_1$ and receiver impedance		$A_1 + C_1 Z_S$
$A_1 B_1 C_1 D_1$ and shunt admittance at receiver		$A_1 + B_1 Y_R$
$A_1 B_1 C_1 D_1$ and shunt admittance at sending end		A_1

ABCD constants for different types of networks

B	C	D
Z	0	1
0	Y	1
$Z_T\left(1 + \dfrac{Z_T Y_T}{4}\right)$	Y_T	$1 + \dfrac{Z_T Y_T}{2}$
0	0	N
$\sqrt{Z/Y}\,\sinh\sqrt{ZY} =$ $Z\left(1 + \dfrac{ZY}{6} + \dfrac{Z^2 Y^2}{120} + \cdots\right)$	$\sqrt{Y/Z}\,\sinh\sqrt{ZY} =$ $Y\left(1 + \dfrac{ZY}{6} + \dfrac{Z^2 Y^2}{120} + \cdots\right)$	Same as A
$B_1 + A_1 Z$	C_1	$D_1 + C_1 Z$
$B_1 + D_1 Z$	C_1	D_1
$B_1 + A_1 Z_R + D_1 Z_S + C_1 Z_S Z_R$	C_1	$D_1 + C_1 Z_R$
B_1	$C_1 + D_1 Y_R$	D_1
B_1	$C_1 + A_1 Y_S$	$D_1 + B_1 Y_S$

Table 7-3

Type of network		A
$A_1B_1C_1D_1$ and shunt admittance at both ends		$A_1 + B_1Y_R$
$A_1B_1C_1D_1$ in series with $A_2B_2C_2D_2$		$A_1A_2 + C_1B_2$
Two general networks with series impedance		$A_1A_2 + C_1B_2 + C_1A_2Z$
Two general networks in parallel		$\dfrac{A_1B_2 + B_1A_2}{B_1 + B_2}$

*z = ohms/mile; $Z = sz$, where s = miles; $Y = sy$, total susceptance.

ABCD constants for different types of networks

B	C	D
B_1	$C_1 + A_1 Y_S + D_1 Y_R + B_1 Y_S Y_R$	$D_1 + B_1 Y_S$
$B_1 A_2 + D_1 B_2$	$A_1 C_2 + C_1 D_2$	$B_1 C_2 + D_1 D_2$
$B_1 A_2 + D_1 B_2 + D_1 A_2 Z$	$A_1 C_2 + C_1 D_2 + C_1 C_2 Z$	$B_1 C_2 + D_1 D_2 + D_1 C_2 Z$
$\dfrac{B_1 B_2}{B_1 + B_2}$	$\dfrac{C_1 + C_2 + (A_1 - A_2)(D_2 - D_1)}{B_1 + B_2}$	$\dfrac{B_1 D_2 + D_1 B_2}{B_1 + B_2}$

Table 7-4. Conversion Formulas for Transmission-type Networks

To Convert from

To Convert to		ABCD	Impedance	Equivalent pi	Equivalent T	Nomenclature
ABCD	$A =$	ABCD constants $E_s = AE_R + BI_R$ $I_s = CE_R + DI_R$ $E_R = DE_s - BI_s$ $I_R = -CE_s + AI_s$	Z_{22}/Z_{12}	$1 + ZY_R$	$1 + Z_sY$	
	$B =$		$(Z_{11}Z_{22} - Z_{12}^2)/Z_{12}$	Z	$Z_R + Z_s + YZ_RZ_s$	
	$C =$		$1/Z_{12}$	$Y_R + Y_s + ZY_RY_s$	Y	
	$D =$		Z_{11}/Z_{12}	$1 + ZY_s$	$1 + Z_RY$	
Impedance	$Z_{11} =$	$\dfrac{D}{C}$	Impedance constants	$\dfrac{1 + ZY_s}{Y_R + Y_s + ZY_RY_s}$	$Z_R + \dfrac{1}{Y}$	
	$Z_{12} =$	$\dfrac{1}{C}$	$E_1 = Z_{11}I_1 + Z_{12}I_2$	$\dfrac{1}{Y_R + Y_s + ZY_RY_s}$	$\dfrac{1}{Y}$	
	$Z_{22} =$	$\dfrac{A}{C}$	$E_2 = Z_{12}I_1 + Z_{22}I_2$	$\dfrac{1 + ZY_R}{Y_R + Y_s + ZY_RY_s}$	$Z_s + \dfrac{1}{Y}$	
Equiv pi	$Y_R =$	$\dfrac{A-1}{B}$	$\dfrac{Z_{22} - Z_{12}}{Z_{11}Z_{22} - Z_{12}^2}$	Equivalent pi	$\dfrac{YZ_s}{Z_R + Z_s + YZ_RZ_s}$	
	$Z =$	B	$\dfrac{Z_{11}Z_{22} - Z_{12}^2}{Z_{12}}$		$Z_R + Z_s + YZ_RZ_s$	
	$Y_s =$	$\dfrac{D-1}{B}$	$\dfrac{Z_{11} - Z_{12}}{Z_{11}Z_{22} - Z_{12}^2}$		$\dfrac{YZ_R}{Z_R + Z_s + YZ_RZ_s}$	
Equiv T	$Z_R =$	$\dfrac{D-1}{C}$	$Z_{11} - Z_{12}$	$\dfrac{ZY_s}{Y_R + Y_s + ZY_RY_s}$	Equivalent T	
	$Y =$	C	$\dfrac{1}{Z_{12}}$	$Y_R + Y_s + ZY_RY_s$		
	$Z_s =$	$\dfrac{A-1}{C}$	$Z_{22} - Z_{12}$	$\dfrac{ZY_R}{Y_R + Y_s + ZY_RY_s}$		

Nomenclature (circuit diagrams):
- ABCD network: $P_s + jQ_s$, I_s, E_s — $A\ B\ C\ D$ — I_R, E_R, $P_R + jQ_R$
- Impedance network: $P_2 + jQ_2$, I_2, E_2 — $Z_{22}\ Z_{12}\ Z_{11}$ — I_1, E_1, $P_1 + jQ_1$
- Equivalent pi: $P_s + jQ_s$, I_s, E_s — Y_s, Z, Y_R — I_R, E_R, $P_R + jQ_R$
- Equivalent T: $P_s + jQ_s$, I_s, E_s — Z_s, Y, Z_R — I_R, E_R, $P_R + jQ_R$

Table 7-5. Equations for Plotting Circle Diagrams

Type of network	Sending end circle			Receiving end circle		
	Power input*	Vector to center, C_s†	Radius vector, $R_{s\theta}$	Power output	Vector to center, C_R	Radius vector, R_{R0}
ABCD	$P_s + jQ_s$	$\dfrac{\hat{D}}{\hat{B}}\bar{E}_s^2$	$-\dfrac{\bar{E}_R\bar{E}_s\epsilon^{+j\theta}}{\hat{B}}$	$P_R + jQ_R$	$-\dfrac{\hat{A}}{\hat{B}}\bar{E}_R^2$	$+\dfrac{\bar{E}_R\bar{E}_s\epsilon^{-j\theta}}{\hat{B}}$
Equivalent pi	$P_s + jQ_s$	$\left(\dfrac{1}{\hat{Z}}+\hat{Y}_s\right)\bar{E}_s^2$	$-\dfrac{\bar{E}_R\bar{E}_s\epsilon^{+j\theta}}{\hat{Z}}$	$P_R + jQ_R$	$-\left(\dfrac{1}{\hat{Z}}+\hat{Y}_r\right)\bar{E}_R^2$	$+\dfrac{\bar{E}_R\bar{E}_s\epsilon^{-j\theta}}{\hat{Z}}$
Equivalent T	$P_s + jQ_s$	$\dfrac{(1+\hat{Z}_R\hat{Y})\bar{E}_s^2}{\hat{Z}_R+\hat{Z}_s+\hat{Y}\hat{Z}_R\hat{Z}_s}$	$-\dfrac{\bar{E}_R\bar{E}_s\epsilon^{+j\theta}}{\hat{Z}_R+\hat{Z}_s+\hat{Y}\hat{Z}_R\hat{Z}_s}$	$P_R + jQ_R$	$-\dfrac{(1+\hat{Z}_s\hat{Y})\bar{E}_R^2}{\hat{Z}_R+\hat{Z}_s+\hat{Y}\hat{Z}_R\hat{Z}_s}$	$+\dfrac{\bar{E}_R\bar{E}_s\epsilon^{-j\theta}}{\hat{Z}_R+\hat{Z}_s+\hat{Y}\hat{Z}_R\hat{Z}_s}$
Mesh impedance	$P_2 + jQ_2$	$\dfrac{\hat{Z}_{11}\bar{E}_2^2}{\hat{Z}_{11}\hat{Z}_{22}-\hat{Z}_{12}^2}$	$-\dfrac{\hat{Z}_{12}\bar{E}_1\bar{E}_2\epsilon^{+j\theta}}{\hat{Z}_{11}\hat{Z}_{22}-\hat{Z}_{12}^2}$	$P_1 + jQ_1$	$\dfrac{\hat{Z}_{22}\bar{E}_1^2}{\hat{Z}_{11}\hat{Z}_{22}-\hat{Z}_{12}^2}$	$-\dfrac{\hat{Z}_{12}\bar{E}_1\bar{E}_2\epsilon^{-j\theta}}{\hat{Z}_{11}\hat{Z}_{22}-\hat{Z}_{12}^2}$

* For P and Q in megawatts and megavolt amperes, use E_s and E_R in kilovolts line-to-line.
† Bar over E_s and E_R indicates scalar values; ^ over constants indicates conjugates.

Multistation systems can be treated as two-station systems when there is a single path for power flow. For example, suppose circle diagrams are to be constructed for interconnected stations A, B, and C. First consider stations A and B as a two-station system with power flow to or from C remaining constant. Then, with known conditions at B, treat B to C as a two-station system.

Steady-state Stability. Steady-state stability limit is defined as the maximum power flow possible through some point in the system when the entire system or the part of the system to which the stability limit refers is operating with stability. For a simple two-machine system, neglecting losses, the steady-state limit is reached when

$$P = \bar{E}_g \bar{E}_m / X \qquad \text{watts} \qquad (7\text{-}47)$$

where P = three-phase power, watts

E_g = line-to-line internal volts of generator

E_m = line-to-line internal volts of motor

X = reactance between generator and motor internal voltages, ohms/phase

A single generator connected to an infinite bus has a per-unit pull-out torque (POT) (assuming constant speed) of

$$\text{POT} = E_i E_s / (X_g + X_s) \qquad \text{per unit} \qquad (7\text{-}48)$$

where E_i = internal voltage of generator, volts

E_t = generator terminal voltage, volts

E_s = infinite system voltage per unit

X_g = per-unit generator reactance

X_s = per-unit infinite system reactance

Pull-out torque of single machine and infinite bus by the *air-gap voltage method* is given by

$$\text{POT} = E_{ag} E_s / (X_d + X_s) \qquad \text{per unit} \qquad (7\text{-}49)$$

where E_{ag} = per-unit air-gap voltage of generator

X_d = per-unit synchronous reactance of generator

Pull-out torque by *synchronous-reactance method*

$$\text{POT} = E_d E_s / (X_d + X_s) \qquad \text{per unit} \qquad (7\text{-}50)$$

where E_d is the p-u voltage behind synchronous reactance, $E_d = E_t + I X_d$.

Short-circuit ratio (SCR) is the ratio of field current required to produce rated voltage on the no-load saturation curve to the field current required to produce rated armature current with a three-phase short circuit at the generator terminals.

$$\text{POT} = E_i E_s / (1/\text{SCR} + X_s) \qquad \text{per unit} \qquad (7\text{-}51)$$

where $E_i = E_t + I(1/\text{SCR})$ \qquad per unit

Table 7-6. Reactance Constants of Synchronous Machines, Typical Normal Values, Per Cent

Type of machine	Synchronous* direct axis X_d	Transient† X'_d	Subtransient‡ X''_d	Negative-¶ sequence X_2
Turbogenerator:				
3,600 rpm.............	110	15	9	9
1,800 rpm.............	110	23	15	15
Salient-pole generator:				
With dampers.........	115	37	24	24
Without dampers.......	115	35	32	55
Synchronous condenser....	180	40	25	24

* Unsaturated-current values.
† Rated-current values, use stability calculations.
‡ Short-circuit-current values, use three-phase and unbalanced-fault calculations.
¶ Short-circuit-current values, use unbalanced-fault calculations.

Transient Stability. Transient stability limit refers to the maximum power that can be transmitted over a given system during a system disturbance and maintain synchronism.

The *natural frequency* of synchronous machines connected to an infinite bus and shaft-connected to reciprocating machinery is given by

$$f_n = (35,200/n) \sqrt{P_r f/WR^2} \quad \text{cpm} \tag{7-52}$$

where f_n = natural frequency, cycles/min
n = speed of machine, rpm
P_r = synchronizing power = shaft power in kilowatts divided by angular displacement of rotor in electrical radians, kw/δ
f = frequency of circuit, cps
WR^2 = moment of inertia of synchronous machine and shaft-connected prime mover or load, lb-ft²

$$\delta = \tan^{-1} (IX_q \cos \phi/E_t + \bar{I}X_q \sin \phi) \quad \text{radians} \tag{7-53}$$

where δ = rotor displacement angle, electrical radians
$\bar{I}$ = per-unit armature current
E_t = per-unit armature terminal voltage
ϕ = power-factor angle
X_q = per-unit quadrature-axis synchronous reactance

Inertia constant of synchronous machines is given by

$$H = \text{kw-sec/kva} = 0.231(WR^2 \text{ rpm}^2 \times 10^{-6})/\text{kva} \tag{7-54}$$

where WR^2 = moment of inertia, lb-ft²
rpm = speed in revolutions per minute

The *equivalent inertia constant* for reducing a two-machine system to a single machine and an infinite bus is

$$H_{eq\,a} = H_a/(1 + H_a \text{ kva}_a/H_b \text{ kva}_b) \tag{7-55}$$

where H_a = inertia constant of machine a

H_b = inertia constant of machine b

kva$_a$ = capacity machine a, kva

kva$_b$ = capacity machine b, kva

$H_{eq\,a}$ = equivalent inertia constant for machine a

The *acceleration of a synchronous generator* when subjected to an accelerating or decelerating power ΔP is given by

$$\alpha = 180f \,\Delta P/H \text{ kva} \qquad \text{deg/sec}^2 \qquad (7\text{-}56)$$

where α = acceleration or deceleration, electrical deg/sec^2

f = system frequency, cps

ΔP = accelerating or decelerating power, kw

Symmetrical Components. Vector a is of unit length and is oriented 120° in a positive (counterclockwise) direction from the reference direction. A vector operated upon by a is not changed in magnitude, but simply rotated 120° in the positive direction.

Properties of the vector operator a

$1 + j0 = \epsilon^{j0}$

$a = -\frac{1}{2} + j\,\frac{1}{2}\sqrt{3} = \epsilon^{j120}$

$a^2 = -\frac{1}{2} - j\,\frac{1}{2}\sqrt{3} = \epsilon^{j240}$

$a^3 = 1 + j0 = \epsilon^{j0}$

$a^4 = a \qquad a^5 = a^2$

$1 + a + a^2 = 0$

$a + a^2 = -1 = \epsilon^{j180}$

$a - a^2 = j\sqrt{3} = \sqrt{3}\,\epsilon^{j90}$

$a^2 - a = -j\sqrt{3} = \sqrt{3}\,\epsilon^{j270}$

$1 - a = \frac{3}{2} - j\,\frac{1}{2}\sqrt{3} = \sqrt{3}\,\epsilon^{j330}$

$1 - a^2 = \frac{3}{2} + j\,\frac{1}{2}\sqrt{3} = \sqrt{3}\,\epsilon^{j30}$

$a - 1 = -\frac{3}{2} + j\,\frac{1}{2}\sqrt{3} = \sqrt{3}\,\epsilon^{j150}$

$a^2 - 1 = -\frac{3}{2} - j\,\frac{1}{2}\sqrt{3} = \sqrt{3}\,\epsilon^{j210}$

$1 + a = \frac{1}{2} + j\,\frac{1}{2}\sqrt{3} = \epsilon^{j60}$

$1 + a^2 = \frac{1}{2} - j\,\frac{1}{2}\sqrt{3} = \epsilon^{j300}$

$(1 + a)(1 + a)^2 = 1 = \epsilon^{j0}$

$(1 - a)(1 - a^2) = 3 = 3\epsilon^{j0}$

$(1 + a)/(1 + a^2) = a = \epsilon^{j120}$

$(1 - a)/(1 - a^2) = -a = \epsilon^{j300}$

$(1 + a)^2 = a = \epsilon^{j120}$

$(1 + a^2)^2 = a^2 = \epsilon^{j240}$

Resolution of *three unbalanced vectors* into balanced symmetrical components, zero, positive, and negative sequence, can be done as follows:

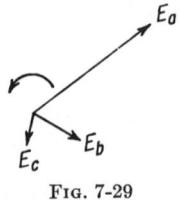

Fig. 7-29

$E_0 = \frac{1}{3}(E_a + E_b + E_c)$ zero sequence, volts

$E_1 = \frac{1}{3}(E_a + aE_b + a^2E_c)$ positive sequence, volts

$E_2 = \frac{1}{3}(E_a + a^2E_b + aE_c)$ negative sequence, volts

This resolution applies to both voltages and currents in three-phase systems.

The unbalanced vectors can be expressed as functions of the balanced

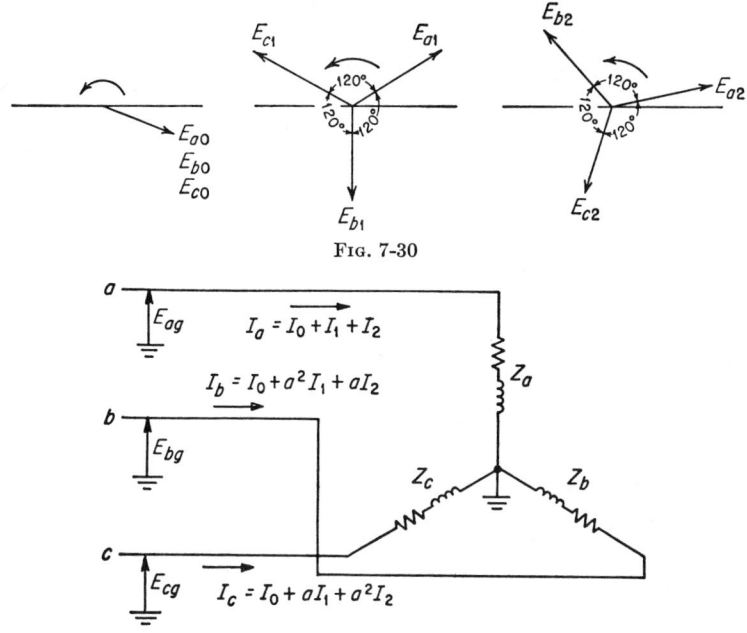

FIG. 7-30

FIG. 7-31

components

$$E_a = E_{a0} + E_{a1} + E_{a2} = E_0 + E_1 + E_2 \qquad \text{volts}$$
$$E_b = E_{b0} + E_{b1} + E_{b2} = E_0 + a^2E_1 + aE_2 \qquad \text{volts}$$
$$E_c = E_{c0} + E_{c1} + E_{c2} = E_0 + aE_1 + a^2E_2 \qquad \text{volts}$$

Unbalanced impedances as shown in Fig. 7-31 can also be broken into symmetrical components.

$$Z_0 = \tfrac{1}{3}(Z_a + Z_b + Z_c) \quad \text{ohms} \quad E_0 = I_0Z_0 + I_1Z_2 + I_2Z_1 \quad \text{volts}$$
$$Z_1 = \tfrac{1}{3}(Z_a + aZ_b + a^2Z_c) \quad \text{ohms} \quad E_1 = I_0Z_1 + I_1Z_0 + I_2Z_2 \quad \text{volts}$$
$$Z_2 = \tfrac{1}{3}(Z_a + a^2Z_b + aZ_c) \quad \text{ohms} \quad E_2 = I_0Z_2 + I_1Z_1 + I_2Z_0 \quad \text{volts}$$

If $Z_a = Z_b = Z_c$, then $Z_1 = Z_2 = 0$ and $Z_0 = Z_a$, so that

$$E_0 = I_0Z_0 \qquad E_1 = I_1Z_0 \qquad E_2 = I_2Z_0 \qquad \text{volts}$$

Mutual impedances between phases (Fig. 7-32) can also be resolved into symmetrical components.

$$Z_{m0} = \tfrac{1}{3}(Z_{mbc} + Z_{mca} + Z_{mab}) \qquad \text{ohms}$$
$$Z_{m1} = \tfrac{1}{3}(Z_{mbc} + aZ_{mca} + a^2Z_{mab}) \qquad \text{ohms}$$
$$Z_{m2} = \tfrac{1}{3}(Z_{mbc} + a^2Z_{mca} + aZ_{mab}) \qquad \text{ohms}$$

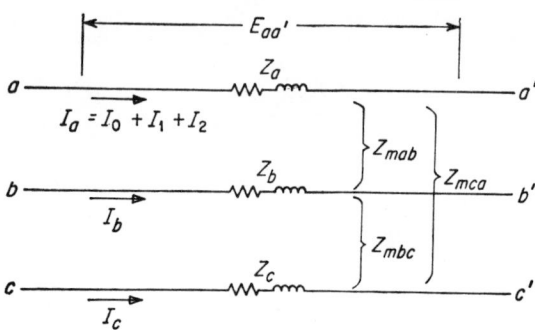

FIG. 7-32

The associated voltage drops are

$$E_0 = \tfrac{1}{3}(E_{aa'} + E_{bb'} + E_{cc'}) \qquad \text{volts}$$
$$= I_0(Z_0 + 2Z_{m0}) + I_1(Z_2 - Z_{m2}) + I_2(Z_1 - Z_{m1}) \qquad \text{volts}$$
$$E_1 = \tfrac{1}{3}(E_{aa'} + aE_{bb'} + a^2E_{cc'}) \qquad \text{volts}$$
$$= I_0(Z_1 - Z_{m1}) + I_1(Z_0 - Z_{m0}) + I_2(Z_2 + 2Z_{m2}) \qquad \text{volts}$$
$$E_2 = \tfrac{1}{3}(E_{aa'} + a^2E_{bb'} + aE_{cc'}) \qquad \text{volts}$$
$$= I_0(Z_2 - Z_{m2}) + I_1(Z_1 + 2Z_{m1}) + I_2(Z_0 - Z_{m0}) \qquad \text{volts}$$

For symmetrical impedance values

$$E_0 = I_0(Z_0 + 2Z_{m0}) = I_0Z_0 \qquad \text{volts}$$
$$E_1 = I_1(Z_0 - Z_{m0}) = I_1Z_1 \qquad \text{volts}$$
$$E_2 = I_2(Z_0 - Z_{m0}) = I_2Z_2 \qquad \text{volts}$$

Three-phase-power expressed in terms of symmetrical components:

$$P = 3(E_0I_0 \cos \theta_0 + E_1I_1 \cos \theta_1 + E_2I_2 \cos \theta_2) \qquad \text{watts} \qquad (7\text{-}57)$$

where θ_0, θ_1, and θ_2 are the angles between E_0 and I_0, E_1 and I_1, and E_2 and I_2 respectively.

Sequence Networks. Sequence networks used for solving fault problems on three-phase systems consist of positive-, negative-, and zero-sequence networks each set up as viewed from the point of fault. The values of positive-, negative-, and zero-sequence impedance to be inserted in each network can be obtained by passing unit current of that sequence through the original three-phase network and calculating or measuring the corresponding voltage drop. In all cases positive current direction must be the same in each sequence network. In many cases complex circuits are lumped to a single equivalent generator and impedance. All quantities are in volts, amperes, and ohms, or all are in per unit.

Three-phase short-circuit sequence network connections (Fig. 7-33)

$$I_{1F} = I_F = E_{a1}/Z_1$$

where $Z_1 = jX_1$ if system resistance is neglected

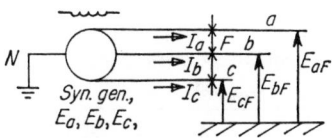

(*a*) Equivalent system for three-phase short circuit

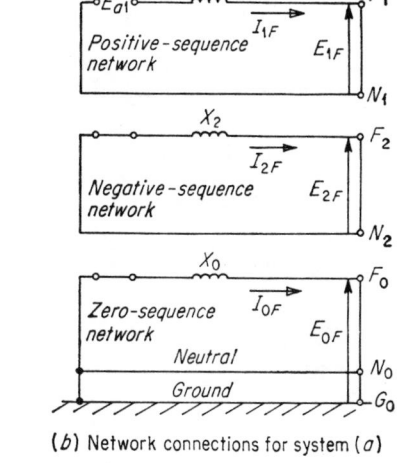

(*b*) Network connections for system (*a*)

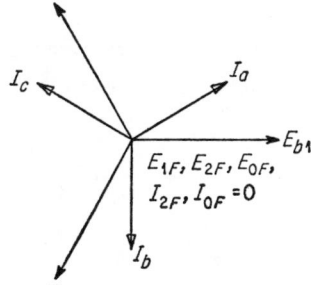

(*c*) Vector diagram for system (*a*)

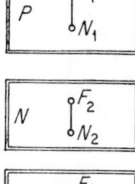

(*d*) Condensed representation of (*b*)

Fig. 7-33

Single-line-to-ground fault on ungrounded generator (Fig. 7-34)

$$I_F = I_{1F} = I_{2F} = I_{0F} = 0$$

$$E_{aF} = 0 \qquad E_{bF} = \sqrt{3}\, E_{b1}\epsilon^{-j30} \qquad E_{cF} = \sqrt{3}\, E_{c1}\epsilon^{j30}$$

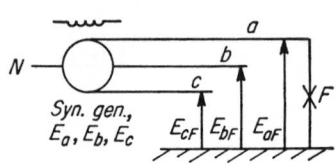

(*a*) Equivalent system for
single-to-ground fault
ungrounded system

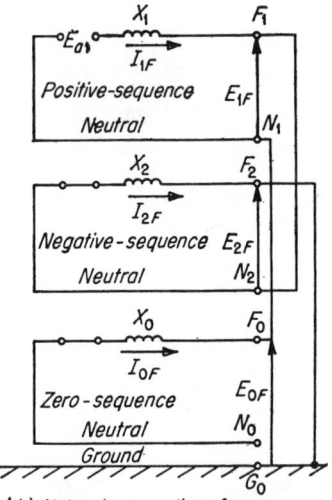

(*b*) Network connections for
system (*a*)

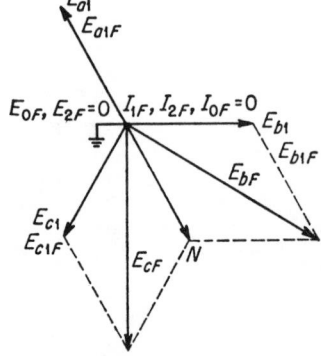

(*c*) Vector diagram for system (*a*)

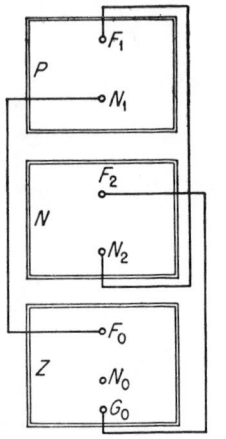

(*d*) Condensed representation
of (*b*)

FIG. 7-34

Single-line-to-ground fault on generator grounded through a neutral reactor (Fig. 7-35)

$$I_{1F} = I_{2F} = I_{0F} = E_{a1}/(Z_1 + Z_2 + Z_0 + j3X_N)$$
$$I_F = I_{1F} + I_{2F} + I_{0F} = 3I_{0F}$$
$$E_{1F} = E_{a1}(Z_2 + Z_0 + j3X_N)/(Z_1 + Z_2 + Z_0 + j3X_N)$$
$$E_{2F} = -E_{a1}Z_2/(Z_1 + Z_2 + Z_0 + j3X_N)$$
$$E_{0F} = -E_{a1}(Z_0 + j3X_N)/(Z_1 + Z_2 + Z_0 + j3X_N)$$

where $Z_1 = jX_1$, $Z_2 = jX_2$, and $Z_0 = jX_0$ if system resistance is neglected.

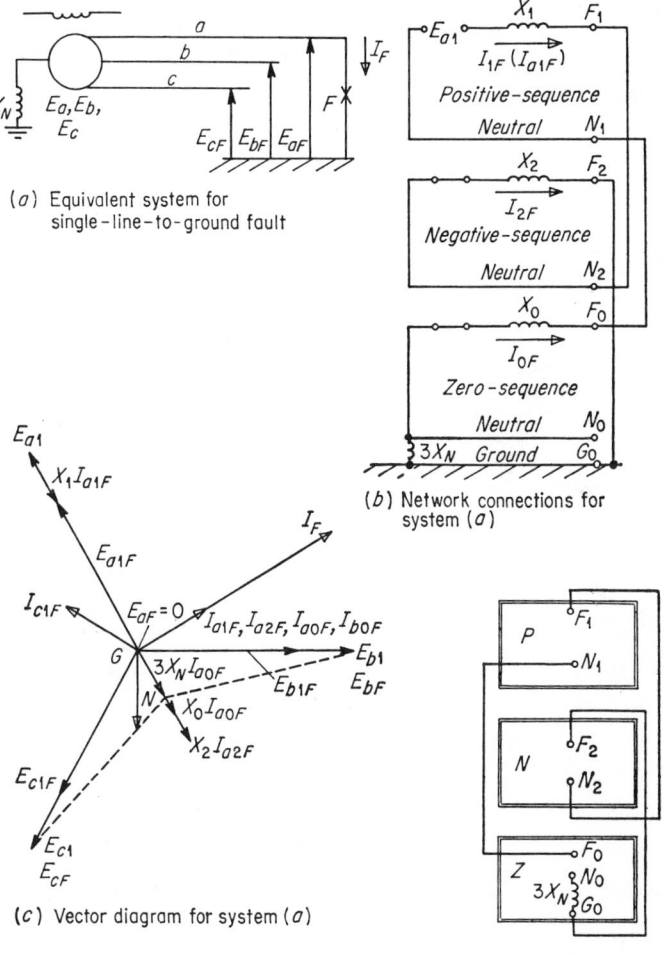

(a) Equivalent system for
single-line-to-ground fault

(b) Network connections for
system (a)

(c) Vector diagram for system (a)

(d) Condensed representation of (b)

FIG. 7-35

Line-to-line fault on grounded or ungrounded generator (Fig. 7-36)

$$I_{1F} = -I_{2F} = E_{a1}/(Z_1 + Z_2)$$
$$I_F = \sqrt{3}\, I_{1F} \qquad E_{1F} = E_{2F} = E_{a1}Z_2/(Z_1 + Z_2)$$

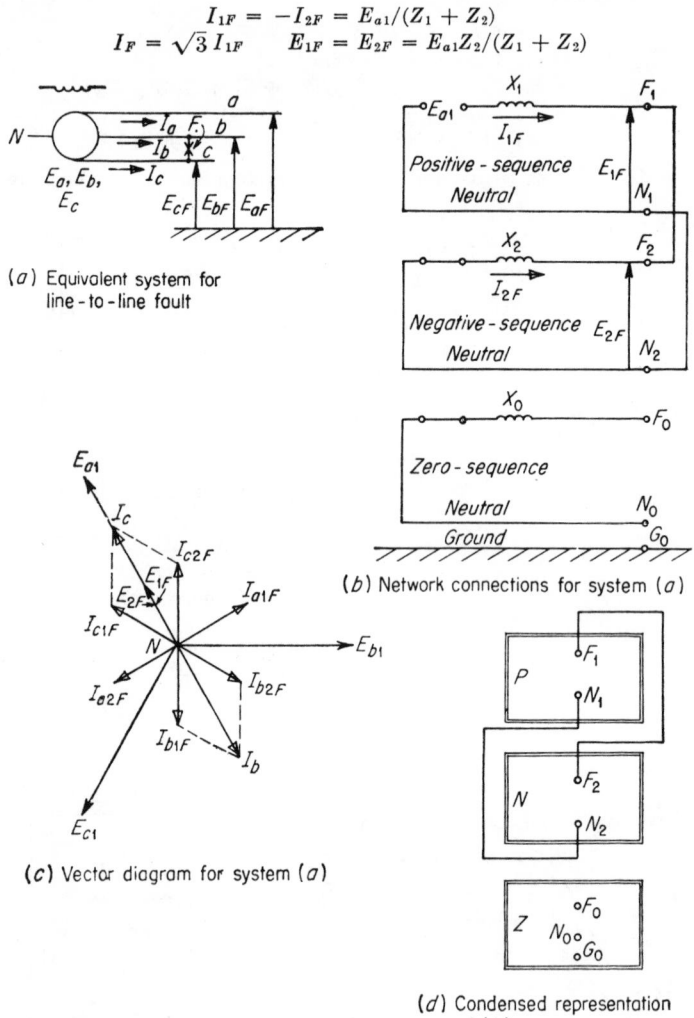

(*a*) Equivalent system for line-to-line fault

(*b*) Network connections for system (*a*)

(*c*) Vector diagram for system (*a*)

(*d*) Condensed representation of (*b*)

Fig. 7-36

Double-line-to-ground fault on generator grounded through a neutral reactor (Fig. 7-37)

$$I_F = I_{1F} + I_{2F} + I_{0F}$$
$$I_{1F} = E_{a1}(Z_2 + Z_0 + j3X_N)/[Z_1Z_2 + Z_1(Z_0 + j3X_N) + Z_2(Z_0 + j3X_N)]$$
$$I_{2F} = -(Z_0 + j3X_N)E_{a1}/[Z_1Z_2 + Z_1(Z_0 + j3X_N) + Z_2(Z_0 + j3X_N)]$$
$$I_{0F} = -Z_2E_{a1}/[Z_1Z_2 + Z_1(Z_0 + j3X_N) + Z_2(Z_0 + j3X_N)]$$
$$E_{1F} = E_{2F} = E_{0F} = \frac{Z_2(Z_0 + j3X_N)E_{a1}}{[Z_1Z_2 + Z_1(Z_0 + j3X_N) + Z_2(Z_0 + j3X_N)]}$$

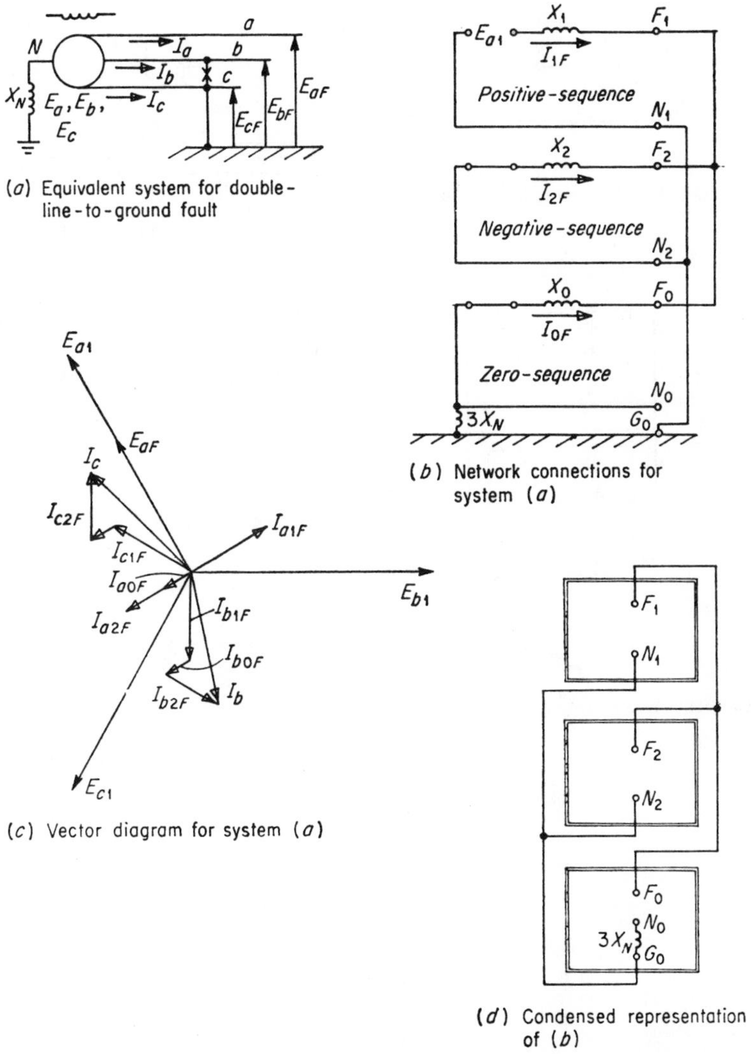

(a) Equivalent system for double-line-to-ground fault

(b) Network connections for system (a)

(c) Vector diagram for system (a)

(d) Condensed representation of (b)

Fig. 7-37

One line open (Fig. 7-38)

$$I_{1F} = E_{a1}(Z_2 + Z_0)/(Z_1Z_2 + Z_1Z_0 + Z_2Z_0)$$
$$I_{2F} = -Z_0E_{a1}/(Z_1Z_2 + Z_1Z_0 + Z_2Z_0)$$
$$I_{0F} = -Z_2E_{a1}/(Z_1Z_2 + Z_1Z_0 + Z_2Z_0)$$

$$E_{1x} - E_{1y} = E_{2x} - E_{2y} = E_{0x} - E_{0y} = \frac{Z_2Z_0E_{a1}}{Z_1Z_2 + Z_1Z_0 + Z_2Z_0}$$

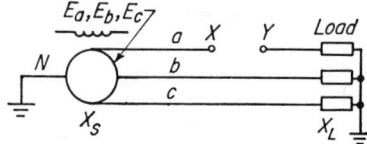

(*a*) Equivalent system for one line open

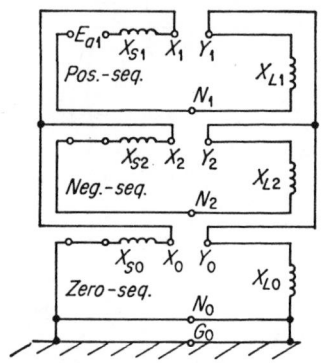

(*b*) Network connections for system (*a*)

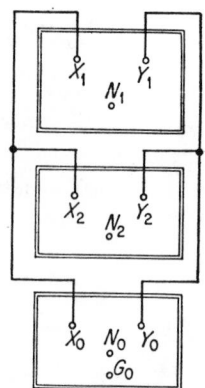

(*c*) Condensed representation of (*b*)

Fɪɢ. 7-38

Two lines open (Fig. 7-39)

$$I_{1F} = I_{2F} = I_{0F} = E_{a1}/(Z_1 + Z_2 + Z_0)$$
$$I_F = I_a = 3I_{0F}$$
$$E_{1x} - E_{1y} = E_{a1}(Z_2 + Z_0)/(Z_1 + Z_2 + Z_0)$$
$$E_{2x} - E_{2y} = -E_{a1}Z_2/(Z_1 + Z_2 + Z_0)$$
$$E_{0x} - E_{0y} = -E_{a1}Z_0/(Z_1 + Z_2 + Z_0)$$

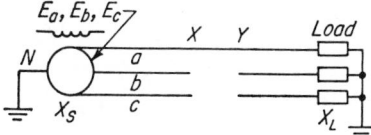

(*a*) Equivalent system for two lines open

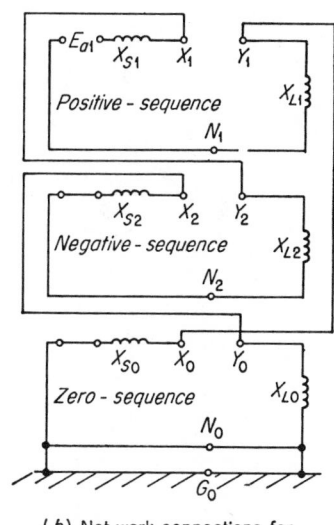

(*b*) Net work connections for system (*a*)

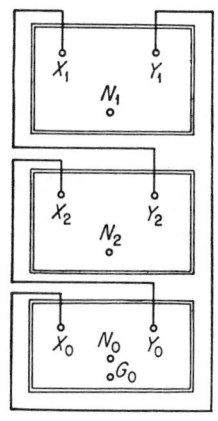

(*c*) Condensed representation of (*b*)

Fig. 7-39

Impedance in one line (Fig. 7-40)

$$I_{1F} = E_{a1}(ZZ_0 + ZZ_2 + 3Z_0Z_2)/(ZZ_1Z_0 + ZZ_1Z_2 + 3Z_1Z_2Z_0 + ZZ_2Z_0)$$
$$I_{2F} = -E_{a1}ZZ_0/(ZZ_1Z_0 + ZZ_1Z_2 + 3Z_1Z_2Z_0 + ZZ_2Z_0)$$
$$I_{0F} = -E_{a1}ZZ_2/(ZZ_1Z_0 + ZZ_1Z_2 + 3Z_1Z_2Z_0 + ZZ_2Z_0)$$

$$E_{1x} - E_{1y} = E_{2x} - E_{2y} = E_{0x} - E_{0y}$$

$$= \frac{E_{a1}ZZ_2Z_0}{ZZ_1Z_0 + ZZ_1Z_2 + 3Z_1Z_2Z_0 + ZZ_2Z_0}$$

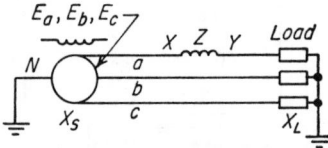

(*a*) Equivalent system for impedance in one line

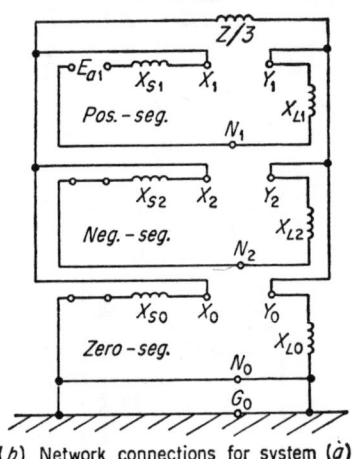

(*b*) Network connections for system (*a*)

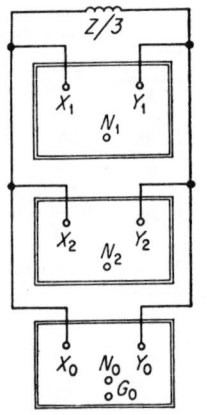

(*c*) Condensed representation of (*b*)

Fig. 7-40

Table 7-7. Transformer Impedances, Typical Normal Values, Per Cent Full-load KVA Base

Voltage class, kv	Single-phase kva rating					
	3	10	25	50	100	500
2.5	2.2	2.2	2.5	2.4	3.3	4.8
15	2.8	2.4	2.3	2.5	3.2	5.0
25	...	5.2	5.2	5.2	5.2	5.2
69	...	...	...	6.5	6.5	6.5
138						
161						
230						

Voltage class, kv	Single-phase kva rating				
	1,000	5,000	10,000	25,000	50,000
2.5					
15	4.5–8.0	4.5–8	4.5–8.0		
25	5.5–9.0	5.5–9	5.5–9.0	5.5–9.0	
69	7.0–11	7.0–11	7.0–11	7.0–11	
138	8.5–17	8.5–17	8.5–17	8.5–17	8.5–17
161	....	9.5–18	9.5–18	9.5–18	9.5–18
230	....	......	11–20	11–20	11–20

Positive- and negative-sequence impedances of three-phase transmission lines can be obtained from Tables 7-8 through 7-11

$$x_1 = x_2 = x_a + x_d \text{ ohms/(phase)(mile)}$$

where x_d = one-third of sum of x_d's from tables for three spacings between line conductors

Zero-sequence impedance of aerial lines is dependent upon a number of factors including the type of grounding, circuit configuration, and the number and type of ground wires. The fundamental equations are quite involved, but can be simplified by defining

$$r_e = 0.00477f \text{ ohms/(phase)(mile)}$$
$$x_e = 0.006985f \log 4.6655 \times 10^6 \rho/f \text{ ohms/(phase)(mile)}$$

where f = frequency, cps
ρ = earth resistivity, ohms/m³

Single three-phase circuit with earth return but without ground wires, zero-sequence impedance

$$z_0 = r_a + r_e + j(x_e + x_a - 2x_d) \qquad \text{ohms/(phase)(mile)}$$

where r_a, r_e, x_e, and x_a are obtained directly from the conductor tables and

$$x_d = \tfrac{1}{3}(x_{d(ab)} + x_{d(bc)} + x_{d(ca)}) \qquad \text{ohms/(phase)(mile)}$$

where $x_{d(ab)} = x_d$ from tables for conductor spacing a to b etc.

Mutual zero-sequence impedance between two three-phase circuits with earth return but without ground wires

$$z_{0(m)} = r_e + j(x_e - 3x_d) \qquad \text{ohms/(phase)(mile)}$$

where $x_d = \tfrac{1}{9}(x_{d(aa')} + x_{d(ab')} + x_{d(ac')} + x_{d(ba')} + x_{d(bb')} + x_{d(bc')}$
$$+ x_{d(ca')} + x_{d(cb')} + x_{d(cc')})$$

$x_{d(aa')} = x_d$ from tables for conductor spacing of a to a', etc.

Single three-phase circuit with ground wire and earth return, zero-sequence impedance

$$z_{0(g)} = 3r_a + r_e + j(x_e + 3x_a) \qquad \text{ohms/(phase)(mile)}$$

Single three-phase circuit with two ground wires and earth return, zero-sequence impedance

$$z_{0(g)} = \tfrac{3}{2}r_a + r_e + j(x_e + \tfrac{3}{2}x_a - \tfrac{3}{2}x_d)$$

where $x_d = x_d$ from table for spacing between ground wires.

Zero-sequence impedance of a three-phase circuit with n ground wires and earth return

$$z_{0(g)} = \frac{3}{n}\,r_a + r_e + j\left[x_e + \frac{3x_a}{n} - \frac{3(n-1)}{n}\,x_d\right] \qquad \text{ohms/(phase)(mile)}$$

where $x_d = (1/n)(n-1)$ (sum of x_d's for all possible distances between all ground wires).

Zero-sequence mutual impedance between one circuit with earth return and n ground wires with earth return

$$z_{0(m)} = r_e + j(x_e - 3x_d) \qquad \text{ohms/(phase)(mile)}$$

where $x_d = (1/3n)(x_{d(ag1)} + x_{d(bg1)} + x_{d(cg1)} + \cdots + x_{d(agn)}$
$$+ x_{d(bgn)} + x_{d(cgn)})$$

Zero-sequence impedance, one three-phase circuit with n ground wires and earth return

$$z_0 = z_{0(a)} - z_0{}^2{}_{(ag)}/z_{0(g)}$$

where $z_{0(a)}$ = zero-sequence impedance of three-phase circuit

$z_{0(g)}$ = zero-sequence impedance of n ground wires

$z_{0(ag)}$ = zero-sequence mutual impedance between three-phase circuit as one group of conductors and ground wires as other conductor group

Shunt capacitive reactance of three-phase circuits can be obtained from Tables 7-8 through 7-11 for positive and negative sequence where

$$x'_1 = x'_2 = x'_a + x'_d \qquad \text{megohms/(phase)(mile)}$$

Divide by number of miles of line to get total reactance.

$x'_d = \frac{1}{3} \times$ sum of x_d's for three distances between line conductors
$$= \frac{1}{3}(x'_{d(ab)} + x'_{d(ac)} + x'_{d(bc)})$$

Zero-sequence shunt capacitive reactance of a single three-phase circuit and earth

$$x'_{0(a)} = x'_a + x'_e - 2x'_d \qquad \text{megohms/(conductor)(mile)}$$

Divide by number of miles of line to get total reactance.

Zero-sequence shunt capacitive reactance of one ground wire and earth

$$x'_{0(g)} = 3x'_{a(g)} + x'_{e(g)} \qquad \text{megohms/(conductor)(mile)}$$
$$x'_e = \frac{12.30}{f} \log 2h \qquad \text{megohms/(conductor)(mile)}$$

where f = frequency, cps
h = height above ground, ft

Zero-sequence capacitive reactance of *two* ground wires and earth

$$x'_{0(g)} = \frac{3}{2}x'_{a(g)} + x'_{e(g)} - \frac{3}{2}x'_d \qquad \text{megohms/(conductor)(mile)}$$

where $x'_d = x'_d$ for distance between ground wires

Zero-sequence capacitive reactonce of n ground wires and earth

$$x'_{0(g)} = x'_e + (3/n)x'_a - [3(n-1)/n]x'_d \qquad \text{megohms/(conductor)(mile)}$$

where $x'_d = \dfrac{2}{n(n-1)}$ sum of all x'_d's for all possible distances between all possible *pairs* of ground wires

or $x'_d = \dfrac{1}{n(n-1)}$ sum of all x'_d's for all possible distances between *all* ground wires

Zero-sequence capacitive reactance between one circuit and earth and n ground wires and earth

$$x'_{0(ag)} = x'_e - 3x'_d \qquad \text{megohms/(conductor)(mile)}$$
$$x'_d = (1/3n)(x'_{d(ag1)} + x'_{d(bg1)} + x'_{d(cg1)} + \cdots + x'_{d(agn)} + x'_{d(bgn)} + x'_{d(cgn)})$$

Zero-sequence capacitive reactance of one circuit with n ground wires

$$x'_0 = x'_{0(a)} - x'_{0(ag)}{}^2/x'_{0(g)} \qquad \text{megohms/(conductor)(mile)}$$

Shunt capacitive reactance of single-phase circuit with identical conductors a and b

$$x' = 2(x'_a + x'_d) \qquad \text{megohms/(mile)(\textit{circuit})}$$
$$x'_d = x'_d \qquad \text{for spacing } a \text{ to } b$$

when a and b conductors are not identical

$$x' = x'_{a(a)} + x'_{a(b)} + 2x'_d \qquad \text{megohms/(mile)}(circuit)$$

Shunt capacitive reactance of one conductor and earth

$$x' = x'_a + \tfrac{1}{3}x'_e \qquad \text{megohms/mile}$$

Table 7-8. Characteristics of Copper Conductors
Hard-drawn, 97.3 Per Cent Conductivity

Conductor size		OD, in.	Wt, lb/mile	Capacity,* amp	x'_a†	r_a‡	x_a¶
Cir mils	Awg or B.&S.						
1,000,000	...	1.152	16,300	1,300	0.0901	0.0685	0.400
900,000	...	1.092	14,670	1,220	.0916	0.0752	.406
800,000	...	1.029	13,040	1,130	.0934	0.0837	.413
750,000	...	0.997	12,230	1,090	.0943	0.0888	.417
700,000	...	.963	11,410	1,040	.0954	0.0947	.422
600,000	...	.891	9,781	940	.0977	0.109	.432
500,000	...	.814	8,151	840	.1004	0.130	.443
450,000	...	.770	7,336	780	.1020	0.144	.451
400,000	...	.726	6,521	730	.1038	0.162	.458
350,000	...	.679	5,706	670	.1058	0.184	.466
300,000	...	.629	4,891	610	.1080	0.215	.476
250,000	...	.574	4,076	540	.1108	0.257	.487
211,600	4/0	.522	3,450	480	.1136	0.303	.503
167,800	3/0	.464	2,736	420	.1171	0.382	.518
133,100	2/0	.414	2,170	360	.1205	0.481	.532
105,500	1/0	.368	1,720	310	.1240	0.607	.546
83,690	1	.328	1,364	270	.1274	0.765	.560
66,370	2	.320	1,071	240	.1281	0.955	.571
52,630	3	.285	850	200	.1315	1.20	.585
41,740	4	.254	674	180	.1349	1.52	.599
33,100	5	.226	534	150	.1384	1.91	.613
26,250	6	.162	420	120	.1483	2.39	.637
20,800	7	.144	333	110	.1517	3.01	.651
16,510	8	.129	264	90	.1552	3.80	.665

* Approximate current-carrying capacity for conductor at 75°C, air at 25°C, wind 1.4 mph (2 fps), 60 cycles.
† x'_a = shunt capacitive reactance at 1 ft, megohms/mile.
‡ r_a = resistance at 50°C, 60 cycles, ohms/(conductor)(mile).
¶ x_a = reactance at 1-ft spacing, 60 cycles, ohms/(conductor)(mile).

Table 7-9. Characteristics of Copperweld and Copperweld-Copper Conductors

Conductor	Cu equiv, cir mils or awg	OD, in.	Wt, lb/mile	Capacity, amp*	x'_a†	r_a‡	x_a¶
			Copperweld-Copper				
350 E	350,000	0.788	7,409	660	0.1012	0.204	0.456
250 E	250,000	.666	5,292	540	.1064	0.278	.476
4/0 E	4/0	.613	4,479	490	.1088	0.326	.486
3/0 E	3/0	.545	3,552	420	.1123	0.406	.501
350 EK	350,000	.735	6,536	680	.1034	0.188	.452
250 EK	250,000	.621	4,669	540	.1084	0.261	.472
4/0 EK	4/0	.571	3,951	490	.1109	0.308	.483
4/0 S	4/0	.633	4,210	490	.1079	0.330	.477
2/0 S	2/0	.502	2,658	360	.1148	0.513	.506
250 V	250,000	.637	4,699	530	.1077	0.278	.480
4/0 V	4/0	.586	3,977	480	.1101	0.325	.490
2/0 V	2/0	.465	2,502	360	.1170	0.505	.518
4/0 F	4/0	.550	3,750	470	.1120	0.320	.505
1/0 F	1/0	.388	1,870	310	.1224	0.627	.547
1 F	1	.346	1,483	270	.1258	0.785	.561
2 F	2	.308	1,176	230	.1293	0.985	.575
2 A	2	.366	1,356	240	.1241	0.978	.591
4 A	4	.290	853	180	.1310	1.544	.620
6 A	6	.230	536	140	.1379	2.44	.648
8 A	8	.199	392	100	.1422	3.87	.666
8 C	8	.179	320	100	.1460	3.87	.678
9½ D	9½	.174	298	85	.1462	5.43	.709
			Copperweld, 30 per cent Conductivity				
19 no. 9	76,000	.572	3,696	370	.1109	0.792	.637
7 no. 4	89,300	.613	4,324	410	.1088	0.672	.629
7 no. 5	70,800	.546	3,429	350	.1122	0.848	.643
7 no. 6	56,100	.486	2,719	300	.1157	1.069	.657
7 no. 7	44,500	.433	2,157	260	.1191	1.348	.671
7 no. 8	35,300	.385	1,710	230	.1226	1.699	.685
7 no. 9	28,000	.343	1,356	200	.1260	2.14	.699
7 no. 10	22,200	.306	1,076	170	.1294	2.70	.713
3 no. 5	30,350	.392	1,467	220	.1221	1.963	.683
3 no. 6	24,100	.349	1,163	190	.1255	2.47	.697
3 no. 7	19,100	.311	922	160	.1289	3.12	.711
3 no. 8	15,150	.277	732	140	.1324	3.93	.725
3 no. 9	12,010	.247	580	120	.1358	4.96	.739
3 no. 10	9,528	.220	460	100	.1392	6.26	.753

* Approximate current-carrying capacity; copperweld at 125°C, copperweld-copper at 75°C, air at 25°C, wind 1.4 mph (2 fps), 60 cycles.
† Shunt capacitive reactance at 1 ft, megohms/mile.
‡ Resistance of copperweld conductors at 25°C, copperweld-copper at 50°C, ohms/(conductor)(mile) at 60 cycles.
¶ Reactance at 1-ft spacing, 60 cycles, ohms/(conductor)(mile).

Table 7-10. Characteristics of Aluminum Cable, Steel-reinforced

Conductor Size, cir mils or Awg	Cu equiv, cir mils or Awg*	OD, in	Wt, lb/mile	Capacity amp†	x'_a‡	r_a§	x_a¶
1,590,000	1000,000	1.545	10,777	1,380	0.0814	0.0684	0.359
1,510,000	950,000	1.506	10,237	1,340	.0821	0.0720	.362
1,431,000	900,000	1.465	9,699	1,300	.0830	0.0760	.365
1,351,000	850,000	1.424	9,160	1,250	.0838	0.0803	.369
1,272,000	800,000	1.382	8,621	1,200	.0847	0.0851	.372
1,192,500	750,000	1.338	8,082	1,160	.0857	0.0906	.376
1,113,000	700,000	1.293	7,544	1,110	.0867	0.0969	.380
1,033,500	650,000	1.246	7,019	1,060	.0878	0.104	.385
954,000	600,000	1.196	6,479	1,010	.0890	0.113	.390
900,000	566,000	1.162	6,112	970	.0898	0.119	.393
874,500	550,000	1.146	5,940	950	.0903	0.123	.395
795,000	500,000	1.093	5,399	900	.0917	0.138	.401
666,000	419,000	1.000	4,527	800	.0943	0.160	.412
636,000	400,000	0.977	4,319	770	.0950	0.169	.414
605,000	380,500	.953	4,109	750	.0957	0.178	.417
556,500	350,000	.927	4,039	730	.0965	0.186	.420
477,000	300,000	.858	3,462	670	.0988	0.216	.430
397,500	250,000	.783	2,885	590	.1015	0.259	.441
336,400	4/0	.721	2,442	530	.1039	0.306	.451
266,800	3/0	.642	1,936	460	.1074	0.385	.465
4/0	2/0	.563	1,542	340	.1113	0.592	.581
3/0	1/0	.502	1,223	300	.1147	0.723	.621
2/0	1	.447	970	270	.1182	0.895	.641
1/0	2	.398	769	230	.1216	1.12	.656
1	3	.355	610	200	.1250	1.38	.665
2	4	.316	484	180	.1285	1.69	.665
4	6	.250	304	140	.1355	2.57	.659

* Based on copper 97 per cent; aluminum 61 per cent.
† Approximate current-carrying capacity for conductor at 75°C, air at 25°C, wind 1.4 mph (2 fps), 60 cycles.
‡ x'_a = capacitive reactance at 1 ft, megohms/mile.
§ Resistance, ohms/(conductor)(mile) at 50°C, 60 cycles.
¶ Reactance at 1-ft spacing, 60 cycles, ohms/(conductor)(mile).

Table 7-11. Reactance Spacing Factors

x_d, Separation in Feet										
Feet	0	1	2	3	4	5	6	7	8	9
0	.....	0.000	0.084	0.133	0.168	0.195	0.217	0.236	0.252	0.267
10	0.279	.291	.302	.311	.320	.329	.336	.344	.351	.357
20	.364	.369	.375	.380	.386	.391	.395	.400	.404	.409
30	.413	.417	.421	.424	.428	.431	.435	.438	.441	.445

x_d, Separation in Inches*										
In.	0	1	2	3	4	5	6	7	8	9
0	.....	$\overline{.302}$	$\overline{.217}$	$\overline{.169}$	$\overline{.134}$	$\overline{.107}$	$\overline{.085}$	$\overline{.066}$	$\overline{.050}$	$\overline{.035}$
10	$\overline{.023}$	$\overline{.011}$	.000	.010	.019	.027	.035	.042	.049	.056
20	.062	.068	.074	.079	.084	.089	.094	.098	.103	.107
30	.111	.115	.119	.123	.126	.130	.133	.137	.140	.143
40	.146	.149	.152	.155	.158	.160	.163	.166	.168	.171

x'_d, Separation in Feet										
Feet	0	1	2	3	4	5	6	7	8	9
0	......	.0000	.0206	.0326	.0411	.0478	.0532	.0577	.0617	.0652
10	.0683	.0711	.0737	.0761	.0783	.0804	.0823	.0841	.0858	.0874
20	.0889	.0903	.0917	.0930	.0943	.0955	.0967	.0978	.0989	.0999
30	.1010	.1020	.1030	.1040	.1050	.1060	.1060	.1070	.1080	.1090

x'_d, Separation in Inches*										
In.	0	1	2	3	4	5	6	7	8	9
0	......	$\overline{.0737}$	$\overline{.0532}$	$\overline{.0411}$	$\overline{.0326}$	$\overline{.0260}$	$\overline{.0206}$	$\overline{.0160}$	$\overline{.0120}$	$\overline{.009}$
10	$\overline{.0050}$	$\overline{.0030}$	.0000	.0023	.0045	.0066	.0085	.0103	.0120	.0136
20	.0151	.0166	.0180	.0193	.0206	.0218	.0229	.0240	.0251	.0262
30	.0272	.0281	.0291	.0300	.0309	.0317	.0326	.0334	.0342	.0349
40	.0357	.0364	.0371	.0378	.0385	.0392	.0398	.0405	.0411	.0417

Values of x_e									
ρ†	1	5	10	50	100	500	1,000	5,000	10,000
x_e	2.05	2.35	2.47	2.77	2.89	3.19	3.31	3.61	3.73

* Bar over number indicates negative value.
† ρ = earth resistivity, meter-ohms.

Table 7-12. 60-Cycle Three-conductor Belted-paper-insulated Cables

Volt-age class, kv	Insulation thickness, mils		Awg (B.&S.) or MCM*	Approx max current-carrying capacity†	Positive and negative sequence		Zero sequence		
	Con-ductor	Belt			Series reactance, ohms/mile‡	Shunt capacitive reactance, ohms/mile¶	Resistance, ohms/mile§	Series reactance, ohms/mile§	Shunt capacitive reactance, ohms/mile¶
3	70	40	6	68	0.192	6,700	9.67	0.322	12,500
	70	40	4	89	.181	5,800	8.06	.298	11,200
	70	40	2	115	.171	5,100	6.39	.278	9,800
	70	40	0	149	.156	4,400	5.06	.256	8,600
	70	40	00	170	.142	3,500	5.69	.259	6,700
	70	40	000	193	.138	2,700	5.28	.246	5,100
	70	40	0000	218	.135	2,400	4.57	.237	4,600
	70	40	350	288	.129	1,800	3.61	.219	3,700
	70	40	500	348	.126	1,500	2.89	.214	3,000
	75	40	750	427	.123	1,300	2.37	.204	2,500
15	170	85	2	106	.217	8,600	4.20	.323	15,000
	160	75	0	138	.193	7,100	3.62	.288	12,800
	155	75	00	156	.185	6,500	3.25	.280	12,000
	155	75	000	178	.180	6,000	2.99	.272	11,300
	155	75	0000	202	.174	5,600	2.64	.263	10,600
	155	75	250	221	.168	5,300	2.50	.256	10,200
	155	75	350	267	.152	5,100	2.54	.250	7,200
	155	75	500	321	.145	4,600	2.26	.239	6,200
	155	75	600	352	.142	4,300	1.97	.231	5,700
	155	75	750	393	.139	4,000	1.77	.226	5,100

* All cables no. 0 Awg and larger have sector-shaped conductors.
† Three similar, loaded, nonshielded cables in a duct bank assumed; earth temperature 20°C, 100 per cent load factor.
‡ For approximate resistance use r_a of conductors of same Awg or MCM from Table 7-8.
¶ For specific inductive capacity of 3.7.
§ Based upon all return current in the sheath, none in ground.

Table 7-13. Dimensions, Weight, and Resistance of Pure Copper Wire

AWG	Diam, in.	Area, d^2, cir mils	Lb/1,000 ft (bare wire)	Ft length/lb	Resistance, 77°F, ohms/1,000 ft (bare wire)
	1.152	1,000,000	3,088	0.3238	0.0108
	1.031	800,000	2,470	0.4048	0.0135
	0.964	700,000	2,161	0.4627	0.0154
	.893	600,000	1,853	0.5397	0.0180
	.813	500,000	1,544	0.6477	0.0216
	.728	400,000	1,235	0.8.97	0.0270
	.575	250,000	772	1.30	0.0431
0000	.4600	211,600	653.3	1.53	0.0509
000	.4096	167,800	518.1	1.93	0.0642
00	.3648	133,100	410.9	2.43	0.0811
0	.3248	105,500	325.8	3.07	0.102
1	.2893	83,690	258.9	3.87	0.129
2	.2576	66,370	204.9	4.88	0.162
3	.2294	52,640	162.5	6.15	0.205
4	.2043	41,740	128.9	7.76	0.259
6	.1620	26,250	81.05	12.34	0.410
8	.1284	16,510	49.98	20.01	0.641
10	.1018	10,380	31.43	31.82	1.018
12	.0808	6,530	19.77	50.59	1.619
14	.0640	4,107	12.43	80.44	2.575
16	.0508	2,583	7.82	127.90	4.094
18	.0403	1,624	4.92	203.40	6.510
20	.0319	1,022	3.09	323.4	10.35
22	.0254	642	1.95	514.2	16.46
24	.0201	404	1.22	817.7	26.17
26	.0159	254	0.77	1,300	41.62
28	.0126	159.8	.48	2,067	66.17
30	.0100	100.5	.30	3,287	105.2
32	.0080	63.2	.19	5,227	167.3
34	.0063	39.7	.12	8,310	266.0
36	.0050	25.0	.076	13,210	423.0
38	.0040	15.7	.047	21,010	672.6
40	.0031	9.89	.030	33,410	1,069
42	.0025	6.22	.019	52,800	1,701
44	.0020	3.91	.012	82,500	2,703
46	.0016	2.46	.008	128,800	4,299
48	.0012	1.55	.004	229,600	6,836
50	.0010	0.97	.003	330,000	10,870

Characteristics of Conductors. Tables 7-8 to 7-13 give resistance and reactance constants of conductors at 60 cycles.

The compactness of the tables is secured by arranging the constants for the different conductors for 1-ft spacing and using additional tables of spacing factors to take care of other spacings. The formulas relating to these constants follow.

Three-phase circuit, impedance to neutral

$$z = r_a + j(x_a + x_d) \qquad \text{ohms/mile}$$

Note: For unsymmetrical spacings, use an effective spacing equal to the cube root of the product of the three spacings.

Example: Determine the impedance to neutral of a 60-cycle line with 795,000 cir mil ACSR conductor, 54 aluminum strands, with conductor separation = 26 ft. From table of ACSR:

$$r_a = 0.138 \qquad \text{and} \qquad x_a = 0.401 \text{ ohms/mile}$$

From reactance-spacing-factor tables:

$$x_d = 0.395 \text{ ohms/mile}$$
$$z = r_a + j(x_a + x_d)$$
$$= 0.138 + j\,0.796 \qquad \text{ohms/mile}$$

Shunt Capacitive Reactance

$$x' = x'_a + x'_d \qquad \text{megohms/mile}$$

Example: Determine shunt capacitive reactance of the above transmission line.

From tables, $\quad x'_a = 0.0917 \quad x'_d = 0.0967$ megohms/mile
$$x' = x'_a + x'_d = 0.1884 \text{ megohms/mile}$$

For total line *divide* by number of miles.

Single-phase circuit, without earth return

$$\text{Total impedance of circuit} = 2[r_a + j(x_a + x_d)] \qquad \text{ohms/mile}$$

With line and neutral wires, the latter grounded:

$$\text{Total impedance} = z_A - m^2/z_N \qquad \text{ohms/mile}$$

where z_A = line wire $z \qquad$ ohms/mile
$\quad z_N$ = neutral wire $z \qquad$ ohms/mile
$\quad z = (r_a + r_e/3) + j(x_e/3 + x_a) \qquad$ ohms/mile
$\quad m = r_e/3 + j(x_e/3 - x_d) \qquad$ ohms/mile

Current-carrying Capacity of Conductors. The current-carrying capacity of conductors can be determined approximately from the I^2R losses and the convection and radiation characteristics of the conductors.

$$I^2R = (W_c + W_r)A \qquad \text{watts} \qquad\qquad (7\text{-}58)$$
or $\qquad\qquad I = \sqrt{(A/R)(W_c + W_r)} \qquad \text{amp}$

where I = conductor current, amp

R = conductor resistance, ohms/ft

W_c = watts/in.² dissipated by convection

W_r = watts/in.² dissipated by radiation

A = conductor surface area, in.²/ft length

and $$W_c = (0.0128 \sqrt{pv}/T_a{}^{0.123} \sqrt{d}) \, \Delta t \qquad \text{watts/in.}^2 \qquad (7\text{-}59)$$

where p = pressure, atm $(p = 1.0$ for atmospheric pressure)

v = air velocity, fps

T_a = average of absolute temperatures of conductor and air, °K

d = outside diameter of conductor, in.

Δt = temperature rise, °C

and $$W_r = 36.8E[(T/1{,}000)^4 - (T_0/1{,}000)^4] \qquad \text{watts/in.}^2 \qquad (7\text{-}60)$$

where E = relative emissivity of conductor surface (1.0 for black body, 0.5 for average oxidized copper)

T = absolute temperature of conductor, °K

T_0 = absolute temperature of surroundings, °K

7-3. Transients in Electric Circuits

D-C Circuits. When a d-c voltage E is impressed on a circuit consisting of a *resistance* of R ohms and *inductance* of L henrys, the transient current i which flows is a function of time and is given by

$$i = (E/R)(1 - \epsilon^{-Rt/L}) + I_0\epsilon^{-Rt/L} \qquad \text{amp} \qquad (7\text{-}61)$$

where I_0 is the current flowing in the circuit at the instant before the voltage E is impressed at $t = 0$. I_0 is positive if flowing in the positive direction of E and negative if flowing in opposition to E. The current I_0 flowing in the circuit at $t = 0$ is the instantaneous value at that time and is consequently a constant and independent of its past time variation. If the source voltage is short-circuited, the current will decay to zero, its value at any time being

$$i = I_0\epsilon^{-Rt/L} \qquad \text{amp} \qquad (7\text{-}62)$$

where I_0 = current flowing at $t = 0$, time at which short-circuit is applied

The *time constant* T of a RL circuit is that value of t required for the current to build up to 63.2 per cent of its final value when the circuit is being energized with zero initial current, or to decay to 36.8 per cent of its initial value when short-circuited.

$$T = L/R \qquad \text{sec} \qquad (7\text{-}63)$$

where R is in ohms and L in henrys.

If a *capacitor* of C farads and a *resistor* of R ohms are connected in series to a d-c voltage E, the transient current i which flows is given by

$$i = [(E - E_c)/R]\epsilon^{-t/RC} \qquad \text{amp} \qquad (7\text{-}64)$$

where E_c is the voltage on the capacitor the instant before the voltage E is applied and may be either plus or minus, depending upon whether it acts in opposition to or conjunction with the impressed voltage. $E - E_c$ represents the net voltage in the direction of positive i.

$$E_c = Q_0/C \qquad \text{volts} \tag{7-65}$$

where Q_0 = initial charge on capacitor C

The *capacitor charge q* is the integral of the current i.

$$q = CE(1 - \epsilon^{-t/RC}) + CE_c\epsilon^{-t/RC} \qquad \text{coulombs} \tag{7-66}$$

The voltage across the capacitor at any time t after the voltage E is impressed is

$$e_c = q/C = E(1 - \epsilon^{-t/RC}) + E_c\epsilon^{-t/RC} \qquad \text{volts} \tag{7-67}$$

The *current i* flowing in an RC circuit when the source voltage is short-circuited and having an initial voltage of E_c is

$$i = (E_c/R)\epsilon^{-t/RC} \qquad \text{amp} \tag{7-68}$$

The *charge q* on C for a short-circuited RC circuit at any time t is

$$q = CE_c\epsilon^{-t/RC} \qquad \text{coulombs} \tag{7-69}$$

The *voltage* across the capacitor under the same conditions is

$$e_c = E_c\epsilon^{-t/RC} \qquad \text{volts} \tag{7-70}$$

The *time constant T* of an RC circuit is that value of t required for the charge to build up to 63.2 per cent of its final value when the circuit is being energized with zero initial charge on the capacitor, or to decay to 36.8 per cent of its initial value when short-circuited.

$$T = RC \text{ sec} \tag{7-71}$$

where R is in ohms and C in farads.

When a circuit consisting of series-connected *resistance, inductance,* and *capacitance RLC* is energized from a d-c source, the transient current is dependent upon the relative magnitudes of R, L, and C.   It may take one of three forms:

1. A damped exponential wave when $R^2/4L^2 > 1/LC$
2. A critically damped exponential wave when $R^2/4L^2 = 1/LC$
3. An exponentially damped sine wave when $R^2/4L^2 < 1/LC$

Case 1. $R^2/4L^2 > 1/LC$

$$i = \left[\frac{E - E_c - (a - b)I_0}{2bL}\right]\epsilon^{-(a-b)t} - \left[\frac{E - E_c - (a + b)I_0}{2bL}\right]\epsilon^{-(a+b)t} \qquad \text{amp}$$

(7-72)

where $a = R/2L$

$\quad b = \sqrt{R^2/4L^2 - 1/LC}$

$\quad E_c = Q_0/C$

$\quad Q_0 = $ initial charge on C

$\quad I_0 = $ initial current in circuit before $t = 0$

If at the time of application of voltage there is no initial current and no initial charge on the capacitor, the expression for the transient current becomes

$$i = (E/2bL)\epsilon^{-at}(\epsilon^{bt} - \epsilon^{-bt}) \qquad \text{amp}$$
$$= (E/bL)\epsilon^{-at} \sinh bt \qquad \text{amp}$$

(7-73)

The time for the current to rise to maximum value is

$$t_m = (1/b) \tanh^{-1} (b/a) \qquad \text{sec}$$

(7-74)

Case 2. $R^2/4L^2 = 1/LC$

$$i = \left[I_0 + \frac{2(E - E_c) - RI_0}{2L} t\right]\epsilon^{-(R/2L)t} \qquad \text{amp}$$

(7-75)

If no initial current or charge is present

$$i = (E/L)t\epsilon^{-(R/2L)t} \qquad \text{amp}$$

(7-76)

Time required for current to reach maximum value:

$$t_m = 2L/R \text{ sec}$$

(7-77)

Maximum current is

$$i_{\text{max}} = 0.736E/R \qquad \text{amp}$$

(7-78)

Case 3. $R^2/4L^2 < 1/LC$

$$i = \left\{\frac{[2(E - E_c) - RI_0]}{2\beta L} \sin \beta t + I_0 \cos \beta t\right\}\epsilon^{-(R/2L)t} \qquad \text{amp}$$

(7-79)

where $\beta = \sqrt{1/LC - R^2/4L^2}$

If no initial current or charge is present, the transient current becomes

$$i = (E/\beta L)\epsilon^{-at} \sin \beta t \qquad \text{amp}$$

(7-80)

where $a = R/2L$

The frequency of oscillation

$$f = (1/2\pi) \sqrt{1/LC - R^2/4L^2} \qquad \text{cps}$$

(7-81)

If $R^2/4L^2$ is negligible, the undamped or natural frequency is

$$f = 1/(2\pi \sqrt{LC}) \qquad \text{cps}$$

(7-82)

Time at which first current maximum occurs

$$t_m = \sigma/\beta \tag{7-83}$$

where $\sigma = \tan^{-1} (\beta/a)$

Any of the positive maximum values of current can be found from

$$I_n = (E \sqrt{LC}/L)\epsilon^{-at_n} \tag{7-84}$$

where t_n = time at which nth current maximum occurs

Numerical decrement is defined as the difference between any two current peaks separated by a complete cycle divided by the larger of the two.

$$\text{Numerical decrement} = 1 - \epsilon^{-R/2Lf} \tag{7-85}$$

Logarithmic decrement is defined as the logarithm of the ratio of two consecutive positive current maxima.

$$\text{Logarithmic decrement} = \log_\epsilon (I_n/I_{n+1}) = R/2Lf \tag{7-86}$$

where f = frequency of oscillation

The *discharge current* which flows when the source voltage is short-circuited is obtained in each of the three cases by setting $E = 0$.

A-C Circuits. If an alternating voltage of the form $e = E_m \sin (\omega t + \lambda)$ is applied to a *RL series circuit*, a current which is made up of two components, steady-state and transient, will flow.

$$
\begin{aligned}
i &= i_s + i_t \\
&= (E_m/Z) \sin (\omega t + \lambda - \theta) - (E_m/Z) \sin (\lambda - \theta)\epsilon^{-(R/L)t}
\end{aligned} \tag{7-87}
$$

where $E_m = \sqrt{2}\, E$

     E = rms value of applied a-c voltage

     $Z = \sqrt{R^2 + (\omega L)^2}$

     $\omega = 2\pi f$

     λ = angular displacement between $e = 0$ and $t = 0$ measured positively from $e = 0$, the zero point for e being at the intersection where e is rising in the positive direction, deg or radians

     $\theta = \tan^{-1} \omega L/R$, the steady-state power-factor angle

If an *alternating voltage* is applied to an RC circuit, the current which flows is

$$i = \frac{E_m}{Z} \sin (\omega t + \lambda - \theta) + [(E_m/R) \sin \theta \cos (\lambda - \theta) + Q_0/RC]\, \epsilon^{-t/RC} \tag{7-88}$$

where $Z = \sqrt{R^2 + (-1/\omega C)^2}$

     $\theta = \tan^{-1} (-1/\omega CR)$

     Q_0 = initial charge on C

If an alternating voltage is applied to a RLC circuit, the current which flows is dependent upon whether $R^2/4L^2$ is greater than, equal to, or less than $1/LC$.

Case 1. $R^2/4L^2 > 1/LC$

$$i = \frac{E_m}{Z} \sin (\omega t + \lambda - \theta) + \epsilon^{-at}[(E_d/bL) \sinh bt - (E_m/Z) \sin (\lambda - \theta)$$
$$\cos bt] \quad (7\text{-}89)$$

where $Z = \sqrt{R^2 + (\omega L - 1/\omega c)^2}$
$\quad\quad\quad \theta = \tan^{-1}[(\omega L - 1/\omega C)/R]$
$\quad\quad\quad a = R/2L$
$\quad\quad\quad b = \sqrt{R^2/4L^2 - 1/LC}$

$$E_d = \left[E_m \sin \lambda - (E_m \omega L/Z) \cos (\lambda - \theta) - \frac{Q_0}{C} - \frac{E_m R}{2Z} \sin (\lambda - \theta) \right]$$
$$(7\text{-}90)$$

Case 2. $R^2/4L^2 = 1/LC$

$$i = (E_m/Z) \sin (\omega t + \lambda - \theta) + \epsilon^{-at}[(E_d/L)t - (E_m/Z) \sin (\lambda - \theta)] \quad (7\text{-}91)$$

Case 3. $R^2/4L^2 < 1/LC$

$$i = (E_m/Z) \sin (\omega t + \lambda - \theta) + \epsilon^{-at}[(E_d/\beta L) \sin \beta t$$
$$- (E_m/Z) \sin (\lambda - \theta) \cos \beta t] \quad (7\text{-}92)$$

where $\quad\quad\quad\quad\quad\quad\quad \beta = \sqrt{1/LC - R^2/4L^2}$

The nature of the *transient response* of a circuit is indicated by the roots of the *determinantal equation* $D(p)$ for that circuit. $D(p)$ for a simple series circuit can be found by first writing the impedance of the circuit in terms of $j\omega$ and then substituting p for $j\omega$ and equating to zero. For example,

$$Z = R + j\omega L + 1/j\omega C \quad\quad\quad (7\text{-}93)$$
$$D(p) = R + pL + 1/pC = 0 \quad\quad\quad (7\text{-}94)$$

For complex networks $D(p)$ can be found from the general expression for D as defined on page 7-16 for the generalized impedance network by substituting p for $j\omega$ in the impedance elements, and then setting $D(p) = 0$ to solve for the values of p.

7-4. Traveling Waves on Transmission Lines

The *surge impedance* of a conductor is equal to

$$Z = \sqrt{L/C} \quad\quad \text{ohms} \quad\quad\quad (7\text{-}95)$$

where L = inductance, henrys/unit length conductor
$\quad\quad\quad C$ = capacitance, farads/unit length conductor
For a single aerial conductor parallel to the earth and with zero earth resistivity,

$$L = 7.410 \times 10^{-4} \log 2h/r \quad\quad \text{henrys/mile} \quad\quad (7\text{-}96)$$
and $\quad\quad\quad\quad C = (3.882 \times 10^{-8})/\log (2h/r) \quad\quad \text{farads/mile} \quad\quad (7\text{-}97)$

where h = height of conductor above ground
$\quad\quad\quad r$ = radius of conductor in same units

For cables

$$L = 7.410 \times 10^{-4} \log (r_2/r_1) \qquad \text{henrys/mile} \qquad (7\text{-}98)$$
$$C = (3.882 \times 10^{-8}\epsilon)/\log (r_2/r_1) \qquad \text{farads/mile} \qquad (7\text{-}99)$$

where r_1 = radius of conductor
r_2 = inner radius of sheath
ϵ = permittivity

The surge impedance of a typical aerial line is approximately 500 ohms and of a typical cable 50 ohms. The relationship between a traveling voltage wave and current wave is

$$e = iZ \qquad (7\text{-}100)$$

The *velocity of propagation* of a surge or traveling wave is

$$v = 1/\sqrt{LC} = 984 \text{ ft/}\mu \text{ sec for aerial conductor} \qquad (7\text{-}101)$$

For cables

$$v = 984/\sqrt{\epsilon} \text{ ft/}\mu\text{sec} \qquad (7\text{-}102)$$

where ϵ has a range of about 2.5 to 4.0.

The *propagation constant* of a conductor when energized with alternating current is

$$\alpha = \sqrt{zy} = \alpha_1 + j\beta \qquad (7\text{-}103)$$

where z = series impedance/(unit length)(phase)
y = shunt admittance/(unit length)(phase to neutral)
α_1 = attenuation constant, nepers/mile
β = wavelength constant, radians/mile

Wavelength

$$\lambda = 2\pi/\beta \qquad \text{miles} \qquad (7\text{-}104)$$

Velocity of propagation of an alternating voltage is

$$v = f\lambda = \omega/\beta \qquad (7\text{-}105)$$

7-5. Nonsinusoidal Periodic Waves

The solution of circuit problems when the applied voltages are *nonsinusoidal periodic waves* can be accomplished by resolving the wave to sinusoidal components by use of *Fourier's series* and applying the superposition theorem. Fourier's theorem states that any function $f(x)$ which within an interval is finite, single-valued, and continuous or has only a finite number of discontinuities may be represented by a series of the form

$$f(x) = A_0/2 + A_1 \cos x + A_2 \cos 2x + \cdots + A_n \cos nx + \cdots$$
$$+ B_1 \sin x + B_2 \sin 2x + \cdots + B_n \sin nx + \cdots$$

$$= A_0/2 + \sum_{n=1}^{n=\infty} A_n \cos nx + \sum_{n=1}^{n=\infty} B_n \sin nx \qquad (7\text{-}106)$$

where $A_n = 1/\pi \int_0^{2\pi} f(x) \cos nx \, dx$

$\qquad B_n = 1/\pi \int_0^{2\pi} f(x) \sin nx \, dx$

$\qquad A_0/2 = 1/2\pi \int_0^{2\pi} f(x) \, dx$

ELECTRICAL MACHINERY

7-6. Rectifiers

For the condition of no grid delay and no overlap, the d-c no-load voltage of a rectifier is given by

$$E_{d0} = \sqrt{2} \, Ep/\pi \sin (\pi/p) \qquad \text{volts} \qquad (7\text{-}107)$$

where E_{d0} = d-c voltage at no load

$\qquad E$ = rms line-to-neutral secondary or anode voltage

$\qquad p$ = number of secondary phases

The *output voltage* of a p-phase rectifier with grid delay but no load is

$$E_d = E_{d0} \cos \alpha \qquad \text{volts} \qquad (7\text{-}108)$$

where α = grid-delay angle

The output voltage of a p-phase rectifier with grid delay and operating under load is

$$E_d = E_{d0} - E_{d0}(1 - \cos \alpha) - (p/2\pi)XI_{dc} \qquad \text{volts} \qquad (7\text{-}109)$$

where X = commutating reactance; reactance to neutral of one anode circuit which includes anode reactors, rectifier transformer, and supply circuit using generator subtransient reactance, ohms

$\qquad I_{dc}$ = load current, amp

The *regulation formula* for a p-phase grid-controlled rectifier:

$$E_d = \begin{matrix} \text{no-load} \\ \text{voltage} \end{matrix} - \begin{matrix} \text{reduction by} \\ \text{grid delay} \end{matrix} - \begin{matrix} \text{reduction} \\ \text{by overlap} \end{matrix} - \begin{matrix} \text{resistance} \\ \text{drop} \end{matrix} - \begin{matrix} \text{arc} \\ \text{drop} \end{matrix}$$

$$ = \quad E_{d0} \quad - E_{d0}(1 - \cos \alpha) - (p/2\pi)XI_{dc} - \quad W/I_{dc} \quad - \quad A \qquad \text{volts}$$
$$(7\text{-}110)$$

where W = total copper losses, watts

$\qquad A$ = arc drop, volts

The *angle of overlap u* without grid control.

$$\cos u = 1 - XI_{dc}/\sqrt{2} \, E \sin (\pi/p) \qquad (7\text{-}111)$$

When grid control is present

$$\cos (u + \alpha) = \cos \alpha - XI_{dc}/\sqrt{2} \, E \sin (\pi/p) \qquad (7\text{-}112)$$

7-7. D-C Motors and Generators

The *emf equation* for a d-c generator is

$$E = Z\phi_a \frac{\text{rpm}}{60} \frac{\text{poles}}{\text{paths}} \times 10^{-8} \qquad \text{volts} \qquad (7\text{-}113)$$

where E = generated voltage between terminals
   Z = total number of active conductors
   ϕ_a = flux per pole which crosses air gap and is cut by armature conductors
   rpm = armature speed in revolutions per minute
   paths = number of parallel circuits through armature

The *terminal voltage* of a d-c generator V

$$V = E - IR \qquad (7\text{-}114)$$

where I = armature current
   R = resistance between brushes
   E = generated voltage between terminals

The *armature torque of a generator*

$$T = 0.1175 Z I \phi_a \frac{\text{poles}}{\text{paths}} \times 10^{-8} \qquad \text{lb-ft} \qquad (7\text{-}115)$$

Power input P_i to a generator

$$\begin{aligned} P_i &= 1.903T \text{ rpm} \times 10^{-4} \qquad \text{hp} \\ &= 0.1420T \text{ rpm} \qquad \text{watts} \\ &= \text{power output of a d-c motor} \end{aligned} \qquad (7\text{-}116)$$

Power output P_0 of a generator

$$\begin{aligned} P_0 &= VI \qquad \text{watts} \\ &= \text{power input to a d-c motor} \end{aligned} \qquad (7\text{-}117)$$

7-8. A-C Motors and Generators

Frequency f of the voltage generated in a synchronous generator.

$$f = p \times \text{rpm}/120 \qquad \text{cps} \qquad (7\text{-}118)$$

where p = number of poles
The internal generated voltage for a full-pitch winding is approximately

$$E = 2.1 f \phi N \times 10^{-8} \qquad \text{volts} \qquad (7\text{-}119)$$

where ϕ = flux per pole, maxwells
   f = frequency, cps
   N = number of series-connected active conductors per phase

The *transient open-circuit time constant T'_{d0}* of a machine is the time in seconds for the field current to build up to 0.632 times its final value after the application of field voltage with the armature open-circuited. The mathematical expression for this relation is

$$I_f = (E_{dc}/R_f)(1 - \epsilon^{-t/T'_{d0}}) \qquad \text{amp} \qquad (7\text{-}120)$$

where E_{dc} = exciter voltage, volts
$\quad R_f$ = resistance of field winding, ohms
$\quad t$ = time, sec
T'_{d0} can be readily found from this expression if an oscillogram of I_f is available.

The *transient short-circuit time constant* T'_d which determines the rate of decay of the transient component of the armature current during short circuit is given by

$$T'_d = (X'_d/X_d)T'_{d0} \qquad \text{sec} \qquad (7\text{-}121)$$

where X'_d = transient reactance
$\quad X_d$ = synchronous reactance

The *subtransient short-circuit time constant* T''_d, which determines the rate of decay of the subtransient component of the armature current during short-circuit, is expressed in

$$\Delta i'' = (i''_d - i'_d)\epsilon^{-t/T''_d} \qquad (7\text{-}122)$$

where $\Delta i''$ can be obtained from short-circuit oscillograms that show the subtransient and transient currents, i''_d and i'_d.

The *armature short-circuit time constant* T_a is given by

$$T_a = X_2/2\pi f R_a \qquad \text{sec} \qquad (7\text{-}123)$$

where X_2 = negative-sequence reactance, ohms
$\quad f$ = frequency, cps.
$\quad R_a$ = armature resistance, ohms

7-9. Induction Motors

The induction-motor equivalent circuit is shown in Fig. 7-41, where
r_s = stator resistance, ohms
X_s = stator leakage reactance at rated frequency, ohms
r_r = rotor resistance, ohms
X_r = rotor leakage reactance at rated frequency, ohms
Z_m = shunt impedance to include the effect of magnetizing current and no-load losses, ohms
E_s = applied voltage, volts
i_s = stator current, amp
i_r = rotor current, amp
S = slip
The slip S of an induction machine is given by

$$S = 1 - \text{rpm}_r/\text{rpm}_{syn} \qquad \text{per unit} \qquad (7\text{-}124)$$

where rpm_r = rotor speed

rpm_{syn} = synchronous speed

Total shaft power of induction motor is

$$P = [(1 - S)/S]3r_r i_r{}^2 \quad \text{watts}$$
$$= (1/746)[(1 - S)/S]3r_r i_r{}^2 \quad \text{hp} \tag{7-125}$$

Induction-motor efficiency, neglecting losses other than rotor copper loss

$$\text{efficiency} = 100(1 - S) \quad \text{per cent} \tag{7-126}$$

Shaft torque is given by

$$T = \frac{7.04}{(\text{rpm})_{syn}} \frac{(3r_r i_r{}^2)_{\text{watts}}}{(S)_{\text{per unit}}} \quad \text{lb-ft} \tag{7-127}$$

or approximately

$$T = \frac{21.12}{\text{rpm}_{syn}} \frac{r_r/S}{(r_s + r_r/S)^2 + (X_s + X_r)^2} \quad \text{lb ft} \tag{7-128}$$

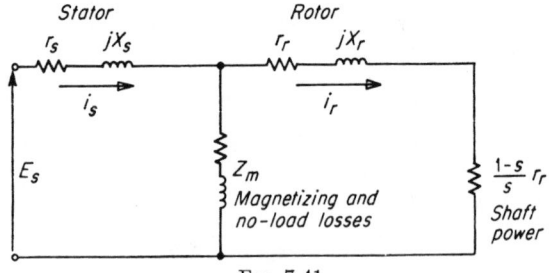

Fig. 7-41

7-10. Transformers

The voltage induced in a transformer winding is given by

$$E = 4.44 f n A B_{\max} \times 10^{-8} \quad \text{volts} \tag{7-129}$$

where f = frequency, cps

n = number of turns in winding

A = cross-sectional area of uniform magnetic circuits, cm^2

$B_{\max}$ = maximum flux density in core, lines/cm^2

A *two-winding transformer* with a primary winding P of n_1 turns and a secondary winding S of n_2 turns has an equivalent circuit as shown in Fig. 7-42. The corresponding vector diagram is shown in Fig. 7-43, where

$N = n_2/n_1$

Z_m = magnetizing impedance, ohms

$Z_p = R_p + j\omega[L_p - (n_1/n_2)M]$ ohms

$Z_s = R_s + j\omega[L_s - (n_2/n_1)M]$ ohms

R_p, R_s = primary and secondary effective winding resistances, ohms

$\omega = 2\pi f$

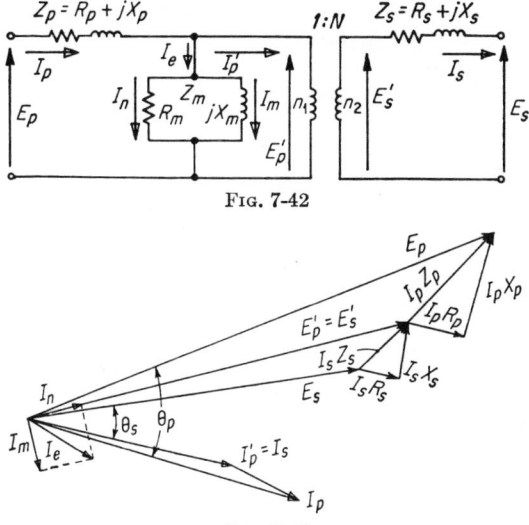

Fig. 7-42

Fig. 7-43

L_p, L_s = primary and secondary winding self-inductance, henrys

M = mutual inductance between windings, henrys

$Z_{ps} = Z_p + (1/N^2)Z_s$ ohms leakage impedance between p and s windings, measured on p winding with s winding short-circuited

In many calculations it is customary to make

$$Z_p = (1/N^2)Z_s = \tfrac{1}{2}Z_{ps} \qquad \text{ohms} \qquad (7\text{-}130)$$

7-11. Decibels

In communications work, it is convenient to consider the transmission characteristic of a system in terms of attenuation, or the decrease in power along the transmission system. The ratio between the voltages, currents, and powers at any two points on such a system is a measure of the attenuation of the circuit between these two points. It is not usually convenient to express these transmission losses or gains in terms of the voltage and current or power ratios directly. The losses so expressed cannot be added to obtain the total loss, but must be *multiplied*. Consequently, these ratios are usually expressed in decibels (db) which can be added directly and can be defined as

$$\text{db} = 10 \log (P_1/P_2) \qquad \text{db} = 20 \log (E_1/E_2) \qquad \text{db} = 20 \log (I_1/I_2)$$

The last two formulas are valid only if the impedance levels of the circuits upon which the two currents or voltages are based are the same.

Various power and voltage or current ratios and the corresponding decibels and efficiencies are shown in the Table 7-14.

Table 7-14. Power, Voltage, and Current Ratios and Their Corresponding Values in Decibels

Power ratio	Voltage or current ratio	Decibels (db)	Efficiency, %
1.26	1.12	1.0	79.5
1.58	1.26	2.0	63.4
2.0	1.41	3.0	50.0
3.16	1.78	5.0	31.6
5.01	2.24	7.0	20.0
10.0	3.16	10.0	10.0
50.12	7.08	17.0	1.99
100.0	10.0	20.0	1.0
1,000.0	31.6	30.0	0.1
10^5	316.2	50.0	.001
10^8	10,000.0	80.0	.000001
10^{10}	100,000.0	100.0	.00000001

7-12. Resistor and Capacitor Color Codes

Table 7-15. Color Code for Fixed Resistors
Values in Ohms

Resistor with axial wire leads   Resistor with radial wire leads

Resistor with radial wire leads....	Body	End	Dot or band	End	
Resistor with axial wire leads.....	1st band	2nd band	3rd band	End band	
Color	Value	Value	Value	Color	Tolerance, %
Black	0	0	None	Gold	± 5
Brown	1	1	0	Silver	± 10
Red	2	2	00	None	± 20
Orange	3	3	000		
Yellow	4	4	0000		
Green	5	5	00000		
Blue	6	6	000000		
Violet	7	7	0000000		
Gray	8	8	00000000		
White	9	9	000000000		

Table 7-16. Color Code for JAN Fixed Mica Capacitors

Color-code scheme for JAN standard fixed mica capacitors. The significance of the letters denoting characteristic will be found in Specification JAN C-5.

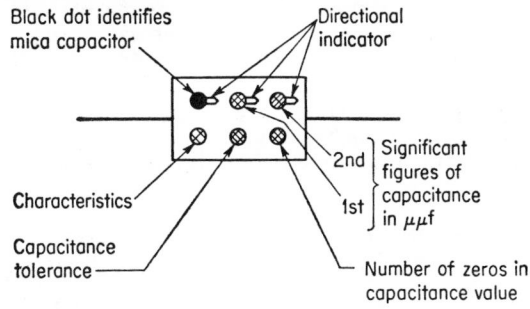

Color	Capacitance, $\mu\mu$f (significant fig)	Decimal multiplier	Tolerance, %	Characteristic
Black......	0	1	20 (M)*	A
Brown.....	1	10	......	B
Red.......	2	100	2 (G)*	C
Orange....	3	1,000	......	D
Yellow.....	4	....	......	E
Green.....	5	....	......	F
Blue.......	6	....	......	G
Violet.....	7			
Gray......	8			
White	9			
Gold......	...	0.1	5 (J)*	
Silver......	...	.01	10 (K)*	

* Code letter for indicated % tolerance.

ILLUMINATION

Definition of Terms

Brightness (*B*) is that property of a light source that specifies the ability of an element of the source to produce luminous effects. It may be expressed in two ways: candles per unit area, such as candles/sq in. (c/in.²), or lumens per unit area.

Footcandle (fc) is the illumination at a point on a surface which is one foot from and perpendicular to a uniform point source of one candle.

Footlambert (fl) is the brightness of a surface emitting or reflecting one lumen per square foot.

Footlambert (fl) = footcandles (fc) × reflection factor

$$= \frac{\text{lumens (incident)} \times \text{reflection factor}}{\text{area (sq ft) of surface}} \quad (7\text{-}131)$$

Illumination (*E*) is the density of luminous flux on a given surface. The unit of measure is the footcandle.

Lambert (*B'*) is the brightness of a surface emitting or reflecting one lumen per square centimeter.

Lumen (lm) is the quantity of light flux falling on a surface of one square foot from a uniform point source of one candle. A one-square-foot section from a sphere of one-foot radius with a one-candle source at its center would be such a surface. The lumen differs from the candle in that it is a measure of light flux, irrespective of direction.

$$\text{Incident lumens} = \text{footcandles} \times \text{area (sq ft)} \quad (7\text{-}132)$$

Luminous flux (*F*) is the time rate of flow of light. The unit of measure is the lumen.

Luminous intensity (*I*) (candlepower) is that property of a light source which specifies its ability as a whole to produce luminous effects. The standard unit of intensity in a given direction is the International Candle. An ordinary wax candle has a luminous intensity of approximately one candle.

$$\text{Candlepower (cp)} = \text{footcandles (fc)} \times \text{distance squared } (D^2) \quad (7\text{-}133)$$

where *D* = distance in feet from light source to illuminated surface.

Mean spherical candlepower (MSCP) is the average candlepower of a source in all directions.

$$\text{MSCP} = \frac{\text{lumens}}{12.57} \quad (7\text{-}134)$$

Inverse-square Law. Illumination decreases inversely as the square of the distance. When the light rays are perpendicular to the surface:

$$\text{Illumination } E = \frac{\text{luminous intensity}}{\text{distance squared}} = \frac{I}{D^2} \quad \text{footcandles} \quad (7\text{-}135)$$

where *I* is the candlepower and *D* is the distance in feet.

When the light rays are not perpendicular to the surface, the horizontal illumination is

$$E_h = \frac{I \times \cos\theta}{D^2} \qquad \text{footcandles} \qquad (7\text{-}136)$$

and the vertical illumination is

$$E_v = \frac{I \times \sin\theta}{D^2} \qquad \text{footcandles} \qquad (7\text{-}137)$$

In both cases θ is measured from the vertical.

Table 7-17. Illumination Conversion Factors

Quantity	Multiply number of	By	To obtain
Brightness...........	blondels	0.0002054	Candles/sq in.
Brightness...........	Candles/sq cm	6.45	Candles/sq in.
Brightness...........	footlamberts	0.002210	Candles/sq in.
Brightness...........	lamberts	2.054	Candles/sq in.
Brightness...........	blondels	0.00003183	Stilbs
Brightness...........	Candles/sq cm	1	Stilbs
Brightness...........	Candles/sq in.	0.1550	Stilbs
Brightness...........	footlamberts	0.0003425	Stilbs
Brightness...........	lamberts	0.3183	Stilbs
Brightness...........	Candles/sq cm	31,416	blondels
Brightness...........	Candles/sq in.	4,870	blondels
Brightness...........	footlamberts	10.76	blondels
Brightness...........	lamberts	10,000	blondels
Brightness...........	Stilbs	31,416	blondels
Brightness...........	blondels	0.0929	footlamberts
Brightness...........	Candles/sq cm	2,919	footlamberts
Brightness...........	Candles/sq in.	452	footlamberts
Brightness...........	lamberts	929	footlamberts
Brightness...........	Stilbs	2,919	footlamberts
Brightness...........	blondels	0.0001	lamberts
Brightness...........	Candles/sq cm	3.1416	lamberts
Brightness...........	Candles/sq in.	0.487	lamberts
Brightness...........	footlamberts	0.001076	lamberts
Illumination........	lumens/sq cm	929	footcandles
Illumination........	lumens/sq meter	0.0929	footcandles
Illumination........	lumens/sq ft	1	footcandles
Illumination........	lux	0.0929	footcandles
Illumination........	phot	929	footcandles
Illumination........	footcandles	10.76	lux
Illumination........	lumens/sq cm	10,000	lux
Illumination........	lumens/sq meter	1	lux
Illumination........	lumens/sq ft	10.76	lux
Illumination........	phot	10,000	lux
Illumination........	foot-candles	0.001076	phot
Illumination........	lumens/sq cm	1	phot
Illumination........	lumens/sq meter	0.0001	phot
Illumination........	lumens/sq ft	0.001076	phot
Illumination........	lux	0.0001	phot
Luminous flux.......	light-watts	680	lumens
Luminous flux.......	youngs	680	lumens

Application.   Generally acceptable lighting levels in terms of footcandles for various types of installations are listed in Table 7-18.   This is the average illumination at the work level.   The number of lamps required to produce a required level of illumination is given by

Number of lamps

$$= \frac{\text{footcandles} \times \text{area}}{\text{lumens per lamp} \times \text{coefficient of utilization} \times \text{maintenance factor}} \quad (7\text{-}138)$$

The lumens per lamp for a number of standard bulbs of incandescent, mercury, and fluorescent types are listed in Tables 7-19 to 7-21.   The coefficient of utilization and maintenance factor (MF) are selected from Table 7-22, corresponding to the luminaire that is to be used.   A luminaire usually consists of a number of lamps.   The total number of luminaires required is

$$\text{Number of luminaires} = \frac{\text{number of lamps}}{\text{lamps per luminaire}} \quad (7\text{-}139)$$

To use Table 7-22 it is first necessary to determine a room index from Table 7-23, which covers a wide variety of room dimensions and light-mounting heights.   Table 7-24 gives average data on diffuse-reflection ratios, and Table 7-25 lists maximum-brightness ratios that are acceptable.

Brightness ratios are determined as follows: Determine the reflection values of the task, desk, floor, walls, and ceilings from Table 7-24.   The brightness of the task and desk is determined by multiplying the average foot-candles by the reflection factor.   Brightness of walls, ceilings, and floor are determined from Table 7-27.

Table 7-18. Illumination Levels, Interior Lighting

	Foot-candles Maintained in Service (Not Initial Values)
Assembly (manufacturing):	
Rough	20
Medium	50
Fine	100
Extra fine	300*
Auditoriums:	
Assembly only	10
Exhibitions	30
Banks:	
Lobby	20
Cages and offices	50
Barber shops and beauty parlors	50
Bathrooms:	
General lighting	5
At mirror (on face)	40
Bedrooms:	
General lighting	5
At mirror (on face)	20
Churches:	
Auditorium	10
Sunday-school rooms	20
Pulpit	20
Classrooms, on desks and chalkboards:	
Typical	30
Sight-saving or special	50
Depots and stations:	
Waiting room	20
Ticket rack and counter	50
Concourse	5
Platforms	5
Dining rooms:	
Homes (general lighting)	5
Hotels and restaurants	10
Drafting rooms	50
Elevators	10
Garages:	
Storage	10
Repair and servicing	50
Gymnasiums:	
Exhibitions and matches	30
General exercise	20
Assemblies	10
Dances	5
Lockers and shower rooms	10
Halls and corridors	5
Homes (see specific rooms)	
Hospitals:	
Private rooms and wards:	
General lighting	5
Supplementary for reading	20
Surgery:	
General lighting	50
Operating table	1800
Obstetrical:	
Delivery room	50
Delivery table	200
Examination table	50
Inspection:	
Rough	20
Medium	50
Fine	100
Extra fine	200 or more*
Ironing	40
Kitchens:	
General lighting	10
Supplementary (at task)	40

Table 7-18. Illumination Levels, Interior Lighting (Continued)

	Foot-candles Maintained in Service (Not Initial Values)
Laboratories:	
General lighting	30
Work tables	50
Close work	100
Living rooms (see also specific visual task):	
General lighting	5
Lobbies	20
Machine shops:	
Rough bench and machine work	20
Medium bench and machine work	50
Fine bench and machine work	100
Extra fine bench and machine work	200 or more*
Mail rooms	30
Museums and art galleries:	
General lighting	10
On displays	50
Offices:	
Casual visual tasks: inactive file rooms, reception rooms, stairways, washrooms, and other service areas	10
Ordinary visual tasks: general office work (except for work classified as "difficult visual tasks"), private office work, general correspondence, conference rooms, active file rooms, mail rooms	30
Difficult visual tasks: auditing and accounting, business-machine operation, transcribing and tabulation, bookkeeping, drafting, designing	50
Reading:	
Short periods, material of reasonably good visibility	20
Prolonged periods or smaller type	40
Proofreading	100
Schools (see specific rooms)	
Sewing:	
Coarse work, high contrast between thread and fabric	20
Light fabrics, occasional periods	40
Light to medium fabrics, prolonged periods	80
Dark fabrics, fine detail, low contrast	150 or more*
Show windows:	
Low surrounding brightness:	
General displays	50
Feature displays	100
Medium surrounding brightness:	
General displays	100
Feature displays	200
High surrounding brightness:	
General displays	200
Feature displays	500
Stairways	10
Storage and stock rooms:	
Rough bulky material	5
Medium material	10
Fine material requiring care	20
Store interiors:	
Circulation areas	20
General merchandising areas	50
Showcases, wall cases, and open-counter displays	100*
Feature displays	200*
Theaters and motion-picture houses:	
Auditorium during intermission	5
Auditorium during picture	0.1
Foyer	5
Lobby	20
Toilets and washrooms	10
Waiting rooms	20
Woodworking:	
Rough sawing and bench work	30
Sizing, planing, rough sanding, veneering, medium machine and bench work	50
Fine bench and machine work, fine sanding and finishing	100
Writing	20

* Usually obtained by supplementary luminaires in combination with general lighting systems providing not less than one-tenth of the recommended value for the task.

SOURCE: "Foot Candle Tables," Bulletin A-4981, p. 3, Westinghouse Electric Corporation, Bloomfield, N.J.

Table 7-19. Incandescent-lamp Data

Watts	Bulb	Base	Finish	Rated avg life, hr	Initial lumens
General-service Lamps					
100	A-21	Med.	I.f	750	1,620
150	A-23	Med.	I.f-cl.	750	2,600
200	PS-30	Med.	I.f.-cl.	750	3,700
300	PS-30	Med.	I.f.-cl.	750	5,900
300	PS-35	Mogul	I.f.-cl.	1,000	5,650
500	PS-40	Mogul	I.f.-cl.	1,000	9,900
750	PS-52	Mogul	I.f.-cl.	1,000	15,600
1,000	PS-52	Mogul	I.f.-cl.	1,000	21,500
1,500	PS-52	Mogul	I.f.-cl.	1,000	33,000
Projector and Reflector Lamps					
75	PAR-38	Med. skt.	Projector spot	1,000	450 (0–15°)
75	PAR-38	Med. skt.	Projector flood	1,000	550 (0–30°)
150	PAR-38	Med. skt.	Projector spot	1,000	1,150 (0–15°)
150	PAR-38	Med. skt.	Projector flood	1,000	1,400 (0–30°)
75	R-30	Med.	Reflector spot	1,000	220 (0–15°)
75	R-30	Med.	Reflector flood	1,000	300 (0–30°)
150	R-40	Med.	Reflector spot	1,000	600 (0–15°)
150	R-40	Med.	Reflector flood	1,000	800 (0–30°)
300	R-40	Med.	Reflector spot	1,000	1,350 (0–15°)
300	R-40	Med.	Reflector flood	1,000	1,600 (0–30°)

SOURCE: "Illumination Design Data for Interiors," p. 6, Westinghouse Electric Corporation, Bloomfield, N.J.

Table 7-20. Mercury-lamp Data

Desig-nation	Watts	Bulb	Base	Ballast loss/lamp, watts	Rated avg life, hr*	Initial lumens
A-H1	400	T-16	Mogul	40†	4,000	16,000
A-H12	1,000	T-28	Mogul	85†	3,000	60,000
A-H9	3,000	T-9½	S.C. term	165‡	5,000	120,000

* Rated average life under specified test conditions at 5 hr per start. At 10 hr/start, rated average life is 6,000 hr.
† Single lamp high PF 110 to 125-volt ballasts. Losses for two-lamp ballasts are generally lower.
‡ Single lamp high PF, 230-volt ballast.
SOURCE: "Illumination Design Data for Interiors," p. 6, Westinghouse Electric Corporation, Bloomfield, N.J

Table 7-21. Fluorescent-lamp Data

Bulb	Watts	Base	Rated avg life, hr	Rated initial lumens*		
				White	Std cool white	Std warm white
Preheat Lamps						
33" T-12	25	Med. bipin	7,500†	1,430	1,370	1,440
48" T-12	40	Med. bipin	7,500†	2,480	2,370	2,500
60" T-17	90	Mog. bipin	7,500†	4,860	4,650	4,900
Instant-start Lamps						
48" T-12	40	Med. bipin	6,000‡	2,480	2,370	2,500
60" T-17	40	Mog. bipin	6,000‡	.....	2,300	
Slimline Lamps¶						
48" T-12	38§	Single pin	6,000‡	2,320	2,200	2,340
	52			3,020	2,870	3,050
72" T-12	59	Single pin	6,000‡	3,660	3,500	3,700
	72			4,300	4,100	4,340
96" T-12	75	Single pin	6,000‡	4,800	4,575	4,850
	96			5,800	5,540	5,860
96" T-8	34	Single pin	6,000‡	2,280	2,180	2,300
	51			3,300	3,150	3,330
	69			4,350	4,150	4,390

* Lumens measured after 100 hr burning at 80°F ambient and under specified test conditions.   The lumen outputs of the de luxe cool white and de luxe warm white lamps are approximately 40 per cent less than those of the corresponding standard cool white and standard warm white.   The lumen values of daylight and soft white lamps are 85 and 73 per cent, respectively, of the white values.

† Life under specified test conditions at 3 burning hours per start.   Lamp life is slightly longer for more burning hours per start.

‡ Life (tentative) under specified test conditions at 12 burning hours per start.   Lamp life is somewhat shorter for fewer burning hours per start.

¶ Slimlines may be operated at any current density within their design range.   The figures listed for the 96" T-8 Slimline are for 120, 200, and 300 ma.   The data listed for the T-12 Slimlines are for 425 and 600 ma.

§ Operates on a standard 40-watt instant-start ballast at 420 ma.

SOURCE: "Illumination Design Data for Interiors," p. 6, Westinghouse Electric Corporation, Bloomfield, N.J.

Table 7-22. Coefficients of Utilization

For Explanation of Symbols, See Notes on Page 7-80

Luminaire	Ceiling.. Room index	75% 50%	75% 30%	75% 10%	50% 50%	50% 30%	50% 10%	30% 30%	30% 10%
MF G−.75↑0 M−.65 P−.55↓79 Direct, RLM dome reflector, MS=1.0 x MH	J	.37	.31	.27	.36	.31	.27	.31	.27
	I	.45	.41	.38	.45	.40	.37	.40	.37
	H	.49	.45	.42	.49	.45	.42	.45	.42
	G	.53	.49	.46	.53	.49	.46	.48	.46
	F	.56	.53	.49	.55	.52	.49	.51	.49
	E	.61	.58	.55	.60	.57	.55	.56	.55
	D	.66	.63	.60	.64	.62	.60	.61	.60
	C	.67	.65	.62	.66	.64	.62	.63	.61
	B	.71	.68	.66	.69	.67	.65	.66	.64
	A	.72	.70	.67	.71	.68	.67	.67	.66
MF G−.75↑0 M−.65 P−.55↓70 Direct, RLM deep-bowl reflector, MS=1.0 x MH	J	.35	.31	.28	.34	.31	.28	.30	.28
	I	.43	.39	.37	.42	.39	.37	.39	.37
	H	.46	.44	.42	.46	.44	.42	.43	.42
	G	.50	.47	.45	.49	.47	.45	.46	.45
	F	.53	.50	.47	.51	.49	.47	.49	.47
	E	.56	.54	.51	.56	.54	.51	.53	.51
	D	.61	.58	.56	.59	.57	.56	.56	.56
	C	.62	.60	.57	.61	.58	.57	.58	.56
	B	.64	.62	.61	.63	.61	.60	.60	.59
	A	.65	.63	.61	.64	.62	.61	.61	.60
MF G−.75↑0 M−.60 P−.40↓75 Direct, high bay, narrow spread, MS=.6 x MH	J	.43	.40	.39	.42	.40	.39	.40	.38
	I	.51	.50	.49	.50	.49	.48	.49	.46
	H	.55	.54	.53	.54	.53	.52	.53	.52
	G	.59	.58	.57	.58	.56	.55	.56	.55
	F	.61	.60	.58	.59	.58	.58	.58	.57
	E	.64	.63	.62	.63	.62	.61	.61	.60
	D	.68	.65	.64	.66	.65	.64	.64	.63
	C	.69	.67	.66	.67	.66	.64	.64	.64
	B	.70	.68	.67	.68	.67	.66	.66	.65
	A	.71	.70	.68	.69	.67	.67	.67	.66
MF G−.75↑0 M−.65 P−.50↓75 Direct, high bay, medium or wide spread, MS=1.0 x MH	J	.40	.36	.34	.39	.36	.34	.36	.33
	I	.48	.45	.43	.47	.44	.43	.44	.42
	H	.52	.50	.48	.51	.49	.47	.49	.47
	G	.55	.53	.52	.55	.52	.51	.52	.51
	F	.58	.56	.53	.56	.55	.53	.55	.53
	E	.62	.60	.56	.61	.59	.57	.58	.57
	D	.66	.63	.61	.64	.62	.61	.62	.61
	C	.67	.65	.62	.66	.64	-62	.63	.62
	B	.69	.67	.66	.67	.65	.64	.65	.64
	A	.70	.68	.67	.69	.67	.65	.66	.64
MF G−.80↑0 M−.72 P−.65↓70 Direct, heavy duty narrow spread, MS=.5 x MH medium spread, MS=.8 x MH	J	.40	.38	.36	.39	.38	.36	.38	.36
	I	.48	.46	.45	.47	.46	.45	.45	.43
	H	.52	.51	.50	.51	.50	.49	.50	.48
	G	.55	.54	.53	.54	.53	.52	.53	.51
	F	.57	.56	.55	.56	.55	.54	.55	.53
	E	.60	.59	.58	.59	.58	.57	.57	.56
	D	.64	.61	.60	.62	.60	.59	.60	.59
	C	.64	.63	.61	.63	.62	.60	.60	.60
	B	.65	.64	.63	.64	.63	.62	.62	.61
	A	.66	.65	.64	.64	.63	.62	.62	.62

Table 7-22. Coefficients of Utilization (Continued)

Luminaire: MF G –.80 ↑0 M –.72 P –.65 ↓70 — Direct, heavy duty, wide spread, MS = 1.1 x MH

Ceiling..	75%			50%			30%	
Walls...	50%	30%	10%	50%	30%	10%	30%	10%
Room index	Coefficient of utilization							
J	.37	.34	.31	.36	.34	.31	.34	.31
I	.45	.42	.41	.44	.41	.40	.41	.39
H	.48	.46	.45	.49	.45	.44	.45	.44
G	.52	.50	.48	.51	.49	.48	.49	.48
F	.55	.52	.51	.50	.51	.50	.51	.50
E	.57	.56	.54	.57	.55	.53	.55	.53
D	.62	.59	.57	.60	.58	.57	.57	.57
C	.63	.61	.58	.62	.59	.58	.59	.57
B	.64	.62	.61	.63	.61	.60	.60	.59
A	.66	.64	.62	.64	.62	.61	.62	.60

Luminaire: MF G –.70 ↑5 M –.60 P –.45 ↓58 — Direct, RLM Glassteel diffuser, MS = 1.0 x MH

Room index	50%	30%	10%	50%	30%	10%	30%	10%
J	.27	.23	.20	.26	.23	.20	.22	.20
I	.34	.30	.28	.33	.29	.27	.29	.27
H	.37	.34	.31	.36	.33	.31	.32	.30
G	.40	.37	.34	.39	.36	.34	.35	.33
F	.42	.39	.37	.40	.38	.36	.37	.36
E	.46	.43	.41	.45	.42	.40	.41	.40
D	.49	.47	.44	.48	.46	.44	.44	.43
C	.51	.49	.46	.49	.47	.46	.46	.44
B	.53	.51	.49	.51	.49	.48	.48	.47
A	.54	.53	.51	.53	.51	.49	.49	.48

Luminaire: MF G –.60 ↑0 M –.50 P –.40 ↓67 — Direct, RLM silvered-bowl diffuser, MS =.8 x MH

Room index	50%	30%	10%	50%	30%	10%	30%	10%
J	.38	.36	.35	.38	.36	.35	.36	.35
I	.46	.45	.44	.45	.44	.43	.44	.42
H	.49	.49	.48	.49	.48	.47	.48	.47
G	.53	.52	.51	.52	.51	.50	.51	.49
F	.55	.54	.53	.53	.53	.52	.53	.51
E	.57	.57	.56	.57	.56	.55	.55	.54
D	.61	.59	.58	.59	.58	.57	.57	.56
C	.62	.61	.59	.60	.59	.58	.58	.57
B	.63	.62	.61	.61	.60	.59	.59	.58
A	.64	.63	.62	.62	.61	.60	.60	.59

Luminaire: MF G –.75 ↑0 M –.65 P –.55 ↓65 — Direct, vapor-tight, wide spread, MS = 1.0 x MH

Room index	50%	30%	10%	50%	30%	10%	30%	10%
J	.31	.26	.23	.30	.26	.23	.26	.23
I	.38	.34	.31	.37	.33	.31	.33	.31
H	.41	.38	.34	.41	.38	.34	.37	.34
G	.45	.41	.39	.44	.41	.39	.40	.39
F	.47	.44	.41	.46	.43	.41	.43	.41
E	.51	.48	.46	.50	.48	.46	.47	.46
D	.55	.52	.50	.54	.52	.50	.51	.50
C	.56	.54	.52	.55	.53	.52	.52	.51
B	.59	.57	.55	.58	.56	.54	.55	.54
A	.60	.58	.56	.59	.57	.56	.56	.55

Luminaire: MF G –.70 ↑0 M –.60 P –.50 ↓53 — Direct, prismatic lens, medium spread, MS =.8 x MH

Room index	50%	30%	10%	50%	30%	10%	30%	10%
J	.25	.22	.20	.24	.22	.20	.22	.20
I	.31	.28	.26	.29	.28	.26	.28	.26
H	.34	.31	.29	.32	.31	.29	.30	.28
G	.36	.33	.32	.34	.33	.31	.32	.30
F	.38	.35	.34	.36	.34	.33	.34	.32
E	.40	.39	.38	.39	.37	.36	.37	.35
D	.43	.41	.40	.42	.40	.39	.39	.38
C	.45	.43	.42	.44	.41	.40	.40	.40
B	.48	.45	.44	.47	.43	.42	.42	.41
A	.50	.47	.46	.48	.46	.45	.45	.42

Table 7-22. Coefficients of Utilization (Continued)

Luminaire	Ceiling..	75%			50%			30%	
	Walls...	50%	30%	10%	50%	30%	10%	30%	10%
	Room index	Coefficient of utilization							

MF-.75 ↑0 ↓62

Direct, PAR-38, 150-watt shielded to 45°, total lamp lumens = 1850, MS=.5 x MH

Room index	50%	30%	10%	50%	30%	10%	30%	10%
J	.52	.49	.47	.51	.49	.47	.48	.47
I	.55	.53	.51	.54	.52	.51	.51	.50
H	.57	.55	.53	.56	.54	.53	.53	.53
G	.58	.57	.55	.57	.56	.55	.55	.54
F	.59	.58	.57	.58	.57	.56	.56	.56
E	.61	.60	.59	.60	.59	.58	.58	.57
D	.63	.62	.61	.61	.61	.60	.60	.59
C	.64	.64	.63	.63	.63	.62	.62	.61
B	.65	.65	.64	.64	.64	.63	.63	.62
A	.66	.66	.65	.65	.65	.64	.64	.63

MF
G -.65 ↑0
M -.55
P -.45 ↓79

Direct, RLM, 2 40-watt lamps, MS = 1.0 x MH

Room index	50%	30%	10%	50%	30%	10%	30%	10%
J	.38	.32	.28	.37	.32	.28	.31	.28
I	.47	.42	.39	.46	.41	.38	.40	.37
H	.51	.47	.44	.50	.47	.43	.46	.43
G	.55	.51	.48	.54	.51	.47	.50	.47
F	.58	.54	.51	.57	.53	.51	.52	.50
E	.63	.60	.57	.62	.59	.56	.58	.55
D	.68	.64	.61	.66	.64	.61	.63	.60
C	.70	.67	.63	.68	.65	.64	.64	.62
B	.73	.70	.68	.71	.68	.67	.67	.66
A	.74	.72	.70	.72	.70	.68	.69	.67

MF
G -.65 ↑0
M -.55
P -.45 ↓72

Direct, RLM, 3 40-watt lamps, MS = 1.0 x MH

Room index	50%	30%	10%	50%	30%	10%	30%	10%
J	.34	.29	.25	.33	.29	.25	.28	.25
I	.42	.38	.35	.41	.37	.34	.37	.34
H	.46	.42	.39	.44	.42	.39	.41	.39
G	.50	.46	.43	.48	.45	.41	.44	.41
F	.53	.49	.46	.51	.47	.44	.47	.44
E	.57	.54	.51	.56	.52	.50	.52	.50
D	.61	.58	.55	.59	.56	.54	.56	.54
C	.63	.60	.57	.61	.58	.56	.58	.56
B	.66	.64	.61	.64	.60	.59	.60	.59
A	.67	.65	.62	.66	.62	.61	.62	.61

MF
G -.60 ↑0
M -.50
P -.45 ↓71

Direct, RLM, 2·85-watt lamps, MS = 1.0 x MH

Room index	50%	30%	10%	50%	30%	10%	30%	10%
J	.33	.28	.25	.33	.28	.25	.28	.25
I	.41	.37	.34	.40	.36	.33	.36	.33
H	.45	.41	.38	.44	.41	.38	.40	.38
G	.48	.45	.42	.48	.45	.42	.43	.42
F	.51	.48	.45	.50	.47	.45	.46	.45
E	.55	.53	.50	.55	.52	.50	.51	.50
D	.60	.57	.54	.58	.56	.54	.55	.54
C	.61	.59	.56	.60	.57	.56	.57	.55
B	.64	.62	.60	.62	.60	.59	.60	.58
A	.65	.63	.61	.64	.62	.60	.61	.60

MF
G -.70 ↑0
M -.65
P -.55 ↓60

Direct, dust and vapor-tight MS = 1.0 x MH

Room index	50%	30%	10%	50%	30%	10%	30%	10%
J	.29	.26	.23	.28	.26	.23	.25	.23
I	.35	.32	.31	.35	.32	.30	.32	.30
H	.38	.36	.34	.38	.36	.34	.35	.34
G	.41	.39	.37	.41	.39	.37	.38	.37
F	.44	.41	.39	.42	.41	.39	.40	.39
E	.46	.45	.42	.46	.44	.42	.44	.42
D	.50	.48	.46	.49	.47	.46	.46	.46
C	.51	.49	.47	.50	.48	.47	.48	.46
B	.53	.51	.50	.52	.50	.49	.49	.49
A	.54	.52	.50	.53	.51	.50	.50	.49

Table 7-22. Coefficients of Utilization (Continued)

Luminaire	Ceiling	75%			50%			30%	
	Walls	50%	30%	10%	50%	30%	10%	30%	10%
	Room index	Coefficient of utilization							
MF G–.70 ↑0 M–.60 P–.50 ↓80 — Direct, 3-kw mercury, MS = 1.0 x MH	J	.38	.32	.28	.37	.32	.28	.31	.28
	I	.47	.42	.39	.46	.41	.38	.41	.38
	H	.51	.47	.43	.50	.47	.43	.46	.43
	G	.55	.51	.47	.54	.51	.47	.49	.47
	F	.58	.54	.51	.56	.53	.81	.52	.51
	E	.63	.59	.55	.62	.59	.56	.58	.56
	D	.67	.64	.61	.66	.63	.61	.63	.61
	C	.69	.67	.64	.67	.65	.63	.64	.63
	B	.72	.70	.67	.71	.68	.67	.67	.66
	A	.74	.71	.69	.72	.70	.68	.69	.67
MF G–.65 ↑0 M–.55 P–.45 ↓64 — Direct, RLM with louvers, MS = .9 x MH	J	.33	.28	.26	.32	.28	.26	.28	.26
	I	.39	.36	.34	.39	.35	.34	.35	.34
	H	.43	.40	.38	.42	.40	.38	.39	.38
	G	.46	.43	.41	.45	.43	.41	.42	.41
	F	.48	.46	.43	.47	.45	.43	.45	.43
	E	.52	.50	.47	.51	.49	.47	.48	.47
	D	.55	.53	.51	.54	.52	.51	.52	.51
	C	.57	.55	.52	.55	.53	.52	.53	.52
	B	.59	.57	.56	.57	.56	.55	.55	.54
	A	.60	.58	.56	.59	.57	.56	.56	.55
MF G–.70 ↑0 M–.60 P–.50 ↓50 — Direct, Troffer, glass, MS = 1.0 x MH	J	.28	.27	.26	.28	.27	.26	.28	.26
	I	.34	.33	.32	.34	.32	.32	.33	.31
	H	.36	.36	.36	.36	.36	.35	.35	.35
	G	.39	.38	.38	.38	.38	.37	.37	.36
	F	.41	.40	.39	.40	.39	.38	.39	.38
	E	.43	.42	.42	.42	.42	.40	.41	.40
	D	.46	.44	.43	.44	.43	.43	.42	.42
	C	.46	.45	.44	.45	.44	.43	.43	.43
	B	.47	.45	.45	.45	.44	.44	.44	.44
	A	.47	.46	.46	.46	.45	.45	.45	.44
MF G–.70 ↑0 M–.60 P–.50 ↓47 — Direct, Troffer, glass, MS = 1.0 x MH	J	.27	.25	.24	.26	.25	.24	.26	.24
	I	.32	.31	.30	.31	.30	.30	.30	.29
	H	.34	.34	.33	.34	.33	.33	.33	.32
	G	.36	.35	.35	.36	.35	.35	.35	.34
	F	.39	.38	.37	.37	.37	.36	.37	.36
	E	.40	.40	.39	.39	.39	.38	.39	.38
	D	.43	.41	.40	.41	.40	.40	.40	.39
	C	.43	.42	.41	.42	.41	.40	.40	.40
	B	.44	.43	.42	.43	.42	.41	.41	.41
	A	.45	.44	.43	.43	.42	.42	.42	.41
MF G–.70 ↑0 M–.60 P–.55 ↓61 — Direct, Troffer, louvers, MS = .8 x MH	J	.33	.31	.30	.33	.31	.30	.30	.29
	I	.40	.38	.38	.39	.38	.37	.38	.36
	H	.43	.42	.41	.42	.41	.41	.41	.40
	G	.46	.45	.44	.46	.44	.43	.44	.43
	F	.49	.47	.46	.47	.46	.45	.46	.45
	E	.51	.50	.49	.50	.49	.48	.49	.47
	D	.55	.52	.51	.53	.52	.50	.51	.50
	C	.55	.54	.52	.54	.53	.52	.52	.51
	B	.56	.55	.54	.55	.53	.53	.53	.52
	A	.57	.56	.55	.56	.55	.53	.54	.53

Table 7-22. Coefficients of Utilization (Continued)

Luminaire	Ceiling..	75%			50%			30%	
	Walls...	50%	30%	10%	50%	30%	10%	30%	10%
	Room index	Coefficient of utilization							
MF G−.75 ↑8 M−.65 ↓50 P−.55 — Semidirect, surface−mounted, MS = 1.0 x MH	J	.21	.17	.14	.20	.16	.14	.16	.14
	I	.26	.22	.20	.25	.21	.19	.21	.19
	H	.29	.25	.23	.28	.25	.22	.24	.22
	G	.32	.28	.25	.30	.27	.25	.26	.24
	F	.34	.30	.28	.33	.30	.27	.29	.27
	E	.38	.34	.31	.36	.33	.31	.32	.30
	D	.41	.37	.34	.39	.36	.34	.35	.33
	C	.42	.39	.36	.41	.38	.36	.37	.35
	B	.45	.42	.39	.42	.40	.39	.39	.38
	A	.47	.44	.41	.45	.42	.40	.41	.39
MF G−.75 ↑9 M−.65 ↓55 P−.55 — Semidirect, surface−mounted, MS = 1.0 x MH	J	.24	.20	.19	.23	.20	.17	.19	.17
	I	.30	.26	.23	.29	.25	.23	.25	.23
	H	.33	.29	.27	.32	.29	.26	.28	.26
	G	.36	.32	.30	.34	.32	.29	.30	.29
	F	.39	.35	.32	.37	.34	.31	.33	.31
	E	.42	.39	.35	.41	.38	.35	.36	.34
	D	.45	.41	.39	.44	.41	.38	.40	.38
	C	.47	.44	.41	.45	.42	.40	.41	.39
	B	.50	.47	.44	.48	.45	.43	.44	.42
	A	.52	.49	.46	.50	.47	.45	.45	.44
MF G−.75 ↑18 M−.65 ↓53 P−.55 — Semidirect, surface−mounted MS = 1.0 x MH	J	.23	.19	.17	.23	.18	.16	.17	.16
	I	.29	.25	.22	.28	.24	.21	.23	.21
	H	.32	.26	.25	.31	.28	.25	.26	.24
	G	.36	.32	.29	.34	.30	.27	.29	.26
	F	.40	.35	.31	.37	.33	.30	.31	.29
	E	.43	.39	.35	.41	.37	.34	.35	.32
	D	.47	.42	.39	.44	.40	.37	.38	.36
	C	.49	.45	.41	.46	.42	.39	.40	.38
	B	.52	.48	.45	.49	.45	.43	.43	.41
	A	.54	.51	.47	.51	.47	.45	.44	.43
MF G−.75 ↑24 M−.65 ↓66 P−.55 — Semidirect, surface−mounted, MS = 1.0 x MH	J	.29	.24	.22	.29	.23	.20	.22	.20
	I	.37	.32	.28	.36	.30	.27	.29	.27
	H	.41	.35	.32	.39	.34	.32	.33	.30
	G	.46	.41	.37	.43	.38	.34	.37	.33
	F	.51	.44	.39	.47	.42	.39	.39	.37
	E	.55	.49	.44	.52	.47	.43	.44	.41
	D	.60	.53	.49	.56	.51	.47	.48	.46
	C	.62	.57	.52	.58	.53	.50	.51	.48
	B	.66	.61	.57	.62	.57	.54	.54	.52
	A	.68	.64	.60	.65	.60	.57	.56	.55
MF G−.75 ↑39 M−.70 ↓45 P−.65 — General diffuse, enclosing globe, MS = 1.2 x MH	J	.24	.20	.16	.22	.18	.16	.17	.15
	I	.30	.25	.23	.27	.23	.21	.22	.19
	H	.33	.29	.26	.31	.27	.24	.25	.22
	G	.37	.33	.30	.34	.30	.27	.27	.25
	F	.41	.36	.32	.36	.33	.31	.31	.27
	E	.45	.41	.37	.41	.37	.33	.33	.30
	D	.49	.44	.40	.44	.40	.37	.36	.33
	C	.51	.47	.43	.46	.42	.39	.38	.35
	B	.55	.51	.47	.49	.45	.43	.40	.38
	A	.57	.53	.50	.51	.47	.45	.42	.40

Table 7-22. Coefficients of Utilization (Continued)

Luminaire	Ceiling..	75%			50%			30%	
	Walls...	50%	30%	10%	50%	30%	10%	30%	10%
	Room index	Coefficient of utilization							

MF
G – .75 ↑30
M – .65
P – .55 ↓59

Semidirect, ceiling – mounted,*
MS = 1.0 x MH

Room index	50%	30%	10%	50%	30%	10%	30%	10%
J	.30	.25	.21	.28	.23	.20	.22	.19
I	.38	.33	.29	.35	.30	.27	.29	.26
H	.42	.37	.34	.39	.35	.32	.33	.30
G	.46	.41	.37	.42	.38	.35	.35	.33
F	.50	.45	.41	.46	.41	.38	.38	.36
E	.55	.50	.46	.50	.46	.43	.43	.40
D	.60	.55	.51	.54	.50	.47	.47	.45
C	.62	.58	.54	.56	.52	.50	.49	.47
B	.66	.62	.59	.60	.56	.54	.52	.50
A	.68	.65	.61	.62	.58	.56	.54	.52

MF
G – .70 ↑19
M – .65
P – .60 ↓49

Semidirect, ceiling – mounted,*
2 or 4 lamps, MS = .9 x MH

Room index	50%	30%	10%	50%	30%	10%	30%	10%
J	.28	.25	.23	.23	.21	.18	.18	.16
I	.34	.31	.29	.28	.26	.25	.22	.21
H	.37	.34	.33	.31	.29	.28	.25	.24
G	.41	.38	.36	.34	.32	.30	.27	.26
F	.43	.41	.38	.36	.33	.32	.29	.27
E	.46	.44	.42	.38	.37	.35	.31	.30
D	.50	.47	.45	.41	.39	.37	.33	.32
C	.52	.49	.46	.42	.40	.39	.34	.33
B	.54	.51	.50	.44	.42	.41	.36	.35
A	.56	.53	.51	.46	.43	.42	.37	.36

MF
G – .70 ↑46
M – .65
P – .60 ↓33

Direct – indirect, suspension-mounted,
2 or 4 lamps, MS = 1.2 x MH

Room index	50%	30%	10%	50%	30%	10%	30%	10%
J	.26	.23	.20	.23	.21	.19	.19	.17
I	.31	.28	.27	.28	.26	.24	.23	.20
H	.35	.32	.30	.31	.28	.27	.26	.24
G	.38	.35	.33	.34	.31	.30	.28	.27
F	.41	.38	.35	.36	.34	.32	.30	.28
E	.44	.42	.39	.39	.37	.35	.32	.31
D	.48	.45	.42	.42	.39	.38	.34	.33
C	.50	.49	.44	.43	.41	.39	.35	.34
B	.53	.50	.48	.45	.43	.42	.37	.36
A	.54	.52	.50	.47	.45	.43	.39	.37

MF
G – .65 ↑20
M – .55
P – .50 ↓47

Semidirect, ceiling – mounted,*
glass bottom, MS = .9 x MH

Room index	50%	30%	10%	50%	30%	10%	30%	10%
J	.28	.23	.21	.23	.20	.18	.17	.16
I	.33	.30	.28	.28	.25	.23	.22	.20
H	.36	.33	.31	.30	.28	.26	.24	.23
G	.39	.36	.34	.33	.30	.29	.26	.25
F	.42	.39	.37	.35	.32	.31	.28	.26
E	.45	.42	.40	.38	.36	.34	.30	.29
D	.48	.45	.43	.40	.38	.36	.32	.31
C	.50	.47	.44	.42	.39	.38	.33	.32
B	.53	.50	.48	.43	.41	.40	.35	.34
A	.54	.52	.49	.45	.43	.41	.36	.35

MF
G – .65 ↑49
M – .55
P – .50 ↓33

Direct – indirect, suspension-mounted,
glass bottom, MS = 1.2 x MH

Room index	50%	30%	10%	50%	30%	10%	30%	10%
J	.27	.24	.22	.24	.22	.21	.21	.19
I	.33	.30	.29	.29	.27	.26	.25	.23
H	.36	.34	.32	.32	.30	.29	.28	.26
G	.39	.37	.35	.36	.33	.32	.30	.28
F	.43	.40	.37	.39	.35	.34	.31	.30
E	.46	.43	.41	.41	.38	.37	.34	.32
D	.50	.46	.44	.43	.41	.39	.36	.35
C	.52	.49	.46	.45	.43	.41	.37	.36
B	.55	.52	.50	.47	.45	.44	.38	.37
A	.56	.54	.52	.49	.47	.45	.40	.38

MF
G – .60 ↑56
M – .50
P – .40 ↓20

Semi-indirect, suspension-mounted,
2 or 4 lamps, MS = 1.2 x MH

Room index	50%	30%	10%	50%	30%	10%	30%	10%
J	.18	.14	.13	.14	.12	.10	.09	.08
I	.22	.19	.17	.18	.15	.14	.12	.11
H	.25	.22	.20	.20	.18	.16	.14	.13
G	.28	.25	.22	.22	.20	.18	.16	.15
F	.30	.27	.24	.24	.22	.20	.17	.16
E	.34	.30	.27	.27	.24	.22	.19	.18
D	.37	.33	.31	.29	.26	.25	.21	.20
C	.39	.36	.33	.30	.28	.26	.22	.21
B	.42	.39	.37	.32	.30	.28	.24	.23
A	.44	.41	.39	.34	.32	.30	.25	.24

* Data based upon photometric curve run with false ceiling plate installed above luminaire in accordance with standard test procedure.

Table 7-22. Coefficients of Utilization (Continued)

Luminaire	Ceiling..	75			50%			30%	
	Walls...	50%	30%	10%	50%	30%	10%	30%	10%
	Room index	\multicolumn{8}{Coefficient of utilization}							

	Room index	75 / 50%			50%			30%	
		50%	30%	10%	50%	30%	10%	30%	10%
MF G −.70 ↑79 M −.60 P −.50 ↓3 Indirect, glass, plastic, or metal, MS = 1.2 x MH	J	.16	.13	.11	.12	.10	.08	.06	.05
	I	.20	.16	.15	.15	.13	.11	.08	.07
	H	.23	.20	.17	.17	.14	.13	.10	.08
	G	.26	.23	.20	.20	.17	.15	.11	.10
	F	.29	.26	.23	.22	.19	.17	.12	.11
	E	.32	.29	.26	.24	.21	.19	.13	.12
	D	.36	.32	.30	.26	.24	.22	.15	.14
	C	.38	.35	.32	.28	.25	.24	.16	.15
	B	.42	.39	.36	.30	.29	.27	.18	.17
	A	.44	.41	.39	.33	.30	.29	.19	.18
MF G −.65 ↑85 M −.60 P −.55 ↓0 Indirect, silvered bowl, MS = 1.2 x MH	J	.17	.14	.12	.13	.11	.09	.07	.06
	I	.21	.17	.16	.16	.14	.12	.09	.08
	H	.24	.21	.18	.18	.15	.14	.11	.09
	G	.27	.24	.21	.21	.18	.16	.12	.11
	F	.30	.27	.23	.23	.20	.18	.13	.12
	E	.33	.30	.27	.25	.22	.20	.14	.13
	D	.37	.33	.31	.27	.25	.23	.16	.15
	C	.39	.36	.33	.29	.26	.25	.17	.16
	B	.43	.40	.37	.31	.30	.28	.19	.18
	A	.45	.42	.40	.34	.31	.30	.20	.19

Typical luminaire	Estimated maintenance factors*	Distribution and max spacing	Room index	Ceiling							
				75%			50%			30%	
				\multicolumn{8}{Walls}							
				50%	30%	10%	50%	30%	10%	30%	10%
Luminous ceiling using thin corrugated plastic diffuser having a reflectance of .40 and transmittance of .50	G −.65 ↑0 M −.65 P −.45 ↓68	Direct	J	.22	.16	.12	Estimates based on calculations with cavity reflectance = 75%, cavity efficiency = 60%, apparent ceiling reflectance = 60%, floor reflectance = 14%				
			I	.27	.22	.19					
			H	.33	.28	.24					
			G	.38	.32	.29					
			F	.41	.37	.33					
			E	.46	.42	.39					
			D	.49	.46	.43					
			C	.52	.49	.46					
			B	.55	.52	.50					
			A	.57	.55	.53					

Typical luminaire	Estimated maintenance factors*	Distribution	Room index	with reflectors shallow cavity 75%			without reflectors shallow cavity 75%		
45° plastic louverall below 2-lamp 40-watt industrial type fluorescent units and bare lamps	G −.70 ↑0 M −.65 P −.55 ↓60	Direct	J	.28	.25	.23	.25	.20	.19
			I	.31	.29	.27	.29	.25	.23
			H	.34	.32	.30	.32	.28	.26
			G	.37	.35	.33	.35	.32	.30
			F	.40	.37	.35	.38	.34	.32
			E	.43	.41	.38	.41	.38	.36
			D	.45	.43	.40	.43	.40	.39
			C	.46	.44	.42	.45	.42	.41
			B	.48	.45	.43	.47	.44	.43
			A	.48	.46	.44	.48	.46	.44
45° white metal louverall	G −.70 ↑0 M −.65 P −.55 ↓50	Direct	J	.23	.20	.19	.23	.19	.18
			I	.27	.24	.22	.26	.23	.21
			H	.30	.27	.25	.29	.26	.24
			G	.32	.29	.28	.32	.29	.27
			F	.34	.31	.30	.34	.31	.29
			E	.36	.33	.32	.36	.33	.32
			D	.38	.35	.34	.38	.35	.34
			C	.39	.37	.36	.39	.37	.36
			B	.41	.39	.38	.41	.38	.38
			A	.42	.40	.39	.42	.40	.39

Table 7-22. Coefficients of Utilization (Continued)

Direct, Troffer, louvers, MS = .8 x MH
MF: G – .70 ↑0, M – .60, P – .55 ↓53

Luminaire / Room index	Ceiling 75%			Ceiling 50%			Ceiling 30%	
Walls	50%	30%	10%	50%	30%	10%	30%	10%
J	.29	.27	.26	.29	.27	.26	.27	.26
I	.35	.34	.33	.35	.33	.33	.33	.31
H	.38	.37	.36	.37	.36	.36	.36	.35
G	.40	.39	.39	.40	.39	.38	.38	.38
F	.43	.42	.42	.41	.40	.39	.40	.39
E	.45	.44	.43	.44	.43	.42	.43	.42
D	.48	.46	.45	.46	.45	.44	.45	.44
C	.48	.47	.45	.47	.46	.45	.45	.45
B	.50	.48	.47	.48	.47	.46	.46	.46
A	.50	.49	.48	.49	.48	.47	.48	.46

Direct, louverall ceiling, shielded to 45°, cavity reflectance 75%
MF: G – .70 ↑0, M – .65 (Metal), P – .55 ↓50 (Metal) / ↑0 ↓59 (Plastic)

Coefficients for plastic louvers based on the use of bare lamps without reflectors.

Room index	METAL Cavity—75%			PLASTIC Cavity—75%		
J	.23	.20	.19	.25	.20	.19
I	.27	.24	.22	.29	.25	.23
H	.30	.27	.25	.32	.28	.26
G	.32	.29	.28	.35	.32	.30
F	.34	.31	.30	.38	.34	.32
E	.36	.33	.32	.41	.38	.36
D	.38	.35	.34	.43	.40	.39
C	.39	.37	.36	.45	.42	.41
B	.41	.39	.38	.47	.44	.43
A	.42	.40	.39	.48	.46	.45

Direct, surface-mounted, 2 or 4 lamps, MS = 1.0 x MH
MF: G – .70 ↑0, M – .60, P – .55 ↓60

Room index	Ceiling 75%			Ceiling 50%			Ceiling 30%	
Walls	50%	30%	10%	50%	30%	10%	30%	10%
J	.29	.26	.23	.28	.26	.23	.25	.23
I	.35	.32	.31	.35	.32	.30	.32	.30
H	.38	.36	.34	.38	.36	.34	.35	.34
G	.41	.39	.37	.41	.39	.37	.38	.37
F	.44	.41	.39	.42	.41	.39	.40	.39
E	.46	.45	.42	.46	.44	.42	.44	.42
D	.50	.48	.46	.49	.47	.46	.46	.46
C	.51	.49	.47	.50	.48	.47	.48	.46
B	.53	.51	.50	.52	.50	.49	.49	.49
A	.54	.52	.50	.53	.51	.50	.50	.49

Semidirect, surface-mounted, MS = 1.0 x MH
MF: G – .70 ↑5, M – .65, P – .60 ↓47

Room index	Ceiling 75%			Ceiling 50%			Ceiling 30%	
Walls	50%	30%	10%	50%	30%	10%	30%	10%
J	.26	.23	.22	.25	.23	.22	.23	.21
I	.31	.29	.28	.30	.28	.27	.28	.26
H	.34	.32	.31	.32	.31	.30	.30	.29
G	.36	.34	.34	.35	.33	.32	.33	.32
F	.38	.36	.35	.36	.35	.34	.35	.33
E	.40	.39	.37	.39	.38	.36	.37	.35
D	.43	.41	.39	.41	.40	.38	.39	.38
C	.45	.44	.41	.42	.41	.39	.40	.39
B	.46	.44	.42	.44	.42	.41	.41	.40
A	.46	.45	.43	.45	.43	.42	.42	.41

NOTES: *Symbols*

MF maintenance factor
G good maintenance factor
M medium maintenance factor

P poor maintenance factor
MS maximum spacing
MH mounting height

Distribution. Curves represent shape and not quantity of light. Fluorescent curves are taken normal to lamp axis.

↑ 48 per cent up
↓ 36 per cent down

$48 + 36 = 84\%$ luminaire efficiency

Table 7-23. Room Index

Ceiling height in feet for semi-indirect and indirect lighting: 9, 9½ | 10–11½ | 12–13½ | 14–16½ | 17–20 | 21–24 | 25–30 | 31–36 | 37–50

Mounting height above floor in feet for direct and semidirect lighting: 7, 7½ | 8, 8½ | 9, 9½ | 10–11½ | 12–13½ | 14–16½ | 17–20 | 21–24 | 25–30 | 31–36 | 37–50

Room width, ft	Room length, ft	7, 7½	8, 8½	9, 9½	10–11½	12–13½	14–16½	17–20	21–24	25–30	31–36	37–50
							Room index*					
9 (8½–9)	8–10	H	I	J	J							
	10–14	H	I	I	J							
	14–20	G	H	I	J	J						
	20–30	G	G	H	I	J	J					
	30–42	F	G	H	I	J	J	J				
	42–up	E	F	G	H	I	J	J				
10 (9½–10½)	10–14	G	H	I	J	J						
	14–20	G	H	I	J	J	J					
	20–30	F	G	H	I	J	J					
	30–42	F	G	G	H	I	J	J				
	42–60	E	F	G	H	I	J	J				
	60–up	E	F	F	H	H	I	J				
12 (11–12½)	10–14	G	H	I	I	J	J					
	14–20	F	G	H	I	J	J					
	20–30	F	G	G	H	I	J	J				
	30–42	E	F	G	H	I	J	J				
	42–60	E	F	F	G	H	I	J				
	60–up	E	E	F	G	H	I	J				
14 (13–15½)	14–20	F	G	H	H	I	J	J				
	20–30	E	F	G	H	I	J	J				
	30–42	E	F	F	G	H	I	J	J			
	42–60	E	E	F	F	H	I	J	J	J		
	60–up	D	E	E	F	F	G	H	J	J	J	
	90–up	D	E	E	F	F	G	I	J	J		
17 (16–18½)	14–20	E	F	G	H	I	J	J				
	20–30	E	F	F	G	H	I	J	J			
	30–42	D	E	E	F	G	H	I	J	J		
	42–60	D	E	E	F	G	H	I	J	J	J	
	60–110	D	E	E	F	G	H	I	J	J	J	
	110–up	C	D	E	E	F	G	H	I	J	J	
20 (19–21½)	20–30	D	E	F	G	H	I	J	J			
	30–42	D	E	E	F	G	H	I	J	J		
	42–60	D	D	E	E	F	G	H	I	J	J	
	60–90	C	D	E	E	F	G	H	I	J	J	
	90–140	C	C	D	E	E	F	F	H	I	J	
	140–up	C	C	D	D	E	E	F	F	H	I	J
24 (22–26)	20–30	D	E	E	F	G	H	I	J	J		
	30–42	C	D	D	E	F	G	H	I	J	J	
	42–60	C	C	D	D	E	F	F	H	I	J	J
	60–90	C	C	D	D	E	F	F	G	H	I	J
	90–140	C	C	C	D	E	E	F	G	H	I	J
	140–up	C	C	D	D	E	E	F	G	H	I	J
30 (27–33)	30–42	C	D	D	E	F	G	H	I	J	J	
	42–60	C	C	C	D	D	F	F	H	H	I	J
	60–90	B	C	C	D	D	E	F	G	H	I	J
	90–140	B	C	C	C	D	E	F	G	H	I	J
	140–180	B	C	C	C	D	E	E	F	G	H	J
	180–up	B	C	C	C	D	E	E	F	G	H	J

Table 7-23. Room Index (Continued)

		C1	C2	C3	C4	C5	C6	C7	C8	C9	C10	C11
Ceiling height in feet for semi-indirect and indirect lighting		9, 9½	10–11½	12–13½	14–16½	17–20	21–24	25–30	31–36	37–50		
Mounting height above floor in feet for direct and semidirect lighting............		7, 7½	8, 8½	9, 9½	10–11½	12–13½	14–16½	17–20	21–24	25–30	31–36	37–50
Room width, ft	Room length, ft	Room index*										
36 (34–39)	30–42	B	C	D	E	F	F	H	I	I	J	
	42–60	B	C	C	D	E	F	G	H	I	J	J
	60–90	A	C	C	C	E	E	F	H	H	J	J
	90–140	A	B	C	C	D	E	F	G	G	I	I
	140–200	A	B	C	C	D	E	F	F	H	I	
	200–up	A	B	C	C	D	E	F	F	G	H	I
42 (40–45)	42–60	A	B	C	C	E	F	G	H	I	J	
	60–90	A	B	B	C	D	E	F	G	H	I	J
	90–140	A	B	B	C	C	D	E	F	G	H	I
	140–200	A	A	B	C	D	D	E	F	H	J	
	200–up	A	A	B	C	D	D	E	F	G	I	
50 (46–55)	42–60	A	A	B	C	D	E	F	G	H	I	J
	60–90	A	A	B	C	C	D	F	F	G	H	I
	90–140	A	A	A	C	C	C	E	F	F	G	I
	140–200	A	A	A	C	C	C	D	E	F	G	I
	200–up	A	A	A	C	C	C	D	E	F	G	H
60 (56–67)	60–90	A	A	A	B	C	D	E	F	G	H	I
	90–140	A	A	A	B	C	C	D	E	F	G	H
	140–200	A	A	A	B	C	C	C	D	E	F	H
	200–up	A	A	A	B	B	C	D	D	E	F	H
75 (68–90)	60–90	A	A	A	A	B	C	D	E	F	G	I
	90–140	A	A	A	A	B	C	D	E	F	G	H
	140–200	A	A	A	A	B	B	C	D	E	F	G
	200–up	A	A	A	A	B	B	C	C	D	E	G

* "Room index" is the classification of a room according to its proportions; large and small rooms of the same proportion have the same index. Hence, for large rooms of dimensions greater than those shown, divide each dimension by the same number and use the index determined for the smaller room.

EXAMPLE: A room 200 by 600 by 40 ft would have the same room index as a room 50 by 150 by 10 ft.

SOURCE: "Essential Data for Lighting Design," p. 2, General Electric Company, Cleveland, Ohio, November, 1951.

Table 7-24. Diffuse-reflection Factors

Color	Average reflection factor	Color	Average reflection factor
White..........	0.88	Medium:	
Very Light:		Blue green....	0.54
Blue green.....	.76	Yellow........	.65
Cream........	.81	Buff..........	.63
Blue..........	.65	Gray.........	.61
Buff..........	.76	Dark:	
Gray..........	.83	Blue.........	.08
Light:		Yellow........	.50
Blue green.....	.72	Brown........	.10
Cream........	.79	Gray.........	.25
Blue..........	.55	Green........	.07
Buff..........	.70	Black.........	.03
Gray..........	.73	Wood Finishes:	
		Maple........	.42
		Walnut.......	.16
		Mahogany....	.12

SOURCE: "Illumination Design Data for Interiors," pp. 2, 6, Westinghouse Electric Corporation, Bloomfield, N.J.

Table 7-25. Brightness Ratios

Area	Max Ratio
Between task and surroundings.............	3:1
Between task and remote surfaces (walls)....	10:1
Between fixtures and adjacent surface.......	20:1
Anywhere in normal field of view...........	40:1

SOURCE: "IES Handbook," Sec. 9, Illuminating Engineering Society, New York, 1952.

Table 7-26. Approximate Ballast Loss per Lamp, Watts

Bulb	Watts	Starter switch no. or current, ma	Approximate ballast loss per lamp, watts					
			110–125 volt				220–250 volt, high PF	
			Single lamp		Two-lamp high PF			
			Low PF	High PF	Series	Lead lag	Single lamp	Two lamp
Preheat Lamps								
48″ T-12	40	FS-4	8.5	11	...	7.8	8.5	9.3
60″ T-17	90	FS-85	....	25	...	19.5	...	16
Rapid-start Lamps								
48″ T-12	40	430	12	12	...	8.5		
Instant-start Lamps								
48″ and 60″	40	415	....	20	11	12		
Slimline Lamps								
72″ T-12	55	425	....	25	16	15		
	67	600	....	...	...	17.5		
96″ T-12	74	425	....	29	16	17.5		
	95	600	....	...	...	29		
96″ T-8	50	200	....	20	...	16		
	69	300	....	25	...	23		

SOURCE: "Illumination Design Data for Interiors," pp. 2, 6, Westinghouse Electric Corporation, Bloomfield, N.J.

Table 7-27. Brightness Ratios for Direct, Uniformly Diffusing, Indirect, and Luminous-ceiling Systems

$$A = \frac{\text{average wall brightness (midway between floor and ceiling)}}{\text{average illumination at work plane}}$$

Ceiling reflectance	0.80				0.70			0.50		
Wall reflectance...	0.80	0.50	0.30	0.10	0.50	0.30	0.10	0.50	0.30	0.10
Room coef*	\multicolumn{10} Luminous Ceilings or Indirect Luminaires (Floor Reflectance: 0.30)									
0.0	0.520	0.325	0.195	0.0650	0.325	0.195	0.0650	0.325	0.195	0.0650
0.1	.536	.332	.198	.0657	.332	.198	.0657	.332	.198	.0656
0.2	.551	.340	.202	.0667	.340	.202	.0667	.340	.202	.0667
0.3	.567	.348	.206	.0680	.348	.206	.0680	.348	.206	.0680
0.4	.583	.357	.212	.0697	.357	.212	.0697	.357	.212	.0696
0.5	.598	.367	.218	.0717	.367	.218	.0717	.367	.218	.0716
0.7	.631	.389	.231	.0765	.388	.231	.0765	.388	.231	.0762
1.0	.681	.426	.256	.0856	.426	.256	.0856	.426	.256	.0851
	\multicolumn{10} Luminous Ceilings or Indirect Luminaires (Floor Reflectance: 0.10)									
0.0	.440	.275	.165	.0550	.275	.165	.0550	.275	.165	.0550
0.1	.463	.288	.172	.0570	.287	.172	.0570	.288	.172	.0570
0.2	.486	.300	.179	.0592	.300	.179	.0592	.300	.179	.0592
0.3	.508	.313	.186	.0616	.313	.186	.0615	.313	.186	.0615
0.4	.530	.326	.194	.0641	.327	.194	.0641	.327	.194	.0641
0.5	.552	.340	.202	.0668	.340	.202	.0668	.340	.202	.0668
0.7	.594	.368	.220	.0728	.368	.220	.0728	.368	.220	.0728
1.0	.655	.413	.249	.0833	.413	.249	.0833	.413	.249	.0833
	\multicolumn{10} Direct Luminaires (Floor Reflectance: 0.30)									
0.0	.218	.137	.082	.0273	.128	.077	.0255	.113	.068	.0225
0.1	.329	.193	.115	.0372	.189	.112	.3640	.182	.100	.0350
0.2	.342	.200	.115	.0367	.197	.113	.3610	.189	.109	.0350
0.3	.363	.205	.117	.0366	.202	.113	.3630	.194	.112	.0353
0.4	.384	.216	.119	.0370	.211	.118	.3670	.205	.115	.0361
0.5	.409	.224	.124	.0384	.220	.123	.3820	.217	.120	.0375
0.7	.415	.253	.139	.0429	.249	.139	.4280	.247	.137	.0424
1.0	.594	.331	.192	.0602	.328	.192	.6020	.327	.191	.0598
	\multicolumn{10} Direct Luminaires (Floor Reflectance: 0.10)									
0.0	.072	.045	.027	.0090	.042	.026	.0085	.038	.023	.0075
0.1	.211	.127	.074	.0242	.125	.073	.0238	.062	.071	.0234
0.2	.239	.140	.080	.0255	.138	.079	.0253	.134	.077	.0249
0.3	.266	.151	.086	.0269	.150	.085	.0268	.146	.083	.0265
0.4	.298	.165	.092	.0287	.164	.089	.0286	.160	.090	.0282
0.5	.329	.181	.100	.0310	.179	.100	.0309	.176	.098	.0308
0.7	.402	.217	.121	.0372	.217	.120	.0372	.214	.119	.0370
1.0	.552	.308	.179	.0565	.307	.179	.0564	.304	.179	.0562
	\multicolumn{10} Uniformly Diffusing Luminaires (Floor Reflectance: 0.30)									
0.0	.351	.220	.132	.0439	.209	.125	.0418	.183	.110	.0367
0.1	.696	.442	.268	.0903	.453	.274	.0925	.478	.289	.0977
0.2	.705	.455	.278	.0945	.464	.284	.0967	.490	.298	.1020
0.3	.714	.466	.287	.0987	.476	.294	.1009	.500	.306	.1063
0.4	.725	.478	.297	.1029	.488	.304	.1052	.512	.313	.1107
0.5	.736	.490	.307	.1074	.500	.314	.1096	.523	.320	.1151
0.7	.757	.514	.328	.1165	.523	.334	.1188	.545	.334	.1245
1.0	.790	.551	.359	.1308	.559	.364	.1329	.576	.354	.1377
	\multicolumn{10} Uniformly Diffusing Luminaires (Floor Reflectance: 0.10)									
0.0	.596	.372	.223	.0744	.363	.218	.0727	.342	.205	.0683
0.1	.653	.415	.252	.0848	.424	.257	.0867	.447	.271	.0913
0.2	.663	.427	.269	.0853	.437	.268	.0912	.460	.282	.0960
0.3	.675	.441	.272	.0906	.450	.278	.0957	.473	.293	.1007
0.4	.688	.454	.283	.0959	.464	.289	.1003	.487	.304	.1055
0.5	.701	.468	.294	.1011	.477	.300	.1051	.500	.315	.1103
0.7	.729	.496	.316	.1115	.505	.322	.1148	.525	.336	.1201
1.0	.769	.538	.350	.1272	.545	.356	.1300	.562	.368	.1348

Table 7-27. Brightness Ratios for Direct, Uniformly Diffusing, Indirect, and Luminous-ceiling Systems (Continued)

$$B = \frac{\text{average ceiling brightness}}{\text{average illumination at work plane}}$$

Ceiling reflectance	0.80				0.70			0.50		
Wall reflectance...	0.80	0.50	0.30	0.10	0.50	0.30	0.10	0.50	0.30	0.10
Room coef*	Luminous Ceilings or Indirect Luminaires (Floor Reflectance: 0.30)									
0.0	1.000	1.000	1.000	1.0000	1.000	1.000	1.0000	1.000	1.000	1.0000
0.1	1.074	1.108	1.129	1.1510	1.108	1.129	1.1510	1.108	1.129	1.1510
0.2	1.153	1.228	1.277	1.3260	1.228	1.277	1.3260	1.228	1.277	1.3260
0.3	1.236	1.363	1.446	1.5280	1.363	1.446	1.5280	1.363	1.446	1.5280
0.4	1.324	1.514	1.638	1.7610	1.514	1.638	1.7610	1.514	1.638	1.7590
0.5	1.418	1.682	1.856	2.0300	1.682	1.856	2.0300	1.682	1.856	2.0270
0.7	1.625	2.078	2.386	2.6990	2.078	2.386	2.6990	2.078	2.386	2.6910
1.0	1.989	2.861	3.481	4.1380	2.861	3.481	4.1380	2.861	3.481	4.1120
	Luminous Ceilings or Indirect Luminaires (Floor Reflectance: 0.10)									
0.0	1.000	1.000	1.000	1.0000	1.000	1.000	1.0000	1.000	1.000	1.0000
0.1	1.086	1.114	1.134	1.1530	1.114	1.134	1.1520	1.114	1.134	1.1520
0.2	1.174	1.241	1.285	1.3280	1.241	1.285	1.3280	1.241	1.285	1.3280
0.3	1.267	1.381	1.457	1.5310	1.381	1.457	1.5310	1.381	1.457	1.5310
0.4	1.364	1.537	1.651	1.7650	1.537	1.651	1.7650	1.537	1.651	1.7650
0.5	1.466	1.710	1.872	2.0350	1.710	1.872	2.0350	1.710	1.872	2.0350
0.7	1.686	2.113	2.406	2.7050	2.113	2.406	2.7050	2.113	2.406	2.7050
1.0	2.067	2.906	3.506	4.1460	2.906	3.506	4.1460	2.905	3.506	4.1460
	Direct Luminaires (Floor Reflectance: 0.30)									
0.0	0.234	0.234	0.234	0.2340	0.210	0.210	0.2100	0.150	0.150	0.1500
0.1	.245	0.232	0.212	0.2020	0.196	0.188	0.1760	.140	.132	0.1260
0.2	.252	0.214	0.190	0.1700	0.186	0.166	0.1480	.133	.118	0.1060
0.3	.264	0.206	0.173	0.1440	0.179	0.151	0.1260	.127	.108	0.0897
0.4	.278	0.202	0.160	0.1230	0.175	0.140	0.1080	.124	.099	0.0769
0.5	.297	0.202	0.151	0.1070	0.175	0.131	0.0938	.124	.093	0.0668
0.7	.338	0.211	0.143	0.0847	0.183	0.125	0.0732	.129	.088	0.0528
1.0	.440	0.357	0.162	0.0737	0.224	0.143	0.0477	.158	.102	0.0460
	Direct Luminaires (Floor Reflectance: 0.10)									
0.0	.080	0.080	0.080	0.0800	0.070	0.070	0.0700	.050	.050	0.0500
0.1	.096	0.084	0.076	0.0689	0.073	0.067	0.0592	.052	.047	0.0430
0.2	.116	0.091	0.075	0.0602	0.079	0.065	0.0526	.056	.046	0.0386
0.3	.140	0.099	0.075	0.0534	0.085	0.065	0.0470	.061	.046	0.0334
0.5	.195	0.121	0.080	0.0451	0.105	0.070	0.0396	.074	.049	0.0285
0.7	.234	0.151	0.092	0.0419	0.131	0.080	0.0368	.094	.057	0.0262
1.0	.394	0.223	0.134	0.0489	0.194	0.117	0.0436	.136	.083	0.0310
	Uniformly Diffusing Luminaires (Floor Reflectance: 0.30)									
0.0	.578	0.578	0.578	0.5780	0.535	0.535	0.5350	.433	.433	0.4330
0.1	.637	0.634	0.633	0.6310	0.589	0.587	0.5860	.479	.477	0.4760
0.2	.689	0.694	0.693	0.6950	0.642	0.643	0.6450	.522	.520	0.5240
0.3	.735	0.748	0.758	0.7670	0.694	0.732	0.7620	.561	.563	0.5770
0.4	.777	0.805	0.826	0.8480	0.745	0.764	0.8490	.602	.606	0.6350
0.5	.817	0.864	0.898	0.9360	0.797	0.830	0.9420	.640	.650	0.6970
0.7	.889	0.982	1.050	1.1340	0.902	0.969	1.1400	.715	.740	0.8330
1.0	.988	1.167	1.310	1.4830	1.062	1.195	1.4850	.825	.878	1.0610
	Uniformly Diffusing Luminaires (Floor Reflectance: 0.10)									
0.0	.889	0.889	0.889	0.8890	0.824	0.824	0.8240	.667	.667	0.6670
0.1	.565	0.564	0.563	0.5610	0.523	0.522	0.5210	.425	.424	0.4230
0.2	.631	0.634	0.637	0.6120	0.589	0.591	0.5930	.478	.480	0.4810
0.3	.689	0.703	0.712	0.6990	0.651	0.660	0.6690	.527	.535	0.5430
0.4	.741	0.769	0.789	0.7920	0.711	0.731	0.7510	.574	.590	0.6070
0.5	.790	0.835	0.869	0.8910	0.771	0.803	0.8380	.619	.645	0.6750
0.7	.878	0.967	1.040	1.1000	0.888	0.953	1.0260	.704	.757	0.8190
1.0	.993	1.166	1.305	1.4650	1.061	1.190	1.3450	.824	.929	1.0550

Table 7-27. Brightness Ratios for Direct, Uniformly Diffusing, Indirect, and Luminous-ceiling Systems (Continued)

$$C = \frac{\text{average floor brightness}}{\text{average illumination at work plane}}$$

Ceiling reflectance	0.80				0.70			0.50		
Wall reflectance...	0.80	0.50	0.30	0.10	0.50	0.30	0.10	0.50	0.30	0.10
Room coef*	Luminous Ceilings or Indirect Luminaires (Floor Reflectance: 0.30)									
0.0	0.300	0.300	0.300	0.3000	0.300	0.300	0.3000	0.300	0.300	0.3000
0.1	.293	.290	.288	.2860	.290	.288	.2860	.290	.288	.2860
0.2	.286	.280	.277	.2730	.280	.277	.2730	.280	.277	.2730
0.3	.279	.271	.266	.2610	.271	.266	.2610	.271	.266	.2610
0.4	.273	.262	.255	.2490	.262	.255	.2490	.262	.255	.2480
0.5	.266	.253	.245	.2370	.253	.245	.2370	.253	.245	.2370
0.7	.254	.236	.226	.2160	.236	.226	.2160	.236	.226	.2150
1.0	.237	.213	.200	.1880	.213	.200	.1880	.213	.200	.1860
	Luminous Ceilings or Indirect Luminaires (Floor Reflectance: 0.10)									
0.0	.100	.100	.100	.1000	.100	.100	.1000	.100	.100	.1000
0.1	.097	.096	.096	.0954	.096	.096	.0954	.096	.096	.0954
0.2	.095	.093	.092	.0910	.093	.092	.0910	.093	.092	.0910
0.3	.092	.090	.088	.0868	.090	.088	.0868	.090	.088	.0868
0.4	.090	.087	.085	.0828	.087	.085	.0828	.087	.085	.0828
0.5	.087	.084	.081	.0790	.084	.081	.0789	.084	.081	.0789
0.7	.083	.078	.075	.0718	.078	.075	.0718	.078	.075	.0718
1.0	.077	.070	.066	.0623	.070	.066	.0623	.070	.066	.0623
	Direct Luminaires (Floor Reflectance: 0.30)									
0.0	.300	.300	.300	.3000	.300	.300	.3000	.300	.300	.3000
0.1	.302	.300	.299	.2980	.301	.300	.2990	.301	.300	.2990
0.2	.302	.300	.299	.2990	.301	.300	.2980	.301	.299	.2980
0.3	.303	.300	.299	.2980	.301	.299	.2970	.302	.300	.2980
0.4	.303	.301	.298	.2970	.301	.299	.2970	.303	.300	.2980
0.5	.303	.302	.300	.2990	.302	.300	.2990	.303	.302	.2990
0.7	.303	.302	.301	.3000	.302	.301	.2990	.305	.303	.3000
1.0	.302	.302	.302	.3010	.303	.302	.3010	.306	.304	.3010
	Direct Luminaires (Floor Reflectance: 0.10)									
0.0	.100	.100	.100	.1000	.100	.100	.1000	.100	.100	.1000
0.1	.101	.100	.100	.1000	.101	.100	.1000	.101	.100	.1000
0.2	.101	.101	.100	.1000	.101	.100	.1000	.101	.100	.1000
0.3	.101	.101	.100	.1000	.101	.100	.1000	.101	.100	.1000
0.4	.101	.101	.100	.1000	.101	.100	.1000	.101	.100	.1000
0.5	.101	.101	.100	.1000	.101	.100	.1000	.101	.100	.1000
0.7	.100	.100	.100	.1000	.101	.100	.1000	.101	.100	.1000
1.0	.100	.100	.100	.1000	.100	.100	.1000	.101	.101	.1000
	Uniformly Diffusing Luminaires (Floor Reflectance: 0.30)									
0.0	.300	.300	.300	.3000	.300	.300	.3000	.300	.300	.3000
0.1	.300	.298	.295	.2930	.298	.296	.2940	.300	.297	.2950
0.2	.300	.295	.291	.2870	.296	.292	.2880	.299	.293	.2910
0.3	.298	.292	.287	.2820	.293	.289	.2840	.298	.289	.2870
0.4	.296	.289	.283	.2770	.291	.285	.2800	.296	.285	.2840
0.5	.293	.286	.280	.2740	.288	.282	.2760	.295	.281	.2810
0.7	.288	.281	.275	.2680	.284	.278	.2710	.292	.274	.2770
1.0	.280	.275	.270	.2630	.279	.274	.2660	.288	.265	.2740
	Uniformly Diffusing Luminaires (Floor Reflectance: 0.10)									
0.0	.100	.100	.100	.1000	.100	.100	.1000	.100	.100	.1000
0.1	.100	.099	.099	.0980	.100	.099	.0982	.100	.099	.0986
0.2	.100	.098	.097	.0920	.099	.098	.0964	.100	.099	.0973
0.3	.099	.097	.096	.0914	.098	.096	.0948	.099	.098	.0960
0.4	.098	.096	.095	.0906	.097	.095	.0934	.099	.097	.0949
0.5	.097	.095	.093	.0898	.096	.094	.0922	.098	.096	.0940
0.7	.095	.093	.091	.0884	.094	.092	.0902	.097	.095	.0925
1.0	.092	.091	.090	.0871	.092	.091	.0887	.095	.094	.0914

* Room coef = $\dfrac{\text{room height} \times (\text{room length} + \text{width})}{2 \times \text{room length} \times \text{width}}$

SOURCE: "IES Handbook," p. 9-35. Illuminating Engineering Society, New York, 1952.

Visual comfort is determined by first calculating the glare factor, which is given by

$$\text{Glare factor} = AB^2/D^2\alpha^2S^{0.6} \qquad (7\text{-}140)$$

where A = apparent area of source, in.^{2}

B = brightness of source, fl, divided by 1,000

D = distance from source to eye, ft, divided by 10

α = angle above horizontal, deg, divided by 10

s = surrounding brightness, fl, divided by 10

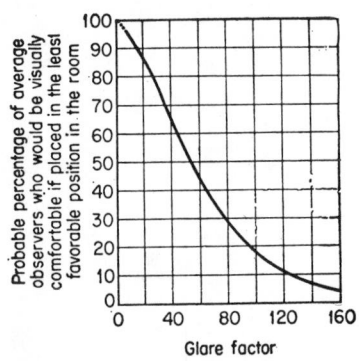

Fig. 7-44. The practical relationship between glare factor and the percentage of occupants who will be visually comfortable.

The total glare factor equals the sum of the glare factors for each fixture in a given reference direction. The total glare factor is entered in the curve of Fig. 7-44 to determine the visual comfort. The values in the equation are found from the physical size of the fixtures (area) and brightness curves. Correct lamp application for color is determined from Tables 7-28 and 7-29. Table 7-26 gives typical losses for fluorescent-lamp ballast, which serves as an aid in the determination of branch-circuit loading.

Table 7-28. Color of Lamps

Lamp type	Basic features	Use
Incandescent....	Oranges emphasized	General lighting, highlighting special areas, lighting meats and meat products
Standard cool white	Deficient in red	Displaying woods and furs, general lighting where the effect of color is not critical
De luxe cool white	Same appearance as cool white with red added	General lighting
Standard warm white	Beige tint emphasizes yellow greens	Home lighting (favorable to complexions)
De luxe warm white	Same as standard warm white with red added	Home lighting (favorable to complexions), use alone where warm red is needed in abundance
White..........	Emphasizes yellows, yellow greens, and oranges	Food-store lighting except for meats, general lighting of schools, offices, etc.
Daylight........	Emphasizes blues and greens, tends to gray red, oranges, and yellows	General lighting, displaying iced foods

Table 7-29. Effect of Colored Light on Colored Objects

Object color	Red light	Blue light	Green light	Yellow light
White.......	Light pink	Very light blue	Very light green	Very light yellow
Black.......	Reddish black	Blue black	Greenish black	Orange black
Red.........	Brilliant red	Dark bluish red	Yellowish red	Bright red
Light blue...	Reddish blue	Bright blue	Greenish blue	Light reddish blue
Dark blue...	Dark reddish purple	Brilliant blue	Dark greenish blue	Light reddish purple
Green.......	Olive green	Green blue	Brilliant green	Yellow green
Yellow......	Red orange	Light reddish brown	Light greenish yellow	Brilliant light orange
Brown.......	Brown red	Bluish brown	Dark olive brown	Brownish orange

SOURCE: "Westinghouse Lighting Handbook," p. 4-16, Westinghouse Electric Corporation, Bloomfield, N.J., 1954.

SECTION 8

MECHANICAL ENGINEERING

Theodore Baumeister, B.S., M.E., P.E.; Stevens Professor Emeritus of Mechanical Engineering, Columbia University; Fellow, American Society of Mechanical Engineers

Eugene A. Avallone, B.M.E., M.S., M.E., P.E.; Associate Professor of Mechanical Engineering, City University of New York; Member, American Society of Mechanical Engineers

CONTENTS

MECHANICS

8-1. Formulas of Motion

Nomenclature

t = time, sec
s = linear displacement, ft
v = linear velocity, fps
V_0 = linear velocity at time zero, fps
a = linear acceleration, ft/sec²
θ = angular displacement, radians
ω = angular velocity, radians/sec
ω_0 = angular velocity at time zero, radians/sec
α = angular acceleration, radians/sec²
w = weight of body, lb mass
f = force of acceleration, lb force
g_c = conversion factor = 32.2 (lb mass)(ft)/(lb force)(sec²)

v = constant	ω = constant	v = variable	ω = variable
$v = s/t$	$\omega = \theta/t$	$v = ds/dt$	$\omega = d\theta/dt$

a = constant	α = constant	a = variable	α = variable
$v = V_0 + at$	$\omega = \omega_0 + \alpha t$	$a = \dfrac{dv}{dt} = \dfrac{d^2s}{dt^2}$	$\alpha = \dfrac{d\omega}{dt} = \dfrac{d^2\theta}{dt^2}$
$s = V_0 t + \frac{1}{2}at^2$	$\theta = \omega_0 t + \frac{1}{2}\alpha t^2$	$v = \int a\,dt$	$\omega = \int \alpha\,dt$
$v = \sqrt{V_0{}^2 + 2as}$	$\omega = \sqrt{\omega_0{}^2 + 2\alpha\theta}$	$s = \int v\,dt$	$\theta = \int \omega\,dt$

For uniform acceleration

$$f = (w/g_c)a \tag{8-1}$$

8-2. Dynamic Similarity (Theory of Models)

Two or more systems are dynamically similar when:
1. They are geometrically similar.
2. The paths of motion in the two systems are similar.

3. The centers of gravity are in the same position.

4. The radii of gyration are proportional.

The times for performing the same motion need not be the same.

8-3. Statics

Any force system in space will be in equilibrium if the resultant force and resultant moment are both equal to zero. This can be expressed by

$$\Sigma F_x = \Sigma F_y = \Sigma F_z = 0 \tag{8-2a}$$
$$\Sigma M_x = \Sigma M_y = \Sigma M_z = 0 \tag{8-2b}$$

where F = force, lb

M = moment, ft-lb

x, y, z = orthogonal axes

Center of Gravity. The center of gravity of a body is that point through which the resultant of all gravity forces acting on the body passes. This point is fixed in the body and is independent of the position of the body.

Law of Motion of the Center of Gravity. The center of gravity of a system of particles or rigid bodies, under the action of several impressed forces, moves exactly as if the whole weight of the system were concentrated there and as if it were acted on by a force equal in magnitude and direction to the vector sum of all impressed forces. The coordinates of the center of gravity of the system being $\bar{x}$, $\bar{y}$, $\bar{z}$, its motion may be determined by the equations:

$$\frac{W}{g_c}\frac{d^2\bar{x}}{dt^2} = \Sigma F_{x_i} \qquad \frac{W}{g_c}\frac{d^2\bar{y}}{dt^2} = \Sigma F_{y_i} \qquad \frac{W}{g_c}\frac{d^2\bar{z}}{dt^2} = \Sigma F_{z_i} \tag{8-3}$$

where W = total weight of system, lb mass

$F_{x_i}, F_{y_i}, F_{z_i}$ = projections of impressed forces on coordinate axes, lb force

t = time, sec

g_c = (lb mass)(ft)/(lb force)(sec²)

Centers of Gravity of Lines[1,2]

Straight line. The center of gravity is at its midpoint.

Circular arc AB, Fig. 8-1. $x_0 = r \sin c/\text{rad } c$ and

$$y_0 = 2r \sin^2 \tfrac{1}{2}c/\text{rad } c$$

Circular arc AC, Fig. 8-2. $x_0 = r \sin c/\text{rad } c$, $y_0 = 0$.

Quadrant AB, Fig. 8-3. $x_0 = y_0 = 2r/\pi = 0.6366r$.

Semicircumference AC Fig. 8-3. $y_0 = 2r/\pi = 0.6366r$, $x_0 = 0$.

Combination of arcs and straight line (Fig. 8-4). AD and BC are two quadrants of radius r.

$$y_0 = \{ABr + 2[0.5\pi r(r - 0.6366r)]\}/[AB + 2(0.5\pi r)], \quad x_0 = 0$$

[1] In this discussion, rad c = angle c measured in radians.

[2] Source: L. S. Marks (ed.), "Mechanical Engineers' Handbook," 5th ed., pp. 195–196, McGraw-Hill Book Company, Inc., New York, 1951.

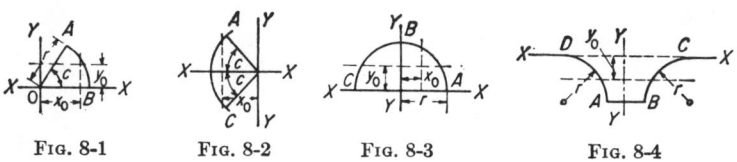

FIG. 8-1   FIG. 8-2   FIG. 8-3   FIG. 8-4

Centers of Gravity of Plane Areas[1,2]

Triangle.   Center of gravity lies at the intersection of the lines joining the vertices with the mid-points of the sides and at a distance from any side equal to one-third of the corresponding altitude.

Parallelogram.   Center of gravity lies at the point of intersection of the diagonals.

Trapezoid (Fig. 8-5).   Center of gravity lies on the line joining the mid-points m and n of the parallel sides.   The distances h_a and h_b are

$$h_a = h(a + 2b)/3(a + b) \qquad h_b = h(2a + b)/3(a + b)$$

Draw $BE = a$ and $CF = b$; EF will then intersect mn at the center of gravity.

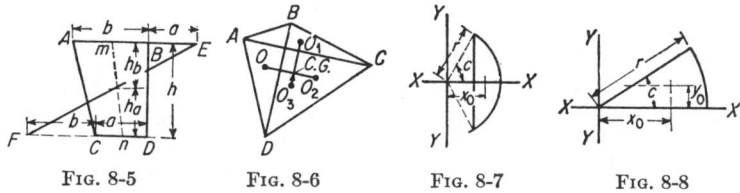

FIG. 8-5   FIG. 8-6   FIG. 8-7   FIG. 8-8

Any quadrilateral.   The center of gravity of any quadrilateral may be determined by the general rule for areas, or graphically by dividing it into two sets of triangles by means of the diagonals.   Find the center of gravity of each of the four triangles and connect the centers of gravity of the triangles belonging to the same set.   The intersection of these lines will be the center of gravity of area.   Thus in Fig. 8-6, O, O_1, O_2, and O_3 are, respectively, the centers of gravity of the triangles ABD, ABC, BDC, and ACD.   The intersection of O_1O_3 with OO_2 is the center of gravity.

Segment of a circle (Fig. 8-7). $x_0 = \frac{2}{3}r \sin^3 c/(\text{rad } c - \cos c \sin c)$.   A segment may be considered to be a sector from which a triangle is subtracted, and the general rule applied.

Sector of a circle (Fig. 8-8). $x_0 = \frac{2}{3}r \sin c/\text{rad } c$, $y_0 = \frac{4}{3}r \sin^2 \frac{1}{2}c/\text{rad } c$.

Semicircle. $x_0 = \frac{4}{3}r/\pi = 0.4244r$, $y_0 = 0$.

Quadrant (90° sector). $x_0 = y_0 = \frac{4}{3}r/\pi = 0.4244r$.

Parabolic half segment, area ABO, Fig. 8-9. $x_0 = \frac{3}{5}x_1$, $y_0 = \frac{3}{8}y_1$.

---

[1] In this dicussion rad c = angle c measured in radians.

[2] Source: L. S. Marks (ed.), "Mechanical Engineers' Handbook," 5th ed., pp., 195–196, McGraw-Hill Book Company, Inc., New York, 1951.

Parabolic spandrel, area AOC, Fig. 8-9. $x'_0 = \frac{3}{10}x_1$, $y'_0 = \frac{3}{4}y_1$.

Quadrant of an ellipse, area OAB, Fig. 8-10. $x_0 = \frac{4}{3}A/\pi$, $y_0 = \frac{4}{3}b/\pi$.

The center of gravity of a figure such as that shown in Fig. 8-11 may be determined as follows: Divide the arm $OABC$ into a number of parts by lines drawn perpendicular to the axis XX, for example, 11, 22, 33, etc. These parts will be approximately triangles, rectangles, or trapezoids. The area

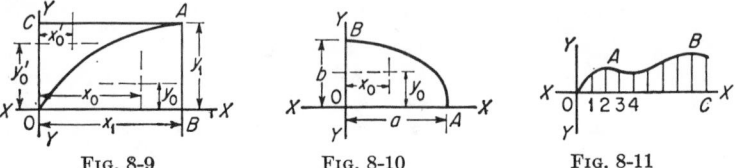

FIG. 8-9   FIG. 8-10   FIG. 8-11

of each division may be obtained by taking the product of its mean height and its base. The center of gravity of each area may be obtained as previously shown. The sum of the moments of all the areas about XX and YY, respectively, divided by the sum of the areas will give approximately the distances from the center of gravity of the whole area to the axes XX and YY. The greater the number of areas taken the more nearly exact the result.

Centers of Gravity of Solids[1]

Prism or cylinder with parallel bases. The center of gravity lies in the center of the line connecting the centers of gravity of the bases.

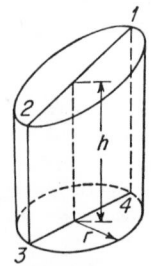

FIG. 8-12

Oblique frustum of a right circular cylinder (Fig. 8-12). Let 1-2-3-4 be the plane of symmetry. The distance from the base to the center of gravity is $\frac{1}{2}h + (r^2 \tan^2 c)/8h$, where c is the angle of inclination of the oblique section to the base. The distance of the center of gravity from the axis of the cylinder is $r^2 \tan c/4h$.

Pyramid or cone. The center of gravity lies in the line connecting the center of gravity of the base with the vertex and at a distance of one-fourth the altitude above the base.

Truncated pyramid. If h is the height of the truncated pyramid and A and B the area of its bases, the distance of the center of gravity from the surface of A is $h(A + 2\sqrt{AB} + 3B)/4(A + \sqrt{AB} + B)$.

Truncated circular cone. If h is the height of the frustum and R and r the radii of the bases, the distance from the surface of the base whose radius is R to the center of gravity is $h(R^2 + 2Rr + 3r^2)/4(R^2 + Rr + r^2)$.

Segment of a sphere, volume ABC, Fig. 8-13. $x_0 = 3(2r - h)^2/4(3r - h)$.

Hemisphere. $x_0 = 3r/8$.

---

[1] Source: L. S. Marks (ed.), "Mechanical Engineers' Handbook," 5th ed., pp. 195–196, McGraw-Hill Book Company, Inc., New York, 1951.

Hollow hemisphere. $x_0 = 3(R^4 - r^4)/8(R^3 - r^3)$, where R and r are the outer and inner radii, respectively.

Sector of a sphere, volume $OABCO$, Fig. 8-13. $x'_0 = \frac{3}{8}(2r - h)$.

Ellipsoid with semiaxes a, b, and c. For each octant, distance from center of gravity to each of the bounding planes equals $\frac{3}{8}$ times the length of semiaxis perpendicular to the plane considered.

The motion of the center of gravity of a system does not change when the internal forces of the system vary. Its motion is not affected when internal forces are created or disappear, as occurs when parts of the system collide or explode.

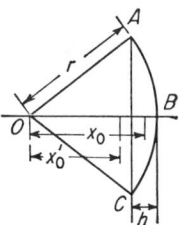

FIG. 8-13

Moment of Inertia. *Rectangular Moment of Inertia.* The rectangular moment of inertia I (Table 8-1) with respect to a given axis is defined by the equations

$$I = \int y^2\, dm \qquad \text{lb-ft}^2 \qquad \text{for solid body} \qquad (8\text{-}4)$$
and
$$I = \int y^2\, dA \qquad ft^4 \qquad \text{for plane area} \qquad (8\text{-}5)$$

where y = distance from elements of mass or area to reference axis, ft
     dm = element of mass, lb
     dA = element of area, ft^2

Radius of Gyration. The radius of gyration is a length K feet such that

$$I = \int y^2\, dm = K^2 m \qquad \text{for solid body} \qquad (8\text{-}6)$$
and
$$I = \int y^2\, dA = K^2 A \qquad \text{for plane area} \qquad (8\text{-}7)$$

where m = total mass, lb
     A = area, ft^2

Rectangular Moments of Inertia and Radii of Gyration about Parallel Axes. Moment of inertia about any reference axis is equal to

$$I = I_{CG} + a^2 m \qquad \text{for solid body} \qquad (8\text{-}8)$$
and
$$I = I_{CG} + a^2 A \qquad \text{for plane area} \qquad (8\text{-}9)$$

where I_{CG} = moment of inertia of solid, lb-ft^2, or area, ft^4, about axis parallel to reference axis and passing through center of gravity
     a = distance between reference axis and axis passing through center of gravity, ft

Likewise, $$K^2 = K^2_{cg} + a^2 \qquad (8\text{-}10)$$

where K_{cg} = radius of gyration through center of gravity, ft

Polar Moment of Inertia. The polar moment of inertia J of an area is taken about an axis perpendicular to the area and is equal to

$$J = I_1 + I_2 \qquad ft^4 \qquad (8\text{-}11)$$

where I_1 and I_2 = moments of inertia about any two mutually perpendicular axes lying in plane of area and intersecting axis perpendicular to plane

Table 8-1. Properties of Various Cross Sections

I = moment of inertia; I/c = section modulus; $r = \sqrt{I/A}$ = radius of gyration

Section	Moment of inertia	Section modulus	Radius of gyration
$I = \dfrac{bh^3}{12}$	$\dfrac{bh^3}{3}$	$\dfrac{b^3h^3}{6(b^2 + h^2)}$	$\dfrac{bh}{12}(h^2 \cos^2 a + b^2 \sin^2 a)$
$\dfrac{I}{c} = \dfrac{bh^2}{6}$	$\dfrac{bh^2}{3}$	$\dfrac{b^2h^2}{6\sqrt{b^2 + h^2}}$	$\dfrac{bh}{6}\left(\dfrac{h^2 \cos^2 a + b^2 \sin^2 a}{h \cos a + b \sin a}\right)$
$r = \dfrac{h}{\sqrt{12}} = 0.289h$	$\dfrac{h}{\sqrt{3}} = 0.577h$	$\dfrac{bh}{\sqrt{6(b^2 + h^2)}}$	$\sqrt{\dfrac{h^2 \cos^2 a + b^2 \sin^2 a}{12}}$
$I = \dfrac{b}{12}(H^3 - h^3)$	$\dfrac{H^4 - h^4}{12}$	$\dfrac{H^4 - h^4}{12}$	$\dfrac{bh^3}{36}; c = \dfrac{2}{3}h$
$\dfrac{I}{c} = \dfrac{b}{6}\dfrac{H^3 - h^3}{H}$	$\dfrac{1}{6}\dfrac{H^4 - h^4}{H}$	$\dfrac{\sqrt{2}}{12}\dfrac{H^4 - h^4}{H}$	$\dfrac{bh^2}{24}$
$r = \sqrt{\dfrac{H^3 - h^3}{12(H - h)}}$	$\sqrt{\dfrac{H^2 + h^2}{12}}$	$\sqrt{\dfrac{H^2 + h^2}{12}}$	$\dfrac{h}{\sqrt{18}}$
$I = \dfrac{bh^3}{12}$		$\dfrac{5\sqrt{3}}{16}R^4$	$\dfrac{1 + 2\sqrt{2}}{6}R^4$
$\dfrac{I}{c} = \dfrac{bh^2}{12}$	$\tfrac{5}{8}R^3$	$\dfrac{5\sqrt{3}}{16}R^3$	$0.6906R^3$
$r = \dfrac{h}{\sqrt{6}}$	$\sqrt{\dfrac{5}{24}}R$		$0.475R$

Table 8-1. Properties of Various Cross Sections (Continued)

Section	Moment of inertia	Section modulus	Radius of gyration
Equilateral polygon A = area R = radius circum-scribed circle r = radius in-scribed circle n = no. sides a = length of side Axis as in preceding section of octagon	$I = \dfrac{A}{24}(6R^2 - a^2)$ $= \dfrac{A}{48}(12r^2 + a^2)$ $= \dfrac{AR^2}{4}$ (approx)	$\dfrac{I}{c} = \dfrac{I}{r}$ $= \dfrac{I}{R\cos\dfrac{180°}{n}}$ $= \dfrac{AR}{4}$ (approx)	$\sqrt{\dfrac{6R^2 - a^2}{24}} \approx \dfrac{R}{2}$ $\sqrt{\dfrac{12r^2 + a^2}{48}}$
	$I = \dfrac{6b^2 + 6bb_1 + b_1{}^2}{36(2b + b_1)}h^3$ $c = \dfrac{1}{3}\dfrac{3b + 2b_1}{2b + b_1}h$	$\dfrac{I}{c} = \dfrac{6b^2 + 6bb_1 + b_1{}^2}{12(3b + 2b_1)}h^2$	$\dfrac{h\sqrt{12b^2 + 12bb_1 + 2b_1{}^2}}{6(2b + b_1)}$
	$I = \dfrac{BH^3 + bh^3}{12}$ $\dfrac{I}{c} = \dfrac{BH^3 + bh^3}{6H}$		$\sqrt{\dfrac{BH^3 + bh^3}{12(BH + bh)}}$
	$I = \dfrac{BH^3 - bh^3}{12}$ $\dfrac{I}{c} = \dfrac{BH^3 - bh^3}{6H}$		$\sqrt{\dfrac{BH^3 - bh^3}{12(BH - bh)}}$
	$I = \frac{1}{3}(Bc_1{}^3 - B_1h^3 + bc_2{}^3 - b_1h_1{}^3)$ $c_1 = \dfrac{1}{2}\dfrac{aH^2 + B_1d^2 + b_1d_1(2H - d_1)}{aH + B_1d + b_1d_1}$	$\sqrt{\dfrac{I}{(Bd + bd_1) + a(h + h_1)}}$	
	$I = \frac{1}{3}(Bc_1{}^3 - bh^3 + ac_2{}^3)$ $c_1 = \dfrac{1}{2}\dfrac{aH^2 + bd^2}{aH + bd}$ $c_2 = H - c_1$ $r = \sqrt{\dfrac{I}{[Bd + a(H - d)]}}$		
	$I = \dfrac{\pi d^4}{64} = \dfrac{\pi r^4}{4} = \dfrac{A}{4}r^2$ $= 0.05d^4$ (approx)	$\dfrac{I}{c} = \dfrac{\pi d^3}{32} = \dfrac{\pi r^3}{4} = \dfrac{A}{4}r$ $= 0.1d^3$ (approx)	$\dfrac{r}{2} = \dfrac{d}{4}$

Table 8-1. Properties of Various Cross Sections (Continued)

Section	Moment of inertia	Section modulus	Radius of gyration
$d_m = \frac{1}{2}(D + d)$ $s = \frac{1}{2}(D - d)$	$I = \frac{\pi}{64}\,(D^4 - d^4)$ $= \frac{\pi}{4}\,(R^4 - r^4)$ $= \frac{1}{4}A(R^2 + r^2)$ $= 0.05(D^4 - d^4)$ (approx)	$\frac{I}{c} = \frac{\pi}{32}\dfrac{D^4 - d^4}{D}$ $= \frac{\pi}{4}\dfrac{R^4 - r^4}{R}$ $= 0.8 d_m{}^2 s$ (approx) when $\frac{s}{d_m}$ is very small	$\dfrac{\sqrt{R^2 + r^2}}{2}$ $= \dfrac{\sqrt{D^2 + d^2}}{4}$
	$I = r^4\left(\dfrac{\pi}{8} - \dfrac{8}{9\pi}\right)$ $= 0.1098 r^4$	$\dfrac{I}{c_2} = 0.1908 r^3$ $\dfrac{I}{c_1} = 0.2587 r^3$ $c_1 = 0.4244 r$	$\dfrac{\sqrt{9\pi^2 - 64}}{6\pi}\,r = 0.264 r$
	$I = 0.1098(R^4 - r^4)$ $\quad - \dfrac{0.283 R^2 r^2 (R - r)}{R + r}$ $= 0.3 t r_1{}^3$ (approx) when $\dfrac{t}{r_1}$ is very small	$c_1 = \dfrac{4}{3\pi}\dfrac{R^2 + Rr + r^2}{R + r}$ $c_2 = R - c_1$	$\sqrt{\dfrac{2I}{\pi(R^2 - r^2)}}$ $= 0.31 r_1$ (approx)
	$I = \dfrac{\pi a^3 b}{4} = 0.7854 a^3 b$	$\dfrac{I}{c} = \dfrac{\pi a^2 b}{4} = 0.7854 a^2 b$	$\dfrac{a}{2}$
	$I = \dfrac{\pi}{4}\,(a^3 b - a_1{}^3 b_1)$ $= \dfrac{\pi}{4}\,a^2(a + 3b)t$ (approx)	$\dfrac{I}{c} = \dfrac{\pi}{4}\,a(a + 3b)t$ (approx)	$\sqrt{\dfrac{I}{(\pi a b - a_1 b_1)}} =$ $\dfrac{a}{2}\sqrt{\dfrac{a + 3b}{a + b}}$ (approx)
	$I = \dfrac{1}{12}\left[\dfrac{3\pi}{16}d^4 + b(h^3 - d^3) + b^3(h - d)\right]$ $\dfrac{I}{c} = \dfrac{1}{6h}\left[\dfrac{3\pi}{16}d^4 + b(h^3 + d^3) + b^3(h - d)\right]$		$\sqrt{\dfrac{I}{\pi\dfrac{d^2}{4} + 2b(h - d)}}$ (approx)

Table 8-1. Properties of Various Cross Sections (Continued)

Section	Moment of inertia	Section modulus	Radius of gyration
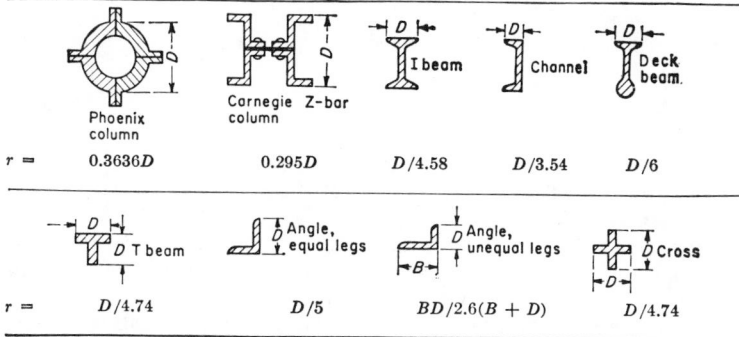	$I = \dfrac{t}{4}\left(\dfrac{\pi B^3}{16} + B^2 h + \dfrac{\pi B h^2}{2} + \dfrac{2}{3}h^3\right)$ $h = H - \tfrac{1}{2}B$ $\dfrac{I}{c} = \dfrac{2I}{H+t}$		$\sqrt{\dfrac{I}{2\left(\dfrac{\pi B}{4} + h\right)t}}$

Section	Moment of inertia and section modulus	Radius of gyration
Corrugated sheet iron, parabolically curved	$I = \dfrac{64}{105}(b_1 h_1{}^3 - b_2 h_2{}^3)$, where $h_1 = \tfrac{1}{2}(H + t)$ | $b_1 = \tfrac{1}{4}(B + 2.6t)$ $h_2 = \tfrac{1}{2}(H - t)$ | $b_2 = \tfrac{1}{4}(B - 2.6t)$ $\dfrac{I}{c} = \dfrac{2I}{H+1}$	$r = \sqrt{\dfrac{3I}{t(2B + 5.2H)}}$

Approximate Values of Least Radius of Gyration r

	Phoenix column	Carnegie Z-bar column	I beam	Channel	Deck beam
$r =$	$0.3636D$	$0.295D$	$D/4.58$	$D/3.54$	$D/6$

	T beam	Angle, equal legs	Angle, unequal legs	Cross
$r =$	$D/4.74$	$D/5$	$BD/2.6(B + D)$	$D/4.74$

NOTE: Square, axis same as first rectangle: side $= h$, $I = h^4/12$, $I/c = h^3/6$, $r = 0.289h$.

Square, diagonal taken as axis: $I = h^4/12$, $I/c = 0.1179h^3$, $r = 0.289h$.

SOURCE: L. S. Marks, (ed.), "Mechanical Engineers' Handbook," 5th ed., pp. 432–435, McGraw-Hill Book Company, Inc., New York, 1951.

Product of Inertia. The product of inertia with respect to two coordinate axes x and y is defined by

$$P_{xy} = \int xy\, dA \qquad \text{ft}^4 \qquad \text{for area} \tag{8-12}$$

and

$$P_{xy} = \int xy\, dm \qquad \text{lb-ft}^2 \qquad \text{for solid body} \tag{8-13}$$

where x, y = distances from element of area or mass to axes x, y

dA = element of area, ft^2

dm = element of mass, lb

Moments of Inertia of Important Solids (*Homogeneous*).[1]

Nomenclature

m = mass per unit volume of body, lb/ft^3

M = total mass of body, lb

r = radius, ft

I = moment of inertia, lb-ft^2

Solid circular cylinder about its axis. $I = \pi r^4 ma/2 = Mr^2/2$, where a is the length of axis of cylinder.

Solid circular cylinder about an axis through the center of gravity and perpendicular to axis of cylinder. $I = M(r^2 + a^2/3)/4$.

Hollow circular cylinder about its axis. $I = \pi ma(r_1{}^4 - r_2{}^4)/2$, where r_1 and r_2 are the outer and inner radii, feet and a is the length (feet).

Thin hollow circular cylinder about its axis. $I = Mr^2$.

Solid sphere about a diameter. $I = 8m\pi r^5/15 = 2Mr^2/5$.

Thin hollow sphere about a diameter. $I = 2Mr^2/3$.

Thick hollow sphere about a diameter. $I = 8m\pi(r_1{}^5 - r_2{}^5)/15$, where r_1 and r_2 are the outer and inner radii (feet).

Rectangular prism about an axis through center of gravity and perpendicular to a face whose dimensions are a and b (feet). $I = M(a^2 + b^2)/12$.

Solid right circular cone about an axis through its apex and perpendicular to its axis. $I = 3M(r^2/4 + h^2)/5$, where h is the altitude of the cone in feet and r is the radius of the base in feet.

Solid right circular cone about its axis of revolution. $I = 3Mr^2/10$.

Ellipsoid with semiaxes a, b, and c.

$$I \text{ about diameter } 2c \ (z \text{ axis}) = 4m\pi abc(a^2 + b^2)/15$$

where the equation of ellipsoid is: $x^2/a^2 + y^2/b^2 + z^2/c^2 = 1$.

Ring with circular section (Fig. 8-14). $I_{yy} = \frac{1}{2}m\pi^2 Ra^2(4R^2 + 3a^2)$, $I_{xx} = m\pi^2 Ra^2[R^2 + (5a^2/4)]$.

Approximate Moments of Inertia of Solids.[1]   In order to determine the moment of inertia of a solid, it is necessary to know all its dimensions.   In the case of a rod of mass M (pounds) and length l (feet) with shape and size of the cross section unknown (Fig. 8-15), making the approximation that the weight is all concentrated along the axis of the rod, the moment of inertia about YY will be $I_{yy} = \int_0^l (M/l)x^2\,dx = Ml^2/3$ lb-ft^2, where x has units of feet.

A thin plate may be treated in the same way (Fig. 8-16).

$$I_{yy} = \int_0^l (M/l)x^2\,dx$$

Here the mass of the plate is assumed to be concentrated at its middle layer.

[1] Source: L. S. Marks (ed.), "Mechanical Engineers' Handbook," 5th ed., pp. 199–200, McGraw-Hill Book Company, Inc., New York, 1951.

Thin ring, or cylinder (Fig. 8-17). Assume the mass M (pounds) of the ring or cylinder to be concentrated at a distance r (feet) from O. The moment of inertia about an axis through O perpendicular to plane of ring or along axis of cylinder will be $I = Mr^2$ lb-ft². This will be greater than the exact moment of inertia, and r is sometimes taken as the distance from O to the center of gravity of the cross section of the rim.

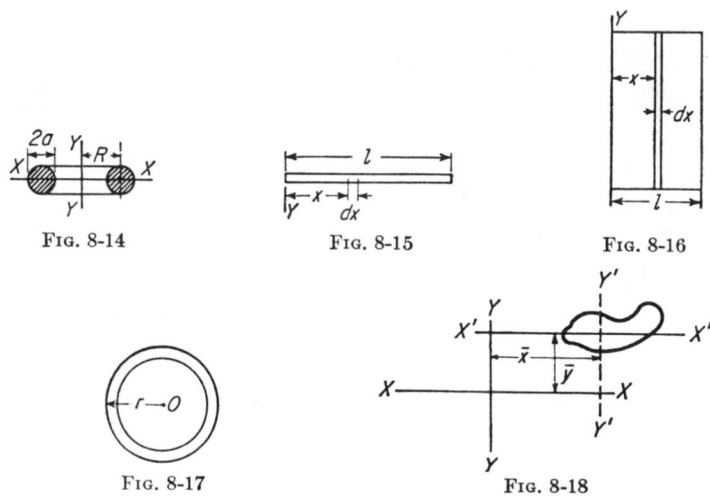

FIG. 8-14   FIG. 8-15   FIG. 8-16

FIG. 8-17   FIG. 8-18

Parallel axis rule for product of inertia (Fig. 8-18).

$$P_{xy} = P_{x'y'} + A\overline{xy} \qquad \text{ft}^4 \qquad (8\text{-}14)$$

and

$$P_{xy} = P_{x'y'} + m\overline{xy} \qquad \text{lb-ft}^2 \qquad (8\text{-}15)$$

where $P_{x'y'}$ = product of inertia through axis through center of gravity

$\bar{x}, \bar{y}$ = coordinates of center of gravity with respect to reference axes

Principal Axes. If the rectangular coordinates axes x, y, z through any point in a body are chosen in such directions that the products of inertia about that point are equal to zero, that is,

$$P_{xz} = \int xz \, dm = 0 \qquad P_{yz} = \int yz \, dm = 0 \qquad P_{xy} = \int xy \, dm = 0 \quad (8\text{-}16)$$

the axes are called *principal axes* of the body at the given point. The corresponding moments of inertia about the point are called *principal moments of inertia*. The three coordinate planes xy, yz, xz are called *principal planes*.

General Rules about Principal Axes

1. The axis perpendicular to a plane of symmetry is the principal axis.
2. For two perpendicular planes of symmetry

$$P_{xz} = P_{xy} = 0 \qquad (8\text{-}17)$$

Therefore if z is a principal axis,

$$P_{zz} = P_{xy} = P_{zy} = 0 \qquad (8\text{-}18)$$

and $0x$, $0y$, $0z$ are all principal axes. The line of intersection of the planes and the two axes in the planes are all principal axes.

3. If a body is in rotation, the axis of rotation is the principal axis, and any other two axes will also be principal axes.

4. The principal axes about which the moments of inertia are maximum and minimum are axes of stable free rotation. The third axis has unstable equilibrium.

5. If a body is rotated about its principal axis, there will be no reactions in the bearings because

$$M_z = P_{xy}\omega^2 = 0 \qquad (8\text{-}19)$$

where ω = angular velocity, radians/sec

P_{xy} = product of inertia about principal (xy) axis, lb-ft^2

M_z = reaction normal to principal axis, lb-ft^2/sec^2

6. Unless a body is rotated about the principal axis through the center of gravity, there will be a bearing reaction due to centrifugal force.

8-4. Kinetics

Energy of a Rigid Body. The *kinetic energy* of a rigid body is the energy possessed by the body by virtue of its motion.

$$\text{Kinetic energy} = \tfrac{1}{2}mv^2 \qquad \text{translation} \qquad (8\text{-}20)$$
$$\text{Kinetic energy} = \tfrac{1}{2}I_0\omega^2 \qquad \text{rotation} \qquad (8\text{-}21)$$

where m = mass, lb

I_0 = moment of inertia about axis of rotation, lb-ft^2

v = velocity, fps

ω = angular velocity, radians/sec

The *potential energy* of a rigid body is the energy possessed by the body by virtue of its position, i.e., that energy which is available to do work.

Free Harmonic Vibrations of Systems with One Degree of Freedom. If an elastic system is disturbed from its position of equilibrium by a force, the elastic restoring forces of the system in the disturbed position will no longer be in equilibrium with the loading, and vibrations will ensue (Fig. 8-19).

Nomenclature

k = spring constant of elastic system, lb force/ft

$v = dx/dt$ = velocity, fps

v_0 = initial velocity, fps

t = time, sec

W = weight (neglecting spring weight as small compared with weight W), lb mass

f = frequency of oscillation, sec^{-1}

p = period of oscillation = $\sqrt{kg_c/W}$, sec^{-1}

t = time for one complete oscillation, sec
ω = p, in the case of rotation, radians/sec
g_c = 32.2 (lb mass)(ft)/(lb force)(sec^2)
x = displacement of W from equilibrium position, ft
x_0 = initial displacement of W from equilibrium position, ft

$$\frac{W}{g_c}\frac{d^2x}{dt^2} - kx = 0 \tag{8-22}$$

$$t = 2\pi/p \qquad f = 1/t = p/2\pi \qquad p = 2\pi f \qquad p = 2\pi/t \tag{8-23}$$

The equation of motion is

$$x = x_0 \cos pt + (v_0/p) \sin pt \tag{8-24}$$

Natural Frequency. If ∂_{ST} is the deflection of the spring caused by the weight W, then $\partial_{ST} = W/k$ and

$$\omega_n = \sqrt{g_c/\partial_{ST}} = \text{number of free oscillations per } 2\pi \text{ sec} \tag{8-25}$$

Then the natural frequency is

$$f_n = 3.14\sqrt{1/\partial_{ST}} \qquad \text{cps} \tag{8-26}$$

Torsional Vibration. If a disk is supported as shown in Fig. 8-20 and subjected to a couple in the plane of the disk which is suddenly removed, free torsional vibrations of the elastic system consisting of the shaft and disk will be produced.

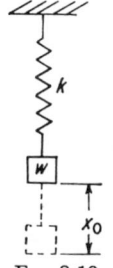
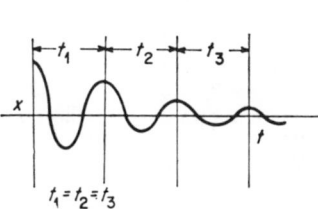

FIG. 8-19   FIG. 8-20   FIG. 8-21   FIG. 8-22

Let ϕ = angle of twist of shaft at any moment, radians
  k = torque moment necessary to produce angle of twist of 1 radian in shaft, lb force–ft
  ω_0 = initial angular velocity, radians/sec
  ϕ_0 = initial angle of twist of shaft, radians
  J = polar moment of inertia of disk (neglecting shaft J as small compared to J of disk), lb mass–ft
and p, f, t, and g_c are as defined above for elastic vibration. The period of the torsional vibration is

$$p = \sqrt{k/J} \tag{8-27}$$

The frequency

$$f = (1/2\pi) \sqrt{kg_c/J} \qquad (8\text{-}28)$$

The equation of motion is

$$\phi = \phi_0 \cos pt + (\omega_0/p) \sin pt \qquad (8\text{-}29)$$

Damped Free Vibrations. Assuming viscous damping, i.e., damping proportional to velocity, such as may exist in dashpots (Fig. 8-21),

$$x = Ae^{(-\alpha+\beta)t} + Be^{(-\alpha-\beta)t} \qquad (8\text{-}30)$$

where[1] $\alpha = cg_c/2W$ $\qquad (8\text{-}31)$

$$\beta = \sqrt{c^2 g_c^2/4W^2 - kg_c/W} \qquad (8\text{-}32)$$

A, B = constants of integration

c = damping coefficient, lb force/ft

When $c^2 g_c^2/4W^2 > kg_c/W$, β is real and positive. The result is exponential decay, in which $x \to 0$ as $t \to \infty$.

When $c^2 g_c^2/4W^2 < kg_c/W$, β is imaginary. This case is more representative of the usual case of damped vibration, the amplitude diminishing after each cycle according to the physical constants of the system. The frequency, however, does not change, that is $t_1 = t_2 = t_3$ in Fig. 8-22.

When $c^2 g_c^2/4W^2 = kg_c/W$, $\beta = 0$. For this condition

$$c = c_{cr} = \sqrt{4Wk/g_c} \qquad (8\text{-}33)$$

or, critical damping (see Fig. 8-23). This is a boundary case and rarely exists.

Forced Vibrations without Damping

P = impressed force, lb force, with frequency ω, sec^{-1}

   = $P_0 \cos \omega t$, where t is time for one vibration, sec

p = natural frequency of system, sec^{-1}, of weight W, lb mass

g_c = 32.2 (lb mass)(ft)/(lb force)(sec^2)

$$x = A \sin pt + B \cos pt + (P_0 g_c/W)[1/(p^2 - \omega^2)] \cos \omega t \qquad (8\text{-}34)$$

where A and B are constants of integration.

In general, the vibrations due to the first two terms die out shortly and only those remain which are due to the forcing frequency ω. At such time, then,

$$x = (P_0 g_c/W)[1/(p^2 - \omega^2)] \cos \omega t \qquad (8\text{-}35)$$

Let $\partial_{ST} = P_0/k$ = static deflection, in feet, resulting from P_0, where k is the system constant, in pounds force per foot, and

$$x_0 = x_{\max} = (P_0 g_c/W)[1/(p^2 - \omega^2)]. \qquad (8\text{-}36)$$

Then $\qquad x_0/\partial_{ST} = [1/(1 - \omega^2/p^2)] = \gamma \qquad (8\text{-}37)$

---

[1] For nomenclature see p. 8-14.

This relation can be plotted as shown in Fig. 8-24. It is seen that:

1. When $\omega/p = 0$, or when ω is small compared to p, $x = \delta_{ST}$ or nearly so.
2. When $\omega/p = \infty$, that is, when ω is very large compared to p, $x = 0$.
3. When $\omega/p = 1$, or $\omega = p$, $x = \infty$. This is the case of resonance.

Figure 8-24 shows that, when the applied forced frequency becomes larger than the natural frequency of the body, the deflection of the body is opposite in direction to that of the force.

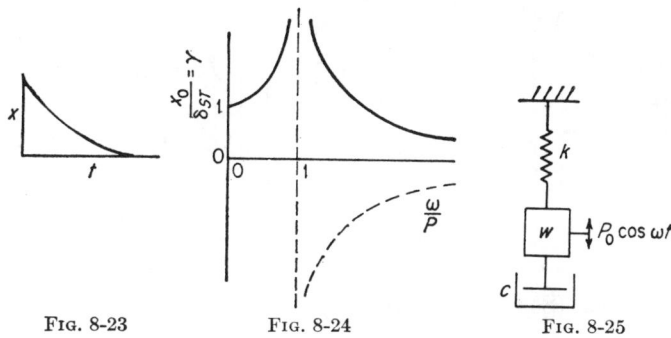

| FIG. 8-23 | FIG. 8-24 | FIG. 8-25 |

In vibration isolation, a quantity known as the transmission ratio is defined as equal to $1/(\omega^2/p^2 - 1)$. For practical vibration isolation, $\omega/p \geq \sqrt{2}$. This is accomplished by supplying a small value of p through use of very soft springs or by increasing the mass of the machine or its foundation.

Forced Vibrations with Damping (Fig. 8-25). The motion of the weight W at any time is

$$x = e^{-\alpha t}(A \cos \beta t + B \sin \beta t) + C \sin \omega t + D \cos \omega t \qquad (8\text{-}38)$$

where A, B, C, and D are constants of integration and α, β are as defined by Eqs. (8-31) and (8-32).

For steady-state application, the last two terms only are of interest, that is,

$$x = C \sin \omega t + D \cos \omega t \qquad (8\text{-}39)$$

where
$$C = \frac{P_0 g_c}{W} \frac{W^2 g_c}{(p^2 - \omega^2)W^2 + c^2 g_c^2 \omega^2} \qquad (8\text{-}40)$$

$$D = \frac{P_0 g_c}{W} \frac{W^2(p^2 - \omega^2)}{(p^2 - \omega^2)^2 W^2 + c^2 g_c^2 \omega^2} \qquad (8\text{-}41)$$

Let
$$R = \sqrt{c^2 + d^2} = \frac{P_0}{k} \frac{1}{\sqrt{(1 - \omega^2/p^2)^2 + (2c\omega/C_{cr}p)^2}} \qquad (8\text{-}42)$$

and
$$\theta = \tan^{-1}(C/D) = \tan^{-1}[cg_c\omega/W(p^2 - \omega^2)] \qquad (8\text{-}43)$$

Figures 8-26 and 8-27 can be drawn:

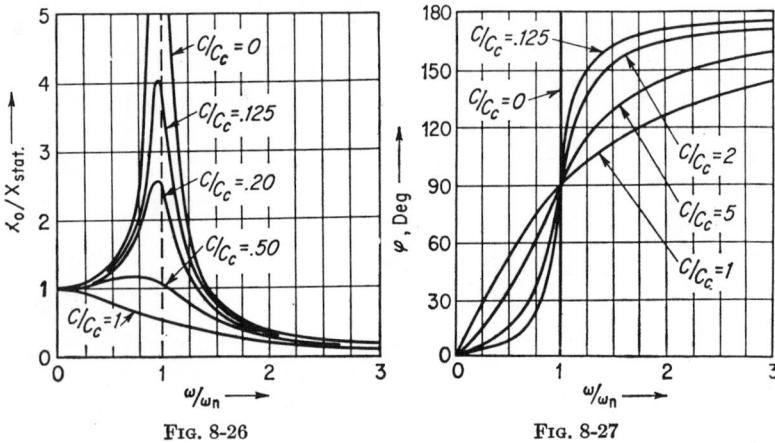

FIG. 8-26   FIG. 8-27

8-5. Torsion (See Table 8-2)

Torsion (Solid Circular Shafts) (See Fig. 8-28)

$$S_v = M_t c / J \qquad (8\text{-}44)$$

where S_v = shear stress, psi

M_t = twisting moment = Pl, in-lb

c = distance from center to stressed surface of interest, in.

J = polar moment of inertia of cross section, in.[4]

Combined Torsion and Bending (Solid Circular Shafts) (Fig. 8-29)

$$\sigma_{\max} = (16/\pi d^3)(M_b + \sqrt{M_b{}^2 + M_t{}^2}) \qquad (8\text{-}45)$$

where $\sigma_{\max}$ = maximum stress, psi

M_t = torque, in-lb.

M_b = moment due to bending load, in-lb = Wx

d = diameter of bar, in.

$$M = \sigma I / c \qquad (8\text{-}46)$$

where M = bending moment, lb-in.

σ = elastic stress at distance c from neutral axis, psi

c = distance from neutral axis to plane at which stress σ is calculated, in.

I = rectangular moment of inertia of cross-sectional area about neutral axis, in.[4]

I/c = section modulus where c is distance to the outermost fiber, in.[3]

Table 8-2. Torsion of Shafts of Various Cross Sections

G = Shear Modulus of Elasticity, psi

Cross section	Torsional resisting moment M_t	Angular deflection, a_1 (length = 1 in., radius = 1 in.)		Work of torsion (V = volume)
		In terms of torsional moment	In terms of max shear	
	$\dfrac{\pi}{16} d^3 S_v$	$\dfrac{M_t}{GJ} = \dfrac{32}{\pi d^4} \dfrac{M_t}{R}$	$2 \dfrac{S_{v_{max}}}{G} \dfrac{1}{d}$	$\dfrac{1}{4} \dfrac{S^2{}_{v_{max}}}{G} V$ (Note 1)
	$\dfrac{\pi}{16} \dfrac{D^4 - d^4}{D} S_v$	$\dfrac{32}{\pi(D^4 - d^4)} \dfrac{M_t}{G}$	$2 \dfrac{S_{v_{max}}}{G} \dfrac{1}{D}$	$\dfrac{1}{4} \dfrac{S^2{}_{v_{max}}}{G} \dfrac{D^2 + d^2}{D^2} V$ (Note 2)
	$\dfrac{\pi}{16} b^2 h S_v$ ($h > b$)	$\dfrac{16}{\pi} \dfrac{b^2 + h^2}{b^3 h^3} \dfrac{M_t}{G}$	$\dfrac{S_{v_{max}}}{G} \dfrac{b^2 + h^2}{bh^2}$	$\dfrac{1}{8} \dfrac{S^2{}_{v_{max}}}{G} \dfrac{b^2 + h^2}{h^2} V$ (Note 3)
	$\tfrac{2}{9} b^2 h S_v$ ($h > b$)	$3.6 \dfrac{b^2 + h^2}{b^3 h^3} \dfrac{M_t}{G}$ *	$0.8 \dfrac{S_{v_{max}}}{G} \dfrac{b^2 + h^2}{bh^2}$ *	$\dfrac{4}{45} \dfrac{S^2{}_{v_{max}}}{G} \dfrac{b^2 + h^2}{h^2} V$ (Note 4)
	$\tfrac{2}{9} h^3 S_v$	$7.2 \dfrac{1}{h^4} \dfrac{M_t}{G}$	$1.6 \dfrac{S_{v_{max}}}{G} \dfrac{1}{h}$	$\dfrac{8}{45} \dfrac{S^2{}_{v_{max}}}{G} V$ (Note 5)
	$\dfrac{b^3}{20} S_v$	$4.62 \dfrac{1}{b^4} \dfrac{M_t}{G}$	$2.31 \dfrac{S_{v_{max}}}{G} \dfrac{1}{b}$	
	$\dfrac{b^3}{1.09} S_v$	$0.967 \dfrac{1}{b^4} \dfrac{M_t}{G}$	$0.9 \dfrac{S_{v_{max}}}{G} \dfrac{1}{b}$	

* When $h/b =$ 1   2   4   8
Coefficient 3.6 becomes = 3.56   3.50   3.35   3.21
Coefficient 0.8 becomes = 0.79   0.78   0.74   0.71
NOTES: (1) $S_{v_{max}}$ at circumference. (2) $S_{v_{max}}$ at outer circumference. (3) $S_{v_{max}}$ at A; $S_{v_B} = 16M_t/\pi bh^2$. (4) $S_{v_{max}}$ at middle of side h; in middle of b, $S_v = 9M_t/2bh^2$. (5) $S_{v_{max}}$ at middle of side.
SOURCE: L. S. Marks (ed.), "Mechanical Engineer's Handbook," 5th ed., p. 452, McGraw-Hill Book Company, Inc., New York. 1951.

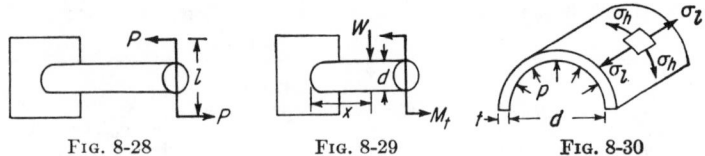

FIG. 8-28   FIG. 8-29   FIG. 8-30

8-6. Cylinder Stresses

Stresses in Thin-walled Tubes or Cylinders (Fig. 8-30)

$$\sigma_h = pd/2t \qquad \sigma_l = pd/4t \tag{8-47}$$

where σ_h = hoop stress, psi

   σ_l = longitudinal stress, psi

   d = internal diameter, in.

   p = internal pressure, psi

   t = thickness of tube wall, in.

Stresses in Thick Cylinders or Tubes (Fig. 8-31)

For internal pressure only:

$$\sigma_r = [a^2 p_i/(b^2 - a^2)](1 - b^2/r^2) \tag{8-48}$$
$$\sigma_t = [a^2 p_i/(b^2 - a^2)](1 + b^2/r^2) \tag{8-49}$$

For external pressure only:

$$\sigma_r = [- p_0 b^2/(b^2 - a^2)](1 - a^2/r^2) \tag{8-50}$$
$$\sigma_t = [- p_0 b^2/(b^2 - a^2)](1 + a^2/r^2) \tag{8-51}$$

where σ_r = stress in radial direction, psi

   σ_t = stress in tangential direction, psi

   a = internal radius of cylinder, in.

   b = external radius of cylinder, in.

   r = radial measurement, in.

   p_i = internal pressure, psi

   p_0 = external pressure, psi

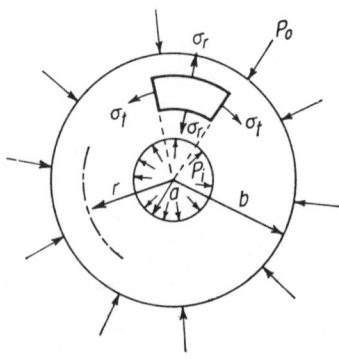

FIG. 8-31

8-7. Columns

Long Columns. Euler's formula for failure by buckling ($l/r > 120$)

$$W = n\pi^2 EI/l^2 \tag{8-52}$$

where $n = \frac{1}{4}$ for one end fixed, one end free; 1 for both ends of column rounded; 4 for both ends fixed; 2 for one end rounded, one fixed
W = load, lb
E = modulus of elasticity, psf
I = rectangular moment of inertia, ft^4
l = length of column, ft
r = least radius of gyration, ft
l/r = slenderness ratio

Short Columns. Rankine's formula ($l/r = 20$ to 120)

$$W = \sigma A/(1 + kl^2/r^2) \tag{8-53}$$

where W = design load, lb
σ = design stress, psf
A = area of cross section, ft^2
l = length, ft
r = least radius of gyration, ft
k = values from Table 8-3, dimensionless

Table 8-3. Values of k (Merriman)

Material	Both ends fixed	Both ends rounded	One end fixed, one end rounded	One end fixed, one end free
Timber..........	1/3,000	1.95/3,000	4/3,000	16/3,000
Cast iron........	1/5,000	1.95/5,000	4/5,000	16/5,000
Wrought iron....	1/36,000	1.95/36,000	4/36,000	16/36,000
Steel..........	1/25,000	1.95/25,000	4/25,000	16/25 000

SOURCE: L. S. Marks (ed.), "Mechanical Engineers' Handbook," 5th ed., p. 466, McGraw-Hill Book Company, Inc, New York, 1951.

MACHINE DESIGN DATA

8-8. Failure

In the broadest sense, a structure or structural element experiences a failure when it can no longer satisfactorily perform its design function. Failure may be due to yielding or fracture, according as the material is ductile or brittle in nature. A ductile failure may result in eventual fracture of the member, though usually the part will have failed long before it breaks. A brittle failure, however, always results in fracture.

8-9. Stress Concentration

A loaded structural member whose design is such that it is subjected to sudden changes in shape and/or stress level must be investigated for the effects of stress concentrations, or stress raisers. The stress raisers may be in the form of notches, fillets, rough surface finish, press fits, inclusions, residual stresses, etc., and their effects are often the most important consideration in design of parts subjected to repeated loading and fatigue failure.

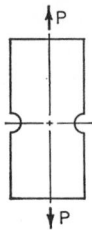

Fig. 8-32. Notched tensile specimen.

The total stress concentration factor, or stress multiplying factor, for a particular design depends on the material as well as type of stress raiser. The disruption in geometry results in a geometrical stress concentration factor, which, by itself, is independent of any variable save the geometry of the discontinuity. That resulting from a relatively simple notch is shown in Figs. 8-32 and 8-33. Note that the geometrical stress concentration factor multiplies the average axial stress $\sigma_n = P/A$ by a factor of 2.

Although some geometrical stress concentration factors can be obtained mathematically for simple notches, most data of this kind are supplied by experimental methods of stress analysis. (See Peterson, "Stress Concentration Design Factors," John Wiley & Sons, Inc., New York, 1953.) The nature of the material enters into the over-all stress concentration factor through its sensitivity to notching, or its index of sensitivity q, ranging between 0 and 1. For $q = 0$, the material experiences no reduction in fatigue strength due to a given notch; on the other hand, if $q = 1$, there is a full reduction in fatigue strength, as indicated by the geometrical stress concentration factor.

8-10. Fatigue

Structural or mechanical members loaded repetitively are subject to fatigue failure if improperly designed. The designer must know the properties of the material which are to be subjected to a particular type and level of repeated loading. Where fatigue data and design are concerned, the following definitions are suggested in the ASTM Manual of Fatigue Testing:

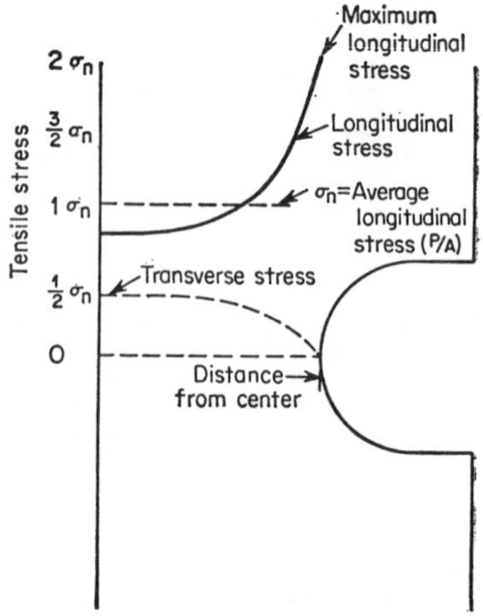

Fig. 8-33. Elastic stress distribution across center of notched specimen shown in Fig. 8-32. A = cross-sectional area at root of notch.

Stress Cycle. A stress cycle is the smallest section of the stress-time function which is repeated periodically and identically.

Figure 8-34 illustrates stress cycles commonly used and indicates, diagrammatically, many of the following terms.

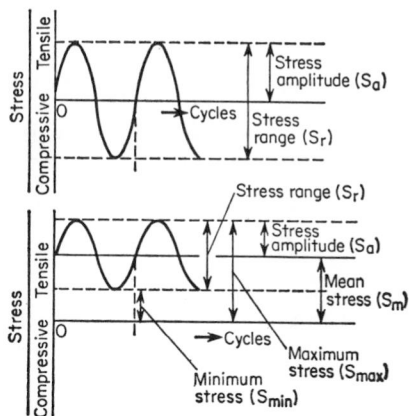

Fig. 8-34. Typical stress cycles in fatigue testing.

Nominal Stress, S. The stress calculated on the net section by simple theory such as $S = P/A$ or $S = Mc/I$ or $S_s = Tc/J$ without taking into account the variation in stress conditions caused by geometrical discontinuities such as holes, grooves, fillets, etc.

Maximum Stress, S_{max}. The highest algebraic value of the stress in the stress cycle, tensile stress being considered positive and compressive stress negative.

Minimum Stress, S_{min}. The lowest algebraic value of the stress in the stress cycle, tensile stress being considered positive and compressive stress negative.

Range of Stress, S_r. The algebraic difference between the maximum and minimum stress in one cycle, that is, $S_r = S_{max} - S_{min}$. For many cases of fatigue testing, the stress varies equally above and below zero stress, but other types of variation may be experienced.

Alternating Stress Amplitude (or Variable Stress Component), S_a. One-half the range of stress, that is, $S_a = S_r/2$.

Mean Stress (or Steady-stress Component), S_m. The algebraic mean of the maximum and minimum stress in one cycle, that is, $S = (S_{max} + S_{min})/2$.

Stress Ratio, R. The algebraic ratio of the minimum stress to the maximum stress in one cycle, that is, $R = S_{min}/S_{max}$.

Stress Cycles Endured, n. The number of cycles which a specimen has endured at any stage of a fatigue test.

Fatigue Life, N. The number of stress cycles which can be sustained for a given test condition.

SN **Diagram.** A plot of stress against number of cycles to failure. It is usually plotted S versus $\log N$, but a plot of $\log S$ versus $\log N$ is sometimes used (Fig. 8-35).

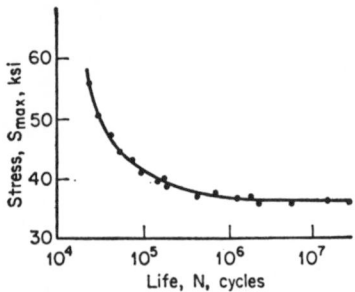

FIG. 8-35. *SN* curve for a steel tested in rotating beam machine. Note well-defined endurance limit at 36 ksi.

Fatigue Limit (or Endurance Limit), S_e. The limiting value of the stress below which a material can presumably endure an infinite number of stress cycles, that is, the stress at which the *SN* diagram becomes horizontal and appears to remain so. It should be noted that certain materials and environment preclude the attainment of a fatigue limit.

If the stress is not completely reversed, it is necessary to state what is meant by the fatigue limit. It may be expressed in terms of the alternating stress amplitude or the maximum stress; whichever method is used, it is also necessary to state the value of the mean stress, minimum stress, or stress ratio.

Most fatigue test data have been obtained through a rotating-beam test which subjects the material to completely reversed bending stresses. Data are usually reported on an *SN* curve (Fig. 8-35). Note that long life is bought at the expense of lowered operating stress level. The material in Fig. 8-35 shows a well-defined endurance limit. For a material whose *SN* curve shows no stress value to which it can be subjected for an infinite number of stress cycles, it is practice to report an endurance strength at a given number of stress cycles, usually between 10^8 and 10^9 cycles. Extensive fatigue data are found in Grover et al., "The Fatigue of Metals and Structures," U.S. Department of the Navy, NAVAER 00-25-534, 1954.

8-11. Gears

$$P_c = \pi D_p / N = \text{circular pitch, in./tooth} \qquad (8\text{-}54)$$
$$P_d = N / D_p = \text{diametral pitch, teeth/in. of pitch diameter} \qquad (8\text{-}55)$$

where N = number of teeth in gear
D_p = pitch diameter, in.

$$\text{Gear ratio} = \frac{N_2}{N_1} = \frac{\text{product of teeth of all driving gears}}{\text{product of teeth of all driven gears}} \qquad (8\text{-}56)$$

$$\text{Pulley ratio} = \frac{N_2}{N_1} = \frac{\text{product of diameters of all driving pulleys}}{\text{product of diameters of all driven pulleys}} \qquad (8\text{-}57)$$

where N_1 = speed of first shaft, rpm
N_2 = speed of last shaft, rpm

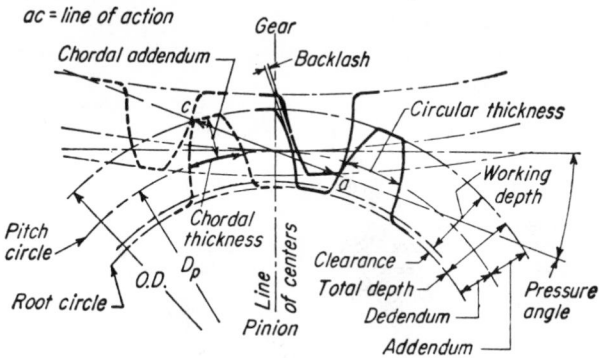

Fɪɢ. 8-36

Table 8-4. Gear Tooth Proportions in Various Systems

Pressure angle..........	$14\frac{1}{2}°$	$20°$	
Depth of tooth.........	Full	Full	Stub
Addendum.............	$1/P_d$	$1/P_d$	$0.8/P_d$
Minimum dedendum including clearance....	$1.157/P_d$	$1.157/P_d$	$1/P_d$
Minimum clearance.....	$0.157/P_d$	$0.157/P_d$	$0.2/P_d$
Minimum total depth...	$2.157/P_d$	$2.157/P_d$	$1.8/P_d$
Outside diameter.......	$(2+N)/P_d$	$(2+N)/P_d$	$(1.6+N)/P_d$

ꜱᴏᴜʀᴄᴇ: L. S. Marks (ed.), "Mechanical Engineers' Handbook," 5th ed., p. 452. McGraw-Hill Book Company, Inc., New York, 1951.

8-12. Screws and Screw Threads

Threaded members are used as fasteners, for power transmission, and to provide adjustments.

Fasteners and adjusting screws generally take the form shown in Fig. 8-37, though in cases where considerable force or power is involved, square or Acme threads are used (Figs. 8-38 and 8-39, Tables 8-5 and 8-6). Power screws are generally of the square or Acme-thread form.

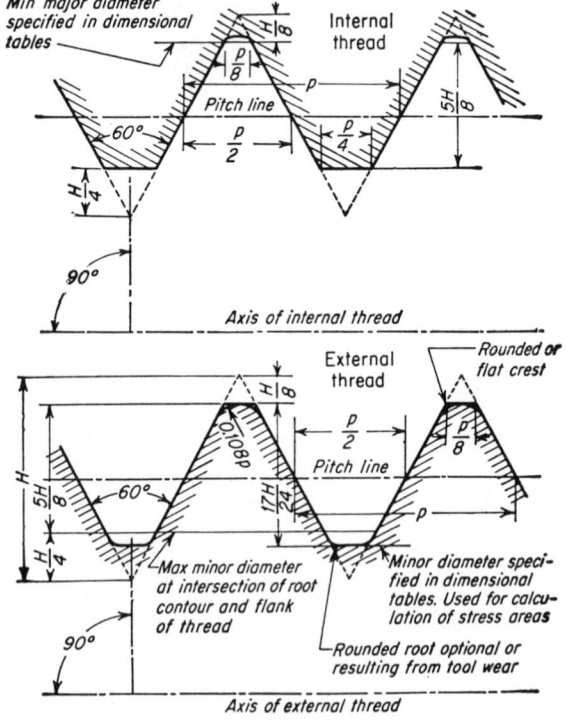

Fig. 8-37. 60° unified thread forms.

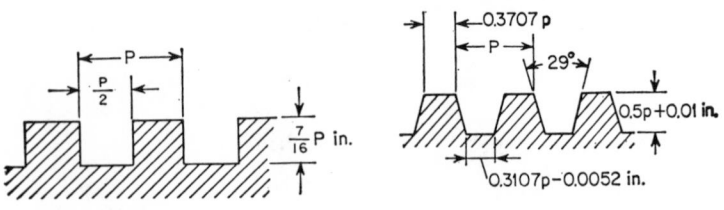

Fig. 8-38. Square thread.   Fig. 8-39. Acme thread.

Table 8-5. Standard Square Threads

Bolt diam., in.	Threads per in.	Root diam., in.	Root area, in.^{2}
¼	10	0.1625	0.0207
⁵⁄₁₆	9	0.2153	0.0375
⅜	8	0.2658	0.0555
⁷⁄₁₆	7	0.3125	0.0767
½	6½	0.3656	0.1049
⁹⁄₁₆	6	0.4167	0.1364
⅝	5½	0.4666	0.1709
¹¹⁄₁₆	5	0.5125	0.2063
¾	5	0.5750	0.2597
¹³⁄₁₆	4½	0.6181	0.3000
⅞	4½	0.6806	0.3638
¹⁵⁄₁₆	4	0.7188	0.4058
1	4	0.7813	0.4804
1⅛	3½	0.8750	0.6013
1¼	3½	1.0000	0.7854
1⅜	3	1.0834	0.9201
1½	3	1.2084	1.1462
1⅝	2¾	1.307	1.3414
1¾	2½	1.400	1.5394
1⅞	2½	1.525	1.8265
2	2¼	1.612	2.0422
2¼	2¼	1.862	2.7245
2½	2	2.063	3.3410
2¾	2	2.313	4.2000
3	1¾	2.500	4.9087
3¼	1¾	2.750	5.9396
3½	1⅝	2.962	6.8930
3¾	1½	3.168	7.8853
4	1½	3.418	9.1756

Table 8-6. Acme Screw Threads

Threads per in.	Depth of thread, in.	Thickness at root of thread, in.
1	0.5100	0.6345
1½	.3850	.4772
2	.2600	.3199
3	.1767	.2150
4	.1350	.1625
5	.1100	.1311
6	.0933	.1101
7	.0814	.0951
8	.0725	.0839
9	.0655	.0751
10	.0600	.0681

The shapes of threaded members are limitless, depending upon the application; the heads, however, are most often of the forms shown in Fig. 8-40.

Set screws prevent motion between two parts by compressive forces set up by driving the end of the set screw tightly against one of the parts. The

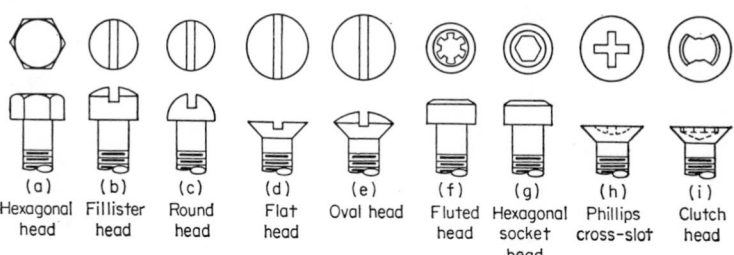

(a) Hexagonal head (b) Fillister head (c) Round head (d) Flat head (e) Oval head (f) Fluted head (g) Hexagonal socket head (h) Phillips cross-slot (i) Clutch head

Fɪɢ. 8-40. Typical head forms for threaded fasteners.

Table 8-7. Thread Form and Formulas, Unified and American

Thread Form	*Formula*
Angle of thread	$2a = 60°$
Half angle of thread	$a = 30°$
Number of threads per inch	$n = 1/p$
Pitch of thread	$p = 1/n$
Height of sharp V thread	$H = 0.86603p$
	$= 0.86603/n$
Height of external thread*	$h_s = 0.61343p$
	$= 0.61343/n$
	$= {}^{17}\!/_{24}H$
Height of internal thread	$h_n = 0.54127p$
	$= 0.54127/n$
	$= {}^5\!/_8 H$
Depth of thread engagement	$h_e = 0.54127p$
	$= 0.54127/n$
Flat at crest of external thread	$F_{cs} = 0.125p$
	$= 0.125/n$
	$= p/8$
Truncation of external-thread crest	$f_{cs} = 0.10825p$
	$= 0.10825/n$
	$= H/8$
Truncation of external-thread rounded root*	$s_{rs} = 0.14434p$
	$= 0.14434/n$
	$= H/6$
Flat at crest of internal thread	$F_{cn} = 0.25p$
	$= 0.25/n$
	$= p/4$
Truncation of internal-thread crest	$f_{cn} = 0.21651p$
	$= 0.21651/n$
	$= H/4$
Flat at root of internal thread	$F_{rn} = 0.125p$
	$= 0.125/n$
	$= p/8$
Truncation of internal-thread root	$f_{rn} = 0.10825p$
	$= 0.10825/n$
	$= H/8$
Addendum of external thread	$h_{as} = 0.32476p$
	$= 0.32476/n$
	$= {}^3\!/_8 H$
Major diameter of external thread (nominal diameter)†	D_s
Pitch diameter of external thread†	$E_s = D - 2h_{as}‡$
	$= D - 0.64952p$
	$= D - 0.64952/n$
Minor diameter of external thread	$K_s = D_s - 2h_s$
	$= D_s - 1.22687p$
	$= D_s - 1.22687/n$
Major diameter of internal thread†	D_n
Pitch diameter of internal thread†	E_n
Minor diameter of internal thread	$K_n = D_n - 2h_n$
	$= D_n - 1.08253p$
	$= D_n - 1.08253/n$

* For calculating minor diameter and stress-area values in tables.
† As external and internal threads have the same basic major diameters and the same basic pitch diameters, hereinafter the subscripts are omitted from D and E.
‡ $2h_{as} = h_b =$ the "basic height" h of the original American National form.
SOURCE: Extracted from American Standard "Unified and American Screw Threads," ASA B1.1—1949. with the permission of the publisher, The American Society of Mechanical Engineers.

most common types of set-screw points are shown in Fig. 8-41. Other variations in point type and ingenious locking features are available from the industry. Data for standard 60°

Oval Cup Cone Dog Flat Hanger

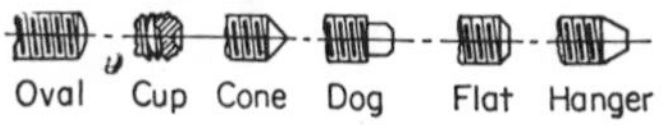

Fig. 8-41. Typical set-screw points.

thread forms are given in Tables 8-7 to 8-10.

Tapping screws have become widely used over the past thirty years. Designed for pierced or drilled holes, they cut or form their own threads as they are driven. Of the types shown in Table 8-11, the drive screw (Type U) is hammered into place; all others are screwed into place. The heads of the latter usually receive a straight or Phillips-head driver or a hexagonal-socket head wrench.

Table 8-8. Coarse-thread Series, UNC and NC, Basic Dimensions

Sizes	Basic major diam, in.	Thds/in.	Basic pitch diam,* in.	Minor diam ext thds, in.	Minor diam int thds, in.	Lead angle at basic pitch diam	Section at minor diam, in.²	Tensile stress area, in.²
	D	n	E	K_s	K_n	λ	at $D - 2h_b$	
1 (0.073)	0.0730	64	0.0629	0.0538	0.0561	4° 31′	0.0022	0.0026
2 (0.086)	0.0860	56	0.0744	0.0641	0.0667	4° 22′	0.0031	0.0036
3 (0.099)	0.0990	48	0.0855	0.0734	0.0764	4° 26′	0.0041	0.0048
4 (0.112)	0.1120	40	0.0958	0.0813	0.0849	4° 45′	0.0050	0.0060
5 (0.125)	0.1250	40	0.1088	0.0943	0.0979	4° 11′	0.0067	0.0079
6 (0.138)	0.1380	32	0.1177	0.0997	0.1042	4° 50′	0.0075	0.0090
8 (0.164)	0.1640	32	0.1437	0.1257	0.1302	3° 58′	0.0120	0.0139
10 (0.190)	0.1900	24	0.1629	0.1389	0.1449	4° 39′	0.0145	0.0174
12 (0.216)	0.2160	24	0.1889	0.1649	0.1709	4° 1′	0.0206	0.0240
1/4	0.2500	20	0.2175	0.1887	0.1959	4° 11′	0.0269	0.0317
5/16	0.3125	18	0.2764	0.2443	0.2524	3° 40′	0.0454	0.0522
3/8	0.3750	16	0.3344	0.2983	0.3073	3° 24′	0.0678	0.0773
7/16	0.4375	14	0.3911	0.3499	0.3602	3° 20′	0.0933	0.1060
1/2	0.5000	13	0.4500	0.4056	0.4167	3° 7′	0.1257	0.1416
9/16	0.5625	12	0.5084	0.4603	0.4723	2° 59′	0.1620	0.1816
5/8	0.6250	11	0.5660	0.5135	0.5266	2° 56′	0.2018	0.2256
3/4	0.7500	10	0.6850	0.6273	0.6417	2° 40′	0.3020	0.3340
7/8	0.8750	9	0.8028	0.7387	0.7547	2° 31′	0.4193	0.4612
1	1.0000	8	0.9188	0.8466	0.8647	2° 29′	0.5510	0.6051
1 1/8	1.1250	7	1.0322	0.9497	0.9704	2° 31′	0.6931	0.7627
1 1/4	1.2500	7	1.1572	1.0747	1.0954	2° 15′	0.8898	0.9684
1 3/8	1.3750	6	1.2667	1.1705	1.1946	2° 24′	1.0541	1.1538
1 1/2	1.5000	6	1.3917	1.2955	1.3196	2° 11′	1.2938	1.4041
1 3/4	1.7500	5	1.6201	1.5046	1.5335	2° 15′	1.7441	1.8983
2	2.0000	4 1/2	1.8557	1.7274	1.7594	2° 11′	2.3001	2.4971
2 1/4	2.2500	4 1/2	2.1057	1.9774	2.0094	1° 55′	3.0212	3.2464
2 1/2	2.5000	4	2.3376	2.1933	2.2294	1° 57′	3.7161	3.9976
2 3/4	2.7500	4	2.5876	2.4433	2.4794	1° 46′	4.6194	4.9326
3	3.0000	4	2.8376	2.6933	2.7294	1° 36′	5.6209	5.9659
3 1/4	3.2500	4	3.0876	2.9433	2.9794	1° 29′	6.7205	7.0992
3 1/2	3.5000	4	3.3376	3.1933	3.2294	1° 22′	7.9183	8.3268
3 3/4	3.7500	4	3.5876	3.4433	3.4794	1° 16′	9.2143	9.6546
4	4.0000	4	3.8376	3.6933	3.7294	1° 11′	10.6084	11.0805

* British: effective diameter.
NOTE: Bold type below rule indicates unified threads, UNC.
SOURCE: Extracted from American Standard "Unified and American Screw Threads," ASA B1.1—1949, with the permission of the publisher, The American Society of Mechanical Engineers.

Table 8-9. Fine-thread Series, UNF and NF, Basic Dimensions

Sizes	Basic major diam., in.	Thds/in.	Basic pitch diam.,* in.	Minor diam ext thds, in.	Minor diam int thds, in.	Lead angle at basic pitch diam	Section at minor diam, in.²	Tensile stress area, in.²
	D	n	E	K_s	K_n	λ	at $D - 2h_b$	
0 (0.060)	0.0600	80	0.0519	0.0447	0.0465	4° 23′	0.0015	0.0018
1 (0.073)	0.0730	72	0.0640	0.0560	0.0580	3° 57′	0.0024	0.0027
2 (0.086)	0.0860	64	0.0759	0.0668	0.0691	3° 45′	0.0034	0.0039
3 (0.099)	0.0990	56	0.0874	0.0771	0.0797	3° 43′	0.0045	0.0052
4 (0.112)	0.1120	48	0.0985	0.0864	0.0894	3° 51′	0.0057	0.0065
5 (0.125)	0.1250	44	0.1102	0.0971	0.1004	3° 45′	0.0072	0.0082
6 (0.138)	0.1380	40	0.1218	0.1073	0.1109	3° 44′	0.0087	0.0101
8 (0.164)	0.1640	36	0.1460	0.1299	0.1339	3° 28′	0.0128	0.0146
10 (0.190)	0.1900	32	0.1697	0.1517	0.1562	3° 21′	0.0175	0.0199
12 (0.216)	0.2160	28	0.1928	0.1722	0.1773	3° 22′	0.0226	0.0257
1/4	0.2500	28	0.2268	0.2062	0.2113	2° 52′	0.0326	0.0362
5/16	0.3125	24	0.2854	0.2614	0.2674	2° 40′	0.0524	0.0579
3/8	0.3750	24	0.3479	0.3239	0.3299	2° 11′	0.0809	0.0876
7/16	0.4375	20	0.4050	0.3762	0.3834	2° 15′	0.1090	0.1185
1/2	0.5000	20	0.4675	0.4387	0.4459	1° 57′	0.1486	0.1597
9/16	0.5625	18	0.5264	0.4943	0.5024	1° 55′	0.1888	0.2026
5/8	0.6250	18	0.5889	0.5568	0.5649	1° 43′	0.2400	0.2555
3/4	0.7500	16	0.7094	0.6733	0.6823	1° 36′	0.3513	0.3724
7/8	0.8750	14	0.8286	0.7874	0.7977	1° 34′	0.4805	0.5088
1	1.0000	14	0.9536	0.9124	0.9227	1° 22′	0.6464	0.6791
1	1.0000	12	0.9459	0.8978	0.9098	1° 36′	0.6245	0.6624
1 1/8	1.1250	12	1.0709	1.0228	1.0348	1° 25′	0.8118	0.8549
1 1/4	1.2500	12	1.1959	1.1478	1.1598	1° 16′	1.0237	1.0721
1 3/8	1.3750	12	1.3209	1.2728	1.2848	1° 9′	1.2602	1.3137
1 1/2	1.5000	12	1.4459	1.3978	1.4098	1° 3′	1.5212	1.5799

* British: effective diameter.
NOTE: Bold type below rules indicates unified threads, UNF.
SOURCE: Extracted from American Standard "Unified and American Screw Threads," ASA B1.1—1949, with the permission of the publisher, The American Society of Mechanical Engineers.

Table 8-10. Extra-fine-thread Series, NEF, Basic Dimensions

Sizes	Basic major diam, in.	Thds/in.	Basic pitch diam,* in.	Minor diam ext thds, in.	Minor diam int thds, in.	Lead angle at basic pitch diam	Section at minor diam, in.²	Tensile stress area, in.
	D	n	E	K_s	K_n	λ	at $D - 2h_b$	
12 (0.216)	0.2160	32	0.1957	0.1777	0.1822	2° 55′	0.0242	0.0269
¼	0.2500	32	0.2297	0.2117	0.2162	2° 29′	0.0344	0.0377
⁵⁄₁₆	0.3125	32	0.2922	0.2742	0.2787	1° 57′	0.0581	0.0622
⅜	0.3750	32	0.3547	0.3367	0.3412	1° 36′	0.0878	0.0929
⁷⁄₁₆	0.4375	28	0.4143	0.3937	0.3988	1° 34′	0.1201	0.1270
½	0.5000	28	0.4768	0.4562	0.4613	1° 22′	0.1616	0.1695
⁹⁄₁₆	0.5625	24	0.5354	0.5114	0.5174	1° 25′	0.2030	0.2134
⅝	0.6250	24	0.5979	0.5739	0.5799	1° 16′	0.2560	0.2676
¹¹⁄₁₆	0.6875	24	0.6604	0.6364	0.6424	1° 9′	0.3151	0.3280
¾	0.7500	20	0.7175	0.6887	0.6959	1° 16′	0.3685	0.3855
¹³⁄₁₆	0.8125	20	0.7800	0.7512	0.7584	1° 10′	0.4388	0.4573
⅞	0.8750	20	0.8425	0.8137	0.8209	1° 5′	0.5153	0.5352
¹⁵⁄₁₆	0.9375	20	0.9050	0.8762	0.8834	1° 0′	0.5979	0.6194
1	1.0000	20	0.9675	0.9387	0.9459	0° 57′	0.6866	0.7095
1¹⁄₁₆	1.0625	18	1.0264	0.9943	1.0024	59′	0.7702	0.7973
1⅛	1.1250	18	1.0889	1.0568	1.0649	56′	0.8705	0.8993
1³⁄₁₆	1.1875	18	1.1514	1.1193	1.1274	53′	0.9770	1.0074
1¼	1.2500	18	1.2139	1.1818	1.1899	50′	1.0895	1.1216
1⁵⁄₁₆	1.3125	18	1.2764	1.2443	1.2524	48′	1.2082	1.2420
1⅜	1.3750	18	1.3389	1.3068	1.3149	45′	1.3330	1.3684
1⁷⁄₁₆	1.4375	18	1.4014	1.3693	1.3774	43′	1.4640	1.5010
1½	1.5000	18	1.4639	1.4318	1.4399	42′	1.6011	1.6397
1⁹⁄₁₆	1.5625	18	1.5264	1.4943	1.5024	40′	1.7444	1.7846
1⅝	1.6250	18	1.5889	1.5568	1.5649	38′	1.8937	1.9357
1¹¹⁄₁₆	1.6875	18	1.6514	1.6193	1.6274	37′	2.0493	2.0929
1¾	1.7500	16	1.7094	1.6733	1.6823	40′	2.1873	2.2382
2	2.0000	16	1.9594	1.9233	1.9323	35′	2.8917	2.9501

* British: effective diameter.
SOURCE: Extracted from American Standard "Unified and American Screw Threads," ASA B1.1—1949, with the permission of the publisher, The American Society of Mechanical Engineers.

8-10. Belts and Sheaves

Belt Lengths

Total belt length $L = 2S \cos \theta + \pi[(R + r) + (R - r)\theta/90]$ in.   (8-58)

where S = center distance between pulleys, in.

     R = radius of large pulley (flat belt) or pitch radius of large pulley (V belt), in.

     r = radius of small pulley (flat belt) or pitch radius of small pulley (V belt), in.

     $\theta = \sin^{-1}[(R - r)/S]$ deg

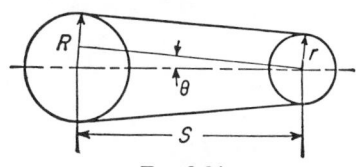

FIG. 8-34

Table 8-11. Standard Tapping Screws

Thread forming

Type B

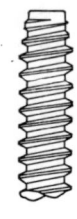

Type A

Spaced thread, gimlet point. Often called sheet-metal screw. Produces strongest joint in light-gauge sheet metal. Used in pierced or punched holes where sharp, starting point is needed and exposed point does not matter. For sheets up to 20 gauge use No. 6 screw; larger screws may be used up to 18 gauge. Do not use on thicknesses larger than 18 gauge (0.048 in.). Fastest driving of all screw types, except for Type U drive screws. Can be used in easily deformed plastics or metals, with pilot hole less than diameter of screw, to increase joint strength.

Spaced thread, blunt point. Used for sheet metals thicker than 18 gauge. Has slight taper on front end insufficient for self-aligning, but when placed in a pilot-hole taper holds screw upright, making it easy to drive. Drives faster than any screw except Types A and U, with less driving torque than A. Can be used in nonferrous castings, plastics, or soft metals.

Type C

Blunt-point screw with threads same pitch as standard machine screw. Used where finer-pitch screw is desirable with chip-free assembly. More engaged thread surface increases frictional resistance to loosening. Small helix angle results in backout torque component under vibration. Obtains higher clamping forces for same applied driving torque.

Type BP

Type U

Spaced thread, same as Type B, but has a cone point. Can be used where holes are slightly misaligned.

Multiple thread, blunt point, metallic drive screw. Threads have high helix angle. Hammered or forced in, this screw has good holding power even when subjected to vibration. Used for permanent fastening, since it is difficult to remove. Do not use in material thinner than 1 diam of the screw. Usually does not have a driving slot or recess.

Thread cutting

Type D

Blunt-point screw with a single narrow flute. Approximate machine-screw thread. Used in same manner as Type C where less driving torque is needed. This screw is very good for low-strength metals and plastics; for high-strength, brittle metals such as cast iron; and for rethreading clogged pretapped holes. Easy starting. Gives the highest clamping force for a given torque of any tapping screw.

Type F

Approximate machine-screw thread, blunt point. Tapered thread may be complete or incomplete at the producer's option. Recommended for same general application conditions as Type C screws but where low driving torque is needed. Because of the five evenly spaced cutting grooves and large chip cavities, this screw is used in a wide range of materials such as aluminum, zinc, die castings, carbon and stainless-steel sheet and shapes, cast iron, brass, plastics, etc. Drives faster than a machine screw and resists vibration. Chip space of the flutes is not suitable for deep penetration because of clogging.

Type BF

Spaced thread same as Type B, blunt point, with five evenly spaced cutting grooves and chip cavities. The grooves of this thread remove only a small part of the material to maintain maximum shear strength in the threaded wall of the hole. Wall thickness should be at least 1½ times the major diameter of the screw. Chip room and cutting-groove design are helpful in brittle plastics and die castings to reduce thread stripping. Used for producing long thread engagement, particularly in blind holes. Permits faster driving than is possible with fine-thread types.

Type G

Blunt point with single through slot which forms two cutting edges. Approximate machine screw threads, front end having incomplete tapered threads. Recommended for same general usage as Type C but where driving torque is required. Has higher percentage of thread and longer thread engagement than Type C, making it useful for low-strength metals and plastics.

Type T

Blunt point with single wide flute. Approximate machine screw threads. Usage same as Type D, except wide flute provides more chip clearance.

Type BG

Spaced thread, blunt point. Single slot has two cutting edges. Especially useful for brittle or friable material where threads that are too close together will cause material to crumble. Since this screw removes the least amount of material from thread wall, maximum stripping strength is maintained in plastics and soft materials. Can produce long thread engagement, particularly in blind holes. Drives faster than fine threads.

Type BT

Spaced thread, blunt point. Same as Type BG except for single wide flute. Flute provides room for twisted curly chips so that they do not cause binding or reaming of the hole.

SOURCE: "Machine Design," Sept. 29, 1960. Copyright 1960, Penton Publishing Co.

8–33

8-13. Bolt Preload and Gasketed Joints

Threaded fasteners develop their holding power by being put into tension as the screw is tightened. The danger of permanently deforming a screw exists if excessive torque is applied in "making up" the joint, with the possibility of breaking the fastener through combined shear and tension. When one of the threaded members is softer than the other, the softer threads may shear or strip.

In practice, the average initial tensile load F_i put on a tightened through-bolt or stud of major diameter $= d$ is approximately

$$F_i = 16,000d \tag{8-58}$$

Thus a $\frac{5}{8}$-11 UNC bolt will be subjected to a 10,000-lb tensile load when tightened or, based on a root area of 0.225 in.^{2}, a direct tensile stress due to tightening alone of 45,000 psi. High-strength fasteners, generally of alloy steel, should be used if high initial tensile preloads are required in high-pressure joints and the like.

A bolted joint consists of two resilient members, the bolt and the gasket. Denote tensile preload force by F_i, external applied load by F_e, and total load by F_t. Then the total bolt load is

$$F_t = KF_e + F_i \tag{8-59}$$

where K, a function of the relative stiffnesses of gasket and bolt, will vary between 0 and 1 (Table 8-12).

Table 8-12. Values of K for Eq. (8-59)

Type of Joint	K
Soft packing with studs	0.90–1.00
Soft packing with through bolts	0.60–0.75
Asbestos	0.50–0.60
Soft-copper gasket with long through bolts	0.40–0.50
Hard-copper gasket with long through bolts	0.20–0.30
Metal-to-metal joints with through bolts	0.00

Obviously, should F_e becomes so large that the gasket loses contact with the faces of the joint, the bolt will be loaded with the entire external load; that is, $F_t = F_e$.

8-14. Shafts and Bearings

A shaft is the fundamental torque-transmitting machine element, and can be subjected separately or simultaneously to torsion, bending, and axial loading. The ASME Code for Design of Transmission Shafting, applicable to ductile materials with ultimate tensile strength about twice the ultimate shear strength, results in the following design equation:

$$d_0{}^3 = \frac{16}{\pi s_s} \sqrt{\left[K_m M + \frac{\alpha F_a d_0 (1 + K^2)}{8} \right]^2 + (K_t T)^2} \; \frac{1}{1 - K^4} \tag{8-60}$$

where d_0 = shaft diameter, in.

F_a = axial tension or compression, lb

K = ratio of inside to outside diameter of hollow shafts

K_m = combined shock and fatigue factor to be applied to computed bending moment (Table 8-13)

K_t = combined shock and fatigue factor to be applied to computed torsional moment (Table 8-13)

M = maximum bending moment, lb-in.

T = maximum torsional moment, lb-in.

s_s = maximum stress permissible in shear, psi

α = ratio of maximum intensity of stress resulting from axial load to average axial stress

$$\alpha = \begin{cases} \dfrac{1}{1 - 0.0044\left(\dfrac{L}{k}\right)} & \text{for } \dfrac{L}{k} < 115 \qquad (8\text{-}61) \\[4mm] \dfrac{s_y}{n\pi^2 E}\left(\dfrac{L}{k}\right)^2 & \text{for } \dfrac{L}{k} \geq 115 \qquad (8\text{-}62) \end{cases}$$

where L = length between bearing, in.

k = radius of gyration of shaft, in.

s_y = compression yield stress, psi

E = modulus of elasticity, psi

$n = 1$ for free (simple) ends; $n = 2.5$–3 for fixed ends (rigid bearings)

A shaft of brittle material loaded in both torsion and bending is designed based on the maximum allowable tensile stress $s_{t,\text{max}}$:

$$d_0{}^3 = \frac{16}{\pi s_t}\left[K_m M + \sqrt{(K_m M)^2 + (K_t T)^2}\right]\frac{1}{1 - K^4} \qquad (8\text{-}63)$$

Table 8-13. Constants for ASME Code Equations for Shafting

Type loading	K_m	K_t
Stationary shafts:		
Gradually applied load........	1.0	1.0
Suddenly applied load.......................	1.5–2.0	1.5–2.0
Rotating shafts:		
Gradually applied or steady load..............	1.5	1.0
Suddenly applied loads, minor shocks only.....	1.5–2.0	1.0–1.5
Suddenly applied loads, heavy shocks..........	2.0–3.0	1.5–3.0

Table 8-14. Maximum Permissible Working Stresses for Shafts

Grade of shafting	Simple bending	Simple torsion	Combined stress
"Commercial steel" shafting without allowance for keyways......................	16,000	8,000	8,000
"Commercial steel" shafting with allowance for keyways...........................	12,000	6,000	6,000
Steel purchased under definite specifications..	60% of the elastic limit but not over 36% of the ultimate in tension	30% of the elastic limit but not over 18% of the ultimate in tension	30% of the elastic limit but not over 18% of the ultimate in tension

Table 8-15. Standard Diameters and Tolerances* of Finished Transmission (T) and Machinery (M) Shafting

All Dimensions Given in Inches

Stock diam of shafting		Diam tolerance†	Stock diam of shafting		Diam tolerance†	Stock diam of shafting		Diam tolerance†
T	M		T	M		T	M	
	½	0.002	1 15/16	1 15/16	0.003		3 ¾	0.004
	9/16	.002		2	.003		3 7/8	.004
	5/8	.002		2 1/16	.004	3 15/16	4	.004
				2 1/8	.004		4 ¼	.005
	11/16	.002						
	¾	.002	2 3/16	2 3/16	.004	4 7/16	4 ½	.005
	13/16	.002		2 ¼	.004		4 ¾	.005
	7/8	.002		2 5/16	.004	4 15/16	5	.005
				2 3/8	.004		5 ¼	.005
15/16	15/16	.002						
	1	.002	2 7/16	2 7/16	.004	5 7/16	5 ½	.005
	1 1/16	.003		2 ½	.004		5 ¾	.005
	1 1/8	.003		2 3/8	.004	5 15/16	6	.005
							6 ¼	.005
1 3/16	1 3/16	.003		2 ¾	.004			
	1 ¼	.003		2 7/8	.004	6 ½	6 ½	.005
	1 5/16	.003	2 15/16	3	.004		6 ¾	.005
	1 3/8	.003		3 1/8	.004	7	7	.005
							7 ¼	.005
1 7/16	1 7/16	.003		3 ¼	.004			
	1 ½	.003		3 3/8	.004	7 ½	7 ½	.005
	1 9/16	.003	3 7/16	3 ½	.004		7 ¾	.005
	1 5/8	.003		3 5/8	.004	8	8	.005
1 11/16	1 11/16	.003						
	1 ¾	.003						
	1 13/16	.003						
	1 7/8	.003						

* Approved by ASA.
† Shaft tolerances are *negative* and represent the maximum allowable variation below the exact nominal size. For example, the maximum diameter of the 1½-in. shaft is 1.500 in. and its minimum allowable diameter is 1.497 in.
SOURCE: L. S. Marks (ed.), "Mechanical Engineers' Handbook," 5th ed., p. 911, McGraw-Hill Book Company, Inc., New York, 1951.

8-15. Keys, Pins, Splines

Keys are used to fasten hubbed members to shafts, and are loaded in shear and compression when transmitting torque from one to the other (Fig. 8-42). Square and Woodruff keys are most commonly used, though many other

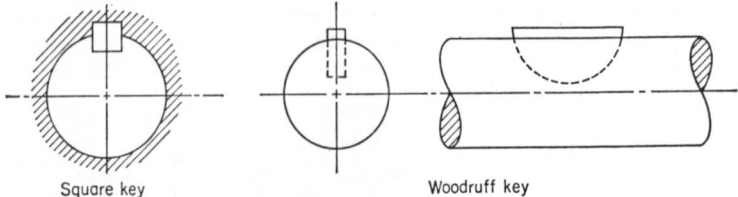

Square key   Woodruff key

FIG. 8-42

types exist. Standard square keys are shown in Table 8-16. Standard key-seats are shown in Table 8-17. Pins are keys positioned at right angles to the shaft center line and are generally round or conical (taper pins) (Fig. 8-43). Hollow spring pins (roll pins) (Fig. 8-44) have come into wide use recently.

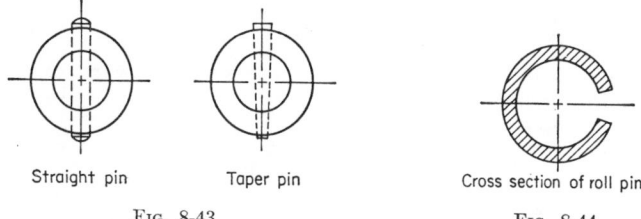

Straight pin   Taper pin   Cross section of roll pin

Fɪɢ. 8-43   Fɪɢ. 8-44

They can replace both solid straight pins and tapered pins because they combine the advantages of both, i.e., simple tooling, ease of removal, ability to be driven from either side.

Splines are effectively a multiplicity of longitudinal keys, either straight or helical, whose teeth are machined integral with the male and female members, in contrast with the common key, which is a third member employed between the male and female elements. The automotive and machine-tool industries employ them extensively in their transmission devices and have caused them to be standardized. Straight-sided standard splines are listed in Table 8-18.

Table 8-16. Dimensions of Square Keys
ASA B17.1-1943

Diam. shaft	Size key	Diam. shaft	Size key	Diam. shaft	Size key
$\frac{1}{2}$ to $\frac{9}{16}$	$\frac{1}{8}$	1 $\frac{7}{16}$ to 1$\frac{3}{4}$	$\frac{3}{8}$	3$\frac{3}{8}$ to 3$\frac{3}{4}$	$\frac{7}{8}$
$\frac{5}{8}$ to $\frac{7}{8}$	$\frac{3}{16}$	1$\frac{13}{16}$ to 2$\frac{1}{4}$	$\frac{1}{2}$	3$\frac{7}{8}$ to 4$\frac{1}{2}$	1
$\frac{15}{16}$ to 1$\frac{1}{4}$	$\frac{1}{4}$	2$\frac{5}{16}$ to 2$\frac{3}{4}$	$\frac{5}{8}$	4$\frac{3}{4}$ to 5$\frac{1}{2}$	1$\frac{1}{4}$
1$\frac{5}{16}$ to 1$\frac{3}{8}$	$\frac{5}{16}$	2$\frac{7}{8}$ to 3$\frac{1}{4}$	$\frac{3}{4}$	5$\frac{3}{4}$ to 6	1$\frac{1}{2}$

Table 8-17. Standard Keyseats

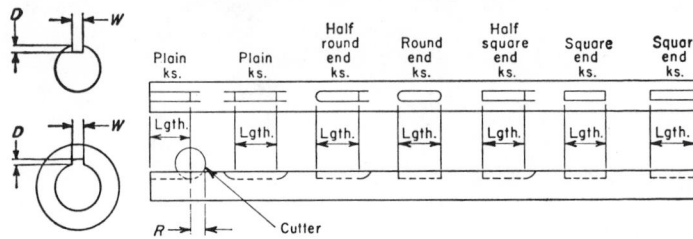

Shaft size	W Width +.002 in. −.000 in.	D* Depth		R Max cutter runout	Max diam of cutter
		Regular	Shallow		
5/16–7/16	3/32	3/64	...	1/2	3 1/4
1/2–9/16	1/8	1/16	...	9/16	3 1/4
5/8–7/8	3/16	3/32	...	11/16	3 1/4
15/16–1 1/4	1/4	1/8	...	13/16	4
1 5/16–1 3/4	3/8	3/16	...	1 1/16	5
1 13/16–2 1/4	1/2	1/4	1/8	1 3/16	5
2 5/16–2 3/4	5/8	5/16	3/16	1 5/16	5
2 13/16–3 1/4	3/4	3/8	3/16	1 9/16	5 1/2
3 5/16–3 3/4	7/8	7/16	1/4	1 11/16	5 1/2
3 13/16–4 1/2	1	1/2	1/4	1 3/4	5 1/2
4 9/16–5 1/2	1 1/4	5/8	1/4	1 13/16	5 1/2
5 9/16–6 1/2	1 1/2	3/4	1/4	2 1/8	5 1/2
6 9/16–7 1/2	1 3/4	3/4	1/4	2 1/8	5 1/2
7 9/16–9	2	3/4	3/8	2 1/8	5 1/2
9 1/16–11	2 1/2	7/8	3/8	2 5/16	6
11 1/16–13	3	1	3/8	2 7/16	6

Shaft keyseat: Always make straight and never taper. Always make regular depth even when shallow depth is used in hub.

Hub keyseat: Make straight unless taper keyseat is specified (see below). Make regular depth unless shallow depth is specified.

Taper keyseat: Should never be used in shafts. Taper is 1/8 in./ft. Depth at large end is equal to D.

* Tolerance on Depth:

+0.010, −0.000 in. for keyseat in shaft.

+0.010, −0.000 in. (preferably +0.010 in.) for straight keyseat in hub.

+0.000, −0.010 in. (preferably −0.010 in.) for taper keyseat in hub.

SOURCE: Extracted from "Engineering Standards-Multiple V-Belt Drives," 1951, with the permission of the publisher, Multiple V-Belt Drive & Mechanical Power Transmission Association, Chicago 3, Illinois.

Table 8-18. SAE Standard Splines

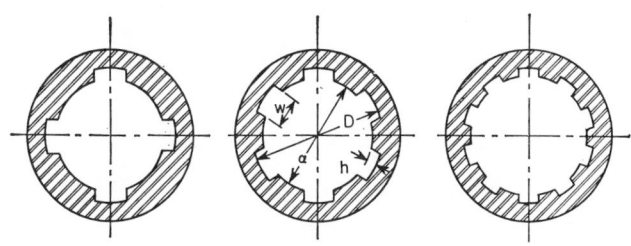

	4 spline	6 spline	10 spline
Permanent fit	$d = 0.85D$ $w = 0.241D$ $h = 0.075D$	$d = 0.90D$ $w = 0.25D$ $h = 0.05D$	$d = 0.91D$ $w = 0.156D$ $h = 0.045D$
To slide when not under load	$d = 0.75D$ $w = 0.241D$ $h = 0.125D$	$d = 0.85D$ $w = 0.25D$ $h = 0.075D$	$d = 0.86D$ $w = 0.156D$ $h = 0.07D$
To slide when under load		$d = 0.80D$ $w = 0.25D$ $h = 0.10D$	$d = 0.81D$ $w = 0.156D$ $h = 0.095D$

NOTE: Shaft dimensions 0.001 in. under nominal for small shafts and 0.002 in. for large shafts.

8-16. Belts and Sheaves

Belt Lengths

Total belt length $L = 2S \cos \theta + \pi[(R + r) + (R - r)\theta/90]$ in.   (8-64)

where S = center distance between pulleys, in.
$\quad\quad R$ = radius of large pulley (flat belt) or pitch
$\quad\quad\quad$ radius of large pulley (V belt), in.
$\quad\quad r$ = radius of small pulley (flat belt) or pitch
$\quad\quad\quad$ radius of small pulley (V belt), in.
$\quad\quad \theta = \sin^{-1}[(R - r)/S]$ deg

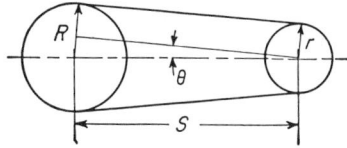

FIG. 8-45

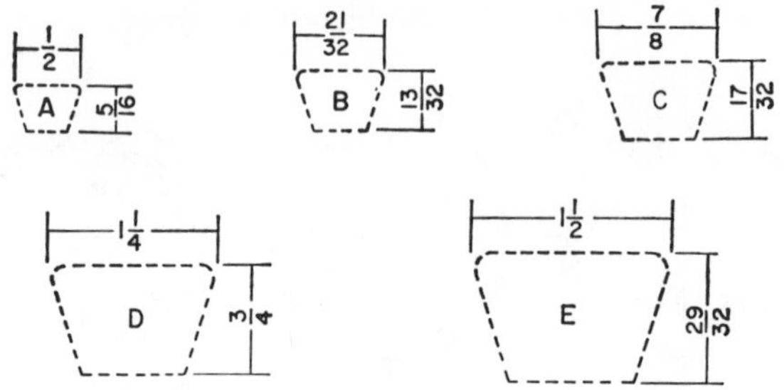

NOTE: The dimensions and cross-sectional shapes are nominal only. Actual cross-sectional dimensions of belts made by one manufacturer may differ from those of the same belt cross section made by another manufacturer. Because of different constructions and different methods of manufacturing, the cross-sectional shapes and the included angle between the side walls may be different for different manufacturers. However, all standard cross sections will operate interchangeably in standard grooves.

SOURCE: Extracted from "Engineering Standards-Multiple V-Belt Drives," 1951, with the permission of the publisher, Multiple V-Belt Drive & Mechanical Power Transmission Association, Chicago 3, Illinois.

FIG. 8-46. V-belt cross sections

Table 8-19. Measuring Tensions

Belt*	Tension,† lb	Belt*	Tension,† lb
A	50	*D*	300
B	65	*E*	400
C	165		

* See Table 8-20.

† The tension specified is the sum of tension in the two strands of the belt.

SOURCE: Extracted from "Engineering Standard-Multiple V-Belt Drives," 1951, with the permission of the publisher, Multiple V-Belt Drive & Mechanical Power Transmission Association, Chicago, Illinois.

Table 8-20. Standard Belt Sizes

For Dimensions and Cross-sectional Shapes See P. 000

Std nominal length	Std pitch lengths, in.					Permissible deviations from std pitch length, in.	Matching limits for one set, in.
	A	B	C	D	E		
26	27.3	.....	.....	.....	.....	+0.7-0.3	0.10
31	32.3	.....	.....	.....	.....	+0.7-0.3	0.10
33	34.3	.....	.....	.....	.....	+0.8-0.4	0.20
35	36.3	36.8	.....	.....	.....	+0.8-0.4	0.20
38	39.3	39.8	.....	.....	.....	+0.8-0.4	0.20
42	43.3	43.8	.....	.....	.....	+0.8-0.4	0.20
46	47.3	47.8	.....	.....	.....	+0.8-0.4	0.20
48	49.3	49.8	.....	.....	.....	+0.9-0.5	0.20
51	52.3	52.8	53.9	.....	.....	+0.9-0.5	0.20
53	54.3	54.8	.....	.....	.....	+0.9-0.5	0.20
55	56.3	56.8	.....	.....	.....	+0.9-0.5	0.20
60	61.3	61.8	62.9	.....	.....	+0.9-0.5	0.20
62	63.3	63.8	.....	.....	.....	+0.9-0.5	0.20
64	65.3	65.8	.....	.....	.....	+0.9-0.5	0.20
66	67.3	67.8	.....	.....	.....	+0.9-0.5	0.20
68	69.3	69.8	70.9	.....	.....	+0.9-0.5	0.20
71	72.3	72.8	.....	.....	.....	+0.9-0.5	0.20
75	76.3	76.8	77.9	.....	.....	+0.9-0.5	0.20
78	79.3	79.8	.....	.....	.....	+1.0-0.5	0.30
80	81.3	.....	.....	.....	.....	+1.0-0.5	0.30
81	.....	82.8	83.9	.....	.....	+1.0-0.5	0.30
83	.....	84.8	.....	.....	.....	+1.0-0.5	0.30
85	86.3	86.8	87.9	.....	.....	+1.0-0.5	0.30
90	91.3	91.8	92.9	.....	.....	+1.0-0.5	0.30
96	97.3	.....	98.9	.....	.....	+1.0-0.5	0.30
97	.....	98.8	.....	.....	.....	+1.0-0.5	0.30
105	106.3	106.8	107.9	.....	.....	+1.1-0.5	0.40
112	113.3	113.8	114.9	.....	.....	+1.1-0.5	0.40
120	121.3	121.8	122.9	123.3	.....	+1.2-0.5	0.40
128	129.3	129.8	130.9	131.3	.....	+1.3-0.6	0.40
136	.....	137.8	138.9	.....	.....	+1.3-0.6	0.40
144	.....	145.8	146.9	147.3	.....	+1.4-0.6	0.40
158	.....	159.8	160.9	161.3	.....	+1.5-0.6	0.40
162	.....	.....	164.9	165.3	.....	+1.6-0.6	0.40
173	.....	174.8	175.9	176.3	.....	+1.7-0.7	0.50
180	.....	181.8	182.9	183.3	184.5	+1.7-0.7	0.50
195	.....	196.8	197.9	198.3	199.5	+1.8-0.8	0.50
210	.....	211.8	212.9	213.3	214.5	+2.0-0.8	0.50
240	.....	240.3	240.9	240.8	241.0	+2.2-0.9	0.50
270	.....	270.3	270.9	270.8	271.0	+2.4-1.0	0.50
300	.....	300.3	300.9	300.8	301.0	+2.5-1.2	0.60
330	.....	.....	330.9	330.8	331.0	+2.5-1.2	0.60
360	.....	.....	360.9	360.8	361.0	+2.5-1.2	0.60
390	.....	.....	390.9	390.8	391.0	+3.0-1.5	0.70
420 —	.....	.....	420.9	420.8	421.0	+3.5-2.0	0.80
480	.....	.....	.....	480.8	481.0	+4.0-2.5	0.90
540	.....	.....	.....	540.8	541.0	+4.5-3.0	1.10
600	.....	.....	.....	600.8	601.0	+5.0-3.5	1.30
660	.....	.....	.....	660.8	661.0	+6.0-4.0	1.50

Table 8-21. Suggested Service Factors

Application	Squirrel cage — Normal torque, line start	Squirrel cage — Normal torque, compensator start	High torque	Wound rotor (slip ring)	Synchronous — Normal torque	Synchronous — High torque	Single phase — Repulsion and split-phase	Single phase — Capacitor	D-c — Shunt wound	D-c — Compound wound	Gas and diesel — 4 or more cyl, above 700 rpm	Gas and diesel — 4 or more cyl, below 700 rpm	Gas and diesel — 3 or less cyl, (refer to factory)	Steam	Line shafts and clutch starting
Agitators, paddle-propeller:															
Liquid	1.0	1.0	1.2												
Semiliquid	1.2	1.0	1.4	1.2											
Brick and clay machinery:															
Auger machine	...	1.2	1.4	1.4	...	...	...	...	1.4	...	...	...	...	...	2.0
De-airing machine	...	1.2	1.4	1.4	...	...	...	...	1.4	...	...	...	...	...	2.0
Cutting table	...	1.2	1.4	1.4	...	...	...	...	...	...	...	...	...	...	2.0
Pug mill	1.5	1.3	1.8	1.5											
Mixer	...	1.2	1.6	1.4											
Granulator	...	1.2	1.6	1.4											
Dry press	...	1.2	1.4	1.4											
Rolls	...	1.2	1.4	1.4											
Bakery machinery:															
Dough mixer	1.2	...	...	...	...	...	1.2	1.0							
Compressors:															
Centrifugal	1.2	1.2	...	1.4	1.4	...	...	...	1.2	...	1.2				
Rotary	1.2	1.2	...	1.4	1.4	...	1.2	1.2	1.2	...	1.2				
Reciprocating:															
3 or more cyl	1.2	1.2	...	1.4	1.4	...	...	...	1.2						
1 or 2 cyl	1.4	1.4	...	1.5	1.5	...	...	...	1.2						
Conveyors:															
Apron	...	1.4	1.6	...	...	...	...	...	1.4	...	...	...	...	...	1.6
Belt (ore, coal, sand)	...	1.2	1.4	...	...	...	...	...	1.2	...	...	...	...	...	1.4
Belt (light package)	...	1.0	1.1	...	...	...	...	...	1.0	...	...	...	...	...	1.2
Oven	...	1.0	1.1	...	...	...	...	...	1.0	...	...	...	...	...	1.2
Screw	...	1.6	1.8	...	...	...	...	...	1.6	...	...	...	...	...	1.8
Bucket	...	1.4	1.6	...	...	...	...	...	1.4	...	...	...	...	...	1.6
Pan	...	1.4	1.6	...	...	...	...	...	1.4	...	...	...	...	...	1.6
Flight	...	1.6	1.8	...	...	...	...	...	1.6	...	...	...	...	...	1.8
Elevator	...	1.4	1.6	...	...	...	...	...	1.4	...	...	...	...	...	1.6
Crushing machinery:															
Jaw crusher	...	1.4	1.6	1.4	...	...	...	...	1.4	1.4	...	...	...	...	1.6
Gyratory crusher	...	1.4	1.6	1.4	1.4	1.6	...	...	1.4	1.4	...	...	...	...	1.6
Cone crusher	...	1.4	1.6	1.4	...	...	...	...	1.6	1.4	...	...	...	...	1.6
Crushing rolls	...	1.4	1.6	1.4	...	...	...	...	1.4	1.4	...	...	...	...	1.6
Ball and pebble mill	...	1.4	1.6	1.4	1.4	1.6	...	...	1.4	1.6	...	...	...	...	1.6
Tube mill	...	1.4	1.6	1.4	1.4	...	...	...	1.4	...	...	...	...	...	1.6
Fans and blowers:															
Centrifugal	1.2	1.2	...	1.4	...	...	...	...	1.2	...	1.2				
Propeller	1.4	1.4	2.0	1.6	...	2.0	...	...	1.4	...	1.4				
Induced draft	1.2	1.2	...	1.4	...	...	...	...	1.4	...	1.4				
Mine fan	1.6	1.4	2.0	...	...	2.0	...	...	...	...	1.6				
Positive blower	1.6	1.6	...	2.0	2.0	2.0	...	...	...	...	1.6				
Exhauster	1.2	1.2	...	1.4	...	...	...	...	1.4	...	...	...	...	1.5	1.5
Flour, feed, cereal-mill machinery:															
Bolter and sifter	...	1.0													
Grinder and hammermill	...	1.4	...	...	...	...	...	...	...	...	1.6				
Purifier and reel	1.2	1.4													
Main line-shaft drive	1.4	1.4	1.6	1.4	1.4	...	...	...	...	...	1.8				
Separator	1.0	1.0													
Roller mill	...	1.4													
Generators and exciters	1.2	...	...	...	...	...	...	...	1.2	...	...	...	...	1.4	1.4

Table 8-21. Suggested Service Factors (Continued)

Application	Electric motors										Engines				
	A-c								D-c		Gas and diesel				
	Squirrel cage				Synchronous		Single phase		Shunt wound	Compound wound	4 or more cyl, above 700 rpm	4 or more cyl, below 700 rpm	3 or less cyl, (refer to factory)	Steam	Line ssafts and clutch starting
	Normal torque, line start	Normal torque, compensator start	High torque]	Wound rotor (slip ring)	Normal torque	High torque	Repulsion and split-phase	Capacitor							
Laundry machinery:															
Washer	1.2									1.2					
Extractor	1.2									1.2					
Tumbler	1.2									1.2					
Dampener	1.2									1.2					
Flat-work ironer	1.2									1.2					
Line shafts	1.4	1.4		1.4	1.4	2.0	1.4	1.4	1.4	1.4	1.6			1.6	1.6
Machine tools:															
Grinder	1.2			1.4			1.2	1.0	1.2	1.2					
Boring mill	1.2			1.4					1.2	1.2					
Lathe	1.0			1.2			1.0	1.0	1.0	1.0					
Milling machine	1.2			1.4					1.2	1.2					
Screw machine	1.0			1.0			1.0	1.0	1.0	1.0					
Cam cutter	1.0			1.0					1.0	1.0					
Planer	1.2			1.4			1.2	1.0	1.2	1.2					
Shaper	1.0			1.0			1.0	1.0	1.0	1.0					
Drill press	1.0			1.0			1.0	1.0	1.0	1.0					
Drop hammer	1.0			1.0			1.0	1.0	1.0	1.0					
Shears	1.2			1.4			1.2	1.2	1.2	1.0					
Mills:															
Pebble		1.4	1.6	1.4						1.4					1.6
Rod		1.4	1.6	1.4						1.4					1.6
Ball		1.4	1.6	1.4						1.4					1.6
Roller		1.4	1.6	1.4						1.4					1.6
Flaking		1.6	1.6	1.4						1.4					1.6
Tumbling barrel		1.6	1.6	1.4						1.4					1.6
Oil-field machinery:															
Slush pump										1.4	1.4	1.6		1.4	1.4
Pumping unit	1.2	1.2	1.4							1.4					1.6
Pipeline pump, centrifugal	1.2	1.2	1.4						1.4	1.4					
Draw works (intermittent)*										1.3		1.0	1.0		
Paper machinery:															
Jordan engine	1.5	1.3	1.8	1.5	1.6	1.8			1.5	1.5					
Beater	1.4	1.4		1.4					1.4	1.4					1.8
Calender	1.2	1.2		1.2					1.2	1.2					
Agitator	1.2	1.0	1.4	1.2					1.2	1.2					1.6
Dryer	1.2	1.2		1.2					1.2	1.2					
Paper machine	1.4	1.4		1.5					1.5	1.5					1.6
Printing machinery:															
Rotary press	1.2	1.2		1.2					1.2						
Embossing press	1.2	1.2		1.2					1.2	1.2					
Folder	1.2	1.2		1.2					1.2						
Paper cutter	1.2	1.2		1.2					1.2	1.2					
Linotype machine	1.2	1.2							1.2						
Flat-bed press	1.2	1.2		1.2					1.2						
Pumps:															
Centrifugal	1.2	1.2	1.4	1.4			1.2	1.2							
Gear	1.2	1.2	1.4	1.4			1.2	1.2							
Rotary	1.2	1.2	1.4	1.4			1.2	1.2	1.2		1.2				
Reciprocating:															
3 or more cyl	1.2	1.2		1.4	1.4	1.6					1.8			1.8	
1 or 2 cyl	1.4	1.4		1.6	1.6	1.8					2.0			2.0	
Dredge pumps	1.4	1.4		1.4							2.0			2.0	

Table 8-21. Suggested Service Factors (Continued)

Application	Electric motors										Engines				
	A-c								D-c		Gas and diesel				
	Squirrel cage				Syn-chronous		Single phase								
	Normal torque, line start	Normal torque, compensator start	High torque	Wound rotor (slip ring)	Normal torque	High torque	Repulsion and split-phase	Capacitor	Shunt wound	Compound wound	4 or more cyl, above 700 rpm	4 or more cyl, below 700 rpm	3 or less cyl, (refer to factory)	Steam	Line shafts and clutch starting
Rubber-plant machinery:															
Calender.....................	1.4	1.4	1.4	1.4	...	1.8	...	...	...	...	...	...	...	2.0	
Banbury mill................	1.4	1.4	1.4	1.4	...	1.8	...	...	...	...	...	...	...	2.0	
Mixer.......................	1.4	1.4	1.4	1.4	...	1.8	...	...	...	...	...	...	...	2.0	
Screens:															
Vibrating...................	1.2	1.2	1.4												
Conical.....................	1.2	1.2													
Revolving...................	1.2	1.2													
Textile machinery:															
Spinning frame..............	1.6	...	1.8												
Twister.....................	1.6	...	1.8												
Loom........................	1.2														
Warper......................	1.2														
Reel........................	1.2														

* Hoisting service factor based on total engine horsepower (continuous rating). Electric drive factor based on continuous rating of motor.

SOURCE: Extracted from "Engineering Standards-Multiple V-Belt Drives," 1951, with the permission of the publisher, Multiple V-Belt Drive & Mechanical Power Transmission Association, Chicago 3, Illinois.

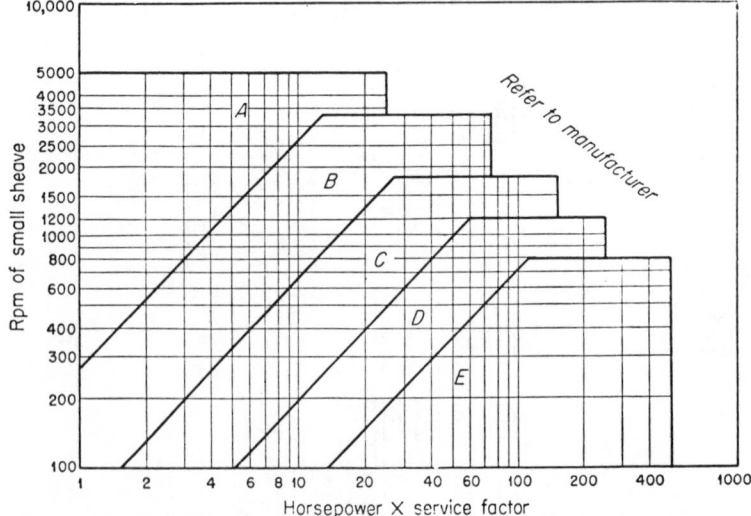

FIG. 8-47. *Source: "Engineering Standards—Multiple V-Belt Drives," 1951, with the permission of the publisher, Multiple V-Belt Drive & Mechanical Power Transmission Association, Chicago, Illinois.*

Sheaves

Table 8-22. Groove Dimensions for V-belt Sheaves

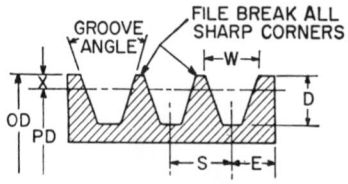

Face Width of Stock and Standard Sheaves
Face width = $S(N - 1) + 2E$

where N = number of grooves

Belt	Min recommended pitch diam	Pitch diam	Groove angle, deg	W	D	X	S	E
			Standard-groove Dimensions					
A	3.0	2.6–5.4 >5.4	34 38	0.494 0.504	0.490	0.125	$\frac{5}{8}$	$\frac{3}{8}$
B	5.4	4.6–7.0 >7.0	34 38	0.637 0.650	0.580	.175	$\frac{3}{4}$	$\frac{1}{2}$
C	9.0	7.0–7.99 8.0–12.0 >12.0	34 36 38	0.879 0.887 0.895	0.780	.200	1	$1\frac{1}{16}$
D	13.0	12.0–12.99 13.0–17.0 >17.0	34 36 38	1.259 1.271 1.283	1.050	.300	$1\frac{7}{16}$	$\frac{7}{8}$
E	21.0	18.0–24.0 >24.0	36 38	1.527 1.542	1.300	.400	$1\frac{3}{4}$	$1\frac{1}{8}$
			Deep-groove Dimensions					
A	3.0	2.6–5.4 >5.4	34 38	0.589 0.611	0.645	.280	$\frac{3}{4}$	$\frac{7}{16}$
B	5.4	4.6–7.0 >7.0	34 38	0.747 0.774	0.760	.355	$\frac{7}{8}$	$\frac{9}{16}$
C	9.0	7.0–7.99 8.0–12.0 >12.0	34 36 38	1.066 1.085 1.105	1.085	.505	$1\frac{1}{4}$	$1\frac{3}{16}$
D	13.0	12.0–12.99 13.0–17.0 >17.0	34 36 38	1.513 1.541 1.569	1.465	.715	$1\frac{3}{4}$	$1\frac{1}{16}$
E	21.0	18.0–24.0 >24.0	36 38	1.816 1.849	1.745	.845	$2\frac{1}{16}$	$1\frac{9}{16}$

SOURCE: Extracted from "Engineering Standards-Multiple V-Belt Drives," 1951, with the permission of the publisher, Multiple V-Belt Drive & Mechanical Power Transmission Association, Chicago 3, Illinois.

Table 8-23. Incline of Belt Conveyors

Material Conveyed	Incline, Deg
Briquets and egg-shaped material	7–12
Wet-mixed concrete	10–15
Sized coal	13–18
Washed and screened gravel	13–18
Loose cement	15–20
Crushed and screened coke	15–20
Sand	15–20
Glass batch	15–20
Run-of-mine coal	17–22
Run-of-bank gravel	17–22
Crushed ore	20–25
Crushed stone	20–26
Tempered foundry sand	20–25
Wood chips	22–28

8-17. Bearings

Table 8-24. Current Practice in Mean Bearing Pressures

Type of bearing	Permissible press., psi, of projected area	Type of bearing	Permissible press., psi, of projected area
Diesel engines, main bearings	800–1,500	Automotive gasoline engines, main bearings	500– 600
Crankpin	1,000–2,000	Crankpin	1,500–2,000
Wrist pin	1,800–2,000	Air compressors, main bearings	120– 240
Electric-motor bearings	100– 200	Crankpin	240– 400
Marine diesel engines, main bearings	400– 600	Crosshead pin	400– 800
Crankpin	1,000–1,400	Aircraft-engine crankpin	700–2,000
Marine line-shaft bearings	25– 35	Centrifugal pumps	80– 100
Steam engines, main bearings	150– 500	Generators, low or medium speed	90– 140
Crankpin	800–1,500	Roll-neck bearings	1,500–2,000
Crosshead pin	1,000–1,800	Locomotive crankpins	1,500–1,900
Flywheel bearings	200– 250	Railway-car-axle bearings	300– 350
Marine steam engine, main bearings	275– 500	Miscellaneous ordinary bearings	80– 150
Crankpin	400– 600	Light line shaft	15– 25
Steam turbines and reduction gears	100– 220	Heavy line shaft	100– 150

SOURCE: L. S. Marks, ed., "Mechanical Engineers' Handbook," 5th ed., p. 967, McGraw-Hill Book Company, Inc., New York, 1951.

8-18. Friction Clutches

Table 8-25. Service Factors for Shock and Variable Load

Type of Service	*Factor*
Driving machine:	
Electric motor, steady load	1.0
Fluctuating load	1.5
Gas engine, single cylinder	1.5
Multiple cylinder	1.0
Diesel engine, high speed	1.5
Large, slow speed	2.0
Driven machine:	
Generator, steady load	1.0
Fluctuating load	1.5
Blower	1.0
Compressor, depending on the number of cylinders	2.0–2.5
Pumps, centrifugal	1.0
Single-acting	2.0
Double-acting	1.5
Line shaft	1.5
Woodworking machinery	1.75
Hoists, elevators, cranes, shovels	2.0
Hammer mills, ball mills, crushers	2.0
Brick machinery	3.0
Rock crushers	3.0

To compensate for high torques required to overcome inertia of driven members upon starting and for the reduced friction torque capacity while the friction surfaces are slipping prior to full engagement, the factors in Table 8-25 are multiplied by 1.5 to 2.0.

8-19. Mechanical Springs

Basically, mechanical springs are resilient structures whose properties depend upon the material used and the shape it is given. Such springs can take an unlimited variety of shapes; the materials most often used are found in Table 8-26. The shape most commonly found is the cylindrical, helical-coiled, round-wire spring, illustrated in Fig. 8-48 with $13\frac{1}{2}$ coils. The treat-

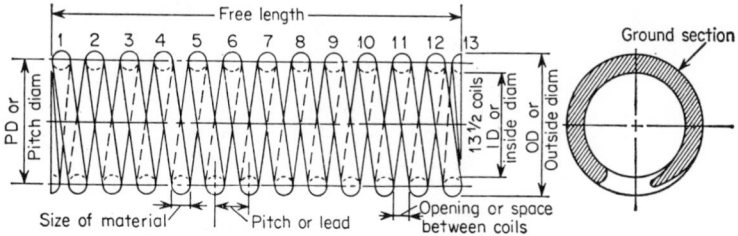

FIG. 8-48. Helical-coil spring.

ment given the ends depends on the spring's intended use; some common types are shown in Figs. 8-49 and 8-50.

MECHANICAL ENGINEERING

Table 8-26. Physical Properties of

	Material	Analysis	Ultimate strength, psi	Elastic limit, psi	Modulus of elasticity
			Tensile properties		
Flat cold-rolled spring steel	Clock spring steel AS 100, SAE 1095	C .90–1.05% Mn .30–.50%	180,000 to 340,000	150,000 to 310,000	30,000,000
	Flat spring steel AS 101, SAE 1074	C .70–.80% Mn .50–.80%	160,000 to 320,000	125,000 to 280,000	30,000,000
	Flat spring steel AS 102, SAE 1060	C .50–.65% Mn .60–.90% P and S .04% max	160,000 to 280,000	120,000 to 180,000	30,000,000
Carbon steel wires	High-carbon wire AS 8	C .85–.95% Mn .25–.60%	200,000 to 250,000	160,000 to 210,000	30,000,000
	Oil-tempered wire AS 10, ASTM A229-41	C .60–.70% Mn .60–.90%	155,000 to 300,000	120,000 to 250,000	30,000,000
	Music wire AS 5, ASTM A228-47	C .70–1.00% Mn .30–.60%	250,000 to 500,000	150,000 to 350,000	30,000,000
	Hard-drawn spring wire AS 20, ASTM A227-47	C .60–.70% Mn .90–1.20%	150,000 to 300,000	100,000 to 200,000	30,000,000
Hot-rolled alloy steel	Silico-manganese alloy steel AS 70, SAE 9260	C .55–.65% Mn .60–.90% Si 1.80–2.20%	200,000 to 250,000	180,000 to 230,000	30,000,000
Alloy and stainless spring materials	Chrome-vanadium alloy steel AS 32, SAE 6150	C .48–.53% Si .20–.35% Mn .70–.90% Cr .80–1.10% P .04 max V .15 min S .04 max subject to standard tolerances	200,000 to 250,000	180,000 to 230,000	30,000,000
	Chrome-silicon alloy steel AS 33, SAE 9254	C .50–.60% Mn .50–.80% Si 1.20–1.60% Cr .50–.80%	250,000 to 325,000	220,000 to 300,000	30,000,000
	18–8 type stainless AS 35, SAE 30302	Cr 17–20% Ni 6–10% C .08–.15% Mn 2% max Si .30–.75%	160,000 to 330,000	60,000 to 260,000	28,000,000
	Type 316 stainless SAE 30316	Cr 16–18% Ni 10–14% C .08% max Mo 2–3% Si 1% max Mn 2% max P .04% max S .03% max	170,000 to 250,000	130,000 to 200,000	28,000,000

Commonly Used Spring Materials

*Rockwell hardness	Torsional properties of wire			Process of manufacture, Chief uses, Special Properties
	Ultimate strength, psi	Elastic limit, psi	Modulus in torsion	
C40–52	Not used	Not used	Not used	Cold-rolled and heat-treated before forming. Clock and motor springs, miscellaneous flat springs.
Annealed B70–85 Temp'd C38–50	Not used	Not used	Not used	Cold-rolled or annealed or tempered. Miscellaneous flat springs. Most popular spring steel.
Annealed B70–85 Temp'd C38–50	Not used	Not used	11,500,000	Use cold-rolled and annealed. Miscellaneous flat springs, static loads.
C44–48	160,000 to 200,000	110,000 to 150,000	11,500,000	Cold-rolled or drawn. High-grade helical springs or wire forms.
C42–46	115,000 to 200,000	80,000 to 130,000	11,500,000	Cold-drawn and heat-treated before coiling. General use.
	150,000 to 300,000	90,000 to 180,000	11,500,000 to 12,000,000 depending on size	Patented and cold-drawn. Miscellaneous small springs of various types—high quality.
	120,000 to 220,000	75,000 to 130,000	11,500,000	Patented and cold-drawn. Same uses as music wire but lower-quality wire.
C42–52	140,000 to 175,000	100,000 to 130,000	11,500,000	Hot- or cold-rolled or drawn. Better heat resistance than chrome-vanadium.
C42–48	140,000 to 175,000	100,000 to 130,000	11,500,000	Cold-rolled or drawn. Special applications.
C47–51	160,000 to 200,000	130,000 to 160,000	11,500,000	Hot- or cold-rolled or drawn. Used at high stresses. Resists heat well to 450°F.
C35–45	120,000 to 240,000	45,000 to 140,000	10,000,000	Cold-rolled or drawn. Best corrosion resistance. Fair temperature resistance.
C35–45	120,000 to 220,000	80,000 to 130,000	11,000,000	Cold-rolled or drawn. Heat-treated after forming. Resists corrosion when polished. Good temperature resistance.

Table 8-26. Physical Properties of Commonly

Material	Analysis	Ultimate strength, psi	Elastic limit, psi	Modulus of elasticity
		Tensile properties		
Spring brass AS 55, AS 155	Cu 64–72% Zn remainder	100,000 to 130,000	40,000 to 60,000	15,000,000
Nickel-silver	Cu 56% Zn 25% Ni 18%	135,000 to 150,000	80,000 to 110,000	16,000,000
Phosphor-bronze AS 60, AS 160	Cu 91–93% Sn 7–9% or Cu 94–96% Sn 4–6%	100,000 to 150,000	60,000 to 110,000	15,000,000
Silicon-bronze AS 46, AS 146 (made under various trade names)	Si 2–3% Small amounts of Sn or Mn, balance copper	100,000 to 150,000	60,000 to 110,000	15,000,000
Monel AS 40, AS 140	Ni (+Co) 63.0–70.0 Cu remainder Mg 2.00 max Fe 2.50 max Si .50 max C .30 max S .024 max	120,000 to 165,000	85,000 to 125,000	26,000,000
K Monel AS 40, AS 140	Ni (+Co) 63.0–70.0 Cu remainder Mg 1.50 max Fe 2.00 max Si 1.00 max Al 2.0–4.0 S .01 max C .25 max Ti .25–1.00	120,000 to 180,000	85,000 to 140,000	26,000,000
Inconel AS 40, AS 140	Ni (+Co) 72.00 min Cu .50 max Mg 1.00 max Fe 6.0–10.0 Si .50 max Cr 14.0–17.0 S .015 max C .15 max	140,000 to 185,000	110,000 to 140,000	31,000,000
Inconel X AS 40, AS 140	Ni (+Co) 70.00 min Cu .50 max Mg 1.00 max Fe 5.0–9.0 Si .50 max Cr 14.0–17.0 S .01 max Al .40–1.0 Ti 2.00–2.50 C .08 max Cb (+Ti) .70–1.20	130,000 to 220,000	90,000 to 150,000	31,000,000
Duranickel AS 40, AS 140	Ni (+Co) 93.00 min Cu .25 max Mg .50 max Fe .60 max Si 1.00 max Al 4.00–4.75 S .01 max C .30 max Ti .25–1.00	125,000 to 205,000	80,000 to 140,000	30,000,000
Beryllium copper AS 45, AS 145	Cu 98% Be 2%	160,000 to 200,000	100,000 to 150,000	16,000,000 to 18,500,000 subject to heat-treatment

Nonferrous spring materials

SOURCE: Handbook of Mechanical Spring Design, Associated Spring Corp., 1955.

Used Spring Materials (Continued)

*Rockwell hardness	Torsional properties of wire			Process of manufacture, Chief uses, Special Properties
	Ultimate strength, psi	Elastic limit, psi	Modulus in torsion	
B90	45,000 to 90,000	30,000 to 60,000	5,500,000	Cold-rolled or drawn. For electrical conductivity at low stresses. For corrosion resistance.
B95–100	85,000 to 100,000	60,000 to 70,000	5,500,000	Cold-rolled or drawn. Better quality than brass. Also used for its color. Corrosion-resistant.
B90–100	80,000 to 105,000	50,000 to 85,000	6,250,000	Cold-rolled or drawn. Used for corrosion resistance and electrical conductivity.
B90–100	80,000 to 105,000	50,000 to 85,000	6,250,000	Cold-rolled or drawn. Used as substitute for phosphor-bronze where lower cost is necessary.
C23–32	85,000 to 110,500	50,000 to 70,000	9,500,000	Cold-rolled or drawn. Resists corrosion. Moderate stresses to 400°F.
C23–35	85,000 to 130,000	50,000 to 75,000	9,500,000	Same as Monel except higher operational stresses can be employed to 450°F. Precipitation-hardened by thermal treatment.
C25–37	95,000 to 130,000	55,000 to 80,000	11,000,000	Cold-rolled or drawn. Resists corrosion. High stresses to 650°F.
C24–46	90,000 to 155,000	50,000 to 90,000	12,000,000	Resists corrosion and oxidation. Can be used to 1000°F for prolonged periods of service; up to 1200°F for short periods of intermittent temperature exposure.
C25–43	85,000 to 145,000	50,000 to 85,000	11,000,000	Cold-rolled or drawn. Precipitation-hardened by heat-treatment. Resists corrosion. High stresses to 600°F.
C35–42	100,000 to 130,000	65,000 to 95,000	6,000,000 to 7,000,000 subject to heat-treatment	Cold-rolled or drawn. Corrosion resistance like copper. High physicals for electrical work. Low hysteresis.

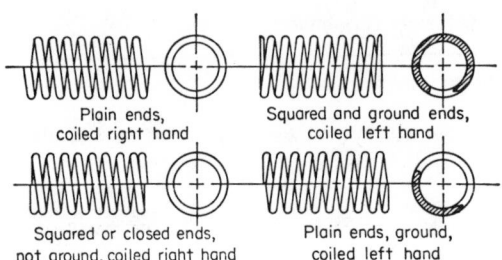

FIG. 8-49. Compression-spring ends.

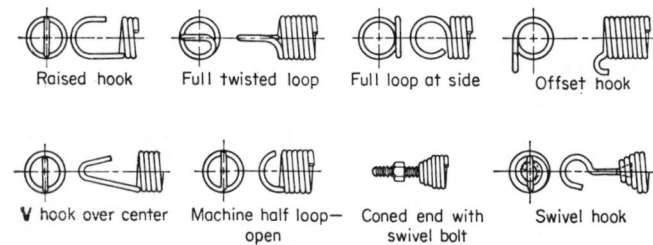

FIG. 8-50. Extension-spring ends.

A coiled spring made of round wire will be subjected to a maximum stress given by

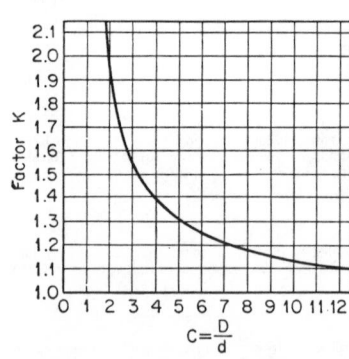

FIG. 8-51. Wahl correction factor.

$$\sigma_{max} = \frac{8PD}{\pi d^3}\left(\frac{4C-1}{4C-4} + \frac{0.615}{C}\right) \tag{8-65}$$

where P = load on spring, lb
D = mean diameter of coil, in. (outside diameter minus the wire diameter)
d = diameter of wire, in.
σ_{max} = torsional stress, psi
$C = D/d$

The expression in parentheses in Eq. (8-65) is the Wahl correction factor K, from Fig. 8-51. It accounts for the added stresses in the coils due to curvature and shear.

8-20. Flywheels

A flywheel is a rotating energy-storing device used to impart more uniform rotation to a machine with fundamentally intermittent operating characteristics (reciprocating machines, punch presses, etc.). Energy is stored in the flywheel by increasing its angular momentum during the time when no external work is done, and then released by a decrease in its angular momentum when external work is done. The degree to which a flywheel succeeds in keeping speed reasonably constant throughout a cycle of operation can be measured by the coefficient of fluctuation C_f, representative values for which in several classes of service are found in Table 8-27.

Table 8-27. Coefficient of Speed Fluctuation

Type of Equipment	C_f
Crushing machinery	0.200
Electrical machinery	0.003
Direct-driven	0.002
Engines with belt transmission	0.030
Flour-milling machinery	0.020
Gear-wheel transmission	0.020
Hammering machinery	0.200
Machine tools	0.030
Papermaking machinery	0.025
Pumping machinery	0.030–0.050
Shearing machinery	0.030–0.050
Spinning machinery	0.010–0.020
Textile machinery	0.025

SOURCE: Kent, "Mechanical Engineer's Handbook," 12th ed., John Wiley & Sons, Inc., New York.

Let ω_{av} = average angular velocity during cycle, radians/sec

$\quad\omega_{min}$ = minimum angular velocity during cycle, radians/sec

$\quad\omega_{max}$ = maximum angular velocity during cycle, radians/sec

$\quad C_f$ = coefficient of speed fluctuation

$\quad I$ = mass moment of inertia of flywheel, lb-ft-sec^2

$\quad\Delta KE$ = energy released from flywheel during working portion of cycle (i.e., while speed changes from ω_{max} to ω_{min}), ft-lb

Then

$$\omega_{av} = \frac{\omega_{max} + \omega_{min}}{2} \tag{8-66}$$

$$C_f = \frac{\omega_{max} - \omega_{min}}{\omega_{av}} \tag{8-67}$$

$$\Delta KE = \tfrac{1}{2}I(\omega_{max}^2 - \omega_{min}^2) \tag{8-68}$$

8-21. Drill and Tap Sizes

Table 8-28. Diameters and Areas of Small Drills
Number, Letter, Metric, and Fractional Drills in Order of Size

No.	Ltr	Mm	In.	Diam, in.	Area, in.²	No.	Ltr	Mm	In.	Diam, in.	Area, in.²
		0.100	...	0.003900	0.0000119	54	...	.....	...	0.055000	0.0023760
		0.150	...	.005900	.0000273			1.400	...	.055100	.0023860
		0.200	...	.007800	.0000477			1.450	...	.057000	.0025440
		0.250	...	.009800	.0000753			1.500	...	.059000	.0027390
		0.300	...	.011800	.0001091	53	...	.....	...	.059500	.0027810
80	...	.....	...	.013500	.0001429			1.550	...	.061000	.0029210
		0.350	...	.013700	.0001468				1/16	.062500	.0030680
79	...	.....	...	.014500	.0001650			1.600	...	.062990	.0031160
			1/64	.015620	.0001920	52	...	.....	...	.063500	.0031670
		0.400	...	.015740	.0001950			1.650	...	.064900	.0033060
78	...	.....	...	.016000	.0002010			1.700	...	.066920	.0035180
		0.450	...	.017700	.0002450	51	...	.....	...	.067000	.0035260
77	...	.....	...	.018000	.0002540			1.750	...	.068800	.0037140
		0.500	...	.019680	.0003040	50	...	.....	...	.070000	.0038480
76	...	.....	...	.020000	.0003140			1.800	...	.070860	.0039440
75	...	.....	...	.021000	.0003460			1.850	...	.072800	.0041620
		0.550	...	.021600	.0003650	49	...	.....	...	.073000	.0041850
74	...	.....	...	.022500	.0003980			1.900	...	.074800	.0043940
		0.600	...	.023620	.0004380	48	...	.....	...	.076000	.0045360
73	...	.....	...	.024000	.0004520			1.950	...	.076700	.0046180
72	...	.....	...	.025000	.0004910				5/64	.078120	.0047940
		0.650	...	.025500	.0005100	47	...	.....	...	.078500	.0048400
71	...	.....	...	.026000	.0005310			2.000	...	.078740	.0048690
		0.700	...	.027560	.0005970			2.050	...	.080700	.0051120
70	...	.....	...	.028000	.0006160	46	...	.....	...	.081000	.0051530
69	...	.....	...	.029250	.0006720	45	...	.....	...	.082000	.0052810
		0.750	...	.029500	.0006830			2.100	...	.082670	.0053690
68	...	.....	...	.031000	.0007550			2.150	...	.084600	.0056150
			1/32	.031250	.0007670	44	...	.....	...	.086000	.0058090
		0.800	...	.031490	.0007790			2.200	...	.086610	.0058920
67	...	.....	...	.032000	.0008040			2.250	...	.088500	.0061490
66	...	.....	...	.033000	.0008550	43	...	.....	...	.089000	.0062210
		0.850	...	.033400	.0008710			2.300	...	.090550	.0064400
65	...	.....	...	.035000	.0009620			2.35	...	.092500	.0067150
		0.900	...	.035430	.0009860	42	...	.....	...	.093500	.0068600
64	...	.....	...	.036000	.0010180				3/32	.093750	.0069030
63	...	.....	...	.037000	.0010750			2.400	...	.094480	.0070120
		0.950	...	.037400	.0010910	41	...	.....	...	.096000	.0072380
62	...	.....	...	.038000	.0011340			2.45	...	.096400	.0072960
61	...	.....	...	.039000	.0011950	40	...	.....	...	.098000	.0075430
		1.000	...	.039370	.0012170			2.50	...	.098420	.0076090
60	...	.....	...	.040000	.0012570	39	...	.....	...	.099500	.0077760
59	...	.....	...	.041000	.0013200	38	...	.....	...	.101500	.0080910
		0.105	...	.041300	.0013510			2.60	...	.102360	.0082290
58	...	.....	...	.042000	.0013850	37	...	.....	...	.104000	.0084900
57	...	.....	...	.043000	.0014520			2.70	...	.106300	.0088750
		1.100	...	.043300	.0014730	36	...	.....	...	.106500	.0089080
		1.150	...	.045200	.0016100			2.75	...	.108200	.0091890
56	...	.....	...	.046500	.0016980				7/64	.109370	.0093960
			3/64	.046870	.0017260	35	...	.....	...	.110000	.0095030
		1.200	...	.047240	.0017530			2.80	...	.110240	.0095440
		1.250	...	.049200	.0019000	34	...	.....	...	.111000	.0096770
		1.300	...	.051181	.0020570	33	...	.....	...	.113000	.0100290
55	...	.....	...	.052000	.0021240			2.90	...	.114170	.0102380
		1.350	...	.053100	.0022060	32	...	.....	...	.116000	.0105680

Table 8-28. Diameters and Areas of Small Drills (Continued)

No.	Ltr	Mm	In.	Diam, in.	Area, in.²	No.	Ltr	Mm	In.	Diam, in.	Area, in.²
		3.00	...	0.118110	0.0109590	7	...	....	....	0.201000	0.0317310
31	...	.....	...	.120000	.0113100				13/64	.203120	.0324030
		3.10	....	.122050	.0116990	6	...	....	....	.204000	.0326850
			1/8	.125000	.0122720			5.20	....	.204730	.0329180
		3.20	....	.125980	.0124660	5	...	.....	....	.205500	.0331681
		3.25	....	.127900	.0128020			5.25	....	.206600	.0335200
30	...			.128500	.0129690			5.30	....	.208600	.0341960
		3.30	....	.129920	.0132570	4	...	.....	....	.209000	.0343070
		3.40	....	.133860	.0140730			5.400	....	.212600	.0354990
29	...			.136000	.0145270	3	...			.213000	.0356330
		3.50	....	.137800	.0149130			5.500	....	.216540	.0368250
28	...	.....		.140500	.0155040				7/32	.218750	.0375830
			9/64	.140620	.0155310			5.600	....	.220470	.0381770
		3.60	....	.141730	.0157770	2	...	.....	....	.221000	.0383600
27	...			.144000	.0162860			5.700	....	.224410	.0395520
		3.70	....	.145670	.0166660			5.750	....	.226300	.0402430
26	...			.147000	.0169720	1	...			.228000	.0408280
		3.75	....	.147600	.0171060			5.800	....	.228350	.0409520
25	...			.149500	.0175540			5.900	....	.232280	.0423770
		3.80	....	.149610	.0175790		A	.....	....	.234000	.0430050
24	...			.152000	.0181460				15/64	.234370	.0431410
		3.90	....	.153540	.0185160			6.000	....	.236220	.0438250
23	...			.154000	.0186270		B	.....	....	.238000	.0444880
			5/32	.156250	.0191750			6.100	....	.240150	.0452990
22	...			.157000	.0193590		C			.242000	.0459960
		4.00	....	.157480	.0194780			6.200	....	.244100	.0467970
21	...	.....		.159000	.0198560		D			.246000	.0475290
20	...	.....		.161000	.0203580			6.250	....	.246060	.0475480
		4.10	....	.161420	.0204640			6.300	....	.248030	.0483170
		4.2	....	.165360	.0214740		E	.....	1/4	.250000	.0490870
19	...			.166000	.0216420			6.400	....	.251970	.0498630
		4.25	....	.167300	.0220560			6.500	....	.255910	.0514340
		4.30	....	.169290	.0225050		F	.....	....	.257000	.0518750
18	...	.....		.169500	.0225650			6.600	....	.259800	.0530280
			11/64	.171875	.0232020		G			.261000	.0535020
17	...			.173000	.0235060			6.700	....	.263700	.0546480
		4.40	....	.173230	.0235680				17/64	.265600	.0554120
16	...			.177000	.0246060			6.750	....	.265700	.0554140
		4.50	....	.177170	.0246520		H	.....	....	.266000	.0555720
15	...			.180000	.0254470			6.800	....	.267720	.0562910
		4.60	....	.181100	.0257600			6.900	....	.271650	.0579590
14	...			.182000	.0260160		I			.272000	.0581070
13	...			.185000	.0268800			7.000	....	.275500	.0596510
		4.70	....	.185040	.0268920		J	.....	....	.277000	.0602630
		4.75	....	.187000	.0274570			7.100	....	.279500	.0613670
			3/16	.187500	.0276120		K	.....	....	.281000	.0620160
		4.80	....	.188980	.0280480				9/32	.281250	.0621260
12	...	.....		.189000	.0280550			7.200	....	.283470	.0631080
11	...	.....		.191000	.0286520			7.250	....	.285400	.0639700
		4.90	....	.192910	.0292290			7.300	....	.287400	.0648740
10	...			.193500	.0294070		L	.....	....	.290000	.0660520
9	...			.196000	.0301720			7.400	....	.291330	.0666630
		5.00	....	.196850	.0304340		M	.....	....	.295000	.0683490
8	...			.199000	.0311030			7.500	....	.295200	.0684770
		5.10	....	.200790	.0316640				19/64	.296875	.0692180

Table 8-28. Diameters and Areas of Small Drills (Continued)

No.	Ltr	Mm	In.	Diam, in.	Area, in.²	No.	Ltr	Mm	In.	Diam, in.	Area, in.²
		7.600	....	0.299220	0.0703150				1/2	0.500000	0.1963500
	N		....	.302000	.0716310			13.00	....	0.511800	.2050700
		7.700	....	.303140	.0721780				33/64	0.515600	.2087500
		7.750	....	.305100	.0730570				17/32	0.531200	.2216600
		7.800	....	.307090	.0740650			13.50	....	0.531400	.2217900
		7.900	....	.311020	.0759760				35/64	0.546800	.2341200
			5/16	.312500	.0766990			14.00	....	0.551100	.2384400
		8.000	....	.314960	.0779120				9/16	0.562500	.2485000
	O		....	.316000	.0784270			14.50	....	0.570800	.2560400
			....	.318890	.0798720				37/64	0.578100	.2624800
		8.100	....	.322830	.0818560			15.00	....	0.590500	.2733900
	P	8.200	....	.323000	.0819400				19/32	0.593700	.2768800
		8.250	....	.324800	.0827810				39/64	0.609300	.2916100
		8.300	....	.326800	.0838650			15.50	....	0.610200	.2922400
			21/64	.328120	.0845580				5/8	0.625000	.3068000
		8.400	....	.330700	.0858980			16.00	....	0.629900	.3117200
	Q		....	.332000	.0865700				41/64	0.640600	.3223200
		8.500	....	.334650	.0879550			16.50	....	0.649600	.3308100
		8.600	....	.338580	.0900370				21/32	0.656200	.3382400
	R		....	.339000	.0902590			17.00	....	0.669200	.3514200
		8.700	....	.342500	.0921430				43/64	0.671800	.3645400
			11/32	.343700	.0928060				11/16	0.687500	.3712200
		8.750	....	.344400	.0929120			17.50	....	0.688900	.3726700
		8.800	....	.346400	.0942740				45/64	0.703100	.3882800
	S		....	.348000	.0951150			18.00	....	0.708600	.3943400
		8.900	....	.350400	.0964280				23/32	0.718700	.4057400
		9.000	....	.354300	.0986070			18.50	....	0.723300	.4165700
	T		....	.358000	.1006600				47/64	0.734300	.4235690
		9.100	....	.358300	.1008110			19.00	....	0.748000	.4393500
			23/64	.359300	.1014340				3/4	0.750000	.4417900
		9.200	....	.362200	.1030390				49/64	0.765600	.4587500
		9.250	....	.364100	.1039860			19.50	....	0.767700	.4623300
		9.300	....	.366100	.1052910				25/32	0.781200	.4793700
	U		....	.368000	.1063620			20.00	....	0.787400	.4858600
		9.400	....	.370100	.1075670				51/64	0.796800	.4977200
		9.500	....	.374020	.1098680			20.50	....	0.807000	.5115800
			3/8	.375000	.1104470				13/16	0.812500	.5184900
	V		....	.377000	.1116230			21.00	....	0.826200	.5368500
		9.600	....	.377950	.1121930				53/64	0.828100	.5386100
		9.700	....	.381800	.1145430				27/32	0.843700	.5591400
		9.750	....	.383800	.1156890			21.50	....	0.846400	.5626600
		9.800	....	.385800	.1169170				55/64	0.859300	.5799200
	W		....	.385900	.1170210			22.00	....	0.866100	.5892000
		9.900	....	.389300	.1193150				7/8	0.875000	.6013200
			29/64	.390620	.1198440			22.50	....	0.885800	.6162900
		10.00	....	.393700	.1217380				57/64	0.890600	.6629700
	X		....	.397000	.1237860			23.00	....	0.905500	.6400700
	Y		....	.404000	.1281900				29/32	0.906200	.6450400
			13/32	.406200	.1296220				59/64	0.921800	.6674600
	Z		....	.413000	.1339650			23.50	....	0.925100	.6722200
		10.50	....	.413300	.1342000				15/16	0.937500	.6902900
			27/64	.421800	.1397200			24.00	....	0.944800	.7011900
		11.00	....	.433000	.1471800				61/64	0.953100	.7150200
			7/16	.437500	.1503300			24.50	....	0.964500	.7297900
		11.50	....	.452700	.1607600				31/32	0.968700	.7370800
			29/64	.453100	.1612400			25.00	....	0.984200	.7614400
			15/32	.468700	.1725700				63/64	0.998430	.7634500
		12.00	....	.472400	.1749000				1.0	1.000000	.7854000
			31/64	.484300	.1842500			25.50	....	1.003000	.7915200
		12.50	....	.492100	.1901400						

SOURCE: Colvin and Stanley, "American Machinists' Handbook," 8th ed., pp. 137–139, McGraw-Hill Book Company, Inc., New York, 1945.

Table 8-29. Tap-drill Sizes for American Standard Screw Threads*

Size, no. or in.	Coarse-thread series Thds/in.	Coarse-thread series Drill size	Fine-thread series Thds/in.	Fine-thread series Drill size	Size, no. or in.	Coarse-thread series Thds/in.	Coarse-thread series D-ill size	Fine-thread series Thds/in.	Fine-thread series Drill size
0	...	......	80	$3/64$	$3/4$	10	$21/32$	16	$11/16$
1	64	No. 53	72	No. 53	$7/8$	9	$49/64$	14	$13/16$
2	56	No. 50	64	No. 50	1	8	$7/8$	14	$15/16$
3	48	No. 47	56	No. 45	$1\,1/8$	7	$63/64$	12	$1\,3/64$
4	40	No. 43	48	No. 42	$1\,1/4$	7	$1\,7/64$	12	$1\,11/64$
5	40	No. 38	44	No. 37	$1\,3/8$	6	$1\,7/32$	12	$1\,19/64$
6	32	No. 36	40	No. 33	$1\,1/2$	6	$1\,21/64$	12	$1\,27/64$
8	32	No. 29	36	No. 29	$1\,3/4$	5	$1\,35/64$		
10	24	No. 25	32	No. 21	2	$4\,1/2$	$1\,25/32$		
12	24	No. 16	28	No. 14	$2\,1/4$	$4\,1/2$	$2\,1/32$		
$1/4$	20	No. 7	28	No. 3	$2\,1/2$	4	$2\,1/4$		
$5/16$	18	F	24	I	$2\,3/4$	4	$2\,1/2$		
$3/8$	16	$5/16$	24	Q	3	4	$2\,3/4$		
$7/16$	14	U	20	$25/64$	$3\,1/4$	4	3		
$1/2$	13	$27/64$	20	$29/64$	$3\,1/2$	4	$3\,1/4$		
$9/16$	12	$31/64$	18	$33/64$	$3\,3/4$	4	$3\,1/2$		
$5/8$	11	$17/32$	18	$37/64$	4	4	$3\,3/4$		

* The sizes listed are the commercial tap drills to produce approx 75 per cent full thread.
source: L. S. Marks, ed., "Mechanical Engineers' Handbook," 5th ed., p. 883. McGraw-Hill Book Company, Inc., New York, 1951.

8-22. Screw Threads for Pipes

American Standard Taper Pipe Thread, ASA B2.1, is shown in Fig. 8-52 and is made to the following specifications: The taper is 1 in. in 16 in. or 0.75 in./ft. The basic length of the effective external taper thread is determined by $L_2 = p(0.8D + 6.8)$, where D is the basic outside diameter of the pipe (Table 8-30).

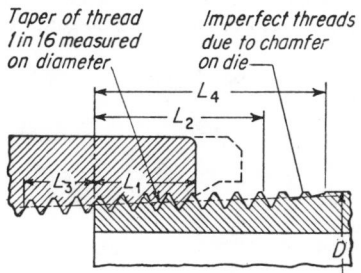

FIG. 8-52. Source: L. S. Marks (ed.), "Mechanical Engineers' Handbook," 5th ed., p. 871, McGraw-Hill Book Company, Inc., New York, 1951.

Table 8-30. ASA Taper Pipe Thread

All Dimensions in Inches

Nominal pipe size	Pipe OD	Thds/in.	Thread pitch, P	L_1*	L_2†	L_3‡	L_4¶
$\frac{1}{16}$	0.3125	27	0.03704	0.160	0.2611	0.1111	0.3896
$\frac{1}{8}$	0.405	27	.03704	0.180	0.2639	.1111	0.3924
$\frac{1}{4}$	0.540	18	.05556	0.200	0.4018	.1667	0.5946
$\frac{3}{8}$	0.675	18	.05556	0.240	0.4078	.1667	0.6006
$\frac{1}{2}$	0.840	14	.07143	0.320	0.5337	.2143	0.7815
$\frac{3}{4}$	1.050	14	.07143	0.339	0.5457	.2143	0.7935
1	1.315	11½	.08696	0.400	0.6828	.2609	0.9845
1¼	1.660	11½	.08696	0.420	0.7068	.2609	1.0085
1½	1.900	11½	.08696	0.420	0.7235	.2609	1.0252
2	2.375	11½	.08696	0.436	0.7565	.2609	1.0582
2½	2.875	8	.12500	0.682	1.1375	.2500	1.5712
3	3.500	8	.12500	0.766	1.2000	.2500	1.6337
3½	4.000	8	.12500	0.821	1.2500	.2500	1.6837
4	4.500	8	.12500	0.844	1.3000	.2500	1.7337
5	5.563	8	.12500	0.937	1.4063	.2500	1.8400
6	6.625	8	.12500	0.958	1.5125	.2500	1.9462
8	8.625	8	.12500	1.063	1.7125	.2500	2.1462
10	10.750	8	.12500	1.210	1.9250	.2500	2.3587
12	12.750	8	.12500	1.360	2.1250	.2500	2.5587
14 OD	14.000	8	.12500	1.562	2.2500	.2500	2.6837
16 OD	16.000	8	.12500	1.812	2.4500	.2500	2.8837
18 OD	18.000	8	.12500	2.000	2.6500	.2500	3.0837
20 OD	20.000	8	.12500	2.125	2.8500	.2500	3.2837
24 OD	24.000	8	.12500	2.375	3.2500	.2500	3.6837

* Hand-tight engagement length.
† Effective thread external length.
‡ Wrench make-up length for internal thread length.
¶ Over-all length external thread.
SOURCE: L. S. Marks, ed., "Mechanical Engineers' Handbook," 5th ed., p. 872, McGraw-Hill Book Company, Inc., New York, 1951.

8-23. Coefficients of Static and Sliding Friction

Coefficients of static and sliding friction are defined as the ratios of frictional force to the normal force between two bodies in contact. (See Table 8-31.)

Table 8-31. Coefficients of Static and Sliding Friction

Materials	Static coef		Sliding coef	
	Dry	Greasy	Dry	Greasy
Hard steel on hard steel............	0.78	0.11	0.42	0.029
	....	.23	....	.081
	....	.15	....	.080
	....	.11	....	.058
	....	.0075	....	.084
	....	.0052	....	.105
	....	......	....	.096
	....	......	....	.108
	....	......	....	.12
Mild steel on mild steel............	0.74	......	0.57	.09
	....	....	....	.19
Hard steel on graphite.............	0.21	.09		
Hard steel on babbitt (ASTM 1)....	0.70	.23	0.33	.16
	....	.15	....	.06
	....	.08	....	.11
	....	.085		
Hard steel on babbitt (ASTM 8)....	0.42	.17	0.35	.14
	....	.11	....	.065
	....	.09	....	.07
	....	.08	....	.08
Hard steel on babbitt (ASTM 10)...	....	.25	....	.13
	....	.12	....	.06
	....	.10	....	.055
	....	.11		
Mild steel on cadmium silver.......	....	......	...	.097
Mild steel on phosphor bronze......	....	......	0.34	.173
Mild steel on copper lead...........	....	......	...	.145
Mild steel on cast iron.............	....	.183	0.23	.133
Mild steel on lead.................	0.95	.5	0.95	.3
Nickel on mild steel................	....	......	0.64	.178
Aluminum on mild steel............	0.61	......	0.47	
Magnesium on mild steel............	....	......	0.42	
Cadmium on mild steel.............	....	......	0.46	
Copper on mild steel...............	0.53	......	0.36	.18
Nickel on nickel...................	1.10	......	0.53	.12
Brass on mild steel................	0.51	......	0.44	
Brass on cast iron.................	....	......	0.30	
Zinc on cast iron..................	0.85	......	0.21	
Magnesium on cast iron............	....	......	0.25	
Copper on cast iron................	1.05	......	0.29	
Tin on cast iron...................	....	......	0.32	
Lead on cast iron..................	....	......	0.43	
Aluminum on aluminum............	1.05	....	1.4	
Glass on glass.....................	0.94	.01	0.40	.09
	....	.005	...	.116
Carbon on glass....................	....	......	.18	
Garnet on mild steel...............	....	......	.39	
Glass on nickel....................	0.78	......	.56	
Copper on glass....................	0.68	......	.53	
Cast iron on cast iron..............	1.10	......	.15	.070
	....	....	...	.064
Bronze on cast iron................	....	......	.22	.077
Oak on oak (parallel to grain)......	0.62	......	.48	.164
	....	....	...	.067
Oak on oak (perpendicular to grain)..	.54	......	.32	.072
Leather on oak (parallel)...........	.61	......	.52	
Cast iron on oak...................	....	......	.49	.075
Leather on cast iron...............	....	......	.56	.36
	....	....	...	.13
Laminated plastic on steel..........	....	......	...	.05
Fluted rubber bearing on steel......	....	......	....	.05

SOURCE: L. S. Marks, ed., "Mechanical Engineers' Handbook," 5th ed., p. 218. McGraw-Hill Book Company, Inc., New York, 1951.

COMPRESSOR, FAN, AND PISTON-MACHINE PERFORMANCE

Nomenclature

a = area of piston (with deductions for piston and tail rods, when present), in.^{2}

C = constant, 12 for 4-cycle engine, 20 for 2-cycle engine

C_p = heat capacity at constant pressure, Btu/(lb)(°F)

C_v = heat capacity at constant volume, Btu/(lb)(°F)

c = clearance, decimal fraction of displacement

D = piston displacement, ft^3/cycle

D' = piston displacement, cfm

d = bore, in.

F = net force at arm bearing point, lb

g_c = conversion factor, 32.2 (lb mass)(ft)/(lb force)(sec^2)

h = enthalpy ($= pv/J + u$), Btu/lb

h_s = static head, ft fluid

h_t = total head, ft fluid

h_v = velocity head, ft fluid

h''_w = head, in. H$_2$O

h_1 = enthalpy at compressor supply, Btu/lb

h_2 = enthalpy at compressor delivery, Btu/lb

J = mechanical equivalent of heat, 778 ft-lb/Btu

k = ratio of specific heats, C_p/C_v

L = length of stroke, ft

= length of brake arm (shaft center line to arm bearing point), ft

l = stroke length, in.

mep = mean effective pressure, psi

N = shaft rpm

= number of stages

n = number cycles completed per minute

= polytropic exponent, pv^n = constant for polytropic process

p = pressure, lb force/ft^2 abs

p_1 = supply pressure, lb force/in.^{2} abs

p_2 = delivery pressure, lb force/in.^{2} abs

R_p = ratio of pressures = p_2/p_1

R_{p1}, R_{p2}, R_{p3} = compression ratio in stages one, two, three, respectively

u = internal or intrinsic energy, Btu/lb

v = volume, ft^3

$\bar{v}$ = specific volume, ft^3/lb

$\bar{w}_f$ = density of fluid, lb/ft^3

$\bar{w}_w$ = density of water, 62.4 lb/ft^3

ΔW = work done on or by fluid, ft-lb force/lb

$_1$ = entering or initial conditions

$_2$ = leaving or final conditions

8-24. Adiabatic (Isentropic) Compressor Standards

The ideal compressor cycle is shown in Fig. 8-53 where there are three phases: (1) admission from a to 1, (2) compression from 1 to 2, and (3) delivery from 2 to b. For a perfect gas with reversible adiabatic (or isentropic) compression (pv^k = const) the work is given as[1]

$$\Delta W_{\text{adiabatic cycle}} = 144 p_1 v_1 [k/(k - 1)](R_p{}^{(k-1)/k} - 1) \qquad (8\text{-}69)$$

If the compression is isentropic and for a real gas, the thermodynamic properties of which are known (as for refrigerants), then for a perfect compressor the work of the cycle is

$$\Delta W_{\text{adiabatic cycle}} = (h_2 - h_1)778 \qquad (8\text{-}70)$$

Equations (8-69) and (8-70) give identical answers for a perfect gas.

8-25. Isothermal Compressor Standards

If compressors are so cooled that temperature is constant during compression, the isothermal standard prevails as shown in Fig. 8-54 (pv = const) and there is a saving in work over the adiabatic value of Eq. (8-69). The work is given as[1]

$$\Delta W_{\text{isothermal}} = 144(p_1 v_1) \log_e R_p \qquad (8\text{-}70a)$$

8-26. Multistage Compressor Standards

The work of a compressor is reduced by the use of multistage compression with intercooling between stages. If cooling is complete and the gas enters the succeeding stage at the same temperature at which it enters the machine, the intercooling is said to be perfect. Minimum work is then obtained with unique values of pressure between the stages, called best receiver pressure. It is determined by[1]

$$R_{p1} = R_{p2} = R_{p3} \cdots = R_p{}^{1/N} \qquad (8\text{-}71)$$

With isentropic compression in each stage, best receiver pressure, and perfect intercooling, the work of the ideal cycle is

$$\Delta W_{\text{multistage}} = 144 N p_1 v_1 [k/(k - 1)](R_p{}^{(k-1)/Nk} - 1) \qquad (8\text{-}72)$$

The isothermal standard of Eq. (8-70a) applies equally well to single- and multiple-stage compression.

8-27. Capacity

Capacity is expressed on a volume basis and for air is given on the "free air" basis. This measures capacity at the ambient pressure, temperature, and humidity.

For a positive-displacement machine without clearance, the volume is represented as $v_1 - v_a$ of Fig. 8-55. This is obtained from the dimensions of the cylinders[1]

[1] For nomenclature see p. 8-60.

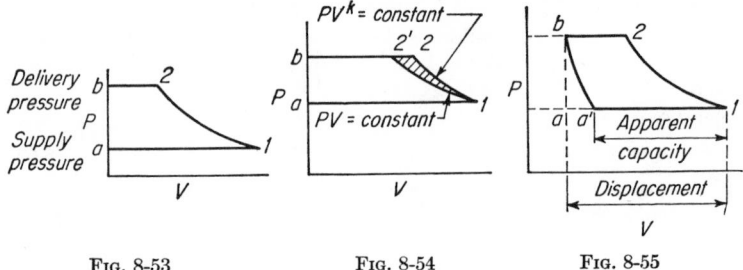

FIG. 8-53   FIG. 8-54   FIG. 8-55

$$\text{Piston displacement, ft}^3/\text{cycle} = D = (\pi d^2/4)(l/1{,}728) \qquad (8\text{-}73)$$

$$D' = \text{piston displacement, cfm} = \frac{\pi d^2}{4} nl \frac{1}{1{,}728} \qquad (8\text{-}74)$$

$$= \frac{d^2 ln}{2{,}200}$$

As the machine contains clearance which runs from 2 to 20 per cent of the displacement, there is a clearance reexpansion loss, so that point a shifts to position a' and the length $v_1 = v'_a$ is less than the displacement $v_1 - v_a$ in Fig. 8-55. This apparent capacity is calculable by

$$\text{Apparent capacity} = D(1 + c - cR_p{}^{1/k}) \qquad (8\text{-}75)$$

The actual capacity, as metered, for a real compressor is less than this apparent value because of suction heating, suction pressure drop, and leakage losses.

Volumetric efficiency is the ratio of capacity to displacement, and if the former is a real metered value, then

$$\text{Actual volumetric eff, \%} = \frac{\text{actual metered capacity}}{\text{piston displacement}} \times 100 \qquad (8\text{-}76)$$

If the apparent capacity is used from Eq. (8-75), then

$$\text{Apparent volumetric eff, \%} = (1 + c - cR_p{}^{1/k}) \times 100 \qquad (8\text{-}77)$$

The relation between these two is called slippage efficiency and is defined as

$$\text{slippage eff, \%} = \frac{\text{actual volumetric eff}}{\text{apparent volumetric eff}} \times 100 \qquad (8\text{-}78)$$

8-28. Ideal Horsepower of Compressors

The equations for ideal work, (8-68), (8-69), (8-70), and (8-72), apply equally well to compressors involving clearance, because work is independent of clearance. For a volume flow rate of 100 cfm the equations can be rewritten as[1]

[1] For nomenclature see p. 8–60.

Isentropic or adiabatic hp/100 cfm $= \dfrac{k}{k-1} \dfrac{p_1}{2.292} (R_p{}^{(k-1)/k} - 1)$ (8-79)

$$= \frac{(h_2 - h_1) \times \text{lb/min}}{0.4242\bar{v}_1}$$ (8-80)

where $\bar{v}_1$ = specific volume, ft³/lb, at supply pressure

Isothermal hp/100 cfm $= (p_1/2.292) \log_e R_p$ (8-81)

In a multistage compressor with perfect intercooling and best receiver pressure:

Isentropic or adiabatic hp/100 cfm $= \dfrac{Np_1}{2.292} \dfrac{k}{k-1} R_p{}^{(k-1)/Nk} - 1)$ (8-82)

These equations for work and horsepower can be conveniently solved by use of Fig. 8-56.

8-29. Compression Efficiency

The actual power required by a compressor can be compared to the ideal power (for the same capacity) to give

$$\text{Compression eff, } \% = \frac{\text{ideal hp}}{\text{actual hp}} \times 100$$ (8-83)

The ideal value may be obtained from Eqs. (8-79) to (8-82) giving adiabatic and isothermal compression efficiencies.

The actual horsepower may be obtained from (1) the compressor-cylinder indicator card, (2) the shaft of the compressor, or (3) it may be actual power input to the motor terminals of an electrically driven unit. Care must be taken to specify the base.

8-30. Fan Performance

A fan is a compressor in which the change in density of the gaseous fluid, on passage through the machine, is negligibly small.

Definitions

Standard air: Air at 68°F, 29.92 in. Hg pressure, and 5 per cent relative humidity. It has a density of 0.07488 lb/ft³ and a specific volume of 13.3 ft³/lb and is the basis for measuring fan performance.

Capacity: The volume delivered by a fan, Q, expressed in cubic feet per minute.

Head: The difference between the pressures on the suction and discharge sides of a fan, variously expressed as feet of fluid, inches of water, pounds per square inch, etc. Conversion is as follows[1]

$h_t = (h''_w/12)(\bar{w}_w/\bar{w}_f)$ ft fluid   (8-84)

$h_t = h''_w \times 69.5$ ft std air   (8-85)

Pressure $= h''_w/27.7$ psi   (8-86)

[1] For nomenclature see p. 8-60.

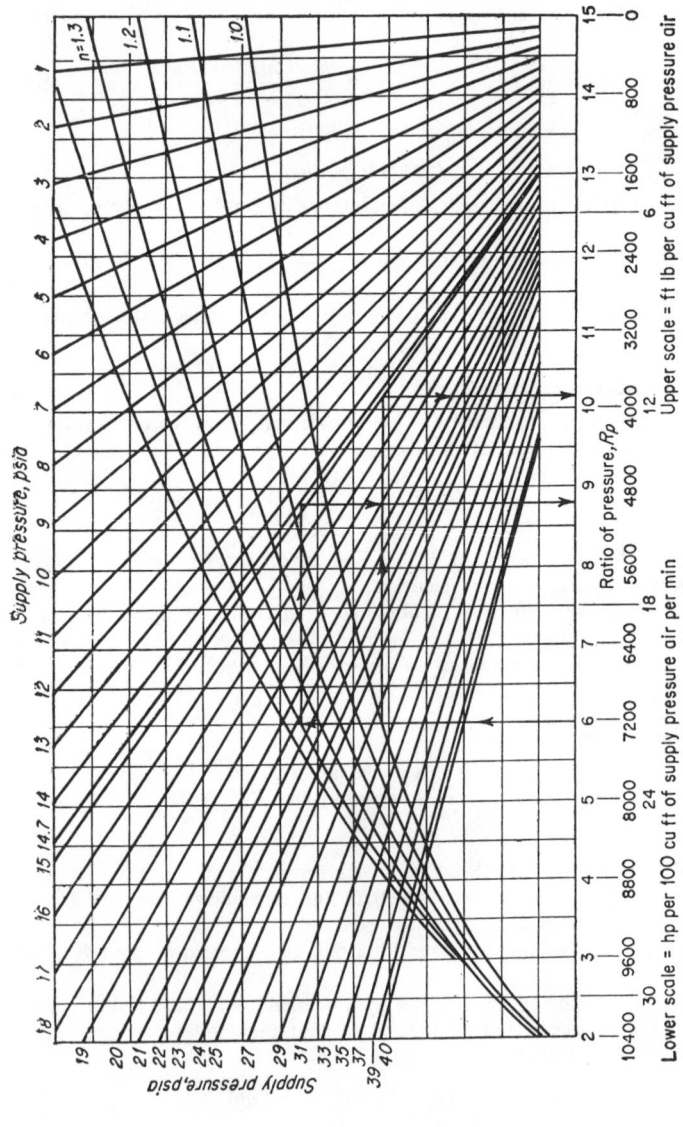

Lower scale = hp per 100 cu ft of supply pressure air per min   Upper scale = ft lb per cu ft of supply pressure air

Work per cubic foot and horsepower per 100 cu ft per minute of supply pressure gas for single-stage compressors

Fig. 8-56

8–64

Static, Velocity, and Total Heads. As shown in Fig. 8-57, three pressures can be read in a fan duct. *Static head* h_s is a directly obtained pressure reading; *velocity head* h_v is obtained from the flow rate in the duct and must be an average value obtained by a traverse. Then *total head*

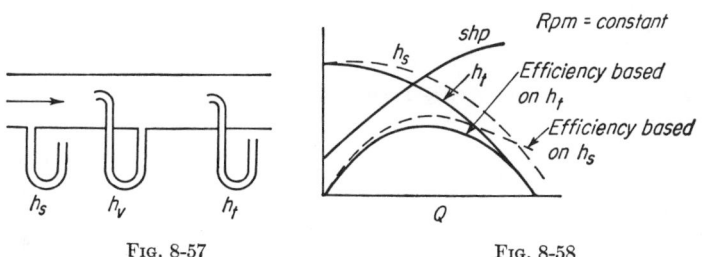

FIG. 8-57   FIG. 8-58

$$h_t = h_s + h_v \tag{8-87}$$

Conversion is by

$$\text{Velocity} = \sqrt{2g_c h_v} \quad \text{fps} \tag{8-88}$$

Substituting the conversion of Eq. (8-84)

$$\text{Velocity} = 1{,}096.2\ \sqrt{h''_w/\overline{w}_f} \quad \text{fpm} \tag{8-89}$$

and if standard air is used

$$\text{Velocity} = 4{,}005\ \sqrt{h''_w} \quad \text{fpm} \tag{8-90}$$

Fan performance is variously based on static and total head, the former being generally more realistic because it is the only form of head usable in overcoming a system resistance.

Horsepower of Fans. The ideal or air horsepower is given by[1]

$$\text{Air hp} = Qh''_w/6{,}355 \tag{8-91}$$

Static or total head may be used, giving two alternative values of ideal horsepower, the latter being larger.

Shaft horsepower (shp). Shaft-horsepower input to drive the fan is measured by a suitable dynamometer. *Fan efficiency* is defined as

$$\text{Fan eff, } \% = \frac{\text{air hp}}{\text{shp}} \times 100 \tag{8-92}$$

This value may be on the static or total basis.

Fan Characteristics. Fans, like other fluid-acceleration machines, operate with characteristic curves. A set of characteristics is plotted in Fig. 8-45 for a representative fan. These curves are exactly definitive, and the fan must operate at some point on the characteristic.

Fan Laws. See pump laws, which are identical to the fan laws.

[1] For nomenclature see p. 8-60.

8-31. Performance Characteristics of Piston Machines

Mean Effective Pressure. In piston and cylinder machines it is convenient to measure performance through the use of mean effective pressure. As illustrated by Fig. 8-59, the mean effective pressure is defined as the difference in pressure on the two sides of the piston, which difference tends to move the piston in an engine or resist its motion in a pump. It can be defined as

Mean effective pressure, mep = mean forward pressure, mfp

$$- \text{ mean back pressure, mbp} \quad (8\text{-}93)$$

Thus in the two illustrations of Fig. 8-59, for a single-acting and a double-acting mechanism, the mep is the same (100 psi) because in A,

$$\text{mep} = 115 - 15 = 100 \text{ psi};$$

in B, mep = 215 − 115 = 100 psi.

These pressures are mean values which can be considered as prevailing throughout the stroke. They may be calculated for ideal cyclic conditions by utilizing the methods of thermodynamics and fluid dynamics. Thus in Fig. 8-60 the area of the $P\text{-}V$ diagram is the work of the cycle, expressible in foot pounds. If that area is divided by the length of the diagram, i.e., by the stroke or displacement, the result is a vertical height for a rectangle of equivalent area, and this height is the mep, as

$$\text{mep} = \frac{\text{work of cycle, ft-lb}}{\text{displacement, ft}^3 \times 144 \text{ in.}^2/\text{ft}^2} = \frac{\text{lb}}{\text{in.}^2} \quad (8\text{-}94)$$

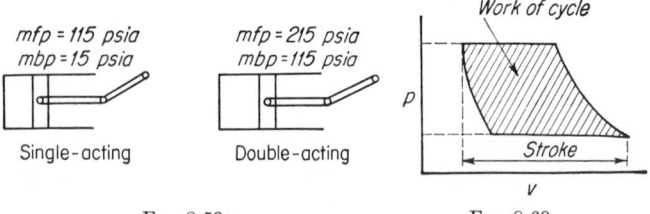

$$\text{Fig. 8-59} \qquad\qquad\qquad \text{Fig. 8-60}$$

Actual mean effective pressure is determined from the planimetered area of the indicator card, dividing by length, and applying spring scale. Thus with Fig. 8-61,

$$\text{mep} = \frac{\text{area, in.}^2}{\text{length, in.}} \times \text{spring scale, lb/(in.}^2)(\text{in.})$$
$$(8\text{-}95)$$

$$\text{Fig. 8-61}$$

Indicated Horsepower. Mean effective pressure is used to calculate the indicated horsepower, thus[1]

$$\text{Indicated hp} = \text{mep } Lan/33{,}000 \quad (8\text{-}96)$$

[1] For nomenclature see p. 8–60.

The items a and L are obtained directly from the bore and stroke. The number of cycles completed per minute depends upon the mechanism construction, i.e., single- or double-acting; number of cylinders; and number of strokes or revolutions needed to complete a cycle (Table 8-32).

Table 8-32. General Data on Engine, Pump, and Compressor Constructions

Machine	Strokes per cycle	Single- or double-acting
Steam engine	2	DA
Air compressors:		
Large	2	DA
Small	2	SA
Refrigeration compressors:		
Large	2	DA
Small	2	SA
Direct-acting pumps	2	DA
Triplex pumps	2	SA
Compressed-air engines:		
Large	2	DA
Small	2	SA
Internal-combustion engines:		
High-speed automotive gasoline	4	SA
Small high-speed gasoline	2 or 4	SA
High-speed diesel	2 or 4	SA
Medium-speed diesel	2 or 4	SA
Low-speed diesel	2 or 4	SA or DA
Natural gas:		
Small	2 or 4	SA
Large	2 or 4	DA

Brake or Shaft Horsepower. As measured on a prony brake or dynamometer, brake or shaft horsepower is determined by[1]

$$\text{hp} = 2\pi \, LFN/33{,}000 \tag{8-97}$$
$$= LFN/5{,}250 \tag{8-98}$$

Brake Mean Effective Pressure, or Brake Mean Pressure. On high-speed engines and compressors it is not possible to take indicator cards, but brake-horsepower readings can be expressed as equivalent brake mean pressure by combining results of Eq. (8-97) in Eq. (8-98), or[1]

$$\text{Brake mean pressure, psi} = \frac{\text{brake hp}}{Lan} \times 33{,}000 \tag{8-99}$$

Mean Friction Pressures. Mean friction pressure measures the losses between cylinders and shaft, or

On engines:

Mean friction pressure, psi = indicated mean effective pressure

$$- \text{ brake mean pressure} \tag{8-100}$$

[1] For nomenclature see p. 8-60.

On compressors and pumps:

Mean friction pressure, psi = brake mean pressure
$$- \text{indicated mean pressure} \quad (8\text{-}101)$$

Mechanical Efficiency.   Mechanical efficiency is another device for expressing the losses between cylinder and shaft, or

On engines:

$$\text{Mechanical eff} = \frac{\text{brake hp}}{\text{indicated hp}} \times 100 \quad (8\text{-}102)$$

On pumps and compressors:

$$\text{Mechanical eff} = \frac{\text{indicated hp}}{\text{brake hp}} \times 100 \quad (8\text{-}103)$$

PUMP PERFORMANCE

8-32. General

Nomenclature

G = capacity, lb/hr
p = head, psi
Q = capacity, gpm
H = head, ft

In American practice, pump sizes generally refer to the discharge-pipe diameter in inches.

Standard Water.   Pump performance is predicated on the use of cold water (less than 85°F).   The specific gravity of water at 60°F is usually referred to as unity, with density of 62.4 lb/ft³ and specific volume of 0.016 ft³/lb.

Capacity.   The capacity of a pump is expressed on a volume basis, generally in gallons per minute (1 United States gallon = 251 in.³).

Head.   The head developed H is expressed in feet of water.   Conversion to pressure p, in pounds per square inch, is computed from

$$p = \frac{H}{2.3} \quad \text{for cold water} \quad (8\text{-}104)$$

The head delivered by a pump is expressed as total dynamic head, which is the sum of the static and velocity heads.   The velocity head is usually a minor item in pump performance.   Conversion of head to velocity v is by

$$\begin{aligned} v &= \sqrt{2g_cH} \\ &= 8.02 \sqrt{H} \quad \text{fps} \end{aligned} \quad (8\text{-}105)$$

Horsepower.   The ideal or water horsepower is given by

$$\text{Water hp} = (QH \times \text{sp gr})/3{,}960 \quad (8\text{-}106)$$
$$= Gp/(857{,}200 \times \text{sp gr}) \quad (8\text{-}107)$$

where sp gr = specific gravity of fluid being pumped.

Shaft Horsepower. The horsepower input to drive the pump is measured by dynamometer.

Pump efficiency is defined as

$$\text{Pump eff, } \% = \frac{\text{water hp}}{\text{shp}} \times 100 \quad (8\text{-}107a)$$

Pump Characteristics. Centrifugal and axial-flow pumps, like fans, must operate at some point on the characteristic curves (Fig. 8-62). These curves are exactly definitive for the performance of a centrifugal or axial-flow pump, and operation must lie on these curves.

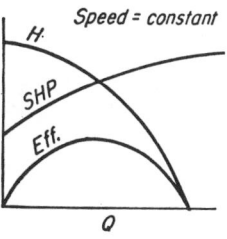

Fig. 8-62

8-33. Pump Laws

For a given centrifugal or axial-flow pump operating at a given point on the efficiency curve, if the speed n (rpm) is changed, then

$$Q \propto n \qquad H \propto n^2 \qquad \text{shp} \propto n^3 \qquad (8\text{-}108)$$

where shp = shaft horsepower

For a series of similar pumps operating at a given point on the efficiency curve, if the size of the pump is changed as measured by the impeller diameter D (feet) for convenience, but with the speed held constant,

$$Q \propto D^3 \qquad H \propto D^2 \qquad \text{shp} \propto D^5 \qquad (8\text{-}109)$$

For a series of similar pumps operating at a given point on the efficiency curve, if the size of the pump is changed as measured by the impeller diameter D but with the tip speed ($u = \pi D n$) held constant

$$Q \propto D^2 \qquad H = \text{const} \qquad \text{shp} \propto D^2 \qquad (8\text{-}110)$$

Specific speed is a useful criterion for defining the adaptability of a pump to a particular service. It is the speed in rpm at which an homologous pump of the series, with suitable diameter, would run in order to deliver 1 gpm at 1 ft head. The specific speed can be plotted as a further characteristic, but the value of the parameter at maximum efficiency is most useful and is always implied. It is derived from the pump-law equations (8-108) and (8-109) by eliminating D from among the four expressions for Q, D, and H to give

$$N_S = \text{specific speed} = \frac{\text{rpm} \times \sqrt{\text{gpm}}}{\text{head}^{3/4}} = \frac{n\sqrt{Q}}{H^{3/4}} \qquad (8\text{-}111)$$

Specific speed is the true criterion for judging high-speed and low-speed pumps. It must be reduced to the single-stage single-inlet-impeller basis. It is related to experience on pump selection as in Fig. 8-63.

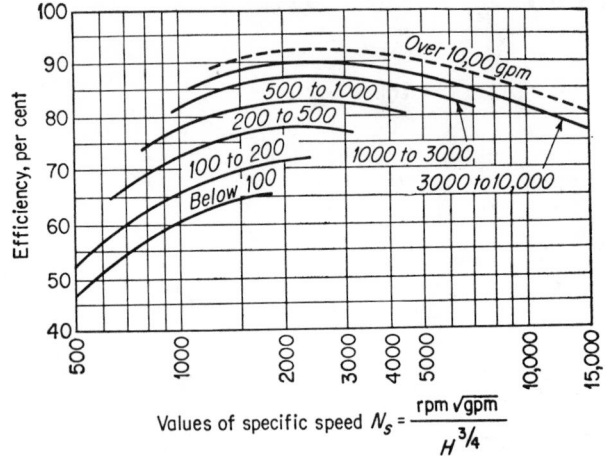

Fig. 8-63. *Source: L. S. Marks (ed.), "Mechanical Engineers' Handbook," 5th ed., p. 1853, McGraw-Hill Book Company, Inc., New York, 1951.*

8-34. Positive-displacement Pumps

The positive-displacement pump may be (1) of a type which is driven through a crank-connecting rod mechanism or (2) of a type which has a steam or compressed-air piston cylinder directly connected through a piston rod to the pump cylinder. In the latter form the stroke is not rigorously fixed. Slip is defined by

$$\text{Slip} = \left(1.00 - \frac{\text{actual volume discharged}}{\text{piston displacement}}\right) \times 100 \qquad \text{per cent} \qquad (8\text{-}112)$$

Speeds are limited on positive-displacement pumps because of the inertia effects of liquid columns. Recommended practice is reflected in the data of Table 8-33.

Table 8-33. Basic Speeds of Standard Pumps

Stroke, in.	Simplex and duplex steam		Duplex and triplex steam		Stroke, in.	Simplex and duplex steam		Duplex and triplex steam	
	Rpm	Fpm	Rpm	Fpm		Rpm	Fpm	Rpm	Fpm
3	74	37	105	52	10	45	75	57	95
4	71	47	90	60	12	41	81	52	104
5	64	53	80	66	15	36	90	47	117
6	60	60	74	74	18	33	99	43	129
8	51	68	64	85	24	27	108	37	148

NOTE: Rpm refers to revolutions per minute of driver, fpm refers to lineal displacement in feet per minute per revolution.
SOURCE: L. S. Marks (ed.), "Mechanical Engineers' Handbook," 5th ed., p. 1838, McGraw-Hill Book Company, Inc., New York, 1951.

Suction Lift and Suction Head. A pump can theoretically operate with either a positive or negative pressure on the suction. The latter condition makes it possible to locate a pump physically above the water level in the sump. The theoretical vertical distance is the barometric height (Table 8-34).

Table 8-34. Barometric Pressure vs. Altitude

Altitude, ft above sea level	Barometer, in. Hg	Altitude, ft above sea level	Barometer, in. Hg
0	29.92	6,000	24.00
1,000	28.84	8,000	22.30
2,000	27.80	10,000	20.72
3,000	26.80	12,000	19.24
4,000	25.83	14,000	17.88
5,000	24.88		

Practical vertical distance or suction lift = (barometric head)
— (velocity head) — (friction losses in pipe fittings and valves
+ pressure of gas in solution + vapor pressure of liquid
+ margin for assuring continuity of liquid column)   (8-113)

The item of vapor pressure is widely variable and is a function of the temperature of the liquid. With water this limitation is reflected in the data of Fig. 8-64.

STATIONARY ENGINEERING

8-35. Hydroelectric Plants and Hydraulic Turbines

Nomenclature

Q = flow, cfs

H = head on site, ft

σ = cavitation coefficient

H_b = barometer head, ft

H_v = vapor pressure, ft

H_s = static suction head, measured positively from tail race to runner-blade periphery, ft

H_e = effective head on unit, ft

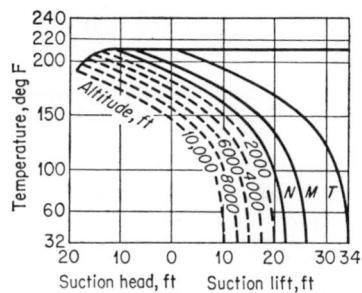

Fig. 8-64. *Source: L. S. Marks (ed.), "Mechanical Engineers' Handbook," 5th ed., p. 1837, McGraw-Hill Book Company, Inc., New York, 1951.*

Water Horsepower. The theoretical power output for a hydro installation is

$$\text{Water hp} = QH/8.8 \qquad (8\text{-}114)$$

or

$$\text{Water kw} = QH/11.8 \qquad (8\text{-}115)$$

Specific Speed. Specific speed in hydraulic-turbine practice is defined differently than for pumps. Here the head on the site and the power output are so related that specific speed is defined as that at which a unit of suitable diameter of an homologous series would run in order to deliver 1 hp under 1 ft head, or

$$N_s = \text{specific speed} = \frac{\text{rpm} \times \text{shp}^{0.5}}{\text{head}^{1.25}} \qquad (8\text{-}116)$$

Experience data on specific speeds of hydraulic turbines are given in Fig. 8-65.

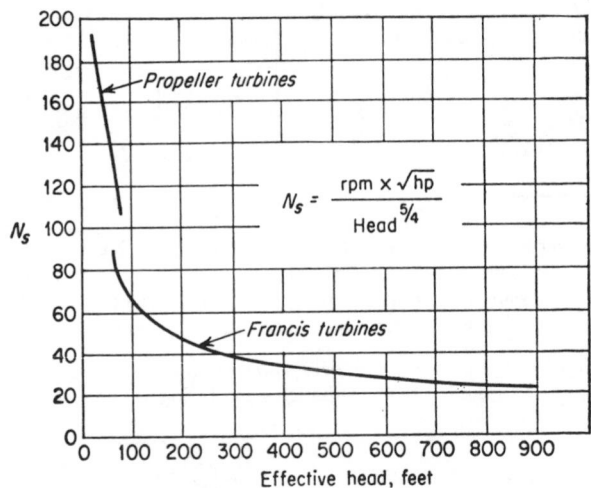

Fig. 8-65. *Source: Kent, "Mechanical Engineers' Handbook—Power," 12th ed., p. 5–30, John Wiley & Sons, Inc., New York, 1950.*

Cavitation. A water wheel must be set with reference to tail-water level at a height that avoids cavitation. A unit must not be designed to operate at lower values of the cavitation coefficient as defined by

$$\sigma = H_b - H_v - H_s/H_e \qquad (8\text{-}117)$$

8-36. Fuels and Combustion

The basic requirements of calculations on fuels and combustion are concerned with evaluation of air needed, the heat of reaction, and analysis of the products of combustion.

Air Requirements. The air requirements are given in Table 8-35 on both gravimetric and volumetric bases. In these and other calculations the air analysis is taken as

Basis	O_2, %	N_2, %
Gravimetric....	23.2	76.8
Volumetric.....	21.0	79.0

N_2 is not entirely chemical nitrogen, but includes all other gases inert to the combustion reaction.

A useful approximate formula for estimating the air requirements for the combustion of coals and oils is

$$\text{Air required, lb/lb fuel} = \frac{\text{higher heating value of fuel, Btu/lb}}{1,300} \quad (8\text{-}118)$$

Heating Value. High or gross heating values of fuels are distinguished from low or net heating values by the condition of the water formed in the products of combustion; if it is condensed to a liquid instead of remaining in the vapor form, the latent heat becomes available. The difference between the high and the low heating values is computed by

$$\text{Difference} = 9H_2(1,090.7 - 0.545t) \quad \text{Btu/lb fuel} \quad (8\text{-}119)$$

where H_2 = weight of hydrogen in fuel, lb/lb

$\quad t$ = temperature of atmosphere, °F

In American practice it is customary to buy fuels, and to guarantee the performance of fuel-burning equipment, on the basis of the high heating value. Heating values are best determined by calorimetric methods, but if such

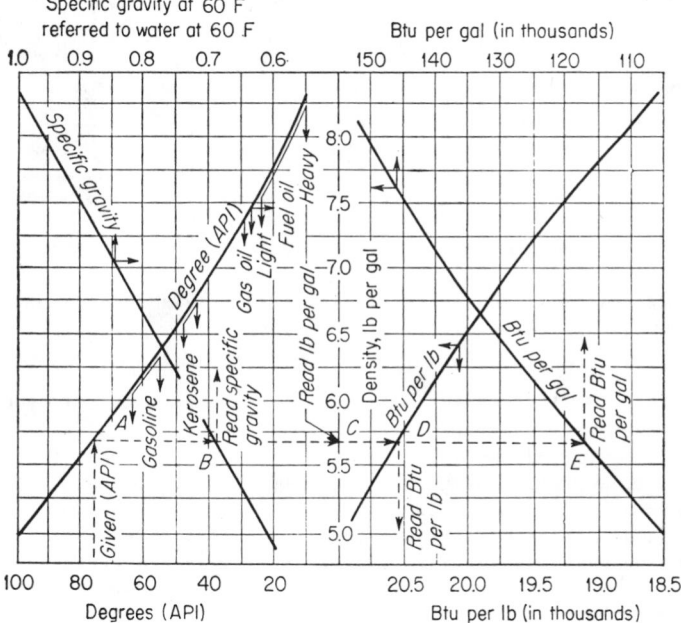

FIG. 8-66. *Source: "Combustion Engineering," p. 25.14, Combustion Engineering, Inc., New York, 1947.*

Table 8-35. Heating Value and the Products of Combustion

Substance	Molecular or atomic wt	Over-all combustion reaction	Heat of combustion*			
			High-heat value		Low-heat value	
			Btu/ lb	Btu/ ft²†	Btu/ lb	Btu/ ft²
1 Graphite............	12.01	$C + O_2 \rightarrow CO_2$	14,087	....	14,087	....
2 Carbon (coal)........	(12.01)	$C + O_2 \rightarrow CO_2$	14,447	....	14,447	....
3 Carbon (coal)........	(12.01)	$C + 0.5O_2 \rightarrow CO$	4,341	....	4,341	....
4 Carbon monoxide.....	28.01	$CO + 0.5O_2 \rightarrow CO_2$	4,344	321	4,344	321
5 Sulfur...............	32.06	$S + O_2 \rightarrow SO_2$	3,980	....	3,980	....
6 Hydrogen...........	2.016	$H_2 + 0.5O_2 \rightarrow H_2O$	60,958	325	51,571	275
7 Hydrogen sulfide......	34.08	$H_2S + 1.5O_2 \rightarrow SO_2 + H_2O$	7,180	639	6,620	589
8 Carbon disulfide......	76.13	$CS_2 + 3O_2 \rightarrow CO_2 + 2SO_2$	12,050	620	12,050	620
9 Ammonia...........	17.03	$2NH_3 + 1.5O_2 \rightarrow N_2 + 3H_2O$	9,668	435	8,001	360
10 Methane............	16.04	$CH_4 + 2O_2 \rightarrow CO_2 + 2H_2O$	23,861	1,011	21,502	911
11 Ethane.............	30.07	$C_2H_6 + 3.5O_2 \rightarrow 2CO_2 + 3H_2O$	22,304	1,772	20,416	1,622
12 Propane............	44.09	$C_3H_8 + 5O_2 \rightarrow 3CO_2 + 4H_2O$	21,646	2,522	19,929	2,322
13 Butane.............	58.12	$C_4H_{10} + 6.5O_2 \rightarrow 4CO_2 + 5H_2O$	21,293	3,270	19,665	3,020
14 Hexane (vapor).......	86.17	$C_6H_{14} + 9.5O_2 \rightarrow 6CO_2 + 7H_2O$	20,928	4,765	19,391	4,414
15 Octane (vapor).......	114.23	$C_8H_{18} + 12.5O_2 \rightarrow 8CO_2 + 9H_2O$	20,747	6,266	19,256	5,812
16 Ethylene............	28.05	$C_2H_4 + 3O_2 \rightarrow 2CO_2 + 2H_2O$	21,625	1,603	20,276	1,503
17 Propylene...........	42.08	$C_3H_6 + 4.5O_2 \rightarrow 3CO_2 + 3H_2O$	21,032	2,338	19,683	2,188
18 Butylene............	56.10	$C_4H_8 + 6O_2 \rightarrow 4CO_2 + 4H_2O$	20,833	3,076	19,484	2,877
19 Acetylene...........	26.04	$C_2H_2 + 2.5O_2 \rightarrow 2CO_2 + H_2O$	21,460	1,473	20,734	1,423
20 Benzene (vapor)......	78.11	$C_6H_6 + 7.5O_2 \rightarrow 6CO_2 + 3H_2O$	18,172	3,745	17,446	3,595
21 Toluene (vapor)......	92.13	$C_7H_8 + 9O_2 \rightarrow 7CO_2 + 4H_2O$	18,422	4,490	17,601	4,285
22 Naphthalene (vapor)..	128.16	$C_{10}H_8 + 12O_2 \rightarrow 10CO_2 + 4H_2O$	17,300	5,854	16,700	5,654
23 Methyl alcohol (vapor)	32.04	$CH_3OH + 1.5O_2 \rightarrow CO_2 + 2H_2O$	10,270	855	9,080	755
24 Ethyl alcohol (vapor)	46.07	$C_2H_5OH + 3O_2 \rightarrow 2CO_2 + 3H_2O$	13,170	1,575	11,930	1,425
25 Lignite‡.............	....	$C_{24}H_{18}O_5 + 28.5O_2 \rightarrow 24CO_2 + 9H_2O$	12,055	....	11,505	....
26 Bituminous coal‡.....	....	$C_{24}H_{20}O_2 + 29.0O_2 \rightarrow 24CO_2 + 10H_2O$	14,550	....	14,055	....
27 Anthracite‡.........	....	$C_{48}H_{18}O + 52O_2 \rightarrow 48CO_2 + 9H_2O$	15,230	....	14,940	....

* Data for heat of combustion for items 1 to 4 and 10 to 21 based on F. D. Rossini et al., Selected Values of Properties of Hydrocarbons, *Natl. Bur. Standards* (*U.S.*) *Circ.* C461, November, 1947. Reactants and products at 25°C (77°F).

† Based upon the standard cubic foot at 60°F and 30 in. Hg of a perfect gas. One lb mole = 379 std ft³.

data are lacking, the high heating value of a coal can be estimated by Dulong's equation

$$\text{Btu/lb} = 14,544C + 62,028(H - O/8) + 4,050S \qquad (8\text{-}120)$$

where C, H, O, and S are the weight percentages of these four elements obtained from the ultimate analysis of the fuel.

The heating values of petroleum and its products can be estimated from the specific gravities, as shown in Fig. 8-66. Combustion data for representative fuels are given in Table 8-35.

Products of Combustion. Flue-gas analyses are made in order to determine the effectiveness of combustion operations and are ordinarily given on the dry, volumetric basis. If the nitrogen content of the fuel is small, then the excess air can be computed from

$$\text{Excess air} = \frac{3.78(O_2 - CO/2)}{N_2 - 3.78(O_2 - CO/2) \times 100} \qquad \text{per cent} \quad (8\text{-}121)$$

of Various Solid, Liquid, and Gaseous Fuels

							Combustion with theoretical amount of air										
Lb/lb							Ft³/ft³							Lb air/ 1,000 Btu		CO₂, % by vol (dry basis)	
Required		Products of combustion					Required		Products of combustion								
O₂	Air	N₂	CO₂	H₂O	SO₂	Total	O₂	Air	N₂	CO₂	H₂O	SO₂	Total	Lhv	Hhv		
2.67	11.50	8.83	3.67	....	....	12.50	....	....	....	....	....	....	....	0.82	0.82	21.0	1
2.67	11.50	8.83	3.67	....	....	12.50	....	....	....	....	....	....	....	0.80	0.80	21.0	2
1.33	5.73	4.40	2.33§	....	....	6.73	....	....	....	....	....	....	....	....	....	....	3
0.57	2.46	1.89	1.57	....	....	3.46	0.50	2.38	1.88	1.00	....	....	2.88	0.57	0.57	34.6	4
1.00	4.31	3.31	....	....	2.00	5.31	....	....	....	....	....	....	....	1.08	1.08	....	5
7.94	34.34	26.40	....	8.98	....	35.38	0.50	2.38	1.88	....	1.00	....	2.88	0.67	0.56	....	6
1.41	6.10	4.69	....	0.53	1.88	7.10	1.50	7.14	5.64	....	1.00	1.00	7.64	.92	.85	....	7
1.26	5.44	4.18	0.58	....	1.68	6.44	3.00	14.28	11.28	1.00	....	2.00	14.28	.45	.45	21.0¶	8
1.41	6.08	5.49	....	....	1.59	7.08	0.75	3.57	3.32	....	1.50	....	4.82	.76	.63	....	9
4.00	17.27	13.27	2.74	2.25	....	18.26	2.00	9.52	7.52	1.00	2.00	....	10.52	.80	.72	11.7	10
3.73	16.12	12.39	2.92	1.80	....	17.11	3.50	16.65	13.15	2.00	3.00	....	18.15	.79	.72	13.2	11
3.64	15.70	12.06	2.99	1.64	....	16.69	5.00	23.80	18.80	3.00	4.00	....	25.80	.79	.72	13.8	12
3.58	15.44	11.86	3.03	1.56	....	16.45	6.50	30.90	24.40	4.00	5.00	....	33.40	.79	.72	14.1	13
3.53	15.21	11.68	3.07	1.46	....	16.21	9.50	45.20	35.70	6.00	7.00	....	48.70	.79	.78	14.4	14
3.50	15.10	11.60	3.08	1.42	....	16.10	12.50	59.50	47.00	8.00	9.00	....	64.00	.78	.78	14.5	15
3.42	14.75	11.33	3.14	1.29	....	15.76	3.00	14.28	11.28	2.00	2.00	....	15.28	.73	.68	15.1	16
3.42	14.75	11.33	3.14	1.29	....	15.76	4.50	21.40	16.90	3.00	3.00	....	22.90	.74	.70	15.1	17
3.42	14.75	11.33	3.14	1.29	....	15.76	6.00	28.55	22.55	4.00	4.00	....	30.55	.76	.71	15.1	18
3.07	13.23	10.16	3.38	0.69	....	14.23	2.50	11.90	9.40	2.00	1.00	....	12.40	.64	.62	17.5	19
3.07	13.23	10.16	3.38	0.69	....	14.23	7.50	35.70	28.20	6.00	3.00	....	37.20	.76	.73	17.5	20
3.13	13.50	10.35	3.35	0.78	....	14.48	9.00	42.80	33.80	7.00	4.00	....	44.80	.77	.73	17.2	21
3.00	12.93	9.93	3.14	0.56	....	13.93	12.00	57.10	45.10	10.00	4.00	....	59.10	.77	.75	18.1	22
1.60	6.90	5.30	1.37	1.13	....	7.80	1.50	7.14	5.64	1.00	2.00	....	8.64	.76	.67	15.1	23
2.08	8.96	6.89	1.91	1.17	....	9.96	3.00	14.28	11.28	2.00	3.00	....	16.28	.75	.68	15.1	24
2.14	9.22	7.08	2.71	0.43	....	10.22	....	....	....	....	....	....	....	.80	.76	19.5	25
2.60	11.21	8.60	3.08	0.52	....	12.21	....	....	....	....	....	....	....	.80	.77	18.6	26
2.74	11.83	9.08	3.46	0.28	....	12.83	....	....	....	....	....	....	....	.79	.78	19.5	27

‡ Computed from average moisture- and ash-free ultimate analysis of 17 lignites, 27 medium and high-volatile coals, and 5 anthracite coals in the United States. The formulas for lignite, bituminous, and lignitic coals, given in the third column, do not represent the true constitution of the coal molecule, which is much more complex, but are adequate for stoichiometric calculations.

¶ $CO_2 + SO_2$. § CO.

SOURCE: Kent, "Mechanical Engineers' Handbook Power," 12th ed., pp. 2–04, 2–05, John Wiley & Sons, Inc. New York, 1950.

where O_2, N_2, and CO are percentages by volume obtained from the flue-gas analysis. Some customary excess-air values are given in Table 8-36.

8-37. Power-plant Performance Factors

Heat rate is defined for the over-all thermal performance as

$$\text{Heat rate, Btu/kwhr} = \frac{\text{heat supplied in fuel for period, Btu}}{\text{energy output for period, kwhr}} \quad (8\text{-}122)$$

$$\text{Thermal eff, \%} = \frac{3{,}412.75}{\text{heat rate}} \times 100 \quad (8\text{-}123)$$

$$\text{Capacity factor, \%} = \frac{\text{average load for period, kw}}{\text{rated capacity, kw}} \times 100 \quad (8\text{-}124)$$

$$\text{Load factor, \%} = \frac{\text{average load for period, kw}}{\text{peak load during period, kw}} \times 100 \quad (8\text{-}125)$$

Table 8-36. Excess Air at Furnace Outlet

Fuel	Excess air, %	Fuel	Excess air, %
Coal................	10–40	Natural gas........	5–10
Coke...............	20–40	Refinery gas.......	8–15
Wood..............	25–50	Blast-furnace gas...	15–25
Bagasse...........	25–45	Coke-oven gas......	5–10
Oil................	8–15		

SOURCE: "Combustion Engineering," 1st ed., 1947, p. 10.3, Combustion Engineering, Inc., New York, N. Y.

8-38. Boiler Performance

Nomenclature

h_{steam} = enthalpy leaving boiler unit (superheater outlet), Btu/lb

$h_{feed\ water}$ = enthalpy of feed water entering boiler unit (economizer inlet), Btu/lb

W_m = moisture content of fuel, lb/lb

t_{fuel} = fuel temperature, °F

t_{fg} = flue-gas temperature, °F

H_2 = lb hydrogen/lb fuel, from ultimate analysis

W_{da} = weight dry air supplied, lb/lb fuel

W_w = weight water vapor/lb dry air

t_a = ambient temperature or temperature of air entering air heater, °F

W_{dg} = weight dry flue gases, lb/lb fuel

C = lb carbon/lb fuel, from ultimate analysis

CO = CO in flue gas, dry volumetric basis, per cent

CO_2 = CO₂ in flue gas, dry volumetric basis, per cent

refuse = lb refuse/lb fuel, as burned in boiler furnace

ash = lb ash/lb fuel, from ultimate analysis

Heat Added to Steam

$$\Delta Q = h_{steam} - h_{feed\ water} \qquad Btu/lb \qquad (8\text{-}126)$$

With a resuperheater, the heat added as reheat must be included and

$$h_{reheat} = h_{leaving\ reheater} - h_{entering\ reheater} \qquad (8\text{-}127)$$

Boiler Rating and Steam Output. Older procedures used the term "developed boiler horsepower" to measure the output of the boiler, or the heat added to the steam, defining it as the evaporation of 34.5 lb water from and at 212°F. Thus,

$$\text{Developed boiler hp} = 34.5 \times 970.4 = 33,479\ Btu/hr \qquad (8\text{-}128)$$

The rated boiler horsepower was defined as

$$\text{Rated boiler hp} = 10\ ft^2\ \text{heating surface} \qquad (8\text{-}129)$$

Thus, $$\text{Per cent rating} = \frac{\text{developed boiler hp}}{\text{rated boiler hp}} \times 100 \qquad (8\text{-}130)$$

Factor of Evaporation, F.E.

$$\text{F.E.} = \frac{\text{actual heat absorbed in converting water to steam}}{\text{latent heat of steam from and at 212°F}}$$

$$= (h_{\text{steam}} - h_{\text{feed water}})/970.4 \qquad (8\text{-}131)$$

Evaporation

$$\begin{array}{l}\text{Actual evaporation, A.E.,} \\ \text{lb steam/lb fuel}\end{array} = \frac{\text{lb steam made during period}}{\text{lb fuel fired during period}} \quad (8\text{-}132)$$

$$\begin{array}{l}\text{Equivalent evaporation, E.E., lb} \\ \text{steam/lb fuel, from and at 212°F}\end{array} = \begin{array}{l}\text{actual evaporation} \\ \times \text{factor of evaporation}\end{array}$$
$$= \text{A.E.} \times \text{F.E.} \qquad (8\text{-}133)$$

Boiler Efficiency

$$\text{Boiler eff} = \frac{\text{heat added to steam over period, Btu}}{\text{heat supplied in fuel over period, Btu}} \qquad (8\text{-}134)$$

In American practice the heat supplied in the fuel is the high or gross heating value on the "as fired basis."

Heat Balance and Losses. By the first law of thermodynamics it is possible to account for all the heat supplied in the fuel by adding all the losses to the heat supplied to the steam.

Loss due to moisture in fuel $= W_m(1,090.7 - t_{\text{fuel}} + 0.455t_{fg})$

Btu/lb fuel (8-135)

Loss due to hydrogen burning to water vapor instead of liquid
$$= 9 \times \text{H}_2(1,090.7 - t_{\text{fuel}} + 0.455t_{fg}) \qquad \text{Btu/lb fuel} \quad (8\text{-}136)$$
Loss due to moisture in air $= W_{da} \times W_w \times 0.47(t_{fg} - t_a)$

Btu/lb fuel (8-137)

Loss due to dry stack gases $= 0.24W_{dg}(t_{fg} - t_a)$ Btu/lb fuel (8-138)
Loss due to incomplete combustion of carbon
$$= 10,160(\text{C} \times \text{CO})/(\text{CO}_2 + \text{CO}) \qquad \text{Btu/lb fuel} \quad (8\text{-}139)$$
Loss due to combustible in refuse $= 14,600(\text{refuse} - \text{ash})$

Btu/lb fuel (8-140)

Loss due to radiation and unaccounted for, Btu/lb fuel
$$= \text{heating value of fuel} - \text{sum of Eqs. (8-135) to (8-140)} \quad (8\text{-}141)$$

8-39. Refrigeration

Nomenclature

h = enthalpy from refrigerant tables, Btu/lb

$\bar{v}_2$ = specific volume of refrigerant at compressor suction pressure ft³/lb

sp gr = specific gravity of coolant

Δt = temperature rise of coolant, °F

The vapor-compression refrigeration cycle is represented on the T-S diagram, Fig. 8-67, where 1-2 is the evaporative phase in the refrigerating coil, 2-3 is the isentropic-compression phase, 3-4-5-6 is the condensation phase in

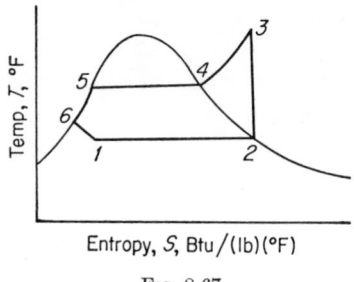

Fɪɢ. 8-67

the condenser, and 6-1 is the constant-enthalpy phase in the expansion valve. For evaporating coils

$$\text{Refrigerating effect} = h_2 - h_1 = h_2 - h_6 \qquad \text{Btu/lb}$$

For compressor, the ideal work of the Rankine cycle is

$$\text{Rankine cycle work} = h_3 - h_2 \qquad \text{Btu/lb}$$

For the condenser

$$\text{Heat removed} = h_3 - h_6 \qquad \text{Btu/lb}$$

At the expansion valve, $h_6 = h_1$. These equations can be modified to tonnage units by including the definition of the ton as the removal of heat in the evaporating coils at a rate of 200 Btu/min, 12,000 Btu/hr, or 288,000 Btu/day.

$$\text{Refrigerant weight required} = 200/(h_2 - h_1) \qquad \text{lb/(min)(ton)} \qquad \text{(8-142)}$$
$$\text{Refrigerant volume required} = [200/(h_2 - h_1)]v_2 \qquad \text{ft}^3/\text{(min)(ton)} \qquad \text{(8-143)}$$

$$\text{Condenser coolant required} = \left[\frac{200}{h_2 - h_1}\right]\left[\frac{h_3 - h_6}{\text{sp gr} \times \Delta T}\right] \qquad \text{lb/(min)(ton)}$$
$$\text{(8-144)}$$

$$\text{Power required based on Rankine cycle} = 42.42[200/(h_2 - h_1)](h_2 - h_2)$$
$$\text{hp/ton} \qquad \text{(8-145)}$$

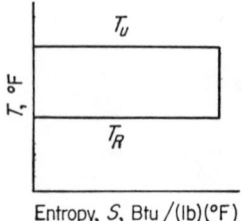

Fɪɢ. 8-68

Coefficient of Performance C.O.P.

$$\text{C.O.P.} = \frac{\text{refrigeration}}{\text{work done}} = \frac{h_2 - h_1}{h_3 - h_2} \qquad \text{as cooling machine} \qquad (8\text{-}146)$$

$$\text{C.O.P.} = \frac{\text{heat delivered to condenser}}{\text{work done}} = \frac{h_3 - h_6}{h_3 - h_2} \qquad \text{as warming machine}$$

$$(8\text{-}147)$$

The maximum value of C.O.P. is given by the Carnot cycle (Fig. 8-68), where the absolute temperatures of the refrigerating coil T_R and the condensing coil T_H prevail instead of enthalpy, since the C.O.P. is independent of the properties of the refrigerant used.

$$\text{C.O.P.} = T_R/(T_H - T_R) \qquad \text{as cooling machine} \qquad (8\text{-}148)$$
$$\text{C.O.P.} = T_H/(T_H - T_R) \qquad \text{as warming machine} \qquad (8\text{-}149)$$

To facilitate calculations on refrigeration cycles it is necessary to have tables and charts showing the thermodynamic properties of the refrigerants. Representative data for several common refrigerants are shown in Fig. 8-69.

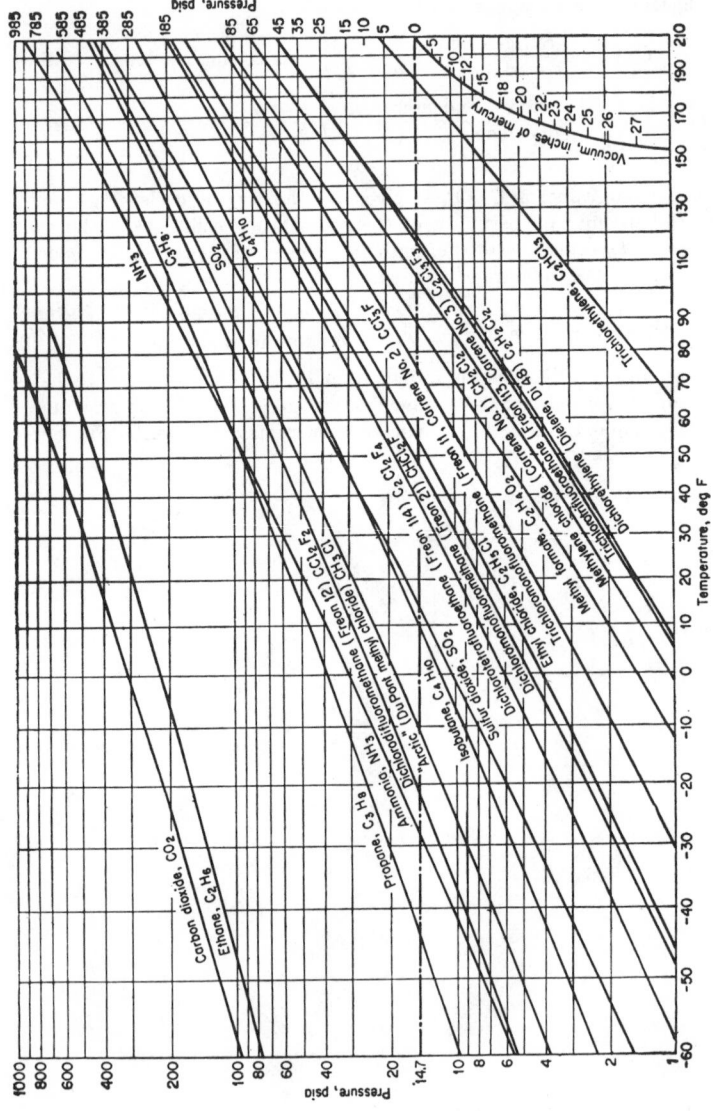

FIG. 8-69. Properties of common refrigerants. *Source: Electrochemicals Department, E. I. du Pont de Nemours & Company, Inc., Wilmington, Delaware.*

8–80

SECTION 9

NUCLEAR ENGINEERING

John W. Bartlett, Ph.D.; Assistant Professor of Chemical and Nuclear Engineering, University of Rochester; Member, American Institute of Chemical Engineers, American Nuclear Society, American Society for Engineering Education, American Association for the Advancement of Science

Stuart McLain, Ph.D.; Professor of Nuclear Engineering, Purdue University; President, McLain Associates, Inc., California Nuclear, Inc., Indiana Research and Development, Inc.; Member, American Nuclear Society, American Society for Engineering Education

Owen H. Gailar, Ph.D.; Associate Professor of Nuclear Engineering, Purdue University; Member, American Nuclear Society

CONTENTS

INTRODUCTION

Nuclear engineering is the utilization of nuclear reactions, particles, and radiations for the benefit of mankind. It is a truly interdisciplinary field that requires application of fundamental principles from many branches of science and engineering to produce an operable nuclear system.

Nuclear systems are of many types. Among the first of these was the atomic bomb, in which principles of nuclear fission were applied—with other engineering principles—to produce an explosive, uncontrolled nuclear fission reaction. In subsequent years, these same nuclear principles have been used, again in conjunction with other engineering effort, in a variety of systems characterized by controlled release of nuclear fission energy.

The major application of controlled fission and nuclear engineering thus far has been production of power for naval propulsion and electric generating stations. In addition, nuclear engineering has come to be an essential part of many diverse fields, such as pasteurization, sterilization, food production, medicine, production and application of radioisotopes, chemical processing, recovery of irradiated nuclear fuels, and disposal or dispersal of radioactive wastes. The prominent nuclear features in each of these areas may differ widely (e.g., use of gamma-ray irradiation to preserve food and use of neutron absorption reactions to produce radioactive isotopes), but all fall within the province of nuclear engineering as it is currently understood.

The emphasis here is placed on principles of nuclear engineering which are fundamental to the design of power-producing systems that are fueled with fissionable materials. In such systems nuclear engineering is involved in designing the fuel-bearing region (known as the *core*), the core-containment vessel, auxiliary systems and components, and shielding. The core and its associated equipment in a nuclear power plant basically replaces the boiler in a conventional system. Components and their design in other portions of the system remain essentially unchanged, and hence are not discussed here.

Core-configuration details are not given because many designs are possible and have been used. Treatment of theoretical development and design methodology is also restricted by space limitations; more details may be found in the literature. Representative references listed at the end of this section are cited for each subject heading.

Requirements for nuclear fission as a source of power deserve brief mention. Projections of the world's power needs in the future indicate that nuclear fission plants will soon be essential. It is significant, however, that today, only eight years after the first nuclear power station in the United States began operation (Shippingport, Pa., in December, 1957), use of nuclear power is already economically justified in many parts of this country and the world.

In the United States, this success has evolved from initial Federal government sponsorship of development and ownership of fuel to the present spectrum of effort in which Federal agencies support development of advanced concepts but many private corporations have the capacity to contract profitably for design and construction of nuclear systems of various types. Simultaneously, responsibility for regulation of nuclear materials and installations has begun to shift, with impetus provided by Washington, from Federal to state control. Thus, although the era of nuclear power is still in its infancy, much progress has already been made toward making it a self-sufficient industry.

9-1. Atomic Structure and Nuclear Particles [1-4]*

Nuclear engineering requires knowledge and manipulation of atoms and the particles that comprise them. An atom is composed of a dense nucleus surrounded by electrons arranged in various orbits. The atom is mostly free space; the atomic radius is on the order of 10^{-8} cm, and the radius of the nucleus is 10^{-12} to 10^{-13} cm.

Ordinary chemical reactions involve changes in the orbital electrons of the atom; nuclear reactions such as fission involve the nucleus. There are great differences in the energy involved in these two types of reactions. For example, the combustion reaction (oxidation of carbon to CO_2) releases 4.1 electron volts (ev) of energy; in contrast, fission of a uranium atom releases approximately 2×10^8 ev (i.e., 200 Mev) of energy.

The physicists have demonstrated that nuclei are composed of many fundamental particles. Relatively few of these particles are, however, of interest in nuclear reactors. These include the neutron and proton (the major constituents of the nucleus, also called nucleons), the electron, and the gamma ray. Gamma rays are high-energy electromagnetic radiation originating in the nucleus; they have neither mass nor charge. Electrons are of low mass [approximately 5.49×10^{-4} atomic mass units (amu), where one amu = 1.66×10^{-24} g on the physical mass scale] and may have either a positive or negative charge. The positively charged electron is called a positron.

The proton has a mass of 1.00759 amu and is positively charged; the neutron is electrically neutral and has a mass of 1.00898 amu. The sum of the number of protons and neutrons in a nucleus defines the mass of an atom; the number of protons defines the atomic number, and therefore the specific element in the periodic table. Individual atoms may possess the same number of protons but different numbers of neutrons (called *isotopes* of a given element) or they may be of the same mass but different charge (*isobars*). Complete designation of an atom therefore requires definition of charge or element and mass. To illustrate the symbolism used, consider uranium, which has an atomic number of 92. The isotope of uranium which has a mass of 238 amu would be designated $_{92}U^{238}$, U^{238}, U 238, or uranium 238.

* Superior numbers correspond to citations in the References given at the end of Sec. 9.

Physicists are still engaged in unraveling the mystery of the structure of the nucleus. The most important aspect of this mystery, from a practical point of view, is that the nucleus, composed of positively charged particles with large repulsive forces between them, manages to be held together as a dense-packed mass. Clearly, a "nuclear glue" characterized by large attractive forces is required. Details of this nuclear glue are not understood. It is characterized, however, by the "binding energy." Experiments have shown that the actual mass of a nucleus is less than the sum of the masses of the constituent nucleons; the binding energy can be shown to correspond to this mass defect.

The binding energy per nucleon is a measure of the stability of a nucleus. When the binding energy per nucleon is high, the nucleus is most stable. Figure 9-1 illustrates the variation of binding energy per nucleon as a function

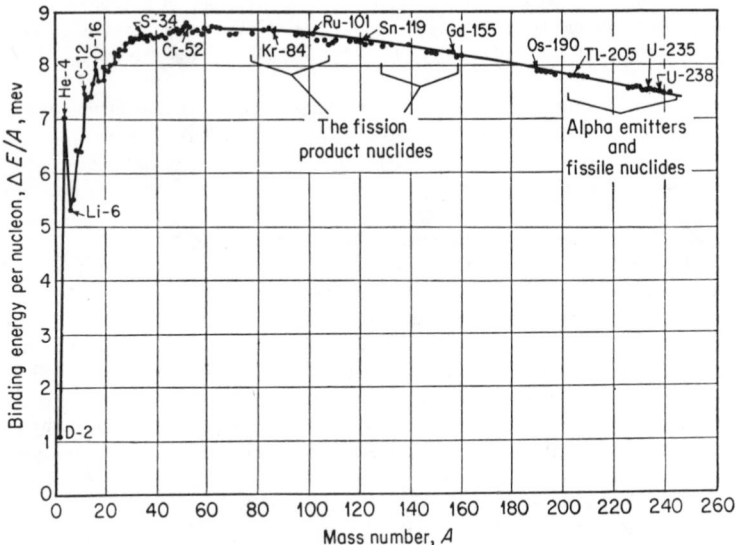

FIG. 9-1. Binding energy per nucleon for stable nuclei. (*After Glasstone and Edlund, "Elements of Reactor Theory," D. Van Nostrand Company, Inc., Princeton, N. J.*, 1952.)

of atomic mass. It can be shown that energy must be released when nuclei of low binding energy per nucleon are converted to nuclei of high binding energy per nucleon. Hence, from Fig. 9-1, combination of light nuclei (fusion) or splitting of heavy nuclei (fission) should release energy.

9-2. Radioactivity [1-10]

A radioactive nucleus contains energy in excess of that characteristic of a stable configuration. To achieve stability, the nucleus must emit the excess energy: the process is called radioactive decay. The energy emission may involve release of a nuclear particle or one or more gamma rays, or both. Several basic modes of decay have been identified, and are discussed below.

The time interval between formation and decay of a single radioactive isotope cannot be predicted. It has been observed, however, that a large number of radioactive isotopes of a given kind will decay at a fixed rate characterized by a quantity known as the decay constant λ. The rate of decay, or alternatively, disintegration, is related to the decay constant by

$$dN/dt = -\lambda N \qquad (9\text{-}1)$$

where N is the number of radioactive atoms present at time t. The units of λ are $(\text{time})^{-1}$. If at time $t = 0$ there were N_0 radioactive atoms present, Eq. (9-1) gives

$$N = N_0 e^{-\lambda t} \qquad (9\text{-}2a)$$

or

$$\ln N/N_0 = -\lambda t \qquad (9\text{-}2b)$$

which shows that λ may be determined as the slope of the straight line obtained with a semilogarithmic plot of disintegration rate vs. time.

Values of λ can be determined only by experiment, and show great variation. It is frequently more convenient to report the half-life $T_{\frac{1}{2}}$, which is defined as the time for the number of radioactive atoms present to decrease by a factor of 2, and may be derived from Eq. (9-2b) in terms of λ as

$$T_{\frac{1}{2}} = \ln (2)/\lambda = 0.693/\lambda \qquad (9\text{-}2c)$$

Measured values of the half-life range from 10^{-7} to 10^{10} years.

Many radioactive nuclides have been identified. Some are naturally occurring, but most have been man-made by bombarding stable nuclei with high-energy particles. Nearly all naturally occurring radioisotopes have mass numbers greater than 80. Man-made isotopes, however, cover the entire spectrum of elements, and many are commercially available.

The quantity λN is known as the disintegration rate, or *activity*. The basic unit of activity is the curie, defined as 3.7×10^{10} disintegrations per second (dis/sec). One curie corresponds approximately to the activity of one gram of radium and is a large amount of activity. More frequently encountered amounts are the millicurie, 3.7×10^7 dis/sec, and the microcurie, 3.7×10^4 dis/sec.

9-3. Modes of Radioactive Decay [1–11]

Two major modes of radioactive decay—alpha-particle emission and beta-particle emission—are of present interest. Decay by emission of beta particles (electrons) characterizes most useful radioisotopes; many of the naturally occurring radioactive nuclides, however, decay by alpha-particle emission. Both modes of decay frequently also involve gamma-ray emission. For nuclear engineering purposes, the properties of the particles and radiations emitted during radioactive decay are of major interest since they govern shielding and personnel-protection requirements.

Alpha Decay. The alpha particle is the nucleus of a helium atom. It is composed of two neutrons and two protons and therefore carries two positive charges. For practical purposes, the initial energy of all alpha particles emitted from a given kind of radioactive nuclide may be assumed to be constant; initial alpha-particle energies range from about 3 to 10 Mev.

Because of their large mass and charge, alpha particles rapidly lose their kinetic energy when passing through a medium by causing ionization of that medium. After sufficient energy has been lost, the slowly moving alpha particle picks up two electrons and becomes a helium atom.

The range of alpha particles from a given source in a given medium is constant since initial energies are essentially constant. This range is not great (approximately 1 in., in air, for a 4-Mev alpha particle) because of the rapid loss of energy by ionization. The range of alpha particles is inversely proportional to the density of the medium; most alpha particles are stopped by a sheet of paper and will not penetrate human skin. Hence alpha particles are not in general a serious external hazard to humans. When ingested into the body, however, they do considerable damage to tissue because of their great ionizing power.

Beta Decay. When a beta particle is emitted from the nucleus during radioactive decay, the transformation in the nucleus may be described by the relation

$$_0N^1 \rightarrow {}_1H^1 + \beta^- + \nu \tag{9-3}$$

i.e., a neutron is converted to a proton, the beta particle, and a neutrino, designated by ν. (The neutrino has never been identified experimentally, but its existence and properties can be demonstrated theoretically.) From Eq. (9-3) it may be inferred that, although little change in total mass of the nucleus has occurred, the mass number of the nucleus has increased by one. Thus the atom is transformed to a different element by beta decay.

The neutrinos carry off different amounts of energy for each transformation, and hence the beta particles from a given radionuclide are found to have a continuous spectrum of energies, terminating in a definite maximum energy E_0. Values of E_0 are of interest for shielding purposes, and it is these values that are tabulated in the literature.

Other modes of beta-particle decay, such as electron capture and positron emission, occur. These are relatively infrequent, however, and are not discussed here.

Because of their low mass and charge, beta particles have much larger ranges than alpha particles (for example, the range of 3 Mev beta particles in air is about 43 ft), although they interact with materials in essentially the same way. In addition, ranges for beta particles are not clearly defined because of secondary interactions with the medium. It is possible, however, to specify the thickness of a given material required to reduce ionization by beta particles nearly to zero. As a first approximation, the thickness required may be assumed to be inversely proportional to the density of the medium.

Gamma Rays. As previously noted, radioactive decay frequently involves

Table 9-1. Common Radioisotopes

Radio-nuclide	Half-life	Beta particle, Mev	Gamma ray, Mev
H^3	12 years	0.018	None
Li^8	0.9 sec	12	Weak
Be^7	54.5 days	K capture	0.48 (12%)
Be^{10}	2.5×10^6 years	0.56	None
B^{12}	0.03 sec	13	Weak
C^{14}	5,800 years	0.155	None
N^{13}	10 min	1.24 (e^+)	None
N^{16}	7.35 sec	10 (18%), 3.8–4.6 (82%)	6.2
O^{15}	2 min	1.68 (e^+)	None
O^{19}	29.4 sec	2.9 (70%), 4.5 (30%)	1.6 (70%)
F^{20}	12 sec	5.1	2.2
Na^{22}	2.8 years	0.575 (e^+)	1.28
Na^{24}	15 hr	1.39	2.76 and 1.38
Mg^{27}	9.6 min	1.8 (80%), 0.9 (20%)	1.01 (20%), 0.84 (100%)
Al^{28}	2.3 min	3.01	1.8
Si^{31}	2.7 hr	1.6	None
P^{32}	14.3 days	1.71	None
S^{35}	87 days	0.167	None
Cl^{36}	4×10^5 years	0.7	Weak
Cl^{38}	38 min	4.81 (53%), 2.77 (16%), 1.11(31%)	1.6 (31%), **2.15 (47%)**
A^{37}	34 days	K capture, L capture	None
A^{41}	1.8 hr	1.2	1.3
K^{42}	12.4 hr	3.58 (75%), 2.04 (25%)	1.51 (25%)
Ca^{45}	152 days	0.25	None
Sc^{46}	85 days	1.49 (2%), 0.36 (98%)	1.12 (98%), 0.89 (100%)
V^{52}	3.9 min	2.3	1.45
Cr^{51}	26.5 days	K capture	0.32 (3%), 0.267 (weak)
Mn^{54}	310 days	K capture	0.84
Mn^{56}	2.6 hr	2.86 (60%), 1.05 (25%), 0.73 (15%)	0.845, 1.81 (25%), 2.13 (15%)
Fe^{55}	2.9 years	K capture	None
Fe^{59}	47 days	0.46 (50%), 0.26 (50%)	1.3 (50%), 1.1 (50%)
Co^{57}	270 days	0.26 (e^+)	0.131
Co^{60}	5.3 years	0.31	1.17 and 1.33
Ni^{63}	85 years	0.06	None
Cu^{64}	12.9 hr	0.57 (35%), 0.65 (e^+ 20%), K capture (45%)	1.34 (1%)
Cu^{66}	4.3 min	2.7	1.32
Zn^{65}	250 days	0.32 (3% e^+), K capture (97%)	1.11 (46%)
Zn^{69}	14 hr	IT*	0.439
Ga^{72}	14 hr	3.17 max (see charts)	2.5 max (see charts)
As^{76}	27 hr	3.12 max (see charts)	2.1 max (see charts)

Table 9-1. Common Radioisotopes (Continued)

Radio-nuclide	Half-life	Beta particle, Mev	Gamma ray, Mev
As^{77}	40 hr	0.7	None
Se^{75}	115 days	K capture	0.405 max (see charts)
Br^{82}	36 hr	0.465	0.547, 0.787, 1.35
Br^{87}	55.6 sec	2 (55%), 8 (45%), delayed neutrons	3
Rb^{86}	19.5 days	1.82 (80%), 0.72 (20%)	1.1 (20%)
Sr^{89}	53 days	1.5	None
Y^{90}	61 hr	2.2	None
Zr^{95}	65 days	0.887 (2%), 0.4 (98%)	0.708 (98%)
Nb^{95}	35 days	0.146	0.758
Mo^{99}	67 hr	1.2 (75%), 0.5 (25%)	0.141, 0.726
Tc^{99}	3×10^5 years	0.30	None
Ru^{97}	2.8 days	K capture	0.23
Ru^{103}	42 days	0.35 (50%), 0.665 (50%)	0.5 (50%)
Pd^{109}	13 hr	0.95	None
Ag^{110}	270 days	2.86 max (see charts)	1.5 max (see charts)
Ag^{111}	7.5 days	1.06	None
Cd^{115}	43 days	1.67	0.5
In^{114}	50 days	IT,* 2.05 (97%), K capture (3%)	0.192, 0.715 (3%), 0.548 (3%)
Sn^{113}	112 days	K capture	0.09
Sb^{124}	60 days	2.37 max (see charts)	2.3 max (see charts)
I^{131}	8 days	0.60 (85%), 0.32 (15%)	0.638 (15%), 0.364 (85%)
I^{135}	6.7 hr	0.47 (35%), 1.0 (40%), 1.4 (25%)	1.3, 1.7
I^{137}	22 sec	Delayed neutrons	
Xe^{135}	9.2 hr	0.93	0.247
Cs^{134}	2.3 years	0.658 (74%), 0.09 (26%)	0.794, 0.602, 0.568 (26%)
Cs^{137}	37 years	1.2 (5%), 0.51 (95%)	0.669 (from 2.6-min Ba^{137})
Ba^{131}	12 days	K capture	0.26, 0.5 (strong)
Ba^{140}	12.8 days	1.022 (60%), 0.48 (40%)	0.54 (40%)
La^{140}	40 hr	2.26 (10%), 1.67 (20%), 1.32 (70%)	2.5 (6%), 1.6 (77%), other low-energy gammas
Ce^{141}	28 days	0.56 (30%), 0.41 (70%)	0.141 (70%)
Ce^{144}	275 days	0.32	0.13 (strong)
Pr^{142}	19 hr	2.15 (96%), 0.64 (4%)	1.57 (4%)
Pr^{143}	13.8 days	0.92	None
Nd^{147}	11 days	0.78 (67%), 0.17 (33%)	0.035 (strong), 0.58 (weak)
Pm^{147}	2.7 years	0.23	None

Table 9-1. Common Radioisotopes (Continued)

Radio-nuclide	Half-life	Beta particle, Mev	Gamma ray, Mev
Sm^{153}	47 hr	0.8 (33%), 0.68 (67%)	0.10, 0.07
Hf^{181}	46 days	0.42	0.34 (22%), 0.48 (78%)
Ta^{182}	122 days	0.50	1.2 max, many others
W^{185}	77 days	0.43	0.134
W^{187}	25 hr	1.32 (30%), 0.63 (70%)	0.68 max, others
Re^{186}	90 hr	1.09 (67%), 0.95 (30%)	0.132 (37%), 0.275 (23%)
Os^{191}	15 days	0.14	0.13, 0.04
Ir^{192}	70 days	0.67	0.65 max, many others
Au^{198}	2.7 days	0.97	0.411
Hg^{197}	2.7 days	K capture	0.077
Hg^{203}	44 days	0.205	0.286
Tl^{204}	2.7 years	0.78	None
Pb^{210}	22 years	0.028	Soft
Bi^{210}	5 days	1.17	None
Po^{210}	138 days	4.95 (alpha)	None
Rn^{222}	3.82 days	5.49 (alpha)	None
Ra^{226}	1,620 years	4.7 (alpha)	0.188
Th^{232}	1.39×10^{10} years	4.1 (alpha)	None
Th^{233}	23.5 min	1.2	None
Th^{234}	24.1 days	0.205 (80%), 0.11 (20%)	0.093 (20%)
Pa^{233}	27.4 days	0.58 (max (see charts)	0.471 max (see charts)
Pa^{234}	1.2 min	2.32 (98%), also IT*	See charts
U^{233}	1.6×10^5 years	4.82 (alpha)	0.04
U^{234}	2.5×10^5 years	4.76 (alpha)	Weak
U^{235}	8.8×10^8 years	4.5 (alpha)	0.17
U^{236}	2.5×10^7 years	4.5 (alpha)	None
U^{238}	4.5×10^9 years	4.18 (alpha)	None
U^{239}	23.5 min	1.2	0.074
U^{240}	14 hr		
Np^{239}	2.3 days	See charts	See charts
Pu^{239}	2.4×10^4 years	5.15 (alpha)	Weak
Pu^{240}	6,600 years	5.1 (alpha)	None

* IT refers to isomeric transitions.
NOTE: "Charts" refers to more complete descriptions such as found in Nuclear Data, *Natl. Bur. Standards* (*U.S.*) *Circ.* 499; also, R. W. King, *Revs. Modern Phys.*, 26: 327 (1954).
SOURCE: R. Stephenson, "Introduction to Nuclear Engineering," p. 372, McGraw-Hill Series in Chemical Engineering, McGraw-Hill Book Company, Inc., New York, 1954.

gamma-ray emission. These gamma rays are of great concern because their high energy and great penetrating power make them difficult to stop by shielding. Gamma rays interact with materials by several processes (described in Sec. 9-18); they also produce ionization, but indirectly.

All disintegrations of a given kind of radioisotope do not always produce the same gamma rays. In other words, although the initial radionuclide and the decay, or "daughter," nucleus may be the same, various decay schemes and various gamma rays may be involved. It is important, again for shielding purposes, that the frequency of each mode of decay, and the gamma rays associated with each, be identified. This is done experimentally, and the data are tabulated in the literature.[11] Properties of some of the more important radioisotopes are summarized in Table 9-1.

9-4. Nuclear Reactions [4-10,12,13]

Many kinds of reactions of incident particles and radiations with an atomic nucleus are possible. Relatively few, however, are of concern in nuclear reactors. The most important are those in which the neutron is the incident particle; fission is an example of these.

Nuclear reactions are of two basic types: scattering reactions, in which the identity of the incident particle is preserved, and absorption reactions, in which the incident particle is absorbed by the nucleus to form a new, highly excited compound nucleus. In absorption reactions the identity of the incident particle is lost; when the excited nucleus loses its energy, new reaction products are formed. In all nuclear reactions, total energy must be conserved either as mass or energy. The equivalence of mass and energy is given by the famous Einstein relation $E = mc^2$, where E is the energy equivalent of the mass m, and c is the velocity of light.

A shorthand notation is widely used to describe absorption reactions. Consider as an example the reaction

$$_0N^1 + Ni^{58} \rightarrow Co^{58} + _1H^1 \tag{9-4}$$

which indicates that absorption of a neutron in the nucleus of a Ni^{58} atom produces a Co^{58} atom and a proton. This reaction is written as $Ni^{58}(n,p)Co^{58}$ in the conventional notation. This form of expression has been adopted because of its simplicity and ease of identifying incident and reaction product particles.

Other types of neutron-induced reactions are (n,n), (n,γ), $(n,2n)$, and (n,f) reactions. The latter designates the fission process. Fission and (n,γ) reactions are most important in nuclear reactors. The (n,γ) reactions are the most predominant mechanism by which radioactive species are produced because energy considerations permit them to occur with relative ease.

Reaction Cross Sections. A measure of the probability of nucleus-particle interaction is required to make quantitative calculations of nuclear reaction rates. The quantity which designates this probability, for a single nucleus, is the microscopic cross section σ. The term *cross section* is derived from the fact that σ is essentially a measure of the effective cross-sectional area the nucleus presents to the incident particle.

As would be expected from the fact that atoms are mostly free-space, cross sections are extremely small. Values of cross sections are reported in the literature in terms of *barns*; one barn is defined as 10^{-24} cm^2. Measured values of σ range from about 10^{-3} to 10^6 barns. Cross sections can be determined only by experimental measurement.

Every nucleus has a specific cross section for each specific kind of nuclear reaction that can occur; i.e., the cross section is different, for a given nucleus, for neutron scattering, neutron absorption, proton absorption, etc. In addition, for each specific kind of reaction, the cross section is a function of the energy of the incident particle. Thus cross sections for a given reaction must be measured at various incident-particle energies of interest.

Of all the nuclear reactions possible, neutron reactions such as scattering, (n,γ), and (n,f) are most important. Hence extensive measurements of σ as a function of energy have been made for these reactions. The data are reported in Ref. 12.

Shorter tabulations of cross sections are also found in the literature (e.g., Table 9-2). Such values are specifically for absorption of so-called "thermal" neutrons. These are neutrons with energies of 0.025 ev (or equivalently, velocities of 2,200 m/sec). The latter values pertain to neutrons of most probable velocity in the Maxwell-Boltzmann distribution for thermal equilibrium at 20°C. If calculations of reaction rates are to be made for other temperatures and, as is the case with nuclear reactors, for environments containing neutrons with a wide spectrum of energies, appropriate corrections to the tabulated values must be made. Correction procedures are described in the literature.[5,6,9,10]

Neutron absorption cross sections show great variation with neutron energy. Typically, at low energies (< 0.1 ev) σ is proportional to $1/v$, where v is the neutron velocity. In the intermediate range (0.1 to 10^3 ev) sharp peaks, or "resonances," occur at specific energies. This is called the resonance region. At high energies, the cross section approaches the geometric cross section of the nucleus. Variations in cross section as a function of neutron energy are illustrated for some nuclides in Fig. 9-2.

Nuclear Reaction Rates. Actual rates at which nuclear reactions occur depend on the cross section for the particular reaction, the number of incident particles available, and the number of target nuclei. In general, calculations must be made for specific reactions for specific isotopes because different isotopes of a given element will have different cross sections and the total cross section for a given isotope is the sum of contributions for various types of reactions such as scattering, (n,γ), etc. Calculation of actual reaction rates in nuclear reactors is a complex process because the reaction rates are a function of material thickness, and the number density of incident particles is spatially dependent. The following procedure, however, is typical for neutron reactions.

The volumetric rate of neutron reaction, R, is given by

$$R = \sigma\phi N_T \qquad (9\text{-}5)$$

where σ = cross section for the particular reaction, cm²
N_T = target nucleus density, atoms/cm³
ϕ = "neutron flux," in neutrons/cm²-sec

Table 9-2. Thermal-neutron-absorption Cross Sections

Element	Isotope	Isotopic abundance, %	Cross section, barns*
H	.....	....	0.33
	H^1	100	0.33
	H^2	0.015	0.46 mb
He	.....	....	Variable
	He^3	0.00013	np 5,200
	He^4	100	0
Li	.....	....	67
	Li^6	7.5	nα 910
	Li^7	92.5	33 mb
Be	Be^9	100	9.0 mb
B	.....	....	750
	B^{10}	18.8	nα 3,990
	B^{11}	81.2	50 mb
C	.....	....	4.5 mb
	C^{12}	98.9	
	C^{13}	1.1	1.0 mb
N	.....	....	1.78
	N^{14}	99.6	np 1.70; nα 0.10
	N^{15}	0.37	0.024 mb
O	.....	....	0.2 mb
	O^{16}	99.76	Very small
	O^{17}	0.037	nα 0.5
	O^{18}	0.20	0.21 mb
F	F^{19}	10C	10 mb
Ne	.....	....	2.8
Na	Na^{23}	100	0.49
Mg	.....	....	59 mb
Al	Al^{27}	100	0.22
Si	.....	....	0.13
P	P^{31}	100	0.19
S	.....	....	0.49
Cl	.....	....	31.6
A	.....	....	0.62
K	.....	....	1.97
Ca	.....	....	0.43
Ti	.....	....	5.6
V	.....	....	4.7
Cr	.....	....	2.9
Mn	Mn^{55}	100	12.6
Fe	.....	....	2.43
Co	Co^{59}	100	34
Ni	.....	....	4.5
Cu	.....	....	3.59
Zn	.....	....	1.06
Zr	.....	....	0.18
Mo	.....	....	2.4
Cd	.....	....	2,400
In	.....	....	190

Table 9-2. Thermal-neutron-absorption Cross Sections (Continued)

Element	Isotope	Isotopic abundance, %	Cross section, barns*
Sn	. . . . .	. . . .	0.65
Xe	. . . . .	. . . .	35
	Xe^{135}	0	3.5×10^6
Sm	. . . . .	. . . .	6,500
	Sm^{149}	13.8	50,000
Eu	. . . . .	. . . .	4,500
Gd	. . . . .	. . . .	44,000
Hf	. . . . .	. . . .	115
Ta	. . . . .	. . . .	21.3
Au	Au^{197}	100	94
Hg	. . . . .	. . . .	380
Pb	. . . . .	. . . .	0.17
Bi	Bi^{209}	100	32 mb
Th	Th^{232}	100	7.0
	Th^{233}	0	1,400
Pa	Pa^{233}	0	37
U	. . . . .	. . . .	nγ 3.50, nf 3.92
	U^{235}	0.714	nγ 101, nf 549
	U^{238}	99.3	2.80
	U^{239}	0	22
Pu	Pu^{239}	0	nγ 361, nf 664

* mb means millibars, or 10^{-3} barns; one mb = 10^{-27} cm².

SOURCE: R. Stephenson, "Introduction to Nuclear Engineering," p. 375, McGraw-Hill Series in Chemical Engineering, McGraw-Hill Book Company, Inc., New York, 1954.

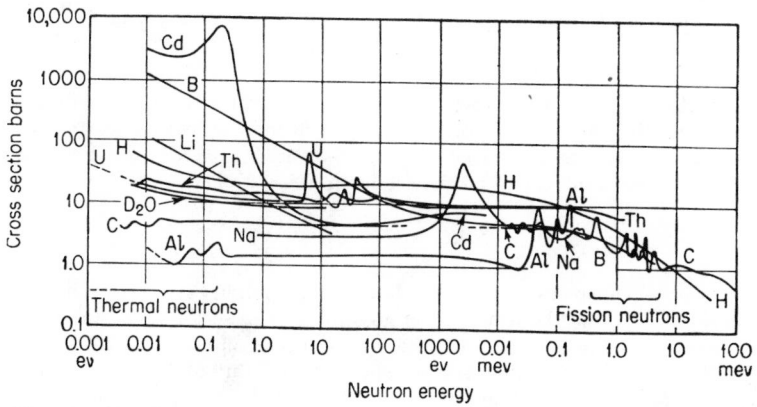

FIG. 9-2. Total neutron cross sections for some reactor materials. ("*Neutron Cross Sections*," *AECU* 2040.)

The neutron flux is properly interpreted as the product nv, where n is the number density of neutrons (neutrons/cm^3) having the velocity v in cm/sec.

Equation (9-5) is frequently written

$$R = \Sigma\phi \qquad (9\text{-}6)$$

where Σ, called the *macroscopic cross section*, is defined by

$$\Sigma = \rho(N_a/A)\sigma \qquad (9\text{-}7)$$

where ρ = mass density, g/cm^3, of specific isotope for which microscopic cross section is σ

N_a = Avogadro's number

A = atomic mass of target isotope, g/g mole.

It is important to recognize potential pitfalls in the use of Eq. (9-5) or (9-6). As previously mentioned, σ is a function of neutron energy, and, in a nuclear reactor—and in many other circumstances—neutrons with a spectrum of energies are present. Hence proper evaluation of the total reaction rate really requires evaluation of the integral of the product $\sigma(E)\phi(E)$, where the argument represents the energy dependence of σ and ϕ, and ϕ is the actual neutron flux in the material in question. An alternative procedure is to use the thermal neutron cross section for the reaction and a properly weighted *effective thermal neutron flux*. The best procedure, however, is to determine experimentally the *activation product* $\sigma\phi$ for the particular system. Even this presents difficulties because ϕ is frequently position-dependent.

To illustrate the use of Eq. (9-5), consider a frequently encountered problem: determination of the amount of radioactive species present as a function of time, when the radionuclide is the product of a neutron absorption reaction. The procedure will be illustrated for the Cu^{63}(n,γ)Cu^{64} reaction, assumed to occur in pure copper exposed to an effective thermal neutron flux of 10^{14} neutrons/cm^2-sec.

The equation describing the amount of Cu^{64} present at any time is

$$dN^{64}/dt = R - \lambda N^{64} \qquad (9\text{-}8)$$

i.e., the number of Cu^{64} atoms present, represented by N^{64}, is the difference between the amount produced by reaction R and the loss by decay. The production rate is obtained from Eq. (9-5) as $R = \sigma\phi N^{63}$, and Eq. (9-8) becomes, when integrated for the condition $N^{64} = 0$ when $t = 0$,

$$N^{64}(t) = \frac{\sigma\phi N^{63}}{\lambda}(1 - e^{-\lambda t}) \qquad (9\text{-}9)$$

Numerical values are obtained as follows: Since an effective thermal neutron flux is given, the thermal neutron absorption cross section from the literature,[13] 4.5 barns, may be used, assuming the reaction occurs at 20°C. The literature[13] also gives the isotopic abundance of Cu^{63} as 69.09 per cent and the half-life of Cu^{64} as 12.9 hrs. Then

$$N^{63} = \frac{0.6909 \text{ g Cu}^{63}}{\text{g Cu}} \times \frac{8.92 \text{ g Cu}}{\text{cm}^3} \times \frac{6.023 \times 10^{23} \text{ atoms Cu}^{63}}{\text{g mole Cu}^{63}}$$

$$\times \frac{1 \text{ g mole Cu}^{63}}{63 \text{ g Cu}^{63}} = 5.9 \times 10^{22} \text{ atoms Cu}^{63}/\text{cm}^3 \quad (9\text{-}10)$$

and from Eq. (9-3),

$$\lambda = \frac{0.693}{T_{1/2}} = \frac{0.693}{12.9(3,600)} = 1.49 \times 10^{-5} \text{ sec}^{-1} \quad (9\text{-}11)$$

Substituting values into Eq. (9-9),

$$N^{64}(t) = \frac{(4.5 \times 10^{-24})(10^{14})(5.9 \times 10^{22})}{1.49 \times 10^{-5}} (1 - e^{-\lambda t})$$

$$= (1.78 \times 10^{18})(1 - e^{-\lambda t}) \text{ atoms Cu}^{64}/\text{cm}^3 \quad (9\text{-}12)$$

At equilibrium $(dN^{64}/dt = 0)$, the atomic density of Cu^{64} is simply 1.78×10^{18} atoms Cu^{64}/cm^3. The activity λN of this amount of Cu^{64} is

$$(1.49 \times 10^{-5})(1.78 \times 10^{18}) = 2.65 \times 10^{13} \text{ disintegrations/sec}$$

or $(2.65 \times 10^{13})/(3.7 \times 10^{10}) = 7.17 \times 10^2$ curies.

9-5. Nuclear Fission [4-6,9,10]

In the (n,f) reaction, the target nucleus splits to form two new nuclei of lighter mass, called *fission fragments,* and, most important to sustaining the reaction in nuclear reactors, several free neutrons. Only three nuclides, U^{235}, U^{233}, and Pu^{239}, are for practical purposes fissionable by neutrons of all energies; they are referred to as *fissile* nuclides. Of these, only U^{235} occurs in nature (its isotopic abundance in natural uranium is 0.72 per cent). The U^{233} and Pu^{239} are produced from Th^{232} and U^{238}, respectively, by neutron absorption; the latter are referred to as *fertile* nuclides.

The mechanism of fission may be explained in terms of the liquid-drop model. The nucleus is viewed as analogous to a drop of liquid; the liquid drop is held together by surface tension forces, and the nucleus is held together by binding energy. When sufficient excitation energy is imparted to the liquid, surface tension forces will be overcome and the drop will split in two. Similarly, when the energy of the excited compound nucleus formed after neutron absorption exceeds the binding energy, the nucleus splits into two fragments. The excess energy is carried off primarily as kinetic energy of the fragments. As previously noted, the total energy released per fission is on the order of 200 Mev, of which about 95 per cent is available for power production. The remainder is carried off by neutrinos.

Important fission properties differ for the various fissile nuclides. For example, the total energy released per fission varies slightly. Similarly, the average number of neutrons released varies, as does the fission cross section, both absolutely and as a fraction of the total neutron absorption cross section.

The latter lead to definition of the regeneration factor η, which has been called "probably the most important single physical constant related to chain

Table 9-3. Properties of the Fissile Nuclides*

	U233	U235	Pu239
Useful energy per fission, Mev†	191	193	201
Total absorption cross section σ_a, barns	578	683	1,028
Fission cross section σ_f, barns	525	575	577
σ_a/σ_f	1.10	1.18	1.39
Fission neutrons per fission	2.51	2.44	2.89
Regeneration factor	2.28	2.07	2.08
Delayed neutron fraction‡	0.0026	0.0065	0.0021

* From H. S. Isbin, "Introductory Nuclear Reactor Theory," p. 461, Reinhold Publishing Corporation, New York. 1963.
† From L. J. Templin (ed.), "Reactor Physics Constants," 2d ed., USAEC, ANL-5800, July, 1963.
‡ From G. R. Keepin, and T. F. Wimett, Reactor Kinetic Functions: A New Evaluation, *Nucleonics*, **16** (10), 89 (1958).

reactors."[9] The average number of neutrons released per fission is conventionally given the symbol ν. The regeneration factor is then defined in terms of ν as

$$\eta = \nu(\Sigma_f/\Sigma_a) \qquad (9\text{-}13)$$

where Σ_f is the macroscopic fission cross section for the fissile nuclide, and

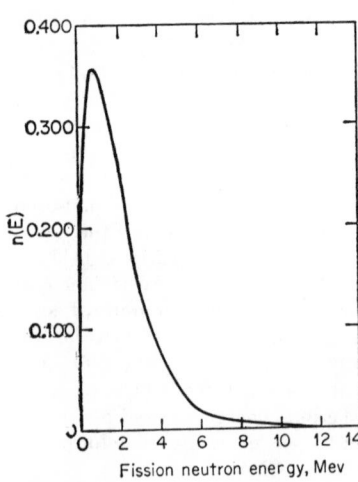

FIG. 9-3. Energy spectrum of prompt fission neutrons. (*Glasstone and Sesonske, "Nuclear Reactor Engineering," D. Van Nostrand Company, Inc., Princeton, N.J.*, 1963.)

Σ_a is the total neutron absorption cross section for the fuel material. In words, η is the number of fission neutrons produced by thermal fission per thermal neutron absorbed in the fuel. This parameter is the key factor in neutron economy (Sec. 9-6). Values of η and other properties of fissile nuclides are given in Table 9-3.

Fission Neutrons. Neutrons released by fission are divided into two fractions, prompt and delayed. As implied by the name, the latter are emitted some time after the fission event, apparently in conjunction with decay of certain of the fission products. Although delayed neutron fractions are very small (Table 9-3), their existence is probably the major factor permitting controlled utilization of nuclear power: they are the key to safe reactor operation (Sec. 9-3).

Prompt fission neutrons are emitted with a spectrum of energies as shown in Fig. 9-3. Most have energies in the range 1 to 2 Mev, but a few have energies in excess of 10 Mev. The latter are an important consideration in shielding.

The delayed neutrons fall into six groups, each characterized by an exponential decay rate. The six groups are the same for the three fissile materials, but the distribution of delayed neutrons in the six groups differs. Half-lives of the groups range between approximately 0.23 and 56 sec. Kr^{87} and Xe^{137} have been identified as the neutron emitters for two of the groups.

Fission Products. The fission process occurs in more than 40 ways, producing fission fragments with mass numbers ranging from about 72 to 160. These fission fragments are highly radioactive, and decay in a succession of steps involving formation of other radionuclides. The nuclei which result from this process—over 200 radioactive species—are known collectively as *fission products.*

The mass distribution of fission products for fissioning of U^{235} by thermal and 14 Mev neutrons is shown in Fig. 9-4. Curves for the other fissile species are similar.[14] It may be noted from Fig. 9-4 that the maximum yield is

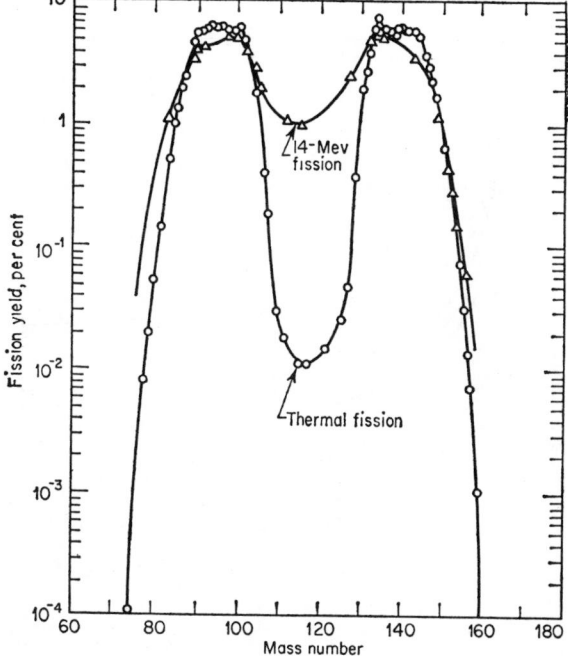

FIG. 9-4. Mass distribution of U^{235} fission products. (*Glasstone and Sesonske, "Nuclear Reactor Engineering,"* D. Van Nostrand Company, Inc., Princeton, N.J., 1963.)

about 6 per cent; the maxima occur at mass numbers of approximately 95 and 135.

The radioactive fission products give off energy as gamma rays and beta particles during decay. In the nuclear reactor, this energy is rapidly manifested as heat, which must be removed to prevent core meltdown. For this reason, and also for proper design of spent-fuel reprocessing facilities, it is important to know the magnitude of this *decay heat power*, as it is called, as a function of time after fission ceases.

The decay heat power can be determined as a fraction of fission power from the expression[15]

$$\frac{P}{P_0} = 6.1 \times 10^{-3}[(\tau - T_0)^{0.2} - \tau^{-0.2}] \qquad (9\text{-}14)$$

where P = decay heat power

P_0 = fission or reactor power (both in arbitrary but identical units)

τ = time in days since cessation of fission

T_0 = number of days for which fission occurred (at constant rate)

As suggested by Eq. (9-13), the ratio P/P_0 is a function of T_0 as well as cooling

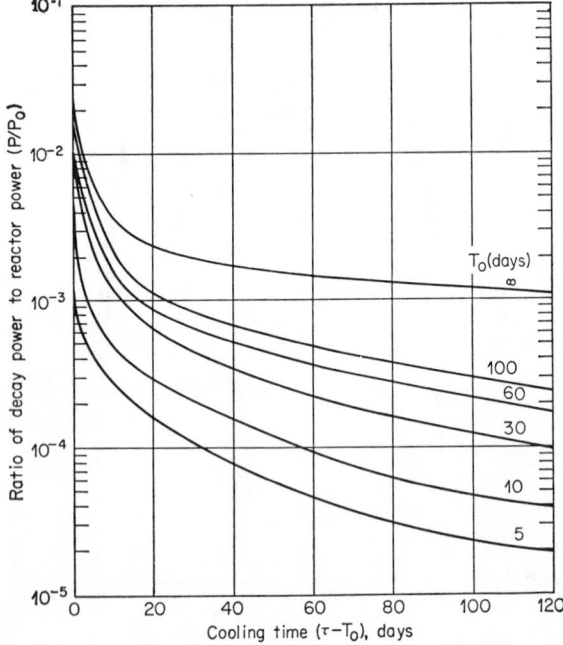

Fig. 9-5. Fission-product-decay heat power. (*Glasstone and Sesonske, "Nuclear Reactor Engineering," D. Van Nostrand Company, Inc., Princeton, N.J.*, 1963.)

time. Equation (9-14) is shown graphically for several values of T_0 in Fig. 9-5.

9-6. Physics of the Nuclear Reactor

From the physicist's point of view, design of a nuclear reactor is a problem of neutron economy. About 2.5 neutrons are produced per fission event (Sec. 9-5), only one of which must be absorbed to produce fission again and thereby sustain a chain reaction. However, many processes compete for neutrons in the reactor. These may be briefly summarized as (1) loss from the system at boundaries, (2) absorption in nonfissionable materials, (3) non-fission absorption in fissile materials, and (4) absorption to produce fission. The physicist's objective is to construct a balance sheet for neutrons which involves these four processes and sustains a chain reaction in the framework of engineering requirements for the reactor (Sec. 9-9).

Classification of Reactors. Nuclear reactors can be classified according to a variety of standards. The most fundamental, however, is the kinetic energy of the neutrons causing most of the fissions. On this basis, there are two major types: *fast* reactors, in which most fissions are caused by neutrons of high energy, and *thermal* reactors, which operate primarily on low-energy thermal neutrons. Since fission neutrons are born at high energies (about 2 Mev; Sec. 9-2), fast reactors operate with neutrons of or near fission energy. In thermal reactors, the fast-fission neutrons are slowed down (to take advantage of the larger cross sections at thermal energies); this slowing down is accomplished by materials known as *moderators* that are put into the core. Thermal reactors predominate in the spectrum of operating reactors in the world today, primarily because of greater design flexibility. In the future, however, fast reactors should become more important in order to make best use of nuclear fuel resources.

Breeding and Conversion. Fast reactors are expected to become important because of their potential for producing more fissionable fuel than they consume, i.e., *breeding*. If new fuel generation involves production of a fissile material different from that being consumed (e.g., a reactor operating on U^{235} produces Pu^{239} from the fertile U^{238}), the process is called *conversion*. Many combinations of types of reactors and fissile and fertile materials have been and are being considered to maximize potential for conversion and breeding. Development of fast reactors for breeding has been slow because of difficult, but apparently soluble, technological problems with heat transfer, materials, and dynamic stability.

Because known world reserves of the only naturally occurring fissile material, U^{235}, are relatively small, breeding and conversion involving the fertile materials Th^{232} and U^{238} are mandatory for effective use of all potential fission energy reserves (which could supply man's needs for a century). The U.S. Atomic Energy Commission has predicted[16] that by 1980 breeder reactors will be the predominant nuclear power source. These plants will necessarily be augmented by thermal convertors burning U^{235} and producing plutonium. The Commission also estimates that in about 40 years nuclear power will provide half the electric generating capacity in the United States.

9-7. Physics Design of Reactor Cores [5–10, 17–20]

The ensuing discussion is directed primarily at thermal reactors because of the importance of neutron slowing-down processes in these systems. Basic concepts such as definition of reactor parameters, method of sizing the core, etc., apply equally well, however, to fast reactors.

Processes that occur for neutrons in a reactor may be described qualitatively as follows: Immediately after birth, the fast-fission neutrons begin to move rapidly through the reactor because of their high kinetic energy. As they do so, they encounter and interact with atoms of materials in the reactor core. These encounters with other atoms may produce one of two results: the neutron may be absorbed in the nucleus of the struck atom, or it may simply suffer a collision in which some of the neutron's kinetic energy is transferred to the struck atom.

These collisions are known as scattering reactions. They are of two types, *elastic* and *inelastic*. In the elastic, or "billiard-ball," collisions, kinetic energy of the neutron-atom pair is conserved. Kinetic energy is not conserved in inelastic collisions, which are generally restricted to nuclei of fairly high mass number and neutrons of energy in excess of 0.1 Mev; the neutron is captured by the nucleus, and part or all of its kinetic energy is converted to excitation energy of the nucleus.

If the neutron is not absorbed during the above processes, its energy is gradually reduced (i.e., moderated—the moderator nuclei are targets for scattering reactions) as a result of the scattering collisions, so that the desired objective, neutrons of thermal energy, is achieved. These thermal neutrons are then available for absorption in fuel to produce fission and thereby re-initiate the above process.

Throughout the foregoing sequence of events, the neutrons are always subject to possible leakage from the system at boundaries. To reduce loss of neutrons by leakage, *reflectors* are placed at the boundaries of reactor cores. The reflectors scatter some of the leaked-out neutrons back into the core so that they remain available to cause fission.

Reactor Parameters. Quantitative calculations of the rate at which the above processes occur are required to size a reactor core. To make these calculations, parameters defined in terms of material properties important to these processes are used. These parameters and their symbols are as follows:

Diffusion Coefficient D. The diffusion coefficient is defined by the equation

$$J = -D \operatorname{grad} \phi \tag{9-15}$$

where J is the neutron current in a particular direction, and ϕ is the neutron flux. A good approximation to D may be obtained from the relation

$$D = \frac{1}{3\Sigma_s(1 - \bar{\mu}_0)} \tag{9-16}$$

where Σ_s is the macroscopic scattering cross section for the medium, and $\bar{\mu}_0$ is the average cosine of the scattering angle per collision, given in terms of the mass number A of the medium by $\bar{\mu}_0 = \frac{2}{3}A$. Note that D has units of length.

Diffusion Length L. The diffusion length is defined by

$$L \equiv \sqrt{D/\Sigma_a} \tag{9-17}$$

where Σ_a is the macroscopic neutron absorption cross section of the medium. It is a measure of the distance a neutron travels from the point where it becomes thermal to the point where it is absorbed.

Average Logarithmic Energy Decrement ξ. This parameter is a measure of the average energy loss the neutron suffers in elastic collisions with nuclei. It is determined to a high degree of accuracy from the relation

$$\xi \cong \frac{2}{A + \frac{2}{3}} \tag{9-18}$$

To minimize the size of the reactor and possibilities of nonfission neutron absorption, it is desirable that ξ have as large a value as possible, i.e., that A be small (hence, moderator materials should be of low atomic mass).

Fermi Age τ. The Fermi age was defined in conjunction with a model in which the slowing down of neutrons, which proceeds in discrete steps of energy loss for each scattering collision, is represented as a continuous process. This parameter is of great practical importance in reactor design (see below). It is a function of neutron energy E, and is defined by the relation

$$\tau(E) \equiv \int_{E_0}^{E} \frac{D}{\xi \Sigma_s E} \, dE \tag{9-19}$$

where E_0 is the energy of the neutrons at the beginning of the slowing-down process. The Fermi age is a measure of the distance (note that the units of τ are length squared) a neutron has traveled from the point of origin to the point where its Fermi age is τ. An important value of τ is τ_{thermal}, corresponding to $E = E_{\text{thermal}}$. This is a measure of the distance the neutron travels to achieve thermal velocity.

Migration Length M. This parameter is a measure of the total distance the neutron travels from birth as a fission neutron to absorption as a thermal neutron. As would be expected, it is defined in terms of L and τ by

$$M \equiv \sqrt{L^2 + \tau} \tag{9-20}$$

The parameter that actually appears in reactor equations is the *migration area M^2*, where

$$M^2 = L^2 + \tau \tag{9-21}$$

Design Methods for the Steady State. The basic problem in reactor design is to devise a useful mathematical model which is descriptive of the physical processes discussed above and utilizes the parameters representative of the effects of reactor geometry and materials on these processes. The ensuing discussion is an outline of the basis for development and use of such models.

The reader is cautioned that in practice, elaborate, complex computer programs are actually used for reactor design. These programs have their origin, however, in the concepts given here.

Neutron behavior in reactors can be described rigorously by Boltzmann transport theory.[6,9,10] The complexity of reactors, however, prohibits detailed solution of the resulting equations. Hence the basis for reactor design lies in an approximation to transport theory known as *diffusion theory*.[5-10] The essential feature of diffusion theory is that neutron leakage from the reactor is described as a diffusional process.

The material balance for neutrons in the reactor must take account of production (by fission) and losses (by leakage and all absorption reactions). In diffusion theory, the neutron balance for steady-state operation takes the form

$$D \nabla^2 \phi - \Sigma_a \phi + S = 0 \qquad (9\text{-}22)$$

where ∇^2 = Laplacian operator

ϕ = neutron flux

Σ_a = effective macroscopic absorption cross section

S = source term

Equation (9-22) is known as the *diffusion equation*, and is the basis of reactor design. It is strictly applicable only in systems containing monoenergetic neutrons, and also at points more than two or three neutron mean free paths from boundaries and strong sources and absorbers. As will be seen, however, these restrictions can be obviated.

To solve Eq. (9-22), it is essential to obtain a representation for the source term S and define reactor geometry and boundary conditions. As the first step in the solution, it is convenient to take as reference a fictitious reactor, infinite in size, so that no neutron leakage occurs. For this system a parameter known as the *infinite multiplication factor* k_∞ is defined. It is given by

$$k_\infty = \frac{\text{no. of fission neutrons produced in a given generation}}{\text{no. of neutrons absorbed in the preceding generation}} \qquad (9\text{-}23)$$

where a "neutron generation" is the fission-birth, slowing-down absorption cycle previously described.

A similar parameter, the *effective multiplication factor* k_{eff}, may now be defined for a finite reactor. It is given in terms of k_∞ and a factor which corrects k_∞ for leakage losses in the finite reactor:

$$k_{\text{eff}} = k_\infty P \qquad (9\text{-}24)$$

where P is defined as the *nonleakage probability*. It should be apparent from these definitions that the reactor is operating at steady state when k_{eff} has a value of exactly unity. When $k_{\text{eff}} = 1$, the reactor is said to be *critical;* when k_{eff} is less than or greater than unity, the reactor is subcritical and supercritical, respectively.

The infinite multiplication factor may be defined in terms of parameters representative of the effect of material properties on physical processes of scattering and absorption that occur during a neutron generation. The relationship is

$$k_\infty = \epsilon p f \eta \tag{9-25}$$

where η is the regeneration factor previously defined (Sec. 9-2), and the other parameters are as defined below. Equation (9-25) is known as the *four-factor equation*. Because of the definitions of ϵ, p, f, and η, it is a powerful means for determining the effect of changes in reactor materials on criticality. These parameters are defined as:

Fast-fission Factor ϵ. This factor accounts for neutron production during the slowing-down process by fissions at high energies. It may be defined as the ratio of the total number of fission neutrons produced by fast and thermal fission to the number produced by thermal fission.

Resonance Escape Probability p. This parameter is the ratio of the number of neutrons leaving the resonance region (Sec. 9-2) at low energies to the number entering at high energies. It is a complex function of the macroscopic absorption and scattering cross sections of the materials in the core.

Thermal Utilization f. This factor is defined as the fraction of all thermal neutrons absorbed that are absorbed in fuel material (which may include nonfissionable material such as U^{238}). The exact definition of f depends on whether the system is homogeneous or heterogeneous; an acceptable general expression for a reactor of volume V is

$$f = \frac{V_F \Sigma_{aF} \phi_F}{V_F \Sigma_{aF} \phi_F + V_m \Sigma_{am} \phi_m + V_i \Sigma_{ai} \phi_i} \tag{9-26}$$

where the subscripts F, m, and i represent fuel, moderator, and impurity (e.g., structural) materials, respectively.

In general, ϵ does not differ much from unity and, as shown in Table 9-3, values of η for the fissile materials are similar. The infinite multiplication factor for a given reactor therefore depends strongly on values of p and f, both of which are dependent on the amount, dispersion, and properties of materials in the reactor.

Solution of the Diffusion Equation. One may take the viewpoint that the objective in solving Eq. (9-22), the diffusion equation, is to obtain an expression for the nonleakage probability P [Eq. (9-24)], in terms of reactor materials and geometry. The actual expression obtained for P depends basically on two factors: the expression used for the source term S and the method of treating the neutron energy spectrum in the core. In practice, the neutron energy spectrum is considered to consist of several groups, each containing monoenergetic neutrons. This leads to a diffusion equation for each group; the source term for each equation is then the neutrons entering that group from the group of next-highest energy neutrons.

The above approach leads to quite complex representations of neutron behavior. The general method by which expressions for P are developed may be illustrated, however, by the following simple model. This model is for an unreflected homogeneous reactor in which all neutrons are considered to have the same energy (i.e., "one-group" theory). The derivation will be illustrated for the steady state, which presupposes that k_{eff} is unity.

For the situation assumed, all neutrons are absorbed at the same energy and at a total rate $\Sigma_a\phi$. Since k_∞ fission neutrons are produced per absorption, the source term is simply $k_\infty\Sigma_a\phi$. Equation (9-22) then becomes

$$D\,\nabla^2\phi - \Sigma_a\phi + k_\infty\Sigma_a\phi = 0 \qquad (9\text{-}27)$$

or upon rearrangement and introduction of the diffusion length [Eq. (9-17)],

$$\nabla^2\phi + \frac{k_\infty - 1}{L^2}\,\phi = 0 \qquad (9\text{-}28)$$

Equation (9-28) indicates only the effect of reactor materials on neutron behavior. It is now necessary to consider the effect of neutron leakage and reactor geometry on the spatial distribution of the neutron flux.

The neutron flux distribution is represented by the relationship

$$\nabla^2\phi + B^2\phi = 0 \qquad (9\text{-}29)$$

which is subject to boundary conditions imposed by the shape of the reactor (e.g., spherical, cylindrical, etc.). The constant B^2 is known as the "buckling," because it measures the bending (i.e., buckling) of the neutron flux.

At this point two operations are possible. First, Eq. (9-29) may be solved independently, with appropriate boundary conditions, to determine the flux distribution on the basis of purely geometrical considerations. Second, it may be noted that Eqs. (9-28) and (9-29) may be satisfied simultaneously if the coefficients of ϕ are identical. Equating coefficients,

$$\frac{k_\infty - 1}{L^2} = B_c^2 \qquad (9\text{-}30)$$

where the subscript on B^2 indicates that the value of B^2 that satisfies Eq. (9-30) is the one for which the reactor is critical. If this value is now made equal to the value obtained by independent solution of Eq. (9-29), the reactor will actually be critical.

Two bucklings may therefore be distinguished. That arising from solution of Eq. (9-29) is known as the *geometric buckling*, and that given by Eq. (9-30) is the *material buckling*. When the reactor is critical, the material and geometric bucklings are identical. Expressions for the geometric buckling for various reactor geometries are given in Table 9-4. It will be noted that these expressions indicate the dimensions of the reactor. When the two bucklings are equal, these are the dimensions for criticality.

Equation (9-30) may be rearranged to

$$\frac{k_\infty}{1 + L^2 B_c^2} = 1 \qquad (9\text{-}31)$$

and it will be recalled that since steady state was assumed, k_{eff} must be unity. Hence

$$\frac{k_\infty}{1 + L^2 B_c^2} = 1 = k_{eff} = k_\infty P \qquad (9\text{-}32)$$

Table 9-4. Geometric Bucklings for Various Reactor Shapes

Geometry	Buckling	Minimum critical volume
Sphere	$\dfrac{\pi^2}{R}$	$\dfrac{130}{B_c{}^3}$
Rectangular parallelepiped	$\dfrac{\pi^2}{a}+\dfrac{\pi^2}{b}+\dfrac{\pi^2}{c}$	$\dfrac{161}{B_c{}^3}\ (a=b=c)$
Finite cylinder	$\dfrac{(2.405)^2}{R}+\dfrac{\pi^2}{H}$	$\dfrac{148}{B_c{}^3}\ (H=1.847R)$

R = radius; a,b,c = length of sides; H = height.

and therefore the nonleakage probability is given by $1/(1 + L^2B_c{}^2)$ according to one-group theory.

Equation (9-31) is known as the *critical equation* for one-group theory. It is, as noted, the result of a very simple model; its predictions of critical size are therefore, at best, approximate. To obtain more reliable estimates of critical dimensions, models that more accurately describe physical processes for the neutrons are required.

Critical equations for two other, more accurate models are as follows: The *age-diffusion model*, which utilizes the Fermi continuous slowing-down approximation mentioned above, gives

$$\frac{k_\infty e^{-B_c{}^2\,\sigma_{\text{thermal}}}}{1 + L^2B_c{}^2} = 1 \tag{9-33}$$

which for a large reactor reduces to

$$\frac{k_\infty}{1 + M^2B_c{}^2} = 1 \tag{9-34}$$

Two-group theory, in which the neutron energy spectrum is divided into a fast group and a thermal group, gives

$$\frac{k_\infty}{(1 + \tau B_c{}^2)(1 + L^2B_c{}^2)} = 1 \tag{9-35}$$

Many *multigroup* methods for determining critical size are also available. These can be quite accurate, but they are also quite elaborate, and require iterative solution on computers. Many of the computer programs, or "codes," used to determine the critical size of reactors are available in the literature.[21]

The above critical equations were derived assuming the reactor is homogeneous. In practice, of course, fuel, moderator, and structural materials are distinct (homogeneous reactors are in development). It is therefore frequently desirable to subdivide the reactor into small "unit cells," each of which may be treated as a homogeneous entity. Such a procedure adds considerably to the complexity—but also the accuracy—of the calculations.

9-8. Reactor Kinetics and Control [5–10, 22–26]

The power output of a nuclear reactor is varied by controlling the neutron flux. Many methods of flux control are available, but the most common is to insert in the core materials which have very large neutron absorption cross sections, called *poisons*. To sustain operation for long periods of time without refueling, the reactor is built with fuel in excess of that required for criticality. The poison materials provide "negative fuel" that compensates for the excess fuel (as fuel is consumed, the poison must gradually be removed) and, in conjunction with the control system, prevent the reactor from becoming supercritical during transient operations such as startup.

Poisons are usually inserted as an array of metallic control rods dispersed throughout the core (see Sec. 9-12 for a discussion of poison materials). The control rods are connected mechanically to drive motors that are actuated as a result of signals received from neutron-detection instruments. Much of the operation of the control system is automatic. An important safety feature is that operator actions which tend to increase the neutron flux are subject to automatic controls built into the system.

Poisons may also be inserted as "burnable" (i.e., gradually depleted) poisons added to the fuel matrix or the coolant. Methods of control other than poisons include addition or removal of fuel, variation of the amount of moderator in the core, and movement of sections of the core or reflector.

Reactor Control Parameters. A fundamental concept in reactor control is the *neutron lifetime* ℓ, which is defined as the average time between successive generations for an infinite reactor. The effective lifetime, defined for a finite reactor, is the neutron lifetime multiplied by the nonleakage probability P. The prompt neutron generation time ℓ^* is defined by

$$\ell^* \equiv \ell/k_\infty \tag{9-36}$$

and characterizes the lifetime of prompt neutrons in the reactor.

Another fundamental concept in reactor control is the reactivity ρ, defined by

$$\rho \equiv \frac{k_{\text{eff}} - 1}{k_{\text{eff}}} = \frac{k_{\text{ex}}}{k_{\text{eff}}} = \frac{\Delta k}{k_{\text{eff}}} \cong \delta k \tag{9-37}$$

The reactivity is frequently taken to be equivalent to Δk, or alternatively, δk.

The significance of these parameters and delayed neutrons in reactor control may be illustrated by considering changes in neutron density in a reactor not operating at steady state. The change in neutron density n with time is given by

$$\frac{dn}{dt} = n\,\frac{\delta k}{\ell} \tag{9-38}$$

which gives, with $n = n_0$ at $t = 0$,

$$n(t) = n_0 e^{(\delta k/\ell)t} = n_0 e^{t/\theta} \tag{9-39}$$

where θ is the reactor period. The effect of the delayed neutrons is to increase the neutron lifetime, and therefore the reactor period, from about 10^{-3} sec, characteristic of the prompt neutrons, to 10^{-1} sec. Thus, by inspection of Eq. (9-39), in a given period of time the neutron density changes by a much smaller amount when delayed neutrons control the reactor period. The neutron density would change at a rate too fast for the electromechanical systems to control if the delayed neutrons did not control the period.

Kinetic-analysis Fundamentals. Because of their powerful influence on reactor dynamics, the delayed-neutron contribution to neutron economy is clearly distinguished in kinetic studies. The one-group diffusion equation for a bare, homogeneous reactor [Eq. (9-22)] becomes

$$D \nabla^2 \phi - \Sigma_a \phi + k_\infty \Sigma_a \phi (1 - \beta) + \sum_{i=1}^{6} \lambda_i C_i = \frac{dn}{dt} \qquad (9\text{-}40)$$

where β is the delayed-neutron fraction (Table 9-3), and $(1 - \beta)$ is therefore the prompt-neutron fraction. The contribution of the six delayed-neutron groups, each characterized by a concentration C_i and decay constant λ_i, is indicated by the summation.

Equation (9-40) may be written

$$\frac{dn}{dt} = \frac{\rho - \beta}{\ell^*} n + \sum_{i=1}^{6} \lambda_i C_i \qquad (9\text{-}41)$$

with which are associated the equations descriptive of delayed-neutron behavior,

$$\frac{dC_i}{dt} = \frac{\beta_i}{\ell^*} n - \lambda_i C_i \qquad i = 1, 2, \ldots, 6 \qquad (9\text{-}42)$$

which, it will be noted, is similar to Eq. (9-8) for neutron reactions.

Equations (9-41) and (9-46) are fundamental to reactor kinetics; they are basic to development of transfer functions descriptive of reactor dynamic response. However, as for steady-state design, relationships used in practice are considerably more complex than those given here. A detailed discussion of methods in use is given by Keepin.[22]

An important aspect of unsteady-state operation that can be extremely dangerous is the "prompt-critical condition," for which $\delta k = \rho = \beta$. The reactor is critical on prompt neutrons alone, and the period is therefore extremely short. The power level could rise at such a rate that the core would melt before corrective action could be taken. Control systems are carefully designed to prevent achievement of the prompt-critical condition.

Temperature Effects. Changes in temperature exert great influence on reactor kinetics because they affect materials density, core dimensions, neutron energy, and cross sections. Temperature effects are basically determined by differentiating the critical equation with respect to temperature (i.e., determining dk_{eff}/dT) and investigating the change with temperature in the range of interest for each resulting term.

Safety considerations require that the reactor temperature coefficient be negative (i.e., if temperature increases, power decreases). It should be noted that a negative coefficient can be achieved only by proper design. Some contributions to the coefficient are positive, and some are negative; the magnitude and sign of each must be determined. All reactors are designed to have negative temperature coefficients, generally on the order of 10^{-5} to 10^{-4} per degree Fahrenheit, at operating temperatures.

A major contributor to the over-all temperature coefficient is the *Doppler coefficient*, which describes the effect of temperature changes on neutron absorption in the resonance region. In general, as the temperature increases, the resonance peaks broaden, and increased neutron absorption occurs. In fissile material, the Doppler coefficient is therefore positive; in other materials it is negative.

Fission-product Poisoning. Two of the fission products—Xe^{135} and Sm^{149}— have very large thermal neutron absorption cross sections (2.7×10^6 and 4.2×10^4 barns, respectively). The magnitudes of these cross sections and the amounts in which the isotopes are formed are sufficient to have an effect on the multiplication factor.

These *fission-product poisons* influence the reactivity of the reactor. The amount of poisons present depends on reactor operating history and the thermal neutron flux. It can be shown, however, that a definite maximum equilibrium *poisoning*, defined as the ratio of the number of neutrons absorbed by the poison to the number absorbed by fuel, exists for operating reactors, as shown in Fig. 9-6.

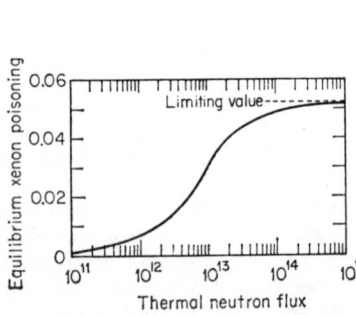

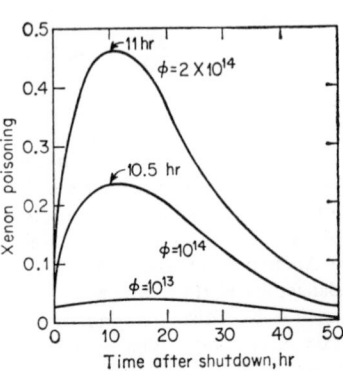

FIG. 9-6. Equilibrium xenon poisoning during reactor operation. (*Glasstone and Sesonske, "Nuclear Reactor Engineering," D. Van Nostrand Company, Inc., Princeton, N.J., 1963.*)

FIG. 9-7. Xenon poisoning after shutdown. (*Glasstone and Sesonske, "Nuclear Reactor Engineering," D. Van Nostrand Company, Inc., Princeton, N.J., 1963.*)

Figure 9-6 shows that the maximum poisoning during operation is relatively small. The poisoning can achieve very large values, however, after reactor shutdown. This phenomenon occurs because the precursor of Xe^{135}, which is I^{135}, has a relatively long half-life (6.7 hr) and hence continues to produce Xe^{135} from its decay after shutdown.

The poisoning achieved after shutdown is a strong function of neutron flux, as shown in Fig. 9-7. The very high value of poisoning achieved for fluxes of 10^{14} and greater is in some cases the limiting factor in operating neutron flux and core life. To restart the reactor when the poisoning is a maximum, the core must have available sufficient excess reactivity (as excess fuel) to "override peak xenon"; near the end of core life this capacity is limited. In ship propulsion reactors, where startup at any time is essential, this limitation becomes quite important.

9-9. Engineering Design of Nuclear Reactors [5–8,27–33]

A unique feature of nuclear power generation is the wide variety of design concepts that may be utilized successfully. Many core configurations, component designs, and materials combinations have been used in the past, and more innovations[33] may be expected for the future. All power reactors have certain common components, however, as outlined below.

Reactor Coolants. The coolant, which removes heat generated by fission and radiation heating of core structures, may be a gas (air, helium, CO_2), molten salt, water (light or heavy), liquid metal, or organic liquid. In some reactor designs, coolant flow through the core is orificed to match the heat-generation distribution.

Reactor Vessel. The core and associated components such as control-rod assemblies, support structures, and reflectors are housed in the reactor vessel. In pressurized, water-cooled reactors the vessel must be able to withstand high operating pressures (up to about 2,000 psig). A major problem in reactor-vessel design is thermal stress; other design problems arise from the need to provide fuel-handling facilities and control-rod drives. Pressure vessels for water-cooled reactors are built in accordance with sec. III of the ASME Code.

Fuel-element Cladding. Individual fuel elements in heterogeneous reactors are sheathed in a cladding which acts as a barrier, preventing escape of fission products from the fuel to the coolant. Cladding materials and properties are detailed in Sec. 9-12.

Thermal Shields. The radiations emitted by nuclear reactions in the core cause extensive heating of adjacent structural materials, including the reactor vessel. To prevent excessive thermal stresses in the vessel as a result of radiation-induced internal heat generation in the region of the core, thermal shields are placed between the core and the vessel. The thermal shields must be cooled (heat generation in the shields is about 3 per cent of the total output of the reactor). The shields must have high absorption coefficients for neutrons and electromagnetic radiation and high thermal conductivities to prevent overheating. Steels are commonly used as shield materials.

Fuel-handling Systems. A system must be provided for loading and unloading fuel in the reactor. The system may also be capable of moving fuel from one position to another in the core. Refueling of water-cooled reactors

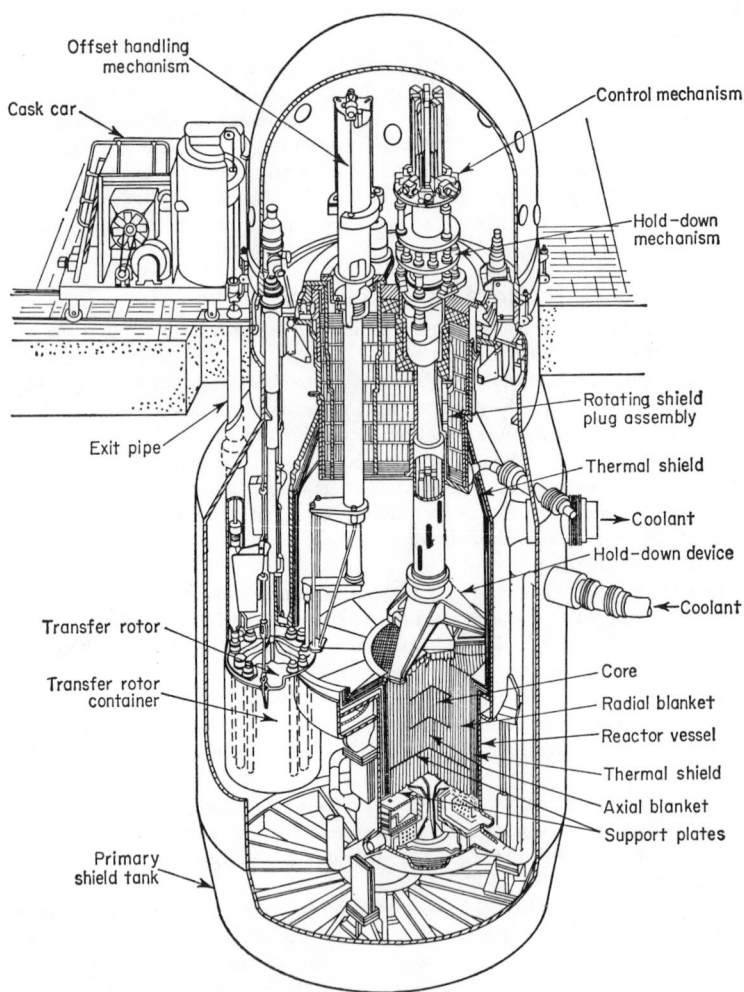

FIG. 9-8. The Enrico Fermi reactor vessel and components. (*Glasstone and Sesonske, "Nuclear Reactor Engineering," D. Van Nostrand Company, Inc., Princeton, N.J., 1963.*)

is usually done with the reactor shut down and the vessel closure head removed. In other systems, however, refueling may be accomplished without costly reactor shutdown. The fuel-handling system and other pressure-vessel components for the Enrico Fermi reactor, a sodium-cooled, fast-breeder sys-

tem, are shown in Fig. 9-8.   For comparison, reactor-vessel components for
the Yankee reactor, a pressurized water system, are shown in Fig. 9-9.

Containment Vessels.   All nuclear power reactors are required to be housed
in containment structures designed to retain fission products and gases that
might be released as a result of the maximum credible accident (see discussion
of hazard analysis below).   In many installations, this structure is a low-
leakage vessel totally enclosing the reactor vessel and associated external
components such as reactor coolant piping and steam generators.   Such

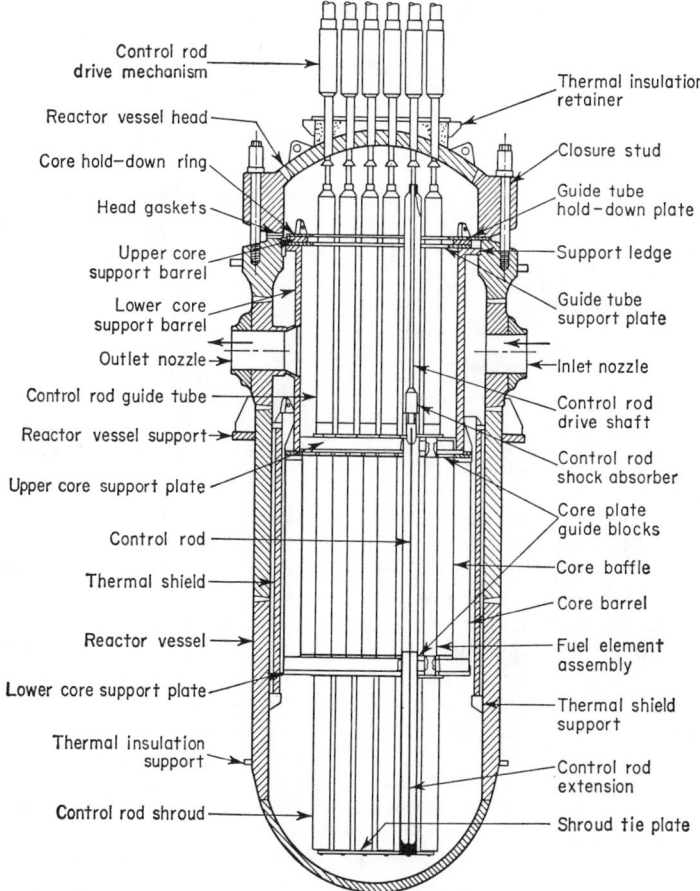

FIG. 9-9. The Yankee reactor vessel and components.   (*Glassstone and Sesonske,*
"Nuclear Reactor Engineering," D. Van Nostrand Company, Inc., Princeton, N.J.,
1963.)

vessels are usually cylindrical or spherical and fabricated from steels not subject to brittle failure.

9-10. Thermal Design of Reactor Cores

Core design objectives for heat transfer and physics are basically at odds. To optimize neutron economy, the core should be small; to ease heat removal, the core should be large. Every operating core represents a compromise of these different objectives.

Nuclear reactors operate with high heat fluxes (on the order of 100,000 and 500,000 Btu/hr-ft^2 in water-cooled and liquid-metal-cooled systems, respectively). To prevent fuel melting and release of fission products, a large number of fuel elements of small cross section is therefore required (for example, the Yankee reactor in Rowe, Mass., contains over 23,000 individual fuel elements; the nuclear ship Savannah contains over 32,000). Power densities in reactors vary considerably for different coolants, as shown in Table 9-5.

Table 9-5. Power Densities for Various Types of Nuclear Reactors

Reactor Type	Power Density, Kw (Thermal)/ft³
Gas-cooled—natural U	15
High-temperature gas	220
Sodium graphite	290
Organic-cooled	390
Heavy water—natural U	510
Boiling water	820
Pressurized water	1,550
Sodium-cooled fast breeder	21,500
Nuclear rocket reactor	280,000
Conventional forced-convection boiler	280

SOURCE: Abstracted from S. Glasstone and A. Sesonske, "Nuclear Reactor Engineering," D. Van Nostrand Company, Inc., Princeton. N.J., 1963.

Standard techniques appropriate for the coolant and heat transfer regime are used to determine heat transfer coefficients (Sec. 5). A detailed, point-by-point heat transfer analysis is required, however, to prevent fuel-element failure. The general procedure is to develop a heat transfer correlation for determining the peak central temperature (PCT) of a fuel element and apply this correlation to individual portions of the core. The correlation must account for the thermal resistance of the fuel, cladding, corrosion-product deposits on the cladding, coolant film, and bulk coolant.

In every reactor core there will be one point in one fuel element which operates at the highest temperature. The thermal analysis must locate this point and assure that fuel-element failure (burnout) will not occur. To achieve this goal, hot-spot analysis involving the so-called *hot-channel factors* is used. The hot-channel factors are of two basic types, nuclear and engineering. They account for variations in neutron flux and design parameters such as fuel-element dimensions, uncertainty in coolant flow rate, uncertainty in the heat transfer film coefficient, etc.

A large number of hot-channel factors may be defined (in general, for a given parameter as the ratio of the maximum-worst-deviation value to the nominal value) and quantitatively determined for a given core. However, they are combined into three basic, over-all factors used in the PCT correlation: (1) the factor for coolant temperature rise, $F_{\Delta T}$; (2) the film temperature-drop factor, F_θ; and (3) the heat generation factor, F_q.

The method by which individual hot-channel factors are combined to determine the over-all factors is a subject of considerable debate. Two basic methods are available: statistical, in which probabilities of occurrence are assigned to each factor, and the "factor-product" method, in which all contributors to each over-all factor are multiplied together. The latter is of course extremely conservative.

9-11. Hazard Analysis

Perhaps the most important single factor bearing on licensing of a nuclear power reactor is the hazard analysis. Details of the analysis are peculiar to a given reactor and reactor site, but in all cases must be presented to the U.S. Atomic Energy Commission (AEC) for review before a construction permit is issued and again before operation may begin. The licensing procedure is outlined in a publication of the Atomic Industrial Forum.[34]

The basis of the hazard analysis is the "maximum credible accident," a phrase indicative of the safety-design philosophy for nuclear plants. For every system, all pertinent design features are analyzed to determine maximum potential for failure and the worst possible consequences of such failure. The plant is then designed to prevent escape of radioactive fission products to the environment under such circumstances.

Specific potential causes for nuclear accidents will depend on the reactor type and location. In general, however, two basic factors (exclusive of external factors such as earthquake, war, etc.) can cause fission-product release: addition of reactivity and insufficient cooling. Each of these factors may be divided into two constituent factors. Addition of reactivity can occur as a result of improper control and, in water-cooled reactors, from a cold-water accident in which high-density water (i.e., moderator) is introduced to the core and causes excessive neutron thermalization and multiplication. Insufficient cooling can occur as a result of loss of coolant or loss of coolant flow. In the latter case, analysis also must be made for reactor shutdown since decay heat removal is essential.

All reactor components, control systems, and instrumentation are designed to minimize the hazard from each of these four accidents. In addition, however, it is assumed that failure which releases fission products will occur, and a system of sequential barriers is used to prevent release to the environment. The first of these barriers is the fuel-element cladding, the second is the boundaries of the reactor system itself (e.g., the reactor vessel and coolant piping), and the third is the containment vessel.

9-12. Nuclear Reactor Materials [5,7,8,26,35—37]

Conventional engineering materials are used in reactors except where special nuclear requirements must be met. Reactor materials must satisfy applicable, conventional criteria such as tensile strength, ductility, corrosion resistance, etc., and those used in the core must also have nuclear properties appropriate to their function.

A choice of materials for each major reactor component is available. There are, however, two general restrictions: materials specifications for reactors are generally more stringent than for nonnuclear applications because interactions with neutrons can affect suitability, and materials that are mutually compatible must be selected.

The combined engineering, nuclear, and compatibility requirements for nuclear materials have led to extensive research and development programs designed to produce new alloys and materials with improved physical properties for reactor use. Results of this work are reported in *Reactor Materials*, a quarterly publication of the U.S. government.[35]

Fuel Materials. Nuclear fuels in common use include natural uranium, slightly enriched uranium (0.95 to $\sim$6.0 per cent U^{235}), and fully enriched uranium (93 per cent U^{235}). The fuel materials also include large amounts of the fertile species U^{238} and Th^{232}. As more and more reactors operate to produce fissile nuclides from these fertile species, it may be expected that Pu^{239} and U^{233} will become important reactor fuels.

Natural uranium is generally used in both heavy-water and in gas-cooled reactors. Reactors cooled and moderated with light water use slightly enriched uranium as fuel; the actual enrichment is dictated by criticality and core-endurance requirements. Fully enriched uranium is used extensively in research and other special-purpose reactors, but thus far has received limited use in nuclear power stations.

Uranium has very poor metallurgical and physical properties.[37] It is dimensionally unstable after irradiation and thermal cycling and fails catastrophically with short exposure to water at 100°C or more. Its apparent physical properties are also extremely sensitive to purity, state of cold work, grain size, and orientation of grains. For these reasons, it is usually desirable to use uranium alloys or compounds as fuel materials; however, in the gas-cooled reactors that are so prevalent in Europe and England it is found economical to use natural uranium metal as fuel.

Reactors that burn slightly or fully enriched uranium use UO_2 or uranium alloys as the fuel material. Common alloying materials include zirconium, aluminum, molybdenum, and stainless steels. UO_2, in spite of low thermal conductivity, is widely used in water-cooled power reactors.

Current nuclear fuel development programs have as their major objectives development of improved fuel-fabrication techniques and better fuel materials. Promising examples of the latter are ceramics, such as UC, UC_2, and UN. These materials show much better resistance to adverse effects of irradiation than uranium metal, and are capable of withstanding long periods of exposure in the core. They have high melting points, reasonably good thermal conductivities, and are easily fabricated but react with water. Successful development of these materials is expected to result in much cheaper production of nuclear power as a result of reduced core-fabrication costs and longer periods of exposure between shutdowns for refueling.

Fuel exposure, or *burnup*, between refuelings is an extremely important factor in determining nuclear power costs. Burnup is usually expressed in megawatt-days of heat energy produced per metric ton (or tonne; equivalent to 2,200 lb) of uranium, abbreviated as Mwt-days/tonne U, or MWD/T. Thermal reactors currently in operation in the United States achieve burnups of about 10,000 MWD/T, with values between 20,000 and 30,000 or more anticipated for the future. The natural uranium-fueled, gas-cooled reactors in England and Europe achieve much lower burnups—on the order of 3,000 MWD/T—primarily because of loss of reactivity in natural uranium.

Radiation effects that limit fuel burnup may be summarized as dimensional instability (elongation or swelling) as a result of accumulation of fission products and gases, adverse changes in mechanical properties, relatively increased parasitic capture of neutrons, and loss of reactivity due to fuel consumption. It is expected that new fuel materials and fabrication techniques (too numerous to detail here) and programmed movement of fuel from one position in the core to another will greatly reduce these adverse effects, and thereby improve burnup and reduce fuel costs in the future.

Moderator Materials. Moderator materials in common use today include light water, heavy water, and graphite. Beryllium, BeO, and lithium 7 are also good moderator materials, but are toxic and highly reactive. Development programs for these materials are in progress.

Graphite is the most commonly used moderator in power reactors. In United States reactors, however, light water is most commonly used; it is cheap, readily available, and serves also as the coolant. Heavy water is actually a better moderator because deuterium has a much lower absorption cross section for parasitic capture of neutrons than hydrogen. Its high present cost ($24.50 per pound), however, has limited its use in power reactors, except where natural uranium can be economically used as fuel. Heavy water is present in natural water to the extent of 140 to 150 ppm; the two species may be separated by distillation, chemical exchange, or electrolysis. The United States maintains large separation plants in Savannah River, Ga.

The graphite used in reactors is of high density (to limit reactor size) and high purity ($\sim$20 ppm total impurities). A highly pure material is required to minimize parasitic capture of neutrons. The product resulting from the graphite-manufacturing process may be easily machined or cast in desired shapes.

Cladding Materials. The cladding must be a high-integrity structural material with good corrosion resistance, high thermal conductivity, and a low neutron absorption cross section. Stainless steels and aluminum are currently the most commonly used cladding materials; however, zirconium alloys are actually superior to these because of their very low neutron absorption cross section ($\sim$0.2 vs. $\sim$3 barns for steel) and excellent corrosion resistance.

Other cladding materials used in thermal reactors include Magnox (a magnesium alloy, used primarily in the United Kingdom gas-cooled reactors), magnesium-zirconium alloys, Incaloy, ceramic coatings, and graphite. Claddings used in fast reactors include stainless steels, zirconium, niobium, and other refractory metals and ceramics. Properties of these and other materials discussed in this section may be found in Sec. 13 of this manual.

Reactor Control Materials. Materials used to control thermal reactors by neutron absorption have as their most important characteristic large neutron absorption cross sections; the elements that contain isotopes suitable for this application include boron, cadmium, europium, and hafnium.

Control materials are used in the reactor in two principal ways. The most common is by control rods, a method that requires the control materials to withstand shock, vibration, and wear. The other method is to use a burnable poison which can be evenly distributed in the fuel, placed in discrete positions in the core, or dissolved in the coolant. Use of burnable poisons requires careful calculation of control-material concentrations; poison burnup and fuel-depletion rates must be comparable.

The control materials may be utilized in various forms. Boron, for example, is used in boron–stainless-steel alloys, as B_4C particles dispersed in zirconium or fuel alloys, and as boric acid added to the coolant. The latter is a commonly used backup safety method in water-cooled reactors. Cadmium is used as a major constituent of silver-indium-cadmium alloys. These alloys have relatively low melting points, however, and poor corrosion resistance in water containing even small amounts ($\sim$5 ppm) of oxygen. They also have poor strength properties.

Hafnium has been found to be an excellent control material. In addition to its good nuclear properties, it has high strength and good corrosion resistance. It is readily shaped and welded as the pure metal. Hafnium is expensive, however. It is obtained only as a by-product of zirconium ores, and processing costs to separate the two elements are high. The separation is essential, because hafnium impurities in zirconium used in reactor cores would greatly increase parasitic capture of neutrons. Hence hafnium is readily available for limited use; but fabrication costs are also quite high because of the need to avoid impurities which adversely affect physical properties of the material.

Most operating power station reactors use boron as the control material. The Shippingport, Pa., reactor and many mobile reactors use hafnium. The Yankee reactor in Rowe, Mass., has used a silver-indium-cadmium alloy, as do many research reactors. The very high cost and metallurgical problems with europium and other lanthanon poisons have prohibited their use except in a few cases.

Reactor Coolants. The basic types of materials available as reactor coolants (water, gases, liquid metals, molten salts, and organic liquids) have previously been mentioned briefly. Of all of these, light water is the most commonly used in the United States because physical-property data are readily available and it is economical. Reactors using the other types of coolants have also been built, however, and several alternatives in each category are available, as outlined below.

Gases. Air, hydrogen, helium, and carbon dioxide are in principle good reactor coolants. Each, however, has certain specific deficiencies: the oxygen in air reacts with reactor materials, hydrogen is extremely hazardous and reacts with many metals, helium is quite expensive, and CO_2 is a relatively poor heat-transfer medium. In general, all gaseous coolants also have the disadvantage of being poor heat-transfer agents compared with liquids.

Carbon dioxide is the most commonly used gas coolant because of the problems with the other gases. Some advanced-concept reactors, however, use helium as the coolant because of superior heat-transfer and physical properties.

Liquid Metals. These materials are virtually a necessity for fast reactors in which coolants with good moderating properties are undesirable. In general, the excellent thermal properties of the liquid metals provide the advantage of operation at high temperatures with high power densities (Table 9-5) and compact cores. On the debit side, however, technological knowledge of the liquid metals is relatively sparse, their cost is high, and their generally high chemical reactivity at elevated temperatures makes selection of compatible materials a problem.

The most meaningful criterion for selection of liquid metals as reactor coolants is the neutron absorption cross section, which must be small to minimize parasitic capture. On this basis, the liquid metals listed in Table 9-6

Table 9-6. Properties of Liquid-metal Reactor Coolants

Metal	σ_a, barns	Melting point, °F
Bismuth.......	0.032	520
Lithium 7......	0.033	367
Lead..........	0.17	621
Sodium........	0.50	208
Tin............	0.65	450
Potassium......	2.0	145
Gallium........	2.7	86
Thallium.......	3.3	576

are found to be suitable reactor coolants. Of these, liquid sodium and the NaK eutectic (22 weight per cent Na), which is liquid at ordinary temperatures, are at present most attractive because they have fewer disadvantages than the others. A major disadvantage of the use of sodium as a reactor coolant is formation of Na^{24} from Na^{23}. The Na^{24} has a significantly long half-life (15 hr) and emits two high-energy gamma rays with decay. Shielding of reactor components is therefore required, and access to the reactor compartment for maintenance may be restricted because of high radiation levels for two or three days.

Molten Salts. These materials have been considered as reactor coolants because they permit economic utilization of all grades of reactor fuels. They are used in a fluid-fueled reactor in which the coolant and fuel are a homogeneous slurry pumped throughout the system. The molten salts are advantageous for fluid-fueled systems because, unlike aqueous fuels, they can be used at low pressures and high temperatures.

Only two molten-salt reactor systems have been built and operated; both had demonstration of feasibility as the major objective. The first was the Aircraft Reactor Experiment, now terminated, and the most recent is the Molten Salt Reactor Experiment (MSRE) located in Oak Ridge, Tenn. The MSRE utilizes a fuel salt which has a composition of 65 mole per cent Li^7F, 29.1 per cent BF_2, 5 per cent ZrF_4 and 0.9 per cent UF_4; its melting point is 842°F. This salt, and other structural materials, were specially developed for the MSRE reactor.

Organic Liquids. Organic liquids have many potential advantages as reactor coolants: the systems may be operated at low pressure; the organics are not highly corrosive; they are good moderators; induced radioactivity is low, and physical properties are well known. It has been found, however, that the organic coolant tends to decompose when exposed to high temperatures and radiation. This characteristic could result in serious operational problems, such as plugging of flow channels and fouling of heat-transfer surfaces. To eliminate these problems decomposed coolant must be removed by purification and replaced with fresh coolant.

Tests have shown that terphenyl, a benzene derivative, is most resistant to decomposition. It is used in the only organic-cooled, power-producing reactor now in operation, located at Piqua, Ohio.

9-13. Corrosion in Reactor Systems [35—40]

Corrosion phenomena in nuclear reactors present several unusual problems relative to conventional systems. In particular, potential problems such as galling of small intricate parts in control-rod drive mechanisms, increased resistance to heat transfer and fluid flow in the core as a result of deposition of corrosion products on core surfaces, and induced radioactivity of corrosion products require careful evaluation. In water-cooled reactors, which are predominant in the United States, careful selection of materials and coolant chemistry conditions is necessary to minimize corrosion problems in the above areas.

Corrosion rates for materials used in reactors are typically extremely low. For example, corrosion of 304 stainless steel, a common reactor structural material, is less than 5 mg/dm^2-mo at reactor operating conditions. The systems are so large, however, (generally on the order of 50,000 ft^2 of surface in contact with reactor coolant) that as much as several pounds of corrosion products is generated each month of operation. These corrosion products distribute throughout the system and exhibit an affinity for deposition on core surfaces. This deposition on core surfaces leads to problems with heat transfer, pressure drop, and induced radioactivity, as mentioned above.

Deposition of corrosion products (or "crud," as it is called) on core surfaces has produced observable increases in heat-transfer resistance and pressure drop. Thus far, these phenomena have not produced serious operational difficulties. Similarly, large amounts of radioactive corrosion products have been produced: the crud deposited on the core becomes highly radioactive as a result of exposure to neutron flux, and a portion of this material is subsequently released to accumulate in low-velocity regions and become incorporated in the adherent corrosion-product film on surfaces.

Again, radioactive crud has not yet produced serious difficulties. Of concern, however, is the possibility that continued production and accumulation of radioactive crud will lead to high radiation fields around reactor components, which would seriously restrict access to the system for maintenance. Possibilities for future difficulties in this area exist because the major contributors to the hazard from radioactive corrosion products are Co^{60}, with a 5.3-year half-life, and Co^{58}, with a 72-day half-life. The Co^{60} is the major radiation hazard, and because of its long half-life, would nominally be expected not to achieve maximum levels until after 20 or 25 years of operation. Reactor operating experience is at present limited to about 8 years; hence there is not yet sufficient information to estimate future hazards from this source.

Several methods are used to combat corrosion problems in reactors. To begin with, materials such as the austenitic stainless steels, which corrode at very low rates, are used as major materials of construction in order to minimize corrosion-product inventories. To further this objective, coolant chemistry conditions are maintained in a manner that experience has indicated serves to minimize corrosion even more. These conditions include maintenance of dissolved hydrogen in the range 10 to 20 ppm (STP) and in some cases an elevated (i.e., basic) coolant pH. The coolant pH is maintained above neutral by addition of LiOH or NH_4OH as pH agents.

The pH agent may be added manually from charging tanks or essentially automatically by a bed of ion-exchange resin. The ion-exchange bed is a necessary portion of the purification system, which is another device used to minimize corrosion problems. In this system a small fraction of the coolant is passed through the bed of ion-exchange resin. The resin bed is usually of the mixed form, so that cations and anions can be removed. The bed also acts effectively as a filter for particulates in the coolant. When the ion-exchange resin serves to maintain an elevated pH in the coolant, the cation exchanger releases a lithium ion or an ammonium ion, and the anion exchanger releases hydroxyl ions. This mode of operation will maintain a coolant pH of about 10 with lithium and about 9 with ammonia.

Attempts to curb crud radioactivity problems have led also to considering use of materials that do not contain elemental cobalt [the Co^{60} is formed primarily by the $Co^{59}(n,\gamma)Co^{60}$ reaction]. Unfortunately, this approach has thus far proved to be impractical. The cobalt is a tramp impurity associated with elemental nickel, so that the minimum practical cobalt content of stainless steel would appear to be about 0.1 weight per cent. In addition, materials such as the Stellites and Haynes alloys, which contain about 60 per cent cobalt, are still the only suitable alloys for applications where wear resistance is required, such as valve facings and control-rod drive mechanisms. Wear products from this source undoubtedly contribute large amounts of cobalt to the crud.

9-14. Radiation Effects in Reactor Materials [5,26,35,36]

The heavy particles (protons, neutrons, alpha particles, and fission fragments) can produce changes in physical properties of metals by causing displacement of nuclei from their lattice sites. The phenomenon is called *radiation damage.*

The mechanisms of radiation damage are not completely understood. It is known, however, that when about 25 ev or more of energy is transferred to a struck nucleus by collision with an incoming particle, the struck atom will be displaced from its lattice site. It then becomes a "primary knock-on." If the energy transferred to the primary knock-on is well in excess of 25 ev (a frequent occurrence, since many of the incident particles have energies of 1 Mev or more), secondary displacements will be caused by the primary knock-on so that a cascade of knock-ons is produced. The number of atoms that may be displaced by a primary knock-on is quite large; for example, the calculated average number of displacements in carbon and iron resulting from an incident 1-Mev neutron are 900 and 390 atoms, respectively.

As the primary knock-on and other displaced nuclei travel through the lattice, they cause extensive ionization of the surrounding material. The knock-ons lose energy as a result of these ionizing interactions and eventually come essentially to rest either in an interstitial location or in a normal lattice vacancy.

The slowing down of knock-ons may produce a *displacement spike.* In this type of damage a large amount of lattice distortion is produced in a volume containing a few thousand atoms as a result of rapid dissipation of the knock-on's energy. Some of the atoms in the volume acquire sufficient vibrational energy to be displaced from their lattice sites.

A *thermal spike* is produced when few, if any, of the vibrationally excited atoms leave their lattice sites. In this situation a region containing on the order of a thousand atoms is subjected to the equivalent of heating to a temperature of about 1800°F for a period of about 10^{-10} sec. Distortion of the lattice and some displacement of atoms result, so that residual stresses may be produced.

9-15. Physical Effects of Radiation

The effects of the damage phenomena discussed above vary with the material and operating conditions. In general, operation at elevated temperatures reduces adverse effects of radiation. High temperatures permit more rapid movement and diffusion of atoms, and therefore produce the same effects as annealing.

Radiation Effects in Metals. Neutron-induced changes in properties of steel are illustrated by Fig. 9-10, which also shows that the significant independent variable is the integrated flux, or flux-time product. The effects shown in Fig. 9-10 are typical; most metals exhibit an increase in strength and hardness and a reduction in ductility with prolonged radiation exposure. It should be noted that materials used in the core of reactor plants may be subjected to integrated fluxes of 10^{21} neutrons/cm² or more.

The radiation effect of most consequence in steels is the increase in nil-ductility transition temperature. This phenomenon could limit the useful

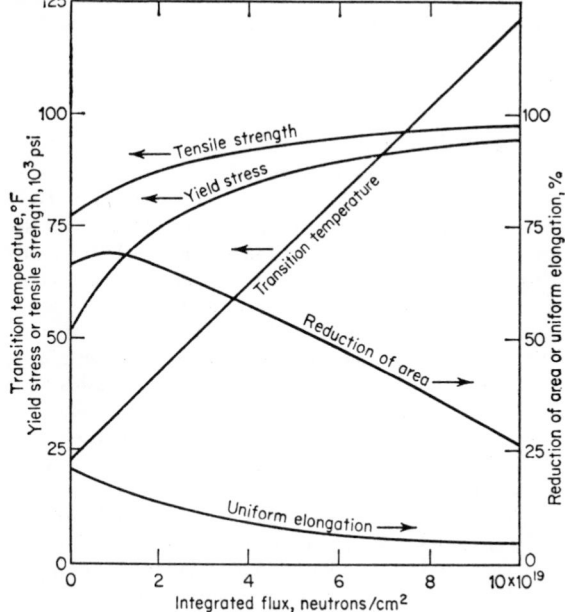

FIG. 9-10. Effect of fast-neutron exposure on properties of steel. (*Glasstone and Sesonske, "Nuclear Reactor Engineering," D. Van Nostrand Company, Inc., Princeton, N.J., 1963.*)

life span of reactor pressure vessels because, with sufficient exposure to radiation, the transition temperature is raised to normal environmental temperatures. Reactor vessels are exposed to considerably lower neutron fluxes than core materials because of protection provided by the thermal shields and distance from the core. However, these factors serve only to increase the time span required for radiation effects to become significant, and increases in transition temperature are already of concern for some reactors with long operating experience.

Other Materials. Radiation effects in other commonly used reactor materials are similar to those for metals. Graphite, for example, exhibits swelling and increases in thermal resistance. Organic liquids decompose, as described in Sec. 9-12, and organic solids polymerize and show increased hardness and brittleness.   Effects of radiation on fuel materials are described briefly in Sec. 9-12.

9-16. Shielding [5,14,41—44]

The many particulate and electromagnetic radiations in the reactor environment require a variety of amounts and types of shielding to protect personnel from hazardous exposure.   Shieldings used vary from sheets of paper (all that is required to shield against alpha particles) to several feet of materials such as lead, steel, or high-density concrete.   Since alpha and beta particles (stopped by a $\frac{1}{4}$-in. thickness of aluminum or equivalent) are easily shielded, attention here is focused on shielding of neutrons and gamma rays.

9-17. Shielding of Neutrons

Requirements for shielding neutrons may be divided into two components: slowing down of fast neutrons and capture of slow neutrons.   To slow down neutrons effectively, heavy nuclei, which efficiently slow down neutrons to about 1 Mev by inelastic collisions, and light nuclei, which are effective for slowing neutrons from 1 Mev to thermal energies, are frequently used together. Elements such as iron and lead are effective as heavy nuclei for these purposes; they will decrease the neutron energy to about 1 Mev in a single inelastic collision.   The light elements (in particular, hydrogen in the form of water) then provide moderation to thermal energies via elastic collisions. Light elements may be used alone as neutron shield materials.   The heavy elements, however, are not effective neutron shields when used alone because they require many collisions to thermalize from energies of about 1 Mev (see Secs. 9-6 and 9-12).

Capture of slow neutrons is accomplished most effectively by hydrogenous materials.   Hence materials such as water and concrete, which contains about 10 weight per cent water, are widely used as neutron shielding materials. Boron is also effective because of its large capture cross section for neutrons, and may be used in a variety of forms.   For example, some reactors have utilized borated polyethylene as a neutron shield; this material has a high hydrogen density, as well as providing efficient neutron capture by the boron.

A potential problem that must be taken into account when selecting slow-neutron capture materials is gamma-ray emissions associated with the capture reaction.   Capture of a neutron by hydrogen, for example, results in a 2.2-Mev gamma photon, for which shielding must be provided.   Similarly, neutron capture by iron produces a 7.6-Mev gamma ray; the high energy of this photon makes iron a less satisfactory neutron shield material because of the additional gamma-ray shielding required.

9-18. Shielding of Gamma Rays

Gamma rays are the most penetrating radiation of concern and hence require extensive shielding.   In general, the effectiveness of materials as gamma-ray shields is proportional to density; however, it is also dependent on the energy of the incident photon and the mechanism of interaction of the photon with the material.   These factors are discussed briefly below.

Gamma rays interact with materials in at least three ways, all of which involve the orbital electrons surrounding the nucleus. The mechanism of interaction at low energies is known as the *photoelectric effect*, in which all the gamma-ray energy is transferred to the orbital electron and the latter is ejected from the atom. At intermediate energies the *Compton effect* predominates; this process involves elastic scattering of the photon by the electron and transfer of energy between them. At high energies the gamma ray is annihilated and an electron-positron pair is formed. This process is called *pair production* and is restricted to photon energies of 1.02 Mev (the energy equivalent of the electron-positron mass) and above.

These interactions attenuate the photon flux so that its intensity decreases exponentially. The capacity of a material to attenuate gamma radiation is measured by the *linear attenuation coefficient* μ, defined by the relationship

$$\frac{dI}{I} = -\mu\,dx \tag{9-43}$$

where I is the radiation intensity, and dx is the thickness of the material.

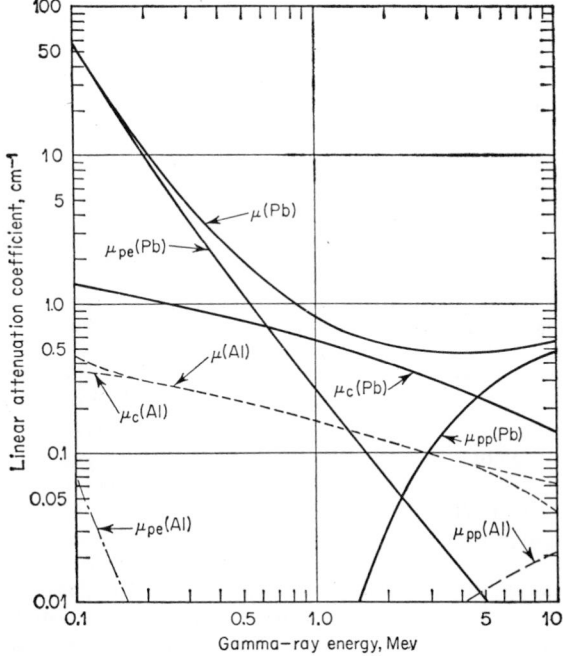

Fig. 9-11. Linear attenuation coefficients of aluminum and lead. (*Glasstone and Sesonske, "Nuclear Reactor Engineering," D. Van Nostrand Company, Inc., Princeton, N.J.*, 1963.)

Equation 9-43 applies only to thin sections of material placed in a collimated beam of monoenergetic photons, and values of μ are dependent on photon energy.

The linear attenuation coefficient for a given material is determined experimentally as a function of photon energy. Typical results are illustrated by Fig. 9-11, which shows the contributions of the three interaction mechanisms described above to the total linear attenuation coefficients for lead and aluminum. Values for other materials are given in reference manuals such as the AEC shielding handbook.[41]

Because of the nature of the interaction phenomena, high electron density is required for effective shielding of gamma rays. Consequently, materials with high mass density and high atomic weight are commonly used. Lead and concrete are typical because they are inexpensive, easily shaped, and structurally suitable. Concrete is particularly advantageous for power stations where low cost is important and shield volume is relatively unimportant. Conversely, lead is convenient for mobile reactors such as ships, where high shield density and low volume are essential.

Various high-density concretes have been developed for shielding applications. In particular, concretes containing materials such as iron punchings, iron ore, lead shot, and barium compounds are available for special applications, such as research reactors, where thinner shields are desirable.

9-19. Shielding Design

The design of shields for reactor systems is an extremely complex process requiring procedures too detailed to give here. In brief, it is necessary to account for effects of radiation source geometry, the energy and type of radiation, the attenuation properties and thickness of the shield material, the effects of radiation heating of the shield material, and requirements for radiation field intensity outside the shield. The complexity of these factors precludes a wholly analytical approach to shield design; semiempirical methods and experimental data are therefore utilized extensively. Some of the major concepts involved in shielding design are outlined below.

Source Strength and Geometry. An analytical expression which gives the intensity of a radiation field as a function of distance from the source is frequently required. To obtain such an expression, it is necessary, first, to define the magnitude and geometry of the source. The source strength is expressed as a flux of photons or neutrons per unit area per unit time. The source strength for fast neutrons is calculated on the basis of the known fissioning rate in the core and the fission-neutron energy spectrum. Source strengths for gamma rays must account for two phenomena: primary radiation, originating from phenomena within the core, and secondary radiation, which is produced from neutron interactions with materials external to the core. An example of the latter is the 2.2-Mev gamma produced by neutron capture in hydrogen, as mentioned above. In general, because attenuation coefficients are a function of photon energy, the gamma-ray flux is divided into several energy groups, and contributions to each group are accounted for as successively different materials are encountered with increasing distance from the core. Figure 9-12 illustrates typical variations in gamma flux as a function of radial distance from the core center line. The flux intensity is expressed in Fig. 9-12 as a dose rate, in milliroentgens per hour (Sec. 9-9).

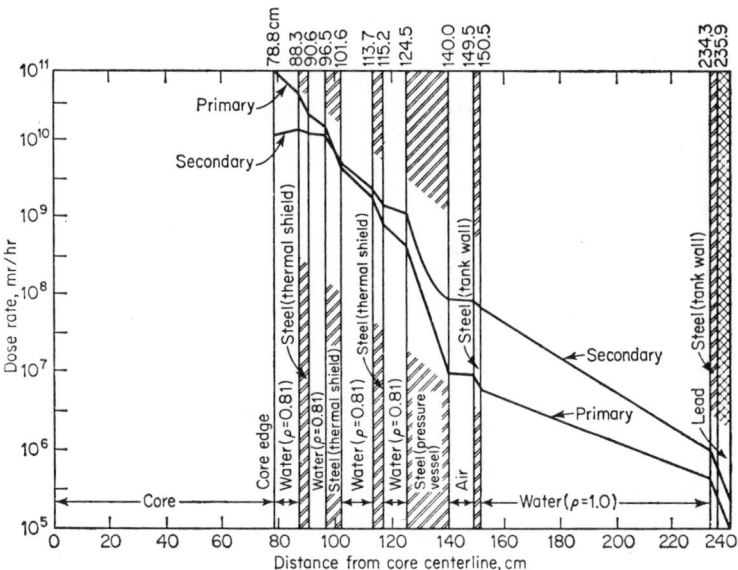

Fig. 9-12. Radial variation in gamma-ray dose rates from a reactor. (*Glasstone and Sesonske, "Nuclear Reactor Engineering," D. Van Nostrand Company, Inc., Princeton, N.J., 1963.*)

Source-geometry effects are handled by defining mathematical functions which express the source intensity for various shapes (known as *distributed sources*), such as spheres and cylinders as an integral of point sources. These expressions and their derivation are given in standard references.[41,42]

Effects of Shield Geometry. The shield itself can introduce complex problems in shielding design. Some factors depend strongly on design details for the individual shield. For example, the presence of ducts and voids will produce local, high-intensity radiation fields outside the shield; the strength and shape of the field will depend on the geometry of the duct or void, and usually can be determined accurately only by experiment.

More general than the above, however, are effects of shield thickness. In brief, the simple exponential relationship

$$I = I_0 e^{-\mu x} \tag{9-44}$$

which results from integration of Eq. (9-43) with $I = I_0$ at $x = 0$, does not apply to thick shields because radiation scattered from the incident beam by interaction with the material, instead of being lost from the beam path as is usual for thin layers of material, may be scattered back into the emergent beam as a result of successive interactions. This phenomenon is accounted for by introducing the so-called *buildup factors*, so that Eq. (9-44) becomes

$$I = B(\mu x)I_0 e^{-\mu x} \tag{9-45}$$

where $B(\mu x)$ is the appropriate buildup factor. As suggested by the symbolism, the buildup factor is a function of the linear attenuation coefficient (and therefore of photon energy) and shield thickness. Buildup factors may be calculated theoretically, and are tabulated in the literature as a function of photon energy, material, and the parameter μx. For shielding materials and photon energies of common interest, buildup-factor values range from just over unity to about 50.

Use of buildup factors is generally reserved for gamma-ray attenuation. For fast-neutron attenuation, an analogous concept, the *removal cross section*, is used. This parameter is similar to the neutron absorption cross section (Sec. 9-4), but applies strictly to compound shields consisting of a thin layer of solid material and a thick layer of water, with the solid between the radiation source and the water (a commonly encountered shield design). Fast neutrons are slowed down in the solid primarily by inelastic scattering, and slowed down more, and captured, in the water; the removal cross section is a measure of the probability of occurrence of this process.

Heat Generation in Shields. An important consideration in shielding design is the fact that absorption of radiation energy leads to production of an equivalent amount of heat (1.519×10^{-16} Btu = 1 Mev). Hence shields must frequently be cooled to prevent overheating and development of thermal stresses.

Heat-generation rates are readily calculable from attenuation data derived from the shield design; methods used to provide cooling will vary in accordance with local requirements. The thermal shields in the reactor vessel (Sec. 9-9) are cooled, for example, by reactor coolant diverted from the core. Heating rates and cooling requirements for these shields are quite high. Conversely, shields and other components located at a relatively large distance from the reactor so that energy absorption rates are low may require no cooling other than normal ventilation or natural convection.

9-20. Radiation Protection [45-49]

The purpose of the shielding described briefly above is to prevent hazardous exposure of personnel to radiation. To achieve this goal, it is necessary to specify how much exposure to radiation is permissible and to measure quantitatively amounts of radiation of various types and the effects of these radiations on the human body.

Amounts of radiation absorbed by a material are determined in terms of energy deposited per unit mass. Certain standard definitions have been universally adopted:

Roentgen (R). The Roentgen measures only X-ray- or gamma-ray-induced ionization of air. It is defined as that radiation which produces 83 ergs of energy absorbed per gram of dry air (STP).

Roentgen Equivalent Physical (rep). The rep accounts for absorption of energy from either electromagnetic or particulate radiation in soft body tissue or, equivalently, water. One rep is defined as energy absorption of 93 ergs/g of soft tissue.

Radiation Absorbed Dose (rad). The rad is a more general unit, defined as absorption of 100 ergs of energy (any type of radiation) per gram of material (any medium). It has replaced the rep in common usage.

Roentgen Equivalent Man (rem). This unit was devised to describe more accurately the physical effects in the human body of the various types of radiation. It is defined as that quantity of radiation of any type that produces the same biological effects in man as those resulting from absorption of one R of X or gamma radiation.

Relative Biological Effectiveness (RBE). This unit was defined in association with the rem. It is given by a ratio,

$$\text{RBE} = \frac{\text{physical dose of 200 kev X rays to produce given effect}}{\text{physical dose of other radiation to produce same effect}}$$

the value of which may depend on a variety of factors, such as the dose rate, the kind and degree of effect, and the type of tissue. Because of these variables, it is common practice to use the single, most conservative (i.e., highest) value of the RBE for each type of radiation. Current values are listed in Table 9-7.

Table 9-7. RBE Factors for Various Radiations

Energy and Type of Radiation	RBE
X rays	1
Gamma rays	1
1-Mev beta particle	1
0.1-Mev beta particle	1.08
Thermal neutron	2.5
1-Mev proton	8.5
0.1-Mev proton	10
Fast neutron	10
5-Mev alpha particle	15
1-Mev alpha particle	20

The above definitions lead to the relationship

$$\text{Dose in rems} = \text{RBE} \times \text{dose in rads} \qquad (9\text{-}46)$$

which is especially useful because it indicates, for different radiations and RBE values, variations in rad doses required to produce physically equivalent doses in rems. Biological effects of rem doses from different radiations are additive, whereas those from rad doses are not.

9-21. Determination of Doses

To determine rem doses the rad dose must first be established. This is accomplished by (1) determining the *rad-dose-rate* equivalent of the radiation flux (the radiation flux is the quantity usually known) and (2) expressing the rad dose as the product of the rad dose rate, usually given in milliroentgens per hour (mr/hr) and the period of exposure in hours.

The rad-dose-rate equivalence of radiation flux is a complex function of the type and energy of the radiation. The relationship has been calculated for photon and neutron fluxes of various energies, as shown in Fig. 9-13.

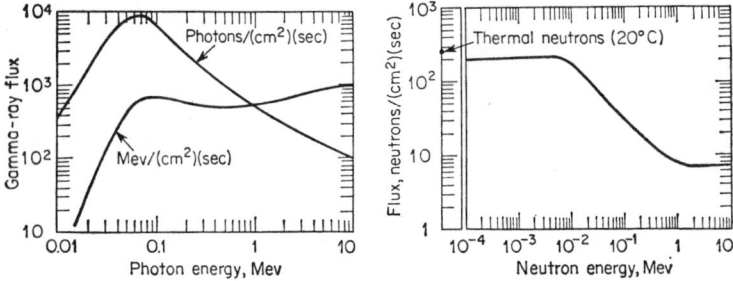

FIG. 9-13. Flux equivalents of 1 mr/hr dose rates. (*Glasstone and Sesonske*, "*Nuclear Reactor Engineering*," *D. Van Nostrand Company, Inc., Princeton, N.J.,* 1963.)

9-22. Types of Doses and Exposure

There are two basic types of radiation doses. A *chronic dose* is a low-level dose accumulated over a relatively long period of time; an *acute dose* involves high-level exposure in a short period of time. In general, an acute dose, when administered to the whole body, causes greater adverse biological effects than chronic doses. However, acute doses, when administered to small localized portions of the body, can be beneficial, as in radiation therapy.

As suggested by the above, it is important to specify type of exposure as well as type of dose. Exposures are conveniently classified as whole-body, fractional (part of the body), continuous or noncontinuous, and excessive. In the case of fractional exposure it is also necessary to specify the part of the body exposed, since certain organs are more critically affected by radiation than others. In particular, the skin, gonads, bone marrow, and lens of the eye have been defined as critical organs for which exposure is severely limited.

9-23. Radiation Protection Standards

Using experimental data as a guide, national and international agencies have established standards for exposure to radiation that are designed to prevent ill effects in any segment of the population. These standards basically establish rates of dose accumulation for the general population and occupationally exposed personnel; they are reviewed periodically and revised if necessary. Present standards are given in detail in Ref. 45 and summarized below.

For occupationally exposed persons, the total accumulated rem dose over

core, which in turn causes a decrease in reactivity; i.e., the reactor tends to shut down. This problem can be eliminated by several methods,[27] but all involve modifications to the basic cycle and a concomitant increase in capital costs.

Dual-cycle Boiling-water Reactors. The dual-cycle type of plant obviates the low power density and poor load response characteristics of the direct-cycle system by increasing and varying the amount of subcooling of the reactor inlet water.

The essential features of the dual-cycle plant are shown in Fig. 9-14. The external steam separator and the secondary steam generator shown are the

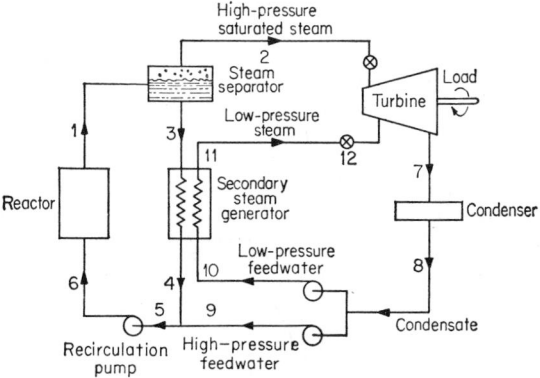

FIG. 9-14. Schematic diagram of a dual-cycle boiling-water reactor. (*El-Wakil,* "*Nuclear Power Engineering,*" *McGraw-Hill Book Company, New York, 1962.*)

components which provide the advantages of this type of system over the direct-cycle system. The external steam separator permits operating with a smaller fraction of the coolant in the core as steam; consequently, the coolant-moderator density—and therefore the power density—in the core is greater.

The secondary steam generator provides greater subcooling of reactor inlet water than is possible in a direct-cycle system. This feature gives the reactor load-following response characteristics in the following manner: When the turbine load is increased, a greater flow of low-pressure steam to the turbine is provided by increasing steam flow through the throttle valve at point 12 in Fig. 9-14. More heat is then extracted from coolant flowing in the high-pressure recirculation line (from point 3 to point 4), and water entering the reactor is consequently cooler. The coolant-moderator density in the core is therefore increased, and the power output of the reactor increases because of greater thermalization of neutrons.

In spite of the drawbacks mentioned above, boiling-water reactors are, and are expected to continue to be, economically attractive. Technical problems are minimal. and new advances continue to reduce power costs. For example, the Oyster Creek reactor in Lacey Township, N.J., scheduled for completion in 1967, is a direct-cycle plant that utilizes variable-speed pumps to overcome load-following problems. This and other improvements are expected to result in power costs as low as 4 mills/kwhr. Similarly, a companion reactor to the now operating dual-cycle Dresden plant in Morris, Ill., is in design. Meanwhile, development work to provide economical nuclear superheat is in progress. Also, many modifications to these basic types of boiling-water plants are being considered.[27]

Pressurized-water Reactors. The PWRs are most numerous in the spectrum of United States nuclear plants because they, exclusively, are used for nuclear naval propulsion. They are also competitive for use in central power stations. They are relatively simple in design, the technology is well established, cores are compact, and thermal efficiencies are reasonably good.

Figure 9-15 is a schematic diagram of the major components in a PWR system. It is apparent that the reactor coolant is not the working fluid in

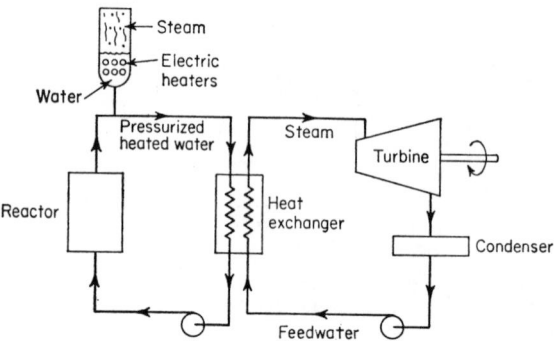

FIG. 9-15. Schematic diagram of a pressurized-water reactor system. (*El-Wakil, "Nuclear Power Engineering," McGraw-Hill Book Company, New York, 1962.*)

this type of system; this feature is necessitated by the fact that boiling generally is not permitted in the core of PWRs (recent designs, however, permit some bulk boiling). The systems operate at pressures of about 2,000 psia; the pressure is maintained by a pressurizer as indicated in Fig. 9-15. These high pressures demand thick-walled reactor vessels and other components and the attendant cost and design problems. A feature of PWRs not shown by Fig. 9-15 is that these plants are built with multiple coolant loops serving the core. This concept permits continued operation in the event of pump or turbine failure in a single loop.

The coolant moderator serving the core of PWRs is known as the *primary coolant*. Total flow is on the order of 10^7 lb mass/hr at a velocity of 15 to 35 fps and an average temperature of about 500°F. Sealed-motor, centrifugal pumps of special (i.e., expensive) design and high capacity (up to 40,000 gpm) are used.

Sealed pumps are required to avoid leakage of radioactive coolant. The coolant picks up tramp activity from various sources such as dissolved solids, corrosion products, and, in the event of fuel-element failure, fission products. The coolant itself also becomes radioactive as a result of transport through the core. The radioactive species produced from coolant activation (N^{13}, N^{16}, N^{17}, F^{18}, and O^{19}) have very short half-lives, and are therefore not an after-shutdown radiation hazard, as is Na^{24}. The N^{16}, however, emits two high-energy gamma rays on decay, and this isotope is a major factor in shielding design for water-cooled reactors.

Pressurized-water reactors also appear to have a bright future. The long-established technology and new developments[33,52] to produce improved component design, materials, and fuel endurance have led to power-cost estimates for these systems on the order of 5 mills/kwhr. Many new PWRs are now in construction and design throughout the world.

Gas-cooled Reactors. Components of gas-cooled reactor systems are similar to those of pressurized-water reactors (Fig. 9-15); a gas simply replaces water as the primary coolant. Steam conditions in gas-cooled and PWR reactors are comparable. There are, however, some major differences in the primary coolant circuit. The gas-cooled systems can achieve higher reactor operating temperatures at lower pressure. In addition, coolant temperature rise through the core in a gas-cooled reactor will be several hundred degrees Farenheit; in PWRs, it is limited to about 30°F. Power densities in gas-cooled systems are extremely low; the increase in cost this necessitates is, however, compensated for in the United Kingdom reactors by use of inexpensive fuel (natural uranium).

Other major advantages of gas-cooled reactors include easy handling of coolant, good neutron economy, low coolant activities, and flexibility of design. These advantages are compensated, however, by very high coolant pumping requirements, low heat transfer rates, and the relatively high capital costs associated with the necessarily large system. Also, design procedures for gas-cooled systems are more complex and difficult than for water-cooled systems.

Despite these difficulties, gas-cooled systems are an attractive reactor concept, even in the United States. They offer potential for attaining modern steam conditions and utilizing modern turbines that boiling-water and PWR systems cannot readily achieve with today's technology. Great progress has been made in gas-cooled-reactor technology, and it is significant that the United Kingdom has again selected gas-cooled systems (new, advanced designs) for their second generation of reactors. This selection is based on anticipated power costs of about 5 mills/kwhr, which is comparable with values predicted for the two projected gas-cooled power reactors in the United States (Peach Bottom, Pa., in construction; Colorado, in design). The U.S. reactors are expected to supply 1000°F, 1,500-psia steam at thermal efficiencies of 35 to 40 per cent, rather than the 28 to 32 per cent that is common for present nuclear plants.

Liquid-metal-cooled Reactors. As previously mentioned, liquid-metal-cooled systems appear to be the only feasible way to achieve good breeding and conversion and thereby utilize fertile materials effectively. Possible future needs for breeding[16] and the inherently high power densities and thermal efficiencies of liquid-metal-cooled systems therefore practically demand development of this reactor concept. However, technical problems are formidable and costs are high.

The coolant (assumed here to be liquid sodium, or NaK) is central to the technical problems. It is expensive and highly chemically active and develops high induced radioactivity. The radioactivity and chemical activity necessitate extensive shielding and an intermediate loop between the primary coolant and the working fluid; thus thermal efficiencies are less than potentially possible.

Liquid-metal coolants are highly corrosive to many reactor materials. In addition, sodium oxide (Na_2O), which is even more corrosive than sodium, is formed if oxygen is present in the coolant. It also tends to deposit out of the coolant and possibly plug narrow passages. These problems necessitate enclosing the reactor system in an inert-gas blanket to prevent formation of Na_2O.

There are also special problems associated with design of the compact cores permitted by liquid-metal coolants. Negative temperature coefficients (Sec. 9-3) are hard to achieve, decay-heat removal is difficult, and core hardware such as control rods, fuel-handling mechanisms, and instrumentation must be elaborate and carefully designed.

Liquid metals may be used as the coolant for either fast or thermal reactors, although the fast reactors take advantage of their natural characteristics. In liquid-metal-cooled thermal reactors, neutron moderation is accomplished by materials other than the coolant; graphite is generally used for this purpose. The graphite must be isolated from the coolant by canning, because it is readily attacked by sodium.

Despite severe technical problems, sodium-cooled reactors have been built and successfully operated. There are, however, only five such systems now operating in the world. It is at present easier and cheaper to build water-cooled reactors. If, however, fast breeders become imperative (and not all authorities agree that they will be required), liquid-metal-cooled systems will become more important and numerous.

Other Reactors. Many other reactor concepts, too numerous to discuss here in detail, have been considered. Most have as their objective elimination of some of the costly characteristics of present nuclear plants. For example, organic-liquid-cooled reactors eliminate the need for high pressure associated with PWRs. Similarly, new concepts such as the pebble-bed reactor[27] and various homogeneous systems (e.g., aqueous homogeneous, liquid-metal-fueled, and molten salt) would eliminate costs and difficulties of fabrication and refueling of heterogeneous systems. Prototype or experimental systems for these reactor concepts have been built, but no use in power stations has yet been proposed.

Special-purpose reactors[5,51] are an important adjunct of the nuclear power industry. Like the power reactors, they are of many types. Some are primarily low- or high-flux neutron sources used for research and training, some are primarily used to irradiate and test materials, and still others are used for testing core configurations. These reactors are located primarily at the National Reactor Testing Station at Arco, Idaho, and at various national laboratories and universities throughout the United States. Multiple-purpose test reactors have also been built by private corporations, and are available on a fee-for-use basis.

9-26. Nuclear Power Costs [5,33,52—55]

Costs of nuclear power are changing very rapidly as more experience is gained and technical improvements are made; quantitative cost figures therefore will not be given here. The basis for cost estimates[53] and some cost figures for present systems[52] are available in the literature.

In comparison with conventional fossil-fired plants, nuclear systems have high capital costs (about 50 per cent more than fossil-fired plants) and low fuel costs. The high capital costs are due in part to sheer system complexity, but are also partially the result of extremely conservative design practice. Increasing experience and technical improvements are serving to reduce costs incurred from both factors.

Since capital and fixed costs for nuclear plants are high, fuel costs must be lower if nuclear and fossil-fired plants are to compete economically. Hence fuel costs are possibly the most important—and, in practice, the most uncertain—cost variable. The fuel in the reactor at a given time is but a part of a cycle involving new-fuel manufacture, spent-fuel processing, fuel storage, and reactor consumption. Costs associated with each portion of the cycle must be carefully assessed to determine accurately actual fuel costs. One important possibility for major reduction in fuel-cycle costs is achievement of high fuel burnup (Sec. 9-5). It has been calculated[5] that increasing burnup from 5,000 to 10,000 MWD/T can reduce fuel-cycle costs by about 50 per cent; costs for a burnup of 25,000 MWD/T would be about a factor of 3 less than those for 5,000 MWD/T.

The U.S. Atomic Energy Commission defines six categories for fuel-cycle costs: fabrication, depletion, use charge, plutonium credit, transportation, and reprocessing. Costs in each category will depend on the size, type of fuel, and location of the reactor. At present, the AEC owns all nuclear fuels (hence the "use charge") and controls price policy. However, plans for private ownership and a free market are well under way.

9-27. Nuclear Fuel Reprocessing [56—58]

The increasing rate at which reactors are being built and operated will produce increasing need for recovery of unburned fuel and fissile species produced from fertile materials (Sec. 9-6). These recovery operations are known as fuel reprocessing; they are essential if effective utilization of nuclear fuel reserves and low fuel costs are to be obtained.

There are several basic processes by which useful materials are recovered from spent fuel.[56] Methods such as precipitation and ion exchange have been used, but solvent-extraction processes (Sec. 5) are most common.

Extraction processes differ according to the materials to be separated. The Redox and Purex processes separate plutonium, uranium, and fission products; they differ primarily in the solvent used (hexone and tributyl phosphate, respectively). The Thorex process, which also uses tributyl phosphate as the solvent, separates thorium, uranium, and fission products. In each process, each chemical species of fuel and fertile material is produced as a separated and decontaminated product.

Fuel-reprocessing plants are extremely elaborate and costly because of the large amounts of radioactivity handled. All operations must be performed remotely from outside thick shielding walls, and special provisions must be made for decontaminating, replacing, and repairing process equipment. Facilities for long-term storage of highly radioactive fuel elements before processing and waste liquors from the process must also be provided.

In the typical process, spent fuel elements are first stored under water for several months to permit some fission-product decay before processing. The elements are then chopped up mechanically, and the fuel material is selectively separated from the cladding by dissolution. The solution of fuel materials is fed to a series of extraction columns in which the separation of species is accomplished; decontamination factors on the order of 10^6 to 10^8 are achieved. The purified fuel species are shipped as a nitrate solution, which is used to initiate fabrication of new fuel elements.

To date, all fuel processing in the United States has been done by the Atomic Energy Commission. However, the world's first privately owned fuel-reprocessing plant was expected to begin commercial operation in West Valley, N.Y., in January, 1966.[58] This plant uses the Purex process, and is capable of handling all commonly used fuels.

Fuel reprocessing and many other activities in the nuclear industry produce a variety of radioactive wastes. Disposal of these materials is carefully controlled by Federal regulations; some states (at present, Arkansas, California, Florida, Kentucky, Mississippi, New York, North Carolina, and Texas) also have autonomous regulatory power. Proper authorities should always be consulted before handling, transporting, or disposing of radioactive materials.

References

1. I. Kaplan: "Nuclear Physics," Addison-Wesley Publishing Company, Inc., Reading, Mass., 1955.
2. O. H. Blackwood, T. H. Osgood, and A. E. Ruark: "An Outline of Atomic Physics," John Wiley & Sons, Inc., New York, 1955.
3. R. E. Lapp and H. L. Andrews: "Nuclear Radiation Physics," 2d ed., Prentice-Hall, Inc., Englewood Cliffs, N.J., 1954.
4. W. E. Burcham: "Nuclear Physics: An Introduction," McGraw-Hill Book Company, New York, 1963.
5. S. Glasstone and A. Sesonske: "Nuclear Reactor Engineering," D. Van Nostrand Company, Inc., Princeton, N.J., 1963.

6. S. Glasstone and M. C. Edlund: "The Elements of Nuclear Reactor Theory," D. Van Nostrand Company, Inc., Princeton, N.J., 1952.
7. R. L. Murray: "Introduction to Nuclear Engineering," Prentice-Hall, Inc., Englewood Cliffs, N.J., 1961.
8. R. Stephenson: "Introduction to Nuclear Engineering," 2d ed., McGraw-Hill Book Company, New York, 1958.
9. A. M. Weinberg and E. P. Wigner: "The Physical Theory of Neutron Chain Reactors," The University of Chicago Press, Chicago, 1958.
10. H. S. Isbin: "Introductory Nuclear Reactor Theory," Reinhold Publishing Corporation, New York, 1963.
11. D. Strominger and J. M. Hollander: "Decay Schemes," URCL-8289, 1958.
12. D. J. Hughes and R. B. Schwartz: "Neutron Cross Sections," 2d ed., BNL-325, 1958.
13. D. T. Goldman and J. R. Stehn: "Chart of the Nuclides," Knolls Atomic Power Laboratory, 1961; available from General Electric Co., Dept. MWH, Educational Relations, Schenectady, N.Y.
14. "Handbook of Nuclear Technology," a collection of papers reprinted from *Nucleonics*, McGraw-Hill, Inc., New York.
15. K. Way and E. P. Wigner: *Phys. Rev.*, **73**, 1318 (1948).
16. "Report to the President on Civilian Power," USAEC, November, 1962.
17. H. Etherington (ed.): "Nuclear Engineering Handbook," McGraw-Hill Book Company, New York, 1958.
18. A. Radkowsky (ed.): "Naval Reactors Physics Handbook," vol. I, "Selected Basic Techniques," USAEC, 1964.
19. H. Soodak (ed.): "Reactor Handbook," vol. 3, part A, Physics, Interscience Publishers, Inc., New York, 1962.
20. L. J. Templin (ed.): "Reactor Physics Constants," 2d ed., ANL-5800, USAEC, July, 1963.
21. A few examples of reactor codes in use are:
    "PDQ: An IBM-704 Code to Solve the Two-dimensional Few-group Neutron Diffusion Equation," WAPD-TM-70, August, 1957.
    "EQUIPOISE: An IBM-709 Code for the Solution of Two-group, Two-dimensional Neutron Diffusion Equations in Cylindrical Geometry," ORNL-2967, November, 1960.
    "FEVER: A One-dimensional Few-group Depletion Program for Reactor Analysis," GA-2749, November, 1962.
    "The TWENTY-GRAND Program for the Numerical Solution of Few-group Neutron Diffusion Equations in Two Dimensions," ORNL-3200, February, 1962.
    For code listings, see:
    Nucleonics, **19**, 154 (November, 1961); also **20**, 132 (August, 1962).
    Code abstracts published in *Nuclear Science and Engineering* (American Nuclear Society).
    Current compilations, AEC Computing Facility, New York University, New York.
22. G. R. Keepin: "Physics of Nuclear Kinetics," Addison-Wesley Publishing Company, Inc., Reading, Mass., 1965.
23. M. A. Schultz: "Control of Nuclear Reactors and Power Plants," 2d ed., McGraw-Hill Book Company, New York, 1961.
24. J. M. Harrer: "Nuclear Reactor Control Engineering," D. Van Nostrand Company, Inc., Princeton, N.J., 1963.
25. "Reactor Kinetics and Control," Proceedings of a symposium held at the University of Arizona, Mar. 25–27, 1963; available from U.S. Dept. of Commerce, Office of Technical Services.
26. W. K. Anderson and J. S. Theilacker (eds.): "Neutron Absorber Materials for Reactor Control," USAEC, 1962.

27. M. M. El-Wakil: "Nuclear Power Engineering," McGraw-Hill Book Company, New York, 1962.
28. C. M. Nicholls (ed.): "Progress in Nuclear Energy," ser. IV, Technology, Engineering, and Safety, Pergamon Press, New York. Four volumes are currently available.
29. J. R. Dietrich and W. H. Zinn: "Solid Fuel Reactors," Addison-Wesley Publishing Company, Inc., Reading, Mass., 1958.
30. A. W. Kramer: "Boiling Water Reactors," Addison-Wesley Publishing Company, Inc., Reading, Mass., 1958.
31. J. A. Lane, H. G. MacPherson, and Frank Maslan: "Fluid Fuel Reactors," Addison-Wesley Publishing Company, Inc., Reading, Mass., 1958.
32. C. Starr and R. W. Dickinson: "Sodium Graphite Reactors," Addison-Wesley Publishing Company, Inc., Reading, Mass., 1958.
33. *Power Reactor Technology*, a quarterly review of recent developments in engineering design of power reactors, available from the U.S. Government Printing Office, publ. 20402.
34. "Background Information on Atomic Power Safety," Atomic Industrial Forum, Inc., New York.
35. *Reactor Materials*, a quarterly review of recent developments, available from the U.S. Government Printing Office, publ. 20402.
36. H. M. Finniston, and J. P. Howe (eds.); ser. V, Metallurgy and Fuels, "Progress in Nuclear Energy," Pergamon Press, New York.
37. A. N. Holden: "Physical Metallurgy of Uranium," Addison-Wesley Publishing Company, Inc., Reading, Mass., 1958.
38. D. J. DePaul (ed.): "Corrosion and Wear Handbook for Water Cooled Reactors," U.S. Atomic Energy Commission, TID-7006, 1957.
39. "Corrosion of Reactor Materials," vols. I and II, International Atomic Energy Agency, Vienna, 1962.
40. J. E. Draley, et al.: "Corrosion in Aqueous Systems," Proceedings of the Third International Conference on Peaceful Uses of Atomic Energy, paper 243, Geneva, 1964.
41. Theodore Rockwell, III (ed.); "Reactor Shielding Design Manual," U.S. Atomic Energy Commission, TID-7004, 1956.
42. E. P. Blizard (ed.): "Reactor Handbook," vol. III, part B, Shielding, Interscience Publishers, Inc., New York, 1962.
43. H. Goldstein: "Fundamental Aspects of Reactor Shielding," Addison-Wesley Publishing Company, Inc., Reading, Mass., 1959.
44. H. Goldstein: "The Attenuation of Gamma Rays and Neutrons in Reactor Shields," U.S. Government Printing Office, 1957.
45. "Standard for Protection Against Radiation," Code of Federal Regulations, 10 CFR Part 20; available from the U.S. Government Printing Office.
46. "Maximum Permissible Body Burdens and Maximum Permissible Concentrations of Radionuclides in Air and Water for Occupational Exposure," National Bureau of Standards Handbook 69, 1959.
47. *Nuclear Safety*, a quarterly review of recent developments, available from the U.S. Government Printing Office, publ. 20402.
48. "Measurement of Absorbed Dose of Neutrons and Mixtures of Neutrons and Gamma Rays," U.S. Bureau of Standards Handbook 75, 1961.
49. W. J. Price: "Nuclear Radiation Detection," 2d ed., McGraw-Hill Book Company, New York, 1964.
50. C. D. Gregg King: "Nuclear Power Systems," The Macmillan Company, New York, 1964.
51. Reactor Tables, published annually in the August issue of *Nucleonics*, a McGraw-Hill, Inc., monthly publication.
52. L. M. Olmsted: Tenth Nuclear Report: Power Boom Takes Off, *Electrical World*, June 14, 1965, pp. 85–104.

53. "Nuclear Power Plants Cost Evaluation Handbook," vols. I–V, U.S. Atomic Energy Commission, 1962.
54. G. Young: The Fueling of Nuclear Power Complexes, *Nuclear News*, November, 1964, pp. 23–30.
55. "Nuclear Power Economics: Analysis and Comments—1964," Joint Commission on Atomic Energy, October, 1964; available from the U.S. Government Printing Office.
56. M. Benedict and T. Pigford: "Nuclear Chemical Engineering," McGraw-Hill Book Company, New York, 1957.
57. *Reactor Fuel Processing*, a quarterly review of recent developments, available from the U.S. Government Printing Office, publ. 20402.
58. NFS Reprocessing Plant Is 97% Completed, *Nucleonics*, **23** (7), 28, 29 (July, 1965).

INDEX

1